FROM ARLINGTON TO APPOMATTOX

Robert E. Lee's Civil War, Day by Day, 1861-1865

Charles R. Knight

Savas Beatie
California

© 2021 by Charles R. Knight

All rights reserved. No part of this work may be reproduced, stored in a retrieval system, or transmitted, in any form or by any means, electronic, mechanical, photocopying, recording, or otherwise, without the prior written permission of the publisher.

Library of Congress Cataloging-in-Publication Data

Names: Knight, Charles R., author.

Title: From Arlington to Appomattox: Robert E. Lee's Civil War, Day by Day, 1861-1865 / Charles R. Knight.
Other titles: Robert E. Lee's Civil War

Description: El Dorado Hills : Savas Beatie LLC, 2021. | Includes bibliographical references and index. |

Summary: "Lost in all of the military histories of the war, and even in most of the Lee biographies, is what the general was doing when he was out of history's "public" eye. Focusing on where he was, who he was with, and what he was doing day by day offers an entirely different appreciation for Lee. Readers will come away with a fresh sense of his struggles, both personal and professional, and discover many things about Lee for the first time using his own correspondence and papers from his family, his staff, his lieutenants, and the men of his army." — provided by publisher.

Identifiers: LCCN 2020035968 | ISBN 9781611215021 (hardcover) | ISBN 9781611215038 (ebook)
Subjects: LCSH: Lee, Robert E. (Robert Edward), 1807-1870—Chronology. | Generals–Confederate States of America—Biography. | Confederate States of America. Army—Biography. | United States—History—Civil War, 1861-1865—Chronology.

Classification: LCC E467.1.L4 K65 2020 | DDC 973.7/3092 [B]—dc23
LC record available at https://lccn.loc.gov/2020035968

First edition, first printing

ISBN-13: 978-161121-502-1
eISBN: 978-1-61121-503-8

SB

Savas Beatie
989 Governor Drive, Suite 102
El Dorado Hills, CA 95762
Phone: 916-941-6896
(E-mail) sales@savasbeatie.com

Savas Beatie titles are available at special discounts for bulk purchases in the United States by corporations, institutions, and other organizations. E-mail us at sales@savasbeatie.com, or click over for a visit to our website at www.savasbeatie.com for additional information.

For that one particular archivist who could just never understand that yes, I DO in fact really need to see the entire Lee collection . . .

General Robert E. Lee

This photograph was taken by Julian Vannerson in Richmond, Virginia, in early 1864, just before the beginning of the spring campaign that began in the Wilderness, carved its bloody course down to and then beyond the James River to Petersburg, and, nearly 10 months later, finally ended in April 1865 at Appomattox Court House. *LOC*

Table of Contents

Foreword by Robert E. L. Krick   vii

Introduction & Acknowledgments   ix

1861

April   1

May   10

June   27

July   39

August   51

September   60

October   70

November   75

December   84

1862

January   90

February   94

March   100

April   111

May   125

June   143

July   163

August   175

September   188

October   205

November   213

December   223

1863

January   232

February   239

March   244

April   250

May   261

June   276

July   290

August   303

September   309

October   318

November   326

December   337

1864

January   343

TABLE OF CONTENTS (continued)

February 350

March 357

April 366

May 376

June 396

July 411

August 423

September 432

October 441

November 449

December 456

1865

January 462

February 468

March 477

April 488

Epilogue 503

Bibliography 505

Index 531

Photographs

A collection of photographs can be found in the gallery following page 238.

List of Maps

These maps will be found at the end of the gallery of photographs following page 238:

Virginia

Western Virginia Theater

Southeast Atlantic Coast

Richmond Area

Northern Virginia: The Maryland and Pennsylvania Theater

Central Virginia

Petersburg Area

Appomattox Campaign

Foreword

Writers working in the field of military history probably labor as much for themselves as for any audience. Many of us relish the process: gathering material, wrestling it into some sort of order, interpreting it, and then converting the results of all that labor into prose, captured for posterity on a printed page. That generalization cannot apply to the noble genre of reference work. Compilers toil for everyone—for themselves, certainly, but indisputably, too, for their colleagues and for future users as yet unborn.

A first superficial glance at *From Arlington to Appomattox* might provoke derisive hoots from certain quarters on the grounds that yet another Robert E. Lee book has arrived to further burden a saturated market. In fact this is no standard biography, nor is it like anything produced before in the comprehensive Lee literature. Instead it is an interpreted collection of facts—a gigantic piece of research that addresses all four years of Lee's Civil War service in an entirely new and useful way. It inevitably will serve as a keystone source for all future Lee books, and for much other historical work on his army and its campaigns.

When R. E. Lee ascended to command of the Army of Northern Virginia on June 1, 1862, he already had fourteen months of significant wartime duty on his record. That service reached into the mountains of western Virginia and the coastal lowlands of South Carolina and Georgia. Lee also exercised country-wide influence and power from his position in Richmond in the opening months of 1862. Admirable scholarship exists on those topics and on nearly every other feature of the general's Civil War experience, but largely, and almost unavoidably, in thematic isolation.

The "day by day" concept employed here probably works best for a soldier of broad responsibility. Through this lens we see the vast scope of Lee's duties, the multitude of diverse topics that occupied and fretted the general on a daily basis, even in winter quarters. By virtually any standard March 9, 1865, was a pedestrian, now-forgotten day in Virginia's Civil War. In *From Arlington to Appomattox*, we find that, at a minimum, Lee concerned himself with desertion rates among North Carolina soldiers; minor military operations in North Carolina and Virginia; and the overall state of the war effort, especially the critical subject of dwindling supplies. Having accomplished all that via the written word, Lee visited his lines of defense around Petersburg and did not return until after midnight.

In active and mobile operations, that grinding stress grew even greater. When the war entered its fourth spring in Virginia, the pressure on Lee reached previously unseen levels, particularly in May 1864, when he staved off Union offensives on three separate fronts. For years historians have remarked on the physical toll those responsibilities took on a 57-year-old man. On tours across the May battlefields, some of us have cited a remark from the army's medical director, Dr. Lafayette Guild, in which he stated that Lee "had not from the 5th to 25th had two hours consecutive sleep." That has been one of the few quantifiable examples of the burden of command on the general. With all the available evidence neatly marshaled here, we can see the exhausting daily routine Lee followed, and can better appreciate its crushing cumulative weight. See, for instance, the reconstruction of his activities on May 21-22, 1864, a period in which the armies moved rather than fought. Lee apparently slept little, if at all, for nearly 48 hours as he coordinated his army's march southward from Spotsylvania. Within a day of that ordeal, sickness felled Lee and famously kept him tent-bound during a critical period of missed opportunities on the North Anna River. The cause and its effect seem startlingly clear in this format.

From Arlington to Appomattox will become the standard reference work on R. E. Lee's daily wartime experiences, and should last until the braying Jacobins of our century succeed in devising legislation to make ownership of Confederate-themed books a felony.

Robert E. L. Krick
Glen Allen, Virginia
author of *Staff Officers in Gray*

Introduction

Douglas Southall Freeman, the Pulitzer Prize-winning biographer of Robert E. Lee, once boasted that he "could account for every hour of Lee's life from the day Lee went to West Point until his death. . . ."[1] Freeman was exaggerating, of course, but not by much. By his own estimation he spent more than 6,100 hours writing his Lee biography, which encompasses more than one million words.[2] His four-volume *R. E. Lee* remains the standard biographical work on the general. Add in his three volumes of *Lee's Lieutenants: A Study in Command*, the previously unpublished correspondence in *Lee's Dispatches* that Freeman edited, and the decades of Lee research that went into those and other works and it is easy to see why Freeman would make such a boast. He probably knew more about certain aspects of Lee's life than even some of the general's family. After all, Freeman's research mantra was, "when you do a thing, do it thoroughly . . . so that not a new word can be said."[3]

But new words "can be said." That is not meant as a knock against Freeman, whose exhaustive research was beyond thorough. As with any episode in history, new sources come to light as time passes, and "old" sources are subject to reinterpretation. Freeman was not truly able to account for every hour of the general's life, but many of the untold hours he could not account for consisted of minutia outside the scope of his work. *From Arlington to Appomattox* fills in many of the gaps in Freeman's *R. E. Lee* by reconstructing the general on a daily basis. It is not intended as an analytical biography. Instead, it focuses on where he was, what he did, who he met with or wrote to, and in some cases even what he ate.

Finding all these minute details made for a fascinating journey. Every historian worth his salts knows it is imperative to study the subject's own words and the words of those closest to him. "You must go to the sources," Freeman directed. "There and there only, patiently and not always consciously, you get perspective, you grasp the spirit of the times in which your subject lived, and you learn the credibility of the witnesses whose testimony you are to cite."[4] For Lee, this meant his own letters, personal and official, and those of his staff and his family.

Unfortunately, Lee did not write his memoirs or a history of the war, although he intended to do the latter and gathered some materials for the project during the few years of life he had left after Appomattox.[5] Gen. John B. Gordon, who commanded half of Lee's infantry at the end, lamented,

---

1 John M. Virden to Burke Davis, May 13, 1956, Burke Davis papers, UNC. The remainder of the quote is, "but I never presumed to know what General Lee was thinking about." ibid.

2 David E. Johnson, *Douglas Southall Freeman* (Gretna, LA, 2002), 163.

3 Ibid., 66.

4 Ibid., 118.

5 Four months before his death Lee wrote his cousin, "A history of the military events of the period would be . . . desirable, and I have had it in view to write one of the campaigns in Virginia in which I was more particularly engaged. I

"It is a great loss to history and to posterity that General Lee did not write his own recollections as General [Ulysses S.] Grant did."[6] Several members of Lee's family and some within his close military circle, however, did put their recollections to paper.

Walter Herron Taylor, who served as an aide to Lee for nearly the entire war, authored two books of his wartime experiences and many of his letters are preserved; most of the wartime letters were published in 1995. "Because of his close relations with General Lee," explained Freeman, "Colonel Taylor became in time an unofficial court of appeals on controversies that related to the Army of Northern Virginia. . . . His conclusions seldom are subject to dispute, because he possessed a memory that was both tenacious and accurate."[7]

Charles Marshall, the only officer to accompany Lee into the McLean house and the author of Lee's farewell order, never completed his contemplated Lee history, but his papers and notes were published in 1927 by Major General Sir Frederick Maurice of the British Army.

The scholarly Charles Scott Venable, with whom perhaps Lee was the closest personally of all his long-serving staff officers, has two vast collections of wartime papers including an unfinished memoir that reveals many unknown details of Lee's wartime service. Lee's military secretary Armistead Lindsay Long overcame postwar blindness to write a lengthy memoir of Lee. The general's youngest son, Rob Jr., wrote a memoir of his father's entire life, and former Army of Northern Virginia cavalry corps commander Fitzhugh Lee also penned a biography of his famous uncle. Much of what is known about Lee during the war years comes to us from these six men, as well as from Lee's own letters.

Other members of Lee's inner circle left accounts, but their writings were less prolific than their comrades mentioned above. T. M. R. Talcott, John A. Washington, Giles B. Cooke, Robert H. Chilton all, to some extent, recorded details of Lee during the war—some of it for public consumption, and some not.

Lee's staff officers had a unique vantage point for their observations of the general. Whereas most of the soldiers in the ranks rarely saw the army commander, those at headquarters were around him constantly. Such close quarters bred a familiarity with Lee that few others experienced. Taylor observed:

> In our small circle of the personal staff, there was between General Lee and his military family a degree of camaraderie that was perfectly delightful. Our conversation, especially at table, was free from restraint, unreserved as between equals, and often of a bright and jocular vein. He was very fond of a joke, and not infrequently indulged in the pastime of teasing those about him in a mild way. While it would never occur to any one of us to be otherwise than perfectly deferential in our manner toward him, and respectful in our deportment toward each other in his presence, there was an utter absence of the rigid formality and the

---

have already collected some materials for the work, but lack so much that I wish to obtain that I have not commenced the narrative." REL to Cassius Lee, June 6, 1870, Lee papers, SH.

6 John B. Gordon, *Reminiscences of the Civil War* (Dayton, OH, 1985), 166.

7 Douglas S. Freeman, *The South to Posterity: An Introduction to the Writing of Confederate History* (Baton Rouge, LA, 1998), 65.

irksome ceremonial regarded by some as essential features of the military etiquette appertaining to the station of the commander-in-chief of the army.[8]

Shortly after Lee's death in 1870, his eldest son Custis asked Charles Marshall to write an article about his father for a memorial volume to be published by Washington & Lee University.[9] Marshall balked at the short turn-around time and complexity of the subject matter. He wrote to a Lee cousin that doing full justice to Lee requires

> that the author should have access to the most authentic proof of all he may state, that he should have ample time to collect all facts and that he should omit nothing that bears upon the subject. I had not, nor have I now the means of writing the more extensive work, though I am using every means to prepare myself at some future time to do so.... I am preparing a life of the General which I hope to present within a year or eighteen months, provided I can get the materials. If I can do no more, I shall collect all I can, and write all I know to be used by some future biographer.[10]

Marshall died before he completed his book, but his son passed along all his father's papers to Gen. Frederick Maurice for eventual publication, so Marshall did ultimately succeed in his secondary goal.

The first of Walter Taylor's two books, *Four Years with General Lee*, appeared in 1877. Despite its title, it is more a history of the campaigns of the Army of Northern Virginia than any sort of personal memoir of Taylor's time alongside Lee. One Lee admirer, knowing that Taylor could offer insight no one else could, attempted to draw the more human side of Lee out of Taylor:

> We have no book that shows Gen. Lee at close range, as a person. All of you have treated him as a 'General.' Fitz Lee also. Now it seems to me that ... hereafter, humanity will hunger and crave more of 'Lee as the Man.' As a military captain we have the data to study, but his personal life ... is strangely hid from the world.... I hoped that Col. Marshall's book would give us much of this, but alas—he was called before it was finished. You were with him night and day, for much of that trying period; is it not possible for you to write of Lee as your friend? I crave more of the personality of the man, and it strangely hides itself. You who were with him, and unconsciously drank all of this in, cannot imagine how we fellows outside envy you?[11]

This plea (among others) led to the publication of Taylor's much more Lee-oriented *General Lee: His Campaigns in Virginia, 1861-1865* in 1906.

But for all the works that have been written about Lee, most of them focus on one particular aspect of his life: Lee the soldier, Lee the educator, Lee the Southern icon, Lee the man. None have

---

8 Walter H. Taylor, *General Lee: His Campaigns in Virginia, 1861-1865* (Dayton, OH, 1975), 157.

9 Known during Lee's tenure as Washington College, it was renamed Washington & Lee University almost immediately after Lee's death. Custis Lee succeeded his father as president of the university, a position he held until 1897.

10 Charles Marshall to Cassius Lee, July 20, 1871, Lee family papers, VHS.

11 C. C. Perrick to Taylor, January 13, 1904, WHT papers, NPL.

truly given more than a brief glimpse into his daily life, although Taylor and Freeman came closest to giving us a sense of his daily routine. Often lost in the study of Lee the soldier is the fact that during this four-year period, he had other obligations and duties besides those to the Confederacy. Lee remained a father, a husband, and a friend—in addition to being a general. In addition to all the demands of the war during 1861-65, Lee lost a daughter, a daughter-in-law (although he thought of Charlotte Wickham Lee more as another daughter), and two grandchildren; his own son was wounded and snatched from his sickbed by Federal cavalry and then held hostage; Lee watched helplessly as his beloved wife became a wheelchair-bound invalid; he lost his home and most of his possessions, had to deal with his father-in-law's will, and he endured the rapid deterioration of his own health. In the wake of the battle of Sharpsburg, Lee's daughter Annie died unexpectedly. While Lee's lines collapsed at Petersburg under the strain of Grant's massive final offensive, Lee repeatedly apologized to his daughter Agnes for not being able to see her while she was in town and agonized over her safe return to Richmond. Throughout the war Lee was tugged in different directions by his myriad responsibilities.

Had Lee kept a diary, of course we would have such a daily journal of his activities during the war. In truth he did not have the time, and he probably did not have the interest. Had he done so, there would be little need for this volume. Recreating someone's daily life a century and a half after the fact is a considerable undertaking, regardless of how famous and well-documented the life. During my research at one Lee repository, I was introduced by an archivist as the historian "trying to do the impossible—Lee day by day."

As the title implies, *From Arlington to Appomattox: Robert E. Lee's Civil War Day by Day, 1861-1865*, is a daily study of Lee during the four years of the Civil War. It covers 208 weeks of Lee's life, from Virginia's secession through his return to Richmond after Appomattox. This is not intended to be an all-encompassing study; tracking down every piece of Lee correspondence and every reference to him in published books and unpublished papers would indeed be "trying to do the impossible." It took the Lincoln Centennial Association and its successor organizations decades to compile the three-volume *Lincoln Day by Day*.[12] Readers will find this Lee volume somewhere in between the Lincoln work and John Schildt's *Stonewall Jackson Day by Day* in terms of detail.[13]

Every historical work is limited by the source material available. Much of what occurred at Lee's headquarters was never written down or has been lost. Much more occurred at headquarters and/or around Lee on a given day, of course, than is noted here. Some incidents are recorded, but cannot be pinned down to a specific day. A prime example of this is Lee's acquisition of his horses Traveller and Lucy Long. A rough time period is known for both, but not the exact date for either. In cases like this, I include the incident in the lead-in material to the appropriate chapter. Conflicting or disputed events are addressed in footnotes rather than in the main text. Times of day are typically not addressed unless particularly important, and the order in which items are presented in the text should not be taken to mean that is how they occurred chronologically. In many cases, we simply do not

---

[12] Unlike this study, the Lincoln work covers the entire life of the 16th president; it was republished by Morningside as one large volume in 1988.

[13] Schildt's slim volume, published in 1980, draws almost exclusively from Jed Hotchkiss' writings, Jackson's own letters, and the *Official Records*. At only 135 pages it is far from exhaustive. Its glaring weakness is the almost nonexistent citations.

know. Walter Taylor rightfully cautioned about trying to remember the specific time an event took place:

> If there is one thing above all others that I have learned to be cautious about, in speaking of our 'late unpleasantness' it is the time of day. Day followed day so rapidly, events so crowded upon each other, my own movements were so dependent upon the varying chances and conditions of battle during the periods of active operations, that I find it a very difficult matter to determine the time of day of any particular incident.[14]

Lee was in almost daily contact with his primary lieutenants and department chiefs. But these briefings, if they can be called such, were more often than not verbal and thus not recorded.[15] Lee's discussions with officials in Richmond, especially early in the war before he assumed command of the Army of Northern Virginia, often went unrecorded. In April and May of 1861 Lee was beset by an overwhelming number of office seekers, and very few of these meetings were memorialized in writing. Only those for which documentation survives are included herein.

Source material for Lee before he assumed command of the Army of Northern Virginia Lee is rather limited, especially for his time in western Virginia. During that time there were few in a position to record anything beyond Walter Taylor and Lee himself, and the general had not yet risen to the fame he would soon achieve. To most of the men in the Army of the Northwest and the Army of the Kanawha, there was little reason to take special note of just another general. Unfortunately for history, Taylor's letters from that period do not survive, but a small handful from Lee's other aide, John Washington, do exist and, although scattered, are an absolute gold mine of detail.

Lee's time on the southeast Atlantic coast is likewise almost devoid of source material. The general himself notes that he went on inspection tours but recorded little to no detail about them. Official correspondence for this time period can be confusing because Lee maintained department headquarters at Coosawhatchie, South Carolina, but was often in Savannah, Charleston, or elsewhere. As a result, correspondence from his South Carolina headquarters over an aide's signature does not mean Lee was present at headquarters at that time.

It was not until Lee returned to Richmond in early March 1862 that source material begins to become abundant. Still, there are periods in which little is known of his movements and activities. Winter encampments are relatively quiet times and usually sparsely documented; somewhat surprisingly, the weeks after the army's return from Maryland following the Battle of Sharpsburg comprises another long dry stretch of documentation.

As a general rule, I have not included Lee's endorsements on communications. Some are included due to their noteworthy nature, while others of a more general nature are included as a representative sampling. Locating and including every endorsement would be far too time-consuming and add little of value or interest. Especially early in the war in his role as commander of Virginia's forces, the amount of paperwork that crossed Lee's desk was astonishing.

---

14 WHT to EPA, June 28, 1894, WHT papers, NPL.

15 "The chiefs of the several departments of the service attached to his staff moved, camped, and messed apart from him, though always within call and reporting to him daily for orders." Taylor, *General Lee*, 57.

Although the paperwork diminished as his number of staff officers increased, much of it still required his perusal and signature.

Weather plays an oft-overlooked role in military operations. Accordingly, I have included mention of adverse weather conditions in Lee's immediate vicinity whenever possible.

I have not attempted to retrace Lee's exact footsteps when he was on the move. The general route he followed can usually be inferred from the towns through which he passed along the way, but the reader will not find here a turn-by-turn route for Lee's movements.

* * *

My own interest in Lee runs as far back as I can remember. Growing up in Richmond, the Civil War was everywhere. I can't recall my first encounter with Lee, but I do remember my first trip to a battlefield: Petersburg. The Crater fascinated me. It was the first of many battlefield journeys.

One episode in particular stands out in my mind for its connection to Lee. My dad and I were coming back home from Spotsylvania in the early 1990s. Since it was just the two of us that time, the conversation was geared toward what all high school guys and their fathers talk about: the Civil War and trains. As we drove south on US 1—Dad absolutely HATED I-95 and avoided it whenever possible—we approached the North Anna River. I had crossed those ugly old aquamarine truss bridges many times, but this time as we ascended from the river bottom he pointed to the old brick house off to the right of the road and said something along the lines of, "You know, Lee was almost killed at that house. It was his headquarters during the fighting here at the North Anna. Yankee artillery fire drove him away." (It wasn't really Lee's headquarters, but Dad was close.) We had driven by that house on countless occasions, and this was the first time he had volunteered anything about its history.

I shouldn't have been surprised because Dad found a way of working Robert E. Lee into just about any trip in or around town. A trip to downtown to Dad's Richmond office required walking past Capitol Square. We would usually detour a block or so west so he could point out an old brick house on Franklin Street where the Lees resided. Visiting my grandparents at their house near Mechanicsville always included a reminder that Lee watched part of the Seven Days' Battles from "right over there." Returning from frequent trips to Hampton Roads usually included a hand gesture in the direction of a large Confederate flag flying beside I-295 at a farm called Powhite—another of Lee's headquarters, I was told—or, if we decided to return through the city, my Dad would point over to what was then Henrico County Police headquarters on Nine Mile Road and say, "Lee met with Stonewall there to plan the Seven Days' Battles." Lee was everywhere, and not only around Richmond; Lee connections spanned much of the state of Virginia.

Some of the sites Dad pointed out are gone, such as the Clarke house, Lockwood at Atlee, where Lee met with President Jefferson Davis and Gen. P. G. T. Beauregard, or the battlefield at Totopotomoy Creek. I find it quite timely that the Fox house, Ellington, overlooking the North Anna at Hanover Junction—the one Dad mentioned where Lee was nearly killed by Union artillery fire—is, as of this writing, being targeted for preservation by the American Battlefield Trust.

The genesis of this project began when my publisher, Theodore P. Savas, pitched me to undertake it. "Charlie, this needs to be done," he urged, "and you are the guy to do it." I was honored and humbled at the same time. What Ted forgot to pass along (and laughs about now) is that I had no idea what I was getting into. I told him that recently, and he replied, "Well, if you had known, would you have done it? You can't get there without getting there, and getting there is most of the fun. It is a giant contribution to the literature, and I am glad you undertook it." Ted was right. This mammoth undertaking turned into the most enjoyable project I've ever tackled.

It is my sincere hope this volume provides a greater understanding and appreciation for Robert E. Lee during the four most turbulent years of his life.

Acknowledgments

No historian works in a vacuum and I owe a great deal to a number of people who assisted in tracking down source material, reviewing portions of the manuscript, answering questions, or otherwise offering support and encouragement.

Without Robert E. L. Krick this would certainly be a much weaker volume. His guidance to Lee source material and comments on the manuscript were invaluable. He also graciously contributed the Foreword, for which I am extremely grateful.

Clark Hall offered his encyclopedic knowledge of Culpeper and Orange, and to him I owe a great deal.

My good friend Michael Hardy was always willing to answer questions at all hours of the day and share his research on Lee's Headquarters Guard, the 39th Virginia Cavalry Battalion.

Other friends and colleagues who helped along the way, in no particular order, include: Harry Smeltzer, Craig Swain, Eric Wittenberg, Dave Powell, Wade Sokolosky, Patrick Schroeder, Byron Faidley, Tom Clemens, Ted Alexander, Rick Allen, Suzanne Muriel Pegley, Jim Hessler, Eric Lindblade, Chris Kolakowski, Jerry Holsworth, Greg Starbuck, Mark Wade, Gloria Bushong, Hunter Lesser, Marc Ramsey, Kris White, Michael Jordan, Jason Amico, Robert Moore, Frank O'Reilly, Terry Lowry, Scott Mingus, Garry Adelman, Robert Wynstra, Stephen Recker, Jim Burgess, Kevin Pawlak, Bert Dunkerly, Rob Orrison, John Fox, Horace Mewborn, Stephen Bockmiller, Teej Smith, Mike Gorman, Alexander Rossino, Eric Mink, Peter Carmichael, Barbara Winters, Frank Clark, Monte Lewis, Tim McKinney, and Jeff Wert.

The staffs at the Virginia Historical Society, Library of Virginia, Southern Historical Collection at the University of North Carolina, Rubenstein Library at Duke University, and the State Archives of North Carolina were of great assistance, as were the Inter-Library Loan folks with the Wake County Public Library. Also Robert Hitchings and Troy Valos at the Norfolk Public Library; Tom Camden, Byron Faidley, Lisa McCown, and Seth McCormick-Goodhart at Washington & Lee; Theresa Roane at the Museum of the Confederacy; Judy Hynson at Stratford Hall; Diane Jacob and Mary Laura Kludy at Virginia Military Institute; Meghan Bryant and Karen King at William & Mary; Jennifer Rouse, Dianna Jowers, and Aaron Bradford at the Coastal Heritage Society; Laura Christiansen with the Thomas Balch Library; Shannon Johnson and Rick Hatcher at Fort Sumter National Monument; Jayne Blair with the Orange County Historical Society; Michelle Lee with Miles Lehane Co.; Tal Nadan with the New York Public Library; Robbie Smith at Colonial National Historical Park; Don Silvius with the Berkeley County Historical Society; Jeanne Meldeon with the Castletown Foundation; Lori Schexnayder at Tulane University; Bettina Helms and Ben Ritter with Handley Library; Mary Morris and Nathan Stalvey with the Clarke County Historical Association;

Joel Cadoff and Talley Kirkland at Fort Pulaski National Monument; Brittany Mayo with the Georgia Historical Society; Elizabeth Howe and John Frye with the Washington County Library; Erin Clark with the Fauquier County Historical Society; Doug Perks at the Jefferson County Museum; Michael Whitaker with the Amelia County Historical Society; Lavonne Allen with the New Kent Historical Society; Eric Blevins at the North Carolina Museum of History; Bethany Sullivan of the James Madison Museum; and Krista Markstrom with the Washington County Historical Society.

A giant thank you to Theodore P. Savas, who proposed the idea for this book to me as a great piggyback to my ongoing William Mahone biography. I would also like to thank the rest of the great crew at Savas Beatie, including marketing director Sarah Keeney, Lisa Murphy, Donna Endacott, Lois Olechny, and Sarah Closson. Thanks also to Lee Meredith for indexing my book, and Hal Jespersen for his outstanding maps.

And the most sincere and important thanks goes to Sara, Carter, and Virginia, who put up with my countless weekends spent in libraries or in front of the computer.

Charles R. Knight

From Arlington to Appomattox

Robert E. Lee's Civil War, Day by Day,
1861-1865

Robert E. Lee and Traveller. Lee was an avid horseman throughout his life, and Traveller was his favorite mount during and after the war. This image of horse and rider was probably taken during the siege of Petersburg, though some contend it was postwar Lexington. *W&L*

April 1861

The election of Abraham Lincoln as president in 1860 led to the secession of seven Southern states. Resignations of officers from states comprising the new Confederacy flooded the War and Navy departments in Washington, D.C. The fate of the Upper South and border states remained in question in April when the Rebels fired on Fort Sumter in Charleston, South Carolina All eyes looked to Virginia, for it was widely believed many of these states would follow her lead.

Colonel Robert E. Lee, one of the most gifted officers in the U.S. Army, watched with sorrow as the Union disintegrated. He did not believe in secession but looked at his native Virginia as his true home. Virginia's course would determine his own.

Lee's was a distinguished career. The son of Revolutionary War hero Henry "Light Horse Harry" Lee graduated second in the West Point class of 1829, was an engineer of great ability, and served with distinction on commanding general Winfield Scott's staff during the Mexican War. Lee had served as the superintendent of West Point, and had recently led the forces that captured John Brown at Harpers Ferry. In early March 1861 he returned to Arlington, the plantation overlooking Washington that his wife Mary Anna Randolph Custis—great-granddaughter of Martha Custis Washington—inherited from her father, George Washington Parke Custis. Several weeks after his arrival Lee was promoted to colonel of the 1st Cavalry Regiment. Rumors circulated that he was marked for higher command should war come.

On or about April 1, Lee went to Washington to discuss his future with Brevet Lieutenant General Winfield Scott, commanding general of the Army. Like Lee, Scott was a native of Virginia; but unlike Lee Scott did not intend to follow his state out of the Union. Although exactly what transpired at this meeting is not recorded, it is known that Lee received a cold reception from Scott's military secretary, Massachusetts-born Lieutenant Colonel Erasmus Keyes, with whom Lee had previously enjoyed a cordial relationship. Keyes felt Lee too sympathetic toward secession, an accusation which must have rankled Lee.[1]

In Virginia's capital Richmond on April 4, a special convention rejected an ordinance of secession by nearly two to one. On April 12 open hostilities erupted with the firing on Fort Sumter. On the 15th President Lincoln issued a call for volunteers to put down the Southern rebellion, prompting Virginia's Governor John Letcher to tell Lincoln that his state would not comply. Two days later the convention met again. This time it voted 88-55 in favor of secession, pending a public referendum on May 23. Virginia would join the Confederacy.[2]

Lee's daughter Agnes captured the feeling at Arlington: "We are all very sad here at the present state of affairs.... I learned ... Virginia had seceded. I cannot yet realize it, it seems so dreadful. But she had to take one side or the other and truly I hope she has chosen the right one. It is a very solemn step and I fear we will have to go through a great deal of suffering."[3]

* * *

1 Douglas S. Freeman, *R.E. Lee: A Biography*, 4 vols. (New York, 1934-5), vol. 1, 431-2.

2 E. B. Long, *The Civil War Day by Day: An Almanac, 1861-1865* (New York, 1971), 53, 59-60.

3 Agnes Lee to Mildred Lee, April 19, 1861, Mary Coulling Papers, W&L.

April 17, Wednesday (Arlington): Lee receives invitations from General Scott and Francis P. Blair, advisor to President Abraham Lincoln, to call on them in Washington tomorrow. Blair's note is delivered by Lee's cousin, John Lee. Rain during the night.[4]

April 18, Thursday (Arlington/Washington): Lee meets for several hours with Francis Blair at the Blair home on Pennsylvania Avenue in Washington. Secretary of War Simon Cameron (and possibly President Lincoln himself) asked Blair to offer Lee command of the U.S. Army in putting down the rebellion. Lee tells Blair that although he is not in favor of secession and hopes that peace may yet be restored, he cannot take up arms against the Southern states or his native Virginia. Lee then calls upon Gen. Scott at the War Department to inform him of the discussion with Blair. When he learns why Lee turned down the offer of command, Scott advises Lee to resign from the Army.

After meeting with Scott, Lee visits his brother Sidney Smith Lee, who is stationed in Washington, to discuss the offer of command of the Army vs. resignation from it, as well as Smith's future with the U.S. Navy. No firm decisions are reached, and Lee returns to Arlington after dark.[5]

April 19, Friday (Arlington/Alexandria): Lee goes to Alexandria in the morning with his wife and eldest daughter, Mary, where they learn of Virginia's secession; Lee tells another, "I am one of those dull creatures that cannot see the good of secession." That evening friends and relatives are at Arlington, but Lee spends most of the evening by himself, walking the grounds and later upstairs in his bedroom. Mrs. Lee reportedly hears him pacing for hours, several times kneeling in prayer.[6]

April 20, Saturday (Arlington): In the very early hours of the morning Lee writes his resignation from the U.S. Army, sending a very succinct one-sentence letter of resignation to Secretary of War Simon Cameron. In a longer letter to Gen. Scott, Lee writes "save in defense of my native state, I never desire again to draw my sword" and thanks Scott for all he has done for Lee. This letter is delivered to Scott by Perry Parks, one of the Arlington slaves. Lee writes also to his brother Smith, sister Anne Marshall in Baltimore, and cousin Roger Jones informing them of his decision.[7]

---

4 Freeman, *Lee*, vol. 1, 435; Emory M. Thomas, *Robert E. Lee* (New York, 1995), 187-8; Burke Davis, *Gray Fox* (New York, 1956), 12-3; Robert K. Krick, *Civil War Weather in Virginia* (Tuscaloosa, AL, 2007), 23.

5 Freeman, *Lee*, vol. 1, 435-8, 633-6; J. William Jones, *Personal Reminiscences, Letters, and Anecdotes of Gen. Robert E. Lee* (New York, 1875), 141; Elizabeth B. Pryor, "Thou Knowest Not the Time of Thy Visitation," *Virginia Magazine of History and Biography*, vol. 119, no. 3, 289. The meeting with Blair occurred at his son Montgomery Blair's residence at 1651 Pennsylvania Ave., on Lafayette Square. William Allan, "Memoranda of Conversations with General Robert E. Lee," in Gary W. Gallagher, ed., *Lee the Soldier* (Lincoln, NE, 1996), 10, 20. Scott's aide Col. E. D. Townsend attempted to leave Lee and Scott alone to confer in Scott's second floor office but Scott requested him to stay. Freeman, *Lee*, vol 1, 636-7. Scott told Lee "You have made the greatest mistake of your life but I feared it would be so." Davis, *Gray Fox*, 13-4. Lee's daughter wrote that Secretary of State William Seward and Secretary of War Simon Cameron also met with Lee (her phrasing suggests that they were present with Gen. Scott), but Lee wrote that he met only with Blair and Scott. Pryor, "Thou Knowest Not the Time," 289. Appendix 1-1 in Freeman *Lee* vol. 1 examines the offer of command extended to Lee.

6 Agnes to Mildred, April 19, 1861, Coulling papers, W&L; Freeman, *Lee*, vol. 1, 439; Davis, *Gray Fox*, 15; William J. Johnson, *Robert E. Lee the Christian* (Arlington Heights, IL, 1993), 61; Murray H. Nelligan, *Custis-Lee Mansion: The Robert E. Lee Memorial* (Washington, DC, 1962), 19, 37; George L. Upshur, "General Robert E. Lee and Arlington," Jan. 19, 1932, George L. Upshur papers, UNC. Upshur's dramatic account has been widely accepted by authors for decades, but much of it is called into question by the discovery of an account of this period written by Lee's eldest daughter Mary. See Pryor, "Thou Knowest Not the Time."

7 Upshur, "Lee and Arlington," Upshur papers; Nelligan, *Custis-Lee Mansion*, 19; R.E. Lee to Simon Cameron, April 20, 1861, RG-94, Records of the Adjutant General, NA; Freeman, *Lee*, vol. 1, 440-1; Jones, *Personal Reminiscences of REL*, 138-40; REL to Roger Jones, April 20, 1861, REL papers, VHS; Pryor, "Thou Knowest Not the Time," 290. Sidney Smith Lee joined the Confederate Navy, though with a much less distinguished career than his brother. Roger Jones did not resign from the Army although two of his brothers, Catesby and Charles, both served in the Confederate Navy. Mrs. Lee wrote that this decision was "the severest struggle of his life to resign a commission he had held for more than 30 years." Robert E. L. deButts, Jr., ed., "Mary Custis Lee's 'Reminiscences of the War,'" *VMHB*, vol. 109, no. 3, 314. One writer proposed that it was Orton Williams who carried Lee's letter directly to Gen. Scott, but Mary's letter clearly

Immediately after finishing breakfast Henry Daingerfield of Alexandria and another man come to Arlington to meet with Lee. The three men retire into his office, where they inform Lee of the riot that occurred in Baltimore the previous day and show him a copy of the Baltimore *Sun*. Lee passes the newspaper on to his daughter Mary because it contains an account of the killing of her friend Robert W. Davis in the riots. After the visitors depart, Lee calls his wife and daughters into his office and reads to them a copy of his letter to Scott. He is met with silence, which he interprets to mean they think he has done wrong. Daughter Mary eventually breaks the silence, telling him, "I don't think you have done wrong at all."

Several visitors from Washington ride to Arlington, but Lee does not see any of them. Cousin Orton Williams, who is serving on Gen. Winfield Scott's staff, arrives in the afternoon and tells the family that Lee's resignation has caused quite a stir in the nation's capital, and that Gen. Scott took it particularly hard— laying on a sofa and refusing to see anyone, "mourn[ing] as for the loss of a son." During the afternoon, Lee's eldest son, George Washington Custis, arrives to discuss his future course with the U. S. Army. Lee gets a message from Judge John Robertson of Richmond requesting an audience with him, to which Lee replies that he will meet Robertson at 1:00 p.m. the next day in Alexandria. The Alexandria *Gazette* promptly publishes an editorial urging Virginia officials in Richmond to immediately appoint Robert E. Lee as the head of the commonwealth's military forces.[8]

April 21, Sunday (Arlington/Alexandria): Upon going to Alexandria in the morning, Lee learns of a prevalent rumor then circulating that he had been arrested upon resigning. The Lees attend service at Christ Church in Alexandria in the morning. Lee waits in the churchyard for Judge Robertson, who he is supposed to meet with him at 1:00 p.m.; Robertson, however, has been detained in Washington, where he meets with Gen. Winfield Scott in a failed attempt to lure the aging general to follow the state of Virginia.[9]

Lee goes for a walk after church with his cousin Cassius F. Lee, discussing the political situation and Lee's future. Afterward, Lee joins his daughter who went to the nearby home of John Lloyd to wait for her father; upon departing Lee requests a kiss from Lloyd's daughter who refuses unless Lee promises to take command of the state's forces. With no word from Judge Robertson, the Lees return to Arlington.

After dark, Judge Robertson sends word to Arlington that Governor Letcher wants to see Lee in Richmond the next day. Lee replies that he will join Robertson at the train station in Alexandria the next morning to go to Richmond together. Virginia's "Council of Three"—comprised of Francis H. Smith, Matthew F. Maury, and Judge John J. Allen—advise Governor

---

states that the letter was entrusted to Perry. Richard B. McCaslin, *Lee in the Shadow of Washington* (Baton Rouge, LA, 2001), 73-4.

8 Upshur, "Lee and Arlington," Upshur papers; Pryor, "Thou Knowest Not the Time," 290; Mary P. Coulling, *The Lee Girls*, (Winston-Salem, NC, 1987), 82-3; Thomas, *Lee*, 188; George G. Kundahl, *Alexandria Goes to War: Beyond Robert E. Lee* (Knoxville, TN, 2004), 26. The Lee family was largely anti-secession; daughter Mary was the only one of the immediate family who leaned toward secession. She wrote an account in late 1870 or early 1871 for Charles Marshall of her father's struggles with secession and his resignation which changes much of what has been accepted as fact about Lee during these few days in April 1861. Elizabeth Pryor used this letter as the basis for her article in *VMHB* cited above (the article includes Mary's letter verbatim). Mary wrote that Lee made it clear to his family that he made his decision to resign *before* learning of the Baltimore riot and that it played no role in his decision. Custis was at the time a first lieutenant in the Corps of Engineers, stationed at Fort Washington on the Maryland shore of the Potomac.

9 Pryor, "Thou Knowest Not the Time," 291; Freeman, *Lee*, vol. 1, 445-6; John Robertson to John Letcher, April 23, 1861, Executive Papers of Governor John Letcher, LVA. Mary did not specify who went with Lee to Alexandria but makes it clear that it was more than just her and her father as has previously been accepted. She also mentioned that the rumor of Lee's arrest caused her brother William Henry Fitzhugh "Rooney" Lee to detain several Northern boats and their crews at his Pamunkey River estate White House, east of Richmond. Her account also suggests that Judge Robertson did not begin looking for Lee until the 21st rather than on the 20th as has long been accepted. The end of her account is missing so it is impossible to gauge her version of Judge Robertson. Pryor, "Thou Knowest Not the Time,"289-91. It is not known exactly who accompanied Lee to church, as various accounts have different daughters with him; it was likely Agnes and/or Mary. Elizabeth B. Pryor, *Reading the Man: A Portrait of Robert E. Lee Through His Private Letters* (New York, 2008), 294.

Letcher to make Lee the commander of Virginia's military forces.[10]

April 22, Monday (Arlington/Alexandria/ Richmond): Lee leaves Arlington and joins Robertson at the Orange & Alexandria station in Alexandria. Robertson discusses Lee joining Virginia's forces, but does not mention Letcher's offer of the supreme command. Lee makes short public appearances along the way at Orange, Culpeper, Gordonsville, and Louisa.

Upon arriving in Richmond in late afternoon, he and Robertson are met by Virginia Adjutant General William H. Richardson, who escorts Lee to the Spotswood Hotel. Lee meets with Governor Letcher and accepts command of the state's forces. A large crowd gathers at the Spotswood in the evening calling for Lee to make a speech; Richmond Mayor Joseph Mayo emerges and tells the crowd that Lee is too busy at present to do so.[11]

April 23, Tuesday (Richmond): Lee establishes his Richmond headquarters and issues General Order [GO] 1, announcing himself as major general commanding Virginia's forces. He is interrupted by a delegation of the state's secession convention led by Marmaduke Johnson, who escorted Lee to the Capitol about noon. The group arrives early and waits in the Rotunda outside the House of Delegates chamber around the George Washington statue, where Lee tells one of the group, "I hope we have seen the last of secession." Lee enters the chamber where convention president John Janney reads an eloquent address welcoming him, after which Lee is formally given command. He humbly replies, "I would have much preferred your choice fallen upon an abler man. Trusting in Almighty God, an approving conscience, and the aid of my fellow citizens, I devote myself to the service of my native State, in whose behalf alone will I ever again draw my sword."[12]

---

10 Ludwell Lee Montague, ed., "Memoir of Mrs. Harriotte Lee Taliaferro Concerning Events in Virginia, April 11-21, 1861," *VMHB* (Oct. 1949), vol. 57, no. 4, 419-20; Coulling, *Lee Girls*, 83; Freeman, *Lee*, vol. 1, 445-7; Thomas, *Lee*, 188-9; Davis, *Gray Fox*, 17-8; John Robertson to Letcher, April 23, 1861, Letcher papers, LVA; Mary Lindsey, *Historic Homes and Landmarks of Alexandria, Virginia* (Alexandria, VA, 1962), 11; *The War of the Rebellion: A Compilation of the Official Records of the Union and Confederate Armies*, 128 vols. (Washington, DC, 1880-1901), Series 1, vol. 51, pt. 2, 21 (hereafter *OR*; all references are to Series 1 unless otherwise indicated). One of Cassius's daughters wrote 40 years later that Lee was approached in the churchyard by a delegation from Richmond. Sarah L. Lee, "War Time in Alexandria, Virginia," *South Atlantic Quarterly* (Winter 1905), 235. John Lloyd's wife was a Lee cousin and the Lees often visited the Lloyd residence at 220 N Washington St. after church; the building today houses the Office of Historic Alexandria. The "Council of Three" served as Governor Letcher's advisory council.

11 Freeman, *Lee*, vol. 1, 448, 462-4; Robertson to Letcher, April 23, 1861, Letcher papers, LVA; Davis, *Gray Fox*, 17-8; Patricia J. Hurst, *Soldiers, Stories, Sites and Fights: Orange County, Virginia 1861-1865 and the Aftermath* (Rapidan, VA, 1998), 10; J. William Jones, *Life & Letters of Gen. Robert Edward Lee* (Harrisonburg, VA, 1986), 136-7; Richmond *Dispatch*, April 23, 1861; Thomas, *Lee*, 189-91. Although Lee went to Alexandria and Washington after the war, there is no evidence he ever returned to Arlington. According to Freeman, Gov. Letcher sent a messenger to Lee on the 21st informing him of his selection to command, but the message never reached Lee. *Lee*, vol. 1, 463-4. It has been proposed Lee must have known the reason for the summons to Richmond and possibly had already agreed to command Virginia's army. Alan T. Nolan, *Lee Considered: General Robert E. Lee and Civil War History* (Chapel Hill, NC, 1991), 42-5. An observer at Culpeper noted: "The train arrived, the crowd surged around it, with enthusiastic calls for 'Lee, Lee.' At first he declined to appear, but the call was so persistent that he had to yield. He appeared on the rear platform of the coach, dressed in citizen's apparel.... He simply bowed to the crowd, said no word, re-entered the car, and the train passed on." W. W. Scott, "Some Personal Memories of General Robert E. Lee," *William and Mary Quarterly* (Oct. 1906), vol. 6, no. 4, 280. Richardson, a War of 1812 veteran, served as Virginia's AG for decades. Jennings C. Wise, *The Military History of the Virginia Military Institute from 1839 to 1865* (Lynchburg, VA, 1915), 50. The popular Spotswood Hotel was located at the intersection of 8th Street and Main Street in Richmond. It is uncertain whether the meeting with Gov. Letcher occurred in the capitol building or at the adjacent Governor's Mansion. William Seale, *Virginia's Executive Mansion* (Richmond, VA, 1988), 70-1.

12 Thomas, *Lee*, 191-4; Davis, *Gray Fox*, 20-2; *OR* 2, 775-6; *OR* 51, pt. 2, 27; Jones, *Personal Reminiscences of REL*, 140-1; William P. Snow, *Lee and His Generals* (New York, 1996), 42-4; Armistead L. Long, *Memoirs of Robert E. Lee* (Secaucus, NJ, 1983), 96-8. Freeman put Lee's initial office at either the city post office or the old state General Court building, and moving to Mechanics Hall very soon thereafter, possibly within only a few days. *Lee*, vol. 1, 464, 489. Jeffry Wert wrote that Lee was at Mechanics Hall "within three days of his appointment." Jeffry D. Wert, "Lee's First Year of the War," in *Robert E. Lee: Recollections and Vignettes with an Appraisal by Glenn Tucker* (no place, no date), no pagination. Mechanics Hall was at the corner of 9th and Bank streets; it later became the Confederate War Department and was destroyed in

After the ceremony, around 1:00 p.m., Alexander Stephens, the vice president of the Confederate States of America, meets with Governor Letcher, Lee, the Council of Three, and most of the convention members to discuss Virginia joining the Confederacy. Lee then returns to his office, where he receives a summons from Stephens to discuss Virginia's military situation. In the evening Lee goes to the vice president's room at the Ballard House, where the Georgian explains that since Virginia will be joining the Confederacy, Lee will very soon have no command as its troops will fall under the command of the new Confederacy and its officers, rather than Virginia state officers. A band comes to the Spotswood to serenade Lee, unaware he is away at the Ballard House.[13]

April 24, Wednesday (Richmond): Lee begins planning for the defense of Virginia's rivers and discusses a defensive-only posture with Governor Letcher. In the morning Lee meets with cousin Charles Lee Jones regarding a commission in Virginia's forces. He sends instructions to Brigadier General Daniel Ruggles at Fredericksburg to act solely on defensive, and to Brig. Gen. Philip St. George Cocke at Alexandria placing batteries along the Potomac River and Aquia Creek under his command, but reiterates that Cocke is to act solely on the defensive: "Let it be known that you intend no attack, but invasion of our soil will be considered an act of war." Cocke replies that he can remove channel markers and other navigational aids along the Potomac River without military force. Lee is in favor of this, as it will solidify the blockade of the Potomac, but he refers the final decision to Governor Letcher. Lee accepts via telegram General P. G. T. Beauregard's offer of two shot furnaces from Charleston for use on the Potomac. Rain.[14]

April 25, Thursday (Richmond): Lee's resignation from the U.S. Army becomes official and Virginia temporarily joins the Confederacy, pending public vote May 23. Lee writes to his friend and former mentor Andrew Talcott—now serving as Virginia's chief engineer—regarding the defenses in and around Norfolk and the important naval facilities there. Virginia's chief of ordnance Col. Charles Dimmock informs Lee that the Richmond Arsenal cannot provide heavy artillery at present and that such must come from the supplies recently captured at Norfolk. Lee, however, deems it "not safe" at present to move heavy artillery from Norfolk to the Potomac. He submits to the governor a list of officers with recommended ranks for service in the state's armed forces, including Joseph E. Johnston as major general, John B. Magruder and Robert S. Garnett as colonels, and Henry Heth and Richard S. Ewell as

---

the evacuation fire April 2-3, 1865. Lee had no staff or aides at this time and wrote GO1 himself. Marmaduke Johnson was former commonwealth's attorney and later commanded an artillery battery in the Army of Northern Virginia. Michael B. Chesson, *Richmond After the War: 1865-1900* (Richmond, VA, 1981), 21.

13 Thomas, *Lee*, 191-4; Davis, *Gray Fox*, 20-2; *OR* 1, Series 4, 242; Stanley F. Horn, *The Robert E. Lee Reader* (New York, 1949), 108-9; Myrta L. Avary, ed., *Recollections of Alexander H. Stephens* (New York, 1910), 80; REL notes, Robert W. Winston papers, UNC. The best account of the ceremony for Lee's acceptance of command is in Snow, *Lee and His Generals*, 42-4. That ceremony was the first time Alexander Stephens met Lee; following their discussion that evening, Stephens wrote of Lee: "I had admired him in the morning, but I took his hand that night at parting with feelings of respect and almost reverence, never yet effaced." Horn, *Lee Reader,* 109.

14 George W. Munford to REL, April 23, 1861, Letcher papers, LVA; Charles Lee Jones to REL, April 24, 1861, Letcher papers, LVA; *OR* 2, 777-8; *OR* 51, pt. 2, 30; Krick, *CW Weather*, 21. Lee's defensive proposal centered around Alexandria and not provoking Lincoln into sending troops to seize Arlington Heights and Alexandria; it then grew into a larger overall defensive strategy. Lee very likely recognized that it was only a matter of time before Alexandria and Arlington Heights would be seized, given their proximity to Washington and the fact that guns placed around Arlington could shell the capital city. Charles Lee Jones was the former adjutant general of the Washington, D.C., militia and had commanded the DC battalion during the Mexican War. Lee recommended Jones for a lieutenant colonel's commission but for now unknown reasons it was not issued. Jones became all but destitute during the war and multiple times sought positions with the Confederate government, but rumors of drunkenness seem to have intervened. See Jones's Confederate Civilian File, NA. Ruggles was a native of Massachusetts but married into a Virginia family; he spent most of the war in the western theater. Ezra J. Warner, *Generals in Gray: Lives of the Confederate Commanders* (Baton Rouge, LA, 1959), 265-6. Cocke was from Fluvanna County, VA, and a noted agriculturist; he resigned in late 1861 and committed suicide Dec. 26, 1861. Warner, *Generals in Gray,* 56-7. Letcher ultimately approved removing navigational aids along the Potomac.

lieutenant colonels. Garnett is then assigned to Lee as his first staff officer.[15]

Lee writes to Richmond attorney James Lyons declining his offer to serve on Lee's staff, telling him "Nothing is organized yet. My personal staff will necessarily be small" and must be qualified to hold their positions and free up the commanding general for other tasks. Lee receives a letter from Peter V. Daniel, Jr., president of the Richmond, Fredericksburg & Potomac Railroad, detailing what his railroad can do for the war effort. Impressed with Daniel's ideas, Lee recommends that the letter be distributed to all railroads.

Lee receives a letter from his cousin Cassius Lee which reads in part: "I hoped your connection with the Virginia forces . . . might lead to some peaceful settlement of our difficulties. I hoped this from the friendship between yourself and Gen. Scott. I . . . offer my earnest prayer that God may make you instrumental in saving our land from this dreadful strife." Cassius encloses a letter from a friend which reads in part "Col. Lee . . . might, by God's blessing, bring peace to our distracted country. O how my heart leaped at the thought. How many thousands, yea millions, would rise up to bless the man that should bring this to pass. . . . Should Col. Lee be a leader in this matter or place his native state in this grand position . . . he will have an honor never reached by Napoleon or Wellington." Lee replies to Cassius's letter regretting that he cannot give his nephew a position on his staff, but also regretful that he could not spend more time with Cassius before leaving for Richmond. He also writes to his wife hoping that war can yet be avoided, "to resist aggression and allow time to allay the passions and permit Reason to resume her sway," and if it cannot that the South's best hope for success is to act on the defensive.[16]

April 26, Friday (Richmond): Col. Garnett assumes his duties as Gen. Lee's adjutant, taking over the drafting of orders and handling much of Lee's outgoing correspondence. At Lee's request, Navy lieutenant John M. Brooke is also assigned to his staff as a naval aide, and Major James R. Crenshaw assumes charge of the general's commissary department.

Lee sends instructions to Maj. Gen. Kenton Harper, commanding at Harpers Ferry, regarding the arms and armory machinery there, and orders Lt. Col. D.A. Langhorne to take command at Lynchburg and prepare a camp for the garrison and incoming recruits. Lee submits another recommended list of officers to Governor Letcher, including Samuel Jones as lieutenant colonel and Lunsford Lomax as captain. He names Walter Gwynn as commander at Norfolk and Joseph Johnston as commander at Richmond, and meets with D. G. Duncan of the Confederate War Department, urging restraint as Virginia's forces are nowhere near combat ready and that Maryland is "helpless" to join the Confederacy. Lee sends a circular to the heads of all the railroads in the state, outlining steps he would like to see them all adopt for the safety of the railroads and their cooperation in the defense of Virginia. Lee writes to Mary that she must leave Arlington immediately, taking the Washington family pieces from Mount Vernon with her— "war is

---

15 Frederick Maurice, *Robert E. Lee: The Soldier* (New York, 1925), 55; Freeman, *Lee*, vol. 1, 442, 487; *OR* 2, 781; Charles Dimmock to REL, April 25, 1861, Charles Dimmock, Compiled Service Record, NA; *OR* 51, pt. 2, 35-6, 38-9; Robert S. Garnett CSR. Andrew Talcott was one of the U.S. Army's most gifted engineers before resigning in the mid-1830s to pursue a railroad career, including construction of the Richmond & Danville Railroad in the 1840s. Talcott was a native of Connecticut, but did not fight during the war apart from assisting Lee in the early weeks of the war in his role as Virginia's chief engineer; instead Talcott went to Mexico to work on a railroad there to avoid having to choose sides. One of his sons, Charles, was superintendent of the Richmond & Danville during the war, and another of his sons, Thomas, served on Lee's staff and later was colonel of the 1st CS Engineer Regiment. This Charles Dimmock should not be confused with his son of the same name, who was a noted Confederate engineer and laid out the defensive lines around Petersburg, VA. Garnett was Lee's adjutant when he was West Point superintendent. It is possible that Lee met with Col. J. T. L. Preston of VMI on this date regarding how the institute would function during hostilities. See Randolph R. Shaffner, *The Father of Virginia Military Institute: A Biography of Colonel J. T. L. Preston, CSA* (Jefferson, NC, 2014), 139.

16 REL to James Lyons, April 25, 1861, Robert A. Brock collection, Huntington Library; *OR* 1, Series 4, 240-1; Cassius F. Lee to REL, April 23, 1861, Lee papers, SH; James May to Cassius F. Lee, April 22, 1861, Lee papers, SH; REL to Cassius F. Lee, April 25, 1861, Lee papers, SH; Johnson, *Lee the Christian*, 68-9. James Lyons was a former member of the Virginia legislature, and served in the Confederate Congress later in the war. On this date Lieutenant Walter H. Taylor wrote to his uncle in Richmond seeking a staff position. WHT to Richard Taylor, April 25, 1861, Letcher papers, VHS. One week later Taylor was assigned to Lee's staff.

inevitable [and] there is no telling when it will burst around you."¹⁷

April 27, Saturday (Richmond): Lee focuses on Harpers Ferry, meeting with Governor Letcher and Col. Thomas J. Jackson regarding the latter's assignment to command there. Col. Dimmock gives his recommendations to Lee regarding the removal of the valuable firearms manufacturing machinery at Harpers Ferry, and for the organization of the state's ordnance department. Lee gives Jackson written instructions to organize the troops at the ferry into battalions under their senior captains until field officers are appointed, and to send the arsenal machinery to Richmond.

In response to concerns from residents of the lower Shenandoah Valley over their safety, Lee writes to several prominent citizens of that area that Jackson has been ordered to take command at Harpers Ferry and will organize the assortment of companies and militia officers there. Lee issues orders regarding responsibility for the state's artillery, placing Dimmock in charge of all field ordnance and Capt. George Minor of the Virginia Navy in charge of all fixed position ordnance. Lee inquires of Governor Letcher where and how he is to procure horses and wagons. Joseph R. Anderson, head of Richmond's Tredegar Iron Works, offers Lee the use of his family's pew at St. Paul's Episcopal Church.¹⁸

April 28, Sunday (Richmond): Lee meets with Armistead T. M. Rust of Loudoun County who was referred by Cassius regarding a commission. He relieves Kenton Harper and his militia from duty at Harpers Ferry with Jackson now in command of the post and instructs that all weapons taken from the armory by the militia are to be turned over to Jackson. U.S. Brig. Gen. William S. Harney arrives in Richmond as a prisoner in the evening and visits with Lee.¹⁹

17 Freeman, *Lee*, vol. 1, 489; George M. Brooke, Jr., *John M. Brooke: Naval Scientist and Educator* (Charlottesville, VA, 1980), 228; Robert E. L. Krick, *Staff Officers in Gray: A Biographical Register of the Staff Officers in the Army of Northern Virginia* (Chapel Hill, NC, 2003), 105; OR 2, 781-3; OR 51, pt. 2, 39-41; "Circular to Railroad Presidents," April 26, 1861, Records of the Virginia Forces, RG-109, NA; Clifford Dowdey and Louis H. Manarin, eds., *The Wartime Papers of R. E. Lee* (New York, 1961), 12-3. Garnett likely began working with Lee on the 25th, although he was not officially announced until today; at least one letter on the 25th was written and signed by him. Garnett to Kenton Harper, April 25, 1861, VAF, NA. Crenshaw served as a department head only briefly, as he was gone by July 1 when he became lieutenant colonel of the 15th VA; he later became a Confederate commissary agent in the Bahamas. Krick, *Staff Officers in Gray*, 105. Harper was appointed colonel of the 5th Va. Inf. in May; he resigned in September to return home to be with his dying wife. Bruce S. Allardice, *More Generals in Gray* (Baton Rouge, LA, 2005), 117. Daniel A. Langhorne became lieutenant colonel of the 42nd VA. Robert K. Krick, *Lee's Colonels: A Biographical Register of the Field Officers of the Army of Northern Virginia* (Dayton, OH, 1996), 230. Gwynn came from one of Virginia's oldest families, a 10-year army veteran, and a very accomplished antebellum railroad engineer. Allardice, *More Generals in Gray*, 110. Lee was almost daily sending to the governor lists of recommendations for officers commissions–only the noteworthy highlights from these lists are mentioned here. Mary's father inherited much of his grandparents'–George and Martha Washington–furnishings from Mount Vernon. Lee feared for the safety of these items if left behind at Arlington, as their Washington connection would surely make them targets for souvenir hunters. It was very likely on this date when Lee met with Joe Johnston; but as Johnston gives no date for the meeting, it could have occurred on the 25th. Joseph E. Johnston, *Narrative of Military Operations during the Civil War* (New York, 1990), 12. Brooke wrote at this time, "Gen. Lee is a second Washington if there ever was one." Brooke, *John M. Brooke*, 228.

18 Undated clipping of Richmond *Whig*, acc # 23476bb, LVA; Dimmock to REL, April 27, 1861, Dimmock CSR; OR 2, 784-5; REL to Robert Conrad, James Marshall, Edmund Pendleton, Hugh Nelson & Alfred Barbour, April 27, 1861, REL papers, MOC; OR 51, pt. 2, 49; OR 2, 784; J. R. Anderson to REL, April 27, 1861, Letcher papers, LVA. Jackson was at this time stationed at Camp Lee in Richmond with the cadets from the Virginia Military Institute. It is possible that Francis H. Smith, superintendent of VMI and one of the governor's "Council of Three," and/or Adjutant General Richardson also were included in the meeting with Jackson–the wording of the original article is vague in this regard. Undated clipping of Richmond *Whig*, acc # 23476bb, LVA. Garnett must have erred in the numbering for General Orders because he issued GO3 twice: once on the 26th announcing Joe Johnston's command of Richmond, and the orders concerning Dimmock and Minor on the 27th are also headed as GO3. St. Paul's is located on Grace St. at the northeast corner of Capitol Square; Lee and Jefferson Davis often attended service there during the war.

19 Cassius Lee to REL, April 27, 1861, Letcher papers, LVA; OR 2, 786-7; Richmond *Daily Dispatch*, May 6, 1861. Rust was colonel of the 57th VA Militia and was subsequently appointed colonel of the 19th VA Inf.; he later served as a military judge in the Department of Southwest Virginia. Rust CSR. Harney was captured at Harpers Ferry on the 25th, en route to Washington from Missouri by rail; he and Lee knew each other from the antebellum army. Upon Harney's

April 29, Monday (Richmond): Lee's trunk with much of his clothing and his sword arrive from Arlington. He instructs Col. Talcott to lay out defensive works on the James River at Burwell's Bay near Smithfield, and more works at the mouth of the Appomattox River near City Point, assisted by Capt. H. H. Cocke and Lt. Catesby Ap. R Jones of the Navy. Lee instructs Maj. Powhatan R. Page to muster in the companies from Gloucester County and assist with the fortifications at Gloucester Point.

Turning his attention to western Virginia, the general orders Maj. Alonzo Loring at Wheeling and Maj. Francis M. Boykin at Grafton to raise whatever troops they can in their respective vicinities and to do all they can to protect the Baltimore & Ohio Railroad, and Lt. Col. John McCausland to raise a regiment in the Kanawha Valley. All three officers are reminded that they are to act on the defensive only.[20]

Lee's efforts at organizing the troops are hampered by ignorance of military regulations among the volunteers, which leads to the issuance today of several General Orders: GO4—regarding the proper filing of returns with Richmond; GO5—regarding the authorization and keeping of records for all expenditures; GO6—announcing Lt. Col. Henry Heth as quartermaster general and Maj. James Crenshaw as commissary general. In the afternoon Lee receives an invitation to dinner from a Mr. Rutherford, but due to the hour at which it was received he declines. Lee's "personal effects and uniforms" are shipped by Adams Express from Alexandria to Richmond by order of Gen. Scott and at the expense of the U.S. Army.[21]

April 30, Tuesday (Richmond): Lee receives a request from Governor Letcher for a report on the number of the state's forces; in reply Lee concedes that he only has that information for Harpers Ferry, but hopes to have it from all other points in a few days.

Lee receives authorization to issue state arms to whatever parties he deems necessary and subsequently issues instructions to Dimmock to send small arms and artillery to the Kanawha Valley. Lee asks Gen. Gwynn at Norfolk if defenses are planned for the mouth of the Nansemond River as it affords an avenue of approach to the Navy Yard.[22]

Lee writes to Talcott offering him a commission in Virginia's forces, and that he will defer to Talcott's discretion for placement of defenses along the James. Lee also mentions having a conversation with Talcott's son Charles today. Lee places Lt. Col. William Mahone in charge of a battery at Burwell's Bay and mustering a regiment to garrison it, and instructs Maj. John P. Wilson to do likewise for Fort Powhatan. Lee orders the withdrawal of all Confederate troops from between Long

---

arrival in Richmond, Letcher ordered his immediate release and offered a guard to escort him to Washington, which Harney declined. Harney, one of only four generals in the antebellum army, was a native Tennessean—his arrival in Virginia sparked rumors he would join the Confederacy. It is possible that Lee broached the subject with him; however, Harney returned to his command in Missouri and retired in 1863. Ezra J. Warner, *Generals in Blue: Lives of the Union Commanders* (Baton Rouge, LA, 1999), 208-9; Richmond *Daily Dispatch*, May 6, 1861. Lee very likely attended church at St. Paul's in the morning, but there is no concrete evidence of this, only Anderson's offer of his pew on the 27th.

20 Dowdey, *Wartime Papers*, 14-5; REL to P. R. Page, April 29, 1861, VAF, NA; *OR* 2, 788; REL to Boykin, April 29, 1861, Francis M. Boykin papers, VMI. Page's regiment became the 26th VA; he was killed at Petersburg, June 17, 1864. Krick, *Lee's Colonels*, 296. Boykin was major and later lieutenant colonel of the 31st VA; he lost his position in the Spring 1862 reorganization and later commanded a company in the 25th VA Battalion. Krick, *Lee's Colonels*, 64-5. McCausland was a professor at VMI; his regiment would be designated the 36th VA, with him as colonel. He was later promoted to brigadier general and is most noted for burning Chambersburg, PA, in July 1864. Warner, *Generals in Gray*, 197-8.

21 GO4 & GO6, April 29, 1861, Boykin papers, VMI; *OR* 51, pt. 2, 52-3; REL to "Mr. Rutherford," April 29, 1861, REL papers, W&L; Adams Express Company receipt, April 29, 1862, (Acc. #2004.20.14) Clarke County Historical Association. Heth offered his services to Jefferson Davis on the 17th; Davis noted in his endorsement that Heth was a "first rate soldier" and worthy of "special attention." Heth to Davis, April 17, 1861, Heth CSR. Heth succeeded William Mahone as quartermaster, who was appointed on or about the 23rd, but Mahone may never have actually performed the duties of the office before he was reassigned. William Mahone biographical sketch, William Mahone papers, VMI. The identity of "Mr. Rutherford" is not known.

22 REL to Letcher, April 30, 1861, VAF, NA; *OR* 51, pt. 2, 54-6; *OR* 2, 791. Apparently Lee lacked copies of nearly every form used in the army except muster rolls, as Garnett wrote to Confederate Adjutant General Samuel Cooper on this date requesting copies "of each of the forms" the AG supplied. Garnett to Cooper, April 30, 1861, VAF, NA.

Bridge and Alexandria. Maj. Robert Johnston joins Lee's staff.

Lee writes to Mary, again urging her to leave Arlington immediately with what she can, and that he has told their youngest son Robert Jr. to remain in school for the present rather than enlist.[23]

---

23 REL to Talcott, April 30, 1861, Talcott papers, VHS; REL to Mahone, April 30, 1861, VAF, NA; REL to J. P. Wilson, April 30, 1861, VAF, NA; Jed Hotchkiss, *Virginia*–vol. 3 in Clement Evans, ed., *Confederate Military History* (Secaucus, NJ, 1975), 92; Krick, *Staff Officers in Gray*, 174; Dowdey, *Wartime Papers*, 15. Wilson commanded what became the 5th VA Battalion and later served in the 9th and 13th VA regiments. Krick, *Lee's Colonels*, 402. Johnston remained on Lee's staff only until mid-June when he was appointed colonel of the 3rd VA Cav. Krick, *Staff Officers in Gray*, 174. Rob was a student at the University of Virginia; he eventually joined the Rockbridge Artillery and later served on his brother Rooney's staff.

May 1861

Robert E. Lee settled into his role as commander of Virginia's forces that May. His was a daunting task, however, because of supply shortages and poorly trained officers and men. Lee was in essence building an army from scratch while at the same time scraping together troops to defend strategic points. None were more important than Norfolk with its Gosport Navy Yard, and Harpers Ferry and the Federal arsenal there. The heavy guns captured at Norfolk were vital to river and coastal defense, and its shipbuilding facilities were critical to the nascent Virginia and Confederate navies. Although the weapons captured at Harpers Ferry helped arm the influx of volunteers, more important was the machinery for the production of more firearms. The town of Harpers Ferry itself was indefensible because of the surrounding mountains that commanded the place, but Lee knew it had to be held long enough for the vital machinery to be removed. Accordingly, these two points received priority. Lee described his own efforts: "Since my arrival I have used every exertion to organize troops and prepare resistance against immediate invasion, which has appeared imminent, and as almost everything had to be created except the guns found at the Gosport Navy Yard, these preparations have absorbed all the means I can command."[1]

Lee's staff began to come together; joining him in May were Walter H. Taylor, John A. Washington, and Francis W. Smith. Of his new staff duties, Taylor wrote:

> There is a great difference between my present work and what I was required to at [the] bank; I now begin in the morning after breakfast and am kept constantly at it until 10 or 11, only allowing myself intermission for meals. The most amusing part of it is that 'tis all for Love and Glory; but everybody must exert themselves and make any sacrifice now for the good of the Old Commonwealth. . . . I do not object to the hard work for many reasons, not the least of which is that the General [Lee] does the same.[2]

Inspection tours took Lee away from Richmond for several days, first to Norfolk and then to Manassas. In neither instance did he like what he found, and both trips resulted in command changes. These were not the only changes. Lee also sought to replace militia commanders and officers sometimes unknown to him with men he knew he could trust. Harpers Ferry—which was first seized by Virginia militia under militia officers—was perhaps the best example of this. Lee sent Col. Thomas J. Jackson—the future "Stonewall"—to replace the militia general on site, followed by his longtime friend Brig. Gen. Joseph E. Johnston.

Federal movements around Newport News in the latter half of the month caused quite a stir as Lee and others feared that it portended an impending move against Norfolk, Yorktown, or both. He knew the troops, and in far too many cases, their commanders as well, were not ready to meet an attack in southeast Virginia or elsewhere. Lee struggled in the fight to make the politicians and the

---

1 OR 51, pt. 2, 105-6. Lee's aide Walter Taylor wrote a friend in Norfolk, "Our General is making every preparation to give our enemies a warm reception, one or two weeks more and then let them come if they dare. . . . You have greater facilities for defending yourselves than any other city or portion of the state." WHT to Eli Barron, May 13, 1861, WHT papers, NPL. Gosport was technically in Portsmouth, across the Elizabeth River from Norfolk.

2 WHT to Eli Barron, May 13, 1861, WHT papers, NPL. Lee handled very little "routine" letter writing after May 1, with Garnett and naval aides John M. Brooke and Thomas Page handling most of it.

population at large realize this. Urging caution was not a popular stance, regardless of whether it was the right one militarily.[3]

Lee's daily routine included meetings with office seekers—some known to him, others strangers—and often meetings with Governor John Letcher and his advisory council and other department heads.[4] One Richmond newspaper editor wrote of Lee during this time: "He sat almost daily in the military council with Governor Letcher and others; here performed an amount of labor that was almost incredible, yet always working with ease and exactness, and he made the reputation of a skillful organizer of armies, before he commenced the career of active commander in the field."[5]

On May 23, Virginia's voters took the commonwealth out of the Union.[6] Six days later Confederate President Jefferson Davis arrived in Richmond following a vote by the Confederate Congress to relocate the capital from Montgomery, Alabama, to Virginia.[7] Although for a brief period he was placed in command of all Confederate troops in the state, Lee's authority quickly diminished when the Confederacy's highest ranking officials arrived in Richmond.

Lee's eldest two sons followed him out of the U.S. Army and into Virginia's and, ultimately, the Confederacy's. The decision left them without a home. Because of Arlington's commanding position on the southern bank of the Potomac River overlooking Washington, the estate was seized by Federal troops on the night of the 23rd. Most of the family possessions were lost; some have never been recovered while others eventually found their way back to the family or the estate during the last century and a half.[8]

* * *

[3] One officer observed: "Lee is doing everything in his power to get things in order here but . . . I think he a little uneasy. He thinks the troops are too eager for a fight and need more discipline before they are ready." Peter W. Hairston to Fanny Hairston, May 9, 1861, P. W. Hairston papers, UNC.

[4] Although there are references to these "daily" or "almost daily" meetings, records are not extant for many of them, so only those which can be documented are included here. Lee probably saw Francis Smith and Charles Dimmock almost daily, but documentation can be found for only handful of such meetings.

[5] Edward A. Pollard, *Lee and His Lieutenants Comprising the Early Life, Public Services, and Campaigns of General Robert E. Lee and His Companions in Arms* (New York, 1867), 56-7.

[6] Long, *CW Day by Day*, 77. The vote was 96,750 for vs. 32,134 against.

[7] Ibid., 79. The decision to move the capital was made on the 20th.

[8] Allen W. Moger, "Letters to General Lee after the War," *VMHB* (Jan. 1956), 63-4. The items not looted by occupation troops were taken to the U.S. Patent Office in Washington for safe-keeping. Rooney's son George Bolling Lee described the "Mount Vernon relics," many of which were left at Arlington: "These so called 'relics' were pictures, furniture, etc. taken from Arlington at the beginning of the war and stored in Washington by the United States Government. They originally came from Mount Vernon but were in Arlington, and therefore the property of my Uncle Custis, he having inherited Arlington from his mother. These 'relics' were returned to my aunt, Mary Custis Lee, by President [William] McKinley, by the advice of his Attorney-General, and were in her possession at the time of her death." G. B. Lee to John Wayland, Dec. 18, 1935, John W. Wayland papers, Duke.

May 1, Wednesday (Richmond): One of Lee's uniform coats arrives from Arlington today. Lee directs Jackson at Harpers Ferry to call out volunteers from lower Valley counties and to be on the lookout for an attack coming from Pennsylvania; the bridge over the Potomac may be destroyed if necessary but Jackson must get the weapons and machinery removed from the arsenal as quickly as possible. Lee informs Kenton Harper that he has been appointed colonel and is to report to Jackson. Lee notifies Benjamin S. Ewell that he has been appointed major and instructs him to raise six companies from James City County and fortify a position defending Williamsburg.[9]

Lee notifies J. W. Allan, William H. Harman, and W. T. H. Baylor of their commissions in Virginia's forces and orders them all to report to Jackson at Harpers Ferry, and informs Jackson to which regiment each should be assigned. Lee requests Edward Marshall, president of the Manassas Gap Railroad, to alter the schedule on his line to coincide with that of the Orange & Alexandria and the Winchester & Potomac railroads to facilitate travel between Richmond and Harpers Ferry; Lee subsequently informs W. L. Clarke, president of the W&P, of the desire to have the trip between Richmond and Harpers Ferry take no more than 24 hours.[10]

May 2, Thursday (Richmond): Lee advises Gen. Philip Cocke that weapons and ammunition are being sent to Alexandria for his use and that he is to place Lt. Col. Algernon S. Taylor in command of the troops at that point. Cocke is also to make arrangements with Orange & Alexandria Railroad officials for the removal of locomotives and rolling stock from Alexandria and destruction of track in the event the city is evacuated. Lee learns from Dimmock that much of the vital machinery at the Harpers Ferry arsenal has not yet been removed. Instructions are sent to Gen. Gwynn at Norfolk to remove all surplus material there as an attack is feared imminent. Lee assigns Lt. Col. Robert H. Chilton as "Superintendent of the Recruiting Service" for the state's forces and charges him with assigning commands to junior officers. Lee issues orders regarding railroad company charges to transport state military personnel and supplies.[11]

An invitation arrives from Dr. J. J. Simkins of Norfolk inviting Lee to visit the city and stay with Simkins, but the general declines the invitation due to the pressing nature of his duties which "require his constant attention and presence." Lee writes to the Reverend Cornelius Walker of Alexandria's Christ Church thanking him for his good wishes. He writes also to Mary, advising her not to go to the Valley, that it is too exposed to the enemy, and requests that Perry, one of their slaves, be sent to him. Lee notes as well that he made his resignation on April 20, not the 25th which is the effective date the Army has—he refuses to accept pay for the intervening days. Lt. Walter H. Taylor is ordered to join Lee's staff as aide de camp. Custis resigns from the U.S. Army.[12]

May 3, Friday (Richmond): Governor Letcher puts out his first official call for volunteers for Virginia's armed forces. Lee has breakfast at the Spotswood, after which he informs the Governor's Council of

---

9 Dowdey, *Wartime Papers*, 17-8; REL to Jackson, May 1, 1861, VAF, NA; REL to Kenton Harper, May 1, 1861, Heritage Auctions, June 12-13, 2015 auction, lot 47567; REL to B. S. Ewell, May 1, 1861, VAF, NA. Benjamin Ewell was the older brother of Richard Ewell, and president of William & Mary College. Krick, *Lee's Colonels*, 133.

10 REL to J. W. Allan, May 1, 1861, VAF, NA; REL to W. H. Harman, May 1, 1861, VAF, NA; REL to W. T. H. Baylor, May 1, 1861, VAF, NA; REL to Jackson, May 1, 1861, VAF, NA; REL to Edward Marshall, May 1, 1861, VAF, NA; REL to W. L. Clarke, May 1, 1861, VAF, NA.

11 *OR* 2, 794-5; Dimmock to REL, May 2, 1861, Dimmock CSR; Garnett to R. H. Chilton, May 2, 1861, VAF, NA; *OR* 1 Series 4, 274-5. Algernon Taylor was a nephew of Zachary Taylor and served most of the war as a quartermaster. A. S. Taylor CSR. It is impossible to overstate Dimmock's concern for the machinery at the Harpers Ferry arsenal; his correspondence with Lee reveals his deep concern that everything of value be removed from Harpers Ferry before the town was captured or evacuated. Chilton would later join Lee's staff.

12 Garnett to J. J. Simkins, May 2, 1861, VAF, NA: Johnson, *Lee the Christian*, 71-2; Dowdey, *Wartime Papers*, 18-9; R. L. Page to WHT, WHT papers, SH; Bernice-Marie Yates, *The Perfect Gentleman*, 2 vols. (Maitland, FL, 2003), vol. 1, 213.

the necessity for a railroad connecting Winchester and Strasburg. He later has a meeting with Charles Talcott, who offers the locomotives and rolling stock of his Richmond & Danville Railroad to remove ordnance from the Norfolk Navy Yard to the state's interior. Lee orders Walter Gwynn to remove all excess guns and ammunition from the Navy Yard and mentions Talcott's offer. Gwynn and Cocke are ordered to muster companies raised in their areas into regiments.[13]

Lee informs William B. Taliaferro of his appointment as colonel and instructs him to take command at Gloucester Point and cooperate with the Navy in the construction of fortifications there. Similar notification is sent to Christopher Q. Tompkins and that he is take command of the troops being mustered in the Kanawha Valley, including those under McCausland. Lee forwards to Governor Letcher a letter from Gwynn requesting 5,000 troops to properly defend Norfolk; Lee notes that he has ordered all Georgia and Alabama troops currently in Virginia to report to Gwynn. He attempts to sort out difficulties at Norfolk between Gwynn and the naval commander, Commodore French Forrest, by putting Gwynn in overall command there, but with Forrest retaining command of all naval operations, personnel, and institutions in and around the important city. Lt. Col. John A. Washington is ordered to report to Lee as an aide de camp.[14]

May 4, Saturday (Richmond): Lee and Governor Letcher meet with Andrew Talcott. The Governor's Council requests Lee to procure a percussion cap machine from New York for state use. Lee sends instructions to Jackson to call out additional troops from the central Valley, and tells Maj. Loring that he has authority to call out troops only from counties around Wheeling. Lee orders Col. George Porterfield to take command at Grafton, and instructs Gen. Ruggles to use the troops he is mustering at Fredericksburg for defense along the lower Potomac, Rappahannock, and Aquia Creek. Lee receives a proposal from J. B. Tree of Norfolk regarding a telegraph system.[15]

---

13 Freeman, *Lee*, vol. 1, 492-3; Taylor, *General Lee*, 21; Edward Marshall to Letcher, May 3, 1861, Letcher papers, LVA; *OR* 51, pt. 2, 69; *OR* 2, 798-9. Walter Taylor first saw Lee on this date and wrote of this first encounter: "I had not previously known General Lee. I then saw him for the first time on the morning of my arrival at Richmond and before my assignment to duty. I was at breakfast at the Spotswood Hotel when he entered the room, and was at once attracted and greatly impressed by his appearance.... He appeared every inch a soldier and a man born to command." *General Lee*, 21-2. At that time a spur line, the Winchester & Potomac RR, ran from the B&O at Harpers Ferry to Winchester; the western portion of the Manassas Gap RR extended from Strasburg south to Mount Jackson. The roughly 20-mile line which Lee proposed connecting Winchester to Strasburg would not be built until 1870. Talcott's offer of the R&D to remove supplies from Norfolk is curious in that that line did not go to Norfolk, which was serviced by William Mahone's Norfolk & Petersburg RR and indirectly by the Seaboard & Roanoke RR, which Gwynn helped build in the 1830s. Nor did the R&D connect directly with either of those lines, and of the two only the N&P was the same gauge track as the R&D.

14 *OR* 2, 799-801; REL to Gwynn, May 3, 1861, VAF, NA; John A. Washington CSR. Taliaferro was a native of Gloucester County; he was commissioned colonel of the 23rd VA and rose to brigade command under Jackson in the Shenandoah Valley before being transferred to the western theater. Warner, *Generals in Gray*, 297-8. The earthworks that Taliaferro's men constructed at Gloucester Point were in part built atop British works from the 1781 siege of Yorktown; the site had been fortified in some fashion since the 17th century. A portion of the remaining earthworks is currently a county park. Martha W. McCartney, *With Reverence for the Past: Gloucester County, Virginia* (Richmond, VA, 2001), 73. Tompkins was brother of noted Confederate nurse Sally Louisa Tompkins and heavily involved in the iron business at Richmond and the Kanawha Valley. He was colonel of the 22nd VA but resigned in November 1861 over a disagreement with Brig. Gen. John B. Floyd. Krick, *Lee's Colonels*, 373-4. John Augustine Washington III was the great grand-nephew of George Washington and the last owner of Mount Vernon. When he inherited the estate in 1855 it was anything but financially stable; plagued by poor harvests and a constant stream of sightseers, Washington sold Mount Vernon to the Mount Vernon Ladies Association in 1858. Gerald W. Johnson, *Mount Vernon: The Story of a Shrine* (Mount Vernon, VA, 1991), 19-26; Millard K. Bushong, *Historic Jefferson County* (Boyce, VA, 1972), 443-4. It is not known precisely when Washington reported for duty; the first known document from Lee's HQ with his signature is dated May 2 (JAW to Anthony A. Fraser, May 2, 1861, VAF, NA) but he was not formally announced until May 13.

15 Talcott diary, May 4, 1861, VHS; T. Goldmarks to Cyrus Bradley, May 4, 1861, Letcher papers, LVA; *OR* 2, 802-3; Garnett to J. B. Tree, May 4, 1861, VAF, NA. Tree was superintendent of the Norfolk & Petersburg Telegraph Company; later in the war he became superintendent of the Southern Telegraph Co. and treasurer of the Norfolk & Petersburg RR.

Lee orders all Georgia troops in Virginia to Norfolk, and instructs Walter Taylor to report to Adjutant General Richardson for assignment to headquarters. Orton Williams comes to Arlington to warn Mary that Federal troops will seize the estate tomorrow and that she needs to pack what she can and evacuate.[16]

May 5, Sunday (Richmond): John Bell Hood reports to Lee for duty, Lee tells him "I am glad to see you. I want you to help me." Lee answers the letter of an unidentified young Northern female admirer, who requested a photo of him. He sends word to Gwynn that 25,000 of the 100,000 rounds he requested have been ordered to him, Gwynn will have to fabricate the remainder from supplies on-hand at Norfolk. Garnett issues GO10 regarding the mustering and acceptance of companies, and GO11 concerning the creation of muster rolls and issuance of arms and equipment. Mary writes to Gen. Scott thanking him for his kindness to Lee and includes a newspaper account of Lee's reception in Richmond.[17]

May 6, Monday (Richmond): Lee directs Gen. Cocke to personally see to the defense of Manassas and writes to Jackson to establish an outpost at Martinsburg, advising a move against the B&O and the Chesapeake & Ohio canal. He also suggests making contacts in Maryland to destroy the B&O bridge over the Monocacy River near Frederick or to drain the C&O canal. Col. Jubal Early is ordered to take command of all the troops being mustered at Lynchburg; Lt. Col. Langhorne is notified that Early will take command of the post. Langhorne is also advised that some of the troops he is mustering into service are intended to go to northern Virginia, and others will remain at Lynchburg. Lee orders Lt. Col. John Echols to organize a pair of regiments at Staunton from companies raised in southwestern .[18]

Gen. Ruggles is ordered to assist the Navy in establishing a battery on the Potomac and to destroy the Richmond, Fredericksburg & Potomac Railroad in the event of a withdrawal. Lee receives a proposal from Gen. John H. Cocke regarding the field uniform to be adopted by the state's forces. Rooney is commissioned as a captain. Orton Williams comes to Arlington in the morning to see Agnes; in the afternoon he is arrested when attempting to resign his commission in the U.S. Army.[19]

"The Retirement of Mr. Tree," *The Telegraph Age,* (Sept. 1903), vol. 20, No. 17, 433. Garnett informed Tree that "at present [Lee's] time is so much occupied that he is unable to examine" the proposal. Garnett to Tree, May 4, 1861, VAF, NA.

16 OR 2, 803-4; SO17, May 4, 1861, WHT papers, SH; DeButts, "Mary Lee's Reminiscences," 315. There is some confusion as to the date of Williams's warning; one writer puts it at May 1, but that seems too early. Juanita Allen, "Agnes Lee's Sweetheart: William Orton Williams, CSA," *UDC Magazine* (June/July 1992), 27. Lee's daughter Mary described the incident in detail, but did not record the date on which it occurred. As she recalled, she was painting in her room when Orton arrived and his manner was so different from his usual that it "startled" her. She was convinced that Gen. Scott had sent him to warn the family: "There was little time to deliberate. The family plate so long treasured, especially that portion of it which my father inherited from Mount Vernon was first secured, then our own, the Washington letters and papers and some small gems, family relics, and mementoes were sent into Alexandria very early in the morning to be forwarded to Richmond." DeButts, "Mary Lee's Reminiscences," 315.

17 John B. Hood, *Advance and Retreat* (New York, 1993), 16-7; Richmond *Daily Dispatch*, Aug. 13, 1861; OR 2, 804; OR 51, pt. 2, 67-8; Jones, *Life and Letters of REL*, 140. Hood later wrote of this meeting: "He had around him, it seemed to me, every cobbler in Richmond, giving them instructions as to the manner of making cartridge boxes, haversacks, bayonet scabbards, etc. He was studiously applying his great mind to this apparently trivial but most important work." *Advance and Retreat*, 16-7. Hood's biographer Richard McMurray disputed Hood's timeline, writing that this incident occurred several weeks later, probably sometime May 27-30. Richard M. McMurray, *John Bell Hood and the War for Southern Independence* (Lincoln, NE, 1992), 25, 208-9.

18 Freeman, *Lee*, vol. 1, 505; OR 2, 806-8; Dowdey, *Wartime Papers,* 20. Echols served in the 27th VA and was wounded at Kernstown March 23, 1862; he was promoted to brigadier general soon after and served in western Virginia. Warner, *Generals in Gray*, 80.

19 OR 2, 807-8; JAW to J. H. Cocke, May 6, 1861, VAF, NA; Mary B. Daughtry, *Gray Cavalier: The Life and Wars of General W. H. F. "Rooney" Lee* (New York, 2002), 53; Agnes to Annie Lee, May 10, 1861, Coulling papers, W&L. John H. Cocke

May 7, Tuesday (Richmond): Andrew Talcott meets with Lee and Governor Letcher. Lee telegraphs President Davis that Joe Johnston is ill and Lee is too busy at present to leave Richmond but Senator R. M. T. Hunter is en route to Montgomery to brief him on the situation at Norfolk. Lee also tells the president that "my commission in Virginia [is] satisfactory." Governor Letcher places Lee in command of troops from other states stationed within the borders of Virginia unless President Davis specifies otherwise. Lee advises Jackson that he can accept volunteers from Maryland if they are willing to serve in Virginia units. Lee orders Maj. John M. Patton to take command at Jamestown Island, and Col. J. B. Baldwin to muster in troops from central Virginia at Richmond. He inquires of Cocke his effective strength and reminds him that per orders that information must be submitted to headquarters by the first of each month.[20]

May 8, Wednesday (Richmond): Lee sends instructions to Col. Taliaferro at Gloucester Point that if an enemy vessel attempts to pass he is only to engage if it does not stop in response to warning shots. Lee responds to a complaint by Gen. Cocke about Lt. Col. A. S. Taylor—according to Cocke, Taylor violated orders in his evacuation of Alexandria on the 5th; Cocke wants to arrest Taylor but Lee will not allow him to do so and insists that Taylor provide an explanation before any further action is taken. Lee writes to George Mason of Alexandria attempting to assuage the fears of many in that region about the lack of troops there to defend them. He writes as well to Gen. Ruggles regarding the fortifications guarding Aquia Creek. Lee informs Col. A. G. Blanchard that Lee has been given authority over non-Virginia troops in the commonwealth and that Blanchard is to take his 1st Louisiana to reinforce Gwynn at Norfolk. He informs Confederate Adjutant General Samuel Cooper that he instructed Early and Langhorne at Lynchburg to deal only with Virginia troops, not those from other states sent there by the Confederate government in Montgomery.[21]

Lee announces the assignment of Col. John B. Magruder to command around Richmond and recommends to Governor Letcher that William Allen be allowed to resign his current commission in order to take command of a battery he raised at Jamestown Island. Lee writes to Capt. James R. Branch, thanking his company for adopting the name "Lee's Life Guard" to honor him. Lee's daughters Mary and Agnes leave Arlington and go to Ravensworth, home of their Fitzhugh cousins in nearby Fairfax County, taking along a piano and many of the paintings, wines, and other valuables. They leave behind their younger sister Mildred's kitten, Tom, who they entrust to one of the house slaves, "Uncle George." Mrs. Lee and Custis remain behind for the time being. Lee writes to his wife, grieving that they have to leave Arlington.[22]

---

was the father of Brig. Gen. Philip St. George Cocke, who was responsible for the defense of Richmond during the War of 1812. Jennifer R. Loux, "John Hartwell Cocke," *Dictionary of Virginia Biography*, www.lva.virginia.gov/public/dvb/bio.asp?b=Cocke_John_Hartwell_1780-1866. Williams's visit is likely the one Mary recalled when he advised that the planned move to seize Arlington Heights had been indefinitely postponed. DeButts, "Mary Lee's Reminiscences," 315-6.

20 Talcott diary, May 7, 1861, VHS; *OR* 51, pt. 2, 69-71; *OR* 2, 813-4; T. J. Jackson to Letcher, May 3, 1861, Alfred and Elizabeth Brand collection of Civil War and Lee family papers, Duke.

21 Dowdey, *Wartime Papers*, 21; *OR* 2, 26, 815-7; *OR* 51, pt. 2, 73. Taliaferro wrote to Lee on the 6th asking guidance in how he should proceed; his inquiry was timely as he exchanged fire with USS *Yankee* on May 9. Long, *Civil War Day by Day*, 72. It is possible Taliaferro's inquiry was prompted by an earlier encounter with the *Yankee*, as another source has it firing on Gloucester Point on May 3. John V. Quarstein, *Hampton and Newport News in the Civil War: War Comes to the Peninsula* (Lynchburg, VA, 1998), 19. Albert Blanchard was a Northerner by birth but lived in New Orleans for 20 years before the war; in 1862 he was removed from field command amidst charges of incompetence. Warner, *Generals in Gray*, 27.

22 *OR* 2, 817; REL to Letcher, May 8, 1861, VAF, NA; Garnett to W. B. Hamlin, May 8, 1861, VAF, NA; Coulling, *Lee Girls*, 87; John Perry, *Mrs. Robert E. Lee: The Lady of Arlington* (Colorado Springs, CO, 2001), 225; Johnson, *Lee the Christian*, 70. Lee's Life Guard became Company K of the 16th VA. Benjamin H. Trask, *16th Virginia Infantry* (Lynchburg, VA, 1986), 3. Mrs. Lee wrote to her youngest daughter: "We have received information from a friend that the government troops are to take possession of these heights in a few days and as they will not . . . be allowed to remain here if the South

May 9, Thursday (Richmond): A delegation from the Richmond city council meets with Lee to discuss constructing fortifications around Richmond. Lee interviews Thomas S. Knox of Fredericksburg regarding a possible quartermaster position. Lee writes to Jackson advising him "not to intrude upon the soil of Maryland unless compelled by the necessities of war." He adds that arms, ammunition, and artillery under Capt. William N. Pendleton are en route to Harpers Ferry. Cocke is advised that several companies under Col. J. T. L. Preston and Samuel Garland have been ordered to him.[23]

Jubal Early is notified that Col. R. C. Radford will assume command of the troops at Lynchburg that are designated for Cocke in northern Virginia. Lee informs William E. Jones at Abingdon that he has been appointed to major and that he should muster troops from southwest Virginia at Abingdon. Lee also notifies Col. George Porterfield at Grafton and Maj. Michael Harman at Staunton that he has ordered arms and ammunition to be sent to Staunton from the arsenal at Lexington, and that when they arrive, they are to be issued to Porterfield's troops. The general also writes to James Barbour of Culpeper, informing him that the county's troops will not be returned from Harpers Ferry until other troops are designated to be posted to the ferry and arrive to assume their place.[24]

May 10, Friday (Richmond): The War Department orders Lee to "assume control of the forces of the Confederate States in Virginia and assign them to such duties as you may indicate, until further orders." Lee orders Cocke and Col. George H. Terrett to withdraw from towns in northern Virginia and place the men in camps "where their instruction may be uninterrupted and rigid discipline established;" Cocke is to send Preston's and Garland's regiments to reinforce the Manassas line. Lee chides Jackson for occupying Maryland Heights as "premature," and it may invite an attack. Lee tells the commanders at Staunton and Lynchburg to send troops to reinforce Jackson as soon as possible. With supply problems at Lynchburg, Langhorne is directed to forward companies to their destination once ready and able to make the move, without waiting for them to be fully formed into regiments.[25]

---

can dislodge them, I fear this will be the scene of conflict and my beautiful home endeared by a thousand associations may become a field of carnage." Mrs. REL to Mildred, May 9, 1861, Coulling papers, W&L. To the general, Mary confided, "I was very unwilling to do this, but Orton was urgent and even intimated that the day was fixed for taking possession of these heights.... I did not feel it was prudent to risk articles that could never be replaced." Mrs. REL to REL, May 9, 1861, ibid. Ravensworth was located on Braddock Road near Annandale; Lee's mother, Anne Carter Lee, died at Ravensworth in 1829. The house burned down in 1926 and the site was lost to suburban development in the 1960s. Eleanor Lee Templeman, *Virginia Homes of the Lees* (Annandale, VA, n.d.), 17.

23 Richard M. Lee, *General Lee's City: An Illustrated Guide to the Historic Sites of Confederate Richmond* (McLean, VA, 1987), 171; A. M. Randolph to REL, May 8, 1861, Letcher papers, LVA; Dowdey, *Wartime Papers*, 22; OR 2, 821-2. Jackson wanted to occupy Maryland Heights, which commanded Harpers Ferry. William Pendleton graduated West Point in 1830, but after a short career in the U. S. Army entered the Episcopal ministry; he was rector of Grace Church in Lexington, VA, and elected captain of the Rockbridge Artillery. Pendleton bore a striking physical resemblance to Lee and was often mistaken for him; he became one of Lee's staunchest defenders after the war and was one of the leaders of the anti-Longstreet faction. Warner, *Generals in Gray*, 234. John T. L. Preston was one of the founders of VMI, and was Jackson's brother in law; he served briefly as lieutenant colonel of the 9th VA and on Jackson's staff but spent most of the war at VMI. Krick, *Staff Officers in Gray*, 246. Garland was a Lynchburg lawyer and VMI graduate; he became colonel of the 11th VA and later commanded a brigade under D. H. Hill and was killed at the Battle of South Mountain. Warner, *Generals in Gray*, 98.

24 OR 2, 822-3; REL to Porterfield, May 9, 1861, VAF, NA; REL to M. G. Harman, May 9, 1861, VAF, NA; JAW to James Barbour, May 9, 1861, VAF, NA. Richard C. W. Radford was colonel of the 2nd VA Cav.. Krick, *Lee's Colonels*, 312. Jones, known as "Grumble" because of his irascible personality, was one of the most gifted (and often overlooked) cavalry commanders of the entire war, but extremely difficult to work with. Jones rose to colonel of the 1st VA Cav. and later the 7th VA Cav., and was made a brigadier general in September of 1862. He was killed at the Battle of Piedmont on June 5, 1864. Warner, *Generals in Gray*, 166-7. Barbour was president of the Orange & Alexandria Railroad; he wrote to Lee on April 24 complaining about the defenseless condition of Culpeper. JAW to Barbour, May 9, 1861, VAF, NA.

25 Freeman, *Lee*, vol. 1, 501, 515; Dowdey, *Wartime Papers*, 23-5; OR 2, 824-6. The government in Montgomery placed Lee in command of all troops in Virginia, but this "authority" was ignored on multiple occasions as troop movements were often dictated from Montgomery and were often at odds with Lee's orders. Freeman, *Lee*, vol. 1, 515.

Lee writes to Francis H. Smith relaying a request from Jackson to have a detachment of VMI cadets assigned to him at Harpers Ferry; Lee defers this decision to Smith, but requests that Smith let him know his decision so that he may notify Jackson accordingly. Lee announces his new authority over all Confederate forces in Virginia, and also Ruggles as commander of all troops around Fredericksburg and Jackson in charge of all troops at Harpers Ferry and Staunton; he publishes also the parameters for free travel on railroads, boats, etc. for official use. Custis is commissioned major of engineers in Virginia's forces.[26]

May 11, Saturday (Richmond): Lee meets in morning with Andrew Talcott discussing the defenses along the James and the approaches to Richmond. Following this Lee meets with the Richmond city council briefing them on the plans for the city's defenses and asking that they furnish Talcott with any assistance he may require. Later in the day he provides the council with a written summation of the conversation. Dimmock advises Lee that he is running out of powder supplies in Richmond which must be replenished. In response Lee orders Dimmock to enlarge his laboratory and production facilities to keep up with the increasing demand. Lee writes to B. M. Jones of Danville acknowledging the military merits of his idea for a railroad connecting Keysville and Clarksville but that the state does not have the funds to undertake its construction.[27]

He advises Maj. Boykin at Grafton that although Boykin is having difficulty in his recruiting efforts he must do it, as Lee does not want to send troops there from elsewhere. Lee urges Taliaferro to complete the Gloucester Point fortifications without delay and Col. Robert T. Preston is ordered to report to Early at Lynchburg. Lee informs Gen. Gwynn and militia Brig. Gen. William B. Shands that he is forwarding to Gwynn the muster rolls for the "Nansemond Rangers," which Shands raised without authority, to call them into service if desired. Lee writes to Mary telling her of Custis's commission; when he comes to Richmond, because of the scarcity of such supplies in the city, Custis will need to bring mess equipment not only for himself but for Lee, Perry, and Custis's servant Billy. Lee sends to Lexington the family valuables that Mary sent from Arlington; the only items he keeps in Richmond are his own personal papers and a sword which belonged to George Washington.[28]

May 12, Sunday (Richmond): Lee orders Gwynn to strengthen his defenses and to send 10 barrels of gunpowder to Richmond immediately. He advises Jackson that additional weapons have been sent him today, but questions Jackson's need for still more: "You know our limited resources, and must abstain from all provocation for attack as long as possible." Lee writes to Early briefing him on the mustering instructions previously given Langhorne. Lee informs "Grumble" Jones that he deems Jones too

---

26 REL to F. H. Smith, May 10, 1861, F. H. Smith papers, VMI; *OR* 2, 827-8; *OR* 51, pt. 2, 79; James L. Howe, "George Washington Custis Lee," *VMHB* (Oct. 1940), 320. The letter to Smith is somewhat confusing in that Lee dated it May 10 in one location and May 14 in another; he also noted on it that he neglected to give it to Smith in person when they spoke on the 15th and subsequently had it delivered to him. Lee and Smith saw each other almost daily during this period, so it is difficult to reconcile the five-day delay, although based on context it does seem to have been written on the 10th.

27 Talcott diary, May 11, 1861, VHS; REL to "Msrrs Wynne, Hill and Glazebrook," May 11, 1861, Gilder Lehrman collection; Dimmock to REL, May 11, 1861, Dimmock CSR; *OR* 1, Series 4, 314; *OR* 2, 830-1.

28 *OR* 2, 830-1; SO45, May 11, 1861, Robert T. Preston papers, VT; REL to W. B. Shands, May 11, 1861, VAF, NA; REL to Walter Gwynn, May 11, 1861, VAF, NA; Dowdey, *Wartime Papers*, 25-6; Coulling, *Lee Girls*, 87; McCaslin, *Lee in the Shadow of Washington*, 79-80. Robert Preston became colonel of the 28th VA. Krick, *Lee's Colonels*, 310. The Nansemond Rangers became Company F, 3rd VA. Lee A. Wallace, *3rd Virginia Infantry* (Lynchburg, VA, 1986), 13. Shands commanded the local militia in Southampton County and served in the state legislature before the war. Thomas C. Parramore, *Southampton County, Virginia* (Charlottesville, VA, 1978), 153, 190. A post-war visitor to the Lee residence at Washington College wrote that the items buried in Lexington for safe keeping during the war included letters and portraits of the Washington family, some of which were heavily damaged by water and mold. Christiana Bond, *Memories of General Robert E. Lee* (Baltimore, MD, 1926), 47.

valuable to the service to decline his promotion to major, and strongly urges Jones to reconsider.[29]

May 13, Monday (Richmond): As part of a re-organization of the state's forces, several high-ranking officers have been reduced in rank by one grade; Lee sends a lengthy letter to Cocke, who was reduced to colonel, explaining why such a move was made and that it does not reflect in any way upon his performance. Lee writes also to Boykin advising that additional arms are being sent him, and to Gwynn authorizing him to raise an additional cavalry company if needed. Lee informs Governor Letcher that he has ordered guards detailed for all the public property in Richmond.[30]

Lee urges Capt. Ed Bradford to reconsider his declining of a promotion to major, telling him he would be of much more use as a field officer than commanding his company. Lee writes to John G. Meem of Lynchburg requesting information about a gunpowder mill Meem is reported to be constructing. Lee issues orders that the chain of command must be followed at all times; that inspections will be made periodically to ensure that ammunition is not being wasted; that returns are to be filed with Lee's headquarters tri-monthly; and announcing Lt. Col. Washington as Lee's newest aide-de-camp. Lee is writing to Mary when interrupted by the arrival of Bishop William Meade.[31]

May 14, Tuesday (Richmond): Lee is named brigadier general in the regular Confederate Army—the highest rank at the time. Edmund Ruffin comes to Lee's office to complain about Capt. Harrison H. Cocke, commander of Fort Powhatan. Lee requests Ruffin to submit his complaints in writing so that they can be investigated. Lee informs Secretary of War Leroy Pope Walker that in accordance with Walker's instructions Lee has taken command of all Confederate troops in Virginia, but a quartermaster in Richmond responded that Lee's instructions interfere with those he received from Walker directly; Lee would like clarification and instructions from Walker.[32]

Lee meets with Governor Letcher concerning rumors of a Federal advance from Fort Monroe, near Hampton and he directs Gwynn at Norfolk and Col. Benjamin S. Ewell at Williamsburg to investigate reports of supplies being landed at Fort Monroe and to determine if the rumors of an advance are true. Gwynn is advised that there are no additional troops that can be sent to Norfolk at present, nor are there any tents available in Richmond. Lee also expresses to Gwynn his concern

---

29 Dowdey, *Wartime Papers*, 26-7; *OR* 2, 835; REL to W. E. Jones, May 12, 1861, VAF, NA.

30 *OR* 2, 836-8; *OR* 51, pt. 2, 87-8; REL to S. B. French, May 13, 1861, VAF, NA. Cocke was quite upset by what he perceived as a personal affront in his demotion. Lee's letter to him is, for Lee, an extremely lengthy one, explaining that Lee had nothing to do with the decision and that it is in the greater good of Virginia. It is a great example of Lee's ability to smooth the ruffled feathers of proud officers who endured what they perceived as a personal affront. Other notable officers also reduced in rank included Joe Johnston, Walter Gwynn, and Daniel Ruggles.

31 REL to E. Bradford, May 13, 1861, VAF, NA; REL to J. G. Meem, May 13, 1861, VAF, NA; *OR* 51, pt. 2, 87-8; Johnson, *Lee the Christian*, 72. Bradford is likely Capt. Edmund M. Bradford of the 6th VA; if so, his war record is all but non-existent: his CSR consists of 3 pages, and lists him in both Co. F and Co. G of the 6th and notes that he was promoted to major May 20, 1861, and transferred to another unit but does not state which unit. He does not appear as serving with any other units of Mahone's brigade. E. M. Bradford CSR. Bradford is mentioned later in a letter to Huger stating that it was intended for Bradford to serve as major of Mahone's 6th VA. Garnett to Benjamin Huger, May 31, 1861, VAF, NA. That Lee had to remind the officers under his command of the necessity for such military basics as following the chain of command is very reflective of the difficulties he faced during these early weeks of the war. Rev. William Meade was the Episcopal Bishop of Virginia and a friend of Lee; he was in town for the Episcopal Church Convention.

32 Freeman, *Lee*, vol. 1, 501; William K. Scarborough, ed., *The Diary of Edmund Ruffin*, 3 vols. (Baton Rouge, LA, 1977), vol. 2, 27; REL to L. P. Walker, May 14, 1861, VAF, NA. Ruffin, a noted agriculturalist, was also one of the leading secessionists not only in Virginia but the entire South; he is credited with firing the first shot against Fort Sumter. Ruffin originally sought an audience with Governor Letcher and failing in that, attempted to speak with his Council but Francis Smith referred Ruffin and his complaint to Lee. Ruffin told Lee that Capt. Cocke was "incompetent, worthless for command;" within days Cocke was removed from command—it is possible that Ruffin's complaint played a role.

over the condition of Fort Norfolk and Fort Nelson and orders that they be rectified immediately. He expresses to Jackson concerns over the lack of volunteers coming in from the northwestern part of Virginia, and that if Jackson can spare any troops without endangering Harpers Ferry, Porterfield is in need of troops. Lee recommends to the Governor's Council that they accept the offer of J. H. Debaws to establish a powder mill near Richmond.[33]

Lee orders that if any troops ready for the field are awaiting orders at Lynchburg they should be sent to Richmond; if not ready for the field they are to be retained at Lynchburg until ready. Dimmock complains that he cannot fill Army requisitions at present and Navy requisitions are furthering hampering his efforts; even though Lee issued orders removing Dimmock from responsibility for the Navy, he continues to receive requisitions from naval officers. Lee responds that he will discuss the situation with Navy officials.

Lee receives a map of Fairfax County from a Capt. W. H. Dulany, and requests that he send a map of Loudoun County as well. Mary departs Arlington for Ravensworth; even though some of the family's possessions had been sent either to Lee in Richmond or already taken by the girls to Ravensworth, most of what the Lee family owned was left behind in the mansion.[34]

May 15, Wednesday (Richmond): Lee meets with Francis Smith in the morning regarding applicants for positions. Lee calls on North Carolina Governor John Ellis, who is visiting Richmond, to discuss the possibility of getting gun carriages from the North Carolina Arsenal at Fayetteville; Ellis, however, is absent when Lee calls. Lee orders Col. George Terrett at Alexandria to limit a Federal advance no further inland than Alexandria rather than to attempt to defend the city itself. He requests Cocke to send troops to Manassas Junction and assures him that now that Norfolk and Harpers Ferry have been fortified, more troops can be spared for service in northern Virginia. Lee informs A. G. Graham of Jonesboro, Tennessee, that he has no authority to accept troops from other states into Virginia service, but if Graham's company is already mustered and equipped, Lee can order it to Harpers Ferry.[35]

Lee informs John M. Speed that he has no information regarding the machinery from the Harpers Ferry arsenal being moved south to North Carolina. Lee issues orders delineating how to discharge troops from state service, and decreeing that the polls be opened for troops to vote in Virginia's secession election. The general attends the Episcopal convention, where Bishop Meade delivers the sermon, which includes a reading from *Genesis* 47:8.[36]

---

33   B. S. Ewell to Letcher, May 13, 1861, REL papers, MOC; Dowdey, *Wartime Papers*, 28; REL to Walter Gwynn, May 14, 1861, VAF, NA; *OR* 2, 838-40; J. H. Debaws to J. M. Brooke, May 13, 1861, Letcher papers, LVA. Benjamin S. Ewell was the older brother of Richard S. Ewell, and president of William & Mary College in Williamsburg. He was colonel of the 32nd VA early in the war and later served on Joe Johnston's staff. Krick, *Lee's Colonels*, 133. Debaws previously acquired a percussion cap machine for Virginia. Debaws to Brooke, May 13, 1861, Letcher papers, LVA.

34   *OR* 2, 840; Dimmock to REL, May 14, 1861, Dimmock CSR; JAW to W. H. Dulany, May 14, 1861, VAF, NA; Freeman, *Lee*, vol. 1, 510. Lynchburg was becoming somewhat of a choke point for troops in Virginia; as eastern terminus of the Virginia & Tennessee RR, troops from across southern Virginia as well as the Deep South were arriving there. Mrs. Lee wrote of the items left behind: "The books were all packed in two locked closets except a few left on the shelves in the dining room and in another locked closet on the staircase were placed our engravings, ornamental books, and treasures of various sorts. The [Society of the] Cincinnati and state china from Mount Vernon was carefully put away and nailed up in boxes in the cellar." She expected to return in a short time; instead she would only see her family's home once more in her life and was so distressed by what she saw then that she did not leave her carriage to go inside the house. DeButts, "Mary Lee's Reminiscences," 317-8. Another source puts Mary's departure on the 19th. Pryor, *Reading the Man*, 302.

35   REL to F. H. Smith, May 15, 1861, F. H. Smith papers, VMI; *OR* 51, pt. 2, 91-2; Garnett to A. G. Graham, May 15, 1861, VAF, NA. Lee forgot to give Smith a request from Jackson for a detachment of VMI cadets for Harpers Ferry, and sent it later in the day (see May 10). Unable to speak with Governor Ellis in person, Lee sent his request in writing.

36   REL to J. M. Speed, May 15, 1861, VAF, NA; *OR* 2, 845-6; *OR* 1, Series 4, 325; Dowdey, *Wartime Papers*, 31. Speed was a former state legislator from Lynchburg. Thomas Speed, *Records and Memorials of the Speed Family* (Louisville, KY, 1892), 169. The referendum for secession was May 23.

May 16, Thursday (Richmond/Petersburg/Norfolk): Lee leaves Richmond for the first time since taking command. He sends a brief letter to Mary and authorizes Col. Terrett to accept Marylanders coming through the lines to enlist. In the afternoon, he leaves on an inspection tour of Norfolk, taking the Richmond & Petersburg and the Norfolk & Petersburg railroads.[37]

May 17, Friday (Norfolk): Lee continues his inspection tour of Norfolk, accompanied by Francis Smith.[38]

May 18, Saturday (Norfolk): Lee continues his inspection tour of Norfolk, with Francis Smith.[39]

May 19, Sunday (Norfolk/Richmond): Lee returns from his inspection tour in the evening. Lee instructs Col. Taliaferro to recruit a full regiment from Gloucester, King & Queen, and Mathews counties, but cautions him to construct a temporary structure for a hospital rather than taking over private residences for that purpose. Lee tells Taliaferro that he cannot fill Taliaferro's request for engineers to lay out more defensive works at Gloucester Point but rather to use the naval officers already present and that "the laboring force in the neighborhood will be sufficient to perform the work required" in erecting the fortifications. Lee writes to John T. Seawall of Gloucester Court House to allay Seawall's concerns about the exposed condition of the Middle Peninsula, informing him that Gloucester Point is the best defensible point on the lower York River and that there are no troops available to erect works elsewhere, also that Taliaferro is forming a regiment in Gloucester to defend that region.[40]

Lee warns Col. Terrett at Alexandria that the entire line of the Alexandria, Loudoun & Hampshire Railroad is exposed and that its locomotives and rolling stock should be secured immediately; Terrett is to work with the heads of the AL&H and the Orange & Alexandria to construct a temporary track connecting their two lines and run off the AL&H engines and cars under the cover of night. Porterfield is advised that additional troops and arms have been ordered to him. Lee makes several command changes: Brig. Gen. T. T. Fauntleroy replaces Magruder in command around Richmond; Lt. Col. Robert H. Chilton to command the cavalry camp at Ashland in place of Lt. Col. Richard S. Ewell who will be in charge of cavalry instruction at Culpeper Court House; Lt. Col. Joseph Selden to replace Chilton in charge of recruiting. Lee informs a Mr. Lindsey of Staunton that his son's company can be mustered in at Staunton if they are willing to join a Virginia unit. He sends a similar advisement to G. W. L. Crook of Memphis, who wishes to bring his company to Lynchburg. Rain all day.[41]

---

37 Dowdey, *Wartime Papers*, 31; *OR* 2, 851; *OR* 51, pt. 2, 92; Freeman, *Lee*, vol. 1, 507-8. The purpose for Lee's visit was two-fold: he wanted to see for himself the defenses in and around Norfolk, but he also wanted to assess Gwynn's fitness for continued command at one of the most vital points in Virginia.

38 Raleigh E. Colston to "My dear little darling Lou," May 17, 1861, R. E. Colston papers, UNC. Precise details of Lee's tour are not known, nor is it known if Smith accompanied him from Richmond or if they traveled separately.

39 Ibid. Despite his responsibility for much of the James River defenses and his familiarity with those at Norfolk, Andrew Talcott was not with Lee on this inspection tour. Talcott diary, May 18, 1861, VHS.

40 *OR* 51, pt. 2, 96; Dowdey, *Wartime Papers*, 31-2; *OR* 2, 857.

41 *OR* 2, 856-8; *OR* 51, pt. 2, 95; REL to A. Lindsey, May 19, 1861, VAF, NA: REL to G. W. L. Crook, May 19, 1861, VAF, NA; Krick, *CW Weather*, 24. The AL&H was to connect Alexandria to Harpers Ferry but by April 1861 extended only as far west as Leesburg and had three locomotives; the connection with the O&A would be made, but by the Federals after the capture of Alexandria. Ames W. Williams, *Washington & Old Dominion Railroad, 1847-1966* (Alexandria, VA, 1977), 7, 13. Fauntleroy began his military career in the War of 1812; he commanded at Richmond only until late August when he was relieved at his own request. He spent the remainder of the war as a civilian; he was father in law of Union Surgeon General Joseph Barnes. Allardice, *More Generals in Gray*, 84-5. Chilton served both as a field and staff officer in the antebellum Army and was paymaster when he resigned in April 1861. He would serve much of the war as Lee's chief of staff, rising to brigadier general, before being reassigned at his own request to the adjutant general's department in Richmond. Warner, *Generals in Gray*, 49. Chilton was not well thought of by the other members of Lee's staff and his abilities have been called into question ever since the war. One recent study of Chancellorsville states of him: "Chilton was

May 20, Monday (Richmond): The Confederate Congress votes to move the capital to Richmond. Instructions are sent to Early to form a regiment and forward it to Culpeper Court House; no experienced staff officers are available so Early will have to do the best he can. Lee informs Taliaferro that an additional recruiting officer will be sent him and that arms will be available for his use upon request. Lee orders Dimmock to send arms and ammunition to Col. Ewell at Williamsburg. Lee writes to Ewell letting him know these are on the way and clarifying the command structure on the lower Peninsula: the batteries at West Point, Gloucester, and Yorktown are under Navy control, but everything below Yorktown is under Ewell's orders, including all active militia; no cadets, however, are available for training purposes. Lee informs John F. Segar that he must apply to Ewell for arms for his company rather than directly to Richmond. Rain continues.[42]

May 21, Tuesday (Richmond): Lee meets with his cousin Col. Hill Carter, commander of the 52nd Virginia Militia, in the morning regarding the status of his regiment; afterwards Lee sends him word that one of his companies from Charles City County has been mustered in as part of Col. Ewell's forces at Williamsburg. Lee makes several command changes: Brig. Gen. Milledge Bonham is given command in northern Virginia, superseding Cocke; and Col. J. B. Magruder given command over the Peninsula, superseding Ben Ewell. Lee writes to James Mason of Winchester about Mason's visit to Harpers Ferry and informs him of the steps taken to protect northwest Virginia. Lee orders Early to send three regiments to Culpeper, and requests the promotion of Andrew Talcott's son Thomas Mann Randolph Talcott. Lee orders that one company of the Tredegar Battalion be detailed to guard the ironworks.[43]

May 22, Wednesday (Richmond): Lee authorizes Gwynn to call upon North Carolina Governor Ellis for troops, and reiterates to Bonham the defensive posture to be adhered to and that Manassas Junction must be held. Supply shortages continue as there are no tents to send to northern Virginia, so Bonham is instructed to have his men construct wooden huts. Terrett is ordered to have a connecting line between the AL&H and O&A railroads built and to get the AL&H rolling stock to safety. Lee appoints Col. William B. Blair as Virginia's new commissary general, and orders that all mounted troops must provide their own horse and its equipment. In the evening Lee meets with Dimmock regarding the movement of the machinery from the Harpers Ferry arsenal. Custis leaves Arlington for Richmond.[44]

---

either the unluckiest staff officer of the war on either side, or the worst. On more than one occasion during the Peninsula campaign, he botched orders from Lee.... During the Maryland campaign, Chilton lost Special Order 191.... Chilton was in over his head." Chris MacKowski and Kristopher D. White, *Chancellorsville's Forgotten Front: The Battles of Second Fredericksburg and Salem Church, May 3, 1863* (El Dorado Hills, CA, 2013), 137. In fairness to Chilton it should be noted that his culpability for the "Lost Order" prior to the Battle of Sharpsburg has never been clearly established. Lindsey's letter to Lee was not located so it is not known what state his company was from.

42 Thomas, *Lee*, 197; *OR* 2, 858-60; REL to J. F. Segar, May 20, 1861, VAF, NA; Krick, *CW Weather*, 24.

43 REL to Hill Carter, May 21, 1862, VAF, NA; *OR* 2, 860, 865; Dowdey, *Wartime Papers*, 32-3; REL to F. H. Smith, May 21, 1861, Sara Smith papers, VHS; Charles B. Dew, *Ironmaker to the Confederacy: Joseph R. Anderson and the Tredegar Iron Works* (Richmond, VA, 1999), 95. Bonham was a Congressman from South Carolina; when the state seceded he was named commander of its army (much the same role Lee filled in Virginia). He resigned his Confederate commission in January 1862 to take a seat in the C.S. Congress, and was governor of SC 1863-5. Warner, *Generals in Gray*, 28-9. T. M. R. Talcott was later assigned to Lee's staff. The Tredegar Battalion was a militia unit consisting of 350 of the ironworks' employees organized into four companies under the command of Joseph R. Anderson. As a result of a failed arson attempt against the works on May 18, Anderson asked the governor to accept the battalion into state service and use it to guard the facility. The matter was referred to Lee, who ordered that only one of the companies be used for that purpose. Co. D of the battalion later stood watch at the factory, and there were no further incidents. Dew, *Ironmaker to the Confederacy*, 94-5.

44 *OR* 2, 866; Dowdey, *Wartime Papers*, 33-4; *OR* 51, pt. 2, 100; Dimmock to REL, May 23, 1861, Letcher papers, LVA; Yates, *Perfect Gentleman*, vol. 1, 226. Lee could not have made North Carolina troops available to Gwynn without himself being authorized to do so, so clearly he communicated with Governor Ellis on this subject. Blair served as commissary

May 23, Thursday (Richmond): Virginia voters approve secession in popular election. Lee and Andrew Talcott drive to Marion Hill on Richmond's eastern outskirts, then to Tredegar Iron Works. Lee forwards to Governor Letcher Dimmock's opinion on the ultimate destination of the Harpers Ferry Arsenal machinery. He advises Early that no field artillery is available for two companies at Lynchburg awaiting their guns; they can be sent to the lower James to man heavy batteries or they may switch to infantry—if neither is acceptable they must be mustered out. Walter Gwynn resigns amid rumors he is going to be replaced; at 10pm Lee orders Brig. Gen. Benjamin Huger to Norfolk as his replacement. After dark Union troops under Brig. Gen. Charles W. Sandford seize Arlington.[45]

May 24, Friday (Richmond): Lee learns of the Federal occupation of Arlington. Lee orders Bonham to have the AL&H Railroad bridges destroyed as close to Alexandria as possible, and meets with D. G. Duncan of the Confederate War Department to discuss the situation along the Potomac. Lee expresses his concern to Col. Porterfield over the lack of recruits in his part of the state: "I hope that the true men of that region have been encouraged to come out into the service of the State." Lee advises John McCausland in the Kanawha Valley that ammunition is being sent to him by way of Staunton. Lee sends a lengthy letter to Brig. Gen. Henry Wise regarding the preparations made for the defense of Norfolk, mentioning all the defensive works being erected there as well as Huger's assignment to command. Lee receives the recommendations of chief commissary William Blair regarding the organization of that department and forwards the suggestions along to Governor Letcher. Lee announces 18 as the minimum enlistment age.[46]

May 25, Saturday (Richmond): Lee briefs the Richmond city council on progress of the city's defenses; the first works to be constructed guard the southeast approaches along the Osborne Turnpike and Darbytown Road. Lee writes to Secretary of War Leroy P. Walker to request that troops ordered to Virginia come fully armed and equipped as, due to the state's own supply shortage, those articles cannot be provided from Richmond. Lee advises Bonham that additional infantry and engineers are being sent to him, and he orders Dimmock to send ammunition to Bonham for those troops.

Lee writes to Huger expressing concern that Craney Island is "the least prepared for defense" out of all the Norfolk fortifications. Lee requests an update on Williamsburg's defenses from Ben Ewell,

---

until December 1861 when he was relieved due to ill health. He later returned to duty in the Trans-Mississippi theater; he was an instructor at VMI after the war. Krick, *Staff Officers in Gray*, 75.

45 Long, *CW Day by Day*, 77; Talcott diary, May 23, 1861, VHS; Dimmock to REL, May 23, 1861, Letcher papers, LVA; *OR* 51, pt. 2, 102; Jeffrey L. Rhoades, *Scapegoat General: The Story of Major General Benjamin Huger, C.S.A.* (Hamden, CT, 1985), 30; *OR* 2, 867; DeButts, "Mary Lee's Reminiscences," 319. Secession was approved by a three-to-one margin. Marion Hill overlooks Rocketts Landing; Lee and Talcott were likely scouting the area as a possible location for fortifications defending either the river approach or the Williamsburg Road approach to the city. Talcott noted in his diary that they departed after he had cast his vote in favor of secession; he also recorded that the journey cost 10 cents in tolls. Gwynn was subsequently commissioned a brigadier general in North Carolina's state forces and assigned to command along the coast; he resigned in 1863. Alladrice, *More Generals in Gray*, 110. Before the war, Huger commanded the Harpers Ferry Arsenal; he happened to be in Richmond procuring supplies for the heavy guns to be emplaced around Harpers Ferry when Gwynn's surprise resignation arrived in Richmond. It is likely that Lee met with him in person, especially given the late hour at which written orders for him to take command at Norfolk were issued; Lee probably met with him first then provided a written synopsis. Lee's instructions to Huger read: "You will soon see what is to be done and will know how to do it. Put all things to rights and keep everybody hard at work. We have not an hour to lose." Rhoades, *Scapegoat General*, 29-30. Federal Brig. Gen. Irvin McDowell issued orders to the troops occupying Arlington Heights that they were to leave Arlington house itself alone. Coulling, *Lee Girls*, 88.

46 Freeman, *Lee*, vol. 1, 510; *OR* 2, 872-3; *OR* 51, pt. 2, 104-6; Dowdey, *Wartime Papers*, 34; W. B. Blair to Garnett, May 24, 1861, Letcher papers, LVA. Henry Wise, a former governor of Virginia, would be a thorn in Lee's side on multiple occasions; this appears to have been the first of those. Wise wrote to Lee on the 3rd expounding upon what Wise perceived to be the lack of attention given to Norfolk and how, as a result, it had been left vulnerable. Wise's political influence coupled with his lack of military knowledge made him a difficult individual to handle.

and also informs him that regimental adjutants can only be selected from among the regimental lieutenants; they cannot come from the ranks.[47]

Lee informs Magruder that he does not think the Federals intend an advance from Fort Monroe in immediate future, but that he must use his cavalry to keep watch on them; in any case, Magruder must finish completion of the defensive lines on the lower Peninsula and at Williamsburg. More cavalry will be sent to Magruder, but he must procure wagons locally and he is to muster Col. D. H. Hill's 1st North Carolina into Confederate service. Taliaferro is urged to complete the works at Gloucester Point as rapidly as possible. Lee forwards to Governor Letcher an application of Francis W. Smith for a commission, and recommends it; Smith is later assigned to Lee's staff as military secretary. He writes to Mary telling her not to return to Arlington regardless of her feelings of sorrow at its loss.[48]

May 26, Sunday (Richmond): Lee writes to Georgia Governor Joseph Brown requesting that in future Georgia troops be sent fully armed due to Virginia's supply shortage, and also asking for any spare cavalry weapons that Georgia may have as Virginia's supply has been exhausted. Lee receives and forwards a complaint from a local civilian regarding the condition of the troops along Aquia Creek. Lee explains to Bonham the geographic boundaries of his command and asks for a report on the extent of damage done to the Alexandria, Loudoun & Hampshire Railroad. In response to a letter from Magruder, Lee informs him that because of the terrain and lack of forage on the Peninsula the amount of additional cavalry being sent him will be reduced.[49]

Lee inquires of Ruggles the number of troops mustered into service from the lower Potomac and Rappahannock counties and advises that if additional troops are needed on that front they will have to be raised locally. Lee establishes Richmond, Norfolk, Fredericksburg, Harpers Ferry, Alexandria, and Hampton as "separate departments." Lee thanks William Morrison of Petersburg for his offer of galvanic batteries and promises to call for them should a need for their use arise. Lee thanks Judge H. W. Sheffey of Staunton for his well wishes and assures Sheffey that his friend Dr. Thomas A. Berkeley will receive an appointment.[50]

May 27, Monday (Richmond): A Union force sent to Newport News from Fort Monroe causes considerable alarm at headquarters, prompting Lee to write to Huger cautioning that they may cross the James to Smithfield or move up the Nansemond to Suffolk to interdict the Norfolk & Petersburg Railroad; accordingly, Huger should telegraph Governor Ellis to forward promised North Carolina troops. He warns Magruder they may intend to move against Yorktown via Warwick Court House, and that J. B. Hood has been ordered to him as a cavalry instructor. Troops are ordered from Fort Powhatan to Zuni on the N&P; and Capt. John M. Brooke to arrange with N&P president William Mahone for the defense of the railroad. Capt. Edmund Ruffin, Jr. is sent to Burwell's Bay to provide advance warning of any movement against the railroad. Lee orders cavalry and artillery dispatched from Lynchburg and Richmond to the Peninsula and Norfolk.[51]

---

47 Lee, *General Lee's City*, 171, 176; Dowdey, *Wartime Papers*, 35-7; *OR* 2, 872-3, 875. The works which Lee described for the city council become Forts 2 and 3, and are not far from the area which he and Talcott reconnoitered on the 23rd. Craney Island is located at the mouth of the Elizabeth River; the wartime island is largely lost, being used as a city landfill and a deposit site for material dredged from the port of Hampton Roads.

48 REL to J. B. Magruder, May 25, 1861, VAF, NA; *OR* 2, 875-7; Francis W. Smith to John Letcher, May 24, 1861, F. W. Smith papers, VHS; F. W. Smith CSR; Dowdey, *Wartime Papers*, 36-7. Francis W. Smith was the nephew of VMI Superintendent Francis H. Smith. Krick, *Lee's Colonels*, 350.

49 *OR* 1, Series 4, 356; REL to "A Soldier's Wife," May 26, 1861, VAF, NA; *OR* 2, 879-80.

50 *OR* 2, 880-882; REL to W. E. Morrison, May 26, 1861, VAF, NA; REL to H. W. Sheffey, May 26, 1861, VAF, NA.

51 Dowdey, *Wartime Papers*, 38; *OR* 2, 882-5. Mahone at that time was colonel of the 6th VA stationed in Norfolk; he retained the presidency of the N&P throughout the war.

Lee informs Joe Johnston that Maj. Arnold Elzey will be sent to him as ordnance officer but that in the interim Jackson can fulfill that role, and informs Early that no cavalry weapons are available in Richmond except for a small number of obsolete flintlock pistols. Lee notifies Porterfield that arms are being sent him and that troops are being recruited around Beverly for his use. Lee issues orders regarding the acceptance of Marylanders into Virginia service and also concerning the movement of troops by rail, as well as announcing Francis W. Smith as his new military secretary. Lee writes again to Judge Hugh W. Sheffey thanking him for his well wishes and informs him that his friend Dr. Thomas A. Berkeley has received a commission and is on duty at Harpers Ferry. Lee informs James L. Perrin of Westmoreland County that he has no vacancies on his staff but will forward his letter to Governor Letcher for possible service elsewhere.[52]

May 28, Tuesday (Richmond/Gordonsville/Manassas): Lee leaves in the morning for an inspection tour of Manassas; Garnett remains at headquarters in Richmond. Before Lee departs, he receives information from Dimmock that the Richmond Arsenal is running out of ammunition and it will be necessary to send elsewhere to supply troops; he orders a guard posted at Bellona Arsenal. As his train passes through Orange Court House, an observer notes the Lee "gave the ladies at the depot an excellent rebuke, said they ought to stay away from such places, not to add to the already too great excitement."[53]

Arriving at Manassas in the afternoon, Lee inspects the works around the Junction. In the evening Lt. Col. J. M. Heck meets with Lee, giving a briefing on the conditions of Porterfield's force at Grafton; Lee replies that he can do little for Porterfield because of threats in northern and southeastern Virginia other than to send additional arms and authorize the creation of another regiment in that quarter. He and Bonham visit the camp of the 2nd South Carolina near Manassas during the evening. Lee sends instructions to Garnett to send troops to Jamestown and Yorktown and have a steamer ready to shuttle troops across the James if necessary. Lee writes to Mary letter telling her he is in Manassas; he encloses $100 and advises her against coming to Richmond as he doesn't think his station there will be permanent. Brig. Gen. Irvin McDowell takes over command at Arlington.[54]

May 29, Wednesday (Manassas/Fairfax Court House): President Jefferson Davis arrives in Richmond in the morning. Lee continues his inspection visit in northern Virginia. Lee telegraphs to Garnett in the evening that the number of troops at Manassas needs to be almost doubled. Custis reports for duty to Col. Talcott, together they go Marion Hill to survey fortification sites.[55]

---

52 *OR* 2, 883-6; *OR* 51, pt. 2, 114; REL to H. W. Sheffey, May 27, 1861, VAF, NA; REL to J. L Perrin, May 27, 1861, VAF, NA. Johnston succeeded Jackson as commander at Harpers Ferry on May 15. Long, *CW Day by Day*, 75. Elzey soon after this became colonel of the 1st MD; he was later promoted major general and given command of Richmond before being sent to the Army of Tennessee as its chief of artillery. Warner, *Generals in Gray*, 82-3. This letter to Sheffey is almost identical to the one to him on the 26th, the only substantial difference being the part about Dr. Berkeley; however, Lee makes no mention of it being a second letter.

53 *OR* 2, 888-91; Charles Dimmock to REL, May 27, 1861, and Dimmock to REL, May 28, 1861, Dimmock CSR; James W. Cortada, ed., *1861 Diary of Miss Fannie Page Hume, Orange, Virginia* (Orange, VA, 1983), 38. Bellona Arsenal was located in Chesterfield County on the south shore of the James River, several miles upstream from Richmond. The Bellona complex consisted of Bellona Foundry and the adjacent Federal Bellona Arsenal. The foundry dated to 1810, the arsenal to 1816; the Army withdrew from the Arsenal in the mid-1830s. Both the foundry and arsenal were used by the Confederate government during the war. A portion of the facility remains, part in ruins, part converted to private residences. Bellona Arsenal, National Register of Historic Places nomination, Dec. 18, 1970.

54 *OR* 2, 254; Mac Wyckoff, *The Civil War Letters of Alexander McNeill, 2nd South Carolina Infantry Regiment* (Columbia, SC, 2016), 25; Freeman, *Lee*, vol. 1, 512; *OR* 51, pt. 2, 119; *OR* 2, 888-9; Dowdey, *Wartime Papers*, 39-40, 45; DeButts, "Mary Lee's Reminiscences," 319. Heck served in the 25th VA. Krick, *Lee's Colonels*, 188-9.

55 *OR* 2, 891; Freeman, *Lee*, vol. 1, 512; *Charleston Mercury*, June 6, 1861; Talcott diary, May 29, 1861, VHS. In a letter written on the 29th to Joe Johnston, Garnett described Lee's trip to Manassas as "a hasty visit," suggesting that it was not

May 30, Thursday (Manassas/Orange/Gordonsville/Richmond): Lee returns to Richmond; when his train arrives at Orange Court House, a crowd demands a speech from Lee—he dismisses them saying that both they and he have better things to be doing. Upon his return to Richmond, he writes to Joe Johnston at Harpers Ferry of the dispositions Lee himself made in northern Virginia, particularly the creation of an observation post under Richard Ewell at Fairfax Court House and a similar post under Eppa Hunton at Dranesville. Lee tells Johnston that if the Federals advance upon Leesburg, Johnston is to join forces with Bonham's army from Manassas to meet them. Lee also advises Johnston that there are no percussion caps to be had in Richmond; as soon as some are available they will be sent to Harpers Ferry.

Lee informs Governor Letcher that there are approximately 36,000 troops presently in Virginia. Lee informs Capt. Marcellus Moorman of the Beauregard Artillery at Norfolk that sights for his guns will be sent as soon as the artisan responsible for them completes his work at Fredericksburg.[56]

May 31, Friday (Richmond): Lee meets for several hours with President Davis and Gen. Beauregard about the conditions in northern Virginia. As a result of this conference, Beauregard is sent to command that front. Lee sends Maj. Thomas G. Rhett to Bonham to assist in the training of his army. Lee conditionally approves of a proposal from Col. F. J. Thomas at Suffolk to prepare transports to cross the James and attack the Federal force at Newport News; he cannot launch this attack, however, unless he is absolutely positive of its success and has cooperation from Yorktown.[57]

Lee suggests to Governor Ellis moving North Carolina's camp of instruction from Weldon to Suffolk so as to aid in the defense of the Norfolk area, and asks if any artillery equipment is available. He also informs the governor that a portion of the machinery from Harpers Ferry will be sent to the

---

pre-planned and was driven by concern over affairs on that front. *OR* 2, 891. Lee was not pleased with the situation he found at Manassas, in addition to there being too few troops, those that were present were very poorly armed—if at all—and officers and men alike were lacking in training. Unsatisfied with troop dispositions, Lee personally repositioned some of the units, establishing at least one advanced observation post. Freeman, *Lee*, vol. 1, 512-3. Within days of Lee's return to Richmond, command on this front was given to P. G. T. Beauregard. A reporter for the *Mercury* noted that Lee "indicates no purpose to advance, but taking impregnable positions, seems resolved to throw the onus of action upon them." Charleston *Mercury*, June 6, 1861. At least one Lee biography has him returning to Richmond the evening of the 29th. Thomas, *Lee*, 197.

56 Freeman, *Lee*, vol. 1, 514; Dowdey, *Wartime Papers*, 40; *OR* 2, 894-5; REL to M. N. Moorman, May 30, 1861, VAF, NA. Lee noted in this letter to Johnston that there was an ammunition shortage across the board and inadequate means for producing it in Richmond. It certainly must have troubled the meticulous Lee that due to incomplete reporting by the commanders in the field, he truly had no idea of the exact number of troops in the field; the 36,000 figure provided was his best guess. Garnett had earlier provided an estimate of the number of troops in the field to the governor's council and noted "It is impossible to get returns from these volunteers." Garnett to F. H. Smith, May 30, 1861, VAF, NA. It speaks volumes to the condition of Virginia's forces that there was apparently only one individual who could fabricate and install cannon sights as Lee explained to Moorman. On the 30th Gen. McDowell wrote to Mrs. Lee: "With respect to the occupation of Arlington by the United States troops, I beg to say it has been done by my predecessor with every regard for the preservation of the place. I am here temporarily in camp on the grounds, preferring this to sleeping in the house under the circumstances which the painful state of the country places me with respect to these properties. I assure you it will be my earnest endeavor to have all things so ordered that on your return you will find things as little disturbed as possible.... When you desire to return every facility will be given you for doing so. I trust, Madam, you will not consider it an intrusion when I say I have the most sincere sympathy for your distress, and, so far as compatible with my duty, I shall always be ready to do whatever may alleviate it. PS – I am informed it was the order of the General in Chief if the troops on coming here should have found the family in the house, that no one should enter it, but that a guard should be placed for its protection." Fitzhugh Lee, *General Lee: A Biography of Robert E. Lee* (New York, 1994), 106-7.

57 Alfred Roman, *The Military Operations of General Beauregard*, 2 vols. (New York, 1994), vol. 1, 66; REL to M. L. Bonham, May 31, 1861, VAF, NA; *OR* 2, 896. Beauregard arrived in Richmond on the 30th. Roman wrote that it was originally intended for Beauregard to be assigned to command at Norfolk, but Lee's report changed Davis's mind. Beauregard's biographer T. Harry Williams, however, wrote that Davis had not yet determined where to assign Beauregard at the time of this meeting. T. Harry Williams, *P.G.T. Beauregard: Napoleon in Gray* (Baton Rouge, LA, 1995), 66-7. Whatever the case, Beauregard departed for Manassas on June 1.

arsenal at Fayetteville. Lee decrees that the Confederate quartermaster general and commissary general supersede their state counterparts. Lee writes to Joe Johnston regarding difficulties in procuring percussion caps. Lee apologizes to Rev. Moses Hoge for not taking him along on the recent inspection trip to Manassas, as Lee did not receive his request until he returned to Richmond. Walter Taylor is promoted to captain.[58]

---

58 Hotchkiss, *Virginia*, 133; OR 51, pt. 2, 121-2; OR 2, 896; REL to J. E. Johnston, May 31, 1861, VAF, NA; REL to M. D. Hoge, May 31, 1861, VAF, NA; WHT commission, WHT papers, SH. The Confederate quartermaster general was Col. A. C. Myers and the commissary general was Col. Lucius B. Northrop. Lee and Northrop butted heads repeatedly during the war. Rev. Hoge was pastor of 2nd Presbyterian Church in Richmond.

June 1861

Throughout June, Lee continued to focus on river defense and building up garrisons to protect the most vital points in Virginia, as the Federals gathered forces to attack those same points. He realized, although most civilians and politicians did not, that there was not enough manpower to defend every vulnerable part of the state. Decisions had to be made about how best to utilize the resources at hand. Lee and the government heard from those areas that were not to be defended—such as the Middle Peninsula and parts of the Northern Neck. The general himself conducted an inspection tour of the defenses of the James and York rivers and continued planning the defenses around the capital.

Although his wife had not yet found a permanent residence, Lee enjoyed visits with several of his children. Rob had not determined his future course, and Lee complained that his daughter Agnes did not seem to grasp the severity of war. Still, having at least some of his family nearby gave him comfort.

In early June Lee was effectively left without a command when Virginia's forces were formally absorbed into the Confederate Army. He also lost his first aide, Robert Garnett, who was given command of Confederate forces in northwestern Virginia. Garnett's departure left Lee to write nearly all of his own correspondence.[1]

Leaving the staff as well was John Brooke. Now that the Confederate Navy Department was being organized, Brooke went to work designing what would become the CSS *Virginia*.[2] Although Lee submitted his report on the state's mobilization for war to Governor Letcher, he was forced to admit that he was not certain of the final numbers because shoddy recordkeeping by some of the field commanders forced him into guesswork.

* * *

---

[1] See outgoing correspondence, VAF, NA. From the 7th through the 16th, Lee wrote or signed almost every letter himself. It is not known why Washington or Taylor did not perform this duty, as much of it was of such a mundane nature that the commanding general had no business devoting his time to it. Lee must have done nothing on June 10 but write/sign orders and correspondence due to the number of letters he wrote that day.

[2] Brooke, *Brooke*, 232-3.

June 1, Saturday (Richmond): Lee sends a lengthy letter to Joe Johnston attempting to allay Johnston's fears about holding Harpers Ferry: "The arrangements made and positions taken . . . are judicious." He adds that Beauregard will take command at Manassas and that reinforcements are en route from Staunton; he instructs that if Johnston is forced to evacuate he is to destroy what he cannot remove and resist any advance up the Valley. Lee reprimands Daniel Ruggles at Fredericksburg for circumventing the chain of command by sending a request for ammunition directly to Gov. Letcher, and also points out that Ruggles would not need that ammunition had he not engaged in a pointless and wasteful exchange of fire with Union gunboats on the Potomac River, which revealed his position and strength but served absolutely no purpose.

Lee requests an update from Col. Eppa Hunton on the destruction of the Hampshire Railroad and how much of its rolling stock has been removed. Lee authorizes James L. Lockridge of Huntersville to raise a mounted company from Pocahontas County. He informs former Congressman Waddy Thompson he will happily promote Thompson's son should the opportunity arise.[3]

June 2, Sunday (Richmond): The city of Richmond presents a horse to Lee as a gift, which Lee names "Richmond." Lee writes to North Carolina Governor Ellis regarding the use of railroad lines in his state, explaining that although priority is to be given to government personnel and supplies, no railroad has been taken over by the government. He notifies Col. Benjamin Ewell that artillery is being sent him for the Williamsburg line. Lee sends clarification to Huger at Norfolk that he can do whatever he wishes with officers of Virginia's provisional army under his command, and that Lee will send an answer regarding authority over Confederate Army officers under his command once that answer is known at headquarters. Lee also relays to Huger a complaint from former Governor Henry Wise that despite orders prohibiting it, he witnessed large amounts of liquor being taken into the camps in Norfolk.[4]

Lee receives from Joseph R. Anderson, head of Tredegar Iron Works, a proposal to muster the Tredegar Battalion into state service to guard the facility. Lee replies that he has referred Anderson's proposal to the governor but has ordered a military guard for it in the interim. Lee informs Mr. "A. Morrison" of New Kent County that he regrets that so many young men are choosing to enroll at Virginia Military Institute rather than enlisting in the army. Lee writes to Dr. Dinwiddie B. Phillips at Woodville, Rappahannock County, about two possible spies who were found in that area and whom Lee has referred to Beauregard.[5]

June 3, Monday (Richmond): Lee and Andrew Talcott spend the morning inspecting the defenses around Richmond. Lee discusses with his aide and former Navy officer John Brooke about going onto active duty with the Navy. Lee directs Johnston to occupy Martinsburg to protect his flank and provides an update on affairs in northwestern Virginia. Lee directs Gen. Ruggles to station a regiment at the mouth of Aquia Creek to provide

---

3 Dowdey, *Wartime Papers*, 41-2; OR 2, 898; REL to Eppa Hunton, June 1, 1861, VAF, NA; REL to J. L. Lockridge, June 1, 1861, VAF, NA; REL to Waddy Thompson, June 1, 1861, VAF, NA. Thompson was former Congressman from South Carolina and minister to Mexico prior to the Mexican War; his son was William Butler Thompson, but no record could be found for his war service.

4 Richmond *Daily Dispatch*, June 3, 1861; REL to Ellis, June 2, 1861, Kate Mason Rowland papers, MOC; OR 2, 900; REL to Benjamin Huger, June 2, 1861, VAF, NA. It is possible that the horse was given to the general a day or two earlier, but the *Dispatch* was usually very prompt in reporting such matters, so the date of June 2 is likely correct. Huger was not the only one unclear on the authority of PAVA officers over PACS officers—as evidenced by this message, Lee himself did not know. Lee was granted special authority over all troops in Virginia by President Davis, so his authority was unquestioned. The issue Huger raised not only had not been addressed, seemingly it had not even been considered by the Confederate War Department. The issue was resolved when Virginia's forces transferred to the Confederate army on June 8.

5 REL to J. R. Anderson, June 2, 1861, VAF, NA; REL to A. Morrison, June 2, 1861, VAF, NA; REL to D. B. Phillips, REL papers, MOC. See May 21 entry for more on the Tredegar Battalion.

advance warning of a movement from that direction upon Fredericksburg.⁶

June 4, Tuesday (Richmond/Fort Powhatan): Lee and Talcott embark on an inspection tour of the James River defenses, spending the night near Fort Powhatan. Mary and the girls move from Ravensworth to her uncle Calvert Stuart's home, Chantilly.⁷

June 5, Wednesday (Fort Powhatan/Jamestown/ Williamsburg/Yorktown): Lee and Talcott tour Fort Powhatan, then cross the river to Jamestown Island. There they are taken on an inspection tour of Fort Pocahontas and the other smaller works on the island by post commander Navy Lt. Catesby Jones and engineer Lt. Emmett M. Morrison. Leaving Jamestown Lee and Talcott ride to Williamsburg where, joined by Col. Benjamin Ewell, they go over the Williamsburg defenses, including Fort Magruder. In late afternoon or evening the pair departs for Yorktown, where they spend the night.⁸

June 6, Thursday (Yorktown/Gloucester Point/West Point): Lee and Talcott tour the works at Yorktown and review the 1st North Carolina. Afterwards they cross the York to inspect Taliaferro's works at Gloucester Point. From there they venture upstream to West Point, arriving there in the evening. Garnett is promoted to brigadier general and given command in western Virginia; his last known official act on Lee's staff is ordering several regiments to Staunton.⁹

---

6   Talcott diary, June 3, 1861, VHS; George M. Brooke, Jr., ed., *Ironclads and Big Guns of the Confederacy: The Journal and Letters of John M. Brooke* (Columbia, SC, 2002), 17; *OR* 2, 901; REL to Ruggles, June 3, 1861, VAF, NA. Talcott did not record precisely where he and Lee went. Brooke wrote, "I dislike the idea of leaving Gen. Lee and yet I wish to do something in the ordnance line." Brooke, *Ironclads and Big Guns*, 17.

7   Talcott diary, June 4, 1861, VHS; deButts, "Mary Lee's Reminiscences," 319. It is not known which, if any, of Lee's staff accompanied him on this trip—Garnett stayed behind at HQ; nothing is documented regarding the others, although it is likely they too stayed behind. Fort Powhatan—the subject of Edmund Ruffin's visit to Lee on May 14—was located on the south side of the James River in Prince George County. It was a second system masonry fort dating to 1808, which replaced an earlier Revolutionary War-era earthwork on the site. It was abandoned in the 1830s and was in considerable disrepair by 1861. Virginia forces occupied it and set about rebuilding and rearming it. It was seized by Union forces in 1863 and was abandoned at the end of the war. The fort currently is in ruins and is inaccessible on private property. Freeman has the dates of this inspection tour wrong, recording it as June 6-8. *Lee*, vol. 1, 520. It seems Freeman misinterpreted Lee when he wrote he had just returned from this tour; Talcott's diary has the correct dates. This error is addressed in detail in David F. Riggs, *Embattled Shrine: Jamestown in the Civil War* (Shippensburg, PA, 1997), 163 n54. A message from Garnett to Joe Johnston on the 5th states that Lee was then absent on an inspection tour down the Peninsula. Garnett to J. E. Johnston, June 5, 1861, VAF, NA. Chantilly was constructed ca. 1817 and was described as "one of the finest farms between Alexandria and Middleburg." By the fall of 1862 the house was deserted and ransacked by Union troops camped on the grounds; it was burned by Yankee troops in early 1863. Robert S. Gamble, *Sully: The Biography of a House* (Chantilly, VA, 1973), 59, 105. It stood on the Little River Turnpike—modern U.S. 50—directly across from the Chantilly Regional Library; eventually the surrounding area became known as "Chantilly."

8   Riggs, *Embattled Shrine*, 35; Carol K. Dubbs, *Defend this Old Town: Williamsburg During the Civil War* (Baton Rouge, LA, 2002), 25; Les Jensen, *32nd Virginia Infantry* (Lynchburg, VA, 1990), 5; *OR* 2, 970; Talcott diary, June 5, 1861, VHS. A 100-man guard escorted Lee's party around Fort Pocahontas, the main work on Jamestown Island. It was erected atop the site of the original 1607 James Fort. The Confederates erected five works on Jamestown Island; only two of them are publicly accessible although all remain today either on NPS or Preservation Virginia property. Part of Fort Pocahontas has eroded into the James, and additional portions of it were destroyed as a result of the excavations of James Fort, but much of it remains amidst the 17th and 18th century town site. As a result of this visit, engineer Col. Alfred M. Rives was sent to Williamsburg to take charge of the construction of its defenses. Jensen, *32nd Virginia*, 5.

9   Riggs, *Embattled Shrine*, 35; Daniel W. Barefoot, *General Robert F. Hoke: Lee's Modest Warrior* (Winston-Salem, NC, 2001), 231; Talcott diary, June 6, 1861, VHS; Clayton R. Newell, *Lee vs. McClellan: The First Campaign* (Washington, DC, 1996), 109-10; *OR* 51, pt. 2, 135. Much of the Confederate works at Yorktown were either built atop or incorporated the 1781 British fortifications; nearly all of the Revolutionary War earthworks present today are reconstructions, but the Confederate works are original. Thomas A. Wheat, *A Guide to Civil War Yorktown* (Knoxville, TN, 1997), 21. Hoke claimed that Lee's review of his regiment was shortly after the Battle of Big Bethel (June 10), but he must have been mistaken as this was Lee's only visit to Yorktown. Talcott recorded that the two of them had supper at West Point at the cost of 50 cents. Garnett was sent to take command in the wake of the Confederate defeat at the Battle of Philippi on the 3rd, which raised questions about George Porterfield's ability to command; a court of inquiry found Porterfield in part responsible.

June 7, Friday (West Point/Richmond): Lee and Talcott depart West Point after breakfast, stopping at Rooney's estate White House to visit with Rooney's wife Charlotte and Lee's daughter Annie who is visiting her sister-in-law. Lee is briefly reunited with Rooney, who arrives just as the general is leaving. Lee and Talcott return to Richmond around 2:00 p. m. and Lee meets with President Davis at the Executive Mansion in late afternoon.[10]

After this meeting Lee writes to Maj. Michael G. Harman at Staunton thanking him for all his efforts at supplying the troops in the western portion of the state and noting that Garnett has been sent to take command in that region. Lee sends instructions to Joe Johnston to hold the Valley, noting that Garnett has been sent to take charge of the troops on Johnston's left flank to guard against an attack from Ohio, leaving Johnston to focus only on a Federal advance from Pennsylvania. Lee sends instructions to the commander at West Point to transfer an artillery battery to Gloucester Point, and updates Magruder on rations and other supplies sent him.[11]

June 8, Saturday (Richmond): Virginia's forces are formally absorbed into the Confederate Army; although Lee has a commission as a brigadier general in the regular Confederate Army, he is now left without a command. Lee details Lt. Col. Crenshaw from his post as Virginia commissary general to duty with the 23rd Virginia, and he gives D. H. Hill his opinion on how to proceed with officers in his command who have been commissioned at higher ranks in other North Carolina units. He also writes to Jubal Early regarding a company which may or may not have been mustered into service and informs him that his regiment will be designated the 24th Virginia. Lee notes the scarceness of army manuals, particularly the regulations of the U.S. Army, in Richmond.[12]

June 9, Sunday (Richmond): Lee writes to his wife mentioning his visit to White House several days earlier, but largely pondering his future now that he has no command. "I do not know what my position will be. I should like to retire to private life, so that I could be with you and the children, but if I can be of service to the State or her cause, I must continue." Lee receives a copy of the Cincinnati *Enquirer* sent by Thomas Matthews of Lewisburg and sends his thanks.[13]

---

10 Talcott diary, June 7, 1861, VHS; Freeman, *Lee*, vol. 1, 521; Dowdey, *Wartime Papers*, 43-6; Riggs, *Embattled Shrine*, 35. It is possible that Lee and Talcott parted company at some point on the return; Talcott however does not mention this. He did note that lodging and breakfast cost him $1.50. It is not known how they returned to Richmond from West Point; the fact that Lee did not stop (or at least there is no mention of it) at Romancoke, Rooney's other plantation just outside of West Point, is curious. The Richmond & York River RR directly connected West Point to Richmond and passed by both Romancoke and White House. Both White House and Romancoke were owned by George Washington; his marriage to Martha Dandridge may have taken place at White House, although Mrs. Lee thought it was at nearby St. Peter's Church. Arthur Gray, "The White House: Washington's Marriage Place," *VMHB* (July 1934), 229, 240; Mrs. REL to unknown, [1873], Lee papers, SH. The discussion with President Davis likely concerned the Shenandoah Valley, and almost certainly Lee reported on what he had observed on the James and York rivers; the main reason for the meeting was probably discussing arrangements for Virginia's forces being absorbed into the Confederate army.

11 OR 2, 910; REL to H. B. Tomlin, June 7, 1861, VAF, NA; REL to Magruder, June 7, 1861, VAF, NA. Harman was one of several brothers in Confederate service; he subsequently served as lieutenant colonel and colonel of the 52nd VA and as Jackson's quartermaster briefly in 1862. Krick, *Staff Officers in Gray*, 149.

12 OR 2, 911-2; Crenshaw CSR; REL to D. H. Hill, June 8, 1861, VAF, NA; REL to Early, June 8, 1861, (2 messages) VAF, NA; REL to R. L. Preston, June 8, 1861, VAF, NA. The wording of the orders suggests that Crenshaw was already serving with the 23rd and this merely extended that arrangement. Lee answered several letters from civilians around the state on this date and some back-dated to the 7th, received while he was away from Richmond, but the brevity of his answers makes it impossible to understand them without seeing the original letters he received; nearly all the correspondence from the 7th through the 16th was written by Lee himself rather than the staff, no doubt caused by Garnett's departure; see outgoing correspondence book in VAF, NA.

13 Dowdey, *Wartime Papers*, 45-6; REL to Thomas Matthews, June 9, 1861, VAF, NA. Lee's phrase "I have just returned from" his inspection tour in this letter to Mary is what confused Freeman regarding the dates of the Peninsula trip. Mary had moved yet again; this letter is addressed to her at Kinloch, home of Lee's cousin Edward Turner in Fauquier County.

June 10, Monday (Richmond): Son Rob, although ill, travels to Richmond for a visit with his father, seeking his advice as to whether he should remain at UVA or transfer to VMI. Lee writes to Brig. Gen. Theophilus H. Holmes, now commanding at Fredericksburg, suggesting that he employ railroad rails as armor to protect his artillery batteries along Aquia Creek; Lee includes a very detailed description and a diagram of how Holmes could best protect his smoothbore guns from the superior rifled pieces of the U.S. Navy.

Col. Eppa Hunton at Leesburg is directed to destroy the bridges of the Alexandria, Loudon & Hampshire, and to remove or destroy all of its rolling stock as well as to target the locks and dams of the Chesapeake & Ohio canal. Lee adds that because General Beauregard is now in command in northern Virginia, all future correspondence should be directed through him. Lee sends word to John Magruder that he approves of all measures he had taken on the Virginia Peninsula, and that several dozen wagons are being sent to him. Lee reiterates his earlier order to transfer the King & Queen Artillery from West Point to Gloucester Point, and writes to Joe Johnston regarding confusion over what regiment Col. Alfred C. Cummings commands.[14]

Lee writes to Cary C. Cocke of Fluvanna County advising that he has been appointed lieutenant colonel and assigned to Hunton's 8th Virginia Infnatry. Lee explains to Richard G. Morris of the Richmond city council all the steps taken for the protection of the Richmond & York River Railroad. He explains to Governor Letcher that overcoats are being issued to the troops in and around Norfolk as quickly as they can be procured. Lee informs Col. Josiah W. Ware that he has been appointed colonel of the 34th Virginia and to report to Johnston.[15]

June 11, Tuesday (Richmond): Rob is still with his father, and daughter Agnes is in Richmond with friends. Lee receives a letter from his wife, the first in some time, and writes a lengthy one in reply to her. He is worried that their letters are going astray and that she has not gotten his last one. Lee hopes that Mary can find a quiet spot to live, away from the front, and adds that White House is not that spot. Lee had originally wanted the servant Billy in Richmond with him and Custis, but Mary would like to keep him with her, so Lee writes that he will get Meredith from White House instead. He orders Huger to strengthen Craney Island and Sewell's Point, noting than when he was there in May "these points were in a weak condition and feebly garrisoned." Pig Point at the mouth of the Nansemond could also be targeted since a landing there would cut Huger off from Richmond, so it too should be strengthened. He adds that a force from

---

She traveled from Ravensworth to Eastern View, home of the Randolphs near Warrenton, and then to Kinloch. Perry, *Mrs. REL*, 238. The 2,000-acre Kinloch estate outside The Plains is owned by the Currier family, of Currier & Ives fame.

14 Dowdey, *Wartime Papers*, 46-8; *OR* 2, 917-8; REL to H. B. Tomlin, June 10, 1861, VAF, NA; REL to Johnston, June 10, 1861, VAF, NA. Holmes superseded Ruggles on June 5 at the direction of the president. Meriwether Stuart, "The Military Orders of Daniel Ruggles, Department of Fredericksburg, April 22-June 5, 1861," *VMHB* (April 1961), 150. Hunton was a member of the secession convention and colonel of the 8th VA, later rising to brigadier general; he was wounded at Gettysburg and captured at Sayler's Creek. Warner, *Generals in Gray*, 146. Hunton's men "so thoroughly impaired the upper sections of the railroad by burning bridges and trestles and tearing up tracks that the line was useless beyond Vienna Station for the balance of the war." Williams, *Washington & Old Dominion Railroad*, 8. Arthur Cummings was originally assigned to command the 2nd VA, which was re-designated the 10th VA, but he apparently was never given command of that unit, hence Lee's confusion. Cummings was eventually given the 33rd VA of the Stonewall Brigade, but spent most of the war serving in the Virginia legislature. REL to J. E. Johnston, June 10, 1861, VAF, NA; Krick, *Lee's Colonels*, 108.

15 REL to Cocke, June 10, 1861, REL papers, UVA; REL to R. G. Morris, June 10, 1861, VAF, NA; REL to S. B. French, June 10, 1861, VAF, NA; REL to J. W. Ware, June 10, 1861, VAF, NA. C. C. Cocke resided at Bremo (Mary spent time there during the war also) and was brother of Phillip St. George Cocke. Apparently Capt. David Weisiger had requested overcoats for his company directly from the governor instead of through the QM at Norfolk, hence Letcher and Lee's involvement. Josiah Ware of Berryville was a long-tenured colonel in the Virginia militia; there is no evidence that he ever commanded the 34th VA Inf. His CSR suggests that he commanded the 34th VA Militia, which was not associated with the 34th VA. J. W. Ware CSR, NA.

North Carolina is being sent to Suffolk to guard his rear.[16]

Lee explains to Lt. Col. D. A. Langhorne that his duties consist solely of mustering new troops into service at Lynchburg, and that another officer will be sent to replace Jubal Early as commander of the post. Lee informs E. H. Gill that arms cannot be provided at the present time for the company he has raised to guard the Virginia & Tennessee Railroad, but the general requests that Gill not disband his men because arms may be available in near future, and the men can assist in the protection of the railroad regardless. Lee explains to T. S. Stuart that troops in southwest Virginia can be more effectively trained at Richmond than at Abingdon, and commissions for Home Guard units are not being issued. Lee informs D. G. Lamar of Augusta, Georgia, that he will do what he can regarding the promotion of his son.[17]

June 12, Wednesday (Richmond): Lee formally accepts his brigadier general's commission in the C.S. Army. Rob leaves Richmond to go back to UVA, and Agnes leaves for White House. Lee requests returns from all major commands detailing the number of units, guns, etc. McHenry Howard and several other Marylanders call upon Lee in the afternoon to complain that their company, as well as several other Maryland companies, was mustered into service "for the war" rather than for one year. Howard noted that they had difficulty gaining admittance to see the general and that Lee "seemed not at all pleased at being interrupted and told us he did not see what could be done, adding sharply that the Maryland troops had already given more trouble than five times as many others." Lee rebukes Capt. Edmund Ruffin, Jr., for protesting orders given him by Gen. Huger, and informs Dr. S. B. Morrison of Rockbridge County that no guerrilla organization is authorized by Virginia or the Confederacy.[18]

June 13, Thursday (Richmond): Lee writes to Porterfield advising him of Garnett's appointment to command; to Magruder congratulating him for his victory at Big Bethel; to Col. R. C. W. Radford at Lynchburg to send cavalry to Manassas by quickest route but that there are no cavalry arms available in Richmond for them. Lee cautions the commander at West Point to be cautious in whom he arrests on grounds of being "suspicious;" that being Northern by birth is not sufficient cause. Lee advises Lt. Col. D. A. Langhorne that he is temporarily in command at Lynchburg but as soon as a vacancy is found in a regiment he will be transferred into the field. Lee sends Col. Charles Smith several drill manuals and muster forms and requests to know the number of men under Smith's command, and he informs Col. B. S. Ewell that several cannon and small arms belonging to the New Kent County militia will be made available for his use.[19]

---

16 Dowdey, *Wartime Papers*, 47-8; OR 2, 919-20; REL to Huger, June 11, 1861, VAF, NA.

17 REL to Langhorne, June 11, 1861, VAF, NA; REL to E. H. Gill, June 11, 1861, VAF, NA; REL to T. S. Stuart, June 11, 1861, VAF, NA; REL to D. G. Lamar, June 11, 1861, VAF, NA. Gill was superintendent of the VA & TN RR; from the context of Lee's letter it is likely that the troops in question were railroad employees.

18 Dowdey, *Wartime Papers*, 48; REL to Huger, June 12, 1861, VAF, NA (this letter includes notation that the same request was sent to Holmes, Magruder, Beauregard, and Johnston); McHenry Howard, *Recollections of a Maryland Confederate Soldier, 1861-1866* (Dayton, OH, 1975), 24; REL to Edmund Ruffin, June 12, 1861, VAF, NA; REL to S. B. Morrison, June 12, 1861, VAF, NA. Howard and his comrades came from a meeting with President Davis to air the same grievance; Howard noted that gaining access to Davis was much easier than with Lee, and Davis seemed much more concerned. On or about June 18, the Marylanders' enlistments were changed to reflect the one-year term rather than "for the war." Howard was unsure of the date, stating that he thought it was the 12th but could have been the 13th; either is plausible, as his company formally mustered on the 12th. Howard was the grandson of Francis Scott Key; he served on the staff of several Maryland generals in the Army of Northern Virginia: Charles Winder, Isaac Trimble, and George Steuart. He was appointed to Custis's staff in early 1865. Krick, *Staff Officers in Gray*, 164-5. The details of Ruffin's protest are not specified in Lee's reply.

19 Dowdey, *Wartime Papers*, 49; OR 2, 926; REL to H. B. Tomlin, June 13, 1861, VAF, NA; REL to D. A. Langhorne, June 13, 1861, VAF, NA; REL to Charles Smith, June 13, 1861, VAF, NA; REL to Vuloski Vaiden, June 13, 1861, VAF,

June 14, Friday (Richmond): Lee's commission as full general in the regular Confederate Army ranks from today. Lee suggests to Governor Letcher that since the Richmond defenses are progressing so slowly, the city council should provide black laborers and that "all available persons in and about" the city be organized for its defense. Lee writes Adjutant General Samuel Cooper regarding conflicting orders given to the Varina Artillery: Lee ordered them to Jamestown Island, which has no artillerymen currently, but the secretary of war ordered them to Fort Powhatan, which already has a garrison. Lee lists for Gen. Holmes the officers to be assigned to 30th and 40th Virginia regiments, and instructs Col. Dimmock as to where to send the remaining artillery pieces he has.[20]

June 15, Saturday (Richmond): Lee submits to Governor Letcher his report on Virginia's mobilization. He estimates that approximately 35,000 troops from Virginia are in the field, but laments that the call for volunteers in the western part of the state "has been feebly responded to." Lee inquires of Col. Ewell how much nitric acid can be procured from the laboratory at William & Mary for use in manufacturing percussion caps. Lee writes to Adjutant General Cooper regarding the issuance of clothing to the troops, and he informs Francis L. Campbell that troops are to be issued a $21 clothing allowance. Lt. Col. George Deas joins Lee's staff.[21]

June 16, Sunday (Richmond): Lee writes to Magruder advising that Yorktown must be held and that reinforcements will be sent when available, and that he has ordered construction of a battery at Day's Point. He instructs Huger to proceed with the construction of a battery at Burwell's Bay now that there are troops enough at Suffolk to protect it. He writes also to Commander Samuel Barron regarding the garrison at Jamestown Island and requests of Navy Secretary Stephen Mallory the use of the steamer CSS *Teaser* as an observation vessel in the lower James. Lee explains to Lt. Gov. Robert L. Montague why a battery was not originally constructed at Burwell's Bay, but now that forces are at Suffolk the work shall be undertaken.[22]

June 17, Monday (Richmond): Lee meets with President Davis, Secretary of War Leroy P. Walker, and Secretary of the Navy Stephen R. Mallory regarding secret service operations in the Northern Neck. Lee instructs Gen. Holmes not to reduce his strength around Fredericksburg and to fortify Mathias Point on the Potomac. Lee writes to Francis Smith regarding a "Lt. Col. A. Jackson" who Huger refused to accept into his command on account of rumors that he is a man "of bad habits;" Lee would like Jackson's commission refused by state authorities as soon as possible as the easiest way to resolve the matter.[23]

NA; REL to B. S. Ewell, June 13, 1861, VAF, NA. Smith commanded the 39th VA Inf., which was formed on the Eastern Shore; when efforts to transfer the regiment across the Chesapeake Bay to join Huger failed, it was disbanded.

20 REL CSR; Dowdey, *Wartime Papers*, 50; REL to Cooper, June 14, 1861, VAF, NA; REL to Holmes, June 14, 1861, VAF, NA; REL to Charles Dimmock, June 14, 1861, VAF, NA.

21 Freeman, *Lee*, vol. 1, 529; *OR* 2, 927-9; REL to B. S. Ewell, June 15, 1861, VAF, NA; REL to Cooper, June 15, 1861, VAF, NA; REL to F. L. Campbell, June 15, 1861, VAF, NA; Krick, *Staff Officers in Gray*, 112. Lee almost certainly delivered this report in person and went over its contents in detail with the governor, most likely on the 15th or possibly the 16th. This may be the Francis Lee Campbell who served as a field officer with the 13th LA Inf., but that regiment served exclusively in the Western Theater of operations and Lee's letter does not include any sort of military rank, post, etc.; it is simply addressed to "Francis Lee Campbell" with no other identifying details. Deas was gone by January 27, 1862, when he became an assistant to Adjutant General Cooper; he was the brother in law of James Longstreet. Krick, *Staff Officers in Gray*, 112.

22 Dowdey, *Wartime Papers*, 53-4; REL to Huger, June 16, 1861, VAF, NA; REL to Samuel Barron, June 16, 1861, Cocke family papers, VHS; REL to S. F. Mallory, June 16, 1861, VAF, NA; REL to R. L. Montague, June 16, 1861, VAF, NA. Day's Point is at the mouth of the Pagan River near Smithfield, just downriver from Burwell's Bay; the works eventually constructed there were Fort Boykin and Fort Huger, both of which are presently county parks.

23 H. H. Sims to Matthew F. Maury, June 17, 1861, Letcher papers; *OR* 2, 932; REL to F. H. Smith, June 17, 1861, F. H. Smith papers, VMI. Little is known about Confederate secret service operations, which appear to have been quite active in

Lee writes to Beauregard regarding the formation of the 19th Virginia and any surplus companies left over and to Magruder regarding "misconduct" by a zouave unit under his command. Lee issues orders for all mustering officers, regimental commanders, and district commanders to send to him a report of the troops and officers under their command in accordance with the transfer of Virginia's forces to the Confederacy.[24]

June 18, Tuesday (Richmond): Lee informs Magruder that additional heavy guns and transports are being sent to him and troops will be sent when available; no facility exists in Richmond for making artillery fuses as requested, but Lee can have complete shells sent him instead. Lee orders Lt. Robert R. Carter, commander of CSS *Teaser*, to take his boat to Jamestown Island to serve as a lookout vessel. Lee writes to D. N. Ingraham, chief of the Bureau of Ordnance and Hydrography, concerning the York River defenses. He writes to Edmund T. Morris of the military necessity of connecting all the railroads in Richmond and Petersburg, to William C. Parks that the only arms available are obsolete flintlocks, and to Garnett regarding opening communications between Staunton and Philippi, and to T. H. Holmes regarding the organization of the 30th Virginia.[25]

Lee explains to a Mrs. J. A. Breeden of Richmond that if her son is under 18 he can be discharged upon proof of his age, but if he is over 18 a substitute must be provided before he can be released from service. He authorizes Maj. Michael Harman, commanding at Staunton, to use militia and home guard to guard the public property in the town. Lee recommends to Governor Letcher that the state purchase a large number of flintlock muskets previously sold to Joseph R. Anderson. Lee thanks Samuel M. Garland of Amherst and the officers and men of the Southern Rights Guard for the offer to serve as his personal bodyguard.[26]

June 19, Wednesday (Richmond): Lee writes to Robert M. T. Hunter, A. B. Evans, and P. W. Woodward explaining that now that time and manpower permit, additional works will be erected in Essex and Middlesex counties and elsewhere along the Rappahannock. Lee forwards to Governor Letcher a request from Col. Roger A. Pryor for a court of inquiry regarding an officer formerly in Pryor's 3rd Virginia. Lee writes to Capt. William H. Werth, lamenting his decision to resign his commission, and orders Col. B. S. Ewell to send the nitric acid at William & Mary's science laboratory to Richmond for use by the ordnance department.[27]

---

the Northern Neck and southern Maryland, as well as Canada; the best two sources on the subject are William Tidwell, *Come Retribution* (Jackson, MS, 1988) and Tidwell, *April '65* (Kent, OH, 1995). Mathias Point is near modern Dahlgren, VA. Lt. Col. Jackson's identity is not known; Lee's language used in describing him was his usual code for drunkenness.

24 REL to Beauregard, June 17, 1861, VAF, NA; REL to Magruder, June 17, 1861, VAF, NA; GO27, June 17, 1861, Order Book, VAF, NA. The details of the offenses as well as the identity of the zouave unit are not known.

25 *OR* 2, 935-7; *OR* 51, pt. 2, 141; REL to Garnett, June 18, 1861, VAF, NA; REL to Holmes, June 18, 1861, VAF, NA. Robert Carter was a Lee cousin; *Teaser*, a tugboat armed with two 32-pound rifles, was one of the original vessels of the small state navy and later made naval history as one of the first minelayers and arguably the first aircraft carrier. John M. Coski, *Capital Navy: The Men, Ships and Operations of the James River Squadron* (Campbell, CA, 1996), 8, 50-1. Both Morris and Parks were members of Virginia's secession convention.

26 REL to Mrs. J. A. Breeden, June 18, 1861, VAF, NA; REL to M. G. Harman, June 18, 1861, VAF, NA; REL to John Letcher, June 18, 1861, VAF, NA; REL to S. M. Garland, June 18, 1861, VAF, NA. Anderson presumably purchased the muskets for use by the Tredegar Battalion; he indicated to Lee that he was willing to sell them back to the state for the price he paid for them. Garland was a member of Virginia's Secession Convention; the Southern Rights Guard became Co. H, 19th VA Inf.

27 *OR* 2, 941; REL to A. B. Evans, June 19, 1861, VAF, NA; REL to P. W. Woodward, June 19, 1861, VAF, NA; R. A. Pryor to L. L. Anderson, June 14, 1861, Letcher papers; REL to W. H. Werth, June 19, 1861, VAF, NA; REL to B. S. Ewell, June 19, 1861, VAF, NA; REL to Josiah Gorgas, June 19, 1861, VAF, NA. Hunter was a former U.S. Senator and Speaker of the House of Representatives from Tappahannock, VA. He was Confederate Secretary of State for several months in 1861-2; he resigned upon his election as Senator from Virginia. As President Pro Temp of the Confederate Senate, Hunter was a very outspoken critic of the Davis administration. As the company to which the officer Pryor

Lee informs Col. J. W. Ware that despite his earlier orders to report to Harpers Ferry and take command of the 34th Virginia, he has since learned that that regiment does not yet exist so Ware will have to wait until companies are gathered to form that unit. Lee informs William G. Paine, an official of the Richmond & York River Railroad, that as that line is far removed from the frontlines of the war, troops cannot be permanently detailed for its safety; those currently detailed to guard the Pamunkey and Chickahominy river bridges are only there temporarily until the railroad can provide personnel to protect them. Lee thanks superintendent H. D. Bird of the Southside Railroad for the offer to provide rolling stock to transport troops to Norfolk, and tells Bir that he will refer the offer to Gen. Huger. Lee informs Robert E. Farrar of Amelia County that he does not know how long his son will be stationed at the Camp of Instruction in Richmond.[28]

June 20, Thursday (Richmond): Lee tours the Richmond Armory with Col. Dimmock. Lee informs Holmes that if he does not have troops enough to defend a battery at Mathias Point he should not construct it, but the troops there must be sheltered from the enemy and not fire on them. Lee reminds the officers and men that proper vigilance must be used to prevent surprise attacks and troops must be careful so as not to avoid friendly fire. Lee writes to Surgeon General David C. DeLeon regarding the creation of a hospital for measles patients at Fredericksburg, and orders Maj. Nathan G. Evans to report to Beauregard at Manassas. J. M. Brooke is ordered to naval duties, relieving him from Lee's staff.[29]

June 21, Friday (Richmond): President Davis and Gen. Lee review and observe drill of the Washington Artillery of New Orleans. An observer takes note that Lee's "horse stood fire so badly that the General had to ride off for fear of running into the ladies," but even under such conditions "he is a magnificent rider." Lee writes to Joe Johnston regarding the condition of two regiments recently sent to Harpers Ferry from Lynchburg. The units, he explains, were sent because the War Department assumed them to be fully equipped and ready for the field, but as they were in Lynchburg they were not personally observed by Lee, Davis, or anyone in the War Department. Lee informs Col. J. Warren Hutt of the 111th Virginia Militia that he has no arms to send, and writes to state legislator Addison Hall regarding the defense of the lower Northern Neck. Lee authorizes Danville Mayor William T. Sutherlin to turn over to the Commonwealth of Virginia 20 muskets in the town's possession. Lee recommends against connecting the Manassas Gap to the Winchester & Potomac railroad, citing "the present

---

complained about had been disbanded, Lee wanted the matter dropped. Pryor served in the U.S. House of Representatives before the war, and reportedly declined the honor of firing the first shot on Fort Sumter; he was elected to the Confederate Congress but resigned to accept a commission as colonel of the 3rd VA and eventually rose to brigadier general. Pryor's brigade was broken up and its regiments assigned to other brigades, leaving him without a command; he then joined the 3rd VA Cav. as a private and functioned as a scout until captured late in the war. Warner, *Generals in Gray*, 247-8. Werth was colonel of the 101st VA militia before the war and was elected captain of the Chatham Grays, part of Montague's Battalion and later the 53rd VA Inf.; his resignation became effective July 14, 1861. W. H. Werth CSR.

28 REL to J. W. Ware, June 19, 1861, REL papers, UVA; REL to W. G. Paine, June 19, 1861, VAF, NA; REL to H. D. Bird, June 19, 1861, VAF, NA; REL to R. E. Farrar, June 19, 1861, VAF, NA. Lee received a request from the York River RR either the 18th or 19th asking for protection, which he referred to the governor for a decision; it is not known if he met with Letcher in person to discuss or not. W. G. Paine to REL, June 18, 1861, VAF, NA. Farrar's son was Lt. Fernandes R. Farrar, Co. H. 44th VA; he resigned in the Fall of 1861. Farrar CSR.

29 REL to Letcher, June 26, 1861, VAF, NA; *OR* 2, 941-3; REL to D. C. DeLeon, June 20, 1861, VAF, NA; SO198 Gilder-Lehrman; Brooke, *Ironclads and Big Guns*, 20. Evans was colonel of the 4th SC and commanded a brigade at Manassas and at Ball's Bluff; promoted to brigadier, he bounced back and forth between Virginia and the Carolinas where allegations of drunkenness derailed his career. Jeffry D. Wert, "Nathan George Evans," in William C. Davis, ed., *The Confederate General*, 6 vols. (Harrisonburg, PA, 1990), vol. 2, 107-8. A court of inquiry, under the command of Col. W. B. Taliaferro, convened at Beverly starting on the 20th to look into Porterfield's defeat at Philippi. *OR* 2, 72-4.

conditions of military operations in the Shenandoah Valley."[30]

June 22, Saturday (Richmond): Agnes comes from White House to Richmond to visit her father. Lee requests that North Carolina Governor Ellis send an artillery battery to Suffolk to man the works along Burwell's Bay. Lee writes to Magruder that he needs to have better soldiers serving as videttes so as to avoid false alarms such as recently befell him on a rumored movement against Yorktown. Magruder also needs enough wagons to evacuate his forward positions in the event of a real advance. Lee informs the commander at Fort Powhatan that the defenses there must be completed as soon as possible and that there are no additional artillery units or guns that can be sent; if more gunners are needed he should employ an infantry company as artillerists. Lee sends instructions to the Camp of Instruction regarding appointment of regimental staff officers.[31]

June 23, Sunday (Richmond): Annie and Charlotte come to visit Lee on their way to Charlotte's family's estate Hickory Hill. Lee writes to Capt. W. C. Whittle regarding keeping a steamer at Yorktown to facilitate communication and transportation with Gloucester Point and West Point. Lee meets with Andrew Talcott in the afternoon.[32]

June 24, Monday (Richmond): Lee writes to Johnston inquiring if he has authorized Brig. Gen. Gilbert S. Meem of the militia to call out a portion of his command as Meem has informed the governor. Lee is concerned about Meem's fitness for command and notes also that the area from which that militia is raised is not the most loyal. Lee informs Garnett that reinforcements and camp equipage is being sent him. Lee relays to Huger information received from several deserters from Fort Monroe regarding enemy strength there. Lee reviews the case of a Private William R. Musser of Lynchburg who works for a company supplying tents to the army and requests a discharge. He also informs Miss Rosa V. Bondurant of Farmville that he cannot discharge her brother from service unless he provides a substitute or can otherwise provide cause. Lee writes a lengthy letter to Mary, full of family information; he notes, "My movements are very uncertain, and I wish to take the field as soon as certain arrangements can be made. I may go at any moment, and to any point where it may be necessary."[33]

June 25, Tuesday (Richmond): Lee writes to Col. Charles A. Crump at Gloucester Point advising that additional heavy artillery has been ordered there. He instructs Capt. George D. Davis in Mecklenburg County to bring his company as fully equipped as possible to Richmond to be mustered in to service, and informs Garnett that an additional battalion has been sent him, bringing along for his command all tents and blankets that are available. He writes to Magruder regarding a trouble-making zouave unit in

---

30 Graham T. Dozier, ed., *A Gunner in Lee's Army: The Civil War Letters of Thomas Henry Carter* (Chapel Hill, NC, 2014), 23; *OR* 2, 945; REL to J. W. Hutt, June 21, 1861, VAF, NA; REL to Addison Hall, June 21, 1861, VAF, NA; W. T. Sutherlin to REL, June 20, 1861, VAF, NA; REL endorsement on Virginia Convention Ordinance, June 18, 1861. This drill was deemed less than satisfactory by the same observing officer owing to the horses being untrained. Lee's horse at this event was likely "Richmond." Hutt commanded the Westmoreland County militia. Sutherlin's mansion was used by Jefferson Davis after fleeing Richmond in April 1865 and is regarded as the last capitol of the Confederacy.

31 Dowdey, *Wartime Papers*, 53-4; REL to Ellis, June 2, 1861, VAF, NA; *OR* 2, 946; REL to J. P. Wilson, June 22, 1861, VAF, VA; REL to William Gilham, June 22, 1861, VAF, NA.

32 Dowdey, *Wartime Papers*, 54; REL to W. C. Whittle, June 23, 1861, VAF, NA; Talcott diary, June 23, 1861, VHS. Hickory Hill was an expansive estate in Hanover County belonging to the Wickham family; the original house, constructed in 1827, was destroyed by fire in 1875. Charlotte's cousin, Williams C. Wickham, was a Confederate brigadier general. Calder Loth, ed., *The Virginia Landmarks Register* (Charlottesville, VA, 1986), 193. Talcott spent the previous several days inspecting works around Richmond. Talcott diary, VHS.

33 *OR* 2, 947-8; REL to Huger, June 24, 1861, VAF, NA: Maurice Langhorn to John Letcher, June 19, 1861, Letcher papers; REL to R. V. Bondurant, June 24, 1861, VAF, NA; Dowdey, *Wartime Papers*, 53-4. Gilbert Meem was a former member of the VA House of Delegates, who lived at Mount Airy in Shenandoah County. Rumors of Meem's alcoholism prompted Lee's apprehension. Allardice, *More Generals in Gray*, 165.

Magruder's force and to J. Marshall McCue regarding the sick at Harpers Ferry. Rain in the evening.[34]

June 26, Wednesday (Richmond): Lee explains to Governor Letcher why Capt. Briscoe Baldwin was reassigned from Col. Dimmock at the Richmond Arsenal to Maj. Josiah Gorgas, the chief of ordnance. Lee requests that Navy Secretary Mallory order the rifling of several large caliber naval guns at Gosport, pointing out that it was being done at the Brooklyn Navy Yard and that Lee thinks it possible with the machinery at Richmond and Norfolk. Lee informs Gen. Theophilus H. Holmes that all his currently unassigned companies will be formed into the 49th Virginia, though they need not be physically united at present.[35] Lee writes also to Joe Johnston regarding the formation of the 43rd Virginia under Col. R. M. Conn, and Lee also sends Conn his commission and orders to form his regiment from companies then at Harpers Ferry. Lee writes to Maj. Gorgas, explaining that Lee mistakenly requisitioned artillery and implements for Garnett's force, but failed to include ammunition for same; he would like Gorgas to send the needed ammunition to Garnett. Lee informs Rev. Thomas Preston of Lexington that he will assign him to whatever regiment he desires, provided it does not already have a chaplain.[36]

June 27, Thursday (Richmond): Lee meets with President Davis in the morning; one of the topics discussed is Yorktown. Lee writes to Col. Talcott his concerns that the location for the battery at Burwell's Bay is too far removed from the channel. He also requests Huger to procure a map of the James said to be at the Lighthouse Inspection Office in Norfolk for Talcott's use.[37]

He writes Maj. Thomas H. Williamson regarding a map of the Manassas fortifications and requests Gorgas to send artillery ammunition to Williamsburg. Lee instructs Gen. Winder to release from arrest a "suspicious character" identified only as "Selby," but cautions that "he is not to leave the city during the war."[38]

June 28, Friday (Richmond): Lee meets twice, once in the morning at Lee's office and then again in the evening at Lee's residence, with his former aide John Brooke, probably to discuss the projectile Brooke is working on. Lee instructs Holmes that if erecting a battery at Evansport is as good as one at Mathias Point, then to choose Evansport. He is to do so, however, only after consulting with the Navy, but to do nothing at either place that will reveal his purpose. Lee writes to Col. J. W. Ware regarding the difficulties Ware is having in forming his 34th Virginia regiment—Johnston has no unassigned

---

34 OR 2, 949-51; REL to J. M. McCue, June 25, 1861, VAF, NA; Edward Porter Alexander to Bettie Alexander, June 25, 1861, E. P. Alexander papers, UNC. Charles Crump served with the 16th VA and 26th VA; he was killed at Second Manassas on August 30, 1862. Krick, *Lee's Colonels*, 106. McCue was an officer in the Virginia militia from Augusta County. John N. McCue, *The McCues of the Old Dominion* (Mexico, MO, 1912), 39.

35 REL to John Letcher, June 26, 1861, VAF, NA; REL to Stephen Mallory, June 26, 1861, VAF, NA; REL to Holmes, June 26, 1861, VAF, NA. Josiah Gorgas was another Northern-born Confederate; married to the daughter of the governor of Alabama, he followed her state into the Confederacy. He rose to brigadier general in late 1864; Joe Johnston said of Gorgas, "He created the ordnance department out of nothing." Warner, *Generals in Gray*, 112. Lee misunderstood Dimmock's wishes regarding Baldwin and mistakenly ordered him away. REL to Letcher, June 26, 1861, VAF, NA.

36 REL to Johnston, June 26, 1861, VAF, NA; REL to R. M. Conn, June 26, 1861, VAF, NA; OR 2, 954-5; REL to T. L. Preston, June 26, 1861, VAF, NA. The 43rd VA Inf. was never created; Col. Conn was commander of the 43rd VA Militia and it may have been intended for his militia to be mustered into Confederate service along with other Shenandoah Valley units. There is no record of Conn serving beyond the first few months of 1861. Conn CSR.

37 REL endorsement on "Lt. Col. Johnston" to REL, June 27, 1861, VAF, NA; REL to Andrew Talcott, June 27, 1861, VAF, NA; REL to Huger, June 27, 1861, VAF, NA. Lee's endorsement on Johnston's letter suggests that Gen. Cooper was also present for the meeting with Davis; "Lt. Col. Johnston" is probably Robert Johnston, as the document concerns a commander for Magruder's cavalry, which position Robert Johnston held. Krick, *Lee's Colonels*, 212.

38 REL to T. H. Williamson, June 27, 1861, VAF, NA; REL to Gorgas, June 27, 1861, VAF, NA; W. M. Ward to REL, July 27, 1861, VAF, NA. Williamson was a professor at VMI for nearly 40 years, including during the war; he was an engineer on Beauregard's and later Jackson's staff but never received a commission in the Confederate forces, only in the Virginia forces. Krick, *Staff Officers in Gray*, 305.

companies and Lee has none at Richmond that can be given to him. Lee writes to Garnett as well regarding Porterfield's difficulties in mustering companies, that one has gone AWOL, one is massively over-strength, and several are under-strength.[39]

June 29, Saturday (Richmond): Lee joins President Davis, Senator Louis T. Wigfall of Texas, and the President's nephew, Lt. Col. Joseph R. Davis in reviewing a portion of the troops in Richmond. Lee instructs Beauregard to form any surplus companies into a temporary battalion until a new regiment can be formed. Lee explains to Capt. M. Dulaney Ball that the Confederate and United States' governments have not yet established any sort of formal protocol regarding prisoners of war and their parole or exchange. Lee inquires of Charles Talcott, superintendent of the Richmond & Danville Railroad, what facilities exist in Danville that could be used as a POW depot.[40]

Lee informs Thomas H. Wynne, president of the Richmond & Petersburg Railroad, that his employees will be exempted from militia duty. Lee writes to Maj. M. G. Harman at Staunton regarding the status of the 27th Virginia and directing him to call out one company of militia to guard government property until more volunteers arrive. Lee writes to his daughter Mildred, who has joined her mother at Kinloch, with the latest family news and mentioning a recent visit by Col. Washington's daughter; he also mentions Mildred's cat Tom, who "no doubt lords it in a high manner . . . at Arlington. He will have strange things to tell you when you next see him."[41]

June 30, Sunday (Richmond): Lee's 30th wedding anniversary. Lee meets with Talcott in the morning to discuss the Norfolk defenses, which Talcott just inspected. Lee instructs Huger to move Col. Roger Pryor's 3rd Virginia to protect Fort Boykin at Day's Point. Lee writes to Holmes further about selecting either Evansport or Mathias Point for a Potomac battery and tells Lt. Eugene W. Baylor of New Orleans that he has no place on his staff for him.[42]

---

39 Brooke, *Ironclads and Big Guns,* 25; *OR* 2, 959; REL to J. W. Ware, REL papers, UVA; REL to Garnett, June 28, 1861, VAF, NA. Evansport is modern-day Quantico.

40 C. Vann Woodward, ed., *Mary Chesnut's Civil War* (New York, 1994), 84; REL to Beauregard, June 29, 1861, VAF, NA; REL to M. D. Ball, June 29, 1861, VAF, NA; REL to Charles Talcott, June 29, 1861, VAF, NA. Wigfall was a career politician from South Carolina; he served as an aide to Beauregard during the bombardment of Fort Sumter. Wigfall was commissioned colonel of the 1st TX Inf. and later brigadier general; he resigned in early 1862 to serve in the Senate, where he was one of the most outspoken opponents of Jefferson Davis. Warner, *Generals in Gray,* 336-7. Joseph Davis was lieutenant colonel of the 10th MS Inf., but served most of the war in Virginia first as an aide to his uncle, then as a brigade commander in the Army of Northern Virginia. Warner, *Generals in Gray,* 68. It is not known what troops Lee, et. al. reviewed. Ball was a captain in the 11th VA Cav. and rose to lieutenant colonel of that regiment. Krick, *Lee's Colonels,* 44.

41 REL to T. H. Wynne, June 29, 1861, VAF, NA; REL to M. G. Harman, (2 messages) June 29, 1861, VAF, NA; Dowdey, *Wartime Papers,* 54-5. Mildred had just finished her first year at St. Mary's School in Raleigh, NC.

42 Dowdey, *Wartime Papers,* 812; Talcott diary, June 30, 1861, VHS; REL to Huger, June 30, 1861, VAF, NA; *OR* 2, 961; REL to E. W. Baylor, June 30, 1861, VAF, NA.

July 1861

Throughout July, Union forces continued to build up in northern Virginia and on the Peninsula, increasing the fears of an impending attack. Gen. P. G. T. Beauregard, in command at Manassas, unveiled a plan to Gen. Lee and President Davis to clear the Yankees from the northern part of the state entirely, and to follow that up by capturing Washington and ending the war. Beauregard's plan was as delusional as it was grandiose, and Lee told him as much by citing the green condition of the troops and the fortifications around Washington behind which the Federals could take position.

Lee's attention turned increasingly toward the mountains of western Virginia during the early summer. He likely considered affairs there largely settled when his former aide Robert Garnett took command, but the situation changed when Garnett was killed in his first action at Corrick's Ford—making him the first general officer to be killed in the war. Lee sent William Loring as a replacement and planned to assume command himself; the Battle of Manassas delayed those plans.

President Davis traveled to Manassas when he learned of the battle there. Lee wanted desperately to go as well, but Davis ordered him to remain in Richmond. The battle confirmed much of what Lee said earlier: the well-intentioned army was not yet a fully conditioned fighting force, and after its defeat the Union army did indeed shelter inside the fortifications of Washington.

A week later Lee went to the mountains to take command in western Virginia, trading his Franklin Street quarters for a tent that he shared with his two aides, Col. John Washington and Capt. Walter Taylor. Before leaving, Washington purchased mess equipment for the three of them.[1]

Not knowing exactly what the future had in store for him, Lee wrote to a cousin a summation of his views on the war thus far, and all that he had done to date:

> As far as my voice and counsel go they will be continued on our side as long as there is one horse than can carry his rider or one rider that can wield a sword. I prefer annihilation to submission, they may destroy, but I trust will never conquer us. I bear no malice, have no animosities to indulge, no selfish purpose to gratify. My only object is to repel the invaders of our peace and the spoilers of our homes. I hope in future they will see the inequity of their course and return to their better nature. Since my arrival here [Richmond] I have been laboring assiduously to organize and equip armies, fortify the entrances of our rivers, and prepare for the struggle which I know was approaching. The battle of the 21st July [sic] was some evidence of our strength. I should have preferred rather to have been there than here, not that I could have done as well as was done, but I could have struck for my home and my country. The President however desired me here and I am happy in believing that all was done that could have been done.[2]

* * *

---

1 REL to Charles Dimmock, July 27, 1861, VAF, NA; Thomas, *REL*, 198. Lee's letter to Dimmock mentions "his lodgings on Franklin Street;" which indicates he moved from the Spotswood Hotel much earlier than previously thought. JAW to Gustavus A. Myers, Sept. 8, 1861, G. A. Myers papers, College of William & Mary. Washington forgot to pay for these items before leaving Richmond and had to get an acquaintance in the city to settle his account later. Washington explained that he expected the trip to western Virginia to be but a short one and intended to pay himself, "but as far as I can see we are as far off as ever." Ibid.

2 REL to Anne Lee Loyd, undated, Edward G. W. Butler papers, Duke.

July 1, Monday (Richmond): Lee writes to Robert Garnett approving of his proposed operations in western Virginia, which Lee has submitted to the president for approval; Lee notes that "capture of the railroad at Cheat River would be worth to us an army" and two more regiments have been ordered to Garnett. He cautions John Magruder not to station troops too far in advance of his main lines around Yorktown. Lee sends clarification to Joe Johnston regarding Gilbert Meem's militia explaining that Lee was only seeking information not trying to censure in any way. Lee writes to the commander at West Point regarding the sale of liquor to the troops, and to the commander of the 39th Virginia Militia regarding acquisition of muskets for his use. He directs Benjamin Huger to swap several guns at Fort Norfolk for those destined for Fort Boykin. Custis is commissioned as captain of engineers.[3]

July 2, Tuesday (Richmond): Lee meets with Andrew Talcott in morning, likely discussing defenses along the Rappahannock. Lee informs Huger that an unnamed individual jailed for "treasonous conduct" at Norfolk should be held for trial by a military court, and that Lee has referred the matter to the secretary of war. He writes to Mary, expressing concern about Agnes's apparent desire to fill her calendar with social visits "as if enjoyment was the order of the day.... These are serious times and our chief pleasure must be what is necessary and proper for the occasion." He tells Mary not to accept currency drawn on banks which are now behind Union lines: "No one receives them here, nor will any of the banks. Wheeling is considered to have gone over to the enemy." Lee laments that Custis is being sent to North Carolina on an inspection tour: "My greatest comfort is therefore taken from me." Custis formally accepts his commission.[4]

July 3, Wednesday (Richmond): In the morning Lee meets with former Governor Wyndham Robertson regarding his son Francis who is currently enrolled at VMI but wants to enlist. Lee orders him relieved from duty at VMI and sends a copy of the orders to Governor Robertson. Lee notifies Jackson that he has been promoted to brigadier general.[5]

July 4, Thursday (Richmond): A young boy named Henry and his father visit Lee and present him a four-volume version of the Bible. Lee informs Huger that per Governor Letcher's wishes, Col. Francis H. Smith, Lt. Col. J. T. L. Preston, and Maj. Stapleton Crutchfield—all of VMI—are being assigned to him for field service. Lee responds to a complaint from D. H. Hill about being placed under Magruder's command; Hill thought himself senior to Magruder and did not realize that Magruder had been promoted to brigadier general.[6]

---

3 OR 2, 239; REL to Magruder, July 1, 1861, VAF, NA; OR 2, 962; REL to H. B. Tomlin, July 1, 1861, VAF, NA; REL to E. S. Brackett, July 1, 1861, VAF, NA; G. W. Custis Lee CSR. Based on the letter to Johnston, it would seem Johnston had taken offense at the inquiry, causing Lee to assure Johnston he meant no interference in Johnston's authority. Custis's commission ranked from March 16.

4 Talcott diary, July 2, 1861, VHS; REL to Huger, July 2, 1861, VAF, NA; Dowdey, *Wartime Papers*, 55-6; Custis CSR. Shortly after this meeting, Talcott went to the Rappahannock, thus the conclusion that that region was the topic of discussion.

5 Robert J. Trout, ed., *In the Saddle with Stuart: The Story of Frank Smith Robertson of Jeb Stuart's Staff* (Gettysburg, PA, 1998), 12; Robert L. Dabney, *Life and Campaigns of Lt. General T. J. (Stonewall) Jackson* (Harrisonburg, VA, 1983), 204. Wyndham Robertson was acting governor in 1836-7 upon the resignation of Littleton W. Tazewell; he was a direct descendant of Pocahontas and John Rolfe. A Whig, Robertson was very Unionist prior to Lincoln's call for volunteers; during Reconstruction he was heavily involved in the readmission of Virginia to the Union. Matthew P. Andrews, *Virginia: The Old Dominion* (Richmond, VA, 1949), 451, 543. Francis Robertson served as a lieutenant in the 48th VA then on the staffs of Stuart and Rooney Lee. Krick, *Staff Officers in Gray*, 255.

6 Jones, *Personal Reminiscences of REL*, 409-10; REL to Huger, July 4, 1861, VAF, NA; REL to D. H. Hill, July 4, 1861, VAF, NA. Henry and his father were initially turned away by one of Lee's staff, claiming the general was too busy to see them. Lee overheard the conversation and admitted them to his office; several days later Lee visited the boy and gave him an inscribed copy of "Light Horse Harry" Lee's *Recollections of General Washington*. Jones, *Personal Reminiscences of REL*, 409-10. Lee recommended that Huger form a new regiment and assign all three VMI officers to it; all three were assigned to the 9th VA Inf. at Craney Island. REL to Huger, July 4, 1861, VAF, NA; Krick, *Lee's Colonels*, 107, 309, 350.

Lee forwards to Col. Dimmock concerns about fire hazards around several of the ordnance department buildings, and directs that it be corrected if true. Lee releases the results of the Philippi court of inquiry, which blames Porterfield for the defeat. Lee writes to several officials of the Baptist Church in Culpeper Courthouse regarding complaints against the troops stationed in the town. Lee recommends to Richmond Mayor Joseph Mayo that he avail himself of an opportunity to employ black laborers on the construction of the city's defenses.[7]

July 5, Friday (Richmond): Lee meets with Governor Letcher's aide Richard H. Catlett concerning the status of Virginia's forces and additional officers required. Lee writes to Sen. R. M. T. Hunter regarding the defenses of the lower Rappahannock region and Northern Neck, and informs several state officers their commissions in Virginia's forces will likely be vacated because Virginia's forces are being absorbed by the Confederacy. Lee writes to Brig. Gen. John H. Winder to revoke the paroles and imprison three Union officers in retaliation for the indictment of the crew of the privateer *Savannah* in New York for treason and piracy.[8]

He also forwards to Huger an opinion from Virginia's Attorney General John R. Tucker regarding the arrest of those accused of treason. Lee approves Magruder's actions to suppress Union raiding parties against Peninsula civilians, and informs him that light field guns are preferable to siege guns for field use. Lee notifies Garnett that three additional regiments are being sent to him, and opines to Capt. J. Lyle Clark that he hopes enough Marylanders will enlist that a second Maryland regiment can be formed, and thus Lee does not want Clark's company joining a Virginia regiment. Lee clarifies for Huger his earlier orders concerning Francis Smith and the others from VMI being assigned to Norfolk. Lee arranges to have 200 tons of raw metal in the Valley moved to Bellona Arsenal via the Orange & Alexandria Railroad. He also orders the temporary exemption of a number of employees of the Manassas Gap Railroad.[9]

July 6, Saturday (Richmond): Lee informs Beauregard that no official POW exchange agreement exists, but if he is able to do a 1 for 1 exchange he is authorized to do so. He relays to Navy Secretary Mallory an inquiry from Huger regarding detailing Army personnel to work at the Navy Yard, and instructs Magruder not to move heavy guns from Gloucester Point to Yorktown as D. H. Hill wishes to do. Lee instructs Holmes that a battery at Mathias Point is not necessary as long as the batteries upriver from there are held, but that the enemy cannot be allowed to occupy Mathias Point.[10]

Lee informs Brig. Gen. Henry Wise that since the transfer of Virginia's forces to the Confederacy, the authority to appoint field and staff officers rests with the president alone. He also clarifies for Maj.

---

7 REL to Dimmock, July 4, 1861, VAF, NA; *OR* 2, 72-4; REL to "Messers T. Latham and others," July 4, 1861, VAF, NA; REL endorsement on Richard Raines to REL, undated, VAF, NA. Lee took no further action against Porterfield, who was left in command of the troops at Beverly, under Garnett's overall control. Newell, *Lee vs. McClellan*, 100.

8 R. H. Catlett to William N. Pendleton, July 5, 1861, W. N. Pendleton papers, UNC; REL to R. M. T. Hunter, July 5, 1861, VAF, NA; REL to Julian Fairfax, July 5, 1861, VAF, NA; REL to J. H. Chamberlayne, July 5, 1861, VAF, NA; *OR* 3, Series 2, 689-90. Catlett was a lawyer from Rockbridge County; he later served on the staff of Gens. John Echols and James Kemper. Krick, *Staff Officers in Gray*, 93. Catlett told Pendleton: "Gen. Lee complains that our officers will not make their returns and that he cannot get the forces regularly organized. . . . [H]e says that with more regiments than he has officers, he cannot ascertain where officers are required." Winder was provost marshal of Richmond and responsible for its prisons. He later was placed in charge of all prisons east of the Mississippi River; he was vilified by Northerners for the living conditions of Union prisoners. He did not survive the war, dying in early 1865. Warner, *Generals in Gray*, 340-1.

9 REL to Huger, July 5, 1861, VAF, NA; REL to Magruder, July 5, 1861, VAF, NA; Dowdey, *Wartime Papers*, 57-8; *OR* 2, 240; REL to J. L. Clark, July 5, 1861, VAF, NA; REL to Thomas A. Dodamead, July 5, 1861, Lee papers, Brock collection; REL to J. M. Goldsborough, July 5, 1861, VAF, NA. Clark was commander of the "Maryland Guards," which became part of the 21st VA Inf.; Clark himself later commanded the 30th VA Battalion. Krick, *Lee's Colonels*, 92.

10 REL to Beauregard, July 6, 1861, VAF, NA; REL to Huger, July 6, 1861, VAF, NA; REL to Magruder, July 6, 1861, VAF, NA; *OR* 2, 963-4.

Michael Harman his earlier instructions to use militia to guard the government property in Staunton. Lee informs Richmond & York River Railroad officials that while some railroad personnel can be exempted from military service, conductors are not exempted under the present law. Lee complains to Governor Letcher that because of incomplete returns from commanders in the field, he does not know what units still need field officers and what field officers are without commands.[11]

July 7, Sunday (Richmond): Lee informs W. A. Smith of Middlesex County that, despite his long service in the state militia, because of a surplus of officers at the present time, he cannot be commissioned.[12]

July 8, Monday (Richmond): Lee instructs Huger to assign the three VMI officers—Smith, Preston, and Crutchfield—to the 9th Virginia so as to keep them together. He instructs Magruder to form the 32nd Virginia from companies at Williamsburg and to put Col. B. S. Ewell in command of it, and reassigns Lt. Col. D. A. Langhorne from mustering officer at Lynchburg to the 42nd Virginia, informing Langhorne that he will be promoted to colonel when a vacancy occurs.[13] Lee writes to Col. Alfred Beckley concerning his commission and the organization of the 35th Virginia, sends Jesse Burks his commission as colonel and assigns him to command of the 42nd Virginia, and informs Lt. Col. William J. Green that another officer has already been given command of the 47th Virginia. He opines that the staff of Eastern State Asylum in Williamsburg is not subject to exemption from military duty, but if they can provide substitutes they can be discharged if essential to the hospital.

He writes as well to Mary that he is still concerned over where she and the girls will reside during the war; he mentions that he cannot give Orton Williams a place on his staff, so he is having Williams sent to Tennessee to serve with Maj. Gen. Leonidas Polk.[14]

July 9, Tuesday (Richmond): Lee informs Garnett that Lt. Col. William L. Jackson and Maj. Pearson B. Adams of his command were intended by Governor Letcher to be assigned to the 35th Virginia, so if he can spare them they are to report to Col. Beckley. The general also informs Gen. Huger of several field officers assigned to his command, including Lee's aide Maj. Francis W. Smith. He writes to Col. John A. Campbell at Abingdon, urging him to finish the organization of his regiment as quickly as possible.[15]

---

11 REL to H. A. Wise, July 6, 1861, VAF, NA; REL to M. G. Harman, July 6, 1861, VAF, NA; REL endorsement on R. H. Temple to REL, undated, VAF, NA; REL endorsement on John R. Chambliss and David Weisiger to unknown, undated, VAF, NA. Lee's comment on Chambliss and Weisiger's letter was, "There are several Majors on duty with troops, who are not assigned to regiments. Until returns are made from the different commands, it is impossible to state whether more officers are needed or not."

12 REL to W. A. Smith, July 7, 1861, VAF, NA. The letter is addressed to "W. A. Smith," but the cover is addressed to "W. A. Street;" he is listed as being lieutenant colonel of the 109th VA Militia, but no records could be found for the 109th nor could any Confederate service record be located for either Smith or Street.

13 REL to Huger, July 8, 1861, VAF, NA; REL to Magruder, July 8, 1861, VAF, NA; REL to Langhorne, July 8, 1861, VAF, NA.

14 REL to Beckley, July 8, 1861, REL papers, VHS; REL to W. J. Green, July 8, 1861, VAF, NA; REL to Robert Saunders, July 8, 1861, VAF, NA; REL to Mrs. REL, July 8, 1861, Lee papers, VHS. Beckley was unable to recruit enough men thus the 35th never formed and his commission was not confirmed. He continued in the field in his role as a militia brigadier general until early 1862. Allardice, *More Generals in Gray*, 34-5. Green was lieutenant colonel of the 47th VA; he was not reelected in May 1862 and was killed during the Seven Days while serving as an aide to Col. Dorsey Pender. Krick, *Lee's Colonels*, 168.

15 REL to Garnett, July 9, 1861, VAF, NA; REL to Huger, July 9, 1861, VAF, NA; REL to J. A. Campbell, July 9, 1861, VAF, NA. Jackson became colonel of the 31st VA and rose to brigadier general. Warner, *Generals in Gray*, 153-4. Adams became major of the 42nd VA, but was not reelected in April 1862. Krick, *Lee's Colonels*, 30. Smith was assigned to the 41st VA. REL to Huger, July 9, 1861, VAF, NA. Campbell's regiment became the 48th VA. He was wounded in the Valley at Winchester in May 1862 and resigned in the fall of that year when he was not promoted to permanent brigade command. Krick, *Lee's Colonels*, 81-2.

July 10, Wednesday (Richmond): Lee places Capt. George N. Hollins of the Navy in command of the James River defenses and instructs him to focus on the portion of river between Day's Point and Mulberry Island. Lee writes to Magruder lamenting the death of Lt. Col. Charles Dreux and noting that additional guns have been sent to him today. Lee adds that the creation of the battery at Day's Point has lessened the chances of the Federals landing at Carters Grove, and that Gloucester Point must be strengthened to prevent passage of the York. He also sends Magruder two opinions by the Virginia attorney general regarding the detention of suspicious persons.[16]

Lee informs Lt. Col. Langhorne that there are no firearms in Richmond, thus he should arm the troops in Lynchburg with whatever flintlocks are on hand there, and inquires of Dimmock why he is sending unmounted cannon barrels to Magruder. Lee requests a meeting with Edmund Fontaine of the Virginia Central to discuss increased facilities for troop movement, and requests that the Orange & Alexandria adjust its schedule to give priority to troop trains.[17]

July 11, Thursday (Richmond): Lee receives two letters from Garnett regarding enemy intentions around Parkersburg; Garnett believes that region to be more threatened than the Kanawha Valley and thus would like Brig. Gen. Henry Wise's force to be diverted northward from the Kanawha. Lee replies with his thoughts on the matter and informs him of officers newly appointed to regiments under Garnett's command. Lee relays Gen. Garnett's views regarding the Kanawha and Parkersburg to Gen. Wise. He writes as well to Gen. Holmes, scolding him for having troops openly firing on enemy shipping from Mathias Point before his position was fortified and strongly defended; Lee worries that Holmes has now made the Federals aware of the importance of Mathias Point, and they will now endeavor to capture it.

Lee forwards the attorney general's opinions regarding suspicious persons to Secretary of the Commonwealth George Munford. Lee tells Rev. G. H. Wortham of Nomini Grove that he does not have enough troops to garrison all parts of the vulnerable Northern Neck, but that if Mathias Point and the Richmond, Fredericksburg, & Potomac Railroad are held, it will do much to keep Union forces out.[18]

Lee endorses John R. C. Lewis for an artillery commission, noting the young man's relationship to George Washington. The general also writes to Francis W. Smith who left this morning for a new assignment on Huger's staff; he is not only upset at what he perceives as the young officer's lack of social graces, but also points out that although he was ordered to report to Huger, Smith had not yet received orders relieving him from duty on Lee's staff; Lee subsequently issues those orders.[19]

---

16 *OR* 2, 972-3; REL to Magruder, July 10, 1861, VAF, NA. Dreux was commander of the 1st LA Battalion; he was killed in a skirmish July 5 on Smith's farm. He had been New Orleans district attorney and state legislator; his funeral procession was witnessed by more than 30,000. Mark St. John Erickson, "Cedar Lane Skirmishes Taught Early Civil War Lessons," Hampton *Daily Press*, July 11, 2016.

17 REL to Langhorne, July 10, 1861, VAF, NA; REL to Dimmock, July 10, 1861, VAF, NA; REL to Edward Fontaine, July 10, 1861, VAF, NA; REL to J. S. Barbour, July 10, 1861, VAF, NA.

18 *OR* 2, 242-4, 974; REL to G. W. Munford, July 11, 1861, VAF, NA; REL to G. H. Wortham, July 11, 1861, VAF, NA.

19 REL endorsement on J. R. C. Lewis to REL, undated, VAF, NA; REL to F. W. Smith, F. W. Smith papers, VHS. Lewis was nephew of Washington's grandson; he served in the Bedford Light Artillery, rising to major before transferring to the Western Theater in 1863. Krick, *Lee's Colonels*, 238. Smith wrote to Lee on the 13th that Lee was mistaken, that he did not actually leave Richmond on the 11th but rather on the 12th. It seems lost on Smith that regardless of *when* he left, he did not have the necessary orders and he should have checked out with Lee before going. F. W. Smith to REL, July 13, 1861, F. W. Smith papers. Although Smith wrote that he was moving on to Huger's staff, his record does not show that he ever served in that role. Joseph H. Crute, Jr., *Confederate Staff Officers, 1861-1865* (Powhatan, VA, 1982), 91-2. Smith briefly served as major of the 41st VA, aide to Gen. William Mahone, and commander at Drewry's Bluff; he was mortally wounded April 5, 1865, on the retreat from Petersburg. Krick, *Staff Officers in Gray*, 268-9. Apparently Beauregard requested Smith's services, as on the 12th Lee informed him that Smith had been assigned to the 41st VA at Norfolk. REL to Beauregard, July 12, 1861, VAF, NA.

July 12, Friday (Richmond): Lee and Davis review the newly arrived 6th North Carolina at Capitol Square. Lee tells Governor Letcher understrength companies should be brought up to minimum strength regardless of their enlistment period. Lee replies to an inquiry from Virginia Adj. Gen. William Richardson regarding Col. George Richardson's assignment to command the 47th Virginia and Col. Francis H. Smith assuming command at Craney Island in his place. Lee requests Richmond Mayor Joseph Mayo provide 300 "laborers" to construct fortifications around the capital.[20]

Lee informs Magruder that several more heavy guns will be sent for the Gloucester Point works, but that no additional troops can be spared. Lee also urges him to press on with completion of the Williamsburg defenses. Lee orders that troop trains will run on schedule henceforth, so officers will have their men and supplies at the depot in time for this to happen. He instructs Maj. Harman to muster into service every company he has at Staunton, but to retain one militia company there as guards. Lee writes to Mary explaining that he has heard nothing about his own appointment as "Commander-in-Chief of the Southern Army, nor have I any expectation or wish for it. President Davis holds that position." He mentions as well that Rob has been made captain of a cadet company at UVA and needs a sword and sash; Lee can provide a sword but he has no extra sash.[21]

July 13, Saturday (Richmond): Gen. Garnett is killed at the Battle of Corricks Ford.[22]

July 14, Sunday (Richmond): Lee learns of Garnett's death and defeat at Rich Mountain and orders Brig. Gen. Henry R. Jackson to move with his brigade to the relief of Garnett's army, and for Gorgas "to send a full supply" of ammunition to Wise. Around 3:30 p. m. Col. James R. Chesnut arrives from Manassas with a proposal of operations from Beauregard. President Davis is ill when Chesnut arrives, but agrees to meet with him later that evening. That evening at the Executive Mansion, Chesnut reveals to the president, Gen. Cooper, and Lee a radical idea from Beauregard to join his force with Johnston's Valley army and together first clear the Federals out of northern Virginia, then have Johnston drive the enemy from the Shenandoah Valley and join with Garnett's army and cross the Potomac River into Maryland to attack Washington from the rear while Beauregard attacks in front from Virginia. Davis and Lee both point out the impracticability of the plan because of Johnston's shortage of manpower and the fact that the Federals would almost certainly fall back into their fortifications around Washington rather than risk an open-field battle. The meeting continues into the 15th.[23]

---

20 A. C. Avery, "Additional Sketch Sixth Regiment," in Walter Clark, ed., *Histories of the Several Regiments and Battalions from North Carolina in the Great War, 1861-'65*, 5 vols. (Raleigh, NC, 1901), vol. 1, 339; Richard W. Iobst, *The Bloody Sixth: The Sixth North Carolina Regiment, Confederate States of America* (Raleigh, NC, 1965), 17; Charleston *Mercury*, July 16, 1861; REL endorsement on S. B. French to REL, undated, VAF, NA; REL to W. G. Richardson, July 12, 1861, VAF, NA; REL to Joseph Mayo, July 12, 1861, VAF, NA. The *Mercury's* account of the 6th NC review places it on the 13th, but this is impossible given the regiment's timeline set out by both Clark and Iobst. Gov. Letcher's aide Bassett French tells Lee that "many companies" being formed were balking at the three-year enlistment required. French to REL, undated, VAF, NA.

21 OR 2, 975; OR 51, pt. 2, 163; Frederick Maurice, ed., *Lee's Aide-de-Camp: Charles Marshall* (Lincoln, NE, 2000), 6; REL to M. G. Harman, July 12, 1861, VAF, NA; Fitz Lee, *General Lee*, 108. UVA had just established a military education program of which Rob was a part.

22 Warner, *Generals in Gray*, 100. Garnett was forced to evacuate his positions atop Rich Mountain and Laurel Hill by Union troops under generals George B. McClellan and William S. Rosecrans. He was shot from his horse while directing the rear guard at the crossing of the Cheat River. His body was taken by troops of the 7th Indiana, whose commander, Col. Ebenezer Dumont, served with Garnett during the Mexican War, who had it returned to Garnett's family. Newell, *Lee vs. McClellan*, 138-40. Garnett's death created a command vacuum in western Virginia that directly impacted Lee in the coming weeks.

23 Freeman, *Lee*, vol. 1, 535; OR 2, 245, 506-11; Fitz Lee, *General Lee*, 110; Roman, *Military Operations of Beauregard*, vol. 1, 85-8. Henry Jackson was a member of the Georgia secession convention, and briefly served as a Confederate judge before accepting a brigadier's commission; he resigned in December 1861 to command Georgia state troops and later

July 15, Monday (Richmond): The meeting with President Davis, Gen. Cooper, and Col. Chesnut continues; Beauregard's plan is not approved and Chesnut returns to convey this to Beauregard. Lee sends his congratulations to Magruder for J. B. Hood's recent victory at Smith's farm. Holmes is instructed to construct a battery at Gray's Point on the lower Rappahannock; Talcott will oversee the actual construction and Lee reiterates not to draw attention to this work.[24]

Lee orders Cols. A. C. Moore and J. A. Campbell to finalize the organization of their regiments at Abingdon and proceed to Staunton upon completion, and similar orders to Jesse Burks at Lynchburg. Lee informs Col. Tompkins that Wise will be joining him in the Kanawha and that more officers will soon be appointed for his command. Lee informs ordnance chief Gorgas that the 3rd Arkansas was sent to the front without ammunition, so to send 40,000 rounds for it to Staunton, as well as ammunition and equipment for an additional three regiments forming there. Lee writes to the Virginia auditor regarding several companies engaged in manufacturing arms.[25]

July 16, Tuesday (Richmond): Lee writes Magruder concerning the defenses at Jamestown Island; Lee does not want guns to be removed from there and used elsewhere on the Peninsula. Lee explains to Adjutant General Cooper that by sending Col. William Gilham into the field with the 21st Virginia, the Camp of Instruction at the Richmond Fairgrounds will be left without a commander; Lee recommends Brig. Gen. Henry Winder as the new commander. Lee orders Henry Jackson to defend the passes of Cheat Mountain and guard the approaches to the Virginia Central RR; he informs Jackson that additional troops are being sent to northwest Virginia and that Lee himself will leave Richmond on the 18th to take command there. He orders Dimmock to have two field guns sent to Cumberland Gap.[26]

July 17, Wednesday (Richmond): Holmes is ordered to send a portion of his force to Beauregard. Commissions for Jeb Stuart and Turner Ashby are sent to Johnston. Rooney is commissioned as a cavalry major.[27]

July 18, Thursday (Richmond): Enemy movements in northern Virginia prevent Lee's planned departure for Staunton and the mountains. Lee explains to Col. William Smith that regimental adjutants are chosen by their colonels, but the positions of regimental

---

commanded a brigade in the Army of Tennessee; he was captured at Nashville in December 1864. Warner, *Generals in Gray*, 149-50. Col. John S. Preston of Beauregard's staff was also present for this meeting. OR 2, 509-11. Preston was dispatched a day before Chesnut on a similar mission to Richmond; it appears that Preston let Chesnut handle the actual presentation to Davis et al. Roman, *Military Operations of Beauregard*, vol. 1, 84. Cooper's account of this meeting places it in the parlor of the Spotswood Hotel (he also placed it a day earlier), but that seems extremely unlikely because of the lack of privacy and also given Davis's illness. OR 2, 512-3. Chesnut's wife also has this meeting on the 13th in her "diary." Woodward, *Mary Chesnut's Civil War*, 99-100. Woodward's edited version of her diary however notes that she was off by 24 hours. Ibid., 225.

24 OR 2, 298, 509-11, 978-9. Lee's lingering irritation with Holmes over the Mathias Point battery was evident in the instructions regarding Gray's Point (located on the Middle Peninsula where state route 3 crosses the Rappahannock).

25 REL to A. C. Moore, July 15, 1861, Gilder-Lehrman; REL to J. A. Campbell, July 15, 1861, VAF, NA; REL to Jesse Burks, July 15, 1861, VAF, NA; REL to Gorgas, (2 messages) July 15, 1861, VAF, NA; REL to J. M. Bennett, July 15, 1861, VAF, NA. Alfred C. Moore was a former member of the NC legislature; he was colonel of the 29th VA until resigning in April 1863 due to poor health. Krick, *Lee's Colonels*, 276.

26 OR 2, 254; REL to Cooper, July 16, 1861, VAF, NA; OR 2, 979; REL to Dimmock, July 16, 1861, VAF, NA. Gilham was previously commandant of cadets at Virginia Military Institute and was both commander of Camp Lee and colonel of the 21st VA; his *Manual of Instructions for Volunteers and Militia* was widely used in the Army of Northern Virginia; he returned to VMI in early 1862. Krick, *Lee's Colonels*, 156. Lee must have discussed with Davis taking command in the mountains; it is possible that this was part of the discussion with Chesnut or possibly after Chesnut's return to Beauregard on the 15th while Lee was still with the President.

27 OR 2, 980-1; George Deas to J. E. Johnston, July 7, 1861, VAF, NA; Rooney CSR. All known correspondence written on the 17th and 18th was written and signed by Deas, suggesting that Lee was otherwise occupied.

quartermaster, commissary, and surgeon are appointed by the secretary of war.[28]

July 19, Friday (Richmond): Lee informs Beauregard that the governor no longer issues commissions, since the transfer of Virginia's troops to the Confederacy, so any such requests must go to the secretary of war. Lee informs the commander at Tappahannock that he wants work suspended on the fortifications at Gray's Point and the guns earmarked for there can be employed wherever desired along that stretch of the Rappahannock. Lee requests information from Maj. Harman regarding the roads through the mountains west and northwest of Staunton, as Lee's maps do not agree with reports he has received from locals. Dabney Maury reports to Lee and is commissioned a colonel.[29]

July 20, Saturday (Richmond): William W. Loring, Armistead L. Long, Carter Stevenson, and James Deshler all call upon Lee today for assignments. Lee sends Loring to take command of the Army of the Northwest; the others are assigned to Loring's staff. Lee explains to Charlottesville lawyer Allan B. Magruder the necessity of calling out the local militia: "The question seems to me to be, shall we remain quiet until driven from our homes, or shall we turn out and endeavor to drive our invader from the state."[30]

July 21, Sunday (Richmond): Lee remains in Richmond while President Davis goes to the front at Manassas; Lee learns of Johnston's and Beauregard's victory there in the evening via a telegram from the president. Lee advises Loring and Harman that reinforcements will be sent and recommends that they be stationed at Millboro to cover the western end of the Virginia Central Railroad; he also wishes Loring to occupy Cheat Mountain if possible, but ultimately to use his own discretion in selecting his position.[31]

Lee thanks Pocahontas County attorney William Skeen for information about that region and requests that he urge the people in his jurisdiction to cooperate with Loring. Lee explains to Elias Edmonds that the troops from Lancaster County

---

28 JAW to Edward Turner, July 19, 1861, J. A. Washington papers, LVA; George Deas to William Smith, July 18, 1861, VAF, NA. Washington wrote, "General Lee . . . intended leaving here yesterday but the anticipated fight at Manassas which has since begun prevented his going as the President was unwilling for him to leave here. I am uncertain when we shall go and whether to Staunton and the West or elsewhere, but we are packed and ready to start at a moment's notice." Smith was a former Congressman Virginia governor known as "Extra Billy" for payments from his private mail service; he was colonel of the 49th VA, rising to major general before taking office as governor in 1864. Warner, *Generals in Gray*, 284-5.

29 REL to Beauregard, July 19, 1861, VAF, NA; REL to W. N. Ward, July 19, 1861, VAF, NA; REL to M. G. Harman, July 19, 1861, VAF, NA; Dabney H. Maury, *Recollections of a Virginian in the Mexican, Indian, and Civil Wars* (New York, 1894), 143. Maury, nephew of famed oceanographer Matthew F. Maury, was a member of the celebrated class of 1846 at West Point; he served most of the war in the Western Theater and was the founder of the Southern Historical Society after the war. Warner, *Generals in Gray*, 215. Maury wrote of this meeting, "I was much impressed by the grave and anxious aspect of General Lee, and remarked . . . that it surprised and depressed me." Maury, *Recollections of a Virginian*, 143.

30 Long, *Memoirs of REL*, 111-2; *OR* 2, 986; REL to A. B. Magruder, July 20, 1861, VAF, NA. Loring lost an arm in the Mexican War; he out-ranked Lee in the antebellum U.S. Army which caused some friction between the two. He served all over the Confederacy; after the war he went to Egypt where he became a general. Warner, *Generals in Gray*, 193-4. The commissions of Long, Stevenson, and Deshler all are dated July 21st; although originally given staff roles, all three become generals. Crute, *Confederate Staff Officers*, 125-6. Long served with Loring only for a few months before he was assigned to Lee's staff; he eventually became Lee's military secretary. He was promoted to brigadier general and named chief of artillery of the Second Corps in 1863. After the war he lost his eyesight, yet wrote an invaluable work on Lee. Warner, *Generals in Gray*, 191-2. Stevenson was briefly colonel of the 53rd VA and served as Gen. Loring's chief of staff; in early 1862 he was promoted to brigadier general and sent to the Western Theater, rising to major general. Ibid., 292-3. Deshler apparently never resigned from the U.S. Army; he simply left while on leave. He was assigned to western Virginia and was wounded in December 1861, after which he was assigned to the staff of Theophilus Holmes; he was promoted to brigadier general in July 1863 and killed less than two months later at Chickamauga when an artillery round struck him in the chest. Ibid., 71-2. Magruder was the brother of Gen. John Bankhead Magruder, and served for a time on his brother's staff; he later wrote a biography of Chief Justice John Marshall. Krick, *Staff Officers in Gray*, 212.

31 Freeman, *Lee*, vol. 1, 537; *OR* 2, 986-7; REL to M. G. Harman, July 21, 1861, REL papers, University of Georgia.

cannot be returned to the Northern Neck to defend their home region. He instructs Huger to send several heavy guns from Norfolk to Magruder via Petersburg and Richmond.[32]

July 22, Monday (Richmond): Lee requests Huger to send an orphan Kentucky company at Norfolk to Richmond to be grouped with other companies from that state. Lee informs Alexander B. Hood of King George County that he already ordered the occupation of Mathias Point but has no more troops to send. Loring leaves Richmond for western Virginia. Heavy rain.[33]

July 23, Tuesday (Richmond): Lee meets with John Brooke regarding Brooke's experimental projectile, for which Lee urges speedy completion. Lee receives a package of books from Thomas H. Ellis. He writes to Henry Jackson advising that ammunition and equipment has been ordered to him, although it was mistakenly sent to Thomas Jackson at Harpers Ferry, 10 more regiments will soon join the Army of Northwest, and Loring has been appointed Garnett's successor.[34]

Lee informs Commissary General Lucius Northrop that there is inadequate amount of supplies at Staunton for the troops there currently, and adds that the equivalent of another division will need to be supplied from there as well. Lee refers to the secretary of war a request from Huger for additional North Carolina units to be sent to Suffolk. The general also writes to Col. George W. Lay regarding his resignation, and sends Dr. J. C. Cummings to Manassas to help with the wounded.[35]

July 24, Wednesday (Richmond): Loring assumes command at Monterey. Lee advises Henry Wise that he shared Wise's report of the engagement at Scary Creek with the president and that Loring is now in command and Wise may be required to link up with Loring's Army of the Northwest. Lee requests Gorgas to send ammunition to Wise's command and inquires of Dimmock if any artillery can be sent to Wise. Lee sends his congratulations to both Beauregard and Johnston for the victory at Manassas; "I almost wept for joy at the glorious victory achieved," he tells Johnston.[36] Lee inquires of Johnston about the Kentucky troops serving with him, as Lee has several companies at Richmond he would like to unite with them, and also advises that per President Davis's instructions Co. A of the 1st Georgia will be converted to an artillery battery using guns captured at Manassas. Lee directs Holmes to proceed with the delayed fortifications at Gray's Point and Cherry Point on the Rappahannock, advising that militia can be used either for that

---

32 REL to William Skeen, July 21, 1861, VAF, NA; REL to Elias Edmonds, July 21, 1861, VAF, NA; REL to Huger, July 21, 1861, VAF, NA. Edmonds was from one of the oldest and most prominent families in Lancaster Co. See Carolyn H. Jett, *Lancaster County, Virginia: Where the River Meets the Bay* (Lancaster, VA, 2003).

33 REL to Huger, July 22, 1861, VAF, NA; REL to A. B. Hood, July 22, 1861, VAF, NA; Long, *Memoirs of REL*, 117; Krick, *CW Weather*, 29.

34 Brooke, *Ironclads and Big Guns*, 27; REL to T. H. Ellis, July 24, 1861, REL papers, W&L; *OR 2*, 993. Ellis was president of the James River & Kanawha Company. Langhorne Gibson, Jr., *Cabell's Canal: The Story of the James River and Kanawha* (Richmond, VA, 2000), 259.

35 REL to L. B. Northrop, July 23, 1861, VAF, NA; REL to Huger, July 23, 1861, VAF, NA; REL to G. W. Lay, July 23, 1861, VAF, NA; J. C. Cummings pass, Stephen D. Lee papers, UNC. Lee and Northrop butted heads repeatedly during the war over supplies; the tone of Lee's letter to him suggests that their relations were already strained at this early point. Lee's aide George Deas notified Northrop on the 20th of this supply shortage at Staunton, but apparently Northrop had done nothing about it hence this somewhat terse note from Lee, which lacks the general's usual tact. Lay was an aide to Winfield Scott before the war and served on Miledge Bonham's staff early in the war; he later served as an aide to Joe Johnston and then in the Bureau of Conscription. Krick, *Staff Officers in Gray*, 198-9. Lee noted that Lay's original letter was delivered to him by Gen. Robert Toombs; whether Toombs had business to discuss with Lee or just happened to be in Richmond is not known. REL to G. W. Lay, July 23, 1861, VAF, NA.

36 Newell, *Lee vs. McClellan*, 174; *OR 2*, 996; REL to Gorgas, July 24, 1861, VAF, NA; REL to Dimmock, July 24, 1861, VAF, NA; Roman, *Military Operations of Beauregard*, vol. 1, 201; REL to Johnston, July 24, 1861, REL papers, UVA. Wise temporarily halted the advance of a Federal force under Brig. Gen. Jacob Cox at Scary Creek on July 17.

purpose or to free up other troops, and Col. Talcott will be sent to oversee the work. Lee thanks Thomas Ellis for the books received yesterday.[37]

July 25, Thursday (Richmond): Lee mildly rebukes Gen. Holmes for having a number of local companies serving in his district that have not been mustered into service, and adds that these men should be used to garrison his river fortifications. Lee directs Gen. Magruder to either route all requests for arms and ammunition through his ordnance officer, or if he does not have one, to appoint one. Lee forwards to Governor Letcher several recommendations for the promotion of Lt. Edwin G. Lee, adding his own recommendation.[38]

July 26, Friday (Richmond): Lee informs several citizens of Scott County that he is very sensitive to the danger posed to their region by Union forces operating out of Kentucky and he has ordered a substantial force to the area. He thanks the loyal citizens of east Tennessee for their pledge to protect the railroads from disloyal citizens, and he assures the citizens of Greenbrier County that Loring and his army will protect them.[39]

Lee writes to Gen. Huger regarding the Norfolk fortifications and informs the aging general that several additional heavy guns will be sent to him. Lee advises Wise that a force has been dispatched to Scott and Lee counties to deal with the enemy on Wise's southern flank. Lee inquires of Lt. Col. Charles Field which of his cavalry companies should receive the handful of carbines now available in Richmond. He also requests that the Tredegar Iron Works make four large caliber rifled guns to be ready for service the following week.[40]

July 27, Saturday (Richmond): Lee meets with President Davis in the morning to discuss the situation in western Virginia and almost certainly Lee's intent to leave for that region the following day. Lee instructs Holmes to hurry completion of the works at Gray's Point and Cherry Point on the lower Rappahannock and garrison them with local troops. Lee sends a major's commission to his cousin, Edwin G. Lee, and writes to Capt. F. S. Hale in Carroll County regarding his uncertainty of the forces then at Wytheville.[41]

Lee informs Col. Dimmock that Loring has two artillery batteries with less than half their complement of guns, thus to send any available pieces, and he informs Huger that there are no artillery officers available at present to take command of his field guns. Lee also requests a report from Dimmock on the troops at the Camp of Instruction. He writes to Mary regretting that he was not able to be present for the fight at Manassas: "I wished to partake in the . . . struggle, and am mortified at my absence, but the president thought it more important I should be here." He mentions as well that he leaves tomorrow for the mountains: "I wished to go before . . . and was all prepared, but the

---

37 REL to J. E. Johnston, (2 messages) July 24, 1861, VAF, NA; REL to T. H. Holmes, July 24, 1861, VAF, NA; REL to T. H. Ellis, July 24, 1861, REL papers, W&L. Gray's Point and Cherry Point are at the south and north ends, respectively, of the route 3 bridge over the Rappahannock.

38 REL to Holmes, July 25, 1861, VAF, NA; REL to Magruder, July 25, 1861, VAF, NA; REL to E. G. Lee, July 25, 1861, VAF, NA. Lee wanted to end the practice of ordnance requests from Magruder's command being submitted by various regimental and brigade commanders. Edwin Gray Lee was a distant cousin of REL; he was then serving in the 2nd VA and was promoted to major on the 26th. His CSR states that he was assigned to the 10th VA, but he served with the 33rd VA; he married William Nelson Pendleton's daughter, but was plagued by poor health and twice resigned his commission due to his inability to remain in the field. Warner, *Generals in Gray*, 177-8.

39 REL to J. L Shoemaker and others, July 26, 1861, VAF, NA; REL to L. D. Stout, July 26, 1861, VAF, NA; REL to "Messers Mattham and Price," July 26, 1861, VAF, NA.

40 *OR* 2, 1001-2; REL to Charles Field, July 26, 1861, VAF, NA; REL to J. R. Anderson, July 26, 1861, VAF, NA.

41 REL to Gorgas, July 27, 1861, VAF, NA; *OR* 2, 1003; REL to E. G. Lee, July 27, 1861, WNP papers, UNC; REL to F. S. Hale, July 27, 1861, VAF, NA. Lee's meeting with Davis is referred to in the letter to Gorgas referenced above; the subject was not mentioned, but given Lee's intent to leave Richmond on the 28th it must have been western Virginia. Not only was Lee unsure if any forces remained at Wytheville, he didn't know if a mustering officer was there or not, and so sent Capt. Hale all the required forms to muster forces himself if needed. REL to Hale, July 27, 1861, VAF, NA.

indications were so evident of the coming battle, and in the uncertainty of the result, the president forbade my departure. Now it is necessary and he consents."⁴²

July 28, Sunday (Richmond): Lee does not depart for western Virginia as he had intended to do. Instead, he updates Governor Letcher on two regiments being organized at Staunton, one to be led by Col. William Stuart, and the other to be commanded by Col. Daniel Ruggles.⁴³

July 29, Monday (Richmond/Staunton): Lee leaves Richmond for western Virginia, accompanied by aides Washington and Taylor and servants Perry and Meredith. They travel via the Virginia Central, arriving in Staunton on the evening mail train. The general and his entourage are saluted by a Georgia artillery battery camped on the Middlebrook Road just outside of town.⁴⁴

July 30, Tuesday (Staunton): Lee meets with Col. J. B. Baldwin, who Lee is considering for colonel of a new regiment being formed at Staunton, and instructs Maj. Michael Harman to hurry the completion of the unit. Lee further instructs Harman that if the governor's quota has been met, the militia on duty at Staunton can be sent home; otherwise, they must be sent to the front for service. Lee informs Governor Letcher that another regiment is nearing completion, but he has concerns the officer proposed to command it will not be acceptable to its officers and men. Lee suggests Baldwin as a replacement. Lee visits Virginia Sen. Alexander H. H. Stuart at his home on Church Street.⁴⁵

July 31, Wednesday (Staunton/Monterey): Lee and party ride westward along the Staunton-Parkersburg Turnpike to Monterey, setting up headquarters in a house at the center of town. At Monterey Lee confers with Brig. Gen. Henry R. Jackson and finds

---

42 REL to Dimmock, (2 messages) July 27, 1861, VAF, NA; REL to Huger, July 27, 1861, VAF, NA; Robert E. Lee, Jr., *Recollections and Letters of Robert E. Lee* (Old Saybrook, CT, n.d.), 37. Lee's request to Dimmock regarding the Camp of Instruction states that he wanted the results sent to him at "his lodgings on Franklin Street." At least one author has proposed that President Davis kept Lee behind in Richmond rather than sending him to Manassas to keep him in the background and minimize his contributions. Stanley Kimmel, *Mr. Davis's Richmond* (New York, 1958), 65. While Davis no doubt wanted to lay claim to being on the victorious field of battle himself, arguing without evidence that he did so at Lee's expense is ludicrous.

43 REL to Letcher, July 28, 1861, VAF, NA. The two regiments mentioned were the 52nd and 53rd, however the officers Lee named did not command either one – John Baldwin was given command of the 52nd, and Carter Stevenson became colonel of the 53rd. William Stuart took command of the 56th VA, and Ruggles was promoted to brigadier general and sent to the West. It is not known what business detained Lee in Richmond for an extra day. Freeman placed Lee's departure on the 28th, citing Lee's letter to Mary that he intended to leave on that date, and every writer since has followed suit. *Lee*, vol. 1, 541-3. However, a prominent resident of Staunton put Lee's arrival in that town on the 29th and John Washington's timeline for the trip confirms that they did not leave Richmond until the 29th (although Washington did not specifically state what day they left, one can follow his timetable backwards).

44 Joseph A. Waddell diary, July 29, 1861, Valley of the Shadow project, http://valley.lib.virginia.edu/papers/AD1500; Freeman, *Lee*, vol. 1, 541-3; Newell, *Lee vs. McClellan*, 182. Lee lamented that he was not able to see Rob at UVA as they passed through Charlottesville. Dowdey, *Wartime Papers*, 62. The Georgia artillery unit was probably the Troup Artillery which was en route to the mountains at that time.

45 REL to Letcher, July 30, 1861, Letcher papers, LVA; REL to Harman, July 30, 1861, REL papers, VHS; Margaret Briscoe Stuart Robertson, *My Childhood Recollections of the War: Life in the Confederate Stronghold of Staunton, Virginia, During the War Between the States* (Staunton, VA, 2013), 13. The regiment became the 52nd VA, and Baldwin was indeed its colonel when it took the field. Lee mentioned discussing the matter of its commander in detail with *someone* but did not say whom, but it was likely Michael Harman that he consulted, or possibly Sen. Stuart. Lee did not identify the unpopular officer slated to command the regiment, but presumably it was William Stuart or Daniel Ruggles. Baldwin was a member of the state's secession convention; he was not reelected colonel in 1862 and served in the Virginia legislature 1862-5. Krick, *Lee's Colonels*, 43. Stuart's daughter recalled Lee visiting during the war, but while she did not put a date to it she suggested that it was during Jubal Early's tenure in command in the Valley but Lee was not in Staunton in 1864. It is this author's contention that July 30, 1861, is the only plausible date for this visit and the passage of 50 years clouded Miss Stuart's memories of the event. John Washington wrote that Lee's party remained in Staunton for one full day after their arrival. JAW to Gustavus A. Myers, Aug. 12, 1861, Myers papers, W&M.

the remnants of Garnett's command to be in deplorable condition. Lee writes to Gen. Cooper advising that he has ordered John Floyd to advance to Lewisburg in support of Henry Wise who has been forced to withdraw up the Kanawha. He writes also to Harman regarding the militia at Staunton.[46]

---

46 JAW to G. A. Myers, Aug. 12, 1861, Myers papers, W&M; Freeman, *Lee*, vol. 1, 543-5; Oren F. Morton, *A History of Highland County, Virginia* (Monterey, VA, 1911), 121; REL to Cooper, July 31, 1861, REL papers, VHS: REL to M. G. Harman, July 31, 1861, REL papers, VHS. The location of Lee's HQ was directly opposite the Methodist Church at the crossroads at the center of town; it is no longer standing and a convenience store is on the site. Unfortunately the source for this does not record the name of the family who owned the house. Morton, *History of Highland County*, 121. Floyd and Wise refused to cooperate, which led to Lee eventually going to the Kanawha himself; the situation did not improve even after Lee's arrival on the scene. Lee wrote of this portion of the trip: "I traveled from Staunton on horseback. A part of the road, as far as Buffalo Gap, I passed over in the summer of 1840, on my return to St. Louis. . . . If anyone had then told me that the next time I travelled that road would have been on my present errand, I should have supposed him insane. I enjoyed the mountains as I rode along. The views were magnificent. The valleys so beautiful, the scenery so peaceful." Dowdey, *Wartime Papers*, 62.

August 1861

The beginning of August found Gen. Lee, Col. Washington, and Capt. Taylor, along with Perry and Meredith, at Monterey in Highland County on the way to join William Loring's Army of the Northwest.

Once Lee joined Loring's command, he spent nearly every day scouting the surrounding terrain in an effort to discover a way to get at the Federals. In at least one instance he went so far forward he was "captured" by pickets from the 48th Virginia Infantry before they discovered who it was they were stopping.

"General Lee," wrote his future military secretary Armistead Long,

> had been distinguished in the Mexican War as a reconnoitering officer, and [Winfield] Scott had been mainly indebted to his bold reconnaissances for the brilliant success of his Mexican campaigns. Rank and age had not impaired the qualities that had formerly rendered him so distinguished. He brought them with him to the mountains of Virginia. There was not a day when it was possible for him to be out that the general, with either Colonel Washington or Captain Taylor, might not be seen crossing the mountains, climbing over rocks and crags, to get a view of the Federal position. Ever mindful of the safety of his men, he would never spare himself toil or fatigue when seeking the means to prevent unnecessary loss of life.[1]

The Union army was almost less of an enemy than was the weather; it rained almost every day. "When not raining, it is going to rain or just done and about to rain again," complained Col. Washington. "I have been damp ever since I have been here. Our tent is moist, the ground we sleep on positively wet, and everything betokens the everlasting abundance of water vapor that prevails. And this is the dry season."[2] The roads turned to impenetrable mud; supply shortages resulted. A short time later sickness broke out in the camps. "The roads became almost impassable, the whole earth seemed full of water with springs bubbling up in our tents," recalled a North Carolinian. "The measles broke out in camp, and transportation being short, the mountain was converted into a sick camp."[3]

Gen. Lee conducted a review of the troops soon after his arrival and was disappointed by what the review uncovered. The army was in no way fit for battle.[4] In the words of historian Robert K. Krick, "General R. E. Lee could make no headway against either the Yankees or the weather under these frustrating circumstances."[5]

Lee and his two aides shared a single tent. Washington led morning and evening prayer, and all three took their meals together.[6] Breakfast was eaten at 6:00 a.m., and a combined lunch and dinner

---

1 Long, *Reminiscences of REL*, 121-2.

2 JAW to Gustavus A. Myers, Aug. 12, 1861, Myers papers, W&M.

3 George H. Mills, *History of the Sixteenth North Carolina Regiment in the Civil War* (Rutherfordton, NC, 1901), 5.

4 Garnett Andrews, "A Battle Planned but not Fought," *CV* (June 1897), vol. 5, 293.

5 Krick, *CW Weather*, 31. One of Loring's men recorded, "It was indeed a fearful summer. We were camped on Valley Mountain 43 days, and it rained 37 days out of that number." Ibid.

6 Transcript of undated address to REL Camp Confederate Veterans, WHT papers, NPL.

at 6:00 p.m. Washington noted their hardtack—a cracker or biscuit so hard that it often had to be soaked in water or coffee to be rendered edible—was sufficiently softened by the dampness in the air.[7]

Regardless of the weather, rampant illness, and poorly supplied troops, Lee and Loring were determined to get at the Federals in their front. Col. William L. Jackson of the 31st Virginia Infantry recorded his first impression of Lee: "I have great confidence in General Lee. He sees the difficulty of his position, and is preparing to meet the emergency. When he does move success is ours. . . . The movements of Gen. Lee are very secret. He keeps everything to himself."[8]

Nearly everyone in the army shared Jackson's confidence.

* * *

---

[7] JAW to G. A. Myers, Aug. 12, 1861, Myers papers, W&M.

[8] W. L. Jackson to wife, Aug. 27, 1861, Roy Bird Cook papers, WVU. Jackson was a cousin of Thomas J. "Stonewall" Jackson; he would not achieve the fame of his cousin and his nickname of "Mudwall" reflected that. He was colonel of the 31st VA, and later recruited the 19th VA Cav.; he rose to brigadier general and was among the last to surrender, in late July 1865 at Brownsville, TX. Warner, *Generals in Gray*, 153-4.

August 1, Thursday (Monterey): A soldier in the 21st Virginia writes today: "General Lee is at Monterey to take command of our army and if that is so have no doubt but he will have a large force under his command very soon as he is too big a man for a small command." Rain throughout the day.[9]

August 2, Friday (Monterey): Lee instructs H. R. Jackson to send a force of infantry and artillery to Huntersville, and to call on Harman for more ammunition. Rain continues.[10]

August 3, Saturday (Monterey/Huntersville): Lee moves headquarters from Monterey to Huntersville, arriving there in the afternoon. At Huntersville he joins Loring, who is none too pleased at Lee's apparently unexpected arrival. Lee receives instructions from President Davis to propose a prisoner exchange with the Federals to recoup prisoners lost at Rich Mountain.[11]

He orders Henry Wise and John Floyd to unite their commands at White Sulphur Springs and occupy Lewisburg, and informs Gen. Cooper of the dispositions of their forces and his plans for Gen. Loring's. Rain throughout the day.[12]

August 4, Sunday (Huntersville): Lee writes to Col. Beckley rebuking him for not keeping Lee apprised of the progress in organizing the 35th Virginia. Lee opines to Gen. Henry Jackson at Monterey that the enemy forces reported moving against Monterey and Huntersville are likely feints and that the real Union advance is against Lewisburg. Lee writes to state Senator Allen Caperton at Union requesting him to determine the intentions of the Federals at Fayette Court House as Lee fears they may be enroute to the Virginia & Tennessee Railroad.

Lee writes also to his wife Mary, telling her of his journey from Richmond and of the situation he found: "The points from which we can be attacked are numerous, and their means are unlimited. . . . My uneasiness on these points brought me out here." Rain.[13]

August 5, Monday (Huntersville): Lee places Brig. Gen. Samuel R. Anderson in command of a Tennessee brigade in Loring's army, and writes to Wise acknowledging his plan to move to Meadow Bluff but notes that movements proposed for Floyd are not practical. Lee informs Gen. Cooper of the arrival of reinforcements and the overall strengthening of the army, and mentions that he will go to Valley Mountain tomorrow. Steady rain.[14]

---

9 Richard H. Cunningham to mother, Aug. 1, 1861, R. H. Cunningham papers, VHS; Dowdey, *Wartime Papers*, 63.

10 REL to H. R. Jackson, Aug 2, 1861, written on W. W. Loring to George Deas, Aug. 1, 1861, REL papers, UGA; Dowdey, *Wartime Papers*, 63. Washington noted that Lee inspected the troops stationed at Monterey during their stay there, but did not give dates or details; he did note that Lee "remedied some few evils that were prevailing at that post." JAW to G. A. Myers, Aug. 12, 1861, Myers papers, W&M.

11 Freeman, *Lee*, vol. 1, 549-51; Dowdey, *Wartime Papers*, 61; Long, *Memoirs of REL*, 120; Taylor, *General Lee*, 28; Robert Josselyn to REL, July 29, 1861, REL papers, VHS. Long wrote of Lee's arrival at Huntersville: "When Lee arrived at Huntersville, he found General Loring busily engaged in forming his depot of supplies and organizing his transportation train. Several days had already elapsed, and several days more would be necessary before he could complete his preparations for an advance. The arrival of Lee at Huntersville as commander of the department took Loring by surprise. Having been his superior in rank in the old army, he could not suppress a feeling of jealousy." Long, *Memoirs of REL*, 120.

12 OR 5, 768; OR 51, pt. 2, 211; REL to Samuel Cooper, Aug. 3, 1861 (2 letters), REL papers, VHS; Dowdey, *Wartime Papers*, 61. One of the letters to Cooper states that he arrived at Huntersville on the 2nd, but in a letter to Mary on the 4th he states that he arrived on the 3rd, which is supported by both Long and Taylor; Freeman also put his arrival on the 3rd. Washington gave a detailed itinerary of the journey, laying out a timeline which places the arrival on the 3rd.

13 REL to A. M. Beckley, Aug. 4, 1861, REL papers, VHS; REL to H. R. Jackson, Aug. 4, 1861, REL papers, VHS; REL to Allen Caperton, Aug. 4, 1861, REL papers, VHS; Dowdey, *Wartime Papers*, 61-3.

14 OR 5, 770-2; REL to Cooper, Aug. 5, 1861, REL papers, VHS; Fitz Lee, *General Lee*, 117. Samuel Read Anderson was postmaster of Nashville before the war; poor health forced his resignation from the army in early 1862, although he was recalled to service in 1864 to lead conscription efforts in Tennessee. Warner, *Generals in Gray*, 10-1. Lee's letter to Cooper is very upbeat in tone, suggesting that he no longer viewed the situation to be as bleak as he did only days before.

August 6, Tuesday (Huntersville/Valley Mountain): Lee moves his headquarters to Valley Mountain, a point from which he hopes to launch an attack against Cheat Mountain. He travels extremely light, with only one valise of clothing for Lee and the two aides, and their mess equipment, one large tent, and the general's cot. Rooney's cavalry command is brought along for reconnaissance work. Lee writes to the Federal commander at Huttonsville, Brig. Gen. Joseph J. Reynolds, to request an exchange of prisoners. The rain continues throughout the day.[15]

August 7, Wednesday (Valley Mountain): Gen. Lee and Col. Washington and Capt. Taylor conduct a reconnaissance to find an approach to the Union position on Cheat Mountain. Lee continues to negotiate for a prisoner exchange with Gen. Reynolds, and sends an update on Union dispositions to Gen. Cooper in Richmond. Rain continues.[16]

August 8, Thursday (Valley Mountain): Lee's reconnoitering continues, and he has dinner with Rooney. Lee informs Henry Wise that, since John Floyd is senior to him, Wise will be under Floyd's command whether he likes it or not. Lee also writes to Floyd reiterating the importance of keeping the enemy west of Lewisburg and away from the V&T.[17]

The general writes to Col. Beckley regarding his ongoing difficulties with the creation of his 35th Virginia, and instructs Brig. Gen. Augustus A. Chapman to report with his 1,500 militia to Floyd. He writes to Allen Caperton thanking him for his reports on enemy movements near Raleigh Court House but regretting that Lee has neither any troops nor an experienced commander to send there. Lee reports to Cooper the continuing difficulties between Wise and Floyd, including several instances of Wise by-passing the chain of command and communicating directly with the president to request transfer from Floyd. Rain continues.[18]

August 9, Friday (Valley Mountain): Lee visits the camp of the 42nd Virginia and meets with its commander, Col. Jesse Burks. The general orders Loring to investigate the arrest of Col. James Ramsey. Lee finds time to write to his wife Mary and complain about the incessant wet weather while commenting also on the natural beauty of the region. He notes that the Federal commander opposing him is Joseph Reynolds, who in friendlier times served as

---

15 Freeman, *Lee*, vol. 1, 554-5; JAW to G. A. Myers, Aug. 12, 1861, Myers papers, W&M; Long, *Memoirs of REL*, 120-1; *OR* 3, Series 2, 25-6. Maj. William H. Kirker may have joined Lee's staff in some capacity on this date: he is listed as being quartermaster to Lee effective Aug. 6, but very little is known of his service, particularly as it relates to Lee. Kirker was on Loring's staff by early 1862, and later served on Jeb Stuart's staff. (Kirker's entry in the best reference work on ANV staff officers states, "Victim of a fuzzy official military record.") Krick, *Staff Officers in Gray*, 194-5. Taylor on several different occasions after the war listed every officer who served on Lee's staff in some capacity and he never mentioned Kirker so it is very doubtful that he ever assumed this post. Their tent measured only 9' x 11' and served as sleeping quarters for all three officers, as well their headquarters office; as Col. Washington noted, "We could not have entertained many guests for the night" given the cramped quarters. The only furniture was apparently Lee's cot, as Washington noted that both he and Taylor slept on the ground. Their mess equipment consisted of one large wash basin, three tin cups, three tin plates, three large tin dishes, and knife, fork, and spoon for each officer. JAW to G. A. Myers, Aug. 12, 1861, Myers papers, W&M.

16 Freeman, *Lee*, vol. 1, 555; Long, *Reminiscences of REL*, 121; REL to Cooper, Aug. 8, 1861, REL papers, VHS; REL to Cooper, Aug. 7, 1861, REL papers, VHS. Freeman, citing Long as his source, wrote that Washington often accompanied Lee and Taylor on these scouting missions; Long—who was not with Lee at that time—may have been incorrect or Freeman embellished for dramatic effect, as Lee himself wrote that Sept. 13 "was the first day I assented" to Washington going. Dowdey, *Wartime Papers*, 74.

17 Long, *Memoirs of REL*, 121-2; Fitz Lee, *General Lee*, 117; *OR* 5, 774; *OR* 51, pt. 2, 220-1.

18 WHT to A. M. Beckley, Aug. 8, 1861, WHT papers, SH; A. T. Caperton to REL, Aug. 5, 1861, REL papers, VHS; REL to Cooper, Aug. 8, 1861, REL papers, VHS. Augustus Chapman was a member of both the Virginia legislature and a former U. S. Congressman; he played little military role in the war beyond 1861. Allardice, *More Generals in Gray*, 55. Raleigh Court House is modern-day Beckley, WV.

an instructor at West Point while Lee was its superintendent. Very severe rain and wind.[19]

August 10, Saturday (Valley Mountain): Lee informs Richmond that there should be a sufficient number of companies at Lynchburg to form a regiment, and asks Maj. Hugh L. Clay at Lynchburg to confirm this; he requests that Edmond Goode be given command of the newly formed regiment.[20]

August 11, Sunday (Valley Mountain): Lee writes to both Governor Letcher and Gen. H. R. Jackson recommending against accepting the resignation of Maj. Alexander C. Jones. The headquarters wagon finally arrives with the rest of their clothing, camp furniture, etc.[21]

August 12, Monday (Valley Mountain): In the morning Lee gets a copy of the August 10 Richmond *Daily Dispatch* which has an article about a victory Lee recently achieved over Rosecrans at Rich Spring; as this is completely false, it proves amusing at headquarters. Lee writes to Wise, glad that he can join Floyd so soon but instructing him that requests for arms and equipment should be directed to Richmond. Lee complains to Cooper about Wise and the state of his command, specifically that the Wise Legion was formed with the understanding that it would come armed but Lee has discovered that not to be the case and that Wise is now requesting weapons from the government. Compounding Lee's frustration with Wise is the fact that Wise has not filed any reports with Lee so he has no idea of its numbers or needs. Lee forwards to Cooper copies of his correspondence with Gen. Reynolds regarding the prisoner exchange—Lee cannot agree to the terms Reynolds proposes. Lee inquires of Maj. Harman the progress of the units being organized at Staunton. He informs Mrs. Willie M. Spencer that he cannot order her husband discharged from service as she has requested.[22]

August 13, Tuesday (Valley Mountain): Lee writes to Cooper requesting winter clothing for the Army of the Northwest. Snow at high elevations.[23]

---

19 Thomas W. Penn to "Ma," Aug.10, 1861, Green W. Penn papers, Duke; J. N. Ramsey to REL, Aug. 5, 1861, REL papers, VHS; Dowdey, *Wartime Papers*, 63-4. Burks was the first commander of the 42nd VA and suffered a wound at Kernstown in March 1862 that forced his resignation. Krick, *Lee's Colonels,* 76. Ramsey was commander of the 1st Georgia (there were three different regiments claiming this numeric designation, the Regular 1st GA, Charles Olmstead's 1st GA, and Ramsey's 1st GA); his arrest was a minor incident as he continued to serve until his regiment was disbanded in 1862. J. N. Ramsey CSR. Lee wrote of the weather: "It has rained . . . some portion of every day since I left Staunton. Now it is pouring, and the wind . . . has veered around to every point of the compass." Dowdey, *Wartime Papers*, 63.

20 REL to George Deas, Aug. 10, 1861, REL papers, VHS; REL to H. L. Clay, Aug. 10, 1861, REL papers, VHS. Clay was the brother of Sen. Clement Clay, and later served on the staff of Edward Kirby Smith and Harry Heth. Krick, *Staff Officers in Gray*, 98. Goode was serving as adjutant of the 28th VA at the time that Lee made this recommendation; he was appointed colonel of the 58th VA upon its formation per Lee's request. Krick, *Lee's Colonels*, 162.

21 REL to Letcher, Aug. 11, 1861, REL papers, VHS; REL to H. R. Jackson, Aug. 11, 1861, REL papers, VHS; JAW to G. A. Myers, Aug. 12, 1861, Myers papers, W&M. Jones was major of the 44th Virginia; he resigned under a misunderstanding of orders from Jackson detailing him to cavalry command. Kevin C. Ruffner, *44th Virginia Infantry* (Lynchburg, VA, 1987), 15. Jones was adjutant general of Minnesota before the war; he was wounded at Gaines' Mill in June 1862 and subsequently assigned to conscription duty in Richmond, before transferring at his own request to the Trans-Mississippi. In May 1865 Jones may have been the last Confederate general appointed, but because of the collapse of the government he was never confirmed. Allardice, *More Generals in Gray*, 137-8. Washington noted that with the arrival of the rest of their baggage, "We are now keeping tent on quite a grand scale compared with our late humble establishment." JAW to G. A. Myers, Aug. 12, 1861, Myers papers, W&M.

22 JAW to G. A. Myers, Aug. 12, 1861, Myers papers, W&M; *OR* 5, 781-2; REL to Cooper, Aug. 12, 1861, (2 letters) REL papers, VHS; REL to M. G. Harman, Aug. 12, 1861, REL papers, VHS; REL to Mrs. W. M. Spencer, Aug. 12, 1861, REL papers, VHS. Of Lee's supposed victory at Rich Spring, Washington wrote, "We think it strange we had not heard of [this] before. However, as it terminated satisfactorily for us, we suppose we must have had the fight in our sleep and forgot . . . about it." JAW to G. A. Myers, Aug. 12, 1861, Myers papers, W&M.

23 REL to Cooper, Aug. 13, 1861, REL papers, VHS; Lesser, W. Hunter, *Rebels at the Gate: Lee and McClellan on the Front Line of a Nation Divided* (Naperville, IL, 2004), 168-70.

August 14, Wednesday (Valley Mountain): Lee instructs Wise to cooperate with Floyd and assures Wise that Floyd meant no offense by going outside the chain of command giving orders directly to Wise's units; Lee points out that as the commanding officer Floyd can redistribute units under his command as he sees fit. Lee adds that the bad weather prohibits further supply coming from Richmond. He writes to Floyd reaffirming that Wise is under Floyd's orders and while it is preferable to keep Wise's command intact, Floyd may detach any portion of it as may be required. Clear during the day, temperatures below freezing during the night.[24]

August 15, Thursday (Valley Mountain): Lee writes to Josiah W. Ware of Berryville, Virginia, regarding complaints about Col. James Allen; Lee is sorry to hear of this but it is outside his scope and he can do nothing. Lee writes to Dr. George W. Bayless of Louisville, Kentucky, thanking him for his offer of coming to care for the wounded in the Army of the Northwest; his services are not needed at present, but should the occasion arise Lee will take him up on his offer. Rain and cold temperatures continue.[25]

August 17, Saturday (Valley Mountain): Lee writes to Col. Charles Tompkins attempting to calm him down over conditions in his regiment and the rest of the Kanawha troops; Lee tells him everything is the best it can be under the circumstances. In response, Lee writes to Floyd concerned about the conditions of Tompkins's men. Lee writes to Col. John Baldwin urging him to get his regiment into the field as quickly as possible and hoping that Baldwin can use his influence to raise additional troops. He writes also to Loring regarding the resignation of a lieutenant in the 1st Georgia.[26]

August 19, Monday (Valley Mountain): Lee writes to Henry Jackson regarding tensions between him and Loring resulting from the arrest of Col. Ramsey of the 1st Georgia. He informs Miss Mary S. Saunders of Lunenburg County that he regrets that he cannot order her brother, James A. Saunders, discharged from service unless he provides a substitute or a compelling military reason presents itself: "A family that has furnished five sons to the Army deserves much consideration and their patriotism and zeal will be gratefully felt by the whole country."[27]

August 20, Tuesday (Valley Mountain): Lee receives a request from Washington College that Company I, 4th Virginia—which is largely composed of students from the college—be disbanded.[28]

August 21, Wednesday (Valley Mountain): Lee orders Wise to command only the Wise Legion as requested, but includes a lengthy lesson in military protocol for Wise; Tompkins's 22nd Virginia and McCausland's 36th Virginia are detached from Wise's immediate command as is the local militia. Lee informs Tompkins, who had been increasingly caught in the feud between Wise and Floyd, that he was correct in obeying orders given him by Floyd.

---

24 *OR* 5, 785; *OR* 51, pt. 2, 232; Freeman, *Lee*, vol. 1, 557; JAW to G. A. Myers, Aug. 14, 1861, Myers papers, W&M. So rare was the lack of rain today that Washington wrote, "We have a clear day at last!"

25 REL to J. W. Ware, Aug. 15, 1861, REL papers, VHS; REL to G. W. Bayless, Aug. 15, 1861, REL papers, VHS; Freeman, *Lee*, vol. 1, 557. Allen was colonel of the 2nd VA; he was wounded at Manassas and killed at Gaines' Mill. Krick, *Lee's Colonels*, 32.

26 REL to C. Q. Tompkins, Aug. 17, 1861, REL papers, VHS; *OR* 51, pt. 2, 239; REL to J. B. Baldwin, Aug. 17, 1861, REL papers, VHS; REL to Loring, Aug. 17, 1861, REL papers, VHS. The officer was 1st Lt. George W. Atkinson; his resignation became effective Sept. 2. His resignation letter is not found in his CSR, which states that the reason for his resignation is not known; there were multiple soldiers of this name and according to his CSR his future military service is unknown for that reason.

27 REL to H. R. Jackson, Aug. 19, 1861, REL papers, VHS; REL to Mary S. Saunders, Aug. 19, 1861, REL papers, VHS.

28 J. L. Campbell et al to REL, Aug. 14, 1861, REL papers, VHS. Known as the "Liberty Hall Volunteers" after one of the college's antecedents, this company had a large number of divinity students on its rolls. James I. Robertson, Jr., *The Stonewall Brigade* (Baton Rouge, LA, 1991), 16.

Lee alerts Floyd that Augustus Chapman has discharged his militia, and that much of it was insubordinate and of questionable loyalty.[29] Lee writes to Cooper complaining about Wise and offering his opinion on the movements of the Army of the Potomac. He sends instructions to Maj. Clay at Lynchburg for mustering troops there and denies the request from Washington College officials to release the Liberty Hall Volunteers from service.[30]

August 22, Thursday (Valley Mountain): Lee writes to Floyd approving of Floyd's usage of Tompkins's regiment.[31]

August 23, Friday (Valley Mountain): Lee visits the camp of the 48th Virginia at Big Spring. He receives a request from Brig. Gen. Thomas Fauntleroy to be relieved of command of the camps of instruction around Richmond, and writes to John L. Powell of Loudoun County regarding the impressment of wagons by Confederate quartermasters. Rain.[32]

August 24, Saturday (Valley Mountain): Lee writes to Col. Beckley regarding continuing difficulties with the formation of the 35th Virginia. Rain continues.[33]

August 25, Sunday (Valley Mountain): Lee sends orders to Richmond relieving Thomas Fauntleroy from command at Camp Lee and proposing Andrew Talcott as his replacement. He informs Richmond that the rain has brought operations in the mountains to a complete standstill and is severely hampering supply efforts. He forwards to Floyd a letter from Beckley regarding his latest organizational woes, in particular militia companies which will not agree to muster into the 35th.[34]

The general informs Col. Baldwin in Staunton that he needs to complete his regiment for field service, and orders Maj. Clay to send four companies to Staunton armed or not. Lee writes to Maj. Harman to differentiate between prisoners of war and civilian political prisoners being held at Staunton; Lee regrets that Harman's brother's company cannot be transferred to Harman's 52nd Virginia as it is already part of the 5th Virginia. Lee informs Capt. John Miller that his company cannot transfer from the infantry to artillery as there are no guns available for any additional artillery batteries. Rain continues.[35]

August 26, Monday (Valley Mountain): Lee writes to Floyd approving of his advance thus far and giving suggestions for future operations. Rain continues.[36]

August 27, Tuesday (Valley Mountain): Lee informs Wise that he will not be removed from Floyd's command, and notifies Floyd that two additional regiments are en route to him. Lee tells Cooper that he cannot recommend Wise's request to be transferred unless those forces can be immediately

---

29 *OR* 5, 799-800; REL to C. Q. Tompkins, Aug. 21, 1861, REL papers, VHS; *OR* 51, pt. 2, 230-1.

30 REL to Cooper, Aug. 21, 1861, (2 letters), REL papers, VHS; REL to H. L. Clay, Aug. 21, 1861, REL papers, VHS; REL to A. L. Nelson, C. J. Harris, and J. L. Campbell, Aug. 21, 1861, REL papers, VHS. Lee's frustration with Wise was becoming increasingly evident in his communications both with that officer and with Cooper; that other officers were being caught up in the Wise-Floyd feud must have been especially irksome to Lee.

31 REL to J. B. Floyd, Aug. 22, 1861, REL papers, VHS. The 22nd VA was previously under Wise's command, but Floyd issued orders directly to Tompkins which sent Wise into a fury.

32 John A. Cooke to father, Aug. 24, 1861, J. A. Cooke papers, VHS; T. T. Fauntleroy to REL, Aug. 17, 1861, REL papers, VHS; REL to J. L. Powell, Aug. 23, 1861, REL papers, VHS; *OR* 5, 807.

33 WHT to Alfred Beckley, Aug. 24, 1861, WHT papers, SH; *OR* 5, 807. The 35th never formed; this eventuality was likely becoming increasingly evident to Lee by this time, who placed Beckley under Floyd's command on this date.

34 *OR* 5, 807; REL to George Deas, Aug. 25, 1861, REL papers, VHS; *OR* 51, pt. 2, 244-5.

35 REL to J. B. Baldwin, Aug. 25, 1861, REL papers, VHS; REL to H. L. Clay, Aug. 25, 1861, REL papers, VHS; REL to M. G. Harman, Aug. 25, 1861, REL papers, VHS; REL to John Miller, Aug. 25, 1861, REL papers, VHS.

36 *OR* 51, pt. 2, 253-4; Freeman, *Lee*, vol. 1, 557.

replaced; he also points out Wise's repeated failures to provide returns. Rain continues.³⁷

August 28, Wednesday (Valley Mountain): Lee informs Sgt. James W. Baldwin of the 8th Alabama that he cannot order his discharge but proposes that Baldwin request through his commanding officer a transfer to a Virginia unit. Lee receives a request from Rabbi Maximillian J. Michelbacher to furlough Jewish soldiers to observe holy services in September. Rain continues.³⁸

August 29, Thursday (Valley Mountain): Lee writes to Rabbi Michelbacher that although he would like to grant the request to furlough all Jewish soldiers to attend religious services, he cannot do so; he recommends that they individually request leave from their respective commanding officers. He receives a letter from Annie and Agnes and writes back about the miserable weather but is confident that the enemy cannot reach Richmond from that direction: "Although we may be too weak to break through their lines, I feel well satisfied that the enemy cannot at present reach Richmond by either of the three routes leading to Staunton, Millboro, or Covington. He must find some other way." Rooney joins Lee for dinner. Rain and cold temperatures.³⁹

August 30, Friday (Valley Mountain): Lee tells Governor Letcher and Adjutant General Cooper that he wants the Highland County militia disbanded once its numbers are reported to him. He informs Maj. James E. Conoway that since he is away from Richmond, he is not familiar with current officer needs and asks Conoway to send a copy of his commission to Valley Mountain. Sunny, cold temperatures at night.⁴⁰

August 31, Saturday (Valley Mountain): Lee is confirmed by the Confederate Senate as a full general, to rank from June 14. Lee receives a very lengthy letter from Wise outlining his recent operations; Lee responds by congratulating Wise for his success at Gauley Bridge and with a reminder that he must work with Floyd for the success of all: "By your united efforts you will be able to drive back to Ohio [the enemy's] whole force." Lee also sends his congratulations to Floyd and suggests a move against an enemy column under Jacob Cox. Lee writes to Richmond regarding a request made directly to President Davis by a Wilson Henry to have his two sons transferred to the 23rd Virginia.⁴¹

Lee writes to Cooper that the rain continues to hinder transportation and that disease is now ravaging the camps. Lee informs Secretary of War Walker that he thinks a Dr. William M. Post would be of better service in a South Carolina regiment than in western Virginia. Lee's aide Col. Washington writes: "Have become so used to being wet and damp that I hardly think of drying or trying to dry

---

37 *OR* 5, 810; *OR* 51, pt. 2, 256; REL to Cooper, Aug. 27, 1861, REL papers, VHS.

38 REL to J. W. Baldwin, Aug. 28, 1861, REL papers, VHS; REL to M. J. Michelbacher, Aug. 29, 1861, REL papers, VHS; Freeman, *Lee*, vol. 1, 557. Baldwin was a native of Virginia who was in Alabama and enlisted in a regiment there prior to Virginia's secession; he wished to join a Virginia unit and requested Lee's assistance.

39 REL to Michelbacher, Aug. 29, 1861, REL papers, VHS; Dowdey, *Wartime Papers*, 67-8. Lee wrote "It rains here all the time, literally. There has not been sunshine enough since my arrival to dry my clothes.... But the worst of the rain is, that the ground has become so saturated with water that the constant travel on the roads have made them almost impassable, so that I cannot get up sufficient supplies for the troops to move.... I have on all my winter clothes and am writing in my overcoat." Dowdey, *Wartime Papers*, 67.

40 REL to Cooper, Aug. 30, 1861, REL papers, VHS; REL to J. E. Conoway, Aug. 30, 1861, REL papers, VHS; Dowdey, *Wartime Papers*, 70; Krick, *CW Weather*, 31. Details of Conoway's service could not be located.

41 *Journal of the Congress of the Confederate States of America, 1861-1865*, 7 vols. (Washington, D.C., 1904-1905), vol. 1, 464; *OR* 5, 823-4; *OR* 51, pt. 2, 264; WHT to Geoge Deas, Aug. 31, 1861, REL papers, VHS. Of the original five full generals, Lee ranked third: Samuel Cooper (May 16), Albert Sidney Johnston (May 30), Lee, Joseph E. Johnston (July 4), P. G. T. Beauregard (July 21). There was no such thing as a short letter from Henry Wise—when he was making a point, he prepared a legal brief with considerable documentation to support his case. There is no one with the last name Henry on the rolls for the 23rd Virginia, so one must conclude that this transfer never occurred. See Thomas M. Rankin, *23rd Virginia Infantry* (Lynchburg, VA, 1985).

myself. At night I am waked up with the cold and cannot sleep continuously for it, even wrapped in two blankets and a great coat. . . . Our fare is bread and mutton or beef, rice and tea or coffee, a little brown sugar. We have been out of butter and potatoes for some time and am now getting short of sugar, coffee, and salt. . . . The country has no idea of our condition, and it is carefully concealed for fear of its reaching the enemy through some of our newspapers, which seem to me to delight in telling everything they ought not."

Custis is promoted to colonel and assigned as an aide to President Davis. Sunny but cold.[42]

---

42 REL to Cooper, Aug. 31, 1861, REL papers, VHS; REL to L. P. Walker, Aug. 31, 1861, REL papers, VHS; JAW to aunt, Aug. 31, 1861, JAW papers, VHS; Custis CSR. Dr. Post of South Carolina offered his services to the Army of the Northwest, but Lee preferred him to serve with a regiment from his own state. Washington wrote of the mountain weather: "The roads are in a condition that almost precludes transportation. We now have bright weather which I hope will last but no one can tell in this most treacherous climate what is coming–from a clear sky everything will be overcast and raining hard in fifteen minutes. You may see the mountains and valleys in clearly defined outline for thirty miles and no appearance of mist. In ten minutes a thick fog has enveloped everything and you can't see fifty yards. So that now I have even ceased to conjecture to myself about the weather and make no plan or calculation based upon its probabilities." JAW to aunt, Aug. 31, 1861, JAW papers, VHS.

September 1861

The weather continued to be an obstacle for Robert E. Lee as summer turned to autumn. The rains continued and temperatures dipped close to freezing. Sickness continued to plague the men and the nearly constant rainfall washed out bridges and mountainside roads. "The deluge of rain flooded the mountains," wrote one Virginia soldier, "and the overflowing rivulets, numerous and terrific, cut off our supplies."[1]

Amidst these conditions Lee continued to plan an offensive. He was ready by the second week of September, but his plan proved much too complicated for his novice officers to implement. Rather than the decisive stroke he had envisioned, the operation fizzled to almost nothing. Close on the heels of this disappointment came the loss of John Washington. The tentmate of Lee and Taylor was killed while on a scouting mission with Rooney Lee. If the war had not hit home yet for Gen. Lee, his failed offensive, Washington's death, and a near-miss of his own certainly brought home that realization. Lee came under fire during the action around Cheat Mountain for what was probably the first time during the war. He and Loring were using a house in the valley south of Elkwater as their headquarters, and the flurry of activity around the dwelling drew the attention of enemy gunners. The artillery fire prompted Lee to send a detachment of the 16th North Carolina to drive them away.[2]

His time in western Virginia made it clear to Lee that the inability of John Floyd and Henry Wise to work together required his personal attention. After sending a preliminary report to Richmond about the failure at Cheat Mountain, Lee and Taylor moved 60 miles south. Unfortunately, neither man recorded Gen. Lee's initial reaction to the situation upon their arrival, but the childish behavior exhibited by Gens. Floyd and Wise surely disgusted Lee.[3]

Each general (Floyd and Wise) believed his respective position was the strongest and the most threatened and refused to aid the other. Lee knew nothing good could from such a situation, but he did not have a solution to the problem. Luckily for him the matter resolved itself when Wise was recalled to Richmond. Lee, meanwhile, had his troops working hard to fortify their positions.

While at Sewell Mountain Lee took a liking to a horse that belonged to an officer in the Wise Legion. Lee, an avid horseman, was so taken with the animal that he called it "my colt" whenever he encountered horse and rider. The horse was called "Jeff Davis" or "Greenbrier" and belonged to Capt. Thomas L. Broun. Lee jokingly told the officer on at least one occasion that he would need the horse before the war was over. Within several months Lee would purchase the horse and rename him "Traveller."[4]

---

1 Krick, *CW Weather*, 35.

2 Mills, *History of the 16th NC*, 7. The exact date of this incident was not recorded, but it probably on the 13th when Lee rejoined Loring in Tygart Valley. Hunter Lesser, email to author, June 12, 2019.

3 Wise's son, John, summed up the situation: "[Floyd] ranked my father and ordered him to withdraw.... This my father flatly refused to do, and his insubordination led to an angry controversy, necessitating the presence of General Lee.... It was evident that two civilians like Wise and Floyd could not cooperate in harmony, and both were ordered elsewhere." John S. Wise, *The End of an Era* (Boston, 1900), 170-1.

4 Thomas L. Broun, "General R. E. Lee's War-Horse," *CV* (July 1898), vol. 6, no. 7, 292. The tree under which Lee supposedly first saw Traveller became known as "Lee's Tree," and was heavily damaged in later years by souvenir hunters

Matters of a graver nature, meanwhile, unfolded in Richmond, where Secretary of War Leroy P. Walker resigned from President Davis' cabinet. Lee's name was discussed by the president and the rest of the cabinet members as Walker's possible replacement.[5] Lee's candidacy may have been one of the reasons Davis asked Lee to return to Richmond from the western Virginia mountains as soon as possible.

* * *

---

who cut so many pieces from it that it had to be removed. Robert M. Pendleton, *Traveller: General Robert E. Lee's Favorite Greenbrier War Horse* (Lutz, FL, 2005), 14.

5 Stephen R. Mallory diary, Sept. 16, 1861, UNC. Other candidates were Leonidas Polk and Lawrence Branch. The only qualifications of Polk, an Episcopal Bishop turned general, would seem to be his close friendship with President Davis; he commanded a corps in the Western Theater until his death during the Atlanta campaign. Branch was a Congressman from North Carolina, who turned down a position in James Buchanan's cabinet; at this time he was colonel of the 33rd NC. Branch eventually commanded a brigade in A. P. Hill's Light Division until his death at Sharpsburg. Warner, *Generals in Gray*, 31. The post went to Judah P. Benjamin, Davis's original attorney general.

September 1, Sunday (Valley Mountain): Lee receives a letter from Mary, who is now at Audley in Clarke County. He writes back that he sees Rooney often and that there is a great deal of sickness in the ranks and mentions that the rains have paralyzed all operations. "The sick list would form an army." Sunny and cold.[6]

September 2, Monday (Valley Mountain): Lee writes to the adjutant general's office requesting clarification for Maj. Clay's authority in mustering troops at Lynchburg, and informs Clay that he is awaiting word from Richmond on Clay's status. Lee forwards to Loring a request from Maj. James Conoway for a position in the field. He writes to Harman at Staunton acknowledging his suggestion of operations, but Lee does not know where troops can be found to execute it. Sunny, but cold.[7]

September 3, Tuesday (Valley Mountain): Lee is writing a letter to Custis when Rooney arrives and interrupts him. Lee's letter is full of fatherly advice and updates on the situation in the mountains. Lee stoically comments on recent reverses on the Outer Banks of North Carolina: "The disaster at Cape Hatteras was a hard blow to us, but we must expect them, struggle against them, prepare for them. We cannot be always successful and reverses must come." Sunny but cold.[8]

September 4, Wednesday (Valley Mountain): General Cooper writes Lee that President Davis is satisfied with all that he has done in western Virginia, but would like to have him back in Richmond as soon as practicable: "Whenever, in your judgment, circumstances will justify it, you will consider yourself authorized to return." Lee inquires of Floyd about the possibility of getting salt in the Kanawha Valley and alerts him to the danger of his position being flanked. He writes to Lt. Hugh H. Lee at Huntersville that he has not seen orders dismissing officers from state service, so he is not familiar with what the officer refers to; accordingly he should continue his duties for the present.[9]

September 5, Thursday (Valley Mountain): Lee orders the 29th Virginia and 52nd Virginia to western Virginia; he informs the adjutant general's office that the 29th needs field officers, and that he has several superfluous majors with his force.[10]

September 6, Friday (Valley Mountain): Lee receives a letter from Gen. Floyd, who is concerned about possible enemy atrocities in the Kanawha region.[11]

---

6 Dowdey, *Wartime Papers*, 68-70. Audley is near Berryville; it was constructed ca. 1795 for Warner Washington, Jr., a cousin of George Washington. Long Marsh Run Rural Historic District, National Register of Historic Places registration form, Sept. 9, 1996. Mary relocated to Audley, home of her cousin Lorenzo Lewis, in late August. Dorothy Lee, "Mary Anne Randolph Custis Lee: Wife of General Robert E. Lee," Honors Thesis, University of Richmond, 1930, 18.

7 REL to George Deas, Sept. 2, 1861, REL papers, VHS; REL to H. L. Clay, Sept. 2, 1861, REL papers, VHS; J. E. Conway to REL, Aug. 31, 1861, REL papers, VHS; REL to M. G. Harman, Sept. 2, 1861, REL papers, VHS; Dowdey, *Wartime Papers,* 70. Harman's letter to Lee is not in this collection so it is not known exactly what he had proposed to Lee.

8 Dowdey, *Wartime Papers*, 69-70. Union forces under Maj. Gen. Benjamin Butler captured Fort Clark on Hatteras Island without opposition on Aug. 27; Fort Hatteras was captured on the 28th. Long, *CW Day by Day*, 112.

9 *OR* 5, 828-9; *OR* 51, pt 2, 270-1; WHT to H. H. Lee, Sept. 4, 1861, REL papers, VHS. Hugh Holmes Lee was no relation to the general; he was serving as ordnance officer at Huntersville, but his service record notes that he was "discontinued" Sept. 1, 1861. He may have gone back to the 31st VA of which he was a member at that time; he appears again as a staff officer to Stonewall Jackson in April 1862. Krick, *Staff Officers in Gray*, 199.

10 REL to A. C. Moore, Sept. 5, 1861, REL papers, VHS; REL to J. B. Baldwin, Sept. 5, 1861, REL papers, VHS; REL to George Deas, Sept. 5, 1861, REL papers, VHS. The 29th was at Abingdon and the 52nd was at Staunton.

11 REL to Floyd, Sept. 7, 1861, REL papers, VHS. It may be this date when Col. Albert Rust and a local citizen reported to Lee the results of their surveying the approach to the enemy lines on Cheat Mountain as described by Taylor, who did not give a date; if not the 6th then certainly it was the 7th. Walter H. Taylor, *Four Years with General Lee* (Bloomington, IN, 1996), 22. Rust was a former Arkansas Congressman, who was colonel of the 3rd AR. After service in Virginia early in the war, Rust was sent west, where he spent the remainder of the war. Warner, *Generals in Gray*, 266.

September 7, Saturday (Valley Mountain): Lee responds to Floyd's letter, "I cannot believe that the enemy will carry out their threat of burning and laying waste the country. It is intended to intimidate. The sentiment in America will not tolerate it." Lee writes to Joseph R. Anderson, owner of the Tredegar Iron Works in Richmond, about the promotion of his son, Archer, and informs Maj. James Conoway there is no vacancy for him among the Virginia units, at present. Taylor informs Floyd that transfers from one unit to another have to go through proper channels before Lee will consider signing off on them. Rain.[12]

September 8, Sunday (Valley Mountain): Lee finalizes his plan of attack against the Federal position on Cheat Mountain and issues orders to the Army of the Northwest to attack on the 12th. Lee informs Floyd of a growing enemy force at Sutton which threatens his position, recommending that Floyd fall back across the Gauley River to a safer position. He writes to Cooper with an update: "I regret to be unable to give you a more favorable report of the condition of this army than in my last. The rain has continued. The roads are worse. In fact continuous tracks of mud, in which the wagons . . . plunge to their axles. The sick have not diminished."[13]

Lee writes to Maj. Harman regarding the continuing mustering of troops at Staunton. Lee publishes a dramatic call to arms to accompany the attack orders, which reads as follows: "The general commanding [takes] the opportunity of exhorting the troops to keep steadily in view the great principles for which they contend, and to manifest to the world their determination to maintain them. The eyes of the country are upon you. The safety of your homes, and the lives of all you hold dear, depend upon your courage and exertions. Let each man resolve to be victorious, and that the right of self-government, liberty and peace, shall in him find a defender. The progress of this army must be forward." In the evening Lee receives a letter from Mary. Rain continues.[14]

September 9, Monday (Valley Mountain): Lee receives word from Richmond that "the Governor considers you still the Commanding General of the State Forces." Lee informs Gen. Floyd that Loring will take the offensive on the 12th, and that Lee would like Floyd's cooperation. Lee tells Gen. Wise once again that he will not be transferred from the Kanawha because it would greatly reduce troop strength there: "I must tell you, in candor, I cannot recommend the division of the Army of the Kanawha. We must endure everything in the cause we maintain."[15]

Lee informs Col. Angus McDonald that the enemy is reported to be withdrawing from Romney, so McDonald should seize the B&O. Lee writes to his wife Mary that he is too busy with military affairs to make decisions for her and the girls, so she must make them herself; he also tells her also to ignore the negative press about him. "I never write private

---

12 REL to Floyd, Sept. 7, 1861, REL papers, VHS; REL to J. R. Anderson, Sept. 7, 1861, JRA papers, LVA; WHT to J. E. Conoway, Sept. 7, 1861, REL papers, VHS; WHT to Floyd, Sept. 7, 1861, WHT papers, SH; REL to Cooper, Sept. 8, 1861, REL papers, VHS. Archer Anderson, a partner in his father's Tredegar Iron Works, enlisted as a private in the 21st VA. He was promoted to captain and assigned to the staff of Brig. Gen. Isaac Trimble in early September 1861 and later served in staff roles in the Western Theater. Krick, *Staff Officers in Gray*, 61.

13 REL to Loring, Sept. 8, 1861, REL papers, VHS; Taylor, *Four Years with Lee*, 24-6; *OR* 51, pt 2, 281-2; REL to Cooper, Sept. 8, 1861, REL papers, VHS.

14 REL to M. G. Harman, Sept. 8, 1861, REL papers, VHS; Dowdey, *Wartime Papers*, 70; *OR* 5, 192. Lee's appeal to the troops in *OR* and Dowdey, *Wartime Papers,* is misdated Sept. 9; Taylor has the correct date of the 8th in *Four Years with Lee*, and an original copy in Telamon Cuyler papers also bears date of the 8th. The plan of attack was a very complicated one, dividing the Confederate forces into multiple columns and placing them on opposite sides of Cheat Mountain. Col. Albert Rust was to begin the attack at dawn with his 3rd AR, attacking the Federals atop the mountain, reinforced by Henry Jackson's brigade. Upon hearing the sound of Rust's attack, the rest of the force—with Lee and Loring—in the Tygart Valley were to attack the Union force at Elkwater. The entire plan hinged on Rust's dawn attack.

15 George Deas to REL, Sept. 6, 1861, REL papers, VHS: *OR* 51, pt 2, 284; *OR* 5, 842. Based on the letter from Col. Deas, Lee at this time was uncertain of his authority and position within Virginia's forces and asked for clarification.

letters for the public eye. . . . I am content to take no notice of the slanders you speak of but to let them die out. Everybody is slandered, even the good," Lee continued. "How should I escape?" The rain continues.[16]

September 10, Tuesday (Valley Mountain): Lee requests that provisions for the Army of the Northwest be sent to Staunton and Millboro, and that Col. McDonald be formally ordered to move against the B&O. He informs Richmond "I begin to advance today."[17]

September 11, Wednesday (Valley Mountain/ Elkwater): Lee, Washington, and Taylor accompany Gen. Samuel R. Anderson's troops to their jump-off point atop the mountain for tomorrow's attack. On the way Lee possibly witnesses a skirmish at Conrad's Mill on Tygart River. Lee and his aides spend the night in the woods near Elkwater encamped along Becky Creek. Rain throughout the day.[18]

September 12, Thursday (Elkwater): At sunrise Lee rides to join Gen. Daniel Donelson's brigade but is nearly captured when he encounters Union cavalry on Becky Creek Road, but the Federals fell back when they discovered the Confederates. He joins Donelson soon after sunrise, and waits for Col. Albert Rust to open the attack. With no action by or word from Rust, around 10:00 a. m. Lee orders Donelson to retreat back down the mountain. By noon the offensive is over, having achieved nothing. Constant rain and heavy fog in the morning.[19]

September 13, Friday (Elkwater): Lee learns what happened yesterday on Cheat Mountain: that Rust deemed the enemy too numerous and the works too strong to assault. Lee explores options to get at the Federals and sends Rooney and Washington to scout along Elkwater Fork. Their party is ambushed—Washington is killed, Rooney's horse is mortally wounded and he escapes on Washington's horse with two soldiers from Rooney's command who accompanied them. A courier brings a report from Washington to Lee only moments before Rooney arrives and informs Lee of Washington's death. Per instructions from President Davis, Lee writes to Union Gen. Reynolds regarding the arrest and execution of two Pocahontas County civilians, Andrew J. Moore and Ellis Houchin; Davis and Lee want to know whether this is true and, if so, they want those responsible for it delivered to Confederate lines as "criminals."[20]

---

16 REL to A. W. McDonald, Sept. 9, 1861, REL papers, VHS; Dowdey, *Wartime Papers*, 70-2. McDonald was colonel of the 7th VA Cav.; his age/health prevented him from serving long in the field. He was replaced by Turner Ashby.

17 *OR* 5, 846.

18 Marcus B. Toney, *The Privations of a Private* (Nashville, TN, 1907), 23; Freeman, *Lee*, vol. 1, 565-6; Thomas, *Lee*, 206; Lesser, *Rebels at the Gate*, 195. According to Freeman the skirmish at Conrad's Mill was the first action Lee saw during the war. Freeman, *Lee*, vol. 1, 565. However, Freeman wrote that Lee accompanied Loring's column along the river but gives no source for this, while one of Anderson's men wrote that Lee was with that column atop the mountain. Toney, *Privations of a Private*, 23. If Lee was indeed with Anderson he may not have been able to see the fighting below at Conrad's Mill.

19 *Supplement to the Official Records of the Union and Confederate Armies*, 100 vols. (Wilmington, NC, 1996), vol. 1, 381; Taylor, *Four Years with Lee*, 28-9; "A Member of the Bar" [Joseph Carrigan], *Cheat Mountain: Unwritten Chapter of the Late War* (Nashville, TN, 1885), 79-82; John H. Savage, *The Life of John H. Savage: Citizen, Soldier, Lawyer, Congressman* (Nashville, TN, 1903), 99; Freeman, *Lee*, vol. 1, 566-8. Donelson, the former speaker of the Tennessee House of Representatives, was sent west after the western Virginia campaign and died in April 1863 days before his promotion to maj. gen. Warner, *Generals in Gray*, 74-5. Rust began moving as ordered, but believed prisoners who exaggerated their numbers and stopped; no other officers questioned his decision. Newell, *Lee vs. McClellan*, 229-30. Rooney wrote of his father's disgust at Rust's failure to take the works on the mountain: "In the opinion of my father, it could have and ought to have been taken." Rooney Lee to W. F. Wickham, Oct. 6, 1861, Wickham family papers, VHS.

20 Freeman, *Lee*, vol. 1, 568; Newell, *Lee vs. McClellan*, 231; Joseph Bryan to WHT, April 29, 1903, WHT papers, NPL; *OR* 2, Series 2, 1379-80. It is unclear if Lee got Rust's report from Rust or through Loring; Taylor claims Rust reported in person (*Four Years with Lee*, 29), but Freeman thought he reported to Loring, who informed Lee (*Lee*, vol. 1, 570). Adam Bell, 9th VA Cavalry, was one of the other two soldiers with Washington; Rooney, Bell, and Washington rode in front when fired upon "from ambush without challenge." Bell grabbed Washington's fleeing horse and gave it to Rooney to

September 14, Saturday (Elkwater): Lee sends a letter under flag of truce by Col. William E. Starke to the Federals to request the return of Washington's body, or some news of his condition if he is not in fact dead; Starke meets a detachment of Federals who are bearing Washington's remains to be conveyed through the lines. Lee sends the body on to their cousin Edward Turner at Kinloch with the request that Turner tend to its proper burial, and then he writes a letter of condolence to Washington's daughter Louisa.[21]

Lee orders Loring's army to return to its former position and expresses satisfaction with the "forced reconnaissance" at Cheat Mountain. He receives a reply from Reynolds to yesterday's inquiry about the execution of two civilians: Reynolds states the report of their execution is incorrect and he is offended by the Lee's language; Lee forwards this on to Cooper.[22]

---

replace his fallen mount. Bryan to WHT, April 29, 1903, WHT papers, NPL. Three bullets struck Washington. Salie W. S. Hoover, "Colonel John Augustine Washington, C.S.A.," *CV* (Jan. 1926), vol. 34, 97. Washington's belongings were captured: his field glasses given to Gen. Reynolds, his gauntlets, revolver, knife, spurs, and powder flask taken by soldiers of the 17th Indiana. Another revolver was presented to Secretary of War Simon Cameron. The Federals marked the spot of his death by carving in an adjacent tree: "Under this tree, on the 13th of Sept., 1861, fell Col. John A. Washington, the degenerate descendant of the Father of his Country." Hunter Lesser, *The First Campaign: A Guide to Civil War in the Mountains of West Virginia, 1861* (Charleston, WV, 2011), 62-3. Lee kept the note he received from Washington just before his death; Lee's handwriting on the back reads: "Col. J. A. Washington reports results of his reconnaissance. Recd [sic] a few moments before the arrival of Major [Rooney] Lee announcing his death." Lee sent this note to Washington's daughter in August 1865: "I have kept the accompanying letter for you during the whole war. It is the last that was written by your dear father, and was sent from the road down Elkwater, a few moments before he met his death. You know how I have sorrowed at his loss, but you cannot know what great love I feel towards you, your sisters and brothers." REL to Louisa F. Washington, Aug. 31, 1865 (letter undated; date on envelope), L. F. Washington papers, W&L.

21 Freeman, *Lee*, vol. 1, 569; Arthur H. Noll, ed., *Doctor Quintard: Chaplain C.S.A. and Second Bishop of Tennessee* (Sewanee, TN, 1905), 30; REL to "U.S. Commander at Huttonsville," Sept. 14, 1861, REL papers, VHS; REL to E. C. Turner, Sept. 14, 1861, REL papers, UVA; REL to Louisa F. Washington, Sept. 14, 1861, L. F. Washington papers, W&L. Starke was once an aide to Garnett and was serving in that role to either Lee or Loring at this time. He would become colonel of the 60th VA, rise to brigadier, and be killed at Sharpsburg. Warner, *Generals in Gray*, 289. A note with Washington's body read: "I forward under flag of truce the remains of Col. John A. Washington that his friends may with more certainty obtain them; there was not time last night after his recognition to communicate." George S. Rose to REL, Sept. 14, 1861, REL papers, VHS. Lee gave Turner the details that he knew about Washington's death, including that Rooney saved his sword. Lee's sense of loss was evident: "I fear [he] was carried too far by his zeal for the cause of the South which he had so much at heart. Before they were aware they were fired upon by a concealed party who fired about 40 shots at four men. He was the only person struck and fell dead from his horse. . . . I received his body through the courtesy of the Commanding General of the [enemy] troops under a flag of truce this morning and now forward it to Manassas Junction where I hope you will meet it and have it interred as his family desires. His death is a grievous affliction to me, but what must it be to his bereaved children and distressed relatives. The country has met with a great loss in his death. Our enemies have started [hole in paper] their attack upon our rights with additional infamy and by killing the lineal descendant and representative of him who under the guidance of Almighty God established them and by his virtue rendered our Republic immortal. . . . May God have mercy on them all." REL to Turner, Sept. 14, 1861, REL papers, UVA. Lee told Washington's daughter, "He fell in the cause to which he had devoted all his energies and in which his noble heart was enlisted. My intimate association with him for some months has more fully disclosed to me his great worth than double as many years of ordinary intercourse would have been sufficient to reveal. We had shared the same tent and morning and evening has his earnest devotion to Almighty God elicited my grateful admiration." The complete text of Lee's letter to Louisa is in Freeman, *Lee*, vol. 1, 569 (though incorrectly dated the 16th); the original was acquired by W&L. Taylor later said of Washington's death: "I was greatly shocked in the contemplation of my noble companion and friend cold in death; and as I looked upon his inanimate form as it lay there on the side of Valley Mountain, I thought of that other valley, of the shadow of death, through which he had just passed never to return; I thought of those dear little girls of his and of the utter desolation that had so suddenly come to their happy home; and I began to realize something of the horrors of war." WHT, undated transcript of address to REL Confederate Veterans Camp, WHT papers, NPL. More than 30 years later a local farmer, A. C. Logan of Mingo Flats, tried to get Washington's family to pay $25 for a coffin he claimed to have provided, but the body was not placed in a coffin until it got to the VA Central RR depot at Millboro. R. J. Washington, adjutant of the 9th VA Cav. who escorted the body from Lee's HQ to Millboro, stated it was carried in a covered wagon to the depot at Millboro and there placed in a coffin. Lawrence Washington to WHT, April 17, 1894, WHT papers, NPL.

22 *OR* 5, 192-3; *OR* 2, Series 2, 1379-80. By styling the failed offensive a "forced reconnaissance" Lee was trying to put the best spin possible on it.

September 16, Monday (Elkwater/Valley Mountain): Lee returns to his former camp at Valley Mountain. Lee receives authorization from Richmond to transfer Wise "to any other command than that of General Floyd . . . in order to produce harmony of action—it being clearly evident that the commands of Generals Floyd and Wise cannot cooperate." Lee informs Cooper of the debacle at Cheat Mountain and of Washington's death. Taylor explains to Floyd that no "express" mail service between his and Lee's headquarters was created by Lee, but Loring had made some sort of similar arrangement, so refers him to Loring for details. Lee's name comes up in today's cabinet meeting as a potential secretary of war.[23]

September 17, Tuesday (Valley Mountain): Lee sends his preliminary report of Cheat Mountain, with details of Washington's death, to Governor Letcher; "We must try again," he concludes. He gives instructions to Loring for the disposition of the army, as he is considering going to the Kanawha Valley. He writes to wife Mary, who is now at Hot Springs, to inform her of the defeat at Cheat Mountain and of the death of Washington. "I cannot tell you my regret and mortification at the untoward events that caused the failure of the plan. I had taken every precaution to ensure success and counted on it." He mentions that he may be going to the Kanawha front and is desperately in need of cotton socks.[24]

September 18, Wednesday (Valley Mountain): Lee informs Cooper that he is going to the Kanawha Valley: "Feeling no apprehension for the security of the lines of communication through Monterey and Huntersville, I now purpose proceeding to the Army of the Kanawha to endeavor to produce concert of action between the commands there, which at this distance appear greatly to jeopardize the interests of the service." He informs Loring in writing that he is going to Floyd's army and that Loring is to keep Lee apprised of developments on this front, and to have the roads repaired and kept in operable condition.[25]

September 20, Friday (Valley Mountain/Frankford): Lee and Taylor, with a small cavalry escort, depart Valley Mountain for Floyd's army. They spend the night at Frankford, several miles north of Lewisburg. From there Lee writes to Floyd advising that he fears the enemy preparing for an attack on Floyd.[26]

September 21, Saturday (Frankford/Lewisburg/Meadow Bluff): Lee and his party pass through Lewisburg in the morning, much to the delight of the locals. They arrive at Gen. Floyd's headquarters at the Deitz farm at Meadow Bluff late that afternoon; Lee establishes his headquarters at the farm. He and Floyd spend the rest of the day inspecting the position at Meadow Bluff. Lee writes to Gen. Wise about his displeasure at not finding his forces united with Floyd's: "I beg therefore if not too late that the troops be united, and that we conquer or die together."[27]

---

23 Freeman, *Lee*, vol. 1, 571; Samuel Cooper to REL, Sept. 12, 1861, REL papers, VHS; REL to Cooper, Sept. 16, 1861, REL papers, VHS; WHT to Floyd, Sept. 16, 1861, WHT papers, SH; S. R. Mallory diary, Sept. 16, 1861, UNC. The exact date of the return to Valley Mountain is not recorded, although it seems to be the 16th; the lack of correspondence on the 15th however suggests Lee could have been in transit that day; in either case he was at Valley Mountain by the 17th. Lee's major hesitation at transferring Wise and his troops was not having replacements for them—Cooper informed him the 20th MS and Phillips Legion could be made available for that purpose.

24 Dowdey, *Wartime Papers*, 73-6; REL to Loring, Sept. 17, 1861, REL papers, VHS. Lee requested that the governor not show this letter to anyone; Letcher indeed did not share the letter with anyone during Lee's lifetime. Richmond *Whig*, undated clipping, LVA.

25 REL to Cooper, Sept. 18, 1861, REL papers, VHS; REL to Loring, Sept. 18, 1861, (2 letters), REL papers, VHS.

26 Freeman, *Lee*, vol. 1, 574; Richmond *Daily Dispatch*, Sept. 27, 1861; OR 51, pt. 2, 304.

27 OR 5, 870; Richmond *Daily Dispatch*, Sept. 27, 1861; William C. Childers, ed., "A Virginian's Dilemma: The Civil War Diary of Isaac Noyes Smith in Which He Describes the Activities of the 22nd Regiment of Virginia Volunteers, Sept. to Nov., 1861," *West Virginia History* (April 1966), vol. 27, no. 3, 183; Tim McKinney, *Robert E. Lee at Sewell Mountain: The West Virginia Campaign* (Charleston, WV, 1990), 40; OR 5, 868. The Deitz farmhouse was constructed in 1840 and is situated

September 22, Sunday (Meadow Bluff/Sewell Mountain): The officers of the 22nd Virginia visit Lee's headquarters to pay their respects to the general in the morning. After this is finished, Lee and Taylor ride forward to Gen. Wise's position, "Camp Defiance," at Sewell Mountain. Wise and many of his senior officers greet Lee upon his arrival. Lee and Wise spend several hours together inspecting the position as skirmishing occurs in the distance. After completing their inspection, Lee and Taylor return to the Deitz farm.[28]

September 23, Monday (Deitz farm): Lee receives word from Gen. Wise that he is about to be attacked, and thus cannot withdraw to Meadow Bluff; Lee urges Wise to fall back, but does not order it as he concedes that he does not know the true circumstances in Wise's front. Lee also informs Wise that Col. Tompkins is being sent to make an inspection of the weapons in Wise's command, and directs Gen. Loring to detach whatever troops he safely can to join Lee and Floyd. The general writes to Maj. Harman that he will have Richmond assign officers to the new regiment at Staunton, and Lee informs the governor that Harman has a regiment nearly complete that needs its field officers. Lee also recommends George Pickett and Lewis Armistead for its command.[29]

September 24, Tuesday (Deitz farm/Sewell Mountain): Before dawn Lee writes to Wise regarding his numbers and is worried that Wise is too isolated from any possible support if the enemy attacks him. Lee also sends instructions to Gen. Loring to send reinforcements to Meadow Bluff, and advises him that a battle is imminent. Lee then moves up to Camp Defiance with four of Gen. Floyd's regiments. The general is forced to sleep out in the open with

---

beside the James River & Kanawha Turnpike, overlooking the Meadow River. Floyd established his HQ in the house upon his arrival at Meadow Bluff; it is possible that Lee and Taylor also used the house. It was later used as a hospital and after Union troops occupied the area it was used at various times as HQ of Gens. Alfred Duffie and George Crook. Trenches built by Floyd's troops remain around the house, which is still owned by the Deitz family, although it has fallen into disrepair. Deitz Farm, National Register of Historic Places registration form, Feb. 13, 1992. Lee's presence was immediately known to the men in Floyd's army, although the purpose was not immediately known. An officer in the Goochland Light Artillery wrote: "Gen. Lee is now at this place, for what purpose he came I know not; I can merely suppose. I think this visit is to give instructions to Floyd and Wise. You know they have been at logger heads about something for some time. I hope Lee will smooth over all that for I desire to see them act together." John Guerrant to sister, Sept. 21, 1861, John Guerrant papers, VHS.

28 Childers, "Virginian's Dilemma," 183-4; Freeman, *Lee*, vol. 1, 589; Richmond *Daily Dispatch*, Oct. 1, 1864; McKinney, *REL at Sewell Mountain*, 41. Lee was comparing the positions of Floyd and Wise to determine which should be held; he found Wise's position at Sewell Mountain strong but vulnerable to being flanked. Maj. Isaac N. Smith of the 22nd VA recorded his initial impression of Lee: "He was known to be the most talented man in the U.S. Army after Gen. Scott.... Decidedly the handsomest figure I ever saw.... Courteous and perfectly easy in his manners, and with the most remarkable faculty of keeping his own counsel I have ever known–perfectly circumspect in all he says, answering all questions civilly, but with good care that no one shall find out more than he intends them to know.... Not the least symptom of the politician appears in his manners or conversation but on the contrary everything that characterizes a gentleman. We shall all feel every confidence in his opinions and directions, and the whole army will act willingly upon his suggestions. We are not advised what his course will be, whether he will remain here or return immediately to his command. It is probable he will straighten up matters here, set these two political generals on the right course in the right way and then leave us." Childers, "Virginian's Dilemma," 183-4. Smith developed an intense hatred for John B. Floyd both because of Floyd's lack of military skill and probably more significantly Floyd's accusation that Smith was a Unionist; this led to Smith's resignation in late October 1861. Terry D. Lowry, *22nd Virginia Infantry* (Lynchburg, VA, 1988), 195. An officer in the 60th VA at Sewell Mountain also recorded a favorable initial impression of Lee: "I had never seen him, and knowing our critical position I was anxious for his presence.... I returned to camp and saw him.... There was a kindliness in his expression most unusual in one possessing eyes so dark and brilliant. He was dignified and courtly.... He appeared so unconscious of his merits, so courteous, so kind, so considerate, that anyone who approached him must have felt that Lee was his very particular friend." McKinney, *REL at Sewell Mountain*, 41.

29 Freeman, *Lee*, vol. 1, 589-90; *OR* 5, 874; REL to H. A. Wise, Sept. 23, 1861, REL papers, VHS; REL to Loring, Sept. 23, 1861, REL papers, VHS; REL to M. G. Harman, Sept. 23, 1861, REL papers, VHS; REL to Letcher, Sept. 23, 1861, REL papers, VHS. Command of the 57th VA went to Armistead, with Pickett assigned to command the defenses of the lower Rappahannock.

only his overcoat, as the headquarters wagon has not yet arrived with the tent and camp equipage. Rain.[30]

September 25, Wednesday (Sewell Mountain): Lee determines that the Federals are concentrating against Wise's position and not Floyd's; while Lee contemplates how best to counter this, he receives a message from Floyd that Wise has orders to report to Richmond. Upon receipt of these orders, Wise consults with Lee as to whether or not he should comply, with the enemy seemingly preparing to attack. Lee urges him to obey orders; Wise departs in the afternoon, turning his command over to Floyd. After riding along the lines again and observing the enemy camps himself, Lee tells Floyd "This [Sewell Mountain] is a strong point, if they will fight us here." He requests Floyd to send forward additional troops and supplies. Lee again sleeps in the rain and cold without a tent.[31]

September 26, Thursday (Sewell Mountain): Lee's wagon with his camp equipment finally catches up with him. He personally interrogates two Yankee prisoners, and writes to Floyd that several units of his army have arrived at Sewell Mountain but they came without rations and there are none to spare, so unless Floyd can send forward supplies for them, Lee will have to return the troops to Meadow Bluff. He receives several letters from Mary and writes back of family news, particularly that Rob must decide for himself whether to return to UVA or switch to VMI, although Lee favors UVA; he sends her a check for $200 and mentions that he needs socks not only for himself but for the troops as well. Rainy and cold.[32]

September 27, Friday (Sewell Mountain): Heavy rains wash out several bridges, isolating Camp Defiance from Meadow Bluff. Lee orders Floyd to send forward more artillery and provisions, and instructs Loring to come in person with the troops he is sending. Lee writes to Harman requesting an update on the troops at Staunton, and to Samuel B. Finley of Mount Sidney regarding the impressment of civilian animals for military use.[33]

September 28, Saturday (Sewell Mountain): Because the regular route of communication between Lee and Floyd is flooded out, Lee sends couriers to find the best alternate route. He orders excess baggage sent to the rear at Lewisburg, and that while in the presence of the enemy the troops are to be provisioned each night and wagons to be ready to move in the morning. Salt supplies at Meadow Bluff

---

30 *OR* 5, 878; REL to Loring, Sept. 24, 1861, REL papers, VHS; Freeman, *Lee*, vol. 1, 590-1; McKinney, *REL at Sewell Mountain*, 51. Lee found Wise's entire force to be extremely unorganized; he lost his temper in an encounter with Lt. T. C. Morton of the 26th Virginia Battalion: Morton had been sent to bring up supplies for his unit from the supply train, the location of which he did not know. In searching for it, he was referred to Lee who happened to be warming himself beside a nearby fire. Morton approached Lee and inquired as to the identity of the ordnance officer and the location of the ordnance train. Morton recalled that immediately he "wished he hadn't." Lee snapped in reply: "I think it very strange, lieutenant, that an officer of this command, which has been here a week, should come to me, who am just arrived, to ask who his ordnance officer is and where to find his ammunition. This is in keeping with everything else I find here: no order, no organization, nobody knows where anything is, no one understands his duty, officers and men alike are equally ignorant. This will not do." Thomas C. Morton, "Anecdotes of General R. E. Lee," *Southern Historical Society Papers*, 52 vols. (Wilmington, NC, 1990), vol. 11, 518-9. Some early histories incorrectly claimed that Lee (and Union Gen. William S. Rosecrans) made HQ at the Tyree Tavern near Ravens Eye, apparently confusing Lee's with Floyd's earlier headquarters. J. T. Peters and H. B. Carden, *History of Fayette County, West Virginia* (Parsons, WV, 1972), 138-9; McKinney, *REL at Sewell Mountain*, 5.

31 *OR* 5, 879; *OR* 51, pt. 2, 312; Freeman, *Lee*, vol. 1, 592-4; REL to Floyd, Sept. 25, 1861, Lee papers, SH; Dowdey, *Wartime Papers*, 78. Freeman noted that Wise was away at the front when Lee received the orders for him to report to Richmond. Lee must have been ecstatic to learn of these orders which, in effect, solved the Floyd-Wise problem for him.

32 Dowdey, *Wartime Papers*, 78; McKinney, *REL at Sewell Mountain*, 63; *OR* 51, pt. 2, 312.

33 Freeman, *Lee*, vol. 1, 594-5; *OR* 51, pt. 2, 318; REL to Loring, Sept. 27, 1861, REL papers, VHS; REL to M. G. Harman, Sept. 27, 1861, REL papers, VHS; REL to S. B. Finley, Sept. 27, 1861, REL papers, VHS. Floyd wrote of the weather, "At this season of the year I do not remember to have seen such a storm in the mountains of Virginia. It has put an almost absolute stop to all locomotion." *OR* 51, pt. 2, 317.

are dwindling, so Lee instructs Floyd to draw from the supply at White Sulphur Springs. Rain continues.[34]

September 29, Sunday (Sewell Mountain): Loring and the lead elements of his force arrive at Camp Defiance in the evening. Lee writes to Floyd urging him to bring his own troops up and to bring any spare wagons that he has, as keeping the troops supplied is becoming increasingly difficult. No rain for the first time in many days.[35]

September 30, Monday (Sewell Mountain): Lee's thoughts turn toward taking the offensive, as the Federals show no signs of attacking. He opines to Floyd that no attack is forthcoming so Floyd will have to take the battle to the enemy. Maj. Isaac Smith meets with Lee prior to inspecting the outlying picket posts and suggests the because of the number and difficulty of access to some of them, that only those "next to the enemy" be inspected; Lee approves his suggestion. Lee informs Cooper that the Wise Legion does not have its full complement of officers and suggests that since Wise himself is now in Richmond, now is "a convenient time for arranging this matter." Sunny for second consecutive day.[36]

---

[34] WHT to Floyd, Sept. 28, 1861, Lee papers, SH; *OR* 51, pt. 2, 321-2; WHT to Floyd, Sept. 28, 1861, WHT papers, SH; McKinney, *REL at Sewell Mountain*, 66.

[35] *OR* 51, pt. 2, 324; McKinney, *REL at Sewell Mountain*, 75. It was probably on this date that an incident occurred that illustrated the informality of the mountain troops. A private named William Catterton wanted change for a five-dollar bill and, spotting Lee nearby, walked up to the general and extended his hand rather than saluting. Catterton inquired about Lee's family (whom he did not know) and asked for change. Lee did not have change, and referred the private to several staff officers nearby, one of whom produced the desired result. McKinney, *REL at Sewell Mountain*, 75-6.

[36] Freeman, *Lee*, vol. 1, 596; *OR* 51, pt. 2, 325-6; Childers, "Virginian's Dilemma," 188; REL to Cooper, Sept. 30, 1861, REL papers, VHS; McKinney, *REL at Sewell Mountain*, 78.

October 1861

Generals Lee and Loring spent the first few days of October preparing for an attack by Brig. Gen. William S. Rosecrans that never came. Instead of assaulting, he retreated. The same conditions hampering Lee's efforts to keep the army supplied now stood in the way of his pursuit of Rosecrans: the rain ruined the roads, and combined with a lack of supplies ended his pursuit almost as soon as it began. The cold reality was that the Federals had escaped him—again.

Southern newspapers began to pronounce Lee a failure–the same Lee they had only months earlier lifted up as the one who would bring about a short and decisive victory. One such detractor was John M. Daniel, editor of the Richmond *Examiner*, who was also an officer on the staff of Brig. Gen. John B. Floyd. Henry Heth, who commanded one of Floyd's brigades, remembered an instance where Daniel told him "that it was a d— [sic] shame for Davis to send Lee to supersede a man like Floyd; that Lee was no more to be compared to Floyd than the moon was to the sun; that Floyd had forgotten more about strategy, grand tactics, and handling troops on the field of battle, than Lee knew or ever would know. . . . It would have done very well to have sent Lee to report to Floyd to dig ditches where Floyd wanted them."[1] According to the Richmond correspondent of the Charleston *Mercury*, "People here begin to say hard things about Lee. They seem to think that his great forte consists in throwing up dirt at a safe distance from the enemy."[2]

The negative press didn't seem to bother Lee: "I know they can regulate matters satisfactorily to themselves on paper. I wish they could do so in the field. No one wishes them more success than I do."[3] One of his men commented on the matter: "My quarters being 50 yards from Lee's tent, I had a good opportunity to study him," he recalled. "When the daily mail came I would pass and re-pass his quarters to see the effect of the press and the public clamor against him. He would frequently sit for an hour in the cold autumn sun on a large log near his tent reading the newspapers. I never observed the least change in his appearance. He was ever the same, quiet, self-possessed gentleman."[4]

When Lee left Richmond for western Virginia at the end of July he was clean-shaven. At some point during his time there he had stopped shaving and grew the gray beard he would sport for the rest of his life.[5] Lee joked with family and friends that they would not recognize him now.

When he returned to Richmond at month's end, Lee probably expected a period of relative quiet in the capital city, not an almost immediate return to the field.

* * *

---

1 James L. Morrison, ed., *The Memoirs of Henry Heth* (Westport, CT, 1974), 156.

2 Charleston *Mercury*, Oct. 8, 1861. The same correspondent recounted another incident: "A story is told of a pretty sour rebuke which Lee received accidentally from one of his officers. . . . This officer, when asked by a friend if there was any prospect of a forward movement, replied, 'None in the world unless somebody puts a coal of fire on the back of that old terrapin Lee.' It so happened that Lee and Loring stood immediately behind him, and overheard every word. Lee smiled good humouredly, but Loring, unable to contain himself, burst into a loud laugh." Charleston *Mercury*, Oct. 25, 1861.

3 Dowdey, *Wartime Papers*, 80.

4 Daniel J. Crooks, Jr., *Lee in the Low Country: Defending Charleston & Savannah, 1861-1862* (Charleston, SC, 2008), 36-7.

5 Freeman, *Lee*, vol. 1, 577. Freeman states that the first reference to a bearded Lee was on October 20 when he saw Rob; this must be a mistake, as they did not see each other again until the 30th. Ibid., 577n78.

October 1, Tuesday (Sewell Mountain): With Wise out of the picture, Floyd's reluctance to move to Sewell Mountain evaporates and he moves his headquarters there and meets with Lee to discuss campaign strategy. Lee sends Gen. Cooper an update on the situation in western Virginia, and requests from the governor authorization to hire black laborers to fix and maintain the roads, as he cannot spare troops from the army for this purpose. Sunny and clear.[6]

October 2, Wednesday (Sewell Mountain): Lee writes to Gen. Samuel Anderson regarding Anderson's displeasure with the published accounts of his brigade's role during the Cheat Mountain operation. Rain resumes.[7]

October 3, Thursday (Sewell Mountain): Lee shifts some troops around, positioning the 50th Virginia near his headquarters, and clarifying for Loring the desired disposition of his forces. Cloudy.[8]

October 4, Friday (Sewell Mountain): Lee receives five copies of the C.S. ordnance manual from Col. Gorgas, and writes to Loring regarding supplying his troops with fresh beef given the difficulties in getting supplies from Richmond and Staunton. He writes also to F. D. Cleary specifying that wagons used in transporting grain are not to be impressed for any other use.[9]

October 5, Saturday (Sewell Mountain): Lee and Loring ascend to a mountain peak from which they can view the enemy position. A pair of soldiers from the 46th Virginia are already there looking around; after completing their official observations, Lee hands his field glasses to the two soldiers for them to have a better view. Lee writes to Maj. Harman authorizing him to send troops from Staunton elsewhere if Harman has instructions from proper authority in Richmond to do so. During the night, pickets report that the Federals are placing artillery for an attack.[10]

October 6, Sunday (Sewell Mountain): Instead of preparing to attack, Lee discovers that the Federals abandoned their position during the night. He sends his cavalry to determine where the enemy has gone, but lack of supplies, the weather, and the condition of the roads prevent any large-scale pursuit. In preparation for a new offensive Lee orders the Lewisburg Turnpike repaired, and rescinds orders calling for excess baggage to be sent to the rear.[11]

He receives a letter from Mary, which includes four pairs of socks, but he is too busy to read it. In the evening Lee meets with Harry Heth—his former quartermaster, now colonel of the 45th Virginia, and acting brigade commander under Floyd—to discuss strategy; Heth tells Lee he thinks Floyd to be completely incompetent. Heavy rain.[12]

---

6 OR 51, pt. 2, 326; McKinney, *REL at Sewell Mountain*, 82; REL to Cooper, Oct. 1, 1861, REL papers, VHS; REL to Letcher, Oct. 1, 1861, Gilder-Lehrman.

7 REL to S. R. Anderson, Oct. 2, 1861, REL papers, VHS; McKinney, *REL at Sewell Mountain*, 83.

8 OR 51, pt. 2, 333; REL to Loring, Oct. 3, 1861, REL papers, VHS; McKinney, *REL at Sewell Mountain*, 84.

9 Josiah Gorgas to REL, Sept. 28, 1861, REL papers, VHS; REL to Loring, Oct. 4, 1861, REL papers, VHS; REL to F. D. Cleary, Oct. 4, 1861, REL papers, VHS.

10 McKinney, *REL at Sewell Mountain*, 91; REL to M. G. Harman, Oct. 5, 1861, REL papers, VHS; Freeman, *Lee*, vol. 1, 596-7. One of the two soldiers described the encounter: "Who should come walking up while we were there but General Lee and General Loring. They had a pair of field glasses and had come to view the Union troops. . . . After they looked at the troops with their field glasses for some moments, General Lee tendered them to my brother saying 'Wouldn't you like to look at them?' When he returned them, the General also handed them to me. I was delighted at his thoughtfulness for even a mere boy like myself." McKinney, *REL at Sewell Mountain*, 91.

11 Freeman, *Lee*, vol. 1, 597-8; OR 51, pt. 2, 335; SO Oct. 6, 1861, WHT papers, SH.

12 Dowdey, *Wartime Papers*, 79; Morrison, *Heth Memoirs*, 156-7; McKinney, *REL at Sewell Mountain*, 94. As with most incidents that Heth recalled, he did not put a specific date, so it is possible that his meeting with Lee may have occurred a day or two to either side, but it seems to have been on this date. "I had a long talk with General Lee and expressed to him

October 7, Monday (Sewell Mountain): Lee has breakfast with Heth and continue their discussion about Floyd. Lee informs Cooper of Rosecrans's withdrawal and the poor state of supply in the Army of the Kanawha. He writes to Governor Letcher again regarding the repair and maintenance of the roads, again requesting authority to hire black laborers for this purpose under engineer officers, and thanks Edmund Fontaine, president of the Virginia Central Railroad, for his suggestions regarding the mountain roads. Lee gives half of the socks he received yesterday from Mary to Perry and half to Meredith.

Lee writes to wife Mary reminding her that they cannot go back to Arlington and that she must find some place to settle down—he suggests Raleigh, North Carolina, since Mildred attends school there and advises against Richmond, believing it will sooner or later become the front lines. He laments the negative press regarding operations in the field and mentions that Floyd has three newspaper editors on his staff. Heavy rain continues.[13]

October 9, Wednesday (Sewell Mountain): Lee informs Gen. Floyd that operations elsewhere in western Virginia make it very likely that Gen. Loring will have to depart the area with his troops soon, which will, of course, have an immediate impact on Floyd's operations. Lee mentions that after Loring leaves, Lee will return to Richmond.[14]

October 10, Thursday (Sewell Mountain): Lee writes Gen. Loring regarding winter quarters for the army, and to Gen. Floyd concerning salt supplies and the routine duties to be performed at Sewell Mountain.[15]

October 11, Friday (Sewell Mountain): Lee informs Gen. Floyd that scouts report seeing the last of the Federals vacating their camps. Lee requests a meeting with Col. William J. Clarke to discuss the sick of Floyd's army.[16]

October 12, Saturday (Sewell Mountain): Lee writes to his son Rooney and mentions that his mother, Mary, has gone to White House with Charlotte, and that Annie and Agnes are in Richmond staying with friends. Lee regrets that the Federals got away and that he was not able to pursue them.[17]

October 14, Monday (Sewell Mountain): Lee orders rumors of an enemy force on the Wilderness Road investigated.[18]

October 15, Tuesday (Sewell Mountain): Ellen W. Tompkins and her daughter Ellen pass through enemy lines for a visit with her husband, Col. Charles Q. Tompkins. Lee sends a cavalry escort to meet them and has the ladies visit his headquarters. Lee informs Gen. Floyd the Federals have reached the vicinity of Gauley Bridge and look to be preparing to spend the winter around Charleston, in western Virginia. He notes that hospitals are overflowing

---

my views as to Floyd's ability to exercise an independent command. . . . If Floyd was given an independent command, it would be merely a question of time when it would be captured; that I did not think the Confederacy could afford to lose three or four thousand men, simply to gratify the ambition of a politician who was as incapable of taking care of his men or fighting them as a baby." Morrison, *Heth Memoirs*, 156-7. Lee forgot his raincoat when going to the front upon learning that Rosecrans's army was gone—he got "thoroughly wet from head to foot" without it. Dowdey, *Wartime Papers*, 79.

13 Morrison, *Heth Memoirs*, 157; REL to Cooper, Oct. 7, 1861, REL papers, VHS; REL to Letcher, Oct. 7, 1861, REL papers, VHS; REL to Edmund Fontaine, Oct. 7, 1861, REL papers, VHS; Dowdey, *Wartime Papers*, 79-80. "We can only get up provisions from day to day, which paralyses our operations," he told Mary. Dowdey, *Wartime Papers*, 80.

14 OR 51, pt. 2, 337-8.

15 REL to Loring, Oct. 10, 1861, REL papers, VHS; WHT to Floyd, Oct. 10, 1861, WHT papers, SH; REL to Floyd, Oct. 10, 1861, J. Ambler Johnston papers, VHS.

16 OR 51, pt. 2, 341; REL to W. J. Clarke, Oct. 11, 1861, Lee-Jackson Foundation papers, W&L. This was probably Col. William John Clarke of the 24th NC, which was part of Floyd's command. Krick, *Lee's Colonels*, 93.

17 REL to Rooney, Oct. 12, 1861, George Bolling Lee papers, VHS.

18 OR 51, pt. 2, 346.

with the sick and as a result, Lee has to send the new cases of illness to facilities far in the rear.[19]

October 16, Wednesday (Sewell Mountain): Lee sends Gen. Cooper an update on the situation in western Virginia. He gives Floyd more details on the Unionists at Gauley Bridge and that the Wise Legion is prostrate from illness and a lack of supplies. His daughter Mary goes to Ravensworth and stops to visit her friends and relatives at Manassas, including Gen. Richard Ewell.[20]

October 17, Thursday (Sewell Mountain): Lee attempts to allay Loring's anxiety for the safety of the Monterey and Huntersville lines.[21]

October 18, Friday (Sewell Mountain): Lee informs Cooper that per instructions from Richmond, Capt. G. S. Magruder and Pvt. A. V. Carter have been sent to Richmond to report to the Henrico County commonwealth's attorney.[22]

October 19, Saturday (Sewell Mountain): Lee orders all wagons at Meadow Bluff to be sent forward to Sewell Mountain. In the evening he receives a report that there are no Federals south of the Kanawha.[23]

October 20, Sunday (Sewell Mountain): Lee orders a withdrawal from Sewell Mountain, sending Wise's former command to Meadow Bluff and Loring and his troops back to Huntersville. He writes to Floyd informing him of these troop movements and also that he has received a report that Rosecrans may be resuming his offensive.[24]

October 21, Monday (Sewell Mountain/Deitz Farm): Lee moves his headquarters from Sewell Mountain back to the Deitz farm at Meadow Bluff. He sends a summary of the current situation to Cooper.[25]

October 26, Saturday (Deitz Farm): Lee grants leave to Capt. William H. Cook, 51st Virginia, to go to Richmond to take his seat in the state legislature. He writes to Col. Thomas R. R. Cobb informing him that the Troup Artillery has been ordered to serve with Cobb's Legion.[26]

October 27, Sunday (Deitz Farm): Lee informs Henry Wise of Lee's intent to reunite him with the Wise Legion but he will not do so as long as it is under Floyd in western Virginia. He writes as well to Governor Letcher's aide, S. Bassett French regarding communication with Virginia's troops.[27]

---

19 Ellen W. Tompkins, ed., "The Colonel's Lady: Some Letters of Ellen Wilkins Tompkins, July-Dec 1861," *VMHB* (Oct. 1961), vol. 69, no. 4, 410-3; *OR* 51, pt. 2, 347. Mrs. Tompkins refused to leave the family's home when Union troops arrived. She insisted on a guard being placed around their residence, and eventually befriended not only the troops encamped on their farm, but the Union commander, Brig. Gen. Jacob Cox, as well, despite her husband being colonel of the 22nd VA. Cox allowed her to correspond with her husband and other family outside Union lines provided she did not reveal any sensitive information. In part because she upheld her end of the deal, Cox and Rosecrans allowed Mrs. Tompkins this foray through the lines for a visit with her husband and family in Richmond.

20 REL to Cooper, Oct. 16, 1861, REL papers, VHS; *OR* 51, pt. 2, 348-9; Dozier, *Gunner in Lee's Army*, 36.

21 REL to Loring, Oct., 17, 1861, REL papers, VHS.

22 REL to Cooper, Oct. 18, 1861, REL papers, VHS. No details could be found regarding this.

23 REL to W. H. Thomas, Oct. 19, 1861, WHT papers, NPL; *OR* 5, 908.

24 Freeman, *Lee*, vol. 1, 577, 598-9; Newell, *Lee vs. McClellan*, 247; REL to Loring, Oct. 20, 1861, REL papers, VHS; *OR* 5, 908-9.

25 McKinney, *REL at Sewell Mountain*, 111; REL to Cooper, Oct. 21, 1861, REL papers, VHS.

26 SO Oct. 26, 1861, WHT papers, SH; REL to T. R. R. Cobb, Oct. 26, 1861, REL papers, VHS. Cook was captain of Co. C, 51st VA, from Patrick County, VA; James A. Davis, *51st Virginia Infantry* (Lynchburg, VA, 1984), 62. Thomas Cobb was the younger brother of Howell Cobb, one of the founders of the Confederate government. Tom was colonel of the Cobb Legion and a brigadier general when killed at Fredericksburg in December 1862. Warner, *Generals in Gray*, 55-6.

27 REL to H. A. Wise, Oct. 27, 1861, REL papers, VHS; REL to S. B. French, Oct. 27, 1861, Gilder-Lehrman.

October 28, Monday (Deitz Farm): Lee receives a letter from Floyd who claims ignorance of Loring being sent back to Huntersville. Lee directs Harman to discontinue the express rider service he established between headquarters and Staunton, and informs Loring that this express line has been abolished so future communication will be by regular mail. Lee attempts to explain to Wise why the Wise Legion must remain for the present in western Virginia and also that its officers cannot transfer to other units as they were elected by the men of the Legion not appointed by Richmond.[28]

October 29, Tuesday (Deitz Farm/Lewisburg/White Sulphur Springs): Lee and Taylor leave Meadow Bluff for good, going to inspect the hospitals at Lewisburg and White Sulphur Springs. Lee reminds Floyd that he was notified of Loring's departure on the 20th, and sends an update on the Wise Legion and the troops at Meadow Bluff as well as the large number of sick troops in the hospitals.[29]

October 30, Wednesday (White Sulphur Springs/Jackson's River Depot/Staunton/Charlottesville): Lee and Taylor depart the mountains for Richmond via the Virginia Central Railroad. They go at least as far as Charlottesville, where Lee visits with Rob at UVA.[30]

October 31, Thursday (Charlottesville/Richmond): Gen. Lee and Walter Taylor arrive in Richmond in the afternoon.[31]

---

[28] McKinney, *REL at Sewell Mountain*, 112; REL to M. G. Harman, Oct. 28, 1861, REL papers, VHS; REL to Loring, Oct. 28, 1861, REL papers, VHS; REL to H. A. Wise, Oct. 28, 1861, REL papers, VHS.

[29] REL to M. G. Harman, Oct. 28, 1861, REL papers, VHS; OR 51, pt. 2, 361-2. It is likely that Lee and Taylor spent the night at White Sulphur Springs. Lee, Taylor, and a Dr. Bedford Brown inspected the hospital at Blue Sulphur Springs several days prior to this, but the date is not known. Bedford Brown to WHT, Dec. 28, 1893, WHT papers, NPL.

[30] Freeman, *Lee*, vol. 1, 602; Davis, *Gray Fox*, 55. Lee and Taylor perhaps spent the night at Charlottesville, as they did not arrive in Richmond until the afternoon of the 31st. Richmond *Daily Dispatch*, Nov. 1, 1861. One author put Lee at a grand review at Fairfax today in company with President Davis, Stonewall Jackson, and James Longstreet but gives no source. Schildt, *Stonewall Day by Day*, 24. However, it seems all but impossible that Lee could have been in Fairfax on this date.

[31] Richmond *Daily Dispatch*, Nov. 1, 1861. No mention is made of their method of return, although it was probably via the Virginia Central. A letter to Mary shortly after returning to Richmond suggests that Lee stayed in the Spotswood Hotel upon his return. Dowdey, *Wartime Papers*, 83-4.

November 1861

When he returned to Richmond from the western Virginia mountains, Robert E. Lee met with President Jefferson Davis and provided him with a full briefing on both the Cheat Mountain campaign and the operations around Sewell Mountain. Although he had provided Governor John Letcher with a brief written synopsis of the failed attack at Cheat Mountain, Lee never filed an official report of his time in western Virginia.

The general likely expected to stay in Richmond for a time and so put off a visit to Mary believing he would soon have another opportunity. Instead, he spent an entire day closeted with Judah P. Benjamin, the new Confederate secretary of war, during which he was briefed on his new assignment along the south Atlantic coast. Lee took Walter Taylor and several new additions to his staff with him and made an overnight journey by rail from the capital to Charleston, South Carolina, where he was greeted by a combined Union naval and land force assaulting Port Royal, South Carolina.

Lee found his new assignment, at least militarily speaking, no better than what he had found in the mountains of western Virginia. He described it to his daughter as "another forlorn hope expedition. Worse than western Virginia."[1] The condition of affairs in Col. Arthur Manigault's area of responsibility was typical of Lee's entire department: "This command was necessarily much scattered, and, although a very respectable force when brought together, it would have been a very difficult matter to do so in under three days, owing to the nature of the country, intersected as it was by rivers, creeks, and inlets."[2] Naval Capt. John N. Maffitt, who would join Lee's staff, put the difficulties this way: "Times are squally! And the enemy are active. We are not in condition to meet them—everything is slip shod. 'Tis a hard case, that Gen. Lee should be always thus situated."[3]

The diffusion of his limited forces across such a wide area with so many avenues of approach did indeed make Lee's job extremely difficult. One of the few advantages he had was the Charleston & Savannah Railroad, which linked the two key cities of his command and provided the best way to shift troops to defend the area. Lee decided he should not try to keep the Federals from landing on the coastal islands because he did not have the manpower to do so. Instead, he established observation posts and garrisons at strategic locations to detect and delay Union columns while mobile forces moved along the railroad to counter the enemy movement.

Lee spent much of November inspecting the positions for which he was now responsible. One of them, Fort Pulaski, was very familiar to him because he had been stationed there some three decades earlier. Lee's first assignment out of West Point was to prepare swampy Cockspur Island, downstream from Savannah, for a masonry fortification that became Fort Pulaski. His academy roommate, Jack Mackay, was assigned to his hometown of Savannah at the same time.[4] Lee became

---

1 Dowdey, *Wartime Papers*, 86.

2 R. Lockwood Tower, ed., *A Carolinian Goes to War: The Civil War Narrative of Arthur Middleton Manigault, Brigadier General, CSA* (Columbia, SC, 1992), 12. Manigault had approximately 3,000 men in early November; by the end of December that number had shrunk by 2/3 due to an outbreak of measles. Ibid., 11, 25.

3 Brooke, *Ironclads and Big Guns*, 50.

4 Lillian C. Bragg and Frank B. Screven, "Robert E. Lee in Georgia," *The Georgia Review* (Winter 1962), vol. 16, no. 4, 433.

good friends with the Mackay family, and when he returned there in November 1861, he used one of the Mackay houses in Coosawhatchie, South Carolina, as his headquarters and renewed his friendship with the family.[5] The family of another of Lee's classmates and close friends, Allen Smith Izard, lived nearby and Lee often visited.[6]

The general also visited Fort Sumter on at least one occasion, most likely in mid-November.[7] He also traveled to the far southern reaches of his command at Fernandina, Florida, and almost certainly visited Fort Clinch, where his son Custis had been stationed shortly before the war.[8] Lee was almost constantly in the field; when he was not touring defensive works, he was chasing down reported Union movements. One of the new additions to his staff, Maj. Armistead Long, wrote of him: "The extensive line of operations that demanded his attention caused Lee to be almost constantly on the move, first at one place, and then at another, where important work was in progress. It was remarkable how his quiet, confident manner stimulated the men to exertion whenever he came among them."[9]

Rather than select a comfortable mansion for his headquarters in one of the big cities anchoring the ends of the railroad, Lee settled instead on an abandoned house at the crossroads of Coosawhatchie on the railroad nearly midway between Charleston and Savannah. The house was owned by Jack Mackay's mother, but was empty and available for his use. "The house at Coosawhatchie selected by General Lee for headquarters," wrote Maj. Long,

> was of just sufficient capacity for himself and military family.... The General was as unpretending in the interior arrangement of his quarters as were his exterior surroundings. His simple camp equipage and that of his staff comprised the entire furniture of the house. The table service consisted of a neat set of tin-ware, plates, dishes, and cups made to fit into each other for convenience in packing. The bill of fare corresponded in frugality to the plainness of the furniture. The General occupied the head of his table, and always seasoned the meal with his good humor and pleasant jests, often at the expense of some member of the staff who seemed to miss the luxuries of the table more than himself.[10]

Lt. George E. Manigault of the 4th South Carolina Cavalry had the opportunity to observe Lee during this time and write about it:

> [D]uring the winter months Gen. Lee occupied the little dwelling at Coosawhatchie to which he moved when he first arrived and made occasional visits to Savannah. I saw him twice then—once as he stood in

---

5 Dowdey, *Wartime Papers*, 89. Mackay died in 1848, but Lee remained close friends with his sisters, and spent time visiting with Mackay's mother as well.

6 Robert N. Rosen, *Confederate Charleston: An Illustrated History of the City and the People During the Civil War* (Columbia, SC, 1994), 84.

7 Horn, *REL Reader*, 131-2. The exact date of this visit is not known but likely happened somewhere Nov. 13-16, when Lee conducted his initial inspection of the Charleston defenses. He was in Charleston again for a lengthy stay Dec. 11-17 again touring the defenses, so possibly, if not probably, he returned to Sumter during that time as well.

8 Construction of Fort Clinch began in 1847 but by the beginning of the war only two walls of the five-sided work were completed and it had no guns. Lewis G. Schmidt, *The Civil War in Florida: A Military History*. 4 vols. (Allentown, PA, 1991), vol. 1, pt. 1, 3-4.

9 Long, *Memoirs of REL*, 142.

10 Ibid., 141-2.

the piazza of the house when I passed on horseback, and the other time when he came to the Huguenin encampment on a short visit of observation. He wore then the blue uniform of the U.S. Army with the conical shaped soft hat of the officers, the only part of his beard which was unshaven being a grey mustache. His appearance was striking and soldierly and it was impossible for him not to be noticed wherever he went.[11]

Although his success thus far in the war had been negligible, news of Lee's appointment was well received in Savannah: "All rejoice that General Lee has come—we hope in time to save us," announced Rev. C. C. Jones of Savannah. "You know his reputation in the army: he checkmated Rosecrans in Western Virginia. And he is Miss Kitty Stiles's great friend. Should he make a progress through these regions I should be happy to know and to receive him at our house."[12]

* * *

---

11 Crooks, *REL in the Low Country*, 64.

12 Derek Smith, *Civil War Savannah* (Savannah, GA, 1997), 48. Katherine Clay "Kitty" Stiles later became the Vice-Regent for the Georgia Room of the Confederate Museum, later Museum of the Confederacy, in Richmond.

November 1, Friday (Richmond): Lee meets with President Davis, providing a full verbal report on the operations in western Virginia. He did not file an official written report and did not wish for blame to be attached to Rust or anyone else.[13]

November 2, Saturday (Richmond): In late afternoon Lee attempts to take a boat down the James to Shirley, where Mary is staying; however all the boats have already left and he finds it too close to nightfall to ride and so returns home.[14]

November 4, Monday (Richmond): Lee meets with the new Secretary of War Judah P. Benjamin well into the night. He receives a letter from Mary but due to the meeting with Benjamin is not able to answer until tomorrow. Lee sends Maj. George Jackson his commission in Virginia's forces.[15]

November 5, Tuesday (Richmond): The Department of South Carolina, Georgia, and East Florida is created and Lee assigned to command it; he meets with President Davis in the morning to discuss this new assignment. Lee issues orders abolishing the official District of Richmond, with all remaining troops reporting directly to Virginia Forces headquarters. Lee writes to Mary about his failed attempt to come to Shirley to visit over the weekend; he invites her to come to Richmond to visit him but cautions that he is overwhelmed with paperwork.[16]

November 6, Wednesday (Richmond/Wilmington): Lee, Taylor, Perry, and Meredith depart Richmond in the morning for Charleston. Capt. Thornton A. Washington is assigned to Lee's staff, and likely travels with them. Davis notifies Florida's governor that Lee has been assigned to command, calling Lee "an officer of the highest ability and reputation."[17]

---

13 Davis did not give a date for this meeting, and no documentation places it on this date; however, it is logical that they would discuss this as soon as possible. See Jefferson Davis to WHT, Jan. 31, 1878, WHT papers, SH; and Jefferson Davis, *The Rise and Fall of the Confederate Government*, 2 vols. (New York, 1990), vol. 2, 376-7. Davis wrote "Gen. Lee orally gave me a full account of the movement to surprise the enemy in the Valley.... Gen. Lee was severely and unjustly criticized for that campaign and ... the blame was thrown jointly upon him and myself, but he magnanimously declined to make an official report which would have exonerated himself by throwing the responsibility of the failure upon others. His oral report to me was therefore confidential." Davis to WHT, Jan. 31, 1878, WHT papers, SH.

14 Dowdey, *Wartime Papers*, 83-4. This is almost certainly the same incident described by quartermaster clerk George B. West: "With [Maj. J. B.] Whitfield one evening a gentleman came in to see if there was a boat going down the river that afternoon as he wished to down to Shirley.... He was dressed in a sort of fatigue coat with no mark of rank, and did not give his name. When he went out, all the clerks wondered who he could be ... and we learned it was General R.E. Lee." Parke Rouse, Jr., ed., *When the Yankees Came: Civil War and Reconstruction on the Virginia Peninsula* (Richmond, VA, 1987), 71-2. The quartermaster office was located at the corner of 9th and Main. Ibid. Shirley was the home of Lee's mother, Anne Hill Carter, who married "Light Horse Harry" Lee in the parlor; Lee spent much time there as a child. The mansion itself dates to the mid-18th century and is still owned by the Carter family. Emmie Ferguson Farrar, *Old Virginia Houses Along the James* (New York, 1957), 88-90. Mrs. Lee continued to roam from one temporary domicile to another, usually staying with relatives; she left Hot Springs for Shirley in late October. Lee, "Mary Anne Randolph Custis Lee," 19.

15 Dowdey, *Wartime Papers*, 83-4; REL to George Jackson, Nov. 4, 1861, VAF, NA. Lee wrote that he was with Benjamin until after 11:00 p. m. The letter to Jackson is the final entry in the Records of the VA Forces HQ; why Lee handled such a routine matter rather than George Deas, who handled all such correspondence while Lee was in western Virginia, is not known. Jackson served with the 14th VA Cav. briefly before several staff assignments. Krick, *Lee's Colonels*, 206.

16 OR 6, 309; Freeman, *Lee*, vol. 1, 606-7; GO34, Nov. 5, 1861, Order Book, VAF, NA; Dowdey, *Wartime Papers*, 83-4. Not only did Lee not mention in his letter to his wife Mary a thing about his pending assignment to the south Atlantic coast, but he told her he would try to visit Shirley or White House soon, so this letter was written in the morning before meeting Davis.

17 Freeman, *Lee*, vol. 1, 608; Richmond *Daily Dispatch*, Nov. 7, 1861; Thornton A. Washington CSR; Crooks, *Lee in the Low Country*, 39. Thornton Washington was a cousin of Lee's former aide John Washington and served 12 years in the U.S. Army before the war. He served on the staff of Gen. Earl van Dorn prior to his assignment to Lee; his time with Lee lasted only until April 1862 when he was assigned to quartermaster duties in the Western Theater. Bushong, *Jefferson County*, 444; Krick, *Staff Officers in Gray*, 297. Washington was in Richmond at this time and was announced as a member of Lee's staff immediately upon Lee's assumption of command in SC, hence the assumption that he accompanied Lee and Taylor. No details of the trip to Charleston were recorded by any of the parties involved, but it is most likely that they went by way of

November 7, Thursday (Wilmington/Charleston/Coosawhatchie/Port Royal): Lee and his party arrive in Charleston, South Carolina, in the morning via the Northeastern Railroad, where they are greeted by sound of distant artillery fire. As Lee soon learns, Union naval forces are attacking Port Royal. He boards a special train on the Charleston & Savannah and gets as far as Coosawhatchie, where he detrains and rides on toward the ongoing battle. On his way there he meets Brig. Gen. Roswell Ripley, who briefs Lee on the fighting at Port Royal. They continue forward to the front, and arrive after the firing has stopped. Lee orders Ripley's forces to withdraw from the remains of the coastal fortifications. The Confederate artillerists have been completely outgunned by the powerful Union Navy. Lee and Ripley return to Coosawhatchie, where Lee establishes his headquarters in an abandoned house owned by Mrs. George Chisholm Mackay of Savannah. Lee and Ripley discuss plans and the disposition of the troops and defenses. It likely falls to either Washington or Taylor to organize the headquarters staff.[18]

November 8, Friday (Coosawhatchie): Capt. Washington issues General Order #1, in which Lee assumes formal command and names his staff: Washington as adjutant general; Taylor as assistant adjutant general; Capt. Joseph C. Ives as chief engineer; Lt. Col. William G. Gill as ordnance officer; and Joseph Manigault as a volunteer civilian aide-de-camp. Lee divides the department into five districts under brigadier generals Ripley, Nathan "Shanks" Evans, John C. Pemberton, Thomas F. Drayton, and Col. Arthur Manigault.[19]

---

the Richmond & Petersburg, Petersburg & Weldon, and Wilmington & Weldon railroads. At Wilmington they would have switched to the Wilmington & Manchester and finally the Northeastern RR for the final leg. Robert C. Black, III, *The Railroads of the Confederacy* (Chapel Hill, NC, 1998), xxv. They apparently spent all night on the train or spent the night at some point along the route, for they did not arrive in Charleston until the morning of the 7th. Richmond *Daily Dispatch*, Nov. 8, 1861. Lt. Col. William G. Gill was assigned to Lee on this date as ordnance officer, but it is not known whether he accompanied Lee or joined him in SC. Gill's stay with Lee was very brief as by Dec. 4 he was in command of the Augusta Arsenal. William G. Gill CSR. Lee left his horse "Richmond" behind in the capital as the animal was in poor health and took "Brown Roan" south with him. Custis to Robert A. Brock, Aug. 11, 1891, Lee papers, SH.

18 Richmond *Daily Dispatch*, Nov. 8, 1861; Black, *Railroads of the Confederacy*, 161; Savannah *Republican*, Nov. 8, 1861; Freeman, *Lee*, vol. 1, 608-9; *OR* 6, 312-3; Crooks, *Lee in the Low Country*, 56-8. Ripley was a native Ohioan who married into a prominent Charleston, SC, family after the Mexican War. He commanded Fort Moultrie during the bombardment of Fort Sumter and was given command of Sumter after its surrender; he was one of Lee's most senior subordinates in South Carolina, and later commanded a brigade in the Army of Northern Virginia. Following his wounding at Sharpsburg he was reassigned back to Charleston. Lawrence L. Hewitt, "Roswell Sabine Ripley," *Confederate General*, vol. 5, 89-90. At Port Royal, a Union fleet under Flag Officer Samuel DuPont silenced the guns of Forts Walker and Beauregard, guarding the approaches to Port Royal Sound, clearing the way for the landing of a large Union force under Brig. Gen. Thomas W. Sherman. This action gave the Union its base at Hilton Head Island and Port Royal that would be maintained for the rest of the war. Long, *CW Day by Day*, 136. Coosawhatchie was at the head of navigation of the river of the same name, roughly half-way between Charleston and Savannah and directly on the C&S Railroad; it was described as "quite healthy in the winter season but very sickly in the summer." H. David Stone, Jr., *Vital Rails: The Charleston & Savannah Railroad and the Civil War in Coastal South Carolina* (Columbia, SC, 2008), 73. Mrs. Mackay was the mother of Lee's West Point classmate and close friend Jack Mackay; Lee became close to the family during his assignment to Fort Pulaski in 1829.

19 *OR* 6, 312; Ellison Capers, *South Carolina* – vol. 5 in Clement Evans, ed., *Confederate Military History* (Secaucus, NJ, 1975), 37-8. Ives explored the Colorado River shortly before the war, and served most of the war as an aide to President Davis. Gill's service on Lee's staff was so brief that Taylor apparently forgot him, or at least didn't deem him worthy of inclusion, when listing Lee's staff during this period. WHT to Edwin D. Newton, May 11, 1903, WHT papers, NPL. Pemberton was a Philadelphian who married into a Virginia family; he eventually succeeded Lee as department commander. He rose to lieutenant general and upon his shoulders fell the defense of Vicksburg. When no assignment could be found for him after that commensurate with his rank, he resigned and was re-commissioned lieutenant colonel and commanded heavy artillery batteries in the Richmond defenses. Warner, *Generals in Gray*, 232-3. Drayton was a West Point classmate of Jefferson Davis who left the army to pursue a railroad career. He was president of the Charleston & Savannah at the beginning of the war, a position which he retained for part of the war, and later commanded a brigade in the ANV. Ibid., 75-6. Manigault was an aide to Beauregard at Fort Sumter and was appointed colonel of the 10th SC. He rose to brigadier general and spent most of the war with the Army of Tennessee; he was severely wounded at Franklin. Ibid., 210-1.

November 9, Saturday (Coosawhatchie): Lee sends to Secretary Benjamin a detailed report of all he has done since arriving, including the defensive measures taken to protect the C&S, and how to counter Union access to a host of inland waterways.[20]

November 10, Sunday (Coosawhatchie/ Savannah): Lee inquires of Sec. Benjamin whether he can temporarily commandeer troops passing through his department. The general leaves for Savannah, Georgia, in the evening to inspect the city's defenses.[21]

November 11, Monday (Savannah): Lee, accompanied by Georgia Governor Joseph Brown, Brig. Gen. Alexander Lawton, and Commodore Josiah Tattnall, takes the steamer *Ida* from Savannah to Cockspur Island to inspect Fort Pulaski. Upon disembarking from the boat, Lee encounters its captain Francis J. Cercopoly, who had ferried Lee to the island 30 years before when Lee was engaged in the construction of Fort Pulaski; instantly recognizing him, Lee introduced Cercopoly to the rest of the entourage. Maj. Charles H. Olmstead, commander of the fort, conducts the party on a tour, during which Lee tells Olmstead that the Federals "will make it very warm for you with shells from that point [Tybee Island] but they cannot breach your walls at that distance." Lee dispatches several officers to scout the Federals at Port Royal and others to oversee construction of river defenses around Savannah, and informs Secretary Benjamin of the steps being taken to prevent Union incursions into the interior. Capt. John N. Maffitt joins Lee's staff as a naval aide, and is charged with creating maps of the region and placing river obstructions.[22]

---

20 OR 6, 312-3. The region around Charleston has a number of waterways which reach to the railroad; Lee realized that there was no way to defend every vulnerable point and devised a plan to keep a mobile force on the railroad to be sent to any threatened point.

21 OR 6, 314; Charleston *Mercury*, Nov. 13, 1861; Rogers W. Young, *Robert E. Lee and Fort Pulaski* (Washington, D.C., 1941), 19.

22 Charles H. Olmstead to wife, Nov. 21, 1861, C. H. Olmstead papers, UNC; Young, *REL and Fort Pulaski*, 19-23; OR 53, 186-7; Emma M. Maffitt, "The Confederate Navy," *CV*, (May 1917), vol. 25, no. 5, 219. Lawton served in the Georgia legislature and was president of the Augusta & Savannah RR; he commanded at Savannah and later led a brigade and division in the ANV before being appointed quartermaster general. Warner, *Generals in Gray*, 175-6. Tattnall was a veteran of the War of 1812 and commander of Georgia's navy; he commanded the James River fleet during the battle of Hampton Roads in March 1862. Olmstead commanded the 1st GA Volunteers (not to be confused with the two other 1st GA regiments). Ralston B. Lattimore, *Fort Pulaski National Monument, Georgia* (Washington, D.C., 1954), 19-23. Lee could not have been more wrong in telling Olmstead the walls could not be breached from Tybee Island as rifled Union artillery on Tybee did indeed breach the fort's walls in only a matter of hours in April. Olmstead recalled that Cercopoly "was delighted on the day of Gen. Lee's visit to the Fort. It seems that he was employed here in some capacity twenty-eight years ago when Lee, then a young lieutenant just from West Point, had charge of the work.... The steamer arrived at the wharf, the escort I had sent down presented arms and then led the way up to the Fort, then came Gens Lee and Lawton, arm in arm, then Gov Brown and Com Tattnall then some ten or twelve army and navy officers of high rank. Old Cercopoly stood at the gate to see if he would be recognized as the cortege came with a few steps of him, Lee stopped and said 'I ought to know that man. Why Francis, is that you?' He went up to him, shook him warmly by the hand, then turning to the other gentlemen introduced the happy Captain to every one of them, just as he would have done the highest dignitary of the land. Cercopoly treasures up every word of the interview and it will doubtless be a tradition in his family for many a year to come 'how Gen Lee met Grandfather.'" Olmstead to wife, Nov. 21, 1861, UNC. Maffitt wrote of his duties: "I am well–hard at work–and my duty is of a general character–surveying–erecting batteries–placing obstructions–I have not resigned from the Navy but am Naval Aide to Gen. Lee–on temporary duty as such, until all is arranged here for a general defense–I am much pleased thus far, and my duties are highly appreciated." John N. Maffitt to "girls," Dec. 20, 1861, J. N. Maffitt papers, UNC. Maffitt would command the commerce raider *CSS Florida* and the ironclad *CSS Albemarle*. He recorded "Many interesting events personal to myself occurred during my very agreeable association with Gen. Lea [sic]—but as they were comical and not in consonance with my present feeling of sadness and despondency, I do not feel the inclination to record them." Maffitt journal, Maffitt papers, UNC. One wonders what he was referring to, and can only wish he had recorded the "many interesting events." Maffitt joined Lee's staff under a cloud: Tattnall had suspended Maffitt from command of his *CSS Savannah* for his actions during the Port Royal engagement. Lee specifically requested Maffitt's services; whether Lee first approached Maffitt or vice versa is not known. Royce G. Shingleton, *High Seas Confederate: The Life and Times of John Newland Maffitt* (Columbia, SC, 1994), 36-7.

November 12, Tuesday (Savannah): Lee remains in Savannah inspecting and planning other defenses around the city. He sends instructions to the commander at Fernandina, Florida, for arming and manning the batteries there, and sends Ives and Manigault of his staff with a cavalry escort to scout Union forces at Beaufort.[23]

November 13, Wednesday (Savannah/ Charleston): Lee departs for Charleston via the C&S Railroad, arriving there in the afternoon, to inspect the harbor defenses.[24]

November 14, Thursday (Charleston): Lee inspects the defenses around sprawling Charleston harbor. One observer notes of him, "He is never hopeful and does not seem in particular good humor concerning things here."[25]

November 15, Friday (Charleston): Lee writes to his daughter Mildred at Winchester, telling her to tend to her studies; he mentions that his current assignment is "another forlorn hope expedition. Worse than western Virginia."[26]

November 16, Saturday (Charleston/ Coosawhatchie): Lee places Capt. D. N. Ingraham of the Navy in charge of the preparation and arming of the batteries around Charleston harbor, and issues instructions for the mustering of South Carolina troops into Confederate service. In the evening he departs for his headquarters at Coosawhatchie.[27]

November 17, Sunday (Coosawhatchie/Savannah): Lee orders Brig. Gen. James H. Trapier to take command at Fernandina, Florida. Lee also writes to Governor Pickens regarding the number of troops that are required from the state of South Carolina, and instructs him that arms arriving on the blockade runner *Fingal* are only for troops whose enlistments are for the duration of the war, and not for troops who are on the books for a shorter period. That night Lee departs for Savannah, arriving there after midnight.[28]

November 18, Monday (Savannah): In the early hours of the morning, Gen. Lee arrives in Savannah, Georgia. Before breakfast, he writes a short letter to his wife Mary. In it, he mentions that the Federals "have been quiescent, apparently confining themselves to Hilton Head, where they are apparently fortifying."[29]

---

23 Richmond *Daily Dispatch*, Nov. 13, 1861; *OR* 53, 187; Charleston *Mercury*, Nov. 13, 1861. It may be this date that Lee inspects the defenses of Green Island, at the mouth of the Little Ogeechee River south of the city. An officer stationed there recalled Lee's visit, but not the specific date other than putting it after Dec. 11, which does not fit with the rest of his narrative of the visit being part of Lee's initial familiarization tour. William S. Basinger, *The Savannah Volunteer Guards, 1858-1882*, pp. 93, in William S. Basinger collection, UGA.

24 Charleston *Mercury*, Nov. 15, 1861. Lee would have a problem with the Charleston and Savannah newspapers revealing military information; a Savannah paper wrote on this date that Lee and Ripley "are now busily engaged in locating and building batteries at various points so as to protect the railroad communication between Charleston and Savannah." Savannah *Daily Morning News*, Nov. 13, 1861.

25 Woodward, *Mary Chesnut's CW*, 237; Charleston *Mercury*, Nov. 15, 1861. At some point during this stay in Charleston, Lee met with South Carolina Governor Francis Pickens; the exact date is not known. Freeman, *Lee*, vol. 1, 611-3. It is likely also either on or about this date that Lee inspected Castle Pinckney. The wife of Capt. C. E. Chichester, commanding officer of the fort, remembered: "He made a very minute examination of every department and before leaving, remarked that he found the castle in better condition, in every respect than any of the other forts, and complimented the garrison on its fine military appearance, and the order and discipline which prevailed in every department." Crook, *REL in the Low Country*, 86.

26 Dowdey, *Wartime Papers*, 86.

27 *OR* 6, 322; Dowdey, *Wartime Papers*, 87.

28 *OR* 6, 323; *OR* 53, 187-8; Dowdey, *Wartime Papers*, 87.

29 Dowdey, *Wartime Papers*, 87.

November 19, Tuesday (Brunswick): Lee inspects the works in and around Brunswick, Georgia.[30]

November 20, Wednesday (Fernandina): Lee inspects the defenses at Fernandina and Amelia Island, Florida.[31]

November 21, Thursday (Savannah): Lee returns to Savannah from his inspection trip along the coast. He writes a report of his findings and recommendations to Gen. Cooper; he recommends more guns and ammunition and laments the lack of trained artillerists at all posts. Orders are issued not to load weapons unless in the presence of the enemy, and to respect private property: "The General hopes that it will only be necessary to remind the troops that they are citizens as well as soldiers, and that, as they take up arms to repel the enemy from our soil, they should still be more careful to preserve it sacred from their own depredations."[32]

November 22, Friday (Savannah): Lee writes to Agnes and Annie who are staying with the family of Dr. Richard Stuart at Cleydael in King George County. The girls have recently been to Stratford Hall, which prompts Lee to mention his desire to purchase his ancestral home. "It is endeared to me by many recollections and it has always been a great desire of my life to be able to purchase it. Now that we have no other home, and the one we so loved has been so foully polluted, the desire is stronger with me than ever." He mentions having seen Mrs. Mackay and several other friends in Savannah, and concedes that all of the coastal defenses are "poor indeed. . . . I hope our enemy will be polite enough to wait for us" to improve them.[33]

November 23, Saturday (Coosawhatchie): Lee returns to headquarters at Coosawhatchie. He writes to Sec. Benjamin explaining the disposition of the arms and equipment from the blockade runner *Fingal*, and relays his difficulties in organizing the commands as there are both Confederate and state troops in the field. He desperately needs more field artillery and cavalry, as well as at least one more brigadier general, preferably Henry Heth.[34]

November 24, Sunday (Coosawhatchie): Lee writes to President Davis regarding Beauregard's report of the Battle of Manassas, and sends instructions to Ripley regarding people coming and going from Charleston. He writes as well to Mathilda Rhett, thanking her for her recent letter and hopes that reverses along the coast can soon be reversed.[35]

---

30 Charleston *Mercury*, Nov. 20, 1861. It is not known when he arrived in Brunswick, or precisely who was with him. The *Mercury* reported several days later that Gen. Lawton accompanied him, but this not only doesn't make sense as Lawton's command was limited to Savannah, but also Washington sent word to Lawton in Savannah on this date that Ripley reported a Federal advance in his front. Charleston *Mercury*, Nov. 23, 1861; T. A. Washington to Lawton, Nov. 18, 1861, REL papers, MOC. Washington remained behind at Coosawhatchie to run HQ during this trip; see OR 6, 327-8 and Washington to Lawton, Nov. 19, 1861, REL papers, MOC.

31 OR 6, 327. Lee's precise movements on this date are not known, especially his arrival and departure times.

32 Charleston *Mercury*, Nov. 23, 1861; OR 6, 327-8.

33 Dowdey, *Wartime Papers*, 88-9. Cleydael, built in 1859, was the summer home of Dr. Stuart, a distant Lee cousin. On April 23, 1865, John Wilkes Booth and David Herold showed up at Cleydael, sent there by Dr. Samuel Mudd. Dr. Stuart likely suspected who his visitors were and made them leave after providing them a quick meal. Michael W. Kauffman, *American Brutus: John Wilkes Booth and the Lincoln Conspiracies* (New York, 2004), 299-301.

34 OR 53, 190-1.

35 Dunbar Rowland, ed., *Jefferson Davis, Constitutionalist: His Letters, Papers, and Speeches*. 10 vols. (Jackson, MS, 1923), vol. 5, 176-7; OR 53, 191; REL to M. M. Rhett, Nov. 24, 1861, Gilder-Lehrman. Lee noted in the letter to Rhett that he had not seen Mary since he left Arlington. The Federals occupied Tybee Island on this date, causing Maj. Olmstead to tell his wife: "It is nothing more than we have expected ever since we gave up Tybee, its occupation by the enemy. I see in it no cause for alarm and I trust my dear wife that you will not allow yourself to be influenced by the excitement which I know will seize the good people of Savannah. The fact that the vessels kept out of the range of our guns shows that they fear us." Olmstead to wife, Nov. 25, 1861, Olmstead papers, UNC.

November 25, Monday (Coosawhatchie): Lee issues instructions that no civilian can leave Charleston without written permission from Mayor Charles MacBeth.[36]

November 26, Tuesday (Coosawhatchie): Lee addresses concerns by Ripley that the enemy can come and go at will on the coastal islands; Lee tells him that while he is correct, the Federals have neither the strength nor any reason to occupy coastal islands after raiding them, thus more river obstructions are necessary to limit the range and frequency of these incursions.[37]

November 29, Friday (Savannah): Lee submits his report of the Federal occupation of Tybee Island to Sec. Benjamin in Richmond.[38]

---

36 Charleston *Mercury*, Nov. 26, 1861.

37 OR 6, 329.

38 OR 6, 32-3.

December 1861

Robert E. Lee must have felt a sense of *déjà vu* during the winter of 1861-2 as he once again scrambled to assemble, equip, and train an army to keep away a threatening enemy in proximity. "I am laboring night and day to organize and equip and bring into the field all the troops I can," he explained to son Rooney.[1] It was not an easy task, as Capt. Maffitt observed: "The troops were raw, badly clad, and almost without organization."[2]

The general continued to tour his department, inspecting and improving defenses. "I am here but little myself," he wrote Mary from his headquarters in Coosawhatchie. "The days I am not away, I visit some point exposed to the enemy and after our dinner at early candle light, am engaged in writing till 11 or 12 at night."[3] His routine was usually breakfast at 8:00 a.m., lunch—if any—was whatever he or his officers could scrounge, dinner at 6:00 p.m., and into bed around 11:00 p.m.; meals were cooked by Meredith and served by Perry.[4]

An inspection tour of Charleston took him to that city just in time for the Great Fire. Lee and several members of his staff watched from a rooftop as more than 500 acres of the historic seaport burned.

One notable addition to Lee's military family during this time, although not yet official, was an acquaintance Lee had met in western Virginia: the horse "Jeff Davis" and "Greenbrier." The 60th Virginia Infantry was again serving under Lee's command—thankfully for Lee, this time without Henry Wise—and Capt. Joseph Broun brought with him the horse to which Lee had taken such a liking only a few weeks before. Lee arranged to borrow the horse for a time as a trial run before purchasing him, using the mount on some of his inspection rides.

* * *

1 REL to Rooney, Dec. 23, 1861, G. B. Lee papers, VHS.

2 Shingleton, *High Seas Confederate*, 38.

3 Dowdey, *Wartime Papers*, 94.

4 REL to Mary, Dec. 22, 1861, REL papers, LOC.

December 1, Sunday (Coosawhatchie): Lee receives a letter from Mary.[5]

December 2, Monday (Coosawhatchie/Port Royal Sound): Lee ventures down the Broad River to Port Royal Sound to cope with marauding parties raiding local plantations. He writes to Mary, glad that she is reunited with Annie and Agnes at White House, and that Rooney's reassignment now has him close by as well.[6]

December 3, Tuesday (Port Royal Sound/Coosawhatchie): Lee returns to headquarters from his trip downriver and informs Secretary of War Benjamin of the results. He also informs Benjamin of the poor recruiting efforts in South Carolina and asks if arms in his department can be issued to troops from other states. He requests Col. John S. Preston, in charge of the state's recruiting to bring the bleak recruiting state of affairs to the attention of the governor: "My great desire is to get a force in the field to resist the landing of the enemy, and to confine him if possible to his ships. They are in great force, and we have nothing to oppose them."

Lee informs a committee of citizens from near Beaufort that he will not declare martial law along the coast as they request: "There is as yet no operation of the enemy to justify the interruption of the civil laws. . . . In no part of the Confederacy has it yet been found necessary to arrest the due course of the laws of a State. It should only be resorted to as a last extremity, which I do not see has yet arrived in South Carolina." Lee receives a gift of "bedding" from the Soldiers Relief Association in Charleston for him and his staff.[7]

December 4, Wednesday (Coosawhatchie): Gen. Lee conditionally approves of Ripley's plan to occupy Edisto Island, provided he has sufficient strength to hold it and means of evacuating it quickly. Lee writes to the Charleston Soldiers Relief Association thanking them for the bedding sent him.[8]

December 5, Thursday (Coosawhatchie/Palmetto Point): Lee goes downriver to Palmetto Point to observe the Union fleet. Upon his return he writes to Governor Pickens giving him an update on the defenses at Charleston and elsewhere, but regrets that he cannot issue recently received Enfield rifles to units unless they enlist for the duration of the war.[9]

December 7, Saturday (Coosawhatchie): Gen. Lee tells Roswell Ripley that defending the rivers is of vital importance as doing so prevents the enemy from striking the Charleston & Savannah Railroad. Lee issues orders concerning purchasing supplies and camp hygiene.[10]

December 8, Sunday (Coosawhatchie): Lee writes to Col. James Jones complaining of poor vigilance by the guards at Port Royal Ferry and notes slaves from area plantations are escaping downriver to the enemy, and he is to round up all boats to put a stop to it. Lee writes to Annie, mainly family news and he encloses some pressed violets picked from the yard at his headquarters.[11]

December 9, Monday (Coosawhatchie): Lee sends the 12th and 13th South Carolina infantry regiments to intercept an enemy landing at Cunningham Point.

---

5 Dowdey, *Wartime Papers*, 89. Mary was then at Rooney's plantation, White House, east of Richmond.

6 OR 6, 335; Dowdey, *Wartime Papers*, 89-90. Coosawhatchie was at the head of navigation on the Coosawatchie River, which flows into the Broad River.

7 OR 53, 193-4; OR 6, 335; REL to Richard Caldwell, Dec. 4, 1861, REL papers, W&L.

8 OR 6, 335-6; REL to Richard Caldwell, Dec. 4, 1861, REL papers, W&L.

9 OR 53, 194-5. Palmetto Point is on St. Helena Island in the vicinity of the postwar Fort Fremont.

10 OR 6, 339-40.

11 OR 53, 195; Dowdey, *Wartime Papers*, 90-1. Jones was colonel of the 14th SC; he resigned in April 1862 and became South Carolina's quartermaster general. Krick, *Lee's Colonels*, 214. Annie was still at White House with her mother and Agnes.

He writes to Roswell Ripley regarding the river defenses and obstructions being constructed. Lee's letter of December 4 thanking the Soldiers Relief Association of Charleston is read aloud at their meeting.[12]

December 10, Tuesday (Coosawhatchie): Lee writes to John Pemberton regarding the obstructions in the Combahee and Ashepoo rivers. Lee makes official the command structure in the department, formally announcing the creation of five separate military districts. Taylor's promotion to captain ranks from today.[13]

December 11, Wednesday (Coosawhatchie/Charleston): Lee, Taylor, and Ives go to Charleston, crossing the Ashley River in a rowboat in the evening. They arrive at the Mills House Hotel, where they are joined by Maj. Armistead Long, who has been assigned to Lee's staff. Around dinnertime, they notice quite a commotion outside as a fire spreads across part of the city. Lee, Long, and others climb to the roof of the hotel, where they observe the raging fire spread until it reaches the immediate vicinity of the hotel itself. The four officers flee the building, accompanied by the wives of both Long and Thornton Washington, who are in the hotel with them; Lee and Long each carry a small child out of the building in the wild confusion. They find a carriage outside that carries their party to the home of Charles Alston several blocks away, where they remain for the night.[14]

December 12, Thursday (Charleston): Lee and his party survey the damage to the city from the previous night's fire. They return to the Mills House, which narrowly survived the blaze.[15]

December 13, Friday (Charleston): Ives is officially named chief engineer of the department.[16]

December 14, Saturday (Charleston): Lee informs former Florida Sen. David Yulee that he has sent officers to oversee the work on the defenses at Fernandina and that he will send all the reinforcements he can. Lee writes to William H. Stiles regarding a military appointment for his son Robert.[17]

December 15, Sunday (Charleston): Lee spends the day in the field inspecting the defenses around the

---

12 OR 6, 343-4; OR 53, 196; Charleston *Mercury*, Dec. 11, 1861.

13 OR 6, 344; OR 53, 197-8; SO17, Dec. 10, 1861, REL papers, MOC; Krick, *Staff Officers in Gray*, 283. SO17 formalized the command structure Lee had already put in place on Nov. 8 upon assuming command. Taylor was already a captain in Virginia's forces; his C.S. captain's commission was issued on Dec. 31, 1861, but to rank from today. Apparently Taylor's pay was not in accord with his grade and assignment, as Robert Chilton in the adjutant general's office in Richmond wrote to Taylor to explain what pay he was entitled to and why. Chilton to WHT, Dec. 10, 1861, WHT papers, SH.

14 Taylor, *General Lee*, 40; Long, *Memoirs of REL*, 134-6. Mrs. Washington was present with the party although her husband was not, having been left to run headquarters at Coosawhatchie; see letter of WHT to Washington, Dec. 11, 1861, REL papers, MOC. The Edmondston-Alston house is located at 21 E Battery St., and was Beauregard's vantage point for the bombardment of Fort Sumter. Clint Johnson, *In the Footsteps of Robert E. Lee* (Winston-Salem, NC, 2001), 150-1. Taylor and Long's accounts differ slightly as to the time the party evacuated the hotel: Taylor wrote that it was just after they sat down to dinner; Long remembered it being several hours afterward. In either case, both left vivid accounts of that night.

15 Taylor, *General Lee*, 40; Long, *Memoirs of REL*, 136. The fire swept across the Charleston peninsula from the Cooper to the Ashley, destroying 575 homes over some 540 acres; damages were estimated from $5 million to $8 million. Somehow no lives were lost in the conflagration. Walter J. Fraser, Jr., *Charleston! Charleston! The History of a Southern City* (Columbia, SC, 1989), 254. Lee donated $300 to the fire relief fund. Thomas, *Lee*, 214.

16 Ives CSR. Washington joined Lee's party in Charleston either Thursday or Friday, as he wrote to Gen. Donelson from Charleston on this date. OR 6, 346. Lee likely continued his inspection tour on this date.

17 REL to D. L. Yulee, Dec. 14, 1861, David Yulee papers, University of Florida; REL to W. H. Stiles, Dec. 14, 1861, REL papers, VMI. Yulee served in the Florida legislature as well as both houses of the U.S. Congress. He lived in Fernandina so was quite concerned with its defense. Stiles was married to Jack Mackay's sister. Lee presumably toured more of Charleston's defenses on this date.

city. In the evening he visits with Andrew Talcott and his family, who are temporarily in Charleston.[18]

December 16, Monday (Charleston): Lee assures Governor Pickens that the Federals will not be able to take Charleston by the water approaches, but tells him "We have need of all the resources of the state." He also asks the governor if there are any "for the war" South Carolina units ready, as Lee can only issue arms to those enlisting for the war. Lee informs Yulee that there are no troops at Brunswick that can be sent to Fernandina, so Florida troops will have to be sent there. He informs Gen. Trapier, commanding at Fernandina, of the same but that Lee will go himself to Savannah to see what might be spared from there. He provides Sec. Benjamin with an update on the Charleston defenses and requests more artillery. He also thanks G. B. Stacy in Richmond for a mattress he gave Lee shortly before he left there for Charleston.[19]

December 17, Tuesday (Charleston/ Coosawhatchie): Lee returns to Coosawhatchie during the day, where he learns that Richmond has ordered substantial reinforcements to his department. He telegraphs Benjamin to request additional field guns.[20]

December 18, Wednesday (Coosawhatchie): Lee makes some administrative changes within the department with Nathan Evans formally assuming command of his district, R. A. Kinloch being assigned as medical director, and Armistead Long replacing Gill as ordnance officer.[21]

December 19, Thursday (Coosawhatchie): Lee recommends to the War Department in Richmond that the Atlantic & Gulf and Pensacola & Georgia railroads be connected.[22]

December 20, Friday (Coosawhatchie): Ripley advises Lee that the Federal Navy sank about a dozen ships laden with stone in one of the shipping channels in Charleston harbor; Lee replies that this act reveals the Federal intent to isolate Charleston rather than attempt a direct water-borne assault against it. Lee informs Benjamin of this "stone fleet," and again requests more heavy guns for defensive works. With Long assuming the role of ordnance officer, all brigade and district commanders are ordered to provide returns to him.[23]

December 21, Saturday (Coosawhatchie): Lee informs Benjamin that he will begin arming individual "for the war" companies once all "for the war" regiments and battalions have been armed. In the evening he receives a letter from Mary.[24]

December 22, Sunday (Coosawhatchie): Lee writes to Mary, sending early Christmas greetings. He tells her of the great fire in Charleston, and seeing the Talcotts while there. He is glad that Rooney is able to be with her for Christmas, but is very upset at what he perceives as lack of commitment by most of the population to the war effort: "It will require misfortune, suffering I fear to induce us to do what we ought." He also complains about his two servants: Perry is "very lackydaisical in his

---

18 REL to Mrs. REL, Dec. 22, 1861, REL papers, Library of Congress. Talcott was on his way to Mexico to continue his railroad career.

19 *OR* 53, 198-9; REL to Yulee, Dec. 16, 1861, Yulee papers; REL to Trapier, Dec. 16, 1861, REL papers, MOC; REL to Yulee and Trapier, Dec. 16, 1861, REL papers, LVA; *OR* 6, 346-7; REL to G. B. Stacy, Dec. 16, 1861, REL papers, MOC.

20 Freeman, *Lee*, vol. 1, 617; *OR* 6, 347.

21 *OR* 6, 347; GO6, Dec. 18, 1861, REL papers, MOC.

22 *OR* 1, Series 4, 777-8. At the beginning of the war, Florida's railroads were isolated from the rest of the Confederacy, without a single link tying the systems together. The roadbed for the connection Lee proposed was completed by the end of 1862, but finding iron for the rails was problematic—eventually other railroads had to be cannibalized for its completion. Black, *Railroads of the Confederacy*, 208.

23 Freeman, *Lee*, vol. 1, 618; *OR* 53, 201; *OR* 6, 42-3, 348; SO Dec. 20, 1861, REL papers, MOC.

24 *OR* 6, 349; REL to Mrs. REL, Dec. 22, 1861, REL papers, LOC.

operations" and Meredith has potential but no one to teach or watch over him.[25]

December 23, Monday (Coosawhatchie): Lee orders reinforcements sent to Pemberton's command, and acknowledges the progress that Ripley has made with river obstructions. He writes to son Rooney worrying about the Federals—he recently counted 80 ships at Port Royal; while he is angry about the "stone fleet" at Charleston he is positive the water will soon carve a new channel, negating the attempt at closing the harbor. He tells Rooney "I grieved to leave you there [western Virginia] and believe it was your presence and vicinity that retained me in that country so willingly."[26]

December 24, Tuesday (Coosawhatchie): Lee sends to Governor Pickens a lengthy list of recommendations for the overall defense of South Carolina, stating that the total military strength of the state must be called out and employed for the duration of the war. He emphasizes that the best qualified men be selected as officers, and that "special corps and separate commands"—such as the Wise Legion and other similar units—should be avoided. He confesses that due to some units not filing returns he does not know the number of troops under his command at present. He is also very concerned that the enlistments of the 12-month units will end just as the spring campaign starts. He tells Lawton in Savannah that he has no troops to send there, so any further requests for additional troops will have to be made directly to Governor Joseph Brown. He inquires of Ripley the number and strength of units under his command and informs Evans that reinforcements are en route to him.[27]

December 25, Wednesday (Coosawhatchie): Lee presents gifts to the children of several of his officers as well as to Perry and Meredith. During the day he writes to his daughters and in the evening he writes to Mary, describing his headquarters and routine for her. He tells her to accept that Arlington and everything in it is gone: "If not destroyed it will be difficult ever to be recognized. Even if the enemy had wished to preserve it, it would almost have been impossible. . . . It is vain to think of its being in a habitable condition. I fear too books, furniture, and the relics of Mount Vernon will be gone. It is better to make up our minds to a general loss." He brings up again the idea of buying Stratford Hall, and asks her to have Rooney look into the possibility. He tells her as well to ignore reports of British intervention in the newspapers: "We must make up our minds to fight our battles and win our independence alone. No one will help us. We require no extraneous aid, if true to ourselves."[28]

December 26, Thursday (Coosawhatchie): Lee writes to Virginia's Governor Letcher advocating for a general draft of all Virginia soldiers who choose not to reenlist.[29]

December 27, Friday (Coosawhatchie): Lee reports to Governor Pickens that the number of available non-garrison troops in the department is approximately 10,000. He instructs Gen. Ripley as to the organization of new units, urges the speedy completion of the defenses around Charleston, and issues orders for a year-end muster on December 31.[30]

December 28, Saturday (Coosawhatchie/Edisto Island): Lee spends the day inspecting the defenses

---

25 REL to Mrs. REL, Dec. 22, 1861, REL papers, LOC. Mary was still at White House.

26 SO24, Dec. 23, 1861, REL papers, MOC; *OR* 6, 349; REL to Rooney, Dec. 23, 1861, G. B. Lee papers, VHS.

27 *OR* 6, 349-52; *OR* 53, 202-3. Lee's concern over the 12-month units proved correct, only he would have to confront this problem in Virginia rather than South Carolina.

28 Freeman, *Lee*, vol. 1, 618-21; Dowdey, *Wartime Papers*, 95-7. The *Mercury* on this date published a list of donors to the Committee for Relief for the Charleston fire; Lee's name was included with a donation of $300.

29 Freeman, *Lee*, vol. 2, 25.

30 *OR* 6, 356-9; SO Dec. 27, 1861, REL papers, MOC.

on and around Edisto Island. He notes that he covered 115 miles, but only 35 of them on horseback riding "Greenbrier." He does not return to Coosawhatchie until 11:00 p.m.[31]

December 29, Sunday (Coosawhatchie): Lee requests several heavy guns from Wilmington be sent to Charleston. He attempts to sort out conflicting orders regarding a battery on Cumberland Island—Trapier wants its guns removed to Fernandina, but Lee himself ordered the construction of the battery at Cumberland. He reviews the case of an underage soldier in the 15th South Carolina, and instructs Capt. Maffitt to call upon Ripley for a boat for his surveying work, but to make sure that the troops along the rivers are aware that it is a friendly vessel so it is not fired upon.

He writes to Rooney's wife Charlotte with family news and a request that she and Lee's daughters make clothes for the army. He sends a lengthy letter to Custis in Richmond regarding finding temporary quarters in Richmond. Lee mentions that he would like to have Custis with him as an aide as he needs an additional experienced officer on his staff: "Every day I have reports of [the enemy] landing in force, marching, etc., which turns out to be some marauding party. . . . He is threatening every avenue. Pillaging, burning, and robbing where he can venture with impunity and alarming women and children."[32]

December 30, Monday (Coosawhatchie/Edisto Island): Lee returns to Edisto Island observing the Federal fleet. He informs Drayton that he can send him no additional troops at present.[33]

December 31, Tuesday (Coosawhatchie/Savannah): Lee informs South Carolina Adjutant General Col. S. R. Gist that Charleston's defenses are very nearly completed but that he lacks men to garrison them fully; he asks when additional South Carolina troops might be coming. He leaves for Savannah in the afternoon. Walter Taylor is promoted to captain, to rank from December 10.[34]

---

31 Dowdey, *Wartime Papers*, 98-9. This is the first known reference to Lee actually riding "Greenbrier" aka Traveller. Before purchasing Greenbrier/Traveller, Lee borrowed him from owner Capt. Joseph Broun for about a month "to learn its qualities." This is almost certainly part of that trial period, as Broun wrote that Lee did not purchase the animal until February 1862. Pendleton, *Traveller*, 15-6. Lee noted that he had two horses with him at this time; one of them must have been Greenbrier/Traveller, and the other was likely Brown Roan, because the horse named Richmond did not go to South Carolina as Custis was using Richmond at this time. Dowdey, *Wartime Papers*, 99.

32 OR 53, 204-5; REL to Trapier, Dec. 29, 1861, REL papers, MOC; REL to Maffitt, Dec. 29, 1861, Maffitt papers, UNC; Jones, *Personal Reminiscences of REL*, 386-7; Dowdey, *Wartime Papers*, 97-9. The underage soldier was Pvt. John R. Gladney.

33 Snow, *Lee and his Generals*, 49; OR 53, 205. Lee's concerns over the dissolution of units mustered in for less than the war were exemplified with the expiration of the enlistment term of the Rutledge Mounted Riflemen, whom he ordered discharged from service on this date. SO, Dec. 30, 1861, REL papers, MOC.

34 OR 6, 364; WHT commission, Dec. 30, 1861, WHT papers, SH. The uniquely-named States Rights Gist was later promoted to brigadier general and killed leading a brigade at Franklin in November 1864. Warner, *Generals in Gray*, 106-7. Lee requested a meeting with Gist upon his return from Charleston; it is not known on what date they met. OR 6, 364; Walter B. Cisco, *States Rights Gist: A South Carolina General of the Civil War* (Gretna, LA, 2008), 68.

January 1862

The Federals continued to build up their strength in South Carolina and Georgia and threatened attacks at both Charleston and Savannah. These threats kept Lee moving along the railroad trying to determine enemy intentions. Although no attack materialized, the Federal Navy continued their efforts to close Charleston's harbor to shipping, and removed obstructions from the water approaches to Savannah. "General Lee is a capital commander," lauded Senator David Yulee of Florida. If his observation was any indication, Lee seemed to have gained the trust of most of those in the department.[1]

In mid-January Lee journeyed south once more to Fernandina on another inspection tour. During this trip he visited Dungeness on Cumberland Island, where his father Henry "Light-Horse Harry" Lee was buried. The son described the visit to his father's grave in great detail to Mary and Custis, although he did not record the date. "It was my first visit to the house [Dungeness] and I had the gratification at length of visiting my father's grave. . . . The spot is marked by a plain marble slab."[2]

Lee conducted a much more in-depth inspection of Savannah's fortifications, likely during the second week of January. Evidence exists that he and Gen. Alexander Lawton spent the better part of a day at Green Island, but no date—or even a hint at one—can be found. According to the commander of the fort, Lee meticulously "inspected the guard, man by man. He then went into the fort and examined that carefully, gun by gun, and the magazines."[3]

Several sizeable gaps exist as far as Lee's January movements. One is the aforementioned trip to Fernandina; during the other, he appears to have traveled to Charleston. Little is known of his stays there for January. Indeed, this is one of the least documented periods of Lee during the entire war.

* * *

1 OR 53, 214. See Chapter 3 of Robert Carse, *Department of the South: Hilton Head Island in the Civil War* (Hilton Head Island, SC, 1987).

2 Dowdey, *Wartime Papers*, 103. Dungeness was the home of Gen. Nathaniel Greene. Lee's father "Light Horse Harry" Lee was on his way to Virginia from the West Indies when he became gravely ill and stopped at Cumberland Island where he was cared for by Greene's family. He did not recover, dying on March 15, 1818, and was buried on the plantation grounds with full military honors. Karl A. Bickel, "Robert E. Lee in Florida," in *Florida Historical Quarterly* (July 1948), vol. 27, no. 1, 61. His remains were moved to Washington & Lee University in 1913. Dungeness was abandoned at the time of the war, although Lee noted that much of the furniture remained. It burned shortly after the war; it was later purchased by the Carnegie family who built a new Dungeness mansion, which also later burned. Currently the property is part of Cumberland Island National Seashore. It is believed that this was Lee's first visit to the grave. However, multiple articles in the *Virginia Magazine of History and Biography* address this topic and the contention that Lee visited during his assignment to Cockspur Island in 1830. See John M. Dederer, "Robert E. Lee's First Visit to His Father's Grave," *VMHB* (Jan. 1994), vol. 102, no. 1, pp. 73-88; J. Anderson Thomson, Jr., and Carlos Michael Santos, "The Mystery in the Coffin: Another View of Lee's Visit to His Father's Grave," *VMHB* (Jan. 1995), vol. 103, no. 1, pp. 75-94; John Dederer, "In Search of the Unknown Soldier: A Critique of 'The Mystery in the Coffin,'" *VMHB* (Jan. 1995), vol. 103, no. 1, pp. 95-112; Alan T. Nolan, "Grave Thoughts," *VMHB* (Jan. 1995), vol. 103, no. 1, pp. 113-116; Gary W. Gallagher, "Robert E. Lee at Cumberland Island and on the Analyst's Couch," *VMHB* (Jan. 1995), vol. 103, no. 1, pp. 117-123. One early article published by the Georgia Historical Society asserts that Lee visited the gravesite while stationed at Cockspur Island in 1829 or 1830 without attribution and also that the date of this wartime visit was Jan. 17, again without source, however he was in Coosawhatchie on the 17th. B. N. Nightingale, "Dungeness," *Georgia Historical Quarterly* (Dec. 1938), vol. 22, no. 4, 381. See also McCaslin, *Lee in the Shadow of Washington*, 93 n53 for additional debate.

3 Basinger, *Savannah Volunteer Guards*, 94.

January 1, Wednesday (Savannah): 3,000 more Union troops land at Port Royal, heightening Lee's concerns about their ability to land and concentrate wherever they chose by water. Thornton Washington is promoted to major.[4]

January 2, Thursday (Savannah/Coosawhatchie): Lee returns to Coosawhatchie in the morning. He writes to Governor Pickens acknowledging the authority granted him to use slaves on the fortifications around Charleston, and reaffirming the need for more troops. He inquires of Gen. Trapier the current status of a battery being built on the south end of Cumberland Island across from Fort Clinch.[5]

January 3, Friday (Coosawhatchie): Lee writes to Governor Pickens regarding troop strength in South Carolina and hopes some discontent among some of the officers in South Carolina units will soon be settled. He instructs Maj. Gen. Henry Jackson to keep his Georgia division in readiness for Lee's or Lawton's call for them.[6]

January 4, Saturday (Coosawhatchie): Lee writes to son Custis concerning conditions of George Washington Parke Custis's will, and particularly the emancipation of the slaves and the payment of legacies to Lee's daughters. Lee's horse "Richmond," which is currently with Custis, is not well and Lee sends advice for the care of the animal.[7]

January 6, Monday (Coosawhatchie): Lee orders the court martial of Col. John Dunovant.[8]

January 7, Tuesday (Savannah): Lee and Gen. Lawton inspect progress at Fort Pulaski. Governor Pickens writes to President Davis about the friction that exists between Lee and Roswell Ripley: "the two are in contrast," he notes, and "the feeling of General Ripley toward General Lee may do injury to the public service."[9]

January 8, Wednesday (Savannah): Lee writes to Gen. Cooper: he may have been misunderstood or misrepresented by the newspapers, and thus the War Department, as to his strength and ability to keep the enemy away from the Charleston & Savannah Railroad: "Our works are not yet finished. Their progress is slow." He reaffirms his desire to draw the enemy inland out of range of their gunboats, but worries their superior numbers will enable them to move inland and sever the line and thus capture either city at will unless reinforcements are sent.[10]

January 10, Friday (Savannah): Lee orders 20 students from the College of Charleston discharged from military service.[11]

---

4 Freeman, *Lee*, vol. 1, 622; Krick, *Staff Officers in Gray*, 297.

5 Savannah *Daily Morning News*, Jan. 3, 1862; OR 6, 364-5.

6 REL to Francis Pickens, Jan. 3, 1862, REL papers, MOC; OR 6, 365-6. This is the same Henry Jackson who served under Lee in western VA; he resigned his Confederate commission in early December and accepted a commission as a major general in Georgia's state forces. Warner, *Generals in Gray*, 150.

7 Dowdey, *Wartime Papers*, 99-101.

8 SO 6, Jan 6, 1862, REL papers, MOC. It is possible that Lee himself was in Savannah as the orders were signed by Thornton who was left to run HQ at Coosawhatchie. The reason for Dunovant's court martial was not specified; he was later cashiered for drunkenness in June 1862. Warner, *Generals in Gray*, 78.

9 At least one writer placed Lee's inspection of Fort Pulaski on the 6th; while not impossible, the 7th seems more likely. Smith, *CW Savannah*, 62; Charleston *Mercury*, Jan. 8, 1862; OR 6, 366. A quick summary of Pickens's letter is that Lee was everything an officer and gentleman was expected to be—and then there was Ripley. For a contrary view of Ripley and a detailed explanation about why the governor's letters (and future historians) exaggerated the differences between the two men, see Chet Bennett, *Resolute Rebel: General Roswell S. Ripley, Charleston's Gallant Defender* (University of South Carolina Press, 2017). This study is especially useful for Ripley's prewar and postwar activities, and his actions around Charleston.

10 OR 6, 367.

11 SO 9, Jan. 10, 1862, REL papers, MOC.

January 11, Saturday (Fernandina): Lee observes the Union fleet off Amelia Island and inspects the island's defenses.[12]

January 13, Monday (Fernandina): Lee reviews the troops stationed at Amelia Island.[13]

January 14, Tuesday (Savannah?): Capt. Robert W. Memminger is assigned to Lee's staff.[14]

January 15, Wednesday (Savannah): Lee writes to Confederate ordnance chief Josiah Gorgas requesting several additional heavy guns in addition to those already sent; Lee also requests Gorgas to inform him what is being sent to his department because he is currently unaware of what ordnance-related supplies are being sent directly to his subordinates. He again urges Trapier to construct a battery on the south end of Cumberland Island.[15]

January 16, Thursday (Savannah/ Coosawhatchie): Lee returns to his Coosawhatchie headquarters from an inspection tour through Georgia and Florida. He receives a letter from Mary.[16]

January 17, Friday (Coosawhatchie): Lee meets with Brig. Gen. Nathan Evans who fears an assault against him is impending. He writes to Ripley regarding Evans's concerns and also clarifies for Ripley that Lee's approval for Ripley's Edisto operation was conditional and that the field commander must judge. Lee advises Trapier that ammunition will be sent to Florida by steamer but that guns must be posted to cover the landings, and informs Benjamin that Trapier has been notified to expect the landing of blockade runners. He tells Charleston city commissioner Charles M. Furman that he will comply with the request to provide advance warning if possible when enemy forces invade vulnerable areas to allow for removal of property from their path. Lee tells his cousin Shirley T. Carter in Charleston, "I shall endeavor to defend it [Charleston] to the last extremity and trust [the enemy] may never put foot within it."[17]

January 18, Saturday (Coosawhatchie): Lee writes to his wife Mary about family news and some friends he had visited while in Savannah, and also offers details of his recent visit to his father's gravesite on Cumberland Island.[18]

January 19, Sunday (Coosawhatchie): Lee's 55th birthday. He writes to Custis that he fears the war means personal economic ruin for him with the loss of Arlington. All his bonds are for Northern railroads and interests, he explains, and he has to use what remains to settle G. W. P. Custis's estate. Lee also inquires about one of Custis's friends who is engaged to the daughter of one of Lee's friends, inquiring as to the young man's character. Lee updates his son on enemy movements along the south Atlantic coast and observes, "No civilized

---

12 Schmidt, *CW in Florida*, vol. 1, pt. 1, 61.

13 Arch Frederic Blakey, Ann Smith Lainhart, and Winston Bryant Stephens, Jr., eds., *Rose Cottage Chronicles: Civil War Letters of the Bryant-Stephens Families of North Florida* (Gainesville, FL, 1998), 93. Lee complimented the 4th FL as being the best-drilled regiment. Ibid.

14 R. W. Memminger CSR. Memminger was the son of Christopher Memminger, the principal author of the provisional Confederate Constitution (1861) and the first Confederate secretary of the treasury. The younger Memminger remained behind in SC when Lee departed in March and would serve on Gen. John Pemberton's staff. Ibid.

15 OR 6, 367-8. In both letters written on this date Lee mentioned a "recent" trip to Fernandina—that is undoubtedly where he was sometime during the span January 10-14. Exactly when, however, cannot be determined.

16 Freeman, *Lee*, vol. 1, 623; Dowdey, *Wartime Papers*, 103. Few details are known about this trip. He went to Fernandina and visited his father's grave at Dungeness; the date that he left HQ as well as the date he visited Cumberland Island are not known. The lack of details about the visit to his father's grave have caused historians and Lee biographers much consternation over the years.

17 OR 6, 369-70; OR 53, 214-5; REL to S. T. Carter, Jan. 17, 1862, Heritage Auctions, May 11, 2017, auction, lot # 47050.

18 Dowdey, *Wartime Papers*, 103-4.

nation . . . has ever carried on war as the United States government has against us."[19]

January 22, Tuesday (Charleston): Lee warns Ripley of rumors that spies are planning to burn bridges along the Charleston & Savannah Railroad, and to take necessary measures to guard against this.[20]

January 23, Wednesday (Charleston): Lee fears an attack on Charleston harbor, however a storm obscures his view of the Federal fleet.[21]

January 25, Friday (Charleston/Sullivan's Island): Lee observes enemy efforts from Sullivan's Island, including preparations for the sinking of a second stone fleet in another channel of the harbor.[22]

January 26, Saturday (Charleston/Sullivan's Island): Lee returns to Sullivan's Island to observe the sinking of the stone fleet.[23]

January 27, Sunday (Charleston/Coosawhatchie): Lee returns to Coosawhatchie.[24]

January 28, Tuesday (Coosawhatchie/Savannah): Lee informs Brig. Gen. Joseph Anderson at Cape Fear, North Carolina, that he will do what he can to provide aid to Anderson should the Federals assault him, but that an attack appears imminent against Savannah so Lee can do nothing at present. Lee requests Commodore Josiah Tattnall to have his "Mosquito Fleet" escort transports carrying six months' supply of provisions down the Savannah River to Fort Pulaski.

Lee writes to Mary of war news at both Charleston and Savannah: "There are so many points of attack, and so little means to meet them on water, that there is but little rest." Among other family news, he is worried that Rob will not be able to continue at the University of Virginia because of interruptions to the curriculum. In the evening Lee goes to Savannah.[25]

January 29, Wednesday (Savannah): Lee oversees placement of river obstructions around Savannah. He informs Adjutant General Cooper that the Navy is unable to prevent enemy gunboats from removing river obstructions, but that he has had more placed today in hopes of slowing their approach.[26]

January 30, Thursday (Savannah): Lee orders that one 4-horse wagon be issued to each cavalry company. The Savannah city council agrees to provide Lee with several hundred black laborers for construction of fortifications at Causton's Bluff and elsewhere around the city.[27]

---

19 Ibid., 104-6. Lee mentioned going to his father's grave in this letter as well, but not to the level of detail he did in his earlier letter to Mary. Lee's accepted birthday is Jan. 19, 1807, but some doubt surrounds that date stemming from the family Bible and his West Point records. See Pryor, *Reading the Man*, 55-6, 498 n2.

20 *OR* 6, 370-1. It is not known when Lee went to Charleston.

21 Freeman, *Lee*, vol. 1, 623.

22 Ibid.

23 Ibid. The Union Navy sank 12 old merchant ships in the Maffitt channel.

24 Dowdey, *Wartime Papers*, 107.

25 *OR* 9, 423-4; Charles C. Jones, Jr., *The Life and Services of Commodore Josiah Tattnall* (Savannah, GA, 1878), 144; Dowdey, *Wartime Papers*, 107-8; Freeman, *Lee*, vol. 1, 623. Washington was again left behind at Coosawhatchie. Washington to REL, Jan. 30 & Feb. 1, 1862, REL papers, MOC.

26 Richmond *Daily Dispatch*, Feb. 1, 1862; *OR* 6, 85. The obstructions placed on this date were at Wilmington Narrows, west of the city.

27 REL to Washington, Jan. 30, 1862, REL papers, MOC; Rogers W. Young, "Two Years at Fort Bartow, 1862-1864," *Georgia Historical Quarterly* (Sept. 1939), vol. 23, no. 3, 254. The work at Causton's Bluff became Fort Bartow. When Lee was away from Coosawhatchie, Thornton Washington was usually left to tend to headquarters; he telegraphed Lee from there on this date regarding issuing quartermaster wagons to cavalry companies. T. A. Washington to REL, Jan. 30, 1862, REL papers, MOC.

February 1862

The build-up of troops around Savannah suggested an attack against the city at any time. Accordingly, Gen. Lee spent the entire month there urging along completion of its defenses and trying to alert the politicians to the predicament they were facing. With Union forces moving against Gen. Albert Sidney Johnston's forces in Tennessee and against the Outer Banks of North Carolina, however, there were no reinforcements available for Lee. His situation was made worse by Governor Joe Brown of Georgia, who refused to allow state troops, i.e., those who had not been taken into Confederate service, to cross the state's borders into South Carolina or Florida. Try as he might, Lee was unable to make Brown understand that Florida was the backdoor into Georgia, and that a move against Savannah would follow on the heels of any move against Charleston.[1]

Although he privately harbored fears for the safety of Savannah, Lee did everything in his power to make the city ready to meet an attack. "General Lee and Brigadier General Lawton are in motion day and night," observed a Georgia soldier, "strengthening our defenses and making arrangements for the rapid concentration of troops at any given point."[2]

When he was not inspecting the defenses or responding to threatened enemy landings, Lee enjoyed the hospitality of his friends in the city. He often saw the Mackay and the Stiles families and dined with them and other members of the city's social elite on several occasions.[3]

The general finally completed his drawn-out acquisition of the horse "Greenbrier." Following his trial period in December and January, Lee determined he must have the animal. Capt. Broun offered to give the horse to Lee as a gift, but Lee insisted on purchasing it for the sum of $200. Lee renamed him "Traveller," and together they would remain for the rest of Lee's life.[4]

A popular story told around Savannah was that Lee was nearly killed during a visit to Fort Bartow during February, where he had gone to observe the testing of a new Columbiad from the Tredegar Iron Works. The gun exploded upon firing, and a large jagged iron chunk narrowly missed him. There is some question as to whether or not this occurred in the manner described, but if it did indeed happen, it was almost certainly closer to the end of the month.[5]

---

1 Brown was heavily anti-Davis administration in nearly every conceivable way. "Governor Joseph Brown had little use for CSA President Jefferson Davis or the unceasing demands of the would-be new country he led," wrote one historian. "Early in the war Brown showed that he would resist in equal measure the incursion of Yankees into Georgia and the demands of Richmond . . . for men and arms." Jacqueline E. Jones, *Saving Savannah: The City and the Civil War* (New York, 2008), 140.

2 Savannah *Daily Morning News*, Feb. 12, 1862.

3 Freeman, *Lee*, vol. 1, 623-4.

4 Pendleton, *Traveller*, 15-6. Broun paid $175 for the animal in western Virginia; Lee paid $25 more than that to cover inflation. Ibid.

5 Michael L. Jordan, *Hidden History of Civil War Savannah* (Charleston, SC, 2017), 46-7. A large chunk of a Columbiad was removed from the river near Fort Bartow in 2000 and is currently on exhibit at Fort Jackson. Ibid. That a gun exploded at Fort Bartow during the war is not in question; the debatable part is Lee's involvement. He made no mention of this episode officially or otherwise, and neither C.S. ordnance chief Josiah Gorgas, Long, or Taylor mentioned it. Long, as departmental ordnance chief, would have been aware and presumably present. Joseph Anderson at Tredegar does not mention one of his guns exploding with Lee in proximity, and the Savannah newspapers are silent about it as well. Two postwar accounts mention a cannon exploding at Causton's Bluff/Fort Bartow, but the details are quite different and only one has Lee present. According to a postwar account by the son of Gen. William W. Mackall, Lee took Francis Sorrel

Sometime toward the end of the month Lee met with Commodore Josiah Tattnall, who was about to move north and assume command of the CSS *Virginia* at Norfolk. The officers discussed the possibility of relieving Fort Pulaski by an attack upon the Federal works on Oakley Island. By occupying the island, which was situated in the Savannah River between the city and the fort, the Federals had effectively isolated the Pulaski from the rest of Lee's forces. Neither Lee nor Tattnall favored such an attack, and that seemed to be the end of it. Tattnall, however, had heard rumors of derogatory remarks about the navy attributed to Lee, which apparently led the flag officer to make the impulsive decision to attempt just such an assault. Lee learned what Tattnall was planning only hours before the scheduled attack and met with the commodore to express his concerns about what the failure of such an assault would mean for the security of Savannah. Tattnall agreed to put the decision to a council of war. His officers submitted their opinion to him on February 28: they believed the attack would likely fail, and even if it was successful, "would be attended with great loss of life and vessels . . . and a fearfully depressing morale effect produced" that would achieve little substantial gain.[6] Their unanimous opposition settled it and the attack never occurred.

The old rumors of Lee being named secretary of war reared up again, this time much stronger than before. Although a gifted politician, Judah Benjamin had few of the skills required to run the War Department. By the end of February it was commonly assumed that Benjamin would be replaced by Gen. Lee.[7]

* * *

(with whom he was staying at the time) and Sorrel's grandson, the younger Mackall, to witness the test firing of a new cannon at Causton's Bluff. According to Mackall, the cannon failed to fire on the first try and on the second attempt burst, injuring several. Mackall, however, places this incident "after the capture of Fort Pulaski," but Lee had been in Richmond more than a month before Pulaski was captured; there was also no such experimental cannon at Savannah at the time. William W. Mackall, *A Son's Recollections of his Father* (New York, 1930), 222-3. Capt. William S. Basinger, commander of the Savannah Volunteer Guards, recorded the explosion of a faulty gun at Causton's Bluff, killing and wounding several, but did not put a date to it, nor did he have Lee involved in any way. Basinger, *Savannah Volunteer Guards*, 92-3. See "Cannon that Exploded near Lee is Pulled from Wilmington River," Athens *Banner-Herald*, Jan. 13, 2000; and "Historic Cannon Recovered off Causton Bluff", Savannah *Morning News*, Jan. 12, 2000. Derek Smith mentions the incident in his work on Savannah during the war, but does not give a source. Smith, *CW Savannah*, 89. In the absence of better evidence, it seems reasonable to conclude that a cannon that exploded at Causton's Bluff somehow later gained an association with Lee. This story may well be a co-mingling of the Savannah gun incident and Lee's well-documented close encounter with a Parrott Rifle that burst at Fredericksburg in December 1862.

6 Jones, *Life and Services of Josiah Tattnall*, 145-7.

7 Charleston *Mercury*, Feb. 27, 1862; Charleston *Mercury*, Feb. 28, 1862.

February 1, Saturday (Savannah): Lee remains in Savannah in preparation for defending against Union attack.[8]

February 2, Sunday (Savannah): Lee instructs John Pemberton not to antagonize Thomas Drayton by putting the Charleston & Savannah Railroad under military control, posting guards on passenger trains, or hindering mail or passenger service. He also authorizes Pemberton to discharge any company whose term of enlistment has expired and puts Gen. S. R. Gist in charge of collecting their arms.[9]

February 3, Monday (Savannah): Lee formally moves department headquarters to Savannah.[10]

February 4, Tuesday (Savannah): Lee communicates with Drayton and Pemberton regarding an enemy raiding party ascending the Savannah River and threatening Drayton's position near Hardeeville. Lee instructs Drayton to withdraw far enough inland as to be out of range of Union gunboats and to delay the advance of ground forces long enough for assistance to arrive from Pemberton. Lee also requests details from Pemberton as to the number of cannon in his command, and to have two guns sent from Charleston to Pocataligo. Taylor informs Washington at Coosawhatchie that they will be detained in Savannah longer than anticipated; "The General's presence is necessary to infuse the proper energy in this apathetic community."[11]

February 5, Wednesday (Savannah): Lee requests more heavy artillery from Gorgas, and brings to the attention of the secretary of war price gouging by some merchants in Savannah.[12]

February 6, Thursday (Savannah): Lee alerts Sec. Benjamin to the pending expiration of one-year enlistments among the Georgia units. He also requests a general officer be assigned him for command in Georgia, specifically requesting Henry Heth or Carter Stevenson.[13]

February 8, Saturday (Savannah): Lee writes to Mary, expressing his fear that the Federals will use the creeks and tidal marshes to bypass Fort Pulaski; the works protecting Savannah above Pulaski are not finished and most lack guns, causing him to privately fear for the safety of the city. "I have more here than I can do, and more, I fear, than I can well accomplish." He mentions seeing Gen. Jeremy Gilmer's wife recently amid reports that Gilmer was captured in Tennessee: "The news from Kentucky and Tennessee is not favorable, but we must make

---

8 Freeman, *Lee*, vol. 1, 623-4. Washington was still at Coosawhatchie as he telegraphed Lee on this date regarding a supplier contract. T. A. Washington to REL, Feb. 1, 1862, REL papers, MOC.

9 Stone, *Vital Rails*, 85; WHT to Pemberton, Feb. 2, 1862, REL papers, MOC. Lee recognized the need to remain on good terms with the railroad, as it was absolutely essential to defending the region; he feared that Pemberton was not aware of or capable of effectively handling this sensitive relationship. Drayton presented an unintentional obstacle since he was both president of the railroad and, like Pemberton, one of Lee's district commanders; Pemberton however was senior to and thus outranked Drayton. The Drayton issue was resolved within days of Lee's admonishment to Pemberton when Drayton was replaced as C&S president by William McGrath on Feb. 12. Stone, *Vital Rails*, 87.

10 Freeman, *Lee*, vol. 1, 623-4. Although Freeman made this conclusion, there is some doubt as to its veracity. Washington continued to remain at Coosawhatchie, and Taylor informed him on the 4th "We remain here contrary to my expectations. There is much to be done & it [follows?—illegible] that the General's presence is necessary to infuse the proper energy into this apathetic community. The General says please make Meredith wash his clothes and place them in his room." WHT to T. A. Washington, Feb. 4, 1862, REL papers, MOC. This shows that Lee obviously intended to return to Coosawhatchie. Meredith was left at Coosawhatchie, but Perry was present with Lee in Savannah. Dowdey, *Wartime Papers*, 112. The location of his headquarters in Savannah is not known, but may have been the Sorrel home as he was known to stay there at times.

11 OR 6, 374-5; REL to Pemberton, Feb. 4, 1862, REL papers, MOC; REL to F. L. Childes, Feb. 4, 1862, REL papers, MOC; WHT to T. A. Washington, Feb. 4, 1862, REL papers, MOC.

12 OR 6, 375-6.

13 OR 6, 376.

up our minds to meet with reverses and to overcome them. . . . The contest must be long and severe, and the whole country has to go through much suffering."[14]

February 10, Monday (Savannah): Lee informs Benjamin of his orders to abandon Jekyl Island and Saint Simon's Island, east of Brunswick, as both of these points are vulnerable to capture by the Union Navy. He explains to both Benjamin and Georgia Governor Joseph Brown that since Brunswick, which these two points defend, has already been evacuated there is no major loss by withdrawing into the interior to a more defensible point.[15]

February 12, Wednesday (Savannah): Lee writes to Benjamin regarding his supply of gunpowder, and instructs that all commanders report any machinists and gunsmiths in their commands.[16]

February 14, Friday (Savannah): Lee advises Ripley that the enemy is landing on Edisto Island and thus to send reinforcements to Evans. He informs Trapier of the abandonment of Jekyl Island to strengthen Savannah, but that two guns have been sent him for use on the St. John's River. He writes as well to Maj. George Rains to find best locations for obstructions in the Savannah River below Augusta.[17]

February 15, Saturday (Savannah): Lee thanks Governor Brown and Augusta Mayor Robert May for their suggestion to have obstructions placed in the Savannah River to guard the approaches to Augusta and informs them that he is already having it done. Lee asks Governor Brown for any available artillery to protect these and other obstructions to prevent their removal, and writes to his former ordnance officer, Lt. Col. William Gill (now in command at the Augusta Arsenal) regarding the river obstructions. Lee tells Ripley that the enemy is swarming about the Savannah area but exhibits no indications of attacking—are there signs of a pending attack against Charleston? Lee explains to Evans that there are not sufficient troops to guard the entire coast line, so he must buy time for reinforcements to arrive from elsewhere. He also orders a man detailed from Pemberton's command to serve as a clerk at headquarters.[18]

February 16, Sunday (Savannah): Lee writes to Rooney with fatherly advice and growing concern over the manumission of the Custis slaves: "If the war continues I do not see how it can be accomplished, but they can be hired out and the funds raised applied to their establishment hereafter. If however you cannot otherwise carry on your farm they might continue as they are until circumstances permit me to emancipate them."[19]

February 17, Monday (Savannah): Lee provides Col. Charles Olmstead, commanding at Fort Pulaski, specific instructions on how to improve the fort defensively. Washington notifies Lee that Pemberton's commission as major general has arrived at headquarters.[20]

February 18, Tuesday (Savannah): Lee writes to Adjutant General Cooper and Governor Brown to

---

14 Dowdey, *Wartime Papers*, 111-2.

15 OR 6, 379-80.

16 REL to Benjamin, Feb. 12, 1862, REL papers, MOC; SO, Feb. 12, 1862, REL papers, MOC.

17 OR 6, 380-5.

18 OR 6, 384-6; T. A. Washington to Pemberton, Feb. 15, 1862, REL papers, MOC.

19 REL to Rooney, Feb. 16, 1862, G. B. Lee papers, VHS. The slaves were to be freed in accordance with Lee's father-in-law's will.

20 OR 6, 389; T. A. Washington to REL, Feb. 17, 1862, REL papers, MOC. The instructions to Olmstead are so detailed as to suggest a very recent personal inspection of the fort by Lee. For some unspecified reason, Pemberton wished to meet with Lee in Savannah, but Lee informed him there was "nothing special calling you here at this time." WHT to Pemberton, Feb. 17, 1862, REL papers, MOC.

inform them that the troops and guns from Jekyl Island and Saint Simon's Island have been withdrawn to better protect Savannah and the C&S railroad. As a result Brunswick is left undefended; however its civilian population already evacuated thus leaving the town empty. Lee would like approval to destroy the town to deny the enemy its use as a base. Lee tells Ripley to construct casemates around his water batteries using railroad iron if possible.[21]

February 19, Wednesday (Savannah): Lee instructs Gens. Ripley and Trapier to make preparations to abandon outlying positions and withdraw to more contracted positions inland. He advises Florida Governor John Milton that he has no troops to send to Trapier or elsewhere in Florida: "Unless troops can be organized in Florida for its defense, I know not whose they can obtain." Lee sends a brief note of congratulations to Pemberton on his promotion to major general. In a Cabinet meeting today attended by Gen. Joe Johnston, President Davis mentions recalling Lee to Richmond, but given the threat to Savannah "it was left undecided."[22]

February 20, Thursday (Savannah): Lee writes again to Evans that if the enemy does land on Edisto as Evans fears they will, he should have forces positioned to provide early warning, and that he should make sure everything of value has been removed from his front. Should the Yankees appear Evans is to notify Pemberton and Ripley immediately so that they may come to his relief. Lee informs Pemberton of Evans's alarm and instructs him to be in readiness to aid Evans.[23]

February 21, Friday (Savannah): Lee alerts each of his district commanders in South Carolina that a Union force departed Warsaw Island yesterday by water and was headed north.[24]

February 22, Saturday (Savannah): Lee goes to St. John's Episcopal Church, to observe a day of fasting and prayer, where Bishop Stephen Elliott "gave a most beautiful prayer for the President." Lee writes to Governor Brown advising that Charleston & Savannah railroad is "precarious" and that it is only a matter of time before the Federals launch an attack to seize it. In order to properly defend Charleston, Augusta, and Savannah, Lee urges that the Augusta & Savannah be connected at Augusta to either the Georgia Railroad or the South Carolina Railroad. Lee notes that the A&S is willing to pay if it can choose the route, or it will follow a route selected by the city of Augusta provided the city pays. Given the military necessity of this connection, Lee requests the Governor to use his influence to make it happen.[25]

February 23, Sunday (Savannah): Lee visits Fort Jackson just east of Savannah, and orders Maj. George Rains to proceed with sinking obstructions in the river below Augusta. He writes to Mary with latest news of mutual friends in Savannah and war news: "Disasters seem to be thickening around us." He writes as well to Custis with latest military developments and regret at hearing about the poor condition of his horse "Richmond."[26]

---

21 OR 6, 390-1. Governor Brown replied to Lee's request on the 21st: "If my own house were in Brunswick I would certainly set fire to it . . . rather than see it used by them [Federals] as a shelter." OR 6, 396.

22 OR 6, 393-4; WHT to Pemberton, Feb. 19, 1862, REL papers, MOC; Thomas Bragg diary, Feb. 19, 1862, UNC. Attorney General Thomas Bragg noted, "Gen. Lee has said if they do not attack before the middle of next week . . . he could repulse them." Bragg diary, Feb. 19, 1862, UNC. Thomas Bragg was the brother of Gen. Braxton Bragg.

23 OR 6, 394-5.

24 REL to Pemberton, Feb. 21, 1861, REL papers, MOC; REL to Ripley, Feb. 21, 1861, REL papers, MOC; REL to N. G. Evans, Feb. 21, 1861, REL papers, MOC; REL to T. F. Drayton, Feb. 21, 1861, REL papers, MOC; REL to A. M. Manigault, Feb. 21, 1861, REL papers, MOC.

25 Dowdey, *Wartime Papers*, 118-9; OR 6, 397.

26 Freeman, *Lee*, vol. 1, 627; OR 6, 397-8; Dowdey, *Wartime Papers*, 118-9; REL to Custis, Feb. 23, 1862, REL papers, MOC. Fort Jackson was a second system fort on the Savannah River; it is currently a state park.

February 24, Monday (Savannah): Benjamin orders Lee to withdraw all troops from coastal Florida and send them to Gen. A. S. Johnston's army. Accordingly Lee orders Trapier to withdraw from Cumberland and Amelia islands, then explains this move to Florida Governor Milton, and informs him that Florida is responsible for providing its own troops for defense as Governor Brown refuses to allow Georgia state troops to serve outside of Georgia. Lee requests arms and ammunition for Trapier's command in hopes that more Florida troops are forthcoming.[27]

February 25, Tuesday (Savannah): Davis's cabinet meets and discusses the military situation in Virginia and elsewhere and once again talks about the possibility of Lee's recall to Virginia. Attorney General Thomas Bragg notes, "If Gen. Lee could be spared from South Carolina he would be called here. I wish it were possible and that he could be made Commander in Chief."[28]

February 26, Wednesday (Savannah): Lee writes to youngest daughter Mildred wishing her a happy 16th birthday.[29]

February 27, Thursday (Savannah): President Davis signs into law a measure authorizing an army general to be appointed secretary of war.[30]

February 28, Friday (Savannah): Lee informs Pemberton that the steamer *John A. Moore* will depart from Coosawhatchie on March 4 and run the blockade through to Charleston; Pemberton is to have his troops on alert and to render all assistance possible. Lee writes to William J. Magrath, new president of the Charleston & Savannah, regarding the use of his railroad by the military.[31]

---

27 *OR* 6, 398-400.

28 Bragg diary, Feb. 25, 1862, UNC.

29 Jones, *Personal Reminiscences of REL*, 388-9.

30 Freeman, *Lee*, vol. 2, 4. Freeman concluded that this measure was done specifically with Lee in mind. Ibid. Attorney General Bragg recorded, "A bill has passed Congress ... allowing any General Officer to be appointed Secretary of War, not losing his rank, but only his pay as a General while acting as Secretary of War, this looks to Gen. Lee, but he can't be spared from the field just now. His services here would be great, as a Commander in Chief, for which there is also a bill before Congress." Bragg diary, Feb 27, 1862, UNC. Joe Johnston prematurely mentioned in a letter to one of his subordinates today that Lee had been made Secretary of War. *OR* 5, 1082-3.

31 REL to Pemberton, Feb. 28, 1862, REL papers, MOC; REL to W. J. Magrath, Feb. 28, 1862, REL papers, W&L. Magrath was elected president of the railroad on Feb. 12 to replace Thomas Drayton, whose military duties occupied his time and attention. Stone, *Vital Rails*, 87.

March 1862

Robert E. Lee did not get to see first-hand the results of his efforts along the south Atlantic seaboard. Just five weeks before Gen. Quincy Gillmore's Federals launched their long-anticipated attack on Savannah, Lee was called back to Richmond. His nephew Fitzhugh Lee wrote about his uncle's time in command of the Department of South Carolina, Georgia, and Florida: "His four months' labor in this department brought prominently into view his skill. Exposed points were no longer in danger. Well-conceived defensive works rose rapidly. Public confidence in that department was permanently restored, and with it came to Lee a new accession of popularity and esteem."[1] Lee's aide Armistead Long observed that the defensive line Lee established "offered an impenetrable barrier to the combined federal forces operating on the coast, until they were carried by General Sherman . . . near the close of the war."[2]

Lee left Savannah with Walter Taylor and both Perry and Meredith; Thornton Washington and Armistead Long soon rejoined their chief in the Confederate capital. For weeks many believed Lee was to be elevated into the cabinet as the next secretary of war, but Jefferson Davis had another role in mind for the general, which was not made known to Lee until he arrived in Richmond. "I have been called here very unexpectedly to me and have . . . been placed on duty at this place under the direction of the President," he wrote to his cousin Cassius. "I am willing to do anything I can do to help the noble cause we are engaged in, and to take any position; but the lower and more humble the position the more agreeable to me and the better qualified I should feel to fill it. I fear I shall be able to do little in the position assigned me and cannot hope to satisfy the feverish and excited expectation of our good people."[3]

Technically, Lee's new role was as commander of the Confederate armies, but in reality he was military advisor to the president. His role and duties were so poorly defined that to the public he was nearly invisible. A Charleston *Mercury* editorial questioned what, exactly, Lee's new role was in an editorial titled "What is Gen. Lee?"[4] After the war Taylor conceded, "Very little was known and very little has since been made public of the character of the service then rendered by General Lee."[5] Douglas Freeman summed up this portion of Lee's career thusly: "In his whole career there was not a period of more thankless service, but there were few, if any, during which he contributed more to sustain the Confederate cause."[6]

When he arrived in Richmond Lee once more took up residence, albeit briefly, at the Spotswood Hotel, before moving to a rented townhouse on Franklin Street. His office was at Mechanics Hall.[7]

---

1 Fitz Lee, *General Lee*, 128.

2 Armistead Long, "Seacoast Defenses of South Carolina and Georgia," *SHSP*, vol. 1, 107.

3 REL to Cassius Lee, March 14, 1862, REL papers, W&L.

4 Charleston *Mercury*, March 19, 1862.

5 Taylor, *General Lee*, 43.

6 Freeman, *Lee*, vol. 2, 7.

7 Ibid., 13. Freeman and others since wrote that Lee remained at the Spotswood Hotel until his assumption of command of the ANV, at which time he moved to the Dabbs House named High Meadows. Lee's own correspondence, however,

He attended prayer breakfast nearly every morning at 7:00 a.m.[8] His official family grew with the addition of Charles Marshall, who would remain with Lee for the rest of the war.

Lee was reunited with his family soon after arriving back in Richmond. He journeyed to White House and spent a day with Mary. Custis's duties kept him in Richmond; Annie and Agnes were in Richmond with friends by mid-March, and Rob came to the city briefly before enlisting in the Confederate Army.[9]

Lee likely missed his old friends and the social scene in Savannah, but soon after he arrived in the Confederate capital one of his Georgia friends, Eleanor Lytle "Nellie" Kinzie Gordon, visited him. Nellie wanted to see her husband William, an officer in one of Jeb Stuart's cavalry regiments, and hoped Lee could assist her. Lee had breakfast with Nellie at the residence of the Haxalls, with whom she was staying, and provided an escort for her to Gordonsville, which was close to where her husband's regiment was stationed.[10]

Several new crises greeted Lee almost immediately upon assumption of his new duties. An amphibious force under Ambrose Burnside defeated a small Confederate command near New Bern, North Carolina, and captured the strategic port town. From there, Burnside threatened not only the rest of coastal North Carolina but the interior as well, and was well-poised for a strike against the rail hub of Goldsboro. Just days later a large Federal force appeared at Fort Monroe, threatening both Norfolk and the Virginia Peninsula. Lee had to scramble to find troops to simultaneously combat these threatened areas.

* * *

reveals that his time at the Spotswood was brief and he and Custis resided in a townhouse at 707 E Franklin St., which they were renting from John Stewart of Brook Hill. It is possible, although there is no evidence to support it, that Lee never resided at the Spotswood and went straight to the Stewart house upon his return from Charleston. Lee appears to be at the Stewart house by March 14. See May 13 entry for additional discussion about the Stewart house.

8 Freeman, *Lee*, vol. 2, 251.

9 Dowdey, *Wartime Papers*, 128.

10 Gladys D. Shultz and Daisy G. Lawrence, *Lady from Savannah: The Life of Juliette Low* (New York, 1988), 78-9; Mary D. Robertson, ed., "The Journal of Nellie Kinzie Gordon, Savannah, 1862," *Georgia Historical Quarterly*, (Fall 1986), vol. 70, no. 3, 488-9. Eleanor Gordon was the mother of Juliette Gordon Low, founder of the Girl Scouts; William Gordon served in the Georgia Hussars, part of the Jeff Davis Legion, and was related to the Stiles family. Alexander M. Duncan, *Roll of Officers and Members of the Georgia Hussars* (Savannah, GA, 1906), 325.

March 1, Saturday (Savannah): Lee informs Gen. James Trapier that his troops are needed as soon as possible by Gen. A. S. Johnston in Tennessee/northern Mississippi to offset the capture of the garrison at Fort Donelson. Trapier is to transfer to Johnston everyone except those on the Apalachicola River. Lee informs Sec. Benjamin that he is executing the War Department's orders to strip Florida of troops and send them to Johnston.[11]

March 2, Sunday (Savannah): President Davis summons Lee to Richmond "with the least delay." Lee replies that he will leave Tuesday for the capital. Lee writes to Annie, despairing over the local population's apathy toward the war effort and the steady approach of the enemy toward the city. He mentions that Elizabeth Mackay Stiles has become his seamstress, and that he sees her family quite often. He also jokingly observes that since Mildred is still upset about having to leave her cat "Tom" behind at Arlington, "I shall have to get Gen. [Joe] Johnston to send in a flag of truce and make inquiries."[12]

March 3, Monday (Savannah/Coosawhatchie): Lee meets with Gens. Pemberton and Lawton in the latter's office to discuss defensive measures to be taken during his absence, and places Pemberton in temporary command of the department. He provides specific written instructions for Lawton regarding the completion of batteries and river obstructions, and leaves Maj. Long, Capt. Ives, and Capt. Tattnall of his staff behind to superintend this work. Lee also informs Pemberton and Lawton that he wants a special train in constant readiness on the C&S to ferry troops to any threatened point. In the evening Lee departs for Coosawhatchie with Capt. Taylor and Perry.[13]

March 4, Tuesday (Coosawhatchie/Charleston): Lee and Taylor go to Charleston, accompanied by Perry and Meredith. Gen. John C. Pemberton assumes command of the Department of South Carolina, Georgia, and East Florida.[14]

March 5, Wednesday (Charleston): Lee makes final preparations to go to Richmond.[15]

March 6, Thursday (Charleston/Florence/Wilmington/Weldon): Lee and Taylor, with the two slaves, leave Charleston for the long train ride to Richmond.[16]

March 7, Friday (Weldon/Petersburg/Richmond): Lee and his party arrive in Richmond. He has a lengthy meeting with President Davis and the

---

11 OR 6, 400, 403-4.

12 OR 6, 400; OR 53, 221; Dowdey, *Wartime Papers*, 121-3.

13 Freeman, *Lee*, vol. 1, 628; A. R. Lawton to father, March 8, 1862, Lawton papers, UNC; SO March 3, 1862; REL papers, MOC; OR 6, 401-2. The orders placing Pemberton in charge read that it was just during the "temporary absence of the commanding general," suggesting that he intended to return. Lawton, however, confided to his father, "my private opinion is that he will not return to this command." Lawton to father, March 8, 1862, Lawton papers, UNC. Upon his return to Coosawhatchie, Lee wrote to an unknown individual thanking him for a box of meats recently received. Lee to unknown, March 3, 1862, REL papers, W&L.

14 Freeman, *Lee*, vol. 1, 628; Charleston *Mercury*, March 5, 1862; OR 6, 402. Presumably Lee met with Pemberton at some point during the day.

15 Freeman, *Lee*, vol. 1, 628. Freeman puts Lee's departure today and his arrival in the Confederate capital on the 6th, and historians have since followed suit. A Savannah newspaper, however, suggests that his departure was on the 6th. Savannah *Daily Morning News*, March 6, 1862. The Richmond *Dispatch* puts his arrival in that city on the 7th. Richmond *Daily Dispatch*, March 8, 1862. A note from Lee to Joe Johnston from Richmond dated March 5 is in OR 5, 1090, but this document is clearly misdated because Lee was not in Richmond on the 5th and it concerns movements during the Peninsula Campaign. The actual date for this message is either May 3 or 5, and most likely the latter. It also appears with the date of May 3 in OR 11, pt. 3, 493.

16 Freeman, *Lee*, vol. 1, 628; Savannah *Daily Morning News*, March 6, 1862. Freeman is very likely off by one day for Lee's travel to Richmond; he certainly arrives there on the 7th, which makes it logical that he left Charleston on the 6th rather than the 5th. Where Lee spent the night while in transit is not known.

cabinet about conditions at Savannah and Charleston, then Fort Donelson and Norfolk.[17]

March 8, Saturday (Richmond): Mary writes to Elizabeth Mackay Stiles that she is pleased Gen. Lee is in Mrs. Stiles's care while in Savannah: "Tonight . . . a letter from Mr. Lee to Annie [March 3] informed me that you were in Savannah and had taken my husband and his wardrobe in charge. I could not delay a moment to express my satisfaction. I have heard nothing that has given me so much pleasure since our last success. I know now that he is in good hands and will be well taken care of. If I could only be with you all."[18]

March 9, Sunday (Richmond/White House): Lee is reunited with Mary after nearly a year apart, making a quick visit to White House.[19]

March 10, Monday (Richmond): Lee joins the president and the cabinet, discussing Joe Johnston and the Army of Northern Virginia. President Davis vetoes a bill to create a Commanding General of the Army—which had been passed with Lee in mind; this leads to the creation of the post of military advisor to the president.[20]

March 11, Tuesday (Richmond): Mary writes, "I heard from my husband today and he is expecting to be sent off to Norfolk. . . . He has sent for me to go up to Richmond for a little while and I shall go to be with him though I fear I shall see but little of him, for this is indeed an anxious time to us all."[21]

March 12, Wednesday (Richmond): Lee meets with President Davis to discuss the situation in southwest Virginia and Brig. Gen. Humphrey Marshall's potential advance into Kentucky.[22]

March 13, Thursday (Richmond): Lee is placed in command of all Confederate military operations. He informs Maj. Gen. John B. Magruder in command on the Peninsula, that the CSS *Virginia* has gone into dock for repairs. Lee inquires of Brig. Gen. Henry Heth at Lewisburg his effective strength and how much militia he can call out. He authorizes Gen.

---

17 Richmond *Daily Dispatch*, March 8, 1862; Freeman, *Lee*, vol. 2, 251; Bragg diary, March 7, 1862, UNC. Taylor's request for quarters has a beginning date of today, suggesting that they arrive in the city today rather than yesterday. WHT Commutation of Quarters, March 31, 1862, WHT CSR. Attorney General Bragg wrote, "The General was told he was wanted here [Richmond]. He seemed not to have expected it, but came expecting to return" to South Carolina. Bragg diary, March 7, 1862, UNC. Per Bragg's account, this cabinet meeting seems to have been especially critical of Benjamin Huger, whom many held responsible for the loss of Roanoke Island. Someone present—Bragg did not say who—called Huger an "imbecile" and should be replaced immediately, a sentiment with which Davis did not disagree but hesitated only because he did not have a replacement for Huger. Ibid.

18 Mrs. REL to Mrs. William Henry Stiles, March 8, 1862, Lee papers, SH. Mary obviously wrote this before she was aware of her husband's return to Richmond.

19 Mrs. REL to Mrs. W. H. Stiles, March 11, 1862 addendum to March 8 letter, Lee papers, SH. She wrote of their reunion, "He looks well in spite of his cares and I see by the papers that he is put in charge of the armies of the Confederacy. Now [that] they have got into trouble they send for him to help them out, and yet he never gets any credit for what he has done. I wish he could have remained longer with you. . . . He never complains or seems to desire anything more than to perform his duty but I may be excused for wishing him to reap the reward of his labors." Ibid. Lee wrote simply of this encounter, "found her better than expected." REL to Charles Carter Lee, March 14, 1862, REL papers, W&L. It is not known if he stayed the night or returned to Richmond.

20 Bragg diary, March 10, 1862, UNC; Freeman, *Lee*, vol. 2, 4-5. Bragg wrote that Lee "had not been informed of it [Johnston's withdrawal], I suppose, and to me it seemed he did not approve of the movement. He is trying to reorganize the Army. But what with conflicting laws of Congress and the Legislature of this State, all is confusion–I really do not see how it is to be done." Bragg diary, March 10, 1862, UNC. Of the Commanding General legislation, one Lee biographer concluded, "There was never a chance that Davis would do anything except veto this measure. It came too close to invading his realm of authority as commander in chief." Clifford Dowdey, *Lee* (Gettysburg, PA, 1991), 181.

21 Mrs. REL to Mrs. W. H. Stiles, March 11, 1862 addendum to March 8 letter, Lee papers, SH. There is no evidence that she went to Richmond as invited.

22 *OR* 10, pt. 2, 321-2. Marshall was a former Kentucky congressman; he served without distinction until his resignation in the summer of 1863, he later served in the Confederate Congress. Warner, *Generals in Gray*, 212-3.

Marshall to call out militia in his district provided it does not interfere with Heth's efforts to do so in his area; his movement into Kentucky is approved provided he can come up with the troops required.[23]

Lee clarifies for Trapier his earlier orders to transfer most of his command to Sidney Johnston; Lee wants to retain as many of them as possible for Florida. Lee informs Florida Governor Milton of the reasons for the transfer of so many troops, and that their place must be taken by Florida troops. Lee, Agnes, and Annie are all invited to dinner with the Lyons family; only Agnes is able to go. Around 6:30 p.m. the ailing Bishop William Meade, an old friend of Lee's, summons Lee to his deathbed to give his blessing and say goodbye; he dies several hours later.[24]

March 14, Friday (Richmond): Lee assumes his new duties as military advisor. In the morning Lee meets with Brig. Gen. Samuel G. French to discuss the situation in North Carolina and he sends French to take command at New Bern. Lee informs Pemberton that he will now be in permanent command of the Department of South Carolina, Georgia, and East Florida, and that Lee requires several of his staff officers and important papers left behind there. Lee instructs Theophilus Holmes that if Fort Lowry, east of Tappahannock, is not the best position to block ascent of the Rappahannock then he is to determine what is and to fortify that point.

He also tells Holmes to see to provisions from the Northern Neck and assist in moving supplies from there.[25]

Lee writes to his brother Carter telling of his new duties, seeing Mary for the first time in nearly a year, and of Bishop Meade's death last night. He writes also to Mary, telling her that Rob is with him, and of Bishop Meade's death. Of his new duties, he tells her: "I have been placed on duty here to conduct operations under the direction of the President. It will give me great pleasure to do everything I can to relieve him & serve the country, but I do not see either advantage or pleasure in my duties." Lee returns home (707 Franklin) after 11:00 p.m. and learns from Custis that Rob has come to Richmond to enlist and is staying at the Spotswood.[26]

March 15, Saturday (Richmond): Lee expected to be sent to North Carolina today, but President Davis changed his mind. In the morning Lee goes with Rob to procure a uniform and equipment, after which Rob goes to the adjutant general's office and enlists in the Rockbridge Artillery. Lee meets with Capt. Augustus Drewry to discuss constructing a fort on the James just downstream from Richmond. Lee orders Magruder to fortify along the Warwick River from Yorktown across the Peninsula to Mulberry Island.[27] He writes to Edmund Kirby Smith at Knoxville advising of Humphrey Marshall's proposed movement into Kentucky and suggests

---

23 *OR* 5, 1098-9; *OR* 9, 64; *OR* 10, pt. 2, 322-3.

24 *OR* 6, 406; *OR* 53, 222-3; Dowdey, *Wartime Papers*, 127-9. Rev. Meade was the Episcopalian Bishop of Virginia; he had known Lee for decades from their time in Alexandria. Freeman has the Bishop Meade incident occurring on the 14th, but Lee clearly wrote that it was the evening of the 13th. Freeman, *Lee*, vol. 2, 251.

25 Dowdey, *Wartime Papers*, 127-9; Samuel G. French, *Two Wars: The Autobiography of Gen. Samuel G. French, CSA* (Huntington, WV, 1999), 143; REL to Pemberton, March 14, 1862, REL papers, MOC; *OR* 5, 1099-1100. French wrote that the meeting occurred at "Lee's home," which strongly suggests that he had already moved from the Spotswood Hotel to the Stewart house at 707 E Franklin. New Bern, where French was ordered to take command, was captured by Federals under Ambrose Burnside on this date; either while meeting with Lee or very soon after leaving him, French learned of this fact. French, *Two Wars*, 143. Lee informed Pemberton that he needed Thornton Washington immediately and Armistead Long and Joseph Ives once they completed the projects they were engaged in; the others were to remain with Pemberton. REL to Pemberton, March 14, 1862, REL papers, MOC. North Carolina's adjutant general James G. Martin was in Richmond at this time and may have been included in the meeting with French. Bragg diary, March 13, 1862, UNC.

26 REL to C. C. Lee, March 14, 1862, REL papers, W&L; Dowdey, *Wartime Papers*, 127-9. Lee told Mary he expected to be sent to North Carolina or Norfolk on the 15th. Dowdey, *Wartime Papers*, 129.

27 Dowdey, *Wartime Papers*, 129; Lee, *Recollections and Letters of REL*, 70; William I. Clopton, "New Light on the Great Drewry's Bluff Fight," *SHSP*, vol. 34, 83-4; *OR* 9, 68.

that they work together. He relays to Brig. Gen. Edward Johnson at Monterey Governor Letcher's instructions to call out the militia in the surrounding counties. He tells Maj. Gen. Samuel Jones at Mobile that President Davis does not want martial law declared there. In the evening Lee writes to Mary that he is not going to North Carolina as he had thought yesterday, and that he took Rob shopping: "I hope our son will do his duty and make a good soldier." Very heavy rain.[28]

March 16, Sunday (Richmond): Lee tells Holmes that a Union advance against him is inevitable, but to hold Fredericksburg: Johnston is aware of his plight and may be able to reinforce him.[29]

March 17, Monday (Richmond): Lee tells Holmes that it was not intended for him to amass more supplies than he could effectively handle or use, but since he has done so to send the bulk of it to Hanover Junction. He informs Johnston of Holmes's fear of an imminent attack and his inability to hold Fredericksburg once the enemy occupies Stafford Heights on the north side of the Rappahannock. He also requests Johnston to transfer any available cavalry to Magruder. He informs Magruder that there are no troops to be had at Richmond but once there are they will be sent on to the Peninsula; he adds as well that Suffolk does not appear to be threatened any more as Burnside has remained at New Bern. He informs Pemberton that troops that are being sent from South Carolina to Goldsboro, North Carolina, will be replaced by Georgia troops.[30]

March 18, Tuesday (Richmond): Lee tells Magruder he does not think the enemy intends a serious attack upon him yet but instead is simply making a reconnaissance of his position; reinforcements are being sent him in any case. He includes his recommendations on how to fight the *Monitor*: either hold fire until she runs out a gun from her turret and concentrate all fire on the exposed gun to disable it, or to coordinate concentrated fire on her turret to generate enough force to capsize her. He writes to Huger regarding inter-service squabbles at Fort Huger near Smithfield: "This is not a time to squabble about rank." Lee tells Adjutant General Cooper that Heth would like to swap the 8th Virginia Cavalry, which he has no use for, for one of Kirby Smith's or Marshall's infantry regiments, and orders it sent to Marshall.[31]

March 19, Wednesday (Richmond): Lee orders Huger to send several regiments from Suffolk to Goldsboro and advises Sam French that they are on the way. Manigault is ordered to send a regiment to Wilmington, and Lee inquires if Johnston can spare James Longstreet, even temporarily, to take command in North Carolina.[32]

Lee advises Maj. Gen. Earl Van Dorn in Arkansas that reinforcements are being sent him, and reminds Humphrey Marshall that he may call out militia to join him provided it does not interfere

---

28 OR 10, pt. 2, 330-1; OR 5, 1101; REL to Samuel Jones, March 15, 1862, telegram book, R.E. Lee Headquarters papers, VHS; Dowdey, *Wartime Papers*, 129; Bragg diary, March 15, 1862, UNC. Sam Jones had just taken over command of the Department of Alabama and West Florida from Braxton Bragg; he served in nearly every theater and state in the Confederacy before the war was over. Warner, *Generals in Gray*, 166. Ed Johnson commanded a brigade in the mountains west of Staunton; he became a division commander in the ANV in 1863. Ibid, 158-9.

29 OR 5, 1103; REL to T. H. Holmes, March 16, 1862, telegram book, REL HQ papers, VHS.

30 OR 5, 1104-5; OR 9, 70-1; REL to Pemberton, March 17, 1861, telegram book, REL HQ papers, VHS.

31 OR 11, pt. 3 384-6; REL to Magruder, March 18, 1862, telegram book, REL HQ papers, VHS; OR 51, pt. 2, 494-5; REL to Heth, March 18, 1862, telegram book, REL HQ papers, VHS. Fort Huger was one of the works laid out by Andrew Talcott in the early months of the war; it is located directly across the James from Magruder's right flank at Mulberry Island and is currently a county park.

32 REL to Huger, March 19, 1862, (2 telegrams), telegram book, REL HQ papers, VHS; REL to S. G. French, March 19, 1862, telegram book, REL HQ papers, VHS; REL to J. R. Anderson, March 19, 1862, telegram book, REL HQ papers, VHS; REL to A. M. Manigault, March 19, 1862, telegram book, REL HQ papers, VHS; REL to J. E. Johnston, March 19, 1862, (2 telegrams), telegram book, REL HQ papers, VHS.

with Heth's militia. He sends Johnston a report on the Rappahannock defenses. Thornton Washington is relieved from duty in South Carolina and ordered to report to Lee.[33]

March 20, Thursday (Richmond): Lee issues orders establishing railroad schedules and tells Johnston that President Davis wants Longstreet sent to North Carolina immediately, and that Davis wants to meet with Johnston in Gordonsville tomorrow. Lee informs Johnston he has conflicting reports—one has the Army of the Potomac moving to Fort Monroe, another has it instead withdrawing to Washington: "Can you by a rapid forward movement threaten Washington and thus recall [the] enemy? If not can you reinforce Norfolk?"[34]

Lee orders additional militia to Huger's assistance; he also chides Huger for posting one regiment in an exposed position on the Roanoke River—"What use is one regiment at Hamilton. It can be taken at pleasure by the enemy." Lee asks Holmes if the troops reported to be arriving at Fort Monroe came from his front, and asks Brig. Gen. Joseph Anderson at Goldsboro what information he has regarding the enemy at New Bern. Lee approves a request from John B. Hood to have the 18th Georgia added to his Texas brigade, but Lee reminds Johnston and Hood of the president's policy of brigading troops by state.[35]

March 21, Friday (Richmond): Lee issues orders regarding recruiting and mustering instructions for Virginia units, and informs Johnston that President Davis is on his way to Gordonsville to meet with him. Lee notifies President Davis that the Union fleet has left Hampton Roads apparently bound for North Carolina "where a great battle is to be fought. Our troops are gathering but we want a commander. Disaster there would be ruinous. I recommend that Longstreet or G. W. Smith be sent at once."[36]

Lee acknowledges Huger's belated transfer of troops to Goldsboro, and forwards to him a letter from Norfolk city officials concerned and confused over Huger's creation of a military government in that city. Lee informs Magruder that Johnston can send him no cavalry. Lee advises Edward Johnson to fortify and hold Shenandoah Mountain to guard the western approaches to Staunton.[37]

Lee recommends to Samuel Cooper that all excess supplies be removed from east Tennessee due to the strong Unionist sentiment there, and to send reinforcements to the area. Lee requests a naval officer assist in the obstruction of the James River near Smithfield. Lt. Charles Marshall joins Lee's staff as aide de camp.[38]

March 22, Saturday (Richmond): President Davis orders Lee to go to North Carolina tomorrow. Lee advises Magruder that the Union fleet from Hampton Roads has gone to reinforce Burnside or possibly farther south along the coast; with them now gone Magruder should place obstructions in the James. Lee advises Huger that the governor and attorney general have serious concerns over Huger's creation of a military government at Norfolk and Portsmouth; both Lee and President Davis want only a provost marshal as exists in Richmond. Lee informs George W. Munford, secretary of the

---

33 *OR* 8, 791; *OR* 10, pt. 2, 349; *OR* 12, pt. 3, 830-2; Thornton A. Washington CSR.

34 *OR* 1, Series 4, 1010-1; REL to J. E. Johnston, March 20, 1862, (2 telegrams), telegram book, REL HQ papers, VHS.

35 REL to "Col. Farmer," March 20, 1862, telegram book, REL HQ papers, VHS; REL to Huger, March 20, 1862, (2 telegrams), telegram book, REL HQ papers, VHS; REL to T. H. Holmes, March 20, 1862, telegram book, REL HQ papers, VHS ; REL to J. R. Anderson, March 20, 1862, telegram book, REL HQ papers, VHS; REL to J. E. Johnston, March 20, 1862, REL HQ papers, VHS.

36 *OR* 1, Series 4, 1011-2; REL to J. E. Johnston, March 21, 1862, telegram book, REL HQ papers, VHS; *OR* 51, pt. 2, 512.

37 *OR* 9, 449-50; REL to Huger, March 21, 1862; REL HQ papers, VHS; *OR* 11, pt. 3, 391; *OR* 12, pt. 3, 833-4.

38 *OR* 10, pt. 2, 321; REL to S. R. Mallory, March 21, 1862, telegram book, REL HQ papers, VHS; Maurice, *Lee's Aide de Camp*, 3, 28. Marshall repeatedly gives the 21st as the date he joined Lee's staff; Krick places it on the 22nd—it is possible that one is the date of the orders the other is the date he physically joined Lee. Krick, *Staff Officers in Gray*, 214.

commonwealth, that he will discuss Huger's military government with President Davis when he returns from the field. Lee forwards Huger a letter from Maj. Benjamin Allston complaining about the scattered condition of his command; Lee informs Huger that it was his intent that experienced officers such as Allston be placed in positions where they could train new troops and that if this cannot be done with Allston then to transfer him somewhere he can be put to that use.[39]

Lee informs President Davis and Joe Johnston that 17 regiments are reported to have left Winchester and headed east. Lee suggests to Roswell Ripley the creation of a floating battery in Charleston harbor.[40]

He informs Joseph Anderson that a cavalry regiment is on its way to him at Goldsboro, and approves of Heth's defensive measures at Lewisburg but tells him he has no additional troops to send him. He writes to Mary that he had hoped to spend tomorrow with her but President Davis has ordered him to leave for North Carolina first thing in the morning, a move which he thinks will impede his efforts to gather troops to all the threatened points; he includes several of his shirts which need mending yet comments on Mary's poor abilities as a seamstress. Rob departs Richmond for the camp of the Rockbridge Artillery.[41]

March 23, Sunday (Richmond/Fredericksburg): Instead of North Carolina Lee heads to Fredericksburg to meet with President Davis and Gen. Johnston to discuss the situation in North Carolina and inspect Johnston's new line along the Rappahannock. Lee orders Holmes to take his troops to Goldsboro and to take command there. Lee advises Kirby Smith that the governor of Alabama has been requested to send every available man to Chattanooga, so Kirby Smith is to collect all his forces and hold the railroad there. Brig. Gen. George W. Randolph becomes secretary of war, ending the rumors of Lee's appointment to that post.[42]

March 24, Monday (Richmond): Lee is visited in the morning by Lucilla Mason, who requests his assistance in becoming a recorder for the Confederate Congress; after her visit he writes to Howell Cobb, whose support Mason also requests. Lee learns from Huger and Magruder that Federals are landing in large numbers at Fort Monroe. Lee telegraphs Holmes at Goldsboro that at least one division has landed at Newport News, so Holmes is to halt his troops at Weldon until enemy intentions become clear. Lee informs Kirby Smith to go ahead with his recruiting efforts and that pikes will be sent for the new troops if nothing else can be gotten.[43]

March 25, Tuesday (Richmond): Lee asks Johnston what troops he can send to the Virginia Peninsula east of the capital, or Norfolk, as Lee is not yet sure which point the Federals intend to attack with the force now at Fort Monroe. He informs Johnston that President Davis wishes to leave a portion of Johnston's army in northern Virginia and move the remainder to the capital. Lee tells Gen. Huger that if

---

39 Dowdey, *Wartime Papers*, 133-4; *OR* 11, pt. 3, 391; *OR* 51, pt. 2, 513-4; REL to G. W. Munford, March 22, 1862, Letcher papers, LVA; REL to Huger, March 22, 1862, REL HQ papers, VHS. Allston is likely Benjamin Allston of Charleston, SC, of the antebellum army; he seems to have held many commands briefly in the early part of the war before settling into a staff role with Kirby Smith. Krick, *Lee's Colonels*, 33.

40 REL to Davis, March 22, 1862, telegram book, REL HQ papers, VHS; REL to J. E. Johnston, March 22, 1862, telegram book, REL HQ papers, VHS; REL to Ripley, March 22, 1863, telegram book, REL HQ papers, VHS.

41 *OR* 51, pt. 2, 542; *OR* 12, pt. 3, 836; Dowdey, *Wartime Papers*, 133-4; Thomas, *REL*, 217.

42 Jeffry D. Wert, *General James Longstreet: The Confederacy's Most Controversial Soldier* (New York, 1993), 99; *OR* 9, 450; REL to E. Kirby Smith, March 23, 1862, telegram book, REL HQ papers, VHS; Bragg diary, March 23, 1862, UNC. Lee and likely Davis also returned to Richmond in the evening, as he was back in Richmond the following morning. REL to Howell Cobb, March 24, 1862, REL papers, UGA.

43 REL to Howell Cobb, March 24, 1862, REL papers, UGA; Freeman, *Lee*, vol. 2, 13; REL to T. H. Holmes, March 24, 1862, telegram book, REL HQ papers, VHS; REL to E. Kirby Smith, March 24, 1862, telegram book, REL HQ papers, VHS. It is not known if Lee returned to Richmond the evening of the 23rd or early on the 24th.

the Federals move against him at Norfolk, Magruder and Johnston will send help; if Magruder is attacked, Huger will be expected to come to his assistance, but he will be expected to furnish his own means of transportation across the James. Lee informs Kirby Smith that several regiments are headed to him from Georgia, and Lee requests quartermaster general Col. A. C. Myers to send equipment for them.[44]

Lee clarifies for Humphrey Marshall that he is not ordered to act in concert with Kirby Smith for the Kentucky operation and to raise all the troops he can in Kentucky. Lee requests Georgia Governor Brown to send a regiment to Knoxville, and forwards to Virginia Governor Letcher a formal complaint from Norfolk officials regarding Huger's military government there. Lee's staff is authorized to be increased commensurate with his new role.[45]

March 26, Wednesday (Richmond): Lee advises Gen. John Magruder that the Federals concentrating at Fort Monroe appear to be coming from Johnston's front in northern Virginia and that they intend either to attack Norfolk or to move up the Peninsula to seize Richmond; until they show their hand no concentration to defend either point will be effected. However, cautions Lee, Magruder must be ready to reinforce Gen. Huger in Norfolk just as Huger will be ready to reinforce him. Lee cautions Magruder that his position is vulnerable to being turned via either the James or York rivers, so he should begin identifying defensible positions in his rear and be prepared to fall back up the Peninsula quickly. Lee also advises him not to send details via telegraph because they may be intercepted, and reiterates that Magruder's strongest position is the Warwick River line. Lee, meanwhile, advises Huger that there are several batteries in Richmond that will be sent him once they are issued their cannon, thus offsetting the loss of the batteries he dispatched to North Carolina; Lee advises Henry Heth that arms are being sent for his command at Lewisburg. The general informs Quartermaster General Myers that the large amount of provisions along the Roanoke River in North Carolina are in danger of being captured unless they are promptly removed, and that the owners are willing to give these provisions to the Confederate Army—but that it will require government transportation to remove them.[46]

March 27, Thursday (Richmond): Magruder reports the enemy advancing on him; Lee instructs him to "hold the Warwick River line." Lee then notifies Huger that Magruder is the target and orders that Gen. Raleigh Colston's infantry brigade at Smithfield be sent north across the James River. Lee also instructs Gen. Cadmus Wilcox at Weldon to join Magruder with his infantry brigade, and informs Gen. Holmes that he has sent Wilcox to the Peninsula, but that several regiments will be sent from Raleigh, North Carolina, to replace him.[47]

Taylor informs Magruder that several additional Alabama regiments will be sent to him from Richmond over the next two days, and that according to Secretary of the Navy Mallory, the CSS *Virginia* "is now about ready to come out." Lee finalizes the organization of the 26th Alabama, which is in the capital awaiting its orders. Lee notifies Johnston that Thomas "Stonewall" Jackson is threatened in the Shenandoah Valley, but that if Jackson is reinforced and launches an offensive, the operation may draw the Federals away from Magruder. Lee warns Commissary General Lucius Northrop that 10,000 troops from Johnston's army are expected to arrive in Richmond beginning today, and they will be in need of provisions. Holmes requests Lee to come to North Carolina himself or to

---

44 *OR* 11, pt. 3, 396-7; REL to E. Kirby Smith, March 25, 1862, telegram book, REL HQ papers, VHS; *OR* 10, pt. 2, 364.

45 *OR* 10, pt. 2, 364-5; REL to Joseph Brown, March 25, 1862, telegram book, REL HQ papers, VHS; REL to Letcher, March 25, 1862, REL HQ papers, VHS; Maurice, *Lee's Aide de Camp*, 7.

46 *OR* 11, pt. 3, 398-400; *OR* 12, pt. 3, 838-9; *OR* 51, pt. 2, 515.

47 REL to Magruder, March 27, 1862, telegram book, REL HQ papers, VHS; REL to Huger, March 27, 1862, telegram book, REL HQ papers, VHS; REL to Cadmus Wilcox, March 27, 1862, telegram book, REL HQ papers, VHS; REL to T. H. Holmes, March 27, 1862, telegram book, REL HQ papers, VHS; REL to Henry T. Clark, March 27, 1862, telegram book, REL HQ papers, VHS.

send Maj. Gen. G. W. Smith instead to "straighten out this tangled yarn."[48]

March 28, Friday (Richmond): Lee writes to Joe Johnston at 1:00 a. m. ordering him to begin withdrawing his army to Richmond, but later cautions him not to do so if it will entail the loss of the Virginia Central Railroad and cut off communications with Jackson, Edward Johnson, and Humphrey Marshall. Lee adds that if Johnston has any questions or doubts as to the best course he should come to Richmond to consult with Lee and Davis, but that Johnston will know the situation in his front better than they will in Richmond. Lee tells Gen. Colston a boat will be sent him to enable him to cross the James River to aid Gen. Magruder, but cautions Colston that he should not do so until it becomes absolutely clear that Magruder, and not Norfolk, is the target. Accordingly, Lee instructs Holmes to ascertain the purpose of the enemy in his front.[49]

Lee also instructs Maj. Harman at Staunton to get the recruits at Lynchburg to Jackson however he is able to do so. Lee tells Nathan Evans that Col. Richard DeTreville, whom Evans recommended for promotion, cannot be made a general at present, because States Rrights Gist was just made a brigadier and there are no more South Carolina appointments available. Lee explains to Gen. Braxton Bragg that Samuel Jones was promoted and given Bragg's former command because it was deemed necessary to have a Regular Army officer in command there instead of state militia generals; Lee also inquires whether it is absolutely necessary for Bragg to have Jones back with him.[50]

March 29, Saturday (Richmond): Lee informs Magruder that reinforcements are on the way and that Colston's Brigade is available. If and when McClellan attacks Magruder, all available troops will be sent to the Peninsula. Lee attempts to allay Gen. Huger's fears about his command being too scattered, and informs him that if the enemy moves against Norfolk, Magruder is prepared to come to his aid. Lee also orders Huger to abolish his military government at Norfolk and Portsmouth and to appoint a provost marshal; Lee goes into detail explaining how martial law works. The general instructs Holmes to use his discretion regarding how to position his forces to protect the Weldon Railroad, and to be prepared to reinforce Huger at Norfolk, if needed.[51]

Lee explains to North Carolina Governor Clark that the arms sent to Goldsboro are intended for the four unarmed regiments currently at Raleigh, who once armed are to be sent north to Holmes. Lee asks Gen. Pemberton if Alexander Lawton can be spared for service in Tennessee, and directs Capt. A. S. Rives to send one observation balloon to Holmes at Goldsboro and another to Magruder at Yorktown. Lee endorses Thornton Washington's application for a commissary position.[52]

March 30, Sunday (Richmond): Lee writes to Huger regarding a prisoner exchange proposed by Union Maj. Gen. John Wool, and informs Humphrey Marshall that there are no arms that can be sent to him at present other than pikes, but that he is authorized to purchase weapons if he can do so. Lee

---

48 OR 11, pt. 3, 404-5; REL to John Gill Shorter, March 27, 1862, telegram book, REL HQ papers, VHS; REL to J. E. Johnston, March 27, 1862, telegram book, REL HQ papers, VHS; Walter C. Hilderman, *Theophilus Hunter Holmes: A North Carolina General in the Civil War* (Jefferson, NC, 2013), 75.

49 OR 11, pt. 3, 408-9; REL to J. E. Johnston, March 28, 1862, telegram book, REL HQ papers, VHS; REL to T. H. Holmes, March 28, 1862, telegram book, REL HQ papers, VHS.

50 REL to M. G. Harman, March 28, 1862, telegram book, REL HQ papers, VHS; REL to N. G. Evans, March 28, 1862, REL papers, VHS; REL to Braxton Bragg, March 28, 1862, telegram book, REL HQ papers, VHS.

51 OR 11, pt. 3, 411-2; OR 51, pt. 2, 518-9; OR 9, 454.

52 REL to H. T. Clark, March 29, 1862, telegram book, REL HQ papers, VHS; REL to Pemberton, March 29, 1862, telegram book, REL HQ papers, VHS; REL to A. S. Rives, March 29, 1862, telegram book, REL HQ papers, VHS; Thornton A. Washington to REL, March 28, 1862, TAW CSR. Lee's endorsement for Washington reads in part: "I have known him in service for many years and for the last five months he has been chief of my staff."

also telegraphs P. G. T. Beauregard regarding reinforcements sent him.[53]

March 31, Monday (Richmond): Lee writes to the presidents of all Southern railroads requesting that they establish uniform schedules to minimize wear on equipment. He informs Magruder that no further troops or artillery will be sent to him until it becomes clear that attack is imminent; Lee still thinks Norfolk to be their target rather than the Peninsula. He orders Huger to issue firearms only to his infantry, even if that means issuing pikes to other units; he also approves Huger's prisoner exchange with Wool.[54]

Lee pressures North Carolina Governor Clark for additional troops and arms for Holmes, and instructs Alexander Lawton to have a signal officer placed at Fort Pulaski. Lee instructs Sam Jones at Pensacola to hold that city and its navy yard but if he cannot he is to remove everything of value when he evacuates. Lee warns Kirby Smith of the disloyalty of the population in east Tennessee and the need for martial law, and above all to protect the East Tennessee and Virginia Railroad.[55]

---

[53] OR 1, Series 2, 102-3; OR 10, pt. 2, 374; REL to Beauregard, March 30, 1862, telegram book, REL HQ papers, VHS. Joe Johnston arrived in Richmond on this date and almost certainly met with Lee. Charleston *Mercury*, April 5, 1862.

[54] REL to railroad presidents, March 31, 1862, REL papers, VHS; OR 11, pt. 3, 412-3; OR 1, Series 2, 102-3.

[55] REL to H. T. Clark, March 31, 1862, telegram book, REL HQ papers, VHS; REL to Lawton, March 31, 1862, telegram book, REL HQ papers, VHS; OR 6, 868; OR 10, pt. 2, 376-7.

April 1862

The water-borne transfer of George McClellan's army from northern Virginia to the Virginia Peninsula changed the strategic situation in Virginia. For weeks, Gens. John B. Magruder and Benjamin Huger were convinced the increased activity in Hampton Roads and Fort Monroe portended an attack on either or both of their departments. Lee shared their concerns—enemy activity in eastern North Carolina alarmed him as well—but was unwilling to commit to a concentration of forces until he knew for certain where that concentration should be effected.

McClellan began his offensive against Magruder on April 4. The Confederates quickly reacted by shifting Joe Johnston's army south from the Rappahannock River to Richmond and then east down the Peninsula, and by stripping the Carolinas of troops. The decision to move Johnston's army was not unanimous. Lee spent hours in conference with Jefferson Davis, Secretary of War Randolph, and Gens. Johnston, James Longstreet, and Gustavus W. Smith. Johnston wanted no part in the attempt to hold the Peninsula, which he considered indefensible because of the James and York rivers on either flank. His reluctance to adopt this policy, coupled with his unwillingness to keep Richmond informed once tasked with the job, ultimately led to his undoing. Lee recognized that confronting McClellan directly was only part of the solution, and that a counter-offensive must be launched somewhere else to draw Union strength and attention away from the Peninsula. Lee looked to the Shenandoah Valley and Stonewall Jackson for the solution.

McClellan was but the closest of several serious problems with which Lee had to contend. No matter how much Lee reassured him that no offensive was looming, Theophilus Holmes in North Carolina remained convinced the interior of that state was directly threatened. New Orleans, meanwhile, by far the South's largest city and a critically important seaport, was under threat of naval invasion and its capture appeared imminent. Gen. Albert Sidney Johnston was killed on the first day of fighting at Shiloh on the 6th. Johnston's successor, P. G. T. Beauregard, stood and fought the second day but the army was driven off the battlefield in defeat and withdrew to Corinth in northern Mississippi, where Beauregard would soon run into trouble.

The Union army was not Lee's only problem. The initial one-year enlistments of many troops, especially among Virginian units, were expiring. The possibility existed that the army could dissolve if the men did not reenlist. One of the most important steps to combat this was the passage of a conscription bill that largely composed by Lee's aide and former lawyer, Maj. Charles Marshall, based on input from Lee.

One of the main weaknesses facing any army trying to hold the Peninsula, which Johnston expressed repeatedly, was its vulnerability on both flanks. The CSS *Virginia*'s position off Norfolk just south of Hampton Roads largely guarded the mouth of the James, but the York flank was exceedingly vulnerable. If Magruder was forced to abandon the lines at Yorktown, Norfolk must also be evacuated, and to do entailed the almost certain loss of the *Virginia*. To protect the river approach to Richmond, Lee and Navy Secretary Stephen R. Mallory began making daily visits to Drewry's Bluff, several miles below the capital, to check on the progress of the fortifications being erected there.[1]

---

1 Newton, *Johnston and the Defense of Richmond*, 158.

Lee met frequently with the president and/or Secretary Randolph. "Many and long were the conferences they held in the office of the President, over movements recommended by General Lee or suggested by some other officer," recalled Lee's aide Charles Marshall.[2] "Gen. Lee is calm," wrote John B. Jones, an observant and opinionated clerk working in the bowels of the War Department, "but the work of preparation goes on night and day."[3] By the end of the month Lee was confident that McClellan could not get to the capital. "There is no possibility of the Federal army reaching Richmond," he confidently informed a friend.[4]

Lee's staff underwent a major reorganization during the second April of the war. Long gone were the western Virginia days of only two overworked aides helping him. Armistead Long rejoined Lee from South Carolina and took over the duties of military secretary. Thomas Mann Randolph Talcott, the son of Lee's mentor Andrew Talcott, joined the general as an aide-de-camp, and an invitation was extended to University of Virginia professor Charles S. Venable to join Lee's staff. Thornton Washington departed from headquarters for the Western Theater; Walter Taylor assumed many of his duties.

* * *

---

2   Maurice, *Lee's Aide de Camp*, 7.

3   John B. Jones, *A Rebel War Clerk's Diary*, 2 vols. (Philadelphia, 1866), vol. 1, 121.

4   REL to Mary Triplett, April 26, 1862, Lee papers, SH.

April 1, Tuesday (Richmond): Lee tells Theophilus Holmes in North Carolina that McClellan's move to Fort Monroe is probably the northern half of a pincer movement against Norfolk, with Burnside's force in North Carolina being the southern arm. Accordingly Holmes is to keep watch on Burnside and to be prepared to guard both Norfolk and Wilmington, keeping a mobile reserve at Weldon. Lee telegraphs Georgia Governor Joseph Brown of the need for troops in North Carolina and reminding of the secretary of war's request to send three regiments to Goldsboro. A bill providing for conscription to fill the ranks of the army, drafted by Charles Marshall, is read in the Senate.[5]

April 2, Wednesday (Richmond): Lee meets with President Davis and Joe Johnston to discuss the situation in North Carolina and on the Peninsula. Lee receives a telegram from South Carolina Governor Francis Pickens concerned about enemy access to Charleston via the Stono River. Lee forwards the governor's concerns to Pemberton with instructions to hold Cole's Island if possible until an interior line is completed, and replies to Pickens that he has forwarded the telegram on to Pemberton, but that Pemberton will know of the situation much better than Lee in Richmond.[6]

Lee requests Georgia Governor Brown to have all state troops retained for the duration of the war. Lee advises Huger that Magruder reports more Federals landing at Newport News, thus he should be prepared to cross over to the Peninsula, and to place obstructions in the Elizabeth River and informs Holmes of the buildup of enemy forces in Hampton Roads so to hold his troops in readiness to go to Suffolk or Weldon if not needed at Greensboro to oppose Burnside.[7] Lee orders Magruder to return Colston's Brigade to Smithfield and to hold Wilcox's Brigade in readiness to cross the James. He notifies John H. Forney of his promotion to brigadier general and orders him to report to Sam Jones at Mobile for duty assignment.[8]

April 3, Thursday (Richmond): Lee meets with Navy Secretary Stephen Mallory in the morning to discuss the cooperation of the James River fleet with Magruder's army. He writes to Huger regarding a possible swap of heavy artillery from some of the James River fortifications with that of the ironclads under construction. Lee writes to Magruder regarding reports of poor conditions at the Gloucester Point batteries. He also advises Magruder of a report that the Federals have left small pox-infected clothing at Young's Mill, attempting to infect his troops. Lee orders that guns should be emplaced at Fort Powhatan and the river obstructed there immediately, but if the guns destined for there can be put to better use at Fort Boykin or Mulberry Island they can be used there instead.[9]

Lee writes Huger regarding a proposed POW exchange—Gen. Wool has objected to the officers involved and Lee knows of no officer who can be substituted of whom Wool may approve. Lee telegraphs Holmes to use his own discretion in

---

[5] *OR* 9, 455; REL to Joseph Brown, April 1, 1862, telegram book, REL HQ papers, VHS; Maurice, *Lee's Aide de Camp*, 30. Marshall did not provide an exact date for when the conscription bill was drafted, writing only that he drafted it "a few days earlier." It stipulated that all males ages 18-35 (later raised to 45) were subject to military service for the duration of the war. It passed the Senate on April 16. Maurice, *Lee's Aide de Camp*, 30-1.

[6] Thomas R. Sharp diary, VT; *OR* 6, 423-4; REL to Francis Pickens, April 2, 1862, telegram book, REL HQ papers, VHS. It is possible that William Loring participated in this meeting of Davis, Lee, and Johnston as he was briefly stationed at Suffolk during this time; indeed, the Charleston *Mercury* reported him as part of this meeting. *Mercury*, April 8, 1862.

[7] REL to Joseph Brown, April 2, 1862, telegram book, REL HQ papers, VHS; REL to Huger, April 2, 1862, (2 telegrams), telegram book, REL HQ papers, VHS; REL to T. H. Holmes, April 2, 1862, telegram book, REL HQ papers, VHS.

[8] REL to Magruder, April 2, 1862, telegram book, REL HQ papers, VHS; REL to J. H. Forney, April 2, 1865, REL papers, W&L. Forney was colonel of the 10th AL and rose to major general, serving most of the war in the Western Theater. Warner, *Generals in Gray*, 90-1.

[9] *OR* 51, pt. 2, 528; Magruder to REL, April 1, 1862, telegram book, REL HQ papers, VHS; *OR* 11, pt. 3, 418; REL to Magruder, April 3, 1862, telegram book, REL HQ papers, VHS.

sending troops to Weldon or Suffolk but "do not create alarm" with whatever action he pursues, and provides Johnston an update on the situation in the Valley.[10]

The general advises James Longstreet at Rapidan that Johnston has returned to Fredericksburg and that Longstreet is now free to operate with whatever discretion Johnston has given him. Lee informs Alexander Lawton that his Georgia troops should be retained for the duration of the war, preferably by Confederate enlistment if possible, but if not then by the state of Georgia. Lee visits with eldest daughter Mary, who is in Richmond for a visit; they enjoy a horseback ride around the city, Mary riding on Brown Roan.[11]

April 4, Friday (Richmond): John Magruder sends word to Gen. Lee that the enemy is emerging from Fort Monroe and heading up the Peninsula; Jeb Stuart also sends word that a large number of transports are headed down the Potomac River. Thus, Lee notifies Johnston that the shift south to the Peninsula must be made immediately. He cautions Gen. Magruder not to overreact because the Federals cannot be in all the places they are reported in such great numbers, and that for the present time, Magruder is the strongest force in front of Richmond.[12]

Lee orders Holmes to send Cobb's Brigade to Petersburg and instructs Longstreet to send his forces to Richmond immediately, but again reminds Holmes to not create undue alarm. He also orders Huger to send Colston's Brigade to Magruder right away and also requests that Col. Gorgas of the ordnance department send additional artillery pieces to fortify Drewry's Bluff and Mulberry Island.[13]

Gen. Lee reiterates to John Pemberton his instructions to hold Cole's Island and reiterates the governor's concerns about abandoning it. Lee approves of Kirby Smith's dispositions in the mountains and informs him that additional weapons are being sent to him. Lee opines that men belonging to units captured at Roanoke Island are not free to join other units until the expiration of their enlistment. He refers to the War Department a question regarding the exemption of plantation overseers from military service; Lee is not in favor of their exemption unless their duties are specifically military in nature, but he admits that he is not at all certain about his opinion.

Lee writes to wife Mary advising her to leave White House because McClellan's Federal army is ascending the Peninsula and if they ascend the Pamunkey River, that plantation would be their likely landing point. He tells her of daughter Mary's recent visit and passes along latest news of Rooney. Because of McClellan's movements, he will not be able to see her tomorrow as planned. "Everything is so unsettled . . . and no telling what a day may bring forth, that I do not feel I ought to be out of the way."[14]

April 5, Saturday (Richmond): Gen. Lee telegraphs Joe Johnston that President Davis wants Johnston himself to go to the Virginia Peninsula with as much of his force as he can take and assume command there. Lee also orders Howell Cobb to join Gen. Magruder by way of Grove Wharf, and the general also advises Magruder that Cobb and Johnston's forces are being sent to the Peninsula, and that a train

---

10 OR 1, Series 2, 103; REL to T. H. Holmes, April 3, 1862, telegram book, REL HQ papers, VHS; REL to J. E. Johnston, April 3, 1862, telegram book, REL HQ papers, VHS.

11 REL to James Longstreet, April 3, 1862, telegram book, REL HQ papers, VHS; OR 6, 424; Dowdey, *Wartime Papers*, 142. Joe Johnston left Richmond for Fredericksburg via a special train at 10:00 a.m. Sharp diary, VT.

12 Freeman, *Lee*, vol. 2, 18-9; OR 11, pt. 3, 420; REL to Magruder, April 4, 1862, telegram book, REL HQ papers, VHS.

13 REL to T. H. Holmes, April 4, 1862 (2 telegrams) telegram book, REL HQ papers, VHS; REL to Longstreet, April 4, 1862, telegram book, REL HQ papers, VHS; REL to Huger, April 4, 1862, telegram book, REL HQ papers, VHS; OR 11, pt. 3, 421.

14 OR 6, 424-5; OR 10, pt. 2, 393; REL to "Capt. J. Taylor," April 4, 1862, telegram book, REL HQ papers, VHS; REL to Hill Carter, April 4, 1862, telegram book, REL HQ papers, VHS; Dowdey, *Wartime Papers*, 142-3.

of ammunition for his army will leave that afternoon to supply them.[15]

April 7, Monday (Richmond): Lee notifies Johnston that Magruder reports an attack upon his Warwick River line imminent. Lee writes to Huger regarding the defenses on the Nansemond River: they are currently too small and scattered. Lee wants them condensed into several major works. He also orders Huger to send all unserviceable guns to the Richmond Armory to be recast, as "iron is in great demand for guns etc., and difficult to be obtained." He authorizes Holmes to keep the horses from the Cobb's Legion cavalry in North Carolina.[16]

Lee advises Kirby Smith that martial law will be declared in east Tennessee as requested and asks if Smith can exchange three of his Tennessee regiments for three in Johnston's army that will re-enlist only if they are allowed to serve in their native state. Lee orders Maj. M. L. Clark in Little Rock to suspend, for the present, the removal of the weapons machinery from the arsenal there, and advises Beauregard of the same. Capt. Taylor submits a request for 500 envelopes and two boxes of steel pens for use at headquarters.[17]

April 8, Tuesday (Richmond): Lee advises Navy Secretary Mallory he believes McClellan is changing his base from the James to the York due to the threat posed by the CSS *Virginia*. Magruder believes they are establishing a base at Poquoson, so Lee proposes moving the ironclad to the York on a night raid to destroy transports and supply ships there and slip back to Norfolk under cover of darkness. Lee advises Magruder various reinforcements are being sent him, ammunition is in short supply in Richmond, and he should use his troops to fortify his position rather than wait for black laborers for that purpose. Lee advises Johnston to bring as much ammunition with him to the Peninsula as possible. The commissary department is advised it needs to provide for 30,000 more troops on the Peninsula.[18]

Lee advises Joseph Finegan that he has been promoted to brigadier general and given command in Florida. Lee writes to Florida Governor John Milton explaining that J. Patton Anderson was the first choice to replace Trapier in command in Florida, but Anderson could not be taken from his current assignment, so the billet was given to Joe Finegan. Lee writes also to the adjutant general's office requesting that orders be drafted assigning Trapier to Beauregard and States Rights Gist to Pemberton. Rain in the evening.[19]

April 9, Wednesday (Richmond): Lee clarifies his orders of March 26 to Magruder: he is not to abandon the Williamsburg lines unless compelled to do so, and he should remain north of the Chickahominy River if forced to retreat toward Richmond. Lee tells Magruder that "all that is possible is being done toward supplying your necessities," but cautions ammunition is in such short supply that it will be necessary to issue orders to conserve it. Lee tells Joe Johnston to have his wagons go by way of Hanover Court House and Williamsburg and avoid the choke point at Richmond, and advises James Longstreet that no bread can be found in Richmond for his troops but there is plenty of raw flour available at Gordonsville that he can use.

---

15 REL to J. E. Johnston, April 5, 1862, telegram book, REL HQ papers, VHS; REL to Howell Cobb, April 5, 1862, telegram book, REL HQ papers, VHS; REL to Magruder, April 5, 1862, (2 telegrams), telegram book, REL HQ papers, VHS. Grove Wharf was at Carter's Grove about midway between Jamestown Island and Mulberry Island.

16 REL to J. E. Johnston, April 7, 1862, telegram book, REL HQ papers, VHS; *OR* 11, pt. 3, 425-6; REL to Huger; April 7, 1862, telegram book, REL HQ papers, VHS; REL to T. H. Holmes, April 7, 1862, telegram book, REL HQ papers.

17 *OR* 10, pt. 2, 397-8; REL to M. L. Clark, April 7, 1862, telegram book, REL HQ papers, VHS; REL to Beauregard, April 7, 1862, telegram book, REL HQ papers, VHS; WHT requisition, April 7, 1862, WHT CSR.

18 *OR* 11, pt. 3, 429-30; REL to Magruder, April 8, 1862, (3 telegrams), telegram book, REL HQ papers, VHS; REL to J. E. Johnston, April 8, 1862, telegram book, REL HQ papers, VHS.

19 REL to Joseph Finegan, April 8, 1862, telegram book, REL HQ papers, VHS; *OR* 6, 429; REL to Samuel Cooper, April 8, 1862, REL papers, VHS; Brooke, *Ironclads and Big Guns*, 87. Finegan was a railroad pioneer in Florida, a member of its secession convention, and commanded there until 1864, when he joined the ANV. Warner, *Generals in Gray*, 88-9.

Lee informs Holmes of a report of several thousand Federal troops landing at Elizabeth City, and of Lee's belief that a movement will be made against Norfolk from that region. Lee adds that more troops will be sent to Goldsboro from Georgia and that hopefully more will be furnished by North Carolina; if possible Holmes should arrange a POW exchange with Burnside.[20]

Lee requests that Josiah Gorgas send 1,000 pikes to Jackson in the Shenandoah Valley, and also informs him of an offer by a church congregation in Liberty, Virginia, to contribute their bell to the war effort. Lee orders Sam Jones to report to Gen. Beauregard at Corinth, Mississippi, and turn over his command in Alabama to Gen. Forney. Lee informs Beauregard that Jones and Trapier have been ordered to report to him and that Lee will gladly promote those whose actions at Shiloh warrant it if Beauregard will provide him a list of names.[21]

April 10, Thursday (Richmond): Lee orders Pemberton to send Donelson's Brigade to Beauregard at Corinth, noting "If Mississippi Valley is lost Atlantic states will be ruined," and advises Beauregard that reinforcements are en route. Lee at first denies a request from Roswell Ripley to issue furloughs to Johnson Hagood's brigade, but then relents on the condition that the men return immediately in case of attack. Lee informs Maj. Clark in Little Rock that since the arsenal machinery is already packed and ready to be moved, to go ahead and do so, advising Beauregard of this change.[22]

April 11, Friday (Richmond): Lee decrees that Virginia troops who do not voluntarily reenlist will immediately be put into state service per Governor Letcher's orders. He instructs Holmes to send engineer Capt. Richard K. Meade to Magruder, and advises Kirby Smith that President Davis wishes him to continue in command in east Tennessee.[23]

Lee informs Pemberton and Beauregard that six regiments will be sent from South Carolina to Corinth for temporary duty. Taylor submits a requisition for "one small pass book for use of Gen. Lee's headquarters."[24]

April 12, Saturday (Richmond): Lee meets with President Davis, Secretary of War Randolph, and Gen. Johnston regarding the situation on the Virginia Peninsula. As a result of this meeting, both Magruder's and Huger's departments are placed under Johnston's overall command. Lee writes to Florida Governor Milton asking if Florida can raise and equip cavalry for use at Pensacola because there is none to spare elsewhere.[25]

April 13, Sunday (Richmond): Lee advises Huger that Johnston has departed for the Peninsula and a

---

20 OR 11, pt. 3, 433-4; REL to J. E. Johnston, April 9, 1862, telegram book, REL HQ papers, VHS; REL to Longstreet, April 9, 1862, telegram book, REL HQ papers, VHS; OR 9, 457.

21 OR 12, pt. 3, 844-5; REL to Gorgas, April 9, 1862, telegram book, REL HQ papers, VHS; OR 6, 881; REL to Beauregard, April 9, 1862, telegram book, REL HQ papers, VHS.

22 OR 6, 432; REL to Beauregard, April 10, 1862, (2 telegrams), telegram book, REL HQ papers, VHS; REL to Roswell Ripley, April 10, 1862, (2 telegrams), telegram book, REL HQ papers, VHS; REL to M. L. Clark, April 10, 1862, telegram book, REL HQ papers, VHS. Lee's own sense of duty is evident in his initial response to Ripley: "Men will surely not leave while in face of the enemy." He would not leave under such conditions; he could not fathom that others would.

23 OR 11, pt. 3, 683; OR 51, pt. 2, 534; REL to T. H. Holmes, April 11, 1862, telegram book, REL HQ papers, VHS; REL to Edmund Kirby Smith, April 11, 1862, telegram book, REL HQ papers, VHS. Meade resigned late from the U.S. Army and was present in blue inside Fort Sumter in April 1861; he worked with Magruder on the defenses of the Peninsula early in the war before his assignment to North Carolina. Krick, *Staff Officers in Gray*, 219.

24 OR 6, 433-4; REL to Beauregard, April 11, 1862, telegram book, REL HQ papers, VHS; WHT requisition, April 11, 1862, WHT CSR.

25 Steven H. Newton, *Joseph E. Johnston and the Defense of Richmond* (Lawrence, KS, 1998), 87-8; OR 11, pt. 3, 438; OR 53, 234. Both Davis and Johnston described this meeting in their memoirs, but neither put a date to it. Johnston, *Narrative of Military Operations*, 110-6, and Davis, *Rise and Fall*, vol. 2, 70. Thomas Cobb noted that Johnston arrived on the Peninsula front the night of the 12th which supports Johnston's recollection of departing immediately after the meeting. Thomas R. R. Cobb, "Extracts from Letters to his Wife, February 3, 1861-December 10, 1862," *SHSP*, vol. 28, 291.

portion of his army is also en route. That afternoon, Lee informs Johnston by telegraph what elements of his army have been ordered to join Magruder.[26]

April 14, Monday (Richmond): Johnston returns early in the morning from his inspection tour of the Peninsula and goes straight to President Davis's office at the Treasury Building. Once he hears Johnston's report, Davis pauses the meeting so Lee and Sec. Randolph can join. Johnston asks that Longstreet and G. W. Smith also participate. The meeting reconvenes between 10:00 and 11:00 a. m., and continues—at times quite heated—until 6:00 p.m., when they recess for dinner. The council resumes at 7:00 p. m. in the Executive Mansion and continues until 1:00 a. m. Tuesday morning. Longstreet listens most of the meeting and contributes little, and Smith falls ill during the evening portion, excuses himself, and lies down on a couch in an adjoining room, where he falls asleep.[27]

Either before joining the meeting or during the brief evening recess, Lee instructs Pemberton that Georgia state troops at Savannah must be kept in service, and also writes to Nathan Evans encouraging him to keep up his efforts and promotion will come in time. He also telegraphs Maj. Gen. Mansfield Lovell at New Orleans that the state of Louisiana has a regiment's worth of weapons but no troops to issue them to, so Lovell is to raise a battalion for this purpose.[28]

April 15, Tuesday (Richmond): Lee's meeting with the president concludes at approximately 1:00 a. m. After a brief rest, Lee meets with Johnston and Adjutant General Cooper to work out the logistics of moving Johnston's army to the Peninsula. Later, he meets with Lt. Cicero Primrose, 1st North Carolina Artillery, who escaped the besieged Fort Macon outside Beaufort, North Carolina, to deliver word of the garrison's plight to Richmond. Lee writes to Holmes regarding the situation at Fort Macon, where on top of the approaching enemy, a mutiny is brewing; Lee wants Holmes to evacuate the garrison before it is too late.[29]

Lee informs Brig. Gen. Charles Field at Fredericksburg that the enemy force landing at Tappahannock is likely just a raiding party; once they depart, Field is to place obstructions in the Rappahannock above the town. Lee authorizes Kirby Smith to move against Nashville if he can gather sufficient force to do so. Lee alerts Lovell that a Union fleet is headed down the Mississippi toward him; if not needed at New Orleans, he is to send the ironclad CSS *Louisiana* upriver to intercept. Lee

---

26 *OR* 11, pt. 3, 438-9; REL to J. E. Johnston, April 13, 1862, telegram book, REL HQ papers, VHS. Edmund Ruffin recorded a rumor that Lee accompanied Johnston down the Peninsula but this was not true. Scarborough, *Diary of Edmund Ruffin*, vol. 2, 280.

27 Joseph L. Harsh, *Confederate Tide Rising: Robert E. Lee and the Making of Southern Strategy, 1861-1862* (Kent, OH, 1998), 36-7; Newton, *Johnston and Defense of Richmond*, 96-8; Douglas S. Freeman, *Lee's Lieutenants: A Study in Command*, 3 vols. (New York, 1970), vol. 1, 149. Harsh called this meeting "the most impressive war council ever held in the Confederacy." Harsh, *Confederate Tide Rising*, 36. Johnston was not in favor of reinforcing Magruder or attempting to hold the Peninsula, wanting instead to concentrate everything from Virginia, the Carolinas, and Georgia at Richmond and fight McClellan there or to mount an offensive with that force to draw McClellan away. Smith sided with Johnston, and Longstreet, by his own admission, contributed little. Lee and Randolph argued that fighting McClellan on the Peninsula would buy time for forces to be concentrated at Richmond. Randolph added that giving up the Peninsula would also entail the loss of Norfolk and its navy yard and with it the ironclad *Virginia*. Davis eventually sided with Lee and Randolph. Freeman, *Lee*, vol. 2, 21-2. Davis, Johnston, and Longstreet all gave various accounts of this meeting. Davis, *Rise and Fall*, vol. 2, 86-8; Johnston, *Narrative of Military Operations*, 113-6; James Longstreet, *From Manassas to Appomattox* (New York, 1992), 66. Johnston's statement in his memoirs, "The belief that events on the Peninsula would soon compel the Confederate Government to adopt my method of opposing the Federal army, reconciled me somewhat to the necessity of obeying the President's order," is curious to say the least. Johnston, *Narrative of Military Operations*, 116.

28 WHT to Pemberton, April 14, 1862, REL papers, MOC; REL to Nathan Evans, April 14, 1862, REL papers, VHS; REL to Mansfield Lovell, April 14, 1862, telegram book, REL HQ papers, VHS. Lovell commanded at New Orleans and later led a corps under Beauregard. Warner, *Generals in Gray*, 194-5.

29 Newton, *Johnston and Defense of Richmond*, 115; Paul Branch, Jr., *The Siege of Fort Macon* (Morehead City, NC, 1982), 60; Clark, *Several Regiments from North Carolina*, vol. 1, 507; *OR* 9, 458. Lee was very familiar with Fort Macon, having conducted a thorough inspection of the fort in late 1840. Paul Branch, *Fort Macon: A History* (Charleston, SC, 1999), 68-70.

informs Beauregard that John C. Breckinridge and Thomas C. Hindman have been promoted to major general, and others have been promoted to lesser grades per Beauregard's request.[30]

April 16, Wednesday (Richmond): Lee meets with Henry Wise, who wants command of a brigade on the Peninsula. Lee writes to Beauregard regarding Kirby Smith's proposed movement against Nashville: all disposable troops available to Kirby Smith have been ordered by Beauregard to join him at Corinth. Lee also suggests to Beauregard that Union Gen. Benjamin Prentiss be proposed as an exchange for Maj. Gen. Simon Buckner. Lee orders the 45th, 50th, and 51st Virginia regiments to join Kirby Smith, noting that there is nothing else to send him from Virginia.[31]

Lee instructs Lovell to request weapons from the state of Louisiana to equip all unarmed men under his command. Lee opines that President Davis does not have the power to commission officers in a Tennessee state unit, that only the governor of each state has authority over commissioning officers in state units. The Senate passes the conscription bill.[32]

April 17, Thursday (Richmond): Lee again requests of Navy Secretary Mallory that the CSS *Virginia* be dispatched to the York River, and writes to Magruder regarding reinforcements and supplies being sent him. Lee informs Field that now that the enemy gunboats have passed back down the Rappahannock now is the time to place river obstructions. Lee authorizes Maj. Gen. Richard Ewell to go on the offensive on the upper Rappahannock if it does not conflict with his orders from Johnston, as more action along that line will likely give the Federals pause. Lee instructs Humphrey Marshall on how to bring militia into service, and outlines for Adjutant General Cooper the dispositions of Holmes's forces in North Carolina.[33] Lee telegraphs Sam Jones at Mobile that he cannot leave his post until his replacement arrives. Lee expresses his displeasure to Florida Governor Milton that he is keeping more troops than he should in Florida, rather than sending most to Beauregard at Corinth. Thornton Washington switches from adjutant general to quartermaster on Lee's staff. Johnston departs Richmond to take command on the Peninsula.[34]

April 18, Friday (Richmond): Lee informs Governor Letcher that many of his concerns regarding the reenlistment of Virginia troops will be addressed by the conscription bill. Lee informs Edward Johnson that Jackson is falling back toward Staunton; if Stonewall moves east out of the Valley to link up with Ewell, Johnson must move to Staunton or Waynesboro. Lee informs Heth of the possibility that Staunton will be lost; if that is the case then Heth must move toward Lynchburg, linking up

---

30 OR 12, pt. 3, 850; OR 10, pt. 2, 422; REL to Lovell, April 15, 1862, telegram book, REL HQ papers, VHS; REL to Beauregard, April 15, 1862, telegram book, REL HQ papers, VHS. Field commanded a brigade in what would soon become A. P. Hill's "Light Division," and would later command a division under Longstreet. Warner, *Generals in Gray*, 87-8. Breckinridge was former vice president and presidential candidate in 1860; he served in the Western Theater until 1864, when brought to Virginia as a combat commander and later became the last Confederate secretary of war. Warner, *Generals in Gray*, 34. Hindman was an Arkansas congressman who served with mixed results in the Western and Trans-Mississippi theaters. Ibid., 137-8.

31 OR 51, pt. 2, 539; OR 10, pt. 2, 424-6; OR 3, Series 2, 845; REL to Kirby Smith, April 16, 1862, telegram book, REL HQ papers, VHS. Buckner was adjutant general of Kentucky at the beginning of the war; although third in command behind John B. Floyd and Gideon J. Pillow at Fort Donelson, those two officers had left Buckner to surrender the fort. Warner, *Generals in Gray*, 38.

32 REL to Lovell, April 16, 1862, telegram book, REL HQ papers, VHS; REL to "Lt. Col. Haynes," April 16, 1862, telegram book, REL HQ papers, VHS; Maurice, *Lee's Aide de Camp*, 30. It is possible that Lee met with Joe Johnston who was still in Richmond. Newton, *Johnston and Defense of Richmond*, 116.

33 OR 51, pt. 2, 538-9, 541; OR 11, pt. 3, 446-7; OR 12, pt. 3, 851-2; OR 10, pt. 2, 427-8.

34 REL to Samuel Jones, April 17, 1862, telegram book, REL HQ papers, VHS; REL to John Milton, April 17, 1862, telegram book, REL HQ papers, VHS; Krick, *Staff Officers in Gray*, 297; Freeman, *Lee*, vol. 2, 23, 31; Newton, *Johnston and Defense of Richmond*, 116.

with Humphrey Marshall, and guard the Virginia & Tennessee Railroad. Lee sends similar notice to Marshall, who is instructed to fall back toward Abingdon and link up with Heth. Lee telegraphs Johnston that additional ammunition is being sent to the Peninsula, and requests that Beauregard report on his strength.[35]

April 19, Saturday (Richmond): Lee writes to Field regarding reports that Fredericksburg has been evacuated and also directs him to prevent the enemy from advancing beyond there. Field is also to keep watch for any movements from Urbana or Tappahannock toward West Point. Lee orders Holmes to send the 60th Virginia to Richmond, and Pemberton to send the 1st South Carolina Rifles to Richmond, both of which will be replaced by newly created regiments.[36]

Lee urges North Carolina Adjutant General James G. Martin to have the new regiments at Raleigh be made ready as soon as possible as they are needed in the field to replace older units being sent elsewhere. Lee orders Finegan to send a regiment to Beauregard at Corinth immediately and notifies Beauregard that all available troops in Florida have now been ordered to him. Lee directs Kirby Smith to send several hundred enemy troops captured in Tennessee to Milledgeville, Georgia. He notes that he is "willing to consider all men borne on enemy's rolls as prisoners of war provided men on our rolls are similarly recognized."[37] Lee informs Governor Brown and Gen. Lawton that these prisoners are on the way, and that they are to make necessary arrangements to quarter and feed them. Lee writes to Thomas M. R. Talcott, son of Andrew Talcott, regarding a position on Lee's staff. He informs Armistead Long that he has requested his promotion and appointment as Lee's military secretary.[38]

April 20, Sunday (Richmond): Lee learns in the morning from Huger of the engagement at South Mills, North Carolina. He instructs Huger not to send a large force but only a "corps of observation" to that point to see if it is a precursor to a larger movement against Norfolk from Roanoke Island. Lee telegraphs Holmes informing him of the enemy presence at Elizabeth City; if they are part of the force at New Bern, Holmes is to detach a portion of his force to go to Huger. Lee also addresses what he views as Holmes's injudicious distribution of the limited numbers of Enfield rifles—in order to get them in the hands of his best troops he will have to take them from some troops and reissue pikes. Holmes is also to send the 60th Virginia north as previously directed; Lee assures him that he is not being singled out, as other departments are also being weakened for the defense of Richmond. Lee orders Pemberton to send a brigade from South Carolina to the capital. He visits with daughter Mary, who is not well.[39]

April 21, Monday (Richmond): Lee's staff is reorganized commensurate with his new position. Walter Taylor and Charles Marshall are promoted to major, and Maj. T. M. R. Talcott joins them as aide de camp. Maj. Charles S. Venable is also appointed to Lee's staff as another aide de camp, however he will not actually join the headquarters staff for

---

35 REL to Letcher, April 17, 1862, telegram book, REL HQ papers, VHS; *OR* 12, pt. 3, 853-5; *OR* 10, pt. 2, 428; REL to J. E. Johnston, April 17, 1862, telegram book, REL HQ papers, VHS; REL to Beauregard, April 17, 1862, REL CSR. Johnston's assumption of command on the Peninsula allowed Lee to focus more of his attention on the Shenandoah Valley.

36 *OR* 12, pt. 1, 433; *OR* 12, pt. 3, 855-6; REL to T. H. Holmes, April 19, 1862, telegram book, REL HQ papers, VHS; REL to J. C. Pemberton, April 19, 1862, telegram book, REL HQ papers, VHS.

37 *OR* 9, 459; REL to J. E. Finegan, April 19, 1862, telegram book, REL HQ papers, VHS; REL to Beauregard, April 19, 1862, telegram book, REL HQ papers, VHS; REL to Kirby Smith, April 19, 1862, telegram book, REL HQ papers, VHS.

38 REL to Joseph Brown, April 19, 1862, telegram book, REL HQ papers, VHS; REL to A. R. Lawton, April 19, 1862, telegram book, REL HQ papers, VHS; REL to T. M. R. Talcott, April 19, 1862, Talcott papers, VHS; Long, *Memoirs of REL*, 5.

39 *OR* 9, 331; REL to T. H. Holmes, April 20, 1862, telegram book, REL HQ papers, VHS; *OR* 9, 461-2; *OR* 14, 480; Dowdey, *Wartime Papers*, 153.

several weeks. Thornton Washington leaves the staff, having been promoted and assigned to quartermaster duty in Texas.[40]

Lee writes to Stonewall Jackson advising of the capture of Falmouth and probable fall of Fredericksburg; if he can join forces with Ewell's division and attack Union Gen. Nathaniel Banks in the Valley it would "prove a great relief" to Johnston and Field but if he does not intend to join with Ewell then Ewell's forces will likely be moved to join with Field or to Richmond. Lee sends a similar message to Ewell, strongly hinting at a move against Banks. Lee advises Field that reinforcements from the Deep South are en route and that he should keep his force as close to the enemy as possible. Lee clarifies for Humphrey Marshall the process of enlisting militia, and instructs Holmes to send along the 60th Virginia and also for Pemberton to send a brigade from Charleston.[41]

He informs Finegan that all available weapons have been sent to Beauregard at Corinth; his new Florida units will have to wait until the next shipment arrives through the blockade. Lee notifies Florida Governor Milton that over-age substitutes can be accepted into the service, and defines for him the geographic limits of Beauregard's command. Lee advises Governor Brown and Lawton that the POWs previously ordered to Milledgeville cannot be handled there, so to stop them at Atlanta.[42] Lee explains to several members of the Charleston city council why troops are being taken from there to defend Richmond. Lee forwards to Secretary Randolph a request from the 11th Mississippi to transfer to their native state; Lee recommends it be denied as that regiment is currently on the Peninsula in front of the enemy. Lee notifies Johnston that the enemy is pressing Field at Fredericksburg and if possible he should reinforce Field. He also provides Johnston with the latest intelligence on the naval situation on the lower James River.[43]

April 22, Tuesday (Richmond): Lee concurs in Holmes's opinion that the Federals are not going to advance from New Bern, thus Lee wants additional troops transferred from North Carolina to Field. He acknowledges receipt of Huger's preliminary report on the engagement at South Mills and advises that wounded prisoners may be released on parole. He orders Gorgas to send additional heavy artillery to Drewry's Bluff and Mulberry Island, as well as to Beauregard at Corinth. Lee orders Pemberton to transfer Brig. Gen. Maxcy Gregg's brigade to Richmond, upon Governor Pickens's recommendation, and notifies Pickens that Gregg will be sent.[44]

Lee instructs Sam Jones to send heavy artillery from Mobile to Lovell at New Orleans to free up the ironclads there, and advises Lovell that it will be sent but that there are no small arms available to send him. He receives a letter from Mary in the morning and writes back in the evening, passing along latest news of Mary and of Rob. He recommends again

---

[40] Krick, *Staff Officers in Gray*, 214, 279, 283, 292-3; C. S. Venable CSR; T. A. Washington CSR. Venable at this time was serving on the staff of Maj. Gen. Martin L. Smith at Vicksburg; through a miscarriage of orders, he remained there until June. Venable CSR.

[41] OR 12, pt. 3, 858-60; OR 10, pt. 2, 432-3; REL to T. H. Holmes, April 21, 1862, telegram book, REL HQ papers, VHS; OR 11, pt. 3, 453-5. Freeman referred to Lee's message to Jackson as "one of his most historic of all his military dispatches." Freeman, *Lee*, vol. 2, 36-7.

[42] REL to J. E. Finegan, April 21, 1862, telegram book, REL HQ papers, VHS; REL to John Milton, April 21, 1862, telegram book, REL HQ papers, VHS; REL to J. E. Brown, April 21, 1862, telegram book, REL HQ papers, VHS; REL to A. R. Lawton, April 21, 1862, telegram book, REL HQ papers, VHS.

[43] REL to "Messrs Barnwell & Orr," April 21, 1862, telegram book, REL HQ papers, VHS; REL to G. W. Randolph, April 21, 1862, telegram book, REL HQ papers, VHS; REL to J. E. Johnston, April 21, 1862, telegram book, REL HQ papers, VHS.

[44] OR 9, 331, 462; OR 11, pt. 3, 455; REL to J. C. Pemberton, April 22, 1862, telegram book, REL HQ papers, VHS; REL to Francis Pickens, April 22, 1862, telegram book, REL HQ papers, VHS. Gregg was colonel of the 1st SC until his promotion to brigade command; he served in A. P. Hill's Light Division until his mortal wounding at Fredericksburg. Warner, *Generals in Gray*, 119-20.

that she leave White House, as it will likely soon be behind Union lines; he suggests she go somewhere in the Carolinas or Georgia.[45]

April 23, Wednesday (Richmond): Lee meets with Henry Wise, who is still lobbying to regain command of the Wise Legion. Lee informs Field that is very likely only a small force in his front, but that reinforcements are being sent to Fredericksburg; it is crucial that Field complete the obstruction of the Rappahannock. Lee tells Johnston that the Federals have not yet crossed the Rappahannock but are likely to once they realize the weakness of Field's force opposing them. He provides the latest news regarding Jackson, mentions the fight at South Mills and that the bridges over the Chickahominy will be repaired. Lee informs Sam French, now in command at Wilmington, that all available arms have been sent to Holmes already; if necessary French is to re-arm his heavy artillery units with pikes and redistribute their rifles to his front-line infantry. Lee complains to Edward Johnson about civilians passing through the lines sharing military information.[46]

Lee instructs Lovell to gather what information he can about Brig. Gen. Henry H. Sibley's campaign in New Mexico. Lee informs Lawton that the Union prisoners from Tennessee have arrived in Atlanta, but the quartermaster there has nothing for them; Lawton is to see to their needs. Lee answers complaints to Governor Letcher about civilians being detained when coming into Virginia—Lee has issued orders for all commanders "on the frontier" to closely examine all those coming into the state from the North and detain those they deem necessary.[47]

April 24, Thursday (Richmond): Lee meets again with Henry Wise, who is not pleased with the command given him by the War Department. Lee informs James Martin in Raleigh that North Carolina will need to provide more troops than their original quota called for; however, there are no arms for them in Richmond. Lee orders Lovell to give all aid he can to the removal of the funds from the New Orleans banks, and explains to Pemberton that privately-owned blockade runners are free to carry any cargo they desire. Lee favorably endorses a request from Brig. Gen. William Mahone to have Lee's former military secretary Francis W. Smith commissioned in the artillery.[48]

April 25, Friday (Richmond): Lee writes to both Jackson and Ewell again urging a combined move by the two of them against Banks to relieve pressure elsewhere, and that if not possible then Ewell is to join with Field. Lee instructs Joseph R. Anderson to move his brigade to Fredericksburg and take command of all forces there from Field, and to place obstructions in the Rappahannock. Lee writes to Holmes regarding poor behavior by the 2nd North Carolina Cavalry in a skirmish on the 13th: Holmes and Brig. Gen. Robert Ransom both want the officers stripped of their rank and the men sentenced to hard labor; Lee does not concur in this, preferring instead courts martial to determine individual culpability and breaking up the offending companies, while subjecting all to increased drill and discipline. Lee warns Beauregard that the New York *Herald* recently printed a coded letter from

---

45 OR 6, 881-2; Dowdey, *Wartime Papers*, 153-4.

46 OR 51, pt. 2, 544-6; OR 12, pt. 3, 864-5; OR 11, pt. 3, 458-9; OR 9, 463.

47 REL to Lovell, April 23, 1862, telegram book, REL HQ papers, VHS; REL to A. R. Lawton, April 23, 1862, telegram book, REL HQ papers, VHS; REL to Letcher, April 23, 1862, telegram book, REL HQ papers, VHS. Sibley launched an invasion of New Mexico Territory in early March; he was soundly defeated at Glorietta Pass on March 28, and retreated back to Texas with the remnants of his force. Long, *CW Day by Day*, 189-90.

48 OR 51, pt. 2, 543-6; REL to Lovell, April 24, 1862, telegram book, REL HQ papers, VHS; REL to J. C. Pemberton, April 24, 1862, telegram book, REL HQ papers, VHS; REL to G. W. Randolph, April 24, 1862, telegram book, REL HQ papers, VHS. Smith briefly served as major of the 41st VA, but was not re-elected at the regiment's reorganization; he was then serving as an aide on Mahone's staff but without a permanent command assignment. Sometime around the 20th Lee met with Randolph to try to get Smith an appointment of some sort. WHT to F. W. Smith, April 26, 1862, F. W. Smith papers, VHS.

Beauregard to Cooper and thus he should change his cipher.[49]

Lee tries to soothe over Governor Milton's hurt feelings at not having his recommendation for commander in Florida followed; Lee hopes that Milton and Finegan can work together. Lee informs Sam Jones that he is needed with Beauregard immediately, so get Forney there to relieve him without delay. Lee authorizes Humphrey Marshall to visit Richmond. Rain throughout the day.[50]

April 26, Saturday (Richmond): Lee informs Holmes that a shipment of arms was just received at Wilmington, a portion of which is for his use; once they are distributed this will allow another brigade to be sent to Fredericksburg. He requests Gorgas to send an ordnance officer to Wilmington to distribute this shipment of arms. Lee informs Beauregard that Sam Jones has been ordered to report to him immediately.[51]

He instructs Finegan to assist with the unloading of a recently arrived blockade runner. He informs Johnston that heavy artillery has been sent to him from Richmond, and again instructs Field to place obstructions in Rappahannock. Lee congratulates John Maffitt on his recent blockade running successes, and asks Pemberton and Georgia Governor Brown the number of unarmed troops in South Carolina and Georgia.[52]

He orders Holmes to transfer the Cobb Legion cavalry to Fredericksburg. Lee relays to Field the concerns of F. V. Daniel, president of the Richmond, Fredericksburg & Potomac Railroad, about adequately picketing the railroad to prevent damage or capture of trains. Lee tells Charles S. Venable that he would like to have him as an aide on his staff; the nomination has already been submitted and approved, thus the decision is Venable's.[53]

Lee receives a letter from daughter Agnes in the morning; he writes back to her in the evening with latest family news, glad that she and Charlotte have gone to Hickory Hill. He writes also to Charlotte, with much the same news as to Agnes, but also includes latest military news from New Orleans, which he expects to fall very soon. Steady rain since yesterday.[54]

April 27, Sunday (Richmond): Lee writes to Gen. Ewell, clarifying his message of the 25th regarding Ewell joining either Gen. Jackson or Gen. Field. He instructs Sam Jones to remove everything not necessary for defense of Pensacola and prepare to concentrate his force at Mobile, sending any extra heavy artillery to Finegan, and instructs Lovell to gather all forces he can for the defense of New Orleans. Lee informs Henry Heth that he thinks the Federals have abandoned most of western Virginia; Heth is to investigate this and report to Lee the situation.[55]

April 28, Monday (Richmond): Lee meets with President Davis, Commissary General Lucius B.

---

[49] *OR* 12, pt. 3, 865-7; *OR* 9, 303; *OR* 10, pt. 2, 439-40.

[50] *OR* 14, 483; REL to Samuel Jones, April 25, 1862, telegram book, REL HQ papers, VHS; REL to Humphrey Marshall, April 25, 1862, telegram book, REL HQ papers, VHS; REL to Mary Triplett, April 26, 1862, Lee papers, SH.

[51] *OR* 9, 464-5; *OR* 51, pt. 2, 547; *OR* 10, pt. 2, 450.

[52] REL to J. E. Finegan, April 26, 1862, telegram book, REL HQ papers, VHS; REL to J. E. Johnston, April 26, 1862, telegram book, REL HQ papers, VHS; REL to C. W. Field, April 26, 1862, telegram book, REL HQ papers, VHS; REL to J. N. Maffitt, April 26, 1862, telegram book, REL HQ papers, VHS; REL to J. C. Pemberton, April 26, 1862, telegram book, REL HQ papers, VHS; REL to Joseph Brown, April 26, 1862, telegram book, REL HQ papers, VHS.

[53] REL to T. H. Holmes, April 26, 1862, telegram book, REL HQ papers, VHS; F. V. Daniel to REL, April 25, 1862, telegram book, REL HQ papers, VHS; *Memoir of Margaret Cantey McDowell Venable*, McDowell-Miller-Warner papers, UVA.

[54] Dowdey, *Wartime Papers*, 158; REL to Charlotte, April 26, 1862, G. B. Lee papers, VHS; Charleston *Mercury*, April 29, 1862.

[55] *OR* 12, vol. 3, 869; *OR* 6, 884; REL to Mansfield Lovell, April 27, 1862, telegram book, REL HQ papers, VHS; *OR* 12, pt. 3, 869-70.

Northrop, and Johnston's commissary Lt. Col. Archibald Cole concerning rations for Johnston's army; he follows up with a letter to Northrop that additional forces have been sent to Fredericksburg so the supplies going there must be increased in addition to those for the Peninsula. Lee writes to Holmes overruling his objections to weakening the forces in North Carolina; Lee reiterates that the loss of the brigade ordered to Fredericksburg will be offset by the new troops from Raleigh who are to be armed with the weapons just received at Wilmington. Lee telegraphs Johnston an updated report on the heavy artillery and ammunition being sent him. He also asks Johnston if Longstreet can be spared from his army to command the troops at Fredericksburg, or if not him who can Johnston send there?[56]

Lee informs Joseph Anderson, who has succeeded Field on the Rappahannock, that Maxcy Gregg's brigade is being sent him from South Carolina. Lee informs Governor Milton that more troops are still needed at Pensacola. Lee writes to Frances Cazenove Minor regarding a staff appointment for her husband, Charles Landon Carter Minor. Col. Long and Maj. Talcott are formally assigned to Lee's staff.[57]

April 29, Tuesday (Richmond): Lee informs Jackson that he has no troops to send to the Valley beyond Ewell's Division and Edward Johnson's force west of Staunton. He cautions that it may be necessary to send a portion of Ewell's force, and possibly Ewell himself, to Fredericksburg. Lee informs Gorgas that Johnston does not need any additional heavy guns or ammunition at Yorktown, and notifies Huger that he received his report of South Mills, but the only reinforcements available to help at Suffolk are local militia.[58]

Lee informs Pemberton that he would like the Virginia units serving in South Carolina sent back to Virginia, and that several thousand firearms are en route to him. Lee explains to Heth that the latter misunderstood his instructions—he was merely to protect the Virginia & Tennessee Railroad, not fall back to it. Lee informs Finegan that he has no arms to send to Florida at present, that if Finegan has unarmed troops he must collect private weapons to arm them.[59]

Lee informs Kirby Smith and Governors Joe Brown of Georgia and John G. Shorter of Alabama that weapons are being sent them, and also tells Gov. Brown that troops at Chattanooga will tend to the safety of the Western & Atlantic Railroad.[60]

April 30, Wednesday (Richmond): Lee informs Huger that the enemy movements near Elizabeth City are likely feints, and that if Johnston's army is forced to give up the lower Peninsula the Federals will then have control of the James, necessitating the evacuation of Norfolk. Lee informs Holmes that there are no indications of an advance against Goldsboro, so Holmes's current force is more than adequate to hold that region. Accordingly he is to send Ransom's Brigade to Fredericksburg as previously instructed, and not to send the raw recruits from Raleigh—these are to take Ransom's place; Johnston Pettigrew cannot be spared to command this new brigade, so the only options to command it are Henry Wise or Roger Pryor.

---

56 *OR* 51, pt. 2, 674; *OR* 12, pt. 3, 871; *OR* 9, 467; REL to J. E. Johnston, April 28, 1862, (2 messages), telegram book, REL HQ papers, VHS.

57 REL to J. R. Anderson, April 28, 1862, telegram book, REL HQ papers, VHS; REL to John Milton, April 28, 1862, telegram book, REL HQ papers, VHS; REL to Frances Cazenove Minor, April 28, 1862, Cazenove papers, VHS; *OR* 51, pt. 2, 548. Minor served in the 2nd VA Cavalry; he eventually was assigned as ordnance officer to Brig. Gen. Albert G. Jenkins and Samuel Jones, before being assigned to the Richmond Arsenal. Krick, *Staff Officers in Gray*, 222.

58 Dowdey, *Wartime Papers*, 160-1; *OR* 11, pt. 3, 475; *OR* 9, 332.

59 REL to J. C. Pemberton, April 29, 1862, REL papers, MOC; WHT to J. C. Pemberton, April 29, 1862, REL papers, MOC; *OR* 12, pt. 3, 873-5; *OR* 14, 484-5.

60 REL to Kirby Smith, (2 messages), April 29, 1862, telegram book, REL HQ papers, VHS; REL to Joseph Brown, April 29, 1862, telegram book, REL HQ papers, VHS; REL to J. G. Shorter, April 29, 1862, telegram book, REL HQ papers, VHS; REL to Joseph Brown, April 29, 1862, REL papers, UGA.

Lee informs Johnston of his and Secretary Mallory's desire to have the CSS *Virginia* make a nighttime sortie into the York. He writes to Jackson that nothing from Fredericksburg can be sent him, so his only sources of reinforcement are Ewell and Ed Johnson. Lee writes Anderson his belief that the Federals will likely raid the Northern Neck rather than cross the Rappahannock now, but if they do cross the river it will be at Port Royal rather than Fredericksburg. Lee informs Pemberton that President Davis will declare martial law at Charleston. Rain.[61]

---

61 *OR* 11, pt. 3, 476-7; *OR* 9, 467-8; *OR* 12, pt. 3, 875-6; REL to J. C. Pemberton, April 30, 1862, telegram book, REL HQ papers, VHS; Charleston *Mercury*, May 3, 1862. Commodore Josiah Tattnall, who previously commanded the small fleet at Savannah alongside Lee, now commanded the James River fleet. Circumstances around Hampton and Norfolk called for inter-service cooperation, but Tattnall was extremely touchy regarding his ships. Tattnall wrote to Navy Sec. Mallory on the 29th: "These are times, Mr. Mallory, for frankness, and without it discord between the two arms, produced by misconception, may be fatal. If, therefore, I am to be placed under the command of an army officer, and, being a seaman, and am to hold my action and reputation subject to the judgment of a landsman, who can know nothing of the complicated nature of naval service, I earnestly solicit to be promptly relieved from my command." Jones, *Life and Services of Josiah Tattnall*, 169. Tattnall also pointed out to Mallory that he had received intelligence that the Federals were expecting the *Virginia* to make a move into the York and had placed obstructions and guns to prevent such a move. Ibid., 172.

May 1862

The defensive effort on the eastern end of the Virginia Peninsula, first by Maj. Gen. John B. Magruder and then Gen. Joseph E. Johnston, bought precious time the Confederates desperately needed to gather troops and resources against Union Maj. Gen. George B. McClellan's Army of the Potomac. By the beginning of May, that time was running out.

McClellan stopped his advance when he came up against Magruder's entrenchments—even though he enjoyed a heavy advantage in numbers and probably could have broken through before Johnston arrived with reinforcements—and began siege operations to overcome the Confederates deployed across his front. No one, including Robert E. Lee, expected the combined forces of Johnston and Magruder would be able to withstand a siege at Yorktown and along the Warwick River line. Johnston asked Maj. Gen. Daniel H. Hill, who commanded the Yorktown sector, how long Hill expected he could hold his position once McClellan's heavy guns began pounding his front. Hill's answer—"about two days"—prompted Johnston to reply that he "had supposed about two hours."[1]

Johnston evacuated the Warwick and Yorktown lines on the night of May 3. Heavy rains impeded his westward march and he was forced to fight a rear guard action at Williamsburg on the 5th. As Johnston retreated, President Jefferson Davis, Secretary of War George Randolph, Secretary of the Navy Stephen Mallory, and Robert E. Lee scrambled to figure out how to save what they could from Norfolk. Johnston's retreat was not unexpected, but it came sooner than Richmond expected—and without much advance notice, either. They worried that not only would they lose the stockpiles of ordnance and other supplies housed at Norfolk and Portsmouth, but that the troops and artillery stationed there under Maj. Gen. Benjamin Huger, would be cut off and captured. Richmond's justified concern for the safety of Huger's troops led to a series of unpleasant exchanges between Lee and Johnston; the former had a much better overall grasp on the situation than did the latter, and issued orders to ensure that Huger's line of retreat remained open—orders that contradicted those issued by Johnston and drove him into a fit of ill-humor directed at Lee and Lee's aide Walter Taylor.

The evacuation of Norfolk and the defenses along the lower James River, coupled with the loss of the CSS *Virginia*, which was too heavy to clear the sand bars and make it up the James to Richmond, opened the river to the Federal Navy almost all the way to the capital. For several days the city was in a near panic, its populace expecting Union gunboats to shell Richmond at any moment. Lee and others hastened to complete obstructions and fortifications at Drewry's Bluff several miles downstream from Richmond. On May 15, the Union flotilla appeared there and was turned back by heavy artillery fire. Lee and the president were on scene as the guns fell silent.

As the Army of the Potomac drew closer to Richmond, first Romancoke and then White House came within the Union lines. Mary Lee and the girls left White House before the Federals arrived, but not without leaving a note on the door for the Yankees. They did not make it far before being discovered by Union patrols and placed under house arrest. At the same time, White House became

---

1 Stephen Sears, *To the Gates of Richmond: The Peninsula Campaign* (New York, 1992), 59.

the main base of supply for McClellan's army. McClellan personally ordered guards posted to protect the property.[2]

The victory at Drewry's Bluff saved Richmond in the short term, but McClellan's army to the east posed a serious threat. Johnston showed no signs of offering serious battle short of the shadows of the capital. Worse yet, he had not offered any plans to Davis, Randolph, or Lee. The men working in the Executive Mansion didn't appreciate Johnston's silence, and President Davis relayed his frustration to Lee, who tried to extract from his old friend any sort of plan of action he could then present to Davis on his behalf. Johnston stubbornly kept his own council.

Lee believed an offensive elsewhere in Virginia would draw off McClellan. In order to take advantage of President Lincoln's fears for the safety of his own capital, Lee urged Thomas "Stonewall" Jackson to gather the forces of Maj. Gen. Richard S. Ewell and Brig. Gen. Edward Johnson and strike the enemy in the Shenandoah Valley. And strike Jackson did at McDowell, Front Royal, and Winchester, a sweeping campaign that carried his small army all the way to the Potomac itself. Jackson's campaign convinced Lincoln to call off Maj. Gen. Irvin McDowell's column that was moving south from Fredericksburg to link up with McClellan's army outside Richmond. McClellan would later claim that McDowell's recall crippled his own campaign against Richmond.

McClellan made a major error when he straddled his army across the Chickahominy River. Several bridges crossed the swampy watercourse, but heavy rains in late May raised the river above flood stage and threatened to sever the two Federal wings. The weather gave Johnston an opportunity and he finally revealed to Lee that he intended to strike McClellan's right flank near Mechanicsville on May 29. Davis and Lee both ventured into the field to observe the battle, but the advance and attack failed to materialize. Johnston had called off the attack when he learned that McDowell had turned back toward Fredericksburg and no longer threatened his left flank. He failed to inform Davis or Lee, and—if Davis is to be believed—any of the commanders involved.[3]

On May 31, however, Johnston finally attacked on the other flank and the effort went horribly awry from the start. The offensive was hours behind schedule, a large portion of the attacking column took the wrong road, and other commands never arrived at all. And the fight spun out of control once it finally got underway. Historian Stephen Sears described the Battle of Fair Oaks/Seven Pines as a "comic opera;" Douglas Freeman described it as "a battle of strange errors."[4]

Much to Joe Johnston's chagrin, Lee and Davis were on hand to witness the confused situation. The fighting proved inconclusive, but one aspect of the battle changed the course of the war in Virginia (and arguably the war itself): Johnston was seriously wounded near the end of the first day, leaving the Virginia army without a reliable commander.

* * *

---

2 OR 11, pt. 3, 202-3. Custis warned his mother in early May: "On any day you may be without our lines and within those of the enemy. What is to become of you and the girls God only knows.... How you are to obtain funds when cut off from us, is a question that disturbs me greatly. I would feel much easier if you would all come here [Richmond] and go further south.... You had best move at once, and not linger until the last moment when the roads may be blocked with wagons and troops. Whatever you may determine upon do at once." Custis to Mrs. REL, May 2, 1862, REL papers, Duke.

3 Davis, *Rise and Fall*, vol. 2, 100-1.

4 Sears, *To the Gates of Richmond*, 123; Freeman, *Lee's Lieutenants*, vol. 1, 225.

May 1, Thursday (Richmond): Lee authorizes Jackson to absorb Edward Johnson's command and attack the Federals in the mountains west of Staunton, and then deal with Nathaniel Banks's force in the Shenandoah itself. Lee advises Ewell that the plan he and Jackson have discussed is approved, and that therefore Ewell is to move to the Valley. Lee notifies Johnston that his proposal to advance to the Potomac has been presented to President Davis, but that having Beauregard invade Ohio is not practicable at this time. Lee informs Johnston that the services of one of his engineers and a portion of his labor force is needed for river defense. He adds that the repair of the Chickahominy bridges is very nearly complete, and that government river boats have been placed at his disposal as requested.[5]

Lee informs Theophilus Holmes that a brigade can be sent him if necessary. Lee requests North Carolina Governor Clark to send all available regiments in Raleigh to Holmes and the best efforts will be made to arm them all. Lee continues his attempts to explain to Humphrey Marshall how to enlist militia, and adds that if Marshall desires that martial law be declared in his region, he needs to specify which counties so that the government can proclaim it.[6]

Lee notifies Alabama Governor Shorter and Brig. Gen. Danville Leadbetter of the transfer of two new Alabama regiments to Chattanooga, where they will be armed and equipped. Lee inquires of Beauregard if he has a brigade to which Henry Wise can be assigned.[7]

May 2, Friday (Richmond): Lee informs Sec. Randolph that Johnston intends to withdraw to Williamsburg tonight and has ordered the evacuation of Norfolk and the forts and garrisons along the lower James, and naval vessels will withdraw to Richmond: "This sudden movement may produce haste and involve the loss of material that cannot be replaced unless you can give directions that will save it. By maintaining positions on the water and . . . sending the CSS *Virginia* to Hampton Roads and gunboats to James River . . . much may be secured. Gen. Johnston will be urged to hold positions to gain time." This message prompts Randolph to go to Norfolk. Lee orders Johnston to hold the Yorktown/Warwick River line a bit longer to buy time to evacuate Norfolk, and advises that Randolph has gone there in person to oversee its evacuation. The unfinished gunboats at the navy yard will be moved upriver to Richmond; Lee presses for the *Virginia* to be dispatched to the York River to destroy Union shipping. He orders a company of sappers/miners to Drewry's Bluff to assist in building its fortifications.[8]

Lee informs Humphrey Marshall that men joining already-existing companies are entitled to an enlistment bounty, and then informs Kirby Smith that what few troops are available in North Carolina and Alabama have been ordered to join him. Taylor notifies John Pemberton that he is entitled to two aides, and that Taylor's brother John is interested in a staff position with Pemberton.[9]

May 3, Saturday (Richmond): Lee explains to Gen. Holmes that the evacuation of Norfolk is under consideration in Richmond, and in light of that he

---

5 *OR* 12, pt. 3, 877-8; *OR* 11, pt. 3, 485-6; REL to J. E. Johnston, May 1, 1862 (2 messages), telegram book, REL HQ papers, VHS.

6 REL to T. H. Holmes, May 1, 1862, telegram book, REL HQ papers, VHS; REL to H. T. Clark, May 1, 1862, telegram book, REL HQ papers, VHS; *OR* 10, pt. 2, 479-80.

7 *OR* 10, pt. 2, 479; REL to J. G. Shorter, May 1, 1862, telegram book, REL HQ papers, VHS; REL to Beauregard, May 1, 1862, telegram book, REL HQ papers, VHS. Leadbetter was primarily an engineer officer, but exercised short periods of field command in the Western Theater. Warner, *Generals in Gray*, 176-7.

8 REL to G. W. Randolph, May 2, 1862, telegram book, REL HQ papers, VHS; Dowdey, *Wartime Papers*, 164; *OR* 11, pt. 3, 488; Newton, *Johnston and the Defense of Richmond*, 158.

9 REL to Humphrey Marshall, May 2, 1862, telegram book, REL HQ papers, VHS; *OR* 10, pt. 2, 483; REL to E. Kirby Smith, May 2, 1862, telegram book, REL HQ papers, VHS; WHT to J. C. Pemberton, May 2, 1862, telegram book, REL HQ papers, VHS. John C. Taylor was Walter Taylor's younger brother; he served as an aide to Mahone before joining the 5th VA Cavalry, and joined Pemberton's staff May 10, 1862. Krick, *Staff Officers in Gray*, 282.

should not make a movement toward Wilmington at present, but instead be prepared to strike at Ambrose Burnside, who will likely make a move toward Norfolk upon its evacuation. At the same time Lee acknowledges Holmes's complaints against reducing his force any further, but informs the aging general that the situation in Virginia requires it. Lee promises him to write to North Carolina Governor Clark to free up troops from Raleigh for Holmes's use. Lee denies a request from William W. Loring to have troops that were sent to reinforce Huger returned to him by explaining that the situation "renders reinforcements to Gen. Huger necessary."

Lee informs Johnston that reports have reached the War Department that soldiers from Johnston's army going on sick leave, furlough, etc. are not turning in their weapons before departing and are subsequently being lost. Due to the shortage of weapons this is unacceptable, so an ordnance officer is being sent to rectify this; Johnston is also reminded that per regulations he is to have ordnance officers at regiment, brigade, and division level. Lee informs Joseph Anderson that there are no additional troops to be sent to the Fredericksburg front, and that due to the scarcity of Enfield rifles, they are not to be issued to entire regiments but rather only the flank companies. Lee informs Alexander Dudley, president of the Richmond & York River Railroad, that Dudley will have to communicate directly with Johnston regarding obstructions in the York and the removal of rails from his line.[10]

Lee informs Gen. Pemberton that he cannot send reinforcements to Charleston at present, and that the quartermaster department requires his surplus wagons in Richmond. Lee informs Florida Governor Milton that several thousand small arms have been ordered to Florida, and notifies Henry Heth that Federals are reported advancing toward him, and under the circumstances he can keep the forces currently under his command to oppose them. Lee writes to John B. Floyd advising that contrary to Floyd's belief, Lee has not censured him for granting furloughs to his men.[11]

May 4, Sunday (Richmond): Lee learns of Johnston's withdrawal from Yorktown and the Warwick River line. He instructs Holmes to send a brigade of infantry to Richmond immediately, but to make certain provisions and cooking utensils go with all the troops, and he informs Gen. Jackson that the transportation he requested has been sent.[12]

May 5, Monday (Richmond): Lee orders Johnston to send a battery with infantry support to block ascent of the Pamunkey, as Union gunboats are reported to be at West Point. Lee cautions Huger to secure all boats around Norfolk so as to prevent spies and "traitors" from carrying information across Hampton Roads to the enemy. Lee endorses a proposal from Col. Hill Carter to construct a canal across Dutch Gap—Lee thinks Carter can do it but fears that the James would subsequently dam it back up without constant maintenance.[13]

---

10 OR 9, 469-70; REL to T. H. Holmes, May 3, 1862, telegram book, REL HQ papers, VHS; OR 11, pt. 3, 491-3. The Richmond & York River RR was completed only a month before the war and ran from the capital to West Point, where the Pamunkey and Mattaponi rivers join to form the York. It became McClellan's main supply line during the middle stage of the Peninsula Campaign. Angus J. Johnston, *Virginia Railroads in the Civil War* (Chapel Hill, NC, 1961), 6, 57. After dark Johnston abandoned the Yorktown/Warwick River line and fell back on Williamsburg. Long, *CW Day by Day*, 206.

11 OR 14, 491; OR 53, 242-3; REL to Henry Heth, May 3, 1862, telegram book, REL HQ paper, VHS; REL to J. B. Floyd, May 3, 1862, REL papers, Brock collection.

12 Freeman, *Lee*, vol. 2, 43; REL to T. H. Holmes, May 4, 1862 (2 messages), telegram book, REL HQ papers, VHS; REL to Jackson, May 4, 1862, telegram book, REL HQ papers, VHS.

13 OR 5, 1090; REL to Huger, May 5, telegram book, REL HQ papers, VHS; REL to A. L. Rives, May 5, telegram book, REL HQ papers, VHS. The orders to Johnston regarding a battery on the Pamunkey appear in the ORs twice with different dates, neither of which seems correct. They are dated March 5 in OR 5, 1090, which is obviously wrong for a multitude of reasons; OR 11, pt. 3, 493, has them dated May 3, which seems too early as Johnston still held the works at Yorktown and Gloucester, which would have prevented any passage to West Point. Lee's "3" closely resembled—and could be mistaken for—a "5", and that is likely what happened here. May 5 is the only possible date that makes sense for this order. See Sears, *To the Gates of Richmond*, 67-8, 85, for details of McClellan's plan to land Franklin's division at West

Lee notifies Ewell that Lawrence Branch's brigade has been ordered to him, but Lee wishes it stationed at Gordonsville rather than going with Ewell to Swift Run Gap, so as to have a presence in central Virginia. Lee informs Alexander Lawton that there is no heavy artillery in Richmond that can be sent south to Savannah at that time, but he requests John Forney at Mobile, Alabama, to send any available Columbiads there for Lawton's use.[14]

Lee asks Georgia Governor Brown's approval for the declaration of martial law at Augusta and Savannah. Lee orders Heth to move to Wytheville and take command of all forces there, and orders Col. Gabriel Wharton to take the 50th and 51st Virginia to Wytheville to join Heth. Lee informs Capt. Woodville G. Latham that he cannot transfer Latham's battery to Virginia as Pemberton needs them in South Carolina at present.[15]

May 6, Tuesday (Richmond): Lee urges completion of the obstructions in the James and the removal of the heavy guns from Norfolk to Richmond while using the CSS *Virginia* to guard the mouth of James as long as possible. He advises Jackson that the Federal evacuation of Harrisonburg may indicate a concentration at Fredericksburg. Lee notifies Ewell that if the Yankees withdraw from the upper Valley there is no reason for him to remain at Conrad's Store.[16]

Lee orders a company of infantry to the York River Railroad to assist in removing valuable supplies and blocking the river, and instructs Gen. Kirby Smith to ensure that public stores passing through Knoxville, Tennessee, are forwarded to their destination. Lee orders Gen. Pemberton to reunite the various sections of the Staunton Hill Artillery at Goldsboro so that it can hold elections for its officers.[17]

Lee orders a court of inquiry to investigate Stonewall Jackson's charges against Brig. Gen. Richard Garnett. Rain in the morning.[18]

Point to intercept Johnston's retreat. Lee's advice to Huger was spot on; it was a Northern tug boat captain who on May 8 carried to the Federals at Fort Monroe the details of Norfolk's pending evacuation. Ibid., 90. The idea of a canal at Dutch Gap to cut-off a loop of the James was not new. It was first tried soon after the settlement of the region in 1611. Union forces under Maj. Gen. Benjamin Butler attempted it again in August 1864; it was not completed and made passable until after the war. Louis H. Manarin and Clifford Dowdey, *The History of Henrico County* (Charlottesville, VA, 1984), 298, 309.

14 OR 12, pt. 3, 880-1; REL to A. R. Lawton, May 5, telegram book, REL HQ papers, VHS; REL to J. H. Forney, May 5, telegram book, REL HQ papers, VHS.

15 REL to Joseph Brown, May 5, telegram book, REL HQ papers, VHS; REL to Henry Heth, May 5, telegram book, REL HQ papers, VHS; REL to G. C. Wharton, May 5, telegram book, REL HQ papers, VHS; REL to W. G. Latham, May 5, 1862, REL papers, MOC. The mayor of Augusta requested martial law for his city and Pemberton wanted it declared in Savannah. Wharton was major of the 45th VA briefly before being appointed colonel of the 51st VA; he became brigadier general in July 1863, spending nearly the entire war in western Virginia. Warner, *Generals in Gray*, 331. Latham commanded the Nelson Light Artillery. Latham CSR. Lt. Charles S. Venable, serving on the staff of Maj. Gen. Martin L. Smith, learned of his appointment to Lee's staff on this date: "On the day of our arrival at Vicksburg, the 5th of May, I received a letter from General R.E. Lee offering me a position on his staff as one of the four aide-de-camps assigned to him as general in chief of the Confederate armies. Although this was a promotion to the rank of major, General Smith said it would not be etiquette for me to leave the post of Vicksburg where the city was threatened with an attack to accept a position in Richmond so I remained until June 15th." Charles S. Venable, *Personal Reminiscences of the Confederate War*, McDowell-Miller-Warner papers, UVA.

16 Freeman, *Lee*, vol. 2, 44; REL to Jackson, May 6, 1862, telegram book, REL HQ papers, VHS; OR 12, pt. 3, 881. Conrad's Store is modern Elkton.

17 REL to Alexander Dudley, May 6, 1862, telegram book, REL HQ papers, VHS; REL to Capt. J. C. Hawood, May 6, 1862, telegram book, REL HQ papers, VHS; REL to E. Kirby Smith, May 6, 1862, telegram book, REL HQ papers, VHS; REL to J. C. Pemberton, May 6, 1862, REL papers, MOC.

18 Freeman, *Lee's Lieutenants*, vol. 2, 7-8; *OR Supplement*, part 3, vol. 2, 269-70; REL to Samuel Cooper, May 6, 1862, telegram book, REL HQ papers, VHS; Krick, *CW Weather*, 58. Jackson's charges against Garnett stemmed from the Battle of Kernstown, March 23, 1862; Garnett was Jackson's successor in command of the Stonewall Brigade and Garnett ordered the unit to retreat at Kernstown without Jackson's approval. Lee wrote, "It [is] necessary as an act of justice to Gen. Garnett and the service to bring it to trial." REL to Cooper, May 6, 1862, telegram book, REL HQ papers, VHS.

May 7, Wednesday (Richmond): Lee sends evacuation instructions to Huger, including returning a portion of Holmes's force to guard Weldon. Huger is to remove as much of the heavy artillery as possible and then send his troops along the Norfolk & Petersburg Railroad to its western terminus; Huger himself is to report in person at Richmond. Lee notifies Holmes that Huger has been instructed to send a portion of the troops he received from Holmes and that Lee wishes them deployed at Weldon to guard the railroad bridge there. William Loring is instructed to hold Suffolk until all of Huger's force passes through that point.[19]

Lee sends instructions to Johnston regarding not just the retreat of his army but also Huger's and Loring's forces; Lee however is called out of the office before signing this order, so it is completed and signed by Maj. Taylor. Lee orders the destruction of all rolling stock and bridges on the York River Railroad below White House. Lee orders Brig. Gen. William Mahone's brigade to Gordonsville to join Ewell, and forwards to Sec. Randolph complaints of insubordination against Col. Turner Ashby's cavalry.[20]

Lee assigns Henry Wise to command of a Virginia brigade, including part of the Wise Legion, and mentions that Beauregard has a brigade for Wise in Mississippi but Lee would rather keep the former governor in Virginia. Lee informs Mansfield Lovell that there are no weapons in Richmond, thus Lovell will have to arm the 3rd Mississippi himself. Lee inquires of Pemberton if city officials in Savannah desire martial law.[21]

May 8, Thursday (Richmond): Lee sends more detailed withdrawal instructions to Huger to move his forces to Richmond via the Norfolk & Petersburg Railroad, and that the CSS *Virginia* should be stationed at the mouth of the James rather than in the Elizabeth off Craney Island so as to protect the garrisons farther up the James. Lee later relays to Huger a request from Navy Sec. Mallory that Huger delay his retreat as long as possible to allow for the removal of as much of the Navy's materiel as possible.

Lee sends a long letter to Johnston about why the orders of yesterday regarding the withdrawal were issued and why they were signed by Maj. Taylor. Lee reassures Johnston that Johnston has command on both sides of the James as well as northern Virginia. Lee requests that Johnston send engineer Maj. Walter H. Stevens to Richmond if possible, and sends his congratulations for the victory at Eltham's Landing.[22]

Lee orders the quartermaster at White House landing to place obstructions and sink all empty vessels in the Pamunkey to prevent Union vessels from reaching the railroad bridge near White House. Lee writes to Jackson and Ewell that Nathaniel Banks's Federals appear to be withdrawing from the

---

19 OR 11, pt. 3, 497; REL to Huger, May 7, 1862, telegram book, REL HQ papers, VHS; OR 9, 470; REL to W. W. Loring, May 7, 1862, telegram book, REL HQ papers, VHS.

20 Freeman, *Lee's Lieutenants*, vol. 1, 204-5; REL to Capt. R. P. Archer, May 7, 1862, telegram book, REL HQ papers, VHS; OR 12, pt. 3, 880, 883. The order to Johnston signed by Taylor had considerable unintended consequences, for Johnston took offense at having his authority questioned and his orders to Loring and Huger overturned by Maj. Walter Taylor. Freeman wrote that receipt of this set of orders bearing Taylor's signature "if it did not enrage General Johnston, ruffled him" and prompted Johnston to fire off a testy letter to Lee that did little to further Johnston's relations with President Davis and caused Lee to waste valuable time in convincing Johnston that no offense was intended and his authority not questioned, that Lee simply wanted to ensure that Huger's force was not cut off by early withdrawal of Loring from Suffolk. See Freeman, *Lee's Lieutenants*, vol. 1, 204-5, for details of this exchange.

21 OR 51, pt. 2, 553; REL to Mansfield Lovell, May 7, 1862, telegram book, REL HQ papers, VHS; REL to L. A. Millan, May 7, 1862, telegram book, REL HQ papers, VHS; REL to J. C. Pemberton, May 7, 1862, telegram book, REL HQ papers, VHS. It is curious that Lee did not avail himself of this opportunity to be rid of Wise.

22 OR 11, pt. 3, 499-501; REL to Huger, May 8, 1862, telegram book, REL HQ papers, VHS. John B. Hood's brigade defeated elements of William Franklin's division which landed at Eltham's Landing, opposite West Point, and threatened Johnston's line of retreat on May 7. Long, *CW Day by Day*, 208. Walter Husted Stevens was a very gifted army engineer; he was chief engineer of Johnston's army and Lee later put him in charge of the Richmond defenses. He was promoted to brigadier general in August 1864 and made chief engineer of the ANV. Warner, *Generals in Gray*, 292.

Valley and heading to Fredericksburg; Lee would like them, if possible, to strike Banks on the move. He adds that the brigades of William Mahone and Lawrence Branch have been ordered to join Gen. Ewell at Gordonsville. Lee explains to North Carolina adjutant general James Martin that Confederate law prohibits the acceptance of any state units larger than a regiment, and so he cannot accept the offer of a division of North Carolina state troops with Martin in command. In addition, Lee explains that he could not guarantee that the state command would be kept intact, and President Davis did not desire the appointment of any additional major generals at that time.[23]

Lee notifies Joseph Anderson that Spanish diplomat Louis de Podestad will be passing through the lines on his way to Washington. Lee acknowledges receipt of Gen. Lovell's preliminary report on the fall of New Orleans, telling him, "The loss of this city is a very severe blow to us, and one that we cannot fail to feel most sensibly, but it is believed that with the means of defense at your disposal you have done all in your power." Lee advises Brig. Gen. Albert Pike that reinforcements are being sent from Louisiana to Little Rock, Arkansas, for his use. Rain in the evening.[24]

May 9, Friday (Richmond): Lee writes to Johnston advising of Jackson's victory at McDowell yesterday and mentions that Union warships attacked Sewell's Point and attempted to ascend the James but the emergence of the CSS *Virginia* turned them back. Lee writes to Huger approving of his evacuation plans and suggests Petersburg as a rendezvous point for all of Huger's scattered commands, adding that Huger is to remain in close communication with Holmes regarding the troops in North Carolina.[25]

Lee directs that if York River Railroad officials will pledge to destroy the Pamunkey bridge themselves then the army will trust them to do so. Lee explains to Loring, who yesterday was appointed to command in southwest Virginia, his role there and not to "interfere" with Humphrey Marshall's plans to invade Kentucky. Lee inquires again of Pemberton if city officials in Savannah request martial law.[26]

May 10, Saturday (Richmond/Drewry's Bluff): Lee goes to Drewry's Bluff to see the progress on the fortifications and river obstructions there, and writes to Johnston with an update on Drewry's Bluff and advising that a commander is needed for the "Army of the Rappahannock," which is currently under its senior brigadier, Joseph Anderson. President Davis would like either James Longstreet or Gustavus W. Smith from Johnston's army assigned to command on the Rappahannock River so that force may undertake offensive operations. Lee asks Johnston if he would like several field artillery batteries forwarded to him, or if they should be kept back in Richmond. Maj. Taylor sends a letter to Johnston that 14 Union ships had just been sighted on the James River at City Point; Taylor adds, "the General is absent, and I send you the above unofficially,

---

23 REL to Charles S. Carrington, May 8, 1862 (2 messages), telegram book, REL HQ papers, VHS; *OR* 12, pt. 3, 883-5; *OR* 9, 471.

24 REL to J. R. Anderson, May 8, 1862, REL papers, MOC; *OR* 6, 652; *OR* 13, 824; Krick, *CW Weather*, 58. Albert Pike was a man of many talents, but his Civil War career was rather dismal and included a poor showing by his command of American Indians at Pea Ridge. Pike was charged by a fellow general with mishandling money and supplies, and, facing arrest, fled into the hills of Arkansas. His resignation was accepted on July 12, 1862, and he played little or no further role in the war. Warner, *Generals in Gray*, 240.

25 *OR* 51, pt. 2, 553-4; *OR* 11, pt. 3, 502; REL to Huger, May 9, 1862, telegram book, REL HQ papers, VHS. Jackson defeated a portion of John Fremont's army at the small Highland County town of McDowell on May 8. Jackson's notification to Richmond read simply, "God blessed our arms with victory at McDowell yesterday." Richard L. Armstrong, *The Battle of McDowell: March 11 – May 18, 1862* (Lynchburg, VA, 1990), 90.

26 REL to C. S. Carrington, May 9, 1862, telegram book, REL HQ papers, VHS; *OR* 10, pt. 2, 508; *OR* 14, 497. Pemberton apparently did not understand the root of Lee's inquires about martial law—Pemberton evaded the question previously by telling Lee that Gov. Brown assented to it, but he did not address Lee's initial inquiry about whether it was wanted by Savannah officials. Lee had to explain to Pemberton that President Davis did not wish to declare it unless specifically requested by the city government. *OR* 14, 497.

knowing that you would like to hear all that is going on."[27]

Lee orders Richmond provost marshal John H. Winder to round up Johnston's troops in the city and send them armed via the York River Railroad to Summit Station, near the Chickahominy bridge. Lee informs Joseph Anderson that a portion of Huger's force will be sent to him, and cautions him to watch out for a Union crossing downstream at Port Royal. Lee inquires of John Forncy if any heavy guns can be moved from Pensacola to the Mississippi, and also informs him that the president does not wish to declare martial law unless civil authorities request it.[28] In addition two cavalry companies have been ordered to join Forney; he is to notify Florida Governor Milton when they arrive.

Lee informs Lovell that no weapons are available in Richmond so to request them from Beauregard or gather privately owned weapons from the countryside. The adjutant general's office officially announces Lee's staff as consisting of Col. Armistead Long, and Majors Walter H. Taylor, T. M. R. Talcott, Charles Venable, and Charles Marshall.[29]

May 11, Sunday (Richmond): Lee advises Samuel S. Wilson, president of the Seaboard & Roanoke Railroad, that Norfolk and Portsmouth have been evacuated, but connections to the south will be maintained through Weldon, North Carolina; Lee wants locomotives and rolling stock of the S&R removed for use on other lines. Lee orders six heavy artillery companies to Chaffin's Bluff to erect fortifications there, and informs Joseph Anderson that "a secret agent" has just returned from behind enemy lines at Fredericksburg and reports the force opposing Anderson to be nothing more than a diversion.[30]

Lee instructs Pemberton to effect a POW exchange, and cautions Jackson not to overextend in his pursuit of Fremont: "Be careful not to be led too far. It has become necessary to concentrate." Mrs. Lee, Annie, and Mildred leave White House, posting a note on the front door reading: "Northern soldiers who profess to reverence [sic] Washington, forbear to desecrate the home of his first married life, the property of his wife, now owned by her descendants. [signed] A Grand-daughter of Mrs. Washington."[31]

---

27 Dowdey, *Wartime Papers*, 169-70; Freeman, *Lee*, vol. 2, 47; *OR* 11, pt. 3, 505-6; REL to J. E. Johnston, May 10, 1862, telegram book, REL HQ papers, VHS. Lee did not specifically state that he went to Drewry's today, but it can be inferred from his report on the works in his letter to Johnston. That, coupled with Taylor's revelation that Lee was away from HQ at some point during the day, strongly suggests a visit to the works. Freeman concluded that sometime during this period Lee and Davis went to Drewry's at least twice before the battle on the 15th, but he could not determine the exact dates. Freeman, *Lee*, vol. 2, 47. Judith McGuire, *Diary of a Southern Refugee During the War, by a Lady of Virginia* (New York, 1867), 112-5, wrote on May 14 of Davis mentioning a recent visit to Drewry's Bluff accompanied by Lee, but did not affix a date to it. From her description it appears to be later than the 10th and closer to the battle on the 15th.

28 *OR* 11, pt. 3, 505; *OR* 12, pt. 3, 885-6; REL to J. H. Forney, May 10 (3 messages), telegram book, REL HQ papers, VHS.

29 REL to John Milton, May 10, telegram book, REL HQ papers, VHS; REL to Mansfield Lovell, May 10, telegram book, REL HQ papers, VHS; *OR* 51, pt. 2, 554. Venable was still in Mississippi at this time.

30 *OR* 11, pt. 3, 508; Newton, *Johnston and Defense of Richmond*, 158; *OR* 12, pt. 3, 886-7. Chaffin's Bluff is located almost directly across the James from Drewry's Bluff.

31 *OR* 3, Series 2, 868; REL to Jackson, May 11, 1862, telegram book, REL HQ papers, VHS; Coulling, *Lee Girls*, 102; Perry, *Mrs. REL*, 249. Where exactly Mary and the girls went upon leaving White House is something of a mystery. Freeman thought it possible that they went to Mount Prospect, the nearby home of Dr. William H. Macon. Freeman, *Lee*, vol. 2, 252n11. This makes little sense as that estate was adjacent to, and actually once part of, White House. Freeman was actually mistaken regarding Mount Prospect—Dr. Macon and family fled from there about the same time the Lees left White House, and were staying at Ingleside, the home of Macon's wife's family. Macon's daughter later told Freeman that her mother—who was friends with Mrs. Lee—maintained that the Lees went straight from White House to Edmund Ruffin's estate Marlbourne. J. Ambler Johnston, *Echoes of 1861-1961* (Richmond, VA, 1971), 58-9, 64-5. Johnston includes an interesting anecdote about when and how he learned this from his mother, and their middle of the night trip to inform Freeman of it. Ibid, 64-5. Johnston placed that incident around 1930, so if true, it is odd that Freeman did not include this information in either *Lee* or *Lee's Lieutenants*, apparently discounting it entirely by placing Mrs. Lee at Mount Prospect. Mary Coulling and John Perry both wrote that the Lees went to another New Kent estate, Criss Cross. Coulling, *Lee Girls*, 102; Perry, *Mrs. REL*, 249. Where they got this information is not specified, as Perry does not cite that reference (although

May 12, Monday (Richmond): President Davis and Lee meet with Johnston at his headquarters in the evening; they arrive while Johnston is out on the lines, so their meeting lasts well into the night. Because of the lateness of the hour, Davis and Lee spend the night at Johnston's headquarters. This trip was preceded by a 4:00 a.m. letter to Johnston explaining the troop dispositions in Virginia and asking him directly how far he plans to retreat and where he plans to concentrate.[32]

Lee sends his approval to Ewell of his decision to stay put at Conrad's Store and await Jackson's return from his pursuit of Fremont. Lee advises Pemberton that another brigade may be needed from Charleston, and directs Sam French to inquire if any railroad iron can be obtained from Charleston. Later Lee informs French that Navy Sec. Mallory has authorized transfer of requested iron from the Navy's supplies. Lee instructs Alexander Lawton to send a force from Savannah to Atlanta to guard government property there, and informs Lovell that the only weapons available anywhere in the Confederacy at present are pikes and knives from the state of Georgia. Elements of the 6th U.S. Cavalry arrive at White House, where they quickly learn from slaves that it is Gen. Lee's property; Gen. McClellan orders a guard posted there and the house protected from looting.[33]

May 13, Tuesday (Richmond): Lee and Davis return to Richmond from Johnston's headquarters in the morning. They then meet for several hours with Commissary General Lucius Northrop, and Maj. Archibald Cole regarding provisions for Johnston's army. Lee informs Johnston where other supply depots are located should Richmond fall. Lee acknowledges Holmes's report of Union reinforcements at New Bern and approves of Holmes's decision to retain troops at Murfreesboro rather than Weldon. Lee informs Holmes that

---

it is likely from Coulling), and the source Coulling cites (George H. Lyman, "Some Aspects of the Medical Service in the Armies of the United States during the War of the Rebellion," in *Papers of the Military Historical Society of Massachusetts*, 14 vols. (Boston, 1881-1918), vol. 13, 193-4 [she wrongly places this in vol. 8 rather than vol. 13 in citation]) makes absolutely no mention of Criss Cross at all. Criss Cross is one of the oldest houses in Virginia, the oldest portion dating to approximately 1690; it was owned by the Poindexter family for nearly 150 years before being sold to S. P. Marsters, who owned it during the war. Criss Cross, National Register of Historic Places Nomination Form, May 11, 1973. Criss Cross still stands near the intersection of VA 155 and Interstate 64. They would have gained little through this relocation, as although they were no longer directly on the Pamunkey River, they were now only about five miles away, located just off the New Kent Road—the main road both armies used on the march to Richmond. There is no known blood connection with the Poindexters or the Marsters, so why they would have gone there is unclear. Lacking definitive evidence that they went to either Mount Prospect or Criss Cross, it seems very likely that they proceeded directly to Marlbourne (see entry for May 23).

32 Varina Davis, *Jefferson Davis: A Memoir by his Wife*, 2 vols. (Baltimore, 1990), 270; Sears, *To the Gates of Richmond*, 89; Newton, *Johnston and Defense of Richmond*, 153; Joseph L. Brent, *Memoirs of the War Between the States* (New Orleans, 1940), 120; *OR* 11, pt. 3, 510-1. Magruder's aide Joseph Brent gave the location of Johnston's HQ as Baltimore Cross Roads until the 17th, but he was mistaken as to the date that Johnston left as that area was behind Union lines by 17th; it is possible that Brent had the location completely wrong. There is some confusion over the date of Davis and Lee's visit to Johnston's HQ; Sears and Newton (cited above) place the visit on this date, but Joseph Harsh in his chart of every known strategy meeting Lee participated in during 1861-2 puts it on the 13th. *Sounding the Shallows: A Confederate Companion for the Maryland Campaign of 1862* (Kent, OH, 2000), 223. Lee and Davis did indeed meet on the 13th but it was in Richmond to discuss supply efforts (see entry for May 13 for details). Freeman puts it "about" May 14. Lee, vol. 2, 60. Freeman was still unsure of the date years later in *Lee's Lieutenants*, writing "It would seem probable that the conference was on May 14.... There is possibility of an error of one or two days." Freeman, *Lee's Lieutenants*, vol. 1, 230. An eyewitness puts Lee and Davis along the Chickahominy on this date. Charleston *Mercury*, May 16, 1862. Davis left a detailed account of the meeting in his memoirs, but did not date it. *Rise and Fall*, vol. 2, 84. Varina Davis quoted a letter from her husband dated the 13th that states the meeting occurred "yesterday." *Jefferson Davis*, vol. 2, 270. Johnston does not mention this meeting at all in his memoirs.

33 *OR* 11, pt. 3, 511-2; REL to S. G. French, May 12, 1862 (2 messages), telegram book, REL HQ papers, VHS; REL to A. R. Lawton, May 12, 1862, telegram book, REL HQ papers, VHS; REL to Mansfield Lovell, May 12, 1862, telegram book, REL HQ papers, VHS; John J. Fox, III, *Stuart's Finest Hour: The Ride Around McClellan, June 1862* (Winchester, VA, 2014), 13. A response was left to Mary's note on the door of White House: "Lady, a Northern Officer has protected your property in sight of the enemy, and at the request of your overseer." Farrar, *Old Virginia Houses*, 197.

McClellan's approach requires further reduction of his force but that the losses will offset by new troops in Raleigh taking the field under newly promoted brigadier generals Thomas Clingman and James Martin. Lee advises North Carolina Governor Clark that he has been forced to call away more of Holmes's force so it is imperative to get new the new regiments into the field as quickly as possible. Lee assures the governor that the best way to defend North Carolina is to drive the Yankees out of Virginia. Lee orders an additional battery sent to Chaffin's Bluff, and sends his approval of Humphrey Marshall's defensive measures.[34]

Lee instructs Kirby Smith to forward to Georgia a shipment of Enfields that is being sent via Knoxville, and explains to Governor Brown how they are to be distributed. Lee writes to Nathan Evans regarding the election of officers in one of Evans's regiments, and advises Judge A. G. Magrath of Charleston that a supply of ice there should be turned over to the medical department for use in the hospitals.[35]

Lee inquires of John Forney if there is a better line to defend Mobile than Fort Gaines and Fort Morgan. He orders Joseph Finegan to send an additional regiment from Florida to Beauregard at Corinth. Lee writes to Mary in the evening, relating the alarm that the loss of the CSS *Virginia* has caused in Richmond; much of the letter deals with money for Mary and the girls, which Lee states he will leave with John Stewart "whose house we occupy."[36]

May 14, Wednesday (Richmond): Lee joins a cabinet meeting discussing what to do if Richmond falls. Lee informs President Davis and his advisors that the next defensive line is along the Staunton River approximately 100 miles southwest of the capital. Lee emotionally tells those present "Richmond must not be given up; it shall not be given up!" He orders Huger to send Mahone's Brigade to Drewry's Bluff and, as Union vessels are reported to have put ashore landing parties on each side of the James several miles below the Bluff, Huger is to have infantry stationed along both sides of the river. Lee informs Johnston that as requested guards will be posted along the railroad to arrest deserters, and the Washington Artillery is being sent to him.[37]

---

34 *OR* 11, pt. 3, 512-3; *OR* 9, 471-2; *OR* 51, pt. 2, 555; *OR* 10, pt. 2, 521-2. Clingman was a pre-war lawyer and former member of both the Senate and House of Representatives; he was colonel of the 25th NC until his promotion and he served most of the war in the Carolinas. Warner, *Generals in Gray*, 54-5. Martin was Adjutant General of North Carolina, with whom Lee corresponded often.

35 REL to E. Kirby Smith, May 13, 1862, telegram book, REL HQ papers, VHS; *OR* 53, 244-5; REL to N. G. Evans, May 13, 1862, telegram book, REL HQ papers, VHS; REL to A. G. Magrath, May 13, 1862, telegram book, REL HQ papers, VHS.

36 REL to J. H. Forney, May 13, 1862, telegram book, REL HQ papers, VHS; REL to J. E. Finegan, May 13, 1862, telegram book, REL HQ papers, VHS; Dowdey, *Wartime Papers*, 172. The *Virginia* was scuttled on the 11th, her crew unable to lighten her enough to get her up the James to Richmond. Long, *CW Day by Day*, 210. The Stewart house is at 707 E Franklin St. less than two blocks from the Capitol; John Stewart rented it to Lee and Custis. Once Lee moved into the field, Custis and several other officers lived there, dubbing it the "bachelors mess" until 1864 when his mother and sisters moved in. The Lees resided there for several months after the war, before moving to Derwent in Powhatan Co. The famous image of Lee, Custis, and Walter Taylor was taken on the back porch of the Franklin St. house. For about 60 years the Virginia Historical Society occupied the house, which is currently the offices of the Homebuilders Association of Virginia. It is not known precisely when Lee moved from the Spotswood to the Stewart house but it was apparently soon after his arrival in the capital in 1861. Stewart-Lee House, National Historical Register of Historic Places Nomination Form, May 5, 1972.

37 Freeman, *Lee*, vol. 2, 48; John H. Reagan, *Memoirs with Special Reference to Secession and the Civil War* (New York, 1906), 139; *OR* 11, pt. 2, 514-6; REL to Huger, May 14, 1862 (3 messages), telegram book, REL HQ papers, VHS. It is possible that Lee went to Drewry's Bluff today with Davis, but that would make for a very busy schedule for both men given the cabinet meeting today. McGuire, *Diary of a Refugee*, 113-5. McGuire recounted a meeting involving Davis, Lee, Navy Sec. Mallory, and others in which Davis mentioned having just visited Drewry's with Lee; no date was provided, but she mentioned that it occurred the same day the *Patrick Henry* was sunk at Drewry's. The *Patrick Henry* was not sunk, but its sister ship, *Jamestown*, was indeed sunk as an obstruction below the Bluff on the 14th. Robert Wright, "Sinking of the *Jamestown*: How it was Done at Drewry's Bluff," *SHSP*, vol. 29, 371-2. It should be noted as well that the date for the cabinet meeting is not certain, but most historians have followed Freeman's lead in placing it today. He noted: "The date

Lee congratulates Jackson on his victory at McDowell and urges a junction with Ewell to move against Banks in the Valley, and instructs Ewell to stay at Conrad's Store until Jackson returns unless Banks leaves the Valley completely. Lee informs Beauregard that the 4th Florida is being sent him, and chides Gen. Finegan for hoarding arms in Florida for future use by Florida troops instructing him to send them to Corinth where Beauregard has thousands of unarmed troops. Lee writes to Annie regarding her financial matters. Rain in the evening.[38]

May 15, Thursday (Richmond/Drewry's Bluff): Lee embarks on an inspection trip down the James in the morning, which is interrupted by gunfire from the direction of Drewry's Bluff. Lee orders Mahone to take command at Drewry's Bluff. While Lee is out, Walter Taylor sends Johnston the latest information from Drewry's and adds that he meant no breach of etiquette in signing Lee's letters on the 7th, about which Johnston had complained. Lee, and possibly President Davis as well, arrive at Drewry's either just as the engagement ends or shortly after its conclusion. After inspecting the damage to the fort and talking with Mahone and the naval officers there, Lee returns to Richmond.

Lee sends Johnston a brief report on the day's action at the Bluff—the ironclads USS *Monitor* and USS *Galena* and several other wooden ships attacked but were repulsed. He adds that Ewell is moving down the Valley in pursuit of Banks. Lee writes to Ewell advising that Jackson is returning to the Valley and urging upon Ewell the need for him to join with Jackson and drive down the Valley to relieve pressure on Richmond and Johnston.[39]

Lee instructs Huger at Petersburg to destroy the wharves and warehouses there if the Federals approach the city, and he asks if Mahone can be supplied from Petersburg or whether provisions for his brigade will have to come from Richmond. Lee writes to South Carolina Governor Pickens regarding disputes between department commander Maj. Gen. John Pemberton and Charleston district commander Brig. Gen. Roswell Ripley: "One or the other must be removed," Lee concludes in his message to Pickens; Lee favors relieving Ripley despite his intricate knowledge of the city's defenses. Lee also informs Congressman William P. Miles and several other prominent Charlestonians that Ripley's command cannot be made independent from Pemberton as proposed; because Ripley has requested a transfer, Lee favors taking that route in the handling of the delicate matter, but would like Miles's opinion. Lee instructs Mansfield Lovell to recruit a partisan ranger command in his department. Rain most of the day.[40]

May 16, Friday (Richmond): Lee informs Gen. Jackson that Nathaniel Banks is falling back to the northern reaches of the Valley, and is possibly bound for Fredericksburg or Alexandria, and that an attack on Banks by Jackson and Ewell would do much to alleviate pressure on Richmond, as would a vigorous campaign to the Potomac. Lee also informs Jackson that he has received no application for promotion of Stapleton Crutchfield, nor is Lee familiar with Crutchfield's current command, thus he needs more details before he can act. Lee writes to Huger that Gen. McClellan's intent is not yet clear, so Huger should keep his command "light and movable" so as

---

of this meeting, as of many incidents during the exciting days of May 1862 cannot be fixed with certainty. Although there is no date into which all the related facts fit so well as approximately May 14, it is possible that the incident came later." Freeman, *Lee*, vol. 2, 48 n45. Postmaster General John Reagan left a detailed but undated account of the meeting. Reagan, *Memoirs*, 139. Only two of Mahone's regiments had left for Gordonsville; the bulk of his brigade remained at Petersburg.

38 *OR* 12, pt. 3, 889; REL to Beauregard, May 14, 1862, telegram book, REL HQ papers, VHS; REL to J. E. Finegan, May 14, 1862, telegram book, REL HQ papers, VHS; REL to Annie, May 14, 1862, REL papers, LOC; Krick, *CW Weather*, 55.

39 *OR* 11, pt. 3, 518-9; Freeman, *Lee*, vol. 2, 48-9; Clopton, "New Light on Drewry's Bluff," 95; *OR* 12, pt. 3, 891. It is unclear exactly when Lee arrived at Drewry's Bluff and if Davis was with him; equally unclear is who was actually in command during the battle, as Mahone's arrival time is not known for certain. Commodore Ebenezer Farrand commanded the post until Mahone's arrival. Freeman addresses Lee's presence at the battle in *Lee*, vol. 2, 49 n46.

40 REL to Huger, May 15, 1862 (2 messages), telegram book, REL HQ papers, VHS; *OR* 14, 503-4; REL to Mansfield Lovell, May 15, 1862, telegram book, REL HQ papers, VHS; Krick, *CW Weather*, 55.

to cover Walthall, City Point, Petersburg, or anywhere else in that vicinity that the enemy may land and use locals for information about the area, and explore locations for placing obstructions in the Appomattox River. Lee gives Johnston the latest information regarding Drewry's Bluff and Huger's troops. Lee orders Mahone to send the eight companies of heavy artillery then stationed at Drewry's to Camp Lee to be organized there into a regiment, for their presence at Drewry's Bluff is no longer required now that Mahone and the CSS *Virginia's* crew are there.[41]

Lee informs Beauregard that rifles are being sent him from Florida, and writes to Miss Maria C. Sims thanking her for a pair of socks she sent him recently. Before noon McClellan arrives at White House, and establishes his headquarters there. Rain during the day.[42]

May 17, Saturday (Richmond): Lee warns Johnston that if given time McClellan will resume siege operations therefore a blow must be struck if he moves from the Pamunkey to the James. He adds that several companies of cavalry are being transferred to him from Huger but they will need to be armed. Lee sends the latest intelligence on Union movements in the Valley to Johnston and Joseph Anderson.[43]

The general also tells Anderson that there are arms available for his use in Essex County, Anderson just needs to go get them. Lee informs Huger that his new responsibility is the protection of the Petersburg & Weldon Railroad, the specifics of which will be left to his discretion but his fall-back position will be Drewry's Bluff; he is also to proceed with obstructing the Appomattox River. Lee writes to his brother, Capt. Sydney Smith Lee, who is now in command of the naval forces at Drewry's Bluff, and explains that Mahone is in overall command and he hopes for cordial cooperation between the services. Lee notifies Mansfield Lovell that he has received reports that Union Gen. Ben Butler is demanding the return of the coin and specie that was removed from the New Orleans banks; Secretary of the Treasury Christopher G. Memminger wants it all seized by the Confederate government for safe-keeping.[44]

May 18, Sunday (Richmond): Lee instructs Johnston to make sure his troops respect private property since they are now on the outskirts of Richmond and summons Johnston to Richmond to meet with President Davis. Lee instructs Huger to use his own discretion as he knows better than Lee does the situation on the Southside front, and informs North Carolina Governor Clark that the

---

41 *OR* 12, pt. 3, 892-3; Freeman, *Lee*, vol. 2, 54; REL to Jackson, May 16, 1862, telegram book, REL HQ papers, VHS; *OR* 11, pt. 3, 519-22. Early Lee biographer Sir Frederick Maurice wrote of the message to Stonewall, "This letter of Lee's of May 16th was, in the circumstances in which it was written, a remarkable document. . . . When McClellan was hammering at the gates of Richmond, Lee saw that the way to save the town was to make [Brig. Gen. Irvin] McDowell defend Washington; Johnston looked only to the prospect of a battle with McClellan. There we have a measure of the intellect of the two men." Maurice, *REL The Soldier*, 103-6. Crutchfield graduated first in the VMI Class of 1855, and was major of the 9th VA and lieutenant colonel of the 58th VA; Jackson subsequently made him his artillery chief. He lost a leg at Chancellorsville and was unable to serve in the field but was recalled in early 1865; he was killed at Sailors Creek April 6, 1865. Krick, *Lee's Colonels*, 105.

42 REL to Beauregard, May 16, 1862, telegram book, REL HQ papers, VHS; REL to Maria Sims, May 16, 1862, REL papers, UNC; Jonathan Horn, *The Man Who Would Not be Washington: Robert E. Lee's Civil War and his Decision that Changed American History* (New York, 2015), 152; Krick, *CW Weather*, 55.

43 *OR* 11, pt. 3, 523; *OR* 12, pt. 3, 894; REL to J. R. Anderson, May 17, 1862, REL papers, VHS.

44 REL to J. R. Anderson, May 17, 1862, telegram book, REL HQ papers, VHS; *OR* 11, pt. 3, 524-5, 549; REL to Mansfield Lovell, May 17, 1862, telegram book, REL HQ papers, VHS. Union Maj. Gen. Samuel Heintzelman, commanding the Union III Corps of McClellan's Army of the Potomac, recorded on this date: "Major Lawrence Williams was sent in arrest (and in irons) to Fort Monroe this morning. An aide of General Robert E. Lee was killed, and on his person letters found from Williams proving correspondence with the enemy. I wonder that a court is not ordered and he is not tried here." Hewitt, ed., *OR Supplement*, vol. 2, 55. Williams was a Lee cousin. None of Lee's aides had been killed except for Col. John A. Washington about eight months earlier, so it is not clear who Heintzelman was referencing.

latest shipment of arms received in Richmond does not include anything for North Carolina.⁴⁵

Lee sends instructions to Edward Johnson and Henry Heth to send a force to intercept a Union raiding party near Jackson's River Depot on the Virginia Central Railroad. A Union patrol discovers Mary and the girls residing within their lines, and Mary tells their commander that she is not pleased with what happened with Arlington and she does not want it repeated at White House.⁴⁶

May 19, Monday (Richmond): Lee notifies Holmes that he is now responsible for the protection of Weldon, as Huger's force is being brought to Richmond including those troops currently at Weldon, and requests of Pemberton that Roswell Ripley be sent to Richmond with a brigade. Lee informs Col. William G. M. Davis of the 1st Florida Cavalry that "horses are individual property and must be provided for by individuals. Volunteers who do not keep themselves provided with serviceable horses must serve on foot."⁴⁷

May 20, Tuesday (Richmond): Jackson notifies Lee that he sees an opportunity to attack Banks, but Johnston has ordered Ewell away; will Lee override Johnston's orders? Lee informs Johnston that President Davis will not place the Department of Henrico [i.e., Richmond] under Johnston's command as requested, but he is willing to adjust its borders. Lee urges Huger and Mahone to strengthen the river obstructions in the James and Appomattox, and sends to Heth an update on Edward Johnson's movements. Lee tells Navy Sec. Mallory that there are no laborers available to construct fortifications to cover the river obstructions at Warwick Bar so it would be better to place obstructions where they can be covered by land batteries. Lee writes to Charlotte with the latest family news.⁴⁸

May 21, Wednesday (Richmond): Lee informs Johnston that President Davis wants to know his plans, and strongly suggests that Johnston inform Davis in person. The general replies to Gen. Jackson's inquiry of yesterday, that Johnston has authorized Stonewall to link up with Ewell and defeat Banks, but if the opportunity does not present itself then Ewell is to move to Hanover Court House.⁴⁹

---

45 *OR* 11, pt. 3, 526; REL to Huger, May 18, 1862, telegram book, REL HQ papers, VHS; REL to H. T. Clark, May 18, 1862, REL papers, LVA. Johnston did not reply to this letter or show up in Richmond as requested. Freeman, *Lee*, vol. 2, 60.

46 REL to Edward Johnson, May 18, 1862, telegram book, REL HQ papers, VHS; REL to Henry Heth, May 18, 1862, telegram book, REL HQ papers, VHS; Coulling, *Lee Girls*, 102. Coulling puts this encounter of Mary with the Federals at Criss Cross. Coulling, *Lee Girls*, 102. The Union officer who left the only known account of this meeting did not state where it occurred. Lyman, "Some Aspects of the Medical Service," *MHSM*, 193-4. If it was indeed at Criss Cross, which seems unlikely, the Lee ladies moved very soon afterward to Edmund Ruffin's home, Marlbourne, in Hanover County; the exact date of the move (if it occurred) is not known, but they were there by the 23rd (see entry for that day).

47 *OR* 9, 472; *OR* 14, 505-6; REL to W. G. M. Davis, May 19, 1862, telegram book, REL HQ papers, VHS. Davis was promoted to brigadier general in November 1862 but resigned in May 1863, spending the balance of the war operating blockade runners to Nassau. Warner, *Generals in Gray*, 69. Confederate mounted troops provided their own horses unlike in the Union army where mounts were issued by the government like other equipment.

48 Freeman, *Lee*, vol. 2, 56-7; *OR* 11, pt. 3, 527-8; REL to Henry Heth, May 20, 1862, telegram book, REL HQ papers, VHS; REL to S. R. Mallory, May 20, 1862, telegram book, REL HQ papers, VHS; REL to Charlotte, May 20, 1862, G. B. Lee papers, VHS. Warwick Bar is just upstream of Drewry's Bluff, several miles below Richmond. Union Gen. Heintzelman recorded more details regarding Lee cousin Lawrence Williams (see footnotes for May 17th entry): "I now hear that the story about Lawrence Williams is only partly true. He was arrested and did write a letter, but it was only about General Lee's, or rather Mrs.' Property and not notable, and General McClellan released him and said he should not have been arrested." *OR Supplement*, vol. 2, 57.

49 *OR* 11, pt. 3, 530; REL to Jackson, May 21, 1862, telegram book, REL HQ papers, VHS. Lee was trying his best to relay to his old friend Johnston the level of Davis's frustration with Johnston's silence. This message to Jackson makes it clear that Lee consulted with Johnston on the situation in the Valley; whether it was in person or in writing is not known. Freeman wrote that Lee's reply to Jackson's inquiry of the 20th was not known, but this message is obviously that reply; see *Lee*, vol. 2, 56-7.

May 22, Thursday (Richmond/Mechanicsville): Lee and President Davis ride to the vicinity of Mechanicsville in the afternoon as artillery duels across the Chickahominy valley; they encounter Jeb Stuart and Brig. Gen. Howell Cobb there, but neither can provide information about what is going on. Davis is not pleased with the situation and tells Lee to meet with Johnston as soon as possible. Before leaving Richmond, Lee informs Johnston that everything is in readiness for the construction of a bridge across the James at Drewry's Bluff. He clarifies for the general that his command includes Mahone at Drewry's, and although the Navy is responsible for work on the fort, it is also under his overall control. Lee informs Gen. Sam French at Wilmington that two heavy guns are being sent to him for Fort Fisher. Lee approves Gen. Finegan's proposed POW exchange in Florida, and instructs Holmes to send Huger's detached units to him.[50]

May 23, Friday (Richmond/New Bridge): Lee and the president watch an artillery duel at New Bridge east of Mechanicsville and come under that in the afternoon. Lee informs Johnston that Governor Clark is sending a brigade of North Carolina troops to Petersburg to relieve Huger's troops; once that happens, the entire line of the Weldon Railroad will become Gen. Holmes's responsibility. Lee instructs Gen. John Winder to convert a heavy artillery battalion now at Camp Lee into infantry, and informs Col. Thomas Rhett, ordnance inspector in Richmond, that Lee has no control over Navy guns, so Rhett must adhere to Sec. Mallory's wishes for two guns for the James River defenses and two for Wilmington. Lee instructs Pemberton to send to Richmond a brigade composed of troops "that could not stand summer's campaign on coast."[51]

Lee requests that Col. Gorgas issue new arms to Mahone's and Branch's brigades, and reminds Gen. Beauregard of the president's policy of brigading troops by state as he organizes the new troops he has received. Lee warns John Stewart of Brook Hill plantation on the northern outskirts of Richmond that McClellan's army now occupies Mechanicsville. A patrol conducted by the 13th New York "discovered that Mrs. General Lee was staying at Mrs. Sayer's house, within our picket lines."[52]

May 24, Saturday (Richmond): Johnston finally comes to Richmond to meet with President Davis and Lee but does not reveal any sort of plan of operations. Lee reaffirms his approval of Mansfield Lovell's actions in the failed defense of New Orleans, that once the Union fleet passed the forts guarding the river, Lovell had little choice but to evacuate. Lee informs Loring in southwest Virginia that no reinforcements can be sent him, and he needs to fill up his existing regiments before

---

50 OR 11, pt. 3, 534-6; OR 9, 472; OR 3, Series 2, 876; REL to T. H. Holmes, May 22, 1862, telegram book, REL HQ papers, VHS. A newspaper account places Lee and Davis at New Bridge east of Mechanicsville on the 23rd in response to artillery fire heard in the capital and they came under artillery fire upon arriving. Although some sources argue it is highly unlikely they would make two separate trips on consecutive days to this area, it appears the date in the newspaper is correct. Charleston *Mercury*, May 27, 1862.

51 Charleston *Mercury*, May 27, 1862; Cobb, "Extracts from Letters," 292; OR 11, pt. 3, 536-7, 539, 542; OR 14, 518. Thomas Cobb noted somewhat sarcastically "the papers will no doubt make much ado about the President being under fire." Cobb, "Extracts from Letters," 292. The heavy artillery battalion Lee referred to was composed of the companies recently stationed at Drewry's Bluff.

52 REL to Gorgas, May 23, 1862, REL CSR; REL to Beauregard, May 23, 1862, REL CSR; REL to John Stewart, May 23, 1862, Gilder-Lehrman; OR 11, pt. 1, 737-8. Stewart was the owner of the townhouse Lee rented in Richmond. Brook Hill estate today is an island of undeveloped 19th century Richmond amidst suburban sprawl at the intersection of US 1 and interstate 95. "Mrs. Sayer's house" was Edmund Ruffin's estate, Marlbourne, near Old Church; the estate was at that time home of Ruffin's daughter Mildred and her husband William Sayre. Ruffin recorded in his diary: "Gen. Lee's family (ladies & children) had been making a temporary home at Marlbourne some weeks ago. The report at Hanover CH is that ALL on the farm were under guard as prisoner to the enemy. . . . If they are guarded it must be designed for their protection." He noted also that Mary caused a bit of a scandal in the neighborhood when she laundered some of the General's clothing and hung it out a second floor bedroom window to dry where it was visible to all passing by. Scarborough, *Diary of Edmund Ruffin*, vol. 2, 315. Ruffin's words "some weeks ago" suggest that the Lees had been there some time, making it highly probable that they came directly to Marlbourne upon leaving White House, rather than making intermediate stops at Mount Prospect and/or Criss Cross as others have written.

requesting the formation of new ones. Rain throughout the day.⁵³

May 25, Sunday (Richmond): Lee tells Holmes that Ambrose Burnside is probably going to move his force from eastern North Carolina to the James River so Holmes should move the majority of his command to Petersburg and establish his own headquarters there and base his defense of the Weldon Railroad from that city. Lee asks Col. Jeremy Gilmer if he can come to Richmond to take command of the engineer bureau. Lee asks Pemberton if he needs any brigade commanders for Georgia or South Carolina troops.⁵⁴

May 26, Monday (Richmond): Lee goes to Johnston's headquarters at the Harrison house on Williamsburg Road to get Johnston to reveal his plans, which are to attack McClellan north of the Chickahominy on the 29th. Lee learns of Jackson's recent victories at Front Royal and Winchester, and acknowledges Huger's arrival at Drewry's Bluff telling him that Johnston will send him specific instructions but he must be in readiness to cross the James. Lee requests Holmes to send as many wagons as he can to Richmond, and again tells Loring that no reinforcements are available to send him for southwest Virginia.⁵⁵

Lee tries to prod Beauregard into action in Mississippi, and tells him that Louis Hebert and John C. Moore have been appointed brigadiers for his army. Lee tells Brig. Gen. Paul O. Hebert in Texas that a new department will be created west of the Mississippi and Gen. Magruder will be assigned to command it, but until then Hebert is in command as senior officer present. Col. Ben Rush leads part of the 6th Pennsylvania Cavalry past Marlbourne (Edmund Ruffin's estate) and meets William Sayre on his way to deliver a report to Lee on Yankee activities. Sayre rides with the enemy and convinces Rush he was searching for Federals to guard the estate. His written report is not found; worried he is under suspicion, Sayre does not deliver it to Lee. Rain in evening.⁵⁶

May 27, Tuesday (Richmond): Lee informs Johnston that Holmes reports a severe reduction in Union numbers at New Bern, so Lee has reduced Holmes's force and ordered him to follow Burnside's army where ever it goes. Lee informs Johnston and Huger that Holmes has taken over responsibilities for protecting the Weldon Railroad, freeing up Huger's troops for any duties Johnston

---

53 Freeman, *Lee*, vol. 2, 60; *OR* 6, 652-3; *OR* 12, pt. 3, 899; Susan P. Lee, *Memoirs of William Nelson Pendleton, DD* (Harrisonburg, VA, 1991), 184.

54 REL to T. H. Holmes, May 25, 1862, telegram book, REL HQ papers, VHS; REL to J. F. Gilmer, May 25, 1862, telegram book, REL HQ papers, VHS; REL to J. C. Pemberton, May 25, 1862, telegram book, REL HQ papers, VHS. Gilmer was one of the antebellum army's most talented engineers and brought those talents to the Confederate army; he was wounded at Shiloh while serving as chief engineer of Gen. A. S. Johnston's army. Warner, *Generals in Gray*, 105. Davis recounted a meeting of Lee and Johnston following his and Lee's trip to Mechanicsville on the 22nd, but as with many incidents in his memoirs, there is no date. *Rise and Fall*, vol. 2, 99-100. It is very probable that Lee and Johnston met today to discuss Johnston's plans. The lack of correspondence between the two of them on this date suggests that whatever business they had was conducted face to face. Whenever the meeting occurred, Johnston told Lee of his intent to attack McClellan's right flank north of the Chickahominy on the 29th. Ibid. Johnston's memoirs are silent on all meetings with Davis and Lee during this time. Freeman puts it on the 26th, and lacking any better information it is included here on that date, but just as Freeman was, this author is unconvinced of that date. Freeman, *Lee's Lieutenants*, vol 1, 213 n56.

55 Freeman, *Lee*, vol. 2, 61-2; *OR* 11, pt. 3, 547; REL to T. H. Holmes, May 26, 1862, telegram book, REL HQ papers, VHS; REL to W. W. Loring, May 26, 1862, telegram book, REL HQ papers, VHS. Freeman was unsure of the date of this meeting with Johnston; his best educated guess was that it occurred today. *Lee's Lieutenants*, vol. 1, 213 n56. As has been noted previously, Davis's account did not attach a date to the meeting, and Johnston did not mention it at all.

56 *OR* 9, 713; *OR* 10, pt. 2. 546; REL to Beauregard, May 26, 1862 (2 messages), telegram book, REL HQ papers, VHS; Scarborough, *Diary of Edmund Ruffin*, vol. 2, 318-9; Krick, *CW Weather*, 56. Louis Hebert was colonel of the 3rd LA and captured at Pea Ridge, AR; he served in the West until 1863 when he was assigned to North Carolina. Warner, *Generals in Gray*, 130-1. Moore was colonel of the 2nd TX and was captured at Vicksburg; after his exchange he served on the Gulf coast. Ibid., 219. Paul O. Hebert was cousin of Louis Hebert and prewar governor of Louisiana; he spent the entire war in Louisiana and Texas. Ibid, 131-2.

wishes. Lee sends two regiments from Richmond to Weldon to assist Holmes, but has to clarify for him that his main focus is to oppose Burnside, but his area of command has been extended to Petersburg. Lee notifies Governor Clark that several thousand small arms will be sent to North Carolina tomorrow.[57]

Lee again informs Loring that nothing can be sent him from Richmond, but there are in his district large numbers of men able and willing to serve so he must bring them into service. Lee asks Kirby Smith if the troops ordered to him from Georgia and Alabama have yet reported, and what is his strength at Chattanooga? Lee informs Lovell that his area of responsibility now includes Jackson and Vicksburg, and reprimands Joseph Finegan for countermanding Lee's orders to send arms from Florida to Beauregard at Corinth. Rain throughout the day.[58]

May 28, Wednesday (Richmond): Lee spends most of the day attempting to sort out confusion over whether Huger or Holmes is responsible for the safety of Petersburg, sending a flurry of messages both by courier and over the telegraph wires to Johnston, Huger, Holmes, James Martin, and several brigade commanders. The end result is that one of Holmes's brigades will be stationed at Petersburg, Huger's command will be reunited, Martin will shift troops from Raleigh to Weldon, and Huger will be responsible for supplying Mahone's Brigade.[59]

Lee informs Gen. Lawton that he cannot arm partisan commands if there are regular troops still without arms, but weapons are being sent as soon as they are received through the blockade. Lee sends his congratulations to Jackson for his recent victories in the lower Valley, adding "We rejoice at your brilliant success. If you can make demonstration on Maryland and Washington it will add to its great results." Rain throughout the day.[60]

May 29, Thursday (Richmond): Expecting Johnston to attack McClellan near Mechanicsville today, Lee goes to Johnston's headquarters; Johnston, however, calls off the attack, preferring instead to attack McClellan's left flank on the Williamsburg Road. Lee denies a request from South Carolina Governor Francis Pickens to have Huger replace Pemberton in command of Lee's former department. Lee writes to Pemberton regarding the state of the Charleston harbor forts and the morale of the troops there: "The importance of defending both Charleston and Savannah to the last extremity, particularly Charleston, is earnestly brought to your attention. . . . Let it be distinctly understood by everybody that Charleston and Savannah are to be defended to the last extremity. If the harbors are taken the cities are to be fought street by street and house by house as long as we have a foot of ground to stand upon."[61]

---

57 OR 11, pt. 3, 552-4; REL to T. H. Holmes, May 27, 1862 (2 messages), telegram book, REL HQ papers, VHS; REL to J. G. Martin, May 28, 1862, telegram book, REL HQ papers, VHS.

58 OR 12, pt. 3, 903; OR 10, pt. 2, 553-4; REL to Mansfield Lovell, May 27, 1862, telegram book, REL HQ papers, VHS; OR 53, 245; Freeman, *Lee*, vol. 2, 63. In a letter to Jackson today congratulating him for his recent string of victories, Johnston added a postscript in effect rebuking Jackson for communicating directly with Lee: "Time would be gained and saved by addressing me always–instead of the government." Johnston to Jackson, May 27, 1862, Lee-Jackson Foundation papers, W&L.

59 OR 11, pt. 3, 555-7; REL to T. H. Holmes, May 28, 1862,(2 messages), telegram book, REL HQ papers, VHS; REL to J. J. Walker, May 28, 1862 (2 messages), telegram book, REL HQ papers, VHS; REL to J. G. Martin (2 messages), May 28, 1862, telegram book, REL HQ papers, VHS; REL to Huger (2 messages), May 28, 1862, telegram book, REL HQ papers, VHS. The confusion at Lee's headquarters must have been considerable as he and his aides tried to make sense of the messages that poured in from all the various commanders involved in this mess. It is a wonder that Petersburg, Weldon, and the entire railroad from Richmond to Wilmington was not left unguarded as Lee, Johnston, Huger, and Holmes all attempted to shift troops around.

60 REL to A. R. Lawton, May 28, 1862, telegram book, REL HQ papers, VHS; REL to Jackson, May 28, 1862, telegram book, REL HQ papers, VHS; Freeman, *Lee*, vol. 2, 64.

61 Freeman, *Lee*, vol. 2, 65-6; Johnston, *Narrative of Military Operations*, 131-2; OR 14, 523-4. Johnston determined not to attack upon learning from Jeb Stuart that Irvin McDowell's force moving south from Fredericksburg turned back and

Lee instructs Holmes to bring all available troops north and to be prepared to defend the Southside front or to join Johnston's army, as circumstances may dictate. Lee informs the Virginia Military Institute's superintendent, Maj. Gen. Francis H. Smith, that John Imboden wishes to borrow the institute's two artillery pieces for the defense of Staunton, Virginia. Lee writes to daughter Agnes expressing concern for her mother and sisters, who are under house arrest behind enemy lines at Marlbourne.[62]

May 30, Friday (Richmond/Half Sink): Lee rides north on Telegraph Road to its crossing of the Chickahominy River at John Minor Botts's estate Half Sink, scouting for McClellan's right flank. He visits son Rooney's camp on the way. He sends Col. Long to Joe Johnston's headquarters to offer Lee's services for the coming battle. Long tells Johnston that Lee "would be glad to participate in the battle. He had no desire to interfere with [Johnston's] command, but simply wished to aid him on the field to the best of his ability and in any manner which his services would be of most value. General Johnston expressed gratification at this message, and the hope that General Lee would ride out to the field, with the desire that he would send [Johnston] all the reinforcements he could." Lee declines Georgia Governor Joe Brown's offer of pikes or knives to arm troops at Richmond. Periods of rain during the day and very heavy thunderstorms in the afternoon and night.[63]

May 31, Saturday (Richmond/Seven Pines): In the morning Lee writes several pieces of correspondence: he informs Pemberton that there is no heavy artillery available in Richmond so to ask Gen. Forney in Mobile, and to send two regiments to Virginia; he also tells Paul Hebert to continue to send supplies to the remains of Henry Sibley's New Mexico force.[64]

After completing this around mid-morning, Lee and staff ride to Johnston's headquarters on Williamsburg Road. Finding that Johnston has gone to the front, Lee's party continues on and finds Johnston at Magruder's headquarters on Nine Mile Road. There Lee learns for the first time that an offensive is in the works, but Johnston reveals few details. After spending several hours, perhaps as many as three, with Lee, Johnston rides off in the afternoon toward the sound of firing to the south, which had been faintly audible most of the afternoon.

Just as Johnston departs, President Davis and Postmaster General John Reagan ride up. Davis, Lee, and Magruder all confer while Reagan goes in search of Johnston. Reagan catches up with Johnston but learns little from him, and rides back toward Magruder's headquarters. He finds that President Davis and the two generals have ridden closer to the front at Seven Pines and are under fire in a clearing, and Reagan "protests" about how they are exposing themselves to danger.

Soon after this, about 7:00 p.m., a severely wounded Johnston is carried past the group on a litter. When he learns that Johnston is wounded, Maj. Gen. Gustavus W. Smith arrives and, as the

---

showed no further signs of linking up with McClellan. Although Lee went to Johnston's HQ, Jefferson Davis chose to avoid Johnston and went instead to a vantage point overlooking the Chickahominy bridges.

62 REL to T. H. Holmes, May 29, 1862, telegram book, REL HQ papers, VHS; REL to F. H. Smith, May 29, 1862, telegram book, REL HQ papers, VHS; REL to Agnes, May 29, 1862, Lee papers, VHS.

63 OR 11, pt. 3, 560; Jones, *Personal Reminiscences of REL*, 390; Long, *Memoirs of REL*, 158-9; REL to Joseph Brown, May 30, 1862, telegram book, REL HQ papers, VHS; Krick, *CW Weather*, 56-7. One account claims that Lee spent the night of the 30th at 707 Franklin, but does not give a source for this (although it seems logical). Sally N. Robins, "General Robert E. Lee: Mrs. Lee During the War—Something About 'The Mess' and its Occupants," in Robert A. Brock, ed., *General Robert Edward Lee: Soldier, Citizen and Christian Patriot* (Richmond, VA, 1897), 337-8. William Nelson Pendleton wrote of the weather, "An unusually hard rain yesterday afternoon and last night, wetting the earth very deeply, swelling the streams prodigiously and leaving masses of threatening clouds this morning." W. N. Pendleton to wife, May 31, 1862, WNP papers, UNC.

64 OR 14, 528; OR 9, 716.

ranking officer of the Army of Northern Virginia, is queried by President Davis (in Lee's presence) about his plans for the battle. Smith relates what he knows of Johnston's plan but confesses he knows little beyond his own command and cannot formulate a plan until he learns the state of the other wing of the army. Smith later wrote, in something of an understatement, that "Mr. Davis did not seem pleased with what I said." After this discussion with Smith, President Davis and Gen. Lee ride back to the city together along Nine Mile Road. At some point during the historic journey Davis informs Lee that he will be assigned to command the Army of Northern Virginia.[65]

---

[65] Long, *Memoirs of REL*, 159; Freeman, *Lee*, vol. 2, 68-74; Harsh, *Sounding the Shallows*, 47; Maurice, *Lee's Aide de Camp*, 56-7; Reagan, *Memoirs*, 140-2; Davis, *Rise and Fall*, vol. 2, 100-3; Johnston, *Narrative of Military Operations*, 138-9; Gustavus W. Smith, *The Battle of Seven Pines* (New York, 1891), 103-4. Long put the time of Lee's departure from Richmond at 9:00 a.m. *Memoirs of REL*, 159.

June 1862

President Jefferson Davis's biographer William C. Davis hailed Davis's appointment of Robert E. Lee to command of the Army of Northern Virginia as "the single best decision of his presidency." An officer on John Magruder's staff observed, "In assuming his command, General Lee acted without the least display of ceremony and took up his burdens with tact and energy."[1]

The situation Lee inherited at the beginning of June was hardly an enviable one. His army had just fought a chaotic offensive battle that looked more like a defeat than a victory and revealed a host of glaring command issues. When it ended, the strategic situation remained unchanged. The army still had its back against a figurative wall in the form of the capital. Demoralization afflicted portions of its officer corps including the highest levels. Lee's own record in the field did little to inspire confidence in those who did not know him. Few could have anticipated that the next 30 days would flip entirely the strategic situation of the war in Virginia.

Lee immediately moved his headquarters from Richmond into an empty house on Nine Mile Road several miles outside the city. Some of the most important decisions of the war were made there at High Meadow, the home of Josiah and Catherine Dabbs. Lee's wife Mary and his daughters made a new flag that June that served as Gen. Lee's personal flag, which he flew outside High Meadow to denote it as army headquarters.[2] Lee's military secretary, Col. Armistead Long described the army's new nerve center:

> Our headquarters are very comfortable. The front room on the house floor is the adjutant general's office. The General's private office is in rear of this. There all the confidential business of the army is transacted, the General's usual attendant being his military secretary or some other member of his personal staff. In the front room the general business of the army is transacted by the adjutant general and his assistants. General Lee and his household mess together. The mess arrangements are not very ostentatious. Our meals are served and dispatched without any very great ceremony. The General is always pleasant at meals, and frequently hurls a pleasant jest at some member of his staff. . . . We were visited today by several high officials from Richmond. Their visit was more from curiosity than any special business. The General bears interruption with great equanimity.[3]

The day after officially taking command, Lee met with his senior generals to get a feel for their prevailing opinion of the current state of affairs. When some gave voice to despair, Lee quickly shut it down. He would not tolerate any public leaning toward defeat. His eventual plan for the deliverance of Richmond was already taking shape in his mind, and he would set it in motion by the second week of the month.

---

1 Gallagher, *Lee the Soldier*, 295; Brent, *Memoirs of the WBTS*, 151.

2 Rebecca A. Rose, *Colours of the Gray: An Illustrated Index of Wartime Flags from the Museum of the Confederacy's Collection* (Richmond, VA, 1998), 19. The flag was a First National pattern with the stars arranged in the shape of an "A" and was used by Lee through at least the summer of 1863. It resides in the collection of the Museum of the Confederacy.

3 *Memoirs of REL*, 166.

Lee's opponent, Gen. George McClellan, failed to reposition his vulnerable command even after Johnston's bungled attack revealed the danger posed by straddling his army on either side of a swollen river, which his position placed his army. When Lee's cavalry chief, James Ewell Brown (Jeb) Stuart, reported that McClellan's right flank above the Chickahominy was vulnerable, Lee merged that intelligence with an idea he had been toying with of bringing Stonewall Jackson's army from the Shenandoah Valley to Richmond to strike McClellan's flank. The stakes were high, and Lee was willing to gamble everything on this move.[4]

The general ordered his engineers to lay out and fortify a defensive line in front of Richmond. While the men grumbled about having to perform manual labor, the value of their toil would soon become apparent. Lee intended to strip the lines in front of Richmond in order to mass a strike force north of the Chickahominy. "General Lee was seen almost daily riding over his lines, making suggestions to working parties and encouraging their efforts to put sand-banks between their persons and the enemy's batteries, and they were beginning to appreciate the value of such adjuncts," recalled Gen. James Longstreet. "Above all, they soon began to look eagerly for his daily rides, his pleasing yet commanding presence, and the energy he displayed in speeding their labors."[5]

Joe Johnston's secrecy had contributed mightily to his poor relationship with President Davis. Lee recognized this and understood the president's need to be kept informed of the army's operations and was determined not to repeat his predecessor's mistake. From the start Lee kept Davis informed of his plans, and thereafter Davis seldom interfered with Lee. "The relations between General Lee and Mr. Davis are very friendly," wrote staff officer Col. Long. "The General is ever willing to receive the suggestions of the President, while the President exhibits the greatest confidence in General Lee's experience and ability, and does not hamper him with executive interference."[6]

Toward the end of the month, Lee gathered the key players at his headquarters to disclose his planned offensive. Lee had learned the lesson from Johnston's mistake of not keeping Davis informed, but he had not learned the major lesson of Johnston's attack at Seven Pines/Fair Oaks, i.e., an overly complicated battle plan designed for green troops under inexperienced commanders, was bound to fail. To some degree Lee's plan was a repeat of Cheat Mountain—if the first domino failed to fall, none after it would either. Lee's entire plan was based on Jackson appearing on schedule to turn McClellan out of his prepared position.[7]

---

4 Both James Longstreet and W. H. C. Whiting later claimed that the idea of using Jackson originated with them around June 10. Both claims are preposterous; however, such claims by Longstreet were not uncommon in the postwar years. Supposedly Whiting told Lee, "If you don't move, McClellan will dig you out of Richmond." See James Longstreet, "The Seven Days, including Frayser's Farm," in Robert U. Johnson, ed., *Battles and Leaders of the Civil War*, 4 vols. (Secaucus, NJ, n.d.), vol. 2, 396; and C. B. Denson, *An Address Delivered in Raleigh on Memorial Day 1895 Containing a Memoir of the Late Major General William Henry Chase Whiting of the Confederate Army* (Raleigh, NC, 1895), 27-8.

5 *From Manassas to Appomattox*, 114.

6 *Memoirs of REL*, 167-8.

7 Historians have long debated Jackson's performance during the Seven Days' Battles (June 25 – July 2). He failed to arrive on time, and went on to perform well below expectations. The brilliance he displayed in the Valley was masked on the Peninsula by lethargy and even borderline ineptitude. Repeatedly he failed to arrive when and where he was supposed to show up, yet Lee still achieved a major strategic victory. See Freeman, *Lee's Lieutenants*, vol. 1, 655-63. See footnote 54 for additional details and citations.

Lee massed three divisions to cooperate with Jackson against McClellan's right flank, the V Corps commanded by Brig. Gen. Fitz John Porter, near Mechanicsville. When McClellan launched an attack against Lee's thinned lines in front of Richmond the day before the Confederate offensive was set to begin, Lee feared that McClellan was on to him. However, Lee made no change to his plan. The next day when Jackson failed to turn Porter's flank, A. P. Hill took matters into his own hands; Hill was no Albert Rust, and Mechanicsville would be no Cheat Mountain. Hill's impetuosity cost hundreds of casualties but it put McClellan on his heels. There followed five more days of fighting which forced McClellan from his base on the Pamunkey River at Rooney Lee's estate White House across the Peninsula to the James River and the cover of the Union navy. McClellan's great campaign against Richmond was over.

Lee was ill during the latter days of the month, no doubt brought on by the stress of physical and emotional exertion and lack of sleep during the long active campaign. It was nothing serious, and manifested itself as little more than a cold, but it was enough to tax his physical strength and endurance at the end of the Seven Days' Battles. Lee attributed it to being too heavily clad.[8]

Lee had at least one burden removed from his shoulders that June. His wife, who for a time had been behind enemy lines, was allowed safe passage to Richmond. For the present at least, her nomadic roaming across the state was at an end. But for that single personal gain, Lee suffered two losses: the fortunes of war claimed the family estate White House, burned to the ground by the enemy at the end of the month, and the death of his only grandchild around the same time.

* * *

---

[8] Jack D. Welsh, *Medical Histories of Confederate Generals* (Kent, OH, 1995), 134.

June 1, Sunday (Richmond/Seven Pines/Dabbs House): At approximately 5:00 a.m. Lee receives a message from Maj. Gen. G. W. Smith giving his dispositions for battle and asking for reinforcements. Lee replies, "Your movements are judicious, and determination to strike the enemy right." He adds "you are right in calling upon me for what you want. I wish I could do more. It will be a glorious thing if you can gain a complete victory. Our success on the whole yesterday was good, but not complete." Soon after sending this message to Smith, formal orders arrive from President Davis appointing Lee to command of the Army of Northern Virginia: "The unfortunate casualty which has deprived the army in front of Richmond of its immediate commander, General Johnston, renders it necessary to interfere temporarily with the duties to which you were assigned. . . . You will assume command of the armies in Eastern Virginia and in North Carolina, and give such orders as may be needful and proper." During the morning Lee sends word to Capt. Harry Gilmor that his cavalrymen cannot use government-owned horses; they must furnish their own mounts, and approves of Gen. Loring's troop dispositions in western Virginia, suggesting that Loring coordinate with Edward Johnson.[9]

Around 1:00 p.m. Lee rides to army headquarters on Nine Mile Road, arriving there about 2:00 p.m. President Davis arrives there about a half-hour before Lee, and informs Smith that he has placed Lee in command of the army. President Davis departs soon after Lee's arrival, and the two generals confer for several hours, then about 4:30 they ride to Williamsburg Road to meet with Longstreet, whom they find conferring with Davis and several members of his cabinet. Lee finds Longstreet's command in no condition to resume the offensive, and so orders the army back to its jump-off point. At about 6:00 p.m. Lee and Smith leave Longstreet's front.[10]

Lee establishes his headquarters at High Meadow, the home of Mrs. Catherine W. Dabbs, on Nine Mile Road. Walter Taylor issues SO22 from Dabbs house, announcing Lee as commander of the Army of Northern Virginia. During the evening, Lee meets with artillery chief William N. Pendleton, who writes: "I liked very much his tone and bearing. . . . His head seems clear and his head strong. Few men have ever borne a greater weight than that which now rests upon his shoulders." Taylor submits a requisition for a shovel, axe, and candles for use at headquarters.[11]

---

[9] Gustavus W. Smith, "Two Days of Battle at Seven Pines," in *B&L*, vol. 2, 252; Freeman, *Lee*, vol. 2, 75-9; *OR* 11, pt. 3, 568-9; REL to H. W. Gilmor, June 1, 1862, telegram book, REL HQ papers, VHS; *OR* 12, pt. 3, 904.

[10] Smith, *Seven Pines*, 137-9; Davis, *Rise and Fall*, vol. 2, 106; *OR* 11, pt. 1, 992. The location of Lee's initial meeting with Davis and Smith is unclear; Freeman put it at the "Hughes House," while Smith merely said it was at "the headquarters near Old Tavern." *Lee*, vol. 2, 75; Smith, *Battle of Seven Pines*, 139. As Smith was in command of the ANV, it is possible he was at Johnston's former headquarters rather than his own in order to have access to Johnston's staff and records. Smith's HQ was the Goddin house "about 100 yards on the right of the Nine Mile road and distant about 4 ½ miles from the city." "Howard" to WNP, June 1, 1862, WNP papers, UNC. Both Longstreet and E. P. Alexander put Lee's arrival on the field and subsequent assumption of ANV command at noon, several hours earlier than Smith placed it. Longstreet, *From Manassas to Appomattox*, 109; Gary W. Gallagher, ed., *Fighting for the Confederacy: The Personal Recollections of General Edward Porter Alexander* (Chapel Hill, NC, 1989), 88. Neither Longstreet nor Alexander were present, however, and Alexander almost certainly based his account on Longstreet's. Thus, Smith's 2:00 p.m. arrival is used here.

[11] Hugh D. Pitts, *High Meadow: Where Robert E. Lee Drew his Sword* (Richmond, VA, 1998), 12; Dowdey, *Wartime Papers*, 181-2; WNP to wife, June 3, 1862, WNP papers, UNC; WHT requisition, June 1, 1862, WHT CSR. Lee took his personal staff (Long, Taylor, Marshall, and Talcott) with him into the field, and inherited Lt. Col. Edwin J. Harvie and Capt. A. P. Mason from Joe Johnston's staff (Harvie and Mason remained until November when they rejoined Johnston). Maurice, *Lee's Aide de Camp*, 58; Taylor, *General Lee*, 55; Krick, *Staff Officers in Gray*, 152, 216. High Meadow was the home of Josiah and Catherine Dabbs. Josiah died in January 1862 and fearing the approach of McClellan's army, Catherine fled to Richmond to the home of Mrs. Archibald Thomas at Second and Marshall. The Dabbs house was thus unoccupied and perfectly situated for use by Lee. Pitts, *High Meadow*, 4-6. After the war the house was purchased by Henrico County to serve as the county almshouse and it later became Henrico County Police headquarters. Although enlarged since 1862, it is open for tours and currently serves as the county visitor center, housing a small museum with the portion used by Lee restored to look as it did when it served as his headquarters. Ibid, 98-9.

June 2, Monday (Dabbs House): Lee officially assumes command of the Army of Northern Virginia, and rides Traveller out among the camps of the army. He requests of the War Department permanent commanders for several brigades either operating without permanent commanders or which had lost their commanders during the recent fighting. Lee meets again with Gen. Pendleton and asks him to continue in his role as the army's chief of artillery.[12]

President Davis informs Lee that he is too ill to come to headquarters today but wishes to be kept informed. G. W. Smith falls ill and his aide, Maj. Jasper Whiting, informs Lee that Smith "finds himself utterly unable to endure the mental excitement incident to his actual presence with the Army. Nothing but duty under fire could possibly keep him up. . . . He goes to town today to gain a few days respite and all business, all exciting questions must be kept from him for a while. . . . Since writing the above I have again seen the General and am pained to learn that partial paralysis has already commenced. The case is critical and the danger imminent." Lee writes to Charlotte with news of the Battle of Seven Pines and assures her that Rooney is safe and well. He mentions Johnston's wounding and his own assumption of command of the army: "I wish his mantle had fallen upon an abler man, or that I were able to drive our enemies back to their homes. I have no ambition and desire but for the attainment of this object, and therefore only wish for its accomplishment . . . most speedily and thoroughly." Rain showers early in the day and heavy rain and thunderstorms in the evening.[13]

June 3, Tuesday (Dabbs House/The Chimneys): Lee goes to the front in the morning, riding a portion of the lines with Col. Armistead Long. He holds a lengthy council of war with the senior generals of the Army of Northern Virginia except the ailing G. W. Smith at The Chimneys on Nine Mile Road, where they discuss how best to oppose McClellan and whether to withdraw even closer to Richmond. Several officers urge giving up their present position because it was susceptible to Federal artillery. Lee counters this argument by saying "If we leave this line because they can shell us, we shall have to leave the next for the same reason, and I don't see how we can stop this side of Richmond." President Davis arrives unexpectedly in the midst of this meeting, where Davis observes "the tone of conversation was quite despondent." The council soon adjourns without any decision announced by Lee; he and the president then ride together and discuss options for taking the offensive. Lee returns to his Dabbs house headquarters in late afternoon, and orders the army's chief engineer Maj. Walter H. Stevens to lay out a defensive line.[14]

---

12 OR 11, pt. 3, 571; Douglas S. Freeman, ed., *Lee's Dispatches: Unpublished Letters of General Robert E. Lee, C.S.A. to Jefferson Davis and the War Department of the Confederate States of America, 1862-1865* (Baton Rouge, LA, 1994), 4; Freeman, *Lee's Lieutenants*, vol. 1, 266-7; WHT to WNP, June 2, 1862, WNP papers, UNC; Lee, *Memoirs of WNP*, 187. Although Lee took over field command of the ANV he retained his former duties as well, meaning his attention was divided between the Richmond front and the other armies. To fill the brigade vacancies, Cols. James L. Kemper, Ambrose R. Wright, James J. Archer, and W. Dorsey Pender were promoted to brigadier general. Freeman, *Lee's Lieutenants*, vol. 1, 267.

13 Harsh, *Confederate Tide Rising*, 50; Jasper S. Whiting to REL, June 2, 1862, WNP papers, UNC; REL to Charlotte, June 2, 1862, G. B. Lee papers, VHS; Krick, *CW Weather*, 59. The nature of Smith's ailment seems to have been more mental than physical; most historians agree he suffered some sort of nervous breakdown. William C. Davis: "The exact nature of Smith's disorder can never be known, but the circumstances under which it surfaced lead strongly to the conclusion that he suffered from too big a reputation based on little or no justification, and the closer he came to having it put on the line by action, the more terrified he became." William C. Davis, "Gustavus Woodson Smith," *Confederate General*, vol. 5, 175.

14 Long, *Memoirs of REL*, 165-6; Maurice, *Lee's Aide de Camp*, 77-8; Davis, *Rise and Fall*, vol. 2, 108-9; OR 11, pt. 3, 570-2. Freeman noted that Maj. Gen. William H. C. Whiting was particularly opposed to the army remaining and fighting where it was, and it was during an exchange between Whiting and Lee that Davis arrived. Freeman, *Lee*, vol. 2, 88-9. Whiting was a talented engineer but left much to be desired as a field commander. He ran afoul of Jefferson Davis early in the war, and promotions came slow as a result. Charges of drunkenness followed his poor showing during the Bermuda Hundred Campaign in 1864. Whiting was wounded in the right thigh and hip, captured at Fort Fisher in January 1865, and died of dysentery in Federal captivity two months later. Lawrence L. Hewitt, "William Henry Chase Whiting," *Confederate General*, vol. 6, 132-3. If Davis is to be believed, the strategy for the subsequent Seven Days' Battles—bringing Jackson from the

Lee sends a brief note to President Davis, thanking him for his offer of a horse but Lee points out that he has more than he needs at present. He acknowledges receipt of Gen. Lawrence Branch's report on his fight at Slash Church several days before, and approves of Branch's actions at that battle. Lee forwards to Longstreet a request from Huger to have his brigades returned to him, as they have been detached from his command since Seven Pines; Lee wants an explanation from Longstreet.[15]

Lee informs Gen. Pemberton at Charleston that Gen. Lawton wants to bring a brigade of Georgia troops to Virginia and that reduction of enemy forces in Pemberton's department render this possible. Lee asks Gen. Finegan if the 2nd and 6th Florida regiments are ready for the field, and alerts Gen. Holmes at Goldsboro that he suspects recent arrivals to McClellan's army came from the forces opposing Holmes in North Carolina. Dr. David C. DeLeon is announced as medical director for the Army of Northern Virginia. Heavy rains carry over from last night and into the morning, with clouds and showers for the rest of the day.[16]

June 4, Wednesday (Dabbs House): Lee remains at the Dabbs house, attending to paperwork and familiarizing himself with the organization and position of the army as well as addressing affairs elsewhere in the Confederacy. Curiosity brings "several high officials from Richmond" to headquarters throughout the day, among them Congressman Alexander R. Boteler of Shepherdstown, who was sent by Stonewall Jackson to give Lee a briefing on affairs in the Shenandoah Valley. Lee approves Maj. Stevens's plans for a fortified line around Richmond and he instructs the engineer to pay particular attention to the area along the Richmond & York River Railroad as a potential location for heavy artillery emplacements. To assist with the fortification efforts, Lee orders the creation of a pioneer corps in each division.[17]

Lee opines to Pemberton that the recent battle at Drewry's Bluff illustrates that ironclads cannot pass well-served land batteries and thus Lee does not recommend abandoning Forts Sumter and Moultrie but does agree to the removal of a portion of their armament to be used elsewhere. Lee inquires again of Kirby Smith in Tennessee if the promised regiments from Alabama and Georgia have arrived, and advises that there are no other troops that can be sent except possibly two regiments in Florida if they are ready for the field. Lee instructs Maj. Michael Harman at Staunton to collect all the troops around that city and join Jackson to "shake [Union Gen. James] Shields and make him pause." Col. Robert Chilton joins Lee's headquarters as chief of staff. Showers throughout the day.[18]

Valley to strike at McClellan's right flank north of the Chickahominy—was agreed upon by Lee and Davis on their afternoon ride. Davis, *Rise and Fall*, vol. 2, 108-9.

15 Freeman, *Lee's Dispatches*, 3-5; *OR* 11, pt. 1, 743; *OR* 11, pt. 3, 570. It is curious that Lee declined Davis's offer of a horse as "Brown Roan" was going blind, and Lee was forced to give him to a local farmer during the summer because the animal was no longer fit for field service. Custis to Robert A. Brock, Aug. 11, 1891, Lee papers, SH. Branch was stationed south of Hanover Court House guarding the Virginia Central when he was attacked by a much larger force under Fitz-John Porter on May 27. The engagement is known variously as the Battle of Slash Church, Hanover Court House, or Peake's Turnout.

16 *OR* 14, 536; REL to J. E. Finegan, June 3, 1862, telegram book, REL HQ papers, VHS; REL to T. H. Holmes, June 3, 1862, telegram book, REL HQ papers, VHS; *OR* 11, pt. 3, 572; WNP to wife, June 3, 1862, WNP papers, UNC; Krick, *CW Weather*, 59. According to Sir Frederick Maurice, Lee biographer and editor of Charles Marshall's papers, GO60 announcing DeLeon as medical director was the first reference in official correspondence to the "Army of Northern Virginia" as the name of that field army. Maurice, *Lee's Aide de Camp*, 119. DeLeon's time with Lee's army lasted only several weeks before he was replaced by Lafayette Guild on June 27. DeLeon CSR.

17 Long, *Memoirs of REL*, 166; Pitts, *High Meadow*, 18-9; Harsh, *Confederate Tide Rising*, 77; *OR* 11, pt. 3, 572-3. Freeman was uncertain whether Boteler's visit occurred on the 3rd or 4th, but Hugh Pitts and Joseph Harsh both put it on the 4th. Freeman, *Lee*, vol. 2, 83.

18 *OR* 14, 541-2; *OR* 10, pt. 2, 584; *OR* 11, pt. 3, 574-5; Robert M. Tombes, ed., *When the Peaches Get Ripe: Letters Home from Lt. Robert Gaines Haile, Jr., Essex Sharpshooters, 55th VA., 1862* (Richmond, VA, 1999), 35; Krick, *CW Weather*, 59.

June 5, Thursday (Dabbs House/Oak Grove/Old Tavern): Lee goes to the front lines early in the morning, making a reconnaissance of a portion of McClellan's position. Lee informs Davis that he is preparing a fortified line in front of Richmond which he will hold with a portion of the army freeing up a portion for offensive maneuver: "I am preparing a line that I can hold with part of our forces in front, while with the rest I will endeavor to make a diversion to bring McClellan out." He mentions his efforts to get a railroad gun to use on the York River Railroad and recommends pulling troops from the Carolinas and Georgia to reinforce Jackson who would then launch an offensive across the Potomac. Lee writes to the secretary of war regarding getting reinforcements for Jackson, and to Gen. Holmes ordering him to come to Petersburg with his force if he cannot strike a blow at Ambrose Burnside at New Bern. Lee checks on the progress of an iron-casemated railroad gun with ordnance bureau chief Josiah Gorgas, chief engineer Walter Stevens, and naval ordnance chief George Minor; he tells Minor: "If I could get it in position by daylight tomorrow I could astonish our neighbors."[19]

Lee instructs Brig. Gen. Robert Ransom to proceed ahead of his brigade to Drewry's Bluff and determine if any additional troops besides his brigade will be needed to hold it; once his brigade arrives to relieve the troops there, he is to take over that position himself. Lee orders the creation of a provost guard within each division, authorizes a whiskey ration at the discretion of the division commanders, and instructs staff officers to stay with their commands unless ordered elsewhere. Lee instructs Magruder not to yield ground to the enemy, and to reoccupy James Garnett's farm tomorrow morning, where Magruder's troops were engaged in a skirmish today. Lee informs Kirby Smith that no heavy artillery is available to send him, and informs Pemberton that all guns recently received have already been distributed, so Pemberton must resort to re-issuing those of sick and wounded troops. Cloudy with showers.[20]

June 6, Friday (Dabbs House/Charles City Road/Williamsburg Road): Lee inspects the progress of works along the portion of the lines occupied by Huger, Longstreet, and D. H. Hill; he assures Longstreet that there is no gap in the line, and that the enemy is "all quiet, but . . . working like beavers, making bridges and causeways." Lee writes to John M. Brooke regarding the railroad gun; Lee wants the cannon mounted as soon as possible so the flatcar can be put in position even if the iron shield is not completed. Lee recommends making a POW exchange proposed by McClellan, who wishes a staff officer of one of his brigade commanders returned.[21] Lee asks Stonewall Jackson by what route troops should be sent him, and orders Joseph Finegan to send his two new Florida regiments to Kirby Smith at Chattanooga, notifying Kirby Smith that they are coming to him. Cloudy with periods of rain.[22]

---

19 Long, *Memoirs of REL*, 166; Freeman, *Lee's Dispatches*, 5-10; OR 11, pt. 3, 574-5; REL to T. H. Holmes, June 5, 1862, telegram book, REL HQ papers, VHS. Long recorded that Lee went out on the lines, but did not record where; Lee's subsequent correspondence today regarding the railroad gun for the York River RR suggests he went to the vicinity of Old Tavern and the area around the railroad near Oak Grove. Lee was astute enough to recognize that one of Joe Johnston's biggest failings had been keeping Jefferson Davis in the dark regarding his movements and plans. Lee informed Davis in his letter of today's date, "Our position requires you should know everything and you must excuse my troubling you." Freeman, *Lee's Dispatches*, 9. The railroad gun was an experimental weapon developed by Lee's former aide John M. Brooke. It incorporated sloping iron armor (similar to what Brooke had used on the *CSS Virginia* and other ironclads of her class) protecting a heavy naval or seacoast gun mounted on a railroad flatcar. It first saw action at the Battle of Savage's Station on June 29.

20 REL to Robert Ransom, June 5, 1862, telegram book, REL HQ papers, VHS; GO64, June 5, 1862, EPA papers, UNC; OR 11, pt. 3, 576-7; OR 10, pt. 2, 590; REL to J. C. Pemberton, June 5, 1862, telegram book, REL HQ papers, VHS; Krick, *CW Weather*, 59.

21 Long, *Memoirs of REL*, 167; OR 11, pt. 3, 577; Brooke, *Ironclads and Big Guns*, 93; OR 3, Series 2, 644-5.

22 REL to Jackson, June 6, 1862, telegram book, REL HQ papers, VHS; REL to J. E. Finegan, June 6, 1862, telegram book, REL HQ papers, VHS; REL to E. Kirby Smith, June 6, 1862, telegram book, REL HQ papers, VHS; Krick, *CW Weather*, 59.

June 7, Saturday (Dabbs House): Lee remains at headquarters today, sending Col. Long in the morning to make a reconnaissance around Mechanicsville on the far left; in the afternoon President Davis comes to headquarters. Lee orders military roads to be constructed from each division to Richmond, and reiterates that captured enemy property cannot be kept for personal use but must be turned over to the proper department. Lee writes to President Davis regarding the possible promotion of Brig. Gen. Richard Anderson to division command; Lee doesn't know Anderson personally but if Longstreet thinks enough of him to recommend him, Lee will agree once a vacancy occurs. Lee presents to Davis the reasons for his opposition to Davis's desire to brigading troops by state, but promises to undertake this reorganization but cautions that it will take considerable time to put into effect.[23]

Lee tells Secretary of War Randolph that Robert Ransom cannot be spared to replace Turner Ashby as Jackson's cavalry commander; instead he recommends Thomas Munford or George H. Steuart. Lee advises Kirby Smith of the two Florida regiments being sent him, and that there are two regiments in Georgia and Alabama available for his use but he will have to provide arms for them. Clouds and showers continue.[24]

June 8, Sunday (Dabbs House): Lee and several members of the staff attend church service in the field with the troops. Lee sends his congratulations to Stonewall Jackson for his recent string of victories and that if possible Lee would like to have his forces in Richmond. Lee tells Sec. Randolph that Jackson's current strategic situation seems to rule out an offensive in the Valley, thus "reinforcements will be lost upon him." He also requests that Randolph curtail the practice of detailing able-bodied troops for hospital duties, preferring instead that noncombatants be used. The general also tells Sec. Randolph that no more field artillery is required by his army, so the artillery units forming at Camp Lee should be converted to infantry and the horses assigned to them put to better use. Lee orders Gen. Ransom to move his infantry brigade from Petersburg to Drewry's Bluff, and Lee consolidates his cavalry under Jeb Stuart by ordering the cavalry contingents from the Cobb Legion and Wise Legion to report to Stuart.[25]

June 9, Monday (Dabbs House): Lee orders Theophilus Holmes to bring his available force to Richmond. Lee informs Sec. Randolph of Jackson's victory at Cross Keys and, in an abrupt reversal from yesterday now that Jackson's situation has changed favorably, Lee requests that reinforcements be sent to the Valley. He also sends the secretary a letter from McClellan regarding a POW exchange; Lee proposes putting Brig. Gen. Howell Cobb in charge

---

23 Long, *Memoirs of REL*, 167-8; GO65, June 7, 1862, REL papers, MOC; Freeman, *Lee's Dispatches*, 10-2. Armistead Long noted President Davis's visit, but he did not mention anything that was discussed during the meeting. *Memoirs of REL*, 167-8.

24 *OR* 11, pt. 3, 580; *OR* 10, pt. 2, 597-8; Krick, *CW Weather*, 59. Ashby was killed June 6 in a rear guard action outside Harrisonburg; a small marker amidst the sprawl surrounding James Madison University marks the spot of his death. Thomas Munford was colonel of the 2nd VA Cav.; he was repeatedly recommended for promotion to brigadier and frequently led a brigade in action, but never received the much-warranted promotion. Krick, *Lee's Colonels*, 284. George Steuart was a native of Baltimore and one of the more prominent Marylanders in Confederate service. He commanded a portion of Jackson's cavalry earlier in the Valley campaign, though not to Jackson's satisfaction. Jackson put Steuart back in command of an infantry brigade. Steuart's wounding at Cross Keys on June 8 removed him from consideration. Once he recovered, Steuart commanded a brigade in the ANV for much of the war. Jeffry D. Wert, "George Hume Steuart," *Confederate General*, vol. 6, 2-3.

25 Long, *Memoirs of REL*, 168; *OR* 11, pt. 3, 579, 581-3. Which brigade church services were attended by Lee is not known; Long recorded only that it was "at one of the right wing brigades." Long, *Memoirs of REL*, 168. The "Legions" were not unlike a modern regimental combat team, containing infantry, cavalry, and artillery. They were not very practical in the field, which led to their separation into their three respective branches such as Lee did here. As an olive branch to Thomas Cobb for breaking up his command, Lee offered to place the Legion artillery in the brigade of his brother Howell Cobb. *OR* 11, pt. 3, 581-2.

of it as it will occur in his front, or Lee can oversee it personally if Randolph so desires.²⁶

Lee informs Henry Wise that the Navy will assume control of Chaffin's Bluff, where Wise is currently stationed, so he is to join D. H. Hill's division. Lee informs Gen. Lovell that Magruder has been assigned to command west of the Mississippi, for which Lovell is currently responsible, but Magruder "cannot leave yet." Rain continues.²⁷

June 10, Tuesday (Dabbs House): Jeb Stuart comes to Dabbs with a written report from his scout, John S. Mosby, detailing the vulnerability of McClellan's right flank. Mosby discovered the Federal right to be not anchored on either the Pamunkey River or Totopotomoy Creek; Stuart proposes to Lee that he lead a reconnaissance in force to that area, to which Lee consents. Lee proposes to President Davis sending two brigades from the Army of Northern Virginia to Jackson to enable him to "wipe out Fremont" and then to come east to join Lee. Lee requests that tentage of any sort be provided for his army, as the men are suffering from being exposed to the elements. Probably largely influenced by Magruder's recent encounter at the Garnett farm on the 5th, Lee distributes a circular calling for vigilance on the part of all commanders and to prevent small parties of the enemy from advancing. Lee informs the War Department and the officers of Gen. W. H. C. Whiting's brigade that Col. Evander Law is only their temporary commander, that the brigade is still Whiting's and he is only temporarily commanding the division during G. W. Smith's illness.²⁸

Lee orders Holmes to send the 1st North Carolina Cavalry to Richmond to join Stuart, and continues to scrape together reinforcements for Kirby Smith at Chattanooga, ordering three unarmed regiments sent to him.²⁹

Mrs. Lee, Annie, and Mildred pass through the lines at Meadow Bridge in early afternoon; they take up residence at the home of James H. Caskie in Richmond. In the evening Lee writes to Mary glad that she has made it safely through the lines and he will visit as soon as he is able. Rain again today.³⁰

---

26 REL to T. H. Holmes, June 9, 1862, telegram book, REL HQ papers, VHS; *OR* 11, pt. 3, 584; *OR* 3, Series 2, 893.

27 *OR* 11, pt. 3, 584-5; REL to Mansfield Lovell, June 9, 1862, telegram book, REL HQ papers, VHS; Tombes, *When the Peaches Get Ripe*, 41. A letter to Mary dated June 9, 1862, from Dabbs was published in Dowdey, *Wartime Papers*, 229-30, but its content is clearly from after the Seven Days' Battles; its correct date is July 9. Dowdey caught this error and placed the letter in its correct context; the original is in the REL papers, LOC.

28 Fox, *Stuart's Finest Hour*, 60-1; Emory M. Thomas, *Bold Dragoon: The Life of J.E.B. Stuart* (New York, 1988), 111-3; *OR* 51, pt. 2, 1074; *OR* 11, pt. 3, 585-8; REL to Jefferson Davis, June 10, 1862, telegram book, REL HQ papers, VHS. This discussion between Lee and Stuart led to the "Ride around McClellan," for which Lee sent written orders on the 11th.

29 REL to T. H. Holmes, June 10, 1862, telegram book, REL HQ papers, VHS; REL to J. E. Finegan, June 10, 1862, telegram book, REL HQ papers, VHS; REL to E. P. Watkins, June 10, 1862, telegram book, REL HQ papers, VHS; REL to M. L. Woods, June 10, 1862, telegram book, REL HQ papers, VHS; REL to H. W. Hilliard, June 10, 1862, telegram book, REL HQ papers, VHS; REL to E. Kirby Smith, June 10, 1862, telegram book, REL HQ papers, VHS.

30 Tombes, *When the Peaches Get Ripe*, 42; Coulling, *Lee Girls*, 103; Dowdey, *Wartime Papers*, 190; Pitts, *High Meadow*, 27. There are only two known firsthand accounts concerning Mrs. Lee's "exchange," and they are vastly different. Lt. Robert G. Haile of the 55th VA was in command of the picket detail at Meadow Bridge when a flag of truce appeared on the Union side with Mary's carriage and an escort. Col. A. T. A. Torbert was in command of her escort, and explained to Lt. Haile his mission. Torbert and Haile shared a flask while a runner went to bring Col. Francis Mallory of the 55th VA to the bridge. Mallory and one of Brig. Gen. Charles Field's staff officers arrived to receive Mary into Confederate lines, and she was driven into Richmond by Charles F. M. Bayliss of Company F, 55th VA. Tombes, *When the Peaches Get Ripe*, 42-5. That version differs greatly from the account provided long after the war by Maj. W. Roy Mason of Field's staff (who was likely the unnamed staff officer in Haile's account). According to Mason, Gen. Lee himself went to Field's headquarters in the morning and asked specifically for Mason, explaining to the major, "I have some property in the hands of the enemy, and General McClellan has informed me that he would deliver it to me at any time I asked for it." Mason then claims to have been taken blindfolded to Army of the Potomac headquarters, where he conversed with McClellan for some time until a carriage bearing Mrs. Lee appeared. Mason escorted the carriage through the lines to the home of "Mrs. Gooch" near Meadow Bridge, where Lee greeted his wife. W. Roy Mason, "Origin of the Lee Tomatoes," *B&L*, vol. 2, 277. Mason's account is so different from Haile's, and was written so long after the war, that its veracity is questionable. Haile's version was written within hours of the incident, and is followed here. Many writers have followed Freeman's error in assuming

June 11, Wednesday (Dabbs House): Lee issues written orders to Stuart to explore McClellan's right flank. He sends Chase Whiting with two brigades to reinforce Jackson, causing Magruder and D. H. Hill to shift positions to cover his departure; Whiting's troops move through Richmond with no secrecy about their destination, although Lee does request that Secretary of War Randolph instruct the newspapers to be silent about the move. Lee advises Jackson by both telegraph and courier that Whiting is headed to him, as is Lawton with a brigade from Georgia; Jackson is to leave a covering force in the Valley and move with everything else—including these three newly arrived brigades—to Ashland and sweep down the Chickahominy behind McClellan's flank.[31]

Lee writes to Gen. McClellan proposing Howell Cobb as the Confederate representative for the requested prisoner exchange. The general also writes to Governor Letcher's aide, Col. S. Bassett French, regarding Stonewall Jackson's request for the promotion of Col. John R. Jones. Lee explains that, while he does not know Jones and has full confidence in Jackson's judgment when it comes to selecting officers, there is no command for Jones at the present time. Edmund Ruffin visits Mrs. Lee in Richmond, where he learns from her that all his farm implements and crops had been seized by the Federals, and that many of Ruffin's slaves had fled as well. "No depredations as yet on the mansion. But now that Mrs. Lee and her daughters have left no doubt it will be pillaged if not burnt," he wrote in his diary. Charles Venable receives orders from the War Department that he is to report to Gen. Lee for staff duties.[32]

June 12, Thursday (Dabbs House): Lee receives a note from his wife Mary in the afternoon giving the details of her safe arrival within Confederate lines. The general requests that Alabama Governor Shorter dispatch three new regiments to the capital, which will all be armed upon their arrival in Richmond. The general also informs John Letcher, Virginia's governor, to expect the arrival of these troops.[33]

June 13, Friday (Dabbs House): Lee observes the enemy position from a location with Cobb's Brigade along the Nine Mile Road. The general accepts McClellan's proposal for a prisoner exchange to occur on Sunday, but he changes the venue to the Mechanicsville Bridge. The general's June 3 letter to Brig. Gen. Lawrence Branch regarding the Battle of

---

that Mary's arrival in Richmond was the first time Lee saw her since leaving Arlington. Freeman, *Lee*, vol. 2, 252-4; Thomas, *REL*, 231, 434n4. Freeman had access to Haile's letters (which were unpublished and in private hands at that time) and he admits using them to pinpoint the date of Mary's arrival as June 10—yet he still relied upon Mason's account. Freeman, *Lee*, vol. 2, 254n16. There was no carriage at Marlbourne, so the Lees had to borrow one from Dr. Macon at Ingleside, which took them first to McClellan's headquarters at the Trent House near Grapevine Bridge, where they had lunch with the Federal commander, and then on through the lines at Meadow Bridge and into Richmond. Johnston, *Echoes of 1861-1961*, 22-3, 64-5. The Caskie house was at 1100 E Clay St. Mary W. Scott, *Houses of Old Richmond* (Richmond, VA, 1941), 128-31. Early secondary accounts incorrectly state that Mary went straight to 707 Franklin, but she did not move there until early 1864. See Robins, "Mrs. Lee during the War," 327; Lee, "Mary Anne Randolph Custis Lee," 21 n47. Mary herself stated in October 1862, "I am at Mr. James H. Caskie's, corner of Clay and 11th Streets." Mrs. REL to Selina Powell, Oct. 30, 1862, Powell family papers, W&M.

31 OR 11, pt. 3, 589-91, 594; Freeman, *Lee*, vol. 2, 95; REL to Jackson, June 11, 1862, telegram book, REL HQ papers, VHS. President Davis noted that Lee was "overwhelmed with visitors" to headquarters today. Davis's reference is unknown. Rowland, *Jefferson Davis, Constitutionalist*, vol. 5, 274-5.

32 OR 3, Series 2, 674-5; Glenn C. Oldaker, ed., *Centennial Tales: Memoirs of Colonel 'Chester' S. Bassett French, Extra Aide-de-Camp to Generals Lee and Jackson, The Army of Northern Virginia, 1861-1865* (New York, 1962), 58; Scarborough, *Ruffin Diary*, vol. 2, 337; Venable CSR. John R. Jones was the lieutenant colonel of the 33rd VA and would be promoted to brigadier general later in June. Jones later abandoned his command at the Battle of Chancellorsville in early May 1863 and was relieved as a result. Warner, *Generals in Gray*, 165. Venable received Gen. Lee's invitation to serve on his staff in May of 1862, but circumstances kept him at Vicksburg, MS, in the interval; this time he was *ordered* to report to Lee.

33 Pitts, *High Meadow*, 30; REL to J. G. Shorter, June 12, 1862, telegram book, REL HQ papers, VHS; REL to S. B. French, June 12, 1862, telegram book, REL HQ papers, VHS. Unfortunately, Mary's note with details of her passage through the lines has not been found; its existence is noted in an undated letter of Lee to Mary in Lee papers, VHS.

Slash Church is published in today's Richmond *Enquirer*.³⁴

June 14, Saturday (Dabbs House): Lee issues orders that partisan units cannot accept recruits from other units, and announces that Brig. Gen. Howell Cobb will serve as the Confederate commissioner for a POW exchange to occur tomorrow. Lee inquires if Jackson would like for Whiting and Lawton's troops to continue all the way to Staunton, and orders Ransom at Drewry's Bluff to harass enemy shipping as much as he can.³⁵

Lee answers a request from a Mrs. William Taylor for her husband to be transferred to the Albemarle Artillery; he gives his usual response that he cannot grant her request and that it must be made by her husband through proper channels. In the evening, Congressman Alexander Boteler meets with Lee to discuss Jackson's options in the Shenandoah Valley: building up his strength enough for him to launch an offensive across the Potomac, or to bring his entire command east to Richmond and use it against the Army of the Potomac. In the evening, possibly while Boteler is present, Corporal Benjamin T. Doswell of the 4th Virginia Cavalry brings word that Jeb Stuart's force is pinned against the Chickahominy, and the cavalry commander would like for Lee to make a diversion on the Charles City Road to allow Stuart to extricate his forces; due to the lateness of the hour, Lee can do nothing.³⁶

June 15, Sunday (Dabbs House): Before dawn Jeb Stuart arrives at headquarters and reports to Lee the results of his mission. Lee grants John B. Magruder's request to have artillerist Stephen D. Lee assigned to his command. Thunderstorms in the afternoon along the leading edge of a cold front create a 30-degree drop in temperatures once the storms pass.³⁷

June 16, Monday (Dabbs House/Half Sink): Lee sends orders via Congressman Boteler to Stonewall Jackson directing him to leave the Valley and join Lee's army outside Richmond. After this, Lee and Col. Long ride to Half Sink, where Telegraph Road crosses the Chickahominy River to reconnoiter the Federal position north of the stream. Longstreet meets with Lee at Dabbs house to discuss the idea of bringing Jackson from the Valley to strike at McClellan's exposed right flank.³⁸

Lee requests a meeting with Sec. Randolph at the Dabbs house in the afternoon because Lee believed that he should not at this time be away from headquarters to come to the city. Lee informs Mansfield Lovell that there are no troops available to

---

34 Cobb, "Extracts from Letters," 292; *OR* 4, Series 2, 14; REL newspaper references, DSF papers, LVA. Cobb recalled that Daniel H. Hill, Magruder, McLaws, and several brigadiers also visited, but his phrasing suggests they were not with Lee. Much public criticism was aimed at Branch for his defeat at Slash Church.

35 *OR* 11, pt. 3, 599; *OR* 4, Series 2, 773; REL to Jackson, June 14, 1862, telegram book, REL HQ papers, VHS; REL to Robert Ransom, June 14, 1862, telegram book, REL HQ papers, VHS.

36 REL to Mrs. W. E. Taylor, June 14, 1862, Dabbs House Museum; Freeman, *Lee*, vol. 2, 99, 102-3. Jeb Stuart's reconnaissance turned into an almost complete circuit of McClellan's Army of the Potomac, and caused the Union general no little embarrassment. The recent rains had raised the Chickahominy above flood stage, and enemy cavalry pursuing Stuart pinned him against the flooded stream. Stuart barely managed to escape with his command.

37 H. B. McClellan, *The Campaigns of Stuart's Cavalry* (Secaucus, NJ, 1993), 66; *OR* 11, pt. 3, 600; Krick, *CW Weather*, 59-60. Charles Venable left Vicksburg for Richmond on this date. Venable memoirs, McDowell-Miller-Warner papers, UVA.

38 Long, *Memoirs of REL*, 168; Pitts, *High Meadow*, 35; Dowdey, *Wartime Papers*, 194; Longstreet, *From Manassas to Appomattox*, 120. Long wrote that he and Lee went to the Chickahominy, but he did not say where. Given that they were checking the approaches to Porter's V Corps, they must have been either at either Half Sink, Meadow Bridge, or Mechanicsville Bridge. Pitts put their reconnaissance at Half Sink. *High Meadow*, 35. Freeman does not give a location, but states they in fact crossed the river, which would rule out Meadow Bridge and Mechanicsville Bridges because the Federals had outposts at the northern ends of spans. *Lee*, vol. 2, 104-6. Lee had personally reconnoitered the Half Sink area just prior to the Battle of Seven Pines and it was not guarded by the enemy, so it seems the most logical destination. The order in which the events of today occur is open to debate. Freeman put Lee's and Long's Chickahominy scout first, followed by Longstreet's visit. Ibid. Joseph Harsh reverses the order, believing their reconnaissance was a result of the meeting with Longstreet. *Confederate Tide Rising*, 87.

send to him unless Gen. Beauregard can spare some.[39]

June 17, Tuesday (Dabbs House): Lee's daughter Mary and Bishop John Johns come to Dabbs to visit. Lee writes to McClellan establishing an agreement between them that medical personnel are non-combatants and thus not subject to capture. Lee explains to Henry Wise that Chaffin's Bluff is under the command of the Navy, and that because of his station on the extreme right flank of the army, he is to provide protection for the land face of the river battery. Maj. Stevens and his engineers, explains the general, will lay out a line for Wise in rear of Chaffin's, and Jeb Stuart's cavalry will picket Wise's front.[40]

Lee informs Holmes that Burnside reportedly moved with 14,000 men to Fort Monroe, so Holmes is to strip his department and bring nearly everything to Petersburg. Lee telegraphs Jackson that the requested wagons will be made available to him, and instructs the mustering officer in Columbia, South Carolina to use conscripts to fill up the under strength South Carolina regiments in Pemberton's department.[41]

June 18, Wednesday (Dabbs House): Lee sends more detailed instructions to Holmes to concentrate his forces at Petersburg so as to protect Drewry's Bluff from a movement by Burnside. Lee directs that firearms be sent to Mansfield Lovell, and updates Kirby Smith on reinforcements ordered to him.[42]

June 19, Thursday (Dabbs House/Richmond): Lee spends the morning and early afternoon attending to correspondence, before going to Richmond in the afternoon. He tells President Davis that he can spare Benjamin Huger from the ANV to be sent to Charleston, South Carolina, as Gov. Pickens requests. He informs Sec. Randolph of his belief that McClellan has been reinforced by not only Burnside but by troops from Henry Halleck's army in the Western Theater, so now is the time for Braxton Bragg's army to advance against a weakened Halleck. Lee sends to McClellan a list of all the prisoners taken since Seven Pines/Fair Oaks, and also asks the Federal general if reports are true that two Confederate officers currently being held prisoner are to be executed. Lee informs McClellan that if these reports are indeed true two randomly selected Federal officers currently being held will likewise be executed in retaliation.[43]

The general orders the post commander at Lynchburg, Virginia, to send several deserters from the Valley Army being held there to Jackson for trial. In the late afternoon Lee travels into Richmond and meets with President Davis at the Executive Mansion to explain his bold plan of bringing Jackson's army east to strike McClellan's right flank; they agree to meet again on the evening of the 21st at Dabbs. After leaving the Executive Mansion, Lee goes to the Caskie house just a block away to visit with his wife and daughter Mary, where he spends the night.[44]

---

[39] REL to G. W. Randolph, June 16, 1862, REL papers, W&L; *OR* 15, 756. There is no known record of whether Sec. Randolph came to Dabbs as Lee requested.

[40] Pitts, *High Meadow*, 36-7; *OR* 4, Series 2, 45; *OR* 11, pt. 3, 604-6.

[41] REL to T. H. Holmes, June 17, 1862, telegram book, REL HQ papers, VHS; REL to Jackson, June 17, 1862, telegram book, REL HQ papers, VHS; REL to J. S. Preston, June 17, 1862, telegram book, REL HQ papers, VHS.

[42] *OR* 11, pt. 3, 607; REL to Mansfield Lovell, June 18, 1862, telegram book, REL HQ papers, VHS; REL to E. Kirby Smith, June 18, 1862, telegram book, REL HQ papers, VHS.

[43] *OR* 14, 569; *OR* 11, pt. 3, 609; *OR* 4, Series 2, 39; *OR* 9, Series 2, 46-7. The two officers to whom Lee referred were identified only as "Capt. Sprigg" and "Capt. Triplett" of the "Virginia Rangers." McClellan replied on the 21st that Lee's information was incorrect, and that no captive officers were to be executed. *OR* 9, Series 2, 49.

[44] REL to J. M Galt, June 19, 1862, telegram book, REL HQ papers, VHS; Pitts, *High Meadow*, 38-9. Annie and Mildred went with Agnes and Charlotte to Jones Spring near Warrenton, NC, leaving Mrs. Lee and daughter Mary alone at the Caskie house. Pitts, *High Meadow*, 38.

June 20, Friday (Richmond/Dabbs House): Lee returns to headquarters from his overnight stay in Richmond at the Caskie House with his wife and daughter. Lt. Col. James L. Corley joins the army as chief quartermaster.[45]

June 21, Saturday (Dabbs House): Lee requests of Navy Sec. Mallory a naval officer and crew to man the "railroad battery" on the York River Railroad so the gun can be put in position tomorrow. Holmes's command is extended to the James River, making him responsible for all of Southside as well as North Carolina; he is to establish headquarters at Petersburg. Lee informs Gen. Pendleton that Lee's plans "will rely greatly upon the good use of artillery to hold the enemy in check should he advance against our weakened lines" so Pendleton is to place as many guns as he can along the lines.[46]

Lee publishes the procedures for transporting and admitting sick soldiers to the hospitals in Richmond, and requests that Gen. Finegan send one of his Florida regiments to Virginia. Lee meets with President Davis in early evening, discussing further the plans for Lee's offensive. Afterward Lee meets with G. W. Smith to inform him of the planned offensive, and instructing Smith to remain in Richmond to recover his health.[47]

June 22, Sunday (Dabbs House): Lee makes slight adjustments to the ANV command structure: Longstreet is given command of his own and D. H. Hill's division, Magruder resumes command of the three divisions originally comprising the Army of the Peninsula, and the artillery is reorganized into battalions. Lee writes to both Charlotte and Agnes; he tells Charlotte of Stuart's "Ride Around McClellan" and describes his own uniform and mentions that he has gone gray and has a full white beard now; to Agnes he describes his recent visit with her mother and sister, and mentions also that Mrs. Dabbs left her cats at High Meadow in his staff's care: "They do not seem to care how the war goes but enjoy their gambols in perfect serenity."[48]

June 23, Monday (Dabbs House): Lee issues congratulatory orders for Stuart's ride around McClellan's army. Around midday Lee summons Longstreet and the two Hills to headquarters for a meeting that afternoon. Around 3:00 p.m. Jackson arrives at Dabbs, but finding Lee busy and unwilling to interrupt him, he waits in the yard in front of the house. While waiting outside, D. H. Hill arrives, much surprised to see his brother-in-law Jackson, who he (and anyone else) thought nowhere near Richmond. Longstreet and A. P. Hill soon arrive and the four-some meets with Lee in the general's upstairs office. Lee explains to them his plan of having Magruder and Huger hold the lines in front of Richmond with Jackson turning the enemy right flank and Longstreet and the Hills as an assault force upon that flank near Mechanicsville. After explaining the concept to them, Lee withdraws to the next room while his four lieutenants work out the details of its execution. When Lee returns to the office, the four generals have agreed upon June 26 as the date for the attack. The meeting breaks up about nightfall. Maj. Charles Venable at last reports for duty, assuming his position as aide de camp on Lee's staff.[49]

---

45 Pitts, *High Meadow*, 38; Corley CSR. The lack of correspondence on this date suggests that Lee may have spent much of the day in Richmond with his wife and daughter.

46 *OR* 11, pt. 3, 610; *OR* 9, 475; A. P. Mason to WNP, June 21, 1862, WNP papers, UNC.

47 GO4, June 21, 1862, Confederate States Army papers, VHS; *OR* 11, pt. 3, 610-1; Pitts, *High Meadow*, 40; *OR* 51, pt. 2, 593-4.

48 GO71, June 22, 1862, EPA papers, UNC; Dowdey, *Wartime Papers*, 196-7; Pitts, *High Meadow*, 41.

49 Dowdey, *Wartime Papers*, 197-8; Freeman, *Lee*, vol. 2, 107-13; Maurice, *Lee's Aide de Camp*, 84-6; Taylor, *General Lee*, 62; Longstreet, *From Manassas to Appomattox*, 121-2; Venable memoirs, UVA. Charles Marshall wrote that the meeting occurred in Lee's second floor office. Maurice, *Lee's Aide de Camp*, 84. Walter Taylor did not state where in the house the meeting occurred, and Armistead Long did not even mention the meeting at all. It seems logical it would have occurred in Lee's upstairs office because the main room on the lower floor was occupied and being used by his staff. Emory Thomas agreed with Marshall and placed the meeting upstairs. Thomas, *REL*, 233. Freeman was unsure of the location, in part

June 24, Tuesday (Dabbs House): Lee personally drafts the attack orders for the offensive on the 26th and gives them to the staff for copying and distribution. Lee is informed that the railroad gun is ready to be transferred to the Army; as it will no longer be under Navy control, he requests Porter Alexander to get artillerists to man it. Capt. Langdon Cheves meets with Lee in the morning regarding use of his observation balloon; Lee instructs him to report to Alexander. Rain during the day.[50]

June 25, Wednesday (Dabbs House/Oak Grove): Early in the day Lee is tending to his morning correspondence at headquarters when the sound of firing from the area of Williamsburg Road catches his attention. Before mounting and riding for the front, he forwards to President Davis a letter from South Carolina Congressman William Porcher Miles regarding just how extremely unpopular Gen. John Pemberton has become in Charleston. Lee tells Davis, "I hardly see how the removal of Pemberton can be avoided," and offers the suggestion that Magruder be sent to command there, and Pemberton be reassigned to Bragg's army in the Western Theater. Lee sends orders to Jackson outlining his line of march to Ashland and beyond. By noon he is at the front on Williamsburg Road watching an attack on Robert Ransom's brigade at Oak Grove.[51]

While Lee is at the scene, President Davis rides to High Meadow to meet with him, but finding the general absent, returns to Richmond rather than continuing on to the front to meet Lee. The general determines that McClellan has not detected Lee's or Jackson's plans, and that the attack at Oak Grove was limited in nature. When Lee returns to Dabbs, he discovers his staff and servants packing up headquarters in preparation for the move "in the field" with the attack tomorrow, and that the president had ridden out to see him. Lee writes to Davis apologizing for missing his afternoon visit and giving a synopsis of the Williamsburg Road fight: the "general behavior of the troops was good, but the affair on the whole was not well managed." Lee particularly took issue with Huger's absence from his front during the engagement: "I have just sent him an order to take his position with his troops and to remain with them." He tells President Davis that McClellan's attack today was not related to Lee's own plans; accordingly, he continued, "I have determined to make no change in the plan." Regarding his earlier message to the president about Gen. Pemberton and Charleston, Lee explains that he does not know Brig. Gen. William D. Smith, but that he would consent to Smith replacing Pemberton.

During the evening Lt. T. W. Sydnor, a 4th Virginia Cavalry officer from Mechanicsville, brings to Lee information about that area including the presence of quicksand along Beaver Dam Creek near the Old Church Road crossing of that stream, which could seriously impact operations there. After a late dinner around 10:00 p.m. Lee sends wife Mary a quick note apologizing that he will not be able to visit

---

because Longstreet and D. H. Hill incorrectly placed Lee's office on the first floor—no doubt based on Long's description of the dwelling. Freeman, *Lee*, vol. 2, 109n4; Long, *Memoirs of REL*, 166. Pitts, who described June 23 as "the most important day in the history of the Dabbs house during the time it served as Lee's headquarters," wrote only that the meeting occurred in Lee's office. *High Meadow*, 17, 43-5. Jackson biographer G. F. R. Henderson wrote that this was the first time Lee and Jackson had met in person, but it is probable that they met in Richmond within days of Lee's arrival (see April 27, 1861, entry). G. F. R. Henderson, *Stonewall Jackson and the American Civil War*, 2 vols. (New York, 1898), vol. 1, 490.

50 Maurice, *Lee's Aide de Camp*, 86; OR 11, pt. 2, 498-9; George Minor to REL, June 24, 1862, EPA papers, UNC; Robert H. Chilton to Langdon Cheves, June 24, 1862, EPA papers, UNC; Freeman, *Lee*, vol. 2, 116. Lee provided written orders in large part to avoid repeating Johnston's mistake at Seven Pines of relying upon verbal orders, which were not understood by the commanders involved. Marshall wrote that Lee "remained in his room nearly all day" attending to the details of the pending attack. Maurice, *Lee's Aide de Camp*, 86.

51 Louis H. Manarin, *Henrico County: Field of Honor*, 2 vols. (Richmond, VA, 2004), vol. 1, 119; OR 14, 560; REL to Jackson, June 25, 1862, REL papers, MOC. The fighting at Oak Grove marked the beginning of the Seven Days' Battles; McClellan wanted to seize the ground there for placement of a siege battery. Portions of that battlefield remain today amidst the residential and commercial development around the Richmond airport, but as a whole, it as well as the Seven Pines battlefield that it overlaps, are lost.

her because of the skirmishing that has consumed the afternoon. Rain continues.⁵²

June 26, Thursday (Dabbs House/Chickahominy Bluff/Mechanicsville/Ravenswood): Early in the morning Lee notifies President Davis and Secretary Randolph that he will be on the Mechanicsville Turnpike today to direct the battle; he adds that Holmes's troops at Petersburg and Drewry's Bluff as well as Wise at Chaffin's Bluff are on alert to join the ANV if necessary. Before leaving Dabbs, Lee receives a message from Jackson that he is running behind schedule. Lee informs President Davis of Jackson's delay and warns that McClellan may have divined Confederate intentions.⁵³

After sending his message to the president, Lee and staff ride out to Chickahominy Bluffs, overlooking the Mechanicsville Turnpike crossing of that river, where he can observe the action around Mechanicsville. By early afternoon President Davis, Secretary Randolph, Secretary of State Judah Benjamin, and a number of Congressmen arrive at Chickahominy Bluffs to observe the fighting. Stonewall Jackson, however, is much later than Lee anticipated and nothing has been heard from him since morning. Davis, Randolph, Lee, Longstreet, and D. H. Hill sit in the shade along the turnpike waiting to hear Jackson's guns.

About mid-afternoon, A. P. Hill pushes his division across Meadow Bridge several miles upstream from Lee's position and quickly drives the Federals from Mechanicsville, but comes under heavy fire from artillery on the opposite side of Beaverdam Creek east of the town. Lee sends Lt. Thomas Sydnor across the river to tell Hill to halt his advance until further orders, wanting to allow time for D. H. Hill and Longstreet to cross the Mechanicsville bridge in support.⁵⁴

In late afternoon Lee crosses the river into Mechanicsville; he meets A. P. Hill there and learns for the first time that Hill acted on his own initiative and knows nothing of Jackson. Lee then orders Hill to resume his attack, as D. H. Hill's brigades begin to deploy in support. Lee observes Hill's attack from the Binford farm, Waverly, at the intersection of Mechanicsville Turnpike and Cold Harbor Road, coming under artillery fire while near the farm's carriage house. It is likely during this stage of the battle that Lee encounters President Davis and the secretary of war under fire, and he orders them to

---

52 Freeman, *Lee's Dispatches*, 12-4; Freeman, *Lee*, vol. 2, 117-20; Freeman, *Lee's Lieutenants*, vol. 1, 514; Dowdey, *Wartime Papers*, 200-1. Lee's lack of confidence in Gen. Huger was becoming increasingly apparent in his correspondence. William D. Smith was colonel of the 20th GA before his promotion to brigadier. Congressman Miles pushed repeatedly for Smith to replace John Pemberton, but Smith's death from yellow fever in October 1862 intervened. Warner, *Generals in Gray*, 285-6. Gen. D. H. Hill's aide J. W. Ratchford recorded that Lee met with Hill and others for several hours during the evening, but he was likely confused about the date of the council of war on the 23rd. Evelyn Sieburg and James E. Hansen, eds., *Memoirs of a Confederate Staff Officer: From Bethel to Bentonville* (Shippensburg, PA, 1998), 16. The letter to Davis apologizing for missing his visit and mentioning Lee going to the front is misdated June 24; Ransom's fight at Oak Grove was on the 25th, which reveals Lee's mistake in dating the letter. Freeman, *Lee's Dispatches*, 12-3.

53 OR 11, pt. 3, 617; Freeman, *Lee's Dispatches*, 15-7; Dowdey, *Wartime Papers*, 201.

54 Maurice, *Lee's Aide de Camp*, 91; Eli N. Evans, *Judah P. Benjamin: The Jewish Confederate* (New York, 1988), 179; Clark, *Histories of Several Regiments from North Carolina*, vol. 1, 138; Brent, *Memoirs of the WBTS*, 160-4; Taylor, *General Lee*, 64; Freeman, *Lee*, vol. 2, 122-35. Jackson was hours behind schedule and failed to communicate at all with A. P. Hill. He also did not seem to fully understand his role in Lee's plan, and so made no effort to engage once he heard the sound of Hill's guns several miles to the south. Hill grew tired of waiting for Jackson and attacked on his own, expecting Jackson would momentarily arrive as planned and assist him. Jackson's performance in front of Richmond did not mirror the skill and audacity he had recently displayed in the Valley, or on other fields in the coming months. In his history of the Peninsula Campaign, Stephen Sears attributed his poor performance mostly to his unfamiliarity with the ground and physical exhaustion, coupled with the complexity of Lee's plan. Sears, *To the Gates of Richmond*, 199, 287-9, 344. Jackson biographer G. F. R. Henderson took an apologetic view of Jackson's actions and tried to absolve him of any blame. Henderson, *Stonewall Jackson*, 350-1, 379-83. Recent Jackson biographer James Robertson also takes a sympathetic view of his subject's role, and that despite his exhaustion and uncertain ground, Jackson should be complimented for what he accomplished rather than condemned for what he did not. James I. Robertson, *Stonewall Jackson: The Man, The Soldiers, the Legend* (New York, 1997), 504-5. Freeman titled the chapter reviewing the performance of the Confederate high command during the Seven Days' Battles thusly: "The Engima of Jackson's State of Mind." While critical of Jackson's performance, he also cited Jackson's exhaustion and having to learn on the fly. Freeman, *Lee's Lieutenants*, vol. 1, 655-63.

safety; a nearby soldier is killed by a bursting shell as this exchange occurs. Both Davis and Lee—independent of one another—personally order Roswell Ripley's brigade into the fight; Lee is eventually joined at Waverly by Longstreet and D. H. Hill.[55]

After the fighting dies out, Lee meets with Longstreet and the two Hills at the Lumpkin house in Mechanicsville, remaining there until about 11:00 p.m. trying to sort out the day's events and making plans to renew the fight tomorrow morning. After the meeting Lee crosses back to the south side of the Chickahominy and establishes headquarters for the night at Ravenswood, overlooking the bridge just west of the turnpike. Worried that McClellan would now surmise the weakness of Lee's lines in front of Richmond, Lee orders Magruder and Huger to hold their positions "at the point of the bayonet if necessary." He authorizes Huger to call on Wise and Holmes for reinforcement if he is pressed, and tells Magruder to be on the lookout for Lee's wing of the army at New Bridge tomorrow.[56]

June 27, Friday (Ravenswood/Mechanicsville/ Meadow Farm/Walnut Grove Church/Selwyn/New Cold Harbor/Powhite): Around dawn, possibly before, Lee leaves Ravenswood and crosses the Chickahominy to Mechanicsville, which is still under artillery fire from the Federal rear guard along Beaverdam Creek. With still no word from Jackson, Lee sends Walter Taylor to find and guide him into position to turn the Federal right flank, but the enemy retreats before Jackson can get into position. Lee accompanies Longstreet's column in the pursuit and stops briefly at the home of the Sydnor family, Meadow Farm; it may have been here that he learns of Jackson's presence close by at Walnut Grove Church. Lee finds Jackson consulting with A. P. Hill in the churchyard and joins the discussion. When Hill departs, Lee instructs Jackson to move to Cold Harbor, where he will be in position to turn the Federal flank if they take position along Powhite Creek as Lee expects. The two generals depart the church around 11:00 a.m. Lee joins Hill's column on the Cold Harbor Road before stopping at Walker Hogan's house, Selwyn, where he establishes a temporary command post. Lee sits on the porch; Longstreet reclines in the yard eating lunch with several brigade commanders nearby.[57]

Lee sends a message to Huger from Selwyn with the routes of march of Lee's columns, and also his belief that the Federals intend to make a stand behind Powhite Creek; he adds a postscript requesting that the message be forwarded to President Davis. Before or shortly after departing Selwyn, Lee sends Charles Venable to oversee repairs to one of the nearby Chickahominy bridges and establish communication with Magruder on the other side of the river. Brig. Gen. Maxcy Gregg, whose troops are in the lead of Hill's division, meets with Lee as his troops engage the Federals near Gaines's Mill on Powhite Creek. In early afternoon, Lee rejoins Hill's troops near Gaines's Mill and finds that the Federals are making their stand not behind Powhite Creek as he anticipated, but rather about a mile further east behind Boatswain's Swamp. Near

---

55 Freeman, *Lee*, vol. 2, 122-35; Hanover County Historical Society, *Old Homes of Hanover County, Virginia* (Hanover, VA, 2015), 60; Constance Cary Harrison, "Richmond Scenes in '62," *B&L*, vol. 2, 447-8; D. H. Hill, "Lee's Attacks North of the Chickahominy," *B&L*, vol. 2, 361; OR 11, pt. 2, 538; Freeman, *Lee's Lieutenants*, vol. 1, 514-5. Constance Cary Harrison recorded the exchange between Lee and Davis, no doubt with an added dramatic flourish, noting that "General Lee . . . at that moment was more to be dreaded than the enemy's guns." Lee: "Who are all this army of people, and what are they doing here?" Davis: "It is not my army, General." Lee: "It certainly is not MY army, Mr. President, and this is no place for it." Harrison, "Richmond Scenes," 448.

56 Sears, *To the Gates of Richmond*, 208; Maurice, *Lee's Aide de Camp*, 96; Freeman, *Lee*, vol. 2, 135; OR 11, pt. 3, 617; REL to Magruder, June 26, 1862, REL papers, UVA. Commercial development and Interstate 295 destroyed much of this battlefield. Small portions remain, including a gun emplacement at Chickahominy Bluffs and a few acres at Ellerson's Mill on Beaver Dam Creek, both operated by the NPS. Ravensworth is a private home amidst an older residential neighborhood; both Waverly and the Lumpkin house have been lost to development.

57 Maurice, *Lee's Aide de Camp*, 96-8; Freeman, *Lee*, vol. 2, 136-42; HCHS, *Old Homes of Hanover County*, 33-4; Henderson, *Stonewall Jackson*, vol. 2, 36-7n1; Snow, *Lee and his Generals*, 60-1. Meadow Farm was on the old River Road (which no longer exists) immediately behind the Union lines along Beaver Dam Creek. The house no longer stands.

New Cold Harbor, Lee, his staff, and several officers of Capt. Marmaduke Johnson's artillery battery assist in rallying Gregg's troops after they meet stiff resistance. Lee determines to make an immediate assault with Hill and Longstreet's divisions, with Jackson to join as soon as he arrives on the field. Maj. Venable returns from the Chickahominy bridge in the midst of the fighting and discovers "the battle was fiercely raging. I found the General on horseback near the line of battle directing the movement of troops and awaiting anxiously the arrival of General Jackson who did not reach us in time. . . . Impatient for the arrival of Jackson, General Lee galloped across the field in the rear of the line of battle under a sharp artillery fire to the left and met him [Jackson] coming up with his divisions."58

Lee greets Gen. Jackson somewhat coldly: "Ah General, I am very glad to see you. I had hoped to be with you before." When he encounters Gen. John B. Hood, who is commanding one of Chase Whiting's brigades, Lee impresses upon Hood the need to carry the enemy's position, to which Hood replies, "I will try." About 7:00 p.m. Hood's troops breach the Federal line and the Union position crumbles giving Lee his first victory of the war. In the evening he establishes headquarters at Powhite, the home of Dr. William Gaines, where he meets with Jackson, Longstreet, and presumably the Hills and others.59

The general sends a message to President Davis announcing the day's victory as hundreds of prisoners are gathered in the yard outside, under guard of a detachment of the 17th Virginia. Lafayette Guild is assigned to duty as medical director of the ANV, supplanting Dr. DeLeon. Lee's congratulatory message to Stuart of the 23rd is printed in the Richmond *Enquirer*.60

June 28, Saturday (Powhite/Cold Harbor): At dawn Lee, with breakfast of bread and ham in hand, departs headquarters for Jackson's front. As they leave, a cavalry detachment rides into the yard to escort the prisoners who had been corralled there overnight to Richmond. Finding the enemy gone

---

58 Dowdey, *Wartime Papers*, 203; Freeman, *Lee*, vol. 2, 141-53; Venable memoirs, UVA; OR 11, pt. 2, 853; "J. B. M.", "How the Seven Days' Battles around Richmond Began," *SHSP*, vol. 28, 95. Marmaduke Johnson was Lee's escort to the state capitol when he officially took command of Virginia's forces on April 23, 1861. At least one postwar account puts Jefferson Davis present on the field with Lee, but this is in error; Davis remained in Richmond: John Worsham, 21st VA, wrote that he saw Lee and Davis together near New Cold Harbor as his division deployed. John H. Worsham, *One of Jackson's Foot Cavalry* (New York, 1912), 99-100.

59 Horn, *REL Reader*, 191-2; William S. Hamby, "Fourth Texas in Battle of Gaines Mill," *CV*, vol. 14, 183; Hood, *Advance and Retreat*, 25; Thomas N. Page, *Robert E. Lee: Man and Soldier* (New York, 1911), 714-5; Freeman, *Lee*, vol. 2, 153-58. The location of Lee's headquarters on the night of the 27th is somewhat confusing. He undoubtedly used Selwyn for that purpose, albeit only briefly, prior to the battle. Nearly every writer has him returning there after the battle. However, his headquarters on the 28th was next door at Powhite. It seems unlikely he would move headquarters only about half a mile on the 28th, so it is this author's contention that Lee took Powhite as his headquarters the night of the battle. The continued use of Selwyn arises from a postwar statement by Andrew R. Ellerson, a local man serving in the 4th VA Cav. detailed to Longstreet as a guide. Ellerson wrote to Lee biographer Thomas Page in 1908 that both Lee and Longstreet had their headquarters for the night at "Hogan's dwelling," i.e. Selwyn. Freeman used this statement as his basis for asserting that Selwyn was indeed headquarters for the night, and this has been repeated by writers ever since. Freeman, *Lee*, vol. 2, 158. George Wise, who was one of the guards for the Yankee prisoners, wrote only that the location was Lee's headquarters; he did not give the name or owner of the house. George Wise, *Campaigns and Battles of the Army of Northern Virginia* (New York, 1916), 103. Historian Robert E. L. Krick agrees that HQ was at Powhite: "I suspect that when the time came for an overnight HQ, Dr. Gaines's house was nearer, and larger, and nicer. It also was Longstreet's headquarters, which was convenient. I can't think of any particular military or geographic motive that would have caused him to ride farther away from the battlefield to reach Selwyn." Email to the author, June 2, 2017. Selwyn was constructed ca. 1840, the middle of three estates along the River Road: Fairfield, Selwyn, and Powhite. The house is privately owned today and visible from the Cold Harbor Road. HCHS, *Old Homes of Hanover County*, 47-8. Powhite dated to around 1800; during the war it belonged to Dr. William Gaines, whose nearby mill lent its name to the fighting on the 27th. Ibid, 43. Powhite was destroyed in the 1930s. Robert E. L. Krick et al, *A Survey of Civil War Sites in Hanover County, Virginia* (Richmond, VA, 2002), 27.

60 OR 11, pt. 3, 622; Wise, *Campaigns and Battles of the ANV*, 103; DeLeon CSR; REL newspaper references, DSF papers, LVA. Fortunately, much of the Gaines' Mill battlefield has been preserved, largely by the National Park Service and the American Battlefield Trust (formerly the Civil War Trust).

from north of the Chickahominy, Lee and Longstreet confer near the Watt house, where Maj. J. L. Brent of Gen. Magruder's staff finds them and relays information regarding the situation south of the river. Gen. Lee rides to the left and meets with Stonewall Jackson; while on that part of the field he also goes in search of the Rockbridge Artillery to check on his youngest son Rob, who is eventually found asleep under a caisson. It is the first time Lee has seen him since Rob enlisted some months earlier.[61]

In the afternoon, Jeb Stuart reports that the Federals are destroying the York River Railroad, which indicates they are likely abandoning their base at White House. Lee spends the afternoon waiting for more information and sifting through reports to determine the enemy's intentions. During the night, artillerist William N. Pendleton brings Lee a message from President Davis, and Lee sends Pendleton to Magruder to advise that the enemy is gone but Lee is unsure of where they are going.[62]

Late in the evening Gen. Lee meets with Brig. Gen. Richard Taylor, one of Gen. Ewell's brigade commanders who is just returning to duty after an illness incapacitated him for several days. Around 11:00 p.m., Jubal Early arrives at the army's headquarters to report for duty, but he finds Gen. Lee asleep; Longstreet is still awake, so he and Early talk for a time about the recent battles. Heavy rain during the night.[63]

June 29, Sunday (Powhite/Fair Oaks/Williams Farm): Shortly after dawn Gen. Lee learns from two of Longstreet's engineers, Maj. R. K. Meade and Lt. S. R. Johnston, that Gen. McClellan had abandoned his works at the Gouldin farm in front of Gen. Magruder. This is the first conclusive proof Lee has received that McClellan is, in fact, withdrawing his army. About the same time Lee receives the engineers' report, a message arrives from Magruder announcing his intent to immediately attack the Federal position at the Gouldin farm. Lee jokingly instructs Magruder not to injure Maj. Meade and Lt. Johnston, who now occupy those abandoned works. Around this same time, Jubal Early returns to headquarters for his assignment; Lee tells the disappointed general that his former infantry brigade

---

61 Wise, *Campaigns and Battles of the ANV*, 103-4; Brent, *Memoirs of the WBTS*, 175; Mills, *History of the 16th NC*, 18; William T. Poague, *Gunner with Stonewall: Reminiscences of William Thomas Poague* (Lincoln, NE, 1998), 28-9; REL, Jr., *Recollections and Letters of REL*, 73-4. Capt. William Poague, commander of the Rockbridge Artillery, recalled of Gen. Lee's visit: "General Lee, followed by well mounted and well dressed staff, rode up to the battery and asked for Private Robert Lee. He could not be found for some time. At last someone found him asleep under a caisson. As he came up to the General, blinking and rubbing his eyes and as dirty as he well could be, the General broke into a broad smile, saying, 'Why Robert, I scarcely knew you, you've changed so much in appearance.' The staff all grinned and tittered and all of us greatly enjoyed the interview between the splendid looking, handsomely mounted general and his son. If you had looked the company over, you could not have found a more unkempt and 'ornery' looking Reb than Bob Lee, Junior. But he was as good a soldier and as fine a fellow as any in that splendid company." Poague, *Gunner with Stonewall*, 28. Rob himself recalled, "To get some shade and to be out of the way, I had crawled under a caisson, and was busy making up many lost hours of rest. Suddenly I was rudely awakened by a comrade, prodding me with a sponge-staff . . . and was told to get up and come out, that someone wished to see me. Half awake, I staggered out, and found myself face to face with General Lee and his staff. Their fresh uniforms, bright equipments and well-groomed horses contrasted so forcibly with the war-worn appearance of our command that I was completely dazed. It took me a moment or two to realize what it all meant, but when I saw my father's loving eyes and smile it became clear to me that he had ridden by to see if I was safe and to ask how I was getting along. I remember well how curiously those with him gazed at me, and I am sure that it must have struck them as very odd that such a dirty, ragged, unkempt youth could have been the son of this grand-looking victorious commander." Lee, *Recollections and Letters of REL*, 73-4.

62 Freeman, *Lee*, vol. 2, 162-3; Maurice, *Lee's Aide de Camp*, 105; Dowdey, *Wartime Papers*, 204-5.

63 WNP to wife, June 29, 1862, WNP papers, UNC; T. Michael Parrish, *Richard Taylor: Soldier Prince of Dixie* (Chapel Hill, NC, 1992), 233; Richard Taylor, *Destruction and Reconstruction* (Waltham, MA, 1968), 82; Jubal A. Early, *Jubal Early's Memoirs: Autobiographical Sketch and Narrative of the War Between the States* (Baltimore, MD, 1989), 76, 89; Krick, *CW Weather*, 60. Richard Taylor was the son of former president and Mexican War general Zachary Taylor and the brother-in-law of Jefferson Davis. Taylor, who had performed well during Jackson's 1862 Valley Campaign, was sent to command in Louisiana after the battles around Richmond, and ended the war as a lieutenant general. Warner, *Generals in Gray*, 299-300. Jubal Early was wounded at Williamsburg on May 5.

was broken up, and at this time there is no vacancy for him.⁶⁴

Probably in late morning Lee learns from Stuart that White House has been burned to the ground. Lee crosses to the south side of the Chickahominy via New Bridge and meets with Magruder on Nine Mile Road; they ride together to Fair Oaks with Lee explaining his plan to catch McClellan in the act of crossing White Oak Swamp with Magruder attacking the enemy rear guard. Lee continues on to Huger's headquarters at the J. B. Williams farm near the intersection of Williamsburg Road and Charles City Road to explain the plan to Huger; because of its central location, Lee establishes his own headquarters at the Williams farm. While there Maj. Brent arrives with a request from Magruder for support, as he thinks that rather than retreating, the Federals are preparing to attack him. Lee does not believe the report and asks Brent for his opinion, which the staff officer declines to offer but at the same time makes it clear he does not agree with Magruder; Lee agrees to temporarily loan Magruder two of Huger's brigades.⁶⁵

During the afternoon Lee sends Walter Taylor to Magruder for an update, as Lee has heard nothing Magruder since his earlier request via Maj. Brent for reinforcements; Taylor returns with news of a misunderstanding between Magruder and Jackson, that Jackson could not support Magruder in his attack at Savage's Station because he "had other important duty to perform." In the evening Lee scolds Magruder for his relative inaction today and assures him that Jackson has orders to support him: "Regret much that you have made so little progress today in pursuit of the enemy. . . . We must lose no more time or he will escape us entirely."⁶⁶

Lee sends an update to President Davis of the fighting of the past several days, and explaining his intent to intercept McClellan before he can get under cover of the gunboats on the James. An unnamed horse described as a six year old "handsome bay mare" about 15 ½ hands high is stolen from Lee's former headquarters at High Meadow. Heavy thunderstorm during the night.⁶⁷

June 30, Monday (Williams Farm/Savage Station/Glendale): Lee leaves the Williams farm before dawn

---

64 Longstreet, *From Manassas to Appomattox*, 148-9; Maurice, *Lee's Aide de Camp*, 105; Freeman, *Lee*, vol. 2, 166-7; Early, *Memoirs*, 76-7. Lee's message to Magruder about Meade and Johnston was likely delivered by Col. Chilton, who carried instructions to Magruder to meet Lee on Nine Mile Road. Manarin, *Henrico County: Field of Honor*, vol. 1, 157.

65 Freeman, *Lee*, vol. 2, 172; Manarin, *Henrico County: Field of Honor*, vol. 1, 156-9; *OR* 11, pt. 2, 662, 789; Rhoades, *Scapegoat General*, 81-2; Brent, *Memoirs of the WBTS*, 180-1. White House was burned against orders, possibly by a soldier in the 93rd New York. McClellan himself had ordered that the house be protected. Sears, *To the Gates of Richmond*, 258; Farrar, *Old Virginia Houses*, 197; *OR* 11, pt. 2, 333.

66 Taylor, *General Lee*, 74; *OR* 11, pt. 2, 687. Two of Jackson's staff officers, Hunter McGuire and R. L. Dabney, later recalled Jackson and Lee meeting in late afternoon near Grapevine Bridge, but this seems unlikely given the misunderstanding between Jackson and Magruder, and Lee's lack of communication with Magruder during the afternoon. McGuire stated that Jackson crossed the Chickahominy at Grapevine about 5:00 p.m. and met with Lee at Reynoldsville, the home of Dr. Peterfield Trent, which was previously McClellan's headquarters. Freeman, *Lee*, vol. 2, 174 n32. Freeman dismisses this account, written more than 30 years after the fact, as McGuire simply confusing the date and place of another meeting of Lee and Jackson. Jackson himself did cross the river briefly and reconnoiter to the Trent house, but he did not move his troops from the vicinity of Grapevine Bridge. Sears, *To the Gates of Richmond*, 268. Dabney also recalled a meeting of Lee and Jackson somewhere near Grapevine during the afternoon, although he does not place it specifically at the Trent house. Freeman addresses Dabney's account and why it is likely incorrect in great detail in *Lee's Lieutenants*, vol. 1, 562-3 n22. The crux of Freeman's argument is that Dabney was also likely misremembering the event, and that McGuire's later recollection of it was probably influenced by Dabney. Freeman rightly states that it is highly unlikely Lee would have been in proximity to Magruder, as the Trent house or Grapevine Bridge would have put him, and then *not* meet with Magruder. In addition, if Lee had met with Jackson, there would not have been any surprise on Lee's part at receiving (via Walter Taylor) Jackson's statement that he "had other important duty to perform" and could not assist Magruder at Savage Station.

67 Freeman, *Lee's Dispatches*, 19-22; Richmond *Daily Dispatch*, July 5, 1862; Krick, *CW Weather*, 61. A large portion of the Savage Station battlefield was destroyed by the construction of Interstates 64 and 295 and the relocation of the Williamsburg Road. The undeveloped portion that remains is in private hands.

and rides toward Magruder's headquarters near Savage's Station. Before he gets there, he encounters Jackson on the Williamsburg Road; Lee explains his plan to trap McClellan at the crossroads hamlet known as Glendale. Lee arrives at Magruder's headquarters soon after sunrise and explains the plan, then joins Longstreet's troops on Darbytown Road.[68]

In mid-afternoon Lee finds Jefferson Davis with Longstreet and Hill in a small clearing near Glendale while battle rages nearby; Lee tries unsuccessfully to persuade President Davis to move to a place of safety. When enemy artillery fire begins to fall in their vicinity, Hill orders both Lee and Davis away; when they do not move out of range, Hill tells them "Did I not tell you to go away from here, and you not promise to obey my orders? Why, one shot from that battery over yonder may presently deprive the Confederacy of its President and the Army of Northern Virginia of its commander!" Just after this exchange a message arrives from Col. Thomas Rosser that the Federals are in force at Malvern Hill, several miles south of Glendale. This intelligence prompts Lee to go investigate in person, leaving Longstreet in charge of the growing fight at Glendale. Lee heads down Long Bridge Road to River Road, where he meets Theophilus Holmes; Lee orders Holmes to attack the Federals at Malvern Hill. On his return to Glendale, Lee encounters President Davis who upbraids Lee for going himself to reconnoiter instead of sending a staff officer and thus exposing himself to danger; Lee replies that he can only obtain accurate intelligence by going himself. Toward the end of the fighting, a detachment of the 47th Virginia brings captured Union Gen. George McCall to Lee and Longstreet.[69]

At the conclusion of the battle, Jubal Early brings Lee a letter from Sec. Randolph recommending that Early be given command of the brigade formerly commanded by the wounded Arnold Elzey. Lee spends the night in the vicinity of Glendale. Rooney's 2-year old son, Robert E. Lee III, dies unexpectedly in North Carolina.[70]

---

68 Freeman, *Lee*, vol. 2, 179-80; Thomas, *REL*, 241; Freeman, *Lee's Lieutenants*, vol. 1, 568; Robert Stiles, *Four Years Under Marse Robert* (Dayton, OH, 1988), 97-9; Manarin, *Henrico County: Field of Honor*, vol. 1, 204-5. There is some doubt as to the order in which Lee met with Jackson and Magruder in the early morning hours. Freeman put forth the order recounted here, encountering Jackson en route to Magruder; most writers have followed suit. Stephen Sears, however, reverses the order in *To the Gates of Richmond*, 277. Without additional evidence, either version is plausible. Glendale is also known as Riddle's Shop, with various spellings.

69 Longstreet, *From Manassas to Appomattox*, 134; Freeman, *Lee*, vol. 2, 180-82; *OR* 11, pt. 2, 532, 666-7, 675; Manarin, *Henrico County: Field of Honor*, vol. 1, 234-5, 267-8; Davis, *Rise and Fall*, vol. 2, 123; Long, *Memoirs of REL*, 180. McCall, a division commander in Porter's V Corps, mistakenly rode into Confederate lines while trying to organize a counterattack and was taken prisoner by the 47th VA. Most of the Glendale battlefield has been preserved by the Civil War Trust. The exact location of Lee's HQ on the night of the 30th is not known. It is highly unlikely that he remained at the Williams farm since it was so far removed from the new scene of operations; he likely stayed somewhere in the Glendale vicinity.

70 Early, *Memoirs*, 77; Daughtry, *Gray Cavalier*, 83; Mrs. REL to Eliza A. Stiles, July 6, 1862, Stiles family papers, Georgia Historical Society. Mary wrote of the loss of her grandson: "He was a most lovely little fellow... the only green spot in my troubled existence now. I had the care of him all winter and fall and he was so sweet and affectionate." Mrs. REL to Eliza A. Stiles, July 6, 1862, Stiles family papers, GHS.

July 1862

Days of constant fighting wore down Lee physically, and by the time his army approached Malvern Hill on July 1 he worried about his ability to command the army that day. He was not pleased that the Army of the Potomac escaped his grasp at Glendale the day before, but he hoped to still deliver a knock-out blow. However, poor staff work and lack of accurate maps combined to work against the Confederates at Malvern Hill. It must have frustrated Lee, who was an engineering officer, for something as simple as a lack of understanding of the terrain a few miles outside the capital to have such an important impact on his military operations. "The Confederate government had but few officers or facilities for topographical surveys," explained Col. William Allan of the 2nd Virginia, "and . . . up to this time few or no maps were to be had except those in existence before the war."[1]

After being defeated at Malvern Hill, Lee was unable to find a way to get at McClellan's army because it was sheltered at Harrison's Landing under the protection of Union warships. He withdrew the army to its works closer to Richmond and returned his headquarters to the Dabbs house. There was some general disappointment that a more decisive victory was not achieved, but McClellan was no longer within sight of the capital. Lee used the lull following the Seven Days' Battles to reorganize his army. He rid the army of some of the commanders whose performance had not been to his liking and replaced them with others who showed promise. Those whose time with the Army of Northern Virginia had ended included John Magruder, Benjamin Huger, and Theophilus Holmes. Lee elevated, among others, Lafayette McLaws, Richard Anderson, and Jeb Stuart.[2] After consultation with Lee in the middle of the month, Joseph R. Anderson determined that he was of much more value to the Confederacy running the Tredegar Iron Works than he was leading one of A. P. Hill's infantry brigades and left the army.[3]

Lee met with President Davis at least once and almost certainly more as a newspaper reporter wrote that they frequently took meals together. Davis "often takes General Lee to dine with him at six o'clock, p.m. The latter appears to have fattened, and has turned out a tremendous pair of grey whiskers. He is a fine looking old fellow, even in a jeans sack coat."[4]

For a time Lee remained uncertain of McClellan's next move, but his attention began to shift away from the idle Army of the Potomac to a new threat in northern Virginia, where John Pope and the newly formed Army of Virginia was now operating. Lee sent Jackson to confront Pope, but he could not send large detachments away from Richmond as long as McClellan remained a relatively short distance from the capital.

---

1 William Allan, *The Army of Northern Virginia in 1862* (Boston, 1892), 137.

2 Magruder already had orders to go West but they were temporarily suspended because of the pending battle; in his case the timing was coincidental.

3 J. R. Anderson to L. O'B. Branch, July 23, 1862, L. O'B. Branch papers, State Archives of North Carolina.

4 Charleston *Mercury*, July 28, 1862.

The summer months were hard on Lee's horses. One unidentified horse was stolen from its corral at the Dabbs House during the midst of the Seven Days' battles.[5] Another, "Brown Roan," went blind during the fighting and was given to a local farmer.[6] "Richmond," the horse given him by that city, died suddenly at the end of the month.[7]

The break in the fighting allowed for some family time. Lee saw Mary at least once following the fighting, and his son Rob arrived for a visit. The general also saw his brother Smith at Drewry's Bluff at the end of the month. Lee's son Rooney took leave from the army to be with his wife Charlotte after the death of their young son, and Custis and Mary spent some time with Lee's brother Carter at his farm in Powhatan County.[8]

* * *

---

[5] Richmond *Daily Dispatch*, July 5, 1862. The stolen animal likely belonged to one of the staff or a courier as Lee made no known mention of it.

[6] Pitts, *High Meadow*, 54.

[7] Fitz Lee, *General Lee*, 180.

[8] REL to Annie & Agnes, undated, REL papers, LOC.

July 1, Tuesday (Glendale/Willis Church/Smith Blacksmith Shop/Poindexter house): Just after sunrise Lee joins Gens. Magruder, Longstreet, and A. P. Hill on the Long Bridge Road. The officers encounter Union surgeon N. F. Marsh of the 4th Pennsylvania Cavalry, who has charge of a large number of enemy wounded in Willis Church and is in search of supplies for these wounded men. Marsh reveals that the battle yesterday was with McCall's division, something Lee already knew because Gen. McCall himself was now a prisoner; Longstreet jokingly tells the surgeon that McCall is safe in Richmond but were it not for the fight put up by his men, the Confederates would have captured McClellan's entire army.[9]

During the morning Lee reveals to Longstreet that he does not feel well and requests that Longstreet stay with him today should he become unable to command. Continuing on to Willis Church with Longstreet and Magruder, Lee finds D. H. Hill and Jackson; Hill tells Lee that a local resident, Rev. L. W. Allen, considers Malvern Hill to be a very strong position. Hill cautions "If Gen. McClellan is there in force, we had better let him alone," to which Longstreet replies, "Don't get scared now that we have got him whipped." With most of the senior commanders present at Willis Church, Lee orders that they will attack Malvern Hill. He later encounters Jubal Early, who mentions his fear that McClellan will make good his escape; Lee snaps back "Yes, he will get away because I cannot have my orders carried out!" Lee and Longstreet accompany Jackson's column to Malvern Hill, with Lee setting up his command post at the C. W. Smith blacksmith shop, near the Willis Church parsonage, where Jackson and D. H. Hill also have their headquarters.[10]

During the early afternoon, Lee dispatches Longstreet and Lafayette McLaws to scout for artillery positions on the right. Longstreet returns with word that Magruder is on the wrong road and thus marching away from his assigned position, and also that he discovered a good artillery platform on that part of the field and saw a promising position in Jackson's sector as well. Lee instructs Longstreet and Jackson to see to the placement of the guns and issues orders for an assault all along the lines; the signal will be Lewis Armistead's brigade on the right attacking "with a yell."[11]

---

9 Brent, *Memoirs of the WBTS*, 197-203; Freeman, *Lee*, vol. 2, 200-1; Manarin, *Henrico County: Field of Honor*, vol. 1, 294; OR 11, pt. 2, 397. Surgeon Marsh previously encountered Jackson in his quest for supplies, but Stonewall referred him to Lee. OR 11, pt. 2, 397.

10 Manarin, *Henrico County: Field of Honor*, vol. 1, 294-6; Longstreet, *From Manassas to Appomattox*, 142; Freeman, *Lee*, vol. 2, 201-2; Early, *Memoirs*, 77-8; Edward A. Moore, *The Story of a Cannoneer under Stonewall Jackson* (New York, 1907), 89. It should be noted that C. W. Smith's blacksmith shop does not appear on wartime maps. R. E. L. Krick email to author, April 13, 2018.

11 Lafayette McLaws to James Longstreet, November 30, 1885, James Longstreet papers, UNC; Freeman, *Lee*, vol. 2, 204-8; Manarin, *Henrico County: Field of Honor*, vol. 1, 308; OR 11, pt. 2, 677, 680. Once again the lack of accurate maps plagued Confederate leadership at Malvern Hill. The names by which roads were identified on Lee's map did not correspond with the names by which the locals knew them—the Quaker Road being the prime example. Lee's Quaker Road and the locals' Quaker Road were not the same, which was the reason why Magruder had his men on the wrong road. The name of the local Darby family was another problem. The name was pronounced "Darby," but spelled on maps "Enroughty." Lee himself had a copy of the 1853 Smith's Map of Henrico County by Robert P. Smith & C. Carpenter (which is in the MOC collection). Gen. McLaws wrote that he found Lee napping at headquarters at one point during the afternoon, which is plausible given Lee's physical condition during the day. Sears, *To the Gates of Richmond*, 317-8. Less likely is McLaws's statement that President Davis was standing guard over Lee as he slept, to allow him to nap uninterrupted. No other account places Davis at Malvern Hill on the day of the battle. Ibid. Without doubt Lee was not well on this day. According to one biographer, Emory Thomas, "His request that Longstreet stay close with him that morning was an index of how infirm Lee felt even early in the day." *REL*, 243. Poor staff work also was a problem for Lee during this period, but nowhere was it more evident than in Col. Robert Chilton's poorly drafted attack orders for the day: "Batteries have been established to rake the enemy's lines. If it is broken, as is probable, Armistead, who can witness the effect of the fire, has been ordered to charge with a yell. Do the same." OR 11, pt. 2, 677. This order placed the decision of whether or not to launch an attack by the entire army on a single untested brigade commander; and the signal was "a yell." Peninsula Campaign historian Stephen Sears speculates that Lee never saw or approved this written set of orders, and that it may have been written and distributed while Lee was napping at headquarters during the early afternoon. *To the Gates of*

As the troops and guns get into position, Lee meets with Gens. Jackson and Ewell near Willis Church, where Ewell reveals that one of his brigadiers found a way to turn McClellan's right flank. While investigating the veracity of this report with Longstreet around 4:00 p.m., Lee receives word from both Magruder and Chase Whiting that the Federals are abandoning their position atop the hill, intelligence that Lee uses to order an immediate attack without confirming the reports. After nightfall Lee rides over the along the lines and, upon encountering Magruder, asks the general, "Why did you attack?" Magruder, who is not well himself, is confused by Lee's question because he understood Lee's instructions to be peremptory orders to launch an attack. Lee spends the night at the nearby Poindexter house.[12]

July 2, Wednesday (Poindexter House): Jackson comes to headquarters early in the morning to report that the Federals are retreating down River Road. Lee writes to President Davis with the latest information: McClellan is gone from Lee's front, but the worn-out condition of the men and the muddy condition of the roads from the steady rain now falling renders it impossible to pursue today, although Stuart's cavalry is giving chase. Lee then holds a meeting with Longstreet, Jackson, and Stuart in the parlor; President Davis and his nephew and aide Col. Joseph Davis arrive while this meeting is in progress. During this conference Maj. Marshall produces a flask of whiskey given him by the captured Union Gen. McCall several days earlier, from which he offers the president a drink. Davis partakes as does Longstreet, but Lee, Jackson, and Stuart all decline; it is soon finished off by the staff officers present. Once the flask is empty, Stuart jokes that McCall had likely poisoned it, why else would he give it up? Lee issues orders for the army to remain in place to rest the men and tend to the casualties. Steady rain throughout the day.[13]

July 3, Thursday (Poindexter House): Lee receives a report from Stuart in the morning regarding McClellan's position at Harrison's landing, which mentions John Pelham's artillery firing on the Federal camps from a ridge overlooking Evelynton plantation. Lee writes to President Davis that Stuart's information is evidence that McClellan does not intend to cross the James and operate against Petersburg, but as he is not sure of the enemy's intentions he is leaving several divisions near

---

Richmond, 216-8. Magruder's aide Brent later charged that Chilton was also mistaken about the placement of the various divisions in the line, i.e., that Chilton flipped Magruder's and Huger's positions, which led to their brigades being intermingled. Of the "charge with a yell" directive, Brent wrote: "Who ever heard of such an order to bring on a battle?" *Memoirs of the WBTS*, 212-5, 221.

12 Donald C. Pfanz, *Richard S. Ewell: A Soldier's Life* (Chapel Hill, NC, 1998), 232; Terry L. Jones, ed., *Campbell Brown's Civil War with Ewell and the Army of Northern Virginia* (Baton Rouge, LA, 2001), 125; Manarin, *Henrico County: Field of Honor*, vol. 1, 320; Thomas, *REL*, 241-3; Brent, *Memoirs of the WBTS*, 190-2; Freeman, *Lee*, vol. 2, 218-9, 221. One of Jackson's aides wrote that Lee had to directly order Jackson not to place artillery himself as the enemy fire was too hot, and that his artillery chief Stapleton Crutchfield could handle the placement of the guns. Henry Kyd Douglas, *I Rode with Stonewall* (Marietta, GA, 1995), 113-4.

13 Freeman, *Lee*, vol. 2, 220-5; Freeman, *Lee's Dispatches*, 22-4; Henderson, *Stonewall Jackson*, vol. 2, 84-5; Douglas, *I Rode with Stonewall*, 114-5; Special Orders, July 2, 1862, D. H. Hill papers, UNC; William M. Owen, *In Camp and Battle with the Washington Artillery of New Orleans* (Baton Rouge, LA, 1999), 94. Brent claimed that about 9:00 a.m. he found Lee in a wagon converted into a field office by putting a desk in it; this seems odd if Lee's headquarters overnight indeed was the Poindexter house. It is possible that he spent the night at the Smith blacksmith shop and did not move to the Poindexter house until the morning of July 2. Brent, *Memoirs of the WBTS*, 231-2. Jackson's aide Sandie Pendleton, the son of Gen. William Nelson Pendleton, noted that the Poindexter house was "riddled with balls" because the adjacent fields were the location of Stonewall Jackson's artillery during the battle. A. S. Pendleton to mother, July 2, 1862, WNP papers, UNC. It seems logical that Lee's message to President Davis about McClellan's withdrawal prompted the president's visit to Lee's headquarters in the afternoon, although it is possible Davis was coming to the field anyway independent of Lee's message. In the latter case, it is possible that Davis did not receive Lee's communiqué before leaving the capital, although it seems much more likely—especially given the weather—that it was Lee's report that prompted him to ride to headquarters. This conference at the Poindexter house was the first time Davis and Jackson met in person. Robertson, Jr., *Stonewall Jackson*, 506.

Malvern Hill; he mentions his desire to go reconnoiter McClellan's position himself later today. Lee orders the pursuit of McClellan's army, but by a more inland route than River Road, which is in poor condition due to the passage of the Army of the Potomac and also in range of Federal gunboats.[14]

The general begins reorganizing the army, sending Magruder to the Trans-Mississippi and combining Magruder's own division with that of Lafayette McLaws, and moving D. R. Jones's division to Longstreet's command. During the morning Lee receives a message from McClellan concerning Federal wounded; Lee writes to Sec. Randolph that the number of prisoners taken during the last week makes a POW exchange desirable, and he recommends having Howell Cobb negotiate such. Lee sends a detachment of troops to guard his cousins at Shirley, and he meets with Gen. Pendleton regarding superfluous artillery to the rear and captured supplies.[15]

July 4, Friday (Poindexter House/Evelynton Heights/Phillips House): Lee reconnoiters the Federal position at Harrison's Landing and Evelynton Heights, arriving about noon. He joins Longstreet and Jackson near Evelynton; Lee and Jackson go forward to observe, leaving Longstreet, Stuart, and their staff some distance to the rear. Lee finds the position too strong to attack directly and orders Longstreet to stand down. Leaving the front, Lee establishes headquarters at the Phillips house near Salem Church, about four miles north of Evelynton. From there, he writes to President Davis and provides the results of his reconnaissance: "As far as I can now see, there is no way to attack [McClellan] to advantage; nor do I wish to expose the men to the destructive missiles of his gunboats.... I fear he is too secure under cover of his boats to be driven from his position."[16]

Lee assigns D. H. Hill's troops the duty of collecting the wounded and burying the dead at Malvern Hill. He forwards to Sec. Randolph a letter from Union surgeon Dr. John Swinburne requesting that all Federal wounded be concentrated at Savage Station; Lee informs Randolph and Swinburne that he will have them moved as requested and paroled. Porter Alexander reports to Lee what he observed of McClellan's position from a balloon above the James.[17]

July 5, Saturday (Phillips House): Lee informs President Davis that the latest reports have

---

14 Freeman, *Lee,* vol. 2, 225-6; Thomas, *Bold Dragoon,* 136-7; Freeman, *Lee's Dispatches,* 24-5. Stuart's shelling of the entire Army of the Potomac with one lone gun was strongly criticized by some of his contemporaries as well as historians. According to Fitz Lee, Stuart was under the impression that Longstreet and Jackson were not far behind him and Stuart expected them to hold the ridge. In reality, the infantry was miles away. Fitz Lee, *General Lee,* 165-6. Some contend that Stuart's actions revealed to the Federals the importance of holding Evelynton Heights; others argue that Union troops would have occupied that position in due course regardless of Stuart's actions. Thomas, *Bold Dragoon,* 137-8. Lee did not go to Harrison's Landing until the next day.

15 OR 11, pt. 3, 630; Richmond *Daily Dispatch,* July 5, 1862; OR 4, Series 2, 797-8; Lee, *Memoirs of WNP,* 199. The decision to transfer Magruder was made in late May but put on hold because of the operations around Richmond (see May 27 entry). His performance during the Seven Days' Battles, although somewhat lacking, was not the reason for his transfer. Rather, its timing merely coincided with the other performance-based changes Lee implemented. The organization of Magruder's command can be somewhat confusing. He led three divisions commanded by McLaws, David R. Jones, and one under his personal direction. Lee selected Cobb for the POW exchange because of his previous involvement with exchanges. Shirley was the home of Lee's mother; he remained in touch with his Carter cousins there throughout the war.

16 Freeman, *Lee,* vol. 2, 226-9; Taylor, *General Lee,* 82; REL to Mary Anna Morrison Jackson, January 25, 1866, REL papers, MOC; Venable memoirs, UVA; Freeman, *Lee's Dispatches,* 25-7. Venable described Lee's recon at Evelynton: "The position for reconnoitering was in full sight of the Federal sharpshooters and gave the opportunity of General Lee's absolute absorption in his work, he stood with glasses to his eyes, under the fire of the enemy's sharpshooters, while every officer of high rank moved away from the spot, which was best for his safety as a crowd would have attracted more fire." Venable memoirs, UVA. The Phillips house was located on what is now the grounds of a large quarry on Barnetts Road in Charles City County.

17 OR 11, pt. 3, 630; OR 4, Series 2, 798-9, 801; Gallagher, *Fighting for the Confederacy,* 117. Alexander narrowly avoided capture when CSS *Teaser,* which was towing his balloon, ran aground and was seized by the enemy. Gallagher, *Fighting for the Confederacy,* 117.

McClellan reinforced and intending to remain at Harrison's Landing; Union gunboats make it all but impossible to get at him so Lee wishes to withdraw the army closer to Richmond and leave Stuart's cavalry to watch McClellan. Lee confides to Henry Wise, back at Chaffin's Bluff to guard against a possible quick strike up the James, that although Lee doesn't think the Federals intend to move south of the James, he cannot rule out that possibility. "There are so many and such various conflicting reports concerning the movements of the enemy that [I am] unable to ascertain definitely either [McClellan's] strength or intention." In reply to Lee's message of yesterday regarding his personal reconnaissance of the enemy position, Davis writes back: "I will renew my caution to you against personal exposure either in battle or reconnaissance. It is a duty to the cause we serve for the sake of which I reiterate the warning." During the evening Lee instructs Porter Alexander to report on the status of the Reserve Artillery and to prepare it to move tomorrow.[18]

An advertisement is published in the Richmond *Dispatch* offering a $50 reward for the horse stolen from the Dabbs house June 29. The funeral for Rooney and Charlotte's son is held at St. Paul's Episcopal Church in Richmond, after which he is buried in the Wickham family plot in Shockoe Hill Cemetery; neither Lee nor Rooney are present.[19]

July 6, Sunday (Phillips House/Richmond): Lee writes to Union Gens. McClellan and Henry W. Halleck for an explanation regarding the reported execution of two citizens in New Orleans. He also writes Union Gen. John Wool advising that Howell Cobb is Wool's counterpart for a POW exchange discussion.[20]

July 7, Monday (Phillips House): Lee complains to Sec. Randolph that today's edition of the *Daily Dispatch* contains information regarding troop movements which Lee fears will fall into enemy hands; he wants the War Department to put a stop to such things being published. Lee issues congratulatory orders to the ANV for the recent string of victories.[21]

July 8, Tuesday (Phillips House): Lee orders the army to withdraw closer to Richmond at sunset. Lee sees Rooney at some point during the day.[22]

July 9, Wednesday (Phillips house/Dabbs House): Lee returns to the Dabbs house where he receives a letter from Mary with news of the death of their grand-

---

18 Lynda L. Crist et al, eds., *The Papers of Jefferson Davis*, 14 vols. (Baton Rouge, LA, 1971-2015), vol. 8, 278-9; WHT to H. A. Wise, July 5, 1862, WHT CSR; *OR* 11, pt. 3, 634. The letter to Davis is misdated July 6 in the *OR* and the editors of Davis's papers published it with the correct date. *OR* 11, pt. 3, 634-5. Ordinarily any correspondence concerning the Reserve Artillery would have gone to Pendleton; however, the message to Alexander explained that Pendleton could not be found.

19 Richmond *Daily Dispatch*, July 5, 1862; Pitts, *High Meadow*, 54; Daughtry, *Gray Cavalier*, 83. The Richmond *Examiner* announced on this date that Lee had returned to his former headquarters at the Dabbs house. REL newspaper references, DSF papers, LVA. This is curious and is either a mistake or he came back to the city for a very brief period. Lee wrote to McClellan on July 6 with the headline "Dabbs House," although his correspondence makes it clear he remained at the Phillips house until July 9. One of Stuart's staff officers noted that Lee, Longstreet, and Stuart all had their HQ at the Phillips house: "General R.E. Lee, Longstreet, and Stuart had established their headquarters together in the extensive farmyard of a Mr. Phillips. . . . Here for a few days we enjoyed rest and comparative quiet. Our generals were often in council of war, undecided whether or not to attack the enemy." Heros von Borcke, *Memoirs of the Confederate War for Independence* (Nashville, TN, 1999), 54.

20 *OR* 15, 906; *OR* 4, Series 2, 134, 208. The letter to McClellan is headlined "Dabbs House" although Lee was still headquartered at the Phillips house. It is not known when he arrived in Richmond, why he was there, or how long he stayed, or if he even went—it may simply have been a ruse to confuse McClellan.

21 *OR* 11, pt. 3, 635-6; *OR* 11, pt. 2, 500-1. Randolph sent copies of Lee's letter to all of the Richmond papers. Of this, J. M. Brooke noted: "Gen. Lee has pitched into the papers for publishing information about the positions of troops etc. It is time, the Federals in Norfolk say they get all the information they want from the *Examiner* and *Dispatch*. With all their professed patriotism some editors sell their countrymen's lives for a few pennies." Brooke, *Ironclads and Big Guns*, 100.

22 *OR* 11, pt. 3, 636-7; Dowdey, *Wartime Papers*, 189.

child. He writes President Davis giving a summation of the army's activities in the days since Malvern Hill and announces that he reestablished headquarters at High Meadow. Lee likely meets with ANV medical director Lafayette Guild as most of his correspondence and orders today concern the wounded from the Seven Days' Battles. Lee writes to McClellan requesting transportation for the removal of their wounded. Lee informs Randolph that he does not wish to continue communicating with McClellan via flag of truce through the lines but wants a boat to carry messages down the James to Westover. Lee writes to Mary, telling her he is back at Dabbs and lamenting that he did not achieve a more complete victory. He sends her some of his clothes to be laundered, and requests that his trunk that he left with Custis be forwarded to him; he mentions losing his spectacles and needing his spares.[23]

July 10, Thursday (Dabbs House): Lee requests all division commanders forward to headquarters their reports of the Seven Days' campaign, and orders Gen. Pemberton to send a detached company of the Hampton Legion from South Carolina to Virginia to rejoin the rest of the unit. Lee asks Sec. Randolph if Howell Cobb can still be Lee's representative to the POW exchange even though ill health is keeping him from the field, as his previous experience makes him the best to perform this duty. Lee writes to Mary, expressing surprise at the death of their grandson. He sends a key to his trunk so a lighter-weight coat in it may be sent him, and mentions that he is suffering from a cold, "from being too thickly clad. . . . I have not time to be sick."[24]

July 11, Friday (Dabbs House): Lee complains to Sec. Randolph that details are being made from the ANV without his knowledge or consent; he feels that the duties these soldiers are performing could be done by civilians, thus without weakening his army. Lee writes President Davis recommending Richard Anderson and Micah Jenkins for promotion. He instructs Holmes to ascertain the movements of Burnside's army in North Carolina and to make necessary dispositions to oppose him. Rob visits headquarters to see his father in the afternoon. Heavy rains.[25]

July 12, Saturday (Dabbs House/Richmond): Lee writes to Sec. Randolph renewing his complaints about details from the army without his consent, and writes to McClellan regarding details of transporting Federal wounded to their own lines. Lee visits with Mary during the evening.[26]

---

23 Pitts, *High Meadow*, 53-4; Freeman, *Lee's Dispatches,* 28-32; *OR* 4, Series 2, 169, 807; Dowdey, *Wartime Papers*, 229-30. This letter from Mary seems to be the first time Lee learned of the death of his grandson, even though the child had been buried in Richmond several days earlier. Lee misdated his letter to Mary June 9, but its battle content clearly shows it was written July 9; the content suggests he wrote it before receiving Mary's letter. Pitts wrote that Mary was living with Custis on Franklin St. by this time. *High Meadow*, 53-4. However, an undated letter Lee wrote around this time to Annie and Agnes mentions that their mother was living with the Caskies. REL to Annie & Agnes, undated, REL papers, LOC.

24 Circular, July 10, 1862, REL papers, MOC; REL to J. C. Pemberton, July 10, 1862, REL papers, MOC; *OR* 4, Series 2, 807; Dowdey, *Wartime Papers*, 189-90. This letter to Mary is likewise misdated June rather than July. Unlike yesterday's letter, which Dowdey caught and put in its correct context, this one appears chronologically in June in *Wartime Papers*. Lee mentions that not only was he not aware of the child's death, but that Rooney had not heard of it when Lee last saw him on the 8th. It is very odd that Charlotte returned to Richmond from North Carolina with the child's body about a week prior, and both the funeral service and the interment occurred without the child's father being aware of what was taking place. Once Rooney learned of it, he took leave to go be with Charlotte. REL to Annie & Agnes, undated, REL papers, LOC.

25 *OR* 11, pt. 3, 638; Freeman, *Lee's Dispatches*, 33-4; REL to T. H. Holmes, July 11, 1862, telegram book, REL HQ papers, VHS; Pitts, *High Meadow*, 58; Krick, *CW Weather*, 63. Jenkins was colonel of the Palmetto Sharpshooters and distinguished himself at Seven Pines. He would be killed by the same friendly fire that wounded Gen. Longstreet on the second day in the Wilderness, May 6, 1864. Warner, *Generals in Gray*, 155.

26 *OR* 11, pt. 3, 640; *OR* 4, Series 2, 176, 812; Mrs. REL to Eliza Stiles, July 6, 1862 (July 13 addendum), Stiles family papers, GHS. Huger was relieved of his command on this date and reassigned as inspector of artillery. *OR* 11, pt. 3, 640. A. P. Hill wrote to Lee on this date requesting to be transferred from Longstreet's command. Ibid, 639-40. Hill and Longstreet feuded over a series of articles in the Richmond papers regarding their respective roles in the recent fighting.

July 13, Sunday (Dabbs House/Governor's Mansion/Executive Mansion): In the morning Lee and Jackson meet with Governor Letcher at the Governor's Mansion. The two generals then go to the Executive Mansion where, joined by Longstreet and several others, they meet with President Davis. The meeting lasts until after lunch when Lee returns to Dabbs. Lee orders Jackson to proceed to Louisa Court House with his own and Ewell's divisions to oppose a new Union force in Northern Virginia. Lee informs Holmes that an enemy movement against Goldsboro seems unlikely at the present so he should concentrate his forces at Drewry's Bluff to assist in the construction of the defenses there. Lee advises Pemberton that Holmes's shifting of his troops on the Weldon Railroad may interfere with the transfer of troops from South Carolina to Virginia, so Pemberton should use a longer route via Raleigh and Charlotte in getting troops northward. Lee writes to G. W. Smith, glad that Smith's condition is improving and noting that if he requires an extension in his leave he must submit the necessary paperwork.[27]

July 14, Monday (Dabbs House): Lee names Richard Anderson to command Huger's former division, and writes to McClellan that D. H. Hill will be the Confederate representative to work out a POW exchange. Lee informs Richmond provost marshal Gen. John Winder that he is sending along 12 civilian prisoners whom McClellan paroled; Lee does not know what is to be done with them or how to address their status.[28]

July 15, Tuesday (Dabbs House): Lee receives a letter from Fitz Lee regarding the condition of the wounded Federal prisoners; in reply Lee tells his nephew that the enemy wounded are being conveyed to the Army of the Potomac as quickly as possible and that an exchange of the non-wounded prisoners is in the works. Lee writes to Joseph R. Anderson regarding his decision to resign from the army and return to his post at the head of Tredegar Iron Works. Lee meets with D. H. Hill regarding the POW exchange and provides him with written instructions as well as several letters from McClellan. Lee's congratulatory order to the army is published in the Richmond *Enquirer*. Thunderstorms at dusk.[29]

July 16, Wednesday (Dabbs House): Lee meets with Hill again regarding the POW meeting tomorrow.[30]

July 17, Thursday (Dabbs House): Lee instructs Gen. Winder to issue bread rations to the Union prisoners, and inquires of Gen. John Forney in

---

Lee likely went into the city in the evening rather than Mary coming out to HQ, but she did not provide details of the visit. Her letter was written in three installments, beginning July 6 with additions on the 7th and 13th. She concluded the document thusly: "The General is well but I rarely see him and then only for a few moments." Mrs. REL to Eliza Stiles, July 6, 1862 (July 13 addendum), Stiles family papers, GHS.

27 Susan Leigh Blackford and Charles M. Blackford, III, eds., *Letters from Lee's Army* (Lincoln, NE, 1998), 85-7; *OR* 12, pt. 3, 915; *OR* 11, pt. 3, 641; REL to J. C. Pemberton, July 13, 1862, REL papers, MOC; REL to G. W. Smith, July 13, 1862, Raab Collection, Ardmore, PA. Capt. Charles Blackford was among the staff officers waiting for the generals outside the Executive Mansion. Blackford made this observation of Lee when he emerged from the house: "Lee, Jackson, and President Davis came out together, a very distinguished trio, and stood talking on the steps. Lee was elegantly dressed in full uniform, sword and sash, spotless boots, beautiful spurs and by far the most magnificent man I ever saw." Blackford, *Letters from Lee's Army*, 86. Blackford may be wrong in his recollection of the date this event occurred. He is the only source for this incident involving Davis, Lee, and Jackson (despite him mentioning a large number of staff officers being present), but other sources have Jackson attending Second Presbyterian Church during the morning making it likely that Blackford got the date wrong. If the date is correct, Blackford must have been mistaken about this incident occurring in the morning. R. E. L. Krick email to author, April 13, 2018.

28 *OR* 11, pt. 3, 642; *OR* 4, Series 2, 210, 814. Hill replaced the ill Howell Cobb; Hill's Union counterpart was John Dix.

29 Dowdey, *Wartime Papers*, 231-2; REL to J. R. Anderson, July 15, 1862, J. R. Anderson papers, LVA; *OR* 4, Series 2, 815; REL newspaper references, DSF papers, LVA; Krick, *CW Weather*, 63. Hill was originally to meet with Dix at Shirley on the 16th, but that was changed to the 17th at Haxall's Landing. *OR* 4, Series 2, 220.

30 *OR* 4, Series 2, 220.

July 18, Friday (Dabbs House): Lee informs President Davis that he sent Jackson to the line of the Virginia Central Railroad, and with so many conflicting reports regarding enemy movements he is not yet sure what is correct but he is certain that McClellan is being reinforced. Lee notifies Jackson that the Federals appear to be moving from Fredericksburg to Gordonsville and that Stuart is sending cavalry to ascertain for certain their intentions. Lee approves of the POW exchange agreement D. H. Hill drafted, and notifies Gen. Longstreet that he authorized Micah Jenkins to send the captured colors of the 16th Michigan to South Carolina Governor Pickens. Lee authorizes Gen. Winder to appropriate whatever force he needs to guard the prisoners, and to make sure they are issued proper rations. Lee writes to Annie and Agnes with news of their youngest brother.[32]

July 19, Saturday (Dabbs House): Lee writes to Capt. A. L. Rives approving of his location for a bridge. He writes to J. Stevens Mason of Fauquier County to explain the process for gaining a commission, and encloses a letter to the secretary of war recommending him for promotion. He also writes to Col. W. Raymond Lee of the 20th Massachusetts thanking him for advising of the death of Lt. Col. Gustavus A. Bull of the 35th Georgia.[33]

July 21, Monday (Dabbs House): Lee complains to McClellan about citizens being arrested for refusing to take the Oath of Allegiance to the United States, and sends Hill a proposed change to the POW agreement but advises that if the Federals balk at that change Hill is to agree to everything else and leave this matter for later resolution.[34]

July 22, Tuesday (Dabbs House): Lee telegraphs Gen. Jeremy Gilmer in Savannah wondering where Gilmer is, as he was ordered to Richmond. Lee issues orders forbidding any sort of military affairs except inspections on Sundays to allow for rest and religious services.[35]

July 23, Wednesday (Dabbs House): Lee orders Longstreet to take command of the right wing of the army and to post brigades on the Darbytown and River roads to provide early alarm of any movement by McClellan in that sector. Lee writes to Jackson that he cannot send reinforcements until McClellan shows his hand, but as soon as he is able Lee will send additional forces to deal with John Pope's army in northern Virginia. Lee urges William Loring to take the offensive in western Virginia but notes that he can send no reinforcements from Richmond. Lee informs D. H. Hill that he submitted Hill's POW cartel to President Davis, and orders him to disrupt enemy shipping on the James. Lee declines McClellan's offer of medical supplies and personnel for wounded Federal prisoners, as they will very soon be returned to McClellan's army. Lee's cousin Martha "Markie" Custis Williams goes to Arlington in an attempt to remove as much of the Lee's belongings as possible, but the Federal commander

---

31 OR 4, Series 2, 822; REL to J. N. Forney, July 17, 1862, telegram book, REL HQ papers, VHS.

32 OR 51, pt. 2, 1074-5; OR 12, pt. 3, 916; OR 4, Series 2, 822-4; OR 11, pt. 3, 644; Lee, *Recollections and Letters of REL*, 75.

33 OR 11, pt. 3, 645; Emily G. Ramey and John K. Gott, eds., *Years of Anguish: Fauquier County, Virginia, 1861-1865* (Annandale, VA, 1987), 170; John F. Fox, III, *Red Clay to Richmond: Trail of the 35th Georgia Infantry Regiment, CSA* (Winchester, VA, 2006), 50-1. Lee did not specify the location of this bridge, but it is clear from his context that Lee himself had not seen the site. Mason, a grandson of George Mason, lived at Rutledge, in Fauquier County. At this time he was a private in the 17th VA. Ramey, *Years of Anguish*, 170. Bull was wounded and captured at Seven Pines. Fox, *Red Clay*, 47. Col. Lee of the 20th was a very distant cousin of the general. In a letter written on this date, Charles Marshall explained Lee's interpretation of the upper age limit of the conscription bill, specifically that if a conscripted man turns 35 while in service, he should be discharged. Charleston *Mercury*, July 31, 1862.

34 OR 4, Series 2, 251, 824.

35 REL to J. F. Gilmer, July 22, 1862, telegram book, REL HQ papers, VHS; Richmond *Daily Dispatch*, July 25, 1862.

is absent; she is able to do nothing more than make an inventory of what remains in the house.[36]

July 24, Thursday (Dabbs House): Lee orders a cavalry screen established from Malvern Hill to Savage's Station. Lee advises McClellan that Robert Ould is the POW exchange agent; Ould was unable to be at Aiken's Landing today as agreed upon but will be there at noon tomorrow. Lee requests also that McClellan investigate a report that Capt. George D. Walker of the steamer *Theodosia* was captured and is being kept in irons at Fort Columbus, New York.[37]

July 25, Friday (Dabbs House): Lee writes to Jackson regarding the possibility of sending A. P. Hill's division to Jackson (even though Hill is under arrest), should Jackson find an opportunity to strike at Pope. Lee writes to Jefferson Davis with the latest intelligence regarding Pope, including information from two spies in Washington. He writes also to the president regarding the policy of brigading troops by state, and detaching Gen. Richard Taylor from the ANV for service in his native Louisiana. Lee writes to Lafayette McLaws regarding the lack of discipline in the army, opining that the problems can and should be handled at lower levels, thus a general order from ANV headquarters will do no good.[38]

July 26, Saturday (Dabbs House/Drewry's Bluff): Lee advises President Davis that Jackson needs additional troops to confront Pope; Lee favors sending A. P. Hill's division, but with Hill under arrest the division is commanded by its senior brigadier, Lawrence Branch, but "I cannot trust the division to him." Lee opines that reports have Kentucky ripe for invasion, and suggests that Braxton Bragg's army, supported by Kirby Smith, Humphrey Marshall, or William Loring's forces, move into the Bluegrass state. Lee advises James Archer that the War Department hopes to get an additional regiment from Tennessee to add to his brigade, but Archer should detail officers to go to that state to gather recruits to bring his brigade back up to strength. Lee tells Texas Sen. Louis Wigfall of the need for additional recruits to replenish Hood's Texas brigade, and that Lee would like additional regiments from that state to make a second brigade. Lee goes to Drewry's Bluff to inspect the progress made on the fortifications there; he does not return until after midnight.[39]

July 27, Sunday (Dabbs House): Lee orders A. P. Hill to join Jackson at Gordonsville and advises Jackson that Hill's Division is en route, telling Jackson "I want Pope to be suppressed." Lee orders McLaws to move his division toward Mechanicsville to alleviate the crowding and resulting sickness in the camps around Richmond. Lee authorizes Pemberton to keep whatever artillery batteries he requires for field service in his department, and orders D. H. Hill to deal with the Federal threat in North Carolina wherever he finds them in force. Lee also instructs Hill to investigate why posted train schedules are not being adhered to and to rectify it. Lee informs North Carolina Governor Henry Clark that D. H. Hill is now in command in North Carolina and has been ordered to deal with the enemy there.[40]

---

36 OR 11, pt. 3, 646-8; OR 12, pt. 3, 916-7; REL to D. H. Hill, July 23, 1862, REL papers, MOC; OR 4, Series 2, 269, 825-6; Markie to Mrs. REL, July 25, 1862, Lee family papers, VHS. In describing her visit to Arlington, Markie wrote "Oh what a sad, sad visit it was." Ibid.

37 OR 11, pt. 3, 653; OR 4, Series 2, 274-5, 292. Ould, a lawyer from Georgetown, was the prosecutor at Philip Barton Key's murder trial in 1859. The accused killer was future Union general Daniel Sickles. Nat Brandt, *The Congressman Who Got Away with Murder* (Syracuse, NY, 1991), 156. Sometime around the 24th Lee came to Richmond to meet with Davis and called at Caskie's afterward. He did not specify the exact date, but it was on, or a day either side of, the 24th. Dowdey, *Wartime Papers*, 242-3.

38 OR 12, pt. 3, 917; Freeman, *Lee's Dispatches*, 34-7; OR 11, pt. 3, 653-4.

39 Dowdey, *Wartime Papers*, 238, 241; OR 11, pt. 3, 654-5. According to Freeman, it is very likely today was the day Lee released A. P. Hill from arrest and restored him to command of his division. *Lee's Lieutenants*, vol. 1, 668 n46.

40 OR 12, pt. 3, 918-9; OR 11, pt. 3, 656; REL to J. C. Pemberton, July 27, 1862, telegram book, REL HQ papers, VHS; REL to D. H. Hill (2 messages), July 27, 1862, telegram book, REL HQ papers, VHS; REL to H. T. Clark, July 27, 1862,

July 28, Monday (Dabbs House): Lee meets with Gen. Pendleton to explain Pendleton's mission to take several batteries south of the James to a point opposite Harrison's Landing and shell McClellan's camps and disrupt Union shipping. As this operation will occur within D. H. Hill's department, Lee makes Hill aware of it and suggests that he put Gen. Samuel French in overall command of Pendleton's artillery and the infantry support. Lee informs Sec. Randolph of Pendleton's mission and requests that the Richmond newspapers keep quiet about it. Lee writes to Gen. James Martin, regretting Martin's resignation and hoping that he will reconsider as Lee wants him to command the North Carolina portion of Hill's department.[41]

Lee approves of Jeb Stuart's reorganization of his cavalry into two brigades commanded by Wade Hampton and Fitz Lee, but Lee notes that Hampton is the senior of the two thus reversing Stuart's ranking of them. Lee orders A. P. Hill to reduce his wagons as much as possible; wagons will be available for him at Gordonsville, and his excess transportation is needed at Richmond. Lee receives letters from his wife and from daughter Mildred, writing back to both. To Mildred, his letter is full of fatherly advice and family news. To both he laments that one of their Marshall cousins, Louis, is serving on John Pope's staff: "I can forgive [Louis] fighting against us, but not his joining such a miscreant as Pope."[42]

July 29, Tuesday (Dabbs House): Lee informs D. H. Hill that Fort Powhatan is a better position for Pendleton's operation on the James than Hill's preferred location of Coggins Point; Lee again urges that Samuel French be put in command of the mission.[43]

July 30, Wednesday (Dabbs House): Lee writes to President Davis regarding a request from former Virginia Governor Col. William "Extra Billy" Smith that he and his 49th Virginia be made an independent command; Lee is not willing to do this but does offer to transfer Smith and his regiment from Mahone's Brigade to Early's. Lee congratulates Stuart on his promotion to major general and requests that Stuart investigate a rumor that Pope is arresting all males in and around Fredericksburg. Lee directs D. H. Hill to recall his wagon train as it is grossly in excess of the number of permitted wagons and animals. Lee notes that his horse Richmond is breathing heavy and not well.[44]

July 31, Thursday (Dabbs House): Lee writes to both President Davis and Jackson regarding a replacement for Gen. Beverly Robertson as Jackson's cavalry commander; to Davis Lee admits "probably Jackson may expect too much." Lee inquires of Navy Sec. Mallory and Col. Thomas Rhett, commander of the Richmond defenses, if guns can be transferred from the *Patrick Henry* and from the city's fortifications to the land face works at Drewry's Bluff. Lee informs Gen. Lawton that new Georgia units arriving cannot be assigned to his brigade and he instructs Jackson to assign artillery to Lawton's brigade as it arrived in Virginia without any.[45] Lee inquires of Gov. Clark if there is any legal prohibition regarding Gen. James Martin holding office in both the Confederate and state governments concurrently—Clark replies that North Carolina law prohibits such an arrangement,

---

telegram book, REL HQ papers, VHS. Theophilus Holmes was reassigned to the Trans-Mississippi Department on July 16, and D. H. Hill replaced him in command in North Carolina the following day. Anne Bailey, "Theophilus Hunter Holmes," *Confederate General*, vol. 3, 116-7; and Gary W. Gallagher, "Daniel Harvey Hill," *Confederate General*, vol. 3, 103-5.

41 A. P. Mason to WNP, July 28, 1862, WNP papers, UNC; *OR* 11, pt. 2, 936-7; *OR* 11, pt. 3, 657.

42 *OR* 12, pt. 3, 919-20; REL to Mildred, July 28, 1862, REL papers, LOC; Lee, *Recollections and Letters of REL*, 77. Lee expressed similar sentiment regarding Louis Marshall and Pope in both letters; the quote used here is the version he used in the letter to Mildred.

43 *OR* 11, pt. 2, 937.

44 Freeman, *Lee's Dispatches*, 40-1; *OR* 12, pt. 3, 920; *OR* 11, pt. 3, 658; Pitts, *High Meadow*, 79.

45 Freeman, *Lee's Dispatches*, 42-3; *OR* 11, pt. 3, 658-9; *OR* 12, pt. 3, 920-1.

but state militia does not fall under that rule; Lee thus advises Martin that he may continue as a Confederate brigadier general and North Carolina adjutant general. Lee writes to his brother Sydney Smith Lee regarding Fitz Lee's promotion, and mentions that he is returning Smith's overcoat which Lee borrowed. Lee's horse Richmond dies around midday. Rain during the day.[46]

---

46 REL to H. T. Clark, July 31, 1862, telegram book, REL HQ papers, VHS; REL to J. G. Martin, July 31, 1862, telegram book, REL HQ papers, VHS; Dowdey, *Wartime Papers*, 241; Pitts, *High Meadow*, 79-80. Smith Lee was in command at Drewry's Bluff. He likely loaned his brother the overcoat when Lee visited the works there on the 26th.

August 1862

In August, Robert E. Lee completed the strategic reversal of the war in the Virginia theater he began two months earlier. During the first week of the month, George McClellan's Army of the Potomac threatened a renewal of its offensive against Richmond, a thrust quickly parried by Lee. It was the last major action around the capital for almost two years because Lee was about to move the scene of battle north.

While Lee reorganized the Army of Northern Virginia in the wake of the bloody Seven Days' Battles, authorities in Washington also regrouped. President Lincoln bought Maj. Gen. Henry W. Halleck east to command all the Union armies and created a new command, the Army of Virginia, under Maj. Gen. John Pope in northern Virginia. With McClellan stymied at Harrison's Landing on the James River, it was Pope's army that most occupied Lee's attention during the summer.

Pope introduced a new style of warfare to Virginia, one that upset and disgusted Lee the gentleman soldier. The Federal general required all citizens to take the Oath of Allegiance to the United States, and those who did not were expelled from Union lines and their property confiscated. "This order has caused more distress and excitement than any before issued," complained a Warrenton resident. "Justice will meet that bundle of self conceit and braggadocio."[1] Lee called the Federal general a "miscreant" and instructed Stonewall Jackson not to defeat him, but "suppress" him.[2] "Pope," explained Southern writer and newspaperman Clifford Dowdey, "seems to be the only Federal general who aroused [Lee's] personal dislike."[3]

Lee first sent Jackson with the Valley Army to confront Pope, and then as it became apparent that McClellan no longer posed a threat, Lee dispatched more and more of his army to northern Virginia. On August 9, Jackson bested a portion of Pope's army at Cedar Mountain outside Culpeper. Within a week, Lee was on scene himself leading the effort to "suppress" the "miscreant" Pope.

When Pope escaped a trap Lee set for him on the Rapidan River, Lee once again divided his army, sending Jackson on a bold and dangerous march behind Pope's Army of Virginia. Pope promptly lost track of Jackson's whereabouts almost entirely until running into him at the Brawner farm near the old Manassas battlefield.

While Jackson battled part of Pope's army close to where he achieved his immortal moniker the summer before, the fortunes of war smiled down on Lee. The commander had several close calls on the way to join Jackson with the balance of the army. Lee was riding in advance of his columns with just his staff and a handful of couriers when enemy cavalry appeared immediately to their front. Had the commander of the Union detachment been more aggressive, he could have netted quite a haul. Several days later, when Lee arrived at the battlefield near Groveton, a Federal bullet missed him by a fraction of an inch during a reconnaissance.

---

1 John T. Toler, ed., *The Civil War Diary of Betty Fanny Gray, Fauquier County, Virginia* (Warrenton, VA, 2015), 28-9.

2 Lee, *Recollections and Letters of REL*, 77; Dowdey, *Wartime Papers*, 239.

3 Dowdey, *Wartime Papers*, 224.

Personal luck, however, is always fleeting and so it was with Lee. After the sweeping victory over Pope at Second Manassas at the end of the month, Lee seriously injured both wrists in a fall. Unable to ride a horse and hold the reins, Lee was relegated to getting about in an ambulance. Possibly motivated by his brush with capture on the march, Company A of the 6th Virginia Cavalry was detailed to serve as Lee's headquarters guard at the end of the month.[4]

Lee was able to see Custis and daughter Mary before leaving Richmond, but he did not get a chance to see his wife Mary before taking to the field. He wrote of his sadness at riding past Hickory Hill, where she was staying at the time, on the train to Gordonsville and being unable to stop and see her. Lee saw Rooney for the first time in several weeks, but when he encountered Rob on the battlefield at Manassas, he did not recognize his own youngest son.

* * *

---

4 Michael P. Musick, *6th Virginia Cavalry* (Lynchburg, VA, 1990), 21. They continued guarding ANV HQ until the army crossed the Potomac River into Maryland, at which point they were left near Leesburg to steer stragglers and others to Winchester. Luther W. Hopkins, *From Bull Run to Appomattox: A Boy's View* (no place, 2010), 21.

August 1, Friday (Dabbs House): Lee advises Longstreet of the need to tighten up on discipline in his division especially regarding men leaving their commands.5

August 2, Saturday (Dabbs House): Lee meets with Gen. Pendleton for several hours going over the recent night attack on the James; the meeting lasts until early afternoon. Lee advises D. H. Hill that he did not intend for Hill and Pendleton to launch one attack on McClellan's shipping and then retire, but rather to establish a permanent presence at Fort Powhatan. After meeting with Pendleton, Lee orders him and Hill to continue to attack along the river; he tells Hill that he must employ a supporting infantry force but to keep it retired from the river and cautions not to fire on any transports bearing exchanged prisoners, as they are expected at any time.6

Lee asks President Davis for instructions in communicating with McClellan regarding rumored atrocities committed by the Federals in the West and violations of the Dix-Hill POW cartel agreement. He writes to Union General in Chief Henry Halleck regarding the reported execution of a citizen in New Orleans, noting that he wrote to McClellan about this, who referred the inquiry to Washington, but Lee has received no reply. He also complains of Pope's actions, which Lee claims are in direct violation of the prisoner agreement recently reached by D. H. Hill and John Dix. Lee answers a request from Magruder for information regarding his division during the Seven Days, referring Magruder to Longstreet for the details he seeks.7

August 3, Sunday (Dabbs House): Lee sends yesterday's letters to Halleck through the lines via flag of truce in the morning. Lee writes to D. H. Hill regarding the appearance of an enemy force on the south bank of the James River opposite Westover, instructing Hill to defend the position as best he can. He sends two more telegrams to Hill to "drive them if you can" and telling Hill to use his own discretion, that Lee can offer no advice from afar.8 Lee receives a letter from Mary and writes back in the evening with latest family news, mentioning being in the city to meet with President Davis recently and calling on the Caskies afterwards, and the death of his horse Richmond. He writes also to Charlotte and mentions that although he was at Rooney's camp recently they were not able to connect. Rain during the day.9

August 4, Monday (Dabbs House): In the morning Lee meets with Jeremy Gilmer to discuss whether he would prefer to be chief engineer with the ANV in the field or would rather have a desk job in Richmond and command of the entire engineer bureau. Both officers prefer Gilmer in the field with Lee's army, and he is named the army's chief engineer. Lee sends former chief engineer Walter Stevens to Petersburg to lay out the defenses there, and orders D. H. Hill to assist with anything Stevens needs. Lee, McLaws, and Tom Cobb inspect the camps of Cobb's Brigade and afterward drink buttermilk at Cobb's headquarters. Lee approves of

---

5 OR 11, pt. 3, 659. A letter from Lee to Stuart regarding the performance of P. M. B. Young of the Cobb Legion at Malvern Hill and Haxall's Landing, questionably dated Aug. 1 appears in OR 11, pt. 3, 660, but the date appears to be incorrect. In this message Lee references a report by Young of his actions, but this report has never been located. It is believed to be in reference to an engagement later in August; the correct date for this letter to Stuart is not known. Email R. E. L. Krick to author, April 13, 2018.

6 WNP to wife, Aug. 2, 1862 and Aug. 5, 1862, WNP papers, UNC; OR 11, pt. 2, 938-9; OR 11, pt. 3, 660. Hill and Pendleton attacked Union shipping with some 40 guns on the night of July 31/August 1.

7 Freeman, *Lee's Dispatches*, 44; OR 15, 906; OR 4, Series 2, 328-30; OR 11, pt. 2, 684-5. According to Navy Sec. Mallory, at least one of the letters to Halleck was written by Secretary of State Judah Benjamin and merely signed by Lee. Mallory diary, Aug. 15, 1862, UNC.

8 Freeman, *Lee's Dispatches*, 45; OR 11, pt. 3, 660-1; REL to D. H. Hill, Aug. 3, 1862, telegram book, REL HQ papers, VHS.

9 Pitts, *High Meadow*, 81-2; Dowdey, *Wartime Papers*, 242-3; REL to Charlotte, Aug. 3, 1862, G. B. Lee papers, VHS; Krick, *CW Weather*, 66.

Stonewall Jackson's reluctance to attack Pope, and suggests Jackson ascertain what force is at Fredericksburg before making any offensive move, adding he is still unsure of McClellan's intentions.[10]

Lee advises President Davis that he sent the letters to Halleck through the lines yesterday, and he returns to Davis two letters from South Carolina Governor Pickens: one regarding the importance of the Charleston & Savannah Railroad, the other about continuing problems with Gen. Pemberton. Regarding Pemberton, Lee tells Davis, "In my opinion it will be easier to relieve Gen. Pemberton from Charleston than to replace him." Lee suggests that Gustavus W. Smith be sent to Charleston if his health permits, and that Gen. William H. C. Whiting be sent to oversee the fortification of the harbor. Lee complains to Commissary General Northrop about details being made from the ANV for commissary service; Lee wants to know why troops who are not fit for field service are not used instead. Lee writes to Secretary of War Randolph regarding the promotion of engineer Lt. Samuel R. Johnston, and tells Randolph that he will reluctantly send one regiment to Louisiana and one to western Virginia if necessary.[11]

August 5, Tuesday (Dabbs House): Lee meets with John Mosby who informs Lee that Burnside's troops from North Carolina have gone to northern Virginia to reinforce Pope; upon leaving, Mosby gives Lee several lemons. Lee replies to a letter from McClellan regarding a flag of truce violation at Jamestown Island; Lee explains that the firing on Union ships in the James River was unauthorized and was likely done not by soldiers, but rather by locals who "took this method to revenge their grievances" with the Federals. Lee receives a letter from Gen. Jubal Early who is upset with his new brigade; Lee explains that Early's former brigade was broken up because it was comprised of troops from multiple states, and he wants Early in command of an all-Virginia brigade. The one he commands now was the only brigade lacking a commander when Early returned to active duty.[12]

August 6, Wednesday (Dabbs House/Malvern Hill/New Market): Lee and Jeremy Gilmer go to Malvern Hill to reconnoiter as McClellan sallies forth from Harrison Landing. Lee instructs D. H. Hill to monitor enemy movements on the south side of the James, and orders Richard Anderson to hold his division in readiness to cross the river at Drewry's Bluff. Lee decrees that brigades and divisions will be named for their commanders. He spends the night somewhere near Malvern Hill.[13]

---

10 Jeremy Gilmer to wife, Aug. 4, 1862, J. F. Gilmer papers, UNC; *OR* 11, pt. 3, 663-4; Cobb, "Extracts from Letters," 295; *OR* 12, pt. 3, 922-3. Gilmer was wounded at Shiloh; Lee was not certain whether his health had recovered enough for field service, hence the offer of a desk job. Cobb recalled that "Lee was high in his praises" of the brigade. "Extracts from Letters," 295.

11 Freeman, *Lee's Dispatches*, 45, 361-2; REL to Davis, Aug. 4, 1862, endorsements, telegram book, REL HQ papers, VHS; *OR* 11, pt. 3, 663-4; REL to G. W. Randolph, Aug. 4, 1862, S. R. Johnston papers, VHS. Johnston was promoted to captain and assigned to Lee's staff as an engineer on Aug. 12. Krick, *Staff Officers in Gray*, 174.

12 Charles W. Russell, ed., *The Memoirs of Colonel John S. Mosby* (Boston, 1917), 130-5; *OR* 11, pt. 3, 358, 664-5. Mosby was captured several weeks prior and saw the transports ferrying Gen. Burnside's troops as he and other exchanged prisoners were delivered to City Point, Virginia.

13 J. F. Gilmer to wife, Aug. 8, 1862, Gilmer papers, UNC; REL to D. H. Hill, Aug. 6, 1862, telegram book, REL HQ papers, VHS; REL to R. H. Anderson, Aug. 6, 1862, telegram book, REL HQ papers, VHS; GO92, Aug. 6, 1862, EPA papers, UNC. McClellan moved a portion of the Army of the Potomac from Harrison's Landing and reoccupied Malvern Hill. Lee did not officially move army HQ from the Dabbs house; Chilton and possibly others remained there. R. H. Chilton to Samuel Cooper, Aug. 6, 1862, telegram book, REL HQ papers, VHS. Lee seems to have spent the night in the vicinity of New Market crossroads, as his correspondence early on the 7th is from there. At least one account puts Lee at the headquarters of Gen. Robert Toombs during this time, but does not specify *where* Toombs's HQ was located. Maj. Raphael Moses, one of Toombs's staff officers, wrote: "Our headquarters was determined by General Lee the best location for him during the sudden changes that he had to make in the movements of his entire army. He sent his cot down by a wagon and some other things and soon after followed with his staff." Raphael J. Moses, "Autobiography," 59, R. J. Moses papers, UNC.

August 7, Thursday (New Market/Malvern Hill/Dabbs House): Lee and Jeremy Gilmer again reconnoiter around Malvern Hill. Lee orders Lafayette McLaws to pursue the retreating McClellan but if the Federals are "beyond reach," he should return to his original position. Lee urges D. H. Hill to complete the fortifications around Petersburg and Drewry's Bluff and to return Anderson's Division and Pendleton's artillery to the main army. On the northern front Lee encourages Stuart to work with Jackson to dispose of an enemy column which the cavalryman has intercepted; he is to continue disrupting Pope's communications.[14]

Lee advises Jackson to use his own judgment in dealing with Pope and gives him the latest developments on the Richmond front. Lee suggests to Adjutant General Sam Cooper that all exchanged officers be ordered to report in person to Cooper to speed along the process of getting them returned to duty with Lee's army. Lee tells Col. J. Thompson Brown that Stonewall requires additional artillery; Lee wants Brown to call on Lee at Dabbs tomorrow to discuss details. Lee informs President Davis that McClellan briefly reoccupied Malvern Hill and Lee countered with several divisions, but no fight developed before the Yankees withdrew. After dark Lee returns to Dabbs.[15]

August 8, Friday (Dabbs House): Lee meets with Gilmer, most likely about strengthening the Richmond fortifications, and with Col. Brown regarding additional artillery for Jackson. He also meets with Sec. Randolph to discuss Beverly Robertson and "Grumble" Jones and command of Jackson's cavalry. The general writes to Jackson approving of his plan to strike at the enemy in Culpeper County, but worries that Jackson may have been too "hasty" in his judgment of Robertson. Lee sends a lengthy letter to Governor Clark of North Carolina regarding the defense of his state, noting that there are not men or resources enough to defend every region in the Confederacy, but that by defending Virginia Lee is keeping the enemy from getting to North Carolina from the north. He points out that D. H. Hill will no doubt endeavor to recover the ground lost while Holmes and his force were called to the defense of Richmond.[16]

Lee informs D. H. Hill that he does not foresee a movement against Petersburg, and asks what brigades need commanders and who Hill recommends. Lee orders Hood to move to Hanover Junction with his division, and instructs Roswell Ripley to keep a strong force posted at the Charles City Road crossing of White Oak Swamp. Lee requests that the 8th Virginia Cavalry be transferred to the ANV from southwest Virginia. Lee informs several leading citizens of Gloucester County that he regrets he is unable to do more to defend that region, but with the Federals controlling the York River, they are able to come and go as they please; if he were to send a force there he fears that it would only draw more Federals to the area. He recommends that they move everything of value that they can to a safer location in the interior and that they raise a partisan unit to combat the Federals there. Lee writes to Governor Letcher's aide S. Bassett French wishing him well in his new position with Jackson.[17]

---

14 J. F. Gilmer to wife, Aug. 8, 1862, Gilmer papers, UNC; REL to Lafayette McLaws, Aug, 7, 1862, Lafayette McLaws papers, UNC; *OR* 11, pt. 3, 666-7; *OR* 12, pt. 3, 925.

15 *OR* 12, pt. 3, 925-6; *OR* 11, pt. 3, 666, 956-7; REL to J. T. Brown, Aug., 7, 1862, REL papers, UVA; Pitts, *High Meadow*, 87-8.

16 J. F. Gilmer to wife, Aug. 8, 1862, Gilmer papers, UNC; REL to J. T. Brown, Aug. 7, 1862, REL papers, UVA; *OR* 12, pt. 3, 926; *OR* 9, 478-9. Lee did not specify whether Randolph came to headquarters or if Lee went to Richmond for their meeting. Wherever it occurred, Lee wrote Jackson before they met.

17 *OR* 11, pt. 3, 667-70; *OR* 12, pt. 3, 926-7; REL to S. B. French, Aug. 8, 1862, REL papers, W&L. Ripley was in command of D. H. Hill's former division. Lee told French, "I have regretted my inability to see more of the troops—I have never had time to be with them except at their duties. Their parades, etc., I have been unable to attend. I visit their camps and their lines etc., but I have had to keep them so constantly at work. So much has to be done, and so much is yet to be done, that I have felt I might not take them from it and engross their time with reviews, etc. for my gratification." French was reassigned to to Stonewall Jackson "for special and confidential service;" French did not explain in his memoirs what this service entailed. Oldaker, *Centennial Tales*, 11-2.

August 9, Saturday (Dabbs House): Lee meets with Longstreet about sending him to Gordonsville. Lee replies to a request from Chase Whiting to be promoted to major general by telling him to be patient, that it will likely happen in time. Lee writes to Mrs. R. K. Meade praising her son's actions during the Seven Days and expressing his condolences at his death. He writes also to Annie and Agnes about the recent operations around Malvern Hill and the latest family news.[18]

August 10, Sunday (Dabbs House): G. W. Smith returns to duty and Lee assigns him to the command of what was previously D. H. Hill's division. Lee orders Hill to retain a few field batteries for his command and to send Gen. Pendleton with the remainder back to the main army. Lee writes to a "Mrs. Ritchie" regarding an appointment for her grandson in the signal corps; Lee states he will gladly recommend him for such, and mentions that he intended to add her son to his own staff while stationed in South Carolina, but was ordered away before he could do so. Lee writes to his son Custis regretting that he will not be able to see him today. He also writes to wife Mary offering suggestions for securing the release of two slaves who have been jailed, as well as with current news of the Malvern Hill operations. Rain during the afternoon and night.[19]

August 11, Monday (Dabbs House): Lee meets again with Longstreet to go over his orders prior to leaving for Gordonsville. Lee writes to Adjutant General Cooper asking if conscripts from South Carolina can be divided between two South Carolina brigades rather than all going to one, and if vacancies among regimental officers can be taken care of today. He writes also to Sec. Randolph recommending that all remaining prisoners be paroled as soon as possible. To discourage straggling on the march, Lee orders a provost detachment at the rear of each division while on the move, and that each company detail two men as stretcher bearers in battle.[20]

August 12, Tuesday (Dabbs House): Lee orders G. W. Smith his troops to advance to Malvern Hill to contest a reported enemy advance, and authorizes Fitz Lee to move from Hanover Court House because of the scarcity of provisions there, but tells him to make sure he does not leave the northern approaches to the capital unguarded. Lee sends his congratulations to Jackson for his victory at Cedar Mountain. Lee informs North Carolina Governor Clark, D. H. Hill, and James Martin that Martin's resignation has not been accepted and he will operate under Hill in a dual role of state and Confederate service; Martin will command all the troops in North Carolina and continue his recruiting and conscription efforts. Lee visits with his daughter Mary and Custis briefly today. Capt. Samuel Johnston formally joins Lee's staff as engineer officer.[21]

August 13, Wednesday (Dabbs House): Lee instructs D. H. Hill to verify reports of McClellan's army leaving Harrison's Landing and orders Longstreet and Hood to Gordonsville to link up with

---

18 Harsh, *Confederate Tide Rising*, 198; Denson, *Address Containing Memoir of Whiting*, 34-5; REL newspaper references, DSF papers, LVA; Dowdey, *Wartime Papers*, 250-1. It is possible that the meeting with Longstreet occurred on August 10, but Harsh was unable to determine the precise day. Meade was one of the officers Lee cautioned Magruder not to accidentally harm at the Gouldin farm in late June (see June 29); he succumbed to illness at Petersburg on July 31. Krick, *Staff Officers in Gray*, 219. Annie and Agnes were at Jones Spring in Warren County, NC, at this time.

19 OR 11, pt. 3, 671; REL to "Mrs. Ritchie," Aug. 10, 1862, Harrison family papers, GHS; REL to Custis, Aug. 10, 1862, REL papers, Duke; Pitts, *High Meadow*, 90; Krick, *CW Weather*, 66. The identity of "Mrs. Ritchie" and her grandson is unknown. According to Krick, *Staff Officers in Gray*, there was no Ritchie or Harrison from South Carolina or Georgia in a staff role in the ANV.

20 Harsh, *Sounding the Shallows*, 223; OR 11, pt. 3, 671-2; OR 4, Series 2, 843; OR 12, pt. 3, 928. Lee's letter to Randolph mentions "a recent conversation on the subject" with President Davis, but Lee did not specify when this occurred, and Davis made no mention of it.

21 OR 11, pt. 3, 672-3; OR 12, pt. 2, 185-6; OR 9, 479; REL to Mary, Aug. 13, 1862, REL papers, LOC; Krick, *Staff Officers in Gray*, 174. It is not known if Lee went into the city, or if Mary and Custis visited his HQ.

Jackson against Pope. Lee meets with Pendleton and Stuart regarding the division of the army on the Richmond and Gordonsville/Culpeper fronts. After this meeting, Lee sends written instructions to Stuart to ascertain the truth of Burnside leaving Fredericksburg; if true, he is to move with the majority of his cavalry to join Longstreet at Gordonsville. Lee sends a short note to his wife mentioning his visit with Custis and Mary yesterday, and regretting that he will not be able to see her and he doesn't know where he will be by week's end.[22]

August 14, Thursday (Dabbs House): Lee informs President Davis and Sec. Randolph that McClellan is withdrawing from the Peninsula to reinforce Pope and that Lee himself will go to Gordonsville with a portion of the troops left in front of Richmond. He informs Longstreet and G. W. Smith of his move and places Smith in command around Richmond. He forwards to Randolph the colors of the 12th New York, captured by Longstreet's men, and Magruder's initial report on the Seven Days. He writes to Custis, apologizing for not being able to see him in person before leaving Richmond, and enclosing a vest and hat to be stored in his trunk. Fitz Lee requests that Rob be commissioned and assigned as his brigade ordnance officer.[23]

August 15, Friday (Dabbs House/Richmond/ Gordonsville/Rocklands): Lee and staff depart Richmond at 4:00 a.m. on the Virginia Central for Gordonsville. He is met upon his arrival by Longstreet and Jackson. Lee establishes headquarters for the night at Rocklands, "the very beautiful farm of Mr. Burton Haxall," as Walter Taylor described it. The cabinet discusses Lee's recent correspondence with Union General in Chief Halleck, and the latter's refusal to answer it on the grounds that it was offensive.[24]

August 16, Saturday (Rocklands/Orange Court House/ Meadow Farm): Lee sends President Davis an update on Pope and advises that he is ordering additional Confederate troops away from Richmond. The general also mentions a recent raid by John Imboden's cavalry against the Baltimore & Ohio line, and urges that the CSS *Richmond* be completed so she can clear the Union navy from the James River. Lee establishes headquarters at Meadow Farm, the home of Erasmus Taylor near Orange Court House. Davis's cabinet continues to discuss Lee's correspondence with Gen. Halleck, and the proper response to send to Washington.[25]

---

22 *OR* 11, pt. 3, 673-5; WNP to wife, Aug. 15, 1862, WNP papers, UNC; REL to Mary, Aug. 13, 1862, REL papers, LOC. It is possible that Lee intended to remain at Richmond himself while entrusting the operation against Pope to Longstreet; Harsh examines this in *Confederate Tide Rising*, 197-9.

23 Dowdey, *Wartime Papers*, 253-6; *OR* 11, pt. 3, 674-80; Fitz Lee to G. W. Randolph, Aug. 14, 1862, REL Jr CSR. Lee noted that he gave Magruder's report only "a cursory examination" before sending it to the War Department, only because Prince John's conduct during the campaign was called into question. *OR* 11, pt., 3, 679-80. Son Rob did not accept the position on his cousin's staff. His mother wrote, "He is very well satisfied with his present position in the artillery and has many of his college friends to share his duties." Mrs. REL to Eliza Stiles, Aug. 20, 1862, Stiles family papers, GHS.

24 *OR* 11, pt. 3, 676, 678; Freeman, *Lee*, vol. 2, 279; Douglas, *I Rode with Stonewall*, 132; R. Lockwood Tower, *Lee's Adjutant: The Wartime Letters of Colonel Walter Herron Taylor, 1862-1865* (Columbia, SC, 1995), 38; Hurst, *Soldiers, Stories, Sites and Fights*, 39; Mallory diary, Aug. 15, 1862, UNC. Lee wrote to Mary that he was tempted to stop at Hickory Hill to visit her but due to the early hour there was no sign of life at the house as the train passed. Dowdey, *Wartime Papers*, 257. Rocklands served as the summer residence of the Haxalls, who lived the majority of the time in Richmond. The original house on the property dated to the 1820s. Rocklands, National Register of Historic Places nomination form, July 20, 1982.

25 Dowdey, *Wartime Papers*, 256-7; REL to Davis, Aug. 16, 1862, telegram book, REL HQ papers, VHS; Tower, *Lee's Adjutant*, 38-9; Hurst, *Soldiers, Stories, Sites and Fights*, 39; Ann L. Miller, *Antebellum Orange: The Pre-Civil War Homes, Buildings and Historic Sites of Orange County, Virginia* (Orange, VA, 1988), 115-6; Mallory diary, Aug. 16, 1862, UNC. Meadow Farm comprised some 800 acres and had been owned by the Taylor family since 1722, the wartime house dated to 1855. Jaquelin P. Taylor, "Meadow Farm: Orange County, Virginia," in *VMHB* (July 1938), 231-2. Erasmus Taylor was later an officer on Longstreet's staff. Patricia J. Hurst, *The War Between the States, 1862-1865: Rapidan River Area of Clark Mountain, Orange County, Virginia* (Rapidan, VA, 1989), 44-6; Krick, *Staff Officers in Gray*, 281-2. Walter Taylor, no relation to the

August 17, Sunday (Meadow Farm): Lee meets with Stuart around midday and with Longstreet and Jackson afterwards to discuss how best to strike at Pope. Lee writes to President Davis his doubts about D. H. Hill's fitness for independent command and his belief that Samuel French is a much better choice to command southern Virginia and North Carolina. Lee requests that Sec. Randolph send Hill to Lee's army with all the available troops from around Richmond, and that G. W. Smith send a portion of the reserve artillery. He writes to Mary lamenting that he was not able to see her before leaving Richmond.[26]

August 18, Monday (Meadow Farm/Hawfield): Lee orders Stuart to be prepared to move tomorrow, but later revises those orders due to the jaded condition of Fitz Lee's horses, setting the date for the advance for Wednesday instead. Lee requests that Richmond not send troops via Lynchburg but rather to Orange on the Virginia Central. In response to a Union cavalry raid, he orders troops from Hanover Junction and Richmond to find the enemy raiders near Tolersville, and for the garrison at Gordonsville to be put on the defensive. Headquarters is established at Hawfield, the farm of Capt. William G. Crenshaw, southeast of Clark's Mountain.[27]

August 19, Tuesday (Hawfield/Clark's Mountain): Lee and Longstreet go to the signal station atop Clark's Mountain in the afternoon to observe Pope's army. Lee issues marching orders for the attack on Pope, with Jackson—accompanied by Lee—on the left at Somerville Ford, Longstreet on the right at Raccoon Ford, and Jeb Stuart on the far right at Kelly's Ford to cut off Pope's retreat. Lee advises Sec. Randolph that Union cavalry is moving toward Hanover Junction and that troops from Richmond are the only forces that can intercept. Lee orders Roswell Ripley at Hanover Junction to position troops along the North Anna, and G. W. Smith in Richmond to send McLaws and D. H. Hill to the North Anna as well. The Lee-Halleck correspondence is published in full in today's Richmond *Dispatch*.[28]

August 20, Wednesday (Hawfield/Raccoon Ford/Brandy Station): Lee crosses the Rapidan River at

---

owners of Meadow Farm, noted, "Such charming quarters cannot be long enjoyed . . . [while] the troops are in motion." Tower, *Lee's Adjutant*, 39.

26 Von Borcke, *Memoirs*, 73; John J. Hennessy, *Return to Bull Run: The Campaign and Battle of Second Manassas* (New York, 1993), 43-4; *OR* 51, pt. 2, 1075-6; REL to G. W. Randolph, Aug. 17, 1862, telegram book, REL HQ papers, VHS; REL to G. W. Smith, Aug. 17, 1862, telegram book, REL HQ papers, VHS; Dowdey, *Wartime Papers*, 257-8. Lee told President Davis that D. H. Hill was "not entirely equal to his present position. An excellent executive officer, he does not appear to have much administrative ability. Left to himself he seems embarrassed and backward to act." *OR* 51, pt. 2, 1075-6.

27 *OR* 12, pt. 3, 934-5; REL to "Lt. Col. Magruder," Aug. 18, 1862, telegram book, REL HQ papers, VHS; REL to J. A. Corley, Aug. 18, 1862, telegram book, REL HQ papers, VHS; REL to H. D. Whitcomb, Aug. 18, 1862, telegram book, REL HQ papers, VHS; Archie P. MacDonald, ed., *Make Me a Map of the Valley: The Civil War Journal of Stonewall Jackson's Topographer, Jedediah Hotchkiss* (Dallas, TX, 1973), 69. Tolersville is present-day Mineral. Crenshaw commanded an artillery battery in A. P. Hill's division. Armistead Long wrote that Lee went atop Clark's Mountain to observe Pope's army on this date, but most accounts place this visit on the 19th. *Memoirs of REL*, 186. Charles Marshall recorded that Lee and Jackson made a trip to the top of the mountain, but he did not state the day on which it occurred. Maurice, *Lee's Aide de Camp*, 124. Longstreet also wrote that he and Lee went to the top of the mountain around this time, but gave no date. *From Manassas to Appomattox*, 161-2. Lee himself wrote that he went up the mountain on the 19th. *OR* 12, pt. 2, 728-9. Given that Lee established HQ at the base of the mountain, it is entirely possible he ascended the heights on both days. Hawfield, about midway between Orange and Raccoon Ford, was destroyed by fire in 1938. Scott, *History of Orange County*, 205; *Orange Review*, Dec. 27, 1938.

28 Freeman, *Lee*, vol. 2, 287-8; *OR* 12, pt. 2, 728-9; *OR* 12, pt. 3, 937; REL to Ripley, Aug. 19, 1862, telegram book, REL HQ papers, VHS; REL to G. W. Smith, Aug. 19, 1862, telegram book, REL HQ papers, VHS; REL newspaper references, DSF papers, LVA. The date of Lee's visit to Clark's Mountain has been a source of considerable confusion, even though Lee himself stated that it was on this day in a message to Jeb Stuart, the original of which is in the REL papers at MOC; it is reproduced in *OR*, 12, pt. 2, 728-9. The confusion arises largely from multiple dates put forth by Longstreet in his postwar writings, and from incorrect or incomplete statements by Armistead Long, Charles Marshall, and others. Joseph Harsh tackles these inconsistencies in *Confederate Tide Rising*, 201-2.

Raccoon Ford and establishes his headquarters near Brandy Station.[29]

August 21, Thursday (Brandy Station/Beverly Ford): Stuart and his staff join Lee for breakfast at headquarters, which consists of rye coffee, bread, and honey. Lee informs President Davis via telegraph that the ANV is across the Rapidan and in pursuit of the enemy, who are falling back on Warrenton and Fredericksburg. Lee rides to Beverly Ford on the Rappahannock River to reconnoiter the Federals opposing Jackson's crossing there. The Confederate House of Representatives passes a joint resolution tendering Gen. Lee the "Thanks of Congress" for his victories over Gen. McClellan outside Richmond.[30]

August 22, Friday (Brandy Station/Farley): In the morning Lee approves a proposal from Jeb Stuart to raid the rear of the Federal army, and later moves his headquarters to Farley, the home of Dr. William Welford. The Confederate Senate considers the House resolution for the Thanks of Congress, and the resolution is printed in the Richmond *Whig*. Heavy rains all that afternoon and throughout the night.[31]

August 23, Saturday (Farley): Lee learns of Stuart's raid at Catlett's Station and that he captured Pope's uniform and papers; Stuart shows Pope's uniform to Lee and Jackson. Lee sends a lengthy letter to the president outlining the campaign to date and Lee's desire to remain in northern Virginia, which will require all available troops from Richmond and elsewhere sent to him. He informs Randolph and William Loring that captured communications show that troops are being withdrawn from the Kanawha Valley and Lee urges for a movement by Loring in the mountains in conjunction with Lee's offensive.[32]

August 24, Sunday (Farley/Jeffersonton): Lee meets with Stuart in the morning before leaving Farley. Lee writes President Davis informing him of Pope's papers captured at Catlett's Station, which detail enemy strength and intentions; Lee again states his desire to shift the scene of battle to northern Virginia and that he needs more of G. W. Smith's troops from Richmond. Lee meets with Jackson near Jeffersonton where both establish headquarters.[33]

August 25, Monday (Jeffersonton): Lee telegraphs President Davis that a portion of McClellan's army joined Pope thus Lee needs G. W. Smith's troops as soon as possible. He forwards the papers captured

---

29 Clark Hall, "Gen. Robert E. Lee in Culpeper," Brandy Station Foundation, www.brandystationfoundation.com/cse_columns/lee-in-culpeper.htm; Freeman, *Lee*, vol. 2, 289-90. Per the original attack plan, Lee intended to accompany Jackson's troops via Somerville Ford; when Pope retreated Lee shifted his own movements eastward, probably to be closer to Pope. By crossing at Raccoon Ford, it is likely Lee went to Brandy Station via Stevensburg rather than through Culpeper, but there is no known evidence to trace his exact route. The precise location of his HQ at Brandy is unknown, although it was almost certainly somewhere on Fleetwood Hill.

30 Von Borcke, *Memoirs*, 82; W. W. Blackford, *War Years with Jeb Stuart* (New York, 1945), 98; *OR* 51, pt. 2, 609; Freeman, *Lee*, vol. 2, 291-2; *Journal of the Congress of the CSA*, vol. 5, 306.

31 Hennessy, *Return to Bull Run*, 67; McDonald, *Make Me a Map*, 71; *Journal of the Congress of the CSA*, vol. 2, 237; REL newspaper references, DSF papers, LVA; Krick, *CW Weather*, 66. Farley, built ca. 1801, overlooks the Hazel River just north of Brandy Station; it was used by Union Maj. Gen. John Sedgwick as his HQ during the winter of 1863-4.

32 Freeman, *Lee*, vol. 2, 296-7; Oldaker, *Centennial Tales*, 30; *OR* 12, pt. 3, 940-2. S. Bassett French claimed to be present when Stuart arrived with Pope's uniform. While he did not state the location, he did note—likely with no little exaggeration—that all three generals were mounted and apparently near the front somewhere as their party came under fire soon after Stuart's arrival, with a solid shot passing between Lee and Jackson and coming to rest under Stuart's horse. Oldaker, *Centennial Tales*, 30.

33 Von Borcke, *Memoirs*, 91; *OR* 12, pt. 3, 942; Henderson, *Stonewall Jackson*, vol. 2, 152; Freeman, *Lee*, vol. 2, 300-1. Freeman called this conference with Jackson "one of the most important Lee ever held." In that meeting, Lee instructed Jackson to take his command into Pope's rear and cut his communications with Washington. Ibid. Jackson aide Henry Kyd Douglas recalled Longstreet and Stuart also being involved in this meeting, but according to Freeman there are no other known accounts putting the four of them together on this date. *I Rode with Stonewall*, 135; *Lee's Lieutenants*, vol. 2, 82 n9. Joseph Harsh, however, sided with Douglas and has all four generals in conference. *Sounding the Shallows*, 223.

from Pope's headquarters wagon to Sec. Randolph and again urges an offensive by Loring in western Virginia; he also requests that the 2nd North Carolina Cavalry be transferred to the ANV. Lee orders Jeremy Gilmer to "perfect" the Richmond defenses so they can be manned by a minimum of troops, but notes he has no additional engineers to send. Stuart's aide Heros von Borcke joins Lee for dinner, having delivered more of Pope's captured papers. Stuart also comes to headquarters during the evening; Lee orders him to take all of his mounted force and accompany Jackson's wing of the army. Rooney visits for a time briefly in the evening also, the first time Lee has seen his son in more than a month. Lee writes to Mary with news of the campaign including Rooney's role in the Catlett's Station raid, and mentions that he saw Rob about a week previous.[34]

August 26, Tuesday (Jeffersonton/Orlean/Edgeworth): Before breaking camp at Jeffersonton, Lee writes to Charlotte with news of Rooney and mentions that cousin Louis Marshall, an aide on Pope's staff, escaped Rooney's clutches at Catlett's Station. He sends to Richmond a captured letter written by Union officer A. A. Tomlinson containing details of Jackson's fight at Cedar Mountain. He instructs D. H. Hill to bring his division to join Lee's army, but if McClellan moves it will be Hill's responsibility to deal with the threat. Lee accompanies Longstreet's column across the Rappahannock where he and Longstreet establish headquarters at Orlean. In the evening the two generals and their staff are invited to dine at Edgeworth, home of the Marshall family.[35]

August 27, Wednesday (Edgeworth/Salem/White Plains): Mrs. Marshall provides breakfast for Lee, Longstreet, and their staff officers before dawn at Edgeworth. "About sunrise" a courier arrives from Jackson with news of his capture of Bristoe Station; shortly after this Lee departs. He is nearly captured or killed near the village of Ada while riding with only his staff far in advance of Longstreet's column when enemy cavalry appears in their immediate front; his staff officers quickly deploy in line of battle to screen the general and the enemy horsemen withdraw without engaging. Shortly after this incident, Lee and his entourage encounter a horseless carriage and several stranded ladies—the same Federal cavalry Lee just encountered had taken their horses. One of the ladies tells Lee that losing her horses was worth the opportunity to speak with the general. At Salem Lee telegraphs President Davis of Jackson's capture of Bristoe Station and Manassas Junction. Lee establishes headquarters at the home of James W. Foster, just west of White Plains.[36]

---

34 Dowdey, *Wartime Papers*, 264-5; OR 12, pt. 3, 943-5; von Borcke, *Memoirs*, 93-4; Freeman, *Lee*, vol. 2, 304-5; Jones, *Personal Reminiscences*, 392. During dinner, von Borcke related many details of the Catlett's Station raid; his story of one of the prisoners turning out to be a woman caused "a good deal of merriment." von Borcke, *Memoirs*, 93-4.

35 REL to Charlotte, Aug. 26, 1862, G. B. Lee papers, VHS; Freeman, *Lee's Dispatches*, 53; REL to D. H. Hill, Aug. 26, 1862, telegram book, REL HQ papers, VHS; Long, *Memoirs of REL*, 191-2. Edgeworth is about two miles north of Orlean; the original portion of the house was constructed ca. 1780 for James Markham Marshall, brother of Chief Justice John Marshall, and was enlarged in 1837. "Former Marshall Home Sells for $900,000," *Fauquier Democrat*, July 9, 1981. Freeman suggests that Lee spent the night at the Marshall home, which can indeed be inferred from Long's account. *Lee*, vol. 2, 307; *Memoirs of REL*, 191-2. Long is the only one of the staff who recorded this incident, so it cannot be determined for certain whether Lee stayed at Edgeworth or if he returned to the HQ complex closer to town. Based on Long's account, it seems safe to conclude that Lee stayed with the Marshalls for the night.

36 Long, *Memoirs of REL*, 192; Statement of Hon. H. W. Lewis, undated, James Vass papers, LVA; Maurice, *Lee's Aide de Camp*, 134; Long, *Memoirs of REL*, 192-3; Freeman, *Lee's Dispatches*, 54; Freeman, *Lee*, vol. 2, 310. Jackson's courier was H. W. Lewis of the Blackhorse Cavalry (Co. H, 4th VA Cavalry), which was detailed to act as couriers for Jackson due to their familiarity with that region of northern Virginia. Statement of H. W. Lewis, Vass papers, LVA. The enemy cavalry Lee encountered was likely a detachment of the 9th New York; they met somewhere in the vicinity of the intersection CR 647 and CR 635. Newel Cheney, *History of the Ninth Regiment, New York Volunteer Cavalry, War of 1861 to 1865* (Poland Center, NY, 1901), 53-4. Long left a detailed account of the incident in *Memoirs of REL*, 192-3. Lee had no more than a dozen staff officers and couriers with him at the time. It is possible the Union commander thought this group of mounted men was the advance of a much larger force (which indeed was true). Long's statement that this "was the only case during the war in which the Confederate leader was in imminent danger of capture" ignores a similar encounter Lee, Stuart, and A. P. Hill

August 28, Thursday (White Plains/ Thoroughfare Gap/ Avenel): Edward Turner of Kinloch comes to visit Lee in the morning; while Turner is there a civilian informs Lee that Federals are advancing toward Thoroughfare Gap from Warrenton. Around midday Lee and Longstreet arrive at Thoroughfare Gap and discover the Federals occupy it. As Longstreet's troops attack a courier from Jackson arrives around 2:00 p.m. and briefs Lee on Stonewall's developing fight near Groveton. Lee and Longstreet watch the fighting around the Gap from a hill just to the west when they receive an invitation to dine with the Robison family. According to Long, "this meal was partaken of with as good an appetite and with as much geniality of manner as if the occasion was an ordinary one, not a moment in which victory or ruin hung trembling in the balance." Lee spends the night at Avenel, the estate of William Beverly, where he and the staff are treated to another meal.[37]

August 29, Friday (Avenel/Thoroughfare Gap/ Haymarket/Gainesville/Groveton): Lee and staff have breakfast at Avenel, and as they leave Lee lets young William Beverly, Jr., ride with him on Traveller. Charles Marshall is ill and so remains behind when the others leave; Lee and his entourage ride about 100 yards in advance of Longstreet's troops to keep the dust from their horses from choking those at the head of the column.[38]

At the crest of Thoroughfare Gap, Lee finds an orphan cavalry company; lacking any other cavalry he sends this and a handful of other hastily gathered mounted troops to scout toward Warrenton under the command of one of Stuart's staff officers. Between Haymarket and Gainesville, Stuart arrives and briefs Lee and Longstreet on Jackson's situation; after a short discussion Stuart guides the column to the battlefield. As they approach Groveton, Lee goes forward on foot and alone to reconnoiter and is very nearly killed when a bullet grazes his face. He establishes headquarters on a small hill south of the Warrenton Pike, and meets with Longstreet, Jackson, and Stuart.[39]

Finding Pope's left flank in the air, Lee orders Gen. Longstreet to attack it before Pope becomes

---

experienced just prior to the Wilderness, but speaks volumes as to how dire the situation was for Lee and his staff. The women in the carriage were likely the residents of Glenaire, a nearby farm. Johnson, *In the Footsteps of REL*, 35-7. Salem is modern-day Marshall; White Plains is modern-day The Plains.

37 Ramey, *Years of Anguish*, 19; Hennessy, *Return to Bull Run*, 153, 158; Statement of James Vass, May 6, 1903, James Vass papers, LVA; Long, *Memoirs of REL*, 194; Jane Eliza Carter Beverly reminiscences, LVA. Long put their arrival at Thoroughfare Gap "about noon." *Memoirs of REL*, 193. Hennessy put their arrival closer to 2:00. *Return to Bull Run*, 153. Jackson's courier James Vass noted that when he arrived "about 2 o'clock" that "skirmishing was then going on in the gap," so Lee's arrival was likely between noon and 2:00 p.m. Statement of James Vass, Vass papers, LVA. The identity of "Mr. Robison" is a mystery. Mrs. Beverly recorded that Lee "was the life of the whole crowd and kept everyone laughing and in good spirits" at dinner. The general and his staff occupied three upstairs rooms for the night; Lee was up until 3:00 a.m. when a courier brought news from Jackson. JEC Beverly reminiscences, LVA. A postwar letter from Marshall to Taylor puts Lee's stay with Beverly a night earlier, but it seems his recollections were off by a day. Charles Marshall to WHT, June 9, 1869, WHT papers, SH. Mrs. Beverly's account does not give a specific date for the stay, nor does a 1930s WPA account by William Beverly, Jr., who was 10 years old in 1862. Susan R. Morton, "Thoroughfare Gap and Environs," Works Progress Administration of Virginia Historical Inventory, Aug. 6, 1937. John Hennessy puts the stay at Avenel on the night of the 28th. *Historical Report on the Troop Movements for the Second Battle of Manassas, August 28, 1862 through August 30, 1862*, NPS, 1985, 56.

38 JEC Beverly reminiscences, LVA; Morton, "Thoroughfare Gap," WPA; Charles Marshall to WHT, June 9, 1869, WHT papers, SH; Blackford, *War Years with Stuart*, 125. Marshall rejoined Lee on the 30th. Marshall to WHT, June 9, 1869, WHT papers, SH. Mrs. Beverly noted that she did not join Lee and the others for breakfast due to the early hour, but she did watch him depart. JEC Beverly reminiscences, LVA.

39 Freeman, *Lee*, vol. 2, 317; *OR* 12, pt. 2, 740; Charles S. Venable, "Personal Memoirs of the Confederate War," McDowell-Miller-Warner papers, UVA; Maurice, *Lee's Aide de Camp*, 137. Venable's memoir is the only known account of Lee's close call: "On reaching the field of Jackson's fight of the 28th . . . [Lee] ordered his staff to remain at the edge of the woods out of sight of the enemy while he went forward on foot to Jackson's skirmish line . . . and made his own observation of the condition of things on Jackson's right. On his return to the edge of the woods . . . he swiftly remarked, 'a sharpshooter came near killing me just now.' We saw how near it was as his cheek had been grazed by the bullet of the sharpshooter." Venable memoir, UVA.

aware of the serious danger he is in; Longstreet demurs because he thinks it is premature. In response to Longstreet's concerns, Lee makes a personal reconnaissance of Pope's flank in the afternoon. Also during the afternoon, Lee summons Jackson to report to headquarters after the fighting ends. Stonewall arrives before Lee returns to camp and falls asleep on Venable's cot. The exhausted Jackson spends the night at Lee's headquarters. At 9:00 p.m., Lee telegraphs President Davis about the result of the day's fighting. A rain shower during the evening.[40]

August 30, Saturday (Groveton): Lee confers with Jackson first thing in the morning. Lee writes to President Davis with more details of the battle, including the arrival of Richard Anderson's division and Stephen Lee's artillery from Richmond. He then meets with Longstreet, Jackson, and Stuart later in the morning. Around midday Col. Robert Bolling rides up in an ambulance which contains lunch for Lee and the staff.[41]

Around 3:00 p.m. William Nelson Pendleton arrives from Richmond with several messages for Lee from President Davis; as Pendleton is ill, Lee instructs him to find somewhere to rest rather than resume his official duties. Lee spends much of the afternoon in rear of Anderson's Division, often conversing with Anderson and other generals; when Pope launches an attack on Jackson in the afternoon, Lee tells Longstreet "Those people must be driven back!"

Lee accompanies Longstreet's men in their attack, but Longstreet personally redirects Lee into a ravine to avoid enemy fire. Longstreet's sweeping assault, which would turn out to be the largest ever launched by the Army of Northern Virginia, crushes Pope's exposed left and drives his army from the field. At the conclusion of the fighting Lee rides up to the Rockbridge Artillery to observe Pope's retreating Union troops and fails to recognize his son Rob manning the gun beside his father. Hood encounters Gen. Lee during the night and takes note of his commander's "high spirits." At 10:00 p.m. Lee sends word to Richmond of the complete victory over the "miscreant" Pope. Lee spends the night in an apple orchard. Periods of rain during the afternoon.[42]

August 31, Sunday (Groveton/Stone Bridge/Sudley): Lee seeks shelter from the morning rain, recalls Venable, "in a small vacant cottage across the threshold of which lay a dead Yankee." Lee and Jackson cross Bull Run at or near the Stone Bridge on the Warrenton Turnpike on a limited reconnaissance, and are fired upon by enemy pickets. Upon their return, they find Jeb Stuart's aide Heros von Borcke at the Stone Bridge, who recounts being detained as a spy while carrying a message for Jackson. James Longstreet joins Gens. Lee and Jackson in conference at or near the Stone Bridge to discuss the best manner to pursue the beaten John Pope.[43]

---

40 Taylor, *General Lee*, 107-10; Hennessy, *Return to Bull Run*, 287-8; Hood, *Advance and Retreat*, 34-5; Venable memoirs, UVA; Freeman, *Lee's Dispatches*, 55; Krick, *CW Weather*, 66.

41 Venable memoirs, UVA; Freeman, *Lee's Dispatches*, 56-9; Scott C. Patchan, *Second Manassas: Longstreet's Attack and the Struggle for Chinn Ridge* (Washington, DC, 2011), 17; Westwood A. Todd reminiscences, UNC. Bolling was from one of the leading families of Petersburg.

42 WNP to wife, August 31, 1862, WNP papers, UNC; George S. Bernard, *War Talks of Confederate Veterans* (Dayton, OH, 2003), 15-6; Freeman, *Lee*, vol. 2, 335; Lee, *Recollections and Letters of REL*, 76-7; Hood, *Advance and Retreat*, 38; Freeman, *Lee's Dispatches*, 59-60; Venable memoirs, UVA; Krick, *CW Weather*, 66. Venable was sent to bring Jackson to HQ during an artillery duel; Lee instructed his aide precisely on the route to follow to minimize exposure to the enemy fire. When Venable returned with Jackson, he attempted to retrace his steps; Jackson, however, insisted they take a more direct route that exposed them to the fire Lee wished them to avoid. Jackson's only comment to Venable was, "I prefer to ride here sir." Venable memoirs, UVA.

43 Venable memoirs, UVA; Longstreet, *From Manassas to Appomattox*, 191; von Borcke, *Memoirs*, 116; Taylor, *General Lee*, 115. Venable did not note the location of either this cottage or the apple orchard where Lee spent the night. His recollection of a dead Federal in the doorway is curious, but it likely places the structure somewhere behind Union lines during the battle.

In mid-morning Lee is severely injured, breaking one wrist and severely spraining the other when he either slips in the mud or is pulled or knocked down by his horse Traveller. A surgeon, probably Dr. N. S. Walker of the 44th Georgia Infantry, is summoned to treat Lee's injuries. The doctor puts splints on both of Lee's injured wrists and one arm in a sling, which prevents Lee from being able to ride his horse in the midst of an ongoing campaign. The frustrated general is forced to ride in an ambulance.

Despite his injuries Lee continues to plan with Longstreet and Jackson. He directs Jackson to lead the pursuit by way of Sudley Springs Ford to get on Pope's flank. Lee denies a request from Pope for a truce, but accedes to a request for the removal of Federal wounded to Union lines. Periods of rain throughout the day.[44]

---

44 Henry W. Thomas, *History of the Doles-Cook Brigade, Army of Northern Virginia, CSA* (Atlanta, GA, 1903), 469; Welsh, *Medical Histories of Confederate Generals*, 134; Freeman, *Lee*, vol. 2, 338-9; OR 12, pt. 3, 779; McDonald, *Make Me a Map*, 75-6. Details regarding Lee's injury vary greatly, with little common elements among the various accounts other than Lee injured both wrists; even the location where it happened is not known with certainty. The location that most often appears in secondary sources is the "Stewart farm," which comes from Henry Thomas, *Doles-Cook Brigade*, 469. Thomas, however, was not present when it happened, and Lee was nowhere near the Stewart farm, which was located outside Chantilly. Walter Taylor wrote that it occurred near a railroad embankment. *General Lee*, 115-6. Armistead Long placed it near the Stone Bridge. *Memoirs of REL*, 206. Charles Venable stated only that it was on the southern bank of Bull Run. Memoirs, UVA. Jackson's aide Henry Kyd Douglas was present, but did not provide a location. *I Rode with Stonewall*, 145. Longstreet's aide G. Moxley Sorrell was apparently present as well, but wrote only that it happened in a thick woodlot. G. Moxley Sorrell, *Recollections of a Confederate Staff Officer* (Dayton, OH, 1978), 102-3. How it happened is also unclear and varies by writer, but most accounts agree that Traveller was involved somehow, most likely being spooked and somehow knocking Lee down. Joseph Harsh analyzed Lee's injury in *Confederate Tide Rising*, 205-8, and compares all the known accounts (13) except for Venable's. Harsh concluded that it occurred in the vicinity of the Stone Bridge between 9:00 and 10:00 a.m. Ibid, 208. Freeman, however, followed Thomas's secondhand account placing the incident at the Stewart farm, and nearly all writers since then have followed Freeman's lead. Harsh convincingly proved why that could not have been the location. Lee was placed in an ambulance captured from McClellan's army on the Peninsula; somehow the spurs he wore at the time of the injury were misplaced and later found in the ambulance after he ceased using it to get around. Wise, *Campaigns & Battles of the ANV*, 199-200. The location of Lee's headquarters on the night of August 31 is not known. Jed Hotchkiss, however, saw Lee near Sudley Springs Ford, so it seems logical that Lee encamped in that vicinity for the night, as the rain and mud prevented much of a pursuit. McDonald, *Make Me a Map*, 75-6.

September 1862

Lee followed up the victory at Second Manassas with a battle in a downpour at Ox Hill (Chantilly) on September 1. The fighting was tactically inconclusive but a strategic victory by ending Pope's threat and opening the route north into Maryland for Lee. Manassas and Ox Hill forced the Union army back on Washington and handed Lee an undisputed grasp of the strategic initiative. The general knew his army could not mount a direct assault against the combined forces of Gens. Pope, McClellan, and Burnside in the entrenchments surrounding Washington. This left him only a handful of options: stay put in northern Virginia; fall back into north-central Virginia; move west into to the lower Shenandoah Valley, or cross the Potomac River and invade Maryland. It took Lee a couple days before he finally decided on the latter course: he would take the war into the North.

Lee was not a politician, but neither did he lack political savvy. He recognized that a move across the river would change the tone of the war. Accordingly, he sought the approval of President Jefferson Davis, but asked for former Maryland Governor Enoch Lowe, then living in semi-exile in Richmond, to accompany the army into Maryland and help explain its reason for being there, i.e. to liberate the Southern state from Lincoln's control.[1]

Lee found himself quite the celebrity when he arrived in Frederick, with admirers clamoring to visit or at least catch a glimpse of him. An officer of the Washington Artillery recorded the visit of one group: "The young ladies are wild to see Gen. Lee, and we agree to find him for them; so in the afternoon a caravan is made up of all the old family carriages in the country, and filled with pretty girls, and we escort them to where 'Uncle Robert' is resting. He is immediately surrounded, and kissed, and hugged, until the old gentleman gets very red in the face, and cries for mercy."[2]

The army's stay in western Maryland did not produce the results Lee hoped for, and few recruits came into the ranks. Lee was thrown another curveball when Federal garrisons in the northern reaches of the Shenandoah Valley did not evacuate as he expected they would; he could not rely on the Valley as his supply route with the enemy in possession of Martinsburg and Harpers Ferry. His old nemesis, George McClellan, had assumed command of the now-combined Federal forces around Washington and was now moving the Army of the Potomac west in search of the invading Confederates. Lee thought he had the luxury of time to deal with the Valley situation and divided his army to capture Harpers Ferry. Fate intervened and changed the course of the Maryland Campaign when a copy of Lee's orders detaching Jackson with more than half the army to eliminate the Valley threat fell into McClellan's hands at Frederick on September 13.

Lee's plan to move the army to Hagerstown and Pennsylvania beyond was dashed when a reinvigorated McClellan moved against a thin Confederate screen attempting to hold the passes of South Mountain on the 14th, threatening to break through and destroy Lee's army in detail. Lee decided to regroup at Sharpsburg, a small village on the banks of Antietam Creek in preparation for a retreat back over the Potomac one mile behind him. Jackson, however, captured the Ferry and was

---

1 Lee, of course banked on Davis's approval and support for his bold operation, and had already ordered the army into Maryland. If Davis had objected, it would have been too late to change course.

2 Owen, *Washington Artillery*, 130.

on his way to reinforce Lee, which convinced the general to make a stand on the rolling land around Sharpsburg. With his back to the wide river his army fought for its very existence on September 17; it would not come as close to complete disaster again until May of 1864. Only the timely arrival of A. P. Hill's "Light" Division from Harpers Ferry and McClellan's innate caution saved the Army of Northern Virginia.

After dark, Lee met with several of his top commanders and, against the advice of some of them, decided to remain in position that night and through the 18th to meet McClellan should he wish to renew the fighting. Often left unsaid is that it was a practical impossibility for Lee to withdraw his artillery, wagons, troops, and thousands of wounded back safely across the Potomac before dawn. Lee was unsure of the extent of his line, the position of all of his units, and even who was in command of them. Being caught at daylight with part of his army straddled across the wide the river was a greater risk than consolidating his position, bringing up ammunition, and remaining on the defensive on the 18th. To Lee's relief, McClellan declined to renew the contest. The general personally supervised the crossing of his army back into Virginia, but did not yet recognize that it also marked the end of the campaign. It was not until Lee reviewed the field returns that he fully understood how roughly the Army of Northern Virginia had been handled and that it was in no condition to continue. It needed an extensive period to rest and refit. During the latter part of the month Lee kept his army in the lower Shenandoah Valley, where it regained its strength.

For the first half of the month Lee was confined to an ambulance, his injured wrists preventing him from riding a horse and other simple tasks as well. He wasn't rid of the slings, and was unable to sign his name again until the end of the month.[3] The pain from these injuries, several sleepless nights, and the pressure of his duties riled Lee somewhat, and there are several instances recorded of him losing his temper or being disagreeable in general during this time. Perhaps the most revealing account comes from Walter Taylor during the early days of the month:

> I am writing at night, all my comrades are asleep and everything is as peaceful and quiet as if war did not reign in the land. I have time to write during the day and tomorrow will be Sunday and I have determined to write tonight with the hope that I MIGHT get to church service in the morning. This privilege I now rarely enjoy. A poor Adjutant General can claim no privileges. If anybody is to be waked at night, to receive the innumerable dispatches, to remain in camp when all else are away, 'tis the AAG. . . . I do have to work pretty hard, but for this I care not, I am only too happy to know and feel that I am of some use. But I never worked so hard to please anyone, and with so little effect as with General Lee. He is so UNNAPPRECIATIVE—everybody else makes me flattering speeches but I want to satisfy HIM. They all say he appreciates my efforts but I don't believe it, you know how silly and sensitive I am? . . . Where Joe Johnston and Beauregard and others have 10, 20, and 30 Adjut. Generals [sic], this army has only one, and I assure you at times I can hardly stand up under the pressure of work. Now I don't care a great deal for rank, but I do want to hear that I please MY GENERAL. When everybody else on the staff goes on leave of absence and I cannot, I am not satisfied to hear others say 'tis because my presence here is necessary. I want him to tell me so, then I'll be satisfied.[4]

---

3 REL to unknown, Sept. 30, 1862, REL papers, LOC.

4 WHT to Bettie, undated but probably Sept. 6, 1862, WHT papers, NPL.

Lee lost his cool several times during the fighting at Sharpsburg on the 17th, and especially directed his ire toward individual soldiers shirking their duties. During an afternoon lull in the fighting, for example, Lee encountered a sergeant from George Anderson's brigade emptying an apple orchard of its contents against orders; the general gave the NCO a thorough tongue-lashing and had the provost escort him back to the front lines.[5] In another well-known instance, Lee ran across a soldier with a stolen pig and, "determined to make an example of this skulking pilferer," ordered the man arrested and shot. When he was delivered by the provost to Jackson for execution, Stonewall instead placed the man "in the front ranks of the army at the most threatened point [to] let the enemy perform the work assigned to him."[6] In a very uncharacteristic move for Lee, when troops on his right flank broke in the face of attacks by Burnside's IX Corps, he ordered his staff to fire on them if they did not rally.[7]

Raphael Moses, a staff officer in one of Longstreet's divisions, witnessed Lee rebuke a courier for mistreating his horse, probably on the 14th at Boonsboro:

> A young cavalryman came dashing up to where General Lee was sitting surrounded by several officers. When he reached the spot he saluted the General, jerked his horse back on his haunches, and delivered what he considered an important piece of news. . . . After he had delivered himself he expected to be overwhelmed with thanks. General Lee said very quietly, 'Young man don't champ that bit so, you are worrying your horse. What command do you belong to?' The young man having answered, General Lee said, 'You had better join your command.'[8]

Col. Armistead Long, who was usually in charge of establishing army headquarters, experienced for himself the ungratefulness Taylor complained about to a friend while setting up army headquarters north of Winchester. The good locations had already been taken by units that had arrived earlier, making Long's search "a long and fatiguing" one. He eventually found a house with a shady yard whose occupants were eager to have Lee stay there. As the tents were being erected in the yard and the wagons emptied, Lee arrived, balked at the location, and ordered Long to relocate his headquarters. "Being vexed at having to look for another place," Long intentionally selected a rock-covered field.[9]

Visiting British officer Garnet Wolseley left a vivid description of the ANV's nerve center:

> Lee's headquarters consisted of about seven or eight pole tents, pitched with their backs to a stake fence, upon a piece of ground so rocky that it was unpleasant to ride over it—its only recommendation being a little stream of good water which flowed close by the General's tent. In front of the tents were some three

---

5 John M. Priest, *Antietam: The Soldier's Battle* (New York, 1993), 292. The man was Sgt. William H. Andrews of the 1st Georgia. Ibid.

6 Long, *Memoirs of REL*, 222. According to Long, the unidentified soldier "was not wanting in courage, and behaved gallantly. He redeemed his credit by his bravery, and came through the thick of the fight unscathed." Ibid.

7 Charles Venable, "Civil War notes," McDowell-Miller-Warner papers, UVA.

8 Moses *Autobiography*, 58.

9 Long, *Memoirs of REL*, 227. This almost certainly describes the camp established near Stephenson's Depot on/about the 27th. Long's passive-aggression backfired because the army remained in place for nearly a month. Long's description of a rocky field is echoed by British officer Garnet Wolseley, who visited HQ in early October. James A. Rawley, ed., *The American Civil War: An English View—The Writings of Field Marshal Viscount Wolseley* (Mechanicsburg, PA, 2002), 34.

or four wheeled wagons, drawn up without any regularity, and a number of horses roamed loose about the field. . . . No guard or sentries were to be seen in the vicinity; no crowd of aides de camp loitering about.[10]

As the army recuperated in Virginia, Custis joined Lee at his headquarters and assisted his father while his wrists healed. While the addition of Custis to the headquarters mess was only temporary, its stables grew when Jeb Stuart presented Lee with a mare named Lucy Long, which the cavalier had acquired from the Dandridge family.[11]

* * *

---

10 Rawley, *English View*, 34.

11 Susan Anthony-Tolbert, *Lucy Long, Robert E. Lee's Other Warhorse: The Mare with Mysteries* (Heathsville, VA, 2012), 23-4. The Dandridges owned one of Stuart's favorite haunts, The Bower, in Jefferson County, VA (later West Virginia). Of Lucy Long, Lee wrote "I rode her frequently after the return of the Army from Maryland to Virginia in 1862." Ibid, 32. The exact date Stuart gave Lee the mare is not known, but can be narrowed to a two-week period (Sept. 28-Oct. 10). *The Bower*, National Register of Historic Places nomination form, Nov. 1, 1981.

September 1, Monday (Sudley/Chantilly): Lee's ambulance sets out for Chantilly around midday and he establishes his headquarters in a house on the Little River Turnpike between Chantilly and Ox Hill. Lee attempts to find a vantage point from which to observe the fighting going on near Chantilly, but his injuries greatly limit his mobility and he returns to his headquarters where he plays no role in the battle. Jeb Stuart and his aide W. W. Blackford are at Lee's headquarters talking about Blackford's horse, Comet, which was wounded in the recent fighting, when a courier brings word of the death of Union Gen. Philip Kearny. In late afternoon Lee meets with Col. Thomas Munford and assigns the cavalryman the task of protecting Leesburg. Lee and Charles Marshall are returning to headquarters at one point during the afternoon when a guard, Pvt. Benjamin F. Peake, detains them because they do not have a pass signed by Lee admitting them to headquarters. Heavy rain throughout the day.[12]

September 2, Tuesday (Chantilly): Lee spends the morning in consultation with Longstreet and Jackson, eventually issuing verbal orders for them to move to Dranesville. Lee has Kearny's body sent through the lines to be returned to his family. He orders all cavalrymen with unserviceable horses to be detailed to gather arms and equipment from the recent battlefields and then to Richmond to be re-shod. Union Medical Inspector Richard H. Coolidge, captured in a hospital in Centreville, is brought to headquarters by Maj. T. M. R. Talcott to seek assistance for the Federal wounded under his care. Coolidge does not meet with Lee directly, Talcott serves as intermediary; Lee relates that he and Pope corresponded on this matter and that ambulances will be allowed to remove Union wounded. Charles Marshall, still not recovered from his illness of the past few days, leaves for Warrenton.[13]

September 3, Wednesday (Chantilly/Dranesville): Lee sends his preliminary report of the Battle of Second Manassas to President Davis, and also informs Davis of his intent to cross the Potomac River into Maryland. Lee suggests that Braxton Bragg's Army of Mississippi (soon to be renamed the Army of Tennessee) be brought east to join Lee. He also informs Sec. Randolph that conscripts can now be gotten from northern Virginia counties that were

---

12 Joseph L. Harsh, *Taken at the Flood: Robert E. Lee and Confederate Strategy in the Maryland Campaign of 1862* (Kent, OH, 1999), 13; Blackford, *War Years with Stuart*, 137; Harsh, *Confederate Tide Rising*, 172; Musick, *6th Virginia Cavalry*, 21; Freeman, *Lee*, vol. 2, 342; Krick, *CW Weather*, 69. Harsh wrote of Lee on this date: "Lee's movements on Sept. 1 are not well chronicled. Likely he was in great pain from the accident of the previous day.... He may have spent the forenoon confined to his tent." *Taken at the Flood*, 13. Bassett French wrote that he encountered Lee and staff "in an open space near a farmhouse" during the height of the battle, and French chided the general for being too exposed to enemy fire, causing Lee to ride away. French's account, however, is likely a fabrication of French's imagination. Oldaker, *Centennial Tales*, 45. Phil Kearny, a division commander in the Federal III Corps, mistakenly rode into Confederate lines and was killed near the end of the action. Hennessy, *Return to Bull Run*, 449-50. Lee received a letter in the afternoon from prominent Leesburg resident John Janney, former head of Virginia's Secession convention, that the Unionist Loudoun Rangers threatened to arrest prominent Southern sympathizers in town the next day (Janney was no doubt one of their targets), hence Lee's instructions to Munford. Harsh, *Confederate Tide Rising*, 172. Peake was one of the troopers of the 6th VA Cavalry recently assigned to HQ as guards; he did not recognize Lee. Musick, *6th Virginia Cavalry*, 21. Marshall ignored Peake's order to halt until prompted by Lee to comply; the source for this incident was unsure of the exact date; Freeman put it on Sept. 1. Hopkins, *Bull Run to Appomattox*, 20. Nearly every account of the fighting on Sept. 1 mentions the severity of the weather. One South Carolina soldier recalled, "I never experienced such thunder and lightning, it was almost incessant." Krick, *CW Weather*, 69.

13 Harsh, *Taken at the Flood*, 18; Taylor, *General Lee*, 116; OR 19, pt. 2, 589; OR Supplement, vol. 2, 760-1; Charles Marshall to WHT, June 9, 1869, WHT papers, SH. A note from Lee was sent with Kearny's remains: "The body of General Philip Kearny was brought from the field last night, and he was reported dead. I send it forward under a flag of truce, thinking the possession of his remains may be a consolation to his family." OR 12, pt. 3, 807. Walter Taylor escorted Kearny's body. "It was a sad duty," he wrote. "There was no place for exultation in the contemplation of the death of so gallant a man, and as I accompanied his remains I was conscious of a feeling of deep respect and great admiration for the brave soldier." Taylor, *General Lee*, 116. Marshall did not give a specific reason for going to Warrenton in his letter to Taylor, and a sizeable gap exists in his memoirs beginning right at the time of his leaving the army. He had been unwell on the march to Manassas, so it seems logical that his health was the reason for his departure.

previously occupied by the enemy. Headquarters is established at Dranesville. Unseasonably cold with frost in the morning.[14]

September 4, Thursday (Dranesville/Leesburg/Harrison Hall): Lee arrives in Leesburg around noon and establishes headquarters at Harrison Hall, the residence of Henry Harrison. Dr. Samuel K. Jackson, who lives across the street, examines Lee's injuries and redresses them. Lee writes to President Davis reaffirming his intent to cross the Potomac and asking permission to go into Pennsylvania; he also requests that Davis have former Maryland Governor Enoch Lowe come to the army. Lee issues orders concerning supplies and the conduct of the men while in Maryland, including the provision that all supplies taken from the other side of the Potomac are to be paid for. In the evening Jackson and Col. Bradley Johnson meet with Lee regarding Maryland; Jackson falls asleep in his chair.[15]

September 5, Friday (Harrison Hall): Before breakfast Dr. Jackson returns to re-examine Lee's hand and wrist injuries and places both of the general's arms in slings. At breakfast, with both arms splinted and in slings, Lee is unable to feed himself so one of the Harrison ladies does this for him. Later in the morning Lee informs Longstreet and Jackson of his plan to cross the Potomac River opposite Leesburg; Jeb Stuart joins them in progress. Afterward, Lee, Jackson, and unnamed others hold a brief prayer meeting in the parlor. The general calls on John Janney at his nearby residence on Cornwall Street; Rooney, Rob, and Fitz all visit Lee at Harrison Hall during the day. Lee advises President Davis that his new line of communications will be west of the Blue Ridge and through the Shenandoah Valley. Lee orders Gen. Richard Garnett released from arrest and assigned to serve under Longstreet. Beverly Robertson is relieved from command.[16]

September 6, Saturday (Harrison Hall/White's Ford/Best Farm): Lee departs Harrison Hall early in the morning and crosses the broad Potomac at White's Ford. Once in Maryland, he is joined by Longstreet and together they ride toward Frederick, with the sound of fighting farther upstream clearly audible. Lee sends a telegram to Richmond from north of the river advising that a portion of the army is across, and that he hopes to have the entire army across by the end of the day. Lee arrives outside of Frederick in the afternoon and establishes headquarters at the Best farm. Many curious civilians from Frederick venture out hoping to speak with or at least catch a glimpse of Lee. The general declines

---

14 *OR* 12, pt. 2, 559-60; *OR* 19, pt 2, 589-91; Harsh, *Taken at the Flood*, 54. Lee's suggestion regarding Bragg's army was impractical for a number of reasons, foremost among them that Bragg was undertaking his own offensive into Kentucky at the time. It demonstrates that Lee was unaware a major offensive was underway in the Western Theater, though he would learn about it three days later. It is thought that HQ was in the field immediately across the Leesburg Pike from the Dranesville Tavern. Rob Orrison, email to author, June 6, 2017.

15 D. Scott Hartwig, *To Antietam Creek: The Maryland Campaign of September 1862* (Baltimore, MD, 2012), 96; "General Lee's Visit to Leesburg and Harrison Hall," Thomas Balch Library, Leesburg, VA; *OR* 19, pt. 2, 591-3; Harsh, *Taken at the Flood*, 81. Harrison Hall, later renamed Glenfiddich, is located at 205 N King St. The oldest portion of the house dates to ca. 1780, but the more prominent Italianate portion was constructed in the 1850s. Author James Dickey later lived in the house during the 1960s and wrote *Deliverance* there. Margaret Morton, "A Large Piece of Leesburg's History Goes up for Sale," *Loudon Now*, Sept. 2, 2016. Lee occupied the second floor bedroom above the dining room; the first floor parlor served as his meeting room. "Lee's Visit to Leesburg," Balch Library. Lowe was governor of Maryland 1851-4 and lived in Richmond during the war. Bradley Johnson was a native of Frederick, MD, and was very active in the Democratic party prior to the war. He was at this time colonel of the 1st MD and would rise to the rank of brigadier general before the end of the war. Warner, *Generals in Gray*, 156-7. Johnson was very familiar with the part of Maryland Lee's army would enter. Lee hoped Lowe and Johnson could influence the citizens of western Maryland to support Lee's army and swell its thinned ranks. Given that Gen. Lewis Armistead was named as provost marshal on this date, it is likely today that he met with Lee at Harrison Hall.

16 Harsh, *Taken at the Flood*, 85-6, 93; *OR* 19, pt. 2, 593-5. Von Borcke placed Stuart's arrival at about 10:00 a.m. It is possible that Jackson had already left by that time to oversee his lead elements crossing the Potomac. Stuart and Lee discussed Beverly Robertson, and the decision was reached to reassign him to North Carolina and place Munford in temporary command of Robertson's brigade. Hartwig, *To Antietam Creek*, 102-3.

to see most of them, but he does make an exception for the mother of Henry Kyd Douglas.[17]

During the afternoon Lee meets with Jackson and later with Stuart, who brings several messages from Richmond. Lee informs Stuart of a secret cache of several hundred dollars in greenbacks he can use to pay informants. From Stuart's messages Lee learns for the first time of the Confederate invasion of Kentucky, and publishes an order to the army announcing Kirby Smith's victory at Richmond, Kentucky. During the late afternoon Col. S. Bassett French of Jackson's staff visits with Lee, whom he finds alone at headquarters with all the staff away in Frederick and even the cook Bryan Lynch absent; when French mentions his horse was wounded at Manassas, Lee tells him to get one from the quartermaster and chides French for suggesting he will steal one in Pennsylvania.[18]

September 7, Sunday (Best Farm): Lee advises President Davis that the entire army has crossed the Potomac and is along the line of the Monocacy River. He reiterates his desire to have Governor Lowe join him to assist with the political side of things. In a second letter to President Davis, Lee complains of the number of poor quality soldiers in the army and the evils of straggling; he proposes creating a permanent provost and inspector general to correct these ills. He sends Sec. Randolph an update on the campaign, and tells G. W. Smith that he is confident that the Federals will draw troops from Norfolk and Suffolk in response to his move into Maryland and that Smith should be able to retake Norfolk once the CSS *Richmond* is completed.[19]

September 8, Monday (Best Farm): Lee issues a proclamation "To the People of Maryland," written by Charles Marshall, that the ANV has come to liberate the state from Lincoln's control. Lee sends two letters to President Davis: one that the enemy is concentrating around Washington; the other suggesting that the time has come to propose to Lincoln that he accept Confederate independence. Lee requests that all recruits, convalescents, etc., bound for his army be retained in Richmond and sent in organized bodies rather than in small leaderless groups as they are at present. Lee meets with Pendleton who has recovered from his illness and reports back for duty. The Richmond *Daily Dispatch* publishes word of Lee's injury after Second Manassas.[20]

---

17 Harsh, *Taken at the Flood*, 104; Longstreet, *From Manassas to Appomattox*, 201; Dowdey, *Wartime Papers*, 296; Douglas, *I Rode with Stonewall*, 149-50. According to Longstreet it was on this ride, while listening to the sounds of George B. Anderson's engagement at Point of Rocks, that Lee first mentioned the idea of capturing Harpers Ferry and proposed that Longstreet do so. *From Manassas to Appomattox*, 201-2. It is possible, if not probable, that Douglas remembered the date wrong for this incident because it seems unlikely that his mother would have learned of his pending arrival in Frederick so quickly. One history of the campaign puts this incident on Sept. 9. John Michael Priest, *Before Antietam: The Battle for South Mountain* (New York, 1992), 50.

18 Harsh, *Taken at the Flood*, 105-8; Hartwig, *To Antietam Creek*, 111; OR 19, pt. 2, 596; Oldaker, *Centennial Tales*, 57-9: Lee, Longstreet, Jackson, Stuart, and D. H. Hill had their HQ at the Best farm. Lee's HQ was located directly across the Urbana Pike from the modern-day Monocacy Battlefield Visitors Center. Best's farm was originally known as "L'Hermitage" and settled in the 1790s by a wealthy French family fleeing a slave revolt in Haiti. The Best family spent the war as tenant farmers on the southern portion of L'Hermitage. Their farm was at the center of the fighting in the Battle of Monocacy in July 1864. Best Farm, NPS booklet (n.d.) Bassett French wrote that Jackson's HQ was 200 yards from Lee's. Oldaker, *Centennial Tales*, 57.

19 OR 19, pt. 2, 596-9; OR 19, pt. 1, 139-40. On either the 6th or the 7th Stuart and Capt. Elijah "Lige" White got into an argument over the role of White's cavalry in the Maryland Campaign. (White's Ford on the Potomac was part of Lige White's farm.) When White refused to obey Stuart's orders, the two went to Lee to decide the issue; Lee ordered White to operate independently of Stuart for the rest of the campaign. Frank M. Myers, *The Comanches: A History of White's Battalion, Virginia Cavalry* (Baltimore, MD, 1871), 107-9. Myers, a member of White's Battalion, was left south of the Potomac to look after worn-out horses and to recruit, and was not present with White's cavalry when this incident occurred. This means he got this information second- or even third-hand. It is possible the incident occurred several days later and, according to historian Horace Mewborn, "probably closer to September 10." Email to author, April 9, 2018.

20 OR 19, pt. 2, 600-2; Harsh, *Taken at the Flood*, 124; WNP to wife, Sept. 10, 1862, WNP papers, UNC; REL newspaper references, DSF papers, LVA. Prominent Baltimorean Gen. Columbus O'Donnell, a veteran of the War of 1812, was

September 9, Tuesday (Best Farm): Lee receives the unwelcome word from Jefferson Davis that he wants to join Lee's army in Maryland, and promptly dispatches Walter Taylor to meet the president and former Maryland Governor Lowe at Warrenton. Lee meets with Gens. Longstreet, Jackson, John Walker, Lafayette McLaws, and Richard Anderson to go over their roles in the complex operation to capture Harpers Ferry. Lee writes to President Davis discouraging him from traveling to Leesburg or beyond, and advises the president in another letter of the difficulty of procuring food for the army in Maryland. Lee issues Special Order 191 that outlines the roles for the Harpers Ferry operation. Curious local residents continue to visit Lee including Catherine Markell, who notes that both of the general's hands are completely bandaged all the way to the fingertips.[21]

September 10, Wednesday (Best Farm/Frederick/Middletown): Lee moves westward, most likely accompanying Gen. James Longstreet's infantry column and establishes his new headquarters for the night at or near Middletown.[22]

September 11, Thursday (Middletown/Boonsboro/Funkstown/Hagerstown): Lee moves west across South Mountain to Hagerstown with Longstreet's column in response to reports of a Federal force moving south from Pennsylvania. A citizen in Funkstown observes Lee as he passes: "General Lee, who was an elegant looking gentleman, passed through the town in a very common ambulance. The Palmetto flag

---

traveling home and came to Lee's headquarters to request a pass; Charles Marshall denied O'Donnell an audience with Lee but procured the requested pass. Richmond *Daily Dispatch*, Sept. 15, 1862. Both Longstreet and John Walker wrote that they met with Lee to go over the Harpers Ferry operation. Longstreet, *From Manassas to Appomattox*, 202; John G. Walker, "Jackson's Capture of Harper's Ferry," *B&L*, vol. 2, 604-6. Most historians agree that these and other Harpers Ferry-related meetings occurred on the 9th.

21 Thomas, *REL*, 257; Thomas G. Clemens, ed., *The Maryland Campaign of September 1862*, 3 vols. (El Dorado Hills, CA, 2010-2017) vol. 1, 109-10; Hartwig, *To Antietam Creek*, 119-21; Joseph C. Eliott, *Lt. Gen. Richard Heron Anderson: Lee's Noble Soldier* (Dayton, OH, 1985), 58-9; *OR* 19, vol. 2, 602-4; John W. Schildt, *Frederick in the Civil War* (Charleston, SC, 2010), 144 n20. Davis wrote to Lee on the 7th that he and Lowe were en route to the ANV; they got at least as far as Rapidan Station. (Davis's letter has never been found.) Harsh, *Taken at the Flood*, 131. Davis turned back when he learned the army had left Leesburg. Hartwig, *To Antietam Creek*, 117. Lowe lingered in northern Virginia for a time and made a speech in Winchester predicting that some 25,000 Marylanders "would flock" to Lee's banners and a new pro-Confederate government would be established in Maryland. Clemens, *MD Campaign*, vol. 1, 110. The meetings with the various commanders took place throughout the day, but it seems that Lee met with Gen. Walker first in the morning or early afternoon, but probably did not go into the Harpers Ferry operation and in fact may not have yet decided to make a move against its garrison when he met with Walker. Despite what Walker wrote after the war, at this meeting Lee likely instructed him to do nothing more than retrace his steps back to the aqueduct carrying the Chesapeake & Ohio Canal over the Monocacy River and destroy it. Harsh, *Taken at the Flood*, 134-5. Lee received a report from Lige White in the afternoon that the Federals had not evacuated Martinsburg or Harpers Ferry; it was this report that convinced Lee of the need to clear out the lower Shenandoah Valley. Ibid, 146-8. Lee next met with Jackson, who would be in charge of the forces operating against Harpers Ferry; Longstreet was not invited to this meeting but happened to show up at HQ while it was in progress and joined it. Hartwig, *To Antietam Creek*, 121-2. McLaws was informed next, followed by Anderson. Diary clipping in McLaws papers, UNC; Harsh, *Taken at the Flood*, 164-5. Anderson was the only non-independent commander who received instructions directly from Gen. Lee, which apparently caused him to ask if Lee was mistaken as to whether he or McLaws was the senior officer. Eliott, *Anderson*, 58-9. SO191 laid out the composition of each piece of the army and their destination; it also included a provision for Walter Taylor going to Leesburg to arrange for the removal of the sick and wounded there. This portion regarding Taylor was likely a cover story disguising his true mission to go there to rendezvous with Davis. Harsh, *Taken at the Flood*, 155-7. SO191 did not, however, indicate the strength of Lee's army.

22 Harsh, *Taken at the Flood*, 178. Little is known of Lee's movements on this date: "The doings of Robert E. Lee on Sept. 10 have been lost to history. It is not known at what hour he struck his headquarters tent, which part of the army he accompanied, when he passed through Frederick, how far he traveled, or where he stopped for the night.... He probably rode with Longstreet's command . . . and encamped just beyond Middletown with the bulk of the army." Ibid. Walter Taylor arrived in Leesburg to meet Davis and Lowe, but discovered that Davis turned back to Richmond, and Lowe had gone to the lower Valley; Taylor stayed at Harrison Hall—Lee's headquarters a week earlier. *OR* 51, pt. 2, 617; Hartwig, *To Antietam Creek*, 117.

floating over it and guarded by six soldiers armed to the teeth. His arm was in a sling." The general establishes his headquarters "in a beautiful grove near" Hagerstown, though the exact location is not known. Rain during the day.[23]

September 12, Friday (Hagerstown): Lee sends President Davis copies of his Maryland proclamation and SO191 and explains that he expected the Federals to evacuate Martinsburg and Harpers Ferry upon his occupation of Frederick but since they did not he sent Jackson and McLaws to dispose of them. Lee learns from Stuart that the enemy is advancing on Frederick and that Burnside's army has joined them. In early afternoon he writes to Stuart that he has heard nothing from McLaws and Walker and that Lee is at currently Hagerstown with Longstreet's force rather than at Boonsboro as he expected to be; accordingly he instructs Stuart not to retire too quickly. Sometime after writing to Davis, Lee learns from Jackson that the Federals evacuated Martinsburg and are headed for Harpers Ferry. The Confederate House of Representatives approves the "Thanks of Congress" to Lee and his army for the victory at Second Manassas. Rain in the afternoon.[24]

September 13, Saturday (Hagerstown): Lee writes to President Davis and mentions the heavy straggling plaguing the army and his fear that the wounded in the hospitals at Gordonsville are exposed to capture unless G. W. Smith can send a covering force. He sends another letter to Davis acknowledging that the president will not be joining the army; Lee laments that he will not have the benefit of Davis's opinion in the field. Lee requests an update from McLaws regarding his progress and advises that Jackson is closing in on Harpers Ferry and McClellan occupied Frederick. Lee learns from Stuart that the Federals are advancing quickly toward South Mountain.[25]

In early afternoon Lee tells Stuart to call upon D. H. Hill at Boonsboro for support if the enemy presence is more than a reconnaissance. After nightfall Lee receives another message from Stuart that a large enemy force is headed for Harpers Ferry via Crampton's Gap; around the same time D. H. Hill reports a large enemy force in front of Turner's Gap. In response, Lee summons Longstreet to headquarters; when he arrives, he finds Lee studying a map. Lee wants to return to Boonsboro to make a stand with Longstreet and Hill at Turner's Gap, and overrules Longstreet, who wants to fall back behind Antietam Creek to fall on McClellan's flank if he moves toward Harpers Ferry. At 10:00 p.m. Lee sends a message to McLaws cautioning that an enemy force is threatening his rear and thus to hurry his operations in Pleasant Valley and move to Sharpsburg once complete.[26]

In addition to the message to McLaws, Lee advises Jackson and D. H. Hill of the developing threat. Around midnight, perhaps after, Lee receives a message from Stuart that a Southern sympathizer happened to be at McClellan's headquarters when a

---

23 Gallagher, *Fighting for the Confederacy*, 142; Freeman, *Lee*, vol. 2, 364-6; S. Roger Keller, ed., *Crossroads of War: Washington County, Maryland, in the Civil War* (Shippensburg, PA, 1997), 20, 59; Harsh, *Sounding the Shallows*, 13-4. Joseph Harsh noted "For the second day in a row, Lee's activities are obscured by a lack of evidence." *Taken at the Flood*, 183. Taylor arrived in Winchester on this date in pursuit of Gov. Lowe. Tower, *Lee's Adjutant*, 43.

24 OR 19, pt. 2, 604-5; Freeman, *Lee*, vol. 2, 366; Hartwig, *To Antietam Creek*, 295; Harsh, *Taken at the Flood*, 196; *Journal of the Congress of the CSA*, vol. 5, 371-2; Harsh, *Sounding the Shallows*, 15.

25 OR 19, pt. 2, 605-6; REL to JD, Sept. 13, 1862, REL papers, LVA; Freeman, *Lee*, vol. 2, 367. Lee received a letter from Davis, which does not survive, and its contents are not known. Harsh, *Taken at the Flood*, 215-9. The lack of material regarding Lee's personal movements and doings during the Maryland Campaign is surprising and in marked contrast to other times during the war. Harsh noted of today: "There is no evidence that Robert E Lee left the confines of his camp on the outskirts of Hagerstown." *Taken at the Flood*, 242.

26 Hartwig, To Antietam Creek, 296; Harsh, Taken at the Flood, 244-5; Longstreet, From Manassas to Appomattox, 219-20; OR 19, pt. 2, 607. Most historians argue that McClellan's activity was spurred on by the capture of a copy of SO191 (see note 27). Steven Stotelmyer, in his recent *Too Useful to Sacrifice: Reconsidering George B. McClellan's Generalship in the Maryland Campaign from South Mountain to Antietam* (Savas Beatie, 2019), in a chapter essay entitled "Fallacies of the Lost Orders," 1-45, argues forcefully that McClellan was already moving fast when the orders were found, and their impact on the campaign was minimal, at best.

captured piece of intelligence was delivered to the Federal commander which turns out to be a copy of SO191 found by Federal troops at either the Best farm or the Myers farm near Frederick.²⁷

September 14, Sunday (Hagerstown/Boonsboro): Lee advises McLaws that Longstreet is moving to Boonsboro, then departs Hagerstown "early" in the morning for Boonsboro. He is accompanied by Porter Alexander and possibly Longstreet; when nearing Turner's Gap, they notice a group of people atop a tower near the pass. Perceiving it to be an enemy signal corps detachment, Lee sends Alexander with a handful of troops to capture them, but Alexander finds them to be a group of local civilians watching the fighting in the gap from an old windmill. Upon his arrival at the base of the mountain, Lee sends forward Col. Long and Maj. Marshall to reconnoiter the ground. The general himself never ascends the mountain, remaining at its western base establishing temporary headquarters at the home of the Widow Herr, leaving direction of the fighting to Longstreet.²⁸

Lee sends Talcott and Venable to serve with Longstreet for the day, leaving Col. Chilton as his only aide for much of the afternoon. As Hood's Division passes Lee, his troops chant "Give us Hood," as their commander was then under arrest; Lee grants Hood a temporary reprieve and restores him to command for the battle. Pendleton arrives with the reserve artillery in late afternoon, and Lee sends him to establish a line on Beaver Creek near Boonsboro. After nightfall Longstreet, Hill, and Hood ride to Lee's headquarters and discuss whether to resume the fight on the mountain tomorrow or to withdraw during the night; the dire picture painted by his lieutenants convinces Lee to withdraw toward Sharpsburg.²⁹

This conference ends around 8:00 p.m. immediately after which orders are sent to McLaws advising that "the day has gone against us" and to give up the Harpers Ferry operation. Around 10:00 p.m. Lee learns from Col. Thomas Munford that the Federals drove the Confederates from Crampton's Gap, opening the way to Harpers Ferry—and McLaws. Munford is then ordered to hold the road at Rohersville at the western base of Crampton's Gap to allow McLaws an avenue to escape and rejoin the main army. As Lee is making plans to return to Virginia he receives word from Jackson that Harpers

---

27 Harsh, *Taken at the Flood*, 153, 247-9; *OR* 19, pt. 1, 42; *Best Farm*, 14-5. Of the orders Lee sent during the night, only the one to McLaws survives. Harsh, *Taken at the Flood*, 247-8. When and how Lee learned of McClellan's capture of SO191, the "Lost Order," is a hotly debated topic. Stuart informed Lee that McClellan had *something* that revealed Confederate intentions. Whether Stuart or his source knew exactly what document was in Federal hands is not known, in large part because his message to Lee has vanished. Harsh, *Taken at the Flood*, 249. Charles Marshall was adamant that Lee did not learn of the capture of a copy of SO191 until reading McClellan's report of the campaign in the summer of 1863. Maurice, *Lee's Aide de Camp*, 160; Marshall to Ezra Carman, Nov. 22, 1900, Ezra A. Carman papers, New York Public Library. News of the discovery of a copy of the order appeared in the Washington newspapers on Sept. 15; it is very possible (and indeed likely) that a copy made its way to Lee's headquarters. Clemens, *Maryland Campaign*, vol. 1, 293 n22. Lee and D. H. Hill (to whom the lost copy was addressed) exchanged somewhat heated letters on the topic after the war. For Lee's recollections on SO191, see Gallagher, *Lee the Soldier*. Freeman changed his opinion between the writing of his biography *Lee* and leadership study *Lee's Lieutenants* of when his subject learned about McClellan's finding the order.

28 *OR* 19, pt. 2, 608; Clemens, *Maryland Campaign*, vol. 1, 295; Gallagher, *Fighting for the Confederacy*, 142; Long, *Memoirs of REL*, 215; Venable memoirs, UVA; Harsh, *Taken at the Flood*, 287. Freeman wrote that Lee was again riding on horseback today, but Marshall stated that Lee was still in his ambulance. *Lee*, vol. 2, 369; Marshall to Carman, Nov. 22, 1900, Carman papers, NYPL. Harsh examines Lee's mode of travel in *Sounding the Shallows*, 176, 193. Freeman has Lee accompanying Longstreet on the ride from Hagerstown to Boonsboro, which is quite probably the case. Longstreet, however, did not mention anything about the march, and Alexander did not mention Longstreet's presence. Freeman put Lee's arrival at the western base of Turner's Gap around 3:00 p.m. Freeman, *Lee*, vol. 2, 370.

29 Venable memoirs, UVA; Hood, *Advance and Retreat*, 39-41; Harsh, *Taken at the Flood*, 284-5; Longstreet, *From Manassas to Appomattox*, 227. Confined to his ambulance, Lee played almost no role at all in the fighting at South Mountain. Harsh summed up Lee's situation: "Never would Lee be so helpless as he was this afternoon at South Mountain. He would have no feel for whatsoever for the dispositions of Hill or the enemy, and he would exert absolutely no influence over the placement of the reinforcements." *Taken at the Flood*, 256. At one point during the afternoon Lee assumed the role of traffic cop, directing wagon traffic. Edgar Warfield, *Manassas to Appomattox: The Civil War Memoirs of Pvt. Edgar Warfield, 17th Virginia Infantry* (McLean, VA, 1996), 94-5.

Ferry will be surrendered tomorrow, convincing Lee to order a concentration at Sharpsburg. Around 11:30 p.m. Lee boards his ambulance and, with Marshall riding ahead of it to clear a path through the troops, heads for Sharpsburg. Around midnight Lee sends Gen. Pendleton with most of the artillery to take up a position covering the Potomac River crossings around Shepherdstown, and instructs E. P. Alexander to take the ordnance train into Virginia.[30]

September 15, Monday (Boonsboro/Keedysville/ Sharpsburg/Grove House): Lee does not get much if any sleep during the night. He arrives in Keedysville around first light, and remains in the town for probably less than an hour. While there he learns from Munford there is no direct road from McLaws's position to Keedysville, and his engineers report that the terrain around Keedysville is not conducive to a defensive stand. He decides to concentrate the army at Sharpsburg and sends a message to McLaws, in case some or all of yesterday's messages did not make it through, to march there. "About sunrise" Lee arrives at Antietam Creek and moves on foot to a hill top—most likely on the Pry farm—to view the surrounding area. As Lee looks around, a local woman (probably Mrs. Pry) provides coffee for the general and his staff. Lee crosses the Antietam in his ambulance between 7:00 and 8:00 a.m.[31]

He spends much of the morning on the hill near the Lutheran Church cemetery and is joined there by Longstreet around 9:30 a.m. Around noon a courier brings word from Jackson of the capture of Harpers Ferry. Stuart arrives in early afternoon with details of the surrender.[32]

During the afternoon Lee and Longstreet establish their headquarters at the home of Jacob Grove in Sharpsburg. From there, Lee writes to Gustavus W. Smith instructing him to send a force to the Rappahannock and recover the wounded gathered at Warrenton. Walter Taylor rejoins Lee sometime during the day.[33]

---

30 Harsh, *Sounding the Shallows*, 181; Dowdey, *Wartime Papers*, 307-8; Harsh, *Taken at the Flood*, 291; *OR* 19, pt. 2, 608-9; Freeman, *Lee*, vol. 2, 375-6; Marshall to Carman, Nov. 22, 1900, Carman papers, NYPL; Gallagher, *Fighting for the Confederacy*, 144; Pendleton, *Memoirs of WNP*, 212-3. Marshall wrote that Lee left South Mountain about 10:00 p.m., but based on the surviving correspondence to Munford and McLaws, it was likely closer to 11:30 p.m. Marshall to Carman, Nov. 22, 1900, Carman papers, NYPL; Hartwig, *To Antietam Creek*, 480. At some point after the close of the battle Capt. A. P. Mason wrote SO193. This order formally released Hood from arrest and directed Lt. Maurice Garland to escort the body of his cousin, Brig. Gen. Samuel Garland, home to Lynchburg, VA. *OR* 19, pt. 2, 609. Garland, one of D. H. Hill's promising brigadiers, was killed at Fox's Gap, which is just south of Turner's Gap.

31 Venable memoirs, UVA; Harsh, *Taken at the Flood*, 298-301; *OR* 19, pt. 2, 609-10; Marshall to Carman, Nov. 22, 1900, Carman papers, NYPL. While Lee was reconnoitering at the Pry farm, Marshall took a nap against a haystack; Lee directed his mess steward, presumably Bryan Lynch or Perry, to save enough coffee for Marshall to have some when he awoke. Marshall to Carman, Nov. 22, 1900, Carman papers, NYPL. While Lee was still on the road, he sent Venable ahead to Sharpsburg to ascertain if the enemy occupied the town; Venable encountered some of Stuart's cavalry who reported Yankee cavalry in Sharpsburg and reported this back to Lee, who instructed the aide to get troops from Brig. Gen. Robert Rodes's brigade nearby and clear the Federals out. As this was transpiring "not much before daybreak," Col. Chilton appeared: "Here a rather ridiculous scene occurred. Adjutant General Chilton . . . rode up and in a rather rough manner asked why we were retreating behind the bivouac assigned by General Lee to us. His words and manner were not agreeable to me and I answered in a manner that did not regard the deference due to a superior officer. For this my friend Rhodes [sic] reproached me with a half-smile on his face and ordered me to accompany [Col. John B.] Gordon" on his advance toward the town. Venable memoirs, UVA. It is likely that Lee was at the Pry farm when he received Jackson's message that Harpers Ferry had surrendered. Gallagher, *Lee the Soldier*, 346. The Pry house later served as McClellan's headquarters and is currently operated as a field hospital museum by the National Museum of Civil War Medicine.

32 Clark, *North Carolina in the Great War*, vol. 1, 307; Clemens, *Maryland Campaign*, vol. 1, 391-2; Hartwig, *To Antietam Creek*, 480-4; Long, *Memoirs of REL*, 216; Harsh, *Taken at the Flood*, 322. Harsh puts Stuart's arrival at approximately 1:00 p.m., and notes that Lee was still at Cemetery Hill at the time. Freeman put Stuart's arrival in the evening and at Lee's headquarters. *Lee*, vol. 2, 380-1.

33 Owen, *Washington Artillery*, 139; Harsh, *Taken at the Flood*, 326; *OR* 19, pt. 2, 609; Harsh, *Sounding the Shallows*, 188; Taylor, *General Lee*, 122. Freeman has Lee at the Grove house by 2:00 p.m. *Lee*, vol. 2, 379. The Grove house is at the southwest corner of the intersection of Main and Mechanic streets. Harsh contends that the letter to G. W. Smith was begun on the 13th and not finished and sent until today. *Sounding the Shallows*, 188. Harsh, citing Owen (see above),

September 16, Tuesday (Sharpsburg): Lee rises before dawn and has breakfast at the Grove house then goes to Cemetery Hill. Today is the first day he is able to ride on horseback, but he is still unable to mount/dismount without help, nor can he handle the reins himself; Traveller must be led. Early morning fog prevents any observation, and Lee dismounts and walks amongst the guns of the nearby Washington Artillery.

During the morning, Jackson and John Walker join Lee and Longstreet on Cemetery Hill. Lee moves headquarters to a woodlot on the western edge of Sharpsburg, where he is joined by Longstreet, Jackson, and other officers for a conference.[34]

The meeting breaks up early in the afternoon, likely in response to artillery fire from east of town. As Lee walks Traveller through the streets he comes under artillery fire and instructs the Washington Artillery not to waste their ammunition in a long-distance duel with Union guns across Antietam Creek. Lee, Longstreet, and Jackson reconvene at the Grove house around 3:00 p.m. where they are joined by Stuart who brings news of the Federals crossing the Antietam beyond Lee's left.[35]

During the evening, Gen. Hood asks Lee to pull his troops off the front lines so they can rest and refit; Lee refers him to Jackson. Late in the evening Lee meets with Longstreet, Jackson, Stuart, Alexander Lawton, Porter Alexander, and others. Lee sends Alexander to Harpers Ferry to oversee the removal of the captured ordnance to Winchester near the northern end of the Valley, and orders Gen. Pendleton to have a bridge constructed over the C&O canal at Boteler's Ford. At some point during the day Lee sends President Davis a summary of the action over the past few days, with details of the fighting at South Mountain. Rain during the evening.[36]

September 17, Wednesday (Sharpsburg): Lee rises early—around 4:00 a.m.—and he and the staff get breakfast at the residence of "Dr. Miller" in town. At 4:30 a.m. Lee orders Gen. Pendleton to station artillery to cover the nearby Potomac crossings. "Just after day light" McLaws rides up and reports to Lee, who is in his shirtsleeves and washing his face when the division commander arrives. Lee tells his lieutenant, "We have, I believe, a hard day's work before us."[37]

Lee is at Cemetery Hill when the fighting begins on Jackson's front about 5:30 a.m., and he spends much of the day on the hill. During the early stages of the battle Lee and Longstreet are both there

---

concluded that Lee spent the night of the 15th in the Grove house with Longstreet. *Sounding the Shallows*, 193. Hartwig has Lee spending the night in his tent in the woodlot on the western edge of Sharpsburg. *To Antietam Creek*, 596. Long after the war, Walter Taylor wrote the Lee did not use any particular house in Sharpsburg as his HQ, but did take at least one meal at the home of a "Mr. Miller" in town. WHT to Jed Hotchkiss, April 9, 1905, WHT papers, NPL. Uncertainty remains as to both Lee's location the night of the 15th and whether the Grove house or a woodlot west of town was his actual HQ.

34 Harsh, *Taken at the Flood*, 330-6. Henry K. Douglas, while describing the arrival of Jackson at Sharpsburg, recounted Lee's presence in the area that became the Sharpsburg National Cemetery. Jackson's staff officer included mention of what became known as "Lee's Rock" in the aftermath of the battle. Douglas, *I Rode with Stonewall*, 164. A myth developed that a large boulder—which was amongst a clump of trees in September 1862—was Lee's vantage point leading up to and during the battle of the 17th. See Calvin Fisher, "Antietam Cemetery and the Problem of Lee's Rock," online at www.crossroadsofwar.org.

35 Owen, *Washington Artillery*, 141; Harsh, *Taken at the Flood*, 343-4; Hotchkiss, *Virginia*, 347; Clemens, *Maryland Campaign*, vol. 2, 30. The enemy movement reported by Jeb Stuart proved to be Gen. Joseph Hooker's I Corps.

36 Hood, *Advance and Retreat*, 42; Von Borcke, *Memoirs*, 160; Gallagher, *Fighting for the Confederacy*, 148; Lee, *Memoirs of WNP*, 224; *OR* 19, pt. 1, 140-1; Freeman, *Lee*, vol. 2, 383. Harsh put the incident with Hood around 8:00 p.m. *Taken at the Flood*, 362-3. Von Borcke wrote only that the conference that night was "late in the evening." *Memoirs*, 160. Alexander put it around midnight. Gallagher, *Fighting for the Confederacy*, 148.

37 Harsh, *Taken at the Flood*, 368; Venable memoirs, UVA, *OR* 19, pt. 2, 619; John C. Oeffinger, ed., *A Soldier's General: The Civil War Letters of Major General Lafayette McLaws* (Chapel Hill, NC, 2002), 182-3; Hartwig, *To Antietam Creek*, 636. Venable wrote that Miller's "pretty auburn haired daughter dispensed the hospitality of occasion most kindly and pleasantly." Venable memoirs, UVA.

observing the unfolding action on foot when D. H. Hill rides up. An enemy artillery battery fires on them. One shell narrowly misses Lee and strikes Hill's horse, taking off its front legs. While Jackson's troops are heavily engaged on the far left, Lee encounters Capt. Thomas Carter of the King William Artillery and instructs him to take his guns along with any others he can find and take up a position on Reel Ridge in support of Jackson. Lee rides to the ridge himself.[38]

About 9:00 a.m. Lee rides to D. H. Hill's position near the center of his long extended line along a sunken road and is joined by Hill. The pair ride along the sunken lane and encounter Col. John B. Gordon of the 6th Alabama, who tells Lee: "These men are going to stay here, General, till the sun goes down or victory is won." Leaving the road, Lee goes back to the left before returning to town and Cemetery Hill.

Around midday, Lee is among the guns of the Washington Artillery when he learns of an enemy force crossing the Antietam downstream from the Lower (aka Burnside's) Bridge. None of Lee's staff are present, so he presses Lt. William Owen, adjutant of the Washington Artillery, into service to carry orders to shift troops to meet this new threat. It is likely around this same time that Lee personally encounters Capt. James Nisbet of the 21st Georgia and Capt. Thomas Garrett of the 5th North Carolina in Sharpsburg, and instructs them to round up all the stragglers they can find in the town; Nisbet is to form a sort of provost guard near Lee's headquarters to prevent anyone except the wounded from retreating to the ford at Shepherdstown, while Garrett is to gather all able-bodied men and rejoin the fighting.[39]

During a lull in the early afternoon Lee encounters the Rockbridge Artillery near the Dunker Church on the left of the army. After ordering the battery back into the fight, he exchanges a few quick words with his son Rob. Following this, Lee meets with Jackson and discusses the possible collapse of the right, and the potential for taking the offensive on Stonewall's front.

Lee is on a knoll south of town when his right flank collapses. Seeing a column of troops approaching from the south (his right-rear), Lee asks a nearby artillery officer, Lt. John Ramsay, 1st North Carolina Artillery, to identify them. Ramsay offers Lee his field glasses, but Lee holds up his bandaged hands to show he cannot hold them; Ramsay informs him one column is the enemy, the other is Confederate. A. P. Hill rides ahead of this column and reports to Lee around 2:30 p.m. Shortly before Hill's troops arrive Lee rides among the broken troops on the right and orders his staff to fire on them if they do not halt and reform.[40]

---

38 Long, *Memoirs of REL*, 221; Longstreet, *From Manassas to Appomattox*, 254-5; Harsh, *Sounding the Shallows*, 203; *OR* 19, pt. 1, 1030; Harsh, *Taken at the flood*, 381-2. When the artillery shell incident occurred is uncertain. Longstreet suggests it was early afternoon in *Manassas to Appomattox*, 254; Long did not give a time in *Memoirs of REL*, 221. Longstreet's aide Moxley Sorrel wrote it was "in the early afternoon." *Recollections*, 111. Harsh: around 7:30 a.m., in *Sounding the Shallows*, 203.

39 Harsh, *Taken at the Flood*, 383, 401-4; Gordon, *Reminiscences*, 84; Owen, *Washington Artillery*, 150-1; *OR* 19, pt. 1, 1043-5.

40 Poague, *Gunner with Stonewall*, 48; Lee, *Recollections and Letters of REL*, 78; Harsh, *Taken at the Flood*, 406-8; Clark, *North Carolina in the Great War*, vol. 1, 575; *OR* 19, pt. 1, 981; Venable, "Civil War notes," box 5, McDowell-Miller-Warner papers, UVA. Poague put the time of the encounter with Rob around 11:00 a.m.; Rob did not give a time. Poague, *Gunner with Stonewall*, 48; Lee, *Recollections and Letters of REL*, 78. Harsh concluded that it probably happened around 1:30 p.m. *Sounding the Shallows*, 206-7. Lee ordering his staff to fire on broken troops is extremely out of character for him, and this is the only known incident of him doing so during the entire war. Venable recorded it *twice* in the random collection of "Civil War notes" found among his wife's papers. One note reads in part: "This was the only time in all the war that Lee ever gave orders to his staff to fire on those who faltered in the charge and showed a disposition to advance." A longer note reads: "On our right center near Gen. Lee's personal position, some troops gave way. The General joined in rallying them and in his great anger at their behavior ordered Marshall of his staff to fire on them. They were soon rallied and as they moved up again in reformed line, General [Montgomery D.] Corse [then colonel of the 17th Virginia] whom they had left wounded on the field raised himself on his elbow and beckoned them to come on." Marshall, specifically mentioned by Venable, wrote nothing about this incident. Artillery officer Thomas Carter either witnessed or heard about this incident but stopped short of mentioning Lee's drastic orders to his staff. He did, however, note Lee's excitement. His wording suggests that Lee acted unusually at Sharpsburg: "I never saw Gen. Lee so anxious as he was at Sharpsburg during the battle.... Gen. Lee exposed himself entirely too much. He got down and endeavored to rally some of D. R. Jones's men but in vain. They ran like hounds. The truth is they were utterly broken down." Dozier, *Gunner in Lee's Army*, 142-3.

After nightfall Lee has a meeting with his senior commanders, including Jackson, both Hills, Hood, D. R. Jones, and Jubal Early. Longstreet is the last to arrive at this meeting, and Lee greets him with, "Here is my old war horse at last!" Although some favor crossing the Potomac during the night, Lee announces that the army shall remain in place to meet McClellan if he resumes the fight tomorrow. Stuart meets with Lee after the others have left. During the night Lee orders Pendleton to send up 15-20 guns and whatever troops have been collected at the fords. Lee's address to the people of Maryland is printed in the Richmond *Dispatch*.[41]

September 18, Thursday (Sharpsburg/Shepherdstown): Lee advises President Davis in the morning of yesterday's battle. Lee sends artilleryman Stephen D. Lee to confer with Jackson regarding the practicality of launching an attack against McClellan's right flank and Lee discusses the same with Jackson and Stuart.[42] After determining that the army cannot take the offensive, Lee meets first with Jackson then with Longstreet regarding crossing the Potomac during the night, and at some point he meets with Congressman Alexander Boteler regarding the battle and the campaign as a whole. Lee places Charles Venable and Maj. John Harman in charge of the Potomac crossing at Boteler's Ford, while he himself watches from the Maryland shore. It is likely well after midnight when Lee himself crosses to Virginia. Rain during the night.[43]

September 19, Friday (Shepherdstown/Smoketown): Lee avoids the congestion in Shepherdstown itself and rides around the town to Smoketown on the Martinsburg Pike, where he then establishes headquarters. During the morning he meets with Gen. Pendleton who is in command of the rear guard along the Potomac River. Later in the day Lee sends written instructions to Pendleton to withdraw from the river if pressed by the enemy. After dark the Federals attack Pendleton and capture much of his artillery; a distraught Pendleton eventually finds Lee around midnight, but Lee "determined to do nothing till next morning."[44]

September 20, Saturday (Smoketown/Shepherdstown): Lee is awakened around midnight by Pendleton and briefed on the disaster at the fords. Lee dictates a message to President Davis informing him of the crossing and the Federal pursuit. At daylight Lee goes in search of Jackson to organize a counterattack, but is unable to find him, and winds up at D. H. Hill's headquarters. After Jackson pushes

---

41 Freeman, *Lee*, vol. 2, 403-4; Owen, *Washington Artillery*, 156-7; Longstreet, *From Manassas to Appomattox*, 262; Hotchkiss, *Virginia*, 356-7; Blackford, *War Years with Stuart*, 151; OR 19, pt. 2, 610; REL newspaper references, DSF papers, LVA. Although many accounts have Lee's meeting with his senior officers occurring at the Grove house, it was likely at his headquarters tent west of town. Harsh, *Taken at the Flood*, 424. Little is known about Lee's activities during the evening of the 17th: Harsh: "Less is known about Lee at sunset and the hours immediately following than at any other time of the day. He neither sent nor received any written messages that have survived; nor, so far as can be determined, did he venture forth from the field across the road from his tent on the Shepherdstown road." Ibid.

42 OR 19, pt. 1, 141; Henderson, *Stonewall Jackson*, vol. 2, 325-7; Harsh, *Sounding the Shallows*, 214-5; von Borcke, *Memoirs*, 166.

43 Harsh, *Taken at the Flood*, 445; Richmond *Daily Dispatch*, Sept. 22, 1862; Venable, "Civil War notes" McDowell-Miller-Warner papers, UVA; Wise, *Campaigns of the ANV*, 445; Freeman, *Lee*, vol. 2, 405-6; Harsh, *Sounding the Shallows*, 21. Little is known of Lee's personal movements on the 18th: "Far less is known about Lee's activities at any time on the 18th than on the day of the battle," wrote Harsh, "and almost nothing certain has survived of his movements during the early morning." Harsh, *Taken at the Flood*, 434. Boteler gave a speech in Winchester the evening of the 19th about the state of Lee's army; it is possible that he met with Lee the morning of the 19th, as he mentioned the army's return to Virginia in his remarks, though that would have necessitated a rather hurried ride to Winchester to organize a public program for that night. Richmond *Daily Dispatch*, Sept. 22, 1862. Harman was Jackson's quartermaster. Artillerist Thomas Carter wrote of the crossing: "Gen. Lee and staff worked unremittingly all night." Dozier, *Gunner in Lee's Army*, 143.

44 Harsh, *Taken at the Flood*, 458, 460; Lee, *Memoirs of WNP*, 213-4, 225. Lee's HQ was likely at the Martinsburg Pike (Rt. 45) crossing of Opequon Creek, just east of Martinsburg. Email Don Silvius (Berkley County Historical Society) to author, June 15, 2017. Longstreet sent his aide, Capt. Osmun Latrobe, to inform Lee of Pendleton's predicament, but Latrobe "hunted . . . ineffectually" for hours searching for Lee. Osmun Latrobe diary, Sept. 20, 1862, VHS.

the Federals back across the Potomac, Lee meets with Jackson and Longstreet at Shepherdstown to discuss whether to continue the campaign and re-cross the river back into Maryland elsewhere. The general orders that field returns showing the effective strength of the army be submitted to headquarters tomorrow, and that all officer vacancies be filled "immediately." Custis departs Richmond to join his father's army bearing several messages from President Davis.[45]

September 21, Sunday (Smoketown): Lee meets with Pendleton in the morning for an explanation of what went wrong at the river. Gen. George Steuart and medical officer R. K. Shriver report to Lee from Richmond and bring with them news of Bragg's Kentucky campaign. Lee sends President Davis a more detailed account of Pendleton's affair at the Potomac River crossing as well as the strength of the army during the entire campaign. The general writes to Jackson regarding the troops and supplies in Winchester, and issues orders for George Steuart to take command there. Lee requests shoes and clothing for the destitute army and complains to Sec. Randolph about "speculators" driving up costs of materiel needed to properly supply, equip and feed his command, particularly medical supplies. Lee writes to Texas Senator Louis T. Wigfall concerning the recruitment of additional regiments from his state for Lee's Virginia army.[46]

September 22, Monday (Smoketown): Lee writes a lengthy letter to President Davis regarding stragglers and he requests that an inspector general be assigned to his army, specifically requesting Lt. Col. Edwin J. Harvie if available. He sends very detailed instructions to Longstreet and Jackson regarding inspections, returns, and efforts to prevent straggling.[47]

September 23, Tuesday (Smoketown): Lee writes to Davis regarding how to strengthen the army: Lee suggests that unfit men be dropped from the rolls so they can be replaced, requesting that unarmed men in the West be sent to his army as he now has weapons on hand for them, and inquiring about conscription efforts in the areas now occupied by his army. He adds that he is keeping the army stationary for the present in an effort to collect stragglers and recovered wounded. He suggests to Sec. Randolph that a law be passed allowing for the demotion of ineffective officers, and writes to Adjutant General Cooper regarding the large number of paroled prisoners, requesting that a prisoner exchange be affected as soon as possible to allow these men to return to the ranks.

The general writes to Pendleton regarding using the woolen factories in the army's vicinity and the need for more artillery horses, and also orders that Pegram's and Fleet's batteries, which were broken up prior to the recent battles, be reconstituted per the wishes of A. P. Hill. Lee writes to Mrs. Lucy A. Cardwell regretting that he cannot give her son a furlough, and thanks an unknown individual for a bouquet of flowers sent to him but apologizing that he can do nothing for depredations done by stragglers. Lee also sends a letter to one of his daughters with a brief synopsis of the Maryland Campaign, noting that the army was not beaten, and lamenting the death of his friend, Union XII Corps commander Gen. Joseph Mansfield. He adds that doctors estimate "it will be three or four weeks yet"

---

45 Harsh, *Taken at the Flood*, 460-2; OR 19, pt. 1, 142; Hal Bridges, *Lee's Maverick General: Daniel Harvey Hill* (Lincoln, NE, 1991), 139; Harsh, *Sounding the Shallows*, 224; General Order, Sept. 20, 1862, REL papers, Duke; Jeremy Gilmer to wife, Sept. 21, 1862, Gilmer papers, UNC.

46 Lee, *Memoirs of WNP*, 215; Harsh, *Sounding the Shallows*, 221; OR 19, pt. 1, 142-3; Lee to Jackson, Sept. 21, 1862, Stonewall Jackson papers, MOC; OR 19, pt. 2, 614-5; Joseph B. Polley, *Hood's Texas Brigade: Its Marches, Its Battles, Its Achievements* (New York, 1910), 135. According to Freeman, Lee moved his HQ to Falling Waters today. That does not appear to be the case, as his correspondence indicates he remained at Smoketown through at least the 25th, and possibly as late as the 27th. *Lee*, vol. 2, 422.

47 OR 19, pt. 2, 617-9. Harvie was a graduate of VMI and was Joe Johnston's inspector general; he left the ANV to rejoin Johnston in the Western Theater in November 1862. After the war Harvie assisted the U.S. government in organizing the Confederate war records. Krick, *Staff Officers in Gray*, 152.

before he is able to regain the use of his writing hand.⁴⁸

September 24, Wednesday (Smoketown): Lee informs G. W. Smith that significant numbers of arms and equipment have been collected from the recent battlefields and forwarded to Richmond, and also that Lee hopes to operate in the Shenandoah Valley if he cannot return to Maryland. Orders are published concerning stragglers and absenteeism. Rain late in the day.⁴⁹

September 25, Thursday (Smoketown): Lee writes to William Loring congratulating him for his recent successes in the Kanawha Valley; he suggests that rather than moving on Ravenswood, Loring move against the B&O at Clarksburg and through Morgantown into western Pennsylvania, possibly joining with Lee's army north of the Potomac. Lee informs President Davis that the Federals have re-occupied Harpers Ferry and that Lee intends to "occupy and detain" McClellan in the Valley. He explains that while he intended to cross the Potomac at Williamsport and continue his campaign in the North, the condition of the army prevents it at present, although he does not rule out joint operations with Loring's army. Lee instructs G. W. Smith to finish evacuating the wounded from Warrenton and to move supplies gathered at Culpeper to Gordonsville where they will be less exposed to capture.⁵⁰

September 26, Friday (Smoketown): Lee issues orders for the army to move up the Valley to Bunker Hill tomorrow morning.⁵¹

September 27, Saturday (Smoketown/Stephenson's Depot): Lee moves south to the vicinity of Stephenson's Depot.⁵²

September 28, Sunday (Stephenson's Depot): Lee writes to Sec. Randolph requesting the consolidation of some artillery batteries due to manpower and horse shortage as well as poor-performing officers. Lee sends President Davis an update on the location and condition of the army. He tells Davis, "History records but few examples of a greater amount of labor and fighting than has been done by this army during the present campaign."⁵³

---

48 *OR* 19, pt. 2, 621-4; REL to Lucy Cardwell, Sept. 23, 1862, REL papers, VHS; REL to unknown, Sept. 23, 1862, LJF papers, W&L; Emily V. Mason, *Popular Life of General Robert E. Lee* (Baltimore, MD, 1872), 147-8.

49 *OR* 19, pt. 2, 624-5; GO110, Sept. 24, 1862, REL papers, MOC; Harsh, *Sounding the Shallows*, 27. John H. Richardson was commissioned major on this date and assigned to command of the 39th Battalion VA Cav., which was assigned to ANV HQ as HQ escort and couriers. Richardson was the lieutenant colonel of the 46th VA but lost his position during the May 1862 reorganization. Krick, *Lee's Colonels*, 320. The 39th was raised not as a combat unit, but as a HQ support unit, and consisted of just four companies.

50 *OR* 19, pt. 2, 625-7.

51 *OR* 19, pt. 2, 628-9.

52 Tower, *Lee's Adjutant*, 45. Taylor wrote only that the new camp was "between Martinsburg and Winchester." Ibid. Lee headlined nearly all of his correspondence from this location as "Camp on Washington Run." Washington's Spring is immediately west of Clearbrook, just to the north of wartime Stephenson's Depot; the creek flowing from it appears on modern maps as "Clearbrook Run," but it seems logical it would have been known as Washington's Run. E. Porter Alexander wrote of his camp "near Stephenson's Depot . . . a few hundred yards from the station to the northeast," and that Lee's camp "was within 100 yards of mine in the meadow," although later Lee "moved out of the meadow, to a small wooded hill very near by to the southeast." Gallagher, *Fighting for the Confederacy*, 155. Alexander's wording in describing the location of camp is somewhat muddled. He could mean his camp was northeast of the depot, or that the depot was northeast of his camp. If the depot was to the northeast, then Lee's camp was likely in what is now a trailer park southwest of Stephenson between US 11 and Interstate 81, or in the open field adjacent to the north. If the camp was northeast of the depot, the site is either lost to a large quarrying operation, or in an open field immediately south of the quarry.

53 *OR* 19, pt. 2, 632-3. Lee's letter to Sec. Randolph is headlined "Lick River, WV." This is unusual because nearly all of his letters from this location are headlined "Camp on Washington Run." Lick Run is just south of Stephenson. No doubt with memories of Joe Johnston, Lee ended the letter to Davis, "There is nothing of interest to report, but I desire to keep you always advised of the condition of the army, its proceedings, and prospects."

September 29, Monday (Stephenson's Depot): Lee informs Sec. Randolph that certain parts of northwestern Virginia are not accepting Confederate currency as payment for supplies for the army, and also forwards a report of stragglers in/around Winchester and a report by Gen. John Imboden on his operations in northwestern Virginia. Lee authorizes a court martial to convene October 1, while the army is stationary. Lee dictates to Custis a letter to Mary strongly suggesting that she and the girls leave Richmond: "I see no benefit of your being constantly on the move and in peril, and as I am so situated that I cannot either see you or counsel you or help you, it adds to my anxiety and trouble."[54]

September 30, Tuesday (Stephenson's Depot): Lee places Gen. George Steuart in charge of organizing recruits from Maryland and explains to Sec. Randolph what is being done with these Marylanders. Lee dictates to Custis a letter to Agnes and Annie, mentioning that he has regained use of his left hand and can again mount his horse, but he can do but little with his right hand still. "The bones in my right hand have united but it is still powerless. I wish you had been with me to assist me in my feebleness. Think of my being left to the graceful ministration of Perry, who had to dress, feed, and array me."[55]

---

54 OR 19, pt. 2, 629-32, 635; GO113, Sept. 29, 1862, REL papers, MOC; REL to Mary, Sept. 29, 1862, Lee family papers, VHS. Custis left Richmond on the 20th. It is not known when he arrived at Lee's HQ (see Sept. 20 entry). While at HQ, Custis wrote most if not all of Lee's personal correspondence and assisted his father while his injured hands continued to heal.

55 OR 19, pt. 2, 636-7; REL to Agnes & Annie, Sept. 30, 1862, Lee family papers, VHS. Lee noted in a letter to an unknown recipient that he was rid of the sling for his arm at last, and could once again sign his own name. REL to unknown, Sept. 30, 1862, REL papers, LOC.

October 1862

The weeks the Army of Northern Virginia spent in the lower Shenandoah Valley following Sharpsburg comprises one of the least-documented periods of the war for its commander. Gen. Lee spent much of this time at his headquarters near Stephenson's Depot while he and his exhausted army recovered from their travails. Walter Taylor, Lee's chief aide-de-camp, recounted that in mid-October they were "still quietly resting in camp near Winchester, our army much improved and largely increased since our battles in Maryland."[1]

Custis remained at headquarters for much of the month aiding his father with correspondence and other tasks.[2] He had already left for Richmond when Lee learned of the birth of his son Rooney's second child, and thereafter the unexpected news of the death of his daughter Annie, which struck Lee very hard, but as he always did, the Virginian continued performing his duties.

The simmering feud between Stonewall Jackson and A. P. Hill dating back to the days of the Cedar Mountain campaign reared its head again when Jackson brought formal charges against Hill on October 4.[3] Lee hoped Jackson would simply drop the matter, but once formal charges were made Lee met with the officers at the Boyd house at Bunker Hill in an effort to resolve the dispute.[4]

The headquarters staff changed slightly when Robert Chilton shifted from chief of staff to inspector general, and Maj. Henry Peyton joined as Chilton's assistant. The chief of staff position was never officially refilled.

Gen. McClellan finally stirred in the middle of the month and sent a force to Charlestown. Lee had another narrow escape (though nowhere near as close a call as that near Thoroughfare Gap a month before) when an enemy cavalry patrol missed the general by only a few minutes as they explored the area between the armies.

Toward the end of the month Lee repositioned the army; Longstreet's command moved across the Blue Ridge Mountains to Culpeper, while Jackson's remained in the lower Valley. Although this dangerously divided the Army of Northern Virginia, it also blocked McClellan's direct route to Richmond and put a strong force in position to threaten his flank and rear. Lee accompanied Longstreet's troops to Culpeper, leaving Jackson once again the master of the Valley. Unfortunately, it is all but impossible to track Lee's movements from Stephenson's Depot to Culpeper because of a lack of documentation.

* * *

1 Tower, *Lee's Adjutant*, 47-8.

2 Custis's friend Jeremy Gilmer wrote that Custis preferred being in the field, but did not think it proper to ask for a transfer. Custis "is now with his Father near Winchester, where he writes he can be of service, and Mr. Davis permits him to remain. The truth is Custis is restive in his position, and feels that he ought to be in the field. History is being acted now, and he does not like to have the record made that Capt. G. W. C. Lee of the Engineers saw no service with the armies of his country during the struggle for independence. He has told me twice that his preference is to be on his proper duty, but that he does not think it would be proper for him to resign his position with the President, or ask to be relieved." Gilmer to wife, Oct. 12, 1862, Gilmer papers, UNC.

3 Jackson to A. P. Hill, Oct. 4, 1862, Stonewall Jackson papers, UNC. Jackson listed eight specific incidents of Hill's "neglect of duty." There is no indication on this document as to when Lee received it.

4 Johnson, *In the Footsteps of REL*, 110. It is not known when this meeting took place.

October 1, Wednesday (Stephenson's Depot): Lee forwards to President Davis copies of the September 22 and 29 Baltimore *American* containing accounts of Sharpsburg and the destruction of Gen. Richard Taylor's Louisiana plantation. Of the Federal version of the recent battle, Lee notes, "it will be seen how little ground they have to claim a victory, even from their own version of the engagement." He writes to Secretary of War Randolph and to G. W. Smith regarding his belief that McClellan will move up the Valley whenever he ventures forth from his camps, and cautions that a force in central Virginia may be planning to move on Gordonsville. Lee responds to a complaint from D. H. Hill regarding the number of wagons allotted to his division, explaining that the orders regarding transportation came from Lee himself not from the quartermaster as Hill supposes, so the orders will stand. Lee issues orders concerning the care and well-being of the army's horses. In the evening he receives a letter from President Davis regarding the condition of the army.[5]

October 2, Thursday (Stephenson's Depot): Lee sends a lengthy letter to President Davis recommending Longstreet and Jackson for promotion to lieutenant general, noting, "My opinion of the merits of General Jackson has been greatly enhanced during this expedition." Lee states that only two corps commanders are needed for his army but he also mentions Edmund Kirby Smith and A. P. Hill as being excellent officers; "Next to these two officers [Longstreet & Jackson], I consider General A. P. Hill the best commander with me." He comments also on prospects in Maryland, Kentucky, and Louisiana, and thinks that Maryland may yet rise up against Lincoln's government. He writes to McClellan regarding the wagons loaned him following the surrender of Harpers Ferry for use in transporting the baggage of the garrison's officers. He congratulates Jeb Stuart for a victory at Martinsburg yesterday and sends a report of the affair to Adjutant General Cooper.[6] Lee instructs W. N. Pendleton to move the horses of the reserve artillery farther south toward Millwood or Front Royal for better foraging, and issues GO116 congratulating the army for its victories from Richmond to Maryland. He sends a letter to Martha "Markie" Custis Williams with the latest family news.[7]

October 3, Friday (Stephenson's Depot): Lee orders Gen. Pendleton to take a leave of absence until his health has recovered. Rooney is promoted to brigadier general.[8]

October 4, Saturday (Stephenson's Depot): Lee sends Union Gen. Philip Kearny's sword, horse, and saddle through the lines with a personal letter of condolence for his widow. Lee instructs G. W. Smith to investigate why the surgeon in charge at Warrenton did not evacuate the wounded from there as ordered, as the men were subsequently captured. He also rebukes Smith for removing several thousand stand of small arms from Gordonsville which belonged to the wounded troops there. Lee receives Pendleton's report of the Maryland Campaign. Lee advises Sec. Randolph that he has reorganized the artillery of the army, and details of the restructuring are announced to the army.[9]

---

5 Freeman, *Lee's Dispatches*, 362-3; OR 19, pt. 2, 640-3.

6 OR 19, pt. 2, 12, 378, 643-4; REL to Stuart, Oct. 2, 1862, REL papers, MOC.

7 REL to WNP, Oct. 2, 1862, WNP papers, UNC; OR 19, pt. 2, 644-5; REL to M. C. Williams, Oct. 2, 1862, REL papers, VHS.

8 REL to WNP, Oct. 3, 1863, WNP papers, UNC; Daughtry, *Gray Cavalier*, 103. Much criticism was directed at Pendleton after he bungled the defense at Shepherdstown. "Pendleton is Lee's weakness," complained one artillerist. "[Pendleton] is like the elephant, we have him and we don't know what on earth to do with him, and it costs a devil of a sight to feed him." Gary W. Gallagher, ed., *The Antietam Campaign* (Chapel Hill, NC, 1999), 260. This may have been Lee's tactful way of allowing Pendleton time and space for the incident to blow over. Rooney's commission ranked from Sept. 15, 1862.

9 OR 19, pt. 2, 381, 646-7, 652-4; Lee, *Memoirs of WNP*, 229. At the same time that Lee dispatched the articles for Mrs. Kearny to McClellan, he also wrote to Sec. Randolph asking for permission to do so. Randolph did not grant permission until Oct. 8, which was *after* they had already been received by McClellan. OR 19, pt. 2, 645. Lee advised Randolph on the

October 5, Sunday (Stephenson's Depot): Lee orders the removal of supplies and ordnance to Staunton.[10]

October 6, Monday (Stephenson's Depot): Lee congratulates Gen. John Imboden for a recent cavalry raid and also dispatches a brief report of the mounted operation to Sec. Randolph. Maj. Henry Peyton joins the general's staff as assistant inspector general.[11]

October 7, Tuesday (Stephenson's Depot/Bunker Hill): Lee meets with Jackson in the morning at Stonewall's headquarters at Bunker Hill. Jackson's aide Jed Hotchkiss notes that they closely examine "my maps of Maryland and Pennsylvania. No doubt another expedition is on foot." Lee requests that McClellan send the borrowed wagons to the picket post on the Charlestown-Harpers Ferry road. The general also requests that Brig. Gen. William Mackall be appointed chief of staff for the ANV. Lee also meets with Stephen D. Lee in the evening regarding sending damaged artillery pieces to Staunton. Lee writes to Nannette Lee Peyton concerning the illness of her nephew, who serves in the Rockbridge Artillery.[12]

October 8, Wednesday (Stephenson's Depot): Lee orders Jeb Stuart to cross the Potomac to destroy a railroad bridge near Chambersburg, Pennsylvania. Lee requests that the sending of conscripts to his army should be suspended for the present because upon arrival with the army, nearly all of them take ill immediately and thus drain the Virginia army's resources. Instead, he would like them kept at camps of instruction long enough for the camp diseases to take their course. The Senate Committee on Military Affairs returns HR4—Thanks of Congress for the Seven Days' Battles—to the full Senate. Weather unseasonably hot.[13]

October 9, Thursday (Stephenson's Depot): Lee writes to G. W. Smith to allay Smith's fears of a pending attack on Richmond. Lee states that he will be ready to move east if and when McClellan does, but he does not see that happening in the immediate future. He recommends that Smith form a reserve corps out of the conscripts gathered in Richmond as an emergency guard for the capital. Lee informs Sec. Randolph that despite reverses in Florida he will not accede to Governor Milton's request to return Florida units currently serving with Lee's army and asks instead for additional Florida troops for the ANV. He tells Randolph also that prisoners recently captured by Imboden are being sent to Richmond rather than paroled because the enemy refuses to parole troops captured from Imboden's command.

6th that he had already sent Kearny's items through the lines, and explained that he did so because of the likelihood of the army moving very soon; Lee noted that he was prepared to reimburse the government for the articles if his actions were not approved. Ibid, 654-5.

10 SO210, Oct. 5, 1862, EPA papers, UNC. With the army stationary it is all but certain that Lee attended church services *somewhere*. There is no known record of him doing so, but the closest Episcopal Church was Christ Church on Boscawen Street in Winchester. "We have never had any proof of the fact that General Robert E. Lee was in Winchester during the war," observed Winchester historian Garland Quarles. "After the Antietam and Gettysburg campaigns . . . we know that he was close to Winchester . . . but no diarist or local observer or official record places him inside the town." Garland R. Quarles, *Occupied Winchester 1861-1865* (Winchester, VA, 1991), 28. Quarles, however, is incorrect; Lee made his HQ at Hollingsworth Mill at Winchester after Gettysburg (see July 21, 1863 entry).

11 OR 19, pt. 24-5; Krick, *Staff Officers in Gray*, 242. Peyton remained with the army through Appomattox.

12 McDonald, *Make Me a Map*, 87; OR 19, pt. 2, 396-7, 658; Jeremy Gilmer to wife, Oct. 8, 1862, Gilmer papers, UNC; REL to N. L. Peyton, Oct. 7, 1862, Peyton family papers, VHS. Mackall had served on Albert S. Johnston's staff earlier in the war and was captured at Island No. 10 in April 1862. At this time (Oct. 7) he was in Richmond awaiting assignment. He eventually became chief of staff for the Army of Tennessee and would serve both Braxton Bragg and Joe Johnston. Gilmer to wife, Oct. 8, 1862, Gilmer papers, UNC; Warner, *Generals in Gray*, 203-4. Robert Chilton, who held the post of chief of staff, was reassigned as inspector general around this same time—possibly in anticipation of Mackall assuming the chief of staff duties. See Peter S. Carmichael, ed., *Audacity Personified: The Generalship of Robert E. Lee* (Baton Rouge, LA, 2004), 91.

13 OR 19, pt. 2, 55, 657; *Journal of the Congress of the CSA*, vol. 2, 442-3; Krick, *CW Weather*, 72. Randolph suspended the flow of conscripts to the ANV on Oct. 14. OR 19, pt. 2, 657.

Lee meets with visiting British officer Garnet Wolseley; they discuss the Maryland Campaign and the war overall.[14]

October 10, Friday (Stephenson's Depot): Lee instructs Pendleton to gather all information he can regarding roads and fords in the vicinity of Front Royal.[15]

October 11, Saturday (Stephenson's Depot): Lee informs Sec. Randolph that information from his scouts negates the rumors of McClellan moving on Richmond: "Whatever may be Gen. McClellan's ultimate intentions, I see no evidence as yet of any advance upon Richmond." Lee explains to Jubal Early why some of his artillery was affected by the recent reorganization and stresses that it should only be temporary.[16]

October 12, Sunday (Stephenson's Depot): Lee attends a grand review of the army, accompanied by Longstreet and Jackson. Lee writes to Mary, mentioning seeing Rob during the battle at Sharpsburg, and providing an update on his own condition: "My hands are improving slowly, and with my left hand I am able to dress and undress myself, which is a great comfort. My right is becoming of some assistance too, though it is still swollen and sometimes painful; the bandages have been removed and my thumb and forefinger being less injured than any part of my hand. I am now able to sign my name. It has been six weeks today since I was injured, and I have at last discarded the sling." Rain at times during the day.[17]

October 13, Monday (Stephenson's Depot): Lee informs Randolph that McClellan's army is still stationary around Sharpsburg and Harpers Ferry.[18]

October 14, Tuesday (Stephenson's Depot): Lee sends Randolph a report of Stuart's Pennsylvania raid, accompanied by several Harrisburg and Baltimore newspapers.[19]

October 15, Wednesday (Stephenson's Depot): Lee informs Randolph that William Loring's forces must protect the Kanawha Valley, and he tells Loring that as long as the salt works at Charleston are protected, Lee will defer to Loring's judgment as he is on the ground and knows the situation better than Lee. He adds that the proposed movement by Loring into western Pennsylvania should be abandoned for the present. Rain during the night.[20]

October 16, Thursday (Stephenson's Depot): Lee learns that a sizeable enemy force is across the Potomac at Shepherdstown and headed toward Lee's army. Lee writes again to Gen. Loring stressing

---

14 OR 19, pt. 2, 658-9; OR 4, Series 2, 913; Rawley, *English View*, 30, 44. Wolseley did not put a specific date to anything in his writings, but he mentioned that he arrived at Lee's HQ on the day that Stuart left on his Chambersburg raid. Stuart's raid began on the 9th so assuming Wolseley was correct, his visit with Lee was today or possibly a day to either side.

15 REL to WNP, Oct. 10, 1862, REL papers, W&L.

16 OR 19, pt. 2, 662-3.

17 Untitled & undated account of 3rd Georgia [possibly a fragment of a regimental history], Charles H. Andrews papers, UNC; REL to Mary, Oct. 12, 1862, Lee family papers, VHS; Schildt, *Stonewall Day by Day*, 81. It is not known where this review occurred or if it took place at all. Andrews's account of the review may be wrong in recording that the entire army was involved. According to Cadmus Wilcox's biographer, the review was of an ad hoc division under Wilcox consisting of a portion of his own and George Pickett's commands, staged to impress visiting British dignitaries, which seems far more likely given the silence of other sources about a grand review of the entire army. Gerard A. Patterson, *From Blue to Gray: The Life of Confederate General Cadmus M. Wilcox* (Mechanicsburg, PA, 2001), 49.

18 OR 19, pt. 2, 663.

19 OR 19, pt. 2, 51.

20 OR 19, pt. 2, 666; Krick, *CW Weather*, 72. William Loring was removed as commander in western Virginia on this date and replaced by Brig. Gen. John Echols, largely because Loring disregarded Lee's instructions to protect the Kanawha Valley. Tim McKinney, *The Civil War in Fayette County, West Virginia* (Charleston, WV, 1988), 168. Loring was a difficult subordinate, which he would prove again soon enough in Mississippi during the Vicksburg Campaign.

that he should use his own judgment so long as he protects the Kanawha Valley and the Virginia & Tennessee Railroad, and that he should regard Lee's correspondence as suggestions rather than direct orders. Lee again complains to Sec. Randolph about the refusal of locals in northwestern Virginia to accept Confederate currency in return for supplies, and at the same time issues orders setting uniform prices for the army's quartermaster supplies. He informs Randolph and G. W. Smith that he has no credible reports of the enemy moving to Norfolk and does not fear for Richmond's safety. Thus, he will not move the entire army back to the capital, but will detach troops for its defense, if needed, and that either Rooney or Fitz Lee can be sent to take command of the cavalry around Richmond.[21]

October 17, Friday (Stephenson's Depot/ Leetown): In the early morning Lee joins Longstreet, Jackson, and Stuart in a reconnaissance around Leetown and narrowly misses an enemy cavalry patrol in the vicinity of the village itself. Lee instructs Pendleton to prepare the reserve artillery to move as Lee "does not design delivering battle about Winchester, wishing to draw the enemy up the Valley."[22]

October 18, Saturday (Stephenson's Depot): Lee forwards to the adjutant general Stuart's report of his Pennsylvania raid and informs Sec. Randolph of the recent enemy movements around Charlestown over the past two days. He instructs George Steuart in Winchester to move the worst cases of sick and wounded to Staunton and to return those who have recovered to their units as the army will move soon. He requests the War Department make Col. Chilton the army's inspector general and recommends that John Echols be retained in command of what had been William Loring's army in western Virginia; Lee points out that he has no place for Gen. Loring in the Army of Northern Virginia.[23]

Lee cryptically informs Secretary of State Judah Benjamin that a "foreigner . . . has been sent back to Richmond. I saw nothing to confirm the suspicion against him." He orders a court of inquiry to convene on the 20th to investigate Lawton's Brigade abandoning Boteler's Ford during the night of Sept. 19. He receives letters from his wife and Charlotte. A recruitment ad for the 39th Virginia Cavalry Battalion is published in the Richmond *Dispatch*.[24]

October 19, Sunday (Stephenson's Depot): Lee instructs Longstreet to have McLaws continue the destruction of the Winchester & Potomac Railroad and expand his efforts to the B&O if possible. He orders Imboden to continue gathering all the livestock and supplies he can from the mountains and do what damage he can to the B&O. He also advises Imboden that Brig. Gen. Albert Jenkins's brigade should be near Imboden so the two of them are to cooperate and gather what intelligence they can as to the enemy presence in that region. Lee sends Gen. Cooper a brief report of Imboden's activities and writes to his wife and to Charlotte, the first letters he has written himself since his injury. He tells Mary that Custis is still with him in camp: "His presence is a great comfort to me." Rooney and Charlotte's second child, Charlotte Carter Lee, is born at Hickory Hill.[25]

---

21 Freeman, *Lee*, vol. 2, 423-4; *OR* 19, pt. 2, 667-9; GO119, Oct. 16, 1862, EPA papers, UNC.

22 Blackford, *Letters from Lee's Army*, 129; von Borcke, *Memoirs*, 218-20; *OR* 19, pt. 2, 670. Von Borcke placed Lee near The Bower around 9:00 a.m., and wrote that Lee's close call occurred on the Kearneysville-Smithfield Road midway between those two towns (which would be somewhere near Leetown). According to von Borcke, the Yankee patrol arrived "just 10 minutes after General Lee with a very small escort had passed by. Our Commander-in-Chief had thus very narrowly escaped falling into the hands of the enemy." Von Borcke, *Memoirs*, 218-20. Smithfield is now Middleway.

23 REL to Sam Cooper, Oct. 18, 1862, REL papers, MOC; *OR* 19, pt. 2, 89, 671; REL to Randolph, Oct. 18, 1862, telegram book, REL HQ papers, VHS.

24 REL to J. P. Benjamin, Oct. 18, 1862, telegram book, REL HQ papers, VHS; *OR* 19, pt. 2, 671-2; REL to Mrs. REL, Oct. 19, 1862, Lee family papers, VHS; REL to Charlotte, Oct. 19, 1862, G. B. Lee papers, VHS; Richmond *Daily Dispatch*, Oct. 18, 1862. Nothing is known about the individual referred to in this message to Benjamin.

25 *OR* 19, pt. 2, 672-3; REL to Charlotte, Oct. 19, 1862, G. B. Lee papers, VHS; REL to Mrs. REL, Oct. 19, 1862, Lee family papers, VHS. Very little is known regarding the brief life of Lee's second grandchild; even her birth date is not

October 20, Monday (Stephenson's Depot): Lee commends Stuart for his recent raid and sends him a copy of Lee's letter of the 18th to Cooper regarding it. Lee writes to Sec. Randolph regarding a "Mr. Kirby, an Englishman or Canadian" who requested a pass to Richmond. Chilton is promoted to brigadier general. Lee's daughter Annie dies suddenly near Warrenton, North Carolina.[26]

October 21, Tuesday (Stephenson's Depot): Lee clarifies for Maj. H. M. Bell, quartermaster at Staunton, what materials are to be retained there for Lee's army and what is to be sent to Richmond.[27]

October 22, Wednesday (Stephenson's Depot/ Bunker Hill): Lee reviews D. R. Jones's division near Bunker Hill. He orders Longstreet to send John Walker's division to Upperville to establish an infantry presence on the east side of the Blue Ridge, and orders Stuart to provide cavalry to cooperate with Walker. Lee explains to President Davis that he prefers to keep part of the army in the Valley and part on the Rappahannock for the winter. He adds that lack of transportation prevented him from removing the much needed iron from the B&O and Winchester & Potomac railroads for use on Southern lines. Lee instructs Jackson to transfer a Maryland battery to serve with George Steuart's Maryland troops, and he tells Sec. Randolph that John Echols can remain as Loring's temporary replacement, but if Ed Johnson has recovered, Lee wants him promoted and given the command.[28]

October 23, Thursday (Stephenson's Depot): Lee reviews Hood's Division and meets with W. N. Pendleton regarding the strength of the artillery. Lee forwards to Sec. Randolph the battle flags of the 11th Pennsylvania and 103rd New York and an accompanying letter from Gen. James Kemper. Lee informs Col. Robert Chambliss, commanding the cavalry along the Rappahannock, of Walker's move to Upperville so their pickets can connect. Lee instructs Imboden to continue his supply-gathering operations and to act in concert with any move Echols may make.[29]

October 24, Friday (Stephenson's Depot): Lee sends a lengthy letter to G. W. Smith regarding McClellan's lack of movement and what to do with conscripts: Lee does not want them until camp diseases have run their course and Smith doesn't want them because he does not have officers to command them. Lee suggests to Randolph that officers and men on furlough not be allowed to draw pay, and also tactfully informs the secretary that Lee does not want Chase Whiting with his army and suggests that

---

known with certainty. Her gravestone does not have a birth date, nor does Washington & Lee have it among their Lee family records. The only place an exact date could be found is findagrave.com. The only biography of Rooney suggests the child was born prematurely, and that Charlotte was left in a very poor state as a result of the birth. Daughtry, *Gray Cavalier*, 104.

26 REL to Stuart, Oct 20, 1862, REL papers, MOC; *OR* 19, pt. 2, 707; Chilton CSR; Freeman, *Lee*, vol. 2, 421. It is possible that "Mr. Kirby" is the "foreigner" Lee referred to in his letter of the 18th to Benjamin. Chilton's promotion was not confirmed by the Senate, probably because of his allegations against John Magruder in the wake of the Seven Days' Battles. Annie was stricken ill very suddenly, probably with typhoid fever, and it is possible she suffered from spinal meningitis and a ruptured appendix as well. Her mother and sister Agnes were with her when she died. Mary confided to a friend that she was unaware of the severity of her daughter's illness, even though Dr. William Selden of Norfolk checked on her three times daily, and "she was very deaf and could neither read nor listen." Mrs. REL to Selina Powell, Oct. 30, 1862, Powell family papers, W&M. The best description of Annie's last days can be found in Coulling, *Lee Girls*, 108-10.

27 *OR* 19, pt. 2, 674. A lengthy list of court martial verdicts and sentences appears in the ANV Order Book under this date; almost certainly Lee reviewed and signed off on them, which may account for the lack of any other correspondence today. ANV Order Book, MOC.

28 George Wise, *History of the Seventeenth Virginia Infantry, CSA* (Baltimore, MD, 1870), 121; *OR* 19, pt. 2, 674-7. Edward Johnson was wounded at the Battle of McDowell on May 8, 1862.

29 William W. Pierson, Jr., ed., *The Diary of Bartlett Yancey Malone* (Chapel Hill, NC, 1919), 25; Lee, *Memoirs of WNP*, 231; *OR* 19, pt. 2, 677-9. The national colors of the 11th Pennsylvania were captured by Pvt. Samuel Coleman of the 17th VA at Second Manassas. The regimental colors of the 103rd NY were captured by Lt. William Athey of the 17th VA at Sharpsburg. *OR* 19, pt. 2, 677.

he would be of better use as an engineer at Charleston, Savannah, or Mobile. Rain during the night.[30]

October 25, Saturday (Stephenson's Depot): Lee reviews Kershaw's Brigade in the afternoon. He urges Randolph to have the Piedmont Railroad completed as soon as possible, and telegraphs a shorter version of his wishes regarding Whiting. Lee writes to Louisa Washington, the daughter of his former aide Col. John A. Washington, to apologize for not visiting her despite being near her home: "I am only now beginning to use my right hand and write with difficulty and pain. . . . Custis has left me now and I presume you would not be afraid even to come to camp. I will not let any of the young men look at you."[31]

October 26, Sunday (Stephenson's Depot): In the morning Lee learns of Annie's death. He writes letters to his wife and brother Charles about her death, and sends word of her passing to Rob. Returning his attention to military operations, he instructs Imboden to continue his operations against the B&O and gathering supplies and urges Imboden to strike a blow at the forces opposing him. He recommends Isaac Trimble for promotion to major general and division command. Lee orders cloth requisitioned by the Confederate quartermaster released to Francis Smith for uniforms for Virginia Military Institute.[32]

October 27, Monday (Stephenson's Depot): Lee sends Sec. Randolph a lengthy order of battle for the army down to brigade level. This accounting includes Lee's recommendations for promotions to fill vacancies. Gen. W. H. C. Whiting is ordered to report to Richmond for reassignment.[33]

October 28, Tuesday (unknown): Lee divides the army with Jackson remaining in the lower Valley near Berryville, with Longstreet and Pendleton moving across the Blue Ridge to Culpeper. Lee will go to Culpeper with Longstreet's wing and Stuart will provide cavalry for both. Lee authorizes G. W. Smith to pull troops from the Rappahannock line if he needs them at Richmond. Lee and Longstreet review McLaws's Division in the afternoon. Col. Chilton is

---

30   OR 19, pt. 2, 679-80; Guy R. Everson and Edward W. Simpson, Jr., eds., *Far, Far from Home: The Wartime Letters of Dick and Tally Simpson, 3rd South Carolina Volunteers* (New York, 1994), 156-7. Gen. Whiting went on a leave of absence after the Seven Days' Battles and John B. Hood assumed command of his troops. Although Whiting was now available to return to duty, Lee did not want him to supplant Hood, who Lee considered a much better fighter and more reliable in the field than Whiting.

31   Everson, *Far from Home*, 157; OR 19, pt. 2, 681; REL to L. F. Washington, Oct. 25, 1862, L. F. Washington papers, W&L. Lee may not have reviewed Kershaw's Brigade. The South Carolinian who mentioned it may have misdated his letter. What is known is that Lee reviewed McLaws's Division on the 28th, so it seems odd that Kershaw's troops would have been reviewed separately from the rest of the division.

32   Taylor, *Four Years*, 76; Freeman, *Lee*, vol. 2, 421; Lee, *Recollections and Letters of REL*, 79; OR 19, pt. 2, 682; William W. Goldsborough, *The Maryland Line in the Confederate Army, 1861-1865* (Baltimore, MD, 1900), 349; Margaretta B. Colt, *Defend the Valley: A Shenandoah Family in the Civil War* (New York, 1999), 191. Taylor was the only one of the staff to record Lee's reaction to the news of his daughter's death, but did not record the day the sad news was received. Taylor remembered that Lee received his usual personal letters with the morning mail, but did not have any unusual reaction while Taylor was still present handling the routine army business. When Taylor returned to Lee's tent a few minutes later, however, he found the general "overcome with grief, an open letter in his hands." *Four Years*, 76. Rob also wrote of his sister's death, but he did not include a date when his father learned of it. He recalled that his father sent him a message by courier, which he received during the afternoon. *Recollections and Letters of REL*, 79. "I never even heard of poor Annie's illness until I heard she was dead," wrote Rob to his mother. Coulling, *Lee Girls*, 111. Lee described the impact of his daughter's death when he wrote: "To know that I shall never see her again on earth, that her place in our circle, which I always hoped one day to enjoy, is forever vacant, is agonizing in the extreme." Lee, *Recollections and Letters of REL*, 79. It is possible that Lee received this news a day or two earlier, but based on the lack of any known mention by him of it prior to the 26th, it seems almost certain this is the day he learned of Annie's passing.

33   OR 19, pt. 2 683-4. Porter Alexander wrote that Lee broke camp on or about the 27th to move to Culpeper. Gallagher, *Fighting for the Confederacy*, 158. The exact date is not known, as none of Lee's correspondence—official or personal—for the rest of October gives his location. He was certainly still somewhere around Winchester, but where exactly cannot be determined.

announced as the army's new inspector general, thus leaving the post of chief of staff vacant; his former duties will be performed by Capt. A. P. Mason for the present.[34]

October 29, Wednesday (Front Royal/unknown): Lee moves through Front Royal and across the Blue Ridge via Chester's Gap.[35]

October 30, Thursday (Culpeper/Gordonsville/Richmond): Lee moves from Culpeper to Richmond via Gordonsville. He writes to G. W. Smith regarding the shifting of units from Smith to the ANV. Rob is appointed 1st lieutenant on Rooney's staff, but President Davis refuses to nominate him for the commission due to his age.[36]

October 31, Friday (Richmond): Lee arrives in Richmond to meet with President Davis; he stays with Mary at the Caskie house.[37]

---

34 OR 19, pt. 2, 685-8; REL to G. W. Smith, Oct. 28, 1862, telegram book, REL HQ papers, VHS; Wyckoff, *CW Letters of Alexander McNeill*, 150. It is not known where Lee's HQ was located on this date, nor where the review of McLaws's Division took place. A letter from Rob to his mother suggests that Lee did not inform his son of Annie's death until today, but it seems unlikely that he would have sat on that information for at least two days. Rob to Mrs. REL, Oct. 30, 1862, Lee family papers, VHS.

35 Laura V. Hale, *Four Valiant Years in the Lower Shenandoah Valley 1861-1865* (Strasburg, VA, 1973), 198. This account places Lee at Front Royal early in the morning; there is nothing to contradict it, but it does mean Lee was in quite a hurry because he was seen in Gordonsville roughly 36 hours later, a distance of approximately 70 miles.

36 T. H. Pearce, ed., *Diary of Captain Henry A. Chambers* (Wendell, NC, 1983), 66; OR 19, pt. 2, 689; REL Jr. CSR. It is not known when Lee arrived in Culpeper. Venable was the only staff officer who mentioned it at all, and he did so only in his misc. notes: "During our brief stay in camp near Culpeper Gen. Lee went to Richmond." "Civil War notes," McDowell-Miller-Warner papers, UVA. An officer stationed in Gordonsville observed it was "a little after dark" when Lee passed through town on his way to Richmond. Pearce, *Chambers Diary*, 66. He did not state if Lee arrived by horse or rail, but he almost certainly went by rail from there to the capital.

37 Charleston *Mercury*, Nov. 5, 1862; Mrs. REL to Selina Powell, Oct. 30, 1862, Powell family papers, W&M (Mary obviously completed this letter after Lee returned to the army, although she did not put additional dates beyond the 30th, which is when she started it). Given the hour at which Lee arrived in Gordonsville, it must have been very late on the night of the 30th or early on the morning of the 31st when he reached Richmond; nothing has been found that states when he arrived in the capital. Braxton Bragg and Edmund Kirby Smith were both in Richmond at this time, and it is conceivable that one or both met with Lee. Thomas Bragg diary, Oct. 30, 1862, UNC.

November 1862

Federal operations in North Carolina occupied Lee's attention for the first few days of November as he met with President Davis about how best to defend the Old North State. When the general arrived in Richmond, Davis had just concluded discussions with Braxton Bragg and Edmund Kirby Smith about their recent failed campaign in Kentucky, leading one newspaper correspondent to write: "The President has been invisible since last Saturday. Up to yesterday he was closeted all the time with Bragg, who returns to his command with the approving smiles of the Executive. Since Bragg's departure, Mr. Davis has been in deep consultation with Generals Lee and Cooper."[1]

The same day that Lee returned to the army at Culpeper, George McClellan was replaced as commander of the Army of the Potomac.[2] His successor, Ambrose Burnside, stole a march on Lee—who was perhaps too focused south of the James River—and appeared at Falmouth directly opposite a lightly defended Fredericksburg along the Rappahannock River. Had luck been with him, Burnside may have slipped across the river and around Lee's right flank before Lee could concentrate his army. Indeed, when Lee learned of the Federal presence at Fredericksburg, he concluded the Union army would be across the river before he could oppose it, and decided to fall back to the North Anna River line and confront Burnside there.[3] Lucky, however, was something Burnside rarely was, and this episode was no exception. The pontoon boats he required to bridge the Rappahannock did not arrive, which gifted Lee the necessary time to reunite the two wings of his army at the historic town.

Lee's reorganization of the army continued during his two week respite at Culpeper with the formal establishment of two army corps under newly promoted lieutenant generals James Longstreet and Thomas Jackson. Some minor changes to his personal and the army's staff were effected as well, the most notable being the transfer of E. Porter Alexander to command an artillery battalion in Longstreet's First Corps.

British politician Francis Lawley, a correspondent for the London *Times*, visited Lee at Culpeper and left a vivid description of his headquarters:

> Of all the spots in which I have seen the headquarters of General Lee established, his present situation, distant about a mile from Culpeper Court House, seems to me the snuggest. It is in the middle of a thick pine wood, so dense that you cannot see the tents till within twelve yards of them, protected altogether from any wind that can blow, and with such an abundance of wood as to make enormous fires possible. In a picturesque kind of Robin Hood bower, General Lee's table, with its simple food, is spread, but as that food is certainly preferable to any that can be procured in the best hotel at Richmond, it will be believed that in the fresh air, after healthy exercise, appetite is not wanting to do justice to it.[4]

---

1 Charleston *Mercury*, Nov. 5, 1862.

2 Long, *CW Day by Day*, 284-5.

3 OR 21, 1020-2.

4 Charleston *Mercury*, Feb. 5, 1863.

Lee departed Culpeper for Fredericksburg accompanied by his son Rob, who had recently been given a position on his brother Rooney's cavalry staff. Gen. Lee spent much of his time at Fredericksburg reconnoitering along the Rappahannock River above and below the town to familiarize himself with defensive positions and potential crossing points. Once he finished, he was confident Gen. Burnside would not attempt a crossing with the Army of Northern Virginia arrayed on the far bank to contest it.

* * *

November 1, Saturday (Richmond): Lee visits the War Department and meets with President Davis and Maj. Gen. Samuel French at the Executive Mansion to discuss the situation in North Carolina.[5]

November 2, Sunday (Richmond): Lee meets with President Davis.[6]

November 3, Monday (Richmond): Lee continues meeting with President Davis and Adjutant General Samuel Cooper. He writes to Mildred regarding Annie's death.[7]

November 4, Tuesday (Richmond): Lee continues discussions with President Davis.[8]

November 5, Wednesday (Richmond/Gordonsville/Culpeper): The general returns to the army at Culpeper, via Gordonsville, in the morning. He arrives in the evening at his camp in the woods on the southeast edge of town. Rain throughout the day.[9]

November 6, Thursday (Culpeper): Lee meets with Gen. Pendleton in the morning, likely discussing reassignments and commanders in the artillery. He meets also with Jed Hotchkiss regarding his status as engineer on Jackson's staff. Lee instructs Longstreet to send a force to Weldon, North Carolina, to guard the railroad and requests clarification from Stuart as to where the Army of the Potomac is headed. He cautions Jackson that McClellan is moving either to get behind Jackson in the Valley or to cut off his line of communication with Longstreet at Culpeper. Lee tells Jackson to make sure all the wounded are evacuated from Winchester before he evacuates the town and to be prepared to pounce on the enemy.[10]

Lee informs the president and the adjutant general that troops will be sent to Weldon and that John Walker and Stephen D. Lee have been ordered to Richmond for service elsewhere. He mentions also that although he wants to promote colonels Carnot Posey and John B. Gordon they are blocked presently, and that Roger Pryor's brigade has been broken up since it contained units from different states; he thus recommends Pryor for service south of the James. He informs G. W. Smith that troops have been sent to Weldon and that several regiments will sent to Richmond, although Lee thinks the enemy movements in North Carolina are merely a diversion. SO234 announces the promotion of Longstreet and Jackson to the newly created grade of lieutenant general, George Pickett and John B. Hood to major general, and a number of new brigadier generals. Lee sends a brief note to his wife.[11]

November 7, Friday (Culpeper): Lee tells Stuart he plans to reunite Longstreet and Jackson east of the mountains and operate in northern Virginia. He notifies Sec. Randolph that the Army of the Potomac has occupied Warrenton and that he intends to have Longstreet and Jackson join somewhere east of the mountains. He also writes to Randolph and P. S. Roller of Mount Crawford regarding the acquisition

---

5 Jones, *Rebel War Clerk's Diary*, vol. 1, 179; French, *Two Wars*, 150. According to Mary, she only saw the general in the evenings. Mrs. REL to Selina Powell, Oct. 30, 1862, Powell family papers, W&M.

6 Charleston *Mercury*, Nov. 5, 1862. Lee likely also attended service at St. Paul's Episcopal Church on Grace Street.

7 Charleston *Mercury*, Nov. 5, 1862; REL to Mildred, Nov. 3, 1862, Lee family papers, VHS. Mildred at this time was at St. Mary's school in Raleigh, North Carolina.

8 Charleston *Mercury*, Nov. 5, 1862.

9 Mrs. REL to Selina Powell, Oct. 30, 1862, Powell family papers, W&M; Pearce, *Chambers Diary*, 68; McDonald, *Make Me a Map*, 92; Gallagher, *Fighting for the Confederacy*, 158; REL to Mrs. REL, Nov. 6, 1862, Lee family papers, VHS.

10 A. P. Mason to WNP, Nov. 6, 1862, WNP papers, UNC; McDonald, *Make Me a Map*, 92; OR 19, pt. 2, 695-7. Hotchkiss was in an odd situation in that he was a volunteer aide to Jackson. There was confusion over whether he was liable to conscription, and thus he sought out Lee for resolution of the matter.

11 OR 19, pt. 2, 697-9; REL to Sam Cooper, Nov. 6, 1862, telegram book, REL HQ papers, VHS; REL to Mrs. REL, Nov. 6, 1862, Lee family papers, VHS. SO 234 formalized the organization of the Army of Northern Virginia into two corps: Longstreet's First Corps and Jackson's Second Corps.

of flour in the Valley for the army's use. Robert Ransom is named to assume command of John Walker's division, and Porter Alexander to take over Stephen D. Lee's artillery battalion; Lee requests that Briscoe Baldwin be assigned to replace Alexander as ordnance chief. Chilton, in his new role as the army's inspector general, publishes orders regarding inspections. Heavy snow, up to eight inches in spots.[12]

November 8, Saturday (Culpeper): Lee advises Jackson that the enemy has occupied Warrenton, with cavalry as far as Rappahannock Station and Jeffersonton, and not only have blocked his route through Chester Gap but may attempt a movement through it into the Valley. Lee appoints "Grumble" Jones to command of Munford's brigade.[13]

November 9, Sunday (Culpeper): Lee informs Stonewall Jackson that he is unclear as to the enemy's intentions: will the enemy enter the Shenandoah Valley around Strasburg and Front Royal, or will the Union army continue operating east of the Blue Ridge? Lee trusts Jackson and grants him significant latitude in how to react, and even authorizing a foray across the Potomac if he deems it necessary. Lee learns during the evening that the Federals have abandoned Ashby's and Snicker's gaps and are concentrating along the Manassas Gap Railroad; he orders Jeb Stuart to determine their intentions. Lee announces that all prisoners delivered to Aiken's Landing as of yesterday are properly exchanged and are to rejoin their commands.[14]

November 10, Monday (Culpeper): Lee learns that Ambrose Burnside has replaced McClellan as commander of the Army of the Potomac. Lee writes several letters to Sec. Randolph giving updates on enemy dispositions as well as his own plans and the condition of the army: he explains that the Army of the Potomac is along the Manassas Gap Railroad and seems poised to move to the Rappahannock, thus Jackson will remain in the Valley to threaten their flank and rear, but if they move against Jackson, Longstreet will thus be in position to threaten their other flank. He forwards a report of a cavalry skirmish near Amissville and notes that Stuart has not found any Federals south of the Rappahannock, but they seem to be in great strength around Warrenton. He points out that the army is in desperate need of blankets and shoes and that the cavalry is in poor condition and it is becoming increasingly difficult to procure replacement horses.[15]

In yet another letter to Sec. Randolph, Lee requests that a "Mr. Kirby," an Englishman or Canadian who had been given a pass to reach Richmond several weeks earlier, be expelled from the Confederacy; this was in response to a letter received at headquarters that Kirby "should be arrested at once. He knows and talks too much." Lee also informs the secretary that assigning the Florida regiments into a brigade under Edward Perry left Roger Pryor without a command, so Lee sent Pryor to Gen. Gustavus W. Smith. Lee corresponds with Smith regarding a troop swap, sending several veteran units to Richmond in exchange for newer and larger North Carolina units. He asks Smith and

---

12 *OR* 19, pt. 2, 699-704; REL to JD, Nov. 7, 1862, telegram book, REL HQ papers, VHS; GO125, Nov. 7, 1862, EPA papers, UNC; Gallagher, *Fighting for the Confederacy*, 159. Alexander recorded that the commanders in S. D. Lee's battalion went to Lee to request that Alexander be assigned to the command, after which Lee summoned Alexander to ask who Alexander recommends should take his place as chief of ordnance. Gallagher, *Fighting for the Confederacy*, 159-60. According to Alexander, this happened on the 8th, but that is clearly in error because the orders for Alexander and his replacement, Baldwin, were issued on the 7th. The meetings Alexander recalled likely occurred on the 6th or possibly on the morning of the 7th.

13 *OR* 19, pt. 2, 704-5; REL to T. J. Jackson, Nov. 8, 1862 (2 messages), telegram book, REL HQ papers, VHS.

14 *OR* 19, pt. 2, 705-7; *OR* 4, Series 2, 937. Lee very likely attended service at St. Stephen's Episcopal Church in Culpeper during the morning, as it is known that he did so while in Culpeper. Hall, "REL in Culpeper."

15 Freeman, *Lee*, vol. 2, 428; *OR* 19, pt. 2, 140, 707-11. President Lincoln ordered McClellan replaced on November 5, but the orders did not reach McClellan until shortly before midnight on the 7th; Burnside fully assumed command two days later. Long, *CW Day by Day*, 284-6.

Col. John Chambliss what troops are stationed along the Rappahannock River and what they know of any Federal presence around Fredericksburg.[16]

During the evening Lee instructs Jackson to unite with Longstreet when holding the Valley is of no further strategic value. Orders are published announcing the dismantling of Pryor's Brigade and the creation of Perry's Florida brigade. Lee writes to Custis regarding his personal finances; he mentions that Rooney has rejoined the army, and also explains briefly his strategic plans. He receives a letter from Mildred and writes back in the evening mentioning his continuing sorrow over the loss of Annie and regretting that his injury still prevents him from writing much.[17]

November 11, Tuesday (Culpeper): Lee advises Jackson that Burnside is advancing around Warrenton but points out that this may give Jackson an opportunity to strike at their rear around Charlestown. Lee gathers all detached cavalry from the upper Valley and inquires of the War Department if a partisan unit at Orange is subject to his orders. He writes to Anne Carter Wickham expressing his regret that her son Williams C. Wickham was wounded but he must return to duty.[18]

November 12, Wednesday (Culpeper): Lee advises Jackson of several thousand Federals rumored to be at McDowell and reiterates the discretion allotted Jackson for his movements in the Valley. He also informs Stonewall that all troops captured and paroled before November 1 are exchanged. Lee instructs Pendleton to send a battery to Fredericksburg to serve with the cavalry stationed there, and requests again of Richmond that Briscoe Baldwin be named as chief of ordnance. He writes to Brig. Gen. Cadmus Wilcox to dissuade him from leaving the ANV.[19]

November 13, Thursday (Culpeper): Lee informs Jackson that Stuart reports the enemy left Amissville and Jeffersonton last night, but there are no indications of a move either across the Rappahannock or on Fredericksburg. He instructs Col. John Critcher, commanding the outpost at Fredericksburg, to closely monitor the Warrenton Road. Lee writes to Mary, mentions seeing Rooney today along the Rappahannock and hoping that Charlotte's baby is doing well.[20]

November 14, Friday (Culpeper): Lee informs Jackson that the latest reports have the Federals concentrated around Warrenton and completely out of the Valley, thus Jackson should determine if he gains any advantage by remaining there; if not he is to join Longstreet as soon as possible. He adds that no Yankees are known to be east of the Orange & Alexandria Railroad, but they are at Bealeton; he is not sure if Fredericksburg is their destination. Lee acknowledges Jackson's need for shoes, which he promises to send when possible, and informs Richmond how many unshod men are in each corps. Lee orders the Richmond, Fredericksburg & Poto-

---

16 OR 19, pt. 2, 707-10; REL to G. W. Smith, Nov. 10, 1862 (2 messages), telegram book, REL HQ papers, VHS; REL to J. R. Chambliss, Nov. 10, 1862, telegram book, REL HQ papers, VHS.

17 OR 19, pt. 2, 710-3; Dowdey, *Wartime Papers*, 333; REL to Mildred, Nov. 10, 1862, REL papers, LOC. In his letter to Mildred, Lee mentioned that he wrote to Rob today as well, but this letter has not been found; presumably its content was much the same as the one to Mildred.

18 OR 19, pt. 2, 714; REL to H. B. Davidson, Nov. 11, 1862, telegram book, REL HQ papers, VHS; REL to G. W. Randolph, Nov. 11, 1862, telegram book, REL HQ papers, VHS; REL to A. C. Wickham, Nov. 11, 1862, REL papers, UVA. The partisan unit to which Lee referred was commanded by Capt. W. G. Brawner; this company was part of the 15th VA Cav., Wickham was wounded in the neck on Nov. 3 in a skirmish near Upperville. OR 19, pt. 2, 143.

19 OR 19, pt. 2, 714-5; REL to Jackson, Nov. 12, 1862, telegram book, REL HQ papers, VHS; A. L. Long to to WNP, Nov. 12, 1862, WNP papers, UNC; A. P. Mason to WNP, Nov. 12, 1862, WNP papers, UNC; REL to G. W. Randolph, Nov. 12, 1862, telegram book, REL HQ papers, VHS; REL to Cadmus Wilcox, Nov. 12, 1862, REL papers, VHS. Wilcox was very dissatisfied as he watched officers far junior to him in the antebellum U.S. Army rising above him in rank. He believed he would have better opportunities for advancement outside the ANV. Patterson, *From Blue to Gray*, 50-2.

20 OR 19, pt. 2, 716; REL to Jackson, Nov. 13, 1862, telegram book, REL HQ papers, VHS; REL to John Critcher, Nov. 13, 1862, telegram book, REL HQ papers, VHS; REL to Mrs. REL, Nov. 13, 1862, Lee family papers, VHS.

mac Railroad destroyed from Fredericksburg north to Aquia and he advises Randolph that he is considering its destruction south to Hanover and also the O&A as far as Gordonsville but is reluctant to do so.[21]

November 15, Saturday (Culpeper): Lee relays to Jackson reports from local citizens that Burnside is moving from Warrenton toward Fredericksburg; Stonewall is to pursue, if possible. Lee orders the 61st Virginia and Norfolk Light Artillery Blues to Fredericksburg to reinforce the small force stationed there. He instructs Col. W. B. Ball at Fredericksburg to save the rails from the RF&P, if possible, for use elsewhere, and grudgingly complies with War Department orders to detail men for work as shoemakers with the quartermaster department.[22]

November 16, Sunday (Culpeper): The general and his staff attend church service at St. Stephen's Episcopal Church in Culpeper. Lee orders Col. Ball at Fredericksburg to ascertain if the reports about Burnside moving on Fredericksburg are true, and orders all remaining cavalry and artillery at Staunton to join the ANV.[23]

November 17, Monday (Culpeper): Lee informs President Davis and Secretary of War Randolph that Burnside is evacuating Warrenton possibly for an advance on either Gordonsville or Fredericksburg, but Lee thinks it more likely the Federals will shift south of the James River. By evening Lee is convinced they are moving to Fredericksburg, notifying Richmond and directing Longstreet to send two divisions to that city. He updates G. W. Smith on the troops at Fredericksburg and instructs that troops be sent from Richmond to guard the railroad bridges over the North and South Anna rivers, and informs Jackson that Burnside left Warrenton and Longstreet is moving to Fredericksburg to counter.[24]

November 18, Tuesday (Culpeper): Lee commits to moving the army to Fredericksburg and begins evacuating supplies from Culpeper. He orders Longstreet to move the rest of his corps to Fredericksburg, with Pendleton's artillery to follow. With Burnside descending the Rappahannock, Lee tells Jackson "I do not see what you can effect in the Valley," thus to begin crossing the mountains to Sperryville or Madison. Lee sends detailed tactical instructions to Col. W. B. Ball, who is the senior officer at Fredericksburg, and instructs Rooney to move with his brigade to that point and take command until Longstreet's troops arrive.[25]

---

21 *OR* 19, pt. 2, 717-21; REL to Jackson, Nov. 14, 1862, telegram book, REL HQ papers, VHS; *OR* 21, 1014. Sometime on or about the 14th President Davis's aide, Col. William M. Browne, called on Lee on unknown business from Richmond. Cobb, "Extracts from Letters," 298.

22 REL to Jackson, Nov. 15, 1862, telegram book, REL HQ papers, VHS; *OR* 21, 1012-4. George Randolph resigned as secretary of war effective on this date. He was so disgusted with the constant interference by Davis that he did not remain until his replacement arrived. Gen. Gustavus W. Smith took over as interim secretary of war. Mallory diary, Nov. 15, 1862, UNC.

23 Lee, *Memoirs of WNP*, 232-3; REL to W. B. Ball, Nov. 16, 1862, telegram book, REL HQ papers, VHS; REL to H. B. Davidson, Nov. 16, 1862, telegram book, REL HQ papers, VHS.

24 *OR* 21, 1014-6; REL to W. B. Ball, Nov. 17, 1862 (2 messages), telegram book, REL HQ papers, VHS; REL to G. W. Smith, Nov. 17, 1862 (2 messages), telegram book, REL HQ papers, VHS; REL to Jackson, Nov. 17, 1862, telegram book, REL HQ papers, VHS. Lee addressed today's correspondence to the War Department to Secretary Randolph, who was no longer secretary of war. Smith was the acting secretary, but Lee did not address him as such either by title, or by using the same deferential tone he had used with previous secretaries. Either Lee did not know Randolph was gone, or he did not like the idea of Smith as acting war secretary because that would make Smith Lee's superior. It is likely that Lee simply did not yet know of Randolph's departure and/or Smith's assumption of his duties. On the 18th, however, Lee began sending information that he had previously sent to the secretary of war to Adjutant General Sam Cooper instead of to Smith.

25 *OR* 21, 1018-20; REL to Jackson, Nov. 18, 1862, telegram book, REL HQ papers, VHS; REL to W. B. Ball, Nov. 18, 1862, telegram book, REL HQ papers, VHS. Lee's instructions to Ball about how to defend a river crossing were painfully

Lee informs Gen. Cooper that Federal cavalry is at Falmouth, directly across the Rappahannock from Fredericksburg, but Ball's cavalry prevented them from crossing; several additional units have since joined Ball and Lee is shifting the army in that direction. He also requests that the quartermaster purchase available supplies around Culpeper while elements of Lee's army are still there. Lee informs G. W. Smith that Longstreet is moving to Fredericksburg thus Smith can have back the units there that were detached from his command, and instructs Col. J. R. Chambliss to pursue the Federals with his cavalry. Lee sends one of his horses to be re-shod and writes to Mary, telling her that Mildred should remain in Raleigh rather than attempt to come to Richmond for the holidays, given the uncertainty of enemy movements in North Carolina and Southside Virginia. Cold rain throughout the day.[26]

November 19, Wednesday (Culpeper/Road to Fredericksburg): Lee informs Jackson that he intends to make a stand on the North Anna River and that Longstreet is concentrating at Fredericksburg; he grants Jackson permission to remain in the Valley as long as it serves a purpose and can get out to unite with Longstreet. He informs President Davis that Burnside is moving on Fredericksburg and that Longstreet is shadowing him in that direction, and also encloses several captured Northern newspapers. Lee cautions Rooney not to take a position which endangers the town of Fredericksburg and to warn the inhabitants that a battle may occur there very soon. Lee leaves for Fredericksburg in the evening, accompanied by Rob, who "walked into my camp, so I put him on one of my horses and brought him along." Constant rain and sleet.[27]

November 20, Thursday (Fredericksburg): Lee arrives in Fredericksburg and establishes headquarters near the intersection of Telegraph Road and Mine Road. He meets with Mayor Montgomery Slaughter and several members of the town council at Snowden. He spends much of the rest of the day reconnoitering, and informs President Davis that the entire Army of the Potomac is gathering at Falmouth. Rain all day.[28]

November 21, Friday (Fredericksburg): Lee conducts an early morning reconnaissance, after which he sends word to Jackson that Army of the Potomac is concentrating opposite Fredericksburg. During the afternoon Lee receives a demand from the Federals that Fredericksburg be surrendered by 5:00 p.m. or they will shell the town tomorrow morning. In reply to this demand, Lee informs

---

simplistic, and from the tone of the exchange it is likely Lee had little confidence in Ball's ability to resist a quick dash by the Federals to seize Fredericksburg—thus his decision to send Rooney to take charge.

26 OR 21, 1017-8; REL to G. W. Smith, Nov. 18, 1862, telegram book, REL HQ papers, VHS; REL to J. R. Chambliss, Nov. 18, 1862, telegram book, REL HQ papers, VHS: REL to "Major Duffy," Nov. 18, 1862, REL papers, UVA; REL to Mrs. REL, Nov. 18, 1862, Lee family papers, VHS; Malone, *Diary*, 26. Lee did not specify which horse was re-shod, and the identity of the farrier, addressed only as "Major Duffy," is not known. Charles Venable was in Fredericksburg and witnessed the skirmish between Ball's forces and enemy cavalry. He did not record when Lee sent him, but it must have been on or about the 17th as Venable noted that it was largely based on his report sent to Lee that the ANV was put in motion for Fredericksburg. He also recounted that the enemy shelled his observation point near a house on the river bank and that a shell fragment took off one of his spurs. Venable, "Civil War notes," McDowell-Miller-Warner papers, UVA.

27 OR 21, 1020-2; REL to Rooney, Nov. 19, 1862, telegram book, REL HQ papers, VHS; OR 51, pt. 2, 648; Dowdey, *Wartime Papers*, 343; Krick, *CW Weather*, 74-5. Lee met with Porter Alexander in the morning, but neither recorded the subject of the meeting. EPA to WNP, Nov. 19, 1862, WNP papers, UNC. It is not known if Lee and company rode all during the night to cover the approximately 40 miles to Fredericksburg, or whether they spent the night somewhere along the road; Lee only recorded that they arrived in Fredericksburg the morning of the 20th. Dowdey, *Wartime Papers*, 343.

28 Dowdey, *Wartime Papers*, 343; WNP to "Nan," Nov. 27, 1862, WNP papers, UNC; Silvanus J. Quinn, *The History of the City of Fredericksburg, Virginia* (Richmond, VA, 1908), 85; Dowdey, *Wartime Papers*, 341; Krick, *CW Weather*, 75. The headquarters location was about a quarter of a mile west of the present intersection of Mine Road and Landsdowne Road. Lee W. Sherrill, *The 21st North Carolina Infantry: A Civil War History with a Roster of Officers* (Jefferson, NC, 2015), 482. This area is largely residential now. Snowden was the home of John L. Stansbury. The house still stands on the grounds of Mary Washington Hospital. James R. Mansfield, *A History of Early Spotsylvania* (Orange, VA, 1977), 172-3.

Mayor Slaughter (through Longstreet) to reply that the ANV will not occupy the town or use it "for military purposes" and that the residents of the town will evacuate. Lee informs Adjutant General Cooper that Stonewall will not part with Jubal Early to take command in western Virginia and that the Federals evacuated Manassas.[29] Lee requests that A. P. Hill transfer engineer Capt. Conway Howard to Lee for temporary duty at Fredericksburg. Lee writes to Joe Johnston, very glad that Johnston is recovered and able to take the field again; Lee will have Capt. A. P. Mason and Lt. Col. E. J. Harvie transferred to rejoin him immediately. Rooney and Rob dine with their father at headquarters. Constant rain.[30]

November 22, Saturday (Fredericksburg): Lee spends much of the day watching the evacuation of Fredericksburg. Lee informs Gen. Cooper that nearly if not all of the Army of the Potomac is at Falmouth and that he has reports that the wharves at Aquia are being rebuilt to serve as Burnside's base of supply. He details the demand for the surrender of the city yesterday and that the enemy has not shelled the city as they threatened. He writes to wife Mary with latest family and army news and laments how poorly clad and supplied Rob is, and that Lee gave him a horse since he will now be on Rooney's staff. Of the evacuation of the town, he writes: "I was moving out the women and children all last night and today. It was a piteous sight. But they have brave hearts. What is to become of them God only knows. I pray he may have mercy on them." Very cold but dry.[31]

November 23, Sunday (Fredericksburg): Lee orders Jackson to move east of Blue Ridge Mountains, but leaves his exact position to Stonewall's discretion. Lee requests G. W. Smith to keep alert for any transports in the James River, as Lee fears a portion of Burnside's army may move elsewhere by water. Pendleton and the reserve artillery arrive at Fredericksburg and Lee orders a portion of it downstream to oppose Federal gunboats. Lee writes to Gooch Raily of Charlottesville, advising the young man not to go against the wishes of his parents and join the army.[32]

November 24, Monday (Fredericksburg): Lee receives a letter from his daughter Mary, and writes back lamenting over Annie's death and sorry that he can do nothing for friends and family behind enemy

---

29 REL to Jackson, Nov. 21, 1862, telegram book, REL HQ papers, VHS; Dowdey, *Wartime Papers*, 342; Longstreet, *From Manassas to Appomattox*, 294; *OR* 21, 1026. There are conflicting accounts regarding the demand for the surrender of the town. Lafayette McLaws wrote that he and Longstreet were at Lee's HQ when the demand was received, and that Lee sent both McLaws and Longstreet to relay Lee's reply to Mayor Slaughter. Oeffinger, *A Soldier's General*, 162. This is somewhat echoed by Longstreet's version, except that he omits Lee entirely and suggests that he handled it entirely on his own. *From Manassas to Appomattox*, 293-4. In a letter to Gen. Cooper, Lee wrote that he sent Longstreet to meet with the civil authorities. Dowdey, *Wartime Papers*, 342. Fredericksburg resident Moncure Conway, however, recounted that Lee, accompanied by Longstreet, met with Mayor Slaughter himself at Snowden, the Stansbury mansion, to discuss the surrender demand. Noel G. Harrison, *Fredericksburg Civil War Sites*, vol. 2 (Lynchburg, VA, 1995), 221-2. Conway seems to be confused because Lee's meeting with the mayor at the Stansbury home occurred *before* the surrender demand was received from the Federals; while they likely did discuss surrendering the town, it was not in response to the Federal threat, as Conway wrote. He seems to have condensed two events into one in his account as the three principal officers involved make it clear that Longstreet met with the mayor, not Lee.

30 REL to A. P. Hill, Nov. 21, 1862, Conway Howard papers, VHS; REL to J. E. Johnston, Nov. 21, 1862, J. E. Johnston papers, W&M; Dowdey, *Wartime Papers*, 343. Lee may have been interested in Howard because of his earlier service along the Rappahannock River in 1861. Krick, *Staff Officers in Gray*, 164. Joe Johnston reported for duty on Nov. 12 and was given command in the Western Theater on the 24th. Johnston, *Narrative of Military Operations*, 147, 149. Mason was relieved from duty with the ANV on this date and formally reassigned to Johnston on the 24th. Mason CSR. Harvie was also relieved on the 21st, but the date of his reassignment to Johnston does not appear in the record; he was formally announced as Johnston's inspector on Dec. 4. Harvie, CSR. James Seddon was named as the new secretary of war on this date. Long, *CW Day by Day*, 288.

31 Dowdey, *Wartime Papers*, 341-3.

32 *OR* 21, 1027-8; *OR* 18, 784; Lee, *Memoirs of WNP*, 235; T. M. R. Talcott to WNP, Nov. 23, 1862, WNP papers, UNC; REL to Gooch Raily, Nov. 23, 1862, REL papers, LVA. It appears Raily was underage and very eager to join the army.

lines on the Northern Neck. Maj. Walter Taylor is named assistant adjutant general for the ANV.[33]

November 25, Tuesday (Fredericksburg): Lee advises President Davis that he believes Burnside intends to advance on the capital from Fredericksburg; he states that destroying the railroads south of Fredericksburg will impede the Federal advance but will not be popular with local citizens. He sends Jackson the latest from Fredericksburg and advises that his corps may be needed there. Later in the day, he recommends that Jackson move to Culpeper to threaten Burnside's flank, but if that is not feasible then to come to Fredericksburg. Lee requests that Col. Josiah Gorgas send heavy artillery to Fredericksburg from Richmond. Lee receives a letter from Roger Pryor requesting that the 1st and 61st Virginia be sent him on the Blackwater River; he responds that due to the situation at Fredericksburg he cannot send them, and suggests that Pryor recruit units in southeastern Virginia to use instead.[34]

Lee requests that Gen. Henry Heth be reassigned to the ANV, and recommends breaking up Thomas Drayton's brigade due to it being composed of troops from multiple states and Drayton's unfitness to command. Lee requests clarification from G. W. Smith regarding details for hospital service in Richmond. Rain throughout the day and night.[35]

November 26, Wednesday (Fredericksburg): Lee orders Jackson to move his corps to Fredericksburg and relays his satisfaction to John Imboden for his recent raid into West Virginia. Lee meets with Gen. Pendleton in the morning and jokes that he "hopes Burnside will eat his turkey and plum pudding elsewhere than in Richmond." Lee favorably endorses requests from Jackson for Jubal Early's promotion to major general, and from Stuart for James B. Gordon to be made colonel of the 3rd North Carolina Cavalry.[36] Lee requests clarification from Richmond on how long a soldier must be AWOL before he is considered a deserter. He requests that the Jeff Davis Legion be brought up to strength rather than broken up and denies a request from the officers of the 18th Georgia for the regiment to be transferred to its home state. Light snow, minor accumulation.[37]

November 27, Thursday (Fredericksburg): Lee writes to Jackson that the inclement weather likely precludes a movement down the Valley to threaten

---

33 Fitz Lee, *General Lee*, 234; Jones, *Personal Reminiscences of REL*, 393-4; OR 21, 1028. Daughter Mary spent much of the war with family on the Northern Neck; Lee seldom corresponded with her for fear that their letters may be intercepted. Taylor was previously aide de camp; this change expanded his scope of responsibilities.

34 OR 21, 1028-32; Freeman, *Lee's Dispatches*, 67; John W. H. Porter, *A Record of Events in Norfolk County, Virginia, from April 19th, 1861, to May 10th, 1862* (Portsmouth, VA, 1892), 175-6. Pryor's Brigade was dismantled earlier, leaving him without a command. He requested the 1st and 61st VA regiments be assigned to him, which the War Department ordered in early November. Lee, however pointed out that those regiments already belonged to Kemper's and Mahone's brigades, respectively, and could not be spared from his army. Pryor's letter to Lee demanded to know why those two regiments were not sent him. Lee tactfully dismissed him, for he did not want Pryor serving with his army.

35 OR 20, pt. 2, 425; OR 21, 1029-30; REL to G. W. Smith, Nov. 25, 1862, REL papers, Brock collection; Herbert M. Schiller, ed., *A Captain's War: The Letters and Diaries of William H. S. Burgwyn, 1861-1865* (Shippensburg, PA, 1993), 36. Gen. Heth wrote to the adjutant general on the 21st requesting reassignment to Lee's army, noting: "Gen. Lee has always been my personal friend and I would much like to join him for many reasons." Heth to Sam Cooper, Nov. 21, 1862, Heth CSR. At this time Heth was stationed at Knoxville with little prospects of active campaigning; he was reassigned to Lee on Jan. 17, 1863. OR 20, pt. 2, 499.

36 OR 21, 1033; OR 19, pt. 2, 159; Lee, *Memoirs of WNP*, 235; REL endorsement on T. J. Jackson to REL, Nov. 21, 1862, endorsement book, REL HQ papers, VHS; REL endorsement on J. E. B. Stuart to REL, Nov. 26, 1862, endorsement book, REL HQ papers, VHS. Lee noted in his endorsement that he had previously recommended Early's promotion to the War Department on Oct. 27.

37 REL endorsement on E. F. Paxton to REL, Nov. 18, 1862, endorsement book, REL HQ papers, VHS; REL endorsement on W. M. Stone to REL, Nov. 25, 1862, endorsement book, REL HQ papers, VHS; REL endorsement on W. T. Wofford to REL, Nov.? 1862, endorsement book, REL HQ papers, VHS; Krick, *CW Weather*, 75. Lee noted that the 18th GA was removed from the Texas Brigade as requested, but was placed in Tom Cobb's Georgia brigade.

Burnside's rear, and informs President Davis that Burnside's Army of the Potomac is concentrated between Fredericksburg and Aquia Creek, and a pontoon train reportedly arrived in the enemy camps at Stafford. Lee writes Postmaster General John Reagan regarding the army's difficulties receiving mail at the present time.[38]

November 28, Friday (Fredericksburg): Lee meets with Roger Pryor, who arrives unexpectedly with a letter from the new secretary of war, James Seddon, regarding obtaining a field command with the ANV. Lee, who does not like Pryor or think much of his abilities, explains to him (and reiterates it in a later reply to Seddon) that the only position open is William Taliaferro's brigade, but it would only be temporary until Taliaferro recovers from his wound. Lee once again recommends Pryor for service in southeastern Virginia, and also recommends that several unattached cavalry commands in Sam French's department be formed into a brigade for Pryor.

Lee informs Jackson that based on a personal reconnaissance of the Rappahannock, he thinks Burnside will likely cross somewhere between Fredericksburg and Port Royal, especially since Union gunboats appeared at the latter point. Accordingly Lee wishes Jackson to take position on Longstreet's right toward Port Royal. Lee informs G. W. Smith that the entire Army of the Potomac is massed opposite Fredericksburg and enemy movements in North Carolina are likely feints; he tells Smith that he cannot send troops to every threatened quarter: "We must risk some points in order to have a sufficient force concentrated, with the hope of dealing a successful blow when opportunity favors." Lee reminds Longstreet to ensure that proper guards are posted around his camps, and writes to Ella Campbell regarding a pass through the lines. Lee writes to Custis regarding arrangements for the manumission of the Arlington and White House slaves and also requests that Custis have a vest made for him in Richmond.[39]

November 29, Saturday (Fredericksburg): Lee oversees the arrival and unloading of two 30-lb Parrott rifles sent by rail from Richmond. Jackson arrives at Lee's headquarters in the evening. Lt. Col. Briscoe Baldwin is assigned as chief of ordnance for the ANV. Company A, 39th Virginia Cavalry Battalion, under Capt. Augustus Pifer arrives at the ANV headquarters, the first of the four companies of the headquarters guard to do so.[40]

November 30, Sunday (Fredericksburg): Lee sends to President Davis a recent New York *Herald*, and congratulates Wade Hampton for his raid on the 28th. Lee inquires of Maj. J. H. Richardson his progress in organizing the 39th Virginia Cavalry Battalion.[41]

---

38 OR 21, 1034-6. Lee mentioned to Jackson on the 28th that he "examined the river some 10 or 12 miles down" looking for potential locations where the Federals could lay pontoon bridges. He did not state when he conducted this reconnaissance, but the lack of correspondence on the 27th, coupled with his report to Davis about Burnside having pontoons, makes it very likely that it occurred on the 27th. OR 21, 1037.

39 OR 21, 1036-9; REL to E. C. Campbell, Nov. 28, 1862, REL papers, VHS; Dowdey, *Wartime Papers*, 350-1. Per the terms of his father-in-law's will, all the former Custis slaves were to be freed by Dec. 31, 1862. Despite the war, Lee was determined to meet this obligation.

40 Everson, *Far From Home*, 161; McDonald, *Make Me a Map*, 96; James P. Smith, "With Stonewall Jackson in the Army of Northern Virginia," *SHSP*, vol. 43, 24-5; *OR* 51, pt. 2, 653; *OR* 21, 1039.

41 REL to JD, Nov. 30, 1862, Lee papers, SH; *OR* 21, 15, 1039.

December 1862

December presented Robert E. Lee an enemy on two fronts: Ambrose Burnside's Army of the Potomac directly across the Rappahannock, and fighting with Richmond to keep his army fed and clothed (which proved to be a much slonger and harder contest). In dealing with the former, Lee spent much of his time along his lines or scouting the river. "Gen. Lee visits the works often," wrote an officer in William Mahone's Virginia brigade on December 4, adding that "Generals Lee, Longstreet, Stuart, and Jackson are all in this vicinity."[1]

Much to Lee's surprise, Burnside forced a crossing of the river at Fredericksburg and launched two frontal assaults. One was against the Confederates on the left of the army along the heights behind the town. While the Federals wrecked themselves in wave after futile wave there against Longstreet's men, they found brief success on Jackson's front on the army's right before being driven back there as well. Even though overwhelming Federal superiority in artillery prevented Lee from following up his tactical success with a counterattack, Fredericksburg was his most lopsided victory of the entire war.

After Burnside withdrew across the Rappahannock River, Lee settled into winter quarters. When he first arrived near Fredericksburg in November, he established headquarters just south of the town along Mine Road. Rather than move from his tent into a more substantial dwelling for the winter, he and the staff remained amidst the cold and snow of the central Virginia winter in their tents. "Although there was a vacant house near which he could have occupied," explained Lee's aide Col. Armistead Long,

> [Lee] preferred . . . to remain in camp, thus giving an example of endurance of hardship that might prove useful to his troops. The headquarters did not present a very imposing appearance. It consisted of four or five wall tents and three or four common tents, situated on the edge of an old pine field, and not far from a fine grove of forest trees, from which was obtained an abundant supply of excellent wood, while the branches of the old field pine served to fortify the tents against the cold of winter and to make shelter for the horses. Though outwardly the winter quarters presented rather a dismal aspect, yet within cheerfulness prevailed.[2]

"The head-quarters tents of General Lee," wrote one of Longstreet's officers, echoing Long, "were in the woods, and far from luxurious. He was advised by his physicians to stay in one of the houses nearby, as many of his officers were doing, but he declined to fare any better than his men did. There was no pomp or circumstance about his headquarters, and no sign of the rank of the

---

1 Richard T. Couture, ed., *Charlie's Letters: The Correspondence of Charles E. DeNoon* (Farmville, VA, 1982), 99.

2 *Memoirs of REL*, 240. Walter Taylor commented on the plain nature not just of this HQ camp, but of nearly every HQ Lee established: "The headquarters camp of General Lee was never of such a character as to proclaim its importance. An unpretentious arrangement of five or six army tents, one or two wagons for transporting equipage and personal effects, with no display of bunting, and no parade of sentinels or guards, only a few orderlies, was all there was of it. General Lee persistently refused to occupy a house, and was content with an ordinary wall tent, but little, if any, larger than those about it." Taylor, *General Lee*, 154.

occupant, other than the Confederate flag displayed in front of the tent of Colonel Taylor, the Adjutant-General."³

Lee suffered yet another personal loss with the death of his second grandchild, Rooney's infant daughter.⁴ In a little more than six months Lee had lost his daughter Annie and two grandchildren to illness.

Unlike the previous year in which Lee spent Christmas apart from his family, this season he enjoyed the company of all three of his sons and a fancy holiday dinner hosted by Stonewall Jackson and William Nelson Pendleton at Moss Neck, one of the finest estates along the Rappahannock.⁵

Honoring the wishes of his father-in-law, Lee granted freedom to all the former Custis family slaves just before the end of the year. Although he complied with one of the largest provisions of George W. P. Custis's will, Lee still struggled with how to fulfill the financial obligations left by Custis's estate, especially regarding money left to the Lee daughters.

*   *   *

---

3 Francis W. Dawson, *Reminiscences of Confederate Service 1861-1865* (Baton Rouge, LA, 1993), 87-8.

4 Daughtry, *Gray Cavalier*, 106. The child's health was such that her death probably came as little surprise to Charlotte and the others at Hickory Hill and Richmond; however, it was a shock to both General Lee and the child's father Rooney.

5 Agnes wrote to a friend, "This was indeed a very different Christmas to us all." Agnes to Hattie Powell, Jan.? 1863, Powell family papers, W&M.

December 1862 | 225

December 1, Monday (Fredericksburg): Lee sends Secretary of War James Seddon the number and disposition of the dismounted cavalrymen in Stuart's command, and recommends that the current practice of using cavalry troopers as couriers be discontinued. Instead Lee proposes that officers be allowed to mount several of their own men thus freeing up the detached cavalrymen to return to their regular commands. Lee instructs Col. Josiah Gorgas to send arms for Jackson's men to Guinea's Station.[6]

December 2, Tuesday (Fredericksburg): Lee sends to Richmond two captured enemy cavalry guidons, and complains to Sec. Seddon about the army's shortage of footwear. He advises Jackson that local citizens report a large body of Federals opposite Port Royal, and that President Lincoln met with Gen. Burnside at Aquia yesterday. Lee writes to his wife regarding her recent visit to New Kent and the ruins of White House.[7]

December 3, Wednesday (Fredericksburg): Lee writes Jackson in regard to distribution of artillery in his corps, and encounters Gen. Dorsey Pender, one of A. P. Hill's brigade commanders, during the day and tells him that he is willing to fall back from Fredericksburg if it would draw Burnside into a fight.[8]

December 4, Thursday (Fredericksburg/Guinea Station): Lee informs Seddon that there is much corn in the upper Rappahannock valley that the quartermaster department needs to procure. He meets with Jackson at Fairfield, Stonewall's headquarters at Guinea Station, in the evening. Briscoe Baldwin is formally announced as the army's new chief of ordnance.[9]

December 5, Friday (Fredericksburg): Lee congratulates Stuart, R. L. T. Beale, and John Pelham for their attack on enemy gunboats at Leeds Ferry and forwards Fitz Lee's report of the engagement to the War Department. Lee clarifies for Sec. Seddon his earlier message regarding dismounted cavalry, explaining that until the men are able to provide a horse they should be attached temporarily to infantry commands. He also requests that in order to improve the artillery arm, all 6-lb guns should be melted down and recast as 12-lb. Napoleons. Lee informs Sec. Seddon, John Imboden, and "Grumble" Jones that the enemy is reported moving on Martinsburg and Winchester and suggests that Imboden and Jones work together in opposing them. Snow with periods of hail.[10]

December 6, Saturday (Fredericksburg): Lee meets with Jackson regarding Burnside's intentions. Lee informs President Davis that the Federals are still opposite Fredericksburg but show no inclination to move, which may indicate operations elsewhere although Lee has no reports of troops leaving the Army of the Potomac. Despite the lack of Federal movements Lee requests that troops be transferred to his army from quiet departments. He tells G. W. Smith that he does not think the enemy will move against Smith but as he is not there he cannot be certain; in any case Lee is not willing to

---

6 OR 21, 1040-1; REL to Gorgas, Dec. 1, 1862, telegram book, REL HQ papers, VHS.

7 OR 21, 15, 1041; Dowdey, *Wartime Papers*, 351; Fitz Lee, *General Lee*, 234. The flags were captured by Wade Hampton's men on the 28th; Lee received them from Stuart on/about Nov. 29. OR 21, 15-6.

8 OR 21, 1043-4; William W. Hassler, ed., *One of Lee's Best Men: The Civil War Letters of General William Dorsey Pender* (Chapel Hill, NC, 1999), 191. Lee had not intended to fight at Fredericksburg, planning instead to fight along the North Anna River; Burnside's delays however gave him time to concentrate at Fredericksburg.

9 REL to J. A. Seddon, Dec. 4, 1862, telegram book, REL HQ papers, VHS; McDonald, *Make Me a Map*, 97; OR 21, 1046. Fairfield was the home of Thomas C. Chandler. Stonewall Jackson would die in an outbuilding at Fairfield following his wounding and the amputation of his arm in early May 1863 at Chancellorsville. Lee was supposed to review Ransom's Brigade today, but did not for reasons today unknown. Schiller, *A Captain's War*, 37-9.

10 OR 21, 28, 38, 1046-51; REL to W. E. Jones, Dec. 5, 1862, telegram book, REL HQ papers, VHS; Dowdey, *Wartime Papers*, 353; McDonald, *Make Me a Map*, 97. An officer in the 21st Virginia recalled today as "one of the most disagreeable days I ever experienced. From early morning till about 3:00 p.m. rain fell rapidly. Then a mixture of rain, hail, and snow." A. D. Kelly to brother, Dec. 7, 1862, Williamson Kelly papers, Duke.

leave the Rappahannock River without dealing with Burnside. Rooney's infant daughter dies. Extremely cold.[11]

December 7, Sunday (Fredericksburg): Lee complains to Sec. Seddon about issues in getting supplies from Richmond via the RF&P: "There is difficulty in getting supplies from Richmond by Railroad. Unless its management is more energetic, I cannot keep the army in its position. Every little obstacle seems able to arrest transportation. Better stop passenger train than arrest supplies of army." Lee requests more details from G. W. Smith regarding enemy transports arriving at Norfolk. Lee writes to his wife bragging of Rooney's recent exploits and tells her of his decision to free the family slaves at the end of the year, but complains about Perry's relative uselessness. The funeral for Rooney's daughter Charlotte is held at St. Paul's Church in Richmond, and she is buried next to her brother at Shockoe Hill Cemetery. Extreme cold continues.[12]

December 8, Monday (Fredericksburg): Lee informs President Davis of a report of an army being built up in New York City to be commanded by Nathaniel Banks rumored to be bound for Texas; Lee doubts that is its destination and again voices his fears that Richmond could be taken in reverse from North Carolina. He reiterates to President Davis his supply problems with the RF&P. Lee instructs Gen. Imboden to cooperate with William "Grumble" Jones, now in command in the Valley, and advises of the availability of forage along the eastern side of the Blue Ridge.[13]

December 9, Tuesday (Fredericksburg): The general finally receives word from his son Rooney about the death of his granddaughter, infant Charlotte.[14]

December 10, Wednesday (Fredericksburg): Maj. J. Horace Lacy of G. W. Smith's staff delivers several messages to Lee and dines with the general at army headquarters: "He kindly invited me to remain as his guest at his headquarters," related Maj. Lacy. "I felt highly honored by the invitation, but the experience of one meal was enough. Rye coffee, heavy biscuits, and poor, tough beef I thought would hardly compensate for the honor of dining with the commander-in-chief." Lee sends his condolences to daughter-in-law Charlotte over the death of her second child. A recruitment ad for the 39th Virginia Cavalry Battalion is published in the Richmond *Dispatch*.[15]

---

11 McDonald, *Make Me a Map*, 97; OR 21, 1049-52; Daughtry, *Gray Cavalier*, 106; Krick, *CW Weather*, 78. Visiting British journalist Francis Lawley witnessed several of Lee's staff fall victim to the general's sense of humor today. As they huddled around a fire in a vain attempt to warm themselves in the morning, one of the aides expressed a desire for a drink, prompting Lee to bring out a jug from his tent and offer it to the young officers "with a twinkle in the old soldier's eye, and a lurking smile upon his mouth." To their chagrin, they soon discovered the contents to be buttermilk. Gallagher, *Lee the Soldier*, 84.

12 REL to Seddon, Dec. 7, 1862, telegram book, REL HQ papers, VHS; REL to G. W. Smith, Dec. 7, 1862, telegram book, REL HQ papers, VHS; Dowdey, *Wartime Papers*, 353-5; Daughtry, *Gray Cavalier*, 106; Krick, *CW Weather*, 78. The superintendent of the RF&P, Samuel Ruth, was a Union sympathizer and a Union informant. Ruth was intentionally slow in making repairs and shipping supplies to Lee's army and was arrested in early 1865 for treason. C. Coleman McGehee, "I've Been Working on the Railroad: The Saga of the Richmond, Fredericksburg and Potomac Railroad Company," Master's Thesis, University of Richmond, 1992, 15-6; Meriwether Stuart, "Samuel Ruth and General R. E. Lee: Disloyalty and the Line to Fredericksburg, 1862-1863," *VMHB* (Jan. 1963), vol. 71, no. 1, pt. 1, 75-7. In his letter to Mary, Lee mentioned that Walter Taylor visited her several days prior; none of Taylor's letters from this period survive, so the details are unknown. Dowdey, *Wartime Papers*, 353-5. Neither Lee nor Rooney attended the funeral and it is almost certain that neither knew at this time of the child's death.

13 OR 21, 1052-4.

14 Jones, *Personal Reminiscences of REL*, 396; Dowdey, *Wartime Papers*, 357. Jed Hotchkiss spent the day mapping the road from Jackson's HQ to Lee's HQ. McDonald, *Make Me a Map*, 98.

15 J. Horace Lacy, "Lee at Fredericksburg," *Century Magazine* (Aug. 1886), 605; Dowdey, *Wartime Papers*, 357; Richmond *Daily Dispatch*, Dec. 19, 1862. Lacy was the owner of both Ellwood and Chatham estates near Fredericksburg, and the brother of Jackson's aide Beverly Tucker Lacy. Chatham served as headquarters for various Union officers during the war

December 11, Thursday (Fredericksburg): Around 5:00 a.m. Federal artillery opens fire from Stafford Heights, providing covering fire for engineers constructing pontoon bridges across the Rappahannock. This fire draws the attention of Lee, who joins Longstreet, Jackson, Stuart, McLaws, and several other generals atop Telegraph Hill but fog obscures their view of the action along the riverfront. Once the fog lifts Lee instructs Pendleton to bring the Parrott rifles recently sent up from Richmond to be placed in position to fire on the bridges. Maj. Lacy joins the officers atop the hill and requests permission to have the artillery shell his home, Chatham, the center of much Federal activity. Lee refuses and pulls Lacy aside and tells him of happier times at the estate, including courting Mary there years before.[16]

Later in the day he advises Sec. Seddon and Gen. Cooper that the Federals laid several bridges across the river and their artillery destroyed much of the town in the process of driving McLaws's troops out. The Federals now occupy Fredericksburg itself, but Lee's army holds the hills in rear of the town. In the evening he writes to Mary, returning an unneeded horse bit, and telling her of the day's action and the destruction of much of the town.[17]

December 12, Friday (Fredericksburg): Lee returns to his vantage point on Telegraph Hill in the morning, and spends much of the day riding along his lines. Around noon, Stuart's aide von Borcke takes Lee and Jackson to a point very close to enemy lines where they observe Union forces opposite Jackson's lines. They are joined by Stuart and conclude that this movement is not a feint, and that the enemy is massing for an attack. Lee advises Richmond that Burnside's troops have crossed to the south bank of the Rappahannock, covered by their guns on Stafford Heights, and that they are burning many of the structures in Fredericksburg. He also informs G. W. Smith of the situation along the Rappahannock and that if Wilmington is threatened, Smith will have to shift troops from South Carolina or Raleigh to confront it.[18]

December 13, Saturday (Fredericksburg): Lee rises early and goes to Telegraph Hill, where early morning fog obscures his view of the enemy. He eats breakfast at Braehead near the base of the hill. Lee telegraphs Wade Hampton at Culpeper (probably after breakfast) that an enemy force is reported to be moving from Harpers Ferry toward Leesburg, after which Lee rides the length of the line accompanied by at least Jackson and Stuart.[19]

By 10:00 a.m., with Union troops beginning the attack against Jackson's front, Lee is back at Telegraph Hill, joined there by Gens. Longstreet, McLaws, George Pickett, and Robert Ransom. The group of officers

---

and was visited at least once by President Lincoln. After being wounded at Chancellorsville, Stonewall Jackson was taken to Ellwood, where his arm was amputated and buried. Both mansions are owned by the NPS, with Chatham serving as the headquarters for the Fredericksburg & Spotsylvania National Military Park.

16 Blackford, *War Years with Stuart*, 189; McClellan, *Campaigns of Stuart's Cavalry*, 191; Schiller, *Captain's War*, 40; OR 21, 1058; Lacy, "Lee at Fredericksburg," 606. Maj. Talcott recalled that as Lee rode toward the heights, they passed a poorly located artillery battery that had been ordered to unlimber there by Robert Chilton. Lee did not disguise his anger at this, remarking, "Colonel Chilton takes a lot upon himself." Freeman, *Lee*, vol. 2, 443. The heights from which Lee observed the action subsequently became known as "Lee's Hill," but are referred to here in this text as "Telegraph Hill." It is preserved as part of Fredericksburg & Spotsylvania NMP.

17 OR 21, 545; Dowdey, *Wartime Papers*, 357-8. John Esten Cooke, one of Stuart's staff, wrote that when the Federal guns opened on the city, Lee remarked, "It is delightful to them to destroy innocent people, without being hurt themselves. *It just suits them* [emphasis in the original]." Charleston *Mercury*, Dec. 29, 1862.

18 McDonald, *Make Me a Map*, 99; McClellan, *Campaigns of Stuart's Cavalry*, 192; Von Borcke, *Memoirs*, 303; OR 21, 545, 1060.

19 Freeman, *Lee*, vol. 2, 451; Harrison, *Fredericksburg CW Sites*, vol. 2, 231; REL to Wade Hampton, Dec. 13, telegram book, REL HQ papers, VHS; Wayland F. Dunaway, *Reminiscences of a Rebel* (Baltimore, MD, 1996), 55-6; Freeman, *Lee*, vol. 2, 455. Braehead was the home of the Howison family; the house is currently a bed & breakfast. Jackson appeared wearing a new uniform and kepi, which was in marked contrast to his usual careworn appearance. This proved a source of amusement to those present, particularly Stuart. Sorrel, *Recollections*, 140. A soldier in Jubal Early's brigade recalled seeing Lee and Jackson together "early in the morning" in the vicinity of Prospect Hill. Samuel D. Buck, *With the Old Confeds: Actual Experiences of a Captain in the Line* (Staunton, VA, 2007), 73.

come under occasional enemy artillery fire, with one shell striking dangerously close to Lee but failing to explode. The general has another scare when a Parrott siege rifle explodes close by, but no one is wounded by the blast.[20]

Early in the afternoon Burnside begins launching waves of infantry attacks against Lee's left on Marye's Heights. Longstreet's troops and artillery have no trouble defeating each attempt. The bloody effort finally ends early on that the cold evening.

That evening Lee's senior generals gather at headquarters; Hood—and probably others—think that Burnside will not attack tomorrow, but Lee disagrees and orders ammunition brought up from the supply depot at Guinea Station to be ready to renew the fight in the morning. Lee sends Longstreet's aide Moxley Sorrel to Burnside to request that the Federals provide burial details for their own casualties.[21]

Lee sends word to Richmond of today's victory, but adds that he expects the fighting to be renewed tomorrow and mentions a raid by Wade Hampton yesterday. He requests the War Department not to send anyone to his army except those personnel attached to it, that "all others are hindrances." He again advises Cooper and G. W. Smith that he cannot provide troops to reinforce Wilmington, that troops must be drawn from Charleston or elsewhere in North Carolina.[22]

December 14, Sunday (Fredericksburg): Lee rides along his line early in the morning to inspect entrenchments dug over night. Around midday Lee, Jackson, Stuart, and Hood ride to Prospect Hill to observe the Federals in that sector but find them doing nothing more than removing wounded and burying their dead. Lee requests that additional ammunition be sent from Richmond without delay, and that all available troops be drawn from the Carolinas to reinforce him. During the evening he sends a preliminary report of the battle to Sec. Seddon. Rain early in the morning and the Northern Lights are visible during the night.[23]

December 15, Monday (Fredericksburg): Lee informs Sec. Seddon that the Federals are collecting their dead and wounded and exhibit no intent to advance, and he notifies Georgia Governor Brown of the death of Gen. Thomas R. R. Cobb. Heavy rain during the night.[24]

December 16, Tuesday (Fredericksburg): In the morning Lee, Jackson, and D. H. Hill go to the vicinity of Hamilton's Crossing to observe in response to a report that the Federals are gone. Lee informs Sec. Seddon that Burnside withdrew his army back across the Rappahannock during the night, and the Confederates again occupy Fredericksburg. He fears that the Federals are likely headed down river to attempt a crossing downriver, so he sends Jackson to Port Royal to block such a move. He advises Wade Hampton at Culpeper of Burnside's retreat and instructs him to keep alert for any signs of movement by the Army of the Potomac. Lee

---

20 Harrison, *Fredericksburg CW Sites*, 154; Robert Ransom, "Ransom's Division at Fredericksburg," *B&L*, vol. 3, 94; Dawson, *Reminiscences*, 192; Longstreet, *From Manassas to Appomattox*, 312; Taylor, *General Lee*, 151. Observing Stuart's horse artillery under 25-year-old Maj. John Pelham on the right flank, Lee reportedly remarked, "It is glorious to see such courage in one so young." Freeman, *Lee*, vol. 2, 456-7. Another of Lee's oft-quoted lines comes from this time: "It is well that war is so terrible, we should grow too fond of it." Thomas, *REL*, 271; John E. Cooke, *A Life of General Robert E. Lee* (New York, 1871), 184. Longstreet's ordnance officer, Capt. Francis Dawson, was among the staff officers atop Telegraph Hill with the generals. He recorded enemy fire striking around them, with one shell wounding three officers standing with him. Dawson, *Reminiscences*, 85.

21 Hood, *Advance and Retreat*, 50; Jones, *Personal Reminiscences of REL*, 155; Sorrel, *Recollections*, 145-7.

22 *OR* 21, 546, 689, 1061; REL to Seddon, Dec. 13, 1862 (2 messages), telegram book, REL HQ papers, VHS; Dowdey, *Wartime Papers*, 360; REL to G. W. Smith, Dec. 13, 1862, telegram book, REL HQ papers, VHS.

23 Freeman, *Lee*, vol. 2, 468; Hood, *Advance and Retreat*, 50-1; Tom Kelley, ed., *The Personal Memoirs of Jonathan Thomas Scharf of the First Maryland Artillery* (Baltimore, MD, 1992), 55; *OR* 21, 546-8; Krick, *CW Weather*, 78. Charles Venable had a near miss today, but he did not state where on the field it happened: "While investigating the Yanks with my glass, a sharp shooter took a deliberate crack at me, missing my head by a very slight distance." CSV to wife, Dec. 22, 1862, Charles S. Venable papers, UNC.

24 *OR* 21, 548; REL to Brown, Dec. 15, 1862, REL papers, UGA; Krick, *CW Weather*, 78.

writes to Mary expressing his sorrow over the death of Rooney and Charlotte's baby, and giving some details on the recent battle. He mentions as well his plans for the family slaves, and that he saw Fitz Lee this morning. Rain during the morning.[25]

December 17, Wednesday (Fredericksburg): Snow during the evening.[26]

December 18, Thursday (Fredericksburg): Lee offers Wade Hampton command of Gen. Maxcy Gregg's brigade and writes to South Carolina Governor Pickens mourning Gregg's death. The general also sends a letter of condolence to Gen. Howell Cobb for his brother Tom's death on the 13th.[27]

December 19, Friday (Fredericksburg): Lee informs Adjutant General Cooper that until Burnside's intentions become clear, he will not detach any troops from the ANV. He advises Sec. Seddon of a Union raid through Gloucester and King & Queen counties, and his belief that once the enemy forces in North Carolina learn of Burnside's retreat across the Rappahannock they will fall back as well. He also forwards to Seddon information printed in the New York *Times* regarding the destination of a force under Nathaniel Banks. He instructs "Grumble" Jones at Strasburg to join forces with Imboden and defeat the Federals in the lower Valley, and thanks W. H. MacFarland of Richmond for a gift of a fur robe. The general explains to Gen. Burnside that Pvt. J. W. Irwin of the 9th Virginia Cavalry, who was captured behind Union lines and about to be tried as a spy, was simply returning to his home to attempt to acquire a horse and is not a spy.[28]

December 20, Saturday (Fredericksburg): Lee forwards to Richmond Wade Hampton's report of his raid on the Occoquan and also a list of casualties from the recent Fredericksburg fighting. He requests that officers detailed for enrolling duty should be those who are wounded and unfit for field service. He also endorses Col. Edwin G. Lee's resignation, noting that he regrets deeply losing his services, and forwards it to the War Department.[29]

December 21, Sunday (Fredericksburg): The general sends a brief message to Sec. Seddon regarding the results of Wade Hampton's raid. He sends further instructions to Gen. William "Grumble" Jones regarding cooperating with Gen. Imboden in the Valley. Lee receives two letters from wife Mary and writes back,

---

25 Pulaski Cowper, ed., *Extracts of Letters of Major General Bryan Grimes to his Wife* (Raleigh, NC, 1883), 27-8; *OR* 21, 548-9; REL to Wade Hampton, Dec. 16, 1862, telegram book, REL HQ papers, VHS; Dowdey, *Wartime Papers*, 364-5; Schiller, *A Captain's War*, 42.

26 Schiller, *A Captain's War*, 43.

27 *OR* 21, 1067-8. Maxcy Gregg commanded one of A. P. Hill's infantry brigades. Gregg was mortally wounded when Federal troops broke through a swampy area in Hill's line on December 13 and caught his brigade by surprise. A bullet pierced his spine and he lingered in agony for two days. Thomas R. R. Cobb commanded one of McLaws's brigades and was mortally wounded in the Sunken Road on the 13th.

28 *OR* 21, 1068; REL to Seddon, Dec. 19, 1862 (2 messages), telegram book, REL HQ papers, VHS; REL to W. E. Jones, Dec. 19, 1862, telegram book, REL HQ papers, VHS; REL newspaper references, DSF papers, LVA; *OR* 5, Series 2, 98. The telegram to Sec. Seddon regarding the raid on the middle of the Virginia Peninsula was printed in the *OR* under the date Dec. 16; it appears in Lee's telegram book dated the 19th; either date is plausible. *OR* 21, 1063. W. H. MacFarland was president of the Farmers Bank of Virginia, secretary of the American Colonization Society, member of the Confederate Congress, and trustee of Hollywood Cemetery in Richmond. He briefly owned James Madison's home Montpelier, apparently in a failed attempt to move Madison's remains to Hollywood. After the war, MacFarland worked as Jefferson Davis's lawyer.

29 *OR* 21, 691, 1069; E. G. Lee to Sam Cooper, Dec. 18, 1862, E. G. Lee CSR. Col. Lee was forced to resign for health issues; REL commented: "I exceedingly regret the loss to the service of Col Lee, who by his merit has risen to his present position. I first made his military acquaintance at Harpers Ferry at the time of the John Brown raid, where, though a youth, he displayed great gallantry. . . . The service could be benefited if some position could be given him at a camp of instruction or elsewhere where without danger to his health he could perform military duty." REL endorsement on E. G. Lee to Cooper, Dec. 18, 1862, E. G. Lee CSR.

mentioning the miserable living conditions in the field, more details regarding his plans for the family slaves, and a recent visit from his brother, Carter Lee.[30]

December 22, Monday (Fredericksburg): Custis comes to headquarters.[31]

December 23, Tuesday (Fredericksburg/Moss Neck): Lee meets with Jackson at the latter's headquarters at Moss Neck. Lee orders Stuart to cross the river into the Federal rear to determine troop locations and inflict as much damage as possible. Lee asks Seddon if any troops are needed from the ANV for the defense of Richmond.[32]

December 24, Wednesday (Fredericksburg): Lee forwards to the War Department Wade Hampton's report on his latest raid, and relays his congratulations and thanks to the cavalry commander.[33]

December 25, Thursday (Fredericksburg/Moss Neck): Lee writes letters to Mary, Mildred, and Charlotte, all containing Christmas greetings and family news. Rooney and Rob visit in the morning, and Custis is still at headquarters, so Lee is able to have all three of his sons with him today. Lee joins Jackson, Stuart, and Pendleton for Christmas dinner at Moss Neck, consisting of turkey, local oysters, and other "good things." Porter Alexander calls at Lee's headquarters, and Lee gives Alexander's teenage servant Charley a dollar as a Christmas present.[34]

December 26, Friday (Fredericksburg): Lee writes to daughter Agnes, mentioning a horse she would like and hoping her health is improved. He sends a donation of $200 to the Fredericksburg Relief Association.[35]

December 27, Saturday (Fredericksburg): Gens. Lee and Longstreet review Robert Ransom's infantry division during the afternoon.[36]

December 28, Sunday (Fredericksburg): The general sends his condolences to Dr. Orlando Fairfax for the death of his son, Randolph, at Fredericksburg, and thanks Col. Chilton's daughter Laura for the gift of a prayer book.[37]

December 29, Monday (Fredericksburg): Lee focuses on the Shenandoah Valley, placing "Grumble" Jones officially in command there. Jones is instructed to work with Imboden and Gen. Sam Jones in driving the

---

30 OR 21, 694-5; REL to W. E. Jones, Dec. 21, 1862, telegram book, REL HQ papers, VHS; Dowdey, *Wartime Papers*, 378-9. Lee mentioned to Mary that his brother "left this morning," but did not say when he arrived.

31 Yates, *Perfect Gentleman*, 262. The date of Custis's arrival at ANV HQ is not certain, but it appears to be the 22nd. It seems from Lee's letter to Mary on the 21st that Custis was not yet with him; he was there by the 25th and likely several days before that. Custis met with Jeb Stuart and von Borcke on the 21st. Von Borcke, *Memoirs*, 336.

32 McDonald, *Make Me a Map*, 103; OR 21, 1075-6; REL to Seddon, Dec. 23, 1862, telegram book, REL HQ papers, VHS. Lee and Jackson may have discussed Gen. D. H. Hill on this occasion, because Stonewall noted that he and Lee met several times to figure out what assignment the difficult Hill was best suited to hold. Jackson to Isabella Morrison Hill, Jan. 24, 1863, T. J. Jackson papers, VMI. Moss Neck was the home of the Corbin family; the estate is currently privately owned.

33 OR 21, 690, 697.

34 Dowdey, *Wartime Papers*, 379-81; REL to Charlotte, Dec. 25, 1862, G. B. Lee papers, VHS; Douglas, *I Rode with Stonewall*, 204; Mary Anna Jackson, *Memoirs of Stonewall Jackson by his Widow* (Louisville, KY, 1895), 379; Gallagher, *Fighting for the Confederacy*, 187.

35 Dowdey, *Wartime Papers*, 382; REL to R. R. Harrison, Dec. 26, 1862, REL papers, MOC.

36 Schiller, *A Captain's War*, 45. The location of the review is not known. An officer in the 49th NC Inf. recalled of Lee at the review: "As he rode along in front of our lines, regiment after regiment made the air resound with cheers for the noble Confederate Chief. We passed twice in review, once at quick time and once at double-quick." Pearce, *Chambers Diary*, 78-9.

37 Constance C. Harrison, *Recollections Grave and Gay* (New York, 1911), 96-7; REL to Laura Chilton, Dec. 28, 1862, REL papers, MOC. Fairfax served in the Rockbridge Artillery and was a friend of Rob's.

Federals under Gen. Robert Milroy north across the Potomac River. The general recommends to Sec. Seddon that a recently captured officer of the 10th West Virginia "be detained as a hostage" in retaliation for Milroy's poor treatment of civilians in the Valley, and Lee orders that all baggage and supplies belonging to the ANV stored at Staunton be shipped to Fredericksburg. Lee forwards to the War Department a guidon captured by Hampton's men. In accordance with G. W. P. Custis's will, Lee sets free the Custis family slaves.[38]

December 30, Tuesday (Fredericksburg): Lt. Col. Edward Murray joins Lee's staff as assistant inspector general.[39]

December 31, Wednesday (Fredericksburg): Lee complains to the adjutant general that minor matters concerning the ANV have been handled by that office without going through proper channels. Lee issues GO138 congratulating the army for the victory at Fredericksburg. Snow during the evening.[40]

---

38 OR 21, 695, 1079-82; Dowdey, *Wartime Papers*, 3; REL Custis Executor document, Dec. 29, 1862, REL papers, MOC.

39 Krick, *Staff Officers in Gray*, 228. Murray remained on the staff until Dec. 3, 1864. Ibid. The Richmond *Daily Dispatch* published a notice today that Lee contributed $200 to the Fredericksburg Relief Fund. REL newspaper references, DSF papers, LVA.

40 REL to Samuel Cooper, Dec. 31, 1862, telegram book, REL HQ papers, VHS; OR 21, 549-50; Schiller, *A Captain's War*, 46.

January 1863

Robert E. Lee still struggled to keep his Army of Northern Virginia supplied in the weeks and months following the Battle of Fredericksburg. He was forced to disperse his cavalry and artillery to keep the animals fed, and to provide cover for the procurement of much-needed foodstuffs from areas outside the control of his main army. When the commissary general, Lucius Northrop, sent an aide to discuss the army's needs, however, Lee declined to meet with him.[1]

Union movements in North Carolina—both real and rumored—reawakened Lee's concern for the safety of the area south of the James River. So great was Lee's concern that he traveled to Richmond in mid-January to meet with President Davis to discuss the state of affairs there. If there was a silver lining to the unsettled situation in North Carolina, however, it was that Lee was finally able to rid himself of two of his more troublesome subordinates: Gustavus W. Smith and Daniel Harvey Hill.[2] Complaints about Smith's fitness for command began on the Virginia Peninsula and led in part to his removal, and Hill's dissatisfaction with the Virginia army led to his reassignment to command in his native state.

Despite the foul weather, which brought movement of men, animals, and vehicles to nearly a standstill, Ambrose Burnside attempted another offensive that abruptly ended Lee's sojourn in the capital. Lee personally moved upstream of Fredericksburg on at least one occasion to observe for enemy movements. Ultimately it was Mother Nature, rather than the Army of Northern Virginia, that brought about the failure of Burnside's "Mud March." The disastrous effort, coming on the heels of the fiasco that was the Battle of Fredericksburg, also ended Burnside's tenure as the commander of the Army of the Potomac.

* * *

1 OR 21, 751, 1088-90. Lee and Northrop never saw eye-to-eye regarding the army's needs and the government's ability to meet them.

2 G. W. Smith remained on duty in Richmond until February 17, 1863, when he resigned his commission as a major general. He would serve as a volunteer aide to Gen. P. G. T. Beauregard for most of the rest of 1863. After a stint as superintendent of the Etowah Iron Works in Rome, Georgia, from late 1863 until the middle of 1864, he was commissioned major general in the Georgia state militia, where he led troops until the end of the war. G. W. Smith CSR.

January 1863

January 1, Thursday (Fredericksburg): Lee advises Jeb Stuart that Williams Wickham's cavalry is across the Rapidan River and Richard Anderson's division is at Chancellorsville if he needs support; should the enemy appear, Stuart is to strike at them.[3]

January 2, Friday (Fredericksburg): Lee informs Secretary of War James Seddon that he has no reports of transports in the James River or the Chesapeake Bay and that the Army of the Potomac shows no signs of moving. Lee orders a court martial to convene at William Pendleton's camp, beginning tomorrow.[4]

January 3, Saturday (Fredericksburg): Lee tells Sec. Seddon that he does not think the large number of vessels in Hampton Roads indicates a movement by water of Burnside's army, pointing out that it is customary for ships to winter there, and he has no reports indicating any movement by the Army of the Potomac. Lee also orders Robert Ransom's division to North Carolina. Heavy rain in the morning.[5]

January 4, Sunday (Fredericksburg): Lee writes G. W. Smith regarding enemy operations in North Carolina, telling Smith: "Partial encroachments of the enemy we must expect, but they can always be recovered, and any defeat of their large army will reinstate everything." He tells Smith also that Ransom's Division is en route and recommends that Smith go take command in North Carolina himself and to hold Wilmington "at all hazards."[6]

January 5, Monday (Fredericksburg): Lee informs Seddon that no offensive can be undertaken in North Carolina at present but he is willing to send D. H. Hill there, if desired. He adds that he is outnumbered at least two to one and is worried Burnside may detach part of his army to operate south of the James. Lee writes North Carolina Gov. Zebulon Vance regarding the defense of his state and offers up D. H. Hill. He instructs Robert Ransom to go in person to Richmond and report to G. W. Smith. Lee writes Custis regarding paying several of the now-freed slaves, and requests another pair of trousers be sent him, either new ones or to send an old pair of cavalry trousers from his trunk.[7]

January 6, Tuesday (Fredericksburg): Lee advises President Davis of his fears for North Carolina and Southside Virginia and requests permission to send D. H. Hill, who he describes as "suffering greatly in health and seems depressed in spirits," to North Carolina to assist in the defense of that state. Lee advises Seddon that Ransom will arrive in Richmond tonight and that the enemy force at New Bern is not as large as originally feared. Rain during the day.[8]

January 7, Wednesday (Fredericksburg): Lee forwards D. H. Hill's resignation, regretting the loss "of so good and faithful an officer." He also pens a letter of recommendation for Walter Taylor.[9]

January 8, Thursday (Fredericksburg): Lee advises the commissary general that the ANV is drawing its

---

3   REL to J.E.B. Stuart, Jan. 1, 1863, telegram book, REL HQ papers, VHS.

4   REL to Seddon, Jan. 2, 1863, telegram book, REL HQ papers, VHS; GO1, Jan. 2, 1863, EPA papers, UNC.

5   OR 18, 817-8; Freeman, *Lee*, vol. 2, 478-9; McDonald, *Make Me a Map*, 106. Lee's letter to Sec. Seddon mentions the general's understanding that the telegraph between Richmond and the army was not in operation at the present time. OR 18, 817-8. Lee's correspondence with Richmond regarding the transfer of Ransom to North Carolina is misdated Feb. 3 rather than Jan. 3. REL to Samuel Cooper, Feb. 3, 1863, telegram book, REL HQ papers, VHS.

6   OR 18, 818-9.

7   OR 18, 819-20; REL to Z. B. Vance, Jan. 5, 1863, Zebulon Vance papers, State Archives of NC; REL to Robert Ransom, Jan. 5, 1863, telegram book, REL HQ papers, VHS; Dowdey, *Wartime Papers*, 385.

8   Dowdey, *Wartime Papers*, 387-8; OR 18, 825; McDonald, *Make Me a Map*, 106. Davis had just returned from a tour of the Western Theater, where the war was not going well for the Confederacy; Lee's letter was largely "welcome back" in its sentiment. Dowdey, *Wartime Papers*, 387-8.

9   Bridges, *Lee's Maverick General*, 163-4; REL to unknown, Jan. 7, 1863, REL papers, MOC. The circumstances of the recommendation for Taylor are not known.

supplies locally as much as possible, but the mills are overworked thus Lee is obliged to call on Richmond for provisions. Lee writes to Mary and admits he does not know where all the family slaves are: "I wish to emancipate the whole whether on the estates or not. Some may still be in the state though absent from the farms. They are all entitled to their freedom and I wish to give it to them." He mentions also that he saw Rooney and Rob recently.[10]

January 9, Friday (Fredericksburg): Lee meets for several hours with Stuart regarding an attempted crossing by Burnside at Beverly's and Kelly's fords near Culpeper, and advises Richmond of the movement. Because of the enemy activity, Lee declines to meet with James Crenshaw, an aide to Commissary General Lucius Northrop, regarding the acquisition of provisions for the army.[11]

January 10, Saturday (Fredericksburg): Lee, Longstreet, and Stuart review Fitz Lee's brigade. Lee expresses to Seddon concern over the strength of the armies and the ignorance of the politicians and civilians at home regarding the need for able-bodied men in the field; he expresses the hope that the Confederate government can communicate the need for more troops: "Blood will be upon the hands of the thousands of able bodied men who remain at home in safety and ease, while their fellow citizens are bravely confronting the enemy in the field, or enduring with noble fortitude the hardships and privations of the march and camp." Lee advises Imboden to hold prisoners from Milroy's command as hostages rather than exchanging them and instructs "you must endeavor to repress his cruelties as much as possible." Lee also recommends to Seddon that Milroy's troops be held as hostages "for the protection of our people against the outrages which he is purported to be committing," and formally complains to Union General-in-Chief Henry Halleck about Milroy's abuses against civilians in the Valley.[12] Lee favorably endorses Jubal Early's recommendation for Robert Hoke's promotion to brigadier general and approves a medical furlough for Capt. Henry Stiles. Heavy rain throughout most of the day.[13]

January 11, Sunday (Fredericksburg): Lee advises President Davis that he wrote to Union Gen. Halleck regarding Milroy's abuses in the Valley. He writes to Mary describing the review of Fitz's brigade yesterday, and to Custis regarding freeing the remaining slaves as he did not have a complete list of them and he fears he may have forgotten some.[14]

January 12, Monday (Fredericksburg): Lee denies A. P. Hill's request for a court martial regarding his continuing issues with Stonewall Jackson: "I do not think that in every case where an officer is arrested there is a necessity for a trial by court martial, and I consider yours one in which such a proceeding is unnecessary." Lee approves Sam Jones's plans to restore his cavalry to full strength, and denies John Imboden's request to keep absentees from the ANV on the rolls of his partisan command.[15]

---

10 OR 51, pt. 2, 667; REL to Mrs. REL, Jan. 8, 1863, REL papers, LOC.

11 OR 21, 751, 1088-90.

12 Blackford, *Letters from Lee's Army*, 157-8; OR 21, 1085-6; OR 3, Series 3, 10-1. Lee wrote of the review: "Though it was raining, and they had marched fourteen miles, they made a very fine appearance, and for their size presented the finest appearance of any cavalry I have ever seen." Jones, *Life and Letters of REL*, 225-6. One witness recalled that, because of the foul weather, the only audience for the review was Gens. Lee, Longstreet, Stuart, Fitz Lee, a handful of staff officers, and one wagon driver. Blackford, *Letters from Lee's Army*, 158.

13 Early to REL, Dec. 29, 1862, Robert F. Hoke CSR; REL to Samuel Cooper, Jan. 10, 1863, telegram book, REL HQ papers, VHS; Jones, *Life and Letters of REL*, 225-6.

14 Freeman, *Lee's Dispatches*, 70; Jones, *Life and Letters of REL*, 225-6, 285-6. Lee mentioned only Perry being with him at HQ, and Billy being with Custis, and both of them being paid wages; no mention was made of Meredith.

15 OR 19, pt. 2, 732; OR 21, 1088; OR 51, pt. 2, 669-70. A. P. Hill wrote to Lee on the 8th requesting a court martial. Robertson, *Stonewall Jackson*, 679. Lee was steadfastly against allowing men in other units to join Imboden's—or other—

Lee advises Sec. Seddon that the army is running low on live beef and it needs provisions of salt beef. Lee informs Howell Cobb that the Cobb Legion needs additional recruits to turn into one regiment each of infantry and cavalry, and suggests that it may return to Georgia if units can be supplied to take its place. Jefferson Davis informs Lee that Governor Vance would like Lee to come to North Carolina, but Davis stops short of ordering him to go.[16]

January 13, Tuesday (Fredericksburg): Lee tells President Davis that Burnside appears to be getting ready to move but Lee does not yet know in what direction; if the Federals retreat, Lee plans to take the offensive in both the Shenandoah Valley and North Carolina, and he will go to the latter as soon as he can. Lee advises Sec. Seddon that he will draw supplies from the counties along the base of the Blue Ridge if Richmond can supply him with additional wagons. He also tells Seddon that contradictory to rumor, Union General John Dix is in New York not North Carolina, and sends a short congratulatory note to "Grumble" Jones for his recent raid into Hardy County. He also denies a request from Jackson to court martial Gen. William Taliaferro for a spat between him and Gen. Frank Paxton.[17]

January 14, Wednesday (Fredericksburg): Lee forwards "Grumble" Jones's report of his Hardy County operations to Sec. Seddon with an explanation of why Jones was placed in command in the Shenandoah Valley and the conditions facing him in that region. Lee requests that the War Department shift Ransom's Division to the Blackwater River to confront the enemy forces in southeastern Virginia, and orders Gen. D. H. Hill to Richmond in preparation for duty in North Carolina. Union Gen. Halleck writes to Lee explaining that Gen. Milroy is not authorized to act as he has threatened in western Virginia and Halleck will investigate further.[18]

January 15, Thursday (Fredericksburg): Gen. Lee forwards to the War Department a report by "Grumble" Jones illustrating the deficiency of his artillery during his recent operations.[19]

January 16, Friday (Richmond): President Davis and Gen. Lee meet in Richmond regarding the situation in North Carolina. Lee telegraphs Longstreet, in temporary command of the army, to send Pender's and Lane's brigades to Richmond.[20]

January 17, Saturday (Richmond): Lee's discussions with President Davis continue. Lee clarifies for Longstreet that Pender and Lane are only to be sent

---

partisan commands on the grounds that it encouraged desertion and drew men away from the infantry, where they were much needed. *OR* 51, pt. 2, 669-70.

16 *OR* 51, pt. 2, 669; REL to Howell Cobb, Jan. 12, 1863, REL papers, W&L; *OR* 21, 1088. According to Freeman, this was Davis's first letter to Lee since the president's return from his Western Theater tour. *Lee's Dispatches*, 69 n1.

17 *OR* 21, 749, 1091-2; *OR* 51, pt. 2, 670; REL to Seddon, Jan. 13, 1863, telegram book, REL HQ papers, VHS; John G. Paxton, ed., *The Civil War Letters of General Frank "Bull" Paxton, CSA: A Lieutenant of Lee & Jackson* (Hillsboro, TX, 1978), 69-70. Taliaferro opened a sealed communication from Paxton to ANV HQ and returned it to Paxton, who then sought to circumvent Taliaferro in the chain of command; Paxton was a favorite of Jackson's, and Stonewall despised Taliaferro, so he requested a court martial. Taliaferro soon thereafter requested to be reassigned and left the ANV permanently. Paxton, *Letters of Bull Paxton*, 69-70.

18 *OR* 21, 1092-3; *OR* 18, 846-7; *OR* 3, Series 3, 15-6. Noah Andre Trudeau placed Lee in Richmond in conference with President Davis on this date, but does not provide a citation; this date seems too early for his arrival in Richmond, but it is not impossible. Noah A. Trudeau, *Robert E. Lee* (New York, 2009), 94.

19 *OR* 21, 748. Lee's movements on this date are largely unknown; it is possible that he left for Richmond, but there is no direct evidence of this other than his lack of correspondence. Freeman put his arrival in the capital on the 16th, which is supported by the available evidence. Freeman, *Lee*, vol. 2, 479.

20 Jones, *War Clerk's Diary*, vol. 1, 239; REL to Longstreet, Jan. 16, 1863, telegram book, REL HQ papers, VHS. It is not known when Lee arrived in Richmond or where they met. Sec. Seddon was certainly included in the discussions with Davis. The two brigades—both composed of North Carolina troops—were to be sent to NC.

if they are not needed on the Rappahannock to confront Burnside.[21]

January 18, Sunday (Richmond/Fredericksburg): Lee returns to the army and tries to discern Burnside's intentions from the latest scouting reports.[22]

January 19, Monday (Fredericksburg/Banks Ford): Lee's 56th birthday. Lee informs President Davis that he is unable to determine what the Federals are up to from reports so he is going to Banks Ford to observe for himself. He states his belief that the Army of the Potomac has been reinforced so he canceled the movement of Pender and Lane to North Carolina. He also forwards Gen. Halleck's letter of the 14th regarding Gen. Milroy, and informs Sec. Seddon of G. W. Smith's movements around Petersburg. Lee criticizes the condition of Pickett's Division and issues orders announcing the promotions of Jubal Early and Isaac Trimble as well as several brigadiers, and the transfer of several regiments to complete same-state brigades.[23]

January 20, Tuesday (Fredericksburg/Moss Neck): Lee reviews Rooney's brigade near Moss Neck around midday, accompanied by Jackson, Stuart, and A. P. Hill. Lee instructs Stuart to have Fitz and Rooney's brigades ready to move as a movement by Burnside appears imminent and warns Wade Hampton that the Federals appear moving in his direction. Lee advises Imboden that he has written to Gen. Halleck regarding Milroy but cautions that taking revenge against Unionist civilians in the same region will not help. Lee proposes to Seddon that the quartermaster trade surplus sugar to locals for provisions rather than purchasing them outright. Rain throughout the day.[24]

January 21, Wednesday (Fredericksburg): Lee informs President Davis that Burnside is preparing to advance and instructs "Grumble" Jones to drive the enemy from the lower Valley and to follow Milroy if he attempts to join Burnside. He instructs Porter Alexander to turn over all "secret service money in your hands" to Briscoe Baldwin, and thanks Mrs. J. B. Meriwether for a hat she recently sent him. Lee writes a short letter to Mary, mentioning having received several gifts from admirers lately. Rain throughout the day.[25]

January 22, Thursday (Fredericksburg): Lee orders Imboden and the garrison at Staunton to join with Jones's force, and advises Imboden that the 25th and 31st Virginia cannot be spared from the ANV to join him but Lee will put in for his promotion to brigadier when he recruits additional units. Lee requests that the ordnance department hurry preparation of the army's needed gun carriages, and urges the War Department to purchase all grain from counties adjacent to the James River & Kanawha Canal. Lee requests Adjutant General Cooper to order that all officers and men in Richmond without authority return to the army immediately, and complains to the Southern Telegraph Company of a delay in

---

21 Longstreet to REL, Jan. 17, 1863, telegram book, REL HQ papers, VHS; REL to Longstreet, Jan. 17, 1863, telegram book, REL HQ papers, VHS; *OR* 21, 1095. War Department clerk John B. Jones noted in his diary that Lee left Richmond today, but that seems incorrect because he was still away from the army for at least the morning of the 18th. Jones, *War Clerk's Diary*, vol. 1, 239. Longstreet was still in command of the ANV for a portion of the 18th. See *OR* 21, 1095-6.

22 Colt, *Defend the Valley*, 215; *OR* 21, 1096-7. It is possible that Lee attended morning service at St. Paul's Church. Accounts of this trip to Richmond are practically non-existent. Longstreet was still issuing orders as acting commander of the ANV. *OR* 21, 1095-6. One of Charles Marshall's cousins visited ANV HQ in late afternoon and noted that Lee was present at that time. Colt, *Defend the Valley*, 215. Precisely when he returned is not known, but it was almost certainly via the RF&P.

23 *OR* 21, 1096-1100; *OR* 3, Series 3, 18; *OR* 18, 852; REL to Longstreet, Jan. 19, 1863, REL HQ papers, VHS. Lee did not specifically state that he went to Banks Ford, only that he was going to the river to observe enemy activity; Burnside planned to cross at Banks Ford on the 20th, so it seems logical Lee rode to that point.

24 Dozier, *Gunner in Lee's Army*, 167; McDonald, *Make Me a Map*, 110; *OR* 21, 1100-2; Dowdey, *Wartime Papers*, 397. The review took place on the plain between the Moss Neck and Hayfield estates. Dozier, *Gunner in Lee's Army*, 167.

25 *OR* 21, 1103-4; R. H. Chilton to EPA, Jan. 21, 1863, EPA papers, UNC; REL newspaper references, DSF papers, LVA; REL to Mrs. REL, Jan. 21, 1863, Lee family papers, VHS; Dowdey, *Wartime Papers*, 397.

transmission of messages from Culpeper. Rain throughout the day.[26]

January 23, Friday (Fredericksburg): Lee reports to President Davis that Burnside is poised for a move and he has reports of large enemy forces both upstream of Fredericksburg as well as downstream at Port Royal. The general wants all men detached from the ANV returned, and advises that if Milroy's forces leave the Valley, "Grumble" Jones follow and unite with Wade Hampton east of the mountains. Lee also relays a complaint from Robert Ransom about G. W. Smith's fitness to command; Lee, who has already found Smith wanting, wants him replaced with either Edmund Kirby Smith or Arnold Elzey. The general recommends that Capt. Thomas Sharp of the quartermaster department be made superintendent of railroads in order to make rail transportation more efficient, and Lee complains to Davis and Seddon that Commissary General Northrop reduced the army's rations. Constant rain.[27]

January 24, Saturday (Fredericksburg/U.S. Mine Ford): Lee spends the entire day above Fredericksburg observing enemy activity.[28]

January 25, Sunday (Fredericksburg): Lee learns that Burnside is in Washington meeting with President Lincoln.[29]

January 26, Monday (Fredericksburg): Lee informs Sec. Seddon of the difficulty in feeding his Virginia army at present, and that two enemy infantry corps had moved upstream but the weather has likely caused Burnside to cancel his offensive. Lee informs Adjutant General Cooper that he received the requests to submit his official reports of the army's engagements, but explains that enemy movements have kept him too busy to draft them.[30]

January 27, Tuesday (Fredericksburg): Lee instructs "Grumble" Jones to gather whatever provisions he can from counties bordering the Valley, and to send a detached company of Stuart's command at Staunton back to the army. Rain throughout the day, turning to snow.[31]

January 28, Wednesday (Fredericksburg): Heavy snow all day.[32]

January 29, Thursday (Fredericksburg): Lee advises Seddon that the weather has thwarted Burnside's planned offensive around Lee's left flank. The general writes to his wife Mary advising of the miserable weather and Burnside's failed offensive; he mentions his recent trip up to U.S. Mine Ford and the need for Mary and the girls to make as many

---

26 OR 21, 1108-10; REL to Samuel Cooper, Jan. 22, 1863, telegram book, REL HQ papers, VHS; REL to D. W. S. Morris, Jan. 22, 1863, telegram book, REL HQ papers, VHS; Dowdey, *Wartime Papers*, 397.

27 OR 21, 1110-1; OR 18, 856; Krick, *CW Weather*, 82. Sharp was a very talented railroad man and worked for a number of lines in Virginia before the war. He was in charge of the removal of locomotives captured by Stonewall Jackson at Harpers Ferry, and later ran the C.S. Locomotive Shop in Raleigh, NC. See David L. Bright, *Locomotives up the Turnpike: The Civil War Career of Quartermaster Captain Thomas R. Sharp, C.S.A.* (Harrisburg, NC, 2017).

28 Dowdey, *Wartime Papers*, 396. Lee specifically mentioned U.S. Mine Ford, but he may have gone to others as well; he did not give a date for this trip, but the lack of correspondence on this date strongly suggests that it was on this day because he wrote that he was gone "from early breakfast" and "did not get back till late at night." Ibid. This may have been the date that Lee visited the Thornton estate Fall Hill just upstream from Fredericksburg. Robert A. Lancaster, *Historic Virginia Homes and Churches* (Philadelphia, 1915), 307.

29 Dowdey, *Wartime Papers*, 396. Burnside presented President Lincoln with an ultimatum that if several senior commanders—Joseph Hooker and William Franklin among them—were not relieved of their commands, he would resign his command of the army. Lincoln responded by replacing Burnside with Hooker, although he did also remove Franklin and Edwin Sumner. Long, *CW Day by Day*, 315.

30 OR 25, pt. 2, 597-8; OR 21, 1113-4.

31 OR 25, pt. 2, 598; Malone, *Diary*, 29.

32 Malone, *Diary*, 29.

gloves as they can for the army. Snow ends in the morning, up to 10" deep.[33]

January 30, Friday (Fredericksburg): Lee writes to Burnside that two British officials would like a pass through Federal lines. He details Brig. Gen. Micah Jenkins to recruiting duty in South Carolina.[34]

January 31, Saturday (Fredericksburg): Lee forwards to the War Department Lige White's report of his operations in Loudoun County, and informs Brig. Gen. Joseph Kershaw that while he is not in favor of the creation of a "battalion of honor" he will forward the proposal to Richmond if desired.[35]

---

[33] OR 21, 755; Dowdey, *Wartime Papers*, 395-6; Malone, *Diary*, 29. He told his wife Mary, "I have got the snow removed from the top and from around my tent and will be dry in a day or two." Dowdey, *Wartime Papers*, 396.

[34] OR 25, pt. 2, 37, 600. Lee was unaware that Burnside no longer commanded the Army of the Potomac; he was replaced by Hooker on the 25th. Long, *CW Day by Day*, 315. Hooker responded on Feb. 4 that per Lincoln's orders foreign officials could enter Union lines only with a pass issued by the War Department upon request of an official representative of their respective government. OR 25, pt. 2, 44-5.

[35] OR 21, 693; OR 25, pt. 2, 600-1. Lee told Gen. Kershaw he thought the idea, which had been proposed by Capt. George B. Cuthbert, 2nd SC., "would reward a few, and leave many equally brave and equally faithful, unnoticed, and perhaps with a feeling that an improper distinction had been made between themselves and their comrades." Ibid.

The Lee Family

Arlington (above). Lee's family left their home on the Virginia shore of the Potomac overlooking Washington a few weeks after Virginia's secession. Union forces occupied the estate soon thereafter, and eventually turned the grounds into a cemetery. *LOC*

Opposite: Mary (wife). By the time of the war, arthritis had all but crippled Mary Anna Randolph Custis Lee, confining her to a wheelchair. Her nomadic lifestyle during the war caused Lee no small concern. *W&L*

Left: General Lee had only a mustache during the first few months of the war, and did not begin sporting a full beard until his time in the mountains of Western Virginia during the latter half of 1861. *LOC*

Left: Mary (daughter). Of all the Lee daughters, Mary—the oldest—was by far the most stubborn and headstrong. *Arlington*

Below: Annie Lee (daughter) sustained a facial injury with a pair of scissors as a child that left her scarred and blind in one eye. This painting is the only known image. *Arlington*

Above: Mildred (daughter), or "Precious Life" as her father called her, was the youngest of the Lee girls and perhaps the most spoiled. *W&L*

Right: Eleanor Agnes Lee (daughter) was regarded as the prettiest of the Lee girls. She never got over the wartime execution of her beloved Orton Williams. *Arlington*

Left: William Henry Fitzhugh Lee (son), better known as "Rooney," served under his father's command for much of the war and was with Lt. Col. John Washington when he was ambushed and killed. *W&L*

Right: Custis Lee (son), pictured here in a seldom seen postwar image, spent most of the war as an aide to President Jefferson Davis, but he longed for a field command. *W&L*

Left: Robert E. Lee, Jr. (son) seen here in a postwar image, served as an aide to his brother Rooney and narrowly escaped capture himself when enemy cavalry took Rooney from his sickbed at Hickory Hill in Hanover County. *W&L*

The Staff

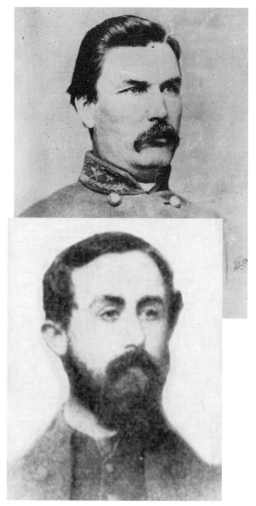

Left: The only known image of Lee's aide, John Augustine Washington III, in Confederate uniform. He connected with Lee on a level better than his other staff. His death pained Lee greatly. *Library of VA*

Below: Armistead Long joined Lee's staff in late 1861 and remained with him through the summer of 1863. His postwar recollections provide deep insight into Lee's inner circle. *LOC*

Above: John Mercer Brooke, in a postwar image, was a noted sailor and scientist before he joined Lee's staff in 1861. He played a prominent role in the conversion of the frigate USS *Merrimack* into the ironclad CSS *Virginia*, and developed a new rifled gun for the Southern Navy that became known as the Brooke Rifle. *Naval History & Heritage Command*

Above: Thomas M. R. Talcott was the son of Lee's mentor and friend, Andrew Talcott. He left the staff for regimental command, but was present with his former chief at the Appomattox surrender. *Photographic History of the Civil War*

Top Left: Walter Herron Taylor attended Virginia Military Institute and worked as a banker in Norfolk before the war. Seen in this previously unpublished image, he served with Lee for nearly the entire war. *Norfolk Public Library*

Top Right: Prewar mathematician Charles S. Venable joined Lee's staff as an aide-de-camp in the spring of 1862 and remained until Appomattox. Some sources claim the general called the native Virginian "Faithful old Venable." *UVA*

Above: Robert S. Garnett served as an aide to Lee at West Point and again in Richmond the first weeks of the war, before taking command in western Virginia. This image is often identified as his cousin, Richard Brooke Garnett. *LOC*

Left: Charles Marshall was present at all of the army's major battles and wrote Lee's after-action reports. He located the Wilmer McLean house for the surrender meeting, and was with Lee when he met with Grant. *Lee's Aide-de-camp*

This composite features General Lee's personal and Army of Northern Virginia staff members. Clockwise, beginning at the top (noon): Walter H. Stevens (chief engineer); Charles Marshall (military secretary); James L. Corley (quartermaster); Briscoe Baldwin (chief of ordnance); Lafayette Guild (medical director); Henry E. Young (judge advocate general); William Nelson Pendleton (chief of artillery); Henry E. Peyton (assistant inspector general); Giles B. Cooke (assistant adjutant general); Walter Herron Taylor (effectively Lee's chief aide-de-camp); A. H. Cole (inspector); Charles Venable (aide-de-camp). With a similar build and white beard, Gen. Pendleton was often mistaken for Lee himself. *W&L*

Politicians, Generals, and Important Places

Top Left: Lee developed a better rapport with Confederate President Jefferson Davis than any other army commander. Lee gained Davis's trust, which earned the general wide latitude in his operations and, until the last few weeks of the war, there was seldom any friction between the two. *LOC*

Above: Like Lee, P. G. T. Beauregard served as an engineer on Winfield Scott's staff in Mexico. Beauregard and Lee worked closely in the war's opening weeks and again in 1864. *NA*

Left: Although one of the Confederacy's most gifted statesmen, Judah Benjamin was an utter failure as head of the War Department. It was his policy of largely ignoring North Carolina in favor of Virginia that was responsible for the loss of the eastern part of that state early in the war. *LOC*

Left: Lee had only a few months to live when he met with his old friend Joe Johnston in Savannah in April 1870. Their friendship dated to their cadet days at West Point. Lee proved far more successful at army command than did Johnston. *LOC*

Right: Despite his lack of military training, John B. Floyd was secretary of war and governor of Virginia before the war. He and Henry Wise despised one another and refused to work together, creating major problems for Lee. *LOC*

Below: A former congressman and governor of Virginia with no military training, Henry Wise was the epitome of a political general and often a thorn in Lee's side. *LOC*

Above: The irascible William Loring was a capable fighter, but difficult to work with. He butted heads with nearly all of his commanding officers including Lee, whom he outranked in the antebellum Army. *NC Museum of History*

Above: The weather seldom cleared enough for Lee to enjoy the breathtaking view from his headquarters on this knoll at Valley Mountain in western Virginia. The almost constant rain and mountainous terrain made getting at the Federals on nearby Cheat Mountain very difficult. *Hunter Lesser*

Above: The remains of the Deitz farm, which was used by both sides during the war as a headquarters and as a hospital. John Floyd made his HQ here in 1861, and Lee joined him here for several days that fall. *Tim McKinney*

Top: The remains of earthworks dug by Lee's men atop Sewell Mountain are still visible today, including these at his headquarters site. *Tim McKinney*

Left: Lee is said to have first seen a horse named Greenbrier standing by this tree near his camp on Sewell Mountain. Several months later, the general purchased the horse and renamed him Traveller. *Hunter Lesser*

Left: Lee and several of his staff witnessed flames sweep across much of Charleston on the evening of December 11, 1861, from the roof of the Mills House, one of the finest hotels in the city. *LOC*

Right: John N. Maffitt provided valuable assistance to Lee with coastal and river fortifications around Savannah while serving as his naval aide in early 1862. He went on to be one of the most successful Confederate privateers. *LOC*

Below: Pennsylvania-born John C. Pemberton replaced Lee as commander of the Department of South Carolina, Georgia, and East Florida, but proved unpopular with officials in Charleston. He served under Lee, albeit much-reduced in rank, during the closing months of the war. *LOC*

Below: Much uncertainty surrounds Lee's visit to his father's grave at Dungeness on Cumberland Island. *Cumberland Island National Seashore*

Left: The Savannah portion of Lee's department was the responsibility of Alexander Lawton, who transferred to the Army of Northern Virginia and was seriously wounded at Sharpsburg. Found wanting, Lee gently rebuffed his effort to return. Lawton did good service behind a desk as quartermaster general for the rest of the war. *LOC*

Right: Gustavus Woodson Smith was one of the earliest major generals in Confederate service. When Joe Johnston fell wounded at Seven Pines, it was Smith who briefly ascended to command of the Army of Northern Virginia. He was unsuited to the task. *LOC*

Below: Lee likely made his headquarters in Savannah in early 1862 at the home of longtime friend Francis Sorrel, father of James Longstreet's aide G. Moxley Sorrel. *LOC*

Above: Mary and the girls moved to White House, Rooney's estate in New Kent County, to avoid the armies in northern Virginia. The war followed them there, forcing them to move again. The house was burned—against orders—by Federal troops. LOC

Above: Students and subordinates alike found Thomas J. "Stonewall" Jackson quite odd and difficult to get along with. Despite his many quirks, he and Lee worked well together and achieved one of the greatest victories of the war at Chancellorsville. LOC

Right: They often differed on matters of strategy and tactics, but Lee's "Old War Horse" James Longstreet was one of his most-trusted lieutenants and a hard fighter on the battlefield. LOC

Above: High Meadow, the home of Catherine and Josiah Dabbs, has been enlarged greatly since the war. Only the right half of the main house existed in 1862 when Lee made his headquarters there. *Author*

Right: Lee said of his cavalry chief James Ewell Brown "Jeb" Stuart, "He never brought me a piece of false information." The flashy Stuart was blamed in many circles for the defeat at Gettysburg. *LOC*

Below: Lee stopped briefly at Selwyn, the home of Walker Hogan, as his army pursued Fitz-John Porter's corps toward Gaines's Mill and Cold Harbor. *Author*

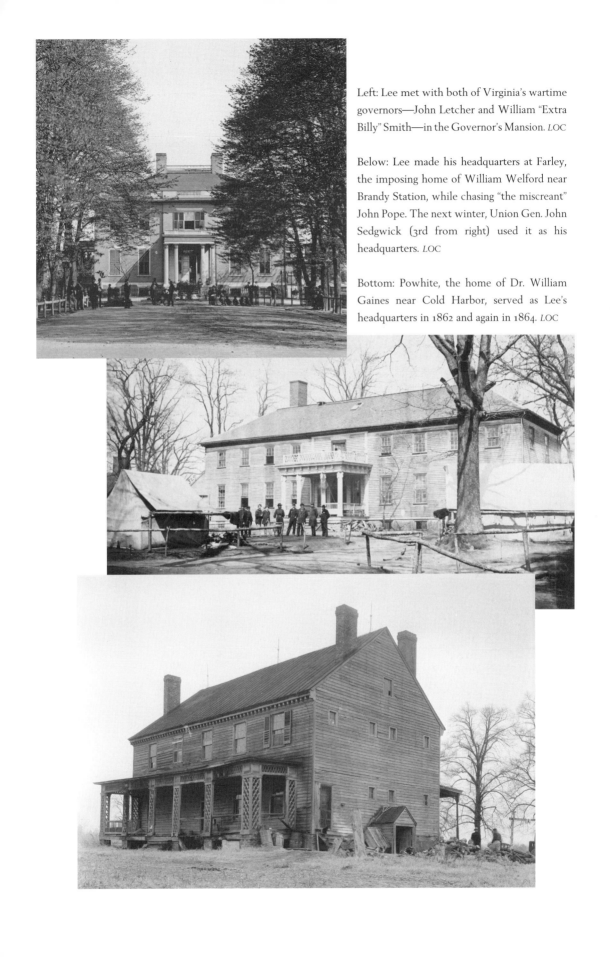

Left: Lee met with both of Virginia's wartime governors—John Letcher and William "Extra Billy" Smith—in the Governor's Mansion. *LOC*

Below: Lee made his headquarters at Farley, the imposing home of William Welford near Brandy Station, while chasing "the miscreant" John Pope. The next winter, Union Gen. John Sedgwick (3rd from right) used it as his headquarters. *LOC*

Bottom: Powhite, the home of Dr. William Gaines near Cold Harbor, served as Lee's headquarters in 1862 and again in 1864. *LOC*

Above: An injured Lee spent several days at Harrison Hall in Leesburg making plans to cross the Potomac and take the war into Maryland and Pennsylvania. *Craig Swain*

Right: On at least three occasions A. P. Hill led the Army of Northern Virginia into a fight prematurely. That same combative nature caused Lee to refer to Hill as one of his best fighters. LOC

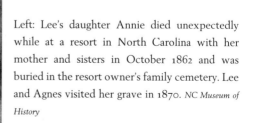

Left: Lee's daughter Annie died unexpectedly while at a resort in North Carolina with her mother and sisters in October 1862 and was buried in the resort owner's family cemetery. Lee and Agnes visited her grave in 1870. *NC Museum of History*

Right: The Brockenbrough Mansion, better known as the "White House of the Confederacy," was President Jefferson Davis's residence. Lee met here with the president, cabinet members, and other officials on many occasions. *LOC*

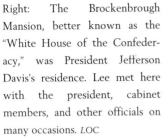

Left: Lee's nephew, Fitzhugh Lee, was one of Jeb Stuart's favorites and rose to command the cavalry corps of the Army of Northern Virginia. Some attributed his rise to his last name rather than great skill on the battlefield. *LOC*

Below: Illness forced Lee to Belvoir, the home of Thomas Yerby, for several weeks in early 1863, where doctor's orders kept him largely confined to his bedroom to rest and recuperate. *Fredericksburg-Spotsylvania National Military Park*

Above: The aptly named Eastern View, which stood in these trees, provided Lee a view of much of Culpeper County. He left his camp in the yard here to go view Stuart's fight at Brandy Station. *Clark Hall*

Left: Idlewild survived heavy fighting in nearby fields during the Fredericksburg Campaign at the Battle of Salem Church and occupation by both sides (including as Lee's headquarters), only to be ravaged by fire in recent years. *Virginia Dept. of Historic Resources*

Above: Lee had breakfast the morning of the Battle of Fredericksburg at Braehead, the home of distant cousin Anne Lee Howison. *Virginia Dept. of Hisstoric Resources*

Above: Clark's Mountain near Orange Court House provided a splendid view of the Federal camps across the Rapidan River in Culpeper County. Lee frequently rode to the signal station here to observe the enemy. *Clark Hall*

Left: Marriage and the loss of his leg at Second Manassas seemed to temper Richard Ewell's fighting spirit. Although he took over Stonewall Jackson's corps, he lacked Jackson's fighting instinct. *LOC*

Below: When Lee left the Shenandoah Valley after Gettysburg, he stopped for a brief rest at Bel Air, the Buck family home in Front Royal. Lucy Buck recalled with pride the general's brief visit. *Shenandoah Valley Battlefields Foundation*

Above Right: Richard Anderson was one of Longstreet's favorites and was a solid fighter at division level. His timely arrival at Spotsylvania was the high point of his stint in corps command. *NA*

Above: When Jefferson Davis visited Lee's army in November 1864, he stayed at Bloomsbury, home of the Jerdone family, very close by Lee's headquarters east of Orange Court House. *Clark Hall*

Below: Five men served as secretary of war in President Davis's cabinet. James A. Seddon held the post the longest, but was unfairly blamed for many of the Confederacy's battlefield losses during the latter half of the war. *NA*

Above: Known as Lee's "bad old man," prewar attorney Jubal Early evolved into one of the Army of Northern Virginia's best tacticians. His irascible personality made him few friends, but Lee trusted him enough by 1864 to take over corps command from an enervated Richard Ewell. *LOC*

Above: Federal skirmishers stumbled upon a surprised Lee, A. P. Hill, Jeb Stuart, and William Pendleton at the Tapp farm in the Wilderness. Later, Lee tried to lead the Texas Brigade in an attack across this field. *Author*

Left: The upper window of Zion Church near Spotsylvania Court House provided an observation post for Lee, and he made his headquarters at the church briefly, as did A. P. Hill and Henry Heth. *Pat Sullivan*

Above: Lee was enjoying a glass of buttermilk on the porch of Ellington, overlooking the North Anna River, when an enemy artillery shell fired from across the river struck the doorframe beside him—but failed to explode. *Hanover County Historical Society*

Above: Weakened by illness and exhausted, Lee moved indoors to the Clarke home, Lockwood, at Atlee. Davis and Beauregard met with him here regarding the threats to Richmond and Petersburg. *Hanover County Historical Society*

Left: Lee's stay in the Beasley house in Petersburg was cut short when a newlywed couple rented it and wanted the headquarters entourage out. Lee probably had his office in a small outbuilding just out of view to the right. *Author*

Below: For the first few months of the siege of Petersburg, Lee made his HQ on the lawn of Violet Bank, as did the Marquis de Lafayette in 1781. *Author*

Top: Walter Taylor begged off from accompanying Lee and Charles Marshall to Wilmer McLean's house at Appomattox Court House to surrender the Army of Northern Virginia on April 9, 1865. *LOC*

Above: This small watercolor by Thomas Conolly of the British Parliament is the only known image of Edge Hill prior to its destruction, where Lee had HQ during the latter stages of the Petersburg siege. *Castletown Foundation*

Right: John B. Gordon was one of only a handful of men with no military experience to rise above brigade command in the Army of Northern Virginia. Lee entrusted him with the attack at Fort Stedman and the breakout attempt at Appomattox. *LOC*

Top Left: John C. Breckinridge proved a capable commander in the Western Theater as well as in Virginia. During his short stint as secretary of war during the last two months of conflict, he met often with Lee and attempted to bring the war to a conclusion. *LOC*

Top Right: Lee and Custis first resided in the townhouse at 707 East Franklin Street in Richmond, seen here ca. 1905; Mary and the girls moved in later. The entire family lived there for a short time after the war ended before moving to Derwent. *LOC*

Left: Five days after returning to Richmond from Appomattox, Lee posed for Matthew Brady on the back porch of his family's residence on Franklin Street with eldest son Custis (left) and longtime aide Walter Taylor (right). *LOC*

From Arlington to Appomattox: A Gallery of Maps

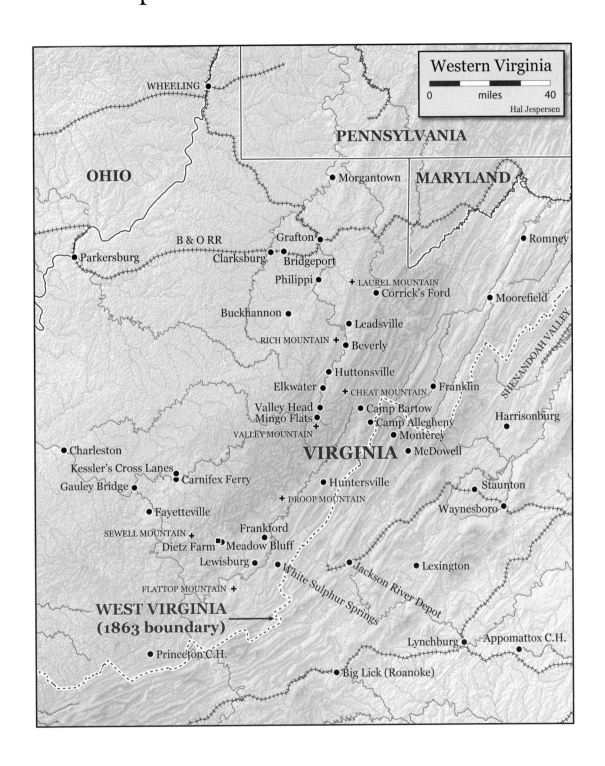

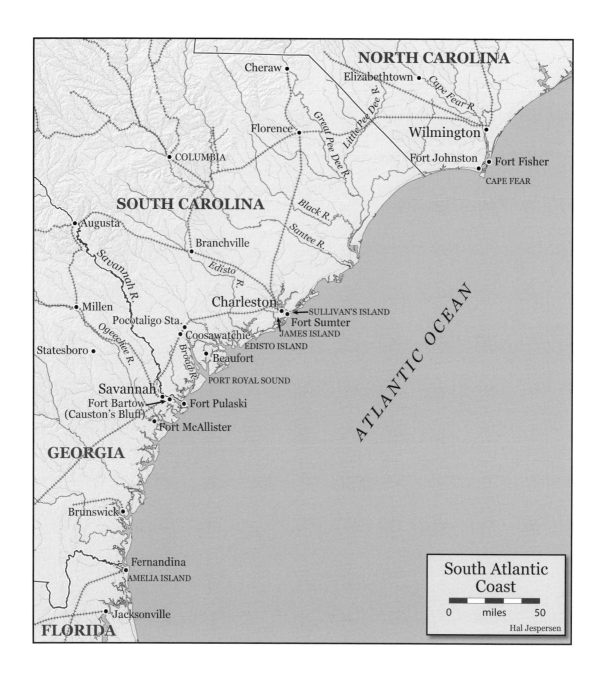

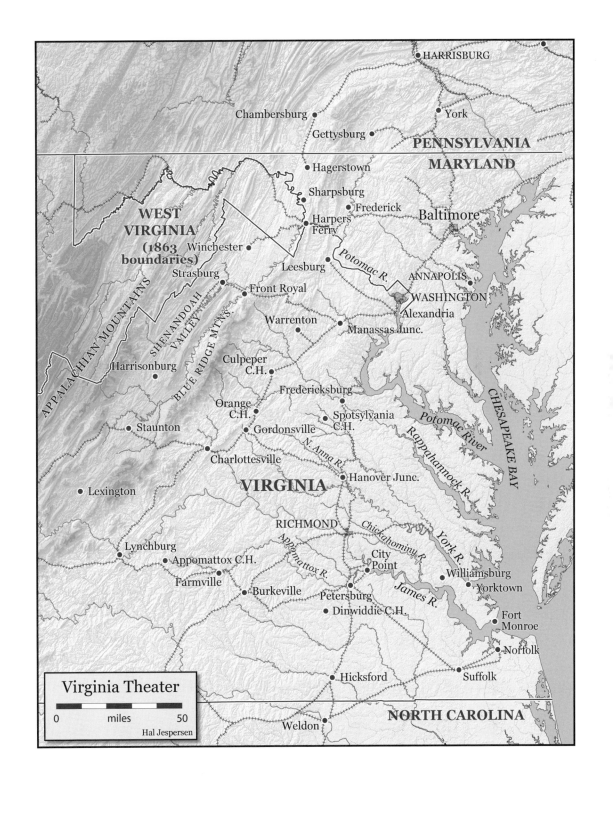

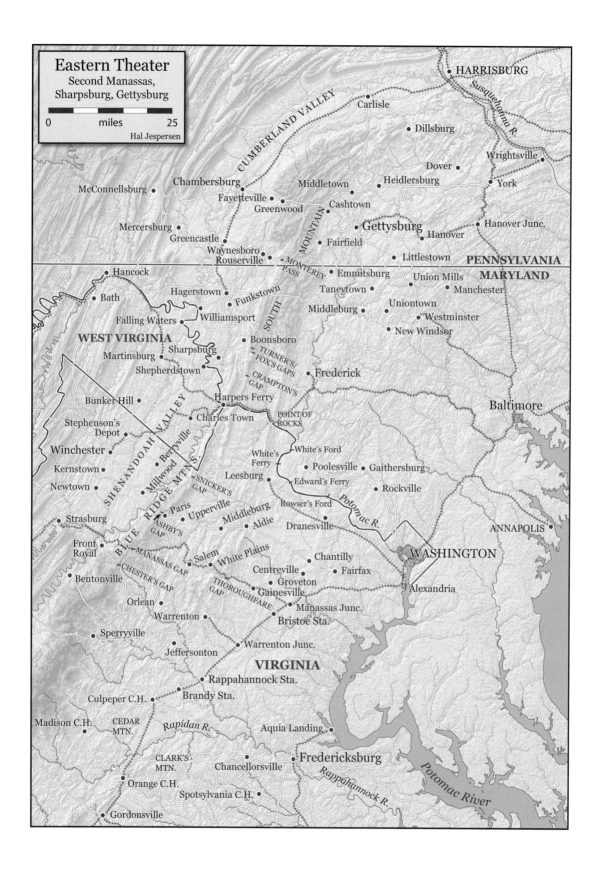

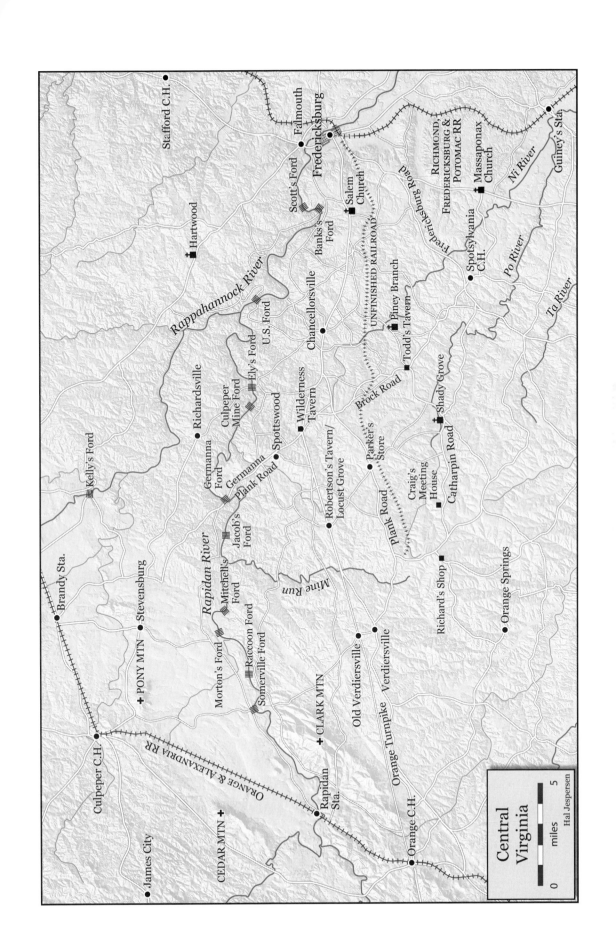

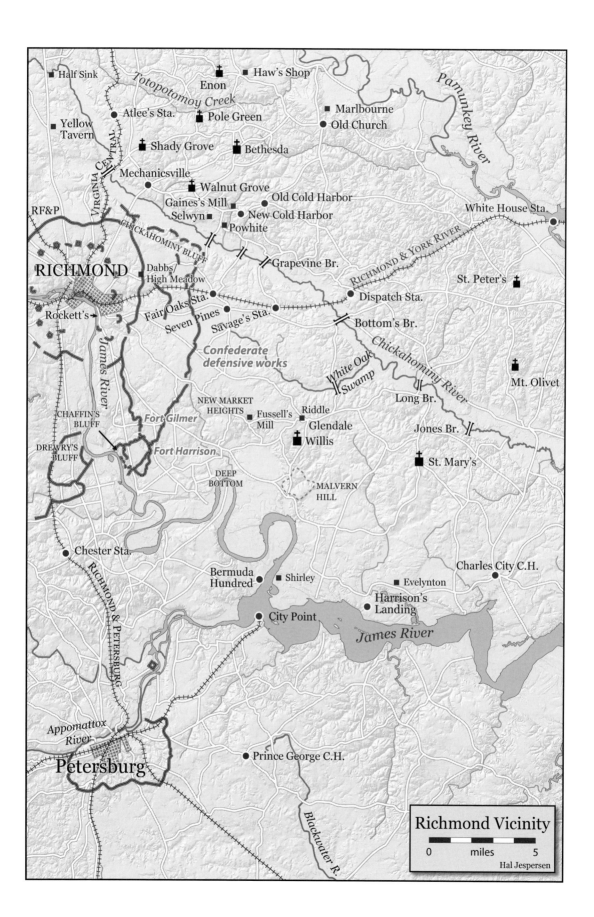

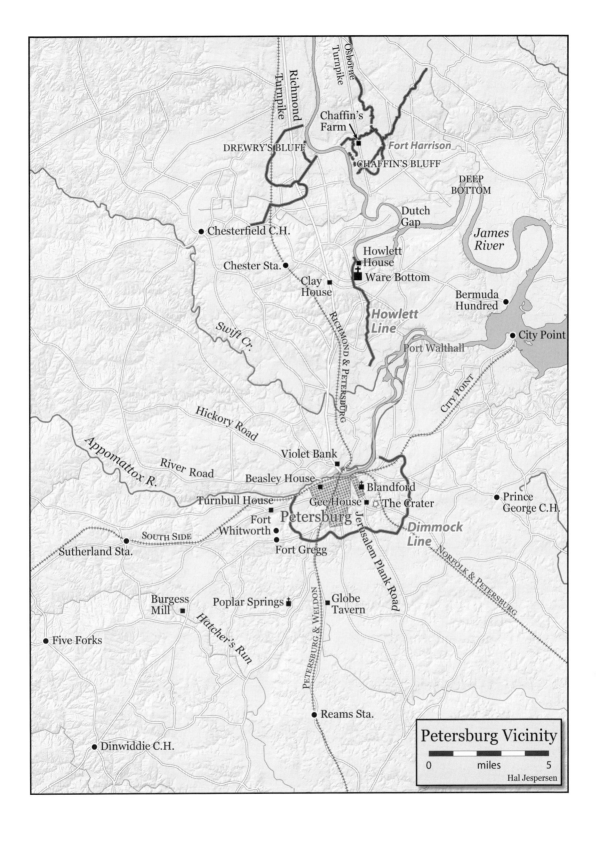

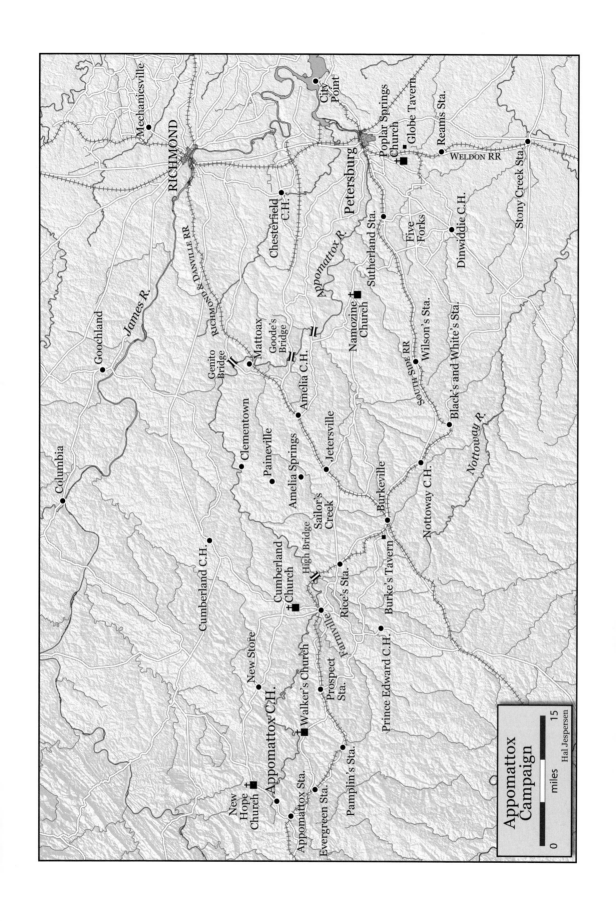

February 1863

Joseph Hooker, the new commander of the Army of the Potomac (or "Mr. F. J. Hooker," as Gen. Lee mockingly referred to him) displayed little inclination to undertake a winter offensive. As a result, Lee and most of the Army of Northern Virginia were finally able to settle into their winter quarters during February.[1] The relative quiet allowed for Lee to complete his campaign reports for the many battles of the previous year, and continue the restructuring of the army's artillery.

Affairs in North Carolina and the Shenandoah Valley, however, continued to trouble Lee. He dispatched a pair of his key subordinates to deal with threats there—Jeb Stuart to the Valley, and James Longstreet to Southside.[2]

Lee's army staff grew by two. Lt. Col. Edward Murray joined as assistant inspector general, and Capt. Henry Young as judge advocate general. Lee added George, a former White House slave, as a camp cook.

* * *

---

1 Dowdey, *Wartime Papers*, 408. Lee's jesting reference was a play on Hooker's nickname "Fighting Joe Hooker," which was mistakenly bestowed upon him by a newspaper during the Peninsula Campaign.

2 *OR* 25, pt. 2, 621-2; *OR* 18, 883-4. The situation in the Shenandoah changed and Stuart ended up not going; Longstreet, however, spent several months at Petersburg and around Suffolk with Hood's and Pickett's divisions on what amounted to a massive forage operation.

February 2, Monday (Fredericksburg): Lee forwards to Secretary of War Seddon a complaint by Congressman Alexander Boteler about Gen. William "Grumble" Jones, and explains the situation facing Jones in the Shenandoah Valley. Lee also makes Jones aware of the complaints against him but affirms his confidence in Jones and his willingness to send a portion of Stuart's cavalry to assist him. Rain in the morning.[3]

February 3, Tuesday (Fredericksburg): Lt. Col. Edward Murray is announced as assistant inspector general. Snow in the morning.[4]

February 4, Wednesday (Fredericksburg): Lee writes to Sec. Seddon again fearing an attack upon either Wilmington or Charleston, but is reluctant to detach troops from his army to either point as Hooker will likely view any weakening of the ANV as an opportunity to advance. Lee also cautions that all telegrams regarding troop movements should be sent in cipher.[5]

February 5, Thursday (Fredericksburg): Lee suggests to President Davis that if Charleston is not attacked troops from there be sent to Wilmington and vice versa, instead of sending troops from Lee's army to either point. Lee approves of "Grumble" Jones's efforts to procure supplies for the army in the Valley and West Virginia and informs Sec. Seddon of the results thus far. Snow all day.[6]

February 6, Friday (Fredericksburg): Lee congratulates John Imboden on his promotion to brigadier general and reminds him that he is to remove all deserters from his ranks and send them to their proper commands. Lee writes to Agnes apologizing for not seeing her when last in Richmond, and complaining about the miserable weather. He mentions receiving a pair of gauntlets recently from cousin Margaret Stuart and is interrupted mid-letter by Maj. Taylor with paperwork. Rain throughout the day.[7]

February 7, Saturday (Fredericksburg): Lee writes to Jackson regarding procuring forage for the animals of his corps and forwards to Stuart a complaint from a resident of Northumberland County regarding his cavalry seizing goods meant for the army, noting that such practices do not encourage those outside the army's lines to bring in supplies for its use. Former White House slave George joins Lee as cook.[8]

February 8, Sunday (Fredericksburg): Lee writes to Mary, mildly admonishing a friend of hers for coming through the lines from Baltimore to visit relatives in the army; Lee fears that they may not be able to return to Maryland and if they do the enemy will lean on them for information. He adds that there is no need for her to continue making gloves, as although the weather is bad they cannot be distributed to the men before spring.[9]

February 9, Monday (Fredericksburg): Lee orders that all cavalrymen detached and serving as couriers at various headquarters are to return to their commands and their places taken by infantrymen who can furnish their own horse. Lee writes to

---

3 OR 25, pt. 2, 604-6; Malone, *Diary*, 29.

4 OR 51, pt. 2, 676; W. P. Cooper diary, Feb. 3, 1863, Cook papers, WVU. Murray was assigned on Dec. 30; it is not known if he did not physically report until later or if there was some other cause for the lengthy delay in his announcement.

5 OR 14, 762-3.

6 OR 14, 766; OR 51, pt. 2, 676-7; Alexander D. Betts, *Experience of a Confederate Chaplain, 1861-1864* (Greenville, SC, n.d.), 27.

7 OR 51, pt. 2, 677; Dowdey, *Wartime Papers*, 400; Betts, *Experience of CS Chaplain*, 27.

8 OR 51, pt. 2, 678-9; OR 25, pt. 2, 608-9; Dowdey, *Wartime Papers*, 402. Lee noted that he paid George and Perry each $8.20 per month. A private in the C.S. Army was paid $11.00 a month at that time.

9 Dowdey, *Wartime Papers*, 401-2.

Custis, enclosing the letter for Mary written yesterday and the pass through the lines for her friend Mrs. Murdock; Lee tells Custis that he fears Hooker is up to something but he doesn't yet know what.[10]

February 10, Tuesday (Fredericksburg): Snow all day.[11]

February 11, Wednesday (Fredericksburg): Lee writes to Sec. Seddon regarding supply difficulties and his suggestions for making it easier to bring supplies up from the Deep South. He also addresses the secretary on the need to increase conscription efforts and to have all absentees and deserters returned to the army. Lee orders Jackson to send a portion of his men "unfit for duty" to Richmond to replace able-bodied men serving in the hospitals there. Snow all day.[12]

February 12, Thursday (Fredericksburg): Gen. Lee writes to his son Custis about the difficulties with bringing the Army of Northern Virginia up to strength: "Every exertion should be made to put the Army . . . on the strongest footing for vigorous work in the spring. Our salvation will depend on the next four months, and yet I cannot even get regular promotions made to fill vacancies in regiments, while Congress seems to be laboring to pass laws to get easy places for some favorites or constituent, or get others out of active service. I shall feel very much obliged to them if they will pass a law relieving me from all duty and legislating someone in my place, better able to do it."[13]

February 13, Friday (Fredericksburg): Lee orders Jeb Stuart to take command in Shenandoah Valley and send detachments from Wade Hampton's and Fitz Lee's brigades for a two-pronged assault against Union Gen. Robert Milroy's forces in the lower (northern) Valley. The general consents to Robert Ransom being given a division in North Carolina.[14]

February 14, Saturday (Fredericksburg): Lee informs Seddon of reports from the Northern Neck of transports loaded with enemy troops passing down the Potomac; Lee thinks they are bound for southeastern Virginia or North Carolina. He orders Pickett's Division to Richmond to counter this threat and holds Hood in readiness to follow if needed. Lee forwards to Gen. Hooker a letter from Mrs. Fannie Scott regarding the fate of her son Benjamin I. Scott of the 18th Virginia, missing since Sharpsburg.[15]

February 15, Sunday (Fredericksburg): Lee tells Stuart that one infantry corps has left Gen. Joe Hooker's Army of the Potomac, and if Stuart finds an opportunity to damage the enemy somewhere east of the Blue Ridge Mountains, he is to do so. The general advises Sec. Seddon that he thinks the enemy is preparing a major offensive against Charleston, South Carolina, and that the troops sent to Fort Monroe at the tip of the Virginia Peninsula are likely part of that, or possibly just a larger garrison; in any case he has no reports of increased activity in North Carolina, but if the Federals do intend to operate south of the James River, "Pickett's division can meet it and beat it wherever it goes." He instructs Gen. Longstreet to have Pickett continue to Richmond and for Hood to start for Hanover

---

10 General Orders, Feb. 9, 1862, REL papers, MOC; Jones, *Life and Letters of REL*, 226. The orders regarding couriers are curious in that the 39th VA Cav. Battalion was formed in part to provide couriers for HQ.

11 Malone, *Diary*, 29.

12 *OR* 25, pt. 2, 612; *OR* 51, pt. 2, 680; Special Orders, Feb. 11, 1863, REL papers, MOC; Malone, *Diary*, 29.

13 Jones, *Life and Letters of REL*, 226.

14 *OR* 25, pt. 2, 621-2; *OR* 18, 875.

15 *OR* 18, 876-7; REL to Joseph Hooker, Feb. 14, 1863, Scott family papers, VHS. Hooker replied on the 16th that he instructed the surgeon general to look for Scott. Hooker to REL, Feb. 16, 1862, Scott family papers, VHS. Scott's CSR notes that he was missing since Sept. 14, 1862, at Boonsboro. He was carried on the company rolls until June 1863, at which time he was dropped with the notation, "presumed killed." Scott CSR.

Junction tomorrow. General Orders 20 unveils the army's new artillery structure. Rain during the day.[16]

February 16, Monday (Fredericksburg): Lee updates President Davis and Secretary of War Randolph on the movements of Pickett and Hood, adding that the condition of the roads and streams prevents any sort of offensive action by the army at present. Rain turning to snow.[17]

February 17, Tuesday (Fredericksburg): Lee orders Longstreet to take command of Pickett and Hood, and advises G. W. Smith in Richmond that they will be passing through his department. Lee informs Seddon that scouts report another Federal corps is moving; Lee is prepared to send the rest of Longstreet's corps to Richmond or elsewhere in response. A mixture of rain, sleet, and snow all day.[18]

February 18, Wednesday (Fredericksburg): Lee provides written orders to Longstreet to accompany Pickett's and Hood's divisions to protect Richmond against any move from Hampton Roads or Suffolk. Lee specifies that Pickett be used to guard Petersburg and if the situation warrants Lee will send the rest of Longstreet's corps. Lee advises President Davis that Hooker is up to something as three corps are rumored to have left the Army of the Potomac. Lee writes to Henry Heth outlining Heth's service under Lee earlier in the war, and informs Mrs. Fannie Scott that he forwarded her letter regarding her son Benjamin Scott through the lines and encloses Hooker's reply. Rain with periods of snow; Lee's tent is flooded out during the night despite trenching around it dug by Perry.[19]

February 19, Thursday (Fredericksburg): Lee solicits input from Longstreet and Jackson regarding promotions in the artillery. Lee receives a letter from Agnes. Rain and snow all day.[20]

February 20, Friday (Fredericksburg): Lee writes to Mrs. Lucy Temple that he is unable to discharge her son from military service as she requested. He writes to Agnes complaining about the weather and giving the latest family news. Rain stops early, sunny for most of the day.[21]

February 21, Saturday (Fredericksburg): Lee goes over the strength of the army with Walter Taylor for several hours, and writes to Sec. Seddon complaining about how details of able-bodied officers and men from his army for government work well behind the lines take a significant toll on the army's strength. Lee suggests again that sick and wounded be put to this work as well as civilians not liable to military service. Eight inches of snow falls during the night and early morning of the 22nd.[22]

February 22, Sunday (Fredericksburg): Lee receives a letter from Agnes. Snow early.[23]

February 23, Monday (Fredericksburg): The general writes to his wife Mary and daughter Agnes, complaining about the weather and giving latest

---

16 OR 25, pt. 2, 623-5; Betts, *Experiences of CS Chaplain*, 27.

17 OR 25, pt. 2, 627; OR 18, 880; Krick, *CW Weather*, 86.

18 Freeman, *Lee*, vol. 2, 483; OR 18, 882; OR 25, pt. 2, 630-1; W. P. Cooper diary, Feb. 17, 1863, Cook papers, WVU.

19 OR 18, 883-4; OR 25, pt. 2, 631-2; REL to Henry Heth, Feb. 18, 1863, Henry Heth papers, MOC; REL to Fannie Scott, Feb. 18, 1863, Scott family papers, VHS; W. P Cooper diary, Feb. 18, 1863, Cook papers, WVU; Dowdey, *Wartime Papers*, 407.

20 Freeman, *Lee's Dispatches*, 74 n1; Dowdey, *Wartime Papers*, 406; W. P. Cooper diary, Feb. 19, 1863, Cook papers, WVU.

21 REL to Lucy Temple, Feb. 20, 1863, REL papers, MOC; Dowdey, *Wartime Papers*, 406-7. The identity of Temple's son is not known.

22 John E. Cooke diary, Feb. 21, 1863, Duke; OR 25, pt. 2, 638-9; Krick, *CW Weather*, 86. Taylor told Cooke he "had been closeted with Gen. Lee for two hours" today. Cooke diary, Duke.

23 William E. Brooks, *Lee of Virginia* (Indianapolis, IN, 1932), 209; Owen, *Washington Artillery*, 205.

family and military news, including the resignation of Gustavus W. Smith.[24]

February 24, Tuesday (Fredericksburg): Lee informs President Davis that he shifted Wade Hampton's brigade across the mountains to Page County due to the scarcity of forage around Culpeper. Lee receives a package from Mary containing a recent sermon by Bishop Stephen Elliott, and he finishes the letter to her he began yesterday. He mentions that "a young French officer" recently arrived but he speaks no English and has no blankets, thus Lee has no idea what to do with him.[25]

February 25, Wednesday (Fredericksburg): Lee sends commissary officer Maj. Raphael Moses to join Longstreet's force in southeast Virginia.[26]

February 26, Thursday (Fredericksburg): Lee advises President Davis of the latest known enemy troop movements and his fears that they will undertake something south of the James and/or in North Carolina, possibly under Ambrose Burnside, as Lee knows the former commander of the Army of the Potomac was given a new command but Lee doesn't know where. He mentions a recent raid by Fitz Lee near Falmouth, and that the weather may impact offensive operations in the spring due to the lack of forage for the animals. He promises to visit Richmond as soon as possible to meet with Davis. Rain.[27]

February 27, Friday (Fredericksburg): Lee addresses complaints from Jackson and his corps artillery chief Col. Stapleton Crutchfield about the number of guns in his corps vs. those allotted to Longstreet and also officers from outside his corps being given positions within it.[28]

February 28, Saturday (Fredericksburg): Lee advises Longstreet that scouts report 20,000 enemy troops from three different corps moved down the Potomac, and updates Sec. Seddon with the latest reports on enemy movements, including the departure of the IX Corps under Burnside. Lee issues a congratulatory order on various cavalry operations during the winter. He writes to Custis complaining about shirkers who avoid military service, requesting a new pair of trousers, and giving the usual updates on the military situation. Capt. Henry E. Young joins the army staff as judge advocate general.[29]

---

24 Dowdey, *Wartime Papers,* 407-8; Brooks, *Lee of Virginia*, 209; G. W. Smith CSR.

25 Freeman, *Lee's Dispatches*, 71-3; Dowdey, *Wartime Papers*, 408.

26 WHT to Longstreet, Feb. 25, 1863, telegram book, REL HQ papers, VHS.

27 OR 25, pt. 2, 642-3.

28 Freeman, *Lee's Dispatches*, 74-5 n1; OR 25 pt. 2, 644-5.

29 OR 18, 898-9; OR 25, pt. 2, 646-7; OR 21, 1114-5; Dowdey, *Wartime Papers*, 410-2; H. E. Young CSR.

March 1863

The foul weather, which shut down Federal operations weeks earlier, continued into March and kept Gen. Lee's men mostly confined to their camps. It also made supplying the army very difficult.[1] Not much is known of Lee's activities during the first half of the month, and even less is known of his trip to Richmond mid-month to meet with President Davis.[2] Enemy movements along the upper Rappahannock River, which resulted in the death of noted artilleryman John Pelham at Kelly's Ford on the 17th, cut short Lee's stay in Richmond and for a time he considered recalling James Longstreet's forces from Suffolk, Virginia.

Rumors that elements of the Army of the Potomac were being sent to the Western Theater as well as to North Carolina plagued Lee's thoughts. Conflicting reports poured into headquarters regarding the locations of different enemy corps, and whenever it seemed Lee had divined the truth, more conflicting reports arrived. Although he was convinced Joe Hooker's army had been reduced by at least one infantry corps and possibly more, Lee worried that if he made any further detachments from his own army, he would be unable to hold the line along the Rappahannock.[3]

During the first half of the month, Lee, Stonewall Jackson, Jeb Stuart, and William Pendleton converged at Hayfield, where the Federals threatened to cross the Rappahannock. After finishing a reconnaissance mission, the generals called on the Taylor family at Hayfield, where they were joined by artillerist John Pelham and a host of other young officers.[4] This was probably the same occasion described by Fannie Lewis Gwathmey, Mrs. Taylor's niece, as follows:

> The first time General Lee came to Hayfield, Bessie and I met him at the door. He asked, 'Are those the little Gwathmey girls?' and we told him we were. He said 'I have two kisses for each of you. Your aunt, Mrs. Caskie, sent them. Are you going to let me give them to you?' We said yes we would be glad for him to kiss us. He gave us two for our aunt and two for himself. General Stuart was standing by with his staff. He said 'General, I don't think it fair for you to get all the kisses. I would like to kiss these little girls too.' I said 'General Stuart, I would love dearly to kiss you but I just can't let anyone take General Lee's kisses off my lips.' His staff bent double laughing. They said, 'Well General this is the first time I ever saw you turned down.' I have always been sorry I didn't kiss him, for I never had another opportunity.[5]

---

1 Krick, *CW Weather*, 89.

2 Around March 5 or 6, Custis went to ANV HQ at the behest of President Davis to discuss with Lee, and presumably Gen. Pendleton and possibly others, the proposed reorganization of the army's artillery. Freeman, *Lee's Dispatches*, 76n1.

3 *OR* 18, 943-4.

4 Smith, "With Stonewall Jackson," 42-3. Hayfield is located near Moss Neck, several miles downstream from Fredericksburg; Lee and Mrs. Taylor were cousins. The mansion was built ca. 1760; it fell into disrepair in the late 20th century but has been restored. It was the boyhood home of actor Judge Reinhold. For more on the history and restoration of the estate see R. W. D. Fenn and J. E. Ellis, *This Very Desirable Estate: The History of Hayfield in Caroline County in the Commonwealth of Virginia* (Bardon Hall, Leicestershire, England, 2007); http://haygenealogy.com/hay/presidents/hayfield.pdf. Lee wrote of this visit on the 24th, but Pelham's presence places it at least a week earlier because Pelham was killed on the 17th at Kelly's Ford. REL to Charles Carter Lee, March 24, 1863, REL papers, UVA.

5 Fannie Lewis Gwathmey Adams, *Reminisces of a Childhood Spent at "Hayfield" Plantation*, Fitzhugh family papers, VHS.

The general continued to receive gifts from admirers, and sometime around March 20 received a pair of gold spurs from "some of his Maryland friends."[6] He had his photograph taken very early in the month, for which he soon began receiving requests.[7]

The constant exposure to the weather took a toll on Lee's health, and by the end of the month he had to be moved indoors to Belvoir and placed under a surgeon's care. It was thought at the time he had pericarditis, as he suffered from chest pains that ranged into his arms and back. It is possible he suffered a heart attack that March. Whatever the specific nature of his ailment, it kept him confined to his room at the Yerby plantation for several weeks.[8]

* * *

---

6 Richmond *Daily Dispatch*, March 20, 1863. These may be the spurs on exhibit at Stratford Hall.

7 REL to Mary, March 6, 1863, REL papers, LOC.

8 Welsh, *Medical Histories*, 134-5. Pericarditis is the swelling and irritation of the thin sac-like membrane surrounding the heart (the pericardium).

March 1, Sunday (Fredericksburg): Lee endorses and forwards Fitz Lee's report of a skirmish at Hartwood Church. Rain in the morning.[9]

March 2, Monday (Fredericksburg): Lee sends President Davis the proposed new artillery organization for the ANV, and informs Adjutant General Cooper that he does not oppose the resignation of Brig. Gen. Robert Toombs.[10]

March 3, Tuesday (Fredericksburg): Lee writes to Custis, giving him the latest on the military situation along the Rappahannock and again requesting another pair of trousers. He also receives a letter from Charlotte and writes back with latest family news. Rain before dawn.[11]

March 4, Wednesday (Fredericksburg): Lee writes to Sec. Seddon acknowledging the instructions to replace "Grumble" Jones as commander in the Shenandoah Valley, but Lee again defends Jones's performance and actions in the Valley. He states that Fitz Lee and his brigade will be sent to the Valley as soon as circumstances permit.[12]

March 5, Thursday (Fredericksburg): Henry Heth joins the ANV and is assigned Charles Field's former brigade in A. P. Hill's division.[13]

March 6, Friday (Fredericksburg): Lee submits his report of the Seven Days' Battles to Gen. Cooper, and requests that chief engineer Jeremy Gilmer provide an engineer for Longstreet in southeast Virginia. He writes wife Mary that he is not well, and fears he may not be physically able to lead the army that spring. He mentions that he recently had his photograph taken and also that George is a much better cook than Meredith although there is little more than ham and coffee to work with.[14]

March 7, Saturday (Fredericksburg): Lee writes to President Davis regarding the reorganization of the

---

9 OR 25, pt. 1, 26; W. P. Cooper diary, March 1, 1863, Cook papers, WVU. Fitz Lee drove Union cavalry from Hartwood Church on Feb. 25 in an effort to locate the main body of the Army of the Potomac.

10 OR 25, pt. 2, 651; REL to Samuel Cooper, March 2, 1863, telegraph book, REL HQ papers, VIIS. The actual telegram to Cooper regarding Toombs's resignation is dated the 3rd, so there must have been some delay between the time it was dictated at HQ to the time it was actually dispatched to Richmond at the telegraph office at Fredericksburg. Toombs CSR. Toombs's resignation was accepted on the 4th. Warner, *Generals in Gray*, 307.

11 Dowdey, *Wartime Papers*, 412; REL to Charlotte, March 3, 1863, G. B. Lee papers, VHS; W. P. Cooper diary, March 3, 1863, Cook papers, WVU.

12 OR 25, pt. 2, 654.

13 OR 25, pt. 2, 654. Heth recalled his arrival at Lee's headquarters: "When I reported to General Lee, there were quite a number of officers near his tent. On the opposite side of the Rappahannock some military display was going on, a review perhaps. An officer said 'I wish I could throw a hundred shells among them and kill them all.' 'Oh no,' said General Lee, 'do not wish that, wish that they were all at their homes with their friends and that they would stay there.'" Morrison, ed., *Heth Memoirs*, 169.

14 OR 11, pt. 2, 489-98; OR 25, pt. 2, 686; REL to Mrs. REL, March 6, 1863, REL papers, LOC. Lee did not personally write his battle reports; that duty fell almost entirely to Charles Marshall, while Lee served more as an editor. Marshall explained the report process in great detail in a postwar address: "It was my duty to prepare the reports of General Lee under his directions. To do this, as he required it to be done, I had first to read all the reports made by the different commanding officers, who always forwarded the reports of all their subordinates, down to company commanders. From all these I prepared a statement with great detail, of course using such information as I possessed from my personal knowledge and observation as a staff officer, and from orders and correspondence. One of the most difficult things I had to do was to reconcile the many conflicting accounts of the same affair. Sometimes this was impossible, and when the matter was important enough to warrant it, I was required to visit the authors of the conflicting reports or they were brought together and required to reconcile or explain their respective narratives. After exhausting every means to attain entire accuracy, a more general report of the whole was prepared and submitted to General Lee, who made such corrections as he thought proper, and directed the omission of such things as he deemed unnecessary for a clear understanding of the subject, and the report was thus verified and corrected as was then written for his signature." Charles Marshall, *Appomattox: An Address Delivered before the Society of the Army and Navy of the Confederate States in the State of Maryland, January 19, 1894* (Baltimore, MD, 1894), 5.

artillery; he favors promoting his aide Armistead Long to serve as Longstreet's artillery chief and moving William Pendleton over to head Jackson's artillery with Arnold Elzey brought in to serve as the army's chief of artillery. Lee advises Longstreet that an attack on Charleston or Savannah is not likely and Wilmington is likely not threatened either, despite reports of Burnside taking three corps to Hampton Roads. Jackson's aide Jed Hotchkiss meets with Lee to discuss whether Hotchkiss is liable to conscription; Lee determines that he is not as he is already performing military service although a civilian.[15]

March 8, Sunday (Fredericksburg): Lee writes to Maj. Gen. Isaac Trimble thanking him for his suggestions for moving into northern Virginia but explains they that are not practicable at present. Lee instructs Brig. Gen. Joseph Kershaw that no communications are to be sent across the Rappahannock unless approved by headquarters. Lee's cook Bryan arrives at headquarters bearing several messages from Lee's wife Mary.[16]

March 9, Monday (Fredericksburg): Lee writes to Mary chastising her for complaining about how seldom he writes: "You forget how much writing, talking, and thinking I have to do when you complain of the interval between my letters." He also mentions having pawned off the ill-prepared French officer on the Federals.[17]

March 10, Tuesday (Fredericksburg): Lee receives a summons from President Davis to come to Richmond "when convenient and practicable." He notifies Adjutant General Cooper of John Mosby's capture of Brig. Gen. Edwin Stoughton. Snow during the day.[18]

March 11, Wednesday (Fredericksburg): Lee sends a short note to the president that the storm continues and greatly hampers transportation and provisioning the army. Lee orders Gen. Samuel Jones in southwest Virginia to cooperate with John Imboden on "a secret expedition" in West Virginia, and agrees to send Imboden the 25th and 31st Virginia regiments from the ANV if either Imboden or Jones will provide units to take their place. Snow continues.[19]

March 12, Thursday (Fredericksburg/ Richmond): Lee meets with Jackson in the morning. He cautions Stuart to be alert for an enemy movement at Rappahannock Station, and also instructs him to deal with Hampton's troopers who are interfering with hay supplies at Staunton. In the afternoon Lee departs for Richmond to meet with President Davis.[20]

March 13, Friday (Richmond): Lee meets with President Davis to discuss the upcoming spring campaign. He writes to Larkin Hundley of Essex

---

15 Freeman, *Lee's Dispatches*, 73-80; *OR* 18, 911-2; McDonald, *Make Me a Map*, 119. Hotchkiss was a volunteer aide and not a military officer, hence his concern over being susceptible to conscription.

16 *OR* 25, pt. 2, 657-8; Dowdey, *Wartime Papers*, 412. Gen. Trimble was recuperating from a wound received at Second Manassas. Joe Kershaw's men were on picket duty along the river; informal truces and trading among the pickets was quite common, though both Lee and Hooker issued orders to curtail it.

17 Dowdey, *Wartime Papers*, 412-3.

18 *OR* 51, pt. 2, 683; REL to Samuel Cooper, March 10, 1863, telegram book, REL HQ papers, VHS; Lee, *Memoirs of WNP*, 253. Mosby with about 30 men entered Fairfax Court House on the night of the 8th and captured Gen. Stoughton, 32 other officers and men, and 58 horses. Mosby personally roused the slumbering general from his bed. Long, *CW Day by Day*, 327.

19 Freeman, *Lee's Dispatches*, 80-1; *OR* 25, pt. 2, 661. Imboden specifically requested the 25th and 31st VA infantry regiments because they were from the area in which he intended to operate.

20 McDonald, *Make Me a Map*, 120; *OR* 25, pt. 2, 664; REL to J.E.B. Stuart, March 12, 1863, telegram book, REL HQ papers, VHS; Thomas, *REL*, 277. During Lee's absence Jackson commanded the army because Longstreet was on detached service, hence the morning conference. Lee presumably went to the capital by rail via the RF&P.

County regarding the use of 50 free blacks to work on the extensive Richmond fortifications.[21]

March 14, Saturday (Richmond): Lee's discussions with President Davis continue. He telegraphs Col. Chilton that no furloughs are to be granted beyond the end of the month, and those issued for medical reasons do not require Lee's personal approval.[22]

March 15, Sunday (Richmond): It is very likely Gen. Lee attended church service at St. Paul's.[23]

March 16, Monday (Richmond): Lee informs Longstreet that only one corps and not three as previously reported have left the Army of the Potomac.[24]

March 17, Tuesday (Richmond): Chilton telegraphs Lee news of the enemy crossing at Kelly's Ford.[25]

March 18, Wednesday (Richmond/ Fredericksburg): Lee departs Richmond in the morning on an extra train on the RF&P. Soon after arriving back at ANV headquarters, Lee informs Adjutant General Cooper that it is not necessary to return Hood and Pickett to the Rappahannock. He instructs Lt. Col. James Howard at Hanover Junction to return to Richmond with his artillery, and advises President Peter Daniel of the RF&P that regular operations of that line can resume. Lee asks Longstreet's opinion as to visiting British officer Lt. Stephen Winthrop and his qualifications for a commission.[26]

March 19, Thursday (Fredericksburg): Lee informs President Davis that the enemy crossing of the Rappahannock yesterday was only a cavalry raid but that Maj. John Pelham, commander of Stuart's horse artillery, was killed in repulsing it. Lee explains to Longstreet that the enemy was driven back across the river and he does not fear an immediate offensive by the Army of the Potomac; instead of returning to the ANV, Longstreet should be vigilant for an offensive in southeast Virginia or North Carolina and focus on gathering supplies from that region. Lee advises Gen. Arnold Elzey in Richmond that the emergency has passed and the troops from the Richmond garrison will be returned. Lee writes to Mary, praising Fitz Lee's actions at Kelly's Ford on

---

21 Thomas, *REL*, 277; REL to Larkin Hundley, March 13, 1863, Hundley family papers, VHS. As with most of Lee's trips to Richmond, few details are extant. He likely either stayed with Custis at the Franklin Street townhouse or with Mary at the Caskie residence.

22 Thomas, *REL*, 277; REL to R. H. Chilton, March 14, 1863, telegram book, REL HQ papers, VHS.

23 Thomas, *REL*, 277.

24 *OR* 18, 921-2. This was the IX Corps under Ambrose Burnside.

25 R. H. Chilton to REL, March 17, 1863, telegram book, REL HQ papers, VHS. Stuart and Fitz Lee turned back this incursion across the Rappahannock, but the young artillerist John Pelham was mortally wounded during the fighting. Jackson ordered a portion of the army in motion, which at least one officer thought was an overreaction: "We received orders to march with despatch [sic] to Hamilton's Crossing but before a start was made the order was countermanded.... Chilton and Jackson are fond of alarms." Dozier, *Gunner in Lee's Army*, 181.

26 Jones, *Rebel War Clerk's Diary*, vol. 1, 276; *OR* 25, pt. 2, 672; REL to James Howard, March 18, 1863, telegram book, REL HQ papers, VHS; REL to P. V. Daniel, March 18, 1863, telegram book, REL HQ papers, VHS; REL to Longstreet, March 18, 1863, Skinner Fine Books & Manuscripts Auction, November 12, 2017, Auction 3040B, Lot 70. Either Cooper did not receive Lee's telegram regarding Longstreet's divisions, or Cooper failed to notify Longstreet, as Walter Taylor responded to an inquiry from Longstreet at 10:00 p.m. on the 18th telling him the orders to move Hood and Pickett were countermanded, and that Cooper should have informed Longstreet of this. WHT to Longstreet, March 18, 1863, telegram book, REL HQ papers, VHS. Whatever happened regarding Longstreet's command, there was a serious breakdown in communication *somewhere* because Hood also never received orders to stand fast and so proceeded to Hanover Junction; Taylor notified him on the 19th that his orders to return to the army had been countermanded and to halt where he was and await further instructions. WHT to Hood, March 19, 1863, telegram book, REL HQ papers, VHS. Lt. Col. Howard commanded the 18th and 20th VA Heavy Artillery battalions of the Richmond garrison. Krick, *Lee's Colonels*, 199. Winthrop joined Longstreet's staff as a volunteer aide-de-camp in February 1863; he was commissioned a captain in late March and served on Longstreet's and later Porter Alexander's staff for much of the rest of the war. Krick, *Staff Officers in Gray*, 307.

the 17th and regretting the loss of Pelham. Snow begins during the night.[27]

March 20, Friday (Fredericksburg): Lee writes to Senator Edward Sparrow regarding changes in the army: "The more simple the organization of our Army, the more suitable in my opinion it will be to our service." Lee provides his view on the number and grade of staff officers required from army headquarters down to brigade and regiment level. Lee forwards to Gen. Cooper a complaint by A. P. Hill against Jackson for interfering with subordinate departments and staff officers; in his endorsement, Lee explains his intent in issuing the orders cited by both Jackson and Hill. Snow continues.[28]

March 21, Saturday (Fredericksburg): Lee explains to President Davis his rationale in wanting to reorganize his staff and support positions in the Virginia army. Lee writes to James Longstreet, explaining that he prefers to keep Hood and Pickett closer than North Carolina in case Hooker's operations necessitate their return. Lee forwards John Mosby's report of his recent raid on Herndon, and suggests to President Davis that Mosby should be promoted.[29]

Lee informs John Imboden and Sam Jones that he cannot reinforce Imboden and urges them to work together, pointing out that a large body of Federals left West Virginia to join William Rosecrans's army. Lee forwards to the War Department Grumble Jones's report of a skirmish at Woodstock, and also sends Sec. Seddon orders he received from Hooker which he thinks violate the existing POW exchange agreement. Lee orders that a list of all slaves serving in the various commands of the ANV be furnished to headquarters.[30]

Lee asks Gen. Cooper to return his Seven Days report to make corrections, and promises to return it the next day. Lee writes to Gen. Trimble hoping that he is recovering quickly and will be able to take the field. He instructs Gen. Pendleton to make sure all his artillery encampments are adequately guarded against enemy cavalry raids, as advance warning of such may not be received, and to finish the reorganization of battalions before the campaign opens. Orders are published canceling future leaves of absence, to send all excess baggage to the rear, and reducing transportation overall. Lee writes to Mary, enclosing a photograph of himself.[31]

March 22, Sunday (Fredericksburg): The general spends much of the day revising his report of the Seven Days' Battles. He names Henry Benning to assume command of Robert Toombs's former brigade.[32]

March 23, Monday (Fredericksburg): Lee instructs Stuart, Imboden, and Grumble Jones that in response to a new policy adopted by the enemy regarding paroles for prisoners, all captives are to be sent to Richmond for the present. He apologizes to

---

27 OR 25, pt. 2, 675; OR 18, 927; Dowdey, *Wartime Papers*, 414-5; Douglas, *I Rode with Stonewall*, 210. Elzey replaced G. W. Smith in command of the troops around Richmond.

28 OR 2, Series 4, 446-7; A. P. Hill to REL, March 11, 1863, Lee papers, SH; Betts, *Experience of CS Chaplain*, 29. Sparrow was chair of the Confederate Senate Committee on Military Affairs.

29 OR 2, Series 4, 447-8; OR 18, 933-4; OR 25, pt. 1, 66; OR 25, pt. 2, 678-9. Lee told Davis: "Our armies are necessarily very large in comparison with those we have heretofore had to manage. Some of our divisions exceed the army Gen. Scott entered the City of Mexico with, and our brigades are larger than his divisions. The greatest difficulty I find is in causing orders and requisitions to be obeyed. This arises not from a spirit of disobedience, but from ignorance. We therefore need a corps of officers to teach others their duty, see to the observances of orders, and to the regularity and precision of all movements." OR 2, Series 4, 447-8.

30 OR 25, pt. 2, 679-80; OR 25, pt. 1, 33; OR 5, Series 2, 854; WHT orders, March 21, 1863, REL papers, MOC.

31 REL to Samuel Cooper, March 21, 1863, telegram book, REL HQ papers, VHS; REL to Isaac Trimble, March 21, 1863, LJF papers, W&L; OR 25, pt. 2, 680-2; Dowdey, *Wartime Papers*, 416. For more on wartime photographs of REL, see Roy Meredith, *The Face of Robert E. Lee in Life and in Legend* (New York, 1947), and the more recent, scholarly, and complete Donald A. Hopkins, *Robert E. Lee in War and Peace: Photographs of a Confederate and American Icon* (El Dorado Hills, CA, 2013).

32 REL to Samuel Cooper, March 21, 1863, telegram book, REL HQ papers, VHS; OR 25, pt. 2, 682.

Jones for mistakenly omitting Jones's Moorefield raid in the recent GO outlining all cavalry successes. Lee congratulates John Mosby on his promotion and orders him to recruit his command up to its new authorized strength. Lee requests that the War Department assign Raleigh Colston to the ANV, and decrees that Friday March 27 will be a day of fasting and prayer per Presidential declaration.[33]

March 24, Tuesday (Fredericksburg): Lee confers with Jackson at William Yerby's house, Stonewall's new headquarters. Lee writes to his brother Carter giving family and military news including a recent visit to Hayfield, home of their cousin Mrs. W. P. Taylor, where it seemed Hooker intended to cross the river. Rain in the afternoon and evening.[34]

March 25, Wednesday (Fredericksburg): Lee informs Sec. Seddon of requests from the Virginia Central Railroad to move a portion of the black workers laboring on the Richmond fortifications over to railroad maintenance: "The necessities of the road are immediate and I see no other way of supplying them." He issues orders regarding preventing scurvy.[35]

March 26, Thursday (Fredericksburg): Lee explains to Imboden and "Grumble" Jones that the weather has prevented him from making any sort of operation east of the mountains in conjunction with their movements in the lower Valley, so it is up to them to do whatever damage they can now while enemy strength there is reduced; Samuel Jones will make a diversion in the Kanawha Valley and send whatever troops he can spare to Imboden. Lee requests the quartermaster in Richmond to send extra wagons to Imboden to carry out any supplies he can gather while on his raid. He notifies Gen. Cooper of a skirmish involving Mosby yesterday, and requests that Tredegar Iron Works continue producing Napoleons until all bronze guns in the ANV have been replaced with them.[36] Lee forwards to Richmond Stuart's GO9 lamenting the loss of Pelham, adding "I feel deeply the loss of the noble dead, and heartily concur in the commendation of the living."

The general denies Nathan "Shanks" Evans's request for his brigade to be transferred to Charleston, South Carolina, explaining that he does not think it is needed there at present, but should the need arise it will be sent. Lee thanks North Carolina Governor Vance for his efforts to fill the ranks of his state's regiments, but mildly rebukes him for not advising Lee that he had declared amnesty for North Carolina deserters. Lee receives from Joe Hooker news of the death of Maj. Gen. Edwin V. Sumner. Lee writes to Maj. M. S. Rives expressing his condolences over the death of Maj. R. K. Meade.[37]

March 27, Friday (Fredericksburg): Lee emphasizes to Longstreet the need to draw all possible supplies from North Carolina and southeast Virginia while undertaking an offensive with the troops already in theater. Lee explains that if he sends any further troops from the ANV he will have to fall back to the North Anna River. Lee informs chief engineer Jeremy Gilmer that he requested some time ago an engineer officer for Longstreet at Petersburg but this has not happened. Lee briefs Sec. Seddon on the provisions gathered by "Grumble" Jones and Longstreet thus far and warns that scurvy is beginning to appear in large numbers. Lee receives

---

33 OR 25, pt. 2, 682-3; OR 51, pt. 2, 688; REL to Samuel Cooper, March 23, 1863, telegram book, REL HQ papers, VHS.

34 McDonald, *Make Me a Map*, 123; REL to Charles Carter Lee, March 24, 1863, REL papers, UVA. Jackson moved his HQ from Moss Neck to Hunter's Ridge, the home of John Yerby, on March 17, putting him much closer to Lee's HQ. McDonald, *Make Me a Map*, 121.

35 OR 25, pt. 2, 683-4; WHT GO March 25, 1863, REL papers, MOC.

36 OR 25, pt. 2, 684-6; REL to A. H. Cole, March 26, 1863, REL CSR; Freeman, *Lee's Dispatches*, 83; Dew, *Ironmaker to the CSA*, 190.

37 OR 25, pt. 1, 60; OR 25, pt. 2, 684; OR 51, pt. 2, 689; Dowdey, *Wartime Papers*, 420; REL to M. S. Rives, March 26, 1863, REL papers, MOC. Sumner was a prewar friend of Lee and commanded the II Corps in the Army of the Potomac. He died March 21, 1863. Armistead Long was Sumner's son-in-law.

Fitz Lee's report of Kelly's Ford and compliments both him and Stuart on their handling of the action. Lee writes to Mary, confessing that he has been unwell for some time; he sends the latest family news and the disposition of many of the former slaves from White House.[38]

March 28, Saturday (Fredericksburg): Lee learns from "Grumble" Jones that Gen. Burnside and the IX Corps were sent west on the B&O, and he advises Samuel Cooper and James Longstreet accordingly. Longstreet requests an experienced artillery officer to serve in southeast Virginia and inquires about E. Porter Alexander; Lee responds that Alexander is president of a court martial at present and thus cannot be spared, but Lee will send Armistead Long instead. Rain all day.[39]

March 29, Sunday (Fredericksburg): Lee's health declines rapidly, and Jackson meets with him in the afternoon likely discussing his temporary command of the army. Lee informs Sec. Seddon that he thinks "Grumble" Jones's report of Burnside going west is wrong, that Burnside's corps is the one at Newport News and that it must be Franz Sigel's corps going to Kentucky, but Lee's scouts cannot penetrate enemy lines to get correct information. Lee notifies Longstreet that Alexander's court duty has concluded and he will be sent as Longstreet requested. Lee receives several shad from a John F. Skaggs and sends a brief note thanking him. Rain continues.[40]

March 30, Monday (Fredericksburg/Belvoir): Lee's illness requires that he be moved indoors and he relocates to an upstairs bedroom at nearby Belvoir, where he is placed under the care of ANV chief surgeon Lafayette Guild and Dr. S. M. Bemiss. Lee asks Longstreet if he can confirm that Burnside left Virginia for the West, and opines that enemy intentions in North Carolina are likely defensive only and the weather precludes taking any sort of offensive along the Rappahannock. Rain continues with periods of snow and hail.[41]

March 31, Tuesday (Belvoir): Lee writes to Wade Hampton regarding the importation of English Blakely rifled cannons through the blockade and the creation of additional horse artillery batteries, and writes to son Custis regarding the employment of the former family slaves. Rain and hail in the morning, turning to snow.[42]

---

38 *OR* 18, 943-4; *OR* 25, pt. 2, 686-7; Dowdey, *Wartime Papers*, 419-20.

39 *OR* 18, 946, *OR* 25, pt. 2, 689; REL to Longstreet, March 28, 1863, telegram book, REL HQ papers, VHS; REL to A. L. Long, March 28, 1863, telegram book, REL HQ papers, VHS; Betts, *Experience of a CS Chaplain*, 30. Long was temporarily in Richmond, so it appears Lee did not consult with him but simply ordered him to go to Longstreet.

40 McDonald, *Make Me a Map*, 124; *OR* 25, pt. 2, 691; REL to Longstreet, March 29, 1863, telegram book, REL HQ papers, VHS; REL to John F. Skaggs, March 29, 1863, REL papers, W&L; Betts, *Experience of a CS Chaplain*, 30.

41 John Hennessy, *Belvoir: The Thomas Yerby Place, Spotsylvania County*, Fredericksburg & Spotsylvania NMP files; Freeman, *Lee*, vol. 2, 502; *OR* 18, 906-7, 949-50; Betts, *Experience of a CS Chaplain*, 30. Belvoir, about two miles from Lee's HQ camp, was a large mansion that dated to the early 19th century and the home of the Thomas Yerby family. It was used as a hospital after the Battle of Fredericksburg, and Gen. Maxcy Gregg died in the house on Dec. 15, 1862. It burned in 1910 and was not rebuilt; the site is overgrown and in private hands. Hennessy, *Belvoir*. Stonewall Jackson's wife later occupied the same room that Lee had when she came to visit her husband with their newborn daughter. Freeman, *Lee's Lieutenants*, vol. 2, 520 n14. Lee's second letter to Longstreet is misdated March 3 in the *OR*. Lee remained at Belvoir for nearly three weeks, returning to HQ April 16. Thomas, *REL*, 278. ANV HQ remained at his camp on Mine Road, and he retained command of the army. Margaret C. M. Venable memoirs, UVA. Perry stayed with Lee at Belvoir, but all of the staff remained at HQ. Dowdey, *Wartime Papers*, 427-9.

42 *OR* 25, pt. 2, 694-5; Jones, *Life and Letters of REL*, 286-7; McDonald, *Make Me a Map*, 124; Betts, *Experience of a CS Chaplain*, 30.

April 1863

As the opening of the spring campaigning season loomed, Robert E. Lee was confined by doctor's orders to a bedroom in Belvoir, the Yerby family plantation house two miles from army headquarters.[1] His staff remained at headquarters, though they checked in with the general often, and Jackson was close by if needed. Lee's servant Perry seems to have been the only one who stayed with him at Belvoir.[2]

Dr. Samuel Bemiss treated Lee during much of his illness and wrote a letter to his children about his impression of the general:

> For over a week past he has been sick and I was first called to see him in consultation then his physician was taken sick and he is now my patient and I visit him every afternoon. Do not be alarmed at supposing him much sick, for he is everyday getting better and will, I doubt not, soon be well again. I wish you could all see him—he is so noble a specimen of man, that even if he were not so distinguished, you would be attracted by his appearance and manners. He is a tall robust fine looking man with white beard all over his face and white hair, always polite and agreeable and thinking less of himself than he ought to and thinking indeed of nothing, hoping and praying for nothing but true success of our cause and the return of a blessed peace.[3]

Lee did not relinquish command of the Army of Northern Virginia during this time, and his staff kept him well-informed. Jeb Stuart visited him at least once and almost certainly more, and it is reasonable to suspect that Stonewall Jackson, who was next in rank if Lee was unable to command, did so as well.[4] During at least part of this time, Lee reviewed the reports on the Fredericksburg and Cedar Mountain campaigns. By the second week of April, Lee was recovered enough to get out and move about the camps, but it was mid-April before he was allowed to return to his tent at headquarters.

Shortly after Lee left Belvoir, Stonewall Jackson's wife took up temporary residence in the room recently occupied by the commanding general. Within a day or two of her arrival Lee called on Mrs. Jackson, who later wrote about the event. "We had a large, comfortable room at Mr. Yerby's," she began,

---

1 Gen. Lafayette McLaws's comments on the timing of Lee's illness no doubt reflected the views of many: Lee "has been sick for some six or ten days, but is getting better so I am informed . . . as it would be a real misfortune for him to be away from us at this time." Oeffinger, *A Soldier's General*, 176.

2 Dowdey, *Wartime Papers*, 427-9.

3 Samuel Bemiss to Eli L. Bemiss, April 10, 1863, Bemiss family papers, VHS. Dr. Bemiss treated Gen. Lee while Dr. Lafayette Guild, the Army of Northern Virginia's medical director, was himself absent sick. Bemiss was a well-known physician in Kentucky prior to the war, received his medical education in New York, and joined the Confederate Army in 1862. He had served with the Army of Tennessee in the Western Theater, and would later become its assistant medical director. Bemiss practiced medicine in New Orleans after the war. www.findagrave.com/memorial/79949105/Samuel-Merrifield-Bemiss; Unknown author, *Biographical and Historical Memoirs of Louisana* (Chicago, 1892), vol. 1, 281-2.

4 Dowdey, *Wartime Papers*, 427-9. James Longstreet was senior to Jackson, but Longstreet was on detached service around Suffolk in southeastern Virginia. It is reasonable to wonder who would have led the army if Hooker had launched his offensive several weeks earlier than he did. Was Lee too incapacitated to command in the field?

which was hospitably furnished with three beds. It seems that General Lee had been an occupant of this room before us, for when he called on me he facetiously alluded to our capacious accommodations, and said he had written to his wife and daughters that if they would come to see him, he could entertain them all in this room! This was the first time I met him, and when the announcement was made that "General Lee and his staff had called to see Mrs. Jackson," I was somewhat awe-struck at the idea of meeting the commander-in-chief, with a retinue of officers, and descended to the parlor with considerable trepidation; but I was met by a face so kind and fatherly, and a greeting so cordial, that I was at once reassured and put at ease. The formidable "staff" consisted of only two or three nice-looking, courteous gentlemen, and the call was greatly enjoyed.[5]

As the month wound to a close, Lee began shifting his army west of Fredericksburg, in response to the long-awaited enemy advance, to a small crossroads known as Chancellorsville.

* * *

---

5 Jackson, *Memoirs of Stonewall Jackson*, 412.

April 1, Wednesday (Belvoir): Lee sends instructions to William Pendleton regarding finding forage for his artillery horses and forwards to Fannie Scott a letter received today from Gen. Hooker regarding the fate of her son Benjamin I. Scott.[6]

April 2, Thursday (Belvoir): Lee informs President Davis and Longstreet that Ambrose Burnside and the IX Corps are in Kentucky and that Union operations along the Blackwater River are just diversions so Longstreet should take the offensive there or return to the ANV. He writes to John B. Hood regarding the rumored murder of two civilians by members of his command, and notifies Rabbi M. J. Michelbacher that he will grant permission for Jewish troops to go to Synagogue when possible as requested.[7]

April 3, Friday (Belvoir): Lee writes to wife Mary, recommending that she and Agnes go to one of the springs in southwest Virginia to improve their health and get away from the stresses of war. He admits that he is in poor health and laments that his forces are scattered and without adequate provisions.[8]

April 4, Saturday (Belvoir): Lee informs Davis that a scout in Maryland confirms that Burnside indeed took his corps west on the B&O, and also notifies President Davis of a fight between Mosby and the 1st Vermont Cavalry at Dranesville. Lee informs Sec. Seddon that he is moving Fitz Lee's brigade into Loudoun County to enable gathering of supplies from that region. He also tells Seddon that the Virginia Central must be repaired, as Lee as urged previously; if slaves cannot be utilized then the War Department needs to find another way to do it. Brig. Gen. Raleigh Colston is appointed to command of William Taliaferro's former brigade. Snow throughout the day.[9]

April 5, Sunday (Belvoir): Lee receives a letter from his wife Mary in the morning, delivered personally by Jeb Stuart. "After breakfast" staff officers bring him some paperwork that needs Lee's attention, which he finishes "by 3 p.m." During the evening the general writes to Mary, advising that he is still quite unwell and confined to his room at Belvoir, but that he has Perry with him to assist. Snow continues.[10]

April 6, Monday (Belvoir): Lee asks Arnold Elzey in Richmond if he can spare Wise's Brigade and artillery to send to Longstreet. Lee writes to Longstreet again, confirming that Burnside is not in Virginia or North Carolina, and that he regrets that part of Pickett's Division was sent to D. H. Hill in North Carolina; Lee can send nothing else from the ANV at present, but Elzey can provide reinforcements if needed. Lee writes to Gen. Pendleton again concerning provender for his artillery horses as well as a commander for the artillery of Hood's Division.[11]

April 7, Tuesday (Belvoir): Lee sends a map to the adjutant general to accompany his report of the Seven Days' Battles from the previous year. The general approves "Grumble" Jones's proposed cavalry raid against the B&O involving his own and John Imboden's troops, but cautions that no troops from the ANV can be spared for the expedition; instead, Lee directs that Jones and Imboden call

---

6 OR 25, pt. 2, 697; C. S. Venable to Fannie Scott, April 1, 1863, Scott family papers, VHS.

7 OR 25, pt. 2, 700-1; Freeman, *Lee's Dispatches*, 84; OR 18, 954; Stephen M. Hood, *John Bell Hood: The Rise, Fall, and Resurrection of a Confederate General* (El Dorado Hills, CA, 2013), 14 n6; Jones, *Personal Reminiscences of REL*, 443-4. Jed Hotchkiss noted today that Lee's physical condition was improving. Hotchkiss to Sara Hotchkiss, April 2, 1863, Valley of the Shadow.

8 Dowdey, *Wartime Papers*, 426-7.

9 OR 25, pt. 2, 702-5; REL to J. F. Davis, April 4, 1863, John S. Mosby papers, VHS; Dowdey, *Wartime Papers*, 428.

10 Dowdey, *Wartime Papers*, 427-9; Krick, *CW Weather*, 92.

11 OR 18, 966-7; OR 25, pt. 2, 709. On this date Sec. Seddon first broached with Lee the subject of sending Gen. Longstreet west to Braxton Bragg's Army of Tennessee. Freeman, *Lee*, vol. 2, 503.

upon Gen. Sam Jones in southwest Virginia for support.[12]

April 8, Wednesday (Belvoir): Capt. Justus Schcibert of the Prussian Army arrives at Lee's headquarters with a letter of introduction from Sec. Seddon. Lee tells Scheibert to use his tent for quarters while he is at Belvoir. Lee sends Maj. Marshall changes to make to the Fredericksburg report, and then goes to Jackson's headquarters in the afternoon.[13]

April 9, Thursday (Belvoir): Lee writes to Seddon regarding reinforcements in the West and the enemy's offensive potential; he proposes that rather than detaching troops from the ANV, the best way to relieve pressure on Joe Johnston and Beauregard is for Lee to cross the Potomac and carry the war north. He also asks if the Navy can send all or part of the James River fleet to cooperate with Longstreet around Suffolk and protect his flank and rear. Lee informs Longstreet that he needs a pontoon train. Lt. Col. William P. Smith is announced as the ANV's new chief engineer.[14]

April 10, Friday (Belvoir): Lee submits his report of the Fredericksburg campaign to the adjutant general, and rides to his headquarters camp and checks in with Surgeon General Guild.[15]

April 11, Saturday (Belvoir): Lee approves of a diversionary movement against Yorktown by Arnold Elzey to draw attention away from Longstreet at Suffolk. He requests that materials for a 350-foot pontoon bridge, with officers to oversee its construction, be sent by rail to Orange Court House and names John B. Gordon to command Alexander Lawton's former brigade. He submits Guild's casualty report for the Seven Days and returns to Maj. Marshall a draft of his Cedar Mountain report for changes. Lee writes to Agnes that he is healing quickly and is upset that Drs. Guild and Bemiss will not allow him to leave Belvoir to return to camp; he regrets that she and Custis are unable to visit.[16]

April 12, Sunday (Belvoir): Lee receives letters from Mildred and his wife Mary, delivered by Mr. Caskie. He writes to Mary that he is much recovered, but still has a cough, and the doctors would not allow him to attend a nearby church service today

---

12 *OR* 11, pt. 2, 500; *OR* 25, pt. 2, 710-2.

13 Justus Scheibert, *Seven Months in the Rebel States During the North American War, 1863* (Tuscaloosa, AL, 1958), 34-5; *OR Supplement*, part 3, vol. 3, 166; McDonald, *Make Me a Map*, 127. Scheibert did not meet Lee in person on this occasion. Scheibert, *Seven Months in the Rebel States*, 38. The purpose of the visit to Jackson is not known. Lee told Marshall, "My head is ringing with quinine and I am otherwise so poorly I do not seem able to think." *OR Supplement*, part 3, vol. 3, 166.

14 *OR* 25, pt. 2, 713-4; *OR* 18, 974; REL to Longstreet, April 9, 1863, telegram book, REL HQ papers, VHS; Orders, April 9, 1863, REL papers, MOC. Smith was a rather well-traveled engineer by this point in the war, having served with several generals in Virginia and North Carolina; he apparently joined the staff on April 2, but was not announced until the 8th. His record is incomplete, but he later served with Jubal Early in the Shenandoah Valley. Krick, *Staff Officers in Gray*, 271. SO99 of this date transferred the 25th and 31st VA regiments to Imboden, even though Lee had told Imboden several days before that he could not send any troops; instead of sending troops directly to Imboden, Sam Jones sent the 50th VA from his command to the ANV to free up the two regiments for Imboden. *OR* 25, pt. 2, 714. Artilleryman Thomas Carter wrote of Lee's illness today: "Gen. Lee is not seriously sick, you can tell Agnes. Gen. Chilton told me on Monday [6th] that he had complained of pain across his chest and camp fever was apprehended but at that time he was not confined to his bed and was performing office duties." Dozier, *A Gunner in Lee's Army*, 188.

15 *OR* 21, 550-6; Samuel Bemiss to children, April 10, 1863, Bemiss family papers, VHS. This report was submitted out of order chronologically due to the arrival and non-arrival of reports from various subordinate officers. *OR* 21, 550-6. Dr. Bemiss noted that Lee was especially "cheerful" this afternoon. Bemiss to children, April 10, 1863, Bemiss family papers, VHS. It may have been on this date that Lee met Capt. Scheibert for the first time; Scheibert did not record the date but mentioned that Lee "visited his headquarters one day as a convalescent." *Seven Months in the Rebel States*, 38.

16 *OR* 18, 979; *OR* 25, pt. 2, 715, 717; *OR* 11, pt. 2, 502; *OR Supplement*, part 3, vol. 3, 166; Dowdey, *Wartime Papers*, 431-2. Neither Lee nor Marshall specifically stated which campaign report this was; Cedar Mountain was the next one Lee submitted, so it was likely that campaign. The next one (Second Manassas) was not completed until early June. Robert Chilton's nomination for brigadier general went before the Senate for confirmation and was rejected on this date. Chilton CSR.

conducted by Rev. Tucker Lacy. Instead, he "had my solitary prayers in my own room and enjoyed a sermon sent me from Hampden-Sydney College preached by the Reverend Mr. [R. L.] Dabney." Rain in the afternoon.[17]

April 13, Monday (Belvoir): Lee meets with Gen. Pendleton and forwards Mosby's report of his operations over the last several weeks. The headquarters camp is relocated "for the benefit of our health," but remains in the same general vicinity.[18]

April 14, Tuesday (Belvoir): Lee meets with Jackson at Stonewall's headquarters. Lee informs "Grumble" Jones that enemy cavalry is moving against him in the Shenandoah Valley, and that Jeb Stuart will assist him. Lee endorses and forwards a letter from Maj. Talcott to the adjutant general seeking appointment in the 1st Engineer regiment; Lee recommends him for lieutenant colonel, and speaks very highly of him both personally and professionally.[19]

April 15, Wednesday (Belvoir): Rain.[20]

April 16, Thursday (Belvoir/Fredericksburg): Lee returns to ANV headquarters camp on Mine Road. Lee informs President Davis that the cavalry of the Army of the Potomac appears poised for a raid as they have tried several times to cross the Rappahannock but were repulsed by Stuart's cavalry. He notes that Stuart thinks the Federal horsemen are bound for the Valley as a feint while Hooker moves the rest of the army to White House or possibly south of the James, but Lee discounts this thinking it very unlikely that Hooker will uncover Washington. Lee proposes to take the offensive around May 1 by moving into the lower Valley and then across the Potomac, but notes that without Longstreet's forces returning to the ANV he lacks the strength to do so. Lee writes to Sam Cooper regarding reinforcing Bragg in Tennessee: Lee is concerned over the disparity of numbers in every theater but especially his own and this concern is made more acute by the absence of Longstreet, whom he does not wish reduced further to reinforce Bragg.

The general sends the official casualty report for the Battle of Fredericksburg to the War Department and announces the newest artillery reorganization for his army. Lee informs Sam Jones that the 25th and 31st Virginia regiments were dispatched to Imboden upon the arrival of the 50th Virginia from Jones's department, and apprises "Grumble" Jones of Jeb Stuart's situation along the upper Rappahannock.[21]

April 17, Friday (Fredericksburg): Lee advises Sec. Seddon that ration shortages are causing sickness among the troops. Lee informs Gen. Longstreet (operating around Suffolk in southeastern Virginia) that he requested that the Navy assist Longstreet, but that he has received no reply, and advises that any requests for additional support must go to Richmond directly because Lee can spare nothing else to send him. The general provides Jeb Stuart with an update on enemy movements and strength, and notifies "Grumble" Jones that the enemy forces

---

17 Dowdey, *Wartime Papers*, 432-3; Schildt, *Stonewall Day by Day*, 105. Agnes noted on this date, "Papa has been quite sick in bed with a violent cold but is much better now." Agnes to Hattie Powell, April 12, 1863, Powell family papers, W&M.

18 Lee, *Memoirs of WNP*, 255-6; *OR* 25, pt. 1, 71-3; Margaret C. M. Venable memoirs, UVA. Pendleton observed that Lee "is now nearly well." Lee, *Memoirs of WNP*, 256. Venable did not record the exact location of the new campsite, but it must have been in the immediate vicinity of the old one. Lee, he wrote, "is better, but still in a house some two miles from us." He added, "My friend [Maj. T. M. R.] Talcott will I think leave us by getting a position in the Engineer Corps. I might possibly have done the same but would have to ask it which I will not do, and besides it is far more agreeable to me to be with Gen. Lee for some time to come." Margaret C. M. Venable memoirs, UVA.

19 McDonald, *Make Me a Map*, 128; *OR* 25, pt. 2, 721; T. M. R. Talcott to Samuel Cooper, April 13, 1863, Talcott CSR.

20 Krick, *CW Weather*, 92. Lee returned to HQ on the 16th, so it is likely he was examined by either Dr. Guild or Dr. Bemiss today.

21 Thomas, *REL*, 278; *OR* 25, pt. 2, 724-30; *OR* 21, 562; REL to Grumble Jones, April 16, 1863, telegram book, REL HQ papers, VHS.

at the upper Rappahannock River crossing points show no signs of going anywhere, so if nothing in the Valley prevents Jones and Imboden from acting, they should move ahead with their plans.[22]

April 18, Saturday (Fredericksburg): Lee submits his report of the Cedar Mountain campaign to the adjutant general's office. Lee writes to Sec. Seddon and Longstreet regarding six "disloyal citizens" of North Carolina arrested by D. H. Hill and sent to Petersburg: three are to be conscripted into service and three to be sent to North Carolina to stand trial. Lee orders the "commanding officer, Valley District" to keep Stuart informed of all enemy movements in the Valley while Jones and Imboden are absent. Maj. Talcott explains to Fannie Scott that Lee will issue her a pass through the lines if she wishes to go to Washington, but that she cannot go via Fredericksburg having to go instead via a truce boat on the James River.[23]

April 19, Sunday (Fredericksburg): Lee attends church service with Brig. Gen. Joseph Kershaw. Lee tells Stuart he has no new information regarding Hooker's intentions and tells him to keep in contact with the forces left in the Valley. He also informs Stuart that he does not need Lee's approval for sending officers and men to Richmond on detached service. Lee writes to Mary thanking her for the letter and package of food he received from her today. She moved to Shirley since her last communication and he hopes that this change of scenery will improve her health. He adds that if the Confederacy can hold on for another year, the Republican Party will be ousted in the 1864 election resulting in peace and Southern independence. Capt. Scheibert leaves Lee's camp for Stuart's headquarters.[24]

April 20, Monday (Fredericksburg): Lee explains to President Davis the need for more cavalry to match the strength of the mounted arm of the Army of the Potomac, and tells Stuart that he has told Richmond multiple times of this need and he is renewing the request. Lee also tells President Davis that he has reports of "enough beef cattle in Florida to supply our entire forces for two years" and he wants the commanders there to devote their efforts to securing these animals before they are captured by the enemy. He writes to a cousin, thanking for her sympathetic thoughts on the loss of Annie. Rain all day.[25]

April 21, Tuesday (Fredericksburg): Lee forwards to Seddon a request from Longstreet that the CSS *Richmond* move to the lower James River in support of his forces at Suffolk. Lee orders Jeb Stuart to determine at which Rappahannock River crossing the enemy is concentrating. Rain in the morning.[26]

April 22, Wednesday (Fredericksburg): Lee forwards to Richmond Fitz Lee's report of operations at Rappahannock Station on the 14th and 15th and instructs Stuart that if Hooker's cavalry crosses the Blue Ridge into the Valley he is to follow them. Lee provides Chilton a summation of his service and mentions that he recommended Chilton for brigadier after Sharpsburg.[27]

---

22 *OR* 25, pt. 2, 730-1; *OR* 18, 996; REL to W. E. Jones, April 17, 1863, telegram book, REL HQ papers, VHS.

23 *OR* 12, pt. 2, 176-9; *OR* 18, 998-9; *OR* 25, pt. 2, 731; T. M. R. Talcott to Fannie Scott, April 18, 1863, Scott family papers, VHS. Jones did not inform Lee who would be in command in the Valley while he was on his raid into western Virginia. Mrs. Scott was still in search of information regarding her son Benjamin Scott of the 18th VA.

24 Gallagher, *Lee the Soldier*, 358; *OR* 25, pt. 2, 736-7; Dowdey, *Wartime Papers*, 437-8; Scheibert, *Seven Months in the Rebel States*, 41. It is not known where Lee and Kershaw attended church, or who else attended with them.

25 *OR* 25, pt. 2, 737-8, 740-1; REL to "Cousin Ellen," April 20, 1863, REL papers, Missouri Historical Society; Betts, *Experience of a CS Chaplain*, 32.

26 *OR* 18, 1009; REL to Stuart, April 21, 1863, telegram book, REL HQ papers, VHS; Betts, *Experience of a CS Chaplain*, 33. Gen. Dorsey Pender commented on Lee's condition today: "Gen. Lee is about again attending to business much to the gratification of all." Hassler, *One of Lee's Best Men*, 227.

27 *OR* 25, pt. 1, 85-7; REL to Stuart, April 22, 1863, telegram book, REL HQ papers, VHS; REL to R. H. Chilton, April 22, 1863, Chilton CSR. Chilton was gathering facts for a court of inquiry as to why his nomination for brigadier general

April 23, Thursday (Fredericksburg): Lee responds to a report by Raleigh Colston of the Federals crossing at Port Royal, telling Jackson and Colston he thinks it to be a feint and that Hooker's real crossing will be upstream of Fredericksburg and so notifies McLaws and Richard Anderson to have their pickets on the lookout for enemy activity. Lee informs Sec. Seddon of the enemy crossing at Port Royal but notes increased Federal activity at the upper Rappahannock fords. Lee inquires of Longstreet what cavalry is available in North Carolina that can be added to Stuart's command. Lee responds to a letter from Lt. Col. St. Clair Dearing who is seeking a new command; Lee tells him he can offer no aid. Lee visits Stonewall Jackson's wife, Mary Anna, and infant daughter Julia at Belvoir. Rain throughout the day.[28]

April 24, Friday (Fredericksburg): Lee advises Sec. Seddon that the Federals crossed at Port Royal yesterday, taking everything of value from in and around the town, but re-crossed before they could be attacked. He writes to Mary, acknowledging letters from her and Agnes; he tells her that his health is much better and relates recent enemy movements. Heavy rains.[29]

April 25, Saturday (Fredericksburg): Lee tells Stuart that if Hooker's cavalry crosses the Blue Ridge, he is to move behind the Union army and damage its rear. He also wants Stuart to investigate reports that the VIII Corps is in Longstreet's front at Suffolk. Lee writes Gen. Pendleton concerning animals and transportation for the artillery: "The destruction of horses in the army is so great that I fear it will be impossible to supply our wants. There are not enough in the country." He adds that Pendleton's duties are more in line with those of a major general than a brigadier and authorizes more equipage for Pendleton if he needs it. Lee declines a request from Jackson to have his photograph taken, noting that he does not have time to get to the photographer.[30]

April 26, Sunday (Fredericksburg): Lee, Jackson, Early, and Joseph Kershaw attend church services conducted by Rev. B. T. Lacy, after which he visits Mrs. Jackson at Belvoir. Lee learns from Stuart that Hooker's cavalry "is in force" around Warrenton.[31]

April 27, Monday (Fredericksburg): Lee updates President Davis on the strength and location of the Army of the Potomac, and wants to know if troops can be shifted from South Carolina to North Carolina to allow Longstreet to return to the ANV.

---

was rejected by the Senate. It is interesting to note that Lee's letters of recommendation for his staff officers seeking promotion were usually very laudatory; his comments on Chilton's service in this letter can best be described as mildly complimentary. The *OR* misdates this letter as 23rd. *OR* 25, pt. 2, 745-6. Dorsey Pender visited HQ today and learned that Gens. Ed Johnson and Chase Whiting had been recommended for promotion to major general rather than him. Pender complained to his wife, "Johnson was my competitor so you see my hope is gone." Pender did not mention if he saw Lee in person, or if he got this information from one of the staff. Hassler, *One of Lee's Best Men*, 228-9.

28 *OR* 25, pt. 2, 744-5, 859; *OR* 18, 1018; REL to St. Clair Dearing, April 23, 1863, REL papers, Duke; Schildt, *Stonewall Day by Day*, 107; McDonald, *Make Me a Map*, 134. Dearing was the lieutenant colonel of the 25th NC, but was not reelected in April 1862. At this time he was in Charleston, SC, without a command. Dearing would recruit black troops in Georgia near the end of the war. Krick, *Lee's Colonels*, 116. Jackson's daughter was baptized today and she and her mother were visited by a number of senior officers during the day. Schildt, *Stonewall Day by Day*, 107.

29 *OR* 25, pt. 2, 749; Dowdey, *Wartime Papers*, 439-40; McDonald, *Make Me a Map*, 134. Mary must have been considering moving to Liberty (modern Bedford) because Lee suddenly began writing about that area in the middle of this letter. Dowdey, *Wartime Papers*, 440. On this date Jackson wrote a formal complaint against A. P. Hill, specifically regarding signal corps orders being not being routed through the proper channels, and requested that Hill be removed from serving under Jackson; it is not known when Lee received this document. Jackson to REL, April 24, 1863, Jackson papers, UNC.

30 *OR* 25, pt. 2, 749-50; REL to Jackson, April 25, 1863, REL papers W&L. For more on Lee's and Jackson's photo session, see Eric J. Mink, "Southern Exposure: Stonewall Sells—The 1863 Jackson Photograph," *Fredericksburg History & Biography* (vol. 11, 2012), 177-83.

31 Jackson, *Memoirs of Stonewall Jackson*, 411; J. William Jones, *Christ in the Camp: The True Story of the Great Revival during the War Between the States* (Harrisonburg, VA, 1986), 488-9; Dowdey, *Wartime Papers*, 440-1. Jed Hotchkiss estimated that the audience for Lacy's sermon was about 2,000. McDonald, *Make Me a Map*, 134.

Lee gives Longstreet the latest intel on Hooker's army and urges against an attack on Suffolk itself, as if it is taken then troops would have to be left to hold it. Lee wants to know when Longstreet expects to return to the Rappahannock and if any of his troops can be spared at present. Capt. J. K. Boswell of Jackson's staff speaks with Lee at headquarters; Lee tells him he thinks Hooker intended to advance last Friday (24th) but only the heavy rains prevented it. Lee meets with Jackson in the afternoon. A court of inquiry is formed to investigate Chilton's rejection as brigadier general.[32]

April 28, Tuesday (Fredericksburg): Porter Alexander visits ANV headquarters in the evening and spends the night. Rain showers during the day.[33]

April 29, Wednesday (Fredericksburg): Lee is awakened before dawn by Jackson's aide Lt. James P. Smith, who informs Lee that the Federals have crossed the Rappahannock River near Fredericksburg. Around 5:30 a.m. Lee meets with Jubal Early, whose troops occupy the ground in the immediate area of the crossing, and then goes to Prospect Hill where he and Jackson attempt to observe the enemy but cannot see them because of the thick morning fog. At 6:30 Lee notifies Gen. Pendleton of the enemy crossing near the mouth of Deep Run and tells him to be alert at other crossing sites used by Burnside in December. Over the next ninety minutes Lee notifies President Davis of the crossing, but is unable to provide many details because of the fog. He requests that any troops not needed south of the James River be forwarded to the ANV. The general also orders Pendleton to send up all batteries in the rear not belonging to Jackson's corps.[34]

More reports arrive throughout the morning and afternoon, including word from Stuart that a large enemy force crossed at Kelly's Ford and appears headed for Gordonsville. Later, Stuart reports at least three corps moving toward Germanna and Ely's fords on the Rapidan River, which prompts Lee to urge Davis to send any available troops to defend Gordonsville. Lee provides updates to the president and Gen. Cooper as he learns new information, sending several messages to each, and requests that Longstreet and his troops be sent back to the ANV. He informs the president, "Their intention I presume is to turn our left and probably to get into our rear. Our scattered condition favors their operations."[35]

In response to the enemy movements Lee orders Jackson to close up his corps on

---

32 *OR* 25, pt. 2, 752-3; *OR* 18, 1024-5; *OR* 4, 514; AIGO SO109, Chilton CSR. Chilton's court consisted of Maj. Gen. Richard Ewell, Brig. Gen. Charles Field, Brig. Gen. Roger Pryor, and Col. George Deas. Ibid.

33 Gallagher, *Fighting for the Confederacy*, 194; Krick, *CW Weather*, 6. Alexander did not mention the purpose of his visit or if he met with Lee at all, only that he visited with the staff. *Fighting for the Confederacy*, 194. Chilton was at the War Department in Richmond today. Jones, *Rebel War Clerk's Diary*, 300.

34 James P. Smith, "Stonewall Jackson's Last Battle," *B&L* vol. 3, 203; Gallagher, *Lee the Soldier*, 361; Mackowski, *Chancellorsville's Forgotten Front*, 86; REL to WNP, April 29, 1863 (2 messages), telegram book, REL HQ papers, VHS; REL to J. F. Davis, April 29, 1863, telegram book, REL HQ papers, VHS. According to J. P. Smith, Maj. Venable deemed his message important enough to wake Lee, who responded, "Well I thought I heard firing and was beginning to think it was time some of you young fellows were coming to tell me what it was all about. Tell your good general that I am sure he knows what to do. I will meet him at the front very soon." Smith, "Stonewall's Last Battle," 203. Jed Hotchkiss recorded a slightly different version of the exchange as told him by Smith: "I thought I heard firing, but was waiting for someone to come and tell me, and you are a good boy for telling me." McDonald, *Make Me a Map*, 136. Smith was not the only one who claimed to have awoken Lee that morning with news of Hooker's army; Lt. Robert T. Hubbard, adjutant of the 3rd VA Cav., wrote that when elements of his regiment detected Federals crossing upstream of Fredericksburg, the courier he sent to headquarters also found Lee still asleep and Maj. Taylor determined his news important enough to wake the general. R. T. Hubbard memoirs, R. T. Hubbard papers, Duke.

35 Freeman, *Lee*, vol. 2, 509-11; Freeman, *Lee's Dispatches*, 84-5; Dowdey, *Wartime Papers*, 441-3; *OR* 25, pt. 2, 756-7. Porter Alexander spent the night at ANV HQ and was still there when the reports of Hooker's movements began to arrive. Gallagher, *Fighting for the Confederacy*, 194-5. He later mentioned that he met with Lee regarding the organization of his battalion, but did not record the exact date other than to say "the day before the commencement of the battles." EPA to WNP, May 8, 1863, WNP papers, UNC. It seems unlikely that they would have discussed this while trying to determine the extent of Hooker's movements, but Alexander recorded no other time around this date when he was with Lee.

Fredericksburg with the lower Rappahannock guarded only by the 15th Virginia Cavalry. During the early evening Lee orders Gen. McLaws to withdraw his troops from Fredericksburg itself to the heights behind the town, and orders Richard Anderson to take his division west toward Chancellorsville to guard the roads approaching the army's left. Fearing that the enemy may have intercepted his earlier messages to Stuart, Lee sends orders to close up on Anderson, and instructions to the commander at Beaver Dam Station to gather up whatever mounted troops he can to watch Anderson's left flank. At 9:00 p.m. Lee sends President Davis a brief report of the day's operations. Periods of rain.[36]

April 30, Thursday (Fredericksburg): Lee informs President Davis that Stuart intercepted an enemy column near Germanna and captured prisoners from three different corps; Lee determines Hooker's "object [is] evidently to turn our left. If [I] had Longstreet's Division[s] I would feel safe." Lee orders Anderson to select and fortify the best position he can find and delay the enemy's advance as long as possible. With Hooker massing a large force on Lee's left, he sends McLaws (minus Barksdale's Brigade) to reinforce Anderson; he tells McLaws that the terrain in Anderson's front is not favorable for artillery so to send his extra guns to the rear. After consulting with Jackson and observing the Federals around Fredericksburg, Lee determines that to be a feint and Hooker's main body to be moving on his left flank. Accordingly he orders Jackson west, leaving behind Jubal Early's division (reinforced by Barksdale) to defend the heights south of the city.[37]

Lee advises Richmond that he has shifted the main body of the army from Fredericksburg into the Wilderness to meet Hooker. Lee orders Col. John Critcher's 15th Virginia Cavalry to watch Early's right flank, and instructs Sam Jones in southwest Virginia to send a portion of his cavalry to Stuart.[38]

Fearing for the safety of central Virginia, Lee orders his pontoon train at Orange to be moved to Gordonsville or Charlottesville and for the handful of troops at Gordonsville to be ready to defend that point against enemy cavalry. Maj. Gen. Edward Johnson is appointed to command of D. H. Hill's former division. Very late during the night Stuart arrives at Lee's headquarters from Kelly's Ford. The Richmond *Daily Dispatch* publishes an article about the meeting of Lee and Rob on the field at Sharpsburg.[39]

---

36 OR 51, pt. 2, 698-9; OR 25, pt. 2, 759-60; Taylor, *General Lee*, 162; REL to JEB Stuart, April 29, 1863, telegram book, REL HQ papers, VHS; REL to J. L. Davis, April 29, 1863, telegram book, REL HQ papers, VHS; REL to Jefferson Davis, April 29, 1863, telegram book, REL HQ papers, VHS; Krick, *CW Weather*, 6. Lee spent much time with McLaws on Marye's Heights; McLaws wrote to his wife: "We had a long conversation with each other, he was very confident of his ability to beat back the enemy should our troops behave as well as they have usually done, and 'General McLaws' he said 'Let them know that it is a stern reality now, it must be, Victory or Death, for defeat would be ruinous." Oeffinger, *A Soldier's General*, 179.

37 OR 25, pt. 2, 761-2; Dowdey, *Wartime Papers*, 447-9; Freeman, *Lee*, vol. 2, 512-3; Freeman, *Lee's Dispatches*, 86. Freeman wrote that Lee was ill this morning, but the general did not mention it himself, nor did any of the staff. Freeman, *Lee*, vol. 2, 512.

38 Dowdey, *Wartime Papers*, 449; Freeman, *Lee's Dispatches*, 86; OR 51, pt. 2, 699; REL to Sam Jones, April 30, 1863, telegram book, REL HQ papers, VHS.

39 REL to H. T. Douglas, April 30, 1863, telegram book, REL HQ papers, VHS; REL to Thomas Rhett, April 30, 1863, telegram book, REL HQ papers, VHS; OR 25, pt. 2, 762; Scheibert, *Seven Months in the Rebel States*, 59; REL newspaper references, DSF papers, LVA.

May 1863

The previous week, observed Lee's aide Walter Taylor, "has been a most eventful one. The operations of this army under Gen. Lee during that time," he predicted with good reason, "will compare favorably with the most brilliant engagements ever recorded."[1] Outnumbered almost three-to-one, Lee and the Army of Northern Virginia turned back "Fighting Joe" Hooker's Army of the Potomac at Chancellorsville by sending Stonewall Jackson's Second Corps crashing into Hooker's exposed right flank, and by blocking and driving back another force under Maj. Gen. John Sedgwick at Salem Church and eventually over the Rappahannock River. What is widely considered Lee's greatest victory, however, came at a high price: Stonewall Jackson, wounded by his own men, succumbed to pneumonia a week later after the amputation of his arm.[2]

James Longstreet rejoined the army with his two divisions shortly after Chancellorsville following his successful large-scale foraging operation in southeastern Virginia that included a failed siege of Suffolk. His return offset the army's recent losses. Jackson's loss deprived Lee of one of his two most trusted lieutenants and led to a revamped Army of Northern Virginia. The reorganization split the two large infantry corps into three smaller corps. Longstreet continued at the head of First Corps. Jackson's two most promising division commanders were promoted to lieutenant general and each given a corps with Richard S. Ewell in charge of Jackson's former Second Corps, and A. P. Hill tapped to lead the new Third Corps. Unfortunately for Lee and the army, neither officer would prove to be a good replacement for the late Stonewall. As new officers moved into division and brigade command positions, Lee availed himself of the opportunity to finally be rid of the talented yet troublesome D. H. Hill. As one historian put it, although he was a tenacious fighter, "there was something about Hill that irritated" Lee.[3]

The victory along the Rappahannock River left Lee in a situation similar to the one he was in the previous summer: He held the strategic initiative and did not wish to surrender it. Richmond, however, did not share his view. President Jefferson Davis and his cabinet secretaries were rightfully worried about the deteriorating situation in the Western Theater and alarmed over Lt. Gen. John Pemberton's inability to hold back Gen. U. S. Grant's Union operation to take control of the Mississippi River by seizing Vicksburg. Davis had a weighty decision to make: send a portion of Lee's army to reinforce Pemberton and put the Army of Northern Virginia in a defensive posture, or reinforce Lee to enable him to undertake another offensive north of the Potomac in the hope of drawing troops away from Mississippi and winning a major victory on Northern soil. Lee met with the president and his cabinet in the middle of the month to debate that very question.[4]

On the personal front, Lee grew increasingly frustrated that his wife and daughters did not understand the pressures and responsibilities of leading an army in wartime. Wife Mary complained

---

[1] Tower, *Lee's Adjutant*, 53.

[2] Jeffry D. Wert, *A Glorious Army: Robert E. Lee's Triumph, 1862-1863* (New York, 2011), 204-5.

[3] Ibid, 178. Longstreet wrote of Hill: "There was never a more plucky or persistent fighter . . . but he could not resist the temptation when it came to criticise [sic]." Ibid. D. H. Hill had been assigned to command in North Carolina, but was still reporting to Gen. Lee.

[4] Freeman, *Lee*, vol. 3, 19.

that he did not write to her often enough, while Mildred seemed oblivious to the fact that there was a war going on at all, and, like most teenagers of every generation, was focused only on herself.[5] Lee may not have known it at the time, but at the end of the month his former Arlington home was formally seized by the U.S. government for the failure to pay taxes.[6]

Once assured by the president that his army would not be weakened to aid Pemberton, Lee spent the latter half of the month reorganizing and seeking reinforcements. He reviewed much of the army, which increasingly came to be viewed by its officers and men (as well as by the public at large) as invincible.[7] After Chancellorsville, the open question was how well the Army of Northern Virginia would do under its new senior leadership.

* * *

---

[5] Dowdey, *Wartime Papers*, 491; REL to Mrs. REL, May 14, 1863, REL papers, LOC.

[6] Robert M. Poole, *On Hallowed Ground: The Story of Arlington National Cemetery* (New York, 2009), 52-3, 55. In June of 1862, the United States Congress passed legislation imposing a property tax on land in "insurrectionary" (i.e., seceded) portions of the United States, and amendments passed in early 1863 required that this tax be paid in person. Mary Lee, who suffered from severe rheumatoid arthritis and was ill behind Confederate lines, could not pay the tax in person so the estate was seized for nonpayment of taxes and auctioned on January 11, 1864. The United States government obtained the property for $26,800.

[7] J. F. J. Caldwell, *A History of a Brigade of South Carolinians Known First as "Gregg's" and Subsequently as "McGowan's Brigade"* (Philadelphia, 1866), 89; Dickert, *History of Kershaw's Brigade*, 225; Wert, *A Glorious Army*, 204-5.

May 1, Friday (Fredericksburg/Zoan Church/Chancellorsville): Around dawn Lee meets with Jeb Stuart and Maj. von Borcke regarding the cavalry's position west of Fredericksburg. After meeting with Stuart, Lee rides to Marye's Heights and Telegraph Hill, accompanied at least part of the time by Stonewall Jackson. Once he determined that the main Federal threat was not at Fredericksburg but rather farther to the west, Lee departs the town late in the morning, leaving Jubal Early in command of the small force left there.[8]

Around midday Lee meets Jackson near Zoan Church on the Orange Turnpike, just as skirmishers became engaged to the southwest along the Plank Road. At the front Lee personally orders Brig. Gen. Dorsey Pender to engage an enemy battery shelling the head of Jackson's column. As the Federals fall back in the face of Jackson's men, Lee personally reconnoiters the Federal left flank, but finds it unassailable.[9]

In late afternoon Lee informs Stuart that he has engaged the V Corps but none of the other corps of Hooker's army which are known to be in the area and instructs the cavalrymen to locate the unaccounted for enemy units. Around sunset Lee and Jackson meet at what becomes Lee's headquarters at the intersection of the Plank Road and Catharine Furnace Road, where they came under fire from both Federal sharpshooters and enemy artillery, which forces them to withdraw into the cover of the nearby woods.[10]

The two confer into the early hours of Saturday morning, and are joined during their discussion by Stuart and A. P. Hill. As the generals discuss options, Lee dispatches Maj. Talcott and Jackson's chief engineer Capt. J. K. Boswell to reconnoiter the Federal position, and receives a report from Fitz Lee that Hooker's right flank is completely in the air.[11]

Talcott and Boswell return before midnight and report that the enemy is too strong in front to be attacked directly. This information, along with Lee's own observations of the enemy's left flank, convinces Lee to send Jackson against Hooker's exposed right flank. During the evening, Lee telegraphs President Davis that he has moved to meet Hooker near Chancellorsville and requests reinforcements.[12]

May 2, Saturday (Chancellorsville): Lee continues to meet with Jackson in the early hours of the morning, and then meets with Rev. Beverly Tucker whom Stuart referred as a guide. After speaking with Rev. Tucker, Lee sleeps for a few hours under a tree before being awakened by Capt. James Smith of Jackson's staff who brings a report of another reconnaissance. Shortly before dawn Jed Hotchkiss

---

8 Freeman, *Lee*, vol. 2, 516-7; Long, *Memoirs of REL*, 251; Gallagher, *Fighting for the Confederacy*, 196; Dowdey, *Wartime Papers*, 450.

9 Freeman, *Lee*, vol. 2, 517-8; Noel G. Harrison, *Chancellorsville Battlefield Sites* (Lynchburg, VA, 1990), 24; William W. Chamberlaine, *Memoirs of the Civil War Between the Northern and Southern Sections of the United States of America, 1861-1865* (Washington, DC, 1912), 57; Gallagher, *Lee the Soldier*, 364. A South Carolina officer recalled Lee and Jackson passing his brigade on the Plank Road around noon while artillery dueled at the front. Caldwell, *A History of a Brigade of South Carolinians*, 73. An artillery officer recalled the cheers the men gave for Lee and Jackson as they passed: "I cannot recall a moment of higher enthusiasm during the four years of the war." Stiles, *Four Years*, 169. During a portion of the afternoon Lee accompanied the 1st TN of Gen. James Archer's Brigade. OR 25, pt. 1, 969.

10 OR 25, pt. 2, 764; Long, *Memoirs of REL*, 254-5; T.M.R. Talcott, "General Lee's Strategy at the Battle of Chancellorsville," *SHSP*, vol. 34, 17; Scheibert, *Seven Months in the Rebel States*, 60. Talcott's article is one of the most complete and detailed accounts of Lee's actions during the night of May 1-2, although he was absent for a portion of the night; it incorporates not only his own recollections, but those of several others present.

11 Smith, "Stonewall's Last Battle," 204; Taylor, *General Lee*, 165; Dabney, *Life and Campaigns*, 672; Gallagher, *Lee the Soldier*, 367; Freeman, *Lee*, vol. 2, 519-20; Dabney, *Life and Campaigns*, 672-3. It was probably during the "lull" as the generals waited for Talcott and Boswell to return when Lee called Prussian army Capt. Justus Scheibert to join them, introducing Scheibert to Jackson and telling him to stay with Jeb Stuart during the fighting. Scheibert, *Seven Months in the Rebel States*, 60-2.

12 Talcott, "Lee's Strategy at Chancellorsville," 16; Long, *Memoirs of REL*, 252; REL to Davis, May 1, 1863, telegraph book, REL HQ papers, VHS.

and Rev. Lacy brief Lee and Jackson on a route for Jackson's troops to get behind Hooker's flank.[13]

Around 7:00 a.m. Lee meets with Jackson at intersection of the Plank Road and Catherine Furnace Road one final time. It is the last time the two of them speak. After this, Lee meets with Gens. Richard Anderson and A. P. Hill, during which the group comes under sporadic small arms fire. Sometime after parting company with Jackson, Lee writes to President Davis to notify him that Hooker is now in force around Chancellorsville, and that the troops at Fredericksburg are just a diversion; he mentions Stonewall Jackson's flank march and the unlikelihood of any of Longstreet's forces arriving before battle is joined.[14]

Lee sends Col. Chilton to Fredericksburg with orders for Early to bring most of his infantry to the Chancellorsville front if he can do so safely. Lee spends much of the day with Anderson's Division, coming under fire while with William Mahone's brigade and personally ordering Mahone to send his skirmishers forward. While conferring with Lafayette McLaws, a shell strikes a tree very close to the generals and another shell causes Traveller to rear, prompting Capt. E. S. McCarthy of the Richmond Howitzers to urge Lee to find safer ground.[15]

When Jackson's troops attack, Lee orders an advance on his front to keep Hooker from reinforcing against Jackson; Lee directs Mahone's Brigade in this assault. Mahone's 6th Virginia captures the colors of the 107th Ohio which they present to Lee. Lee does not go to bed until around midnight at his headquarters at the Plank Road-Catherine Furnace Road intersection.[16]

May 3, Sunday (Chancellorsville/Fairview): Lee is awakened around 2:30 a.m. by Capt. R. E. Wilbourne of Jackson's staff, who brings word both of Jackson's success and his subsequent wounding. About an hour later, Jed Hotchkiss arrives with a similar message and takes breakfast with Lee at about 4:00 a.m. Upon learning of the dispositions of Jackson's men, Lee sends instructions to Stuart—now in temporary command of the Second Corps—to press the enemy and link up with Lee's wing of the army. He also sends a congratulatory note to the wounded Jackson and stating, "I should have chosen for the good of the country to have been disabled in your stead."[17]

---

13 Smith, "Stonewall's Last Battle," 204-5; Freeman, *Lee*, vol. 2, 521; McDonald, *Make Me a Map*, 137-8; Henderson, *Stonewall Jackson*, vol. 2, 531-2. See Appendix II-5 in Freeman, *Lee*, vol. 2 for his analysis of the Lee-Jackson interaction of May 1-2.

14 Freeman, *Lee*, vol. 2, 524; Gallagher, *Lee the Soldier*, 369; Benjamin W. Leigh, "The Wounding of Stonewall Jackson—Extracts from a Letter of Major Benjamin Watkins Leigh," *SHSP*, vol. 3, 230; *OR* 25, pt. 2, 765. At the famed "last meeting" of Lee and Jackson, Freeman wrote that Jackson was mounted but makes no definitive conclusion as to whether Lee was on horseback or on foot. Robert K. Krick concluded that Lee was mounted and Jackson on foot, resting one arm on the neck of Lee's horse. Freeman, *Lee*, vol. 2, 524; Gallagher, *Lee the Soldier*, 369. Maj. Leigh, one of A. P. Hill's staff officers, did not put a time for when he saw Lee with Anderson and Hill, but he did note that "Jackson's corps had already commenced the flank movement." Hill being present suggests that his division, which was the last of Jackson's three in the order of march, had not yet been put in motion, which Leigh places around 9:00 a.m., thus making it appear that Lee's meeting with Anderson and Hill took place sometime between 7:00 and 9:00 a.m. Ibid.

15 Lee, *Memoirs of WNP*, 263-4; Bernard, *War Talks*, 71-3; J. B Minor, "General Robert E. Lee under Fire," *CV*, vol. 17, 333. Chilton delivered Lee's orders to Jubal Early about 11:00 a.m., but completely botched them; Lee meant the orders to be discretionary, but Chilton informed Early they were peremptory, which resulted in Early removing most of his forces from Fredericksburg. When Chilton returned, Lee sent the correct orders to Early, who received them that evening and reoccupied his former position during the night. Early, *Memoirs*, 200-3. See Mackowski & White, *Chancellorsville's Forgotten Front*, for a scathing indictment of Chilton not just on this occasion, but for his performance and abilities throughout the war.

16 Freeman, *Lee*, vol. 2, 531-2; *OR* 25, pt. 1, 864. Lt. Col. Edward Feild of the 12th VA of Mahone's Brigade recalled, "I saw more of Gen. Lee [at Chancellorsville] than during any battle of the war." Bernard, *War Talks*, 73.

17 MacDonald, *Make Me a Map*, 138-9; Cook, *Life of REL*, 238-9; Freeman, *Lee*, vol. 2, 532; *OR* 25, pt. 2, 769. Lee reportedly responded to Wilbourne's news of Jackson's wounding, "Any victory is dearly bought which deprives us of the

Going to the front, Lee observes the attack on Fairview, conversing with the Prussian officer Scheibert; a bullet strikes the ground just in front of the officers which Lee retrieves and gives to Scheibert as a souvenir. Once Stuart seizes the high ground at Hazel Grove, Lee moves his command post there, despite the heavy enemy artillery fire directed at the spot. Lee personally sends Archer's Brigade into battle, effectively establishing a link between his forces and Stuart's. By late morning, with the two wings of the army reunited, Lee rides into the Chancellorsville clearing to thundering cheers. While near the Chancellor mansion a message arrives from Jackson which Maj. Marshall reads to Lee, congratulating the general for his victory.[18]

Around midday Lee telegraphs word of his victory to President Davis, including the wounding of Stonewall Jackson and A. P. Hill. With Joe Hooker temporarily disposed of, Lee confers with Gen. McLaws about sending a force back to reinforce Jubal Early. While they talk, the alarmed chaplain of the 17th Mississippi arrives with word that Early has been driven away from Fredericksburg. In response, the general orders McLaws to take his own division, reinforced by Gen. Mahone's Virginia brigade, back toward Fredericksburg, and instructs Raleigh Colston to take his division toward U.S. Mine Ford.[19]

During the evening the general orders Gens. McLaws and Early to work in concert to attack the Federals at Fredericksburg. He also notifies Richmond that Early was forced to give up Fredericksburg, and requests that reinforcements from North Carolina be sent instead to Hanover Junction to guard against enemy cavalry raids. Lee is joined at his headquarters on the lawn of Fairview in the evening by Stuart and Maj. von Borcke; as they sit around the campfire von Borcke provides several candles for Lee to read incoming messages. One of these is a proposal from Early that he and McLaws attack Fredericksburg from two directions simultaneously, to which Lee accedes telling Early "I think you would demolish them."[20]

---

services of Jackson, even for a short time." Dabney, *Life and Campaigns*, 701-2. Lee's breakfast consisted of ham and crackers. May 15, 1863, Richmond *Enquirer*, REL newspaper references, DSF papers.

18 Scheibert, *Seven Months in the Rebel States*, 75-6; Trout, *In the Saddle with Stuart*, 47; Gallagher, *Lee the Soldier*, 371; OR 25, pt. 1, 925; Maurice, *Lee's Aide de Camp*, 173. Scheibert amused Lee by recounting how he captured half-dozen Yankees of the 6th Ohio on his way from Jeb Stuart to Lee that morning. Scheibert, *Seven Months in the Rebel States*, 69-70. Lt. Col. Feild of the 12th VA recalled of Gen. Lee's arrival at the Chancellor mansion, "I heard no cheer during the war to compare with this." Bernard, *War Talks*, 73. One artilleryman wrote, "I wish you could have seen and heard the boys cheer him [Lee] as he rode down our thinned ranks, after the battle was over. Even a number of Yankees were constrained to cheer him so grand and majestic was his appearance." William S. Harrison, Jr., to "mother," May 8, 1863, William S. Harrison papers, VHS. Although the message from Jackson apparently no longer survives, Marshall was adamant that it did not make mention of the amputation of Jackson's arm. Maurice, *Lee's Aide de Camp*, 173. There is some uncertainty as to Gen. Lee's reply to this message. Freeman wrote that it was the "disabled in your stead" note based on James P. Smith's recollections, but his conclusion is at odds with Hotchkiss's recollections of when that particular note was sent. See Freeman, *Lee*, vol. 2, 543 n51.

19 OR 25, pt. 2, 768; OR 25, pt. 1, 830; Stiles, *Four Years*, 174-8; Raleigh E. Colston, "Lee's Knowledge of Hooker's Movements," B&L, vol. 3, 233. As Lee's telegram to President Davis made no mention of Early at Fredericksburg, it must have been sent around midday before word of Early's action reached Lee. Robert Stiles of the Richmond Howitzers wrote that he was observing a large number of captured Federals when several recognized him from a prewar acquaintance and called out; when he saw this, Lee told Stiles to go amongst the prisoners and see if he could learn anything of importance. Stiles, *Four Years*, 174-5. Stiles was still in the vicinity when Lee learned of Jubal Early's defeat and was amused by Lee's reference to Union Maj. Gen. John Sedgwick, who commanded the Federal wing at Fredericksburg, as "Major Sedgwick"—a reference to Sedgwick's prewar rank. Ibid, 176-8. Colston estimated that Lee learned of Early's fate around 1:00 p.m. and he met with Lee shortly thereafter. "I found [Lee] standing in a small tent pitched by the roadside," Colston wrote. "His plain gray sack coat, with only three stars on the rolling collar, was, like his face, well sprinkled with the dust of the battlefield." "Lee's Knowledge of Hooker's Movements," 233. According to Brig. Gen. Joseph Kershaw, Lee's initial plan was to send Kershaw and Mahone only, but the news from Early changed this plan. OR 25, pt. 1, 830.

20 OR 25, pt. 2, 768-70; Scheibert, *Seven Months in the Rebel States*, 77; Freeman, *Lee*, vol. 2, 549-50. Scheibert wrote that Lee, Stuart, and the wounded A. P. Hill all established headquarters on the lawn of Fairview (he misidentified the property

May 4, Monday (Fairview/Chancellorsville/Salem Church/Idlewild): In the early morning Lee orders Jackson removed to Guiney's Station on the RF&P and a guard placed with him until moved. Lee telegraphs President Davis that he needs two major generals to fill command vacancies and wants Robert Rodes and either Arnold Elzey or Edward Johnson for these billets. Determining Hooker's new position to be too strong to attack without his entire force, Lee turns his attention to John Sedgwick's force, sending Richard Anderson's division to join McLaws and Early around Salem Church. Lee goes to command this force himself, leaving Stuart to watch Hooker with Jackson's three divisions. Lee and Anderson arrive together in mid-morning at the head of Anderson's troops. Inspecting the position and talking with McLaws, Lee finds that McLaws—senior officer on the field prior to Lee's arrival—had done little in the way of preparing for attack and knew even less about the enemy position. Lee then spends the next several hours personally reconnoitering the ground himself, and meeting with Early.[21]

By early afternoon Lee is on Anderson's front in between McLaws on the left and Early on the right; his plan of attack is little changed from what Early proposed yesterday—to turn Sedgwick's flank and drive him into the Rappahannock. Lee watches Early's troops attack around the Downman house, Idlewild, and takes particular notice of Brig. Gen. Robert Hoke's brigade, asking "who the young man was leading that gallant brigade." He establishes his headquarters at Idlewild once the enemy is driven away, and meets with Early there to discuss continuing the attack after nightfall.[22]

At 10:00 p.m. Lee sends a message to McLaws advising him of the success of Anderson and Early and ordering a night attack: "If we let them alone until morning we will find them again entrenched, so I wish to push them over the river tonight." In response to a message from Stuart warning of increased enemy activity, Lee orders Jackson to be moved immediately to the Chandler farm at Guiney's Station, and for corps surgeon Dr. Hunter McGuire to accompany the wounded general.[23]

May 5, Tuesday (Idlewild/Salem Church/Chancellorsville/Fairview): Finding Sedgwick gone from his front at Salem Church, Lee returns to Chancellorsville with McLaws and Anderson's divisions, leaving Early at Fredericksburg to watch Sedgwick. Lee establishes his headquarters at Fairview again, and there meets with Jed Hotchkiss, who brings the latest news on Jackson's condition; Lee queries Hotchkiss

---

as Fairfield); Freeman—using Colston as his source—wrote only that Lee's HQ was on the side of the Plank Road. Freeman, *Lee*, vol. 2, 546. Fairview was at the western edge of the Chancellorsville clearing and used as a hospital after the fighting; it burned several weeks after the battle and little trace remains today on the grounds of Fredericksburg & Spotsylvania NMP. Harrison, *Chancellorsville Battlefield Sites*, 102. Scheibert may have been mistaken about Fairview serving as anything more than a temporary command post, for Rice Bull of the 123rd New York, who was captured in the fighting on the 3rd, mentioned Stuart's HQ as being in the vicinity of Fairview but that Lee's HQ "was two miles on toward Fredericksburg." K. Jack Bauer, ed., *Soldiering: The Civil War Diary of Rice C. Bull* (Novato, CA, 1995), 69, 79.

21 Freeman, *Lee*, vol. 2, 550-1; OR 25, pt. 2, 774; OR 25, pt. 1, 827, 869; Gallagher, *Fighting for the Confederacy*, 213; Early, *Memoirs*, 227-8. The message to Davis bears no time stamp, but as it contains no reference to the fighting at Salem Church on this date, it seems logical that it was sent in the morning before that battle began. Porter Alexander wrote that Lee came to his position on the left of McLaws's line about 10:00 a.m., and noted that Lee was in a very foul mood: "For the first time . . . I saw him in a temper. I could not comprehend at the time whom it was with, or what it was about." Gallagher, *Fighting for the Confederacy*, 213. Presumably Lafayette McLaws' inactivity was the reason for Lee's anger.

22 Freeman, *Lee*, vol. 2, 552-5; Barefoot, *General Hoke*, 84; Early, *Memoirs*, 232; Idlewild National Register of Historic Places registration form, April 23, 2009. Idlewild was completed just before the war in 1859 and was severely damaged by fire in 2003; its burned-out shell stands just south of Route 3 (wartime Plank Road) immediately east of Interstate 95, amidst residential and commercial development. Ibid. Just before the attack began around 6:00 p.m., Lee rode along Hoke's line: "Suddenly we saw passing through the thin woods on the little hill in our rear, Gen. Lee. As soon as his face was well seen . . . every man instantly commenced getting ready. The word soon went down the line, 'All is right, Uncle Robert is here, we will whip them.' There was no cheering, the men leaned on their muskets and looked at him, as he rode along his lines, as tho' a God were passing by." Gallagher, *Lee the Soldier*, 373.

23 OR 25, pt. 2, 860-1; Freeman, *Lee*, vol. 2, 555.

on the roads around U.S. Mine Ford and sends the engineer to gather what information he can. Lee informs President Davis and Secretary Seddon of the fight at Salem Church and Sedgwick's withdrawal across the river, and that Hooker is entrenched in front of U.S. Mine Ford. Heavy rain beginning in the afternoon and during the night.[24]

May 6, Wednesday (Fairview): Shortly before dawn Hotchkiss comes to headquarters bearing word from Stuart that the Federals are gone. Lee is just rising when Hotchkiss arrives and, listening to the engineer's report over coffee, sends him back to Stuart with orders to attack. Dorsey Pender arrives "just at dawn" with confirmation that Hooker's army is indeed gone; Lee in frustration orders Pender to pursue "and damage them all you can." Lee himself goes to confer with Stuart soon after, and the two are joined by A. P. Hill.

Realizing that the Army of the Potomac has escaped, Lee orders Hotchkiss to draft a map of the battlefield and places A. P. Hill in command of Jackson's corps and returns Stuart to the cavalry. He informs Richmond that 5,000 enemy cavalry are running loose in central Virginia threatening the James River & Kanawha Canal and multiple railroads; unless additional cavalry is sent from North Carolina "it will be impossible to arrest these raids, and they will roam through this entire section of country with little or no molestation." He also denies a request by Hooker for a truce to bury his dead, but he assures the Federal commander that his wounded and dead will receive the same care as Lee's own casualties, but medical staff and supplies to assist with the treatment of Yankee wounded would be most welcome. Heavy rain throughout much of the day.[25]

May 7, Thursday (Fairview/Fredericksburg): In the morning, Lee moves headquarters back to his previous camp site on Mine Road outside of Fredericksburg; British journalist Francis Lawley accompanies him on the ride. Rev. Lacy stops at headquarters while in search of Dr. S. B. Morrison to assist Dr. McGuire with Jackson's care; Lacy informs Lee that Jackson's condition is worsening. Lee tells Lacy, "Give him my affectionate regards, and tell him to make haste and get well, and come back to me as soon as he can. He has lost his left arm; but I have lost my right arm." Before leaving the Chancellorsville area, Chaplain Thomas L. Ambrose of the 12th New Hampshire comes to headquarters to request provisions for the Union wounded.

Lee issues a congratulatory order to the army for its recent victories, and has President Davis's letter of congratulations read to each unit. He advises President Davis by telegraph that the army was reunited on the 5th and he attempted to attack Hooker yesterday but the Federals already retreated across the Rappahannock. He also again requests the promotion of Robert Rodes to command D. H. Hill's division and the assignment of Edward

---

24 Hotchkiss, *Virginia*, 392; *OR* 25, pt. 1, 794-5; REL to Seddon, May 5, 1863, telegram book, REL HQ papers, VHS; Krick, *CW Weather*, 95. The telegram to Seddon appears in the *OR* but is dated May 6, which may be the date of its delivery in Richmond as the date in the telegram book is clearly the 5th; it was obviously written before Lee learned around dawn of the 6th of Hooker's withdrawal. *OR* 25, pt. 2, 779. According to Hotchkiss, Lee's HQ was located "at Fairview cemetery." Hotchkiss, *Virginia*, 392. The telegram to Davis is headed "Headquarters, Guiney's"; while this almost certainly refers to the telegraph station at Guiney's Station, which would have been the closest to the ANV at this time, at least one Lee biographer has taken it to mean that Lee himself was at Guiney's Station at some point on the 5th. Dowdey, *Wartime Papers*, 455; Thomas, *REL*, 287. This is a curious interpretation by Thomas, who concedes Lee did not see Jackson at any point after his wounding, but what other reason would Lee have for going to Guiney's Station during this time other than to visit the wounded Stonewall Jackson? It is only about 20 miles, depending on the route taken, from Idlewild to Guiney's Station, so it was physically possible for Lee to have done just that. However, this seems extremely unlikely as not only is there no evidence placing Lee there, but during the afternoon Hotchkiss brought an update on Jackson. If Lee had gone to the Chandler farm at Guiney's Station, he would have been aware of Jackson's condition, thus it is this author's contention that Thomas's assertion that Lee was at Guiney's Station is incorrect.

25 McDonald, *Make Me a Map*, 141-2; Hotchkiss, *Virginia*, 392; *OR* 25, pt. 2, 432, 781-2. When Pender brought Lee the news of Hooker's retreat, Lee reportedly lost his temper and snapped, "Why General Pender! This is the way you young men always do. You allow those people to get away. I tell you what to do, but you don't do it! Go after them and damage them all you can!" Hotchkiss, *Virginia*, 392. The order placing A. P. Hill in command of the Second Corps was the uniquely numbered SO 123 ½. *OR* 25, pt. 2, 782.

Johnson for the other vacant division. He tells President Davis that "unless we can increase the cavalry attached to this army we shall constantly be subject to aggressive expeditions of the enemy similar to those experienced in the last ten days." In addition to more mounted troops, Lee points out that he was outnumbered 3:1 in the recent battle, and must have additional troops as Hooker is being reinforced; he proposes drawing troops from the Atlantic coast and transferring them to Virginia under Beauregard. He also requests that President Davis come to Fredericksburg for consultation, if possible.[26]

Lee advises Seddon that Hooker's cavalry is reportedly heading back toward the Rappahannock, and Stuart is moving to intercept them. Lee informs Longstreet that a forced march by Hood and Pickett is not necessary because the immediate threat from Hooker had passed, but he is to move a division to Tolersville to guard the railroad. Lee writes Hooker granting permission for the Federals to care for their wounded on the field at Chancellorsville; he explains that he denied the request previously because active operations were pending. That evening, Lee goes to Forest Hill, the home of the Hamilton family at Hamilton's Crossing, to pay his respects and visit the grave of distant cousin George Washington Stuart of the Rockbridge Artillery, killed in the recent fighting. Weather "bad."[27]

May 8, Friday (Fredericksburg): Lee thanks President Davis for his congratulatory letter and advises that he ordered it read to every unit in the army; Edward Johnson and Robert Rodes are announced as new division commanders in Jackson's former Second Corps. Lee informs temporary corps commander A. P. Hill that orders coming from Col. Chilton as chief of staff "may be considered as emanating directly from me and executed accordingly," and Lee advises Sec. Seddon that the forces sent from Richmond to guard the Virginia Central will be ordered back as soon as Gen. Hood's division takes their place. Lee answers an inquiry from Joe Hooker regarding medical supplies for the Federal wounded, explaining that the medical director will have them distributed if they can be gotten across the river; he alerts both McLaws and Anderson that the Federals will send ambulances and medical supplies across the river tomorrow morning. James Longstreet is ordered to halt Pickett's Division and to send a force to harass enemy boats reported to be operating in the Pamunkey River.[28]

May 9, Saturday (Fredericksburg): Longstreet rejoins the ANV and he and his staff have lunch with Lee at army headquarters; Lee briefs Longstreet on the recent fighting and the condition of the army. Lee informs Stuart that he may use the army's pontoons at either Orange or Gordonsville although Lee fears they may not be protected once laid down across the river; he adds that he is transferring "Grumble" Jones and his brigade from the Valley to Stuart's division, with Albert Jenkins taking over the Valley. Lee sends the corresponding orders to southwest Virginia for Jenkins and his brigade to go to Staunton, and asks Gen. Samuel Jones his opinion of Jenkins as possible Valley district commander. The general issues a circular requesting a list of vacancies among general and field officers in each

---

26 Gallagher, *Lee the Soldier*, 80-1; Dabney, *Life and Campaigns*, 716; Bauer, *Soldiering*, 79; OR 25, pt. 1, 805; Dowdey, *Wartime Papers*, 457; Freeman, *Lee's Dispatches*, 87-9; OR 25, pt. 2, 782-3. Lawley wrote of this ride: "Even at this intoxicating moment, not a particle of self-exaltation or conscious triumph was discoverable on Lee's features, or traceable in his conversation.... His road lay over ground where the hottest fighting had taken place.... General Lee said, in weariness and anguish, 'All that I want them (the Federals) to do is to leave us what we are, plain Virginian farmers.'" Gallagher, *Lee the Soldier*, 80-1.

27 OR 25, pt. 2, 447, 783; OR 18, 1049; REL to Longstreet, May 7, 1863, telegram book, REL HQ papers, VHS; REL to Mrs. REL, May 14, 1863, REL papers, LOC; Scheibert, *Seven Months in the Rebel States*, 78.

28 OR 25, pt. 2, 448, 785-7; REL to Seddon, May 8, 1863, telegram book, REL HQ papers, VHS; REL to Longstreet, May 8, 1863, telegram book, REL HQ papers, VHS. Having run afoul of Jackson on numerous occasions, Hill was likely seeking guidance to avoid any similar misunderstandings now that he was reporting directly to Lee. GO60 published on this date set forth the most current rules for providing a substitute for military service and noted that each individual case must be signed off by Lee personally. OR 25, pt. 2, 787.

command, as well as a list of officers for promotion.²⁹

May 10, Sunday (Fredericksburg): In the morning Lee, accompanied by Scheibert and others, attends church service led by Rev. Lacy at Second Corps headquarters; the service ends with a prayer for Jackson. Rev. Lacy privately informs Lee that Jackson is not expected to survive the day, to which Lee replies that that cannot be the case, that "God will not take him from us, now that we need him so much." At midday Lee receives a message from Sec. Seddon about sending Pickett's Division to reinforce Pemberton at Vicksburg, to which Lee replies that he strongly opposes this. Rather than weaken his army, which he claims will leave him heavily outnumbered and forced to fall back into the Richmond defenses (the last thing President Davis wants to hear), he should be reinforced.³⁰

Lee answers a message from Hooker regarding families recovering bodies from the battlefield at Chancellorsville, telling him that he will gladly have a search made for specific bodies upon request and have the remains sent across the river. Lee orders Hood to deploy his troops to cover the railroad around Gordonsville, and for the troops there to return to Richmond. He receives a letter from his wife, but has not time to answer it and in the afternoon learns of Jackson's death; he informs Seddon by telegram and requests an honor guard to meet the body in Richmond. He informs A. P. Hill of Jackson's death and orders Jackson's aide Sandie Pendleton to escort the body to the capital.³¹

May 11, Monday (Fredericksburg): Jackson's aide Henry Kyd Douglas meets with Lee to ask permission for the Stonewall Brigade to accompany its former commander's body to Richmond, but Lee tells him that the men cannot be spared and that Lee himself cannot be away long enough to go. General Orders 61 announces to the army the death of Jackson. Lee writes President Davis of recent intelligence regarding the overwhelming strength of the Army of the Potomac thus necessitating reinforcement of the Army of Northern Virginia: "I think you will agree with me that every effort should be made to reinforce this army in order to oppose the large force which the enemy seems to be concentrating against it." He also proposes that Gen. D. H. Hill be given command of North Carolina. Lee orders Stuart to complete his pontoon bridge and move into Culpeper to better observe the Federals, also informing him of Jackson's death. He explains further to Stuart that the troops at Gordonsville were returned to Richmond upon orders from the War Department, otherwise Stuart could have retained them for his own use.³²

Lee cautions Johnston Pettigrew in command at Hanover Junction that Pickett reports Federals moving in that direction from West Point. Lee tells Gen. Alexander Lawton that he is glad Lawton has recovered from his wound, but as Lee feared that Lawton would not be able to resume field command he assigned John B. Gordon to permanent command of Lawton's brigade. Lee writes to Hooker regarding the evacuation of Union wounded to the other side of the Rappahannock, and advises

---

29 James Longstreet, "Lee's Invasion of Pennsylvania," *B&L*, vol. 3, 244-5; Latrobe diary, May 9, 1863, VHS; *OR* 25, pt. 2, 788-90; Circular, May 9, 1863, REL papers, MOC. Osmun Latrobe, one of Longstreet's staff officers, suggested that Lee and Longstreet were in consultation for some time, but Longstreet wrote that they "had very little conversation." Longstreet, "Lee's invasion of PA," 244-5. HQ received a message from Richmond, but it was either incorrectly deciphered by HQ staff or was not encoded correctly in Richmond; it concerned possibly sending Pickett's Division to Pemberton's army at Vicksburg and was properly read on the 10th. *OR* 25, pt. 2, 790.

30 Scheibert, *Seven Months in the Rebel States*, 80-1; Jones, *Personal Reminiscences of REL*, 152-3; Dabney, *Life and Campaigns*, 725; *OR* 25, pt. 2, 790. This message from Sec. Seddon regarding Pickett and Vicksburg was initially received on the 9th but was badly garbled and could not be read, and thus resent on the 10th.

31 *OR* 25, pt. 2, 461, 791; REL to Hood, May 10, 1863, telegram book, REL HQ papers, VHS; REL to Thomas Rhett, May 10, 1863, telegram book, REL HQ papers, VHS; Dowdey, *Wartime Papers*, 484; REL to A. P. Hill, May 10, 1863, WNP papers, UNC.

32 Douglas, *I Rode with Stonewall*, 221; *OR* 25, pt. 2, 791-3; REL to Stuart, May 11, 1863, telegram book, REL HQ papers, VHS.

McLaws to admit Federal ambulances into his lines when they appear. He writes to both his wife and Custis, about Jackson: "I do not know how to replace him." He requests that Custis send him some summer clothing he left in Richmond, and also mentions that he must meet with the president, be it at headquarters or in Richmond.[33]

May 12, Tuesday (Fredericksburg): Lee endorses and forwards to Richmond "Grumble" Jones's report of his recent West Virginia raid.[34]

May 13, Wednesday (Fredericksburg): Lee receives a letter from Mary.[35]

May 14, Thursday (Fredericksburg/Richmond): Lee answers Mary's letter before leaving camp for Richmond, expressing regret over the death of cousins Bernard Hill Carter and George Washington Stuart, both killed at Chancelorsville, and mentions a visit from Lt. Randolph McKim, who came in search of Jeb Stuart's body. He mentions his frustration with Mildred and what he views as her selfishness in doing nothing to help either the family or the war effort: "A life of idleness in times like these is sinful."[36]

May 15, Friday (Richmond): Lee meets with the president and secretary of war regarding reinforcing Vicksburg or Lee's army. War Department clerk J. B. Jones notes that "Lee looked thinner, and a little pale."[37]

May 16, Saturday (Richmond): Lee requests reinforcements from D. H. Hill in North Carolina, but is opposed to exchanging veteran brigades from his army for larger fresh ones from Hill's command; he does consent to exchanging one brigade but points out to Hill that Ransom and Cooke's brigades belong to the ANV and are only on detached service with Hill. Lee orders Samuel Jones to send all cavalry he possibly can to Staunton, and requests Maj. Harman in Staunton to ensure that Jones does not ruin the horses in getting them to Staunton. Lee advises Longstreet by telegram that Pickett's Division passed through Richmond this morning.[38]

---

33 OR 18, 1056; REL to Lawton, May 11, 1863, Lawton papers, UNC; OR 25, pt. 2, 465-6; REL to McLaws, May 11, 1863, McLaws papers, UNC; Jones, *Personal Reminiscences of REL*, 153-4; Dowdey, *Wartime Papers*, 441.

34 OR 25, pt. 1, 115. It is likely that Lee spent much of the 13th and 14th in consultation with Longstreet regarding both a replacement for Jackson and the War Department's desire to send at least one of Lee's divisions to the Western Theater.

35 REL to Mrs. REL, May 14, 1863, REL papers, LOC. On either the 12th or 13th Lee must have made arrangements with President Davis to meet with him in Richmond, and also—likely on the 13th—with Longstreet to command the army in his absence.

36 REL to Mrs. REL, May 14, 1863, REL papers, LOC; Freeman, *Lee*, vol. 3, 19. Freeman wrote that Lee's visit to Richmond began on the 14th, but there is no solid evidence to confirm this. While Lee was seen in Richmond on the 15th, his letter to Mary written on the 14th was from Fredericksburg, and a telegram from the adjutant general was sent to him at Fredericksburg on the 14th. OR 25, pt. 2, 798. It is possible that Lee left for Richmond by train on the morning of the 15th, but without definitive evidence either way this is strictly conjecture. In the absence of concrete evidence, Freeman's date of the 14th is used here.

37 Jones, *War Clerk's Diary*, 325-6. According to clerk Jones, Jeb Stuart and Sam French were also at the War Department on this date, and French wrote that he also saw Richard Ewell and Robert Ransom while in Richmond; it is possible that Lee met with some or all of them while in the city. Ibid; French, *Two Wars*, 168. Longstreet, who was in command of the ANV in Lee's absence, telegraphed Lee requesting that Pickett be sent to Hanover Junction. OR 25, pt. 2, 801. It is possible that Lee did not leave Fredericksburg until the morning of the 15th; none of the accounts placing him in Richmond on the 15th state when he arrived. Whenever he arrived, it is almost certain that he stayed with Custis at the Franklin St. house.

38 OR 18, 1063; REL to D. H. Hill, May 16, 1863, telegram book, REL HQ papers, VHS; OR 25, pt. 2, 805; REL to M. G. Harman, May 16, 1863, telegram book, REL HQ papers, VHS; REL to Longstreet, May 16, 1863, telegram book, REL HQ papers, VHS. The full Davis cabinet met in the morning to consider the Vicksburg question; it is possible that Lee was there briefly at the beginning of the meeting, but he did not participate in the day's discussion. Trudeau, *REL*, 115. Postmaster General John Reagan recorded that the discussion lasted all day and into the evening, but he made no mention of Lee being present. Reagan, *Memoirs*, 121.

May 17, Sunday (Richmond): Lee attends church at St. Paul's and writes to a Dr. S. B. Anderson thanking him for a package of strawberries, bread, and milk.[39]

May 18, Monday (Richmond/Ashland/Fredericksburg): Lee returns to Fredericksburg by the morning train on the RF&P, stopping for breakfast at Ashland, where he visits Judith McGuire and Bishop John Johns, as well as several of Agnes's friends. Upon his return to Fredericksburg, Lee advises Seddon that Union forces under Robert Milroy occupied Front Royal the previous day and may be moving to join Hooker, so quickly send more cavalry to Culpeper to join Jeb Stuart. He instructs Stuart to keep watch on Gen. Milroy's movements.[40]

May 19, Tuesday (Fredericksburg): James Walker and William "Extra Billy" Smith are named to brigade command. A court of inquiry returns its findings regarding Col. Chilton's actions regarding Gen. John Magruder after the Seven Days' Battles, determining that Chilton acted in the best interest of the service and no disciplinary action will be taken against him.[41]

May 20, Wednesday (Fredericksburg): Lee proposes to President Davis reorganizing the ANV into three corps and recommends Richard Ewell and A. P. Hill for corps command, calling Hill "the best soldier of his grade with me," and naming Richard Anderson and J. B. Hood as potential corps commanders in future, also listing recommendations for brigade vacancies. Lee requests that the secretary of war officially name D. H. Hill to command in North Carolina, but transferring Drewry's Bluff from that department to the Department of Richmond; he also orders that Colquitt's Brigade be sent to Hill in North Carolina in exchange for Junius Daniel's Brigade. Lee writes to Isaac Trimble offering him command of the Shenandoah Valley, and requests Gen. Elzey in Richmond to have patrols on the lookout for deserters attempting to cross the James. He writes to Mary Triplett in Richmond apologizing for being unable to attend her party while in Richmond, and also to his wife with the latest family and military news.[42]

May 21, Thursday (Fredericksburg): Lee answers a May 9 letter from Congressman William C. Rives of Albemarle County, thanking him for his congratulations for Chancellorsville but deeply regretting the loss of Jackson. Lee writes also to Hood, glad to have him back with the army and stating, "Our army would be invincible if it could be

---

39 G. Ward Hubbs, ed., *Voices from Company D: Diaries by the Greensboro Guards, 5th Alabama Infantry Regiment, Army of Northern Virginia* (Athens, GA, 2003), 168; REL to S. B. Anderson, May 17, 1863, REL papers, SH. It is possible that Lee visited with Mary, perhaps going to Shirley on this date, as the phrasing of his first letter to her after returning to Fredericksburg suggests that he saw her at some point while in Richmond: "I felt very sad . . . at leaving you in so helpless and suffering a state." Dowdey, *Wartime Papers*, 486. Whenever possible, it was his habit to visit her after church on Sundays when he was in Richmond.

40 Dowdey, *Wartime Papers*, 493; McGuire, *Diary of a Southern Refugee*, 214-5; *OR* 25, pt. 2, 807; REL to Stuart, May 18, 1863, telegram book, REL HQ papers, VHS. McGuire noted that Lee did not go to the hotel in Ashland with the rest of the train's passengers for breakfast, but came to her residence and remained there until "the whistle summoned him to his seat in the cars." McGuire, *Diary of a Southern Refugee*, 214-5.

41 *OR* 25, pt. 2, 809; Chilton CSR. James Walker was expelled from VMI just shy of his graduation in 1852 as a result of charges brought by Professor Thomas J. Jackson. A vengeful Walker attempted to kill Jackson with a brick and apparently considered challenging the future Stonewall to a duel. Walker was one of Jubal Early's favorites and he took command of the Stonewall Brigade after Chancellorsville, leading it until he was wounded at Spotsylvania in May 1864. Robert K. Krick, "James Alexander Walker," *Confederate General*, vol. 6, 86-7; Warner, *Generals in Gray*, 319.

42 *OR* 25, pt. 2, 810-3; *OR* 18, 1066; REL to Mary Triplett, May 20, 1863, REL papers, SH; Dowdey, *Wartime Papers*, 486-7. Lee's letter to Davis suggests that he met with Longstreet that morning, almost certainly to discuss the proposed three corps structure and their commanders, and that it was at this meeting that Lee learned that Longstreet ordered D. H. Hill, Sam French, and Robert Ransom to all report directly to the War Department rather than naming Hill to command the Department of North Carolina, as Lee assumed had been done. Lee's phrasing, however, is vague enough that his dealing with Longstreet that morning may not have been in person but rather in writing, although this seems highly unlikely, especially as any such correspondence is not known to exist. The date of Mary Triplett's soiree is not known.

properly organized and officered. There never were such men in an army before." Lee alerts Seddon to the large number of desertions from North Carolina units, and directs Gen. Pettigrew at Hanover Junction to apprehend them. Lee explains to Sam Jones that the 50th Virginia cannot be returned to him until the 25th and 31st Virginia are returned by Imboden. J. M. Jones is named to brigade command, and D. H. Hill is notified that Colquitt's Brigade is being sent him.[43]

May 22, Friday (Fredericksburg): Lee writes to D. H. Hill, enclosing a copy of his letter of the 16th which Hill never received, adding that no large number of troops has been reported moving from Suffolk to Washington and reminds Hill of the urgency of reinforcing Lee. He asks Elzey if he has any information concerning transports reported at West Point. Lee receives a letter from Mary and an accompanying package of socks. Union Gen. Samuel P. Heintzelman orders his troops to seize Arlington and put freed slaves to work cultivating the land for government use.[44]

May 23, Saturday (Fredericksburg): Lee congratulates Imboden on his recent raid and inquiring as to the number of recruits secured for the 25th and 31st Virginia, urging their return to Lee so he can release the 50th Virginia back to Sam Jones. Lee orders "Grumble" Jones to join Stuart, advising that Albert Jenkins will take his place in the Valley. He instructs Stuart not to undertake a raid at present in favor of resting his troops and horses, and advising that "Grumble" Jones's Brigade as well as Beverly Robertson's new North Carolina brigade will soon join him, although Lee would prefer to have Robertson in command of a cavalry camp of instruction rather than in field command. In the evening Jed Hotchkiss comes to headquarters for a map and visits with Lee for a time. While Hotchkiss is there, Jackson's aide Sandie Pendleton calls on Lee "to ask to be relieved" as he does not want to serve under A. P. Hill, but Lee denies the request on the grounds that Jackson's staff are experienced veterans and know their duties better than any newcomer would. Lee writes to wife Mary, thanking her for the socks, but admonishing her for expecting him to write more often. He gently reminds her that he has an army to command; he includes the latest family news and invites Custis to join him in the field.[45]

May 24, Sunday (Fredericksburg): Lee and Edward Johnson attend church service conducted by Rev. Lacy at Second Corps HQ. Afterwards he meets with A. P. Hill to discuss Hill assuming command of the new Third Corps. Lee writes to his brother Carter, lamenting the loss of Jackson.[46]

May 25, Monday (Fredericksburg): Lee writes to President Davis concerning the promotions of Henry Heth and Dorsey Pender to major general, as Davis misunderstood Lee's desire to promote both of them and thought Lee wanted him to choose between the two of them to succeed A. P. Hill. Lee writes to D. H. Hill regarding returning Ransom's and Jenkins's troops and that if Hill needs reinforcements he is to get them from Beauregard rather than from Lee; he reminds Hill that he needs any cavalry that can be spared, but offers to send Beverly Robertson to North Carolina to command Hill's remaining cavalry if desired. Lee writes to Agnes urging her to take care of her mother and

---

43 REL to W. C. Rives, May 21, 1863, REL papers, MOC; Dowdey, *Wartime Papers*, 490; OR 25, pt. 2, 814-6; REL to J. J. Pettigrew, May 21, 1863, telegram book, REL HQ papers, VHS; REL to D. H. Hill, May 21, 1863, telegram book, REL HQ papers, VHS. John Marshall Jones was an 1841 graduate of West Point whose career in the Confederate Army consisted of staff duty until promoted to brigadier general and given a brigade in Edward Johnson's Division. Jones was wounded at Gettysburg and again at Payne's Farm on November 27, 1863, during the Mine Run Campaign, and killed at the Battle of the Wilderness in early May 1864. Warner, *Generals in Gray*, 164-5.

44 OR 18, 1069-70; Dowdey, *Wartime Papers*, 491; Poole, *On Hallowed Ground*, 52-3.

45 OR 25, pt. 2, 819-21; Sandie Pendleton to mother, May 24, 1863, WNP papers, UNC; McDonald, *Make Me a Map*, 145; Dowdey, *Wartime Papers*, 491-2.

46 McDonald, *Make Me a Map*, 145; James I. Robertson, Jr., *General A. P. Hill: The Story of a Confederate Warrior* (New York, 1992), 193; REL to C. C. Lee, May 24, 1863, REL papers, UVA.

herself, and mentions stopping in Ashland and seeing several of her friends on his return from Richmond.[47]

May 26, Tuesday (Fredericksburg): Lee writes to North Carolina Governor Vance regarding a report he forwarded to Lee of a slave revolt planned for Aug. 1, approving of Vance's reaction to the intelligence; Lee also forwards this information to Richmond. Lee alerts Stuart that the Federal cavalry appears to be preparing for another raid, and requests that Stuart notify Hood and Pickett to be on the alert should he find this to be true. Lee instructs Col. Critcher's 15th Virginia Cavalry to patrol the lower Rappahannock and look for an opportunity to attack enemy gunboats there with artillery stationed at Port Royal.[48]

Lee orders "Grumble" Jones to be on the lookout for deserters from the ANV and to arrest them when found. Lee informs President Davis that due to reassignment of J. B. Gordon, he needs another brigadier general in Rodes's Division, and he explains to Adjutant General Cooper that it was intended for Colquitt's Brigade to acquire wagons for its use in North Carolina, not to have its current vehicles accompany it on the move to Goldsboro.[49]

May 27, Wednesday (Fredericksburg): In early afternoon Lee reviews Early's Division, in company with Ewell, Hill, and Heth. Lee writes to A. P. Hill regarding breaking up his former division into two, and asking for qualifications of Heth, Pender, and Ransom for promotion. Lee warns Arnold Elzey of a possible cavalry raid on Richmond and to make all precautions to meet it. Lee informs Sec. Seddon that he has not had an opportunity to send the secretary's views on POW paroles to Gen. Halleck in Washington, and doesn't think that any benefit would come from Lee discussing the subject with Hooker; instead Lee proposes that Robert Ould meet with his Federal counterpart to discuss the subject. Lee also outlines the known enemy forces in North Carolina and tells Seddon that if D. H. Hill needs reinforcements he should call on Beauregard at Charleston for them.[50]

Lee orders "Grumble" Jones to corral a large number of deserters reported in the vicinity of Stanardsville. The general informs Jeb Stuart that the only reports he has of enemy movements are those from Stuart himself, and instructs him to be prepared to assist Jones at Stanardsville if needed. Lee orders A. G. Jenkins to hurry his men to Staunton to relieve Jones, and instructs Imboden to get his men ready for offensive operations.[51]

---

47 Freeman, *Lee's Dispatches*, 91-2; *OR* 18, 1071; Dowdey, *Wartime Papers*, 492-3.

48 *OR* 18, 1072-3; REL to Stuart, May 26, 1863, telegram book, REL HQ papers, VHS; *OR* 25, pt. 2, 826. In response to orders issued by the Federals that any Confederate captured wearing *any* article of Federal clothing or equipment would be treated as a spy, Lee issued GO67 proclaiming that uniforms and equipment are legitimate spoils of war and may be used as the captors desire, and that "steps will be taken to repress any attempt to treat as spies or punish" any soldier captured wearing them. *OR* 5, Series 2, 733.

49 REL to W. E. Jones, May 26, 1863, telegram book, REL HQ papers, VHS; Freeman, *Lee's Dispatches*, 94-6; REL to Cooper, May 26, 1863, telegram book, REL HQ papers, VHS. Gettysburg historian Edwin B. Coddington, *The Gettysburg Campaign: A Study in Command* (New York, 1997), 7, wrote that Lee was in Richmond again on this date meeting with the president and cabinet members to discuss a move north by the ANV versus going west to relieve Vicksburg. Postmaster General Reagan did not put dates with his account of the meeting[s] with Lee, and Davis did not mention them at all in his memoirs. Davis biographer William C. Davis hinted that Lee may have been in Richmond on the 26th, noting that Lee was "invited" to attend the cabinet meeting on that date. William C. Davis, *Jefferson Davis: The Man and His Hour* (New York, 1992), 505. It doesn't seem likely that Lee had time to go to Richmond, meet with cabinet members for what must have been a lengthy discussion, and then get back to Fredericksburg; his correspondence on this date and the troop reviews on the 27th leave little time for such a trip, and Lee himself made no mention of another Richmond trip around this time.

50 Pierson, *Diary of Yancy Malone*, 33; Iobst, *Bloody Sixth*, 121-2; *OR* 25, pt. 2, 826-7; *OR* Series 2, vol. 5, 959; REL to Seddon, May 27, 1863, telegram book, REL HQ papers, VHS. Kyd Douglas wrote that Lee also reviewed Johnson's Division as well as Early's on this date. Douglas, *I Rode with Stonewall*, 233.

51 REL to W. E. Jones, May 27, 1863, telegram book, REL HQ papers, VHS; *OR* 25, pt. 2, 827-8; REL to Jenkins, May 27, 1863, telegram book, REL HQ papers, VHS; REL to Imboden, May 27, 1863, telegram book, REL HQ papers, VHS.

May 28, Thursday (Fredericksburg): Lee writes to Davis regarding the promotions of Dorsey Pender and Robert Ransom: "I should be very glad to have a division for Ransom and should dislike to lose him from this army—I think he will make a fine division commander." But with only two open divisions and three new major generals Lee recommends sending Ransom to replace Sam French in North Carolina and sending French to Mississippi. Lee orders D. H. Hill to send Micah Jenkins's brigade to Hanover Junction and for Ransom to report in person to Richmond. Lee writes to Adjutant General Cooper that Governor Vance has complained himself and forwarded complaints from the two North Carolina regiments in Colston's Brigade about serving under a Virginian; to address this Lee wants Colston replaced by Marylander George Steuart.[52]

Lee formally assigns Isaac Trimble to command in the Shenandoah Valley, and asks Stuart if he has any reports of enemy movements away from the Rappahannock. Lee informs Gov. Vance that he dispatched an officer to recruit "in counties where the Conscript Act cannot well be enforced," and in early afternoon Lt. Randolph McKim, a distant cousin of Lee's, reports at headquarters and has lunch with Lee.[53]

May 29, Friday (Fredericksburg/Hayfields): Richard Ewell returns to the army and, accompanied by his new wife and two step-children, calls upon Lee at headquarters. The afternoon is spent reviewing Rodes's Division on the grounds of Hayfields, accompanied by Longstreet, Ewell and family, Hill, Early, and Johnson.[54]

---

52 Freeman, *Lee's Dispatches*, 96-9; *OR* 18, 1075-6; *OR* 25, pt. 2, 830. Longstreet was critical of French's actions during the recent Suffolk campaign, and D. H. Hill had little complimentary to say about French, either. Freeman, *Lee's Dispatches*, 96-9. Colston's Brigade was one of the few remaining "mixed" brigades in the ANV, consisting of the 10th, 23rd, and 37th VA and 1st and 3rd NC regiments. Maryland-born George Steuart returned to duty from his Cross Keys wound about this time, presenting Lee with a way to resolve the North Carolina complaints and also remove Colston from field command, for Lee was not satisfied with his performance at Chancellorsville. Colston was relieved of command on this date by SO144 and directed to report to Richmond for orders. *OR* 25, pt. 2, 830.

53 *OR* 25, pt. 2, 830; REL to Stuart, May 28, 1863, telegram book, REL HQ papers, VHS; REL to Vance, May 28, 1863, George H. & Katherine M. Davis collection, Tulane University; Randolph H. McKim, *A Soldier's Recollections: Leaves from the Diary of a Young Confederate* (New York, 1910), 133-4. McKim served on George Steuart's staff and was later chaplain of the 2nd VA Cav., McKim recalled this meeting: "The General received me graciously and asked me to dine with him.... The highest officer in the army would have esteemed it a great honor—what, then, were the feelings of a young 'first lieutenant and A. D. C.' in sitting down at the board of the great soldier who was the idol of the armies and the people of the South? The simple courtesy and genial hospitality of General Lee would have put me at ease if I had been a stranger; but he had several times been a guest at my father's house in Baltimore, when he was in charge of the construction of Fort Sollers [Carroll] in the Patapsco River, so that I felt at home in his presence. Our families were on very friendly and familiar terms. Indeed the General was a cousin of my mother.... As I talked with him after dinner, he cast his eyes across the Rappahannock to the camps of... Hooker's army and said to me, 'I wish I could get at those people over there.'... He was very friendly, talked of the days when he used to visit Belvidere, and inquired after my father and mother and my sisters." McKim, *Soldier's Recollections*, 133-4. The timeline in McKim's memoirs appears somewhat muddled and it is possible that he confused the date of his meeting with Lee, as Lee mentioned meeting with McKim earlier in the month (see May 14 entry), and McKim mentioned in passing being at Chancellorsville looking for the body of a relative about that time. Ibid, 132.

54 Dowdey, *Wartime Papers*, 499; Johnnie P. Pearson, ed., *Lee and Jackson's Bloody Twelfth: The Letters of Irby Goodwin Scott, First Lieutenant, Company G, Putnam Light Infantry, Twelfth Georgia Infantry* (Knoxville, TN, 2010), 120; REL to Mrs. William Taylor, May 29, 1863, REL HQ papers, VHS; William E. Ardrey diary, May 29, 1863, Davidson University. An Alabama officer recalled that the division passed in review before Rodes, then repeated the entire process once Lee and the other dignitaries arrived on the field. Robert E. Park, "War Diary of Capt. Robert Emory Park, Twelfth Alabama Regiment," *SHSP*, 26, 10. One North Carolinian in Rodes's Division who caught a glimpse of Lee when he visited the Virginia Peninsula in June 1861 noted the physical changes he saw in Lee two years later: "I see a great change in the appearance of General Lee. He looks so much older than when I saw him at Yorktown. Then his hair was black. Now he is a gray-headed old man." Louis Leon, *Diary of a Tar Heel Confederate Soldier* (Charlotte, NC, 1913), 28. The review was attended by a large number of those in the vicinity. An officer in the 30th NC wrote, "Many ladies graced the occasion with their presence, who with long feathers in their caps and long skirts reaching almost to the ground their spirited chargers as if they too know 'something of war.'" James J. Harris to "Burton," Aug. 24, 1863, William J. Bone papers, NC Archives. At least a

Lee warns Stuart of a possible enemy cavalry raid, as their mounted pickets along the Rappahannock have been replaced by infantry, and also cautions Albert Jenkins about the new Federal response to Confederate troops captured in Union uniform or equipment. Gen. Lee telegraphs President Davis to complain about D. H. Hill: "I gave Hill discretionary orders. . . . He declined to act and requested positive orders. I gave such orders as I could at this distance. Now he objects. I cannot operate in this manner."[55]

May 30, Saturday (Fredericksburg): The new corps structure of the Army of Northern Virginia is announced to the army via SO146. Lee explains to Trimble what troops are under his command: Albert Jenkins and John Imboden's cavalry, and the Maryland troops which Lee hopes Trimble can grow into a more effective unit. He writes to Jeb Stuart regarding expanding the number of guns in his horse artillery, and that Lee will transfer all the North Carolina mounted units to create a new brigade for Beverly Robertson.

Lee writes to President Davis, elaborating upon yesterday's telegram regarding D. H. Hill; Lee requests that he be relieved of responsibility for Hill's department and points out that Hill is hording troops in North Carolina while another Federal force is marshaling at West Point for a possible move against Richmond. Lee writes to Hill, informing him that all further orders will come from Richmond rather than from Lee, and he points out that many of the enemy troops in North Carolina are reported to now be at West Point thus Hill has far more men than he needs to defend his department. Lee urges Sec. Seddon to form a local defense force in Richmond and to transfer available troops from the Atlantic coast to Virginia.[56]

May 31, Sunday (Fredericksburg): Lee, Ewell, Hill, and Pendleton attend church service conducted by Rev. Lacy, after which Lee and Pendleton have "a long and pleasing talk . . . on the great question of religion." Lee receives several captured New York newspapers from Stuart, and cautions him to keep his force concentrated and rested should Hooker's cavalry undertake a raid; he adds that he will not be able to attend Stuart's review of the cavalry division. He also instructs Stuart to ascertain the veracity of a report that Hooker's infantry has fallen back to Aquia Creek, and sends details regarding the assignment of several captured enemy guns. Lee writes to his wife with the latest family news and rumors of enemy movements; he mentions that he has not time to determine Mildred's future course regarding her schooling so he trusts her and Custis to make a decision.[57]

---

portion of the civilians present were alerted to the review by Lee himself, who wrote to the Taylors at Hayfield inviting them to attend. REL to Mrs. William Taylor, May 29, 1863, REL HQ papers, VHS.

55 REL to Stuart, May 29, 1863, telegram book, REL HQ papers, VHS; *OR* 25, pt. 2, 832; Freeman, *Lee's Dispatches*, 99-100.

56 *OR* 25, pt. 2, 834-7, 840; *OR* 18, 1078-9.

57 Pfanz, *Ewell*, 279; WNP to wife, June 1, 1863, WNP papers, UNC; *OR* 25, pt. 2, 844; REL to Stuart, May 31, 1863 (2 messages), telegram book, REL HQ papers, VHS; Dowdey, *Wartime Papers*, 498-9.

June 1863

There was little time for General Lee's new commanders to become acquainted with their corps, subordinates, and responsibilities before the Army of Northern Virginia embarked on another offensive aimed once more at Pennsylvania. Lee departed Fredericksburg for Culpeper before the first week of June was over. Even as he rode toward the Blue Ridge, he reminded the War Department in Richmond that he needed every available soldier with his army, and pressed for the creation of a new command under Gen. P. G. T. Beauregard to threaten Washington from north-central Virginia while his own army operated north of the Potomac River.[1]

For all Lee's planning and wrangling with the politicians in Richmond, his offensive almost ended before began it began when Union cavalry surprised Jeb Stuart around Culpeper. Stuart staged two reviews of his horsemen in a matter of days at Brandy Station, with Lee attending the second review on the 8th. The gallant pageantry exhausted Stuart's troopers and horses and nearly led to disaster when Union horsemen crossed the Rappahannock River on the morning of June 9 and caught Stuart unawares. Lee and several of his generals were briefly isolated in a house watching the fighting before Rooney's cavalry came to their rescue.[2] Soon thereafter Rooney fell wounded and was sent to Hickory Hill to recuperate.[3] The fighting swirled for hours and although Stuart managed to recover in time to prevent the Federals from discovering Lee's movement toward the Shenandoah Valley, the Battle of Brandy Station was a watershed moment for the Union mounted arm. "The Northern horsemen," concluded noted cavalry historian Eric Wittenberg, "were finally the equals of their Southern counterparts, and they would never look back."[4]

Despite the near-disaster Lee concluded the Federals had not discovered his intentions and continued his planned campaign north. Stonewall Jackson's former corps, now under Richard S. Ewell, led the way into the Valley, where Ewell—in Jackson-like fashion—scored a major victory at Winchester to clear the way to and across the Potomac. It looked as though Ewell had learned well under his former teacher. Lee needed someone he could trust to operate independently, as Jackson had, and the choice to have Ewell lead the Second Corps appeared to be a good one. Lee, meanwhile, remained farther back with the corps of Longstreet and A. P. Hill.

On either June 19 or 21, Stuart met personally with Lee and submitted a plan to have his cavalry cross the Potomac behind (east of) Hooker's army and ride into Maryland to cut Hooker's communications with Washington and Baltimore and create as much havoc as possible. Lee sanctioned the move with a few stipulations. Lee paused in the lower (northern) Shenandoah for a time at Berryville, where he issued strict orders concerning the behavior of his troops in enemy territory. He expected them to behave responsibly and to pay for anything taken from civilians.[5]

---

1 *OR* 27, pt. 2, 293-4.

2 Pfanz, *Ewell*, 281.

3 Daughtry, *Gray Cavalier*, 141.

4 Eric J. Wittenberg, *The Union Cavalry Comes of Age: Hartwood Church to Brandy Station, 1863* (Washington, DC, 2003), 311.

5 Freeman, *Lee*, vol. 3, 40-41; *OR* 27, pt. 3, 912-3. Depredations were committed by his troops despite the orders. In one instance Lee himself discovered a fence torn down against his orders, which he personally rebuilt. "It was the best rebuke that he could have given to the offenders," in the opinion of one witness. Dawson, *Reminiscences*, 92.

Also while at Berryville, Lee and his aide Charles Venable appear to have gotten into some sort of disagreement that induced Maj. Venable to considering leaving the staff: "I get tired of my aideship sometimes and feel like going back on my Lieutenancy of Artillery," complained Venable. "I am too high-tempered to stand a high-tempered man and consequently I become stubborn, sullen, useless and disagreeable. But it makes no difference I suppose after all, provided the Yanks are licked and the old man has much to annoy and worry him and is very kind and considerate after all."[6]

As the Army of Northern Virginia moved into enemy territory, rumors flew regarding its destination and even wilder rumors arose regarding sightings of its commander. One of the more preposterous rumors was that Lee and the Virginia army were in Pennsylvania so he could visit his mulatto mistress in Philadelphia.[7]

At least some of the rumors were true: Ewell was poised to capture Harrisburg. As elements of the Second Corps threatened the capital city, Lee met with Longstreet and Hill at Chambersburg, unaware of enemy movements below the Potomac. Lee had heard nothing from Jeb Stuart regarding Hooker and the Army of the Potomac following him, leaving the general to believe he could operate with relative impunity for the time being. For a while Lee played the role more of military governor at Chambersburg than of army commander, where he spent almost as much time dealing with complaints and requests from local civilians than with planning the movement of his own army.[8] That changed when one of Longstreet's scouts informed him the Federals were moving to meet him across the mountains, forcing Lee to abandon his plan to capture Harrisburg and instead concentrate the army before Maj. Gen. George Meade, who had replaced Hooker at the head of the Army of the Potomac on June 28, could catch his corps and defeat him in detail.

Lee issued his orders for the army to concentrate at the logistical hub of Gettysburg, unaware that only days before, enemy cavalry had raided Hickory Hill and carried away his wounded son Rooney to a Northern prison.

* * *

---

6 Margaret C. M. Venable memoirs, UVA.

7 Mary B. Seifer to "my dear friend," July 14, 1863, Mary B. Seifer papers, Duke. According to one version of this tale, a former slave of Lee's was walking through the streets of Philadelphia when he saw Lee emerge from a house "in which resided a handsome lady of African blood." When the surprised former slave greeted Lee, the general supposedly "called him two very bad names—adjectives denoting the quality of rascal and told him not to dare mention his name or his d____d [sic] brains should be blown out." Instead of silence, the man reported Lee's presence to the mayor, who had Lee's supposed mistress and their children "removed . . . to some obscure locality." Ibid.

8 Sorrel, *Recollections*, 178.

June 1, Monday (Fredericksburg): Lee meets with his senior generals, including Richard Ewell and A. P. Hill, at army headquarters. In the evening, the general goes to visit Ewell in his headquarters at Belvoir. Lee writes to the War Department about procuring cattle for his army, and instructs Gens. Sam Jones and John Imboden to gather cattle in West Virginia and George Pickett to do the same in King & Queen County.[9]

June 2, Tuesday (Fredericksburg): Gen. Lee summons his three corps commanders to headquarters; A. P. Hill, however, is too sick to attend, but James Longstreet and Richard Ewell arrive and meet with Lee to discuss the general movement north. The general writes to Secretary of War Seddon regarding matters in North Carolina and potential reinforcements from that state, but once again turns down Gen. D. H. Hill's offer to exchange new infantry brigades for veteran brigades from Lee's army. Lee writes to President Davis regarding the need for more cavalry and the strategic situation outside of Virginia, and advises Richmond that enemy cavalry raided up the Middle Peninsula, but Pickett safely removed the commissary stores beforehand.[10]

Lee instructs Gen. Pickett to move to Tappahannock, a small town on the Rappahannock River in Essex County, to block the Federals and to attack them along the Piankatank River, if possible. Lee temporarily places Gen. Johnston Pettigrew's brigade at Hanover Junction under Gen. Pickett's orders, but cautions that they make certain that the North Anna River bridge and the railroad are secure before moving away.[11]

Lee declines Jeb Stuart's request to have Wade Hampton ride out and capture what Jeb perceives is an isolated Union force on the Rappahannock, explaining that it would not be there without support, and orders Gen. Imboden to return the 25th and 31st Virginia regiments by way of Hanover Junction. In the evening, the general receives a basket of strawberries from an unknown admirer.[12]

June 3, Wednesday (Fredericksburg): In the afternoon Lee meets with Bishop John Johns regarding the army's "religious improvement to which his example and counsel happily contributed." After this, Lee meets with artillery chief Rev. William N. Pendleton regarding the bishop's visit. Lee once again informs Secretary of War James Seddon that he is not in favor of exchanging his veteran brigades for larger fresh brigades from D. H. Hill in North Carolina. Lee clarifies for Gen. Pickett that he was ordered to Tappahannock to confront the Federals

---

9 McDonald, *Make Me a Map*, 146; Pfanz, *Ewell*, 276; OR 25, pt. 2, 846-7; REL to Imboden, June 1, 1863, telegram book, REL HQ papers, VHS; REL to Pickett, June 1, 1863, telegram book, REL HQ papers, VHS. Hotchkiss wrote only that "There was a conference of generals at General Lee's headquarters," and did not specify names. His context suggests the presence of Ewell and Hill. It is likely that Lee unveiled his plan to move across the Potomac at this "conference of generals," in which case Longstreet would have been present as well. Freeman, however, places that meeting on the 2nd. *Lee*, vol. 3, 26.

10 Samuel J. Martin, *The Road to Glory: Confederate General Richard S. Ewell* (Indianapolis, IN, 1992), 173; Freeman, *Lee*, vol. 3, 26; OR 25, pt. 2, 849; OR 18, 1088-9; REL to James Seddon, June 2, 1863, telegram book, REL HQ papers, VHS. Gen. Lee was particularly upset about the detachment of Gen. Micah Jenkins's brigade from George Pickett's Division and the no-show of Gen. Ransom's brigade, both of which he expected to be returned from North Carolina to his army. OR 25, pt. 2, 849.

11 REL to Pickett, June 2, 1863 (2 messages), telegram book, REL HQ papers, VHS; WHT to J. J. Pettigrew, June 2, 1863, telegram book, REL HQ papers, VHS. The increased enemy activity in Pickett's sector led to problems between Pickett and Lee. Pickett received orders to proceed to "Newton," but he could not find such a place on his maps. He requested clarification from Lee's HQ, but did not receive it in what he viewed as a timely fashion. He complained to Gen. Arnold Elzey in Richmond that he "telegraphed immediately to find out what place was meant. As usual from those headquarters, received no reply." Pickett's biographer noted with considerable understatement that relations between Pickett and Lee "showed signs of serious strain" at this time. Lesely J. Gordon, *General George E. Pickett in Life & Legend* (Chapel Hill, NC, 1998), 103.

12 OR 25, pt. 2, 849-50; WHT to Imboden, June 2, 1863, telegram book, REL HQ papers, VHS; Dowdey, *Wartime Papers*, 500.

in that vicinity, but if the enemy are gone, there is no reason for Pickett and his troops to remain there.[13]

Lee informs Samuel Jones that the 50th Virginia will remain with the ANV for the present, but it will be returned upon request if the situation demands it. Lee inquires of Albert Jenkins how many of his regiments have reached Staunton and how many more he expects, and orders Sam Jones to hurry along the remaining units of Jenkins's brigade. Lee writes to Mary but confesses that he has no news, but is writing because Maj. Venable is going to Richmond and can hand deliver his letter; he encloses a letter from Fitz. He declines an invitation to an ice cream social in the evening.[14]

June 4, Thursday (Fredericksburg): Lee orders the creation of artillery reserve battalions assigned to each of the three infantry corps, replacing the army level reserve artillery, and Maj. D. B. Bridgford's 1st Virginia Battalion is designated the provost for the ANV. Lee requests that the number of inspectors per brigade be expanded to increase unit efficiency.[15] Lee requests that Gov. Vance send recruits to bring Ramseur's Brigade up to full strength, or to send two new regiments to be assigned to the brigade. He asks Richmond to hurry Davis's Brigade to the army, and that returning convalescents from Longstreet's and Ewell's corps be sent to Culpeper rather than Fredericksburg effective immediately.[16] He advises Sec. Seddon that Pickett reports Federals at Urbana and moving toward Hooker, and orders Pickett to return to his previous position once assured that the enemy threat is gone. Jed Hotchkiss brings his completed map of the Chancellorsville battlefield to Lee.[17]

June 5, Friday (Fredericksburg): Lee orders A. P. Hill to hold Fredericksburg with his corps while the other two corps move to Culpeper. Lee intends to accompany the troops to Culpeper today himself, but he remains at Fredericksburg to investigate unexpected enemy movements.[18]

June 6, Saturday (Fredericksburg/Chancellorsville): The general observes Federal movements around Fredericksburg in the morning while accompanied by Gen. Pendleton. In the evening, Lee departs Fredericksburg for Culpeper, once more accompanied by Pendleton. The generals likely spend the night at the Lacy house, Ellwood, in the Wilderness.[19]

---

13 John S. Wood, *The Virginia Bishop: A Yankee Hero of the Confederacy* (Richmond, VA, 1961), 47-8; A. L. Long to WNP, June 3, 1863, WNP papers, UNC; *OR* 25, pt. 2, 851-3. Johns stayed with the Marye family at Brompton and spent much of his visit in company with Gen. Pendleton. Long to WNP, June 3, 1863, WNP papers, UNC. Lee probably also discussed with Pendleton on this occasion the break-up of the Army of Northern Virginia's artillery reserve, and the reassignment of arrtillery batteries to each of the three infantry corps, which became official on June 4, 1863. Freeman, *Lee*, vol. 3, 28.

14 *OR* 25, pt. 2, 852, 858; REL to Jenkins, June 3, 1863, telegram book, REL HQ papers, VHS; Dowdey, *Wartime Papers*, 500-1.

15 *OR* 27, pt. 3, 859; *OR* 51, pt. 2, 720-1; REL to ? [probably Sam Cooper], June 4, 1863, Brand collection, Duke. The 1st VA "Irish" Battalion served under Jackson for the first half of the war, but was so reduced by casualties that it was reassigned to ANV HQ.

16 *OR* 27, pt. 3, 858-9, 871-2; REL to Samuel Cooper, June 4, 1863, telegram book, REL HQ papers, VHS. Joseph Davis, the president's nephew, commanded a brigade of Mississippi and North Carolina troops in Henry Heth's new division.

17 Freeman, *Lee's Dispatches*, 100-1; REL to Pickett, June 4, 1863, telegram book, REL HQ papers, VHS; McDonald, *Make Me a Map*, 147. Hotchkiss did not state precisely when he delivered the map to Lee, but his context suggests it was likely early in the day.

18 *OR* 27, pt. 3, 859-60, 863. Stuart reviewed his cavalry near Brandy Station on this date; Lee declined an earlier invitation to attend. REL to Stuart, May 31, 1863, telegram book, REL HQ papers, VHS.

19 *OR* 27, pt. 2, 293; Lee, *Memoirs of WNP*, 276; Clark B. Hall, "The Battle of Brandy Station," *Essential Civil War Curriculum*, www.essentialcivilwarcurriculum.com/the-battle-of-brandy-station.html. Freeman and Thomas did not give a specific location for Lee's HQ on the night of June 6/7, only that it was beside the road to Culpeper. Freeman, *Lee*, vol. 3, 28; Thomas, *REL*, 290. Ellwood was constructed ca. 1790 on William Jones's 5,000-acre plantation on the edge of the Wilderness. Reportedly, Lee's father "Light Horse Harry" Lee wrote his memoirs in the house, although this is disputed

June 7, Sunday (Chancellorsville/Culpeper/ Eastern View): Lee crosses the Rapidan River at Raccoon Ford in the morning; arriving at Culpeper probably around midday, he establishes headquarters on the lawn of the Freeman home, Eastern View. Lee meets Stuart who, along with his horse, has been adorned with flowers by female admirers in town, of which Lee does not approve and mildly rebukes the cavalryman for it.[20]

The general meets with Longstreet in the afternoon and telegraphs President Davis that the enemy troops at West Point are reported to have joined Joe Hooker, thus eliminating the threat to Richmond from the east. He also tells Davis, "I require all troops that can be spared." He also sends a lengthy letter to President Davis, detailing the troop movements from Fredericksburg to date and his conclusion that Hooker discovered their withdrawal; he also mentions reports that the Army of the Potomac is being reinforced by troops from South Carolina and Georgia, thus troops from Beauregard should be sent either to Virginia or to Joe Johnston in the West.[21]

Lee instructs Imboden and Jenkins to operate in the lower Valley and cooperate with Lee's advance elements that will soon arrive, and requests Sam Jones to send a force into the Kanawha Valley. He also explains to Trimble that he issued orders directly to Imboden and Jenkins as he did not know if Trimble had yet taken command in Staunton; if so, Lee wants Trimble to coordinate their actions and join in Lee's operations.[22]

June 8, Monday (Eastern View/Brandy Station): Lee, Longstreet, Ewell, Hood, and Pendleton review Jeb Stuart's cavalry on the grounds of Auburn plantation near Brandy Station. Lee notes, "The men and horses look well. . . . Stuart was in all his glory."[23]

Lee submits his report of Second Manassas to the War Department and relays complaints from Stuart's command about the quality of carbines and saddles made in Richmond. Lee tells Sec. Seddon that D. H. Hill and Chase Whiting at Wilmington are greatly overestimating enemy strength in North Carolina and are retaining far more troops than they need to defend that region; he cautions that if his

---

by his biographer. See Charles Royster and Robert E. Lee, eds., *The Revolutionary War Memoirs of General Henry Lee* (New York, 1998), iii.. Ellwood was the summer home of J. Horace Lacy, owner of Chatham; Stonewall Jackson's arm is buried on the grounds. The house is now part of Fredericksburg & Spotsylvania NMP. www.nps.gov/frsp/learn/historyculture/ellwood.htm. Ellwood's location at the intersection of the Orange Turnpike and the Germanna Plank Road, as well as its connection with Rev. Lacy's family, make it a logical stopping point for Lee.

20 McDonald, *Make Me a Map*, 149; Hall, "Brandy Station"; William B. Styple, ed., *Writing & Fighting the Confederate War: The Letters of Peter Wellington Alexander, Confederate War Correspondent* (Kearny, NJ, 2002), 146. Eastern View was the home of the widow Sarah Freeman; her home stood on the hill just east of the Culpeper National Cemetery Annex. Clark Hall, email to author, August 25, 2018. Newspaperman Peter W. Alexander recorded this supposed exchange between Lee and Stuart: Lee "surveyed him [Stuart] from head to foot, quietly remarked, 'Do you know General, that Burnside left Washington in like trim for the first battle of Manassas. I hope your fate may not be like his.' Unfortunately Stuart was too much occupied with his flowers to take the hint." Styple, *Writing & Fighting*, 146. It was likely during this encounter that Lee accepted Stuart's invitation to attend another review tomorrow. Thomas, *REL*, 290.

21 Latrobe diary, June 7, 1863, VHS; Freeman, *Lee's Dispatches*, 101-2; OR 27, pt. 2, 293-4. Longstreet's aide Osmun Latrobe noted in his diary that "Lee's staff dined with us," so it seems logical that their generals met during that time. Latrobe diary, June 7, 1863, VHS.

22 OR 27, pt. 3, 865-7.

23 Hall, "Brandy Station"; WNP to wife, June 10, 1863, WNP papers, UNC; Eugene M. Scheel, *Culpeper: A Virginia County's History through 1920* (Culpeper, VA, 1982), 201-2; Dowdey, *Wartime Papers*, 507. Lee's vantage point was on a knoll on the grounds of John Minor Botts's Auburn, about where US 15 Business splits from US 15 north of Culpeper, near the intersection of US 15 and VA 665. Freeman, *Lee's Lieutenants*, vol. 3, 1-4; Scheel, *Culpeper*, 202; Hall, "Brandy Station." Lee saw Rooney and Rob, as well as Fitz. The latter was suffering from what Lee described as "an attack of rheumatism in his knee," and was thus riding in a carriage as a spectator rather than on horseback participating in the review. Dowdey, *Wartime Papers*, 507. Rob wrote of the review: "We had been preparing ourselves for this event for some days, cleaning, mending and polishing, and I remember we were very proud of our appearance. . . . It was a grand sight—about eight thousand well-mounted men riding by their beloved commander, first passing him in a walk and then in a trot." Lee, *Recollections and Letters of REL*, 95-6.

army is further reduced he may be forced into a defensive posture: "There is always hazard in military movements, but we must decide between the positive loss of inactivity and the risk of action."[24]

Lee instructs A. P. Hill to reinforce the garrison at Hanover Junction once Pickett's Division departs, and that if Hooker moves north to send Anderson's Division to Culpeper. The general asks Gen. Elzey in Richmond if it is certain that the Federals are gone from West Point, and declines an offer from the Richmond "Ambulance Committee" to take the field with his army, telling them they would only be needed in the wake of a battle and can be of better service at home for the present.[25]

June 9, Tuesday (Eastern View/Brandy Station/ Hill Mansion): In the morning Lee learns from Capt. W. W. Blackford of the Federal attack on Stuart's cavalry at Brandy Station. Lee sends Maj. Venable to Stuart reminding him to keep the Confederate infantry hidden from the Federals, but that infantry support is nearby if needed. Lee remains at headquarters until early afternoon when he rides toward the firing, arriving at Fleetwood Hill around 3:00 p.m.[26]

Lee, along with Ewell and Rodes, observe the latter stages of the fighting from the cupola atop the Barbour house, Beauregard; when Federal cavalry approaches the house, Ewell suggests that they barricade themselves in and fight to the last but Rooney's men drive them away. Rooney is wounded in this charge and Lee instructs that he be taken to the Hill Mansion in Culpeper, where he is cared for by A. P. Hill's sister in law; Lee visits his wounded son during the night.[27]

Before the battle, Lee writes to Davis a summation of affairs on the Fredericksburg front, and his belief that now enemy reinforcements are bound for either the Peninsula or New Bern, NC. In the evening, Lee advises President Davis that the "enemy crossed Rappahannock at Beverly Ford . . . in large force this morning" and requests that troops be sent to Hanover Junction and the Chickahominy line. He advises Adjutant General Cooper, Arnold Elzey, and A. P. Hill of the fight at Brandy Station and instructs the latter two to be on the alert for further enemy movements. He receives a letter from Custis and writes to Mary thanking her for a new pillowcase she sent, and with details of the cavalry review yesterday.[28]

June 10, Wednesday (Eastern View): Lee writes a lengthy letter to President Davis concerning the rising Peace Party in the North and the reaction of the Southern press to it; he states that the Confederacy should be encouraging this movement rather than condemning it. Lee instructs Ewell to press into the Shenandoah Valley and alerts Jenkins and Imboden to Ewell's movements and to work with him. Rooney is taken by Rob to Hickory Hill to recover; Lee is not able to see his wounded son before he leaves Culpeper, but he sends him a short

---

24 *OR* 12, pt. 2, 551-9; *OR* 27, pt. 3, 868-9, 872-3.

25 *OR* 27, pt. 3, 869, 873; REL to Arnold Elzey, June 8, 1863, telegram book, REL HQ papers, VHS.

26 Trout, *In the Saddle with Stuart*, 59; *OR* 27, pt. 3, 876; Scheibert, *Seven Months in the Rebel States*, 92-3; Blackford, *War Years with Stuart*, 216. One account has Lee personally telling Brig. Gen. Junius Daniel to keep his brigade out of sight behind a hill except in extreme emergency. Clark, *Histories of NC Regiments*, vol. 4, 253.

27 Pfanz, *Ewell*, 281; Hall, "Brandy Station"; Dowdey, *Wartime Papers*, 511; Daughtry, *Gray Cavalier*, 141. Beauregard was owned by Maj. James Barbour, one of Ewell's staff officers and the brother of Orange & Alexandria RR president John Barbour. It is currently a private residence. Krick, *Staff Officers in Gray*, 67. The Hill Mansion was completed in 1857 by Gen. A. P. Hill's brother Edward. It is located at 501 S East St., less than a mile from Lee's HQ at Eastern View, and is currently a private residence. Hill Mansion, National Register of Historic Places nomination form, Dec. 8, 1979. Lee wrote wife Mary of Rooney, "I saw him the night after the battle. Indeed met him on the field as they were bringing him from the front." Dowdey, *Wartime Papers*, 511.

28 *OR* 27, pt. 2, 294; *OR* 27, pt. 3, 874; REL to Cooper, June 9, 1863, telegram book, REL HQ papers, VHS; REL to Elzey, June 9, 1863, telegram book, REL HQ papers, VHS; REL to A. P. Hill, June 9, 1863, telegram book, REL HQ papers, VHS; Dowdey, *Wartime Papers*, 506-7, 509. The letter to Mary was written before he went to Brandy.

note wishing him well. Lee receives a letter from Mary.[29]

June 11, Thursday (Eastern View/Hill Mansion): In the morning Gen. Lee meets with Richard Ewell, and also goes to the Hill Mansion to thank Mrs. Hill for taking care of his wounded son Rooney. Lee interviews Col. Edward O'Neal to determine his fitness for brigade command. It doesn't go well for the colonel. The result of this interview is that the general withdraws his recommendation of O'Neal and instead requests that the position go instead to Col. John T. Morgan. Lee writes to Mary, concerned over her physical condition which confines her to her room at the Caskie's house; he assures her that Rooney is doing well and requests her to give Mr. Caskie a hat given to him by Maj. Venable's family. He writes also to Charlotte about Rooney's wounding and imploring her to take good care of him; he tells her "I want all the husbands in the field, and their wives at home encouraging them, loving them, and praying for them. We have a great work to accomplish, which requires the cordial and united strength of all."[30]

June 12, Friday (Eastern View): Lee explains the dispositions of Albert Jenkins's cavalry to Sam Jones and thanks him for the cattle he sent to Lee's army. Lee informs Hill of an enemy force moving up the Peninsula and instructs him to send Corse's Brigade to Hanover Junction. He also advises Elzey of the same and that Cooke's Brigade has been ordered to Richmond, and that Micah Jenkins and Ransom's brigades can be called on for additional support.[31]

June 13, Saturday (Eastern View): Lee sends Col. Long to Richmond to report to the War Department on conditions in the army and to make the case in person for reinforcements. Lee writes to Sec. Seddon advising of Long's mission and informing him of the difficulty of launching an offensive while at the same time being called on to defend Richmond. Lee learns of the execution of cousin Orton Williams as a spy in Tennessee, and writes to Mary of his sorrow over this loss and to relay his condolences to Orton's sister Markie; he also encloses sketches of Stonewall Jackson and the Chancellorsville battlefield drawn by Scheibert. He writes also to Custis advising that Col. Long will be in Richmond, and his opinion that the enemy force on the Peninsula cannot be that large; he also requests that Custis send him another pair of trousers as those he has are wearing out.[32]

---

29 OR 27, pt. 3, 878-82; Daughtry, *Gray Cavalier*, 141; Dowdey, *Wartime Papers*, 509, 511. Rob was appointed a cadet and acting ordnance officer of Rooney's brigade on this date. REL Jr. CSR, NA.

30 McDonald, *Make Me a Map*, 150; Dowdey, *Wartime Papers*, 511-3; Darrell L. Collins, *Major General Robert E. Rodes of the Army of Northern Virginia: A Biography* (El Dorado Hills, CA, 2008), 305-6; Freeman, *Lee's Dispatches*, 225-6. O'Neal was the colonel of the 26th AL and took over command of Robert Rodes's brigade after Chancellorsville; Rodes, however, was vehemently opposed to O'Neal's promotion, which prompted Lee's interview. Based on his conference with O'Neal and speaking to others about him, Lee rejected O'Neal's promotion. O'Neal was sent to the Western Theater in 1864 and finished the war in his native Alabama. Collins, *Rodes*, 305-6; Warner, *Generals in Gray*, 226. Rodes's biographer was unsure whether Lee met with O'Neal on the 10th or the 11th, but the 11th seems more likely given the lack of Lee correspondence on this date. Collins, *Rodes*, 305-6. Lee's letter to President Davis withdrawing his recommendation of O'Neal was originally dated June 11, 1863, but someone "corrected" the date to 1864 and filed it accordingly; the content clearly places it in 1863, although Freeman used the later date in placing the message in chronological sequence in *Lee's Dispatches*. The original is in the REL papers at Duke. For O'Neal's reaction, see Jerry Frey, *In the Woods Before Dawn: The Samuel Richey Collection of the Southern Confederacy* (Gettysburg, PA, 1994), 93-5. In June 1864, Morgan was under arrest for drunkenness in Georgia and Edward O'Neal was by that time serving with Joe Johnston's Army of Tennessee in Georgia. Arthur W. Bergeron, Jr., "John Tyler Morgan," *Confederate General*, vol. 4, 191; William C. Davis, "Edward Asbury O'Neal," *Confederate General*, vol. 4, 205.

31 OR 27, pt. 3, 885-6; REL to A. P. Hill, June 12, 1863 (2 messages), telegram book, REL HQ papers, VHS; REL to Elzey, June 12, 1863, telegram book, REL HQ papers, VHS.

32 OR 27, pt. 3, 886; Coulling, *Lee Girls*, 122-3; REL to Mrs. REL, June 13, 1863, REL papers, LOC; Dowdey, *Wartime Papers*, 514. The execution of Williams on June 9 is one of the great mysteries of the war. He was captured using an assumed name and historians have never uncovered what he was doing in Tennessee or why he was there. He and Agnes were very close, and possibly engaged, so his death affected her greatly. The Richmond *Examiner* published news of his

June 14, Sunday (Eastern View/Culpeper): Lee attends church at St. Stephens in Culpeper; Gen. Pendleton delivers the sermon. There, Lee consoles Rev. John Cole on his wife's recent death. Hill reports the Federals seem to be abandoning Stafford Heights, so Lee orders Hill to brush aside enemy cavalry and instructs Ewell to use his own judgment regarding the continuation of the advance into the Valley. He writes Mary regarding Orton Williams's death and wants an update on Rooney's condition.[33]

June 15, Monday (Eastern View): Shortly after dawn Lee sends an update to President Davis on the location of his army and of Hooker's army, noting that the uncertainty regarding enemy intentions in North Carolina and southeastern Virginia have slowed his movements. He meets with Longstreet to go over his marching orders, and receives a letter from Sen. R. M. T. Hunter complaining about the withdrawal of troops from the Middle Peninsula, to which Lee replies that it is necessary to concentrate the army and recommends forming home guard units. He endorses and forwards to Richmond Imboden's and Jones's reports of their recent raid, and instructs Gen. Elzey in Richmond to decide if reports of Federals landing at West Point are true.[34]

Lee informs the War Department that future communications for him should be sent via Gordonsville and Staunton, and notifies his corps commanders and garrison commanders at Staunton, Gordonsville, and Lynchburg to send all returning convalescents along the same route to rejoin the army. Lee requests Gen. Simon Buckner at Knoxville to send Col. John T. Morgan to Lee's army, and in late afternoon he advises A. P. Hill that Richard Anderson's Division is across the Rapidan River at Germanna Ford. In the evening Lee learns of Ewell's victory at Winchester and relays the news to President Davis and Longstreet; in acknowledging Ewell's news, Lee tells him simply "Push on."[35]

June 16, Tuesday (Eastern View): Lee informs A. P. Hill that Anderson's Division arrived at Culpeper this morning, and Hill is to follow with the remainder of his corps; he also tells Hill if Lee is not at Culpeper when he arrives, he "will be found in the advance with General Longstreet." He informs Maj. C. R. Collins, commanding the 15th Virginia Cavalry, that with Hooker gone from the Rappahannock it is no longer necessary to picket the river but rather keep watch on the Fredericksburg region. He forwards to President Davis a letter from newspaperman John L. O'Sullivan regarding the Peace movement in the North, and receives Stuart's report of Brandy Station and commends him for his actions in the battle.[36]

June 17, Wednesday (Eastern View/Markham): Lee breaks camp in the morning and rides north, moving

---

execution on this date, so it is very likely Agnes also learned of it on this date as well. Coulling, *Lee Girls*, 122-3; Pryor, *Reading the Man*, 373. Lee's fury over Orton's execution did not abate as the years passed. "My own grief," he told Markie in late 1866, "is as poignant now as on the day of its occurrence, and my blood boils at the thought of the atrocious outrage, against every manly and Christian sentiment which the Great God alone is able to forgive." Avery Craven, ed., *"To Markie:" The Letters of Robert E. Lee to Martha Custis Williams* (Cambridge, MA, 1933), 71-2.

33 Daniel E. Sutherland, *Seasons of War: The Ordeal of a Confederate Community, 1861-1865* (New York, 1995), 260; Freeman, *Lee*, vol. 3, 36; REL to Hill, June 14, 1863, telegram book, REL HQ papers, VHS; REL to Ewell, June 14, 1863, telegram book, REL HQ papers, VHS; REL to Mrs. REL, June 14, 1863, Lee papers, VHS.

34 OR 27, pt. 2, 295; OR 27, pt. 3, 890, 894; OR 25, pt. 1, 105, 121; REL to Elzey, June 15, 1863, telegram book, REL HQ papers, VHS. Charles Marshall wrote that Lee left Culpeper on this date, but none of the dates he recorded on this march are consistent with other accounts. Maurice, *Lee's Aide de Camp*, 195.

35 OR 27, pt. 3, 890-1; REL to S. B. Buckner, June 15, 1863, telegram book, REL HQ papers, VHS; REL to A. P. Hill, June 15, 1863, telegram book, REL HQ papers, VHS; Dowdey, *Wartime Papers*, 515; REL to Ewell, June 15, 1863, telegram book, REL HQ papers. Morgan was to take command of Rodes's Brigade in place of O'Neal, but he declined the promotion. That November he was ordered to take command of it. Warner, *Generals in Gray*, 221-2.

36 OR 27, pt. 3, 896-7; OR 27, pt. 2, 687. Despite what Lee told Hill, he did not accompany Longstreet for long, as they parted company sometime on the 17th. O'Sullivan was an influential figure in the antebellum Democratic Party, and served as minister to Portugal under President Franklin Pierce. It was O'Sullivan who coined the phrase "Manifest Destiny."

through elements of Longstreet's corps. He establishes headquarters at Markham in mid-afternoon, where he receives messages from Longstreet that he deviated from his assigned line of march and has gone across the Blue Ridge, and from Ewell regarding enemy forces at Harpers Ferry. He mildly rebukes Longstreet for changing his route of march, but instructs him to press ahead on to Winchester and relieve Ewell, and informs Ewell that estimates of enemy strength at Harpers Ferry are likely inflated, and he is to press on to Hagerstown, and to pay for all supplies taken in Maryland. Lee dines that evening with Edward C. Marshall's family.[37]

June 18, Thursday (Markham/Paris): The general moves north to Paris, where he establishes headquarters for the night. He notifies Richmond of the capture of Martinsburg by Gen. Rodes, and that Hooker's army seems to be concentrating around Centerville, while Ewell and Longstreet are near the Potomac River with A. P. Hill following them, and Jeb Stuart's cavalry actively guarding the mountain passes.[38]

June 19, Friday (Paris/Millwood/Saratoga): In early morning Lee advises Ewell that Anderson's Division will relieve Early at Winchester and grants Ewell wide latitude to operate north of the Potomac while Longstreet and Hill face Hooker in northern Virginia; he adds that if Hooker crosses the river Longstreet will do so as well. He then breaks camp and travels across Ashby's Gap through Millwood to Gen. Daniel Morgan's estate Saratoga where headquarters is established. Lee writes to President Davis with the latest positions of his army and the Army of the Potomac.[39]

June 20, Saturday (Saratoga/Berryville): Lee moves north to Berryville, encamping on the grounds of the

---

37 James A. Mumper, ed., *I Wrote You Word: The Poignant Letters of Private Holt, John Lee Holt, 1829-1863* (Lynchburg, VA, 1993), 140; *OR* 27, pt. 3, 900-1; Blackford, *Letters from Lee's Army*, 178. Edward Carrington Marshall was the youngest son of Chief Justice John Marshall, a former member of the Virginia General Assembly, and president of the Manassas Gap Railroad. There were several Marshall homes in the area, but Lee likely dined at Innis, north of Markham. Kimberly P. Williams, *A Pride of Place: Rural Residences of Fauquier County, Virginia* (Charlottesville, VA, 2003), 71; Clara S. McCarthy, *The Foothills of the Blue Ridge in Fauquier County, Virginia* (Warrenton, VA, 1974), 104-5, 110. The exact location of Lee's HQ at Markham is not known.

38 Maurice, *Lee's Aide de Camp*, 198; *OR* 27, pt. 2, 295-6. Lee's movements on this date are largely a mystery. He sent only two known pieces of correspondence, which suggests that he was in the saddle for much of the day, and only one of them—a telegram to Gen. Cooper—has a place in the heading, and that is Culpeper, which would have been the closest telegraph station to Lee. While the dates in Charles Marshall's writings for the march to Gettysburg are incorrect, he does seem to have the places/campsites correct and he lists Paris as being Lee's intermediate stop between Markham and Millwood, although he places it on the 21st (Lee was at Berryville on that date). Maurice, *Lee's Aide de Camp*, 198. A courier captured by the Federals told his interrogators that Lee was at Berryville on this date. *OR* 27, pt. 2, 25. Winchester resident Cornelia McDonald wrote that Lee was expected there on the evening of the 18th. Minrose C. Gwin, ed., *A Woman's Civil War: A Diary, with Reminiscences of the War, from March 1862* (Madison, WI, 1992), 162. A distant cousin claimed long after the war that Lee attended the wedding of her aunt Ella Carter at Goodwood in Prince Georges County, MD, on this date, which clearly was impossible. William F. Chaney, *Duty Most Sublime: The Life of Robert E. Lee as Told Through the "Carter Letters"* (Baltimore, MD, 1996), 127-30. The claim did not include the date of the wedding, which comes from Robert W. Johnson, *The Ancestry of Rosalie Morris Johnson, Daughter of George Calvert Morris and Elizabeth Kuhn* (Philadelphia, 1905), 44. A Virginia Department of Historic Resources historical marker (J-14) claims that Lee camped just north of Berryville the night of the 18th, but the Clarke County Historical Association does not know the source used for the marker and has no evidence in its collection to support the claim; further, it does not believe the marker to be correct. Mary Morris, CCHA Archivist, email to author, Sept. 12, 2018. Armistead Long is the only known contemporary source for Berryville on the 18th, and his dates are not concrete. *Memoirs of REL*, 271.

39 *OR* 27, pt. 3, 905; Maurice, *Lee's Aide de Camp*, 198-9; *OR* 27, pt. 2, 296. Freeman wrote that Lee met with Longstreet and Stuart on this date and that Stuart proposed taking three brigades to raid in rear of Hooker's army, to which Lee agreed; Freeman noted however that he was unsure whether this meeting occurred on the 19th or 21st. *Lee*, vol. 3, 40-1. Saratoga was constructed in 1779, possibly by Hessian prisoners of war, and named after Morgan's Revolutionary War victory in New York. During the Civil War, it was occupied by the Burwell family, and after the war was the home of noted writer and former Stuart staffer John Esten Cooke. It stands approximately one mile east of Boyce and is privately owned. Loth, *Virginia Landmarks Register*, 105; Lancaster, *Historic VA Homes*, 458-9.

Beemer farm, Mantua, just north of town. Lee congratulates Imboden for his success in wrecking the B&O and urges him to drive off the Federal garrison at New Creek and to advance on Lee's left flank across the Potomac; he reminds Imboden that everything taken north of the river must be paid for. Lee writes to Sam Jones advising of the Army of Northern Virginia's move into Maryland and Pennsylvania and urging him to make a corresponding move into western Virginia: "A more favorable opportunity will probably not occur during the war." He sends his now daily update to President Davis on the army's movements, including those of Imboden and Jones.[40]

June 21, Sunday (Berryville): Lee, Longstreet, and Charles Venable attend morning church service at Grace Episcopal Church in Berryville, where Gen. Pendleton preaches the sermon. GO72 is published setting forth the guidelines for procuring supplies for the army in enemy territory.[41]

June 22, Monday (Berryville): Lt. Col. Arthur J. L. Fremantle of the British army arrives at Lee's headquarters in the morning and is introduced to most of the staff, but is referred to Longstreet and Winchester for accommodations without meeting the commanding general. Lee authorizes Ewell to move toward the Susquehanna River and capture Harrisburg if possible, and that Stuart is moving across the Potomac and will communicate with him; he authorizes Stuart to take three of his brigades into Maryland and Pennsylvania. Lee encounters Dorsey Pender who finds Lee to be "in fine spirits" yet complaining about straggling.[42]

June 23, Tuesday (Berryville): Lee meets with Longstreet, going over his marching orders and plans for the army once across the Potomac River. Lee writes to President Davis opining again that the Federals do not intend any operations along the coast or in North Carolina, and thus Southern troops there can be utilized to create a new army in central Virginia under Gen. Beauregard that can threaten Washington while Lee operates north of the Potomac. A second letter to President Davis advises that Joe Hooker laid a pontoon bridge at Edward's Ferry east of Leesburg, Jeb Stuart has kept them from breaking through the mountain passes, and Gen. Ewell is in Pennsylvania with Gens. Longstreet and Hill to follow.[43]

Lee again requests of the War Department that Corse and Cooke's brigades be restored to the ANV, and instructs Imboden to continue his foraging but to cross the river and guard Ewell's left flank. Lee writes Isaac Trimble asking him to accompany the ANV north if he is able, although Lee has no command for him other than the Valley District. In late afternoon, Lee authorizes Stuart to take his three brigades around the Army of the Potomac and rejoin the army north of the Potomac.[44]

June 24, Wednesday (Berryville/Martinsburg): The general breaks camp in the morning and rides north to the Martinsburg vicinity. For a portion of the way Lee rides with Brig. Gen. Eppa Hunton, who later claims he was wary of the move into Pennsylvania: "We had a half hour's conversation. . . . General Lee was so enthusiastic about the movement that I threw

---

40 Mary Morris, CCHA Archivist, email to author, Sept. 12, 2018; *OR* 27, pt. 3, 905-6; *OR* 27, pt. 2, 296-7. Mantua was located near the intersection of modern US 340 and the VA 7 bypass (the approximate location of the misdated historical marker J-14 mentioned in note 38); the house itself burned shortly after the turn of the century. Morris, email to author, Sept. 12, 2018. A turn-of-the-century publication noted only that the HQ was located "just north of Berryville, under a large oak tree," and that spot was indicated by a marker. Thomas D. Gold, *History of Clarke County, Virginia, and its Connection with the War Between the States* (Berryville, VA, 1914), 113.

41 Franklin G. Walter diary, June 21, 1863, LVA; Venable memoirs, UVA; Lee, *Memoirs of WNP*, 297; *OR* 27, pt. 3, 912-3.

42 Arthur J. L. Fremantle, *Three Months in the Southern States: April—June 1863* (Lincoln, NE, 1991), 227; *OR* 27, pt. 3, 913-5; Hassler, *One of Lee's Best Men*, 251.

43 *OR* 51, pt. 2, 726; *OR* 27, pt. 3, 924-5; *OR* 27, pt. 2, 297-8.

44 *OR* 27, pt. 1, 77; *OR* 27, pt. 3, 923-4. This order to Stuart was at the center of the scrutiny that surrounded his operations during the subsequent days.

away my doubts and became as enthusiastic as he was."[45]

June 25, Thursday (Martinsburg/Williamsport): In the morning Lee writes to President Davis on a number of subjects, including press reaction to the peace movement in the North, prisoner exchanges, and rumors of enemy troop movements; he proposes that Braxton Bragg and Simon Bucker combine forces to invade Ohio, and reiterates his desire to create a force under Beauregard in Virginia. Lee, Longstreet, Pickett, and Pendleton pass through Martinsburg together with elements of Pickett's Division probably before noon. Lee, Longstreet, and Pickett cross the Potomac at Williamsport in the rain, and their party is greeted by a group of admiring young ladies on the Maryland shore; they try to put a wreath around Traveller's neck but the horse balks and it is given to one of Lee's aides instead. Lee pauses for a time on the north bank of the river to watch the troops cross, with the cortege of female admirers; he establishes headquarters on the roadside about three miles north of Williamsport. While conferring with Longstreet and Hill at headquarters, young Leighton Parks brings a basket of raspberries for the generals; after sharing this snack the officers take turns playing with the youngster and putting him on their horses.[46]

Lee writes again to President Davis in the afternoon, again reiterating his belief that the enemy plans no offensive in North Carolina, thus freeing up troops there for Beauregard's proposed force; he tells Davis that creating that force is the best possible use of troops not on active campaign and also that if Buckner cannot join with Bragg, he and Sam Jones should unite and move into Kentucky: "It should never be forgotten that our concentration at any point compels that of the enemy, and his numbers being limited, tends to relieve all other threatened localities." Lee meets with Trimble in the afternoon as, being a Marylander, Trimble is familiar with the region. Custis is promoted to brigadier general.[47]

June 26, Friday (Williamsport/Hagerstown/Middleburg): Lee leaves camp near Williamsport in late morning, accompanied by Longstreet and Pendleton. Around noon they arrive in Hagerstown in the rain to much applause from the locals. Lee sends Pendleton to investigate the local road network, and confers with Trimble again regarding the roads, and Trimble urges him to send a force to capture Baltimore.[48]

---

[45] F. G. Walter diary, June 24, 1863, LVA; Eppa Hunton, *Autobiography of Eppa Hunton* (Richmond, VA, 1933), 86-7. The location of Lee's camp on the night of the 24th is not certain. F. G. Walter of Lee's HQ Guard (39th VA Cav. Battalion) wrote that they broke camp at 6:00 a.m. and moved via Summit Point to "camp 5 miles south of Martinsburg." It should be noted, however, that Walter wrote that the 39th was not with Lee until the afternoon of the 25th. Walter diary, June 24 and 25, 1863, LVA. Freeman's phrasing suggests that Lee went all the way to Williamsport on the 24th, which does not seem likely distance-wise, and even less likely given that the HQ guard stopped several miles short of Martinsburg. *Lee*, vol. 3, 50. Isaac Trimble wrote that he reported to Lee "on the afternoon of the 24th of June near Berryville." It seems unlikely, however, that Lee was still at Berryville that afternoon, and more likely he left around the same time the HQ guard did that morning. Isaac Trimble, "The Campaign and Battle of Gettysburg," *CV*, vol. 25, 209. Lee mentioned in a June 30 letter that he saw some of Mildred's friends in Smithfield [now Middleway] which reveals at least a portion of his route from Berryville. Dowdey, *Wartime Papers*, 535-6.

[46] OR 27, pt. 3, 930-1; Mabel H. Gardiner, *Chronicles of Old Berkeley: A Narrative History of a Virginia County from its Beginnings to 1926* (Durham, NC, 1938), 161; Dawson, *Reminiscences*, 90-1; Blackford, *Letters from Lee's Army*, 182; S. Roger Keller, *Crossroads of War: Washington County, Maryland in the Civil War* (Shippensburg, PA, 1997), 63-4. Parks wrote that HQ was "in a hickory grove about three miles from Williamsport. The grove was on the top of a small hill, near enough to the pike for the General to see the troops as they marched by." Keller, *Crossroads of War*, 63. Parks had also visited Lee in the wake of the Battle of Sharpsburg the previous year. Freeman, *Lee*, vol. 3, 53-4.

[47] OR 27, pt. 3, 931-3; *OR Supplement* vol. 5, 435; Custis CSR. The 39th VA Battalion rejoined HQ during the afternoon. F. G. Walter diary, June 25, 1863, LVA.

[48] Fremantle, *Three Months*, 236; Charles E. Lippitt diary, June 26, 1863, Valley of the Shadow; L. M. Blackford to William Blackford, June 28, 1863, Valley of the Shadow; Lee, *Memoirs of WNP*, 280; Trimble, "Campaign and Battle of Gettysburg," 210. Franklin Walter of the HQ guard remembered, "A few beautiful ladies on the road cheering our soldiers and anxiously looking for Gen. Lee" all along the line of march, despite the rain. Walter diary, June 26, 1863, LVA.

Gen. Lee meets with George Kealhofer, the president of the Hagerstown Gas Light Company and a noted Southern sympathizer, to glean whatever information Kealhofer can provide regarding enemy activity and the general area; Lee also may have met with another local Southern sympathizer known only as "Dr. Doyle." The general rides on through Middleburg, where he stops with his staff for water at the Martin farm on the northern edge of the town, where a 5-year-old named Alice Martin fetches a cup for him. He and Longstreet camp for the night near Bushtown Dunkard Church, about midway between Middleburg and Greencastle.[49]

Rooney is captured from his sick bed at Hickory Hill by the 11th Pennsylvania Cavalry; Rob escapes capture by hiding in the bushes and his mother, wife, and two youngest sisters are also present as Rooney is literally carried off in the family carriage.[50]

June 27, Saturday (Middleburg/Greencastle/Chambersburg): Gen. Lee departs from his Middleburg camp around 8:00 a.m., passing through Greencastle with little fanfare. The general arrives in Chambersburg around 9:00 a.m. riding at the head of Richard Anderson's Division.[51]

Soon after his arrival in the town, Lee meets with Gen. A. P. Hill in the town square, where he was possibly joined by Longstreet. A local photographer, a "Mr. Bishop," attempts to take a picture of the meeting but the assembled crowd obscures his view.[52]

Lee attempts to meet with the local sheriff regarding the safety of the town, but he cannot be found. Around 11:00 a.m. Gens. Lee, Longstreet, and Hill ride east out of town and Lee sets up his camp in Messersmith's Woods about one mile outside of town around noon.[53]

---

49 Keller, *Crossroads of War*, 61-2, 159; W. P. Conrad and Ted Alexander, *When War Passed This Way* (Greencastle, PA, 1987), 157; L. M. Blackford to William Blackford, June 28, 1863, Valley of the Shadow. Kealhofer's daughter wrote in her diary, "I had the honor of an introduction to Gen. R. E. Lee, Gen. Longstreet, and Gen. Pickett. I shall ever remember and feel proud of having shaken hands with such men." Keller, *Crossroads of War*, 159. Middleburg is modern State Line, PA. A citizen later reported to Gen. George Meade that Lee and Longstreet had had their headquarters at James H. Groves's residence, "just beyond town limits, toward Greencastle," which would be near Bushtown Church. OR 27, pt. 1, 65. Freeman, and nearly every other writer including Coddington, has Lee reaching Chambersburg on this date. Freeman, *Lee*, vol. 3, 54-5; Coddington, *Gettysburg Campaign*, 172. The historical markers in and around Chambersburg also use the date of June 26 for Lee's arrival there. All seem to rely on the postwar account of Chambersburg resident Jacob Hoke as their source. Jacob Hoke, *The Great Invasion of 1863: General Lee in Pennsylvania* (Gettysburg, PA, 1992), 161-4. Numerous military and civilian contemporary sources, however, state that it was the 27th when Lee arrived in Chambersburg. Hoke's account has been widely accepted although it is clearly incorrect.

50 OR 27, pt. 2, 794-7; Coulling, *Lee Girls*, 126; Daughtry, *Gray Cavalier*, 142-5. The Lees, and the Confederates in general, thought Rooney was the specific target of the cavalry raid, but this is not reflected in the surviving Federal reports, which indicate that their objective at that time was the bridges near Hanover Junction and they happened by chance to learn of Rooney's proximity at Hickory Hill. The best recounting of Rooney's capture is in Daughtry, *Gray Cavalier*; Charlotte's aunt's account is in Pryor, *Reading the Man*, 361-3.

51 OR 27, pt. 1, 65; Conrad, *When War Passed this Way*, 158; OR 27, pt. 3, 477; William H. Stewart to WHT, May 1, 1903, WHT papers, NPL. Frank Walter of the HQ guard wrote that his company "marched at sunrise" and then established camp around 10:00 a.m. one mile east of Chambersburg. F. G. Walter diary, June 27, 1863, LVA. As noted in note 49, Lee did not reach the town of Chambersburg until June 27th—despite what appears in much of the Lee and Gettysburg literature.

52 Hoke, *Great Invasion*, 161-4; William H. Stewart, *A Pair of Blankets: Wartime History in Letters* (Wilmington, NC, 1990), 94; William D. Henderson, *12th Virginia Infantry* (Lynchburg, VA, 1984), 55; Rachel Cormany diary, June 27, 1863, Valley of the Shadow. William Stewart, an officer in Mahone's 61st VA, recalled that Ewell was with Lee and Hill, but he was mistaken; Ewell was at Carlisle on this date, so it may have been Longstreet with them. Stewart, *Pair of Blankets*, 94. Mahone's Brigade passed the town square as the generals conferred and gave a rousing cheer for their leaders. Henderson, *12th Virginia*, 55. One of the townspeople observing the conference told another observer, "There ... is perhaps the most important council in the history of this war, and the fate of the government may depend upon it." They quickly relayed Lee's presence to authorities in Harrisburg. Hoke, *Great Invasion*, 164. A historical marker at the town square has the incorrect date of June 26 for the conference.

53 William Heyser diary, June 27, 1863, Valley of the Shadow; Charleston *Mercury*, July 7, 1863; Hoke, *Great Invasion*, 169; Jacob Stouffer to Mary R. Stouffer, July 5, 1863, Valley of the Shadow. Resident William Heyser recalled of Lee as he left

Lee meets with Gen. Trimble again regarding the local area, and issues an order lauding the conduct of his army in enemy territory while condemning actions taken by the Federals against civilians in Virginia. Rooney is admitted to the hospital at Fort Monroe.[54]

June 28, Sunday (Chambersburg): Lee meets with Longstreet and Hill around midday; Capt. Fitzgerald Ross of the Austrian army arrives at headquarters to meet Lee, and presents his letters of introduction to Lee's staff. Ellen McClellan and her daughter call on Lee regarding a shortage of food for the residents of Chambersburg, and they ask for his autograph before leaving; after she leaves he orders flour from a local mill distributed to the townspeople.[55]

Around 10:00 p.m. Lee meets with Henry T. Harrison, one of Longstreet's scouts who brings word that the Army of the Potomac—now commanded by Gen. George Meade—is in Maryland. Charlotte's father writes to Lee about Rooney's capture.[56]

June 29, Monday (Chambersburg): Ewell's aide James P. Smith arrives at Lee's headquarters about dawn and finds Lee mounting his horse to leave; Lee asks Smith if he has any word of Stuart. Dr. J. L Suesserott calls on Lee to request to have his neighbor's blind horse exempted from seizure to which Lee agrees, but the horse is taken while the doctor meets with Lee. Fitzgerald Ross is introduced to Lee who invites Ross to stay for lunch, which Ross describes as "a frugal meal, simply served." Lee reportedly announces to the staff in the afternoon, "Tomorrow, gentlemen, we will not move to Harrisburg, as we expected, but will go over to Gettysburg and see what General Meade is after." Periods of rain during the day.[57]

---

town: "About 11 o'clock Gen. Lee passed with his staff. He is fine looking man, medium size, stoutly built ... grey beard, and mustache, poorly dressed for an officer of his grade. He wore a felt hat, black, and a heavy overcoat with large cape. His horse appeared to be rather an indifferent one, for a man who reputedly is fond of fine stock." Heyser diary, June 27, 1863, Valley of the Shadow. HQ was located in a wooded grove owned by George R. Messersmith, but also sometimes referred to as "Shetter's Woods" after its former owners; the property was the site the town's Independence Day celebrations, and the trees were removed ca. 1886. Hoke, *Great Invasion*, 169. The HQ site was lost to commercial development decades ago; a historical marker at the intersection of U.S. 30 and Coldbrook Ave. indicates the spot, though it has the incorrect date of June 26 for Lee's arrival there. Lee made Chambersburg off-limits to his officers and men, allowing no one into the town without a pass signed by him personally. Scheibert, *Seven Months in the Rebel States*, 110. According to Fremantle, Lee granted permission for very few to enter the town, noting, "I hear of officers of rank being refused this pass." Fremantle, *Three Months*, 242.

54 Freeman, *Lee*, vol. 3, 57-9; *OR* 27, pt. 3, 942-3; Daughtry, *Gray Cavalier*, 146. Trimble claimed that Lee pointed at a map and indicated that he suspected a battle to be fought at Gettysburg; this is a rather dubious claim and reeks of post-war romanticizing by Trimble. Freeman, *Lee*, vol. 3, 58-9.

55 Fitzgerald Ross, *Cities and Camps of the Confederate States* (Urbana, Il, 1997), 37-8; Hoke, *Great Invasion*, 197-9. Freeman placed Mrs. McClellan's visit on the 27th, but that was a result of him having the wrong date for Lee's entry into Chambersburg. *Lee*, vol. 3, 59. (She was no relation to Gen. McClellan.) There is a letter dated 7:30 a.m. June 28 to Ewell instructing him not to come to Chambersburg as ordered "last night," but rather to move to Gettysburg. *OR* 27, pt. 3, 934-4. Randolph McKim argued that this is misdated and should be the 29th, and Freeman agreed. Randolph H. McKim, "General J.E.B. Stuart in the Gettysburg Campaign," *SHSP*, vol. 37, 211-6; Freeman, *Lee*, vol. 3, 62 n40.

56 Maurice, *Lee's Aide de Camp*, 218-20; Sorrel, *Recollections*, 163-4; William F. Wickham to REL, June 28, 1863, REL papers, UVA. Lee initially refused to speak with Harrison, whom he did not know; it was only after conferring with Maj. John Fairfax of Longstreet's staff, who brought Harrison to Lee's HQ, that he agreed to meet with the scout. Freeman, *Lee*, vol. 3, 60-1. It is not known when Lee received Wickham's letter; his letter to Mary on the 30th makes no mention of Rooney's capture, and his first known mention of it to her is in a July 7th letter.

57 James Power Smith, "General Lee at Gettysburg," in *The Gettysburg Papers*, ed. by Ken Bandy and Florence Freeland (Dayton, OH, 1986), 1040; Hoke, *Great Invasion*, 205; Ross, *Cities and Camps*, 42; Freeman, *Lee*, vol. 3, 64; Betts, *Experiences of a CS Chaplain*, 38. Ross described HQ "in a little enclosure of some couple acres of timber. There are about half-a-dozen tents, and as many baggage-wagons and ambulances. The horses and mules from these, besides those of a small escort, are tied up to the trees, or grazing about the place." He remained at HQ for a time conversing with Lee's staff, and Marshall told him he thought the Lost Order during the Maryland campaign a worse blow to the Confederacy than the fall of New Orleans. Ross, *Cities and Camps*, 42. Taylor sent a note to Pickett on this date explaining that Lee tried repeatedly to

June 30, Tuesday (Chambersburg/Fayetteville/Greenwood): Gen. Lee meets with Gen. Longstreet in the morning, who introduces Col. Fremantle to Lee. They break camp that morning and Lee rides with Longstreet. They camp in the early afternoon "near a deserted sawmill" near Greenwood.[58]

The general meets with A. P. Hill and Henry Heth in the afternoon. They inform Lee of the presence of enemy cavalry at Gettysburg. Lee sends a brief note to his wife Mary with family news, and (ironically) how happy he is that everyone is safe at Hickory Hill.

Periods of rain during the day.[59]

---

get the War Department to return Corse's and Jenkins's brigades, and still had hope that at least Corse would rejoin Pickett's Division. *OR* 27, pt. 3, 944-5.

58 Hoke, *Great Invasion*, 226; Fremantle, *Three Months*, 248-50; Longstreet, *From Manassas to Appomattox*, 349; E. Porter Alexander, *Military Memoirs of a Confederate: A Critical Narrative* (Dayton, OH, 2005), 380; Ross, *Cities and Camps*, 44. Greenwood has largely been absorbed by the neighboring village of Fayetteville, but during the war they were two distinct villages separated by about two miles. Hoke, *Great Invasion*, 92. The exact location of Lee's camp is not known.

59 Morrison, *Heth Memoirs*, 174; David G. Martin, *Gettysburg: July 1* (Conshohocken, PA, 1996) 29-31; Dowdey, *Wartime Papers*, 535-6; William Heyser diary, June 30, 1863, Valley of the Shadow. Heth wrote that Lee asked him if he had any news of Stuart. Morrison, ed., *Heth Memoirs*, 174.

July 1863

On the morning of July 1, Robert E. Lee was riding east along the Chambersburg-Gettysburg Road near the crest of South Mountain when the unexpected sound of battle greeted him. He was not expecting a battle that morning, and what he heard was no mere cavalry skirmish. As it turned out, part of his Army of Northern Virginia had stumbled into a meeting engagement outside the small town called Gettysburg, and it was about to escalate into the largest engagement of the Civil War.

Three days of heavy fighting heavily damaged his army and ended Lee's second invasion of the North. The battle also revealed that he would need to monitor some of his corps- and division-level generals much more closely than he was accustomed to doing. In addition to the widespread leadership problems exposed by the new three-corps structure, Lee was himself ill during at least a portion of the battle.[1] Much was written by participants and historians after the war in an effort to figure out where to place the blame for the defeat at Gettysburg; if there was blame to be assigned, Lee believed it should fall upon his shoulders.[2] He clearly recognized that a significant opportunity for victory on Northern soil had slipped through his hands, telling one of his generals, "We must whip these people soon—we old men want to see our wives, and these young men want to see their sweethearts. If we defeat them we are nigh unto peace; I repeat—we must whip these people."[3]

As the army withdrew toward Virginia, rains flooded the Potomac River and prevented the Confederates from crossing. Lee had no choice but to prepare for another battle at Hagerstown. As the army congealed around Hagerstown, an officer recalled seeing Lee and others by the roadside:

> I saw Gen. Lee who had halted with his staff and pitched his tent by the side of a little brook. He was studying a map intensely and Gens. A. P. Hill, Early, and others were near him. It was impossible not to be struck with his calm, composed, and resolute bearing. He seemed to be entirely undisturbed by the trying scenes which he had lately passed through, and by the still more trying ordeal through which he was now passing.[4]

While backed up against the swollen river, Lee learned of Rooney's capture from his sickbed in Hanover; worse still, because Rooney was Lee's son, he was being treated as a hostage rather than as a regular prisoner.[5] The circumstances of Rooney's capture greatly affected Charlotte—who was

---

1 Blackford, *War Years with Stuart*, 230. Lee's illness likely impacted his ability to get around the field; Charles Venable noted in a letter to Walter Taylor concerning Lee's possible attendance at an 1869 reunion at Gettysburg, "You know well that you and I know more of that field than the old man, and could tell more to keep those Yankees straight." Venable to WHT, Aug. 21, 1869, WHT papers, SH. Indeed, when Fitz Lee was preparing his biography of his uncle, he sought out Venable for the details of Lee's actions on the 2nd and 3rd. Fitz Lee to Venable, July 30, 1894, Venable papers, UNC.

2 Dowdey, *Wartime Papers*, 565; George R. Stewart, *Pickett's Charge: A Microhistory of the Final Attack at Gettysburg, July 3, 1863* (Boston, 1987), 257; Glenn Tucker, *Lee and Longstreet at Gettysburg* (Dayton, OH, 1982), 218-21. Jubal Early and William Pendleton viciously attacked Longstreet after the war, pinning the defeat squarely on him, but others targeted Stuart for his absence and Ewell admitted the mistakes he made likely were the cause. Tucker, *Lee and Longstreet*, 207-9.

3 Richmond *Examiner*, July 15, 1863, REL newspaper references, DSF papers, LVA.

4 John W. Daniel, Gettysburg memoir, J. W. Daniel papers, VHS.

5 Daughtry, *Gray Cavalier*, 148-9.

powerless to stop the Federals from carting her husband out of the house—and Lee was astounded to learn that his wife Mary and daughters left Charlotte so soon after the event to go to Hot Springs in the mountains.[6]

Washington County, Maryland, was not without its Southern sympathizers and Lee enjoyed the hospitality of some of them while at Hagerstown. He and the staff dined with Dr. John A. Wroe, and the doctor's children supposedly hid the officers' side arms while they ate.[7]

The army crossed the Potomac once the river had subsided enough to be bridged and forded. The campaign did not end with the crossing, however; once in the northern reaches of the Shenandoah Valley, Lee's army found itself in a high-stakes game of strategic chess against Gen. Meade's Army of the Potomac as both sides raced to control the gaps leading back into north-central Virginia. By the end of the month the Army of Northern Virginia was back near Culpeper, where the offensive began a little more than one month before.[8]

The Confederacy's fortunes suffered across the board that July. In addition to Lee's defeat at Gettysburg, Braxton Bragg's Army of Tennessee was maneuvered out of its namesake state without a major fight in the Tullahoma Campaign, and the important Mississippi River bastion of Vicksburg fell to U. S. Grant's Federals, and with it, John Pemberton's entire army.

* * *

---

[6] REL to Charlotte, July 26, 1863, G. B. Lee papers, VHS; Dowdey, *Wartime Papers*, 559-61. In Mary's defense, Charlotte's parents were with her at Hickory Hill, so she was not completely alone.

[7] Stephen R. Bockmiller, *Hagerstown in the Civil War* (Charleston, SC, 2011), 84. Wroe's home is currently the Hagerstown Women's Club. Ibid.

[8] Recent scholarship argues persuasively that, contrary to longstanding tradition, the campaign did not end once Lee crossed below the Potomac River, and few if any of the men and officers in either army believed that it truly had ended there. For the next two weeks Lee marched south up the Valley in an effort to avoid a dogged Federal pursuit, while Meade shifted east in an effort to capture the gaps and drive west to cut off portions of the crippled Virginia army. Much of this period was punctuated by cavalry skirmishes and infantry fighting that put Lee's command in serious (and long-overlooked) peril. See Jeffrey Wm. Hunt, *Meade and Lee after Gettysburg: The Forgotten Final Stage of the Gettysburg Campaign, from Falling Waters to Culpeper Court House, July 14-31, 1863* (El Dorado Hills, CA, 2017). The Tullahoma affair in Middle Tennessee is the subject of fresh scholarship in David A. Powell and Eric J. Wittenberg, *Tullahoma: The Forgotten Campaign that Changed the Civil War, June 23-July 4, 1863* (El Dorado Hills, CA, 2020).

July 1, Wednesday (Greenwood/Cashtown/Gettysburg): Lee instructs John Imboden to take over from Pickett the duties of protecting the army's rear; he adds that "headquarters for the present will be at Cashtown." Lee and Longstreet leave Greenwood together in the morning; somewhere near the top of South Mountain they hear artillery fire to the east. They part company with Lee riding ahead to Cashtown where he meets with A. P. Hill and Richard Anderson around noon; Hill informs Lee that Heth encountered enemy cavalry at Gettysburg.[9]

While in Cashtown Ewell's aide Campbell Brown arrives to inform Lee that the Second Corps shifted its march toward Gettysburg as ordered; Lee asks if Ewell has any news of Stuart, but Brown tells Lee he knows nothing of Stuart's whereabouts. Lee rides to the front to investigate for himself, arriving at Knoxlyn Ridge in early afternoon where he rejoins Hill. He meets with Heth, who requests permission to attack with his entire force, which Lee at first denies citing his desire to not bring on an engagement until the army is fully concentrated; Heth returns a second time telling Lee that the Federals are massing against Ewell's troops to the left, and Lee consents to Heth attacking. Lee and Hill, joined by Fremantle, observe the final attack from the artillery line on Herr Ridge.[10]

As the Union line collapses, Hill follows his advancing troops and Lee dispatches Walter Taylor to Ewell with orders to pursue them as well and take the hills on the other side of Gettysburg if possible. Longstreet arrives on the field after the Union collapse and meets with Lee on Seminary Ridge, discussing their options. Lee sends Armistead Long to reconnoiter Cemetery Ridge; Longstreet argues for a move to the south, to which Lee reportedly replies "the enemy is there and I am going to attack him there."[11]

During the afternoon, one of Stuart's staff officers reports to Lee on the Chambersburg Pike about Stuart's movements and location; Lee then sends a detachment of the 39th Virginia Cavalry Battalion to find Stuart and bring him to Gettysburg. Headquarters is established at the Widow Thompson house on Seminary Ridge, with the staff setting up their tents in an orchard across the road. In late afternoon or early evening Lee and Longstreet part company, with Lee riding to Ewell's headquarters where he meets with Ewell, Jubal Early, and Robert Rodes.[12]

---

9 OR 27, pt. 3, 947-8; Longstreet, *From Manassas to Appomattox*, 351-2, 357; Taylor, *General Lee*, 187-8. Anderson made no mention of Hill being present when he met with Lee, so presumably they met with him individually. Anderson later told Longstreet that Lee was "very much disturbed and depressed" over not knowing what happened to Stuart and not having any idea of what was in his front at Gettysburg. Longstreet, *From Manassas to Appomattox*, 357.

10 Jones, *Campbell Brown's CW*, 204-5; Maurice, *Lee's Aide de Camp*, 227; Martin, *Gettysburg*, 341; Morrison, Morrison, ed., Heth, *Memoirs*, 174-5; Fremantle, *Three Months*, 254-5. About the time of the Union retreat, Lee learned from W. A. Castleberry, color bearer of the 13th AL, of the disaster that had befallen Archer's Brigade, including the capture of its commander. Martin, *Gettysburg*, 163-4. James Archer was the first general from the Army of Northern Virginia to be captured in battle.

11 Taylor, *General Lee*, 190; Maurice, *Lee's Aide de Camp*, 227-8; James Longstreet, "Lee's Right Wing at Gettysburg," *B&L*, vol. 3, 339-40; Long, *Memoirs of REL*, 276-7. William Oates, colonel of the 15th AL, and Michael Jacobs, a professor at what is now Gettysburg College, wrote that Lee went into the cupola of the Lutheran Seminary to observe, but that has been refuted by a number of writers. William C. Oates, *The War Between the Union and the Confederacy and its Lost Opportunities* (New York, 1905), 204; Michael Jacobs, *Notes on the Rebel Invasion of Maryland and Pennsylvania and the Battle of Gettysburg, July 1st, 2nd, and 3rd, 1863* (Philadelphia, 1864), 41. Freeman was adamant that Lee did not ascend the cupola. *Lee*, vol. 3, 71 n9. Gettysburg historian Carol Reardon wrote only that "it is not certain" if Lee ever went in the cupola. Carol Reardon and Tom Vossler, *A Field Guide to Gettysburg* (Chapel Hill, NC, 2013), 153.

12 Eric J. Wittenberg and J. David Petruzzi, *Plenty of Blame to Go Around: Jeb Stuart's Controversial Ride to Gettysburg* (El Dorado Hills, CA, 2006), 129; Timothy H. Smith, *The Story of Lee's Headquarters, Gettysburg, Pennsylvania* (Gettysburg, PA, 1995), 40-1; Longstreet, *From Manassas to Appomattox*, 361; Early, *Memoirs*, 271. There is considerable debate about whether the Thompson house was actually Lee's HQ, or whether the HQ was located across the road. It seems that Lee himself quartered in the house while the actual army nerve center was across the road. For decades the Thompson house was maintained as a privately-owned museum billed as "Lee's Headquarters Museum" before being acquired by the Civil War Trust in 2015 and restored to its wartime appearance. The NPS headquarters marker for Lee is across the street and

Lee changes his mind several times that evening regarding his plan for the morrow and meets again with Ewell at the Thompson house, and separately with Longstreet. That evening, Lee instructs Pendleton to scout the area south of Gettysburg in preparation for an assault tomorrow. That night, Campbell Brown returns to Lee's headquarters with a message for Lee from Ewell, but finds Lee confined to his quarters by a stomach ailment.[13]

July 2, Thursday (Gettysburg): Gen. Lee rises, eats breakfast, and is "in the saddle before it was fully light." That morning the general meets with Longstreet, Hill, McLaws, Hood, and Heth on Seminary Ridge near his headquarters, where Pendleton and engineer Capt. Samuel R. Johnston report their findings from the reconnaissance recently conducted on the Confederate right.[14]

After making plans for Longstreet to assault south of town, Lee rides to the left to meet with Ewell around 9:00 a.m. The corps commander is absent when the general arrives at his headquarters, but Isaac Trimble is there. Lee and Trimble climb to the cupola of the nearby Adams County Almshouse to observe the enemy lines. Once they finish, they return to Ewell's headquarters to await his return. When Ewell arrives, he is accompanied by staff officer Charles Venable, whom he took with him on a ride of his part of the field. Ewell explains to Lee the difficulties in launching at attack from his sector; they are soon joined by Gens. Early and Rodes, and staff officer Armistead Long.[15]

Leaving Ewell, Lee rides along the lines on Seminary Ridge, encountering Maj. William Poague's artillery and, initially mistaking Poague for part of Longstreet's command, expresses his displeasure

---

states that HQ was in an orchard there. The best analysis of this is Tim Smith, *The Story of Lee's Headquarters*. Also uncertain is the location of the meeting with Ewell and his division commanders, though it is thought to have occurred at the John Blocher house north of town at the intersection of the Biglerville and Table Rock roads. Pfanz, *Ewell*, 312, 581 n40. Ewell and Rodes were present when Lee arrived; Early came soon thereafter and dominated the conversation; Ed Johnson was not in attendance because he was overseeing the deployment of his newly arrived division. Charles C. Osborne, *Jubal: The Life and Times of General Jubal A. Early, CSA, Defender of the Lost Cause* (Baton Rouge, LA, 1994), 193-5. It seems unlikely that Lee would have gone that far east of Gettysburg, but there is a claim that he was at the Daniel Lady farm at Benner's Hill at some point on the evening of July 1. J. David Petruzzi, *The Complete Gettysburg Guide* (El Dorado Hills, CA, 2009), 274.

13 Jones, *Campbell Brown's CW*, 214, 218 n75; Freeman, *Lee's Lieutenants*, vol. 3, 101-3; Thomas, *REL*, 296; Lee, *Memoirs of WNP*, 286-7, 291-2. Lee almost certainly must have met with A. P. Hill at some point during the night, although there is no record of such a meeting. The passage of time and the desire to shift and/or assign blame in postwar accounts makes it difficult to assemble a timeline of Lee's activities on the afternoon and night of July 1. As Coddington observed, "The records are not definite about the sequence of these conferences, but it seems clear that his first [meeting] was with General Ewell." Coddington, *Gettysburg Campaign*, 363. Lee's condition is verified by William Blackford, who wrote that he observed Lee "come out of his tent hurriedly and go to the rear several times while I was there, and he walked so much as if he was weak and in pain that I asked one of the gentlemen present what was the matter with him, and he told me General Lee was suffering a great deal from an attack of diarrhea." Blackford, *War Years with Stuart*, 230. Much has been written about Lee's intentions for July 2 and Longstreet's role therein. Because this falls outside the scope of this work, readers should refer to the publications treating the battle of Gettysburg.

14 Jubal Early to A. L. Long, April 3, 1874, A. L. Long papers, UNC; Fremantle, *Three Months*, 257; Taylor, *General Lee*, 197-8; Longstreet, *From Manassas to Appomattox*, 362; Hood, *Advance and Retreat*, 56-7; Lee, *Memoirs of WNP*, 286-7; Fitzhugh Lee, "A Review of the First Two Days' Operations at Gettysburg and a Reply to General Longstreet," *SHSP*, vol. 5, 183. According to Gen. Hood, Lee appeared at this meeting "with coat buttoned to the throat, sabre-belt buckled round the waist, and field glasses pending at his side—[he] walked up and down in the shade of the large trees near us, halting now and then to observe the enemy. He seemed full of hope, yet, at times, buried in deep thought." *Advance and Retreat*, 56-7. Much has been made of Pendleton's and Johnston's pre-dawn reconnaissance and how it related to Longstreet's attack later that day. The best analysis can be found in David L. Schultz and Scott L. Mingus, Sr., *The Second Day at Gettysburg: The Attack and Defense of Cemetery Ridge, July 2, 1863* (El Dorado Hills, CA, 2015). Schultz and Mingus place Johnston's report to Lee at about 9:00 a.m. Shultz and Mingus, *Second Day*, 143.

15 Maurice, *Lee's Aide de Camp*, 233-4; Trimble, "Campaign and Battle of Gettysburg," 212; Harry W. Pfanz, *Gettysburg: Culp's Hill & Cemetery Hill* (Chapel Hill, NC, 1993), 121-2; Jubal A. Early, "A Review by General Early," *SHSP*, vol. 4, 289; Martin, *Road to Glory*, 231-2; Long, *Memoirs of REL*, 280-1. Jed Hotchkiss claimed that it was only after this meeting with Ewell that Lee settled on his plan of attack for the day: Lee "there planned the movement, though not . . . very sanguine of its success. He feared we would only take it at a great sacrifice of life." McDonald, *Make Me a Map*, 157.

that they were not yet in position. Lee finds Longstreet in late morning and orders him to attack with Hood and McLaws.[16]

Lee rides for time with Longstreet as his troops move into position before finding a vantage point on Seminary Ridge from which to watch the fighting. Lee stops near the Pitzer Farm to speak with Gen. Cadmus Wilcox (Hill's Corps). Lee spends the rest of the afternoon in the rear of John Brockenbrough's Virginia brigade with Gens. Hill and Heth, Col. Long, and foreign observers Fremantle and Scheibert.[17]

Lee returns to headquarters that evening and finds that Jeb Stuart has finally arrived and was waiting for him. The meeting, writes one of Stuart's staff officer, was "painful beyond description." Lee holds no formal meeting with his commanders that night, and of the corps commanders only Hill is known to meet with Lee after the fighting.[18]

July 3, Friday (Gettysburg): Around sunrise, Lee and Longstreet, accompanied by Fremantle, reconnoiter along the right and center of the line, occasionally coming under fire; they are joined during the ride by Hill and Heth, as well as Long, Taylor, and Venable of Lee's staff. Near the Sherfy peach orchard, Lee and Longstreet dismount and move forward alone, drawing enemy fire and warnings from nearby Mississippians to seek cover. While on McLaws's front they speak with Gen. William Wofford about enemy strength in his front and his opinion on success if they attacked again today.[19]

After a discussion with Longstreet about where to attack and what troops to use, Lee determines to strike the Union right-center with Pickett's Division and two of A. P. Hill's divisions, all under Longstreet's direction. During his ride, Lee spies Maj. James Dearing, the commander of Pickett's artillery, far out in advance of his line and chastises him for exposing himself unnecessarily. It is probably around the same time that the general encounters Maj. Dearing that he is also seen in that area with Gens. Hill and Pickett studying the enemy position.[20]

Around midday Lee, Longstreet, and Hill observe the Union position from Heth's line; riding through Pender's Division, Lee tells Trimble— temporarily in command of the division due to Pender's wounding— that many of the men in ranks are not fit for duty and should be sent to the rear. Lee returns to headquarters in the early afternoon and is there when the artillery bombardment before the assault begins; he initially goes across to the north

---

16 Long, *Memoirs of REL*, 281-2; Poague, *Gunner with Stonewall*, 71; Fitz Lee to WHT, Aug. 5, 1894, WHT papers, NPL; Longstreet, *From Manassas to Appomattox*, 363-5. Poague referred Lee to A. P. Hill's artillery chief, Col. R. Lindsay Walker who was nearby; Walker recalled the meeting: "As we rode together Gen. Lee manifested more impatience than I ever saw him show upon any other occasion, seemed very much disappointed and worried that the attack had not opened earlier, and very anxious for Longstreet to attack at the earliest possible moment. He even for a little while placed himself at the head of one of the brigades to hurry the column forward." Quoted in Fitz to WHT, Aug. 5, 1894, WHT papers, NPL.

17 Longstreet, *From Manassas to Appomattox*, 366; Schultz, *Second Day*, 318; Dunaway, *Reminiscences*, 89-90; Fremantle, *Three Months*, 259-60; Morrison, ed., Heth, *Memoirs*, 176-7. Fremantle: Lee "sat quite alone on the stump of a tree. . . . During the whole time the firing continued he only sent one message and only received one report." *Three Months*, 260.

18 Thomas, *Bold Dragoon*, 246; Wittenberg, *Plenty of Blame*, 157; Robertson, *A. P. Hill*, 219-20; Coddington, *Gettysburg*, 455; Reardon, *Field Guide to Gettysburg*, 309. Although no record of the conversation between Lee and Stuart is known to exist, Lee reportedly greeted his cavalry chief with an icy, "Well, Gen. Stuart, you are here at last." Thomas, *Bold Dragoon*, 246; Freeman, *Lee's Lieutenants*, vol. 3, 139.

19 Maurice, *Lee's Aide de Camp*, 238; Fremantle, *Three Months*, 262; Snow, *Lee and his Generals*, 103; Coddington, *Gettysburg*, 458-61; W. Gart Johnson, "Reminiscences of Lee and of Gettysburg," *CV*, vol. 1, 246; Gerald J. Smith, *One of the Most Daring of Men: The Life of Confederate General William Tatum Wofford* (Murfreesboro, TN, 1997), 93. Gart Johnson of the 18th MS observed Lee and Longstreet making their reconnaissance: "Gens. Lee and Longstreet—on foot, no aids [sic], no orderlies or couriers, fifteen or twenty steps apart, field glasses in hand—came walking past us, stopping now and then to take observations. . . . He went on with his observations as calm and serene as if he was viewing a landscape." Johnson, "Reminiscences of Lee," 246.

20 Long, *Memoirs of REL*, 288; Alexander, *Military Memoirs*, 415-6; Poague, *Gunner with Stonewall*, 73-4; Richard F. Selcer, *Lee vs. Pickett: Two Divided by War* (Gettysburg, PA, 1998), 35-6.

side of the railroad cut to observe, but then rides down Seminary Ridge to a point opposite the "copse of trees" to observe.[21]

During the attack, Lee rides through Cutts's artillery and gets a drink from one of the gunners; he forms the slightly wounded into a line to support the artillery. When the attack fails, Lee rides among the survivors rallying them and taking the blame for the loss; he encounters Pickett who dramatically tells Lee "General Lee, I have no division now," and offers words of comfort to Gen. James Kemper as he is carried off the field seriously wounded. Meeting Fremantle, Lee suggests the Englishman seek cover as enemy artillery fire begins to fall; Lee fears a counterattack and orders up several of Anderson's brigades to support the guns, telling Gen. Cadmus Wilcox, "All this has been my fault—it is I that have lost this fight and you must help me out of it in the best way you can." Porter Alexander joins Lee behind the gun line; Lee chastises one of Alexander's aides for whipping his horse and remains there until he is convinced there will be no counterattack.[22]

During the evening, he meets with his corps commanders at Hill's headquarters at the Emmanuel Pitzer farm; Lee issues orders for Ewell to give up the town and pull back to Seminary Ridge. The meeting lasts until after midnight, with Lee returning to his headquarters around 1:00 a.m.[23]

July 4, Saturday (Gettysburg/Black Horse Tavern): Upon his arrival back at the Thompson house in the early hours of the morning, Lee meets with John Imboden and assigns the cavalryman the task of escorting the army's wagons and wounded to the Potomac River. Finishing with Imboden around 2:00 a.m., Lee goes to bed for a few hours but is up by 6:30 a.m. when he sends a request to Meade for a prisoner exchange. He writes a preliminary report of the fighting at Gettysburg, which he entrusts to Imboden to deliver to President Davis.[24]

Englishman Francis Lawley arrives at Lee's headquarters toward midday, where Lee informs him of the decision to retreat. Around the same time Lee issues orders to Imboden regarding the route of the wagon train, and issues orders to the army to withdraw to Williamsport. As the headquarters wagon is being packed, Lee's hen is discovered to be missing; the staff and Lee himself search for their feathered companion, who eventually turns up in the wagon.[25]

When the retreat begins that afternoon, Lee and Hill ride at the head of the column, pausing at Black

---

21 Birkett D. Fry, "Pettigrew's Charge at Gettysburg," *SHSP*, vol. 7, 92; Horn, *REL Reader*, 326; Trudeau, *REL*, 153-4; Walter Harrison, *Pickett's Men: A Fragment of War History* (Baton Rouge, LA, 2000), 92; Taylor, *Four Years*, 104. Col. Fry recalled Lee, Longstreet, and Hill "dismounted, seated themselves on the trunk of a fallen tree some fifty or sixty paces from where I sat on my horse at the right of our division. After an apparently careful examination of a map, and a consultation of some length, they remounted and rode away." Fry, "Pettigrew's Charge," 92. Lee's observation point was near the location of the Virginia monument.

22 Pendleton, *Traveller*, 22; Hewitt, ed., *OR Supplement*, vol. 5, 315; Taylor, *General Lee*, 214; Freeman, *Lee*, vol. 3, 129-30; Fremantle, *Three Months*, 269; Alexander, *Military Memoirs*, 425-6. Fremantle wrote of Lee after the attack: "He was engaged in rallying and in encouraging the broken troops, and was riding about a little in front of the wood, quite alone—the whole of his staff being engaged in a similar manner further to the rear . . . he was addressing to every soldier he met a few words of encouragement." *Three Months*, 267-8. Poague recorded a similar coolness on Lee's part: "He was perfectly calm and self-possessed." Pogue, *Gunner with Stonewall*, 75-6.

23 McDonald, *Make Me a Map*, 157-8; Robertson, *A. P. Hill*, 225; Martin, *Road to Glory*, 243; John D. Imboden, "The Confederate Retreat from Gettysburg," *B&L*, vol. 3, 420. There is some debate about whether Lee met with all three corps commanders together; Trudeau proposes that he met with each of them individually, and Freeman concluded Lee did not meet with Ewell at all. Trudeau, *REL*, 155-6; Freeman, *Lee*, vol. 3, 133.

24 Imboden, "Confederate Retreat from Gettysburg," 420-2; *OR* 27, pt. 3, 514; *OR* 27, pt. 2, 298. The report to President Davis makes no mention of Lee's intent to retreat, so it seems logical that it was written before he issued his retreat orders later in the day.

25 Ross, *Cities and Camps*, 63; *OR* 27, pt. 3, 966-7; *OR* 27, pt. 2, 311; Long, *Memoirs of REL*, 241-2. This same chicken was unknowingly eaten by Lee and the staff during the winter of 1863/4 at Orange Courthouse, when Bryan served it as the main course without informing anyone. Long, *Memoirs of REL*, 242. Widow Thompson later claimed that Jeb Stuart proposed to Lee destroying the town upon their retreat, which seems highly unlikely. Smith, *Lee's HQ*, 42.

Horse Tavern to watch the troops pass. Lee and Longstreet camp together on the roadside "a mile or two" past the tavern. Heavy rain and storms beginning in the afternoon and lasting all night.²⁶

July 5, Sunday (Black Horse Tavern/Fairfield/Monterey Pass): Lee meets with Ewell in the morning regarding his march and the enemy pursuit. Around midday Lee and Longstreet arrive at Fairfield, where Lee lingers for most of the afternoon, meeting with Ewell again later in the afternoon. Ewell is irate over the loss of a portion of his wagons during the night and wants to attack immediately; Lee tells him: "We must let those people alone for the present. We will try them again some other time." Lee moves into Monterey Pass during the night.²⁷

July 6, Monday (Monterey Pass/Rouserville/Waterloo/Hagerstown): Lee meets with Longstreet and Hill in the morning, and stops briefly at the Stephy Tavern in Rouserville. He pauses in Waterloo where he meets with Jed Hotchkiss, instructing him on the route Ewell's corps is to follow to Hagerstown, and instructs him to tell Ewell "If these people keep coming on, turn back and thresh them soundly." Lee arrives in Hagerstown in late afternoon, and establishes headquarters about 2 ½ miles beyond town on the road to Williamsport.²⁸

July 7, Tuesday (Hagerstown): Lee learns of Rooney's capture, which he thinks was the sole object of the enemy raid in Hanover. He meets with Fremantle, who requests a pass through the lines, as he must return to England. Lee, Longstreet, and several other generals make a reconnaissance east and south of Hagerstown. He writes an update on the army's situation to President Davis, mentioning that the rains make the Potomac unfordable. He writes to Mary regarding Rooney's capture, and sends a rent payment for the Caskie house. Rain during the night.²⁹

July 8, Wednesday (Hagerstown): Lee spends nearly all day with his three corps commanders exploring the ground from Hagerstown to the Potomac, escorted by Co. D, 14th Virginia Cavalry. Lee instructs Pickett to ferry the army's wounded across the Potomac and to move his division to Winchester to rest and refit. Lee writes to President Davis that the rains have the army trapped north of the Potomac and he may be forced to give battle; he continues to urge for Beauregard to threaten

---

26 Clark, *Histories of Several Regiments and Battalions*, vol. 2, 661-2; Eric J. Wittenberg, J. David Petruzzi, and Michael F. Nugent, *One Continuous Fight: The Retreat from Gettysburg and the Pursuit of Lee's Army of Northern Virginia, July 4-14, 1863* (El Dorado Hills, CA, 2008), 351; Ross, *Cities and Camps*, 64-5; Owen, *In Camp and Battle*, 256-7; Fremantle, *Three Months*, 274. William Owen of the Washington Artillery was present for a time at Lee and Longstreet's camp and remembered it as one of the very rare occasions when Lee partook of alcohol; Owen attributed it to the cold rain, but Lee's health may also have been a factor. In addition to his intestinal ailments at Gettysburg, it is possible Lee was experiencing a flare-up of malaria. Welsh, *Medical Histories*, 135. Fremantle wrote of the weather: "The night was very bad—thunder and lightning, torrents of rain—the road knee-deep in mud and water, and often blocked up with wagons 'come to grief.'" Fremantle, *Three Months*, 276.

27 McDonald, *Make Me a Map*, 158; Fremantle, *Three Months*, 277; Driver, *39th Virginia Cavalry Battalion*, 57-8; Martin, *Road to Glory*, 245. One of troopers of the 39th VA Cav. Battalion noted that they continued about 10 miles beyond Fairfield and "camped among the mountains." Driver, *39th Virginia Cavalry Battalion*, 57-8. It seems likely that Lee would have been in the vicinity of the HQ guard, and thus near Monterey Pass. For a time he was at the Monterey House Hotel at the pass. Eric J. Wittenberg, message to author, Sept. 25, 2018.

28 Fremantle, *Three Months*, 280; Wittenberg, *One Continuous Fight*, 356; McDonald, *Make Me a Map*, 159; Wittenberg message to author, Sept. 25, 2018; Scheibert, *Seven Months in the Rebel States*, 119-20. The Stephy Tavern stood at the corner of the Waynesboro Pike (PA 16) and Midvale Road (PA 418). Wittenberg, *One Continuous Fight*, 356. For at least a portion of the time at Hagerstown, Lee had his HQ at the home of David Atter, described as being two miles from Hagerstown on the National Road; it is not known if that is the initial and only location or if he moved. Richmond *Daily Dispatch*, July 23, 1863. The location does not match up with Hotchkiss's description of being 2 ½ miles beyond town on the road to Williamsport, and the newspaper account phrasing suggests that Lee was only at Atter's house for two days.

29 Fremantle, *Three Months*, 287; Hermann Schuricht, "Jenkins' Brigade in the Gettysburg Campaign," *SHSP*, vol. 24, 348; F. G. Walter diary, July 7, 1863, LVA; OR 27, pt. 2, 299; Dowdey, *Wartime Papers*, 542; J. B. Clifton diary, July 7, 1863, NC Archives.

Washington from central Virginia. Rain all afternoon.[30]

July 9, Thursday (Hagerstown): During the early morning Lee, Ewell, Hill, Early, and Jed Hotchkiss lay out a defensive line, remaining in the saddle until noon when they return to Lee's headquarters. Lee meets with Imboden regarding assisting with getting the prisoners across the Potomac River and gathering information of enemy movements in West Virginia; Longstreet joins them for part of the discussion. That afternoon Francis Lawley and Fitzgerald Ross call on Lee; the trio discuss the recent battle at Gettysburg, with Lee telling them that if he had known that he faced the entire Army of the Potomac, he would not have fought there, but he believed the results of July 1 warranted it.

Lee sends written orders to Imboden following up their earlier conversation, telling him his main priority is to get the prisoners to Staunton and to let his brother George Imboden handle scouting. Lee advises Stuart that he does not trust Imboden's cavalry to guard the supply wagons, and cautions that much of what was procured was subsequently lost to enemy raids. Lee writes twice to Pickett attempting to assuage Pickett's hurt feelings over being sent to the rear to guard prisoners and wounded. Rain continues.[31]

July 10, Friday (Hagerstown): In the morning Lee meets with Lt. Thomas L. Norwood, 37th North Carolina, who escaped from enemy custody several days prior, and has breakfast with him afterward. Lee meets with all three corps commanders regarding the intelligence brought by Norwood; he shares the same information with Jeb Stuart by letter and instructs the cavalryman to keep watch to the north and east for approaching enemy columns. Lee advises President Davis of the army's situation by letter and telegraph, stating that he has enough ammunition but is running low on provisions. Lee names Brig. Gen. Alfred Iverson as provost marshal at Williamsport.[32]

July 11, Saturday (Hagerstown): The general personally oversees the positioning of Longstreet's corps, and sends written direction to Gen. Ewell regarding the placement of his troops. Lee instructs Jeb Stuart to screen Longstreet's front as long as possible, then to take position on the army's left. He issues GO76 congratulating the army on its performance on the campaign.[33]

July 12, Sunday (Hagerstown): Lee informs President Davis that the Potomac River is falling and that he anticipates crossing tomorrow. He notifies Sam Jones that, per instructions from Richmond, Jones is to move with his forces to Winchester where he will be subject to Lee's orders. Lee instructs Stuart to mass his forces on the left, as Col. Long scouted the enemy position and discovered them massing in

---

30 McDonald, *Make Me a Map*, 159; Schuricht, "Jenkins' Brigade," 348; *OR* 27, pt. 3, 983; *OR* 27, pt. 2, 299-300; Clifton diary, July 8, 1863, NC Archives.

31 McDonald, *Make Me a Map*, 159-60; Imboden, "Retreat from Gettysburg," 428; Ross, *Cities and Camps*, 76; *OR* 27, pt. 3, 985-8; Driver, *39th Virginia Cavalry Battalion*, 58.

32 T. L. Norwood to father, July 16, 1863, Joseph C. Norwood papers, UNC; McDonald, *Make Me a Map*, 160; *OR* 27, pt. 3, 991-4; *OR* 27, pt. 2, 300-1; Dowdey, *Wartime Papers*, 546. Freeman put Lee's interview with Norwood on the 9th, based on Lee's letter to Stuart, the wording of which can be interpreted to mean that. However, Norwood himself told his father he arrived at Lee's HQ "around midnight" the night of the 9th/10th and slept there until his audience with Lee the morning of the 10th. Norwood escaped from a Union hospital at Gettysburg and passed through much of the Army of the Potomac dressed in ill-fitting civilian clothes provided by a Southern sympathizer. He wrote: "General Lee received me very politely, got from me the information I had discovered about the Yankee army—which was very considerable—for I had successfully reconnoitered their position and found out something of their plan of operation. He complimented me upon my adventure and then insisted on my taking breakfast with him, which I accordingly did, sitting by the General in my uncouth garb and feeling at ease." Norwood to father, July 16, 1863, Norwood papers, UNC.

33 Alexander, *Military Memoirs*, 439; REL to Ewell, July 11, 1863, REL papers, U.S. Army War College; *OR* 27, pt. 3, 994-5; *OR* 27, pt. 2, 301. E. Porter Alexander wrote of Lee at this time: "I never before, and never afterward, saw him as I thought visibly anxious over an approaching action; but I did upon this occasion." Alexander, *Military Memoirs*, 439.

front of Longstreet and Hill. He writes to his wife regarding Rooney and Gettysburg.[34]

July 13, Monday (Hagerstown): Lee meets with Gens. Longstreet, Stuart, and Imboden to inform them of their roles in the retreat and Potomac river crossing: Longstreet is to oversee the actual crossing, Stuart is to cover the infantry as it withdraws, and Imboden is to act as guide. The general orders Pendleton to place artillery in position covering the crossing sites, and sends Imboden to investigate reports of Federals in the army's rear in Virginia.[35]

Written instructions are sent to Stuart to relieve the infantry, to which Stuart sends an aide to tell Lee his men need rest. Lee sends Maj. Venable to Williamsport to report on the conditions there; when Venable gives a less than favorable report Lee "spoke pretty hotly to Venable for making a report of an unsatisfactory condition . . . in too loud a tone of voice." Lee soon apologizes by inviting Venable to have a glass of buttermilk. Rain.[36]

July 14, Tuesday (Hagerstown/Falling Waters/Martinsburg): Lee spends much of the night and morning watching the troops cross at Falling Waters. With all of Lee's staff either elsewhere or asleep, Lee presses Maj. Moxley Sorrel of Longstreet's staff into service to urge Hill to hurry his corps across the Potomac. Lee crosses to fix a traffic jam on the Virginia side and leaves Longstreet in charge on the opposite shore; he is eventually joined by Stuart who provides Lee with a cup of coffee.

Lee makes his headquarters for the night at Martinsburg, where he informs President Davis that his army is now south of the Potomac River, although Gen. Pettigrew was seriously wounded in a rear guard action at Falling Waters. He issues marching orders for the Army of Northern Virginia to move to Bunker Hill on the morrow, where it will remain for the time being. Rain continues.[37]

July 15, Wednesday (Martinsburg/Bunker Hill): Lee moves up the Valley Pike to Bunker Hill, where he plans to rest his exhausted command for the near future. His summons of the band of the 26th North Carolina to his headquarters prompts fears among its members that the general is about to order them into the ranks to offset recent heavy losses. Instead, Lee tells the musicians that he considers their band one of the finest in the army and that he wants them to do all they can to boost the morale of the soldiers. Lee writes to his wife Mary about the recent

---

34 *OR* 27, pt. 2, 301-2; *OR* 27, pt. 3, 998-9; Dowdey, *Wartime Papers*, 547-8.

35 Longstreet, *From Manassas to Appomattox*, 429-30; *OR* 27, pt. 3, 1001; Imboden, "Retreat from Gettysburg,", 296-7; Lee, *Memoirs of WNP*, 296-7; REL to Imboden, July 13, 1863, REL papers, W&L. Lee's HQ was at David Atter's house on this date, if not before. Richmond *Daily Dispatch*, July 23, 1863.

36 *OR* 27, pt. 3, 1001; Trout, *In the Saddle with Stuart*, 84-5; Long, *Memoirs of REL*, 301; Dowdey, *Wartime Papers*, 551. Stuart's aide, Frank Robertson, recalled delivering Stuart's message to Lee: "I found General Lee sitting alone in a piece of woods. There was not a staff officer nor anybody around except a lone courier, who held my horse during the interview. Marse Robert greeted me in a kindly, almost fatherly way, and said 'Come boy, what news of the cavalry?' He made me sit down on a camp stool, and sitting down himself after I had delivered my message, he proceeded to ask me all about cavalry matters generally. . . . He looked worn and tired, but his eyes blazed with energy and he seemed to me as nobly and as splendidly defiant and confident as ever—I had seen him many times before, in and out of battle. The conference lasted about 20 minutes. I remember especially his last remark: 'There will be no rest for man or beast until we whip these people.'" Trout, *In the Saddle with Stuart*, 84-5.

37 Sorrel, *Recollections*, 175; Freeman, *Lee*, vol. 3, 142-3; Dowdey, *Wartime Papers*, 550-1; *OR* 27, pt. 3, 1006. Venable was again sent to Williamsport to observe Ewell's crossing there. When Venable returned to Lee at Falling Waters, he fell asleep with the rest of the staff; Lee removed his own poncho and covered Venable, which caused the aide to forgive Lee's outburst of the previous day. Long, *Memoirs of REL*, 301. A soldier in McLaws's Division observed Lee "sitting on the southern bank of the river as we crossed. Still the same expression warmed up his features as when success had attended all his efforts. I could but think that his thoughts and feelings were at variance with his appearance." Wyckoff, *CW Letters of Alexander McNeill*, 314. Lee rode alongside the ambulance carrying the mortally wounded Gen. Pettigrew for a time; it is unclear whether that occurred on the 14th or 15th, although Freeman placed it on the 14th. Clark, *Histories of Several Regiments and Battalions*, vol. 2, 376-7; Freeman, *Lee's Lieutenants*, vol. 3, 192-3. The precise location of his HQ is not known.

campaign, but includes no personal information in the letter.[38]

July 16, Thursday (Bunker Hill): Lee has a lengthy meeting with Stuart, and also meets with Thomas Seddon regarding the army's needs; he gives Seddon a letter to deliver to his brother Secretary of War James Seddon regarding the army's lack of supply. He writes to President Davis that the army needs provisions and that the enemy intercepted some of their correspondence and learned of Lee's proposal to strip coastal garrisons, which are now threatened; Lee explains that if Meade pursues him, he intends to draw the Federals farther up the Valley and attack them. He orders Imboden to quickly deliver the army's prisoners so he can raid the B&O. Lee relieves Alfred Iverson from duty with the army. Heavy rain in the afternoon and evening.[39]

July 17, Friday (Bunker Hill): Lee meets with his corps commanders to discuss the strategic options open to the army. He informs Richmond of a cavalry skirmish the previous day and of Pettigrew's death, and recommends the creation of engineer regiments. Lee writes to ask Sam Jones where he and his men are, since he has not reported in. Rain.[40]

July 18, Saturday (Bunker Hill): Lee asks Stuart to verify that the enemy occupies Snicker's Gap.[41]

July 19, Sunday (Bunker Hill): Lee attends church service at Gen. Carnot Posey's headquarters with both Longstreet and Hill. The general meets with Ewell and his division commanders at Boydville in Martinsburg regarding Ewell's corps attacking the pursuing enemy force. Lee instructs Longstreet to cross his corps over the Blue Ridge at Front Royal and take up a position along the eastern base of the mountains. If Meade moves on Richmond, instructs Lee, Longstreet is to move his command to the Rapidan River and A. P. Hill will support him. Iverson is restored to command, but at the head of Nicholls's Brigade rather than his former North Carolina brigade.[42]

July 20, Monday (Bunker Hill): Lee advises Dick Ewell and Jeb Stuart that A. P. Hill's corps will leave the Shenandoah Valley the next day with Lee accompanying them, but that Ewell and Stuart will remain a few days longer; once they depart only Sam Jones and Imboden's troops will be left in the Valley. He adds that an enemy force is said to be approaching Edward Johnson's division and that Ewell and Stuart are to attack tomorrow. He requests that the adjutant general return several battle reports Lee submitted before he left Fredericksburg so that Lee can complete his own reports.[43]

---

38 Harry H. Hall, *A Johnny Reb Band from Salem: The Pride of Tarhelia* (Raleigh, NC, 2006), 106-7; Dowdey, *Wartime Papers*, 551. This letter to Mary is one of the very few which is solely military in nature, containing no family news. The location of his HQ at Bunker Hill is not known.

39 OR 27, pt. 2, 302-3, 706; OR 27, pt. 3, 1011, 1016; Krick, *CW Weather*, 103. Alfred Iverson performed poorly at Gettysburg, and had remained in the rear while his brigade was surprised and slaughtered on Oak Ridge on July 1; Lee removed him from command temporarily on July 10; SO175 was intended to end his time with the ANV entirely, but this was not the case. See July 19 entry for more details.

40 Martin, *Road to Glory*, 252-3; OR 27, pt. 2, 303; OR 27, pt. 3, 1016-7; Betts, *Experience of CS Chaplain*, 42. SO176 issued on this date ordered all men who had been detailed for engineer service to return to their parent units. OR 27, pt. 3, 1020.

41 OR 27, pt. 3, 1020. A deserter reported to the Federals that Jefferson Davis was at Lee's HQ at Bunker Hill; although incorrect, the Federals regarded the report as true. OR 27, pt. 3, 727, 731.

42 Austin C. Dobbins, ed., *Grandfather's Journal: Company B, Sixteenth Mississippi, Harris' Brigade, Mahone's Division, Hill's Corps, A.N.V.* (Dayton, OH, 1988), 152; Steve French, *Imboden's Brigade in the Gettysburg Campaign* (Berkeley Springs, WV, 2008), 185-6; OR 27, pt. 3, 1024-5. Ewell's aide Campbell Brown, was likely correct in thinking that Iverson brought political pressure to bear in Richmond (his father served in both houses of Congress before the war), thus resulting in his reassignment to command. Jones, *Campbell Brown's CW*, 206-8.

43 OR vol. 27, pt. 3, 1026-7; Dowdey, *Wartime Papers*, 555. A New York cavalry regiment erroneously reported that Lee left Bunker Hill on this date. OR 27, pt. 3, 763.

July 21, Tuesday (Bunker Hill/Winchester/Hollingsworth Mill): Gen. Lee breaks camp in the morning and moves through Winchester to Hollingsworth Mill just outside town. He writes to Sam Jones, Imboden, and Col. Gabriel Wharton to inform them that the ANV is leaving the Shenandoah and that Imboden is in command until Sam Jones arrives. Lee informs Samuel Cooper in Richmond that printed reports of an entire brigade or more being captured at Falling Waters are incorrect, and that it was only stragglers who fell into enemy hands.[44]

July 22, Wednesday (Hollingsworth Mill/Front Royal/unknown): Lee moves with Hill's troops through Front Royal, where he is invited to have refreshments with the Buck family at Bel Air. From there he crosses the Blue Ridge at Chester Gap and camps somewhere east of the mountains for the night.[45]

July 23, Thursday (unknown): T. M. R. Talcott is promoted to the rank of lieutenant colonel in the engineers.[46]

July 24, Friday (Culpeper): Lee arrives at Culpeper Court House in the morning at the head of Longstreet's First Corps. The general advises President Davis of his arrival there, and of his intent to concentrate the army there. He also explains his reasons for evacuating the Shenandoah Valley. Lee advises Stuart that the enemy presence at Manassas Gap may be more important than previously thought. He requests that the War Department reassign Gabriel Wharton's brigade from Sam Jones to the ANV.[47]

July 25, Saturday (Culpeper): Gen. Lee receives a letter from daughter-in-law Charlotte, and sends his regrets to Elizabeth Stiles in Savannah, Georgia, over

---

44 F. G. Walter diary, July 21, 1863, LVA; *OR* 27, pt. 3, 1031-2; *OR* 27, pt. 2, 303-4. There were two Hollingsworth Mills just south of Winchester. One is located on Millwood Pike southeast of town adjacent to the campus of Shenandoah University, and is today operated as a museum by the Winchester-Frederick County Historical Society. The other was located on the Valley Pike about a mile south of town and is now in ruins. Winchester historian Ben Ritter thinks that Gen. Lee camped at the latter location, which was later known as Hahn's Mill after a later owner. Bettina Helms, Handley Library archivist, email to author, June 17, 2019. Without any further detail, Lee could have camped at either mill.

45 Hale, *Four Valiant Years*, 289-90. William Buck met Lee at the pontoon bridges over the Shenandoah River immediately north of Front Royal and invited Lee and staff to his house; Buck's daughter Lucy wrote of the visit: "I shall never forget the grand old chief as he stood on the porch surrounded by his officers, a tall, commanding figure clad in dusty, travel-stained gray, but with a courtly, dignified bearing . . . and the face, earnest and careworn but kind an benevolent in expression, was that of a father rather than that of a warrior. . . . In compliance with a request for Southern songs, my sister and I played and sang while he stood by the piano and listened with as much courteous interest as if his heart had really been in the music and not with his brave troops straining every nerve to reach the desired goal in time. . . . Passing out to the lawn, his quick eye noted under the aspen trees a little carriage in which my baby brother lay asleep. Bending down, he pressed his bearded lips to the little unconscious face, then mounted his horse and with a parting wave of his hat, rode forward from our sight." Hale, *Four Valiant Years*, 289-90. Bel Air was built ca. 1795 and it stands near the intersection of Commerce Ave. and Happy Creek Road. The home is privately owned today, but it is visible from the road. Gen. Lee's movements from Front Royal to Culpeper are unknown, and it is also not known where he spent the night of July 22.

46 Krick, *Staff Officers in Gray*, 279. Lee's whereabouts on this date are unknown; although Freeman wrote that Lee was at Culpeper on this date, Lee himself wrote that he did not arrive there until the morning of the 24th. *Lee*, vol. 3, 146; Freeman, *Lee's Dispatches*, 106. Lee sent a dispatch to Stuart apparently in the morning of the 24th from "Mr. Eggleston's, on the Grade." *OR* 27, pt. 3, 1037. There is no Eggleston listed on the 1850 census for Culpeper, so it is likely Lee was at one of the Eggborn family residences on what is now Eggbornsville Road, as an 1864 map by the Confederate engineer corps refers to this as "Graded Road." Map 47a, "Map of King George Co., and parts of the counties of Caroline, Culpeper, Orange, Spotsylvania, Stafford, and Rappahannock," Jeremy Gilmer map collection, VHS. The Eggborn farms were located near where the Old Richmond Road crossed the Hazel River. Talcott remained on Lee's staff but his duties changed. Krick, *Staff Officers in Gray*, 279.

47 Freeman, *Lee's Dispatches*, 106-7; *OR* 27, pt. 2, 304; *OR* 27, pt. 3, 1037. Wharton's small brigade was the only force that Jones sent into the Valley in response to orders from Richmond; Lee deemed it too small a force to occupy the Valley and wanted it to offset some of his Gettysburg losses. *OR* 27, pt. 3, 1037. The exact location of Lee's HQ in Culpeper is not known; he may have returned to Eastern View.

the death of her daughter, Mary Cowper Stiles Low.[48]

July 26, Sunday (Culpeper): Lee orders all officers and men absent on leave to return to the army immediately, and he writes to Imboden for an exact count of the prisoners he took to Staunton and instructs him to make a raid against the B&O. He writes to Charlotte regarding Rooney and also regretting that the army is losing the service of her cousin Williams Wickham to Congress. He writes to cousin Margaret Stuart, sorry that he cannot visit them because they are behind enemy lines, and also says of Gettysburg: "The army did all it could. I fear I required of it impossibilities." He writes also to his wife, glad that she is at Hot Springs and has Mary, Agnes, and Rob with her, but he is very concerned that by taking them all with her that there is no one left with Charlotte in her time of need.[49]

July 27, Monday (Culpeper): Lee writes to President Davis regarding the failure of conscription to produce large numbers of troops for the army and requesting that Davis issue amnesty for deserters and others AWOL to return to the ranks. He also forwards to Richmond a request from the officers of Nicholls's Brigade for their regiments to return home to recruit, but states that it cannot be spared at present. Lee informs his commanders that he wishes to review all elements of the army. He writes to Mildred, who returned to school in Raleigh, sorry that he could not see her while she was home on break; he mentions the condition of the lower Shenandoah Valley and the plight of its inhabitants: "Poor Winchester has been terribly devastated and the inhabitants plundered of all they possessed."[50]

July 28, Tuesday (Culpeper): In the morning Lee meets briefly with Augusta County farmer Jacob Hildebrand, who is in search of his son in Early's Division. Rain.[51]

July 29, Wednesday (Culpeper): Lee sends President Davis the initial casualty estimates for the Gettysburg Campaign, noting they "will not fall short of 20,000," which has caused the temporary combining of some units until they are back up to strength. The general reports that Meade's losses are likely equal to his own, and that the Army of the Potomac is now massed around Warrenton. He also informs Davis that he does not favor returning to his previous position behind Fredericksburg, but wants to locate more advantageous ground farther south. Lee, who fully understood how to work with the president, asks for Davis's feedback.[52]

July 30, Thursday (Culpeper): Lee meets with Ewell and Jed Hotchkiss, the latter spending the night at ANV headquarters. Lee orders Gabriel Wharton to bring his brigade across the mountains to join Lee's army, and he advises Imboden of this move, telling Imboden to keep Lee informed of developments in the Valley and not to miss an opportunity to strike the enemy a blow. He writes to Sec. Seddon regarding the large number of desertions from Scales's Brigade, and encloses a report from the brigade adjutant with details.[53]

July 31, Friday (Culpeper): In the morning Lee meets with Hotchkiss, discussing the roads around Culpeper. Lee submits his preliminary report of the Gettysburg Campaign, and also forwards Mosby's latest report of his operations. He notifies Richmond

---

48 REL to Charlotte, July 26, 1863, G. B. Lee papers, VHS; REL to Elizabeth Stiles, Lee papers, SH. Mary Stiles was the wife of Savannah merchant Andrew Low. Smith, *CW Savannah*, 57-8.

49 *OR* 27, pt. 3, 1039-40; REL to Charlotte, July 26, 1863, G. B. Lee papers, VHS; Dowdey, *Wartime Papers*, 559-61.

50 *OR* 27, pt. 3, 1013-4, 1040-1; circular, July 27, 1863, REL papers, MOC; Dowdey, *Wartime Papers*, 561-2.

51 John R. Hildebrand, ed., *A Mennonite Journal, 1862-1865: A Father's Account of the Civil War in the Shenandoah Valley* (Shippensburg, PA, 1996), 16; Betts, *Experiences of CS Chaplain*, 43. Hildebrand's brother and son both served in Co. A, 52nd VA. Hildebrand, *Mennonite Journal*, xii.

52 *OR* 27, pt. 3, 1048-9.

53 Martin, *Road to Glory*, 255; McDonald, *Make Me a Map*, 164; *OR* 27, pt. 3, 1051-2.

that Meade is moving toward Fredericksburg and Lee will do so as well. He complains to President Davis about an article in the Charleston *Mercury* which criticizes Heth's actions at Gettysburg, as it can "do us no good either at home or abroad.... No blame can be attached to the army for its failure to accomplish what was projected by me, nor should it be censured for the unreasonable expectations of the public. I am alone to blame, in perhaps expecting too much of its prowess and valor."[54]

---

54 McDonald, *Make Me a Map*, 164; OR 27, pt. 2, 305-11, 992; Dowdey, *Wartime Papers*, 564-6.

August 1863

Once the Gettysburg Campaign ended, both armies settled down in central Virginia. Lee's Army of Northern Virginia took up a position south of the Rapidan River around Orange. "Two months of comparative quiet then ensued," wrote Walter Taylor. "Our camp was a comfortable one and our daily life uneventful. General Lee's habit was to rise early, and after breakfast he would ride to some part of the army" with either Maj. Charles Marshall or Maj. Charles Venable in tow, leaving Taylor behind to man headquarters.[1]

Lee was not well at the beginning of the month and was probably suffering an attack of his recurring rheumatism.[2] Uncertainty over son Rooney's fate only exacerbated his stress. Surprisingly, Lee submitted his resignation to Jefferson Davis early in the month citing, in part, his failing health. The primary factor behind the move was his belief that, because of the defeat in Pennsylvania, he had lost the confidence of the officers and men of the army. "No one is more aware than myself of my inability for the duties of my position," he wrote the president. "I cannot even accomplish what I myself desire. How can I fulfill the expectations of others?"[3] Davis, of course, did not accept the resignation and told the general that replacing him was "to demand an impossibility."[4]

As the army recovered from its Gettysburg losses Lee once more tackled the problem of desertion and caught up on his official campaign reports. He reviewed at least two of his three infantry corps during the latter half of August before traveling to Richmond to discuss the deteriorating situation in the Western Theater, which had taken a dramatic turn for the worse with the fall of Vicksburg and the surrender of Pemberton's Army of Mississippi.[5]

* * *

---

1 Taylor, *General Lee*, 221.

2 Welsh, *Medical Histories*, 135.

3 OR 51, pt. 2, 752-3.

4 OR 29, pt. 2, 640.

5 Dickert, *Kershaw's Brigade*, 262; Goldsborough, *Maryland Line*, 119. The exact dates of the reviews of Longstreet's and Ewell's corps were not specified.

August 1, Saturday (Culpeper): Lee advises President Davis that yesterday's reports of the Army of the Potomac moving to Fredericksburg are incorrect, and that Gen. Meade's army appears to be advancing toward Culpeper. Lee proposes to fight south of the Rapidan River and wants all available troops sent from Richmond to the front. The general proposes reorganizing the army's cavalry arm into two divisions, one under Wade Hampton and the other under his nephew Fitzhugh Lee. Both officers would be promoted to major general; several other officers had been newly promoted to brigade command. Lee also requests that Cadmus Wilcox be promoted and assigned to command Dorsey Pender's former infantry division.[6]

August 2, Sunday (Culpeper): Lee informs Adjutant General Samuel Cooper that the Federals placed pontoon bridges at Kelly's Ford and Rappahannock Station on the night of July 31 and crossed three divisions of cavalry and one of infantry, which pushed Jeb Stuart's horsemen back as far as Brandy Station before themselves being driven back. In the evening, the general requests an update from Stuart regarding enemy movements. He also writes to his wife Mary that he expects Rooney to be exchanged soon but doubts that Charlotte would be permitted to visit him at Fort Monroe, and mentions the enemy's crossing and his fears that a battle seems to be imminent.[7]

August 4, Tuesday (Culpeper/Orange/Meadow Farm): Lee leaves Culpeper for Orange where he meets with Ewell and establishes headquarters at Meadow Farm. He instructs Stuart to hold Culpeper as long as possible then fall back to the Rapidan, and writes to Gen. Cooper explaining that he fell back to the Rapidan because he could not find a good defensive position around Culpeper, but pledges that wherever Meade goes he will oppose him.[8]

August 5, Wednesday (Meadow Farm): Lee informs President Davis of his opposition to the proposed consolidation of some under strength Georgia units as well as sending them to their home state to recruit. He endorses and forwards Gen. Beverly Robertson's request to be sent to North Carolina, but Lee wants him to command a cavalry camp of instruction there instead of Robertson's desired field command: "I know of no one so well qualified for the post." He complains to Commissary General Lucius Northrop about the reduction of rations for his army and proposes that it be extended to all armies rather than only the Army of Northern Virginia. Rain in the evening.[9]

August 6, Thursday (Meadow Farm): Lee orders Fitz Lee to move toward Fredericksburg to ascertain enemy strength in that direction. Steady rain in the evening hours.[10]

August 7, Friday (Meadow Farm): Lee proposes to Sec. Seddon that arms be collected from militia and local reserve forces and issued to unarmed troops in his army, and also recommends Northrop's suggestion that trains carrying army provisions be given priority over other rail traffic. Lee sends his condolences to Gen. William Barksdale's widow over her husband's death at Gettysburg, and writes to Custis regarding the Federal threat to execute

---

6 Dowdey, *Wartime Papers*, 566; *OR* 27, pt. 3, 1068-9; REL to Davis, Aug. 1, 1863, REL papers, LVA. Taylor abruptly closed a letter to his sister written on this date, "The enemy is moving. Whether we will meet him here or near Fredericksburg cannot yet be said. The General's 'Major Taylor' has interrupted me sadly while writing. I am now much hurried." Tower, *Lee's Adjutant*, 65.

7 *OR* 27, pt. 2, 312; Adele H. Mitchell, ed., *The Letters of General James E. B. Stuart* (Richmond, VA, 1990), 334; Dowdey, *Wartime Papers*, 566-7. Rappahannock Station is modern Remington.

8 McDonald, *Make Me a Map*, 164-5; Freeman, *Lee*, vol. 3, 162; *OR* 27, pt. 3, 1075; *OR* 29, pt. 2, 624. It is quite possible that Lee left Culpeper on August 3rd, for his whereabouts cannot be determined on that date. Hotchkiss wrote that Lee reached Orange on the 4th, but his wording is vague regarding when he departed Culpeper. McDonald, *Make Me a Map*, 164-5. Lee also stayed at Meadow Farm, the home of Erasmus Taylor, for several days in mid-August 1862.

9 Freeman, *Lee's Dispatches*, 118-9; *OR* 27, pt. 3, 1007; *OR* 29, pt. 2, 625; J. B. Clifton diary, Aug. 5, 1863, NC Archives.

10 REL to Fitz Lee, Aug. 6, 1863, telegram book, REL HQ papers, VHS; J. B. Clifton diary, Aug. 6, 1863, NC Archives.

Rooney. Lee receives $1,820 in pay for the months of April through July. Heavy rain.[11]

August 8, Saturday (Meadow Farm): Lee writes to President Davis and offers his resignation for the defeat at Gettysburg. Light rain falls throughout the evening.[12]

August 9, Sunday (Meadow Farm/Orange): Lee and Ewell attend service at St. Thomas Episcopal Church in Orange in the morning. He instructs Imboden to be on the alert for an enemy cavalry raid and to remove government property and supplies farther up the Valley if it is threatened. Lee writes to his wife joking about the continued postponement of Custis's wedding: "You have no immediate prospects of acquiring any [new] daughters. . . . You must take good care of your old ones." He also encloses cousin Orton Williams's last letter to Markie Williams, and mentions the possibility of an exchange for Rooney. Rob's trunk arrives at Lee's headquarters but Rob is no longer there, making getting it to him difficult for Lee.[13]

August 10, Monday (Meadow Farm): Lee writes to Sam Jones and Imboden regarding enemy build-up at Moorefield and a possible attack on Staunton from the west; although Lee thinks an enemy move into the upper Valley likely he cautions, "Do not call out militia prematurely or alarm the population." He provides Gen. Cooper the latest reports from West Virginia, and instructs Fitz Lee to send scouts to the Potomac to keep watch for enemy transports.[14] He writes to President Davis regarding shuffling of troops among Early, Johnson, and Pickett's divisions and the promotion of Gabriel Wharton and William H. Forney to brigadier general. He seeks clarification from Imboden regarding what supplies, if any, were left behind when Winchester was evacuated, as he received conflicting reports. Lee writes to Custis complaining about the lack of forage for the horses, and encloses money to be deposited in Lee's account in Richmond.[15]

August 11, Tuesday (Meadow Farm): The general informs Sam Jones that he now doubts that the Federals intend to move on Staunton; instead, he wants Jones and Imboden to join forces and attack them. President Davis responds to Lee's resignation: "Where am I to find that new commander who is to possess the greater ability which you believe to be required? . . . To ask me to substitute for you by someone in my judgment more fit to command, or who would possess more of the confidence of the army, or of the reflecting men of the country, is to demand an impossibility."[16]

August 12, Wednesday (Meadow Farm): Lee announces that all troops absent without leave will be pardoned if they return to the army within 20 days. Rain beginning late afternoon and lasting all night.[17]

August 13, Thursday (Meadow Farm): Lee announces that August 21 will be a day of fasting and prayer, and orders that all arms at Staunton be sent to

---

11 OR 29, pt. 2, 628; Richmond *Daily Dispatch*, Oct. 23, 1863; Daughtry, *Gray Cavalier*, 150; pay receipt Aug. 7, 1863, REL CSR; J. B. Clifton diary, Aug. 7, 1863, NC Archives. Seddon replied on the 9th that confiscation of arms was not necessary and that the required weapons would be sent. OR 29, pt. 2, 631.

12 OR 51, pt. 2, 752-3; J. B. Clifton diary, Aug. 8, 1863, NC Archives. Freeman suggested that this letter was written to be suitable for publication in case Davis accepted Lee's resignation. *Lee*, vol. 3, 157.

13 McDonald, *Make Me a Map*, 166; OR 29, pt. 2, 632; REL to Mrs. REL, Aug. 9, 1863, Lee papers, VHS; Jones, *Personal Reminiscences of REL*, 288. The pew used by Lee is marked and the tree to which Lee supposedly hitched his horse survives to this day. Miller, *Antebellum Orange*, 20. Custis was engaged to Agnes's friend Sally Warwick; they never married.

14 OR 29, pt. 2, 632-3; REL to Imboden, Aug. 10, 1863, telegram book, REL HQ papers, VHS; REL to Fitz, Aug. 10, 1863, telegram book, REL HQ papers, VHS.

15 Freeman, *Lee's Dispatches*, 119-22; OR 29, pt. 2, 633; Jones, *Life and Letters of REL*, 288.

16 OR 29, pt. 2, 639-40.

17 OR 51, pt. 2, 754; J. B. Clifton diary, Aug. 12, 1863, NC Archives.

the army unless there is an immediate threat to the city. He writes to Elizabeth Taylor of Hayfields that he is sorry to learn she is ill, and informing her that her nephew is coming home on leave. Heavy rain in morning.[18]

August 14, Friday (Meadow Farm): Mapmaker Hotchkiss gets a map of Rappahannock County from Lee's headquarters. Thunderstorm in the afternoon.[19]

August 15, Saturday (Meadow Farm): Lee meets with ordnance chief Lt. Col. Briscoe Baldwin in the morning regarding the army's small arms, and dispatches him to Richmond to brief Col. Josiah Gorgas on the subject. He writes to Gorgas regarding the shortage of quality weapons, requesting that a supply of small arms rumored to be at Charleston be sent to the ANV, and writes also to Stuart regarding the state of arms in the army's cavalry. He requests that Gen. Cooper have the Bureau of Conscription find all men absent from the army and return them immediately, and also that a search also be made for all weapons given up by convalescents and deserters. Lee informs Imboden that Sam Jones moved his forces to Monterey in response to Imboden's report but neither Jones nor Lee has heard anything further from Imboden—please report. Thunderstorm in the afternoon.[20]

August 16, Sunday (Meadow Farm): Lee, Richard Ewell, Edward Johnson, and Robert Rodes attend church service preached by Rev. Lacy at Ewell's headquarters in the morning. He writes to Mary at Hot Springs, hoping that the stay will continue to improve her health; he encloses letters from Gen. Pickett and Mrs. Stiles. Thunderstorm after dark.[21]

August 17, Monday (Meadow Farm): Lee complains to President Davis about the high number of desertions and his inability to stop them; he suggests he has done all that he can by issuing amnesty, and that the next step is execution whenever deserters are caught. Lee instructs Gen. Imboden to interdict the B&O to disrupt enemy troop movements, and to return any deserters he comes across.[22]

August 18, Tuesday (Meadow Farm): Lee forwards John Mosby's report of his latest operations; while Lee appreciates his exploits, he notes, "I fear he exercises but little control over his men. . . . His attention has been more directed toward the capture of wagons than military damages to the enemy." He instructs Stuart to have Mosby focus his attention on the railroads rather than wagon trains and sutlers, so as to cause Meade to detach troops to guard the rail lines. Lee updates Sam Jones on Imboden's position and instructs him to take a position to support Imboden at Bridgewater. He writes to Margaret Corker of Waynesboro, Georgia, regarding her husband's capture at Gettysburg, and rides to Ewell's headquarters that evening. He writes to Custis regarding paying his taxes; being in the field, Lee is unsure of who and how to pay, and the amount owed and requests Custis's help. He tells his son the only property he owns is "three horses, a watch, my apparel and camp equipage."[23]

August 19, Wednesday (Meadow Farm): Lee submits his report of the Maryland Campaign to

---

18 Jones, *Personal Reminiscences of REL*, 421-2; REL to H. B. Davidson, Aug. 13, 1863, telegram book, REL HQ papers, VHS; REL to Elizabeth Taylor, Aug. 13, 1863, REL HQ papers, VHS; Clifton diary, Aug. 13, 1863, NC Archives.

19 McDonald, *Make Me a Map*, 167.

20 OR 29, pt. 2, 647-9; REL to Imboden, Aug. 15, 1863, telegram book, REL HQ papers, VHS; McDonald, *Make Me a Map*, 167. Gen. Heth's wife was supposed to have dinner with Lee, but she did not arrive. Tower, *Lee's Adjutant*, 70.

21 Miller, *Antebellum Orange*, 131; REL to Mrs. REL, Aug. 16, 1863, REL papers, LOC; McDonald, *Make Me a Map*, 167. Lee's continued anger over the execution of Orton Williams is very much evident in this letter to Mary.

22 OR 29, pt. 2, 649-51.

23 OR 27, pt. 2, 992; OR 29, pt. 2, 652-3; REL to M. P. Corker, Aug. 18, 1863, Stephen A. & Margaret P. Corker papers, UGA; McDonald, *Make Me a Map*, 168; Dowdey, *Wartime Papers*, 592. Corker was a captain in the 3rd GA; he was captured July 2 and held at Fort Delaware and Johnson's Island until exchanged in early 1865. Corker CSR.

Richmond, and writes to Ewell regarding a bust of Stonewall Jackson by Alexander Galt.[24]

August 20, Thursday (Meadow Farm): Lee requests that Brig. Gen. John Pegram be assigned to the ANV, and issues orders abolishing elections for junior 2nd lieutenant and creating a board of examination for the promotion of field officers. Sam Jones encounters Mrs. Lee, Mary, Agnes and possibly Rob at Hot Springs, noting "All are well as usual."[25]

August 21, Friday (Meadow Farm): Lee attends church service conducted by Rev. Lacy at Dick Ewell's headquarters, accompanied by Gens. Ewell, Johnson, Rodes, Stephen Ramseur, and Robert Hoke.[26]

August 22, Saturday (Meadow Farm): Lee acknowledges President Davis's refusal to accept his resignation: "Beyond such assistance as I can give to an invalid wife and three houseless daughters I have no object in life but to devote myself to the defense of our violated country's rights," he wrote back. The general also sends Davis the latest information regarding enemy dispositions and posits that a major offensive against Charleston, South Carolina, is imminent. Lee writes to Charleston attorney William Whaley regarding his neighbor Maj. Julian Mitchell, who was captured on the retreat from Gettysburg.[27]

August 23, Sunday (Meadow Farm/Orange): Lee writes to Mary and mentions that Erasmus Taylor, on whose farm he is camped, "has been very kind in contributing to our comfort. His wife sends us, every day, buttermilk, loaf bread, ice, and such vegetables as she has. I cannot get her to desist, though I have made two special visits to that effect."[28]

August 24, Monday (Meadow Farm/Orange/Richmond): Lee advises President Davis that one and possibly two enemy infantry corps moved down the Potomac River, and also that the shortage of forage for the army's animals prevents undertaking an offensive at the present time. Lee orders Wharton's and Jenkins's brigades to return to southwest Virginia and advises Sam Jones and the War Department of the move. The general forwards to Richmond John Mosby's report of an engagement near Annandale, and urges an offensive by Sam Jones and John Imboden in the Valley. He receives a message from the president that he is unable to come to Orange to meet with Lee, and requests that Lee come to the capital; Lee leaves in the afternoon for Richmond.[29]

---

24 OR 19, pt. 1, 144-53; REL to Ewell, Aug. 19, 1863, Jackson papers, MOC. Alexander Galt was an upcoming sculptor from Norfolk who began work on his Jackson piece in 1862. Unfortunately, he contracted smallpox while in camp to meet Jackson and died soon thereafter. His most famous works are a large statue of Thomas Jefferson for the University of Virginia, and a bust of Jefferson Davis in the collection of the MOC. George H. Tucker, *Norfolk Highlights: 1584-1881* (Norfolk, VA, 1972), 79-80. Lee received a small medallion with Galt's bust of Jackson on/around this date and wanted Ewell's opinion; presumably Ewell visited HQ to see it within a day or two.

25 REL to Samuel Cooper, Aug. 20, 1863, telegram book, REL HQ papers, VHS; OR 51, pt. 2, 756-7; OR 29, pt. 1, 41.

26 A. W. Hoge diary, Aug. 21, 1863, VHS; Hubbs, *Voices From Company D*, 195. The sermon was from 2nd Kings; Hotchkiss observed that "General Lee . . . spoke to each lady there and to all the children." McDonald, *Make Me a Map*, 168-9.

27 OR 51, pt. 2, 1076; OR 29, pt. 2, 660-1; REL to William Whaley, Aug. 22, 1863, Misc. Manuscript collection, SC Historical Society. Mitchell, a prewar Charleston attorney, served as commissary for Rodes's Division until he was captured on July 4 after the Battle of Gettysburg. He remained in enemy custody until early October 1864. Krick, *Staff Officers*, 222.

28 Lee, *Recollections and Letters of REL*, 109-10. Lee almost certainly attended church at St. Thomas in Orange in the morning, as Taylor recorded only the dates when Lee did *not* attend church during this time period, and he made no mention of this date.

29 OR 29, pt. 2, 664-6; REL to Samuel Jones, Aug. 24, 1863 (2 messages), telegram book, REL HQ papers, VHS; OR 29, pt. 1, 69-70; OR 51, pt. 2, 759; McDonald, *Make Me a Map*, 171. Lee almost certainly traveled by rail; the hour of his departure from Orange and arrival in Richmond are not known.

August 25, Tuesday (Richmond): Lee stays with Custis at the Franklin Street house.[30]

August 27, Thursday (Richmond): War Department clerk John B. Jones notes that Lee "is in town—looking well."[31]

August 29, Saturday (Richmond): Rain.[32]

August 30, Sunday (Richmond): Lee sends a short note to President Davis in the morning that he thinks Sam Jones can undertake an offensive in his department. In the afternoon he meets with President Davis.[33]

August 31, Monday (Richmond): Lee writes to Longstreet that he has been detained in Richmond longer than expected, but the quartermaster promises to increase the amount of forage sent to the army. As a result, Longstreet is to prepare for an offensive to be launched upon Lee's return.[34]

---

[30] Yates, *Perfect Gentleman*, vol. 1, 281. Lee meets with President Davis and Sec. Seddon often during this trip to Richmond, but little is known of the specifics beyond that he stayed with Custis while in the capital. Subsequent events reveal that one of their topics of discussion was the situation in the Western Theater and the possible reinforcement of Braxton Bragg's Army of Tennessee, which was in northern Georgia after being maneuvered out of Tennessee by Rosecrans's Army of the Cumberland in the Tullahoma Campaign.

[31] Jones, *Rebel War Clerk's Diary*, vol. 2, 25.

[32] Krick, *CW Weather*, 105.

[33] Freeman, *Lee's Dispatches*, 125. Lee probably attended church service in the morning at St. Paul's. Clerk J. B. Jones incorrectly noted in his diary that Lee returned to the army on this date, but corrected himself a few pages later. *Rebel War Clerk's Diary*, vol. 2, 28, 32.

[34] *OR* 51, vol. 2, 761. Lee wrote that he expected to leave on Sept. 1, but Davis would not allow it. Ibid. Freeman wrote that Lt. Col. Edward Murray left Lee's staff on this date, but that does not agree with the dates in his compiled service record, which have him with HQ until December 1864. Freeman, *Lee*, vol. 1, 643; Krick, *Staff Officers in Gray*, 228. At least one source has Armistead Long's time on Lee's staff ending on this date, although that seems several weeks premature. Crute, *Confederate Staff Officers*, 116. Long himself wrote that he left the staff "about the last of September." *Memoirs of REL*, 303.

September 1863

For much of the Army of Northern Virginia, the relative quiet of August continued into September. For the army's commander, it was anything but a restive period.

Lee remained in the capital meeting with President Davis to discuss, among other things, the situation in Tennessee—including the possibility of Lee taking command there—and to inspect Richmond's defenses. Rumors swirled that Lee would be going to take command of the Army of Tennessee. One Georgian, who had complete faith in the general, concluded that if Lee went west, "he will show the western boys how to fight and would drive the last Yankee back on their own soil."[1]

Although his wife and daughters were not in the Richmond, he stayed with Custis and saw Rob on at least one occasion. The general saw his friend James Caskie, former Secretary of War George Randolph, and, quite frequently, cousins Margaret and Caroline Stuart. When he returned to Orange, the Stuart girls accompanied him.[2] It was likely the visit of his Stuart cousins that was recounted in an Orange newspaper shortly after the war in article aptly titled "Gen. Lee Plays a Practical Joke:"

> Gen. Lee was visited by two or three young ladies. . . . He sought and obtained for them comfortable quarters at the handsome residence of Mr. [Joseph] Hiden [Montpeliso]. . . . The same day, or very shortly afterwards, Mr. Hiden observed some very unusual proceedings in his yard. A party of officers had taken possession of it and were evidently preparing to hold it permanently. Mr. Hiden's house is situated on a commanding eminence. At a loss what to make of this sudden and almost rude occupation of his private grounds, Mr. Hiden demanded an explanation from Gen. Lee. Looking at him very gravely, Gen. Lee said, "When young ladies visit camp they are often excessively annoyed by the visits of young officers. I am determined to put a stop to these visits and shall hold you personally responsible for any violation of my regulations. No one, upon any pretense whatever, shall visit the young ladies now at your house – no one but myself. To protect the ladies from intrusion and to insure your obedience to my orders (here Gen. Lee's voice became very stern) I have posted this force in your yard, to remain day and night, and instructed the officer in charge, whenever any gentleman is caught in company with the young ladies, your guests, to arrest yourself and every member of your family and to hold them in arrest until further orders." Mr. Hiden is a very astute gentleman, but the idea that Gen. Lee could joke never entered his head and a look of such bland dismay overspread his features that the General, pitying his terror, told him laughingly that the men in his yard were only a portion of the Signal Corps who had selected that position because it was the highest in the surrounding country.[3]

When he returned to the Army of Northern Virginia's headquarters, Lee bid farewell to James Longstreet and much of his First Corps, two divisions of which were about to journey by rail to north Georgia to reinforce Gen. Braxton Bragg's Army of Tennessee. Lee conducted reviews of

---

1 Fox, *Red Clay*, 207.

2 REL to Mrs. REL, Sept. 8, 1863, REL papers, LOC. Rob may have accompanied him back to the army as well.

3 Hurst, *Soldiers, Stories, Sites and Fights*, 164-5. The article incorrectly identified one of the girls as being Lee's daughter, but it almost certainly refers to the Stuart girls.

Richard Ewell's and A. P. Hill's infantry corps, and cautioned Richmond that with his army reduced by about one-third, he may be forced back upon Richmond if the enemy takes the offensive.[4]

When Bragg scored a major victory at Chickamauga—aided significantly by Longstreet and his troops—Lee urged for a concerted advance to retake Tennessee and, if such a move could not or would not be undertaken, to return Old Pete and his men to his own army so he could move against a weakened Army of the Potomac.

In addition to Longstreet's transfer, headquarters lost the services of military secretary Armistead Long, who was made chief of artillery for Ewell's Second Corps.[5]

* * *

---

4 OR 29, pt. 2, 710-2.

5 OR 29, pt. 2, 745.

September 1, Tuesday (Richmond): Lee writes to Longstreet regarding deserters in North Carolina: Gov. Vance wants troops sent south to to deal with a number of deserters hiding in the mountains of the western part of his state and causing trouble there. Lee wants to send either Robert Hoke or Stephen Ramseur and a suitable number of men to deal with the matter.[6]

September 2, Wednesday (Richmond): Gen. Lee spends hours riding along and inspecting the extensive Richmond fortifications with President Davis. At some point during the journey he sees his son Rob.[7]

September 3, Thursday (Richmond): Lee rides around the Richmond defenses with President Davis, and later informs the chief executive that he simply cannot return the Florida Brigade to its home state, as requested by Governor Milton, because Lee intends to assume the offensive when he returns to his army. Lee instructs Richard Ewell to send an infantry brigade to Germanna because he fears that Gen. Meade may be moving part of his army in that direction.[8]

September 4, Friday (Richmond): Lee continues to meet with President Davis and inspect the defenses of Richmond.[9]

September 5, Saturday (Richmond): Both Lee and President Davis continue to ride around the capital's defenses. Wesley Norris, a former slave at Arlington who had been with Lee's army, enters Union lines and tells the Yankees all he had observed of the Confederate troops around Gordonsville.[10]

September 6, Sunday (Richmond): Lee writes to President Davis that he will return to Orange the next day and that arrangements have been made to transport Longstreet and two divisions of his First Corps west by rail. The general agrees that he will take command of the Army of Tennessee if the president orders him to do so, but that he much prefers to remain in Virginia and have an officer already with the Tennessee army promoted to command it.[11]

September 7, Monday (Richmond/Orange/Meadow Farm): Lee returns to his army in the morning, accompanied by cousins Margaret and Carrie Stuart. The general personally escorts the girls to

---

6 *OR* 29, pt. 2, 692. One Tar Heel wrote that Lee attended a review of Ewell's Second Corps at Orange on this date, but this is impossible because Lee was in Richmond until September 7. Ardrey diary, Sept. 1, 1863, Davidson.

7 Edward Younger, ed., *Inside the Confederate Government: The Diary of Robert Garlick Hill Kean* (New York, 1957), 103; Dowdey, *Wartime Papers*, 595. The same soldier who claimed Lee reviewed Ewell's corps on the 1st incorrectly claimed that he reviewed A. P. Hill's Third Corps on the 2nd. Ardrey diary, Sept. 2, 1863, Davidson.

8 Jones, *Rebel War Clerk's Diary*, vol. 2, 32; REL to Davis, Sept. 3, 1863, REL papers, W&L; *OR* 51, pt. 2, 762. Freeman and numerous other writers were confused as to whether Lee was still in Richmond or if he was back with the army and atop Clark's Mountain on this date. The confusion arises from a letter Lee wrote to his wife dated "September 4" that mentions traveling to the mountain the day before for observation purposes; the letter also mentions that Lee was ill and forced to ride in a wagon to get about. This does not match his condition as known in early September, however it *does* match his physical condition in early October, and it is also known that he was at the signal station on Clark's Mountain on Oct. 3. It is thus clear that Lee simply misdated the letter "September 4" when it was actually written on October 4. Dowdey, *Wartime Papers*, 595-6; REL to Mrs. REL, "September 4, 1863," REL papers, LOC. See also Freeman, *Lee*, vol. 3, 164 n21.

9 Jones, *Rebel War Clerk's Diary*, vol. 2, 32; Younger, *Inside the Confederate Government*, 103.

10 Younger, *Inside the Confederate Government*, 103; *OR* 29, pt. 2, 158-9. Wesley Norris and his sister Mary escaped from Arlington before the war and were caught in Maryland and returned. Norris's postwar account of his subsequent treatment by Lee remains a controversial document; the best discussion of Norris is in Pryor, *Reading the Man*, 260-275. Longstreet wrote to Lee on this date proposing a swap to place Longstreet in command of the Army of Tennessee and Braxton Bragg in command of the First Corps in Lee's army. *OR* 29, pt. 2, 699.

11 *OR* 29, pt. 2, 700-1. Lee might have delivered this message to Davis in person, as he told Mary of going to meet with Davis at 10:00 p.m. Sunday night to inform him that he would be leaving Richmond the following day. REL to Mrs. REL, Sept. 8, 1863, REL papers, LOC.

Montpeliso, the home of Joseph Hiden, to request that they be quartered there.[12]

September 8, Tuesday (Meadow Farm): Lee informs Gov. Vance of North Carolina that Brig. Gen. Robert Hoke was dispatched back to the Tar Heel state with two regiments to deal with deserters in the western mountains, as Vance requested.

The general writes to his wife Mary, mentioning his recent trip to Richmond and how much paperwork needs his attention: "My table is piled with letters and papers which it will take some time to work off.... I missed you all when in Richmond very much, though I was occupied as I usually am when in that city. I slept in Custis's room. Breakfasted with the neighbors and dined with the President. I saw Mr. Caskie several times.... I tried to get off every day and at last having got the decision of the President Sunday night, went in about 10 p.m. to announce my departure Monday."[13]

September 9, Wednesday (Meadow Farm/Greenfield): Lee reviews Ewell's corps at Greenfield with Ewell, Hill, Stuart, Early, Rodes, and Johnson; Margaret and Carrie Stuart also are among Lee's party. Lee writes to President Davis regarding the detachment of Longstreet's corps: Hood and McLaws will go to Bragg's army and are already on their way to Hanover Junction, Pickett will go to Richmond to replace troops there going west with Longstreet.[14]

Lee formally announces the reorganization of Stuart's cavalry into two divisions, and forwards to Richmond Lt. Col. Elijah White's report of his operations in northern Virginia. He writes to Sec. Seddon regarding the dissatisfaction of North Carolina troops in the ANV, giving an outline of Carolinians promoted to brigade and higher command, and he notifies Richmond that the telegraph equipment in Fredericksburg is malfunctioning.[15]

September 10, Thursday (Meadow Farm): Lee meets with Longstreet, telling him "Now General you must

---

12 Dowdey, *Wartime Papers*, 598; REL to Mrs. REL, Sept. 8, 1863, REL papers, LOC; Rose Burgess, "General Lee in Orange County," *Orange County Historical Society Newsletter*, Winter 2004-5. Burgess's account, written in 1913, recalled events from her childhood 50 years before. Montpeliso dates to ca. 1819 and was on the western edge of the town during the war; Lafayette stayed in the house during his American tour in 1824. The house has been altered significantly since the war and still stands, although its fields are now a residential neighborhood. Miller, *Antebellum Orange*, 18-9. Gen. Ewell's wife was also staying at Montpeliso at this time. REL to Mrs. REL, Sept. 8, 1863, REL papers, LOC.

13 OR 29, pt. 2, 676; REL to Mrs. REL, Sept. 8, 1863, REL papers, LOC. Lee's reference to dining with the neighbors most likely refers to former Secretary of War George Randolph, who lived next door, as Lee mentioned seeing Mrs. Randolph often and the Stuart girls were staying with the Randolphs. Mrs. Randolph intended to go to Orange with Lee and the Stuart girls, but was apparently not a morning person; she changed her mind when Lee informed her he would be leaving at 5:30 a.m. REL to Mrs. REL, Sept. 8, 1863, REL papers, LOC. There is a letter dated Sept. 8, 1863, to Caroline Stuart among Lee's papers inviting her to come visit the army; this must be misdated since she and her sister accompanied Lee to Orange. REL to Caroline Stuart, Sept. 8, 1863, REL papers, VHS.

14 Leon, *Diary of a Tar Heel*, 47; Hurst, *Soldiers, Stories, Sites and Fights*, 72; OR 29, pt. 2, 706; Freeman, *Lee's Dispatches*, 126. Several writers, both contemporary and modern, recorded that two of Lee's daughters were with him for the review. This is not correct. Daughters Mary and Agnes were with their mother at Hot Springs, Mildred was at school in Raleigh, and Rooney's wife Charlotte (whom Lee referred to as his daughter) was in Charlottesville. Dowdey, *Wartime Papers*, 597-9. The young ladies referred to were almost certainly the two Stuart girls. Although many writers trace the presence of Lee's daughters back to John Worsham, *One of Jackson's Foot Cavalry*, 179-81, he was not the first to make this incorrect assumption. A letter written several days later by a William Campbell reads, in part: "It was a grand sight to see such a large body of men in one field. There were three divisions drawn up one behind the other. Gens. Lee, Ewell and A. P. Hill, each with their staffs, rode around the lines in a gallop, a distance of at least six miles. The bands played 'Hail to the Chief' and other popular airs during the time and besides there was a great many pretty ladies to enliven the scene. *Gen. Lee's two daughters were present* [emphasis added]. One would be very pretty if it was not for her mouth. She shows all her teeth when she laughs. Gen. Ewell's two daughters were there too. They attracted the particular of every Brigadier and Major General present." Partial transcript, William Campbell to unknown, Sept. 12, 1863, eBay listing in Coulling papers, W&L. Greenfield was the home of Thomas Scott on the Orange Turnpike just east of town. The dwelling remains a private residence. Miller, *Antebellum Orange*, 119-20.

15 OR 29, pt. 2, 707, 723-4; OR 29, pt. 1, 92; REL to W. T. Morris, Sept. 9, 1863, telegram book, REL HQ papers, VHS.

beat those people out in the West." Lee informs President Davis which troops Longstreet has designated to be replaced by those from Richmond, and gives Quartermaster General Alexander Lawton the details of which troops are to go where.[16]

Lee instructs John Imboden to investigate complaints brought by numerous civilians about the behavior of Maj. Harry Gilmor's troops; he adds also that he wants to assign a company of Missourians currently in Richmond to Imboden's command. Lee forwards to the War Department but does not endorse favorably a request by Capt. Victor Girardy to raise a partisan command in Georgia. Lee apologizes to Margaret and Carrie Stuart for not seeing them today, they were out when he called; he offers to send a wagon for them tomorrow afternoon to observe the review of Hill's corps. Lee writes to Mildred with latest family news and fatherly advice.[17]

September 11, Friday (Meadow Farm): Lee reviews Hill's corps, joined by Rob, Hill, Anderson, Heth, Wilcox, and several generals from Ewell's corps. He informs President Davis that Richmond's defenses must be completed as soon as possible and recommends keeping Pickett's Division intact around Richmond due to its diminished size; he advises against concentrating all Confederate arsenals in Richmond in case the city falls. Of reports of reinforcements going to George Meade's Army of the Potomac, Lee states: "When he gets all his reinforcements I may be forced back to Richmond. The blow at Rosecrans should be made promptly and Longstreet returned." He also tells President Davis that he cannot spare Brig. Gen. William Wofford and send him to Georgia, as Gov. Joe Brown requests, but he would consent to sending Brig. Gen. Ambrose Wright (another Georgian) in Wofford's place.[18]

September 12, Saturday (Meadow Farm): Lee informs Adjutant General Cooper that Imboden reports he cannot provide mounts for the new Missouri company and proposes sending them on a raid to procure horses, which course Lee does not support "as the parties sent out are too liable to take horses from friends as well as foes."[19]

---

16 Longstreet, *From Manassas to Appomattox*, 437; OR 29, pt. 2, 708; REL to A. R. Lawton, Sept. 10, 1863, telegram book, REL HQ papers, VHS. Longstreet could not recall the date of this final meeting with Lee, but noted that it occurred as he left for Richmond, which he did on the 10th. Longstreet, *From Manassas to Appomattox*, 437; Wert, *James Longstreet*, 303. In a postwar letter to Lee's former chief of staff Robert Chilton, Longstreet confessed that he did not remember the date but recalled that it was a lengthy meeting for which Chilton was present. Longstreet to Chilton, June 2, 1875, R. H. Chilton papers, MOC. Freeman has this meeting occurring on either the 9th or 10th, but the 10th seems more likely given the review of Ewell's corps on the 9th and Longstreet's recollection of it being a lengthy encounter. Freeman, *Lee's Lieutenants*, vol. 3, 224. It is possible that Lee met with Longstreet upon his return from Richmond when the details of the arrangement worked out with the president and War Department were fresh in his mind and Longstreet, intentionally or not, combined them into one meeting.

17 OR 29, pt. 2, 709; Girardy CSR; Jones, *Life and Letters of REL*, 283; Dowdey, *Wartime Papers*, 597-9. One of the complaints against Gilmor was brought by former Virginia senator Robert Y. Conrad. Girardy served on the staff of Brig. Gen. Ambrose Wright for much of the war until he transferred to William Mahone's staff in May 1864. Girardy so distinguished himself at the Battle of the Crater at the end of July 1864 that he was promoted to brigadier general. Unfortunately, he only served in that capacity for two weeks before being killed outside Richmond. Warner, *Generals in Gray*, 105-6. In declining Girardy's request, Lee wrote: "It would be a waste of service of such a man as Capt. Girardy." Girardy CSR.

18 Lee, *Memoirs of WNP*, 302; Fox, *Red Clay*, 200; Lee, *Recollections and Letters of REL*, 106-7; Todd, *Reminiscences*, 147-8; OR 29, pt. 2, 710-2. The location of the review is not known. Margaret and Carrie Stuart probably did not attend despite the invitation from Lee, for by the time they requested the offered transportation it was no longer available. Lee jokingly sent them a note: "Ask Mr. Hiden to close his doors at 10 o'clock. That is the proper time for you to retire your bright eyes from the soldiers' gaze." Jones, *Life and Letters*, 284. Lee's concerns about Longstreet's extended absence were well-founded, for on this date he saw a copy of a New York *Herald* dated Sept. 9 reporting Longstreet's move. William D. Henderson, *The Road to Bristoe Station: Campaigning with Lee and Meade, August 1–October 20, 1863* (Lynchburg, VA, 1987), 32.

19 OR 29, pt. 2, 714. These Missourians were a company of exchanged prisoners from the Western Theater commanded by Capt. Charles Woodson. For more on this unusual unit, see Charles R. Knight, "'Strangers in a Strange Land': Capt. Charles H. Woodson & His Missouri Cavalry in the Valley," *Shenandoah at War* (Spring 2018), 59-63, and Charles R.

September 13, Sunday (Meadow Farm): Federal cavalry crossing the Rappahannock north and east of Culpeper attracts Lee's attention and prevents him from attending church service. Lee writes to Agnes with the latest family news, including his belief that Custis's fiancé has no intention of marrying him and that Carrie Stuart, whom Rob has a crush on, paid him no attention while they were in Orange.[20]

September 14, Monday (Meadow Farm): Lee expresses his concern to the President over leaks in the War Department, since the New York newspapers published that Longstreet was headed west the same day that Hood and McLaws departed. He tells Davis of Stuart's fight yesterday around Culpeper and that he was pushed back to the Rapidan with the loss of several guns. He fears this signals the beginning of an offensive by Meade, who knows of the reduction of Lee's forces: "Everything looks like a concentration of their forces. . . . I begin to fear that we may have lost the use of troops here where they are much needed, and that they have gone where they will do no good. . . . If Gen. Bragg is unable to bring Gen. Rosecrans to battle, I think it would be better to return Gen. Longstreet to this army to enable me to oppose the advance of Gen. Meade with a greater prospect of success."[21]

September 15, Tuesday (Meadow Farm): Lee briefs Sec. Seddon on the measures taken regarding the deserters along the North Carolina–South Carolina border; he sent Hoke with a small brigade to North Carolina and Gov. Bonham dispatched cavalry from South Carolina.[22]

September 16, Wednesday (Meadow Farm): Lee informs President Davis that Meade's army is concentrating around Culpeper, and he proposes putting all the Maryland troops at Hanover Junction under Bradley Johnson's command to free up Cooke's Brigade to move and join Lee. The general also informs Sam Jones that Gen. Albert Jenkins's cavalry might be temporarily brought east. Lee replies to a request from Gen. Raleigh Colston be restored to command in Lee's army by explaining that he was removed after complaints from North Carolinians having to serve under a Virginian, and that there were no vacancies in any of the Virginia brigades to which Colston could be assigned at that time.[23]

September 18, Friday (Meadow Farm): Lee sends President Davis his insight on the situation facing Braxton Bragg's Army of Tennessee and a possible course to prevent the forces of William Rosecrans and Ambrose Burnside from uniting at Chattanooga.

Knight, *Valley Thunder: The Battle of New Market and the Opening of the Shenandoah Valley Campaign, May 1864* (El Dorado Hills, CA, 2010), 291-5.

20 Lee, *Memoirs of WNP*, 302; REL to Agnes, Sept. 13, 1863, REL papers, LOC. The Stuart girls returned to Richmond on the 12th; Lee did not mention if he escorted them to the train station or even bid them farewell in person. Ibid.

21 OR 29, pt. 2, 719-21; OR 29, pt. 1, 134-5.

22 OR 2, Series 4, 768-70. Lee sent a short note to Gen. Pendleton on this date regarding a complaint made by a Maj. Page—probably Thomas J. Page, Jr. of the Hardaway Battalion—about Lee's handling of Pendleton's role at Second Fredericksburg. In the message to Pendleton Lee noted that he "cannot now give the matter much attention." The entire matter is very vague. The circumstances are even more difficult to interpret because both Pendleton's and Page's original letters are lost. OR 29, pt. 2, 724-5.

23 OR 29, pt. 2, 727; REL to Sam Jones, Sept. 16, 1863, telegram book, REL HQ papers, VHS; REL to Colston, Sept. 16, 1863, R. E. Colston papers, UNC. Lee did not want Colston back with his army and the entire letter is a very gentlemanly and Lee-like way of addressing the situation: "From the communication of Governor Vance of the subject of North Carolina regiments, on which my order relieving you was based, I formed the idea that the NC officers objected to a Virginia brigadier and this point had been urged more than once. I am glad to see from the memorial of the NC officers that they take a different view of the matter. I have now no vacancy in the Virginia brigades of this army to which you could be assigned. Your former letter was referred to the commanders of Divisions in the 2nd Corps who desired other arrangements. Pickett's Division is now detached from this army and he has recommended the promotion of Col. [William] Aylett . . . now commanding the brigade to fill Gen. Armistead's place. This recommendation was not concurred in by me as I was not convinced of Gen. Armistead's death. Hoping that you may find a position in which you can do the country good service." Ibid.

In his own front Meade's army is between the Rappahannock and the Rapidan rivers and seems to be gaining reinforcements; the general does not believe the rumors going around that the XI Corps is going west. Lee would like Pickett's Division returned to him, if possible, but regardless he is making plans to fall back closer to the capital because of Meade's overwhelming superiority in numbers. Lee writes to wife Mary with the latest military and family news. Rain.[24]

September 19, Saturday (Meadow Farm/ Richmond?): Gen. Lee may have left Orange and been in Richmond on this day.[25]

September 20, Sunday (Meadow Farm): Lee is not in good health, and blames it on an attack of rheumatism. Lee recommends to President Davis that engineer Col. Walter H. Stevens be sent to Weldon to erect fortifications there as a Union build-up at Norfolk may indicate a move against the railroad. He also urges that the Piedmont Railroad be completed as soon as possible to have a back-up line to the Petersburg & Weldon.[26]

September 21, Monday (Meadow Farm): Lee acknowledges the result of Imboden's investigation into Harry Gilmor's activities, glad to learn that the reported crimes were not done by Gilmor's men but rather deserters; he reiterates that Imboden must put a stop to this lawlessness regardless of the perpetrators. Lee informs Adjutant General Cooper that Sam Jones needs to concentrate his forces and drive the enemy out of his department, and also rebukes one of Cooper's aides for sending an unencrypted message via telegraph. Armistead Long is promoted to brigadier general.[27]

September 22, Tuesday (Meadow Farm/Morton's Ford): Lee learns of Bragg's victory at Chickamauga, and he rides the lines to Morton's Ford, where he tells artilleryman Thomas Carter that the army will take the offensive very soon. Maj. Taylor submits a requisition for paper, envelopes, and pens for HQ use, noting that current "supply exhausted."[28]

September 23, Wednesday (Meadow Farm): Lee writes to President Davis regarding Chickamauga, hoping that Bragg can follow up his victory and that Longstreet can move to east Tennessee to unite with Sam Jones and move against Burnside's forces at Knoxville, then rejoin Lee's army: "No time ought now to be lost or wasted. Everything should be done that can be done at once, so that the troops may be speedily returned to this department. As far as I can judge they will not get here too soon." Lee describes also Stuart turning back an attempt by Meade's cavalry to get around Lee's left flank via Madison. Lee congratulates Stuart on his victory over Pleasanton's men and urges him to pursue them if possible. Lee finally submits his report of the

---

24 OR 29, pt. 2, 730-1; Jones, *Life and Letters of REL*, 285; Milton Koontz diary, Sept. 18, 1863, VT.

25 At least two sources put Lee in Richmond on/about this date, although there is little to corroborate this. Richard Lee (no relation) states that Lee was in the capital "for the first time since Gettysburg" on this date; however, he gives no source for this, and Lee had spent almost two weeks there at the end of August/beginning of September, so this would not have been his first post-Gettysburg trip to the capital. *General Lee's City*, 177. Also, Mary Chesnut puts Lee in conference with Jefferson Davis around the 20th of September, but her dates are not to be trusted when they are even present at all. Woodward, *Mary Chesnut's CW*, 475. Lee himself made no mention of being in Richmond around this time, and the staff officers are silent on it (although Taylor's letters from this period do not survive). While the evidence suggests Lee did not leave Orange, the notion that he was in Richmond on this date cannot be fully discounted without more definitive evidence.

26 Freeman, *Lee*, vol. 3, 170; OR 29, pt. 2, 736. The Piedmont RR bridged a gap between the Richmond & Danville's western terminus and Greensboro on the North Carolina RR. See Black, *Railroads of the Confederacy*, 149-53.

27 OR 29, pt. 2, 739; OR 30, pt. 4, 678; Warner, *Generals in Gray*, 192. As noted earlier, the exact date of Long's departure from the staff is unclear. He was promoted on this date and two days later assigned as Gen. Ewell's chief of artillery. Ibid.; OR 29, pt. 2, 745.

28 OR 29, pt. 2, 742; Dozier, *Gunner in Lee's Army*, 203; requisition, Sept. 22, 1863, WHT CSR. Taylor's requisition was for six reams of paper, 3,000 envelopes, and three boxes of steel pens.

Chancellorsville Campaign, and Armistead Long is reassigned as Ewell's chief of artillery.[29]

September 24, Thursday (Meadow Farm): Lee announces Bragg's victory at Chickamauga to the army and writes to Judge Robert Ould about a letter published in the Richmond newspapers regarding prisoner paroles. Lee informs Imboden that a large enemy force is reported to be at Beverley, which could threaten the Valley. He also informs the War Department that he cannot spare engineer Maj. John J. G. Clarke for service in Georgia as requested.[30]

September 25, Friday (Meadow Farm): Lee advises Arnold Elzey that he fears an advance by Meade is pending and requests that all troops that can be spared from Richmond be sent to him at once. Lee explains to the adjutant general the order in which his official reports should be arranged for their formal presentation to Congress. Lee congratulates Longstreet for the victory at Chickamauga and hopes he will return to Virginia soon: "My whole heart and soul have been with you and your brave corps in your late battle. It was natural to hear of Longstreet and [D. H.] Hill charging side by side, and pleasing to find the armies of the east and west vying with each other in valor and devotion to their country. A complete and glorious victory must ensue under such circumstances." Taylor submits a requisition for more headquarters supplies: paper, envelopes, and ink.[31]

September 26, Saturday (Meadow Farm): Lee informs Sam Jones that an advance by Meade is likely and unless Jones is going to undertake offensive operations immediately Lee wants Corse's Brigade returned. Lee recommends his cousin Charles Lee Jones for a judge advocate position: "I think it important that every man in the Confederacy should be put to some work."[32]

September 27, Sunday (Meadow Farm): Lee notifies Davis that Meade's army continues to concentrate but has not moved forward yet; he requests that if Sam Jones is not going to go on the offensive or link up with Bragg or Longstreet that he return Corse's Brigade to the ANV. He adds that he is very pleased to learn that the rumors of Hood and Wofford's death are not true. He writes also to Custis, noting "I rejoice over Bragg's victory" and giving his views on the situation in Tennessee and Virginia.[33]

September 28, Monday (Meadow Farm): Lee informs Richmond that he has reports of the XI and XII Corps being sent to Chattanooga under Joe Hooker, but he fears it may be false and they are instead bound for the Peninsula to move against Richmond from the east; accordingly he wants Elzey to look for any sign of their arrival on the James. The general writes to Virginia legislator J. M. McCue to explain why John McNeil will not be given an independent command.[34]

September 29, Tuesday (Meadow Farm): Lee informs Davis that he cannot confirm the reports of the two

---

29 OR 29, pt. 2, 742-5; OR 25, pt. 1, 795-805. Lee closed his letter to Davis by writing, "I am gradually losing my best men—Jackson, Pender, Hood!" in response to what turned out to be incorrect reports that both Hood and William Wofford had both been killed at Chickamauga. OR 29, pt. 2, 743.

30 OR 29, pt. 2, 746; OR 6, Series 2, 317; REL to Imboden, Sept. 24, 1863, telegram book, REL HQ papers, VHS; REL to Samuel Cooper, Sept. 24, 1863, telegram book, REL HQ papers, VHS. Clarke supervised much of the fortification along the York and James rivers early in the war and was assigned to Longstreet in May 1863. He was eventually sent to Georgia later in 1863 and rose to become chief engineer of the Army of Tennessee. Krick, *Staff Officers in Gray*, 97.

31 OR 29, pt. 2, 747-9; requisition Sept. 25, 1863, WHT papers, NPL. It is possible that the departure of Col. Long as military secretary had something to do with this additional supply requisition, as this one duplicated much of the earlier one submitted on the 22nd: 6 reams of papers, 2,000 envelopes, and 12 bottles of ink.

32 OR 29, pt. 2, 750; REL to Seddon, Sept. 26, 1863, Charles Lee Jones Confederate citizens file, NA.

33 OR 29, pt. 2, 752-3; REL to Custis, Sept. 27, 1863, REL papers, Duke.

34 OR 29, pt. 2, 753-5.

corps from the Army of the Potomac going to Chattanooga, but Sam Jones reports a portion of Burnside's troops from Knoxville going to Chattanooga. Lee again requests Jones to either move against Knoxville or return Corse, and he tells Imboden that the Federals cannot be guarding every point on the B&O so find a weak spot and attack it. Lee favorably endorses and forwards to Richmond a request from Ewell to appoint Lee's cousin Edwin G. Lee to military court duty.[35]

September 30, Wednesday (Meadow Farm): Lee tells President Davis that the latest reports have the XI and XII corps going to Chattanooga and the rest of Meade's army moving to the Peninsula, although Lee does not believe the latter; he requests that Bragg be informed of the transfer so his cavalry can interdict the railroads to delay their arrival. He forwards to Richmond the personal effects of 32 deceased soldiers that have been sent through the lines, and requests that the War Department have them returned to the men's families. Lee sends his watch to Custis to be repaired in Richmond.[36]

---

35 *OR* 29, pt. 2, 756; REL to Sam Jones, Sept. 29, 1863, telegram book, REL HQ papers, VHS; REL to Imboden, Sept. 29, 1863, telegram book, REL HQ papers, VHS; Ewell to Samuel Cooper, Sept. 28, 1863, E. G. Lee CSR.

36 *OR* 29, pt. 2, 757-8; REL to Custis, Sept. 30, 1863, REL papers, W&L.

October 1863

Illness plagued General Lee for much of October, keeping him out of the saddle and dependent on a wagon for days at a time.¹ It did not, however, keep him confined to camp. Once he was convinced that the Army of the Potomac had been weakened as much as his own army by sending detachments to the Western Theater, Lee embarked on a campaign to cut Gen. Meade's Federals off from Washington, hoping for a repeat of his success against John Pope's Army of Virginia in August 1862.

Pope had played into Lee's hands; George Meade would not. The Union commander was much more competent than the general Lee described as a "miscreant" who must be "suppressed," and the Army of the Potomac escaped from Lee's grasp. Unwilling to let the enemy get away unscathed, Lee pursued his foe into northern Virginia where, for the second time since being promoted to corps command, A. P. Hill stumbled into a fight. Unlike in Pennsylvania, however, where the mistake erupted into a major battle, the action at Bristoe Station was limited to part of Hill's Third Corps. After bloodying Hill, the Federals withdrew into their fortifications around Washington, which Lee was unwilling to attack. Unable to supply his army in that denuded region of the state Lee withdrew below the Rappahannock River and assumed a position with his left near Brandy Station and his right opposite Kelly's Ford. Once in place Lee perhaps thought the active campaign season had come to a close and looked to a quiet period before settling in to winter quarters.²

"For the last few days I have been riding around the different head quarters with Gen. Early [and] during this time we have visited Gen. Lee several times," wrote one of Jubal Early's aides during this time. "He is very dignified and polite, but you can see at once no one can approach him with anything like familiarity. . . . Nothing however minute escapes his attention. Though old and afflicted with rheumatism he will not sleep in a house as he said it would be setting a bad example to his officers who are to be in camp with their men. He sends for his Commissary, Quartermaster, and Chief Engineer every morning," he added, "and has a talk with them to know what they are doing.³

While his own army focused on Meade, Lee also dealt with a threat to Richmond from the lower Virginia Peninsula and complained of the inactivity in southwest Virginia, where he continued to urge an advance into eastern Tennessee. By the end of the month Lee was pressing the War Department for a new commander in southwest Virginia to replace Sam Jones; his dissatisfaction with Arnold Elzey as commander around the capital was also growing.⁴

Lee's exasperation with his wife Mary revealed itself as she left Hot Springs and stayed with friends in Bedford County, where she drew rations from the local quartermaster, which in turn drew a strong rebuke from the general when he learned of it. Here he was complaining to Richmond about the quartermaster general's inability to properly supply his army, and his wife was partaking of the

---

1 Dowdey, *Wartime Papers*, 595.

2 Lee winterized his own tent with a fireplace and chimney constructed by Perry, which suggests he thought his Brandy Station camp to be semi-permanent. Dowdey, *Wartime Papers*, 615-6.

3 P. W. Hairston to Fanny Hairston, Oct. 30, 1863, P. W. Hairston papers, UNC.

4 OR 29, pt. 2, 800-1; REL to Elzey, Oct. 27, 1863, telegram book, REL HQ papers, VHS.

supplies Lee was trying so desperately to increase; this he could not tolerate.[5] Mary's nomadic lifestyle continued when she found lodging in Richmond. To Lee's dismay it was only for herself and their girls; Charlotte was yet again excluded.[6]

* * *

---

[5] Dowdey, *Wartime Papers*, 610-1.

[6] Dowdey, *Wartime Papers*, 615-6.

October 1, Thursday (Meadow Farm): Lee has a lengthy conference with Richard Ewell and Jubal Early, and writes to President Jefferson Davis confirming that the Union XI Corps and XII Corps were sent to Chattanooga and that no effort should be spared to reinforce Bragg. The general writes also to Custis regarding passes through the lines. Rain.[7]

October 2, Friday (Meadow Farm): Lee writes to President Davis recommending Brig. Gen. Alfred Iverson for command in Georgia, and notes that Gens. Ewell and Early both recommend Col. Leroy Stafford to replace him. Lee visits with son Rob during the day. Rain continues.[8]

October 3, Saturday (Meadow Farm/Clark's Mountain): Lee goes to the signal station atop Clark's Mountain with Ewell, A. P. Hill, and Early to observe the Army of the Potomac's camps. Lee informs President Davis that Harry Gilmor confirms the XI and XII Corps travelled along the B&O but that Gilmor was unable to impede their movement despite several attempts to strike the railroad. Lee adds that the troops have not been paid for months and he thinks it would do much for morale if this were rectified. Rainy and windy during the night.[9]

October 4, Sunday (Meadow Farm/Orange): Lee attends church at St. Thomas's in Orange in the morning, the first time in several days that he is able to ride a horse. Lee informs Adj. Gen. Cooper that he ordered Maj. John Clarke to Longstreet as requested, and asks when Gen. John Pegram will arrive, as the brigade intended for him has been without a permanent commander for months. Lee writes to Mary, who left Hot Springs and is now with Charlotte at Buford's Depot, telling her of his physical ailments and that he thinks the danger of an attack by Meade has passed. He notes that Rooney's exchange seems likely, given the prisoners Bragg captured at Chickamauga, and describes his observations of Meade's army yesterday.[10]

October 5, Monday (Meadow Farm): Lee recommends to President Davis that he [Davis] visit Bragg's Army of Tennessee to improve its morale, and also suggests again that Iverson be sent to Georgia and "Grumble" Jones likewise be sent elsewhere due to his inability to get along with Jeb Stuart: "I have lost all hope of his being useful in the cavalry here," he writes of Jones.[11]

October 7, Wednesday (Meadow Farm): Rain in the afternoon. Lee meets with Jed Hotchkiss in the evening.[12]

October 8, Thursday (Meadow Farm): Lee confers with Gens. Ewell and Hill regarding launching an

---

7 Hurst, *Soldiers, Stories, Sites and Fights*, 90; *OR* 29, pt. 2, 766; Jones, *Life and Letters of REL*, 289; Richmond *Daily Dispatch*, Oct. 3, 1863.

8 Freeman, *Lee's Dispatches*, 127-9; REL to Davis, Oct. 2, 1863, telegram book, REL HQ papers, VHS; Dowdey, *Wartime Papers*, 595; Richmond *Daily Dispatch*, Oct. 3, 1863.

9 P. W. Hairston to Fanny Hairston, Oct. 5, 1863, P. W. Hairston papers, UNC; Dowdey, *Wartime Papers*, 595; *OR* 29, pt. 2, 769; Krick, *CW Weather*, 109.

10 Dowdey, *Wartime Papers*, 595-6; REL to Samuel Cooper, Oct. 4, 1863, telegram book, REL HQ papers, VHS. What changed Lee's mind regarding the availability of Maj. Clarke remains unknown, for he told Cooper on Sept. 25 that he could not part with the engineer (see entry, Sept. 25). Lee mistakenly dated this letter to Mary "September 4," and it has been the source of confusion to a number of Lee biographers and historians trying to reconcile how Lee was in Orange and Richmond at the same time; the details of the letter, such as his illness, reference to a recent victory by Bragg, and the visit to Clark's Mountain, make it clear Lee simply misdated it. Buford's Depot is modern-day Montvale, located at the eastern base of the Blue Ridge Mountains in Bedford County.

11 *OR* 29, pt. 2, 771-2.

12 Jed Hotchkiss to Sara Hotchkiss, Oct. 7, 1863, Valley of the Shadow; W. P. Cooper diary, Oct. 7, 1863, R. B. Cook papers, WVU. Hotchkiss did not state the reason for his call on Lee, but Hotchkiss returned from leave the previous day and noted in his diary that he rode with H. D. Whitcomb, superintendent of the Virginia Central, so he may have relayed parts of their conversation to Lee. McDonald, *Make Me a Map*, 179.

offensive. Maj. Gen. Robert Ransom arrives at Orange and meets with Lee, whom he finds "quite unwell from an attack of rheumatism." Lee asks the War Department if a replacement has been named for Iverson, and also informs Elzey that no cavalry can be spared at present from the ANV, to get it from North Carolina.[13]

October 9, Friday (Meadow Farm/Orange/Madison): Lee moves toward Madison Court House, but has to ride in a wagon due to the ongoing pain in his back. The general informs Gens. Cooper and Elzey in Richmond that a raid up the Virginia Peninsula appears likely, but he can spare no troops to help defend Richmond; reinforcements will have to be pulled from south of the James River. Lee urges Sam Jones in southwest Virginia to advance in his theater if only to occupy the enemy in his front and prevent them from going elsewhere, and instructs Gen. Imboden to move north to Strasburg to protect Lee's left and rear.[14]

October 10, Saturday (Madison): Lee is still unable to ride a horse and must travel by wagon. He informs Sec. Seddon that he has reports a major enemy offensive against Charleston is pending.[15]

October 11, Sunday (Madison/Culpeper/Griffinsburg): Lee is well enough to ride a horse again and departs in the morning for Culpeper, but learns enroute that Meade learned of Lee's move to outflank him and pulled back across the Rappahannock River. Lee enters Culpeper to a warm welcome; one woman complains to him about her neighbors, who often visited Union Gen. John Sedgwick's headquarters, to which Lee replies, "I know General Sedgwick very well. It is just like him to be so kindly and considerate and to have his band there to entertain them. . . . You will find that General Sedgwick will have none but agreeable gentlemen about him." The general continues riding on to Griffinsburg, where he establishes headquarters for the night. That evening he meets with Ewell and learns that Jeb Stuart is driving the enemy cavalry. Lee writes to Sec. Seddon complaining that his offensive was reported in the Richmond newspapers and he thinks that is how Meade learned of it.[16]

October 12, Monday (Griffinsburg/Jeffersonton/Warrenton Sulphur Springs): Lee moves with Gen. Ewell's column toward Warrenton, passing through Jeffersonton around midday. In late afternoon the general arrives at the Rappahannock River at Warrenton Sulphur Springs where he, Ewell, and Jeb Stuart watch the action to secure the river crossing. Headquarters is established for the night just south of the Springs.[17]

---

13 Robertson, *A. P. Hill*, 233; *OR* 29, pt. 2, 781; REL to Samuel Cooper, Oct. 8, 1863, telegram book, REL HQ papers, VHS; REL to Elzey, Oct. 8, 1863, telegram book, REL HQ papers, VHS.

14 Dowdey, *Wartime Papers*, 611; *OR* 29, pt. 2, 779-81. Robert Ransom happened to pass through Orange as Lee's offensive was beginning, and wrote "Lee moves today." This is the only known source for Lee actually leaving Orange on this date, although it can be inferred from his own writings. Where he established HQ for the night is not known.

15 Dowdey, *Wartime Papers*, 611; *OR* 29, pt. 2, 782. Lee's exact location and movements on this date are not known. Walter Taylor, who was on leave in Richmond and became engaged to Bettie Saunders, rejoined HQ at Madison Court House during the night. Tower, *Lee's Adjutant*, 74-6. According to a popular Madison County legend, Traveller was re-shod at a blacksmith at Locust Dale as Lee passed by; no timeframe is attached to the story and there are few known times when Lee was in that vicinity. Depending on the route taken, he could have gone through Locust Dale on this march; another possibility is immediately following the Kilpatrick-Dahlgren Raid in early March of 1864. Margaret G. Davis, *Madison County, Virginia: A Revised History* (Madison, VA, 1977), 35.

16 Dowdey, *Wartime Papers*, 611; Tower, *Lee's Adjutant*, 76; Long, *Memoirs of REL*, 306; Freeman, *Lee*, vol. 3, 173; *OR* 29, pt. 1, 405-6. Lee supposedly joked to Ewell about the number of reports he received from Stuart during the day, and told one of Stuart's couriers it was unnecessary to send so many. Freeman, *Lee*, vol. 3, 173. The long-awaited John Pegram was appointed to command of William "Extra Billy" Smith's former Virginia brigade on this date. *OR* 29, pt. 2, 783.

17 Freeman, *Lee*, vol. 3, 174; Henderson, *Bristoe Station*, 127, 131; Tower, *Lee's Adjutant*, 76. For reasons unknown, Walter Taylor was on the skirmish line when the attack on the ford began and "was carried along with them." Tower, *Lee's Adjutant*, 76. From Lee's camp near Griffinsburg (several miles northwest of Culpeper on the Sperryville Turnpike), Lee

October 13, Tuesday (Warrenton Sulphur Springs/ Warrenton): Lee departs the Springs in the morning and establishes headquarters in Warrenton, where he is once again welcomed by the residents. Lee informs Sec. Seddon that he drove Gen. Meade north of the Rappahannock River by moving around his right flank and he intends to push Meade back on Washington.[18]

October 14, Wednesday (Warrenton/Greenwhich/ Bristoe Station): About 1:00 a.m. Lee meets with one of Stuart's scouts, who reports that Stuart is trapped near Auburn between two enemy forces and requests that Lee make a diversion to allow the cavalry to break out. Lee makes plans for Ewell to send a force to Stuart's relief at dawn then goes to bed for a few hours. In the morning Stuart reports in person to Lee that once Ewell's guns opened, he was able to extricate himself. Lee then rides with Ewell and William Pendleton at the head of Ewell's corps toward Bristoe Station. During the afternoon firing becomes audible to the north on A. P. Hill's front, and Lee arrives at Bristoe Station around 4:00 p.m. to discover Hill engaged. Shortly before dark Hill briefs Lee on the fight; Lee sternly rebukes Hill for his impulsiveness in attacking without reconnoitering. Lee establishes headquarters on the battlefield.[19]

October 15, Thursday (Bristoe Station): In the morning Lee rides the battlefield with A. P. Hill and Henry Heth. Hill explains how the fighting unfolded and assumes responsibility for the defeat. Lee orders Hill to destroy the railroad in the vicinity and writes to Sec. Seddon that Gen. Meade outran his army and is now too close to Washington to attack. Rain.[20]

October 16, Friday (Bristoe Station): Lee is again quite unwell and confined to his tent. He writes again to Seddon explaining that no good can come from pursuing Meade further and the condition of the

---

would have had to move against the tide of Hill's corps on the turnpike back to Culpeper, or move cross-country toward Rixeyville to intercept Ewell's column. Warrenton Sulphur Springs (known by several names), was a thriving prewar resort mostly destroyed during the campaign against Pope in 1862. Today it is the Fauquier Springs Country Club.

18 Tower, *Lee's Adjutant*, 76; *OR* 29, pt. 1, 406. The precise location of Lee's HQ in Warrenton is not known.

19 Long, *Memoirs of REL*, 308-10; Freeman, *Lee*, vol. 3, 179; Lee, *Memoirs of WNP*, 302; Henderson, *Bristoe Station*, 187-90; Tower, *Lee's Adjutant*, 77. After Stuart's scout reported to Lee, he gave details of Stuart's situation to Lee's staff; Lee overheard portions of this exchange from inside his tent and sternly ordered the scout not to talk to anyone. Realizing that Lee had misinterpreted the exchange, Maj. Venable explained to the general that the man was only telling them where a diversion would be most effective; Lee emerged from his tent and apologized to the soldier, had coffee and a meal prepared for him, and insisted he use Lee's personal camp stool. Long, *Memoirs of REL*, 309-10. It is possible that Lee went to Auburn with Ewell to personally oversee Stuart's rescue. Henderson, *Bristoe Station*, 150. Taylor is the best source for the march from Madison to Bristoe, but he makes no mention of Stuart or Auburn. A. P. Hill sent two brigades forward against an entire Union corps at Bristoe with disastrous results. Taylor referred to this as a "trifling affair, but nothing worthy of the name of a fight." Tower, *Lee's Adjutant*, 75. The exact location of Lee's HQ is not known; only that it was "a mile or two back" from Broad Run (according to an aide in Ewell's Second Corps). Colt, *Defend the Valley*, 284.

20 Morrison, ed., Heth, *Memoirs*, 180; Freeman, *Lee*, vol. 3, 185; *OR* 29, pt. 1, 406; Jones, *Campbell Brown's CW*, 235. Several versions of Lee's demeanor and the conversation between him and Hill exist. The most common—"Well, General, bury these poor men and let us say no more about it"—can be found in Freeman, *Lee*, vol. 3, 183. Other versions suggest a more animated conversation between Lee and Hill. See, for example, Henderson, *Bristoe Station*, 192-3. Jeffrey Wm. Hunt, the author of the most recent and best treatment of the campaign, *Meade and Lee at Bristoe Station: The Problems of Command and Strategy after Gettysburg, from Brandy Station to the Buckland Races, August 1 to October 31, 1863* (El Dorado Hills, 2019), 375, concluded Lee "barely contained [his] anger." Hunt also uses a passage from a Louisiana staff officer, William J. Seymour, who left the following account: "Lee and Staff came up to a little knoll a few yards in front of our line. The General seemed to be in no good humor and casting a glance over the field thickly strewed with dead Confederates sharply called to Gen. Hill to send immediately for his pioneer corps to bury his unfortunate dead. Gen. Hill recognized a rebuke in the tone and manner of his commander and replied, 'this is all my fault, General.' 'Yes,' said Lee, 'it is your fault; you committed a great blunder yesterday; your line of battle was too short, too thin, and your reserves were too far behind.' Poor Hill, he appeared deeply humiliated by this speech and no doubt wished that he could sink out of sight in the lowest depths of his capacious cavalry boots, and there hide his diminished head." William J. Seymour, Terry L. Jones, ed., *The Civil War Memoirs of Captain William J. Seymour: Reminiscences of a Louisiana Tiger* (El Dorado Hills, CA 2020), 65-66.

roads and railroad prevent the army from sustaining itself in northern Virginia. Rain continues.[21]

October 17, Saturday (Bristoe Station): Lee sends a preliminary report of the campaign to President Davis, noting that he cannot pursue Meade any further as the Army of the Potomac is entrenched and his own army is running out of supplies where it is. Rain continues.[22]

October 18, Sunday (Bristoe Station/ Rappahannock Station): Lee leaves Bristoe and moves south toward the Rappahannock, arriving at the river before noon to discover no pontoon bridge there, which causes a delay of "several hours." In the evening Lee crosses the newly completed bridge and establishes headquarters on a hill near the river. Rain resumes in the evening.[23]

October 19, Monday (opposite Rappahannock Station): Lee informs President Davis that Meade is along Bull Run but Lee cannot tell what his intentions are, and that Lee cannot stay in northern Virginia to directly oppose him because of the difficulty of supplying the army. He also complains that he is not satisfied with the performance of Sam Jones in southwestern Virginia and that if further reductions are to be made to the ANV, Lee would rather the troops went to Bragg at Chattanooga than to Jones. He writes also to Quartermaster General Alexander Lawton thanking him for his efforts to get supplies to the army, but points out that had the army been properly equipped and supplied initially he could have pushed Meade across the Potomac. He instructs Imboden to keep watch on the mountain passes and to confine the enemy to the lower Valley. He congratulates Stuart for his victory over Judson Kilpatrick at Buckland and orders him to provide guards for the parties removing the rails from the Orange & Alexandria. Lee writes a lengthy letter to his wife admonishing her for taking supplies from the commissary in Bedford County: "Everything abstracted from the commissary diminishes the supply for the army which I endeavor to increase as much as possible." He mentions the recent campaign and how he did not personally go beyond Bristoe or Broad Run but he learned that the Federals erected a fortification in the yard of Chantilly. Regarding his own health he writes "I think my rheumatism is a little better. Yet I still suffer." Rain continues through the morning.[24]

October 20, Tuesday (opposite Rappahannock Station/ Kelly's Ford): Lee and Ewell go to Kelly's Ford in the morning. Lee informs Gen. Cooper of Stuart's victory at Buckland, and warns Imboden that the enemy is reported advancing on him from the west.[25]

October 21, Wednesday (opposite Rappahannock Station): Lee dines with Rob, who notes of his father "Found him and his staff very well."[26]

October 23, Friday (opposite Rappahannock Station): Lee sends a preliminary report of the Bristoe Campaign to the War Department and also forwards a request from Stuart to have the 8th and 14th

---

21 Lee, *Memoirs of WNP*, 304; OR 29, pt. 1, 407; Jones, *Campbell Brown's CW*, 235. A courier observed Lee's tent to be just as inundated as the surrounding fields: "I found him with his feet resting on a box, the floor of the tent (sod) being saturated with water." Colt, *Defend the Valley*, 284.

22 OR 29, pt. 1, 407-8; Henderson, *Bristoe Station*, 201.

23 Tower, *Lee's Adjutant*, 79; Henderson, *Bristoe*, 201. The pontoon bridge was at Rappahannock Station and Lee's campsite was somewhere on the high ground just south of the river. Taylor complained about the location but did not specify exactly where it was: "We pitched our tents in our present location, which by the way, being a bare eminence with a northern exposure is by no means a pleasant one whilst this cutting wind prevails; but 'tis one of my commander's idiosyncracies [sic] to suffer any amount of discomfort and inconvenience sooner than to change a camp once established. So the minor lights must submit, quietly, grin and endure." Tower, *Lee's Adjutant*, 79.

24 OR 29, pt. 1, 408-9; OR 29, pt. 2, 794-5; Henderson, *Bristoe Station*, 201; Dowdey, *Wartime Papers*, 610-1.

25 McDonald, *Make Me a Map*, 179; OR 29, pt. 1, 409-10; REL to Imboden, Oct. 20, 183, telegram book, REL HQ papers, VHS.

26 REL Jr. to Mrs. REL, Oct. 21, 1863, Lee family papers VHS.

Virginia Cavalry transferred from southwest Virginia to his command. Lee congratulates Imboden on his success capturing the garrison at Charlestown and notifies Richmond of the victory. He informs Sec. Seddon that if the troops in southwest Virginia were better led they could drive the Federals from that region; he adds that his men need clothing, shoes, and blankets. Rain.[27]

October 24, Saturday (opposite Rappahannock Station): Lee meets with engineer Capt. Oscar Hinrichs regarding mapping the fortifications along the Rapidan. The general informs Sec. Seddon that several miles of railroad iron taken up from the Orange & Alexandria line north of the Rappahannock River is corralled near Brandy Station; if the railroad is not going to use the iron, Lee wants it turned over to the Confederate Navy. Rain continues.[28]

October 25, Sunday (opposite Rappahannock Station): Taylor writes home reflecting on the recent inactivity: "We have had a period of quiet and inactivity, by no means unacceptable, after the exciting race of the previous week." Rain continues.[29]

October 26, Monday (opposite Rappahannock Station): Lee advises Sec. Seddon that he will have the iron rails removed from the Richmond, Fredericksburg & Potomac Railroad north of the Rappahannock, but will need a pontoon bridge to get them back across to Fredericksburg, and cautions that once the enemy learns of the expedition, it will have to be abandoned because he does not have the troops needed to protect the work parties. Lee forwards to Richmond a request from one of Jeb Stuart's brigadiers to have three cavalry units currently in Gen. P. G. T. Beauregard's department transferred north to the ANV.

The general sends letters of congratulations to both James Longstreet and Lt. Gen. Leonidas Polk for the victory at the Battle of Chickamauga in northern Georgia, telling both that he does not think he could be of any service in Tennessee and cites his own poor health. Lee sends President Davis a letter of recommendation for Gov. Letcher's former aide S. Bassett French.[30]

October 27, Tuesday (opposite Rappahannock Station/ Brandy Station): Lee moves headquarters farther back from the river, to "a nice pine thicket" closer to Brandy Station. Lee informs Elzey to concentrate his forces, that the enemy cannot be in strength on both sides of the James.[31]

October 28, Wednesday (near Brandy Station): Lee's servant Perry constructs a chimney for Lee's tent. The general recommends to Sec. Seddon that since the Lincoln administration has suspended prisoner exchanges, that no prisoners be kept at Richmond. Rather, they should be moved to the interior along

---

27 OR 29, pt. 1, 410-1, 492; OR 29, pt. 2, 800-1; REL to Samuel Cooper, Oct. 23, 1863, telegram book, REL HQ papers, VHS; Tower, *Lee's Adjutant*, 80.

28 Richard B. Williams, ed., *Stonewall's Prussian Mapmaker: The Journals of Captain Oscar Hinrichs* (Chapel Hill, NC, 2014), 104-5; REL to Seddon, Oct. 24, 1863, telegram book, REL HQ papers, VHS; Tower, *Lee's Adjutant*, 80. Hinrichs worked for the U.S. Coast Survey prior to the war and entered Confederate service in early 1862, serving on the staffs of Joe Johnston, Richard Ewell, and Thomas "Stonewall" Jackson, among others. His opinions of other officers and keen observations are invaluable. Hinrichs was the great-grandfather of Jim Henson of "Muppets" fame. Krick, *Staff Officers in Gray*, 160.

29 Tower, *Lee's Adjutant*, 79-80.

30 OR 29, pt. 2, 802; OR 51, pt. 2, 773-5; OR 30, pt. 3, 69; OR 52, pt. 2, 549-50; REL to Davis, Oct. 26, 1863, S. B. French CSR, NA. Lee confided to Longstreet: "I have been suffering so much from rheumatism in my back that I could scarcely get about. The first two days of our march I had to be hauled in a wagon, and subsequently every motion of my horse, and indeed of my body, gave much pain. I am rather better now, though still suffering." OR 52, pt. 2, 549-50.

31 Dowdey, *Wartime Papers*, 615; REL to Elzey, Oct. 27, 1863, telegram book, REL HQ papers, VHS. Period maps show very few wooded areas around Brandy Station, but it is unknown precisely where Lee's new camp was located. Taylor noted only that the new camp was "about a mile distant" from the previous one. Tower, *Lee's Adjutant*, 81. It was probably on Fleetwood Hill, but there is no direct evidence for this. Author, conversations with Clark Hall, Oct. 6, 2019.

rail lines. He also complains to the secretary that the orders permitting leaves of absence for members of the Georgia legislature is greatly hampering the number of officers present in some of the Georgia units. Lee writes to his wife Mary that he is glad she has found a house in Richmond, but is unhappy that there is not room enough for Charlotte; he has no idea when son Rooney will be exchanged, and requests that Mary send him some winter clothing because he has none at present. Lee observes that his health is improved, but he is still not well.[32]

October 30, Friday (near Brandy Station): Lee writes to Stuart praising John Mosby's latest exploits, and acknowledges orders from Richmond staying the execution of two soldiers in the 41st Virginia but argues that leniency only encourages further desertion and that it can be stopped only by execution of the offenders.[33]

October 31, Saturday (near Brandy Station): Lee meets with William Pendleton regarding the Maryland Line being assigned to garrison Hanover Junction. Lee asks Gov. Letcher for his assistance regarding several distilleries in Rappahannock County which are buying up all the wheat in that region which is desperately needed for the army's use. He also instructs Stuart to assist in rounding up deserters along the eastern foot of the Blue Ridge.[34]

Lee authorizes Elzey to use the troops at Hanover Junction and to call for reinforcements from North Carolina if needed to defend Richmond; he also rebukes Elzey for sending a message regarding troop strength unencrypted. Lee receives a letter from his wife, and sends one to Mildred mentioning camp life and inviting her to visit. Rain in the morning.[35]

---

32 Dowdey, *Wartime Papers*, 615-6; *OR* 6, Series 2, 438-9; *OR* 51, pt. 2, 779-80. Of his health he told wife Mary: "I have felt very differently since my attack of last spring, from which I have never recovered.... My rheumatism is better, though I still suffer. I hope in time it will pass away." Ibid. Taylor also had a chimney for his tent, and it is presumed the rest of the staff did as well, suggesting that Lee believed they would winter in this location. Tower, *Lee's Adjutant*, 81.

33 Charleston *Mercury*, Nov. 10, 1863; *OR* 29, pt. 2, 806-7.

34 WNP to "Mr. Lee," Oct. 31, 1863, WNP papers, UNC; *OR* 33, 1090; REL to Letcher, Oct. 31, 1863, LJF papers, W&L; *OR* 29, pt. 2, 809.

35 *OR* 29, pt. 2, 809; REL to Mrs. REL, Nov. 1, 1863, REL papers, LOC; REL to Mildred, Oct. 31, 1863, Lee family papers, VHS; Betts, *Experiences of a CS Chaplain*, 48. Lee described the camp for Mildred: "My people have built a nice chimney to my tent and shuttered it with pine walling, so you will be very comfortable and can sleep before the fire.... We have some beef and camp biscuit." REL to Mildred, Oct. 31, 1863, Lee family papers, VHS.

November 1863

Poor health continued to plague Robert E. Lee in early November and kept him from the saddle. He had recovered enough to at least sit on a horse at a review of Jeb Stuart's cavalry attended by Virginia Governor John Letcher on the 5th on the familiar grounds of John Minor Botts's estate at Brandy Station.[1] If Lee entertained thoughts of a quiet autumn along the Rappahannock River, they were dashed two days later when George Meade's Army of the Potomac attacked at Rappahannock Station and Kelly's Ford, capturing hundreds of men and forcing the Army of Northern Virginia's hurried withdrawal. Lee himself had a close call at Rappahannock Station when an officer's horse was killed right beside him.[2]

When Meade failed to press his advantage after securing the river crossings, Lee withdrew behind the Rapidan River and made his headquarters just outside of Orange. A rumor made the rounds that one of Lee's horses was stolen soon after his arrival at Orange. Walter Taylor sarcastically assured his fiancé that it was not true, and that headquarters was well-protected: "The battalion of guides and couriers—Gen. Lee's Body Guard as they are pleased to call themselves—the 'Guides, Scouts, Couriers, Detectives and Scamps' as we call them—always attend our Chief's person and never camp more than a mile from him. . . . I pledge you my word the Tycoon shall not be kidnapped."[3]

Jefferson Davis made a rare visit to the army intending to review the troops, but foul weather forced the cancellation of his public appearances. He did, however, join Lee atop Clark's Mountain during a break in the weather to observe Meade's army. During the several days Davis was at the front he enjoyed much finer quarters than Lee, staying at Bloomsbury estate close by Lee's camp.[4]

This was a period of unrest in Lee's military family. "The truth is Gen. Lee doesn't make our time pleasant here," confided Taylor to a friend.[5] Charles Venable butted heads the most with Lee (if his surviving correspondence is any indication) and went to Richmond to explore other service opportunities away from the commander. Taylor and the others within Lee's inner military circle did not expect Venable to return, but to their surprise he did.[6]

Custis joined his father for much of the month, preceding the president by several days and then returning to Orange at his father's request late in the month when the army once again took to the field. Lee still had no idea when son Rooney would be exchanged. One small piece of good news was that he had been transferred from Fort Monroe to Fort Lafayette in New York harbor—away from any possible harm that might befall him at the hands of Gen. Benjamin Butler.[7] Although Lee had

---

1 Freeman, *Lee*, vol. 3, 189.

2 P. W. Hairston diary, Nov. 7, 1863, UNC.

3 Tower, *Lee's Adjutant*, 85.

4 Miller, *Antebellum Orange*, 115.

5 Tower, *Lee's Adjutant*, 89.

6 Ibid. Venable was gone during most of Davis's visit and may have missed the beginning of the Mine Run operations also. Ibid, 89-91.

7 Agnes to Fanny R. Johnston, Nov. 26, 1863, Lee family papers, LVA.

long since dismissed any thoughts of ever regaining Arlington, the U.S. government announced its intention to auction the estate for unpaid taxes.[8]

Just two days after the president's return to Richmond, Lee learned that Meade was taking the offensive. He was crossing the river beyond Lee's right flank, and, by all appearances, making a dash for Fredericksburg or Spotsylvania. Lee put his army in motion to intercept the enemy columns and was surprised to find Meade moving not east but west, putting the two armies on a collision course. Two corps of the Army of the Potomac ended up on and behind Lee's left flank, where an accidental collision with a lone Confederate division triggered a sharp battle at Payne's farm. Lee fell back west a few miles and entrenched behind Mine Run, between Orange and the Wilderness. Meade followed him there. It seemed a major battle was imminent.

* * *

---

8 Anthony J. Gaughan, *The Last Battle of the Civil War: United States vs. Lee, 1861-1883* (Baton Rouge, LA, 2011), 27.

November 1, Sunday (near Brandy Station): Lee is visited by a South Carolina soldier and his wife, the latter having come from home by rail to hand-deliver a new uniform to her husband. She refused to return home without meeting Lee. Later, Fitz and his two brothers John and Henry call on Lee. Lee writes to Mary, again upset that Charlotte cannot move in with her. He describes the visit with the South Carolina couple as well as the visit from his nephews.[9]

November 2, Monday (near Brandy Station): Lee writes to Sam Jones that he cannot provide reinforcements and suggests Jones either move on Knoxville to divert enemy attention from Virginia or unite with Imboden for a raid into West Virginia. Lee directs Imboden to force the Federals out of Hampshire and Hardy counties, but cautions that he can spare nothing from the ANV to assist; he also orders Imboden to detail a small force under Capt. George W. Stump to interdict traffic on the B&O. Lee sends Stuart a list of deficiencies in the horse artillery found by Col. Chilton on a recent inspection. In response to a letter from Secretary Seddon regarding officers in the Georgia legislature, Lee opines that it would be better if the officers would resign which would allow their places to be filled; he fears that other states will follow Georgia's example which will lead to widespread departure of officers from their commands. Lee orders that a "Mr. Rodebaugh" pass through the lines at Warrenton if his papers are in order. Lee receives pay of $1,365 for the months of August-October.[10]

November 3, Tuesday (near Brandy Station): Lee instructs Sam Jones and Imboden to combine forces and attack an enemy force moving on Lewisburg, and requests the military telegraph office in Richmond to retrieve excess wire with the army.[11]

November 4, Wednesday (near Brandy Station): Lee writes to Adjutant General Cooper arguing against transferring any units from the ANV to Charleston: "I believe the troops of this army have been called upon in winter, spring, and summer to do almost as active service as those of any other department, and I do not see the good of the service will be promoted by scattering its brigades and regiments along all the threatened points of the Confederacy. It is only by the concentration of our troops that we can hope to win any decisive advantage." He also asks again for the 8th and 14th Virginia Cavalry regiments to be transferred from Sam Jones to Stuart in part because Stuart needs more mounted troops and Lee thinks Jones has far too much cavalry in his department. Lee forwards Col. Chilton's report on Hart's Battery to Stuart, which found it deficient in nearly every area. He also writes to Sec. Seddon regarding the treatment of deserters, explaining that courts martial rarely return a death sentence for those who return voluntarily. Lee notifies Gen. Cooper that the sentence of Pvt. Coleman Wells has been stayed temporarily pending the final decision from President Davis. He receives a package from Mary containing several letters for him as well as a new pair of flannel drawers.[12]

November 5, Thursday (near Brandy Station): Lee and Gov. John Letcher review Stuart's cavalry at Brandy Station, the first time in several days that Lee is able to mount a horse; during the review Lee is

---

9 REL to Mrs. REL, Nov. 1, 1863, REL papers, LOC. Unfortunately Lee did not identify the soldier or his wife, only that she was from Abbeville District. John Mason Lee and Henry Carter Lee were the younger brothers of Fitz Lee; Henry served on his brother's staff and John served on Rooney's staff. Krick, *Staff Officers in Gray*, 199.

10 *OR* 29, pt. 2, 814-6; *OR* 51, pt. 2, 782-3; REL to J. Q. A. Nadenbousch, Nov. 2, 1863, telegram book, REL HQ papers, VHS; REL CSR. Stump was captain of Co. B, 18th VA Cav., in John Imboden's command. He delivered a message from Imboden to Lee and took advantage of his audience to suggest that he be detached and allowed to remain on the B&O; Stump was captured and murdered while in enemy custody in early 1865. Roger U. Delauter, *18th Virginia Cavalry* (Lynchburg, VA, 1985), 93.

11 *OR* 20, pt. 2, 817; REL to W. S. Morris, Nov. 3, 1863, telegram book, REL HQ papers, VHS.

12 *OR* 29, pt. 2, 819-21; REL to Samuel Cooper, Nov. 4, 1863, telegram book, REL HQ papers, VHS; Dowdey, *Wartime Papers*, 618. Stuart wanted those two regiments in particular because they were the only ones in Jones's command not formed with the specific promise of serving in their home region.

presented a pair of gold spurs. In response to reports of an enemy movement on Fredericksburg, Lee orders that troops be sent from Hanover Junction to intercept them; later he informs Richmond that this was nothing more than the Federals driving away the work parties removing the rails from the RF&P.[13]

The general instructs John Imboden to leave a screening force in the Shenandoah Valley to report any enemy movements there, and to take the rest of his force to work with Sam Jones; Lee informs Jones of an enemy move against Lewisburg, and that Imboden will work with him to oppose the effort. Lee writes to Mary, mentioning the review and that it gave opportunity to see Rob and Fitz; he adds also that she should wait to make his winter clothing until she has a pattern in-hand so as not to waste material.[14]

November 6, Friday (near Brandy Station): Lee writes to Gov. Letcher requesting that food be sent to Fredericksburg and Culpeper for the families of soldiers, as authorized by the state legislature. The general also writes to John Barbour, president of the Orange & Alexandria Railroad, and asks about the current condition of the line. He also pens a note to to Edwin G. Lee regarding vacancies on the military courts. His son Rob visits with his father during the evening.[15]

November 7, Saturday (near Brandy Station/opposite Rappahannock Station): In the afternoon Lee and Jubal Early ride to the hill directly opposite Rappahannock Station in response to reports of a Federal force approaching Early's outposts across the river. Lee observes the skirmishing from alongside the guns of Dance's Battery while Early rides across the river to his troops guarding the north end of the pontoon bridge. When he returns, Early reports to Lee that a large enemy force is in his front, but little develops beyond an artillery duel and some skirmishing. As Lee, Early, and John Pegram observe the fighting, a Union battery fires on their party, killing the horse of one of Early's staffers. Lee returns to his headquarters when the firing dies out at sunset, thinking the action to be nothing more than a demonstration.[16]

When the general arrives back at headquarters, he learns from Gen. Ewell that the Federals have crossed at Kelly's Ford and captured several regiments guarding the crossing. While considering how to react to this unexpected move, word arrives from Gen. Early that the Federals launched a night attack north of the river at Rappahannock Station and captured his entire force—two veteran infantry brigades. In order to prevent Meade from crossing, Early burned the pontoon bridge. Around 8:00 p.m. Lee meets with Gens. Ewell, Early, Rodes, and Pendleton—and probably others—to determine the scope of Meade's offensive. While the generals meet, the headquarters staff packs up and prepares to move, which they do shortly before midnight; Walter Taylor notes: "We are now on the outposts and this

---

13 Dowdey, *Wartime Papers*, 618-9; REL to "Commanding Officer Hanover Junction," Nov. 5, 1863, telegram book, REL HQ papers, VHS; *OR* 29, pt. 2, 821. These spurs were from several Baltimore ladies and are now in the collection of the Museum of the Confederacy. Freeman, *Lee*, vol. 3, 189 n14. The review occurred on the same field at Inlet Station as the reviews in June.

14 REL to Imboden, Nov. 5, 1863, telegram book, REL HQ papers, VHS; REL to Jones, Nov. 5, 1863, telegram book, REL HQ papers, VHS; Dowdey, *Wartime Papers*, 618-9.

15 *OR* 29, pt. 2, 823-4; REL to E. G. Lee, Nov. 6, 1863, WNP papers, UNC; REL Jr. to Agnes, Nov. 17, 1863, Lee family papers, VHS.

16 Early, *Memoirs*, 309-14; *OR* 29, pt. 1, 619-22; P. W. Hairston diary, Nov. 7, 1863, UNC. Early's aide, Peter Hairston wrote of his close call: "I was in the act of handing them [field glasses] to him [Lee] when my horse was killed by a shell passing through him, having entered his right flank and coming out at his tail, cutting it off entirely. It passed through my saddle blanket and coat tail and did not injure me. I cannot be too thankful for my almost miraculous escape.... The shot was evidently aimed at the party and showed great accuracy in shooting." Hairston diary, Nov. 7, 1863, UNC. One account placed Ewell with the party as well, although he wrote in his report that he did not go the bridge, "knowing that both the general commanding [Lee] and Major General Early were [there]." Robert Hubbard, *Memoirs*, 84, Duke; *OR* 29, pt. 1, 618.

is not exactly the place for the General Commanding."[17]

Lee sends several messages to Richmond regarding both his own situation and that in western Virginia, noting several times that he can send no troops to southwest Virginia. Very cold night.[18]

November 8, Sunday (near Brandy Station/ Culpeper): Lee establishes headquarters just north of Culpeper and positions the army in an arc from Mount Pony to near Chesnut Fork Church. Lee rides the lines, expecting Meade to attack. During the night Lee moves south of the Rapidan, camping along the south bank of the river.[19]

November 9, Monday (Near the Rapidan): A correspondent from the Raleigh *Progress* meets with Lee and writes it up for his readers: "Gen. Lee is in blooming health and spoke hopefully of our cause and confidently of our final triumph in this bloody struggle for Southern independence. He remarked 'It is with us independence or nothing.'" Snow.[20]

November 10, Tuesday (Near Rapidan/Orange/ Middle Hill): Gen. Lee moves closer to Orange and establishes his headquarters at Middle Hill, off the Orange Turnpike east of town on a shoulder of Clark's Mountain. The general sends the details of the Rappahannock Station fight to President Davis and ends the report with the statement, "The army now occupies about the same position as before the recent advance." He also advises Sec. Seddon that he needs shoes for the men and fodder for the animals, and instructs Maj. Robert White to drive the enemy from Hardy County. His cook Bryan Lynch arrives from Richmond with letters and a winter robe for Lee; temperatures dip below freezing and Lee notes that all the water in his tent froze during the night.[21]

---

17 Freeman, *Lee*, vol. 3, 189-92; WHT to WNP, Nov. 7, 1863, WNP papers, UNC; WNP to wife, Nov. 11, 1863, WNP papers, UNC; Tower, *Lee's Adjutant*, 82, 87. Hays's and Hoke's brigades were the commands north of the river. The battlefield has been largely lost to residential development and the relocation of US 15/29. Taylor noted that before leaving they destroyed their recently constructed fireplaces and burned all the firewood, but not before he grabbed a nap by the fire. Tower, *Lee's Adjutant*, 87.

18 *OR* 29, pt. 1, 609; *OR* 29, pt. 2, 825; REL to Seddon, Nov. 7, 1863, telegram book, REL HQ papers, VHS; W. P. Cooper diary, Nov. 7, 1863, R. B. Cook papers, WVU. Lee sent a telegram to Sam Jones and, based on the phrasing of the message, it was just as he learned of Meade's movements. The telegram updated Jones on Imboden's movements. Lee added, almost as a stream of consciousness postscript, that the enemy was beginning "a demonstration" in his front. REL to Jones, Nov. 7, 1863, telegram book, REL HQ papers, VHS.

19 Freeman, *Lee*, vol. 3, 192; *OR* 29, pt. 1, 614; Tower, *Lee's Adjutant*, 82, 87. During his ride Lee encountered Gen. Harry Hays, whose brigade had been largely captured at Rappahannock Station. One of Early's staff officers recorded their exchange: "Gen. Lee rode up to him and said, 'General, this is a sad affair. How do you feel today?' 'I feel, sir, as well as a man can feel who has just lost so many men. But it is all over now and cannot be helped; the only thing is to try to get even with them today.'" P. W. Hairston diary, Nov. 12, 1863, UNC. Nothing is known regarding Lee's withdrawal to the river, the route he took, where he crossed, or where he camped. Taylor is the only known source and he did not provide any details. A description by a visiting newspaperman mentioned it being near "an old meeting house"—this is likely either Mt. Pisgah Meeting House or the old St. Thomas's Parish Glebe along the Old Rapidan Road. Clark Hall, conversation with author, Oct. 6, 2019; Miller, *Antebellum Orange*, 111.

20 Richmond *Examiner*, Nov. 11, 1863, REL newspaper references, DSF papers, LVA; Dowdey, *Wartime Papers*, 622. The journalist described his arrival at Lee's camp, "which consisted of a cluster of cloth tents pitched in a grove of oaks, surrounding an old meeting house. I found Gen. Lee sitting by a log fire at the mouth of his tent, with one of his aides, enjoying a social conversation over a late Yankee newspaper. Upon my approach, the old hero, without any formality, rose and gave me a cordial welcome." Richmond *Examiner*, Nov. 11, 1863, DSF papers, LVA.

21 Tower, *Lee's Adjutant*, 87; Hurst, *Soldiers, Stories, Sites and Fights*, 124-5; *OR* 29, pt. 1, 610-1; *OR* 29, pt. 2, 830; REL to Robert White, Nov. 10, 1863; telegram book, REL HQ papers, VHS; Dowdey, *Wartime Papers*, 622. Taylor bragged to his fiancé that he selected the new camp site, "more central to the army and more convenient to all parties . . . and I am pleased to see it gives general satisfaction." He also hoped it would be their permanent winter location. Tower, *Lee's Adjutant*, 87. Lee apparently refused an offer from Mrs. Taylor of Meadow Farm to use her house for his winter quarters, saying he preferred to have the same accommodations as his men. The exact site was about 100 yards north of the Orange Turnpike about a mile and a half east of town; Lee's tent eventually had a wooden floor and rock fireplace and chimney,

November 11, Wednesday (Middle Hill/Orange): Lee, Hill, and Pendleton ride along a portion of Hill's lines in the morning. Ewell's aide Sandie Pendleton comes to headquarters in the morning to request a furlough, but is told by Lee that no leaves are being granted at present as he expects an attack by Meade in the near future. Lee informs Seddon that he can send no troops to southwest Virginia or east Tennessee at present, and also tells Imboden he must use his own resources, including local reserves if necessary, to defeat the enemy in his front. Lee writes to Mary regarding his need for winter under garments and also his instructions to emancipate the remaining slaves at White House and Romancoke: "They can then hire themselves out and support themselves. Their families . . . can remain at their present homes. I do not know what to do better for them."[22]

November 12, Thursday (Middle Hill): Lee informs President Davis that a move by Meade's army is imminent and that without forage for the horses, he will be hard-pressed to meet it; he adds also that scouts report a pending raid on Richmond so he recommends that the enemy POWs be removed from the city at least temporarily. He complains to the secretary of war about the condition of the Virginia Central Railroad and requests that something be done either by railroad officials or by the War Department to maintain the line as it is now Lee's main supply line. He informs the wounded Gen. Robert Hoke of the disaster that befell his brigade at Rappahannock Station and requests him to ask Gov. Vance for additional troops to bring the unit back up to strength. He also informs Gov. Letcher that he ordered several individuals found harboring deserters to be turned over to authorities at Gordonsville—what should be done with them now? He thanks the Richmond city council for its offer of a house for his use in the capital, but declines: "The house is not necessary for the use of my family, and our duties will prevent my residence in Richmond." Rooney leaves Fort Monroe for Fort Lafayette.[23]

November 13, Friday (Middle Hill): Lee writes to Agnes mentioning that his health is greatly improved and he has "been riding a great deal lately" but has no idea when he will be able to visit Richmond and it is not safe for her to come to the army right now. He writes also to Col. John Washington's daughter Louisa, in response to a letter received from her yesterday; he is very sorry to learn of her cousin's capture and he will write to Judge Robert Ould regarding his possible release for health reasons but cautions that prisoner exchanges have been discontinued for the present.[24]

November 14, Saturday (Middle Hill): Maj. Taylor's tent catches fire while Lee and the staff are eating breakfast, but it is quickly extinguished.[25]

November 15, Sunday (Middle Hill/Raccoon Ford/Morton's Ford): Lee, accompanied by all the staff except Taylor who is left behind to manage headquarters, go to the lower fords in the morning in

---

which were still visible in the 1920s, which allowed later owners of the property to erect a small marker on the exact spot that is today privately owned. Hurst, *Soldiers, Stories, Sites and Fights*, 124-5.

22 Koontz diary, Nov. 11, 1863, VA Tech; Sandie Pendleton to Rose, Nov. 11, 1863, WNP papers, UNC; *OR* 29, pt. 2, 831; REL to Imboden, Nov. 11, 1863, telegram book, REL HQ papers, VHS; Dowdey, *Wartime Papers*, 621-2.

23 *OR* 29, pt. 2, 832-3; REL to Letcher, Nov. 12, 1863, telegram book, REL HQ papers, VHS; Freeman, *Lee*, vol. 3, 210 n12; Yates, *Perfect Gentleman*, vol. 1, 286. Hoke had not returned to duty from his Chancellorsville wound. Gen. Harry Hays spoke with an unidentified member of Lee's staff on this date, who informed Hays that Rappahannock Station "had been discussed at Gen. Lee's headquarters and Gen. Lee said no blame has to be attached to the officers or men who were in the fight and rather intimated that whatever blame there is must attach to [Lee] himself." Hairston diary, Nov. 12, 1863, UNC.

24 Dowdey, *Wartime Papers*, 623-4; REL to Louisa Washington, Nov. 13, 1863, L. F. Washington papers, W&L.

25 Tower, *Lee's Adjutant*, 85. "Whilst we were at breakfast this morning my tent took fire and my wardrobe and me were in great danger, but fortunately the boys extinguished it and save a yard or so of canvas destroyed, no harm was done." Ibid.

response to fighting there, where they are joined by Early, Johnson, and Rodes. Rooney enters Fort Lafayette. Heavy rain in the morning.[26]

November 16, Monday (Middle Hill/Rapidan River): Lee rides along the lines on Ewell's front. Rain continues.[27]

November 17, Tuesday (Middle Hill): Lee forwards to Richmond Mosby's report of his recent operations, and notes that despite Jeb Stuart's request for Mosby's promotion to lieutenant colonel, the strength of Mosby's command does not warrant such a promotion. Lee dispatches Fitz Lee to the Valley with a brigade of cavalry, and instructs Imboden to work with Fitz in turning back a reported enemy advance up the Valley. Custis arrives at Lee's headquarters bearing messages from President Davis.[28]

November 18, Wednesday (Middle Hill/Clark's Mountain): Lee and Early, accompanied by Maj. Taylor and several of Early's aides, go to the signal station atop Clark's Mountain to observe enemy movements. Lee writes to the young daughter of Maj. Andrew L. Pitzer of Early's staff thanking her for several pairs of socks she sent him. Lee requests that President Davis come to Orange to confer and visit the army.[29]

November 19, Thursday (Middle Hill/Mine Run/Bartlett Mill/Zoar Church): Lee and Jubal Early, accompanied by Custis, Col. Chilton, Maj. Marshall, and one of Early's aides, make an extended reconnaissance to the east, primarily on the Raccoon Ford Road and along Mine Run. They pause at Zoar Church, where Lee and Early have a lengthy private discussion. Lee writes to Sec. Seddon regarding impressment to provision the army.[30]

November 20, Friday (Middle Hill): Lee submits his report of Rappahannock Station and Kelly's Ford to the War Department. Lee receives word from Stuart of two privates who captured a number of prisoners very close to Meade's headquarters and passes along his satisfaction and congratulations on their exploit. Jed Hotchkiss calls at headquarters for a map of Albemarle County but finds Lee using it.[31]

November 21, Saturday (Middle Hill/Orange/Bloomsbury): President Davis arrives in Orange on the afternoon train and is greeted at the station by Lee; the two are met with rousing cheers from the troops and civilians present. Davis and his aides, Col. William Browne and Custis, join Lee and his staff for dinner at headquarters, after which Lee escorts Davis to neighboring Bloomsbury plantation where the President stays during his visit to the army.[32]

---

26 Tower, *Lee's Adjutant*, 87-8; McDonald, *Make Me a Map*, 183; Rooney CSR; Hairston diary, Nov. 15, 1863, UNC. Hotchkiss wrote that "there were ten generals present" at Raccoon and Morton's fords, but did not specify any names beyond Lee and Early, the latter being in temporary command of the corps because Ewell was ill. That area was Ed Johnson's sector, so he certainly would have been present, and probably Robert Rodes as well.

27 Alexander S. Patton diary, Nov. 16, 1863, W&L; Krick, *CW Weather*, 111.

28 OR 29, pt. 1, 80-1; REL to Imboden, Nov. 17, 1863, telegram book, REL HQ papers, VHS; Yates, *Perfect Gentleman*, vol. 1, 286.

29 Hairston diary, Nov. 18, 1863, UNC; Yates, *Perfect Gentleman*, vol. 1, 287.

30 Hairston diary, Nov. 19, 1863, UNC; OR 29, pt. 2, 837-8. Early was not with Lee's party originally, and his aide's account makes it sound as though Lee and Early embarked on separate scouting missions that happened to encounter each other; he did not specify where they met up. Early was still in temporary command of the corps; Ewell did not return until Dec. 4. Pfanz, *Ewell*, 348.

31 OR 29, pt. 1, 498, 611-6; McDonald, *Make Me a Map*, 184.

32 Richmond *Daily Dispatch*, Nov. 26, 1863; Couture, *Charlie's Letters*, 203; REL to Elizabeth Stiles, Nov. 25, 1863, Lee papers, SH; Tower, *Lee's Adjutant*, 90-1; Miller, *Antebellum Orange*, 155. An officer in the 41st VA witnessed the president's arrival: "At the court house when Davis made his appearance, Huzza, Huzza was heard from the bystanders. . . . It was not known at that time that Gen. Lee was present. And when that Noble Old Hero's head was seen riding above those of the crowd, as he mounted his war steed, a shouting went up from the crowd that caused the earth almost to tremble beneath

Lee forwards A. P. Hill's report of Bristoe Station to Richmond, noting: "General Hill explains how, in his haste to attack the Third Corps of the enemy, he overlooked the presence of the Second, which was the cause of the disaster that ensued." Lee notifies Early there will be a review of the corps by Davis when weather permits. Lee writes to cousin Caroline Stuart with family news, thanking her for clothing she sent him, adding that Gen. Edward Johnson would like very much to see her. Lee writes to his wife thanking her for the requested garments she sent, glad that Custis is with him temporarily, and happy Rooney is away from Maj. Gen. Benjamin Butler at Fort Monroe. He notes that Davis is visiting the army. The U.S. government announces its intention to auction Arlington in January for unpaid taxes. "Pelting rain" in the afternoon.[33]

November 22, Sunday (Middle Hill/Orange/Bloomsbury): Lee meets President Davis at Bloomsbury in the morning and brings him to army headquarters for breakfast. Afterward they attend church service at St. Thomas's, the sermon delivered by Gen. Pendleton. Davis and Lee spend the afternoon in consultation at Lee's headquarters. After dinner Lee escorts President Davis back to Bloomsbury.[34]

November 23, Monday (Middle Hill/Clark's Mountain/ Bloomsbury): Lee has breakfast with the president after meeting him at Bloomsbury. Once they finish eating, they ride the lines accompanied by Pendleton, and ascend Clark's Mountain to observe Meade's army in the afternoon. In the evening they return to Lee's headquarters for dinner and afterwards are serenaded by the 11th Mississippi's band. Lee again escorts the President to Bloomsbury after dinner.[35] Lee writes to Commissary General Northrop regarding the use of impressment to keep the army fed, and he sends Adjutant General Cooper and Sam Jones the latest intelligence regarding enemy movements around Knoxville and hopes that Jones can work with Longstreet to remove Burnside from east Tennessee. Rain in the morning.[36]

---

our feet." Couture, *Charlie's Letters*, 203. Bloomsbury is one of the oldest and most architecturally unique structures in Orange County. It was built by Col. James Taylor, one of Gov. Alexander Spotswood's "Knights of the Golden Horseshoe," in the early 1720s. When the war began, it was owned by Francis Jerdone. The house sits immediately north of the Orange County airport on the trace of the old Orange Turnpike, and is privately owned. Miller, *Antebellum Orange*, 113-5. A portion of the 39th VA Cav. Battalion was assigned to guard the residence during the president's stay. Hurst, *Soldiers, Stories, Sites and Fights*, 96. Col. Browne and Custis shared a tent with Taylor. Tower, *Lee's Adjutant*, 91. Lee wrote to Francis Jerdone in advance of the president's visit to ask if Davis could stay at Bloomsbury; if it still exists, the letter (the exact date of which is not known, but was probably the 19th or 20th) is thought to be in the possession of the Jerdone family. Bethany Sullivan, James Madison Museum (Orange, VA) Director, email to author, Oct. 8, 2019.

33 *OR* 29, pt. 1, 426-8; Hairston diary, Nov. 21, 1863, UNC; REL to Caroline Stuart, Nov. 21, 1863, REL papers, VHS; Dowdey, *Wartime Papers*, 624-5; Gaughan, *Last Battle of the CW*, 27; Tower, *Lee's Adjutant*, 90. Ed "Allegheny" Johnson met the Stuart girls at one of the reviews of the army in September and was apparently quite taken with the much younger Carrie, who was not at all interested in return—something Lee teased her about on several occasions. Gregg S. Clemmer, *Old Allegheny: The Life and Wars of General Ed Johnson* (Staunton, VA, 2004), 521. Ben Butler was perhaps the most hated man in the entire South and had his headquarters in late 1863 at Fort Monroe; Agnes wrote a friend about her disgust at Butler being involved with her brother's capture, and took offense at Butler adding a needless notation to communications regarding Rooney: "My brother Fitzhugh [ie Rooney] has been sent to Fort Lafayette. Just to think of Butler's adding an autograph postscript to his letter. . . . I think it a disgrace that his handwriting should enter it." Agnes to Fanny R. Johnston, Nov. 26, 1863, Lee family papers, LVA.

34 Hurst, *Soldiers, Stories, Sites and Fights*, 96; Lee, *Memoirs of WNP*, 306; Richmond *Daily Dispatch*, Nov. 26, 1863; WNP to wife, Nov. 23, 1863, WNP papers, UNC; Hairston diary, Nov. 22, 1863; UNC. Lee told Early that Davis would review the corps on Monday, but morning rain prevented it. Hairston diary, Nov. 22, 1863, UNC; Tower, *Lee's Adjutant*, 91.

35 Hurst, *Soldiers, Stories, Sites and Fights*, 96; WNP to wife, Nov. 23, 1863, WNP papers, UNC; Richmond *Daily Dispatch*, Nov. 27, 1863.

36 *OR* 29, pt. 2, 844; REL to Cooper, Nov. 23, 1863, telegram book, REL HQ papers, VHS; REL to Sam Jones, Nov. 23, 1863 (2 messages), telegram book, REL HQ papers, VHS; Tower, *Lee's Adjutant*, 91. The morning rain prevented the scheduled review of Early's [Ewell's] Second Corps, which was rescheduled for Tuesday with A. P. Hill's Third Corps scheduled for Wednesday. Tower, *Lee's Adjutant*, 91.

November 24, Tuesday (Middle Hill/ Bloomsbury/Orange): Lee retrieves President Davis from Bloomsbury and later accompanies him to the train station in Orange, the weather having cut short his attempts to visit and review the troops. Custis returns to Richmond with President Davis and Col. Browne. Lee informs Gen. Cooper that Sam Jones has been directly ordered to send his cavalry to help Longstreet at Knoxville. Rain again cancels the review of the Second Corps.[37]

November 25, Wednesday (Middle Hill): Lee informs President Davis that Meade appears to be preparing to move and he would like Pickett's Division sent to Hanover Junction. He also tells Davis that despite the commissary's promise to increase the fodder for the army's animals, no corn at all was received two of the past four days. Lee issues GO102, to boost the army's morale in the face of a pending attack.[38]

Lee chides Imboden for the incorrect information his scouts are turning in: "Proper dispositions cannot be made to repel these attacks unless the number of the enemy be correctly stated." In the event Meade advances, Lee wants Imboden to operate against the railroad in the Federal rear. He forwards to Richmond two reports from Imboden concerning his own operations and those of Capt. John McNeil's rangers, and writes to Elizabeth Stiles, thanking her for the peach leather that arrived yesterday and also passing along family news and information about the president's visit. He writes also to Mary about Davis's stay and grateful for all the kindness exhibited toward him by the population.[39]

November 26, Thursday (Middle Hill): Lee learns that the Army of the Potomac is moving east toward Germanna Ford and the Wilderness, and so issues orders for the ANV to move east to meet them; he advises Richmond of his intent to meet Meade and requests all troops that can be spared from Richmond, including Custis. Lee advises Imboden of Meade's movements and instructs him to be ready to move.[40] Lee instructs Bradley Johnson to have his forces at Hanover Junction ready to meet the enemy, as Lee does not yet know where Meade is going. Lee writes to R. H. Graves concerning recovering the body of a Capt. H. A. Gordon from Gettysburg, and sends a short note to Mildred, to be delivered by Gen. Hoke, hoping to see her soon. Taylor and the other staff are kept busy well into the night packing up headquarters.[41]

November 27, Friday (Middle Hill/Verdiersville/Mine Run): Lee and staff depart Middle Hill around 3:00 a.m. in bitter cold temperatures, arriving at Verdiersville where Lee meets with Stuart and Early. He establishes headquarters at Catlett Rhodes's house on the Plank Road, reaching there before sunrise in advance of the main body of the army. Lee sends word to Richmond that Meade is crossing at Germanna and Ely's fords and moving toward

---

37 Hurst, *Soldiers, Stories, Sites and Fights*, 96; Tower, *Lee's Adjutant*, 91; REL to Elizabeth Stiles, Nov. 25, 1863, REL papers, SH; *OR* 31, pt. 3, 748.

38 *OR* 29, pt. 2, 846; REL to Davis, Nov. 25, 1863, telegram book, REL HQ papers, VHS; Richmond *Daily Dispatch*, Dec. 5, 1863. The review of A. P. Hill's Third Corps scheduled for today was called off because Davis was no longer with the army. Tower, *Lee's Adjutant*, 91.

39 *OR* 29, pt. 2, 846-7; *OR* 29, pt. 1, 550, 644; REL to Elizabeth Stiles, Nov. 25, 1863, REL papers, SH; Fitz Lee, *General Lee*, 320.

40 *OR* 29, pt. 1, 823-4; *OR* 29, pt. 2, 847; REL to Imboden, Nov. 26, 1863, telegram book, REL HQ papers, VHS. Lee's request for Custis may have been in part because of the absence of Charles Venable, who was offered a position with the Bureau of Conscription and was in Richmond exploring that position; it is not known when Venable returned to the army, but it does not seem plausible that he would have remained in the capital during an active campaign, or that Lee would have allowed him that option. Tower, *Lee's Adjutant*, 91. Davis responded that Custis would be sent to Orange on the 27th; however, Custis's travel payment request states that he left for the Orange on the 26th and remained with the army until Dec. 7. *OR* 51, pt. 2, 787; Custis CSR.

41 REL to Johnson, Nov. 26, 1863, telegram book, REL HQ papers, VHS; REL to R. H. Graves, Nov. 26, 1863, REL papers, UNC; REL to Mildred, Nov. 26, 1863, REL papers, LOC; Tower, *Lee's Adjutant*, 92-3.

Chancellorsville and Lee is concentrating the army to attack them.[42]

Lee is conferring with A. P. Hill at the Rhodes house early in the afternoon when a report arrives from Jeb Stuart that Meade's army is headed not east toward Chancellorsville and Fredericksburg, but rather west toward Orange. Lee rides forward with Heth's Division on the Plank Road to the vicinity of New Hope Church; despite early success, Lee denies Heth's request to press his attack further until he better understands the overall situation, which remains in flux. Lee waits while some of Early's troops (Ed Johnson's Division) engage the enemy on the Raccoon Ford Road at Payne's Farm. Once he determines that the entire Army of the Potomac has been identified, Lee orders his own army to withdraw west behind Mine Run. Rain during the night.[43]

November 28, Saturday (Verdiersville/Mine Run): Lee meets with Early (and presumably Hill) in the morning at HQ and determines to dig in behind Mine Run and await Meade's attack. He informs Richmond that Meade is moving toward Orange rather than Spotsylvania as previously thought. Lee rides the length of the line, making adjustments in the positions of the troops and urging them to entrench quickly. Rain continues.[44]

November 29, Sunday (Verdiersville/Mine Run): In the morning Lee sends an update to Richmond, that the rain yesterday prevented major movements by either army, but Meade's full army is in his front along Mine Run. Lee and Hill, accompanied by their staffs, are riding along the lines in the morning when they encounter a church service in progress; Lee immediately pauses and stays for the remainder of the service, then they continue their ride. During the

---

42 Tower, *Lee's Adjutant*, 93-4; McDonald, *Make Me a Map*, 185; Early, *Memoirs*, 319-20;Hurst, *Soldiers, Stories, Sites and Fights*, 113; Long, *Memoirs of REL*, 313-4; *OR* 51, pt. 2, 788. Taylor wrote that it was so cold that everyone had icicles in their mustaches and beards. Lee, he added, outpaced the infantry on the march: "As usual the General was ahead of everyone else and we arrived at Verdiersville without any army whatever." Tower, *Lee's Adjutant*, 94. Stuart had a close call at Rhodes's house the year before where he was literally caught napping on the porch by enemy cavalry who captured his plumed hat, among other things. Frank S. Walker, *Remembering: A History of Orange County, Virginia* (Orange, VA, 2004); 152-3, 170-1. The small house stood at the intersection of Mine Run Road and Strawberry Hill Road, just east of modern-day Rhoadesville. Hurst, *Soldiers, Stories, Sites and Fights*, 40. Stuart's aide William Blackford noted that Lee was quartered in the house, and that his room "contained little else . . . than the General's camp bed, a small camp writing table, and some camp stools." Blackford, *War Years with Stuart*, 245. Some sources confuse the community of Verdiersville with the two dwellings that lent their names to the village—Old Verdiersville and the newer Verdiersville— and further conflate the Stuart incident at the Rhodes house with Old Verdiersville. See Miller, *Antebellum Orange*, 147-8 for the histories of these two homes and Hurst, *Soldiers, Stories, Sites and Fights*, 40-1, 113 for the Rhodes house.

43 Freeman, *Lee*, vol. 3, 197-8; *OR* 29, pt. 1, 897; Krick, *CW Weather*, 111. The fight at Payne's Farm ended up being the largest of the campaign and was also exceptionally important, even if mostly overlooked and misunderstood by previous writers. William Henry French's Union III Corps and John Sedgwick's VI Corps crossed Jacob's Ford on the Rapidan and after several delays moved down the Widow Morris Road, accidently striking the tail of Johnson's infantry division marching along the Raccoon Ford Road toward Locust Grove. Johnson, who did not know the terrain or who or what he faced, ordered an overly complex double-envelopment that mostly froze French in place. The Rebel attacks were poorly delivered and, if they had been launched against nearly almost any other commander, could have cost Johnson much of his widely separated division. The heavy fighting lasted from 4:00 p.m. to dark, or roughly two hours, and ended in a bloody stalemate with nearly 1,000 Union losses and 550 Confederates. The accidental encounter revealed that two enemy corps were on and essentially behind Lee's exposed left flank with the balance of the Potomac army to his immediate front. If Johnson had been allowed to pass unmolested, or if French (leading the advance) had been just half an hour slower, Lee may not have been able to withdraw behind Mine Run and the entire campaign would have unfolded much differently. For a full discussion of this fascinating battle, including outstanding maps, see Bradley M. Gottfried, *The Maps of the Bristoe Station and Mine Run Campaigns: An Atlas of the Battles and Movements in the Eastern Theater after Gettysburg, Including Rappahannock Station, Kelly's Ford, and Morton's Ford, July 1863–February 1864* (El Dorado Hills, CA, 2013), 126-151. Publisher Theodore P. Savas, together with Richmond native Paul Sacra, rediscovered the battlefield (which had been improperly located in previous works) in the early 1990s. Their work lead to its eventual preservation.

44 Early, *Memoirs*, 322; *OR* 29, pt. 1, 824; Tower, *Lee's Adjutant*, 94; Taylor, *General Lee*, 226; Krick, *CW Weather*, 111. Early mentioned only himself being present for a morning briefing with Lee, but it seems logical that Lee met with both corps commanders and possibly Jeb Stuart as well, if not all together then at the least individually.

day, Richard Ewell reports to Lee expecting to resume command of his corps, but Lee demurs telling him he should not have rushed back so soon, and leaves Early in command of the corps. Lee sends a very long letter to President Davis regarding how to keep the armies in the field and up to strength, recommending cutting exemptions from service to the bare minimum, combining woefully under strength units, creating an invalid corps, and removing unfit officers from the rolls to allow for the promotion of others.[45]

November 30, Monday (Verdiersville/Mine Run): Lee notifies Richmond that the armies continue to face off along Mine Run, and that Meade has not yet attacked; Lee adds that he does not wish to endanger Richmond by pulling additional troops from there. Lee and Stuart make a reconnaissance on the army's right in response to a report by Wade Hampton that Meade's flank can be turned. During the night Lee meets with Hill, Early, and Stuart to discuss attacking the exposed Union flank; when Hill and Early balk at the idea, Lee agrees to remain on the defensive.[46]

---

[45] OR 29, pt. 1, 824; Tower, *Lee's Adjutant*, 94; Taylor, *General Lee*, 226-7; Long, *Memoirs of REL*, 316; Pfanz, *Ewell*, 347; OR 29, pt. 2, 853-4. Although Lee did not allow him to resume command, Ewell went to corps HQ anyway; his influence over Early in an awkward situation, however, seems to have been minimal. Pfanz, *Ewell*, 347.

[46] OR 29, pt. 1, 824; OR 51, pt. 2, 790; McClellan, *Campaigns of Stuart's Cavalry*, 398. Stuart aide Henry McClellan is the only source for the flank reconnaissance and the resulting council of war. He claimed that Ewell was in attendance rather than Early, but he was likely mistaken given the passage of time between the event and when he put it down on paper, and likely simply forgot that Early commanded the Second Corps at that time.

December 1863

The major battle that took shape along Mine Run never came to be. When it looked as though Lee's right flank could be turned George Meade ordered a general attack, but a closer reconnaissance discovered the flank was in fact entrenched, and the assault was called off at the last minute. Meade withdrew before Lee could launch an attack of his own, ending the campaign and the fighting for that year. Instead of a possibly decisive battle, Mine Run proved a great fizzle. The armies returned to their camps.

No sooner had Lee and the army returned to Orange than rumors began to fly that Lee was to succeed Braxton Bragg at the head of the Army of Tennessee. Such things had been said before, but this time there was merit behind them and Lee himself believed them to be true—despite his recommendation that Gen. P. G. T. Beauregard be given the command. When Lee was called to Richmond on the 9th to meet with President Davis, the army commander told Jeb Stuart that he expected to be assigned to the Army of Tennessee in Georgia.[1]

During what must have been intense discussions with the president, Lee convinced Davis to retain him in Virginia and the Army of Tennessee was given not to Beauregard but to Joseph Johnston. With the matter of the Western command settled, at least for the time being, Lee remained in Richmond inspecting the city's defenses and conferring on other matters. Rather than stay in the capital and spend Christmas with his family, however, he returned to Orange several days before the holiday. In all likelihood he later likely wished he had stayed, for Charlotte died on December 26 and he was unable to return for her funeral.[2]

Heavy rains closed out the month as Lee settled in for the winter at Orange.

* * *

---

1   *OR* 29, pt. 2, 858-9, 866. It was widely believed in the Army of Northern Virginia and in Richmond that Lee would be sent to north Georgia to take command, the state of Tennessee by this time having completely fallen to Union forces, and that Gen. P. G. T. Beauregard would be transferred from Charleston, SC, to replace Lee as the head of the Virginia army. Charleston *Mercury*, Dec. 15, 1863.

2   Jones, *Life and Letters of REL*, 296; Dowdey, *Wartime Papers*, 645.

December 1, Tuesday (Verdiersville/Mine Run): Before dawn Capt. W. W. Blackford of Jeb Stuart's staff meets with Lee in the Rhodes house and, as Lee dresses, explains the intelligence gathered by a scout during the night that Gen. Meade intends to launch an attack against Lee's right flank. Lee waits for Meade to launch the attack, and, when it does not come off, decides to take the offensive himself and reconnoiters the ground on his right flank with A. P. Hill and Jeb Stuart. Lee pulls two of Hill's divisions out of line to launch an assault on Meade's flank in the morning. Lee advises Richmond that Meade did not attack him today, but he does not reveal his own intention to do just that himself.[3]

December 2, Wednesday (Verdiersville/Mine Run/Parker's Store/Middle Hill): Lee learns at about dawn that Gen. Meade's army had retreated during the night; he orders an immediate pursuit. The general personally follows the enemy as far as Parker's Store before ordering his army back to its previous camps. Lee returns to his former headquarters location at Middle Hill. Upon his return to Orange, Lee notifies the Richmond authorities that the Army of the Potomac has retreated back across the Rapidan River without a fight, and he submits a preliminary report of the first portion of the Mine Run operations to the adjutant general.[4]

December 3, Thursday (Middle Hill): Lee sends the continuation of his preliminary report of Mine Run to Gen. Cooper. Lee writes to Davis regarding the state of affairs in Tennessee and suggests Gen. Beauregard replace Gen. Bragg in command of the Army of Tennessee, then in northern Georgia.[5]

December 4, Friday (Middle Hill): Lee advises Richmond that Pickett's troops can return to the capital from Hanover Junction when needed, and he orders Ewell to resume command of his corps. Lee writes Mary telling her of the recent movements and noting of his health, "I am much better, though stiff and painful. I fear I will never be better and must be content." The "Freedmen's Village" for former slaves is dedicated by the Federal government at Arlington.[6]

December 5, Saturday (Middle Hill): Lee receives a telegram from Jefferson Davis asking if he would take command of the Army of Tennessee. Lee writes to Mary chiding her for her habit of having her letters to him hand-delivered by private individuals rather than sending through the War Department, which would have them delivered the next day.[7]

December 6, Sunday (Middle Hill/Orange): Lee attends church service at St. Thomas with Gens. A. P. Hill, Jeb Stuart, and Fitz Lee. Gen. Lee notifies the

---

3 Blackford, *War Years with Stuart*, 245-6; Tower, *Lee's Adjutant*, 95; McClellan, *Campaigns of Stuart's Cavalry*, 398-9; Mills, *16th North Carolina*, 44; OR 29, pt. 1, 824. Taylor wrote that he was "constantly awakened this night by couriers who were bringing information of the enemy's movements." Tower, *Lee's Adjutant*, 95.

4 Tower, *Lee's Adjutant*, 95; OR 29, pt. 2, 858; OR 29, pt. 1, 825-6. An officer in McGowan's Brigade observed that Lee "looked very much annoyed" at Meade's escape. Caldwell, *Brigade of South Carolinians*, 120. Lee supposedly complained, "I am too old to command this army. We should never have permitted those people to get away." Freeman, *Lee*, vol. 3, 202.

5 OR 29, pt. 1, 826-7; OR 29, pt. 2, 858-9.

6 OR 29, pt. 2, 859; McDonald, *Make Me a Map*, 187; Dowdey, *Wartime Papers*, 631-2; Gaughan, *Last Battle of the CW*, 30. Gen. Ewell formally resumed command of Second Corps the 5th. Pfanz, *Ewell*, 348.

7 OR 31, pt. 3, 785; REL to Mrs. REL, Dec. 5, 1863, Lee family papers, VHS. From the wording of Davis's telegram, he and Lee obviously discussed Lee going west during the president's visit to the army several weeks earlier. Taylor was privy to the idea, either learning it that day from Lee or possibly earlier when Davis was with the army; he was not in favor of the idea of leaving of Virginia and, like Lee, also thought Beauregard would be a much better choice to command the Army of Tennessee, as he "could render much more service in opposing Grant than in witnessing artillery duels in Charleston Harbor." (Grant had not yet been promoted to lieutenant general and put in command of all Union armies. He would not come east until March of 1864.) Taylor, *Lee's Adjutant*, 95-6. Lee wrote that Custis would return to Richmond on this date, but Custis's own travel vouchers state that he did not return to Richmond until the 7th, so it is likely he stayed the extra days discussing with his father the western command and probably delivered Lee's reply to the president. Dowdey, *Wartime Papers*, 631; Custis CSR, NA.

War Department in Richmond that Meade's Army of the Potomac is crossing the Rapidan River at Morton's Ford and that he needs Rodes's Division returned to him immediately.[8]

December 7, Monday (Middle Hill): Lee informs President Davis by telegraph that he will go west to northern Georgia if ordered, and explains in far more detail in a letter that he does not think he will be of any use out west because he doesn't know any of the commanders in the Army of Tennessee, and that he doesn't know who would replace him in Virginia if he goes. Lee informs the commissary general that he will not use impressment as requested but if something is not done to keep the army fed, it will lead to disaster. He proclaims December 10 to be a day of fasting and prayer.[9]

December 8, Tuesday (Middle Hill): Lee informs John Imboden that he has received a request from several prominent citizens of the lower Shenandoah Valley requesting that the 7th Virginia Cavalry be sent there; he explains that he cannot part with that unit at present and wants to know what Imboden can do to address their concerns. He writes also to Sgt. Maj. Cary Robinson of the 6th Virginia concerning a furlough.[10]

December 9, Wednesday (Middle Hill/Orange/Richmond): Lee receives a summons to Richmond from President Davis in the morning, which he believes to be a sign that he will be reassigned to command of the Army of Tennessee. Before departing, he instructs Jeb Stuart to find good grazing ground for his cavalry mounts that is not too far removed from the front; he tells his cavalry chief: "My heart and thoughts will always be with this army." Upon arriving in Richmond that evening, the general goes to see his wife Mary at her rented house on Leigh St.[11]

December 10, Thursday (Richmond): Lee meets with President Davis and during the afternoon instructs Gen. Ewell by telegraph to send a brigade of cavalry to Luray in the Shenandoah Valley.[12]

December 11, Friday (Richmond): General Lee continues to meet with President Davis. Walter Taylor relays a number of messages between Gens. Lee and Ewell.[13]

December 12, Saturday (Richmond): Lee continues to meet with the president, and writes to Union General in Chief Henry Halleck to decline a proposed prisoner exchange because it does not conform to the agreed-upon POW cartel. The general sends this letter to Walter Taylor to be forwarded through the lines to Gen. Meade and explains that he is being detained much longer than expected in the capital. Lee also advises Taylor to have Jeb Stuart remain extra vigilant in light of reports that the Union XI Corps and XII Corps are

---

8 Richmond *Daily Dispatch*, Dec. 11, 1863; Freeman, *Lee's Dispatches*, 129-30.

9 Freeman, *Lee's Dispatches*, 130; *OR* 29, pt. 2, 861-2; *OR* 51, pt. 2, 793. Lee's detailed response to Davis specifically stated that he did not think Richard Ewell, who was next in rank with James Longstreet still absent from the army, was up to army command. *OR* 29, pt. 2, 861. Whenever Lee was away and Ewell assumed command, observed Freeman, "the work at headquarters was arranged to trouble him little. Usually, decisions not of the first magnitude were made by the staff and were reported to the acting commander." Freeman, *Lee's Lieutenants*, vol. 3, 330. Custis likely returned to Richmond on this date and probably carried Lee's response to Davis. Travel voucher, Dec. 7, 1863, Custis CSR, NA.

10 *OR* 29, pt. 2, 865; REL to Cary Robinson, Dec. 8, 1863, Robinson family papers, VHS. The 7th was specifically requested because it was from that region. Robinson's family somehow knew Lee from before the war; he was killed at Burgess Mill in October 1864. Michael A. Cavanaugh, *6th Virginia Infantry* (Lynchburg, VA, 1988), 121.

11 *OR* 29, pt. 2, 866; McDonald, *Make Me a Map*, 187; Freeman, *Lee*, vol. 3, 207-8. There are conflicting reports as to the location of Mrs. Lee's temporary residence; Rob wrote that it was on Clay Street, Agnes put it at 3rd and Leigh, and several family friends identified the house as being at 210 E Leigh St. Freeman, *Lee*, vol. 3, 208 n5.

12 Charleston *Mercury*, Dec. 17, 1863; *OR* 51, pt. 2, 793.

13 Charleston *Mercury*, Dec. 17, 1863; *OR* 51, pt. 2, 794. Ewell remained at his own headquarters and did not relocate to Lee's although he was in command of the army. Dowdey, *Wartime Papers*, 643.

back in Virginia. Lee also grants Charles Venable's request for leave.[14]

December 13, Sunday (Richmond): Lee attends church service at St. Paul's. He instructs Taylor to send several additional brigades to the Valley in response to reports from Imboden of an enemy move up the Valley.[15]

December 14, Monday (Richmond): The House of Representatives passes a measure inviting Lee to attend a House session. Taylor notifies Lee that the Federals advanced to Strasburg to distract Imboden while another column under William Averell is moving on Staunton from the southwest; Stuart is aware and will react accordingly.[16]

Lee writes to Lucy Minnedgerode and Lou Haxall concerning a furlough for Sgt. Maj. Cary Robinson, and he thanks cousin Nat Burwell for the apples and animal skin he sent. The Charleston *Mercury* reports that there is no further talk of Lee going to the Western Theater.[17]

December 15, Tuesday (Richmond): Lee and President Davis inspect the Richmond defenses. While Lee is out on the lines, House Speaker Thomas Bocock calls at Lee's residence to personally invite him to the House floor. Lee orders Jubal Early to take command in the Valley.[18]

December 16, Wednesday (Richmond): Lee receives the House invitation, and thanks them for the honor but declines. He meets with officials of the Virginia Central Railroad regarding the condition of the railroad and the army's supply needs.[19] Lee receives and forwards Thomas Rosser's report of a skirmish at Ely's Ford, noting that Rosser "has well performed his duty" since his promotion to brigade command. Taylor informs Lee of the situation in the Shenandoah Valley and that Jubal Early arrived in Staunton this morning to take command and Fitz Lee is moving to join Imboden. Walter Taylor also forwards a request for leniency regarding the execution of a private from Johnston's Battery.[20]

December 17, Thursday (Richmond): Lee informs Early that a brigade will be dispatched from Richmond to Lynchburg to guard against Gen. Averell's Union force, and informs him that "Averell must be captured." Lee's letter to House Speaker Thomas S. Bocock is read on the House floor. Lee

---

14 Charleston *Mercury*, Dec. 17, 1863; OR 6, Series 2, 691; REL to WHT, Dec. 12, 1863, Lee papers, SH. Rumor was rampant in Richmond and within the Army of Northern Virginia in the field that Gen. Lee was going to be Braxton Bragg's replacement at the head of the Army of Tennessee, and that Gen. Beauregard would succeed him in command in Virginia. Charleston *Mercury*, Dec. 17, 1863.

15 Woodward, *Mary Chesnut's CW*, 504; OR 51, pt. 2, 795. Taylor was in essence running the army in Lee's absence, meeting often with Gens. Ewell and Stuart and relaying messages between them and Lee. "I desire to keep Gen. Lee fully informed of what really occurs and is important for him to know, and yet he so dislikes to be unnecessarily annoyed by false or exaggerated reports, that I hate to be the medium of conveying uncertain statements." Compounding his problems, only Taylor, Venable, and one other person (who he did not name but was probably Charles Marshall) were present at headquarters, and Venable went on leave on the 14th. Taylor jokingly told his fiancé, "It is such a trial 'playing commanding general,' that I have concluded never to accept that position when the Government awakes to a sense of my merit to tender it beseechingly to me." Tower, *Lee's Adjutant*, 96-7.

16 *Journal of the Congress of the CSA*, vol. 6, 531; Thomas Bocock to REL, Dec. 16 1863, REL papers, Duke; WHT to REL Dec. 14, 1863, telegram book, REL HQ papers, VHS; Dowdey, *Wartime Papers*, 643.

17 REL to Lucy Minnegerode, Dec. 14, 1863, Robinson family papers, VHS; REL to Nat Burwell, Dec. 14, 1863, Burwell family papers, VHS; Charleston *Mercury*, Dec.18, 1863. Joe Johnston was appointed to command of the Army of Tennessee on Dec. 16, 1863, and assumed command on the 27th. Long, *CW Day by Day*, 447, 449.

18 Davis, *Gray Fox*, 270; Thomas Bocock to REL, Dec. 16, 1863, REL papers, Duke; OR 29, pt. 2, 876.

19 Thomas Bocock to REL, Dec. 16, 1863, REL papers, Duke; Richmond *Daily Dispatch*, Dec. 18, 1863; Freeman, *Lee*, vol. 3, 215 n47; OR 33, 1073-4; OR 51, pt. 2, 798.

20 OR 29, pt. 1, 903-5; WHT to REL, Dec. 16, 1863 (3 messages), telegram book, REL HQ papers, VHS. The deserter, Pvt. Dennis Driscoll, was executed by firing squad on the 17th at Rapidan Station. Driscoll CSR.

informs Walter Taylor that no reprieve shall be given the young deserter from Johnston's Battery.[21]

December 18, Friday (Richmond): Lee joins President Davis, James Chesnut, and Gen. Arnold Elzey on an inspection tour of the Richmond defenses. The general writes to Congressman Alexander Boteler to thank him for a hat and gloves he had forwarded to Lee from several "ladies of Shepherdstown." The Charleston *Mercury* reports that Gen. Lee will not be sent west to command the Army of Tennessee, and that Gen. Joe Johnston will replace Bragg.[22]

December 19, Saturday (Richmond): Lee writes to Sec. Seddon to recommend once again that Robert Chilton be promoted to brigadier general, stating he does not know why his promotion was rejected in April.[23]

December 20, Sunday (Richmond): Taylor writes on this date: "My Chief is still in Richmond. Christmas is near so it would be natural for him to remain with his family during the week, but it will be more in accordance with his peculiar character, if he leaves for the Army just before the great anniversary to show how very self-denying he is."[24]

December 21, Monday (Richmond/Orange/Middle Hill): Lee departs Richmond on the morning train and arrives in Orange during the early afternoon.[25]

December 22, Tuesday (Middle Hill): Lee instructs Jubal Early to procure any and all supplies he can in regions out of reach to government purchasing agents, and orders the quartermaster at Staunton to assist him. Lee also instructs one of Jeb Stuart's quartermasters to stop purchasing hay from around Charlottesville, as that area is reserved for other units. He writes to wife Mary advising of his safe return, and he recommends that she take a downstairs room for her bed chamber in order to avoid having to climb stairs.[26]

December 23, Wednesday (Middle Hill): Lee forwards to Richmond a request from the men of the Florida brigade that they be allowed to winter in their home state to recruit; the officers of the brigade are very irritated that they have received no conscripts from Florida to offset their losses and fear that the regiments will be consolidated due to their minimal strength. Gens. Perry, Anderson, and Hill all favor the request as does Lee, provided other troops can be sent to take their place. Snow.[27]

---

21 OR 51, pt. 2, 798; *Journal of the Congress of the CSA*, vol. 6, 539; WHT to R. L. Walker, Dec. 17, 1863, telegram book, REL HQ papers, VHS.

22 Woodward, *Mary Chesnut's CW*, 507; REL to A. R. Boteler, Dec. 18, 1863, A. R. Boteler papers, Duke; Charleston *Mercury*, Dec. 18, 1863. Regarding Bragg's replacement, a newspaper reported: "[T]he order was sent a day or two ago, but it has been kept very secret, for there is nothing of it on the streets. It is pretty certain that Lee intended to visit Georgia, and came down from the army . . . for that purpose, but after close and continued consultation with the President, the present change occurred." Charleston *Mercury*, Dec. 18, 1863. In a message to Ewell on this date, Taylor adopted Lee's usual terminology for the enemy, referring to the Federals as "those people." OR 51, pt. 2, 800.

23 REL to Seddon, Dec. 19, 1863, R. H. Chilton CSR. Taylor wrote that, in addition to Venable likely leaving to take a job in Richmond, Chilton was also thinking of taking another position in the capital. Taylor admitted that Venable would be missed, but he was "indifferent" toward Chilton, adding that Chilton was vocal that if he was not promoted brigadier as he should have been, he would go to Richmond. "I shan't cry" if Chilton left, he added. Tower, *Lee's Adjutant*, 97.

24 Tower, *Lee's Adjutant*, 101. Lee likely attended church at St. Paul's in the morning.

25 Dowdey, *Wartime Papers*, 643-4.

26 OR 29, pt. 2, 890-1; REL to John A. Palmer, Dec. 22, 1863, telegram book, REL HQ papers, VHS; Dowdey, *Wartime Papers*, 643-4. At some point around the beginning of the new year, wife Mary and daughter Agnes moved to Custis's residence at 707 Franklin, although the exact date is not known. Lee's suggestion of a downstairs room suggests that although the move was being contemplated, it had not yet taken place. See Freeman, *Lee*, vol. 3, 262 n16.

27 OR Series 4, vol. 2, 21-3; Betts, *Experiences of CS Chaplain*, 52.

December 24, Thursday (Middle Hill): Lee instructs Early and Fitz Lee to send back whatever cavalry is not needed in the Valley, Rosser can remain there.[28]

December 25, Friday (Middle Hill/Orange): Lee attends church service at St. Thomas's and receives a turkey and socks for the troops from Mary. Fitzgerald Ross and Frank Vizetelly call on Lee after his return and converse about the suffering of civilians; Ross mentions Arlington, but Lee changes the subject. He invites them to join him and the staff for Christmas dinner, but they already accepted an invitation from Stuart. Lee writes Margaret Stuart with the latest family news, and is distraught over Charlotte's rapidly declining health: "I left Richmond with a sad heart. Charlotte, who was so well on my arrival, looking like herself again, so cheerful, affectionate and sweet, was taken sick two or three days before my departure and completely prostrated. . . . The change between my arrival and departure was so sudden and unexpected to me, that I am filled with sadness, yet can do nothing." He writes Mary he is afraid he cannot get to Richmond before Charlotte succumbs to her illness.[29]

December 26, Saturday (Middle Hill): Lee forwards Early's report to Richmond of his unsuccessful effort to catch Averell in the Valley, adding, "high water and erroneous reports" prevented his capture. Custis informs him during the night of Charlotte's death earlier that day.[30]

December 27, Sunday (Middle Hill/Orange): Lee and Taylor attempt to go to church at St. Thomas's only to discover it is canceled due to the weather. Lee sends Stuart the most recent report from the Clark's Mountain signal station, which does not match the reports his scouts have turned in; Lee directs Stuart to go to there in person tomorrow and report his findings. Charlotte is buried beside her two children in the Wickham family plot at Shockoe Hill Cemetery in Richmond. A distraught Lee writes Mary about her death and apologizes that he cannot get away for the funeral. Heavy rains.[31]

December 28, Monday (Middle Hill): Lee informs the secretary of war that the results of a court martial regarding a soldier in the 50th Virginia were forwarded to Richmond a month ago.[32]

December 29, Tuesday (Middle Hill): Lee forwards to Richmond Fitz Lee's report of his role chasing Averell and adds, "the circumstances" preventing Fitz Lee from doing so "were beyond his control." Lee writes to thank Margaret Stuart for pickles she sent and expresses sorrow over Charlotte's death. He writes Mary Jerdone of Bloomsbury thanking her for the handkerchief. Lee receives a letter from his wife that evening and replies right away, mostly regarding Charlotte and how Rooney will react to her death. Rain.[33]

December 30, Wednesday (Middle Hill): Lee notifies Gen. William Hardee at Dalton, Georgia, that leave was granted Maj. Ivey F. Lewis of the Jeff Davis Legion on the 23rd.[34]

December 31, Thursday (Middle Hill): Rain.[35]

---

28 OR 51, pt. 2, 806; REL to Early, Dec. 24, 1863, telegram book, REL HQ papers, VHS; REL to Fitz Lee, Dec. 24, 1863, telegram book, REL HQ papers, VHS.

29 Ross, *Cities and Camps*, 169; Dowdey, *Wartime Papers*, 644-5; Jones, *Life and Letters of REL*, 296.

30 OR 29, pt. 1, 970-1; Dowdey, *Wartime Papers*, 645.

31 Tower, *Lee's Adjutant*, 103; OR 29, pt. 2, 892; Daughtry, *Gray Cavalier*, 162; Dowdey, *Wartime Papers*, 645.

32 REL to Seddon, Dec. 28, 1863, telegram book, REL HQ papers, VHS.

33 OR 29, pt. 1, 971-3; Jones, *Life and Letters of REL*, 297; REL to "Miss Mary," Dec. 29, 1863, REL papers, W&L; Dowdey, *Wartime Papers*, 645-6; Driver, *39th Virginia Cavalry Battalion*, 61.

34 REL to Hardee, Dec. 30, 1863, telegram book, REL HQ papers, VHS.

35 W. P. Cooper diary, Dec. 31, 1863, R. B. Cook papers, WVU.

January 1864

How to keep the army fed and supplied and how to refill its ranks dominated Robert E. Lee's correspondence during the third January of the war as snow and generally frigid weather kept the men largely confined to their quarters. Lee's longtime frustration with Commissary General Lucius Northrop began to turn into open hostility—something not often evident in Lee's correspondence—as rations dwindled and excuses piled up.[1]

When the weather permitted, Lee rode through the camps accompanied usually by either Charles Venable or Charles Marshall.[2] In the evenings, the staff offers often left to visit friends in other commands or occasionally to make social calls in town. Many of the local residents called upon Lee at his headquarters, usually bearing gifts.[3] One local youngster was a frequent visitor at headquarters:

> His home was about ¾ of a mile distant and, being only about five or six years old at the time, he was usually accompanied on these visits by one of the soldiers . . . stationed at his home as guards. Upon one occasion, having gone over on the shoulder of a soldier, when he arrived, he went into the tent without warning and found General Lee handing around a plate of cake to some officers. General Lee asked him to have a slice. . . . My friend then told General Lee that the soldier who had him over was outside and he wished a slice for him. The General took him by the hand, and, going outside, offered the cake to the soldier, who was greatly affected by this courtesy from his commander.[4]

As the family mourned the loss of Charlotte, Mildred concluded her studies in Raleigh and joined her mother and Agnes in Richmond. Around the first of the year, Mary and the girls left their tiny residence on Leigh St. and moved in with Custis on Franklin St.[5]

* * *

---

1   *OR* 33, 1085-8.

2   Freeman, *Lee*, vol. 3, 218.

3   Tower, *Lee's Adjutant*, 109.

4   Burgess, "General Lee in Orange County."

5   Freeman, *Lee*, vol. 3, 262 n16. The exact date of the move is not known, nor whether Mildred ever stayed at the Leigh St. house.

January 1, Friday (Middle Hill): Lee authorizes a 30-day furlough for any enlisted man who brings in a new recruit.[6]

January 2, Saturday (Middle Hill): Lee proposes to President Davis an attack on New Bern noting "I can now spare troops for the purpose, which will not be the case as spring approaches." A bill giving the official thanks of Congress to Lee passes the Senate. Lee receives pay of $910 for November and December.[7]

January 3, Sunday (Middle Hill): Snow, more than 6 inches deep.[8]

January 4, Monday (Middle Hill): Lee writes to the adjutant general regarding efforts to round up deserters along the Blue Ridge Mountains, noting that enrolling and conscription officers in that region are negligent in their duties. Lee instructs Early to arrest any deserters and stragglers he finds in the Valley, and also alerts him that a division of Union cavalry is reported to have gone to the Valley. Lee writes to the War Department regarding the Florida brigade, asking why recruits can't simply be sent to it in Virginia rather than sending the entire brigade home to recruit; he doesn't like the precedent sending it to Florida would establish as then every unit from outside of Virginia would request to return home, and proposes that if it can't be brought back up to strength that it be consolidated into one regiment. The House of Representatives passes the thanks of Congress resolution. Snow continues to fall.[9]

January 5, Tuesday (Middle Hill): Lee sends a very sharply worded letter to Commissary General Lucius Northrop regarding the army's shortage of rations. He asks Sam Jones if any cattle or sheep can be obtained for the army's use in southwest Virginia and when he expects the Virginia & Tennessee Railroad will be back in operation.[10]

January 6, Wednesday (Middle Hill): Lee writes to Early regretting the difficulties that have beset his operations in the Valley and confirms that a division of enemy cavalry moved to Front Royal. Lee informs President Davis that cattle and prisoners from Imboden's raid into Hardy County will reach Early at Harrisonburg today. President Lincoln authorizes the Federal government to purchase Arlington when it goes on auction.[11]

January 7, Thursday (Middle Hill): Lee comments on a letter Governor Vance of North Carolina wrote to Secretary of War Seddon regarding North Carolina units serving in mixed brigades. The topic frustrates Lee, who has addressed the issue multiple times. Vance specifically mentions three regiments that he wants removed from their current brigades to create a new North Carolina brigade. To do so would break up currently effective brigades, so Lee refuses. The thanks of Congress passes and is forwarded on to President Davis.[12]

January 8, Friday (Middle Hill): Lee writes to Sec. Seddon concerning the difficulties of the Virginia Central Railroad. Lee instructs Early and Fitz Lee to rest their men and horses in the Valley and to grant

---

6 OR 33, 1059.

7 OR 33, 1061; *Journal of the Congress of the CSA*, vol. 3, 509; pay voucher, Jan. 2, 1864, REL CSR.

8 Ardrey diary, Jan. 3, 1864, Davidson.

9 OR 33, 1063; REL to Early, Jan. 4, 1864 (2 messages), telegram book, REL HQ papers, VHS; OR 29, pt. 2, 884-6; *Journal of the Congress of the CSA*, vol. 6, 586; Betts, *Experience of a CS Chaplain*, 53.

10 OR 33, 1064-6.

11 OR 33, 1066-7; Gaughan, *Last Battle of the CW*, 28.

12 OR 29, pt. 2, 866-8; *Journal of the Congress of the CSA*, vol. 3, 522. Vance was still concerned about the 1st and 3rd NC regiments, which were in a Virginia brigade commanded by Marylander Gen. George Steuart, and the 55th NC, which was part of Joe Davis's Mississippi brigade. Vance wanted those three regiments and one from Alfred Scales's North Carolina brigade to form a new North Carolina brigade. Lee's irritation at having to address this subject again was apparent, but he remained respectful in his reply.

the companies from the Shenandoah Valley 10 days leave. President Davis approves the Thanks of Congress to Lee and the army for the campaigns of 1862-3.[13]

January 9, Saturday (Middle Hill): Adjutant General Cooper informs Lee that James Longstreet requested to be relieved of command of his corps; Cooper wants to get Gen. Lee's views on swapping Longstreet and Ewell.[14]

January 10, Sunday (Middle Hill): Lee responds to Cooper's inquiry regarding Longstreet, stating that he does not understand Longstreet's request and he will not switch Longstreet and Ewell. He writes to wife Mary complaining about the cold weather and the scarce rations; he thanks her for the latest shipment of socks and gloves she and the girls made for the army and sent to the front via Col. Chilton.[15]

January 11, Monday (Middle Hill): Lee writes to President Davis regarding the shortage of rations and how some are disappearing somewhere between Richmond and the army. He also warns that the Federals appear poised for a raid on the capital, possibly to free the prisoners held there; the general requests that a scout be sent to investigate the reports. Lee informs the War Department that he will not send any troops south to Wilmington, and that the troops there are more than sufficient to meet any Federals force threatening the city. Lee's former home Arlington is purchased at auction by the U.S. government for $26,800.[16]

January 12, Tuesday (Middle Hill): Lee complains to Gen. Cooper about the repeated requests from Gen. Chase Whiting for the need of additional troops at Wilmington, North Carolina: "I cannot see that the enemy is collecting any force against it [Wilmington]. . . . If the defense of Wilmington requires 'the constant presence of an army,' I do not see where it is to come from." He requests confirmation that no supplies will be sent to the army from Lynchburg for four days because of troops being sent along the railroad to Bristol, and instructs Jubal Early to investigate reports of another enemy advance from the mountains.[17]

January 13, Wednesday (Middle Hill): Lee complains to President Davis about the quality of the troops in western and southwest Virginia, specifically their inclination to desert when a unit is moved away from its home region. He mentions in particular Sam Jones and John Imboden's men. Lee requests that Jones be replaced as commander in southwest Virginia, and also that the policy be overhauled that allows men to serve in local units because that contributes to the overall uselessness of those units. Lee also complains to the head of the Conscription Bureau, Col. J. S. Preston, that depleted units are not being reinforced with conscripts as intended because many of those liable to conscription are volunteering for local defense units and serving in backwater areas, in some cases filling those local units far beyond their authorized numbers. Lee argues with Commissary General Northrop about impressments; the general

---

13 OR 33, 1073-4; REL to Fitz Lee, January 8, 1864, telegram book, REL HQ papers, VHS; *Journal of the Congress of the CSA*, vol. 3, 545-6; OR 27, pt. 2, 326.

14 OR 33, 1074. Longstreet wrote to Cooper on Dec. 30 as a result of his disastrous attempt to capture Knoxville in November. He not only failed, but made scapegoats of Lafayette McLaws and Jerome Robertson, the commander of the Texas Brigade. Wert, *Longstreet*, 357-60.

15 OR 32, pt. 2, 541; Dowdey, *Wartime Papers*, 649.

16 OR 33, 1076-7, 1081; OR 29, pt. 2, 910; Gaughan, *Last Battle of the CW*, 28; Freeman, *Lee*, vol. 3, 213-4. The seizure and subsequent sale of the estate led to a lengthy legal fight after the war. Lee attempted to pay the necessary taxes—$92.07, not including penalties—through a cousin, but the government refused the payment on the grounds that Lee must make it himself. Freeman, *Lee*, vol. 3, 213. Lee sought legal advice after the war. "I would be obliged to you if in your power to have the . . . sale examined, and to let me know the fact in the case," he wrote an attorney, and "whether the sale was regular and legal, and what can be done." REL to Francis S. Smith, April 5, 1866, Lee papers, SH.

17 OR 33, 1069-71; REL to Samuel Cooper, Jan. 12, 1864, telegram book, REL HQ papers, VHS; REL to Early, Jan. 12, 1864, telegram book, REL HQ papers, VHS.

January 14, Thursday (Middle Hill): Lee instructs Gen. Wade Hampton to use his cavalry to intercept an enemy raiding party around Fredericksburg.[19]

January 15, Friday (Middle Hill): Lee writes to Mary, thanking her for the latest batch of socks sent for the troops and asking for a pair for himself; he mentions also that he declined several offers to take up quarters in local houses: "They do not know what they ask. I . . . cannot go alone or be alone, as a crowd is always around me." Walter Taylor is promoted to lieutenant colonel.[20]

January 16, Saturday (Middle Hill): Lee sends a lengthy letter to Gen. Longstreet on the overall strategic situation and also responds to Longstreet's suggestion that he mount his entire force on mules: "If Grant could be driven back and Mississippi and Tennessee recovered," explains the general, "it would do more to relieve the country and inspire our people than the mere capture of Washington." Lee dismisses the idea of mounting Longstreet's force because even if enough animals could be found, where would saddles and other tack come from? Lee asks also if Gen. Simon B. Buckner would be an acceptable replacement for Hood as a division commander. Lee informs Sec. Seddon that a recruiting officer for Gen. John H. Morgan is in Richmond enlisting deserters from Lee's army; Lee wants this shut down immediately and the offenders arrested. The general sends Mary Jerdone at neighboring Bloomsbury several partridges.[21]

January 17, Sunday (Middle Hill): Lee requests that Quartermaster General Alexander Lawton send rations to his hungry army as soon as possible. Lee writes a short note to his son Rob with some family news.[22]

January 18, Monday (Middle Hill): Lee writes to Lawton regarding the shortage of shoes and blankets in the army; the general proposes that the army produce its own shoes if supplies and trained men are sent to do so. Lee writes to Richard Ewell that Ewell himself knows best if he is physically able to serve in the field: "I was in constant fear during the last campaign that you would sink under your duties or destroy yourself. In either event injury might have resulted. I last spring asked for your appointment provided you were able to take the field. You now know from experience what you have to undergo," continued Lee, "and can best judge of your ability to

---

[18] OR 33, 1085-8. Lee's missive to Northrop reads like a legal brief, suggesting that it was written at least in part, if not in total, by Charles Marshall.

[19] REL to Hampton, Jan. 14, 1864, telegram book, REL HQ papers, VHS.

[20] Dowdey, *Wartime Papers*, 652; WHT commission, WHT papers, SH. Longstreet's aide T. J. Goree brought Lee several messages from Longstreet during the evening. OR 32, pt. 2, 566. Goree, who was staunchly loyal to Longstreet, recalled one of the meetings with Lee: "Gen. Lee asked me into his tent when he was alone with two or three Northern papers on his table. He remarked that he had just been reading the Northern official reports of the battle of Gettysburg, that he had become satisfied from reading those reports that if he had permitted you to carry out your [Longstreet's] plans on the 3rd day, instead of making the attack [Pickett's Charge] on Cemetery Hill, we would have been successful. He said that the enemy seemed to have anticipated the attack on their center, in consequence of which they had withdrawn the larger part of their forces from the left flank and from Round Top Mountain and that if you had made your flank movement early on the morning of the 3rd day as you desired that you would have met with but little opposition." Goree to Longstreet, May 17, 1875, Longstreet papers, UNC. Lee's letter to Mary was delivered to Richmond by Col. John T. Wood, who met with Lee around this time to discuss his role in a joint Army-Navy operation in eastern North Carolina. The exact date when he met with Lee is not known, but Wood was back in Richmond by the 20th. Dowdey, *Wartime Papers*, 652; Royce G. Shingleton, *John Taylor Wood: Sea Ghost of the Confederacy* (Athens, GA, 1979), 91; OR 33, 1104.

[21] OR 32, pt. 2, 566-7; REL to Seddon, Jan. 16, 1864, telegram book, REL HQ papers, VHS; REL to Mary Jerdone, Jan. 16, 1864, REL papers, W&L. Longstreet needed two new division commanders (Hood had been promoted to lieutenant general and given an infantry corps command in the Army of Tennessee once he had recovered from his Chickamauga wound, and McLaws had been removed from command after Knoxville).

[22] REL to Lawton, Jan. 17, 1864, telegram book, REL HQ papers, VHS; Fitz Lee, *General Lee*, 324-5.

endure it. I fear we cannot anticipate less labor than formerly." Rain.²³

January 19, Tuesday (Middle Hill): Lee's 57th birthday. He meets with Gen. Robert Hoke concerning an operation to liberate New Bern, North Carolina, and informs Gen. Ewell of the mission. Lee complains to President Davis about troops recruited for local service only, specifically South Carolina units around Charleston and Savannah, and how recruits need to be sent to the armies in the field, not to local garrisons. The general provides Lawton more details regarding his proposal to make shoes locally for the army, and requests that Corse's Brigade be sent to Weldon, North Carolina.²⁴

January 20, Wednesday (Middle Hill): Lee instructs Hoke to go ahead of his troops to Petersburg to deliver instructions to George Pickett, who will have overall command of the North Carolina operation, which will also include a naval force under Col. John T. Wood. Lee notifies Chase Whiting at Wilmington of the New Bern mission and requests that a diversion be made to prevent reinforcements being sent against Pickett and Hoke. He arranges with Col. Wood the transportation of his boats and for rail transportation for Hoke's troops to Petersburg so as not to interfere with the army's supply trains, and informs the president of the details of the operation offering to go command it in person if Davis desires, but notes that he prefers to stay with the ANV.²⁵

Lee complains again about John Hunt Morgan's officers recruiting men from Lee's army into Morgan's ranks, and advises Imboden that he has no military authority over civilians in Hardy County and thus Imboden must turn over to civilian authorities a local resident he arrested and imprisoned pending court martial. Lee submits his report of the Gettysburg Campaign.²⁶

January 21, Thursday (Middle Hill): Lee addresses the continuing supply problems with Sec. Seddon, and inquires whether funds already earmarked for overseas purchases can instead be used at home. He instructs Sam Jones to continue gathering supplies in his department, and instructs Early to extend his reach as far as possible into West Virginia for cattle. Lee asks for Mosby's promotion to lieutenant colonel.²⁷

January 22, Friday (Middle Hill): Lee reduces the army's rations due to supply shortage, and warns Seddon of the ill effects this will have on his men physically and that it will lower morale; he requests that the regulation granting officers permission to purchase army supplies for their families be rescinded. Lee denies a request from Wade Hampton that infantry be used for picket outposts, noting that infantry could not escape as quickly as cavalry. Lee forwards a report from Tom Rosser and

---

23 OR 33, 1094-6; Krick, *CW Weather*, 115. William Mahone set up a shoe factory for his brigade and possibly Richard Anderson's entire division, in New Zion Church south of Orange. W. W. Scott, *A History of Orange County, Virginia, From its Formation in 1734 to the End of Reconstruction in 1870* (Richmond, VA, 1907), 49. The letter to Ewell was prompted by Sec. Seddon bluntly asking the general if he could physically serve in the field, because his lieutenant generalship was up for confirmation by the Confederate Senate; Ewell wanted Lee's advice and opinion. Pfanz, *Ewell*, 351.

24 OR 33, 1097-1100. It is possible that Ewell was part of the meeting with Hoke.

25 OR 33, 87, 1101-4; Shingleton, *John Taylor Wood*, 91, 215. A soldier in the 53rd NC recorded that "General Lee and his daughter" rode past his work detail near Orange. This may be a case of mistaken identity because none of Lee's letters indicate that any of his daughters were with him at this time. Leon, *Diary of a Tar Heel*, 56. The identity of Lee's guest is unknown.

26 OR 51, pt. 2, 812; OR 6, Series 2, 862; OR 27, pt. 2, 312-25. John Mosby, a fierce supporter of Jeb Stuart and a vigorous defender of Stuart's role in the Gettysburg Campaign, harshly criticized Lee's official report: "General Lee's report does great injustice to the cavalry.... I do not believe General Lee ever read it, simply signed it mechanically. It is full of errors and contradictions. Charles Marshall wrote all his reports." Adele H. Mitchell, ed., *The Letters of John S. Mosby* (Richmond, VA, 1986), 86. Mosby was correct that Marshall wrote Lee's official reports, but the suggestion that Lee never read the reports in general, or this one in particular, is absurd.

27 OR 33, 1111-4.

Stuart regarding partisan rangers; he does not concur in Rosser's opinion that they are all ineffective or comment on Stuart's endorsement that Mosby is the only effective one. Instead, he recommends "the law authorizing these partisan corps be abolished." Lee sends a letter of recommendation for Henry Heth to Sen. R. M. T. Hunter.[28]

January 23, Saturday (Middle Hill): Lee renews his request for the 8th and 14th Virginia Cavalry regiments to be transferred to his army and also excess mounted units in South Carolina be sent north. Lee informs Hampton that he cannot send any of his units to South Carolina for the winter, but he will allow the rotation of units between the front, Northern Neck, and North Carolina; he consents to Hampton himself transferring to the Army of Mississippi. Lee receives a letter from Rob.[29]

January 24, Sunday (Middle Hill): Lee instructs Stuart to use all his wagons for foraging purposes, and writes to Mary regarding the continuing need for her and the girls to make socks for the army and his distress that the slaves at Romancoke have not yet been freed.[30]

January 25, Monday (Middle Hill): Lee complains vehemently to Sec. Seddon about the authority recently granted by the War Department to several officers to recruit a new unit to operate behind enemy lines, as it will draw men away from other units: "If the system of giving these permissions to raise companies continues as it now exists my efforts to preserve and improve the discipline of the army must be unavailing. . . . No good has resulted from it at all commensurate with its bad effects. I would prefer to see it suppressed entirely, at the expense of losing the men who are rightfully brought into service by it, rather than lose the larger number it draws from the army."[31]

January 26, Tuesday (Middle Hill): Lee informs President Davis that concerns over the vulnerability of southwest Virginia can be better addressed by an increase in organization and discipline in the troops serving in that region than by sending additional troops there, but he will order the return of the 54th and 63rd Virginia infantry to the region from Joe Johnston's army. Lee advises Gens. Arnold Elzey and Wade Hampton of an enemy movement around Williamsburg on the Virginia Peninsula, and instructs them to attack if the opportunity presents, and places the Hanover Junction garrison at their disposal.[32]

January 27, Wednesday (Middle Hill): Lee requests a change of commanders in southwest Virginia, listing Jubal Early, Robert Rodes, Edward Johnson, Cadmus Wilcox, and John Gordon as candidates from his army and Simon Buckner and Robert Ransom as possibilities from outside his command to replace Sam Jones, and he recommends that the Shenandoah Valley be included in that department. "A change . . . is necessary both for the sake of the officers in that department and the interests of the country. . . . The first step to improvement is an energetic, active commander, and no time should be lost in his selection."[33]

January 28, Thursday (Middle Hill): Lee inquires of Elzey if the reports of enemy movement on the Peninsula are correct, as Hampton's scouts do not report anything of the sort; he instructs Hampton to keep watch and if the Federals are moving to strike

---

28 OR 33, 1081-2, 1088-9, 1114-7; Freeman, *Lee*, vol. 3, 231-2. Heth was blamed in some circles for bringing on the fighting at Gettysburg and for blundering into an ambush at Bristoe Station; Lee sought to exonerate his friend.

29 OR 33, 1117-9; Dowdey, *Wartime Papers*, 661.

30 OR 33, 1119; Dowdey, *Wartime Papers*, 660-1.

31 OR 33, 1120-1.

32 OR 33, 1106-7; REL to Elzey, Jan. 26, 1864, telegram book, REL HQ papers, VHS; REL to Hampton, Jan. 26, 1864, telegram book, REL HQ papers, VHS.

33 OR 33, 1124.

them in flank. Lee orders the troops to restore the fences around fields and stay out of the fields to allow for farmers to plant their crops. Charles Marshall goes on leave to Richmond.[34]

January 29, Friday (Middle Hill): Lee writes to Gen. James Kemper regarding supplying the army and criticizing recruiting for local units.[35]

January 30, Saturday (Middle Hill): Lee cautions President Davis that if reports of enemy movements on the Peninsula are true, he may not be able to get troops from his army to Richmond in time to defend it, so recommends that two brigades recently sent from the capital to Charleston be recalled. Lee complains to Quartermaster General Lawton about the quality of shoes being sent to the army from Richmond and Columbus, Georgia; Lee prefers to have the materials sent to Orange and footwear produced locally.[36]

January 31, Sunday (Middle Hill): Lee instructs Stuart to find a body of enemy cavalry supposed to have crossed the Robertson River in the morning. Lee informs Alabama Congressman Thomas J. Foster that he will not transfer Col. Edward O'Neal's 26th Alabama to its home state unless a replacement regiment is sent to take its place. Maj. Gen. John C. Breckinridge is supposed to visit Lee today, but does not arrive.[37]

---

34 OR 33, 1125; REL to Hampton, Jan. 28, 1864, telegram book, REL HQ papers, VHS; OR 33, 1126; Tower, *Lee's Adjutant*, 109. Taylor noted that Chilton and Venable left to socialize elsewhere, leaving him and Lee alone at HQ during the evening. Tower, *Lee's Adjutant*, 109.

35 OR 33, 1127-8. James Kemper recovered from his Gettysburg wound but was no longer fit for field service, so he was assigned to command Virginia's reserve forces. Warner, *Generals in Gray*, 169-70.

36 OR 33, 1131-2.

37 OR 33, 1133-4; Tower, *Lee's Adjutant*, 111. Edward O'Neal was angry about not being promoted and wanted to transfer out of Lee's army. Sam Jones's eventual replacement in southwest Virginia was John C. Breckinridge, who had served as vice president in James Buchanan's administration and was himself a candidate for president in 1860. Breckinridge had proven himself a capable commander in the field and would later become President Davis's secretary of war.

February 1864

Winter was supposed to be a time of relative quiet for Civil War armies, with the bad weather preventing active campaigning. Such was not the case along the Rapidan River in February. The Federals undertook a two-pronged offensive early in the month, crossing a large force at Morton's Ford while another column was supposed to move up the Virginia Peninsula against Richmond. Although the attack against the capital never developed, Arnold Elzey's penchant for constantly believing an attack against the city was imminent—although correct this time—served to keep portions of Lee's army in motion.

It was indeed a winter of change. After his disastrous campaign around Chattanooga in late November 1863, Braxton Bragg resigned as commander of the Army of Tennessee and in February was named military advisor to President Davis, the same post held by Lee two years earlier. Other lesser command changes were in the offing as well, and repeated poor performances by Sam Jones in southwest Virginia and Arnold Elzey at Richmond hastened their exits.

Lee went to Richmond at the end of the month to meet with the president, leaving Richard Ewell in temporary command of the army. When another Federal threat manifested itself during the commander's absence, it was not Ewell—or any other general officer, for that matter—who organized the response but Lee's staff officer Walter Taylor. This action cut Lee's Richmond trip short, and the general narrowly avoided being captured when his train was the last to get through from Richmond to Orange before Yankee cavalry (part of the Kilpatrick-Dahlgren Raid) cut the Virginia Central line.

Lee's wife Mary and his daughters, meanwhile, together with friends and neighbors they could corral into the effort, worked hard knitting socks and gloves for the Virginia army. Although the numbers of garments they produced were minimal when compared with the army's needs, there was much value in the symbolism of their actions. "We paid our respects to Mrs. Lee," penned an unidentified visitor to the Lee residence in early February, who continued:

> Her room was like an Industrial School—everybody with hands busy. Her daughters were all there plying their needles with a lot of ladies. Mrs. Lee showed us a beautiful sword, recently sent the General by some Marylanders. When we came out, one said 'Did you see how the Lees spend their time? What a rebuke to the frivolity and taffy parties.'[1]

Although Lee did not know of them at this time, two significant events occurred that would deeply affect his personal life: President Lincoln approved Rooney's exchange, and Lee's sister Anne died.[2]

* * *

---

1 "Anne Farrar ancestor" diary, Feb. 1864, Coulling papers, W&L.

2 Lincoln endorsement on John M. Flinn to Thomas A. Hendricks, Heritage Auctions, lot #42036 Jan. 24, 2015 auction; Edmund Jennings Lee, *Lee of Virginia, 1642-1892: Biographical and Genealogical Sketches of the Descendants of Colonel Richard Lee* (Philadelphia, 1895), 342.

February 1, Monday (Middle Hill): Lee hosts John C. Breckinridge at headquarters. Lee writes to Sam Jones and Sec. Seddon regarding forage for his department and for the ANV.[3]

February 2, Tuesday (Middle Hill): Lee advises Sam Jones that he can't spare any troops to reinforce southwest Virginia, but that he will send engineers to map the region. Lee inquires how many animals and riding accouterments can be gathered by March 1 to mount Longstreet's force.[4]

February 3, Wednesday (Middle Hill): Lee proposes to President Davis two options for the Spring campaign: reinforcing Longstreet and Sam Jones and moving into east Tennessee and Kentucky, or bring Longstreet back to Virginia and attack Meade. Lee trades messages with Arnold Elzey and the War Department regarding a force moving up the Peninsula, and arranges to have troops sent from his army to the capital.[5]

February 4, Thursday (Middle Hill): Lee orders Wade Hampton to move to Hanover Court House, but is not convinced of the threat to Richmond.[6]

February 5, Friday (Middle Hill): Lee telegraphs Hampton, inquiring about reports of an enemy pontoon train and advises Adjutant General Cooper of a raid by Tom Rosser into Hardy County. He receives a package from Mary with gloves, socks, and coffee.[7]

February 6, Saturday (Middle Hill): Lee meets with Revs. J. William Jones and Beverly T. Lacy to discuss observance of the Sabbath within the ANV. Lee learns from Richard Ewell that a large force of the enemy has crossed the Rapidan River at Morton's Ford in the morning, and he orders Stuart to investigate. Lee orders Armistead Long and R. L. Walker to bring up as much artillery from their commands as possible to the river crossings, and instructs Rodes to rejoin Ewell's corps by rail from Hanover Junction.[8]

Lee informs President Davis that the Federals are crossing at Morton's Ford but he does not yet know the strength, and requests that if Pickett is no longer needed in North Carolina that he be brought closer to Richmond. Lee asks Early if reports of the VIII Corps leaving the lower Valley and going to Chattanooga or the I Corps moving to the Valley are correct. Lee writes to Mary, thanking her for the clothing and coffee, and notes that Perry is sick probably caused by the reduced rations. President Lincoln approves Rooney's exchange.[9]

February 7, Sunday (Middle Hill/Morton's Ford): Lee learns before dawn that Federal cavalry crossed

---

3 Richmond *Daily Dispatch*, Feb. 2, 1864; OR 33, 1140, OR 51, pt. 2, 814. John Breckinridge replaced Gen. Jones as commander in southwest Virginia. Breckinridge was on his way to Richmond at this time. He officially replaced Jones on March 4. Knight, *Valley Thunder*, 20.

4 OR 33, 1141-2; OR 32, pt. 2, 654.

5 OR 32, pt. 2, 667; Freeman, *Lee's Dispatches*, 133-4; REL to Elzey, Feb. 3, 1864 (2 messages), telegram book, REL HQ papers, VHS; REL to Lawton, Feb. 3, 1864, telegram book, REL HQ papers, VHS.

6 OR 33, 1143; REL to Hampton, Feb. 4, 1864, telegram book, REL HQ papers, VHS.

7 REL to Hampton, Feb. 5, 1864, telegram book, REL HQ papers, VHS; REL to Samuel Cooper, Feb. 5, 1864, telegram book, REL HQ papers, VHS; Dowdey, *Wartime Papers*, 667. The message regarding Tom Rosser also appears in *Lee's Dispatches* dated Feb. 7; according to the HQ telegram book, it was sent on the 5th. Freeman, *Lee's Dispatches*, 134-5.

8 Jones, *Christ in Camp*, 49-50; OR 33, 1148; REL to Long, Feb. 6, 1864 (2 messages), telegram book, REL HQ papers, VHS; REL to Walker, Feb. 6, 1864, telegram book, REL HQ papers, VHS; REL to Rodes, Feb. 6, 1864 (2 messages), telegram book, REL HQ papers, VHS. Lee was unsure of the meaning of the Morton's Ford action but would offer battle if pressed: "If his [Meade's] whole army is in motion I will order out Hill's Corps." *OR Supplement*, vol. 3, pt. 3, 421.

9 REL to Davis, Feb. 6, 1864 (2 messages), telegram book, REL HQ papers, VHS; REL to Early, Feb. 6, 1864, telegram book, REL HQ papers, VHS; Dowdey, *Wartime Papers*, 667-8; Lincoln endorsement on John M. Flinn to Thomas A. Hendricks, Heritage Auctions, lot #42036 Jan. 24, 2015 auction. Lee wrote to an unknown person regarding a new commander for Cadmus Wilcox's former brigade. REL to unknown, Feb. 6, 1864, REL papers, Duke.

yesterday at Gold Mine, Ely's, and Barrett's Ford in addition to the main crossing at Morton's Ford. He orders Rodes to send one brigade to Richmond and hold the rest of his division at Hanover Junction until the enemy's intent is clear, and instructs Early to be ready to rejoin the army by railroad. Lee and the staff move toward Morton's Ford at daybreak. After but a few miles word arrives from Ewell that the enemy has re-crossed the river. Lee sends Taylor back to headquarters but continues on to the river himself, and has orders sent to Ewell's and Hill's artillery chiefs to bring only a portion of their guns to Morton's and have others sent to the other crossing points.[10]

By 8:30 a.m., Lee orders a stand-down, ordering most of the artillery back to its camps and cancelling Rodes and Early's movements.[11] Lee notifies President Davis at 8:30 a.m. that the Federals re-crossed the river. After remaining at Morton's Ford for much of the morning, Lee returns back to headquarters, where he issues GO15 regarding the observation of the Sabbath in camps.[12]

February 8, Monday (Middle Hill): Lee sends a preliminary report of Morton's Ford to Richmond and recommends Sec. Seddon that the current law regarding promotion at junior levels be changed to be more inclusive and allow for promotions at company and regimental level to come from outside the unit. Lee instructs Elzey to take his entire force at Richmond and Rodes from Hanover Junction, if warranted, to "clear the Peninsula of enemy," and orders Hampton to move to New Kent and operate with Elzey.[13]

February 9, Tuesday (Middle Hill/Orange): Lee attends a meeting of the Chaplains Association in Orange. Lee reviews reports of the New Bern operation, and grants Rodes leave to visit Richmond.[14]

February 10, Wednesday (Middle Hill/Orange): Lee attends Ash Wednesday service at St. Thomas's, and provides the War Department with a list of the latest units to reenlist for the entire war.[15]

February 11, Thursday (Middle Hill): Lee advises Elzey that the Federals on the Peninsula returned to Yorktown, so to return his troops to camp. Lee inquires of Early if his forces in the Valley can be of further use there, noting that he wants to recall Early and his troops to the army and he forwards to Richmond Early's report of his operations in the Valley. Lee compliments Hoke on his handling of the New Bern operation and directs him to stay in North Carolina for the present to recruit his brigade.[16]

February 12, Friday (Middle Hill): Lee directs Hampton to move to Hanover Court House in response to a report from Elzey of a large enemy

---

10 REL to Rodes, Feb. 7, 1864, telegram book, REL HQ papers, VHS; REL to Early, Feb. 7, 1864, telegram book, REL HQ papers, VHS; Tower, *Lee's Adjutant*, 116. REL to A. L. Long, Feb. 7, 1864, telegram book, REL HQ papers, VHS; REL to R. L. Walker, Feb. 7, 1864, telegram book, REL HQ papers, VHS. Lee's directives to Long and Walker at 6:30 a.m. suggest that he was still quite uncertain as to Meade's intentions. Two hours later, he was convinced no offensive was forthcoming. REL to Long, and REL to Walker, Feb. 7, 1864 (2 messages each) telegram book, REL HQ papers.

11 REL to A. L. Long, Feb. 7, 1864, telegram book, REL HQ papers, VHS; REL to R. L. Walker, Feb. 7, 1864, telegram book, REL HQ papers, VHS; REL to Early, Feb. 7, 1864, telegram book, REL HQ papers, VHS; REL to Hampton, Feb. 7, 1864, telegram book, REL HQ papers, VHS.

12 Freeman, *Lee's Dispatches*, 136; Ardrey diary, Feb. 7, 1864, Davidson; OR 33, 1150.

13 OR 33, 141; OR 3, Series 4, 84; REL to Elzey, Feb. 8, 1864, telegram book, REL HQ papers, VHS; REL to Hampton, Feb. 8, 1864, telegram book, REL HQ papers, VHS. Taylor was critical of Elzey's handling of the campaign outside Richmond, referring to him as "Mr. Excitable Elzey." He was "very easily alarmed and floods us with anxious telegrams. I only wish he would not have put them in cipher, as I have the trouble of interpreting them." Tower, *Lee's Adjutant*, 116.

14 Hurst, *Soldiers, Stories, Sites and Fights*, 154; Betts, *Experiences of a CS Chaplain*, 55; Freeman, *Lee's Dispatches*, 136; REL to Rodes, Feb. 9, 1864; telegram book, REL HQ papers, VHS.

15 Tower, *Lee's Adjutant*, 118; OR 33, 1152.

16 OR 33, 43-5, 1159-61.

force at Barhamsville. Lee receives a package of socks from Eliza Beverly for the army.[17]

February 14, Sunday (Middle Hill): Lee's mail and messages from Richmond are "lost on the train this evening," and he inquires of the War Department if any of it was important. Lee writes to Mary, glad that her health is improving and mentions that he is considering giving Rob a place on his staff although he is not in favor of nepotism.[18]

February 15, Monday (Middle Hill): Lee rebukes Elzey for the erroneous reports of his scouts regarding enemy strength and movements on the Peninsula; Lee tells him he can spare nothing to guard Richmond other than a brigade at Hanover Junction, and he states that the recent enemy movement was likely nothing more than a diversion. Accordingly Lee instructs Rodes to return to the army but to leave one brigade at Hanover Junction, and requests that trains be sent from Richmond to move Rodes's men by rail. Lee informs the War Department that he created a medical inspection commission to assist with returning convalescents to the ranks quicker and asks for approval.[19]

Lee declines a request from Imboden for a court of inquiry in response to complaints made against he and his command by Jubal Early. Lee writes to Early, regretting that Imboden's men were not of better use. He grants Early a short furlough before having to return to the army, although Lee wants Early's infantry left in the Shenandoah Valley for the present. Lee grants a request from Brig. Gen. Pierce M. B. Young to go to South Carolina to recruit for his command. Lee informs Longstreet that John Sedgwick is in temporary command of the Army of the Potomac. Snow.[20]

February 16, Tuesday (Middle Hill): Lee complains to Sec. Seddon regarding the ongoing food shortage and proposes trading cotton and tobacco for provisions, mentioning that this is already being done by some in the Valley with U.S. troops. Lee advises Rodes that rail transportation cannot be provided for his men so they will have to march from Hanover Junction, and he writes to S. F. Cameron regarding a presentation sword. Chilton is promoted to brigadier general.[21]

February 17, Wednesday (Middle Hill): Lee writes to Longstreet explaining that he cannot reinforce him and there are not enough horses and mules to mount Longstreet's force; he mentions also that changes are being made in southwest Virginia and that John Breckinridge will likely be placed in command there, and wonders if Longstreet can work with Johnston and Breckinridge against the Federals in Tennessee. Lee forwards to Richmond the results of William Pendleton's inspection of the horse depot in Lynchburg.[22]

February 18, Thursday (Middle Hill): Lee meets with Gens. Ewell and Edward Johnson regarding mass desertions from Gen. Leroy Stafford's

---

17 REL to Hampton, Feb. 12, 1864, telegram book, REL HQ papers, VHS; Dowdey, *Wartime Papers*, 670.

18 REL to Samuel Cooper, Feb. 14, 1864, telegram book, REL HQ papers, VHS; Dowdey, *Wartime Papers*, 670-1. There is a notation in the HQ telegram book that messages were sent on this date to the president of the Virginia Central and to the station agents between Hanover Junction and Richmond, but nothing was recorded regarding the subject matter. Telegram book, REL HQ papers, VHS. Lee wrote of Rob: "I should prefer Rob's being in the line in an independent position, where he could rise by his own merit and not through the recommendation of his relatives." Dowdey, *Wartime Papers*, 671.

19 OR 33, 1173-5; REL to Rodes, Feb. 15, 1864, telegram book, REL HQ papers, VHS; REL to Lawton, Feb. 15, 1864, telegram book, REL HQ papers, VHS.

20 OR 33, 1153-4, 1167-8, 1174-5; REL to Longstreet, Feb. 15, 1864. Telegram Book, REL HQ Papers, VHS. Mary Chesnut put Lee in Richmond the night of the 15th and morning of the 16th, and Emory Thomas followed suit. Available evidence, however, suggests that he was still in Orange. Woodward, *Mary Chesnut's CW*, 569; Thomas, *REL*, 317.

21 OR 33, 1180-1; REL to Rodes, Feb. 16, 1864, telegram book, REL HQ papers, VHS; REL to Cameron, Feb. 16, 1864, Lee family papers, VHS; Chilton commission, Chilton papers, LVA. Chilton ranked from Dec. 21, 1863.

22 OR 32, pt. 2, 760-1; OR 33, 1182-3.

Louisiana brigade, and writes Gen. Cooper on the same subject. Lee writes to President Davis regarding Longstreet's proposal to attack Knoxville; he favors sending Pickett to join Longstreet and also reinforcing Simon Buckner and drawing the Federals out of the city's fortifications to where they can be attacked: "It is very important to repossess ourselves of Tennessee, as also to take the initiative before our enemies are prepared to open the campaign." Lee requests that the War Department restore several units detached from Gen. Longstreet to his command, but tells Longstreet that reports of Sedgwick's corps going to Knoxville are incorrect, but if he does go west then reinforcements will be sent.[23]

Lee again rebukes Arnold Elzey for the incorrect information provided by his scouts, which resulted in the needless moving of Wade Hampton's cavalry and the wearing down of his horses. Lee approves of Hampton's decision to not move any farther in response to Elzey's reports, and he also approves of Hampton's suggestion to create a small mobile force in King William County drawn from the dismounted troopers of Hampton's command and the Marylanders at Hanover Junction. Lee orders an investigation into Gen. Seth Barton's conduct during the New Bern operations and advises Gen. Pickett that he has done so.[24]

February 19, Friday (Middle Hill): Lee sends the War Department the latest list of units to reenlist for the duration of the war, and notifies James Longstreet that the Philadelphia newspapers report that all of Ambrose Burnside's Pennsylvania units were sent home to raise additional recruits.[25]

February 20, Saturday (Middle Hill): Lee responds to a letter by Cary Robinson regarding his furlough and mentions his daughter-in-law Charlotte's death. The general also writes to his brother Carter lamenting the army's deteriorating supply situation, and passing along family news, including Charlotte's death and the death of cousin Charles Randolph at Kinloch, which Lee attributes to an illness he contracted while a prisoner at Old Capitol Prison. Lee's sister Anne Marshall dies in Baltimore.[26]

February 21, Sunday (Middle Hill): Gen. Lee receives a large package of baked goods from Col. Briscoe Baldwin's aunt and uncle, which he shares with the staff.[27]

February 22, Monday (Middle Hill/Orange/Richmond): In the morning Lee goes to Richmond by train to meet with President Davis and his new military advisor, Gen. Braxton Bragg. Maj. Venable notifies Gen. Ewell that he is in temporary command

---

23 REL to Ewell, Feb. 18, 1864, REL papers, W&L; *OR* 33, 1185-8; *OR* 32, pt. 2, 766; REL to Longstreet, Feb. 18, 1864, telegram book, REL HQ papers, VHS.

24 *OR* 33, 1185-7. Regarding Elzey's repeated cries of wolf, Venable wrote Hampton that Gen. Lee "has been very much annoyed by the false alarms from Richmond, and the distress which it has caused among the men and horses in moving during this winter season." *OR* 33, 1186. The difference in Lee's reaction to Pickett's report of New Bern and Hoke's report of the same operation was stark, praising Hoke's performance while saying little regarding Pickett's; Lee almost certainly intended for Hoke to be in overall command. See Selcer, *Lee vs. Pickett*, 58-62. In his report Pickett blamed Brig. Gen. Seth Barton for the failure. Barton served in the Shenandoah Valley and western Virginia before being transferred to command a brigade in the Western Theater. He was captured at Vicksburg and later given command of Lewis Armistead's former brigade under Pickett. Barton's conduct came under scrutiny once again, this time by Robert Ransom, for his actions at Drewry's Bluff in May 1864. Thereafter, Barton commanded a brigade in the Richmond defenses. Warner, *Generals in Gray*, 18-9.

25 *OR* 33, 1190; REL to Longstreet, Feb. 19, 1864, telegram book, REL HQ papers, VHS.

26 REL to Cary Robinson, Feb. 20, 1864, Robinson family papers, VHS; REL to C. C. Lee, Feb. 20, 1864, REL papers, W&L; Lee, *Lee of Virginia*, 342. Lee did not learn of his sister's death for more than two months. See entry for April 23, 1864.

27 Briscoe Baldwin to William & Mary Donaghe, Feb. 27, 1864, Robertson family papers, VHS. Baldwin informed his relatives that Lee "gave a dinner to his staff and the contents of your box ... was the bill of fare.... [Lee] was very much pleased with it, and especially so with the horse cakes which seemed to afford him more hearty pleasure and amusement than any present I have known him to receive." Ibid.

of the Army of Northern Virginia, and Gen. Chilton will be in charge of headquarters.[28]

February 23, Tuesday (Richmond): Lee joins President Davis and Mississippi Senator James Phelan for breakfast at the Executive Mansion where Phelan subjects Lee to a lengthy lecture on military strategy.[29]

February 24, Wednesday (Richmond): Bragg is officially placed in charge of the military operations of the Confederacy. Taylor telegraphs Lee regarding transportation for the portion of Rodes's command still at Hanover Junction.[30]

February 25, Thursday (Richmond/Drewry's Bluff): Lee, President Davis, Gen. Bragg, and Navy Secretary Stephen Mallory inspect the Richmond defenses, Drewry's Bluff, and a portion of the James River fleet. Marshall and Venable are both promoted to lieutenant colonel.[31]

February 26, Friday (Richmond): Lee meets with the president, and decides to transfer 1,000 men from the Army to the Navy to crew the new ironclads under construction in Richmond and elsewhere.[32]

February 27, Saturday (Richmond): In the morning Taylor notifies Lee that the Clark's Mountain signal station sighted an unusually large enemy column moving toward Madison. During the afternoon Venable goes atop the mountain to observe for himself and reports that it appears to be nothing more than a division changing its camp as no other camps show signs of movement; he adds that Stuart concurs in this assessment and does not regard the move as a serious threat.[33]

February 28, Sunday (Richmond): Lee attends morning church service at St. Paul's, where he is graciously welcomed by all those in attendance. Walter Taylor apprises Lee on the enemy's movements. The clouds obscure the view of the enemy's expansive camps from atop Clark's Mountain, he advises, but "camp fires at Brandy and Mitchell's last night as usual."[34]

---

28 Tower, *Lee's Adjutant*, 123; Venable to Ewell, Feb. 22, 1864, Polk-Ewell-Brown papers, UNC. Taylor complained, "I don't relish . . . old Mr. Ewell will be trotting around here and assuming the airs of General Commanding during the Tycoon's absence." Tower, *Lee's Adjutant*, 123.

29 Woodward, *Mary Chesnut's CW*, 573; Freeman, *Lee*, vol. 3, 218, 221.

30 *OR* 33, 1196; WHT to REL, Feb. 24, 1864, telegram book, REL HQ papers, VHS. Bragg's position was not unlike that which Lee had held in early 1862, the major difference being that the commanders of the three major forces in the field—Lee, Johnston, and Beauregard—all outranked him; unlike Lee in 1862, Bragg could not give these men direct orders.

31 Richmond *Daily Dispatch*, March 1, 1864; Krick, *Staff Officers in Gray*, 214, 292-3.

32 Jones, *Rebel War Clerk's Diary*, vol. 2, 159. Sec. Mallory and probably Sec. Seddon and/or Gen. Bragg were likely also part of this discussion, which was no doubt influenced by the inspection tour of the previous day.

33 WHT to REL, Feb. 27, 1864 (2 messages), telegram book, REL HQ papers, VHS.

34 Charleston *Mercury*, March 4, 1864; "Anne Farrar ancestor" diary, Feb. 28, 1864, Coulling papers, W&L; WHT to REL, Feb. 28, 1864, telegram book, REL HQ papers, VHS. Lee intended to return to the army today, but Taylor convinced him to delay a day to avoid traveling on Sunday. Tower, *Lee's Adjutant*, 128. Taylor was very irritated that Ewell and Chilton took no action regarding the enemy movements, and left it to him to inform Lee and/or make decisions: "In my great care and anxiety to avoid appearing unnecessarily excited or laying myself liable to the charge of being a 'stampeder,' I sometimes fear I may make my dispatches [to Lee] too moderate and sanguine. Gen. Ewell who is supposed to be in command doesn't relieve me at all, nor does my friend Chilton who terms himself 'Chief of Staff.' Neither has volunteered one single suggestion or in any way divided the responsibility. As for Gen. Ewell he is 15 miles away and though I have kept him regularly and constantly informed of the enemy's movements yesterday and today I am yet to hear the first word from him." Tower, *Lee's Adjutant*, 128. Ewell's HQ was at Morton Hall, near Morton's Ford. Pfanz, *Ewell*, 335. As an example of Taylor's initiative, he recalled Jubal Early to the army. WHT to Early, Feb. 28, 1864, telegram book, REL HQ papers, VHS.

February 29, Monday (Richmond/ Orange/ Middle Hill): Lee returns to Orange, narrowly avoiding capture as his train is the last to pass on the Virginia Central before Union cavalry cuts the railroad. He is joined on the train by Charles L. Powell and Edwin G. Lee; Powell notes that the general seems "distracted" and "nervous," constantly looking "through the windows on both sides of the car." Before Lee arrives back at headquarters, Taylor burns up the telegraph wires sending messages in every direction alerting commanders along the railroad of the potential danger and organizing troops to meet the threat; upon Lee's arrival Taylor briefs the general of what he has done and Lee approves. Lee alerts Richmond to the raid, and requests additional troops sent to Lynchburg. Rain.[35]

---

35 Taylor, *General Lee*, 228-9; Charles L. Powell to wife, March 5, 1864, Powell family papers, W&M; Tower, *Lee's Adjutant*, 129-30; *OR* 33, 1200; Richmond *Daily Dispatch*, March 4, 1864. Powell learned later that enemy cavalry struck the railroad at Fredericks Hall about 20 minutes after they passed, and then he understood Lee's curious behavior on the train. C. L. Powell to wife, March 5, 1864, Powell family papers, W&M. Taylor voiced his displeasure with Ewell and Chilton's inaction to Bettie: "I essayed one effort to procure assistance from our 'Chief of Staff,' but his reply to the first question I put to him was so muddy and exhibited such ignorance of the situation that I was convinced I was to receive no help from this quarter. I plucked up the necessary courage and on my own responsibility issued the orders for such movements as in my opinion the emergency required." Taylor was quite nervous about how Lee would react, but "to my infinite gratification and comfort, he had no fault to find." Tower, *Lee's Adjutant*, 130. As evidence of Taylor's activity, there are 15 messages from him (some signed by him and others not, but those had been sent before Lee returned and so must have been Taylor's doing) to various commanders ranging from captains to major generals in the HQ telegram book. REL HQ papers, VHS.

March 1864

The raid led by Union cavalry leaders Judson Kilpatrick and Ulric Dahlgren caused an uproar far out of proportion to the actual number of particants involved. They had come (unintentionally) close to capturing Robert E. Lee on his harried return to the army from Richmond at the end of February. Now that he was back with the army, the general set troops in motion to catch the various Yankee columns. Lee himself accompanied a portion of the army to Madison Court House, but the Federals there had too much of a head start and he abandoned the pursuit of that force after only one day. Back in Orange, he tried to arrange his chess pieces on a distant board to net Dahlgren and Kilpatrick. Ultimately, Dahlgren's force was cornered and its commander killed. Papers found on his body raised the stakes of the war, for they indicated that his mission was to assassinate Jefferson Davis and members of his cabinet, and free the Federal prisoners held in Richmond.[1]

Lee spent several days in Richmond discussing Dahlgren and where efforts should be concentrated for the spring campaigning season that was rapidly approaching. Something that almost certainly came up in the talks was the rumor—which would soon prove to be true—that Ulysses S. Grant was being promoted and he was coming east to lead the Union war effort.[2]

The struggle to keep the army fed and supplied continued, as did efforts to bolster the ranks as much as possible. In this latter effort Lee was aided by North Carolina Governor Zeb Vance, who spent a week with the army encouraging reenlistments and politicking on his own behalf.[3]

Lee's headquarters staff lost the services of Robert Chilton as chief of staff, who departed for a desk job in Richmond. His departure was little mourned by the rest of the staff.[4] Lee urged for the creation of a new engineer command with the Army of Northern Virginia and hoped to have his son Custis head it. At some point during the month Lee observed his engineers practice laying a pontoon bridge on a lake near headquarters. According to one eyewitness:

> General Lee, mounted on Traveller, was on a little hill to the right of the pond. Unattended save by one or two couriers, General Lee watched the men unload the pontoon boats, launch and connect them with the proper parts as the boats were pushed out across the pond. General Lee remained to see the bridge removed and the boats reloaded on the pontoon wagons, no detail of the drill escaping his attention.[5]

Lee climbed Clark's Mountain at least once during the month to observe the enemy's camps across the river in Culpeper County. Because the vista was so splendid he was seldom the only visitor, which made it difficult at times for the signalmen to attend to their duties. "We were in full

---

1 Many point to the "Dahlgren Papers" for justification for the original plot to kidnap Abraham Lincoln later in the war. The authenticity of the papers is still debated today.

2 Tower, *Lee's Adjutant*, 139-40.

3 Edward Warren, *A Doctor's Experiences in Three Continents* (Baltimore, MD, 1885), 314. One of the Governor's aides wrote that Lee told Vance his "visit to the army had been equivalent to its reinforcement by fifty thousand men." Ibid, 316.

4 Tower, *Lee's Adjutant*, 139-40. Chilton had been serving in a dual role of inspector general and chief of staff.

5 Burgess, "General Lee in Orange County." This was most likely "Farrar's Pond" near Meadow Farm.

view of the enemy's camp across the river," one signal officer wrote, "and hundreds of officers, citizens, and ladies used to visit the mountain top and our courtesy would be at times taxed to the utmost to show them the attention we wished to. General Lee would come up and spend hours studying the situation with his splendid glasses."[6]

Perhaps the most pleasing incident of the month of March was son Rooney's return from prison. Although his father could not be there in Richmond to welcome him when he climbed down from the train, President Davis and Governor Smith greeted him when he arrived.[7] Lee's reunion with his son came several days later.[8]

* * *

---

[6] Hurst, *Soldiers, Stories, Sites and Fights*, 165.

[7] Kimmel, *Mr. Davis's Richmond*, 172.

[8] Whether Rooney knew by this time that his wife Charlotte had died is not known; he may have learned of it from his mother or sisters once he arrived at the Franklin St. house.

March 1, Tuesday (Middle Hill/Orange/Mad-ison): Lee pursues one of the enemy columns toward Madison, but halts the pursuit that evening; he and the staff spend the night at an unknown house near Madison. Rooney leaves Fort Lafayette for Fort Monroe. Rain turning to snow in the evening.[9]

March 2, Wednesday (Madison/Orange/Middle Hill): In the morning Lee returns to Middle Hill, and remotely directs efforts to entrap another of the raiding columns in the Richmond vicinity, sending Ed Johnson's division to the Wilderness, Jeb Stuart's cavalry to Parker's Store, and Ambrose Wright's brigade to Fredericks Hall. Lee advises Richmond that he pursued the enemy beyond Madison but they escaped across the Robertson River; currently "All quiet in front."[10]

March 3, Thursday (Middle Hill): Lee fears that Gen. Ben Butler's forces on the Peninsula may be moving on Richmond to aid Kilpatrick's cavalry, so sends Stuart and Heth to reinforce Arnold Elzey at Richmond, but halts their movement when it becomes clear Butler is not moving. He advises Adjutant General Cooper of the steps taken to prevent Kilpatrick's return the way he came and requests to be kept informed of his movements.[11]

Lee instructs Armistead Long to have his artillerymen wintering along the railroad plus the Hanover Junction garrison assist in repairing the damage done by Kilpatrick. Lee advises Imboden that Averell may also attempt another raid and to use local troops to hold the mountain passes to buy time to assemble his forces, and sends Gen. Pendleton to Richmond for special assignment by the adjutant general's office. Lee forwards to Richmond Seth Barton's New Bern report with the notation, "I think it due to General Barton that a court of inquiry be granted him."[12]

Lee informs Gov. Joseph Brown that it is "injurious to the service" to grant furloughs to officers who are also members of the Georgia legislature, as doing so would leave Gen. Ambrose Wright's Georgia brigade under the command of a lieutenant colonel and remove every field officer from the 49th Georgia. "It would be better for members of [the] legislature to resign [their] military commissions," he explained. Rooney arrives at Fort Monroe and is immediately paroled and quartered in the Hygeia Hotel.[13]

March 4, Friday (Middle Hill): Lee advises Richmond of a reported enemy crossing at Ely's Ford near Chancellorsville, and instructs Stuart to investigate, while the troops around Richmond

---

9 Tower, *Lee's Adjutant*, 130-1; Daughtry, *Gray Cavalier*, 164. Walter Taylor was very critical of Lee's handling of this pursuit: "It was indeed piteous to see the heaviness, the indecision of our generals that afternoon. My chief is first rate in his sphere. . . . He has what few others possess, a head capable of planning a campaign and the ability to arrange for a battle, but he is not quick enough for such little affairs. . . . He is too undecided, takes too long to form his conclusions." Tower, *Lee's Adjutant*, 131. The Union activity was the Kilpatrick-Dahlgren raid; the column in Madison made a diversionary attack on Charlottesville before withdrawing, while Kilpatrick's and Dahlgren's separate columns moved on Richmond.

10 Tower, *Lee's Adjutant*, 131-2; *OR* 33, 1205; REL to A. R. Wright, March 2, 1864, telegram book, REL HQ papers, VHS; REL to A. L. Long, March 2, 1864 (3 messages), telegram book, REL HQ papers, VHS; *OR* 33, 1204-5. Taylor learned on this date that Chilton would indeed leave Lee's staff; he had been confirmed as a brigadier general, but the date of his rank was not satisfactory to him. Taylor was concerned that regardless of whom the new chief of staff turned out to be, he would be more difficult to work with than Chilton. Tower, *Lee's Adjutant*, 132.

11 *OR* 33, 1206; REL to Heth, March 3, 1864, telegram book, REL HQ papers, VHS: REL to Samuel Cooper, March 3, 1864, telegram book, REL HQ papers, VHS; REL to Elzey, March 3, 1864, telegram book, REL HQ papers, VHS.

12 REL to Long, March 3, 1864, telegram book, REL HQ papers, VHS: REL to Imboden, March 3, 1864, telegram book, REL HQ papers, VHS; Freeman, *Lee's Dispatches*, 137-8; *OR* 33, 97-100. Barton and Pickett pointed fingers at each other for the failure in North Carolina.

13 REL to Brown, March 3, 1864, telegram book, REL HQ papers, VHS; Daughtry, *Gray Cavalier*, 164; Rooney CSR. Pendleton was sent to the Army of Tennessee to inspect its artillery and advise how best to reorganize and improve its efficiency overall. Lee, *Memoirs of WNP*, 314.

repair the damage done by Kilpatrick to the railroads and telegraph lines.[14]

March 5, Saturday (Middle Hill): Lee informs Gen. Cooper that the enemy is crossing at Ely's Ford and that "troops are there to meet them," and also sends a list of the latest units to reenlist for the war. Lee advises Imboden that scouts report B&O officials being notified of a large troop movement in the immediate future. Sec. Seddon writes to Lee regarding papers found on the body of Union Col. Ulric Dahlgren, ordering the execution of Jefferson Davis and other officials; Seddon favors executing all the prisoners captured from Dahlgren's command and requests Lee's views.[15]

March 6, Sunday (Middle Hill): Lee responds to Seddon regarding the Dahlgren papers: "Formal publication of these papers should be made . . . that our people and the world may know the character of the war our enemies wage against us, and the unchristian and atrocious acts they plot and perpetrate." However, Lee does not support executing the prisoners, as there is no proof that Dahlgren acted with the knowledge of the government.[16]

March 7, Monday (Middle Hill): Lee telegraphs a J. G. Baker in Richmond.[17]

March 8, Tuesday (Middle Hill): Gen. Lee notifies the garrisons at Richmond, Hanover Junction, Fredericks Hall, and Milford of an enemy force reported in King & Queen County. Lee sends James Longstreet a lengthy letter regarding Western Theater issues; The general notes the impossibility of mounting Longstreet's command as the Georgian had proposed, and suggests that Longstreet and Joe Johnston unite to retake Tennessee: "A victory gained there will open the country to you to the Ohio." Lee forwards two of Mosby's reports for recent raids, and approves an extension of William Mahone's leave for the Virginia legislative session.[18]

March 9, Wednesday (Middle Hill/Orange): Lee proposes the creation of five regiments of local reserves along the Blue Ridge range, and advises Armistead Long at Fredericks Hall that the reported enemy raiders are very small in number and that the troops have been ordered back to camp. Lee thanks Rev. Charles Minnigerode for sending a donation to be used in purchasing artificial limbs for amputees. In the evening, the general dines with Gen. and Mrs.

---

14 REL to Cooper, March 4, 1864, telegram book, REL HQ papers, VHS; REL to Stuart, March 4, 1864 (2 messages), telegram book, REL HQ papers, VHS; REL to P. M. B. Young, March 4, 1864, telegram book, REL HQ papers, VHS; REL to A. L. Long, March 4, 1864, telegram book, REL HQ papers, VHS; *OR* 33, 1209.

15 *OR* 33, 1210; Freeman, *Lee's Dispatches*, 138-9; REL to Imboden, March 5, 1864, telegram book, REL HQ papers, VHS; *OR* 33, 218. Dahlgren was turned back just west of Richmond, on the modern-day grounds of the Country Club of Virginia and University of Richmond, by troops commanded by Custis; Dahlgren then skirted north of the capital and was ambushed and killed near King & Queen Court House on the night of March 2, 1864. For more on Dahlgren's Raid see Virgil C. Jones, *Eight Hours Before Richmond* (New York, 1957) and Eric J. Wittenberg, *Like a Meteor Blazing Brightly: The Short but Controversial Life of Colonel Ulric Dahlgren* (El Dorado Hills, 2019).

16 *OR* 33, 222-3.

17 REL to Baker, March 7, 1864, telegram book, REL HQ papers, VHS. Nothing was recorded regarding the contents or the subject of this message. A "J. G. Baker" was affiliated with the American Bible Society and was also involved with the distribution of Bibles to Confederate prisoners held at Point Lookout, so it is quite possible that this was the individual in question. Association of [Gettysburg] Licensed Battlefield Guides, *Battlefield Dispatch* (Dec. 2012), vol. 30, No. 4, 7. It is likely that the general spent much of the day looking through and considering the captured and incendiary Dahlgren papers.

18 REL to Elzey, March 8, 1864, telegram book, REL HQ papers, VHS; REL to Bradley Johnson, March 8, 1864, telegram book, REL HQ papers, VHS; REL to A. L. Long, March 8, 1864, telegram book, REL HQ papers, VHS; REL to Wade Hampton, March 8, 1864, telegram book, REL HQ papers, VHS; *OR* 32, pt. 3, 594-5; *OR* 33, 157-60; WHT to Mahone, March 8, 1864, telegram book, REL HQ papers, VHS. Mahone was named to the Virginia General Assembly in 1863 but remained with the army until it went into winter quarters. John F. Chappo, "William Mahone of Virginia: An Intellectual Biography," PhD Thesis, University of Southern Mississippi, 2007, 118-9.

Stuart, Williams Wickham, and Jeb Stuart's staff at the cavalryman's headquarters.[19]

March 10, Thursday (Middle Hill): Lee thanks Rev. Moses D. Hoge for a Bible. Rain.[20]

March 11, Friday (Middle Hill): Lee forwards the report of Lt. James Pollard, 9th Virginia Cavalry, of the ambush of Dahlgren, commending Pollard for his actions. He writes to Col. Edward S. Willis about the Kilpatrick-Dahlgren raid and hopes to have Willis back with the army soon. Rooney arrives at City Point on a flag of truce steamer, and is greeted by President Davis and Gov. Smith.[21]

March 12, Saturday (Middle Hill/Orange/Richmond): Lee leaves in the morning for Richmond. In the evening Taylor advises Lee by telegram that Hampton reports enemy cavalry burned the King & Queen Courthouse then withdrew to Gloucester.[22]

March 13, Sunday (Richmond): Lee attends church at St. Paul's, where more than a dozen generals are in attendance, including Bragg, Longstreet, and John Hunt Morgan.[23]

March 14, Monday (Richmond): In the morning Lee meets with President Davis, Sec. Seddon, and Gen. Bragg regarding strategy in the West. In the afternoon Lee brings Longstreet into the conversation.[24]

---

19 *OR* 33, 1212; REL to Long, March 9, 1864, telegram book, REL HQ papers, VHS; REL to C. E. Minnigerode, March 9, 1864, REL papers, MOC; J. E. Cooke diary, March 9, 1864, Duke.

20 REL to M. D. Hoge, March 10, 1864, REL papers, MOC; Betts, *Experiences of a CS Chaplain*, 57. This may be the Bible in the Lee collection at W&L, which is signed by both Lee and Hoge.

21 *OR* 33, 208-9; REL to Willis, March 11, 1864, Hunter McGuire papers, VHS; Rooney CSR; Kimmel, *Mr. Davis's Richmond*, 172. A member of Lee's HQ guard wrote that Lee "was visited [by] one of the great generals of the west. I will not give any names, but I will describe him." The description could be several generals who were known to be in or around Richmond at that time, including both John Hunt Morgan and James Longstreet. Thomas G. Lupton to wife, March 12, 1864, T. G. Lupton papers, Handley Library. It seems odd that Longstreet would be referred to as a "western general," but no one on the staff recorded the presence of Morgan, which would have been noteworthy, while Longstreet's presence would not have been unusual. A correspondent for the Charleston *Mercury* noted on the 14th, "Longstreet arrived at Lee's headquarters unexpectedly, just as Lee was about to dispatch a courier to him." Charleston *Mercury*, March 21, 1864. Longstreet and his aide Sorrel both mention that Longstreet was called to Richmond to meet with Lee and Davis, and that Longstreet first met with Lee, so there is strong circumstantial evidence that the mystery visitor was in fact James Longstreet, although the possibility of it being John Hunt Morgan cannot be ruled out. Longstreet, *From Manassas to Appomattox*, 544-5; Sorrel, *Recollections*, 229. Whoever it was stayed overnight at Lee's HQ and left the morning of the 12th. Lupton to wife, March 12, 1864, Lupton papers, Handley Library. Willis, colonel of the 12th GA Infantry, was mortally wounded during the Overland Campaign at Bethesda Church on May 30, 1864, and died the following day. Krick, *Lee's Colonels*, 401.

22 Tower, *Lee's Adjutant*, 135-6; WHT to REL, March 12, 1864, telegram book, REL HQ papers, VHS. A passenger on Lee's train observed that the general "is affable, polite, and unassuming, and shares the discomforts of a crowded railroad coach with ordinary travelers. He travels without staff or other attendant. He is first to rise and offer his seat to ladies, if any difficulty occurs in seating them. He talks freely about affairs generally, but had little to say ... concerning the army and the country. At one station where an eager crowd was gazing at him he suddenly remarked, 'I suppose these people are speculating as to what is on foot now.' He speaks quickly, sometimes brusquely, and with the tone of one who is accustomed to command. . . . He wore a Colonel's coat (three stars without the wreath), a good deal faded, blue pantaloons, high top boots, blue cloth talma and high felt hat, without adornment save a small cord around the crown." Unknown publication, March 19, 1864, REL newspaper references, DSF papers, LVA. Lee stayed at the Franklin St. house, Mary and the girls having moved in with Custis earlier in the year. See entry dated Dec. 22, 1863. Rose M. E. MacDonald, *Mrs. Robert E. Lee* (Arlington, VA, 1973), 176.

23 Woodward, *Mary Chesnut's CW*, 585-6; "Anne Farrar ancestor" diary, March 13, 1864, Coulling papers, W&L; Charleston *Mercury*, March 21, 1864; Jones, *Rebel War Clerk's Diary*, vol. 2, 170-1. Other generals present included Robert Hoke, Thomas Clingman, John Pegram, Arnold Elzey and possibly Chase Whiting and John B. Hood. Woodward, *Mary Chesnut's CW*, 585-6; Charleston *Mercury*, March 21, 1864.

24 Longstreet, *From Manassas to Appomattox*, 544-5; *OR* 32, pt. 3, 641. Longstreet's account of this meeting is tainted against both Davis and Bragg. According to Mrs. Lee's biographer, the general attended church service every morning

March 15, Tuesday (Richmond): Lee continues to meet with President Davis, and is observed walking the streets of the capital with his brother Sydney Smith Lee and Rooney.[25]

March 16, Wednesday (Richmond): Lee remains in Richmond visiting with his family.[26]

March 17, Thursday (Richmond/Orange/Middle Hill): Lee returns to ANV headquarters bringing with him several dozen pairs of socks made by Mary and the girls for the army's use, and finds more socks and several packages of food awaiting him in camp.[27]

March 18, Friday (Middle Hill): Lee writes to Mary that he is back in camp and found more socks and all sorts of food sent him by cousins and admirers. He sends a box of food to her via Bryan, who leaves for Richmond today. He writes also to cousin Julia Calvert Stuart thanking her for the socks, which are distributed to the Stonewall Brigade.[28]

March 19, Saturday (Middle Hill): Lee writes Imboden regarding two "scouts," who claim to have information regarding enemy movements; Lee does not know or trust either of them and orders that one of them not be allowed into Confederate lines and grants Imboden discretion to deal with the other as he chooses. He writes to cousin Carrie Stuart, thanking her for mending his coat and jokes about setting her up with Gen. Ed Johnson.[29]

March 20, Sunday (Middle Hill/Orange): Lee attends church service in the morning at St. Thomas's, accompanied by A. P. Hill, Jeb Stuart, and Edward Johnson. Lee writes to cousin Margaret Stuart with family news, and mentions that both Jubal Early and Ed Johnson asked about her. He writes also to Mary, acknowledging her latest shipment of socks for the Stonewall Brigade, and sends one of his coats to be repaired. Taylor writes of the rumors of U. S. Grant taking command in Virginia, but holds a very low opinion of Grant's abilities, and mentions also that Chilton has left the staff, leaving only himself, Marshall, and Venable.[30]

March 21, Monday (Middle Hill/Clark's Mountain): Lee goes atop Clark's Mountain to observe the Army of the Potomac and rides a portion of the lines along the Rapidan River. He writes to Mrs. Bettie Land of Ninety-Six, South Carolina, declining to excuse her husband from the ranks, explaining, "The time is now near at hand when every good man should be at his post. . . . If he and his fellow soldiers will display as I doubt not they will, the patriotic spirit that animates yourself, I trust the day is not far distant

---

before breakfast during this stay in Richmond because it was Lent, though she did not provide a source for this. MacDonald, *Mrs. REL*, 176.

25 Tower, *Lee's Adjutant*, 136; Woodward, *Mary Chesnut's CW*, 586. Lee intended to return to the army today, but for unknown reasons did not, and possibly did not advise Ewell, Taylor, or anyone else that he changed his plans; Taylor certainly did not know and asked the head of the Virginia Central if Lee was on the morning train for Orange. Tower, *Lee's Adjutant*, 136; WHT to H. D. Whitcomb, March 15, 1864, telegram book, REL HQ papers, VHS.

26 Freeman, *Lee*, vol. 3, 261-2. No documentation has been found for Lee's activities on this date, so Freeman conjectured that he spent the day with his family, although Lee himself lamented that he saw little of Rooney while in Richmond. Dowdey, *Wartime Papers*, 679.

27 Dowdey, *Wartime Papers*, 679.

28 Dowdey, *Wartime Papers*, 679-80; REL to J. C. Stuart, March 18, 1864, REL papers, VHS.

29 *OR* 33, 1233; REL to Carrie Stuart, March 19, 1864, REL papers, VHS. The mention of Carrie Stuart mending Lee's coat suggests that she visited the army again; it is possible that she was the one mistaken for Lee's daughter on Jan. 20. See Leon, *Diary of a Tar Heel*, 56.

30 George M. Coiner to Kate Coiner, March 20, 1864, Coiner family papers, VHS; REL to Margaret Stuart, March 20, 1864, REL papers, UVA; Dowdey, *Wartime Papers*, 680; Tower, *Lee's Adjutant*, 139-40. Chilton departed for Richmond on/about the 18th, but his resignation and separation from Lee's staff did not become official until April 1, 1864. Robert K. Krick, "Robert Hall Chilton," in *Confederate General*, vol. 1, 185.

when they may all return to the homes which it is now their first duty to defend."³¹

March 22, Tuesday (Middle Hill/Orange): Lee attends a chaplain's meeting in Orange. Heavy snow accumulates to 18 inches in places.³²

March 23, Wednesday (Middle Hill): Lee writes to Sec. Seddon requesting the recent Congressional action abolishing military courts in favor of courts martial be reversed and that military courts be reinstated. Lee approves of John C. Breckinridge's plan to fortify the approaches into southwestern Virginia, adding that he does not know where the dividing lines between different departments in that region are: "I have therefore considered the line between them imaginary." Lee issues orders refining the process for applying for furlough, and thanks a Granville G. Elliott for a pipe he recently sent. In the evening Lee receives a letter from Chilton that he is leaving Lee's staff to take a position on Adjutant General Cooper's staff in Richmond.³³

March 24, Thursday (Middle Hill): Lee forwards to the War Department Jeb Stuart's recommendation to promote Rooney to major general to command a new cavalry division, and sends a lengthy letter to Chilton expressing his regret at losing his services. The general writes to a Mrs. J. S. Heiskell thanking her for the use of the table linens she provided for headquarters and apologizes that they have not been returned, but promises to find out what has become of them. He receives a package of socks from Mary, and writes back with latest family news and jokes about Mildred's pet squirrel "Custis Morgan" becoming soup.³⁴

March 25, Friday (Middle Hill): Lee writes to Davis that he thinks the major enemy effort will be made outside of Virginia and based on latest reports from Imboden that they likely intend to concentrate against either Johnston or Longstreet, and he has nothing to indicate a renewed effort against Richmond and suspects that the rumors of Grant taking command in Virginia are a ruse. Governor Vance comes to Orange to meet with the North Carolina troops in Lee's army. Heavy rain and hail in the afternoon.³⁵

March 26, Saturday (Middle Hill): Lee joins Ewell, Hill, Johnson, and Rodes for Gov. Vance's address to Daniel's and Ramseur's brigades. Lee proposes to

---

31 Dowdey, *Wartime Papers*, 681; REL to Bettie Land, March 21, 1864, Robert A. Siegel Auctions, Lot #2073, Dec. 8, 2004 auction.

32 Betts, *Experiences of CS Chaplain*, 57.

33 OR 3, Series 4, 246-7; OR 33, 1239; GO21, March 23, 1864, WHT papers, VMI; REL to G. G. Elliott, March 23, 1864, REL HQ papers, VHS; REL to Chilton, March 24, 1864, Chilton papers, MOC. A member of the HQ Guard noted that there was "heavy skirmishing in camp with snow balls" from yesterday's snow. F. G. Walter diary, March 23, 1864, LVA. This pipe from Elliott is probably the one Lee referenced in a letter to Mary on the 24th: "I have had a present of a very pretty pipe. It is beautifully carved, made by a Mississippian in camp, with his penknife." Dowdey, *Wartime Papers*, 681.

34 Stuart to REL, March 23, 1864, Rooney CSR, NA; REL to Chilton, March 24, 1864, Chilton papers, MOC; REL to J. S. Heiskell, March 24, 1864, REL papers, UVA; Dowdey, *Wartime Papers*, 680-1. Lee told Chilton: "I have as yet thought of no one to succeed you in this army, preferring instead to wait till it should be decided that you would leave it. I shall miss your ever ready aid and regret your departure. You have been untiring in the discharge of your duties, honest in your purpose and earnest in your efforts to promote the good of the service." REL to Chilton, March 24, 1864, Chilton papers, MOC.

35 Dowdey, *Wartime Papers*, 682-4; Charleston *Mercury*, March 25, 1864; F. G. Walter diary, March 25, 1864, LVA. Few details are known about Lee's interaction with Vance during his visit to the army, but certainly Lee would have met with him upon his arrival. For more on Vance's visit to the army, see Max Williams, "The General and the Governor," in Carmichael, *Audacity Personified*, 107-132. The Charleston *Mercury* published a short article on this date about the city of Richmond's offer of a house to Lee: "The papers lately published Gen. Lee's letter, refusing a house which was to be bought for him. The matter was not delicately managed. [The] Common Council voted $60,000 for the house and then a subscription for the furniture was started, which reached $20,000 and there stopped. Meantime, the subject had been noised abroad in the newspapers, placing Gen. Lee in the attitude of a dependent, if not supplicant. His family now resides in one of the largest and handsomest houses in Franklin street." Charleston *Mercury*, March 25, 1864.

Sec. Seddon that bonds be used to pay for certain military expenditures rather than Confederate currency. Dr. Robert Peyton of Fairfax visits Lee in the evening bearing news of his wife and daughters; he spends the night at headquarters.[36]

March 27, Sunday (Middle Hill/Orange): In the morning Lee and Taylor attend church service at St. Thomas's; Fitz Lee returns with them to headquarters and Lee invites three young officers wives with whom they rode out of town to join them for lunch. Lee writes to Mary in the evening, mentioning Gov. Vance's visit to the army, the gifts he receives from admirers including a large box of food from Mrs. W. T. Harmon: "I fear people impoverish themselves on our account." He also chides her for continued incorrect accounting when she sends socks, gloves, and other items and points out that her poor arithmetic puts the courier in a difficult position where he could be blamed for any apparent loss.[37]

March 28, Monday (Middle Hill): Lee and Gov. Vance review all the North Carolina troops in Ewell's and Hill's corps, and Vance delivers a 4-hour oration to the men with Lee turning down a call to speak. Lee writes to Longstreet that he was wrong about Grant, that he is to command in Virginia and that Burnside's corps is at Annapolis; he advises that little can be provided in the way of animal tack for his command and that overall, the growing supply shortage will limit what moves the armies are able to undertake when the spring campaign begins: "The great obstacle everywhere is scarcity of supplies. That is the controlling element to which everything has to yield."[38]

March 29, Tuesday (Middle Hill): Lee writes to Sec. Seddon regarding exporting goods, what can be passed through the lines, and how that could be done. Lee writes to Margaret Stuart with an update on the military situation, and sends a letter to son Custis congratulating him on his nomination to succeed Arnold Elzey as commander of Richmond as well as for command in the Valley. Lee tells him "I would rather have you there [Richmond] than any one I could now select," and offers him the position of the army's chief engineer if he does not want the Richmond command. Rooney returns to duty. Rain.[39]

March 30, Wednesday (Middle Hill): Lee informs the president that he is now convinced Grant is with the Army of the Potomac and will launch a major offensive in Virginia, in addition to a move up the Valley; he argues that if an offensive movement is made in the West it will disrupt Grant's plans but if one is not undertaken Lee needs Longstreet and Hoke returned, and possibly additional troops sent to the Valley. Lee requests the Engineer Bureau to

---

36 Leon, *Diary of a Tar Heel*, 58; Richmond *Daily Dispatch*, March 28, 1864; Hubbs, *Voices from Company D*, 231; OR 3, Series 4, 253-4; REL to Mrs. REL, March 27, 1864, REL papers, LOC.

37 Tower, *Lee's Adjutant*, 143-4; REL to Mrs. REL, March 27, 1864, REL papers, LOC. Vance may have reviewed and addressed Ramseur's Brigade on this date. Gary W. Gallagher, *Stephen Dodson Ramseur: Lee's Gallant General* (Chapel Hill, NC, 1995), 91.

38 Warren, *Doctor's Experiences*, 314-5; Leon, *Diary of a Tar Heel*, 58; Collins, *Rodes*, 340; OR 52, pt. 2, 648-9. It is not known where the review took place, but it may have been at Greenfields, where previous reviews occurred, due to its proximity to both the town and Lee's headquarters.

39 OR 51, pt. 2, 842-3; Lee, *Recollections and Letters of REL*, 123; Dowdey, *Wartime Papers*, 685-7; James A. Graham to mother, April 2, 1864, J. A. Graham papers, UNC. Lee was steadfast against nepotism and wanted his sons to rise on their own merit; Custis being named as a possibility to supersede Imboden in the Shenandoah and Elzey at Richmond were both Jefferson Davis's doing, although Custis declined both offers. Davis wrote years later that he may have consulted with Lee about the Valley command, although he couldn't remember, "but the reason why Custis Lee was not assigned . . . is that he made such objection to it as to cause me to change my purpose. . . . After hearing that I had proposed to assign him to command in western Virginia he silently withdrew to the aide's room and there stated his objection to going in such terms as caused one or more of you to repeat his expressions to me with the hope that the order would be changed." Davis to William P. Johnston, Oct. 6, 1883, in Preston Johnston, "Some Post War Letters from Jefferson Davis to his Former Aide de Camp, William Preston Johnston," *VMHB* (April 1943), 158-9.

assign the 1st Engineer Regiment to the ANV and to create six pioneer companies, all under the command of the chief engineer of the ANV, and that either Maj. Gen. Martin Smith, Col. W. H. Stevens, or Custis be assigned that position. Lee declares April 8 as a day of fasting and prayer, and receives from Adj. Gen. Samuel Cooper copies of the Dahlgren papers and directions to write Meade to determine the authenticity of the documents. Lee dines with Stuart and Rooney, and afterward writes to Mary, thanking her for the latest batch of socks and sharing the latest military news.[40]

---

40 OR 33, 233, 1244-6; Dowdey, *Wartime Papers*, 687. Gov. Vance addressed the North Carolina units of Jeb Stuart's command on this date, but Lee declined to attend. Dowdey, *Wartime Papers*, 687.

April 1864

As the spring campaigning season drew closer, much of Robert E. Lee's time was devoted to sifting through the reports pouring into headquarters of enemy troop movements. The first order of business was to determine where the Federals were concentrating, and where they were vulnerable to attack, which was relatively easy compared to convincing Richmond to shift troops around where Lee believed they were needed. "We have to sift a variety of reports before reaching the truth," was how Lee explained the many conflicting reports to President Davis.[1]

Lee lobbied hard not only for the return of units detached from his army—such as James Longstreet's First Corps troops then operating in Tennessee, and George Pickett's and Robert Hoke's men in North Carolina—but also began to sound somewhat like Gen. P. G. T. Beauregard when he pushed for large-scale concentrations across the map. (Unlike many of Beauregard's similar proposals, however, Lee's were feasible). While some of his detached brigades remained in North Carolina, the return of Longstreet and his two divisions was most welcome. When Lee reviewed these troops in late April, the officers and men made it clear they were just as glad to be back with the Army of Northern Virginia as Lee was to have them once more on his roster.

Supply remained a constant problem and one that increasingly concerned Lee. This issue did not just affect enlisted men, but officers all the way up to the army's headquarters, as one observer noted:

> In General Lee's tent meat was eaten twice a week. His bill of fare was a head of cabbage boiled in salt water, sweet potatoes, and a pone of corn bread; when he invited an officer to dinner, he had to his astonishment four inches of middling—everyone refused from politeness, and the servant excused the smallness of the piece by saying it was borrowed.[2]

Very soon after Longstreet's return, his chief commissary, Maj. Raphael Moses, was dispatched to Georgia in hopes that he might be able to scare up supplies for Lee's army using his personal connections in his home state:

> I carried my furlough to Lee's headquarters . . . which were nearby. There was never any difficulty about approaching Lee. He had very little red tape routine. He was writing in his tent. When I entered he looked up with a friendly smile and said, "Major, what will you have?" I handed him the furlough. He read it and said, "Major I would approve it but really we can't spare you." I then explained to him my plans. He hesitated a moment or two and then said, "Well Major, if you think you can do anything for my poor boys, go and may God crown your effort with success." He approved my furlough and I started for Georgia.[3]

* * *

---

1 OR 33, 1268-9.

2 Varina Davis, *Jefferson Davis*, vol. 2, 532. Middling is a product of the wheat milling process, made from the protein/starchy part of the grain, but is not flour.

3 Moses memoirs, 50-1, UNC. Joe Johnston likely would have balked at this blatant raiding of his source of supplies, and it is odd that Lee did not take this into consideration because he did not hesitate at times from complaining about commissaries procuring supplies outside their areas.

April 1, Friday (Middle Hill): Lee writes to George Meade regarding the papers found on Ulric Dahlgren's body, and recommends to Adjutant General Cooper that all partisan units in Virginia—except Mosby—be disbanded and the men put into regular units. He forwards to Richmond the report of Capt. Thaddeus Fitzhugh, 5th Virginia Cavalry, of a combined raid with the Navy across the Chesapeake Bay to the Eastern Shore, resulting in the capture of several vessels. In the evening Lee meets with Gen. Pendleton for several hours, who just returned from an inspection of the Army of Tennessee's artillery; due to the lateness of the hour and the weather, Lee urges Pendleton to stay the night at headquarters but he declines. Lt. Col. Talcott is promoted to colonel and given command of the 1st Confederate Engineer Regiment. Snow.[4]

April 2, Saturday (Middle Hill): Lt. Samuel B. Davis delivers the original Dahlgren papers to Lee. The general writes to President Davis summing up Pendleton's findings in Joe Johnston's Army of Tennessee and urges again that an offensive be undertaken in the West. He reports increased troop activity on the B&O indicating reinforcements in the Valley and also probably to Meade, and that Longstreet reports Burnside gone from Knoxville; accordingly he wants Longstreet returned to the ANV and reinforcements for Johnston instead to come from the Gulf and Charleston. He sends a short note to Mary, including an update on their sock production: by his count 263 pairs sent by her and the girls have been issued to the Stonewall Brigade. Snow continues.[5]

April 3, Sunday (Middle Hill): Lee asks Joe Johnston if the XI and XII Corps are in his front as Lee's scouts report them on the Rappahannock. Lee acknowledges receipt of the original Dahlgren papers from Richmond, and receives a letter from Agnes. He replies to Agnes advising her against coming to visit him at Orange as a battle could begin any day. He writes also to Mary complaining about the weather, which prevented Gov. Vance from seeing the troops the last few days, and lamenting her inability to correctly count socks.[6]

April 4, Monday (Middle Hill): Lee writes a lengthy letter to the secretary of war objecting to the policy of exempting men from service due to "extreme hardship," stating, "It is impossible to equalize the burdens of this war; some must suffer more than others." Lee informs Treasury Secretary Christopher Memminger that he approves of the transfer of Memminger's son, but those orders must come from the adjutant general in Richmond and not Lee. Heavy rain turns to snow during the night.[7]

April 5, Tuesday (Middle Hill): Gov. Vance leaves the army to return to Raleigh. Lee informs Davis that he thinks it likely that the main Federal effort will be made in Virginia, thus he needs Longstreet's corps returned, and he sends Sec. Seddon his suggestions regarding officer examination boards. Lee issues the specifications regarding transportation and baggage

---

4 OR 33, 178, 232, 1252; OR 32, pt. 3, 736; Krick, *Staff Officers in Gray*, 279; Lee, *Memoirs of WNP*, 319. Meade replied on April 17 that neither he, Kilpatrick, nor anyone in Washington authorized the assassination of Jefferson Davis or any member of his cabinet. OR 33, 180. Freeman wrote that Talcott left Lee on April 3, which may be the date he actually took command of the engineers. Freeman, *Lee*, vol. 1, 642. Chilton's resignation became official on this date. Chilton CSR, NA.

5 OR 33, 224, 1254-5; OR 32, pt. 736-7; Fitz Lee, *General Lee*, 325; Lee, *Memoirs of WNP*, 319. Lee stated only that a "Lt. Davis" of Gen. John Winder's staff delivered the papers; Samuel Boyer Davis is the only "Davis" on Winder's staff, so presumably he is the officer in question. Krick, *Staff Officers in Gray*, 111.

6 REL to Johnston, April 3, 1864, telegram book, REL HQ papers, VHS; OR 33, 224; Dowdey, *Wartime Papers*, 689-90; REL to Mrs. REL, April 3, 1864, REL papers, LOC. Taylor wrote that Lee was somewhat depressed about the outlook for the spring campaign, and the two of them had a long talk in Lee's tent, which concluded with Lee saying, "But Col. we have got to whip them, we must whip them and it has already made me better to think of it." Tower, *Lee's Adjutant*, 148.

7 OR 33, 1256-7; REL to C. G. Memminger, April 4, 1864, telegram book, REL HQ papers, VHS; F. G. Walter diary, April 4, 1864, LVA. Lt. Christopher G. Memminger, Jr., was court-martialed by Gen. Roswell Ripley in March of 1863 and as a result transferred to Virginia, where he served on Gen. Richard Anderson's staff. Memminger received a transfer back to his native South Carolina in late April of 1864. Krick, *Staff Officers in Gray*, 220.

allocations for the coming campaign. Very heavy rain continues, ending during the night.[8]

April 6, Wednesday (Middle Hill): Lee writes to President Davis regarding Col. Edward O'Neal, who continues to complain about being passed over for promotion; Lee cannot spare personnel for a court of inquiry as O'Neal requests, and since O'Neal and his regiment were transferred west two months ago Lee knows nothing about his current situation. Lee has dinner with Jeb Stuart. Rain resumes in the morning, ending in the afternoon.[9]

April 7, Thursday (Middle Hill): Lee informs Braxton Bragg of the various reports from his scouts, and requests again that Gens. Hoke and R. D. Johnston's brigades be returned. He proposes to Custis using Col. J. T. Wood's naval force and the 9th Virginia Cavalry to attack the Union Navy on the St. Mary's River in southeastern Maryland, and sends President Davis a lengthy list of deserters facing execution; Lee wants Davis's concurrence in suspending their sentences. Lee issues a circular to the army regarding what the men should do if captured. The general sends Margaret Stuart a Confederate flag pincushion. Rain.[10]

April 8, Friday (Middle Hill): Lee informs President Davis that he has reliable reports that no large units (ie XI and XII Corps) have joined the Army of the Potomac, although black troops replaced some of the white troops around Washington which are thought to have joined Meade's army. Lee learns from Richmond that Maj. Gen. Martin L. Smith will be his army's new chief engineer, and he receives a package of socks from Mary. Rain.[11]

April 9, Saturday (Middle Hill): Lee tells the president that Mosby reports additional troops going to Meade's army from elsewhere, and requests that a large shipment of cavalry weapons just run through the blockade into Wilmington, North Carolina, be shipped to Orange for Stuart's men. Lee sends a long letter to son Custis: now that Martin L. Smith is chief engineer, he sees no way to have Custis join him; he does not want Custis as chief of staff because of potential charges of nepotism. Lee respects Custis's reasons for declining the Richmond command, but admonishes that he will never be qualified for a field command unless he actually takes one. He mentions also that he thinks Brig. Gen. William Mahone would likely do well in charge of railroads for the government. He writes also to his wife Mary to share family news, and advises that once the Stonewall Brigade has all the socks it requires, Mahone's 61st Virginia will be the next recipient. Rain all day.[12]

April 10, Sunday (Middle Hill): Lee informs Adjutant General Samuel Cooper that he wrote to Union Gen. Meade regarding the Dahlgren papers on April 1 as instructed, but due to the rains the rivers are flooded and so prevented anyone from crossing under a flag of truce. The general does not know when it will be possible to convey the letter across the lines. Rain continues.[13]

---

8 Carmichael, *Audacity Personified*, 108; OR 33, 1260-4; F. G. Walter diary, April 5, 1864, LVA. Lee attended only a few of Gov. Vance's speeches to the troops, while Jeb Stuart attended most and perhaps all of them. J. A. Graham to mother, April 2, 1864, Graham papers, UNC. Stuart brought Lee a pamphlet of some sort in the morning. C. S. Venable to Stuart, April 5, 1864, H. B. McClellan CSR.

9 Freeman, *Lee's Dispatches*, 146-8; OR 33, 1265; F. G. Walter diary, April 6, 1864, LVA. Lee was spotted during the evening riding alone on the Plank Road; this may have been before or after dinner with Stuart. Hubbs, *Voices from Company D*, 239.

10 OR 33, 1265-7; Freeman, *Lee's Dispatches*, 149-54; Long, *Memoirs of REL*, 350-1; Tower, *Lee's Adjutant*, 151.

11 OR 33, 1267; Dowdey, *Wartime Papers*, 694-5; Tower, *Lee's Adjutant*, 151. Smith was appointed on April 6, but Lee was not made aware of this until the 8th. OR 33, 1265.

12 OR 33, 1268-9; REL to A. R. Lawton, April 9, 1864, telegram book, REL HQ papers, VHS; REL to Gorgas, April 9, 1864, telegram book, REL HQ papers, VHS; Dowdey, *Wartime Papers*, 694-6; F. G. Walter diary, April 9, 1864, LVA.

13 OR 33, 224; Tower, *Lee's Adjutant*, 151.

April 11, Monday (Middle Hill): Lee meets with Jed Hotchkiss in the morning, discussing the situation facing the army: Lee "said he wanted every man to his post, that we had hard work to do this year, but by the blessing of Providence he hoped it would turn out well.... The enemy had not as large a force as they had last year, though it was said they were coming with large forces in every direction." Lee briefs Gen. Breckinridge on the latest enemy dispositions, including that two corps left Knoxville, and Lee suggests that Breckinridge and Simon Buckner join forces for a move into east Tennessee, or possibly into West Virginia linking up with Imboden. Lee instructs Imboden to strike the B&O if the opportunity presents and to be prepared to cooperate with John Breckinridge. He also approves of Pickett's plans in North Carolina but instructs that he return Hoke and strengthen the Petersburg defenses, and informs Richmond that supplies for Longstreet should be sent to Charlottesville.[14]

April 12, Tuesday (Middle Hill): Lee complains to Richmond regarding the lack of supplies, telling President Davis "I cannot see how we can operate with our present supplies," which consist of rations for only two days; if not resupplied immediately he cautions that he will have to fall back to North Carolina as central Virginia is barren. He suggests to Sec. Seddon that supplies at Richmond be reserved only for troops on duty there and that prisoners be removed so as not to use up the supplies in the capital; he argues also that the railroads should be devoted primarily to supplying the army: "No private interests [should] be allowed to interfere with the use of all the facilities for transportation that we possess until the wants of the army are provided for. The railroads should be at once devoted exclusively to this purpose, even should it be found necessary to suspend all private travel for business or pleasure upon them for the present." He complains also to the commissary about the difficulty in trading tobacco and cotton, and illegal trade of those items compounds the problem.[15] Lee continues to sift through reports regarding the strength of the Army of the Potomac, informing Richmond and Stuart that Mosby's reports differ greatly from others. He also forwards Mosby a report from Sec. Seddon that the Federals are harassing citizens in Leesburg and surrounding Loudoun County.[16]

April 13, Wednesday (Middle Hill): Lee writes to President Davis regarding the increasing number of desertions and AWOL cases in the army: "Desertion and absence without leave are nearly the only offences ever tried by our Courts. They appear to be almost the only vices in the army." Lee again states that pardons and exonerations only encourage others to desert and that only swift punishment will put a stop to the problem, citing the case of a four-time offender Pvt. Jacob Shomo of the 52nd Virginia. Lee advises Bragg that he sees no prospect of success in North Carolina without a riverine navy so he wants Hoke and Pickett returned, their places taken by troops shifted from the South Atlantic Coast. Lee then reverses course and instructs Pickett to retain Hoke for the present.[17]

---

14 McDonald, *Make Me a Map*, 198-9; *OR* 3, 1272-4; *OR* 51, pt. 2, 855. Lee sent a telegram to Longstreet on this date, but the content was not recorded in the message book and it does not appear in the *OR*. REL to Longstreet, April 11, 1864, telegram book, REL HQ papers, VHS.

15 *OR* 33, 1275-7; *OR* 3, Series 4, 285-7.

16 *OR* 33, 1274-8. John Mosby's information proved remarkably accurate: Troops from the Western Theater were sent to Annapolis, not to Meade's Army of the Potomac; the XI Corps and the XII Corps were combined into one command under Maj. Gen. Joseph Hooker; and Maj. Gen. Philip Sheridan was the new cavalry commander in the Army of the Potomac. Mosby also reported that Sec. Seddon's information was incorrect: the Federals had not occupied Loudoun County. Ibid.

17 Freeman, *Lee's Dispatches*, 154-8; *OR* 33, 1278-9; REL to Pickett, April 13, 1864, telegram book, REL HQ papers, VHS. Lee provided a lengthy explanation of his view of courts martial in general and desertion cases in particular: "In reviewing Court Martial cases, it has been my habit to give the accused the benefit of all extenuating circumstances that could be allowed to operate in their favor without injury to the service.... It is certain that a relaxation of the sternness of discipline as a mere act of indulgence, unsupported by good reasons, is followed by an increase of the number of offenders. The escape of one criminal encourages others to hope for like impunity, and that encouragement can be given as well by a

April 15, Friday (Middle Hill): James Longstreet arrives in Orange and meets with Gen. Lee in the afternoon. Lee informs Richmond that he still has widely conflicting reports regarding enemy troop dispositions, specifically Burnside's IX Corps, the XI Corps and XII Corps, and the VIII Corps from Baltimore and the lower Shenandoah Valley. He tells the president that Gen. Beauregard could cover North Carolina with troops from Charleston and the Gulf Coast, and that Simon Buckner serves no purpose at Bristol, and should unite with either Lee or Joe Johnston. The general replies to a letter from Braxton Bragg regarding North Carolina that enemy moves there are just a feint, and that the real threat will come from north of the James River. Lee forwards a report by Jeb Stuart to the War Department about a skirmish at Catlett's Station on the 11th, and also a request from Stuart for additional forage.[18]

April 16, Saturday (Middle Hill): Lee writes to Bragg regarding reinforcement of his army: he wants Longstreet and Pickett returned and also possibly troops from the Atlantic coast, and Buckner and troops from Mobile sent to Johnston. "At present my hands are tied" without reinforcement; "If I was able to move with the aid of Longstreet and Pickett, the enemy might be driven from the Rappahannock and be obliged to look to the safety of his own capital instead of the assault upon ours." He notes also his increasing supply shortage: "The scarcity of our supplies gives me the greatest uneasiness." Separately Lee informs Bragg of the logistical difficulties of moving Longstreet to Orange—that the railroads can only handle about 1,500 troops at a time to Charlottesville and that they would have to march to Gordonsville to find adequate camp sites. Lee notes that Longstreet detached Evander Law's brigade to Buckner and it was not included in the orders to move to Virginia; Lee wants Law included. He also informs Bragg that contrary to what he and ordnance chief Josiah Gorgas wrote Lee, the Army of Northern Virginia does not have an overabundance of artillery, that in fact it has too few guns.[19]

Lee writes to Stuart regarding the shortage of forage in Albemarle County, and forwards a letter from Stuart on the same topic to the War Department, requesting that the grain allotment for civilians be curtailed somewhat. He orders the artillery brought up to the front from its camps in the rear if sufficient foraging grounds can be found. A sutler with Early's Division complains to Lee that his wagon was raided by men from the 49th Virginia; Lee simply advises him to camp somewhere else. Porter Alexander comes to headquarters in the evening and spends the night. Gen. M. L. Smith assumes the duties of chief engineer.[20]

---

repetition of a general act of amnesty or pardon, as by frequent exercise of clemency toward individuals.... Many more men would be lost to the service if a pardon be extended in a large number of cases, than would be restored to it by the immediate effects of that action." Freeman, *Lee's Dispatches*, 154-8. Shomo (whom Lee misidentified in his letter as "Shomore") was an Augusta County farmer who enlisted in July 1861, but went AWOL for two and a half months in the summer of 1862, one month in the winter of 1862-3, two weeks in May 1863, and again from late July through the end of December 1863. He was apparently pardoned yet again, and killed at Bethesda Church May 30, 1864. Robert J. Driver, Jr., *52nd Virginia Infantry* (Lynchburg, VA, 1986), 148.

18 John W. Daniel diary, April 15, 1864, VHS; *OR* 33, 267-8, 1282-3; Dowdey, *Wartime Papers*, 701; Freeman, *Lee's Dispatches*, 158-9; *OR* 51, pt. 2, 859-60. Lee may not have been expecting Longstreet to arrive on this date, as he sent a telegraph to Longstreet at Charlottesville inquiring when his troops would show up. REL to Longstreet, April 15, 1864, telegram book, REL HQ papers, VHS.

19 *OR* 33, 1284-6. An undertone of frustration at having to deal with Braxton Bragg is evident in Lee's correspondence with him, and it became increasingly evident as the spring campaign wore on. Longstreet blamed Evander Law for several defeats in Tennessee and also denied him command of Hood's Division, even though Law was its senior brigadier and very experienced. As their feud worsened, Longstreet transferred Law to Simon Buckner's division in order to be rid of him, but Lee and Davis intervened. Wert, *Longstreet*, 376-7; J. Gary Laine and Morris M. Penny, *Law's Alabama Brigade in the War between the Union and the Confederacy* (Shippensburg, PA, 1996), 217-8.

20 Dowdey, *Wartime Papers*, 700; *OR* 51, pt. 2, 861; REL to A. L. Long, April 16, 1864, REL papers, W&L; *OR* 33, 1287; Hurst, *Soldiers, Stories, Sites and Fights*, 168; EPA to wife, April 17, 1864, EPA papers, UNC. Lee had little sympathy for the sutlers and the exorbitant prices they charged for their goods.

April 17, Sunday (Middle Hill): Lee spends much of the day in consultation with Longstreet, who departs Orange today.[21]

April 18, Monday (Middle Hill): Lee informs President Davis that reports are clearer regarding enemy dispositions: no additional corps joined Meade's army although it has been reinforced by newly formed regiments, and he thinks it likely that a movement will be made in the Valley at the same time that the Army of the Potomac advances. Lee advises Imboden that he thinks the Federals will launch another raid against the Virginia & Tennessee in the near future, but cannot rule out a move up the Valley: "I hope you and Gen. Breckinridge will be prepared to unite and beat him back wherever he may come, and drive him across the Potomac. I shall be so occupied in all probability that I shall be unable to aid you." Lee receives Meade's reply regarding the Dahlgren papers: neither Meade nor anyone else authorized Davis's assassination. Lee orders all surplus baggage sent to the rear and thanks the Semon sisters of Richmond for the rank insignia they sent him.[22]

April 19, Tuesday (Middle Hill): Lee writes to Sec. Seddon regarding having Navy machine shops construct railroad rolling stock, and informs Breckinridge that reports have Union Gen. William Averell massing a large cavalry force in West Virginia so he should be prepared to work with Imboden in repulsing a movement from west of Staunton. Lee writes to Quartermaster General Lawton regarding a lack of shirts and underclothes among the ANV.[23]

He recommends against a proposal by Lt. Col. Henry D. Capers that the Society of the Cincinnati be established in the army for fear that it would be misunderstood and generate mistrust: "We have now but one thing to do; to establish our independence. We have no time for anything else, and nothing of doubtful bearing on the subject should be risked." He forwards Gen. Thomas Rosser's report of his operations in the Shenandoah Valley during the winter, noting that "Rosser acquitted himself with great credit." Lee declines an offer of one Whitworth cannon in Richmond, and receives a request from James Longstreet to go to Petersburg.[24]

April 20, Wednesday (Middle Hill): Lee meets with Early and forwards to Richmond Stuart's report of a minor affair at Catlett's Station. Lee replies to Longstreet that he needs to hurry along his troops as the enemy is expected to take the offensive any day, and he grants permission to go to Petersburg before rejoining Lee, but insists that Longstreet appoint a temporary commander in his absence. Lee again declines the offer of a Whitworth gun for service with the ANV and suggests that it go to Wilmington instead. Lee advises Imboden that reports of the VI Corps being in the Valley are false, and asks why his scouts think that Averell and his cavalry have gone west.[25]

---

21 J. W. Daniel diary, April 17, 1864, VHS.

22 OR 33, 1290-1; Tower, *Lee's Adjutant*, 152; Freeman, *Lee*, vol. 3, 266; REL newspaper references, DSF papers, LVA.

23 OR 33, 1294-5, 1313. Lee mentioned having discussed the production of railroad rolling stock with Navy Secretary Mallory, but did not say when; it was likely during his most recent trip to Richmond. OR 33, 1294-5.

24 Dowdey, *Wartime Papers*, 704; OR 33, 45-6; REL to Gorgas, April 19, 1864, telegram book, REL HQ papers, VHS; REL to Longstreet, April 20, 1864, REL papers, W&L. The Society of the Cincinnati was formed in 1783 by the officers of the Continental Army with an elite hereditary membership. Capers served in the Treasury Department and on J. B. Magruder's staff early in the war before forming the 12th GA Artillery Battalion. Capers was wounded at Cold Harbor in June of 1864 and retired from field service in December 1864. Krick, *Lee's Colonels*, 82. Longstreet wanted to go to Petersburg in part to disguise the destination of his corps.

25 J. W. Daniel diary, April 20, 1864, VHS; OR 33, 276-7; OR 51, pt. 2, 869; REL to Gorgas, April 20, 1864, telegram book, REL HQ papers, VHS; REL to Imboden, April 20, 1864 (2 messages), telegram book, REL HQ papers, VHS. Jubal Early's aide did not state the reason Lee met with Early, and Early did not mention it in his memoirs. Lee mentioned the Richmond defenses to Longstreet, perhaps hoping that he would make a quick inspection tour of them on his way back to the army: "I have endeavored to push forward the entrenchments around Richmond for years. They are in pretty good condition now except for the injury sustained through the winter and they are connected with Chaffin's Bluff." OR 51, pt.

April 21, Thursday (Middle Hill): Lee instructs Gen. Breckinridge to turn over all deserters he collected from Lee's army to Longstreet's troops as they pass through his department. Lee thanks Neilia Cave of nearby Montebello for an unspecified gift, and writes to wife Mary that more socks are needed for men in the Stonewall Brigade.[26]

April 22, Friday (Middle Hill): Lee writes to President Davis regarding Winchester citizens being arrested by both sides and his desire to break up the Unionist government of Virginia headed by Francis Pierpont. Lee informs Imboden that he has reliable reports that John Sedgwick's VI Corps is in front of the ANV and not in the Valley as Imboden thinks. Lee advises Bragg that Union transports in the Chesapeake are bound for the Peninsula and that a black regiment previously stationed on the Northern Neck is reported to have joined Meade; he mentions that Imboden thinks Sedgwick to be in the Valley although Lee himself believes this to be wrong, and he renews his request for Hoke to rejoin the ANV. Lee writes to Maj. J. B. Ferguson thanking him for a uniform and blanket he attempted to send through blockade.[27]

April 23, Saturday (Middle Hill/Orange): Lee and A. P. Hill review Cadmus Wilcox's division near Orange. Lee advises President Davis that he has so many conflicting reports now of enemy troops shifting around he cannot be certain what is fact and what is rumor; he reiterates his desire to get Hoke's and R. D. Johnston's brigades returned. He advises the War Department that he "cannot spare" Gen. Edward Johnson for duty elsewhere.[28]

Lee requests that Jeb Stuart use his cavalry scouts to determine enemy intentions in the Shenandoah Valley, and worries that publication of several of Stuart's letters may put the lives of his scouts at risk. Lee instructs Col. John Mosby to cooperate with Gen. Imboden in turning back whatever enemy offensive comes out of West Virginia. Lee receives a letter from Nannie Peyton and forwards it to his wife Mary. The letter contains the news of his sister Anne's death in Baltimore. He also tells Mary that "Richmond is not the place for you," and recommends that she go to Halifax, Charlotte, or Bedford counties. Lee also worries about Mildred's squirrel Custis Morgan, and its penchant for biting people. Lee dines with Gens. A. P. Hill, Cadmus Wilcox, and Alfred Scales at the home of "Old Man Graham" in the evening, enjoying a surprisingly lavish spread that includes "plenty of fine wine." Rooney Lee is promoted to major general.[29]

2, 869. Lee specifically mentioned Longstreet needing to name a temporary commander largely because of the unsettled command structure in his corps following John B. Hood's wounding and Longstreet's decision to relieve Lafayette McLaws; Maj. Gen. Charles Field was selected by Jefferson Davis to replace Hood, which was not satisfactory to Longstreet who objected to Field's appointment; McLaws's status at this time was in limbo, and Simon Buckner was also in play to lead one of Longstreet's divisions. Wert, *Longstreet*, 372-6.

26 REL to Breckinridge, April 21, 1864, telegram book, REL HQ papers, VHS; REL to Neilia Cave, April 21, 1864, REL papers, W&L; Fitz Lee, *General Lee*, 325. The Cave family estate Montebello is just across the ridge to the north of Middle Hill. Miller, *Antebellum Orange*, 112. It is not to be confused with another Montebello in southern Orange County near Barboursville, where President Zachary Taylor was born.

27 Freeman, *Lee's Dispatches*, 162-4; REL to Imboden, April 22, 1864, telegram book, REL HQ papers, VHS; OR 33, 1303; REL to Ferguson, April 22, 1864, Coons family papers, VHS. Ferguson was a Confederate purchasing agent in England; the items Ferguson attempted to send Lee in November 1863 were captured, but the letter he sent Lee regarding them was on another vessel that was not captured. "Sketch of Maj. Ferguson," *CV* (March 1899), vol. 7, No. 3, 99-100.

28 Alfred M. Scales to wife, April 24, 1864, A. M. Scales papers, NC Archives; OR 33, 1306-7; Freeman, *Lee's Dispatches*, 164-5. Edward Johnson was under consideration to command in Arkansas, and was requested by that state's Congressional delegation; Johnson wanted out from under Dick Ewell, and did not like Jubal Early. Lee, however, did not want to lose Johnson on the eve of the spring campaign. Clemmer, *Old Alleghany*, 531.

29 OR 33, 1307; REL to Stuart, April 23, 1864, H. B. McClellan papers, VHS; Dowdey, *Wartime Papers*, 705; Scales to wife, April 24, 1864, Scales papers, NC Archives; Daughtry, *Gray Cavalier*, 171. The letter from Dr. Peyton's wife was the first Lee knew of his sister Anne's death two months earlier. It appears the siblings had little or no contact after Lee resigned from the U. S. Army. "Old Man Graham" was possibly William M. Graham. Scott, *History of Orange*, 151.

April 24, Sunday (Middle Hill/Orange): Lee attends church at St. Thomas's where Rev. Charles Minnegerode preaches today's sermon. Lee requests President Davis to come visit the army, if enemy movements and weather permit, and learns from the Clark's Mountain signal station that enemy cavalry is moving toward Germanna Ford, while the pickets at Germanna report an enemy crossing at Ely's Ford after dark. He writes to Rooney, glad he is back and congratulating him on his promotion; Lee is still upset over Charlotte's death. Rain during the night.[30]

April 25, Monday (Middle Hill): Lee meets with Gen. Pendleton, presumably about bringing the reserve artillery back to the army from its distant camps. Lee informs President Davis that Meade's army has not advanced yet despite the cavalry action, which Fitz Lee has been sent to handle, and he reiterates his invitation to have Davis visit the army. He advises also of the need to have some force to protect the people and supplies of the Northern Neck but notes that he has nothing he can send there from his army. Lee recommends to Seddon that officers on detached local duty not be permitted to have their friends also detached with them so as to be near their homes. Lee declines Gen. Francis Smith's offer to have the Virginia Military Institute corps of cadets serve with the ANV, preferring instead to keep them at Lexington in case of need by Breckinridge or Imboden.[31]

April 26, Tuesday (Middle Hill): Lee informs the War Department of difficulty with the local reserves in the Lynchburg area, and denies a request from Porter Alexander to have rations issued to officers for their servants. Lee informs Longstreet that his charges against Gen. Evander Law will be dropped and Law restored to command of his brigade.[32]

April 27, Wednesday (Middle Hill): Lee submits his report of the Mine Run Campaign and learns that President Davis will not be able to come to Orange this week as requested. Lee advises Breckinridge that Averell is at New Creek rather than in the Kanawha Valley as previously reported, and instructs Imboden to keep Breckinridge informed and work with him. Lee writes to Ewell rebuking Early for some transgression but ordering that Early be released from arrest. He writes also to Mary requesting her to send him several more shirts and collars and sending her a check for $1,365.[33]

April 28, Thursday (Middle Hill): Lee sends a lengthy letter to President Davis that he is unsure of Meade's intentions as he now seems to be entrenching around Culpeper; he is glad to learn of Hoke's promotion and sorry to lose his services but Lee still needs his brigade; he suggests that Joe Johnston be reinforced from Mississippi and states again that he cannot spare Ed Johnson and suggests that he could part with Early as either Hoke or Gordon could take his place. Lee explains John Imboden's command to Secretary of War Seddon and the circumstances under which it was raised. Lee asks Breckinridge if he turned over deserters to Longstreet's troops and also informs Gen. Daniel

---

30 Tower, *Lee's Adjutant*, 154; Freeman, *Lee's Dispatches*, 165; Dowdey, *Wartime Papers*, 706; REL to Rooney, April 24, 1864, REL papers, LVA; J. B. Clifton diary, April 24, 1864, NC Archives. Davis declined Lee's invitation to visit the army.

31 WNP to wife, April 27, 1864, WNP papers, UNC; Dowdey, *Wartime Papers*, 705-6; Freeman, *Lee's Dispatches*, 363-4; OR 33, 1311; OR 51, pt. 2, 875. Pendleton did not specify the reason for his meeting with Lee, but as the army was concentrating along the Rapidan River, it seems logical that their discussion involved at least in part the return of batteries dispatched to the rear for better foraging. Breckinridge pressed the VMI cadets into service with his small army to help repel Franz Sigel's army in May.

32 OR 33, 1312-3; REL endorsement on EPA to REL, April 24, 1864, REL papers, W&L; Laine, *Law's Alabama Brigade*, 222. The Longstreet-Law feud was a nasty affair that threatened to rip apart relations between the senior officers in the First Corps; Longstreet's wounding at the Wilderness brought an end to the bickering when Lee and Richmond could not. For details see chapters 11 and 12 in Laine, *Law's Alabama Brigade*.

33 OR 33, 827-30, 1317, 1320-1; REL to Imboden, April 27, 1864, telegram book, REL HQ papers, VHS; REL to Ewell, April 27, 1863, REL papers, MOC; REL to Mrs. REL, April 27, 1864, REL papers, LOC. Little is known regarding Jubal Early's arrest, and he made no mention of it in his memoirs. For discussion on this point, see Freeman, *Lee's Lieutenants*, vol. 3, 333. Early was released from arrest on the 28th by Lee's order. J. W. Daniel diary, April 28, 1864, VHS.

Ruggles that he has no vacancy in the ANV to which he could be assigned. Taylor informs Longstreet that Lee will review his troops tomorrow and to have an officer meet Lee at Gordonsville. Lee writes to cousin Margaret Stuart advising that he will write less frequently as he fears that if the letters are intercepted it may "bring distress" on their intended recipients; he mentions that his daughters may come to Cleydael.[34]

April 29, Friday (Middle Hill/Orange/Gordonsville/Green Springs): Lee reviews Longstreet's First Corps at Green Springs. When Lee returns to headquarters around 9:00 p.m., he is serenaded by the 26th North Carolina's band. The general learns from Jeb Stuart's scout, Frank Stringfellow, that Gen. Burnside had moved through Washington to Alexandria several days ago, and that the XI Corps and XII Corps are no longer in Virginia. He relays this information to Richmond and opines that Burnside is likely bound for the Rappahannock rather than Suffolk or North Carolina as previously thought, thus Lee needs all his detached troops returned immediately. He mentions also that an enemy cavalry force is operating against his left near Madison.[35]

April 30, Saturday (Middle Hill): Lee advises President Davis that Burnside is now on the Rappahannock with Meade, and additional troops from Florida and the coast are reported to be en route; he mentions that the Federals do not appear to have concentrated yet in Tennessee thus presenting an opportunity for Joe Johnston and Leonidas Polk to attack. "Everything indicates a concentrated attack on this front," he writes and again requests that all his detached troops be returned, noting that Beauregard (now in command in southern Virginia) can handle any threat along the James and that Breckinridge and Imboden can defend the Valley. Lee forwards Longstreet's charges against Evander Law to the adjutant general, and explains why he has not acted upon them; upon hearing from Longstreet, he recommends that Law be relieved until an investigation can be held.[36]

Lee complains to Seddon about his battle reports being published; the government may use them, but Lee argues that they should not be made

---

34 OR 33, 1320-1; REL to Breckinridge, April 28, 1864, telegram book, REL HQ papers, VHS; REL to Ruggles, April 28, 1864, telegram book, REL HQ papers, VHS; WHT to Longstreet, April 28, 1864, telegram book, REL HQ papers, VHS; REL to Margaret Stuart, April 28, 1864, Lee papers, VHS. Longstreet requested on the 25th that Lee review his corps, but as Lee expected the president to visit he could not commit at that time; once he knew Davis was not coming the review was scheduled. Despite the unpleasantness surrounding the situation with Evander Law, Lee was very glad to have his capable lieutenant back with the Virginia army. Taylor wrote Longstreet on the 26th that Lee "is anxious to see you, and it will give him much pleasure to meet you and your corps once more. . . . I really am beside myself, General, with joy having you back. It is like the reunion of a family." Helen D. Longstreet, *Lee and Longstreet at High Tide* (Wilmington, NC, 1989), 79. Some part of Taylor's reaction was likely because Longstreet's return meant that Ewell would no longer be in command of the army when Lee was absent.

35 D. Augustus Dickert, *History of Kershaw's Brigade* (Newberry, SC, 1899), 340-1; REL to Mrs. REL, April 30, 1864, REL papers, LOC; Hurst, *Soldiers, Stories, Sites and Fights*, 172; OR 33, 1326. One of Kershaw's men recorded, "We were delighted to see our honored leader. . . . The grey-haired veteran seemed delighted at the warm greeting he received at our hands." Wyckoff, *CW Letters of Alexander McNeill*, 433. Col. William Oates of Law's Brigade wrote that the review took place near Cobham's Station on the Virginia Central Railroad, but that is a heavily wooded area and is not consistent with Capt. Dickert's description of "a very large old field, of perhaps 100 acres or more" two miles south of Longstreet's camp at Mechanicsville [crossing of US 15 and VA 22]. Oates, *War between the Union and the Confederacy*, 339-40; Dickert, *Kershaw's Brigade*, 340. The Green Springs area along US 15 south of VA 22 is largely open and perfect for a review field. Oates also wrote that Lee's daughter Mildred was present with her father at the review, but there is no other account that mentions her, nor is it known how Oates learned this. Reportedly Lt. William Pendleton, Co. B, 50th GA, was the only company officer in Longstreet's two divisions who rendered a correct salute to Lee during the review. James W. Parrish, *Wiregrass to Appomattox: The Untold Story of the 50th Georgia Infantry Regiment, CSA* (Winchester, VA, 2009), 169-70. During the review a chaplain in Longstreet's Corps is said to have asked Charles Venable, "Does it not make the General proud to see how these men love him?" Venable reportedly responded, "Not proud. It awes him." Alexander, *Military Memoirs*, 494.

36 OR 33, 1331-2; Dowdey, *Wartime Papers*, 708; OR 31, pt. 1, 473. Gen. Leonidas Polk was moved from corps command in the Army of Tennessee to command of the Army of Mississippi in late 1863; Gen. Beauregard was assigned to command of the Department of North Carolina & Southern Virginia on April 18. Long, *CW Day by Day* 425, 447, 486-7.

public as the enemy can learn from them. Lee advises Imboden that Rosser and his brigade are needed with the ANV, and writes to Mrs. Blair Robertson returning a chicken she gave him as Lee does not want to take it on active campaigning: "I expect to move my camp soon, and in the journey I am obliged to make, I fear the chicken you were so kind as to give me may suffer and be injured. I have therefore determined to send him to you to keep for me. He will have nice grounds to run in with you, whereas with me he will have to be cooped up and have a dreadful time." Lee writes to Custis with the latest military news, and asking for information regarding Federal strength on the Peninsula and lower James.[37]

Lee writes to his wife, mentioning that he received his repaired coat and new shirts and collars she sent, and about the review of Longstreet's Corps yesterday. Lee draws pay of $1,820 for the first four months of 1864. Showers off and on throughout the day.[38]

---

37 OR 33, 1330-1; REL to Imboden, April 30, 1864, telegram book, REL HQ papers, VHS; REL to Mrs. Blair Robertson, April 30, 1864, REL papers, W&L; Dowdey, *Wartime Papers*, 707-8.

38 REL to Mrs. REL, April 30, 1864, REL papers, LOC; Pay Voucher, April 30, 1864, REL CSR; J. B. Clifton diary, April 30, 1864, NC Archives.

May 1864

Just before General Grant, the new Federal commander of the Union armies, opened his spring 1864 campaign by crossing the Rapidan River, a newspaper reporter asked, "about how long will it take you to get to Richmond?" According to Union staff officer Horace Porter, Grant replied, "I will agree to be there in about four days—that is, if General Lee becomes a party to the agreement; but if he objects, the trip undoubtedly will be prolonged." As it turned out, Gen. Robert E. Lee refused to become a "party to the agreement," and Grant's trip would take nearly a full year.[1]

On May 2, Lee gathered his senior commanders atop Clark's Mountain. The Union army was plainly visible in the fields below on the far side of the river. Lee predicted the Army of the Potomac would cross the Rapidan beyond Lee's right flank at Germanna Ford—just as part of it had the previous November. Once across, and depending on Grant's direction, Lee intended to either attack him in the Wilderness, where the dense woods and difficult terrain would negate the numerical superiority of the Federals, or await an attack in the imposing Mine Run works he used five months earlier. The next day Grant did as Lee expected, but instead of turning west as Gen. Meade had done the previous November before being stymied by the Mine Run entrenchments, Grant intended to move quickly through the Wilderness to reach the more open sprawling farms of Spotsylvania County. When it was obvious the enemy army was underway, the general's winter home outside Orange was broken up and the staff put only necessities into the headquarters wagons.[2]

The armies met in the Wilderness. The fighting the previous May around Chancellorsville included a friendly fire incident that threw the Confederate command structure into turmoil and prevented an even greater Confederate victory. This May was much the same except this time the bullets cut down the recently returned Gen. James Longstreet. His severe wounds would keep him out of action for many months and severely limit his ability to command in the field. Lee himself had several close calls. Enemy skirmishers caught the army commander, A. P. Hill, and Jeb Stuart resting in a field, for example, but the surprised Federals did not realize who they had stumbled upon. The following day, in the same field, Lee attempted to personally lead an attack—the first of three he would attempt in the span of a single week to save his army from the verge of collapse. "It was under such circumstances as this that General Lee, by his readiness to share their dangers, endeared himself to his men," explained Lee's former aide Armistead Long.[3]

Early in the ongoing campaign, as casualties mounted and Grant realized that fighting Lee was not the same as battling John Pemberton or Braxton Bragg out west, the Union commander told his superiors in Washington, "I propose to fight it out on this line if it takes all summer." It would take that, and then some. Indeed, the two armies would remain locked in almost daily combat for the

---

1 Horace Porter, *Campaigning with Grant* (New York, 1991), 43-4.

2 Hurst, *Soldiers, Stories, Sites and Fights*, 247; Burgess, "General Lee in Orange." Lee gave away many of the furnishings he had used over the previous months, including a small writing table to the Rogers family of Middle Hill, several chairs to Mary Jerdone of neighboring Bloomsbury, a candlestick to John White (father of the owner of Middle Hill), and a hat to Mrs. Peyton Grimes of Selma. The hat was a handmade gift to Lee from an unknown admirer that did not fit him; it was later given to the MOC. Ibid.

3 Long, *Memoirs of REL*, 341.

balance of the summer and beyond, up to and through the end of the war in the Eastern Theater.[4] Rather than retreat after the heaving fighting in the Wilderness, as prior generals had done, Grant pressed on until stymied around Spotsylvania Court House. For two weeks the armies battled there. Lee suffered staggering losses, including the capture of an entire division on the 12th. He also lost the intrepid Jeb Stuart, mortally wounded defending Richmond from a raid by the Army of the Potomac's new cavalry commander, Phillip H. Sheridan.

The astonishing casualty lists would only increase. "I think that Grant will soon give it up and go back to Washington. His losses have been enormous. His men are deserting and straggle over the whole country in his rear," Charles Venable wrote to his wife. "Yesterday a very bold attack was led on our lines by a Yankee Col. which gained our rifle pits for ten or 15 [sic] minutes but was repulsed. The Col. was killed and somebody gave me a letter of his wife found in his pocket full of baby talk about their little children. This war is terrible on friend and foe."[5] Four days later Venable wrote of the continuing slaughter: "I saw a poor little young soldier this afternoon . . . crying by his dead comrade. I was afraid it was his brother or father and could not ask him anything about it. May God send us peace and stop this fearful carnage."[6]

The stress of command and long hours in the saddle wore Lee down physically and, although less obvious from the historical record, mentally as well, just as it did his two remaining lieutenant generals—Richard Ewell and A. P. Hill. All three men fell ill during the campaign. According to Venable, Lee got at best five hours of rest (one may be hard-pressed to call it sleep) on most nights, retiring to his cot between 10:00 and 11:00 p.m. each evening and rising at 3:00 a.m. He spent nearly all of his daylight hours along the lines.[7] There are several recorded instances of Lee's temper flaring, usually at his staff or senior commanders. During the Wilderness fighting, Lee berated a courier for mistreating his horse—"'Young man, you should have some feeling for your horse; dismount and rest him!'—he snapped, while at the same time removing a buttered biscuit from the saddle bags and giving half of it, from his own hand, to the young courier's pony."[8]

From Spotsylvania the armies moved southeast to the North Anna River, as Grant continued his attempts to outflank Lee's right. One of the very few opportunities to inflict a serious defeat on the enemy and throw the Federals back presented itself there. Lee set an ingenious trap, but fell seriously ill and was unable to leave his tent and direct the effort. "[A]t one time," confessed Walter Taylor, "it looked as if he would have to give up and retire from the field."[9] A. P. Hill and Richard Ewell were also unwell at the time, which left the army almost leaderless. After the war, Rob reflected on the implications of his father's illness:

> When we learned that General Lee was ill . . . this terrible thought forced itself upon us: Suppose disease should disable him, even for a time, or worse, should take him forever from the front of his men! It could

---

4 Porter, *Campaigning with Grant*, 98.

5 Venable to wife, May 11, 1864, Venable papers, UNC.

6 Venable to wife, May 15, 1864, Venable papers, UNC.

7 Venable, "Lee in the Wilderness," 242.

8 Barker, "Two Anecdotes of Gen. Lee," 328-9.

9 Taylor, *General Lee*, 249.

not be! It was too awful to consider! And we banished any such possibility from our minds. When we saw him out again, on the lines, riding Traveller as usual, it was as if some great crushing weight had been suddenly lifted from our hearts.[10]

The fighting moved from the North Anna to ground more familiar to Lee and many of the army's veterans at Totopotomoy Creek and Cold Harbor, the scene of some of the fighting during the Seven Days' Battles. Unlike George McClellan two years earlier, however, Grant never showed no inclination to retreat.

Grant was not Lee's only concern because an enemy build-up on the Peninsula and an advance south up the Shenandoah Valley were also likely. One would tax Confederate resources; both simultaneously would create potentially catastrophic problems. Luckily for Lee and the Confederacy, the commanders of the two supporting armies—Benjamin Butler in southeastern Virginia and Franz Sigel in the Shenandoah—were not first-string caliber. Butler would not only squander a golden opportunity to capture Petersburg and possibly Richmond, but allowed Gen. P. G. T. Beauregard to contain his Union Army of the James at Bermuda Hundred, several miles south of the capital. Sigel, meanwhile, moved at a glacial pace through the Valley, allowing Gens. John C. Breckinridge and John Imboden to combine forces—which included the cadets of the Virginia Military Institute—and turn him back at New Market. Thereafter, portions from both Beauregard's and Breckinridge's commands joined Lee, offsetting at least some of his losses.

Lee's wife Mary added to his stress by refusing to leave Richmond. The general pointed to the recent Kilpatrick-Dahlgren Raid and Sheridan's raid as reasons why she and the girls were no longer safe in the capital. After defeating Stuart at Yellow Tavern, Sheridan rode to Harrison's Landing on the James River to rest briefly and refit. While there, his men took possession of the neighboring Shirley plantation while Mildred happened to be there visiting her cousins. She was unharmed and released when the Federals left, but the war was beginning to hit too close to home.[11]

* * *

---

10 Lee, *Recollections and Letters of REL*, 127.

11 Dowdey, *Wartime Papers*, 757.

May 1, Sunday (Middle Hill/Orange/Mayhurst): Lee and Walter Taylor attend church in the morning at St. Thomas's, where Rev. Joseph P. Wilmer delivers the sermon. Rooney and Beverly Turner return from church with Lee for lunch at headquarters. Lee also participates in the baptism of A. P. Hill's daughter Lucy, being named as the girl's godfather, at Hill's headquarters, Mayhurst. Lee warns John Breckinridge that reliable reports have Union Gen. William Averell ready to embark on a raid against the Virginia & Tennessee Railroad or Staunton, and that Breckinridge will have to cooperate with John Imboden's forces in the Shenandoah Valley to turn back this threat, as Lee anticipates the Army of the Potomac moving at the same time. Lee receives a letter from Mary with another shipment of socks for the Stonewall Brigade, as well additional shirts and collars for him.[12]

May 2, Monday (Middle Hill/Clark's Mountain): Lee goes to the Clark's Mountain signal station with all three corps commanders and all eight division commanders to observe the Union army, and announces that Grant will cross at either Germanna or Ely's Ford and move around Lee's right flank. Lee telegraphs Braxton Bragg, again requesting that all detached units of the ANV be returned, and also that telegraph lines be kept open at night, adding that he will provide sentinels to keep the operators awake as needed. He writes to Mary and sends his winter clothing to be kept in Richmond, and asks that she send his summer clothes; he also sends along a pair of gloves he recently received as a gift as well as the rank insignia he received from the Semon girls several days earlier. Bad storm in afternoon.[13]

May 3, Tuesday (Middle Hill): Lee meets with Gen. William Pendleton in the morning regarding the artillery's readiness for the upcoming campaign. He writes to the president that enemy troops on the lower James are likely those drawn from the Deep South and they will probably operate on the Peninsula or Southside, adding that Burnside's presence on the Rappahannock is perhaps a change of plans from what was originally intended for his corps. He adds that by all appearances an offensive will be undertaken in the Shenandoah Valley or West Virginia against Staunton. Robert Johnston's brigade at Hanover Junction is released to Lee's control; he orders it to rejoin Rodes's Division on the Rapidan. In the evening Lee receives a letter from daughter Agnes and around midnight he learns from the signal station on Clark's Mountain that the Federals are breaking camp, but the observing officers cannot determine in which direction they are heading.[14]

May 4, Wednesday (Middle Hill/Verdiersville): Soon after daylight Lee learns that Meade's army is headed for Germanna and Ely's Fords, as he predicted. During the late morning, Jeb Stuart and Congressman Alexander R. Boteler meet with Lee, who invites them to take lunch with him; they find headquarters in the process of being packed preparatory to a move. Lee informs Richmond that the Army of the Potomac is moving east, and Lee's

---

12 Tower, *Lee's Adjutant*, 157; Dowdey, *Wartime Papers*, 717-8; Robertson, *A. P. Hill*, 249; *OR* 37, pt. 1, 707. Rev. Richard Davis of St. Thomas's conducted the baptism and Lee held the young girl in his arms for most of the ceremony. Robertson, *A. P. Hill*, 249. Mayhurst was built ca. 1859 and is located just south of Orange; it was the home of the Willis family and was known as Howard Place during the war. It was renamed Mayhurst around the turn of the 20th century, and is better known by that name. Today, it is a bed & breakfast. Miller, *Antebellum Orange*, 27.

13 *OR* 36, pt. 1, 1070; *OR* 51, pt. 2, 885; REL to G. W. Rady, May 2, 1864, telegram book, REL HQ papers, VHS; Dowdey, *Wartime Papers*, 717-8; WNP to wife, May 3, 1864, WNP papers, UNC. Neither Jeb Stuart nor any of his division commanders were included in the war council. One officer who frequented the mountaintop wrote: "It is certainly a grand sight and not soon to be forgotten. The enemy's camps are nearly all in full sight. Their drills, reviews etc. are all plainly visible. It lays before you like a mammoth panorama." N. R. Fitzhugh to sister, April 30, 1864, Montgomery D. Corse papers, UNC.

14 WNP to wife, May 3, 1864, WNP papers, UNC; *OR* 36, pt. 2, 942-3; REL to Robert Ransom, May 3, 1864, telegram book, REL HQ papers, VHS; REL to R. D. Johnston, May 3, 1864, telegram book, REL HQ papers, VHS; REL to Agnes, May 4, 1864, REL papers, LOC; Noah A. Trudeau, *Bloody Roads South: The Wilderness to Cold Harbor, May – June 1864* (Boston, 1989), 30.

army is moving to intercept. Around midday, he departs with Hill at the head of the Third Corps, moving east along the Orange Plank Road.[15]

In late afternoon or early evening Lee arrives at Verdiersville and establishes headquarters in a woodlot across from Catlett Rhodes's house. That evening Lee advises the president that "the long threatened effort to take Richmond has begun"—Lee believes the enemy force on the Peninsula will move now also, thus Beauregard must be brought to Richmond with any troops from North Carolina to defend the capital and Petersburg; Lee is not yet sure of Meade's intentions, whether he intends to attack or flank Lee by way of Fredericksburg, but Lee is occupying the Mine Run works until he determines Federal intentions. During the evening he learns the Federals are advancing in the Shenandoah Valley and a Federal force landed at Bermuda Hundred, between Richmond and Petersburg. After writing to Davis, Lee determines to take the offensive, ordering Ewell to advance along the Orange Turnpike in the morning, adding that the idea is "to bring him [Grant] to battle as soon now as possible;" if the Federals are found to be moving toward Fredericksburg Lee will attack, but if they turn west the army will use the Mine Run works.[16] Lee notifies Breckinridge that Imboden reports a large enemy column moving up the Valley, and Lee wants Breckinridge to oversee operations west of the mountains: "I trust you will drive the enemy back." He adds that if the Federals cross the Blue Ridge and threaten Lee's flank, Breckinridge should leave a guard in the Valley and bring the rest of his force to Orange. Lee writes to Agnes concerning her friend Richard Lee, who wants permission to pass through the lines to visit an unwell sister in Maryland; Lee advises that granting a pass is not in his power, but he advises strongly against it, fearing that the man may be treated as a spy if caught.[17]

May 5, Thursday (Verdiersville/Tapp Farm): At breakfast at the Rhodes house, Lee is "very cheerful" of the situation, joking with the staff that Grant seems not to have learned anything from Joe Hooker's experiences in the Wilderness the previous year. Lee rides with Hill and Stuart at the head of the Third Corps eastward on the Plank Road, receiving messages from Ewell via Campbell Brown and Sandie Pendleton regarding the progress of the Second Corps along the Orange Turnpike. Lee is at the front when contact is made between Hill's troops and the Federals between Mine Run and Parkers Store, and he cautions Ewell not to get too far in advance of Hill.[18]

---

15 REL to Longstreet, May 4, 1864 (2 messages), telegram book, REL HQ papers, VHS; *OR Supplement*, vol. 6, 533-4; *OR* 51, pt. 2, 887; William W. Hassler, *A. P. Hill: Lee's Forgotten General* (Chapel Hill, NC, 1995), 186; Gordon C. Rhea, *The Battle of the Wilderness: May 5 – 6, 1864* (Baton Rouge, LA, 1994), 86. Boteler, who was serving on Stuart's staff, noted: "The General's iron grey horse Traveller was ready for him to mount and . . . he himself is looking remarkably well and as calm, as courteous, and as considerate today as on the most ordinary occasions. No one would suppose from his demeanor that great events are in the gale or vast responsibilities weighing on his mind." *OR Supplement*, vol. 6, 533-4. Lee's initial plan was to re-occupy the works along Mine Run. REL to Bragg, May 4, 1864, telegram book, REL HQ papers, VHS.

16 *OR* 36, pt. 2, 948; Dowdey, *Wartime Papers*, 719-20; Freeman, *Lee*, vol. 3, 274-5. Lee had made his HQ at the Rhodes house as well during the Mine Run campaign in late 1863.

17 *OR* 37, pt. 1, 712-3; REL to Agnes, May 4, 1864, REL papers, LOC. A review of Fitz Lee's division was scheduled for the morning at Hamilton's Crossing; Mrs. Lee, and possibly one of the girls, along with Gov. Smith, journeyed up from Richmond to watch, but enemy movements canceled the review. "Extra Billy" Smith delivered a speech to the assembled crowd before their party returned to Richmond. Rhea, *Battle of the Wilderness*, 80; John M. Priest, *Nowhere to Run: The Wilderness, May 4th & 5th, 1864* (Shippensburg, PA, 1995), 20.

18 Long, *Memoirs of REL*, 327; Charles S. Venable, "General Lee in the Wilderness Campaign," *B&L*, vol. 4, 240-1; Walter B. Barker, "Two Anecdotes of General Lee," *SHSP*, vol. 12, 328; Jones, *Campbell Brown's CW*, 247. Sgt. Walter of the HQ guard wrote that Lee paused at a church four miles from Verdiersville, where initial contact with enemy cavalry was made; this was almost certainly New Hope Church. F. G. Walter diary, May 5, 1864, LVA. One account states that three young women were watching the troops pass from a house probably in the vicinity of Mine Run, and as Lee passed they flagged down a passing officer to give him a package containing several shirts; just as he accepted them, initial contact was made with the Federals. Barker, "Two Anecdotes," 328.

As the generals near the Brock Road intersection, Lee instructs Henry Heth to seize the crossing if he can but not to bring on a general engagement. In early afternoon Lee, Hill, Stuart, Pendleton, and their staffs stop to rest in a field at the Tapp farm. As they sit under a large tree an enemy skirmish line emerges from the woods across the field from them; Lee's party scatters but the Federals withdraw without firing a shot.[19]

Worried about Federals being in the gap between Gens. Ewell and Hill, Lee sends Taylor to bring up Cadmus Wilcox's division to fill the gap; Lee and Stuart remain in the Tapp field near William Poague's guns as Wilcox deploys, where they both establish their headquarters. In early evening after the fighting dies down, Lee informs Ewell of the state of affairs on Hill's front and that the Federals appear to be moving to the Confederate right; he asks Ewell if he can move around the enemy's flank and sever their communications but also be prepared to move to his right. During the night Wilcox requests permission from Lee to adjust his lines in the darkness and entrench, but Lee tells him that it is not necessary because Longstreet and Anderson will relieve Hill's men before dawn.[20]

As Lee is sitting for dinner around 10:00 p.m., Stuart's aide Henry B. McClellan arrives and informs Lee of Charles Field's refusal to come to Hill's relief in response to Lee's verbal orders, requesting written orders instead. Later, Lee informs Richmond of the day's fighting, including the death of Gens. John M. Jones and Leroy Stafford. He also orders Imboden to call out all available forces, including the local reserves and the VMI cadets, and to work with Breckinridge to defend the Valley.[21]

May 6, Friday (Tapp Farm): In the very early hours of the morning both Hill and Wilcox come to headquarters for news of Longstreet's arrival; around the same time Lee sends Pvt. C. C. Taliaferro of the headquarters guard to find Longstreet and hurry him forward. At first light the Federals renew their attack upon Hill, breaking the Third Corps lines and sending the troops racing back toward Lee at the Tapp farm. Fearing the worst, Lee dispatches Taylor to get the wagon train ready to retreat, and sends Venable to bring up Longstreet. Lee assists in rallying Hill's broken troops, and encounters Gen. Wilcox whom he also sends to find Longstreet.[22]

---

19 Morrison, *Heth Memoirs*, 182; Hewitt, ed., *OR Supplement*, vol. 6, 536; William L. Royall, *Some Reminiscences* (New York, 1909), 28; F. G. Walter diary, May 5, 1864, LVA; Venable, "Lee in the Wilderness," 241. Col. W. H. Palmer of A. P. Hill's staff noted that the Yankees were "within pistol shot" of the generals. The skirmishers were likely companies C and K of the 1st PA Reserves. Priest, *Nowhere to Run*, 43-4.

20 Royall, *Some Reminiscences*, 28-9; Caldwell, *History of McGowan's Brigade*, 127; *OR* 36, pt. 2, 952-3; Freeman, *Lee's Lieutenants*, vol. 3, 353. One of Stuart's aides described the heavily wooded country around the Tapp farm: "This is a dreary country . . . not a house, not an open field. Nothing but a wilderness of trees and underbrush and marsh and perfectly flat. We are in a small field by the road side about 2 miles from the scene of battle. And here are Gen. Lee's and Gen. Stuart's headquarters—and an infinity of wagons and artillery." Philip H. Powers to unknown, misdated May 4, 1864, Valley of the Shadow. Gen. Heth had a similar discussion with A. P. Hill regarding adjusting his lines during the night, but Hill refused to let the troops be moved. Morrison, *Heth Memoirs*, 184.

21 Freeman, *Lee*, vol. 3, 283-4; *OR* 36, vol. 1, 1028; REL to Imboden, May 5, 1864, telegram book, REL HQ papers, VHS. On this date sculptor Edward Valentine in Berlin received images of Lee taken at J. Vannerson's Richmond studio to use as the basis for a statue of Lee. Meredith, *Face of REL*, 44. It is not known when the images were taken, but probably during one of his trips to the capital earlier in 1864.

22 Royall, *Some Reminiscences*, 30; Driver, *39th Virginia Cavalry Battalion*, 68-9; Longstreet, *From Manassas to Appomattox*, 560-1; *OR* 36, vol. 1, 1028; Venable, "Lee in the Wilderness," 241; Rhea, *Battle of the Wilderness*, 293; Freeman, *Lee*, vol. 3, 286. Lee encountered Brig. Gen. Samuel McGowan in or near Tapp field as his men fled the field. Lee yelled, "My God! Gen. McGowan is this splendid brigade of yours running like a flock of geese?" McGowan is said to have replied, "No General. The men are not whipped. They just want a place to form and they are ready to fight as ever." Gallagher, *Fighting for the Confederacy*, 357. Engineer Capt. S. R. Johnston later wrote that he provided Lee with "a sketch showing the best route" for Longstreet to get from Gordonsville to the Wilderness, but he did not recall who was to guide Longstreet to the front. Johnston to WHT, July 11, 1879, WHT papers, NPL. Wilcox and many others who encountered Lee after A. P. Hill's lines broke noted an excitement and visible concern Lee rarely displayed on a battlefield. Freeman, *Lee*, vol. 3, 286; Caldwell, *McGowan's Brigade*, 133.

As Poague's guns hold the Federals at bay, Longstreet arrives ahead of his troops, followed by the Texas Brigade, which Lee welcomes with the shout "Hurrah for Texas!" As the Texans form in the Tapp field, Lee rides with them, apparently intending to lead a counterattack himself. When the men become aware of Gen. Lee's presence with them, many—including brigade commander Brig. Gen. John Gregg—attempt to deter him from going into the fight. Many shout "Lee to the rear!" and some grab Traveller's reigns to stop him. Venable eventually succeeds in getting Lee out of immediate danger by demonstrating that Longstreet was nearby and steering him toward the corps commander; Longstreet is also uncomfortable with Lee so close to the front and urges him to go farther to the rear.[23]

Lee places Longstreet in command of the counterattack, has Porter Alexander collect all the artillery with that column and take it to the rear as there is no place for it in the wooded terrain, and himself works with Hill to link up with Ewell's corps on the left. During a lull in the fighting in late morning, Ewell comes to the Tapp farm to brief Lee on the affairs on his front, telling Lee he thinks the Union right flank to be vulnerable.[24]

When a staff officer brings Lee news of the success of Longstreet's flank attack in early afternoon; Lee responds that once Longstreet's entire corps is engaged they will push the Federals into the Rappahannock. During that afternoon lull following Longstreet's attack, Moxley Sorrel informs Lee that Longstreet has been wounded, and Lee quickly arrives on the scene where he comes under sporadic fire, a courier's horse being killed.[25]

Lee assumes personal command of Longstreet's and Hill's troops along the Plank Road for a push against the Brock Road in late afternoon; little is gained. During the evening he sends at least two messages to Richmond to update the day's fighting, including Longstreet's wounding, the death of Micah Jenkins, and the capture of Union Gen. James Wadsworth.[26]

---

23 Poague, *Gunner with Stonewall*, 89-90; Royall, *Some Reminiscences*, 32; Lee, *Memoirs of WNP*, 326; Venable, "Lee in the Wilderness," 241; Taylor, *General Lee*, 234; Bernard, *War Talks*, 102. The "Lee to the Rear" episode was the largest crisis Lee had faced up to that time, and arguably the worst crisis in the life of the Army of Northern Virginia until the final breakthrough at Petersburg. At least a half-dozen soldiers, and probably more, claimed to have grabbed Lee's horse and led him off the field, many of the claims appearing in newspapers and *Confederate Veteran* years after the war. According to artillerist Poague: "This was the first time Gen. Lee ever advanced in a charge with his troops and his action shows how critical the condition was at that juncture. . . . He was perfectly composed, but his face expressed a kind of grim determination I had not observed either at Sharpsburg or Gettysburg. Traveller was quiet but evidently interested in the situation, as indicated by his raised head with ears pointing to the front. But there was no rearing or plunging on the part of the horse and no waving of sword by General Lee." Poague, *Gunner with Stonewall*, 90-1.

24 Gallagher, *Fighting for the Confederacy*, 359; Freeman, *Lee*, vol. 3, 288; Chamberlaine, *Memoirs*, 94-5; Royall, *Some Reminiscences*, 33-4; Martin, *Road to Glory*, 291. A. P. Hill was nearly captured at the Chewning farm, which offered the only vantage point of Ewell's front from the southern portion of the field, and at that time was not yet occupied by either side. Reminiscent of the episode the previous day, enemy troops emerged from the woods close to Hill, who dispatched Col. Palmer of his staff to Lee for one of Anderson's brigades to occupy the Chewning farm. Royall, *Some Reminiscences*, 33-4.

25 Smith, *One of the Most Daring*, 111; Sorrel, *Recollections*, 244-5; Bernard, *War Talks*, 102; Todd, *Reminiscences*, 192-3, Todd papers, UNC. It is possible that Lee met with Longstreet shortly before his wounding, as one artillery officer recalled seeing them together near his guns in the Plank Road along with Gens. Micah Jenkins and William Mahone. J. C. Haskell *Memoirs*, 43, John C. Haskell papers, Duke. E. P. Alexander put Longstreet's wounding around 1:00 p.m., and claimed he he knew almost immediately it was friendly fire from Mahone's Brigade that had felled him. EPA to father, May 29, 1864, EPA papers, UNC. Francis Dawson witnessed Lee's reaction when the wounded Longstreet was carried past in an ambulance: "I shall not soon forget the sadness in his face, and the almost despairing movement of his hands, when he was told that Longstreet had fallen." *Reminiscences*, 116.

26 Long, *Memoirs of REL*, 332; OR 36, pt. 1, 1028; REL to Seddon, May 6, 1864, telegram book, REL HQ papers, VHS. John Gordon wrote that Lee came to Ewell's sector late in the afternoon and gave his personal approval to a proposed flanking attack by Gordon, overriding Jubal Early. Gordon, *Reminiscences*, 253-8. Freeman believed Gordon's account, although it—like so much else in Gordon's memoirs—seems to be a complete fabrication. Biographers of Gordon, Early, and Ewell discount this exchange with Lee and point out that there is no contemporary evidence for Lee being on Ewell's front on May 6. Freeman, *Lee*, vol. 3, 295-7; Ralph L. Eckert, *John Brown Gordon: Soldier, Southerner, American* (Baton Rouge, LA, 1989), 67-8; Osborne, *Jubal*, 235-6; Martin, *Road to Glory*, 293-5; Pfanz, *Ewell*, 591 n36.

May 7, Saturday (Tapp Farm/Parkers Store): "At sunrise" Lee meets with Longstreet's chief of staff Moxley Sorrel regarding a successor to Longstreet at the head of the First Corps. He learns from Jeb Stuart in the morning that the Federals are moving toward Chancellorsville. He directs Stuart to scout the roads toward Spotsylvania Court House and has Gen. Pendleton construct a road parallel to the Brock Road, should the army need to move quickly to Spotsylvania. Lee also meets with Ewell at the Tapp farm in the morning, where he probably learns for the first time the details of John Gordon's flank attack the previous evening against the far right flank of the Army of the Potomac. Lee updates Gen. Bragg on the progress of the fighting, mentioning that Gordon's troops had captured two Union generals.[27]

In the afternoon Lee rides over to Ewell's front on the Orange Turnpike, where he inspects the lines. After meeting with Ewell, Lee stops to confer with A. P. Hill at the Chewning farm, from which point enemy troops can be seen moving toward Spotsylvania. He returns to headquarters around sundown.[28]

Upon his return, Lee informs Richard Anderson that he is to take over command of Longstreet's corps, and is to march for Spotsylvania using Pendleton's military road to head off a move by Grant. Lee orders Stuart to investigate reports of enemy wagons crossing back to the north bank of the Rapidan; he thinks them to be empty and not a sign of a pending withdrawal but wants Stuart to confirm. He notifies Richmond that Gen. Grant removed his pontoon bridge at Ely's Ford on the Rapidan and seems to be moving to Spotsylvania; he also notifies Breckinridge that whatever moves he undertakes in the Shenandoah Valley must be done quickly. Lee orders Ewell to have his corps follow Anderson to Spotsylvania, and moves his own headquarters several miles to the rear to Parkers Store.[29]

May 8, Sunday (Parkers Store/Shady Grove Church/ Spotsylvania Court House): During the morning Lee informs Richmond that he is moving the army to Spotsylvania to mirror Grant's move. He moves to Shady Grove Church by midday; along the way he learns that Hill is too sick to command, and so places Early in temporary command of the Third Corps. When Ewell arrives at Shady Grove, he and Lee ride together to Spotsylvania arriving in mid-afternoon.[30]

Fighting is still going on when Lee arrives, and he informs the War Department that Anderson repulsed the enemy that morning. Lee watches part

---

27 Sorrel, *Recollections*, 248-50; *OR* 36, pt. 2, 967-70; Lee, *Memoirs of WNP*, 327; Pfanz, *Ewell*, 375. Lee had three viable candidates to take over Longstreet's First Corps: Jubal Early, Edward Johnson, and Richard Anderson. Sorrel told Lee that Early may be the best of the three, but he was immensely unpopular; Johnson, a Second Corps man, was an "unknown" to Longstreet's men; Anderson, however, had served in First Corps until the post-Chancellorsville reorganization, and was thus "known" to its officers and men. Sorrel left the meeting expecting that Early would get the assignment. Sorrel, *Recollections*, 248-50. It is worth noting that neither George Pickett nor Lafayette McLaws were under consideration by Lee—the former was on detached service south of the James River, and the latter's situation had not yet been resolved; both were available if Lee chose.

28 F. G. Walter diary, May 7, 1864, LVA; Dowdey, *Wartime Papers*, 723; Royall, *Some Reminiscences*, 35. It is possible that Lee rode with Early and Gordon, and possibly Ewell as well, over the scene of Gordon's flank attack. Gordon recounted a conversation with Lee wherein the commanding general announced that Grant would move to Spotsylvania; this is probably another of Gordon's postwar fabrications because Lee was not yet convinced of Grant's next move. Gordon, *Reminiscences*, 267. Freeman used this conversation (incorrectly placing it in the morning), but added that he was unsure of the veracity of Gordon's account. Freeman, *Lee*, vol. 3, 301-2. Taylor wrote after the war that Lee spent most of the day away from HQ, either riding the lines or meeting with Ewell and Hill; Sgt. Walter of the HQ guard, however, wrote that evening that Lee was present at the Tapp farm until the afternoon and returned "about sundown." Taylor, *General Lee*, 238; F. G. Walter diary, May 7, 1864, LVA.

29 *OR Supplement*, vol. 6, 656; *OR* 36, pt. 2, 966-7; *OR* 37, pt. 1, 722; WHT to Ewell, May 7, 1864, Polk-Ewell-Brown papers, UNC. Mahone took over Anderson's Division as its senior brigadier, and Taylor accompanied Anderson on the march to Spotsylvania. *OR* 36, pt. 2, 967; Taylor, *General Lee*, 238.

30 *OR* 36, pt. 2, 974; *OR* 51, pt. 2, 902-3; Pfanz, *Ewell*, 376-7; Taylor, *General Lee*, 239. John Gordon took over Early's Division, which required shifting Henry Hays's Louisiana brigade to Johnson's Division, because Hays was senior to Gordon. *OR* 36, pt. 2, 974-5.

of the action on Anderson's front from near the Spindle house with Jeb Stuart, where he comes under sporadic fire. He establishes headquarters near Ewell at the Block house on the Shady Grove Road. During the night Lee sends Sec. Seddon a summation of the day's fighting.[31]

May 9, Monday (Spotsylvania Court House): Lee rises early before dawn and rides along the army's lines around Spotsylvania Court House, but is "not favorably impressed" by the army's position. He informs President Davis that he plans to stay between Grant and Richmond but will not attack unless the circumstances are favorable; he also suggests that if Ben Butler's army cannot be directly attacked that his supply line along the James be targeted.[32]

May 10, Tuesday (Spotsylvania Court House): In the morning, Lee and Stuart spend several hours observing Union lines from the upper windows of Zion Church, just south of the courthouse. Lee advises Ewell that all is quiet on Anderson and Early's fronts and sets up his command post in rear of Rodes's lines.[33]

In the early evening Lee learns of a Federal breakthrough of Rodes's lines very close to his headquarters and starts immediately toward the spot until Taylor and others from the staff convince him not to expose himself. Taylor himself leads the counterattack to recover the lost entrenchments, and his horse is shot out from under him. Lee remains near his headquarters, helping to rally survivors and personally sends the gunners of the Staunton Artillery to man recaptured guns in the works.[34]

Lee, Ewell, and many of their aides come under a heavy fire while rallying Rodes's survivors, a bullet striking Lee's saddle, and an observer notes "I looked for him [Lee] to fall every minute." After the lines are retaken, Lee meets with Ewell and his division commanders on the McCoull house porch and indirectly chastises Rodes for allowing the

---

31 OR 36, pt. 1, 1028-9; Gordon C. Rhea, *The Battles for Spotsylvania Court House and Road to Yellow Tavern, May 7-12, 1864* (Baton Rouge, LA, 1997), 357 n20; Long, *Memoirs of REL*, 387; McDonald, *Make Me a Map*, 202; Rhea, *Battles for Spotsylvania CH*, 88; OR 36, pt. 1, 1029. As Lee observed the fighting, "a few bullets cut the limbs and struck the ground near him," prompting an unidentified general to tell him, "General this is no place for you; do go away at once to a safe place." Lee replied, "I wish I knew where my place is on the battlefield; wherever I go someone tells me it is not the place for me to be." Long, *Memoirs of REL*, 387. The Block house was at the intersection of the Shady Grove Road and Old Courthouse Road. Rhea, *Battles for Spotsylvania CH*, 88.

32 Venable, "Lee in the Wilderness," 242; Hotchkiss, *Virginia*, 447; Freeman, *Lee's Dispatches*, 174-7. Lee is said to have remarked of the salient portion of Ewell's front near the McCoull house: "This is a wretched line. I do not see how it can be held." Pfanz, *Ewell*, 378. The location of Lee's HQ on the 9th is not known with certainty; he may have remained at the Block house, or moved to the Harrison house behind Ewell's lines. Some sources have him at Zion Church, just south of the village, but that seems unlikely before the 13th. Michael Aubrecht, *The Civil War in Spotsylvania County: Confederate Campfires at the Crossroads* (Charleston, SC, 2009), 17. The stone marker for Lee's HQ is on the grounds of the courthouse itself, but as far as is known he never camped there; indeed the county history mentions that the courthouse was used as a field hospital but makes no mention of Lee using it or the grounds. James R. Manfield, *A History of Early Spotsylvania* (Orange, VA, 1977), 100. According to Fredericksburg historian Frank O'Reilly, the marker at the courthouse was never intended to mark the exact spot of the HQ, and was placed there in a highly visible location to denote the commander's presence nearby. Frank O'Reilly email to author, Oct. 31, 2017. Venable noted that Lee's command post the following day was "on a knoll about 150 yards in the rear" of the left of the salient; he did not specify if that was where Lee spent the night. Charles S. Venable, "The Campaign from the Wilderness to Petersburg," *SHSP*, vol. 14, 528.

33 Monte Akers, *Year of Desperate Struggle: Jeb Stuart and his Cavalry, from Gettysburg to Yellow Tavern, 1863-1864* (Philadelphia, 2015), 214; REL to Ewell, May 10, 1864, LJF papers, W&L; Venable, "Campaign from Wilderness to Petersburg," 528. Zion Church was A. P. Hill's and Harry Heth's HQ. Hill remained with his troops even though he was too ill to command them; Lee moved his own HQ there on the 13th. Robertson, *A. P. Hill*, 270.

34 Venable, "Campaign from Wilderness to Petersburg," 528; Taylor, *General Lee*, 240; WHT to John W. Daniel, Nov. 29, 1904, WHT papers, NPL; C. C. Taliaferro to WHT, April 25, 1894, WHT papers, NPL; Robert J. Driver, Jr., *The Staunton Artillery-McClanahan's Battery* (Lynchburg, VA, 1988), 35. Taylor recalled that Lee agreed not to lead the counterattack himself, telling the staff, "Then you gentlemen must see that the lines are restored." WHT to Daniel, Nov. 29, 1904, WHT papers, NPL. C. C. Taliaferro of the HQ guard accompanied Taylor in leading the attack. He described it as "the hottest place I was in during the war." Taliaferro to WHT, April 10, 1894, WHT papers, NPL.

breakthrough. He cautions Ewell to remain vigilant during the night, noting that night attacks were "a favorite amusement of [Grant's] at Vicksburg." Lee informs the War Department that both sides are entrenched around Spotsylvania and, apart from Rodes's battle, little fighting has occurred today.[35]

May 11, Wednesday (Spotsylvania Court House): In the morning Lee rides along Rodes's line with chief engineer Gen. M. L. Smith. He sends Jed Hotchkiss to reconnoiter Grant's left; when Hotchkiss reports it exposed, Lee sends him to have Early attack but Hotchkiss is unable to locate Early. Lee learns that Federals under George Crook and William Averell cut the Virginia & Tennessee Railroad at Dublin and notifies Breckinridge that he may have to give up his operations in the Valley and return to southwest Virginia. He requests that Hoke's Division be sent to Guinea Station and sends to Richmond an enemy flag captured yesterday.[36]

In late afternoon Lee meets with Ewell, Rodes, and Armistead Long at Ewell's headquarters at the Harrison house; reports point to Grant's army moving during the night, so he orders the artillery removed from the "Mule Shoe" salient. During the evening Lee rides to Zion Church to meet with Hill, Heth, and others; he informs them of his belief that Grant intends to move to Fredericksburg that night and to be ready to move. Rain in the afternoon and evening.[37]

May 12, Thursday (Spotsylvania Court House): The general rises early that morning and is in the vicinity of the Harrison house when Maj. Robert W. Hunter of Ed Johnson's staff informs him that Johnson's lines at the Mule Shoe have been broken. Lee hurriedly meets with John Gordon near the Harrison house and attempts to lead Gordon's men in a counterattack to retake Johnson's lines. Gordon blocks Lee's path while several officers and men from Pegram's Brigade grab Traveller's reins to lead him to the rear.[38]

After agreeing to remain behind, the general passes through the ranks of the 52nd Virginia and remains near the Harrison house, feeding infantry reinforcements into the fight, at times coming under heavy fire. Dawn allows Lee to grasp the full extent of the disaster that has overtaken his army at the

---

35 Rhea, *Battles for Spotsylvania CH*, 171-2, 187; *OR* 36, pt. 2, 982-3. Ewell's aide and stepson, Campbell Brown, recorded that Lee, Ewell, and their staffs "were under a very hot fire for a time." Brown to his mother Lizinka Ewell, May 11, 1864, Polk-Ewell-Brown papers, UNC. Lee's HQ for the night seems to have been near the Harrison house. Rhea, *Battles for Spotsylvania CH*, 172; Venable, "Lee in the Wilderness," 242.

36 Pfanz, *Ewell*, 382; Freeman, *Lee*, vol. 3, 315; McDonald, *Make Me a Map*, 203; *OR* 37, pt. 1, 728; *OR* 36, pt. 2, 988; *OR* 26, pt. 1, 1029-30. The unidentified flag was captured by Maj. John S. Brooks of the 20th NC and presented by Brooks to Lee, probably very soon after its capture, with the request that it be sent to Raleigh to Gov. Vance; Brooks was killed two days later. Rhea, *Battles for Spotsylvania CH*, 172, 248.

37 Jones, *Campbell Brown's CW*, 253; Morrison, *Heth Memoirs*, 186-7; F. G. Walter diary, May 11, 1864, LVA. One history of the Spotsylvania battles states that Lee met with Ewell and Long at the Harrison house twice: once before his conference at Zion Church, and again after meeting with Hill and Heth. William D. Matter, *If It Takes All Summer: The Battle of Spotsylvania* (Chapel Hill, NC, 1988), 175-7. According to Heth, when A. P. Hill (still too ill to take command, but present) suggested that the army remain behind its fortifications and let Grant continue to attack them, Lee supposedly replied, "This army cannot stand a siege; we must end this business on the battlefield, not in a fortified place." Morrison, *Heth Memoirs*, 186-7.

38 Rhea, *Battles for Spotsylvania*, 230; Matter, *If It Takes All Summer*, 199-201; Taylor, *General Lee*, 242; Gordon, *Reminiscences*, 278-9; Richard B. Kleese, *49th Virginia Infantry* (Lynchburg, VA, 2002), 45; Walbrook D. Swank, ed., *Stonewall Jackson's Foot Cavalry: Company A, 13th Virginia Infantry* (Shippensburg, PA, 2001), 40-1; J. G. Wheeler, "Lee to the Rear," *CV*, vol. 11, 116; J. Catlett Gibson, "The Battle of Spotsylvania Courthouse, May 12, 1864," *SHSP*, vol. 32, 200-4. Unlike the earlier "Lee to the Rear" episode at the Tapp farm, where numerous individuals claimed to lead Lee off the field, Sgt. William A. Compton, Co. D, 49th VA was almost universally identified as the one who did so at the Mule Shoe. Kleese, *49th Virginia*, 45. One witness placed Ewell with Lee during his brief encounter with Gordon. Swank, *Stonewall's Foot Cavalry*, 40. Another unidentified witness placed Lee beside the colors of the 49th as he prepared to lead the charge, perhaps indicating that Lee intended to carry the flag himself. Richmond *Daily Dispatch*, June 2, 1864. Gordon left a detailed account of this episode, but how much of it actually happened and how much was fabricated by Gordon is open to question. Gordon, *Reminiscences*, 278-9.

Mule Shoe, and he dispatches Charles Venable to bring Mahone's Division from the left.[39]

Lee is conferring with Ewell, Rodes, and Gordon behind the Mule Shoe when the first of Mahone's troops (Perrin's Brigade) arrive. Gordon sends Perrin into the fight. When Lee sees Harris's Brigade near the courthouse and leads it to the front himself, an artillery round strikes the ground in front of a rearing Traveller. Lee tries to lead the brigade in its attack, but again remains behind when the men implore him to stay out of the fighting. He instructs Venable to guide them to the front. The fighting continues on Ewell's front; Lee explores the situation on both flanks for an opportunity to relieve pressure on Ewell; he finds the situation in Hill's front favorable to a counterstroke.[40]

During the afternoon Lee observes an attack by Lane's and Mahone's Brigades, coming under heavy fire again at times at his position along Heth's lines. In late afternoon he orders the construction of a new line across the base of the Mule Shoe and goes with Ewell to oversee its construction and around midnight orders the troops withdrawn from the salient into the new line. During the night Lee and Ewell ride along the new line urging the troops to hurry its completion.[41]

During breaks in the fighting Lee advises Richmond of the capture of most of Johnson's Division along with Gens. Johnson and George Steuart, and requests that Gordon be promoted to replace Johnson. He also points out to the president that Ben Butler's army is largely composed of troops drawn from the Atlantic coast so Lee requests that troops be drawn from those areas to oppose Butler and Grant in Virginia. Lee learns of Jeb Stuart's severe wounding at the Battle of Yellow Tavern. Rain, heavy at times, throughout most of the day.[42]

May 13, Friday (Spotsylvania Court House): Lee relocates his headquarters to Zion Church and receives several flags captured by Lane's men yesterday. He rides along his lines and encounters Gen. Stephen Ramseur along Ewell's new line and thanks him for his efforts in averting further disaster. Lee is talking to Col. Willie Pegram when a courier brings news of Jeb Stuart's death from his wounds; Lee remarks of Stuart "I can scarcely think of him without weeping" and "He never brought me a piece of false information."[43]

---

39 Driver, *52nd Virginia*, 55-6; Venable, "Lee in the Wilderness," 243; Stiles, *Four Years*, 259-60; Lawrence R. Laboda, *From Selma to Appomattox: The History of the Jeff Davis Artillery* (New York, 1996), 218-9; Freeman, *Lee*, vol. 3, 319-20. Maj. Stiles of the Richmond Howitzers noted that six of his men were killed as they rushed across the knoll on which Lee sat. *Four Years*, 259-60. Gen. Cullen Battle, a brigadier in Robert Rodes's division, wrote that as his men passed Lee, the army commander "saluted and stood uncovered until the brigade passed." Brandon H. Beck, ed., *Third Alabama: The Civil War Memoir of Brigadier General Cullen Andrews Battle, CSA* (Tuscaloosa, AL, 2002), 110.

40 Rhea, *Battles for Spotsylvania*, 268-70; Nathaniel H. Harris, "General Lee to the Rear—The Incident with Harris' Mississippi Brigade," *SHSP*, vol. 8, 105-7; Venable, "Lee in the Wilderness," 243; Freeman, *Lee*, vol. 3, 322. Several witnesses commented on Lee's calmness throughout the morning, with the adjutant of the Stonewall Brigade noting, Lee "was perfectly composed, superb in all respects." Colt, *Defend the Valley*, 314. This contrasted sharply with Ewell. Lee encountered the Second Corps commander shortly after the breakthrough and upbraided him, "General Ewell, you must restrain yourself; how can you expect to control these men when you have lost control of yourself. If you cannot repress your excitement, you had better retire." Gallagher, "REL at Cumberland Island," 122.

41 Rhea, *Battles for Spotsylvania*, 296; Early, *Memoirs*, 356; Freeman, *Lee*, vol. 3, 325; Pfanz, *Ewell*, 389-90; John O. Casler, *Four Years in the Stonewall Brigade* (Girard, KS, 1906), 214.

42 *OR* 36, pt. 1, 1030; REL to Jefferson Davis, May 12, 1864, telegram book, REL HQ papers, VHS; *OR* 51, pt. 2, 922; Venable, "Lee in the Wilderness," 243n; F. G. Walter diary, May 12, 1864, LVA. Stuart met Philip Sheridan's cavalry several miles north of Richmond at Yellow Tavern on the Brook Turnpike, where Stuart was mortally wounded in the abdomen and taken to Richmond. Venable's wording is vague: "the news of Stuart's fall reached General Lee on the 12th." Venable must mean Stuart's wounding, for Stuart died in Richmond around 7:30 p.m. on the 12th, making it practically impossible for the news to reach Lee by courier on the 12th. Jeffry D. Wert, *Cavalryman of the Lost Cause: A Biography of J. E. B. Stuart* (New York, 2008), 361.

43 Gordon C. Rhea, *To the North Anna River: Grant and Lee, May 13-25, 1864* (Baton Rouge, LA, 2000), 88; *OR* 51, pt. 2, 926; Gallagher, *Ramseur*, 111-2, 194 n61; Lee, *Recollections and Letters of REL*, 124-5; Freeman, *Lee*, vol. 3, 327. The history of Zion UMC states that Lee was asleep on a pew when Lt. James Washington of the 9th VA Cavalry brought him news of

Lee notifies Richmond that no fighting occurred today as the Federals are burying their dead; he renews his request for Hoke's Division to offset his recent losses and points out that "constant labor is impairing the efficiency of the men." The first interments occur at Arlington. Rain continues.[44]

May 14, Saturday (Spotsylvania Court House): Around midday Lt. Robert J. Washington of the 9th Virginia Cavalry brings word that the Army of the Potomac captured the Myers farm, directly east of Spotsylvania Court House; the trooper finds Lee asleep on a bench at Zion Church. Lee advises Gen. Ewell several times during the afternoon that he is not certain what the Federal movement to the right indicates, but he instructs Ewell to determine what is left in his front in late afternoon. The general encounters Gen. Bryan Grimes while riding the lines and thanks him for his efforts during the Mule Shoe fighting. Lee orders the remains of the Virginia brigades from Edward Johnson's division combined under the senior officer, and what is left of both Louisiana brigades combined, all being placed in Jubal Early's division; no successor to Stuart is named, instead all three cavalry divisions will report directly to Lee.[45]

Gen. Lee issues a congratulatory order to this army for its recent successes and resilience in the face of extreme and unrelenting adversity, and requests that Gen. John Breckinridge bring his forces across the mountains to join the Army of Northern Virginia if the enemy in the Shenandoah can be defeated quickly. Lee cautions the War Department that Breckinridge cannot be withdrawn from the Valley unless the forces opposing him there are defeated; he also recommends that all available troops from South Carolina be brought to defend Richmond. Rain continues.[46]

May 15, Sunday (Spotsylvania Court House): While Lee is on the Third Corps lines, Federal artillery opens "as if they had discovered his presence;" an unidentified soldier manhandles the general into a gun pit to protect him from the falling shells. Lee advises President Davis of yesterday's fighting and tells him that Gen. Grant seems to be moving the Union army to the right again. Rain continues.[47]

May 16, Monday (Spotsylvania Court House): Lee informs Richmond that Grant has made no attacks today but shifted to the right toward Massaponax, and advises Ewell that reports of an enemy column moving south on Telegraph Road was only cavalry. He congratulates Breckinridge for his victory over Franz Sigel at New Market and instructs him to push Sigel across the Potomac if possible but if that can't

---

Stuart's death, but no source is given for this (and it seems to confuse news of Stuart's death with Lt. Washington's message of Grant's army moving, which he delivered on the 14th). See Rhea, *To the North Anna*, 81. This does not agree with the eyewitness account given by Gordon McCabe, quoted in Rob's biography of his farther used here. Zion United Methodist Church, http://www.historiczionumc.org/History.

44 *OR* 36, pt. 2, 998; *OR* 51, pt. 2, 925; Perry, *Mrs. REL*, 276; Clifton diary, May 13, 1864, NC Archives. Pvt. William H. Christman, 67th PA Infantry, was the first burial at Arlington; he died of measles on May 11 in a Washington hospital. Poole, *On Hallowed Ground*, 58-9.

45 Rhea, *To the North Anna*, 81; *OR* 51, pt. 2, 929-30; Cowper, *Letters of Grimes*, 54; *OR* 36, pt. 2, 1001. A rather dubious claim was put forth by both of Richard H. Anderson's biographers that Lee asked Anderson to succeed Stuart as the head of the Virginia army's cavalry arm, but that Anderson declined the post and recommended Wade Hampton instead. Neither writer put a date on the conversation, but if it occurred, it must have been on the 13th or 14th. Eliot, *R. H. Anderson*, 88-9; Cornelius I. Walker, *The Life of Lieutenant General Richard Heron Anderson, of the Confederate States Army* (Charleston, SC, 1917), 173.

46 *OR Supplement*, part 3, vol. 3, 508-9; *OR* 37, pt. 1, 735; Dowdey, *Wartime Papers*, 730; Freeman, *Lee's Dispatches*, 177-8; Clifton diary, May 14, 1864, NC Archives.

47 Poague, *Gunner with Stonewall*, 93; Dowdey, *Wartime Papers*, 730; Freeman, *Lee's Dispatches*, 181-2; Clifton diary, May 15, 1864, NC Archives. This was likely the same bombardment Freeman mentioned, although he made no mention of a soldier grabbing Lee, only that he came under heavy fire. *Lee*, vol. 3, 331. Gordon Rhea put this incident on the 17th, but did not explain why he disagreed with Poague's date of the 15th. Rhea, *To the North Anna*, 132. Much of the HQ guard escorted prisoners to Gordonsville on this date, leaving only a handful to serve as couriers. F. G. Walter diary, May 15, 1864, LVA.

be done to bring his force to join Lee. He writes to wife Mary advising that no more socks are needed as the quartermaster finally delivered 30,000 pairs before the army left Orange; he regrets the loss of Stuart and apologizes for not writing more frequently but the constant fighting has prevented it: "As I write I am expecting the sound of the guns every moment." Steady rain continues.[48]

May 17, Tuesday (Spotsylvania Court House): Lee advises Breckinridge that George Crook and William Averell's forces have retired from southwest Virginia, so Breckinridge is to bring his infantry to Hanover Junction. He informs Sec. Seddon that Grant's forces remain quiet with no reported changes in position; he also expresses his elation at Beauregard's victory over Ben Butler as reported in the newspapers. He also requests that Lafayette McLaws not be assigned to duty with the ANV again and be sent elsewhere. In the evening A. P. Hill complains to Lee about Ambrose Wright's poor performance in conducting a reconnaissance in force along the Massaponax Church Road; Lee tells Hill "General Wright is a lawyer, not a soldier," and tells Hill nothing good will come from bringing charges against Wright. Light rain in the evening.[49]

May 18, Wednesday (Spotsylvania Court House): Lee observes an attack made against Ewell and Early in the morning; Charles Marshall is wounded in the head by a shell fragment which knocks the lens from his glasses. Lee sends several messages to President Davis complaining about the army's current situation: "We cannot attack . . . with any prospect of success without great loss of men which I wish to avoid if possible." He points out that Grant is being constantly reinforced while the ANV receives no additional troops, thus he would like some of Beauregard's army sent him: "The question is whether we shall fight the battle here or around Richmond. If the troops are obliged to be retained at Richmond I may be forced back."[50]

Lee advises Gen. Breckinridge that scouts report Franz Sigel's forces leaving the Shenandoah Valley to join Grant, so "you can with safety join me." Lee advises Richmond that he ordered the supplies at Hanover Junction moved to protect them from Sheridan's cavalry, and requests that Col. Clement Evans be promoted to brigadier general command John Gordon's brigade. Lee orders Fitz Lee to gather all the cavalry he can find and follow Phil Sheridan, and he informs Sec. Seddon of the morning's fighting. Steady Showers fall throughout the day.[51]

May 19, Thursday (Spotsylvania Court House): Lee informs Sec. Seddon that Gen. Grant "continues to drift to our right," and that Gen. Ewell located the Federals near Telegraph Road. Turning his attention again to western Virginia, Lee asks Gen. Breckinridge if he can spare any cavalry for service with Lee, and instructs "Grumble" Jones to move into the Shenandoah Valley to support Gen. Imboden, and for Imboden to call out the reserves to

---

48 *OR* 36, pt. 1, 1030; *OR* 36, pt. 2, 1011-2; *OR* 37, pt. 1, 737-8; Dowdey, *Wartime Papers*, 730-1; Thomas, *REL*, 329. In response to the uncertainty regarding Grant's movements and intentions, Lee supposedly told one of the staff on this date, "If my poor friend Stuart were here I should know all about what those people are doing." Trudeau, *Bloody Roads South*, 192.

49 *OR* 37, pt. 1, 738; *OR* 36, pt. 2, 1015; Freeman, *Lee's Dispatches*, 182-3; Rhea, *To the North Anna*, 132; Krick, *CW Weather*, 126. By mentioning the newspapers as his source for Beauregard's victory over Butler, Lee was perhaps making a thinly veiled jab at Sec. Seddon for not keeping him informed. With all the losses in his general officer corps, Lee's request not to have McLaws is a telling indicator of Lee's assessment of that general's abilities in the field. Freeman has the episode with Lee and A. P. Hill occurring on the 15th, but Rhea convincingly argues that it was the 17th. Freeman, *Lee*, vol. 3, 330-1; Rhea, *To the North Anna*, 132, 412 n17.

50 *OR* 36, pt. 2, 1019; F. G. Walter diary, May 18, 1864, LVA; Driver, *39th Virginia Cavalry Battalion*, 72-3; Freeman, *Lee's Dispatches*, 183-6; Dowdey, *Wartime Papers*, 733.

51 *OR* 37, pt. 1, 742; *OR* 51, pt. 2, 942-3; REL to Jefferson Davis, May 18, 1864, telegram book, REL HQ papers, VHS; *OR* 36, pt. 2, 1019; Krick, *CW Weather*, 126. Evans was a former member of the Georgia Senate and colonel of the 31st GA Infantry. After the war, he became active in Confederate veteran organizations and was editor of the 12-volume *Confederate Military History*. Warner, *Generals in Gray*, 83.

augment his force: "The enemy must be beaten back from the Valley and the people can do it."⁵²

May 20, Friday (Spotsylvania Court House): Lee issues a general order announcing Stuart's death: "Among the gallant soldiers who have fallen in this war, General Stuart was second to none in valor, in zeal, and in unflinching devotion to his country." Lee advises Ewell that Grant seems to be at the Telegraph Road crossing of the Ny River—has Ewell discovered any movement in his front or can he strike the enemy flank? In the evening he sends a mild rebuke to Ewell for his silence regarding enemy dispositions in his front and instructs him to move in the morning to the extreme right to counter Grant's latest shift. He informs Seddon of Grant's move to the right but cautions that he is not certain of the Union general's intentions. Lee instructs Breckinridge to be prepared to cooperate with Lee's army upon his arrival at Hanover Junction, and sends a very terse telegram to President Davis regarding the army's position.⁵³

May 21, Saturday (Spotsylvania Court House/ Southworth House/Road to North Anna): Lee is up well before dawn, sifting through reports regarding another movement by Grant. Between 4:30 and 5:00 a.m. Lee sends a number of communications to Richmond, to Hanover Junction, and to his various commanders, regarding the pursuit of Grant's army and the defense of the railroad and bridges at Hanover Junction and Milford. Later in the morning he notifies Seddon that Grant appears headed southeast again and Lee will move along Telegraph Road and look to strike Grant once he crosses the Pamunkey River.⁵⁴

Around midday, Gen. Lee moves his headquarters to the Southworth house, about two miles south of Spotsylvania Court House, and sets his infantry in motion toward Hanover Junction. During the afternoon, A. P. Hill resumes command of the Third Corps and a reconnaissance confirms that the Army of the Potomac is gone from its extensive works around Spotsylvania. In early evening Lee meets with Gens. Anderson, Early, Hill, and Rooney to discuss the march to Hanover Junction and the North Anna River. Well after dark Lee departs for the North Anna, guided by Lt. Eustis C. Moncure and Pvt. W. G. Jesse of the 9th Virginia Cavalry. Their party proceeds via Traveller's Rest to Telegraph Road at Mud Tavern, where they turn south. Rain during the afternoon.⁵⁵

---

52 *OR* 36, pt. 2, 1022; *OR* 37, pt. 1, 743; REL to Jones, May 19, 1864, telegram book, REL HQ papers, VHS; REL to Imboden, May 19, 1864, telegram book, REL HQ papers, VHS. After the war, Lee told William Allan that Ewell "lost all presence of mind" in the fighting at the Harris farm on this day, and that Lee had found Ewell "prostrate on the ground" and incapable of commanding the fight. Ewell's modern biographer, however, contends that this event did not happen because Gen. Lee was not present at the Harris farm, and he probably never left his own headquarters. Pfanz, *Ewell*, 393. In any event, Richard Ewell botched the engagement and lost nearly 1,000 men for no purpose. Freeman, *Lee*, vol. 3, 338-9.

53 *OR* 36, pt. 3, 800-1; *OR* 37, pt. 1, 744-5; Dowdey, *Wartime Papers*, 734. Charles Marshall completed the letter to Breckinridge and noted that Lee left camp before it was finished, hence why it was not signed by Lee; where Lee went is not known. His letter to President Davis reads in part: "Am fully alive to importance of concentration and being near base. . . . My letters give you my views." This is not Lee's usual tone with the president, which suggests that Lee may have taken umbrage with something in some of Davis's communications.

54 J. Michael Miller, *The North Anna Campaign: "Even to Hell Itself" May 21 – 26, 1864* (Lynchburg, VA, 1989), 23; *OR* 36, pt. 3, 801-2; REL endorsement on Birkett Fry to WHT, May 20, 1864, EPA papers, UNC; REL to Fitz Lee, May 21, 1864, telegram book, REL HQ papers, VHS; REL to Breckinridge, May 21, 1864, telegram book, REL HQ papers, VHS; REL to Pickett, May 21, 1864, telegram book, REL HQ papers, VHS; *OR* 36, pt. 3, 812, 815. One cavalry officer claimed that reports were sent to Lee every 15 minutes during the night of the 20th and early morning of the 21st regarding Grant's movements. R. L. T. Beale, *History of the Ninth Virginia Cavalry in the War Between the States* (Richmond, VA, 1899), 120. The Southworth house was located near Snell Bridge over the Po River.

55 Matter, *If It Takes All Summer*, 341; *OR* 36, pt. 3, 813-5; Freeman, *Lee*, vol. 3, 343; E. C. Moncure, "Reminiscences of the Civil War," Moncure papers, LVA; Clifton diary, May 21, 1864, NC Archives. SO 128 restored A. P. Hill to command of his Third Corps with Jubal Early reverting back to his own division. It also combined all of the Virginia units of Ed Johnson's division into a single brigade under Gen. William Terry, and assigned John Gordon to command of the remnants of Johnson's Division. *OR* 36, pt. 3, 813-4. Lee's party rode via Courthouse Road to modern-day Snell, where

May 22, Sunday (Road to North Anna/Hanover Junction): Lee is in the saddle most of the night of the 21st/22nd on the ride south from Spotsylvania. Just past Jerroll's Mill, where Telegraph Road crosses the Ta River, he helps to sort out a traffic snarl of wagons and artillery stuck in the mud. Several miles further, Lee pauses to urge along a group of stragglers asleep beside the road. About 2:00 a.m. Lee arrives at the home of Dr. Joseph A. Flippo where he dismounts and speaks with the doctor for a short time before continuing on to Stevens's Mill Pond, about four miles north of Carmel Church, where he rests for several hours. At 5:00 a.m. Lee writes to President Davis, advising that Pickett and Hoke are near Milford and that all three corps of Lee's army will be on the North Anna today; he thinks Grant may be planning to use the RF&P Railroad as his supply line rather than by water to Port Royal. Shortly after daybreak Lee continues on with Ewell's corps, riding a portion of the way with Jed Hotchkiss.[56]

Around 8:30 a.m. Lee crosses the North Anna at Chesterfield Bridge onto the Fox farm where he meets briefly with Jubal Early and John Breckinridge. Lee joins Breckinridge's aide Maj. J. S. Johnston for breakfast, as Breckinridge is out reconnoitering the ground when Lee arrives, but the Kentuckian returns very soon after Lee's arrival. In mid morning Lee advises Seddon that Ewell's corps arrived at Hanover Junction, and the other two corps will arrive soon. Lee has lunch with Breckinridge and in the afternoon the two of them reconnoiter along the river. Lee establishes headquarters at the Miller house, Whitehall, just north of Hanover Junction, and he receives letters from Mary and Agnes. In the evening he advises Fitz Lee of a report of enemy cavalry headed for White House.[57]

Traveller's Rest was located during the war. The party turned east there on Morris Road to Thornburg, and then south along Telegraph Road. Moncure left a very detailed account of this night march from Spotsylvania to the North Anna, although he recalled the dates incorrectly as the night of 22/23.

56 Moncure, "Reminiscences," LVA; Dowdey, *Wartime Papers*, 745-6; WHT to R. H. Anderson, May 22, 1864, EPA papers, UNC; Freeman, *Lee*, vol. 3, 349. Stevens's Mill Pond was in the vicinity of modern Lake Caroline. At least a portion of the staff preceded Lee and erected several of the HQ tents beside the pond, where the general shared his breakfast of biscuits and coffee with guides Moncure and Jesse. Moncure, "Reminiscences," LVA. Ironically, both Gens. Grant and Meade established their headquarters at Moncure's home Ellerslie near Carmel Church. Rhea, *To the North Anna*, 285.

57 Rhea, *To the North Anna*, 264-5; J. Stoddard Johnston, "Recollections of Robert E. Lee," Louisville *Courier-Journal*, June 3, 1900, REL papers, Duke; *OR* 36, pt. 3, 823; Dowdey, *Wartime Papers*, 748; REL to Fitz Lee, May 22, 1864, telegram book, REL HQ papers, VHS. Lee's meeting with Jubal Early was less than pleasant. When he instructed Early to put his men into position immediately, Early protested that they were tired from marching all night and needed rest, to which Lee replied, "Gen. Early you must not tell me these things, but when I give an order, see that it is executed." Out of earshot of Lee, Early voiced to the others present that the army commander was "much troubled and not well." George W. Booth, *A Maryland Boy in Lee's Army: Personal Reminiscences of a Maryland Soldier in the War Between the States, 1861 – 1865* (Lincoln, NE, 2000), 110-1. Few writers mention Lee's interaction with Breckinridge, so it is not known which meeting, with Early or Breckinridge, occurred first. Johnston's account of the meeting with Breckinridge is very detailed although he is off by one day, incorrectly placing Lee's arrival at Hanover Junction on the 21st. Lt. Moncure rejoined Lee about 11:00 a.m. after carrying a message to Wade Hampton, and noted that Lee was in company with not only Breckinridge, but also President Jefferson Davis and Sec. James Seddon; no other account mentions the presence of either Davis or Seddon. J. Stoddard Johnston, nephew of Albert Sidney Johnston and cousin of John Breckinridge, served as an aide to Braxton Bragg, Simon Buckner, Breckinridge, and John Echols. After the war, Johnston authored the Kentucky volume of the *Confederate Military History* series. Krick, *Staff Officers in Gray*, 173-4. The location of Lee's HQ on the 21st has been the cause of some confusion. Freeman believed it was literally at the junction "in the southwest angle of the crossing" of the RF&P and Virginia Central railroads, based on the 1926 recollections of a local resident who had been a young boy in 1864; this is repeated on the Civil War Trails marker at the site and in the North Anna battlefield tour brochure. Freeman, *Lee*, vol. 3, 350. Overland Campaign historian Gordon Rhea wrote that Lee's HQ was at the Miller house just north of the intersection, which—although Rhea does not cite a source for this—seems much more likely. *To the North Anna*, 265. J. S. Johnston's recollections seem to reinforce Rhea's location, for he notes that Lee's tent was "near and north of" the junction. Jed Hotchkiss wrote of a conference on the 23rd at Lee's HQ "near Mrs. Miller's." McDonald, *Make Me a Map*, 207. Lee met with William N. Pendleton sometime in the morning after his arrival at Hanover Junction and relayed news of the death of Hill Carter's wife, Mary Braxton Randolph Carter, of Shirley, as conveyed by wife Mary's letter. WNP to wife, May 22, 1864, WNP papers, UNC.

May 23, Monday (Hanover Junction): In the morning Lee and Jed Hotchkiss ride along the left half of the army's lines. Around noon, enemy troops appear on the north bank of the river, battling with the South Carolinians stationed at the northern end of Chesterfield Bridge. Lee observes this action from Joe Kershaw's headquarters at the Fox home, Ellington, and owner Thomas H. Fox invites Lee inside; Lee declines the invitation, but asks for a glass of buttermilk. He is standing on the porch when an artillery round from an enemy gun fired from across the river passes right next to him and strikes the doorframe of the house.[58]

During the afternoon Lee goes upstream to Jericho Mills to investigate firing there, but is too ill to ride on horseback. He makes the trip in a carriage and observes the fighting from the position of Chew's Battery. Determining the action to be nothing more than a feint, the general returns to the junction. Lee informs President Davis that the entire army is in position along the North Anna River, and that he would like to have Gen. Beauregard join him with his army for a combined strike against the Army of the Potomac before the Federals reach the Chickahominy River. Lee directs Fitz Lee to move his force to Hanover Court House to guard against Phil Sheridan's approach from the east.[59]

In the evening Gen. Lee meets in the yard of Whitehall with Gens. Ewell, Hill, and Anderson, M. L. Smith, Porter Alexander, Jed Hotchkiss and several other engineers regarding the best defensive position for the army. The meeting is interrupted by a nearby teamster whipping a mule, which Lee puts a stop to. Following the meeting, the general updates Sec. Seddon on the fighting at Chesterfield Bridge and Jericho Mills. He writes to wife Mary with the latest news of the campaign and requests some summer-weight underclothes be sent to him. Storms break out during the evening.[60]

May 24, Tuesday (Hanover Junction/Taylorsville): Lee rises before 6:00 a.m. and meets with several engineer officers, including Gen. Smith and Col. Talcott, regarding the army's position, and notifies Richmond that not all of the elements of Pickett's and Hoke's forces were sent to the North Anna River as he had requested. Lee joins Gens. Ewell and Anderson for breakfast at Anderson's headquarters. Following breakfast, he rides in a carriage to A. P. Hill's front on the left side of the line, where he strongly rebukes Hill for his handling of the fight at Jericho Mills the previous day, telling Hill "Why did you not do as Jackson would have done—thrown your whole force upon these people and driven them back?"[61]

In the afternoon Jed Hotchkiss joins Lee for a snack, and probably accompanies Lee as he rides the right half of his position. Likely as a result of this survey of his position, he shifts Breckinridge's small

---

58 Hotchkiss to WHT, March 4, 1897, WHT papers, NPL; Freeman, *Lee*, vol. 3, 352-3; HCHS, *Old Homes of Hanover*, 78; Miller, *North Anna Campaign*, 56. Freeman recorded the owner of Ellington as W. E. Fox, but this is incorrect; Parson Thomas H. Fox was the owner in 1864. After Lee left the house, Richard Anderson used it as his headquarters; Anderson, Porter Alexander, and several others were resting against the side of the house when more enemy fire struck it, sending part of the chimney toppling down on Alexander's party and killing a courier. The house was later used by Maj. Gen. Winfield S. Hancock as his headquarters. Rhea, *To the North Anna*, 299-300, 332. Ellington was constructed in 1830 and Fox ran a school in an outbuilding before the war. The property was recently purchased by the Civil War Trust. HCHS, *Old Homes of Hanover*, 78.

59 Hassler, *A. P. Hill*, 205; George M. Neese, *Three Years in the Confederate Horse Artillery* (New York, 1911), 274-5; Dowdey, *Wartime Papers*, 747-8; REL to Fitz Lee, May 23, 1864, telegram book, REL HQ papers, VHS. Hotchkiss recalled long after the war that although Lee was quite ill later in the day and became worse over the next few days, he showed no signs of it on their morning ride. Hotchkiss to WHT, March 4, 1897, WHT papers, NPL.

60 McDonald, *Make Me a Map*, 206-7; Gallagher, *Fighting for the Confederacy*, 389-90; Rhea, *To the North Anna*, 323; OR 36, pt. 1, 1030; Dowdey, *Wartime Papers*, 748; Freeman, *Lee*, vol. 3, 355. Lee made no mention to Mary of his failing health.

61 Rhea, *To the North Anna*, 325-6; OR 51, pt. 2, 957; McDonald, *Make Me a Map*, 207; Hotchkiss, *Virginia*, 460. Lee's illness continued, and although he was not able to ride on horseback, he was able to get around. His ailment was characterized at the time as "bilious dysentery." Welsh, *Medical Histories*, 135. A surgeon who examined Lee noted that he had not slept more than two consecutive hours in weeks, and was "cross as an old bear." Rhea, *To the North Anna*, 326.

division to the right and cautions Anderson to guard the road to Atlee.[62]

Lee shifts headquarters about two miles south to Taylorsville at some point during the day. He notifies Sec. Seddon that Brig. Gen. Evander Law was restored to duty and after reviewing the evidence, Lee is convinced that the situation regarding Law was mishandled by Longstreet. During the night he informs Richmond of the day's action: several probing assaults along the line and a successful counterattack by Mahone which captured several enemy colors and an aide to Brig. Gen. James Ledlie. Showers in the evening.[63]

May 25, Wednesday (Taylorsville): Lee rises before dawn but his condition keeps him confined to his tent. Before dawn he sends to Richmond communications between Grant and Ambrose Burnside captured yesterday by some of Mahone's men which confirm that the Federals stripped other theaters to reinforce the Army of the Potomac. He again requests that Beauregard's force be combined with the ANV: "Every available man has been brought to the front [by Grant]. This makes it necessary for us to do likewise." With Breckinridge and much of the western Virginia force along the North Anna, Lee expresses his concern to Richmond and John Imboden regarding the situation in the Valley, telling Sec. Seddon "the case is urgent" to appoint an overall commander in western Virginia in Breckinridge's absence.[64]

Lee tells Richmond he does not however wish to detach Brig. Gen. John Echols from Breckinridge's Division to send him back to western Virginia, and he notifies Imboden to do what he can to resist any enemy move up the Valley and that Breckinridge will be sent back there as soon as possible. In the afternoon he sends M. L. Smith to scout out a new line along the South Anna River. Rain in the evening.[65]

May 26, Thursday (Taylorsville): Lee remains confined to his tent. In late morning he orders probes sent forward to determine if Grant is still

---

62 McDonald, *Make Me a Map*, 207; Rhea, *To the North Anna*, 108; *OR* 51, pt. 2, 672; *OR* 36, pt. 3, 828. Hotchkiss did not comment on Lee's health at this time, and no known source mentions whether Lee was on horseback or in his carriage for his afternoon ride, although it seems likely given his condition that he was not on horseback.

63 *OR* 36, 1030-1; *OR* 52, pt. 2, 672; F. G. Walter diary, May 24, 1864, LVA. The location of Lee's HQ on this date is not certain; his previous location at the Miller house was no longer tenable after the repositioning of the army during the night and morning, as the new line passed through the yard of the house. Krick, *Survey of CW Sites in Hanover*, 41. It is known that he was at Taylorsville on the 25th, so it seems highly likely he relocated there at some point on the 24th. Freeman has him moving to Taylorsville on the 25th, as does Trudeau. Freeman, *Lee*, vol. 3, 359; Trudeau, *Bloody Roads South*, 242. A history of Hanover County also gives the 25th as the date of the move. John M. Gabbert, *Military Operations in Hanover County, Virginia, 1861-1865* (Roanoke, VA, 1989), 74. A misdated note in the *OR* from Venable to Anderson, incorrectly dated May 21, when Lee was still at Spotsylvania, gives the exact location of the HQ at Taylorsville, but offers no clue as to the correct date: Lee's HQ was located "1 ½ miles below [the] Junction, on Telegraph Road, right-hand side, in an orchard near an old house, with a chimney running through the middle." *OR* 36, pt. 3, 814. The 9:30 p.m. telegram to Seddon was headlined "Taylorsville," but that by itself does not prove Lee himself was there, only that the message was sent from the telegraph station there. *OR* 51, pt. 2, 672. Little exists today of the wartime village of Taylorsville, which was where the RF&P and Telegraph Road crossed the Little River. Roseanne G. Shalf, *Ashland, Ashland: The Story of a Turn-of-the-Century Railroad Town* (Lawrenceville, VA, 1994), 61.

64 Lee, *Memoirs of WNP*, 336; Venable, "Campaign from the Wilderness to Petersburg," 535; Dowdey, *Wartime Papers*, 750-1; *OR* 37, pt. 1, 747-8. It is almost certainly on this date that Lee and Venable exchanged words (argument may be too strong) over some unknown matter. Venable emerged from Lee's tent and complained to another aide, "I have just told the old man that he is not fit to command this army, and that he had better send for Beauregard." Freeman, *Lee*, vol. 3, 359. While Venable himself did not record that incident, he did write of Lee's incapacitation at this time: "As he lay in his tent he would say, in his impatience, 'We must strike them! We must never let them pass us again! We must strike them!' He had reports brought to him constantly from the field. But Lee ill in his tent was not Lee at the front." Venable, "Lee in the Wilderness," 244. He did not put a date to this episode, but it almost certainly must have been on the 25th or 26th because Lee was not well enough to organize an attack on Grant's isolated corps on the south bank of the North Anna, and he refused to turn over command of the army to Ewell, Hill, or anyone else.

65 Freeman, *Lee's Dispatches*, 197-8; REL to Imboden, May 25, 1864 (2 messages), telegram book, REL HQ papers, VHS; Miller, *North Anna Campaign*, 128; F. G. Walter diary, May 25, 1864, LVA.

south of the river. Lee forwards to the War Department a request from A. P. Hill for a new commander for McGowan's Brigade and also requests that Col. Bryan Grimes be given command of Junius Daniel's former brigade. In the evening Lee informs Sec. Seddon that Grant did not make an attack today, and he thinks Grant intends to move his army around Lee's left flank. Lee also notes also that Sheridan's cavalry rejoined the Army of the Potomac. Rain in the morning.[66]

May 27, Friday (Taylorsville/Ashland/Belle Farm): Lee is again up before dawn dealing with reports of Grant's withdrawal. When he confirms them and learns Grant is crossing the Pamunkey at Hanovertown, Lee orders the army to move to Ashland. He is unable to ride a horse still, so accompanies Ewell's column in a carriage. He establishes headquarters for the night at Belle Farm, the home of the Jenkins family at the intersection of Telegraph Road and Atlee's Station Road. From there Lee orders the army to move early the next morning to Totopotomoy Creek. Showers during the day.[67]

May 28, Saturday (Belle Farm/Atlee's/Lockwood): Lee has breakfast at Belle Farm and informs President Davis that in response to Grant's move to Hanovertown, he put the army in motion for Atlee's Station and Totopotomoy Creek to block the direct path to Richmond. He fears Grant may move toward Ashland by way of Lee's left flank. Whichever path Grant takes, Lee still wants Beauregard to join him; Lee sends out cavalry to determine Grant's direction. Lee departs for Atlee's in the morning, arrives in late morning, and establishes headquarters at the Clarke house (Lockwood).[68]

Upon his arrival at Atlee's, he sends a message to Gen. Bragg requesting that Meadow Bridge be rebuilt and that a telegraph operator be sent to Atlee's to speed communication with the capital. During the afternoon Lee meets with Breckinridge, and later sends his division to Enon Church to guard the army's rear. In early evening Lee apprises Sec. Seddon that the army is in position from Atlee's to Totopotomoy Creek. Showers during the day.[69]

May 29, Sunday (Lockwood): In the morning Lee receives a letter and "basket of provisions" from

---

66 *OR* 51, pt. 2, 960; *OR* 36, pt. 3, 834; Venable to R. H. Anderson, May 26, 1864, EPA papers, UNC; REL to Jefferson Davis, May 26, 1864 (2 messages), telegram book, REL HQ papers, VHS; Clifton diary, May 26, 1864, NC Archives.

67 *OR* 36, pt. 3 836-9; *OR* 51, pt. 2, 962; F. G. Walter diary, May 27, 1864, LVA; HCHS, *Old Homes of Hanover*, 69-70; Krick, *CW Weather*, 126. Belle Farm was constructed in the early 1850s on 330 acres overlooking Stony Run and owned during the war by Rubin Jenkins. According to Jenkins family lore, one of the Jenkins children was given a ride in Lee's carriage as he approached the house; Mrs. Jenkins prepared Lee's meals while he stayed with the family, and for some reason supposedly Lee's food was examined by his physician before eating it. It was not specified if Lee stayed in the house or in his tent, although Freeman wrote that Lee "rested" on the back porch. HCHS, *Old Homes of Hanover*, 69-70; Freeman, *Lee*, vol. 3, 363 n4. The area has largely been developed but the house still stands north of Lakeridge Parkway (VA 782) opposite Lakeridge Square Apartments, although in extreme disrepair.

68 Dowdey, *Wartime Papers*, 753-4; Freeman, *Lee*, vol. 3, 364; *OR* 36, pt. 3, 844; F. G. Walter diary, May 28, 1864, LVA. Taylor, "on road, near Atlee's," sent marching orders to Breckinridge at 10:30 a.m. A subsequent message to Gen. Bragg at 10:45 a.m. was marked "Hd. Qrs., Atlees," suggesting that Lee arrived at Atlee shortly after 10:30. *OR* 36, pt. 3, 844; Freeman, *Lee's Dispatches*, 201. Lee's illness forced him to stay indoors at Lockwood. Venable, "Lee in the Wilderness," 244. The house stood until 1990, when the property was purchased by Media General to construct offices and a printing facility for Richmond's two newspapers. Several preservation groups attempted unsuccessfully to preserve the structure. See Joe Taylor, "House Where Lee Stayed Sparks Battle," *Washington Post*, April 21, 1990; John F. Harris, "Civil War House Stirs a New Battle in Richmond," *Washington Post*, July 8, 1990; and Land & Community Associates, *Survey of Historic Resources, Hanover County, Virginia* (Charlottesville, VA, 1992), 60. The house site is immediately east of the interchange of US 301 and Interstate 295, near Lockwood Blvd. HCHS, *Old Homes of Hanover*, 30.

69 Freeman, *Lee's Dispatches*, 201; F. G. Walter diary, May 28, 1864, LVA; *OR* 36, pt. 3, 844; *OR* 36, pt. 1, 1031; Krick, *CW Weather*, 126. Lee almost certainly traveled to Atlee's by carriage, although no account specifically mentions this; he admitted to Mary on the 29th that he was unable to ride. Dowdey, *Wartime Papers*, 756. Found among Charles Venable's papers is a cryptic note that reads "Lee's sickness at Atlee's Station." It was likely some sort of reminder to himself for his postwar writings on the Overland Campaign. "Civil War notes," Box 5, McDowell-Miller-Warner papers, UVA. For the short period that Breckinridge was with the ANV, he reported directly to Lee.

Mary. During the morning he sends requests to Beauregard and Bragg for a meeting with Beauregard today at Lockwood. He also notifies Breckinridge that he does not intend any troop movements today, so to take advantage of the respite to rest his troops. Ewell takes ill and Lee appoints Early to command the Second Corps, sending a note to Ewell hoping for a quick recovery; he requests Dr. Hunter McGuire to examine Ewell.[70]

Despite Lee's intentions of not moving any troops and allowing them to rest, he is forced to shift around elements of the army in response to Grant's movements. During the afternoon President Davis comes to headquarters to discuss how best to utilize Beauregard's army. After Davis departs, Beauregard himself arrives and after a lengthy discussion tells Lee he cannot part with any of his 12,000 troops. Afterwards Lee sends a very short two-sentence summary of their meeting to President Davis, concluding "If Gen. Grant advances tomorrow I will engage him with my present force." Lee writes to Mary and admits to being sick but "not . . . very sick" although unable to ride; he mentions that "some kind gentleman has sent some brandy which I am using. I want for nothing. Everybody is so kind that I am overwhelmed by it." He mentions also that he is glad Mildred returned safely from Shirley, where she was briefly detained by Sheridan's men who encamped there; he uses that incident as further reason that she and the girls need to move away from Richmond to a safer locale. Periods of rain.[71]

May 30, Monday (Lockwood/Bethesda Church/Shady Grove Church): In the morning Lee sends a lengthier summation of his meeting with Gen. Beauregard to President Davis. Lee proposes that if he cannot have any of Beauregard's troops, that the Richmond defenses be stripped instead and that its garrison be sent to bolster the Army of Northern Virginia. The general warns Richmond that "if this army is unable to resist Grant, the troops under Gen. Beauregard and in the city will be unable to defend it." He also advises the president that he was promised two battalions of Georgia troops, but that only one arrived—where is the other? In late morning Early proposes attacking a portion of Grant's army on the south side of Totopotomoy Creek; Lee—finally able to ride a horse again—goes to Bethesda Church where he meets with Early, Porter Alexander, and others to survey the field before attacking. In early afternoon Lee orders Anderson to support Early's attack and he is still in the field in late afternoon relaying information from Early to Anderson.[72]

---

70 Dowdey, *Wartime Papers*, 755; OR 36, pt. 3, 846, 848; REL to Ewell, May 29, 1864, Polk-Ewell-Brown papers, UNC; Percy G. Hamlin, *The Making of a Soldier: Letters of General R. S. Ewell* (Richmond, VA, 1935), 127. Although McGuire reported that Ewell would be well enough to resume his duties within four days, Lee used his illness as a basis for replacing him permanently with Early. Hamlin, *Making of a Soldier*, 127-8. As incredible as it seems today, even at this late stage of the war a lack of adequate maps continued to plague the Confederate high command. Lee instructed Taylor on the morning of the 29th to procure an accurate and detailed map of the Richmond vicinity for HQ. Taylor wrote to Pendleton that "Lee has but an indifferent one and is most anxious to get a more complete and correct one." WHT to WNP, May 29, 1864, WNP papers, UNC.

71 OR 36, pt. 3, 846-8; Gordon C. Rhea, *Cold Harbor: Grant and Lee May 26 – June 3, 1864* (Baton Rouge, LA, 2002), 100; Freeman, *Lee*, vol. 3, 368; Dowdey, *Wartime Papers*, 756; Robert Bluford, Jr., *The Battle of Totopotomoy Creek: Polegreen Church and the Prelude to Cold Harbor* (Charleston, SC, 2014), 136. Neither Davis nor Beauregard mentioned this meeting with Lee in their memoirs. Another cryptic note by Venable in his papers reads simply, "the Beauregard incident" (among other incidents from this time). "Civil War notes," Box 5, McDowell-Miller-Warner papers, UVA. Lockwood is probably the only house besides the Executive Mansion and possibly the Virginia Governor's Mansion visited by R. E. Lee, Jefferson Davis, P. G. T. Beauregard, and John C. Breckinridge during the war.

72 Dowdey, *Wartime Papers*, 757; Freeman, *Lee's Dispatches*, 206; Gallagher, *Fighting for the Confederacy*, 397; OR 36, pt. 3, 851; REL to Anderson, May 30, 1864, EPA papers, UNC. Alexander wrote that Lee was present at Bethesda Church with him and Early prior to the attack. Gallagher, *Fighting for the Confederacy*, 397. Freeman was adamant Alexander was wrong and that Lee never left Lockwood on the 30th, calling Alexander's memory a "serious mistake" and "the *Official Records* plainly show that General Lee was not present." Freeman, *Lee*, vol. 3, 371 n38. However, a note to Richard Anderson from Taylor signed by Lee dated 5:45 p.m. from Shady Grove Church backs up Alexander's claim Lee was present for this action. REL to R. H. Anderson, May 30, 1864, EPA papers, UNC. Testimony by a wounded Rebel officer taken captive at

In the afternoon Lee learns one corps of Butler's Army of the James is being sent to Grant, and relays that news to Richmond. After his return to Atlee's, he adjusts his lines and instructs "Grumble" Jones to assemble any force he can and move to Imboden's aid in the Valley. He also instructs Anderson to consult with Field and Kershaw regarding brigade vacancies.[73]

Throughout the day Lee corresponds with Richmond and Beauregard attempting to get reinforcements from Petersburg and Bermuda Hundred transferred to him in light of the information that a portion of Butler's troops are being transferred to Grant. During the evening, he abruptly informs both President Davis and Beauregard that the latter's attempt to sidestep the decision by requesting the War Department to make it for him is irresponsible: "If you cannot determine what troops you can spare, the [War] Department cannot. The result of your delay will be disaster. Butler's troops will be with Grant tomorrow." He all but demands that Hoke's Division be sent to him by dawn.[74]

May 31, Tuesday (Lockwood/Coleman's House): Before dawn Lee sends instructions for Hoke's Division to proceed to Cold Harbor to reinforce Fitz Lee's cavalry. During the afternoon he sends to Richmond a list of officers to be promoted under the newly passed legislation allowing for temporary promotions, including Anderson, Mahone, and Ramseur, as well as permanent promotion for Kershaw. In response to reports from Fitz Lee that enemy infantry is at Cold Harbor, he orders Anderson to extend his corps to link up with Hoke (who arrived at Cold Harbor today) and to take overall command in that sector. In the afternoon he leaves Atlee's for a position closer to the center of his new line, moving by carriage to the area of Shady Grove Church where he establishes headquarters at/near the Coleman house.[75]

Ewell reports he is ready to resume command of his corps, but Lee does not allow him to do so, writing, "I do not think any change [in command] at the present time would be beneficial." He advises him to retire to Richmond or elsewhere to fully restore his health. During the evening Ewell meets with Lee to plead his case in person, but Lee again denies his request.[76]

Bethesda Church confirms Lee was on horseback in the field. OR 36, pt. 3, 392. Lee planned to meet with Anderson at Lockwood in the morning, but it is not known whether he did so. WHT to Anderson, May 29, 1864, EPA papers, UNC.

73 Dowdey, *Wartime Papers*, 758; REL to Breckinridge, May 30, 1864, Jamestown Exhibit Papers, LVA; OR 37, pt. 1, 750; OR 36, pt. 3, 851; REL to Anderson, May 30, 1864, EPA papers, UNC.

74 REL to Beauregard, May 30, 1864 (2 messages) telegram book, REL HQ papers, VHS; OR 36, pt. 3, 850. Taylor noted on this date that Lee's health was significantly better: "The Gen. has been somewhat indisposed and could attend to nothing except what was absolutely necessary for him to know and act upon. . . . He is now improving." Tower, *Lee's Adjutant*, 164.

75 Freeman, *Lee's Dispatches*, 210-1, 364-7; Freeman, *Lee*, vol. 3, 373-7; OR 36, pt. 3, 858; Bluford, *Totopotomoy Creek*, 74. Coleman's house is not on any of Jed Hotchkiss or Jeremy Gilmer's maps of Hanover County, although Walter Taylor put it "on [the] road from Shady Grove Church to Mechanicsville." OR 36, pt. 3, 858. One writer put it at the intersection of the Meadow Bridge and Shady Grove Church roads, but offers no source. Bluford, *Totopotomoy Creek*, 115. Some unnamed dwellings appear on period maps there. Trudeau put HQ at Shady Grove Church as does the official history of the county. Trudeau, *Bloody Roads South*, 261; Martha W. McCartney, *Nature's Bounty, Nation's Glory: The Heritage and History of Hanover County, Virginia* (Hanover, VA, 2009), 216. Taylor: HQ was "near Mechanicsville." Tower, *Lee's Adjutant*, 165.

76 REL to Ewell, May 31, 1864, Polk-Ewell-Brown papers, UNC; Pfanz, *Ewell*, 37. Lee possibly intended to go to Cold Harbor himself, but made it no farther than Shady Grove due to his ongoing poor health. Freeman noted it was around this time that Dr. Lafayette Guild prescribed wine for Lee, but the general refused to use it or any other alcoholic stimulants. Freeman, *Lee*, vol. 3, 377 n9.

June 1864

If Mine Run and Spotsylvania had not taught the value of entrenchments, the slaughter at Cold Harbor on June 3, 1864, certainly did. Gen. U. S. Grant sent several corps into a frontal assault against Robert E. Lee's works that cost him thousands of killed and wounded in a short time. It was one of the few mistakes Grant had made thus far in the campaign. "I have always regretted that the last assault at Cold Harbor was ever made," he wrote years later. "No advantage whatever was gained to compensate for the heavy loss we sustained."[1]

The conflict was changing. Rare would be the battle where men on both sides did not throw up some manner of field works when they halted for a prolonged period. Grant's relentless assaults and flanking operations had driven Lee's army in a giant arc down to the James River. "The time has arrived, in my opinion, when something more is necessary than adhering to lines and defensive positions," Lee told A. P. Hill. "We shall be obliged to go out and prevent the enemy from selecting such positions as he chooses. If he is allowed to continue that course we shall at last be obliged to take refuge behind the works of Richmond and stand a siege, which would be but a work of time."[2]

Whatever ailment had plagued Lee in late May lingered into the first few days of June. Still, he had recovered enough to host a small army of visitors from Jefferson Davis on down through the political hierarchy; such was the cost of being but a short ride from the capital.

Headquarters early in the month was on the old Gaines' Mill battlefield. Former President John Tyler's son, Maj. John Tyler, Jr., accompanied Lee from the beginning of the campaign and told his chief, Maj. Gen. Sterling Price, about how sparse his headquarters was compared to Price's: "Your own headquarters establishment is more numerous and bulky. He rides with only three members of his staff and never takes with him an extra horse or servant, although he is upon the lines usually from daybreak until dark. . . . He eats the ration of the soldier and quarters alone in his tent."[3]

Two signal corps soldiers, doing what soldiers have always done, took the shortest route and had an unexpected encounter with Lee during the lull that followed the heaviest fighting at Cold Harbor:

> Between our camp and the river, the public road made a wide half-circle around the base of a hill that gradually sloped up, for nearly a mile, to a house where General Lee had his headquarters. There was a private road, leading by the house, which cut off this long bend, and we took it. As we neared the house, General Lee, attended by several officers and couriers, rode out and came towards us. We drew to one side to let him pass; but, instead of passing, he stopped and asked where we were going. When we told him, he said: "This is a private way that you have no right to use. Go back to the public road and follow it to your destination." He waved his hand to indicate that we must precede him, and, crestfallen, we started back. The constant going to and from headquarters had pulverized the dry ground, and our horses raised a cloud of dust that enveloped him. Seeing this, my companion, a nervy young thoroughbred, wheeled his horse, saluted, and said: "General we deserve to be punished, but we beg that you will make our punishment less severe by permitting us to ride in the rear, so that you will not get the dust we raise." Instead of making him a captain and me a lieutenant, as the young fellow afterwards said Napoleon would

---

1 Ernest B. Furguson, *Not War But Murder: Cold Harbor, 1864* (New York, 2001), 234.

2 Dowdey, *Wartime Papers*, 759-60.

3 OR 51, pt. 2, 993-5.

have done, General Lee, striving in vain to hide a smile, merely thanked us for wishing to save him from discomfort and made us . . . ride before him and throw dust in his face all the way back to that public road.[4]

While the Army of Northern Virginia was relatively secure behind its entrenchments at Cold Harbor, threats elsewhere reappeared. David Hunter replaced Franz Sigel in the Valley and brushed aside what little resistance remained there, capturing Staunton and Lexington and burning Virginia Military Institute before moving on Lynchburg. Closer to home, Ben Butler found a way to become useful again by becoming in essence a replacement depot for Gen. Meade's Army of the Potomac. Some of Butler's troops were used at Cold Harbor, and others in another effort to take Petersburg.

Lee found Hunter a much simpler problem to deal with, first by sending John Breckinridge's small force and then the entire Second Corps to defend Lynchburg. It was not Ewell who led the corps on its return to the Valley, but Jubal Early. Lee was unsatisfied with Ewell's performance at the head of Jackson's old Valley Army, and when the one-legged general reported to reassume command of his corps in early June following an illness, Lee refused to accept him back and sent him to command at Richmond. It was a disappointing exit for one of the 1862 army's best fighters.

Petersburg was a different story. The city, with its extensive railroad network, was absolutely vital to the survival of Lee's army, and perhaps the entire Confederacy. The only link between Richmond and the port of Wilmington passed through the Cockade City, as did the Southside Railroad, one of the links with southwestern Virginia. Gen. P. G. T. Beauregard had the equivalent of a small corps to defend the city. To the Creole's dismay, Lee viewed his force as a potential source of reinforcement for the Army of Northern Virginia.

When Grant disappeared from Cold Harbor, Lee did not know where he went—but Beauregard did. Lee made only a handful of serious mistakes during the war, but one of the biggest was when he allowed Grant and Meade to steal a march on him and then refused to believe the Army of the Potomac was knocking on Petersburg's door south of the James. Beauregard had contributed to this situation by constantly crying for reinforcements and declaring that the capture of Petersburg was imminent. As a result, when the "wolf" at Petersburg was real, Lee remained skeptical. The hesitation nearly cost Lee the city, and if not for extraordinarily poor leadership on the Federal side, he would have lost Petersburg.[5] Beauregard made up for crying wolf by rising to the challenge in what would be his shining single moment of the war: his flexible and adept defense of Petersburg while waiting and praying that Lee's men would reach him in time.

Although Lee himself came south of the James on the 16th—the day after the assault on Petersburg began—he didn't deem the situation dire enough to require his own presence or that of the entire army until the 18th. Of course, no one knew at the time that the armies would not leave Petersburg until the following April, and then on a path that led to Appomattox Court House.

* * *

---

4 Walbrook D. Swank, ed., *Raw Pork and Hardtack: A Civil War Memoir from Manassas to Appomattox* (Shippensburg, PA, 1996), 71-2. The short cut road was probably modern day Powhite Farm Drive.

5 One historian poetically described the situation at Petersburg on June 15: "An unholy mix-up of orders, lack of rations, poor maps, missed opportunities, and delays by commanders, combined with courageous Southern defense, saved Petersburg and undoubtedly lengthened the war by many months." Long, *CW Day by Day*, 522.

June 1, Wednesday (Coleman's House/Gaines' Mill): Lee learns in the morning that Anderson was unable to dislodge Grant from Cold Harbor, so plans to send Breckinridge's Division there. When enemy movements prevent Breckinridge from moving, Lee instructs Anderson to have Hoke attack at Cold Harbor. Around midday Lee again urges Beauregard to bring most of his force across the James, noting that most of Butler's army is with Grant at Cold Harbor. Later in the afternoon he renews his request for Beauregard's aid and advises that Grant may possibly be headed for the James.[6] Ewell again attempts to resume command of his corps, enlisting the opinion of Dr. Hunter McGuire who finds Ewell well enough to take the field; Lee again denies the request and tells Ewell to take command of the troops in Richmond until the present battle is concluded. In early evening Lee directs Anderson to entrench at Cold Harbor.[7] Lee remains at Coleman's house until well into the evening, sending instructions to "Grumble" Jones regarding his movements in the Valley, and informing Richmond he has no objection to Gen. John Echols returning to southwest Virginia. He also updates the secretary of war on the day's fighting, advising that elements of Butler's army are in Lee's front.[8] During the night Lee goes toward Cold Harbor by carriage and establishes headquarters near Gaines' Mill. During the night Lee meets with Hoke and probably Anderson as well.[9]

June 2, Thursday (Gaines' Mill/Mechanicsville): In the morning Lee goes in search of Breckinridge's Division and finds it in Mechanicsville, its guide having taken the wrong road. During the day Lee continues shifting units from his left to the right around Cold Harbor. During the evening he receives word from Imboden that the enemy drove him from Harrisonburg. During the night Lee updates Sec. Seddon on the fighting around Cold Harbor. Rain the afternoon and evening.[10]

June 3, Friday (Gaines' Mill): Shortly before sunrise Lee sends an update on his position to Richmond and instructs Anderson to make a demonstration against the enemy in his front. Lee's headquarters comes under artillery fire during a heavy Federal assault in the early morning and one of President Davis's aides, Col. William P. Johnston, joins Lee during the fighting. Toward midday Postmaster General John Reagan appears at Lee's headquarters, wanting to see

---

6 Freeman, *Lee*, vol. 3, 377-8; REL to Anderson, June 1, 1864, EPA papers, UNC; OR 36, pt. 3, 863-5. In his midday telegram to Beauregard, Lee offered him "command of right wing" of the ANV—this may have been an appeal to Beauregard's ego, but it also may be an indication of both Lee's inability to take command at Cold Harbor himself and a lack of confidence in Anderson's abilities commanding on that front. OR 36, pt. 3, 863. Taylor noted that Lee was still quite unwell on this date and was more removed from command than usual: "Since the General's indisposition he has remained more quiet and directs movements from a distance." Tower, *Lee's Adjutant*, 165.

7 OR 36, pt. 3, 863; Ewell to WHT, June 1, 1864, Polk-Ewell-Brown papers, UNC; WHT to Ewell, June 1, 1864, Polk-Ewell-Brown papers, UNC; REL to Ewell, June 1, 1864, Polk-Ewell-Brown papers, UNC; REL to Anderson, June 1, 1864, EPA papers, UNC. Ewell complained to Taylor, "I am as able for duty today as at any time since the campaign commenced. I am unwilling to be idle in this crisis." OR 36, pt. 3, 863.

8 REL to W. E. Jones, June 1, 1864, telegram book, REL HQ papers, VHS; Freeman, *Lee's Dispatches*, 211; OR 36, pt. 1, 1031. Lee's message to Davis regarding Echols was dated 8 p.m. from Coleman's house. Freeman, *Lee's Dispatches*, 211. Most writers put his departure for the front in late afternoon, but this message and the orders to Anderson to entrench sent at 6:10 p.m. show he was in the Shady Grove vicinity much later.

9 Rhea, *Cold Harbor*, 268; Lee, *Memoirs of WNP*, 337; Freeman, *Lee*, vol. 3, 378-9; Barefoot, *Robert F. Hoke*, 193. Freeman, piecing together accounts from Maj. Henry B. McClellan, Porter Alexander, and Postmaster General John Reagan, wrote that Lee moved HQ to Gaines' Mill but it is entirely possible that Lee remained near Shady Grove until the morning of the 2nd. See Freeman, *Lee*, vol. 3, 378 n16 and 379 n17. Lee's meeting with Hoke is not concrete: Hoke's biographer cites only Freeman for his assertion that the meeting occurred. Barefoot, *Robert F. Hoke*, 193, 396 n67. Although not 100% certain, HQ may have once again been at Powhite as in 1862, which was on a hill overlooking Gaines' Mill.

10 Freeman, *Lee*, vol. 3, 381-2, 385; William C. Davis, *Breckinridge: Statesman, Soldier, Symbol* (Baton Rouge, LA, 1992), 436; OR 36, pt. 1, 1031-2; Early to REL, June 2, 1864, Venable papers, UNC. Maj. Henry McClellan was the guide assigned to lead Breckinridge into position. Lee later called him to HQ to point out the road to Cold Harbor on his map "and quietly remarked, 'Major, this is the road to Cold Harbor.'" McClellan: "Not another word was spoken, but that quiet reproof sunk deeper and cut more keenly than words of violet vituperation would have done." Freeman, *Lee*, vol. 3, 383.

the fight; Lee is under artillery fire when Reagan arrives but rebuffs his request that he seek shelter.[11]

During the afternoon President Davis and General Bragg ride out to meet with Lee, and Col. Josiah Gorgas also arrives to observe the fighting. Hoke comes to Lee's headquarters after the fighting subsides and notes that Lee's illness seems finally to have passed.[12]

Lee sends reports of the day's action to the president and secretary of war, including the capture of men from Butler's army in Hoke's front. He also issues circulars to the army for the lines to be strengthened as much as possible with and that every available man be in the ranks. He forwards to the War Department a letter from Gen. Breckinridge concerning John Echols as temporary department commander in southwest Virginia, but Lee notes Echols's poor health and his preference for "Grumble" Jones in that capacity. In the evening he receives a letter from Mary and he thanks Mrs. Louis Crenshaw for bread she sent to headquarters.[13]

June 4, Saturday (Gaines' Mill): Lee names Joseph Kershaw as permanent commander of McLaws's Division and temporary promotions for Anderson, Early, Mahone, and Ramseur. He advises Seddon that apart from a night attack on his right there was no action today, and expresses his fears to Anderson and Fitz Lee that Grant is preparing to cross the Chickahominy. Lee writes to Mary informing her of his improved health and urging her to relocate to Fluvanna County. Rain during the night.[14]

June 5, Sunday (Gaines' Mill/Bottom's Bridge): Lee spends most of the day out on the right of his lines, reconnoitering the Chickahominy crossings and going as far downstream as Bottom's Bridge. While in Breckinridge's sector Lee checks on the Kentuckian, who was wounded the previous night. Grant sends a request that he be allowed to retrieve his wounded from between the lines, but stops short of asking for a formal truce.[15]

Lee does not receive Grant's request until his return to headquarters after nightfall, and misinterprets the request and replies that Grant should request a formal truce "as is customary" to avoid "misunderstanding and difficulty." During the night Lee notifies Richmond that "nothing has occurred" today nor can he detect any movement by Grant's army. He learns during the evening of "Grumble" Jones's defeat and death at Piedmont today and informs President Davis that the only force he can spare to go to the Valley is Breckinridge's Division. Rain.[16]

---

11 Dowdey, *Wartime Papers*, 763; WHT to Anderson, June 3, 1864, EPA papers, UNC; Freeman, *Lee*, vol. 3, 387-8; Reagan, *Memoirs*, 191-3. Reagan noted only that Lee's HQ was "on the field at the Gaines Mill farm." *Memoirs*, 192. This coincides with the orders to Anderson which were marked "William Gaines" whose farm Powhite extended from the Chickahominy to Gaines Mill.

12 Furguson, *Not War But Murder*, 172; Frank E. Vandiver, ed., *The Civil War Diary of General Josiah Gorgas* (Tuscaloosa, AL, 1947), 112; Barefoot, *Robert F. Hoke*, 196-7; Freeman, *Lee*, vol. 3, 390. Gorgas wore a blue cape and Lee cautioned him about going too near the front as he might be mistaken for the enemy. Vandiver, *Gorgas Diary*, 112.

13 Dowdey, *Wartime Papers*, 762-4; OR 36, pt. 1, 1032; OR 36, pt. 3, 869-70; OR 51, pt. 2, 981-2; REL to Mrs. Louis Crenshaw, June 3, 1864, REL papers, MOC.

14 OR 36, pt. 3, 873-4; OR 36, pt. 1, 1033; Dowdey, *Wartime Papers*, 764-5; F. G. Walter diary, June 4, 1864, LVA.

15 OR *Supplement* vol. 6, 814; Pearce, *Chambers Diary*, 202; Richmond *Examiner*, June 13, 1864, REL newspaper references, DSF papers, LVA; OR 36, pt. 3, 600. An officer in Matt Ransom's brigade of Hoke's Division wrote that Lee and Ransom spent considerable time at the York River RR bridge across the Chickahominy just upstream from Bottom's Bridge; he noted as well that Jefferson Davis was also in the vicinity but not with Lee's party—it is not known if Lee and Davis met or if they were even aware of their proximity to each other. Pearce, *Chambers Diary*, 202. The *Examiner* article did not mention Breckinridge by name, only referring to a "major general who had been hurt during the previous night;" Breckinridge, whose leg was injured when his horse was killed and fell on top of him, is the only one who matches this description. See Davis, *Breckinridge*, 437-8. The article quoted Lee as saying "we punished them very severely" in the fighting the morning of the 3rd.

16 OR 36, pt. 1, 368, 1033; OR 36, pt. 3, 600; Freeman, *Lee's Dispatches*, 215-6; Clifton diary, June 5, 1864, NC Archives. Col. Theodore Lyman of Meade's staff and Maj. W. G. Mitchell of Winfield Hancock's staff carried Grant's message to

June 6, Monday (Gaines' Mill): In the morning Lee sends a lengthy letter to President Davis recommending that Breckinridge, although slightly injured, be sent with his division to the Valley. He adds that Grant is moving again although he does not know where but prisoners indicate that most if not all of Butler's Army of the James is in Lee's front. By afternoon Breckinridge's troops are ready to depart and Lee again recommends to Davis that the Kentuckian accompany them if he is able. During the day Lee is visited by Rooney and also Mary's physician Dr. Alfred Hughes. Lee exchanges several messages with Grant regarding permission to care for the casualties between the lines but due to misunderstandings and the amount of time in transmitting the messages, no agreement is reached. Lee advises Seddon in the evening that little skirmishing occurred today but that Grant appears to be moving again. In the evening Lee receives a letter from Mary. Rain during the night.[17]

June 7, Tuesday (Gaines' Mill): In the morning Lee instructs Jed Hotchkiss to map out the Confederate position and later defers to Breckinridge for selecting brigade commanders for the Valley force. During the afternoon Lee and Grant finally agree to a truce to care for the wounded from the June 3 battle and he issues a circular announcing that there will be a truce tonight.[18]

During the evening Lee sends his now-daily update to the Richmond War Department, noting "the operations of today have been unimportant." He also informs Bragg that the force that attacked Petersburg must have come from Bermuda Hundred because it did not come from his front. The general takes some time to write wife Mary in the evening, thanking her for forwarding care packages to him. He insists that she first take what she and the girls want before sending them to him; he also mentions to her his visit with Dr. Hughes yesterday.[19]

June 8, Wednesday (Gaines' Mill): Lee has a lengthy meeting with Ewell, still seeking to be restored to command; Lee again denies his request and sends him to Richmond to rest. President Davis comes to headquarters to meet with Lee and together they ride a portion of the lines, including the scene of the heaviest fighting on June 3. Lee instructs A. P. Hill to investigate the capture of enemy flags on May 12, as both William Mahone and James Lane's troops claim to have captured them.[20]

Lee learns that two divisions of enemy cavalry under Phil Sheridan left Grant's army and warns Breckinridge that they may be headed for the Valley. He sends his now routine evening report to the War Department noting the "unusual quiet" displayed by Grant, apart from Sheridan's departure. He receives

---

Lee; when they reached Confederate lines on the Mechanicsville Turnpike they were informed that Lee was "absent from headquarters of his army" and they waited until 10 p.m. for his reply. OR 36, pt. 1, 368.

17 Dowdey, *Wartime Papers*, 767-8; Freeman, *Lee's Dispatches*, 219-20; OR 36, pt. 3, 638-9, 666; OR 36, pt. 1, 1033; Krick, *CW Weather*, 130. Dr. Hughes was from a prominent family of Wheeling, WV, and a member of the Virginia legislature during the war; he was a practitioner of homeopathic medicine and Rooney expressed to his mother his disdain for Hughes's medical practices: "I am afraid Dr. Hughes is not what he represents himself to be. Still if his medicines do you no harm, he is better than the others." Rooney to Mrs. REL, Sept. 25, 1864, Lee family papers, VHS; Egbert Cleave, *Cleave's Biographical Cyclopaedia of Homeopathic Physicians and Surgeons* (Philadelphia, 1873), 412-3.

18 McDonald, *Make Me a Map*, 210; OR 51, pt. 2, 993; OR 36, pt. 3, 667; circular, June 7, 1864, EPA papers, UNC. Four and a half days elapsed since the fighting of June 3 so by the time the truce went into effect at 6 p.m. on the 7th, there were no "wounded" left to care for in between the lines and it became a matter of recovery and burial.

19 OR 36, pt. 1, 1033; REL to Bragg, June 7, 1864, Lee papers, SH; Dowdey, *Wartime Papers*, 768.

20 Pfanz, *Ewell*, 399-400; Hamlin, *Making of a Soldier*, 128-30; Ferguson, *Not War But Murder*, 225; OR 36, pt. 3, 802-3. The details are not known but at some point Robert Rodes protested directly to Lee against Ewell being restored to command. Gallagher, *Lee the Soldier*, 11. The best account of Ewell's departure from the ANV is Chapter 27 in Pfanz, *Ewell*. Ewell assumed command of the Department of Richmond on June 13, 1864. Pfanz, *Ewell*, 405. Mahone claimed that the flags in question were captured by the 12th and 41st VA regiments of his old brigade and he was upset that Lane's men were credited with the capture; Lee forwarded the results of Hill's investigation to the War Department on the 12th to be sorted out in Richmond. OR 36, pt. 3, 803.

a letter from Mary and writes a brief one in reply, noting "It is useless for us to grieve for the calamity at Staunton. . . . We must bear everything with patience that is inflicted on us." He advises her also not to worry about the family silver removed from Arlington and sent to Lexington in the early days of the war—it cannot now be retrieved and if it is discovered by the enemy, there is nothing that can be done.[21]

June 9, Thursday (Gaines' Mill): In the morning Jed Hotchkiss delivers to Lee his map of the Cold Harbor lines. Throughout the afternoon Lee exchanges messages with Bragg and Beauregard regarding an enemy attack on Petersburg today—Lee is adamant that the attacking force was not withdrawn from his front and he reluctantly agrees to return Beauregard's troops if necessary. In a letter to President Davis, he advises that Wade Hampton was sent to intercept Sheridan who probably intends to link up with David Hunter's force in the Valley; he also mentions that John Pope is rumored to be reinforcing with Grant with a force from the western frontier. In his nightly update to the War Department, Lee notes simply "the enemy has been quiet today."[22]

June 10, Friday (Gaines' Mill): Lee and Beauregard differ over what the attack on Petersburg means, with Lee telling Richmond it was nothing more than a reconnaissance. Lee informs Sec. Seddon of increased skirmishing along his front but no moves by Grant; he reiterates his belief that Sheridan's force is headed for Hunter and likely will go after the Southside or Richmond & Danville railroads.[23]

June 11, Saturday (Gaines' Mill): Lee meets with Gen. Arnold Elzey regarding organization of the Maryland troops in Virginia and the possibility of a position with the ANV. Lee forwards to the War Department a proposal from Gen. John Gregg to transfer additional Texas and Arkansas troops from the Trans-Mississippi theater to reinforce Gregg's Texas Brigade; while Lee supports the request he is adamant that Gregg not be allowed to leave his post to go west to recruit. He also informs President Davis and Gen. Bragg of the need to retake the Valley and notes that Breckinridge lacks adequate force to drive the Federals from that region completely, and offers to send a portion of the ANV if necessary: "I acknowledge the advantage of expelling the enemy from the Valley. The only difficulty with me is the means. It would take one corps of this army. If it is deemed prudent to hazard the defense of Richmond…I will do so." Lee sees Rooney and Rob briefly during the day, and his nightly update to the secretary of war reads simply "the enemy has been quiet today, with the usual skirmishing along the lines."[24]

June 12, Sunday (Gaines' Mill): Lee learns of David Hunter's capture of Lexington in the Valley the previous day, and meets with Jubal Early to discuss whether he should send the Second Corps to oppose Hunter. Lee formally requests that the War Department reassign Richard Ewell, recommending he temporarily take command of the Richmond defenses. Lee writes to Mary, regretting deeply the damage done by the enemy at Hickory Hill.[25]

---

21 OR 37, pt. 1, 754; OR 36, pt. 1, 1034; Dowdey, *Wartime Papers*, 769. Union Gen. David Hunter's army defeated "Grumble" Jones at Piedmont on June 5, and then occupied Staunton, looting and destroying parts of the town; Hunter then moved on Lexington.

22 McDonald, *Make Me a Map*, 210; Dowdey, *Wartime Papers*, 770-2; REL to Beauregard, June 9, 1864, telegram book, REL HQ papers, VHS; Freeman, *Lee's Dispatches*, 224-5; OR 36, pt. 1, 1034. Taylor noted "this quiet has been complete and remarkable. I have not heard a gun today, nor did I hear many during the night." Tower, *Lee's Adjutant*, 166. Gen. Quincy Gillmore attacked Petersburg with about 5,000 men and was turned back by a small force under Gen. Henry Wise; it was known as the "Battle of Old Men and Young Boys" owing to the nature of Wise's scratch force. Gillmore's mismanagement likely cost the Federals their best chance to capture Petersburg.

23 REL to Bragg, June 10, 1864, REL papers, VHS; OR 36, pt. 1, 1034; OR 36, pt. 3, 888.

24 OR 40, pt. 2, 650; OR 36, pt. 3, 894-5; OR 51, pt. 2, 1002-3; Dowdey, *Wartime Papers*, 775; OR 36, pt. 1, 1034.

25 Early, *Memoirs*, 371; OR 36, pt. 3, 897-8; Dowdey, *Wartime Papers*, 775.

June 13, Monday (Gaines' Mill/Glendale): In the morning the Federal trenches are found deserted so Lee orders the army—minus Early's corps—across the Chickahominy to block the eastern approaches to the capital. Once the Federals are found near the old Glendale battlefield, Lee personally compliments Col. Martin Gary for preventing them from seizing the strategic crossroads there. President Davis attempts to meet with Lee during the afternoon, but with Lee being on the move they do not connect. He establishes headquarters at "Fisher's house" on the Charles City Road, just north of Glendale.[26]

In early evening Lee informs President Davis of the army's new position and of Early's pre-dawn departure toward Charlottesville. Lee informs Sec. Seddon during the evening that Grant moved southeast the previous night, and also that Hampton defeated Sheridan at Trevilian's Station.[27]

June 14, Tuesday (Glendale/Bottom's Bridge): The arrival of morning once again reveals that Grant has left Lee's front, and the general rides to at least some of the Chickahominy crossings to reconnoiter. By midday Lee knows that Grant is on the James, and thinks he occupies McClellan's fortifications around Harrison's Landing. He writes to President Davis at noon, apologizing for missing him yesterday, and advising of Grant's latest movements; Lee fears that Grant is bound for Petersburg and thus he will send Hoke's Division to the pontoon bridge at Drewry's Bluff to be ready to reinforce Beauregard. By late afternoon Lee learns that the Army of the Potomac is at Westover and Wilcox's Landing, and all reports have the Federals intending to cross the James River and move toward Petersburg; Lee notifies President Davis and Gen. Bragg of the latest developments and that Robert Hoke can be sent to Beauregard. His nightly report to the War Department informs of Grant's presence on the James and that the Federals are no longer using White House as their base of supply, further indicating a shift to Southside. He decides during the evening to withdraw the army closer to Richmond and informs Richmond of his intent.[28]

June 15, Wednesday (Glendale): In the morning Lee sifts through reports from Rooney and A. P. Hill regarding Grant's position and learns from Beauregard that reinforcements from north of the James are in front of Petersburg, prompting Lee to order Hoke to Petersburg. Probably in late morning Lee meets with Beauregard's aide, Col. Samuel Paul, regarding the situation at Petersburg and Bermuda Hundred; Lee informs Col. Paul that he does not think any of Grant's force is present at Petersburg and that Beauregard faces only Butler's Army of the

---

26 WHT to R. H. Anderson, June 13, 1864, EPA papers, UNC; Venable to R. H. Anderson, June 13, 1864, EPA papers, UNC; Marc Ramsey, *The 7th South Carolina Cavalry: To the Defense of Richmond* (Wilmington, NC, 2011), 63; Dowdey, *Wartime Papers*, 777. Lee was not aware that Davis was looking for him until the 14th. Dowdey, *Wartime Papers*, 777. Smith's Map of Henrico (1853) shows a "J. Fisher" house on Charles City Road at its crossing of White Oak Swamp, approximately two miles north of Glendale; a residential neighborhood occupies that area currently. Glendale was also known as "Riddell's Shop" after the blacksmith shop (with several variants of the spelling) at the Glendale crossroads, which is how Lee marked all of his correspondence.

27 Venable to R. H. Anderson, June 14, 1864, EPA papers, UNC; Dowdey, *Wartime Papers*, 782-3; *OR* 36, pt. 1, 1035. Lee's letter to Davis was misdated June 15 but the content places it on the 13th. Dowdey, *Wartime Papers*, 782-3. Hampton and Sheridan's forces met along the Virginia Central between Louisa and Gordonsville in the largest all-cavalry battle of the war on the 11th and 12th.

28 Benjamin W. Jones, *Under the Stars and Bars: A History of the Surry Light Artillery* (Dayton, OH, 1975), 203; Dowdey, *Wartime Papers*, 777-80; *OR* 36, pt. 1, 1035. It appears that once Lee learned the Federals were not in his immediate front he set out in search of them for most of the morning; he was seen at Bottom's Bridge at some point, but it is not known where else he went; an artilleryman at Bottom's Bridge wrote only "General Lee has just passed us here." Jones, *Under the Stars and Bars*, 203. He was back at HQ near the Fisher house no later than noon when he wrote to Davis, and was there for most if not all of the afternoon. See Venable to R. H. Anderson, June 14, 1864, EPA papers, UNC; and Dowdey, *Wartime Papers*, 777-9. A post-war account by one of the army's engineers confirms that Lee was in the field but gives no details of where he went, writing only that Lee "rode some distance down the James." John F. Lanneau, "Field Glimpses of Lee," *Wake Forest Student* (Jan. 1907) vol. 26, no. 5, 327. A partial document by an officer in Scales's Brigade places Lee, Hill, Heth, Wilcox, Hoke, Scales and others together at some point on this date awaiting information on Grant's whereabouts, but the author did not provide any details as to where or when. *OR Supplement*, vol. 7, 325.

James. Lee does concede it likely that Grant intends to cross the James and informs Paul that he ordered Hoke to Petersburg and that he will give all aid he can including coming to Petersburg himself.[29]

After Col. Paul departs, Lee notifies Gen. Bragg of the meeting and of Beauregard's request to have his original force returned to him; he also informs Bragg that he will not withdraw the army closer to Richmond as he intended, and expresses his regret at the death of Gen. Leonidas Polk in Georgia. He also informs Bragg that although he would like a pontoon bridge across the James at Chaffin's Bluff, if there is not enough material for it, he would rather have the one at Drewry's Bluff as it is more protected than one at Chaffin's would be. He then notifies President Davis that he will not move the army closer to Richmond, although he may move his own headquarters closer. Lee sends several additional messages to President Davis during the night regarding the army's location and also requests that the newspapers not print any information about Early; in response to a message from Davis regarding a replacement for Polk in Joe Johnston's army, Lee dismisses the suggestion of William Pendleton and proposes Ewell as he is a favorite of Johnston. His nightly report to Seddon mentions driving away enemy cavalry from Malvern Hill but "nothing else of importance has occurred today." The War Department issues orders placing Lee in overall command in Virginia and North Carolina. U.S. Secretary of War Edwin Stanton orders the official creation of a "Military Cemetery" at Arlington.[30]

June 16, Thursday (Glendale/Drewry's Bluff/Bermuda Hundred): Lee is awakened at 2 a.m. by a messenger from Beauregard informing him that Beauregard abandoned his lines on Bermuda Hundred to concentrate all his forces at Petersburg; he requests Lee to send troops to occupy the vacated fortifications. Immediately upon receipt of this message, Lee orders Pickett's Division across the James to Bermuda Hundred because of Pickett's familiarity with the area. During the early morning hours Lee determines both to send Richard Anderson along with Pickett and to move his own headquarters closer to Drewry's Bluff. Lee himself crosses the James to Drewry's Bluff around 9:30 and informs Beauregard and Bragg of his arrival there with Pickett's Division.[31]

---

29 Freeman, *Lee*, vol. 3, 406-7; Dowdey, *Wartime Papers*, 781; Roman, *Military Operations of Beauregard*, vol. 2, 579-80. Paul wrote that he met with Lee around 1:00 p.m.; Lee however notified Bragg of the meeting at 12:20 p.m. so obviously it occurred earlier than Paul remembered. Roman, *Military Operations of Beauregard*, vol. 2, 579-80; Dowdey, *Wartime Papers*, 781. Porter Alexander was witness to this meeting and noted that "Gen. Lee's air and attitude seemed to me so suggestive of hostility that I drew a mental inference that he, for some cause, disliked either the message or the messenger, or perhaps both." Alexander incorrectly wrote that the encounter took place on the 14th. Gallagher, *Fighting for the Confederacy*, 421. Beauregard wrote that he dispatched Paul on the 14th, but he omits that it took Paul quite some time to get to Lee, not arriving until the morning of the 15th; it is possible that Beauregard's article influenced Alexander's memory of the event. P. G. T. Beauregard, "Four Days of Battle at Petersburg," *B&L*, vol. 4, 540. Paul noted that Lee's HQ "were difficult to find." Roman, *Military Operations of Beauregard*, vol. 2, 579.

30 Dowdey, *Wartime Papers*, 780-3; Freeman, *Lee's Dispatches*, 237-41; *OR* 36, pt. 1, 1035; *OR* 40, pt. 2, 654; Gaughn, *Last Battle of the CW*, 33. Leonidas Polk was killed outside Marietta, GA, on June 14 while observing Sherman's position with Gens. Johnston and Hardee. Warner, *Generals in Gray*, 243. Lee was considering moving his HQ to either the Osborne Turnpike or New Market Road, both of which would put him closer to the bridge at Drewry's. Dowdey, *Wartime Papers*, 780. Venable incorrectly wrote that Lee moved south of the James on this date. "Lee in the Wilderness," 245. Lee's commentary on Pendleton is noteworthy: "As much as I esteem and admire Gen. Pendleton, I would not select him to command a corps in this army. I do not mean to say by that he is not competent, but from what I have seen of him, I do not know that he is." Dowdey, *Wartime Papers*, 783. It is not known when Lee learned of the unified command structure placing him officially over Beauregard. See Freeman, *Lee*, vol. 3, 411.

31 Dowdey, *Wartime Papers*, 785; WHT to R. H. Anderson, June 16, 1864 (2 messages), EPA papers, UNC; *OR* 40, pt. 2, 658-9; Douglas S. Freeman, ed., *A Calendar of Confederate Papers with a Bibliography of Some Confederate Publications* (Richmond, VA, 1908), 62. In addition to the message directly to Lee received at 2 a.m., Beauregard also notified Bragg at 9 p.m. on the 15th that his lines at Petersburg had been broken and that assistance was needed from Lee immediately—this information was not forwarded to Lee thus he was unaware of the crisis unfolding across the James. See Freeman, *Lee*, vol. 3, 409. Lee did not immediately decide to send Anderson with Pickett; his 2 a.m. orders to Anderson to send Pickett survive in Porter Alexander's papers and no mention is made of Anderson himself accompanying the division. It is possible that Lee and

Lee and Beauregard continue to trade messages during the morning, but Beauregard's most important communiqué—that which mentions the presence of Grant's army in front of Petersburg—goes astray thus leaving Lee under the impression that they face nothing but Butler's Army of the James and he remains unwilling to "strip north bank of James River." In response to Beauregard's repeated calls for assistance at Petersburg, Lee orders Field's Division to Bermuda Hundred and cautions Anderson that it may be necessary to send Pickett to the Cockade City. When Butler's troops are found occupying the vacated works on Bermuda Hundred, Lee oversees the retaking of the line.[32]

During the afternoon Lee continues to ask Beauregard for information regarding Grant's location. After Anderson's men push Butler's troops away from the Richmond & Petersburg Railroad, Lee notifies railroad and government officials that trains are not needed at Drewry's Bluff to shift troops to Petersburg because of damage done to the tracks by the enemy. In late afternoon or early evening he establishes headquarters at Drewry's Bluff and instructs Anderson to retake those works still remaining in enemy hands, especially those on the Howlett farm overlooking the James.[33]

During the night Lee informs President Davis of the events of the day, including that the enemy retains the advanced line of entrenchments on Bermuda Hundred and that Lee still does not have definitive information regarding Grant. Lee meets with the Army of Northern Virginia's quartermaster Col. James Corley during the evening regarding difficulties in getting forage for the army's animals. Afterwards, he notifies the president that the fault seems to rest with the railroads rather than the quartermaster department: "It is clear that the railroads are not working energetically and unless some improvement is made, I do not know what will become of us." The general instructs Wade Hampton to keep after Phil Sheridan and destroy him if the opportunity presents. During the night Lee receives word from Gen. Beauregard that Winfield Hancock's II Corps of the Army of the Potomac is in front of Petersburg, but he has "no satisfactory information" regarding the rest of that army.[34]

June 17, Friday (Drewry's Bluff/Bermuda Hundred): Lee is up before dawn and learns not only that Pickett recaptured most of the Howlett Line on Bermuda Hundred during the night and that only a small portion of the railroad is still out of service, but more importantly that Petersburg still remains in Confederate hands. Between 5:30 and 6:00 a.m. he informs the superintendent of the R&P of the remaining gap in the railroad, and advises Beauregard of the status of affairs on Bermuda

---

Anderson met during the early hours of the morning to discuss the situation and Anderson himself was not intended to go until Lee decided to have Charles Field's division also at hand. See Lee's letter to Davis in Dowdey, *Wartime Papers*, 785-6. Although Lee himself was on the south side of the James in the morning, it seems he intended initially to keep ANV HQ on the north bank as Taylor notified Richmond that HQ would be in "the vicinity of Chaffin's Bluff." Unfortunately there is no time stamp on Taylor's message. OR 40, pt. 2, 658. It seems Lee did not decide to move HQ south of the James until the evening. REL to R. H. Anderson, 6 p.m., June 16, 1864, EPA papers, UNC.

32 A. Wilson Greene, *A Campaign of Giants: The Battle for Petersburg* (Chapel Hill, NC, 2018), 125; OR 40, pt. 2, 659; REL to Anderson, 10:45 a.m., June 16, 1864, EPA papers, UNC; Venable, "Lee in the Wilderness," 245. It is difficult to ascertain what Lee knew when in the very fluid situation on June 16. However, it is evident from both his actions and his communications with Beauregard that he remained unaware of Grant's presence in Beauregard's front, although Beauregard had prisoners from Hancock's II Corps. Venable wrote that Lee "superintended personally the retaking of Beauregard's Bermuda Hundred line" on both the 16th and 17th; how much of an active role he took on the 16th is not known, but likely not to the same extent that he did on the 17th. Venable, "Lee in the Wilderness," 245.

33 OR 40, pt. 2, 659-60; REL to Anderson, 6 p.m., June 16, 1864, EPA papers, UNC; Venable to "Dear Sir," Sept. 26, 1876 or 1878 [year is not clear], Venable papers, VHS. HQ was somewhere "on the first bluff above the pontoon bridge" at Drewry's, according to Lee; Venable said only that it was "within a half mile" of Drewry's. REL to Anderson, 6 p.m. June 16, 1864, EPA papers, UNC; Venable to "Dear Sir," Sept. 26, 1876/8, Venable papers, VHS. An undated telegram from Drewry's Bluff from this period gives the location of Lee's HQ as "on this side of the river, just opposite Wilton bridge;" it likely refers to this campsite. Freeman, *Calendar of Confederate Papers*, 72.

34 Dowdey, *Wartime Papers*, 785-6; Freeman, *Lee's Dispatches*, 246-7; OR 36, pt. 3, 901; Freeman, *Lee*, vol. 3, 415.

Hundred; he again inquires if Beauregard knows anything further of Grant's whereabouts. During the morning Lee goes to Bermuda Hundred to direct Pickett and Field's attack to recover the rest of the Howlett Line, establishing his command post at the Clay house. He goes to Battery Dantzler and observes the enemy vessels in the James as well as the obstructions they placed in Trent's Reach to hamper navigation by Confederate ironclads. In mid-morning he reports to President Davis the progress made at Bermuda Hundred and what he knows of the situation at Petersburg.[35]

Lee trades messages with Beauregard regarding the situation on their respective fronts, but little new information about Grant and the rest of the Army of the Potomac is learned and Lee tells him that until he knows more about Grant's location he will not bring more troops south of the James. He tells Beauregard that only the X Corps is at Bermuda Hundred and he has no information regarding the V Corps since the 14th when it was at Westover. With no new information from Petersburg, Lee instructs Rooney to press forward from Malvern Hill to glean what intelligence he can. Lee oversees the fighting along the Howlett Line from the Clay house and it is likely there that he receives a message from Beauregard that prisoners report Grant's army is south of the James and headed for Petersburg.[36]

In response to that intelligence, Lee orders Hill and the other elements of the army still north of the James to move to Chaffin's Bluff unless they have positive information contrary to Beauregard's. About the same time, he orders a final attack to secure the last remaining portion of the Howlett Line still in enemy hands, but calls off the attack when his engineers report that they found a better position; Pickett however does not get the cancellation orders before his men advance. Once Pickett recaptures the works, Lee congratulates Anderson with a joke at Pickett's expense: "We tried very hard to stop Pickett's men from capturing the breastworks of the enemy, but could not do it." He then notifies both President Davis and Gen. Beauregard that the Bermuda Hundred line has been retaken, and only the X Corps is present in his front.[37]

Around 5:30 p.m. Lee sends engineer Col. Walter Stevens to inspect the Howlett Line and returns to his headquarters camp at Drewry's Bluff. During the evening the general continues to receive messages from Gen. Beauregard indicating a rapidly deteriorating situation at Petersburg; first, further confirmation of the presence of the Army of the Potomac, and next word that Beauregard will have to abandon the city all together without reinforcements. In response to these latest reports, Lee orders A. P. Hill across the James River and sends Joe Kershaw's division to Petersburg, and advises Beauregard that help is coming. During the night, Capt. A. R. Chisholm of Beauregard's staff comes to headquarters and gives Lee a detailed account of the fighting at Petersburg over the past three days. Lee reports to Sec. Seddon that the Bermuda Hundred works have been retaken and that Beauregard reports part of his line at Petersburg captured.[38]

---

35 OR 40, pt. 2, 664-5; Venable to "Dear Sir," Sept. 26, 1876/8, Venable papers, VHS; Dowdey, *Wartime Papers*, 787-8. The Clay house is located at the intersection of Old Stage Road and Old Bermuda Hundred Road; it is one of the more architecturally intriguing dwellings in that part of Virginia (although its date of construction is unknown) and it remains a private residence. Jeffrey M. O'Dell, *Chesterfield County: Early Architecture and Historic Sites* (Chesterfield, VA, 1983), 192. Battery Dantzler was the northern anchor of the Howlett Line and commanded the James River; Trent's Reach was the section of the James immediately downstream of Dantzler; both were later bypassed by the Dutch Gap Canal. Although much of the Howlett Line has been lost to development, segments of it remain including Battery Dantzler which is a Chesterfield County park.

36 OR 40, pt. 2, 663-5; David E. Johnston, *The Story of a Confederate Boy in the Civil War* (Portland, OR, 1914), 271; Venable, "Lee in the Wilderness," 245; Freeman, *Lee*, vol. 3, 419.

37 OR 40, pt. 2, 662-5; Venable, "Lee in the Wilderness," 245; Venable, "Campaign from the Wilderness to Petersburg," 538-9; REL to R. H. Anderson, 5:30 p.m., June 17, 1864, EPA papers, UNC; OR 40, pt. 1, 749. Lee spoke to the handful of wounded Pickett sustained as they were taken off the field past the Clay house. Johnston, *Confederate Boy in the CW*, 271.

38 REL to R. H. Anderson, 5:30 p.m., June 17, 1864, EPA papers, UNC; Freeman, *Lee*, vol. 3, 420-2; OR 40, pt. 2, 662-5; Dowdey, *Wartime Papers*, 786-7. The exact time Lee's dispatch to Seddon was written is not known, but since it lacks the

June 18, Saturday (Drewry's Bluff/ Petersburg): Lee goes to bed around midnight but is wakened before 1:00 a.m. by Col. Taylor upon the arrival of Col. Alfred Roman, another of Beauregard's aides, with more evidence of Grant's presence at Petersburg. Taylor denies Roman an audience with the general but relays his messages. About an hour after Roman's departure, another of Beauregard's officers, Maj. Giles Cooke, arrives and meets with Lee, who agrees to move to Petersburg. At 3:30 a.m. Lee informs Anderson that Grant's entire force is at Petersburg and orders him to move his corps to join Beauregard.[39]

Around the same time Lee inquires of R&P officials if the line is restored to Petersburg and requests that trains be sent to move the army to that point. The general then moves to Petersburg, where he arrives around 11:30 a.m. Lee goes straight to Gen. Beauregard's headquarters in the Customs House, and the two remain in deep conference for approximately one hour. Once they finish, the generals emerge together to the cheers of a small crowd gathered outside and then ride to a hill near the city reservoir to observe the terrain to the east and southeast of the city. Afterwards, the pair rides along Beauregard's new line. Beauregard proposes to Lee that he attack Grant's left flank southeast of Petersburg once all of Lee's army arrives, but Lee demurs, explaining that the troops will need rest and that they will assume a defensive posture for the present.[40]

During the afternoon Lee observes the deployment of Anderson's troops east of town and comes under sporadic artillery fire; an officer near him is struck by enemy fire. Lee notifies Bragg that he moved headquarters to Petersburg and informs President Davis that he ordered the rest of the army, less most of the cavalry, to Petersburg and the Richmond defenses are manned by Custis's troops. He also informs Early that "Grant is in front of Petersburg," so Early must either engage the enemy in the Shenandoah Valley or return to Lee "without delay," and advises Hampton that if he cannot bring Sheridan to battle, then he is to come to Petersburg. Headquarters is established in the yard of Violet Bank, the Shippen residence on a hill on the north

---

most dire reports from Petersburg it was likely sent early in the evening before receipt of Beauregard's messages. Freeman incorrectly wrote (and others followed suit) that Lee moved HQ to the Clay house and spent the night of the 17th there. *Lee*, vol. 3, 419-20, 424. However, Lee's afternoon message to Anderson clearly states that he returned to his camp at Drewry's Bluff. REL to RHA, 5:30 p.m., June 17, 1864, EPA papers, UNC. A careful reading of a post-war letter of Venable's also reveals that Lee was at the Clay house during the day only. Venable to "Dear Sir," Sept. 26, 1876/8, Venable papers, VHS. Also, Col. Alfred Roman and Maj. Giles Cooke of Beauregard's staff, both of whom met with Lee in the early hours of June 18, noted that Lee's HQ was "near Drewry's Bluff." Giles B. Cooke, "Col. W. H. Taylor, A.A.G Army of Northern Virginia: An Appreciation," *CV*, vol. 24, 234; Roman, *Military Operations of Beauregard*, vol. 2, 576. It is worth noting that although Beauregard had multiple reports of Grant's entire army being at or on the way to Petersburg, Lee still had reservations: he informed Wade Hampton that "Grant's army is *chiefly* [emphasis added] on south side of James River." *OR* 36, pt. 3, 901.

39 Roman, *Military Operations of Beauregard*, vol. 2, 576-7; Cook, "Col. W. H. Taylor," 234; Giles B. Cooke, "When With General Lee," *CV*, vol. 37, 182; Giles B. Cooke, *Just Before Lee Surrendered*, WHT papers; REL to Anderson, June 18, 1864, EPA papers, UNC. According to Roman, Beauregard's exact words to describe the severity of the situation were, "unless reinforcements were sent before 48 hours, God Almighty alone would save Petersburg and Richmond." Roman, *Military Operations of Beauregard*, vol. 2, 577. Cooke apparently relayed that message to Gen. Lee verbatim, to which the general is said to have replied "I hope God Almighty will save Petersburg." Cooke, "When with General Lee," 182. Cooke had gone to school with Walter Taylor before the war, and he used this friendship to gain his audience with Lee. Cooke, "W. H. Taylor," 234.

40 *OR* 40, pt. 2, 668; Venable, "Lee in the Wilderness," 246; Roman, *Military Operations of Beauregard*, vol. 2, 236; William D. Henderson, *Petersburg in the Civil War: War at the Door* (Lynchburg, VA, 1998), 116-7; Beauregard, "Four Days of Battle at Petersburg," 543-4. Venable stated multiple times that Lee arrived with the head of Kershaw's Division. Venable, "Campaign from the Wilderness to Petersburg," 539; Venable to "Dear Sir," Sept. 26, 1876/8, Venable papers, VHS. However, Lee himself stated that Kershaw and Field preceded him. *OR* 40, pt. 2, 667. Beauregard gave the arrival times of Kershaw as 7:30, Field as 9:30, and noted at 11:30 that "General Lee has just arrived." Roman, *Military Operations of Beauregard*, 236. Beauregard wrote of Lee's arrival: "My welcome to General Lee was most cordial. He was at last where I had, for the past three days, so anxiously hoped to see him—within the limits of Petersburg!" "Four Days of Battle at Petersburg," 543. The Customs House is at the corner of W Tabb St. and N Union St.; it currently serves as the Petersburg City Hall.

side of the Appomattox River overlooking Petersburg.[41]

June 19, Sunday (Violet Bank/Petersburg): Gen. Lee attends church service at St. Paul's Episcopal in Petersburg. Thereafter, he sends a lengthy update to President Davis about what troops still remain in front of Richmond, but adds that as long as the R&P is in service troops can be shuttled back and forth; The general laments how close the new defensive line is to Petersburg itself, and cautions that it will be very difficult if not impossible to keep the Federals off the Petersburg & Weldon Railroad, thus "every effort should be made to secure" the Richmond & Danville Railroad as it will be the only remaining connection leading south. Lee requests that the War Department "accumulate supplies of all kinds in Richmond in anticipation of temporary interruptions. When [rail] roads are broken every aid should be given to the companies to enable them to restore them immediately.... Every... arrangement made to keep the roads in running order."

The general learns that Jubal Early repulsed an attack on Lynchburg, Virginia, yesterday, but the enemy retreated during the night before Early could attack them this morning, and informs Sec. Seddon of Early's situation. He writes to wife Mary, thanking her for the bread she sent him, and notes that while he appreciates the clothes she sent, he cannot use them unless they are gray.[42]

June 20, Monday (Violet Bank): Gen. Lee orders all of his wounded removed from the hospitals in Petersburg because of their exposure to enemy artillery fire.[43]

June 21, Tuesday (Violet Bank): Lee sends a very bleak report to President Davis regarding the army's situation at Petersburg: "The enemy has a strong position, and is able to deal us more injury than from any other point he has ever taken. Still we must try and defeat them. I fear he will not attack us but advance by regular approaches. He is so situated that I cannot attack him." He also warns Seddon that "it will be almost impossible" to preserve the Petersburg & Weldon Railroad so all available locomotives and rolling stock should be transferred to the Richmond & Danville as it will become the main supply line. During the morning Lee learns of an enemy force near Chaffin's Bluff and requests information from Custis about it. His concern over this force grows during the day and he instructs Pickett to send support from the Howlett Line.[44]

June 22, Wednesday (Violet Bank/Petersburg): During the morning Lee rides to his right flank to observe enemy movements near the Weldon Railroad. He meets with Gen. Mahone, who is familiar with the terrain from his time as chief engineer of the Norfolk & Petersburg Railroad, at Mahone's headquarters near the Winfree farm and

---

41 Venable to "Dear Sir," Sept. 26, 1876/8, Venable papers, VHS; Dowdey, *Wartime Papers*, 791-3; Taylor, *General Lee*, 253. Lee apparently gave Rooney his orders in person, and possibly Custis as well, as he related to wife Mary on the 19th that he saw Rooney and Rob on this date. Dowdey, *Wartime Papers*, 793. Violet Bank was constructed in 1815; it stands one block east of U.S. 1 just north of the Appomattox River. Although the grounds of the estate were developed into a residential neighborhood in the early 20th century, the house itself is a city museum. Edward A. Wyatt, IV, *Plantation Houses Around Petersburg in the Counties of Prince George, Chesterfield, and Dinwiddie, Virginia* (Petersburg, VA, 1955), 20-1.

42 Freeman, *Lee*, vol. 3, 448; Dowdey, *Wartime Papers*, 793-5; *OR* 37, pt. 1, 766. Lee regularly attended church services while at Petersburg, usually at St. Paul's but also at Grace Episcopal as well. Greene, *Campaign of Giants*, 328-9. Lee sat in Pew #44 at St. Paul's. Greene, *CW Petersburg*, 314 n76.

43 John H. Claiborne, *Seventy-five Years in Old Virginia* (New York, 1904), 206. Dr. Claiborne, who was superintendent of all military hospitals in the city, could not recall the exact date but wrote that it was "on the 3rd or 4th day of [Lee's] arrival." The 20th seems the more likely as Lee was busy on the 21st with reports of enemy activity north of the James at Deep Bottom.

44 Freeman, *Lee's Dispatches*, 253-7; *OR* 40, pt. 2, 671-4; REL to Pickett, June 21, 1864, telegram book, REL HQ papers, VHS. Freeman noted that this letter to Davis was "the first time Lee admitted that he could not expect victory." *Lee's Dispatches*, 255 n5. Davis visited the Howlett Line on this date but as far as is known did not meet with Lee there or in Petersburg, as he sent a note to Lee complaining about the lack of an engineer overseeing the fortifications there (Lee had appointed one but was not sure why he apparently was not present). *OR* 51, pt. 2, 1023.

sends Mahone's and Wilcox's divisions to drive the Federals away from the railroad. Returning to headquarters, Lee notifies Bragg in early afternoon of enemy cavalry raiding through Dinwiddie County and requesting that forces be sent to protect the Southside and Richmond & Danville railroads, and requests an update from Heth regarding affairs north of the James. Lee receives a letter from Mary and notifies Seddon of Mahone's success south of Petersburg.[45]

June 23, Thursday (Violet Bank/Petersburg): Lee likely reconnoiters Grant's right flank along the Appomattox River and meets with Beauregard to plan an attack on that portion of the lines.[46]

June 24, Friday (Violet Bank/Petersburg): Lee and Beauregard observe Beauregard's attack from high ground near Violet Bank and afterward meet with both division commanders involved: Hoke and Field. During the night Lee reports to Seddon on Mahone's renewed fighting on the 23rd as well as Hoke's morning attack. He writes two letters to Mary, one in the morning thanking her for bread and cheese sent him and also expressing his relief that she is leaving Richmond, and another in the evening requesting some summer clothing from his trunk.[47]

June 25, Saturday (Violet Bank): Lee congratulates Wade Hampton on his victory over Sheridan and instructs him to come to Petersburg as more cavalry is needed to keep the enemy away from the railroads. He advises Secretary of War Seddon that Rooney is in pursuit of the enemy cavalry threatening the R&D and Southside, and also sends him a report on the failed attack east of Petersburg yesterday. Lee opines that flags captured in battle are the property of the Confederate government, not any particular officer or state government.[48]

June 26, Sunday (Violet Bank): Lee learns that the enemy raid along the R&D was turned back at Staunton River Bridge yesterday and Rooney's troopers are in pursuit. He advises Seddon of the victory but again cautions that the Petersburg & Weldon cannot be held and that further reliance will be placed upon the R&D. He instructs Col. Talcott to move his regiment to repair the damage to that

---

45 Edwin C. Bearss, *The Petersburg Campaign*, 2 vols. (El Dorado Hills, CA, 2012, 2014), vol. 1, 154; John D. Smith, *The History of the Nineteenth Regiment of Maine Volunteer Infantry, 1862-1865* (Minneapolis, MN, 1909), 209-10; OR 40, pt. 1, 749-50; OR 40, pt. 2, 680; Dowdey, *Wartime Papers*, 804. Mahone, who was given to extreme exaggeration in his postwar writings, wrote that Lee told him simply to drive the Federals from his front, and then returned to his HQ. Mahone made no mention of A. P. Hill being present or even involved in the attack and claimed Wilcox *requested* to take his division along also. Smith, *19th Maine*, 209-10. Wilcox of course did not "request" to come along but rather was ordered along by Hill. William Palmer to Mahone, February 27, 1872, William Mahone papers, Duke. Freeman wrote that Lee personally directed Mahone's attack but that does not seem to be the case. *Lee's Dispatches*, 258-9 n1 (although he incorrectly dated the action as occurring on the 21st). One of Mahone's couriers noted after the war that Mahone was in command of this fight, as Hill "very gracefully declined command of the field." J. W. Friend to Mahone, February 1, 1872, Mahone papers, Duke. In reporting the results of the attack to Lee, Hill stated "Mahone's three brigades have done it all. Promote him at once." Hill to REL, undated (but the numbers stated are those Lee sent to Seddon, so almost certainly evening of June 22), Venable papers, UNC. Writing to Anderson during the evening, Lee stated "Your statement confirms the opinion that I have had for some time, that if we could get at our enemies we could destroy them." REL to RHA, June 22, 1864, EPA papers, UNC.

46 Nothing is known regarding Lee's actions on the 23rd, however since he placed Beauregard in command of a dawn attack on Grant's northern flank, it seems probable that he studied the ground in some fashion and met at least with Beauregard if not the other officers involved. See Johnson Hagood, *Memoirs of the War of Secession* (Camden, SC, 1997), 274-6; and Bearss, *Petersburg Campaign*, vol. 1, 192. Venable implied that Lee met with Porter Alexander either on the night of the 22nd or morning of the 23rd to plan the artillery portion of the attack on the 24th. Venable, "Campaign from the Wilderness to Petersburg," 539-40.

47 Hagood, *Memoirs*, 274-6; OR 40, pt. 1, 750, 796-8; Dowdey, *Wartime Papers*, 804; REL to Mrs. REL, June 24, 1864, REL papers, LOC. In his second letter to Mary, Lee mentioned going out on the lines but he gave no details.

48 Dowdey, *Wartime Papers*, 805; OR 36, pt. 3, 903; OR 40, pt. 1, 750-1, 769-73. The flag issue stemmed from the capture of two flags by Bushrod Johnson's men on the 16th that Gen. Henry Wise then gave to the Commonwealth. Johnson wrote Beauregard that they should have been turned over to the War Department; Beauregard concurred and passed the issue to Lee. OR 40, pt. 1, 769-73.

railroad done by the enemy raiders, and orders Fitz Lee to move his division south of the James River as well. Lee learns also that David Hunter's enemy force retreated deep into the mountains of West Virginia and so instructs Early to move down the Valley toward the Potomac rather than pursue Hunter.[49]

Lee sends a lengthy letter to President Davis regarding Early's operations in the Valley and also the possibility of a raid on the POW camp at Point Lookout, Maryland. He states that he can hold at Petersburg for the present without Early as Grant seems to have gone over to the defensive and confesses that keeping the army fed is a greater concern that Grant currently: "I am less uneasy about holding our position than about our ability to procure supplies for the army." In response to continued complaints from residents of the Northern Neck about lack of defense of their region, Lee informs both Davis and Seddon that he cannot send troops there and does not relish the idea of making John Mosby responsible for the area either as he could easily be isolated there and proposes instead that a new Mosby-like command be created there. He receives a letter from Dr. Robert Peyton and clothes from Mary, and replies to Mary complaining about how the oppressive heat has shut down military operations for the time being and praises Rooney's recent actions; he also sends her more of his winter clothing for storage.[50]

June 27, Monday (Violet Bank): Gen. Lee requests that several heavy guns and mortars from the Richmond defenses be sent to Petersburg. He names commanders to fill several brigade vacancies: William Terry for James Kemper's brigade, William McRae for Kirkland's Brigade, and John Bratton for Micah Jenkins's brigade. Rain during the afternoon.[51]

June 28, Tuesday (Violet Bank): Lee informs Bragg and Seddon that the local reserve troops may be withdrawn from the Richmond defenses but Heth's troops cannot remain north of the James; Lee agrees with Seddon's suggestion to use dismounted cavalry in the works instead. He provides Seddon an update on the Wilson-Kautz raid and urges prompt repair of the R&D, including taking up rails from other less important railroads to keep the R&D in service, but cautions that once it is back in operation the newspapers must not report on it. He advises Adjutant General Cooper that while Bradley Johnson is worthy of promotion to brigade command, Thomas Munford is likely more acceptable to the officers and men of the brigade. He writes to Mildred, apologizing for not being able to see her and advising her to let her pet squirrel, Custis Morgan, go.[52]

June 29, Wednesday (Violet Bank): Lee writes to President Davis regarding Early and the Valley, again recommending an attempt to liberate the prisoners from Point Lookout. He expresses again his fears over keeping the army supplied at Petersburg: "My greatest present anxiety is to secure regular and constant supplies. At this time I am doing well, but I must look to the future." He mentions that he has implemented a wagon route to bring supplies into from Petersburg from Stony Creek station on the Weldon Railroad. He informs Seddon of Hampton and Mahone's victory over Wilson and Kautz south of Petersburg today, and also informs Gen. Anderson that he agrees Moxley Sorrel is worthy of promotion to brigade command but there is no

---

49 OR 40, pt. 1, 751; OR 40, pt. 2, 689-92; OR 36, pt. 3, 903; REL to Early, June 26, 1864 telegram book, REL HQ papers, VHS. The enemy force under Gens. James H. Wilson and August V. Kautz was turned back by a handful of Pickett's men, convalescents, and local reserves at Staunton River Bridge commanded by Capt. Benjamin Farinholt. Col. T. M. R. Talcott's brother Charles was superintendent of the R&D.

50 OR 37, pt. 1, 766-8; Freeman, *Lee's Dispatches*, 259-60; OR 40, pt. 2, 689; Dowdey, *Wartime Papers*, 808-9.

51 Freeman, *Lee's Dispatches*, 261-2; OR 40, pt. 2, 694; Clifton diary, June 27, 1864, NC Archives.

52 OR 40, pt. 2, 696-9; OR 40, pt. 1, 751-2; REL to Cooper, June 28, 1864, telegram book, REL HQ papers, VHS; Dowdey, *Wartime Papers*, 810. Richmond's local defense troops were clerks, artisans, mechanics, and other government employees; keeping them in the field prevented them from doing their actual jobs.

Georgia brigade in need of a commander at present. He receives a letter from Mary.[53]

June 30, Thursday (Violet Bank): President Davis meets with Lee at Violet Bank. He forwards to Richmond two letters from Chase Whiting regarding Wilmington and cautions that he can send no aid to Whiting but he does not think the rumors of a pending attack there are true. He writes to Mary, glad that her health is improving and mentions that today is their 33rd wedding anniversary; he mentions also the graciousness of his host, Mrs. Shippen, in keeping him and the staff well-fed.[54]

---

53 OR 37, pt. 1, 769-70; OR 40, pt. 1, 752; REL endorsement on RHA to REL, May 29, 1864, Sorrel CSR; Dowdey, *Wartime Papers*, 812. Sorrel was Longstreet's chief of staff; he was promoted to brigadier general in late October 1864 and given command of one of Mahone's brigades. Warner, *Generals in Gray*, 286-7.

54 Dowdey, *Wartime Papers*, 812; Freeman, *Lee's Dispatches*, 263-4. Davis's arrival actually interrupted Lee's letter to Mary. No known record exists of this meeting; Lee's letter to Davis regarding Wilmington makes no mention of their meeting today so it was probably written before President Davis's arrival.

July 1864

After Confederate attempts failed to dislodge the Army of the Potomac from Petersburg in late June, both sides strengthened their fortifications and each looked for ways to bring the other to battle outside of the trenches. For Robert E. Lee, this meant an increased hope that operations in the Shenandoah Valley might tip the scales at Petersburg in his favor, much as Thomas J. "Stonewall" Jackson influenced operations around Richmond two years earlier. For the Federals, it meant going underground—literally.

For a time it looked as though Lee's plan might work. Jubal Early not only cleared the Valley but he moved into Maryland to attack the outskirts of Washington. On July 12, as Early's men engaged in long-range skirmishing with a combination of the green troops of the capital garrison and seasoned veterans rushed north from Petersburg, some may have noticed a tall figure in a black coat and top hat standing among other officers and men on the ramparts of Fort Stevens. If so, they were looking at President Abraham Lincoln, who wanted a view of the Confederates for himself.[1]

As part of Early's campaign, Lee authorized a daring raid to free the prisoners held at Point Lookout, Maryland. In a clandestine operation that sounds more like something from World War II, a small army and navy force from Wilmington, North Carolina, was to make its way up the Chesapeake Bay to the POW camp in southern Maryland, where it would rendezvous with a cavalry force dispatched from Early's Valley army. The plan was to have the thousands of freed prisoners join Early's force near Washington. The complex plan had very little chance of success, but the dwindling manpower reserves for the Confederacy justified the risk. General Lee was not directly involved, but his sons Custis and Rob had a hand in it; Rob was Lee's special messenger to inform Early of his role in the mission, and Custis was part of the Wilmington force and likely the intended commander of the freed prisoners.[2]

In Georgia, meanwhile, William Sherman's army group repeatedly outflanked Joe Johnston's Army of Tennessee, pushing it back to the outskirts of Atlanta. Sherman's playbook was much the same as Grant's, who preferred moving around his enemy rather than trying to go through him. Sherman had his own Cold Harbor (though not as bloody) at Kennesaw Mountain on June 27. but Johnston was unable to stop the Union flanking efforts. His non-communicative habits of early 1862 remained firmly in place, and Jefferson Davis had had enough when it appeared that Johnston would give up Atlanta without a fight. The president demanded a change in Georgia, but his viable options were few. He sought Gen. Lee's opinion on the matter, but promptly ignored his advice and installed John B. Hood at the head of the Army of Tennessee.

To Lee's relief, his Mary wife finally left Richmond to stay with friends in Fluvanna County. Her stubbornness, however, remained firmly in place. Contrary to her doctor's orders, she was determined to walk without assistance and fell, seriously injuring herself.[3]

---

1 Frank E. Vandiver, *Jubal's Raid: General Early's Famous Attack on Washington in 1864* (Lincoln, NE, 1992), 167-8. Early is said to have remarked "We haven't taken Washington, but we've scared Abe Lincoln like Hell." Ibid, 171.

2 Freeman, *Lee's Dispatches*, 275-6; Lee, *Recollections and Letters of REL*, 131. The grand raid never happened although Early did dispatch a cavalry force in that direction that failed to come anywhere near the camp.

3 Dowdey, *Wartime Papers*, 827-8.

Toward the end of the month Grant sent a force north of the James River to threaten Richmond, which forced Lee to counter the move by withdrawing troops used to defend Petersburg. Lee thought it might be a feint, and that rather than moving on the capital, Grant's target was actually the thinly held lines at Bermuda Hundred between Richmond and Petersburg. Lee was partially correct: the force was indeed a diversion, but the target was Petersburg itself.

On July 30, one of the most unique and desperate battles of the war took place southeast of the city when several tons of gunpowder were detonated beneath the Confederate lines. The massive explosion ripped a hole in the line of defenses, which were then stormed by the entire Union IX Corps. The resulting contest to either drive through the gap or seal the breach at "the Crater," as it became known, was a horrific action that involved extensive hand-to-hand fighting. It also catapulted Brig. Gen. William Mahone from relative anonymity to instant Confederate hero, his handling of the defense drawing high praise from Lee and the Richmond newspapers alike.[4] Grant, who called the affair a "stupendous failure," noted, "The chances of success were so great—the failure so utter—that all men who understand the whole matter are paralyzed and petrified."[5] It cost Ambrose Burnside his command and for weeks afterward nervous Confederates thought every strange sound was another Yankee tunnel being dug beneath their feet.

* * *

---

[4] Gens. Lee and Beauregard observed the battle only a few hundred yards away from "the Crater," but played no major role in directing Mahone's fight.

[5] Richard Slotkin, *No Quarter: The Battle of the Crater, 1864* (New York, 2009), 317.

July 1, Friday (Violet Bank): Lee meets with Francis Lawley of the *London Times*. Porter Alexander comes to headquarters and informs Lee of his belief that the Federals are constructing a mine under Elliott's Salient southeast of Petersburg; Lawley remains for the conversation and interjects that the distance involved is too great for such a mine shaft. Lee sends the president several news items from a recent Philadelphia newspaper, and updates the secretary of war on the skirmishing on Beauregard's front. He also stresses to Secretary of War Seddon the importance of keeping the Virginia Central Railroad open and requests that forces be stationed to guard the bridges over the South Anna and Rivanna rivers.[6]

July 2, Saturday (Violet Bank): Lee recommends to President Davis that Wade Hampton should be promoted to command the army's cavalry. He writes to Beauregard that Wilmington, North Carolina, needs more troops, but that Goldsboro and Weldon both must be protected to ensure the rail connection to Petersburg; he also writes to Lt. Gen. Theophilus Holmes regarding the defense of Weldon and Goldsboro. In the evening he meets with Col. John T. Wood to plan a raid on the POW camp at Point Lookout.[7]

July 3, Sunday (Violet Bank): Lee writes to President Davis with plans for the Point Lookout raid, approving of Col. J. T. Wood being placed in overall command of the operation but stating that a general should be sent to command the prisoners once released; he suggests Robert Hoke for this but then notes that he cannot spare him from Petersburg and so suggests having Early send John Gordon with a brigade of cavalry as an escort. Lee advises Seddon that Hampton does not approve of the idea of using dismounted cavalry to man the Richmond defenses as proposed earlier.[8]

July 4, Monday (Violet Bank): Lee is awakened around 2 a.m. by reports from Bushrod Johnson of the enemy moving across his front; Lee instructs Richard Anderson to report on affairs in his front and have Kershaw's Division prepared to intercept whatever movement is afoot. He instructs Ewell to arrange his forces so as to have a mobile force of at least two brigades at Chaffin's Bluff to meet any emergency that arises. Lee orders John Hunt Morgan not to undertake an offensive at present as it would leave southwest Virginia exposed, and writes to VMI superintendent Francis Smith expressing regret over the destruction of the Institute by Hunter's army.[9]

---

6 Alexander, *Military Memoirs*, 564-5; Freeman, *Lee's Dispatches*, 265-7; OR 40, pt. 1, 752; OR 40, pt. 2, 709. On this date Gen. George Meade received a letter addressed to Lee from the widow of Gen. James Wadsworth, who had been killed at the Wilderness, requesting the return of Wadsworth's personal effects. Meade wanted to send it through the lines immediately, but Grant refused, preferring to wait until other matters necessitated a flag of truce, at which time it could be forwarded to Lee. OR 40, pt. 2, 561.

7 Dowdey, *Wartime Papers*, 813; OR 40, pt. 2, 710; REL to T. H. Holmes, July 2, 1864, REL papers, Duke; Freeman, *Lee's Dispatches*, 269. Lee did not immediately appoint a successor to Jeb Stuart; instead, each of the three cavalry divisions reported directly to him.

8 Freeman, *Lee's Dispatches*, 269-71; OR 40, pt. 2, 711. Lee did not attend church service because he believed it was canceled due to the heavy enemy fire in Petersburg. In fact, Rev. William Platt conducted the service in the basement but did not ring the church bell "for fear Gen. Lee might be tempted to come over from his headquarters . . . and it is too dangerous for him to be riding about the streets." Tower, *Lee's Adjutant*, 171; A. Wilson Greene, *Civil War Petersburg: Confederate City in the Crucible of War* (Charlottesville, VA, 2006), 197. It was likely in connection with this proposed Point Lookout operation that Lee summoned Rob to HQ "about July 1st," to carry a special order to Early in the lower Valley. Lee, *Recollections and Letters of REL*, 131. Rob reached Early on July 6 at Sharpsburg. Benjamin F. Cooling, *Jubal Early's Raid on Washington, 1864* (Baltimore, MD, 1989), 39.

9 OR 40, pt. 2, 712-3; REL to J. H. Morgan, July 4, 1864, telegram book, REL HQ papers, VHS; REL to F. H. Smith, July 4, 1864, Sara Smith papers, VHS. Somehow either Anderson or Beauregard, or both, confused Lee's instructions for Anderson to determine what was in his front with orders to attack, prompting Lee to inquire of Anderson what Beauregard meant when he wrote Lee "that General Anderson has an attack to make on his front, similar to the one in front of Elliott." OR 40, pt. 2, 713. Lee told Francis Smith, "I have grieved over the destruction of the Military Institute.

July 5, Tuesday (Violet Bank): Custis and Col. J. T. Wood, with several other officers, visit Lee in the morning to make final preparations for the Point Lookout raid; he provides transportation for them to Wilmington and instructions for Whiting to provide artillery. He informs President Davis of Wood's arrival and his orders to Whiting to assist. In a much longer letter to President Davis, Lee addresses the problem of getting recruits and horses for the cavalry; he proposes the transfer of mounted troops from Georgia and also using cotton and tobacco instead of government funds to purchase horses. He receives a letter from Mildred, and sends her some fresh fruit and again expresses his disgust at her pet squirrel, Custis Morgan.[10]

July 6, Wednesday (Violet Bank): A. P. Hill comes to headquarters to report on what units are in his front, and Lee informs President Davis that Burnside's IX Corps is still at Petersburg. He instructs Ewell to have his men gather all crops within their reach and to drive the enemy away from Deep Bottom and destroy their bridge there. He writes to Gen. Holmes lauding his efforts at getting North Carolina's reserve troops into the field but also chiding him for allowing the destruction of supplies stored at South Quay: "I hope you will take measure to prevent the accumulation of stores at exposed points. Where subsistence is received on the rivers or at other points in eastern North Carolina, it should be sent to a place of security as soon as is possible and I hope you will be able to afford protection to those engaged in receiving and removing it. The presence of even a small force will deter the enemy from making an attempt sometimes, even when the force would not be adequate to resist it if made." Lee tells President Davis that because Europe views the war as a contest over slavery no outside help can be expected: "This war presents to the European world but two aspects: A contest in which one party is contending for abstract slavery and the other against it. The existence of vital rights involved does not seem to be understood or appreciated. As long as this lasts, we can expect neither sympathy or aid. . . . Our safety depends upon ourselves alone."[11]

July 7, Thursday (Violet Bank): Fitz Lee comes to headquarters in the morning, likely regarding enemy movements north of the James. Lee asks Bragg the source for reports of enemy troops moving from Petersburg to Bermuda Hundred, and instructs Martin Gary to locate Sheridan's troopers north of the James. Lee writes to President Davis regarding enemy movements along the James and reactions to Early's campaign, and inquires of Richmond & Danville Railroad Superintendent Charles Talcott when that line will be in operation again. He sends a short note of condolence to Maj. James Breathed regarding his recent wounding and compliments him for his gallantry. He receives a letter from Mary and writes back to remind her that her health will continue to improve if she eats more fruit as her doctors instructed, and he half-jokingly recommends cooking Mildred's pet squirrel.[12]

July 8, Friday (Violet Bank): Lee advises President Davis that word of the Point Lookout raid leaked and Lee will leave it up to Col. Wood and the others whether to proceed. He advises Ewell that rather

---

But the good that has been done to the country cannot be destroyed, nor can its name or fame perish. It will rise stronger than before, and continue to diffuse its benefits to a grateful people." REL to Smith, July 4, 1864, Sara Smith papers, VHS.

10 Freeman, *Lee's Dispatches*, 275-6; Yates, *Perfect Gentleman*, vol. 1, 305-6; Dowdey, *Wartime Papers*, 814-5. Wood's raid was to depart from Wilmington. It was called off when word of it leaked out; Custis, Wood, and the others returned to Richmond several days later, with Custis stopping to visit with his father; the return date is not known. Yates, *Perfect Gentleman*, vol. 1, 305-6. Little is known of this aborted raid, but it seems that Custis may have assumed the role Lee originally intended for Hoke or Gordon.

11 Freeman, *Lee's Dispatches*, 276-7; *OR* 40, pt. 3, 745; REL to T. H. Holmes, July 6, 1864, REL papers, Duke; Dowdey, *Wartime Papers*, 816. South Quay is on the Blackwater River, just south of Franklin, VA.

12 Hewitt, ed., *OR Supplement*, vol. 7, 342; Freeman, *Lee's Dispatches*, 277; REL to Martin Gary, July 7, 1864, telegram book, REL HQ papers, VHS; *OR* 37, pt. 2, 593-4; REL to C. G. Talcott, July 7, 1864, telegram book, REL HQ papers, VHS; Freeman, *Calendar of Confederate Papers*, 327; Dowdey, *Wartime Papers*, 816-7. Breathed led the cavalry's horse artillery.

than establishing permanent batteries along the James to combat enemy gunboats, Lee prefers to use mobile field artillery. Lee admonishes Charles Talcott of the Richmond & Danville Raiload for what he perceives as tardiness on the part of the railroad to repair damage inflicted by the enemy: "Do not see why you are dependent upon [the] Govt more than other roads. Better surrender the road to [the] Govt if you cannot operate it. You have more aid than other roads have." Gen. Lee complains to Secretary Seddon that Talcott is doing "nothing" to repair the railroad and urges that the Confederate government take over the line.[13]

July 9, Saturday (Violet Bank): Lee forwards to the War Department several flags captured by Mahone at Jerusalem Plank Road on June 22. He asks Ewell if troops from Richmond can relieve those from Lee's army at Chaffin's Bluff and notifies John Hunt Morgan that Hunter is reported moving north so Morgan is free to undertake his proposed offensive. He also requests clarification from Richmond regarding whether the new enlistment act applies to Maryland troops. He notifies Talcott of the R&D that he is depending upon railroad officials to keep the line in operation: "The Govt is dependent upon you to operate the road. If you depend upon the Govt, I fear in the present emergency it will not be worked with that energy necessary to prevent disaster to the country. Better that one party should have control and responsibility than both."[14]

July 10, Sunday (Violet Bank): Rev. William H. Platt of St. Paul's Episcopal holds church service on the lawn at Violet Bank in the morning. In attendance are Lee, Taylor, and a number of ladies from Petersburg. The general forwards to President Davis a copy of the July 8 New York *Herald* to illustrate the effect Jubal Early's operations in the Valley are having on the Northern populace: "The people in the U.S. are mystified about our forces on the Potomac." Lee warns Gen. Theophilus Holmes at Weldon that the enemy seems to be concentrating at New Bern, likely for a strike against Kinston or Washington, North Carolina.[15]

Lee informs Grant that he will have Gen. James Wadsworth's personal effects returned to his widow if they can be found. He also communicates that he will inquire as to the status of Col. William Sackett, but that he will not allow Sackett's wife to come within the lines to visit him. The general also advises Grant that he referred the request for a POW exchange to the secretary of war. During the evening, Lee warns Gens. Ewell and Pickett that Grant may in fact be preparing for an attack. Lee writes to wife Mary, mentioning the devastation of Petersburg and also his relief that Mildred's squirrel is missing.[16]

July 11, Monday (Violet Bank): Lee informs the War Department that Rickett's Division of Wright's Union VI Corps left Petersburg and the rest of the corps will likely follow. He notifies Early that Grant

---

13 Freeman, *Lee's Dispatches*, 278; *OR* 40, pt. 3, 749-50; REL to C. G. Talcott, July 8, 1864, telegram book, REL HQ papers, VHS. Seddon replied to Lee on the 9th that the damage to the Richmond and Danville line was far more extensive than Lee realized, and that in addition to Talcott's employees some of Jeremy Gilmer's engineers were also at work to get it back in operation. *OR* 40, pt. 3, 753-4.

14 *OR* 51, pt. 2, 1031-2; *OR* 40, pt. 3, 755-6; REL to J. H. Morgan, July 9, 1864, telegram book, REL HQ papers, VHS; *OR* 3, Series 4, 546-7; REL to C. G. Talcott, July 9, 1864, telegram book, REL HQ papers, VHS.

15 Dowdey, *Wartime Papers*, 817-8; Tower, *Lee's Adjutant*, 173; REL to T. H. Holmes, July 10, 1864, telegram book, REL HQ papers, VHS. Lee was trying to keep the enemy guessing about his personal whereabouts, having requested the War Department not print any of his communications and to be silent on his involvement in affairs at Petersburg. *OR* 51, pt. 2, 1031-2. In the evening Jefferson Davis instructed J. T. Wood to call off the naval raid on Point Lookout. Shingleton, *John Taylor Wood*, 117.

16 *OR* 40, pt. 3, 125; *OR* 7, Series 2, 452; REL to Ewell, July 10, 1864, telegram book, REL HQ papers, VHS; REL to Pickett, July 10, 1864, telegram book, REL HQ papers, VHS; Dowdey, *Wartime Papers*, 818. The two letters were sent through the lines on either the 8th or 9th. *OR* 40, pt. 3, 81. Sackett was colonel of the 9th NY Cavalry and was mortally wounded at Trevilian Station on June 11; he died three days later. On July 14 Sackett's widow was notified by a Confederate surgeon of her husband's death and granted permission later in the month to retrieve his body. Eric J. Wittenberg, *Glory Enough for All: Sheridan's Second Raid and the Battle of Trevilian Station* (Washington, DC, 2002), 327.

is sending troops from Petersburg to counter him north of the Potomac, but Lee assures Early he is free to operate as he chooses and is not locked in to any predetermined course of action. Gen. Lee authorizes Gen. Ewell to place torpedoes [i.e. floating mines] in the James River, and favorably endorses a request from Gen. Mahone for the promotion of Capt. Victor Girardy. Rain in the evening.[17]

July 12, Tuesday (Violet Bank): Jefferson Davis notifies Lee that he intends to replace Joe Johnston as commander of the Army of Tennessee with John B. Hood; Lee replies back that replacing Johnston is not a good idea and he does not recommend Hood: "We may lose Atlanta and the army too. Hood is a bold fighter. I am doubtful as to other qualities necessary." Explaining his thoughts in greater detail in a letter to President Davis that evening, Lee recommends William Hardee rather than Hood as a replacement for Johnston. He also recommends to Davis that Theophilus Holmes be given command of North Carolina's reserve forces, and tells Holmes to use his own discretion regarding the defense of the Weldon Railroad. He looks to Rooney for confirmation that the entire VI Corps departed Petersburg and instructs John Hunt Morgan to strike at the B&O.[18]

July 13, Wednesday (Violet Bank): Lee informs Gen. Ewell that the local reserves will only be called out in absolute emergencies, so he must plan to man the works without them. Lee once again expresses his displeasure that the residents of the Northern Neck continue to complain about the lack of defense of that region, but they do nothing to defend themselves: "If the people will do nothing to defend themselves against such outrages, I can see no remedy for them. . . . They could easily expel such marauding parties if they would exert themselves." He points out that if he were to detach troops from the ANV to the Northern Neck it would only draw even more enemy attention upon the region. He writes to Virginia Burwell regarding the role that women on the home front can play to assist the war effort.[19]

July 14, Thursday (Violet Bank): Grant expresses his concern that General Lee himself may be with Jubal Early's forces in the Shenandoah because the messages sent through the lines over the last few days were addressed to Lee, but came back answered by Beauregard.[20]

July 15, Friday (Violet Bank): Secretary of War Seddon rides to Violet Bank in the morning and meets with Lee for several hours regarding who should replace Joe Johnston at the head of the Army of Tennessee. Lee favorably endorses a request from James Longstreet for the promotion of William Wofford to major general, but Lee regrets that there is no division in need of a commander at the present

---

17 *OR* 37, pt. 2, 594-6; *OR* 40, pt. 3, 764; Mahone to REL, July 7, 1864, Girardy CSR; F. G. Walter diary, July 11, 1864, LVA. Girardy was born in France but grew up in Georgia and New Orleans; at this time he was the lone officer serving on Mahone's staff. Warner, *Generals in Gray*, 105-6.

18 Dowdey, *Wartime Papers*, 821-2; Freeman, *Lee's Dispatches*, 280-2; REL to T. H. Holmes, July 12, 1864, telegram book, REL HQ papers, VHS; REL to Rooney, July 12, 1864, REL papers, Duke; REL to J. H. Morgan, July 12, 1864, telegram book, REL HQ papers, VHS. Davis relieved Johnston and replaced him with Hood on July 17. Long, *CW Day by Day*, 540. William C. Davis, the president's biographer, argues that with the Army of Northern Virginia pinned down in the trenches around Petersburg and Richmond, Lee should have been sent to Georgia and put in command of the Army of Tennessee, and the Virginia army given to P. G. T. Beauregard: "Now was the time to send Lee himself to the West, whether he liked it or not. Beauregard could ably command the defense of the earthworks in Virginia, leaving Davis's best general to try to do something with the only remaining large mobile field army east of the Mississippi." Davis, *Jefferson Davis*, 564.

19 *OR* 40, pt. 3, 772-4; REL to V. B. Burwell, July 13, 1864, Beverly R. Wellford papers, VHS. Virginia Burwell was the younger sister of George Pickett. Edward G. Longacre, *Pickett, Leader of the Charge: A Biography of General George E. Pickett, C.S.A.* (Shippensburg, PA, 1998), 88.

20 *OR* 37, pt. 2, 302. Nothing is known of Lee's activities on this date; the lack of correspondence suggests he spent the day on the lines.

time. The general asks Wade Hampton whether he can make a raid on Grant's sprawling Union supply base at City Point.[21]

July 16, Saturday (Violet Bank/Petersburg): In the morning Lee rides to Rives Salient southeast of Petersburg, where he is joined by A. P. Hill, Anderson, Field, Heth, and Mahone to observe the enemy. Lee informs Hampton that he cannot keep several flags captured by his command, that they are the property of the Confederate government. Lee congratulates Capt. Benjamin Farinholt for his victory at Staunton River Bridge last month, and writes to Mary with latest family news and that he does not need any more clothing at present.[22]

July 17, Sunday (Violet Bank): Lee congratulates Early on his success outside Washington and instructs him to attack Hunter if he returns to the Valley and to gather all supplies he can for the ANV. He updates Sec. Seddon on Early's operations.[23]

July 18, Monday (Violet Bank): Lee learns of John Hood's appointment to command of the Army of Tennessee. He writes to Sec. Seddon regarding the rumored execution of civilians and officers alike by the Federals, stating that he finds retaliation repulsive but something must be done; rather than execute an equal number of POWs, he will execute any captured from the guilty command: "It is true the innocent may sometimes suffer by this course, but it will have a tendency to make those who do not approve the savage usages of their comrades exert all their influence to restrain them." Lee asks Rooney if he can confirm the departure of the VI Corps, and issues orders prohibiting fraternization with enemy pickets.[24]

Lee warns Pendleton of a possible spy in one of his artillery units, and instructs Early to operate against the B&O and to send all horses he can get to Richmond. He also requests Josiah Gorgas to send arms for the North Carolina reserves to Salisbury.[25]

July 19, Tuesday (Violet Bank): Lee forwards to Adjutant General Cooper a circular from the Federals encouraging Lee's men to desert; Lee proposes to produce a similar one to persuade desertion among Grant's troops. He also forwards to Seddon a report from Early on his operations to date, and provides a lengthy justification of why Early was detached. Rain all day.[26]

---

21 Younger, *Inside the CS Government*, 167; Davis, *Rise and Fall*, vol. 2, 474 n5; Smith, *Most Daring of Men*, 128; REL to Hampton, July 15, 1864, telegram book, REL HQ papers, VHS. City Point is located at the confluence of the James and Appomattox rivers. During the long siege, the village swelled in size and became one of the largest ports in the world.

22 Wiley, *Norfolk Blues*, 134; OR 40, pt. 3, 772-3; REL to B. H. Farinholt, July 16, 1864, Whitaker-Snipes papers, UNC; REL to Mrs. REL, REL papers, LOC. A telegram to Charles Talcott of the Richmond & Danville line is noted as being sent, but the content was not recorded. REL to Talcott, July 16, 1864, telegram book, REL HQ papers, VHS. A gunner in Grandy's Battery wrote of the gathered generals: "This morning we had an assembly of rare military talent . . . just in rear of my gun, who were viewing the operations of the enemy and discussing their movements. I felt uncomfortable the whole time they were there, fearing that the enemy might discover the group and throw a shell into it." Wiley, *Norfolk Blues*, 134.

23 REL to Early, July 17, 1864, telegram book, REL HQ papers, VHS; Jones, *War Clerk's Diary*, vol. 2, 251. George Pickett's son was born on this date, and Mrs. Pickett claimed that her husband requested permission to visit her and the baby in Richmond but Lee denied the request. Seth Moyle, ed., *The Heart of a Soldier: Intimate Wartime Letters from General George E. Pickett C.S.A. to his Wife* (Gettysburg, PA, 1995), 148. It should be noted that many of Pickett's letters in that volume were heavily edited, and perhaps outright fabricated, by his widow, and must be used with great caution.

24 Freeman, *Lee*, vol. 3, 462; OR 7, Series 2, 473; REL to Rooney, July 18, 1864, REL papers, Duke; SO 167, July 18, 1864, REL HQ papers, VHS.

25 Charles Marshall to WNP, July 18, 1864, WNP papers, UNC; REL to Early, July 18, 1864 (2 messages), telegram book, REL HQ papers, VHS; REL to Gorgas, July 18, 1864, telegram book, REL HQ papers, VHS. A Joseph Lee of King George County reported that a soldier from the 3rd IN Cav. had infiltrated an unknown artillery unit as a spy; Lee gave little credence to the report, but ordered Pendleton to investigate anyway. Marshall to WNP, July 18, 1864, WNP papers, UNC.

26 OR 40, pt. 3, 781-2; OR 37, pt. 1, 346; F. G. Walter diary, July 19, 1864, LVA.

July 20, Wednesday (Violet Bank): Lee forwards to Richmond two flags captured by the 9th Virginia Cavalry with the request that, if possible, they be given to Gen. Hampton; he also requests that the War Department issue orders explaining what is to be done with captured flags in the future. He advises Gen. Ewell that the torpedoes intended for his use on the James were captured and reverses his earlier stance regarding a permanent battery on the river, wanting to know if one can be erected.[27] He advises the secretary of war of Jubal Early's victory at Snicker's Gap on the 18th, and informs Gov. Vance that the requested weapons will be sent to Salisbury tomorrow. Lee favorably endorses Gen. Mahone's request to have his aide, Victor Girardy, promoted and given command of the Georgia Brigade in his division.[28]

July 21, Thursday (Violet Bank): Lee informs President Davis of the difficulty of getting adequate supplies from the port of Wilmington along the Weldon Railroad, and requests that stockpiles be established in Richmond and elsewhere along the Richmond & Danville line for the Virginia army's use. The general inquires of engineer chief Jeremy Gilmer whether other troops are available to relieve Talcott's regiment working on the R&D, and he thanks Col. Talcott for his assistance in getting the railroad back into operation. Lee also directs Gen. Martin Gary to establish observation posts along the James River and to attack any enemy cavalry operating north of the waterway. Lee requests a new tent from the quartermaster general because the one he is using is now three years old and leaks like a sieve.[29]

July 22, Friday (Violet Bank): Gen. Lee writes to Wade Hampton regarding maintaining a cavalry presence in central Virginia in order to cooperate with Jubal Early.[30]

July 23, Saturday (Violet Bank): Lee chides Ewell for the poor scouting efforts east of Richmond which allow enemy raiding parties to roam at will on the lower Peninsula, and sends Kershaw's Division to Chaffin's Bluff to counter a rumored Federal buildup north of the James. He advises Early that if he cannot keep the Federals detained in the Valley, they will join Grant and he will have to rejoin the ANV at Petersburg, and he informs Sec. Seddon of an attack by Early near Winchester on the 20th.[31]

Lee writes to President Davis regarding bringing corn from Georgia to Richmond, and sends him a lengthy description of the strategic situation in Virginia: he does not think Lincoln will allow troops to be withdrawn from the Valley as long as Early is

---

27 *OR* 40, pt. 3, 785, 788-9. Col. Beale of the 9th VA Cav. gave the captured colors to Hampton, not understanding the procedure for captured flags; Lee countermanded those orders but Beale's actions were the reason for his request they be given to Hampton, if possible. *OR* 40, pt 3, 785.

28 *OR* 37, pt. 1, 346; REL to Josiah Gorgas, July 20, 1864, telegram book, REL HQ papers, VHS; REL to Vance, July 20, 1864, telegram book, REL HQ papers, VHS; Mahone to REL, July 20, 1864, Victor Girardy CSR. Girardy was promoted on Aug. 3 but was killed less than two weeks later at Fussell's Mill. Warner, *Generals in Gray*, 106. Maj. Gen. Martin L. Smith was reassigned as chief engineer of the Army of Tennessee on this date and replaced by Col. Walter H. Stevens. *OR* 40, pt. 3, 787-8.

29 Freeman, *Lee's Dispatches*, 285-6; REL to Gilmer, July 21, 1864, telegram book, REL HQ papers, VHS; REL to T. M. R. Talcott, July 21, 1864, telegram book, REL HQ papers, VHS; REL to Martin Gary, July 21, 1864, telegram book, REL HQ papers, VHS; REL to A. R. Lawton, July 21, 1864, Lawton papers, UNC. Lee's tent was issued prior to taking the field in West Virginia: "My present one was among the first that was made in Richmond in 1861 and has been my principal habitation since wherever I have been." REL to Lawton, July 21, 1864, Lawton papers, UNC.

30 *OR* 37, pt. 2, 598. In a letter to his fiancé on this date, Taylor mentioned several of the more prevalent camp rumors, among them that Burnside's men were digging a mine under the Confederate works, and that the Army of the Potomac's commander, George Meade, had told Gen. Henry Wise that he would switch sides and join the Confederate army if offered a position. Tower, *Lee's Adjutant*, 175.

31 *OR* 40, pt. 3, 794-5; REL to Kershaw, July 23, 1864, telegram book, REL HQ papers, VHS; REL to Early, July 23, 1864, telegram book, REL HQ papers, VHS; *OR* 37, pt. 1, 347. Lee saw Rooney and Rob at some point during the day. Dowdey, *Wartime Papers*, 826.

nearby and mentions his efforts to disrupt Grant's communications on the James.³²

July 24, Sunday (Violet Bank): Rev. William Platt conducts church service at Violet Bank in the morning, attended by both Lee and Gen. Beauregard. Lee orders Gens. Ewell and Kershaw to eradicate the Federal bridgehead north of the James River: "We cannot afford to sit down in front of the enemy and allow him to intrench [sic] himself wherever he pleases."³³

The general writes to son Custis requesting him to use any influence he can to get Ewell to actively interdict enemy navigation of the James River, and mentions the possibility of drawing troops from the Trans-Mississippi theater east to Virginia. Lee sends two letters to his wife, one with family news that mentions having seen Custis, Rooney, and Rob recently, and the other about the morning's church service and the continued kindness that the people of Petersburg show him. A violent storm erupts during the night, which takes down Walter Taylor's tent.³⁴

July 25, Monday (Violet Bank): Gen. Lee tries to identify the source of the troops north of the James River because prisoners taken by Joe Kershaw belong to the Union X Corps of Ben. Butler's Army of the James. Lee instructs Gen. Pickett to determine what enemy is in his front along the Howlett Line, where Lee believed the X Corps was stationed. He explains to Dick Ewell the chain of command regarding torpedoes, and endorses a recommendation from Gen. Pendleton recommending the disbanding of the 1st Virginia Artillery Regiment.³⁵

July 26, Tuesday (Violet Bank): Lee learns of Early's victory at Kernstown on the 24th and informs the War Department of the success.³⁶

July 27, Wednesday (Violet Bank): Lee focuses on the enemy force at Deep Bottom; in response to a request from Kershaw for reinforcements, Lee sends Heth's Division across the James and orders Anderson to take command and drive the Federals across the James and destroy their pontoon bridges. He also congratulates Early for his victory at Kernstown.³⁷

---

32 *OR* 38, pt. 5, 903; *OR* 37, pt. 2, 599. Lee told President Davis that he doubted Early's operations in the Valley or any sort of actions along the James River would force Grant to abandon the Petersburg front: "I have no idea that Grant will evacuate his position unless forced. It is one from which he can attack us at three points . . . and our success will depend upon our early information and celerity of movement, as we have not troops to guard all points." *OR* 37, pt. 2, 599.

33 Tower, *Lee's Adjutant*, 176; George W. Venable to mother, July 24, 1864, G. W. Venable papers, VHS; REL to Kershaw, July 24, 1864, telegram book, REL HQ papers, VHS; *OR* 40, pt. 3, 796. Lee wrote, "During the services I constantly heard the shells crashing among the houses of Petersburg." Jones, *Life and Letters of REL*, 318. Another churchgoer recalled of the scene at Violet Bank: "It is a beautiful place over the river and overlooking the town. . . . Lee and Beauregard sat together and groups of officers and soldiers reclined in the group around the speaker—the ladies occupying the inner enclave. It was a peaceful and picturesque scene while the voice of song went up and mingled with booming of the distant guns." G. W. Venable to mother, July 24, 1864, G. W. Venable papers, VHS.

34 Dowdey, *Wartime Papers*, 825-6; REL to Mrs. REL, July 24, 1864, Lee papers, VHS; Jones, *Life and Letters of REL*, 318; Tower, *Lee's Adjutant*, 177. Some confusion exists regarding the letters to Mary on this date: Rev. Jones and Rob both printed the letter detailing the morning's church service, but Rob incorrectly dated it June 24. Lee, *Recollections and Letters of REL*, 132-3. Another letter exists at VHS that may carry an incorrect date: REL to Mrs. REL, July 24, 1864, Lee papers, VHS. The church service letter writes of the many gifts the people sent him, from clothing to food: "They have given me everything—which I fear they cannot spare—vegetables, bread, milk, ice cream. Today one of them sent me a nice peach—the first one I think I have seen for two years. I sent it to Mrs. Shippen." Jones, *Life and Letters of REL*, 318. Taylor gave a lengthy account of his nighttime ordeal with his collapsed tent. After that, he wrote, "I was compelled to sleep with one eye shut whilst with the other I watched the movements of my traitorous tent pole." Tower, *Lee's Adjutant*, 177.

35 REL to Pickett, July 25, 1864, telegram book, REL HQ papers, VHS; *OR* 40, pt. 3, 797-800. The 1st VA Art. Reg. only existed as such on paper. In reality, its component batteries operated independently, or as part of other artillery battalions.

36 *OR* 37, pt. 1, 347. Early attacked George Crook's army at Kernstown to keep Federal attention on the Valley.

37 REL to Kershaw, July 27, 1864, telegram book, REL HQ papers, VHS; *OR* 40, pt. 3, 809; REL to R. H. Anderson, July 27, 1864, telegram book, REL HQ papers, VHS; REL to Early, July 27, 1864, telegram book, REL HQ papers, VHS.

July 28, Thursday (Violet Bank): Lee's attention is divided between the operations in the Shenandoah and the Richmond front. He is unclear as to who is in command north of the James, and asks Ewell, "are you directing operations" in front of the capital? He informs him and Richard Anderson that more cavalry will be sent north of the James, and he urges an attack upon the Federal flank on Charles City Road. He also meets with Gen. Pendleton regarding the artillery north of the James. Lee intervenes in a dispute between Gens. Beauregard and Bragg concerning troops being retained at Petersburg despite orders from the War Department to send them elsewhere; Lee informs the adjutant general that he is satisfied with Beauregard's explanation, and that he hopes the issue has been resolved.[38]

Lee informs the War Department that Early occupies Martinsburg and the Federals retreated across the Potomac. He informs Early that he approved Robert Ransom's request to be relieved from field command, and asks if John McCausland is an acceptable replacement. He also sends a note to Gen. Thomas Rosser expressing his regret at his wounding and hoping he recovers quickly. Lee also directs John Hunt Morgan not to embark on a proposed raid, that defending the salt and lead works are his primary responsibility; he advises Sec. Seddon that Morgan has been made aware of the exposed condition of southwest Virginia if he departs the area.[39]

July 29, Friday (Violet Bank): Lee's concern over Grant's intentions at Deep Bottom continues to increase and he also begins to fear for Pickett's position on the Howlett Line. Shortly after midnight he informs Anderson of his belief that the force at Varina may be a feint, and that the real blow will come against Pickett, so he should keep his reserves ready to move across the river to Bermuda Hundred. Before dawn he sends Fitz Lee to take charge of all the cavalry north of the James, and tries unsuccessfully to prod both Anderson and Ewell into attacking during the afternoon. Long after nightfall he is still worried that the operations north of the James are a diversion and tells Anderson to keep his men ready to reinforce Pickett.[40]

July 30, Saturday (Violet Bank/Petersburg): Lee learns shortly after 6:00 a.m. from Col. Samuel Paul of Beauregard's staff of the detonation of a mine beneath part of the works held by Gen. Bushrod Johnson's Division. Just as Lee is sitting down to breakfast, Col. Paul arrives with a request from Beauregard to meet him at Johnson's headquarters. The general immediately sends Venable to order Gen. Mahone to seal the breach in the lines and heads by himself for A. P. Hill's headquarters. Lee arrives at Hill's headquarters to find that the corps commander had departed a few minutes earlier to find Mahone; Lee then rides with Hill's aide Col. William Palmer toward Mahone's headquarters. When they reach the high ground south of Petersburg, they see that Mahone's troops are already in motion toward the front and thus part ways, with Palmer continuing on to Mahone, and Lee riding on to Johnson's headquarters at the

---

38 OR 40, pt. 3, 801-3, 813; REL to R. H. Anderson, July 28, 1864, telegram book, REL HQ papers, VHS; Lee, *Memoirs of WNP*, 356. Bragg ordered Beauregard to send the 3rd NC Cavalry south, but Beauregard needed every available soldier he could find and so retained the regiment at Petersburg, which prompted Bragg to escalate matters. OR 40, pt. 3, 801-3. Lee sent a telegram to Postmaster General Reagan but the content was not recorded. REL to Reagan, July 28, 1864, telegram book, REL HQ papers, VHS.

39 OR 37, pt. 1, 347; REL to Early, July 28, 1864, telegram book, REL HQ papers, VHS; REL to Rosser, July 28, 1864, REL papers, UVA; REL to J. H. Morgan, July 28, 1864, telegram book, REL HQ papers, VHS; OR 37, pt. 2, 602. Ransom was Early's cavalry chief but failing health prompted his request and eventually forced his retirement several months later. Jeffry D. Wert, "Robert Ransom, Jr.," *Confederate General*, vol. 5, 81. Early requested Tom Rosser as Ransom's successor, but he was recovering from a wound sustained at Trevilian Station that kept him out of action for several months. REL to Early, July 28, 1864, telegram book, REL HQ papers, VHS; William N. McDonald, *A History of the Laurel Brigade* (Baltimore, MD, 2002), 254.

40 REL to R. H. Anderson, July 29, 1864, EPA papers, UNC; REL to R. H. Anderson, July 29, 1864, telegram book, REL HQ papers, VHS; REL to Ewell, July 29, 1864, telegram book, REL HQ papers, VHS; OR 40, pt. 3, 815. Lee was correct about the Deep Bottom force being a diversion, but it was not to draw attention away from Bermuda Hundred, as Lee suspected, but rather from Burnside's front at Petersburg.

Mingea house near Blandford Cemetery to meet there with Beauregard.⁴¹

When Lee arrives at the Mingea house, Johnson is there but Beauregard is not, having ridden closer to the front to observe what is transpiring. To his dismay, Lee discovers that Johnson knows very little of the situation. Beauregard arrives soon thereafter and the three generals ride to the Gee house several hundred yards west of the Crater to observe Mahone's counterattack; William Pendleton joins their party along the way.⁴²

While the outcome of the fighting is still in doubt, Lee personally orders Capt. James Lamkin of the Nelson Light Artillery to man a pair of abandoned guns beside the Gee house, and he also tells one of Mahone's brigadiers that if they fail to drive the enemy out on their first attempt he will lead them in person on their second. In late morning and early afternoon Lee requests Ewell and Anderson to send any available troops from the Richmond front by rail to Petersburg, and asks what has become of the Federals north of the James.⁴³

---

41 W. Gordon McCabe, "Defense of Petersburg," *SHSP*, vol. 2, 289; Roman, *Military Operations of Beauregard*, vol. 2, 263; Charles Venable to Mahone, April 10, 1872, Mahone papers, Duke; Earl J. Hess, *Into the Crater: The Mine Attack at Petersburg* (Columbia, SC, 2010), 114-5; Chris Calkins, *Auto Tour of Civil War Petersburg, 1861-1865* (Petersburg, VA, 2003), 36. Lee sent orders directly to Mahone, bypassing Hill in the chain of command, due to the urgency of the situation; his intent apparently was to inform Hill of what he had done. Bernard, *War Talks*, 151. Lee did finally meet with Hill, but whether before or after meeting Beauregard at Johnson's HQ is not clear. Ibid., Hassler, *A. P. Hill*, 221; Venable to Mahone, April 10, 1872, Mahone papers, Duke. The Mingea house was located at the southeast corner of Mingea St. and Crater Road (the wartime Jerusalem Plank Rd) opposite Blandford Church; the house was destroyed prior to 1890. Calkins, *CW Petersburg*, 36. The time of Lee's arrival at the Mingea house varies greatly; Johnson's biographer puts the hour at approximately 8:30 a.m., while the definitive study of the Crater puts it significantly earlier around 7:00 a.m. Charles M. Cummings, *Yankee Quaker, Confederate General: The Curious Career of Bushrod Rust Johnson* (Rutherford, NJ, 1971), 298; Hess, *Into the Crater*, 114-5. Taylor remained at Violet Bank and Venable was sent to Mahone as noted and later accompanied Lee to the scene of battle; nothing is known regarding Marshall's whereabouts during this fight. WHT to Mahone, June 3, 1872, Mahone papers, Duke.

42 Bernard, *War Talks*, 178n; Roman, *Military Operations of Beauregard*, vol. 2, 263-4; Bearss, *Petersburg Campaign*, vol. 1, 223; Hess, *Into the Crater*, 114-5; Cummings, *Yankee Quaker, Confederate General*, 298; Lee, *Memoirs of WNP*, 357. Although the mine explosion and subsequent attack was on his front, Bushrod Johnson apparently displayed but little concern, and at the very least his behavior on this date was strange. One officer who was present at Johnson's headquarters from the time of the explosion until Lee's arrival noted that Johnson never left to investigate for himself, despite the breakthrough being only several hundred yards from the Mingea house. Bernard, *War Talks*, 178n. Mahone briefly came to Johnson's HQ before Lee arrived and found Johnson more interested in breakfast than the rapidly developing crisis at the Crater; Mahone also intimated that because of Johnson's lackadaisical attitude, Beauregard put Mahone in charge on that front. Bernard, *War Talks*, 213. Former Governor Henry Wise, the source of much grief for Lee in western Virginia, commanded one of Johnson's brigades, which was positioned immediately to the right of the Crater; Wise's son, John, was extremely critical of Johnson's actions at this battle, noting that "Johnson knew no details of the disaster, or of the dispositions made to repair it. . . . If the enemy had pressed forward at any time within two hours after the explosion, they would in all probability have found General Bushrod Johnson in bed. When General Lee arrived . . . he found [Johnson] actually ignorant of the peril." In another diatribe, the younger Wise wrote of the conversation between Lee and Johnson: "The information obtained from [Johnson] was valueless; he knew nothing of the extent of the disaster, and had not even been to the front. He probably learned more from General Lee than he knew himself." Wise, *End of an Era*, 359, 361. There is debate as to whether or not Johnson accompanied Lee and Beauregard to the Gee house; Venable was present with Lee in the house and made no mention of Johnson being there, but he did not mention Pendleton, either who *was* present. Venable to Mahone, April 10, 1872, Mahone papers, Duke. The Gee house was located near the intersection of the Jerusalem Plank Road and Baxter Road, roughly opposite the modern intersection of the NPS tour road with Crater Road. Calkins, *CW Petersburg*, 37. Capt. Gordon McCabe was also in the Gee house during the fighting and recalled "the whole place was riddled with bullets and [was] being further riddled while we were there." Bernard, *War Talks*, 178n.

43 Hampton Newsome, John Horn, and John G. Selby, eds., *Civil War Talks: Further Reminiscences of George S. Bernard and his Fellow Veterans* (Charlottesville, VA, 2012), 355; Freeman, *Lee*, vol. 3, 475; REL to Ewell, July 30, 1864, EPA papers, UNC; REL to Ewell, July 30, 1864 (2 messages), telegram book, REL HQ papers, VHS; REL to R. H. Anderson, July 30, 1864, telegram book, REL HQ papers, VHS; REL to Fitz Lee, July 30, 1864, telegram book, REL HQ papers, VHS. At the Gee house during the fighting, Capt. McCabe remembered that Lee was "very severe during the morning upon certain officers high in rank;" while McCabe did not mention any names, he was likely referring to Bushrod Johnson. McCabe to Mahone, July 17, 1872, Mahone papers, Duke.

By mid-afternoon the fighting is largely over and at 3:30 Lee notifies Richmond of the mine explosion and the temporary loss of a portion of the lines. By early evening he has preliminary casualty figures for the battle, which he sends to the War Department noting that Mahone captured 12 flags and about 1,000 prisoners including one of Burnside's brigadiers. After the battle he forwards to Seddon a letter from H. D. Whitcomb, the Virginia Central superintendent, regarding the defense of that railroad; Lee notes that he can spare nothing from his army, but local reserve troops are stationed at the North and South Anna bridges with cavalry nearby.[44]

July 31, Sunday (Violet Bank/Petersburg): Gen. Pendleton conducts morning church service at Violet Bank, attended by Lee and A. P. Hill; a small dog joins the gathering and befriends both generals. Meade requests a truce to bury the dead at the Crater, which Lee refers to Beauregard; the truce will go into effect at sunrise tomorrow.[45]

Learning that the immediate threat north of the James is past, Lee orders the return of both cavalry divisions to Petersburg. He writes a long letter to his wife at Bremo in Fluvanna County, telling her of the battle yesterday, noting Mahone "charged into them handsomely." He is glad she has found a place to stay outside of Richmond, but chides her for ignoring her doctor's orders and getting out of bed, which caused her to fall and injure herself rather severely.[46]

---

[44] *OR* 40, pt. 1, 752-3; *OR* 40, pt. 2, 697-8. Mahone claimed after the war that Lee sent him a congratulatory letter for his role at the Crater either immediately following the battle or the next day, but that it was lost when Mahone's HQ wagon was captured on the retreat to Appomattox. He twice wrote to Charles Venable after the war asking if a copy of it was retained at ANV HQ. Mahone to Venable, May 27, 1872, C. S. Venable papers, UNC; Mahone to Venable, August 7, 1876, C. S. Venable papers, VHS.

[45] Lee, *Memoirs of WNP*, 359; Robertson, *A. P. Hill*, 294-5; Tower, *Lee's Adjutant*, 178; Taylor, *General Lee*, 258; *OR* 40, pt. 3, 821. Pendleton requested permission from Mrs. Shiplett to hold a service on her lawn, and she in turn requested permission from Lee, who informed Pendleton that he did not need to ask permission and was always welcome to preach at HQ. WHT to WNP, July 31, 1864, WNP papers, UNC. Pendleton was apparently not as lively a congregation leader as Rev. Platt, as soldier-turned-poet Sidney Lanier recalled Lee falling asleep during one of Pendleton's sermons at headquarters; unfortunately, Lanier did not record the date. Horn, *REL Reader*, 394.

[46] *OR* 40, pt. 3, 821; REL to R. H. Anderson, July 31, 1864, EPA papers, UNC; REL to Fitz Lee, July 31, 1864, telegram book, REL HQ papers, VHS; Dowdey, *Wartime Papers*, 827-8. Mary and the girls were staying with the Cocke family at the Bremo estate on the upper James. Bremo consisted of three houses (Upper Bremo, Lower Bremo, and Bremo Recess), the oldest of which was possibly designed by Thomas Jefferson. Fiske Kimball, "The Building of Bremo," *VMHB* (Jan. 1949), 3-13. The Lees stayed at Upper Bremo, arriving there sometime in mid to late July. Mary wrote of her injury: "A few days after my arrival I had a severe fall from my crutches slipping on the polished floor.... My pains have returned and the prospect of walking seems as far off as ever." Perry, *Mrs. REL*, 277.

August 1864

The war in Virginia expanded to two major fronts in late summer as operations around Petersburg and Richmond settled into a quasi-siege, and both sides sent additional forces to the Shenandoah Valley. When Gen. Lee realized Jubal Early's presence in the lower (northern) Shenandoah deeply concerned President Abraham Lincoln and U. S. Gen. Grant, he dispatched Gen. Richard Anderson with Joe Kershaw's infantry division and Fitz Lee's cavalry to cooperate with Early. Grant countered by sending Gen. Phil Sheridan (with most of his cavalry) to take command in the Valley.[1] These transfers reduced the strength of the Union lines around Petersburg, but Lee was still unable to find the opportunity he desired to strike a meaningful blow.

Lee made several trips to the Howlett Line to investigate for himself several credible reports that Union forces were digging a canal to bypass Confederate defenses on the James River. Once he was convinced these reports were true, Lee tried several times to spur Richard Ewell into action to disrupt or stop it.[2]

Using his numerical superiority to his advantage, Grant repeated his strategy of sending a force north of the James to threaten Richmond in an effort to deflect attention from an offensive south of Petersburg. This time, Lee himself traveled north of the James, leaving Petersburg to P. G. T. Beauregard. Lee witnessed but took little active role in the fighting at Fussell's Mill and Deep Bottom, while Beauregard and A. P. Hill dealt with Grant's main attempt to sever the Weldon Railroad at Globe Tavern.

Lee returned to Petersburg in time to witness the last failed effort to dislodge the Federals from the vital railroad. Its loss severed his direct connection to Wilmington, North Carolina. It was a costly defeat, but he had anticipated the eventual breach of the line and had cautioned the War Department to prepare for it. Supplies still arrived from Wilmington, but they had to travel a roundabout way that involved transferring them to army wagons for part of the journey. They had no choice but to place even greater reliance on the existing lines feeding the capital. Lee was now convinced that Grant would not risk another major frontal assault against Petersburg's heavy works. Instead, he would creep his way west, stretching the Southern lines to the breaking point while cutting vital roads and rail lines until the Confederates could no longer feed or equip themselves.

* * *

---

1 A rumor spread through Early's ranks that Lee would turn over command at Petersburg to Beauregard and take charge in the Valley himself. Wyckoff, *CW Letters of Alexander McNeill*, 451.

2 The Dutch Gap Canal became one of Ben Butler's biggest follies. The Dutch Gap peninsula was less than two football fields in width. When the final berm was detonated to open the canal, however, the remaining soil filled the trench to such a depth as to render it impassible for most vessels. The canal was not completed and opened to water traffic until 1871. O'Dell, *Chesterfield County*, 385.

August 1, Monday (Violet Bank): Lee notifies Jubal Early that the Union VI Corps and XIX Corps remain around Washington and have not been sent to Petersburg, thus he should continue to operate in the Shenandoah: "I think you can do good service in the Valley." The general urges Richard Anderson to attack on the Richmond front when practicable, and requests that Gen. Pendleton complete his report of the Overland Campaign. He writes to Secretary of War Seddon concerning deserters and informing him of the truce during the morning to bury the dead from the Crater fight; he adds that the number of flags captured was incorrect—it was 20 rather than 12.[3]

August 2, Tuesday (Violet Bank): Lee recommends to the War Department that John Hunt Morgan embark on a raid into Pennsylvania rather than into Tennessee and Georgia against Sherman, as going north would keep southwest Virginia protected while going south would leave it open to invasion. Lee issues orders regarding discharge from service due to age, and approves a request from the mayor of Petersburg that rations be made available for sale to the citizens of Petersburg.[4]

August 3, Wednesday (Violet Bank): Lee notifies Richmond authorities that scouts report nearly 50 loaded transports in the James River, and that he fears they are destined for the Valley. He recommends the promotion of Col. A. C. Godwin of the 57th North Carolina for command of Robert Hoke's brigade, and requests a meeting with President Davis.[5]

August 4, Thursday (Violet Bank): Gen. Lee writes to President Davis regarding the strategic picture at Petersburg and in the Shenandoah Valley: If the Union troops afloat on the James River are indeed bound for the Shenandoah Valley, explains the general, he will be forced to send Gens. Joe Kershaw and Charles Field "and that would not leave me a man out of the trenches for any emergency which might arise. . . . I think it better to detach these troops, than to hazard his [Early's] destruction and that of our railroads, etc., north of Richmond."[6]

August 5, Friday (Violet Bank/Richmond): Lee meets with his nephew, Fitz Lee, regarding the possibility of sending him and his cavalry division to operate in the Shenandoah, and informs Wade Hampton that he will have to cover the same territory around Richmond and Petersburg with only two mounted divisions. Lee inquires as to what artillery is operating in the Valley, and orders Gen. Anderson to come to Richmond to meet with him and President Davis. Lee travels to the capital by train in the afternoon and encounters Agnes's friend Mary Triplett while he is on his way to meet with President Davis.[7]

August 6, Saturday (Richmond): Lee and Anderson (and possibly Fitz Lee) meet with President Davis regarding operations in the Valley and in north-central Virginia. Walter Taylor informs Lee via telegraph that at least one enemy cavalry division left Petersburg for the Shenandoah, and an enemy force was reported at Beverly's Ford late the previous day. Lee misses the evening train to Petersburg, so he visits with his daughter Mary, son Custis, and

---

3 REL to Early, Aug. 1, 1864, telegram book, REL HQ papers, VHS; REL to R. H. Anderson, Aug. 1, 1864, telegram book, REL HQ papers, VHS; Charles Marshall to WNP, Aug. 1, 1864, WNP papers, UNC; *OR* 42, pt. 2, 1167; *OR* 40, pt. 1, 753. Walter Taylor took advantage of the brief truce to explore the Crater area and the surrounding fields on either side where heavy fighting took place, noting, "our troops will become used to this mode of warfare as they have to all others." Tower, *Lee's Adjutant*, 179.

4 *OR* 37, pt. 2, 604; *OR* 42, pt. 2, 1157; Freeman, *Calendar of Confederate Papers*, 435-6.

5 REL to Davis, Aug. 3, 1864 (2 messages), telegram book, REL HQ papers, VHS; *OR* 42, pt. 2, 1160.

6 *OR* 42, pt. 2, 1161-2.

7 REL to Fitz, Aug. 5, 1864 (2 messages), telegram book, REL HQ papers, VHS; REL to Hampton, Aug. 5, 1864, telegram book, REL HQ papers, VHS; REL to E. C. Lee, Aug. 5, 1864, telegram book, REL HQ papers, VHS; WHT to R. H. Anderson, Aug. 5, 1864, telegram book, REL HQ papers, VHS; Dowdey, *Wartime Papers*, 829; REL to Agnes, Aug. 12, 1864, Lee family papers, VHS. Fitz may not have met with Lee until the 6th. *OR Supplement*, vol. 7, 596.

brother Smith. Together, he and Smith call on one of Agnes's friends during the evening, but discover that she is not home.[8]

August 7, Sunday (Richmond/Violet Bank): Gen. Lee departs Richmond early in the morning, before anyone else in the house is awake, to return to Petersburg. He informs Jubal Early that U. S. Grant has sent additional troops to oppose him in the Valley, but that Richard Anderson is en route to Culpeper in north-central Virginia with infantry and cavalry. The general writes to wife Mary telling her of his trip to Richmond and shares the latest family news.[9]

August 8, Monday (Violet Bank): Lee instructs Hampton to gather intelligence about the enemy forces sent from Petersburg to oppose Early.[10]

August 9, Tuesday (Violet Bank): Lee learns of an enemy presence at Dutch Gap, and orders Pickett to turn his guns on the Howlett Line on them. He meets with Thomas W. Richards whom Mosby recommends to organize a partisan command in the Northern Neck; Lee drafts a letter to Seddon requesting Richards be commissioned and assigned to that duty and has Richards deliver the message to Richmond in person. Lee complains to President Davis that the army has no soap and despite his requests, Commissary General Lucius Northrop will not procure any. Lee also informs Davis that he will send the senior brigadier from Fitz Lee's division to replace Robert Ransom as Early's cavalry chief. He notifies John Pemberton that he has no artillery to spare for the Richmond defenses.[11]

August 10, Wednesday (Violet Bank): Gen. Lee meets with Wade Hampton and directs him to move his cavalry division north of the James River. Lee asks Dick Ewell if he can attack Dutch Gap while Gen. Pickett and the James River fleet shell it. Still troubled by the growing issue of desertion, the general issues orders calling for all deserters and others legally absent to return to the ranks. Lee informs President Davis that Jubal Early prefers to have John Pegram command his cavalry rather than Lunsford Lomax, who is the senior brigadier, and that whichever officer Davis prefers, should be made a major general so there is no issue regarding rank. Lee also requests that two recently exchanged generals, James J. Archer and George H. Steuart be assigned to serve with his army.[12]

---

8 OR 42, pt. 1, 873; *OR Supplement*, vol. 7, 596; WHT to REL, Aug. 6, 1864 (2 messages), telegraph book, REL HQ papers, VHS; Dowdey, *Wartime Papers*, 829; REL to Agnes, Aug. 12, 1864, Lee family papers, VHS. Sec. Seddon and/or Gen. Bragg also may have been in the meetings; it is not known whether Fitz was included or if he met with Lee separately. *OR Supplement*, vol. 7, 596. Anderson, with Kershaw's Division and Fitz's cavalry, was sent to Culpeper to further threaten Washington. The name of the lady Lee and Smith tried to visit is illegible.

9 Dowdey, *Wartime Papers*, 829-30; REL to Early, Aug. 7, 1864, telegram book, REL HQ papers, VHS. This telegram to Early appears in the *OR* dated Aug. 8, which may be the date it was marked as received. *OR* 43, pt. 1, 990.

10 *OR* 42, pt. 2, 1165.

11 *OR* 42, pt. 2, 1168; *OR* 43 pt. 1, 990-1; Dowdey, *Wartime Papers*, 830-1. It is uncertain when Lee learned of the canal. His first known reference to it is on the 12th, but he likely knew of it at least by the 11th and perhaps sooner. The canal was finished after the war and became the main channel of the James River. Richards, the brother of Mosby favorite Adolphus "Dolly" Richards, served in the 8th VA and 7th VA Cav. prior to joining Mosby. He was unsuccessful on the Northern Neck and returned to Mosby. Hugh C. Keen and Horace Mewborn, *43rd Battalion Virginia Cavalry: Mosby's Command* (Lynchburg, VA, 1993), 361. Following his service at Charleston, where he succeeded Lee in 1862, Pemberton was promoted to lieutenant general and commanded the army at Vicksburg, MS, that surrendered to Grant in July 1863. The public outcry against him was so strong that after his exchange it was politically impossible to give him another major field command. He resigned, was re-commissioned a lieutenant colonel, and placed in command of the artillery in the Richmond defenses. Lawrence L. Hewitt, "John Clifford Pemberton," *Confederate General*, vol. 5, 9.

12 *OR* 51, pt. 2, 1034; *OR* 42, pt. 2, 1169; REL to Davis, Aug. 10, 1864, telegram book, REL HQ papers, VHS; REL to Seddon, Aug. 10, 1864, telegram book, REL HQ papers, VHS. Gen. James Archer was taken prisoner on the first day at Gettysburg—the first general from the Army of Northern Virginia captured during battle. Archer's health suffered during his imprisonment. He died on October 24, 1864; Gen. George H. Steuart was captured in the Mule Shoe at Spotsylvania on May 12, 1864. Warner, *Generals in Gray*, 11, 291.

August 11, Thursday (Violet Bank/Howlett Line): In the morning Lee rides to the Howlett Line and inspects a portion of it with Gen. Pickett and also observes the enemy activity at Dutch Gap. He attempts again unsuccessfully to get Ewell to attack in conjunction with the James River fleet. Lee learns that Gen. Grant went in person to Harpers Ferry and that Phillip Sheridan is the new commander in the Valley, and informs Richmond of the Federal changes in the Valley. He urges Anderson to advance into northern Virginia to threaten Washington and Sheridan's rear: "It is desirable that the presence of our troops be felt beyond the Rappahannock." He officially names Wade Hampton as commander of the ANV's cavalry and sends him to Culpeper to work with Anderson.[13]

Problems continue to plague Early's cavalry and Lee orders Bradley Johnson relieved of his command because of a dismal performance in the mountains of West Virginia; Lee orders Lunsford Lomax to be the new cavalry chief in the Valley and also suggests that Thomas Munford serve as Johnson's replacement. Lee alerts Early to Sheridan taking command of the forces opposing him, and updates Seddon on the situation in the Valley. He receives a letter from his brother Carter.[14]

August 12, Friday (Violet Bank): Lee informs Ewell that a Yankee deserter reports the Federals intend to dig a canal at Dutch Gap; he instructs that if it cannot be stopped then it must be rendered useless by the establishment of new batteries commanding its approaches. Lee informs President Davis of troop dispositions around Virginia and that he named Hampton cavalry commander; he mentions the Dutch Gap canal but does not know its purpose—whether to flank the Howlett Line or lower the water level in the James to disrupt the ironclads. He instructs Early and Anderson to cooperate against Sheridan who is reported to be around Front Royal. He congratulates North Carolina Gov. Vance on his reelection, and writes to Agnes and his brother Carter, telling the latter: "Do not be uneasy about the location of my camp.... The shells do sometime burst over us, but not often, and they have as yet done us no harm. Besides where can we go to get rid of them? They pervade all space for miles, and I cannot be too far away."[15]

August 13, Saturday (Violet Bank/Petersburg/Howlett Line): Lee goes to Mahone's headquarters at the Wilcox farm to receive the flags captured at Battle of the Crater, which he sends on to Richmond by Mahone's adjutant, Lt. B. H. Nash. Lee also rides to the Howlett Line to observe the progress on the Dutch Gap canal and to oversee the bombardment of it from the Howlett battery. The general writes to President Davis regarding a successor to the command of Wade Hampton's cavalry division and complains about the lack of discipline and laxness of officers in some commands. He also mentions that he witnessed the bombardment of Dutch Gap, but notes, "I saw nothing approaching a canal."[16]

---

13 Wise, *17th Virginia*, 194; OR 42, pt. 2, 1170-2. The regimental history of the 17th VA, one of George Pickett's units on the Howlett Line, records Gen. Lee's visit as having occurred on the August 10, but Lee himself wrote on the 12th that it took place on "Thursday morning," or August 11. Wise, *17th Virginia*, 194; OR 42, pt. 2, 1172. According to Pickett, during what must have been an uncomfortable ride, Lee "did not seem in a remarkably good humor." Moyle, *Heart of a Soldier*, 153. Lee's vantage point for his observation of Dutch Gap was from the Howlett farm, which is now the site of the Chesterfield Power Plant.

14 OR 43, pt. 1, 551, 996; REL to R. H. Anderson, Aug. 11, 1864, telegram book, REL HQ papers, VHS; REL to Early, Aug. 11, 1864, telegram book, REL HQ papers, VHS; REL to Charles Carter Lee, Aug. 12, 1864, REL papers, W&L. Johnson's and John McCausland's brigades were routed near Moorefield on the 7th on their return from burning Chambersburg; Johnson was vindicated and remained with Early until that fall. Jeffry D. Wert, "Bradley Tyler Johnson," *Confederate General*, vol. 3, 178.

15 OR 42, pt. 2, 1172-3; OR 43, pt. 1, 997-8; Carmichael, *Audacity Personified*, 115; REL to Agnes, Aug. 12, 1864, Lee family papers, VHS; REL to C. C. Lee, Aug. 12, 1864, REL papers, W&L.

16 OR 40, pt. 1, 753; OR 42, pt. 2, 170, 1176; Wise, *17th Virginia*, 194; Freeman, *Lee's Dispatches*, 368-70. In addition to Mahone's flags Lee also sent to Richmond several flags captured by some of Bushrod Johnson's men, so he likely retrieved those in person as well. There is no known record of when or how he took possession of them, only that they

August 14, Sunday (Violet Bank): Lee is not able to attend church because of an attack against Field's Division north of the James River. Lee informs Gens. Ewell, Field, and son Custis that while he can send no troops from Petersburg he will recall Hampton's troopers; he thinks the action is likely another feint to distract attention from an attack on Petersburg, but directs Ewell to gather all available troops and drive back the Federals.[17]

During the afternoon he alerts George Pickett that the enemy force must have come from Bermuda Hundred because it did not come from the Petersburg front, so he should reinforce Field if he can do so. Lee urges Gen. Ewell to use this opportunity to interrupt the canal work at Dutch Gap if possible, and writes to Seddon about the increasing number of desertions from the army. Lee and Taylor get into an argument, prompting Taylor to complain to his fiancé, "he is so unreasonable and provoking at times."

Lee writes to wife Mary in the evening mentioning that enemy activity prevented him from attending church, and mentions the supposed canal under construction at Dutch Gap. He despairs to Mary over a letter from Rev. John Cole of St. Stephen's Episcopal Church in Culpeper about the destruction that the enemy inflicted to the houses of worship in that region during the winter, with many of them being destroyed and the contents and building materials used elsewhere. Steady rain.[18]

August 15, Monday (Violet Bank/Chaffin's Farm/New Market Heights): Gen. Lee departs Violet Bank "at an early hour" for north of the James River. Before leaving he gives Taylor a peach—the young officer's favorite fruit—to atone for their argument the previous day. As Lee rides the lines along New Market Road he dismounts to reconnoiter and encounters Col. Asbury Coward of the 5th South Carolina who advises him not expose himself to enemy fire; Lee tells him "I think two men would be a better target than one. . . . I must see the whole field," and sends the colonel to cover nearby while he continues to examine the field. He sets up camp for the night at Chaffin's farm.[19]

The general forwards to Richmond a pair of proposals from Wade Hampton. One is for the creation of a cavalry bureau, which Lee recommends Dick Ewell to head, and the second is to establish a cavalry inspector general. Walter Taylor informs Lee that conflicting reports have reached headquarters regarding the location of Winfield Hancock's II Corps—does Lee have any definitive information? Son Rob is wounded in the arm in the cavalry

---

were forwarded to Richmond on this date. *OR* 40, pt. 1, 753. The author of the 17th VA regimental history remembered Lee's return visit to the Howlett Line, but again his date was one day earlier. Wise, *17th Virginia*, 194. Benjamin H. Nash was a former member of the Virginia Senate and served in the 41st VA prior to becoming adjutant of Mahone's Brigade. Krick, *Staff Officers in Gray*, 229. Matthew C. Butler was Hampton's choice to take over his division, and Lee concurred. Butler would be promoted to major general in September. Warner, *Generals in Gray*, 41.

17 Dowdey, *Wartime Papers*, 836; *OR* 42, pt. 2, 1176-7; *OR* 51, pt. 2, 1035; REL to Custis, Aug. 14, 1864, telegram book, REL HQ papers, VHS; REL to Field, Aug. 14, 1864 (2 messages), telegram book, REL HQ papers, VHS; REL to Ewell, Aug. 14, 1864, telegram book, REL HQ papers, VHS. Although Lee directed Gen. Ewell to take charge, Gen. Field remained in command and received no direction or assistance from Ewell: "Though Gen. Ewell commanded the Department of Richmond . . . in fact I commanded," wrote Field after the war, "and made disposition to suit myself, without consultations with him, and received no orders from him." REL to Ewell, Aug. 14, 1864, telegram book, REL HQ papers, VHS; Charles W. Field, "Campaign of 1864 and 1865," *SHSP*, vol. 14, 550.

18 REL to Pickett, Aug. 14, 1864, telegram book, REL HQ papers, VHS; *OR* 42, pt. 2, 1175-6; Tower, *Lee's Adjutant*, 182; Dowdey, *Wartime Papers* 836-7. The circumstances of the argument with Taylor are not known. Regarding the desecration of Culpeper's churches, Lee wrote "We must suffer patiently to the end, when all things will be made right." Dowdey, *Wartime Papers*, 837.

19 Tower, *Lee's Adjutant*, 181-2; John Horn, *The Siege of Petersburg: The Battles for the Weldon Railroad, August 1864* (El Dorado Hills, CA, 2015), 57-58; Taylor, *General Lee*, 261. Lee took Venable and Marshall with him, leaving Taylor behind to run HQ at *Violet Bank*. Tower, *Lee's Adjutant*, 181-2. According to Col. Coward, as Lee turned to leave that portion of the lines, he noticed a young bird had fallen from its nest. He scooped up the baby sparrow and placed it in the fork of a tree. Horn, *The Battles for the Weldon Railroad*, 58. Horn's study is the definitive treatment of the August fighting along the Weldon Railroad. The exact location of Lee's camp at Chaffin's is not known.

skirmishing on the left flank of Charles Field's lines. Rain in the morning.[20]

August 16, Tuesday (Chaffin's Farm/Fussell's Mill): Lee notifies President Davis in mid-morning that Field reports a large enemy force on the Charles City Road; Lee recommends that the Richmond defenses be manned and Hampton's command be sent forward. He then heads for the front near Fussell's Mill on the Darbytown Road, arriving there just as the Federals launch an attack in early afternoon. Lee is in the midst of the fighting, personally sending a South Carolina regiment into the fray, rallying broken troops, and checking on some of the wounded. Even though present on the ground, Lee leaves the direction of the battle to Field.[21]

After the conclusion of the battle Lee informs the secretary of war that the enemy made a "determined attack" on Darbytown and Charles City roads that breached Field's lines briefly, but that they were driven back beyond White Oak Swamp. The general also notifies Seddon of Mosby's latest operations in the lower Valley. During the night, President Davis and Postmaster General John Reagan meet with Lee at Chaffin's farm.[22]

August 17, Wednesday (Chaffin's Farm): The general requests the assistance of the James River fleet in driving away the enemy from Signal Hill.[23]

August 18, Thursday (Chaffin's Farm): Lee moves the ANV headquarters to Chaffin's farm, where he learns from Gen. Beauregard of a large Union force moving against the Weldon line south of Petersburg. During the evening, the general provides the secretary of war with an update of affairs transpiring on both the Richmond and Petersburg fronts.[24]

August 19, Friday (Chaffin's Farm): Lee informs Beauregard in the morning that although the cavalry is in no condition to fight today they can be put in the trenches to free up other troops for offensive operations, but cautions that the force on the Weldon Railroad must be driven away: "I fear if enemy has time to fortify he cannot be dislodged." Determining the threat to Richmond to be over, he returns a portion of the troops to Petersburg and

---

20 OR 42, pt. 2, 1173-5, 1178; Lee, *Recollections and Letters of REL*, 137; Driver, *39th Virginia Cavalry Battalion*, 41. Ewell declined the cavalry position when it was offered to him later in the year. Hamlin, *Making of a Soldier*, 131-2. Son Rob's wound proved not to be too serious, but the injury did keep him out of action for about three weeks. Lee, *Recollections and Letters of REL*, 137.

21 OR 42, pt. 2, 1180; Manarin, *Henrico County: Field of Honor*, vol. 2, 513, 532; Edward B. Williams, ed., *Rebel Brothers: The Civil War Letters of the Truehearts* (College Station, TX, 1995), 106-7, 111-2; Field, "Campaign of 1864," 554. According to the surgeon of the 8th AL, "Gen. Lee rode to & fro on the road . . . to gather information of how the fight was going, from the direction and character of the sounds of strife. Shell and minnies frequently struck or passed very near him, and I was very fearful for his safety. But he seemed quite indifferent to the dangers of the hour. For several hours he remained near where my hospital was." Williams, *Rebel Brothers*, 106. Surgeon Trueheart's letters describing this battle are some of the best contemporary accounts of Lee in battle. When one of Lee's men took a hat from a captured Federal, the prisoner saw Lee nearby and complained; Lee made the soldier return the hat. John E. Davis, "A Federal Soldier's Incident," *SHSP*, vol. 17, 242. Lee, recalled Gen. Field, "was simply a looker-on" and gave no direction during the engagement. Field, "Campaign of 1864," 554.

22 OR 42, pt. 1, 850; OR 43, pt. 1, 633; Reagan, *Memoirs*, 194-5. President Davis and Sec. Reagan went first to Field's HQ near the battlefield, where Field provided one of his staff officers to guide the pair to Lee's HQ several miles away. The officer got lost and almost led the party into enemy lines before nearby Confederate troops saw them riding the wrong way and redirected them. Reagan placed this incident on Aug. 29, but from the context it is clear he is referring to the Fussell's Mill engagement. Reagan, *Memoirs*, 194-5.

23 REL to J. K. Mitchell, Aug. 17, 1864, Gabriella Page papers, VHS. Lee almost certainly went back to Fussell's Mill.

24 OR 42, pt. 2, 1186-7; OR 42, pt. 850-1. Although Lee himself had been at Chaffin's for several days, army HQ officially remained at Violet Bank with Taylor until this date. Gen. Henry Heth incorrectly wrote that Lee was at Petersburg for the latter stages of the Weldon RR fighting at Globe Tavern, which several modern writers have repeated. Morrison, *Heth Memoirs*, 190. Walter Taylor's notification to Gens. Pickett and Wilcox that ANV HQ was moving to Chaffin's farm, in addition to the communications between Beauregard and Lee addressed to Chaffin's Bluff, show that Heth was mistaken in his recollection. OR 42, pt. 2, 1186-7.

authorizes the local reserves to be withdrawn from the defenses. Lee congratulates Wade Hampton for the efforts of his men in the recent operations, and appoints several new brigade commanders in A. P. Hill's and Early's corps. Light rain in the evening.[25]

August 20, Saturday (Chaffin's Farm/Violet Bank): Lee spends much of the day corresponding with Beauregard about what enemy troops remain in front of Richmond and what force can be gathered to attack at Petersburg. Lee concludes that the X Corps and most of the II Corps remain in front of Richmond, so he will not strip the works bare to reinforce Beauregard but instructs "the enemy must be driven from the railroad." He informs Sec. Seddon of Hill's success at Globe Tavern and of Early's most recent victory near Winchester and notifies President Davis of his intent to return to Petersburg tonight. At approximately 8:00 p.m. Lee and the staff depart Chaffin's in the rain and arrive at Violet Bank around 1:00 a.m. on the 21st.[26]

August 21, Sunday (Violet Bank/Globe Tavern): Lee rests for a few hours on the porch at Violet Bank before heading to Globe Tavern, and requests Gen. Field send any troops he can spare to Petersburg. Lee is joined by Beauregard and E. Porter Alexander in observing A. P. Hill's unsuccessful attack along the Weldon Railroad. After one failed attack Lee finds Mahone near the Davis house, and Mahone requests fresh troops to make another assault to which Lee consents but calls off the attack when they do not arrive in time.[27]

In later afternoon Lee informs Gens. Field and Hampton of reports of the enemy re-crossing the James River at Deep Bottom, so they were to move the bulk of their forces to Petersburg. Lee briefs Sec. Seddon on the failure to drive the Federals away from the railroad and their apparent abandonment of Deep Bottom. Shortly before midnight, Lee learns of an enemy cavalry force heading toward Dinwiddie Court House, and the general warns officials of the Richmond & Danville and Southside railroads that Grant may be intending to raid both of those rail lines.[28]

August 22, Monday (Violet Bank): Lee informs the president and secretary of war of the implications of the Federals cutting the Weldon Railroad, but reminds both men that he had cautioned weeks ago that he could not prevent them from doing so. He thinks this signals a change in Grant's strategy: that he will attempt to starve Lee's army rather than risking direct attacks. Lee warns, "It behooves us to do everything in our power to thwart his new plan of reducing us by starvation, and all our energies should be directed to using to its utmost capacity our remaining line of communication with the south." He adds that he will continue to bring supplies along the Weldon as far as Stony Creek and from there into Petersburg via wagon but that the army cannot survive from that alone, and its supply of corn is exhausted as of today. He informs railroad officials that last night's report of a raid against the R&D and/or Southside was a false alarm, there is no danger to either line at present.[29]

August 23, Tuesday (Violet Bank/Petersburg): Lee rides a portion of the lines with A. P. Hill and writes to Sec. Seddon about his army's dwindling numbers. He issues a dire warning that "unless some measures can be devised to replace our losses, the

---

25 REL to Beauregard, Aug. 19, 1864 (2 messages), REL HQ papers, VHS; REL to Ewell, Aug. 19, 1864, telegram book, REL HQ papers, VHS; *OR* 42, pt. 2, 1189-90; Krick, *CW Weather*, 135.

26 REL to Beauregard, Aug. 20, 1864 (5 messages), telegram book, REL HQ papers, VHS; *OR* 42, pt. 1, 552, 851; REL to Davis, Aug. 20, 1864, telegram book, REL HQ papers, VHS; Tower, *Lee's Adjutant*, 184; Hagood, *Memoirs*, 289.

27 Tower, *Lee's Adjutant*, 184; *OR* 42, pt. 2, 1193; Hagood, *Memoirs*, 296; Gallagher, *Fighting for the Confederacy*, 473; Bearss, *Petersburg Campaign*, vol. 1, 315. As at Fussell's Mill several days before, Lee was little more than an observer for the fighting at Globe Tavern, entrusting the handling of the battle to Gens. A. P. Hill, Heth, and Mahone.

28 *OR* 42, pt. 2, 1192-3; Dowdey, *Wartime Papers*, 841; *OR* 42, pt. 1, 851.

29 Dowdey, *Wartime Papers*, 842-3; *OR* 42, pt. 2, 1194-5; REL to C. G. Talcott, Aug. 22, 1864, telegram book, REL HQ papers, VHS; REL to H. D. Bird, Aug. 22, 1864, telegram book, REL HQ papers, VHS.

consequences may be disastrous." He is specifically concerned about the amount of officers and men detailed for conscription service and the lack of results yielded: "Our numbers are daily decreasing, and the time has arrived in my opinion when no man should be excused from service, except for the purpose of doing work absolutely necessary for the support of the army.... Without some increase of our strength, I cannot see how we are to escape the natural military consequences of the enemy's numerical superiority." He also mentions reports that efforts to encourage desertion from the enemy ranks are working and requests that written materials be distributed in German to target the foreign element of Grant's army. Lee writes to Mrs. Mary Tinsley Kindred of Roanoke thanking her for her invitation to have Mary and the girls spend the winter with her.[30]

August 24, Wednesday (Violet Bank/Petersburg): Lee orders Gen. Field to send an additional brigade to Petersburg and for Wade Hampton to report to Hill with his division. Lee and Beauregard ride to the lead works south of town where Hill marshals his forces for an attack tomorrow. Lee advises Sec. Seddon not to interfere with the rumored execution of prisoners at Fort McHenry, pointing out that President Lincoln has not confirmed their sentences.[31]

August 25, Thursday (Violet Bank): Lee instructs Pickett to make a demonstration on his lines to draw attention away from Hill and Hampton at Ream's Station, and informs Seddon that Early pushed the Federals back to Harpers Ferry.[32]

August 26, Friday (Violet Bank): Lee congratulates Early for driving Sheridan to the Potomac, but reminds him that even with Anderson's troops his force is not strong enough to operate north of the river so to focus on the B&O and possibly sending his cavalry on a raid into Pennsylvania. He congratulates Hampton for the victory yesterday, and advises Richmond of the success at Ream's Station.[33]

August 27, Saturday (Violet Bank): Lee forwards to the War Department a letter from the regimental commanders of Seth Barton's former brigade requesting Barton's return to command, and a formal inquiry to disparaging remarks regarding the brigade made by Robert Ransom. Lee comments that he knows "of no ... censure cast upon the men or officers of Barton's brigade," and that George

---

30 OR 42, pt. 2, 451, 1199-200; REL to M. T. Kindred, Aug. 23, 1864, Lee family papers, VHS. Where exactly Lee and Hill rode is not known.

31 OR 42, pt. 2, 474-5, 1201-2; OR 7, Series 2, 674. Lee and Beauregard were seen at the lead works near the intersection of the Vaughn Road and Weldon RR in the afternoon; presumably they were there to confer with A. P. Hill, who was in charge of the strike force. OR 42, pt. 2, 474-5, Bearss, *Petersburg Campaign*, vol. 1, 349. The lead works were located at the Weldon RR crossing of Halifax Street near Dimmock batteries 40 and 41; the modern re-alignment of the railroad destroyed much of the site. Walter Taylor wrote that he and Lee rode somewhere in the morning, but did not record where. Tower, *Lee's Adjutant*, 184-5. According to Gen. Johnson Hagood, on this date Lee seconded Beauregard's recommendation for Hagood's promotion to major general, but this is a significant stretching of the truth. Lee simply forwarded Beauregard's recommendation without comment, which is hardly the ringing endorsement Hagood claimed later. Hagood, *Memoirs*, 297; OR 42, pt. 2, 1196-7. Lee reportedly gave a pair of his gauntlets to Col. William P. Roberts, 2nd NC Cavalry, in recognition of that regiment's performance at Ream's Station on this date, which were delivered by one of Lee's sons. Whether this occurred immediately in the wake of the battle, as Roberts claimed, or later when he was promoted, is unclear. W. P. Roberts, "General Lee's Recognition of Valor," *Wake Forest Student* (Jan. 1905), vol. 26, no. 5, p. 356; Warner, *Generals in Gray*, 259.

32 REL to Pickett, Aug. 25, 1864, telegram book, REL HQ papers, VHS; OR 43, pt. 1, 1006. The directive to Pickett appears in the OR dated the 26th. OR 42, pt. 2, 1202. It is possible Lee was an observer for at least part of the fighting at Ream's Station, but there is no known credible evidence to support this, and it seems likely that someone in the several divisions engaged would have noted his presence.

33 OR 43, pt. 1, 1006; OR 42, pt. 2, 1204-5; OR 42, pt. 1, 851. Sending Richard Anderson away to cooperate with Early created an awkward command situation because Anderson was senior to Early. Lee, however, wanted Early in overall command and explained in this letter to Early that Anderson would operate *under* Early's orders when they were together, or they could continue to operate separately. OR 43, pt. 1, 1006.

Steuart was assigned to its command. The general informs Seddon that the officers requested for a court of inquiry are not available, but suggests several recuperating from wounds who are, adding "officers capable of duty cannot be spared." He receives a letter from Mary, and writes to Custis, jesting at the incorrect newspaper reports of Rooney's mortal wounding several days earlier. Thunderstorm during the night.[34]

August 28, Sunday (Violet Bank/Petersburg): Lee and Taylor attend church service at St. Paul's in the morning. He instructs Martin Gary to determine if the Federals are constructing a bridge over the Chickahominy at Southall's Ferry, and receives a letter from Longstreet. He writes to Mary with the latest family news and of the latest fighting around Petersburg and Richmond.[35]

August 29, Monday (Violet Bank): Lee writes to Anderson clarifying his role in the overall strategic picture in Virginia and to Gov. Vance commending the conduct of the North Carolina troops at Ream's Station. He writes also to Longstreet, glad that he is recovering well and hoping he will rejoin the army soon.[36]

August 30, Tuesday (Violet Bank): Lee forwards to Pendleton a request to have the guns captured at Ream's Station assigned to Pegram's and McIntosh's battalions, and forwards to Beauregard a request from James Archer to have the Tennessee brigade in Johnson's Division consolidated with his own.[37]

August 31, Wednesday (Violet Bank): Lee forwards Ewell a copy of the Union army's signal code and cautions him that the enemy read Confederate signal messages as well.[38]

---

34 *OR* 36, pt. 2, 227-9; REL to, Aug. 27, 1864, telegram book, REL HQ papers, VHS; Dowdey, *Wartime Papers*, 846; Daughtry, *Gray Cavalier*, 210; Krick, *CW Weather*, 136. Gen. Seth Barton, who Pickett had accused months earlier of misconduct in NC, was relieved of his command by Gen. Ransom on similar grounds in May; Col. William Aylett of the 53rd VA commanded the brigade until Gen. Steuart's appointment. Warner, *Generals in Gray*, 18-9; *OR* 36, pt. 2, 227-9. Rooney was suffering from a severe case of poison oak which, spread to his face and swelled his eyes shut. Somehow, this turned into rumors of his mortal wounding in combat, appeared in the Richmond newspapers as such, and reached the desk of U. S. Grant. Daughtry, *Gray Cavalier*, 210.

35 Tower, *Lee's Adjutant*, 186; *OR* 42, pt. 2, 1206; Longstreet, *From Manassas to Appomattox*, 639; Dowdey, *Wartime Papers*, 846-7. Church service may have been conducted at Violet Bank—Taylor's phrasing is unclear. Wherever it was, Taylor was not pleased to find Gen. Pendleton in the pulpit: "I am not so averse to hearing the General as others," he wrote, "but am always sorry to see him officiate." Tower, *Lee's Adjutant*, 186.

36 Walker, *Life of R. H. Anderson*, 186-7; *OR* 42, pt. 2, 1206-7; Longstreet, *From Manassas to Appomattox*, 639-40.

37 *OR* 42, pt. 2, 1205-6, 1284. Both Gens. Heth and Hill were in favor of Archer's request, but the officers and men of Bushrod Johnson's brigade were vehemently opposed to it. *OR* 42, pt. 2, 1284. A telegram was sent to George Steuart on this date, but its content was not recorded. REL to Steuart, Aug. 30, 1864, telegram book, REL HQ papers, VHS.

38 *OR* 42, pt. 2, 1210.

September 1864

Confederate reverses in Virginia and in the Western Theater dominated the headlines during September. When the last railroad into Atlanta was cut, John Bell Hood abandoned Atlanta on September 1, destroying valuable supplies and railroad equipment as he attempted to save his Army of Tennessee. Closer to home, Jubal Early suffered two crushing defeats in the Shenandoah Valley only days apart, first at Winchester (in the Third Battle of Winchester) and then at Fisher's Hill, losing thousands of men in killed, wounded, and captured, dozens of guns, and arguably his best division commander in Robert Rodes.

The lines around Petersburg remained relatively quiet, allowing Gen. Lee to spend time on the lines when he wasn't in Richmond. "General Lee visited my line more frequently than he did others," recalled Gen. Henry Heth. "There was hardly a week that he did not come to my headquarters [Pickeral House]. He would stop and have a chat with Mrs. Heth and play with my little daughter.... When leaving he would request me to accompany him to the lines."[1] Lee's appearances on the Petersburg lines became more frequent after P. G. T. Beauregard was reassigned to Charleston, South Carolina, late in the month.

Lee's struggle to keep men in the ranks continued. His proposals to the War Department placed an increasing reliance on the use of slaves and free blacks in support roles, while seeking to curtail the number of officers and men detailed away from the front and reduce the number of men exempted from military service.

The troopers of the 39th Virginia Cavalry Battalion—the men comprising Lee's headquarters guard—were involved in a rather prevalent rumor that they were about to be sent to join Wade Hampton's cavalry corps. "There has been some talk of this company being transferred to regular cavalry," complained Pvt. George Coiner of the 39th. "In fact," he continued,

> the company officers have been at head quarters to have it put into regular service. I hope however they may not succeed, and if the officers want to leave the command all they have to do is resign their commissions and go. But the idea is this—they (the officers of the company) are getting a little tired of this service, like all upstart officers are never satisfied nowhere, and they don't want to leave their commissions by going anywhere else so if they can get the company away they will still hold their commissions. From what I can understand, Col. Marshall of Gen. Lee's staff has said that the company would not be put into regular service unless the men were all willing to go. There are a few who are anxious to get transfers to the regular service but not by any means a majority of the company. If they should get Gen. Lee to put us in regular service there ain't two men who would be willing to stay in the present company not under Capt. [Samuel B.] Brown nohow, for he has not got sense enough to command the company here where it is.[2]

---

1 Morrison, *Heth Memoirs*, 194.

2 George M. Coiner to Kate Coiner, Sept. 14, 1864, Coiner family papers, VHS. Capt. Brown previously served as an officer in the 52nd VA but a wound at Port Republic in June 1862 ended his infantry career. He was elected captain of Company C of the 39th VA Cav. Battalion only two weeks after resigning his commission in the 52nd. He commanded the 39th when it surrendered at Appomattox. Driver, *39th Virginia Cavalry Battalion*, 132. Coiner also served in the 52nd and was wounded in the arm at McDowell in May 1862 and medically discharged in December 1862; he enlisted in the 39th VA Cav. Battalion in January 1864. Ibid., 144.

Sgt. Franklin Walter of the 39th, while complaining about the increased workload, was definitely not one of those in favor of transferring to a combat unit:

> Our battalion is doing more duty now than it has ever done before. Having more places to guard as well as doing an extra amount of courier duty. When we are not on duty as couriers we are put on guard about every other day. Although some of us sometimes complain of the amount of duty we have to do, yet we can all congratulate ourselves that we are in a much easier place than in regular cavalry besides being less exposed to the bullets of the enemy.... We now remain on courier duty for seven days at a time. Each one of us doing 5 hours guard duty at Gen. Lee's tent during the week.[3]

Lee, the staff, and most of the Army of Northern Virginia's bureau chiefs found time to make their way to J. E. Rockwell's photography studio in Petersburg to be photographed for a composite image of Lee and the headquarters staff. William Pendleton was the last to sit before the camera.[4]

Gen. Richard Anderson was recalled to Petersburg to resume command. He left Kershaw's Division and Fitz Lee's cavalry behind in the Shenandoah. Anderson had barely arrived back to Petersburg when U. S. Grant launched an offensive north of the James River. Lee sent Anderson to work with Gen. Ewell to stop the breakthrough around Chaffin's farm. As the magnitude of the Union offensive became clearer, Lee rode across the river to command operations himself. Although Ewell and Anderson prevented the Federals from seizing the pontoon bridges at Drewry's and Chaffin's, they could not retake Fort Harrison, which necessitated manning a new defensive line closer to Richmond.

* * *

---

3 F. G. Walter diary, Sept. 7, 1864, LVA. Walter was a Marylander and was one of many in the 39th VA Cav. Battalion who did not surrender at Appomattox. Driver, *39th Virginia Cavalry Battalion*, 156.

4 D. B. Bridgeford to WNP, Sept. 23, 1864, WNP papers, UNC. Rockwell's studio was on Sycamore Street; it is not known when Lee or the others were photographed. The image Rockwell wanted to produce is almost certainly the "Military Medallion" of Lee and his officers produced by Rockwell & Cowell in 1865. Donald A. Hopkins, *Robert E. Lee in War and Peace: The Photographic History of a Confederate and American Icon* (El Dorado Hills, CA 2013), is the definitive book on Lee photographs.

September 1, Thursday (Violet Bank): Lee submits a requisition for fodder for two horses for the month of September.[5]

September 2, Friday (Violet Bank): Lee sends to President Davis a lengthy analysis of the Virginia army's manpower problem and Gen. U. S. Grant's overwhelming numbers. He cites as an example Grant's ability to strike heavily on both sides of the James River, forcing Lee to strip one side or the other to meet the threat. He proposes three options for increasing the number of men in the ranks:

(1) Use only blacks as teamsters, cooks, laborers, etc. to free up the soldiers currently detailed to those positions: "It seems to me that we must choose between employing negroes ourselves, and having them employed against us."

(2) A close inspection of the exempted and detailed men: "The time has come when no man capable of bearing arms should be excused, unless it be for controlling reason of public necessity. The safety of the country requires this . . . and hardship to individuals must be disregarded in view of the calamity that would follow to the whole people if our armies meet with disaster."

(3) Employing the reserves of each state for garrison duty and in fortifications to free up veteran troops. Toward the latter point, he writes to Gen. James Kemper, commander of Virginia's reserves, regarding his plan and the number of men available.[6]

September 3, Saturday (Violet Bank/Richmond): Lee inquires of Bragg what service may be available for Gen. Edward Perry as he has returned to duty but his brigade no longer exists, and instructs Hampton to explore routes behind Union lines for possible raids. In the afternoon Lee goes to Richmond to meet with President Davis.[7]

September 4, Sunday (Richmond): Lee continues to meet with the president regarding the situation in Georgia. He visits with the Caskies and Rob brings him a letter from Mary.[8]

September 5, Monday (Richmond/Violet Bank): Lee continues to meet with Davis and Bragg, and writes to North Carolina Gov. Vance thanking him for his efforts for the defense of Wilmington. He writes to Mary regarding the military situation in Virginia and Georgia, the latest family news, and encloses a check for $800. In the evening he returns to Violet Bank. Storms during the night.[9]

September 7, Wednesday (Violet Bank): Lee informs one of A. P. Hill's artillery officers that county justice of the peace is not an office specified by Congress for which a military discharge may be issued.[10]

---

5 Heritage Auctions lot #72098, Dec. 1, 2007 auction. Presumably the animals were Traveller and Ajax, as Lucy Long was sent to southwestern Virginia sometime during the spring to rest. The reasons for Lucy Long's semi-retirement vary from exhaustion to pregnancy. See Freeman, *Lee*, vol. 1, 644-7; Custis to R. A. Brock, Aug. 11, 1891, Lee papers, SH; and Susan Anthony-Tobert, *Lucy Long, Robert E. Lee's Other Warhorse: The Mare with Mysteries* (Heathsville, VA, 2012), 83-5.

6 OR 42, pt. 2, 1228-30.

7 OR 42, pt. 2, 1232-4; Tower, *Lee's Adjutant*, 187. Lee's original intent for his trip to Richmond is not known; he told Mary only, "I came up on some business which I fear I cannot accomplish." Dowdey, *Wartime Papers*, 851. Lee did not know of the fall of Atlanta when he departed HQ for Richmond, and learned of it either en route or immediately upon his arrival in the capital. Taylor suspected that Lee would be sent to take command in Georgia. Tower, *Lee's Adjutant*, 187. According to rumor, Lee "remained closeted with Mr. Davis and General Bragg from 8 o'clock in the evening until 9 o'clock the next morning." Charleston *Mercury*, Sept. 9, 1864.

8 Dowdey, *Wartime Papers*, 850. Taylor confided to his fiancé that HQ must soon be relocated: "Our camp must be moved shortly for we are not much over a mile from the Yankee lines and when the leaves fall will be in plain view. I advocate taking a house in town and running the risk of a stray shell." Tower, *Lee's Adjutant*, 190.

9 Jones, *Rebel War Clerk's Diary*, vol. 2, 277; Carmichael, *Audacity Personified*, 117; Dowdey, *Wartime Papers*, 850-1; Krick, *CW Weather*, 138.

10 OR 3, Series 4, 659. The courts ordered the man, Thomas Vaden, discharged from military service to assume the duties of his elected office. OR 3, Series 4, 660.

September 8, Thursday (Violet Bank): Lee writes to Stonewall Jackson's widow regarding a position for her brother once he recovers from a wound. During the evening Lee receives a proposal from Wade Hampton for a raid on a cattle herd behind Union lines.[11]

September 9, Friday (Violet Bank): Lee proposes to President Davis combining the C.S. Bureau of Conscription and state reserve enrolling departments into one entity under state control thus freeing up Confederate troops currently detailed for conscription efforts. Lee inquires of Gov. Vance how many arms he requires for the state's reserve forces, and approves of Hampton's proposed raid. The Richmond *Whig* prints Lee's August 29 letter to Gov. Vance regarding Tar Heel troops at Ream's Station.[12]

September 10, Saturday (Violet Bank): Lee sends President Davis a letter from Gov. Vance regarding Wilmington: Vance requests the exchange of green troops for veterans and for Beauregard to replace Chase Whiting in command on the Cape Fear; Lee adds that Beauregard is at Wilmington currently on an inspection visit and Lee prefers to assign him there or Charleston. Lee informs Vance that Beauregard is at Wilmington for the present and that additional arms will be sent per Gov. Vance's request, and asks Beauregard if there is any spare artillery at Wilmington that can be sent for use on the James.[13]

Lee writes to Braxton Bragg regarding conscription efforts in Georgia, and requests that the War Department send an inspector to southwest Virginia in response to complaints about lack of organization and discipline among the troops there. Lee forwards to the War Department a report of the recent justice of the peace issue in A. P. Hill's artillery, pointing out the precedent it establishes, adding "the drain upon the strength of the Army by exemption of civil officers, postmasters, clerks and mail carriers, added to the details made for other purposes, is more than it can bear." Lee requests the promotion of Maj. H. E. Peyton, the army's inspector general, and Capt. H. E. Young, assistant inspector general.[14]

September 11, Sunday (Violet Bank/Petersburg): Lee and Taylor attend service at Grace Episcopal Church for the first time; as the congregation exits, Lee speaks with engineer Capt. Charles Dimmock, creator of Petersburg's defenses.[15]

September 12, Monday (Violet Bank/Richmond): Lee writes to Sec. Seddon regarding Virginia's reserve

---

11 REL to Mary Anna Jackson, Sept. 8, 1864, LJF papers, W&L; *OR* 42, pt. 2, 1242. Capt. Joseph G. Morrison was wounded at Drewry's Bluff in May while serving with the 57th NC. Krick, *Staff Officers in Gray*, 226.

12 Freeman, *Lee's Dispatches*, 293-5; REL to Vance, Sept. 9, 1864, telegram book, REL HQ papers, VHS; *OR* 42, pt. 2, 1242; REL newspaper references, DSF papers, LVA. Lee requested a meeting with Wade Hampton to go over the details of the "Beefsteak Raid," but it is not known if the meeting ever took place. See Horace Mewborn, "Herding Yankee Cattle: The Beefsteak Raid, September 14-17, 1864," *Blue & Gray* (Summer 2005), 7-17-, 44-50, for details of this episode.

13 *OR* 42, pt. 2, 1235, 1242; *OR* 51, pt. 2, 1039. Chase Whiting requested Beauregard's presence at Wilmington, NC, in early September. Roman, *Military Operations of Beauregard*, vol. 2, 274. Vance's request offered both Lee and Beauregard a way out of an awkward command situation at Petersburg. See Williams, *Beauregard*, 239-40.

14 Dowdey, *Wartime Papers*, 851-2; *OR* 43, pt. 2, 867; *OR* 3, Series 4, 660-1; REL to Seddon, Sept. 10, 1864, H. E. Peyton CSR. Both Peyton and Young were advanced one grade on Sept. 20. Krick, *Staff Officers in Gray*, 242, 311.

15 Tower, *Lee's Adjutant*, 190-1; Dimmock to Elizabeth Selden, Sept. 11, 1864, C. H. Dimmock papers, VHS. Rev. Churchill Gibson so impressed Taylor on this occasion that he determined to attend Grace rather than St. Paul's. He also complained about the crowds that gathered to catch a glimpse of Lee: "It is quite trying to accompany the General to Church or any public place. Everybody crowds the way and stops on the pavements to have a look. I get separated from him every opportunity that is offered." Tower, *Lee's Adjutant*, 190-1. Out of a number of officers present, Dimmock was the only one Lee acknowledged, an honor not lost upon the young engineer: "As I came out of the doors I halted a moment to speak to Col. [W. W.] Blackford . . . who, with many other officers, was standing near the entrance. As the Gen. passed we all saluted him when to my surprise he advanced to me and extended his hands. This he did to no one else. Such a manifestation of appreciation from Gen. Lee is prized more than any or all promotion." Dimmock to Elizabeth Selden, Sept. 11, 1864, Dimmock papers, VHS.

troops and the detailing of Lee's men for non-combat roles in Richmond, and informs Bragg that he will not send any of his troops to Hood in Georgia. Lee visits Richmond in the afternoon.[16]

September 13, Tuesday (Richmond): Lee meets with Davis and Seddon discussing how to increase the army's ranks.[17]

September 14, Wednesday (Richmond): Lee continues to meet with Davis and Seddon; during these discussions he recommends Col. Edwin G. Lee for command of the reserves west of the Blue Ridge.[18]

September 15, Thursday (Richmond/Violet Bank): Lee encounters ordnance chief Josiah Gorgas in Richmond and receives a letter from Mary as he heads to the train to return to Petersburg in the afternoon. He arrives in Petersburg around nightfall.[19]

September 16, Friday (Violet Bank): Lee informs Gov. Vance that 2,600 muskets have been sent to North Carolina.[20]

September 17, Saturday (Violet Bank): Lee recalls Anderson to resume command of his corps around Richmond, but Kershaw's Division is to remain with Early. He asks for Early's opinion on reorganizing the cavalry in the Valley and if John Breckinridge can be sent back to southwest Virginia; Lee also wants to know if the VIII Corps is still in Early's front as prisoners report it now at Petersburg. The general informs the War Department of Wade Hampton's "Beefsteak Raid" and also requests 5,000 blacks for work on the fortifications and the railroads. He warns the garrison commanders along the Weldon Railroad that several thousand enemy cavalry moved out on the Jerusalem Plank Road today and may be intending to attack the railroad. He sends a letter to Martha Anne Fowlkes of Nottoway County, thanking her for the cloth she sent him.[21]

September 18, Sunday (Violet Bank): Lee meets with Gen. P. G. T. Beauregard, who returns from Wilmington this morning, about the situation there and perhaps also about Beauregard going to Charleston. Lee informs Jubal Early that scouts confirm the Union VIII Corps with Grant: is it at Petersburg or in the Valley? Lee writes to Custis about his meeting with Beauregard and asks for his extra pair of boots, and writes Mary with family news and explains why he does not make his headquarters indoors: "It is from no desire of exposure or hazard that I live in a tent, but from necessity. I must be where I can speedily at all times attend to the duties of my position, and be near or accessible to the officers with whom I have to act. I have been offered rooms in the houses of our citizens, but I could not turn the dwellings of my kind hosts into a barrack, where officers, couriers, distressed women, etc., would be entering day and night."[22]

---

16 OR 42, pt. 2, 1245-6; Dowdey, *Wartime Papers*, 852; Tower, *Lee's Adjutant*, 190.

17 Jones, *War Clerk's Diary*, vol. 2, 282. One study suggests that a major point of discussion during Lee's Richmond stay was a plot to kidnap Abraham Lincoln; the evidence is circumstantial, at best. William A. Tidwell, *Come Retribution: The Confederate Secret Service and the Assassination of Lincoln* (Jackson, MS, 1988), 20-2.

18 Jones, *War Clerk's Diary*, vol. 2, 282; REL endorsement on E. G. Lee to WNP, Sept. 10, 1864, Lee papers, SH.

19 Vandiver, *Gorgas Diary*, 141; Dowdey, *Wartime Papers*, 854-5; Richard Lewis, *Camp Life of a Confederate Boy of Bratton's Brigade, Longstreet's Corps, C.S.A.* (Charleston, SC, 1883), 95.

20 OR 42, pt. 2, 1252.

21 OR 42, pt. 2, 873-5, 1256-8; OR 42, pt. 1, 852; REL to M. A. Fowlkes, Sept. 17, 1864, REL papers, UVA.

22 REL to Custis, Sept. 18, 1864, REL papers, Duke; Williams, *Beauregard*, 240; OR 43, pt. 2, 876; Dowdey, *Wartime Papers*, 854-5. Lee may have attended morning service at Grace Episcopal; Taylor did, but it is not clear from his wording if he accompanied Lee or went alone. Tower, *Lee's Adjutant*, 192. Lee thought Davis was considering Beauregard to replace Hood as commander of the Army of Tennessee and apparently told Beauregard as much on the 18th or 19th; instead, Beauregard was made department commander over Hood, but with little to no authority over Hood's army—an almost

September 19, Monday (Violet Bank): Lee meets again with Gen. Beauregard regarding the situation in Georgia and receives from Beauregard a written confirmation that he is willing to serve in Georgia. The general sends President Davis a summary of their meeting. Lee then writes to John Mosby congratulating him for all of his success, and forwards to Richmond Mosby's report of his operations from March to September. Lee provides feedback on an artillery reorganization proposed by Pendleton.[23]

September 20, Tuesday (Violet Bank): Lee learns of Early's large-scale defeat at Winchester yesterday, including the death of division commander Robert Rodes. He telegraphs Early asking for a condition report while seeking to reassure him that he could change the course of events there. Lee directs Anderson to remain where he is until the situation in the Valley becomes clearer. He notifies the secretary of war about Early's defeat and also recommends that slaves and free blacks be used as army laborers to free up soldiers to rejoin the ranks: "The time has arrived when the public safety requires that we shall employ negro labor with the army in all cases where it can be used to relieve able-bodied white men."[24]

He writes to Rabbi M. J. Michelbacher regarding furloughs for Jewish troops and to Gov. Vance regarding the reassignment of North Carolina troops in James Dearing's brigade. He directs Martin Gary to ascertain enemy strength in Charles City Co. and Williamsburg, and asks the War Department if Gen. Edward Johnson has been assigned to the Army of Tennessee. Lee informs President Davis that Beauregard will depart this afternoon to meet Davis at Burkeville.[25]

September 22, Thursday (Violet Bank): Lee instructs Anderson to move with Kershaw to Charlottesville or Gordonsville and renews the idea of Anderson and Early working in tandem against Sheridan in the Valley. Lee advises Wade Hampton that some of the enemy cavalry may be withdrawn from the Valley in light of Early's defeat at Winchester, and he writes to John M. Brooke regarding the placement of Brooke guns along the Petersburg works. Lee informs Sec. Seddon that since the CSS *Tallahassee* left Wilmington the Union Navy increased its blockading efforts there thus making it more difficult for incoming blockade runners to get through; he suggests that Wilmington be used solely for running supplies through the blockade and that privateers use Charleston as their base.[26]

September 23, Friday (Violet Bank): Lee learns of Early's defeat at Fisher's Hill yesterday and informs the War Department. In light of this second defeat, he abandons the idea of Anderson operating as a separate force and instructs him to send Kershaw's Division and the artillery to join Early and to come to Petersburg himself to resume corps command; Lee tells Early not to give battle again until Kershaw's troops arrive. Beauregard departs Petersburg for

---

equally uncomfortable command arrangement. Roman, *Military Operations of Beauregard*, vol. 2, 274-5; Williams, *Beauregard*, 240.

23 *OR* 39, pt. 2, 846; Roman, *Military Operations of Beauregard*, vol. 2, 274-5; *OR* 43, pt. 2, 876-7; *OR* 33, 248-9; *OR* 36, pt. 3, 880-2.

24 REL to Early, Sept. 20, 1864, telegram book, REL HQ papers, VHS; *OR* 43, pt. 2, 877; *OR* 43, pt. 1, 552; *OR* 42, pt. 2, 1260-1.

25 Jones, *Personal Reminiscences of REL*, 444; REL to Vance, Sept. 20, 1864, REL papers, Duke; REL to Martin Gary, Sept. 20, 1864, REL papers, MOC; REL to Samuel Cooper, Sept. 20, 1864, telegram book, REL HQ papers, VHS; REL to Davis, Sept. 20, 1864, telegram book, REL HQ papers, VHS. Ed Johnson was sent to Georgia after his exchange and commanded a division in Stephen D. Lee's Corps in the Army of Tennessee. Lee probably had wanted him to command Rodes's Division after that officer's death in the Valley. Clemmer, *Old Alleghany*, 581-90. Davis did not leave on the 20th, which prompted Beauregard to delay his departure; they did not meet until Oct. 2. Davis, *Jefferson Davis*, 565; Williams, *Beauregard*, 240-1.

26 *OR* 43, pt. 2, 878; REL to Early, Sept. 22, 1864, telegram book, REL HQ papers, VHS; *OR* 42, pt. 2, 1270; Brooke, *Ironclads and Big Guns*, 189; *OR* 51, pt. 2, 1040-1.

Charleston, taking "an affectionate farewell" of Lee before leaving.[27]

September 24, Saturday (Violet Bank/ Richmond): Lee goes to Richmond to meet with Gen. Breckinridge regarding affairs in southwest Virginia, and reports a victory at Blue Springs, Tennessee, on the 22nd. Lee requests the aid of Gov. Smith in getting out the local reserves to assist Early and advises John Echols in southwest Virginia to call out all local troops and "resist to the last."[28]

September 25, Sunday (Violet Bank/Petersburg): Lee attends church service at St. Paul's where a number of other generals are present for the baptism of Gen. Walter Stevens's infant son; Lee and Porter Alexander are the boy's godfathers. Lee meets with Governor William Smith regarding Early; Smith wants Early replaced as commander in the Valley based on his recent defeats. Lee informs Early that additional cavalry will be sent him if possible and instructs him to crush Sheridan once Kershaw joins him. Lee inquires if Echols needs additional weapons for his force in southwest Virginia.[29]

September 26, Monday (Violet Bank/Petersburg): Lee continues to plead his case to the War Department regarding details for noncombatant roles, telling Bragg: "The enemy are increasing their forces in Virginia…I get no additions. The men coming in do not supply the vacancies caused by sickness, desertions, and other casualties." He informs Early that Hampton cannot be spared but Rosser will be sent him to take command of the Valley cavalry and that Breckinridge will cooperate with him as much as possible. He orders that all men at Lynchburg fit for field service be sent to Breckinridge and tells Echols that the force opposing him cannot be as large as reported.[30]

Lee informs Seddon that Early continues to retreat and is now near Port Republic, and he forwards to the War Department complaints by

---

27 *OR* 43, pt. 1, 552, 557; *OR* 42, pt. 2, 878; Richard J. Sommers, *Richmond Redeemed: The Siege at Petersburg* (El Dorado Hills, CA, 2014), 205; Roman, *Military Operations of Beauregard*, vol. 2, 275. Beauregard left his HQ intact at Petersburg under Col. G. W. Brent and Lt. Col. J. M. Otey for a short time, but he never returned because he assumed command of the Department of the West on Oct. 3; his troops were formally absorbed into Lee's ANV. Sommers, *Richmond Redeemed*, 205.

28 *OR* 42, pt. 2, 1050; J. Stoddard Johnston, "Sketches of Operations of General John C. Breckinridge," *SHSP*, vol. 7, 385; Freeman, *Lee's Dispatches*, 298-9; Dowdey, *Wartime Papers*, 857-8. Gen. Breckinridge was ordered to report to southwest Virginia on Sept. 21 and he arrived at Abingdon on Oct. 1. Davis, *Breckinridge*, 454, 458. Before resuming command, Breckinridge went to Richmond by rail to meet with Lee, as noted by his aide Johnston, who unfortunately did not record the date. Johnston, "Sketches of Operations," 385. Several Union informants reported Lee's presence at the War Department on this date. *OR* 42, pt. 2, 1050. Given that Breckinridge arrived at Abingdon on Oct. 1, this is the only possible date that works for meeting with Lee in Richmond, unless Breckinridge traveled instead to Petersburg, but Johnston makes no mention of that fact, nor does Breckinridge's biographer, and the correspondence regarding southwest Virginia reinforces Lee's attention to that region on this date. Johnston was mistaken about Jefferson Davis being included in the discussions; President Davis was on his way to meet with Hood in Georgia at this time. Davis, *Jefferson Davis*, 565.

29 Pearce, *Chambers Diary*, 219-20; *OR* 43, pt. 2, 879, 893-5; REL to Echols, Sept. 25, 1864, telegram book, REL HQ papers, VHS. Gens. Longstreet, A. P. Hill, Heth, Wilcox, Hoke, and several brigadiers were also present for the service. Pearce, *Chambers Diary*, 219-20. Although Longstreet had not yet reported for duty, he was in Petersburg. Greene, *CW Petersburg*, 314 n76. The meeting with William "Extra Billy" Smith likely occurred at Violet Bank, although neither Lee nor Taylor mentions Smith's presence. It is possible that Lee went to Richmond to meet with Smith, although in a letter written late that afternoon, Taylor mentions Lee's presence at HQ; he either had a very narrow window between church and late afternoon (which seems extremely unlikely), or he may have gone to the capital in the evening. See Tower, *Lee's Adjutant*, 193-4. Smith was not fond of Jubal Early, their poor relationship dating back to his time Smith commanded a brigade under the irascible general. Smith cited very critical reports by a single informant that Early was incompetent and that he lacked the respect of his men: Lee listened to the governor, but was not inclined to remove Early. Scott L. Mingus, Sr., *Confederate General William 'Extra Billy' Smith: From Virginia's Statehouse to Gettysburg Scapegoat* (El Dorado Hills, CA, 2013), 305-7; Osborne, *Jubal*, 352-4.

30 *OR* 42, pt. 2, 1292-3; *OR* 43, pt. 2, 879; REL to Early, Sept. 26, 1864, telegram book, REL HQ papers, VHS; REL to R. E. Colston, Sept. 26, 1864, telegram book, REL HQ papers, VHS; REL to Echols, Sept. 26, 1864, telegram book, REL HQ papers, VHS.

Pickett of continued violations by the enemy of flags of truce during POW exchanges and points out the lack of cooperation between the Army and Navy along the James River. In late afternoon Lee and Hill review Hoke's Division.[31]

September 27, Tuesday (Violet Bank): Lee dines with Richard Anderson, who reports back for duty with the Army of Northern Virginia, during which Lee amuses himself by jesting with several of Anderson's young staff officers during the meal. Lee forwards Early's report to Richmond detailing the Fisher's Hill defeat and requests that the reserves from the Valley counties be sent to Early. He writes to Early, looking to reassure him: "One victory will put all things right. You must do all in your power to reinvigorate your army."[32]

September 28, Wednesday (Violet Bank): Gen. Lee directs Richard Anderson to take command north of the James River, and approves a leave of absence for William Pendleton, with E. Porter Alexander to serve as Lee's artillery chief in his absence. The general also rebukes Gen. Raleigh Colston for his lack of awareness of the troops at Lynchburg, Virginia.[33]

September 29, Thursday (Violet Bank/Chaffin's Farm): Lee learns soon after dawn of an attack upon the lines around Chaffin's Farm and instructs Gen. Ewell to bring out his entire force to meet the threat and take command in person. As the severity of the attack becomes more apparent, Lee requests help from Braxton Bragg and instructs George Pickett to offer whatever assistance he can from the Howlett Line; Lee also advises Ewell that help is on the way, and directs his former corps commander to personally lead the effort to retake Fort Harrison. The general also briefs Charles Field and E. P. Alexander in person at headquarters before sending them across the James with three brigades and several batteries to reinforce Ewell. Lee enlists the aid of Capt. John Mitchell's gunboats in the James in defending the outer line and protecting the pontoon bridge at Chaffin's Bluff.[34]

Lee informs Pickett that prisoners taken are from the XVIII Corps which was in the Bermuda Hundred lines previously, so to send a portion of his force across the river also. Around mid-morning Lee personally goes across the James to take command himself; he meets Ewell in the vicinity of Fort Maury on the Osborne Turnpike and learns that although Fort Harrison was captured, Ewell's patchwork line prevented any further penetration. Field urges an

---

31 *OR* 43, pt. 2, 879; *OR* 42, pt. 2, 1290-2; Hagood, *Memoirs*, 303-4. One of Gen. Hoke's brigade commanders noted that the review "was made a gala occasion by the citizens of the beleaguered town," but that Lee "seemed bored by the ceremon[y] and glad to be through with it. . . . Even his horse looked as if he thought it was all foolishness." Hagood, *Memoirs*, 303-4.

32 Walker, *Life of R. H. Anderson*, 188; Dawson, *Reminiscences*, 125; *OR* 43, pt. 1, 557-9; *OR* 43, pt. 2, 879. Anderson's aide, Lt. Francis Dawson, recalled that this "was the most uncomfortable meal that I ever had in my life. . . . I wished myself anywhere else than at General Lee's headquarters." Dawson, *Reminiscences*, 125. Anderson's most recent biographer put this meeting a day earlier and in Richmond, but did not provide a source for why he differed with Anderson's earlier biographer. Unfortunately Dawson did not give a date, but the context implies that it occurred in Petersburg. Elliott, *Lt. Gen. R. H. Anderson*, 116.

33 *OR* 42, pt. 2, 1298-9; WHT to WNP, Sept. 28, 1864, WNP papers, UNC; REL to Colston, Sept. 28, 1864, telegram book, REL HQ papers, VHS.

34 REL to Ewell, Sept. 29, 1864 (3 messages) telegram book, REL HQ papers, VHS; *OR* 42, pt. 2, 1302-5; Field, "Campaign of 1864 and 1865," 555; EPA to wife, Oct. 3, 1864, EPA papers, UNC; REL to J. K. Mitchell, Sept. 29, 1864, telegram book, REL HQ papers, VHS. Out of all the battlefields around Richmond, Fort Harrison was the first to be preserved, largely through the efforts of Douglas S. Freeman in the 1920s. The fort itself and portions of the adjacent works remain today, but the surrounding land has changed greatly, with portions of it developed into residential neighborhoods and much of it overtaken by tree growth. Douglas Crenshaw, *Fort Harrison and the Battle of Chaffin's Farm* (Charleston, SC, 2013), 100-4. Normally the Richmond reserves would have been commanded by Custis, but he was accompanying President Davis in Georgia, so his troops were led by Brig. Gen. William M. Gardner. *OR* 42, pt. 2, 1302; Yates, *Perfect Gentleman*, vol. 1, 308-9. Gardner was severely wounded at First Manassas leading the 8th GA and was deemed unfit for field service for the remainder of the war; he commanded briefly in Florida before being sent to Richmond in May 1864. William C. Davis, "William Montgomery Gardner," *Confederate General*, vol. 2, 126-3.

immediate counterattack with the troops at hand, but Lee decides to wait until Hoke's Division arrives.³⁵

In late afternoon Lee observes an attack by Pickett's detachment that retakes some of the adjacent works and he determines to attack Harrison tomorrow with Field and Hoke; he camps nearby at Chaffin's farm. During the night he advises Sec. Seddon that Fort Harrison remains in enemy hands but Federal attacks on the adjacent works were repulsed, and provides an update on Early's situation in the Valley. He informs Early of the attack on Richmond and instructs Gen. Lawrence Baker to impress labor and complete the fortifications at Weldon immediately. During the night Gen. John Gregg, commander of the Texas Brigade meets with Lee and comes away with the misunderstanding that Lee intends to launch a night attack to retake Harrison.³⁶

September 30, Friday (Chaffin's Farm/Fort Gilmer): In the morning Lee, Ewell, and Anderson reconnoiter the approaches to Fort Harrison; during their ride, Ewell's horse steps in a hole and throws him, badly injuring his face and prompting Lee to send him to the rear for treatment. Lee watches the attack from Fort Gilmer, and rides out to rally the men after two successive assaults fail to dislodge the Federals from Fort Harrison. That night he informs Seddon that the attempts to retake Harrison failed, and he holds a conference at headquarters and sharply chides John Pemberton who suggests another attempt be made. Rain during the night.³⁷

---

35   OR 42, pt. 2, 1301, 1304; A. O. Wright, "Reminiscence of Holding Traveller," *CV*, vol. 13, 266; Martin, *Road to Glory*, 336; Freeman, *Lee*, vol. 3, 501. Taylor remained behind at Violet Bank and A. P. Hill, as senior officer at Petersburg, relocated his command post there to speed communication between the two fronts. OR 42, pt. 2, 1301-2. Taylor's brother, Maj. Richard C. Taylor, commanded at Fort Harrison, where he was wounded and captured. Manarin, *Henrico County: Field of Honor*, vol. 2, 612-3. The hour of Lee's arrival north of the James River is not known; Campbell Brown, Ewell's aide and son-in-law, placed Lee on the ground in the afternoon. Jones, *Campbell Brown's CW*, 270.

36   Freeman, *Lee*, vol. 3, 502; Gallagher, *Fighting for the Confederacy*, 479; OR 42, pt. 2, 1301, 1305-6; OR 43, pt. 1, 552; REL to Early, Sept. 29, 1864, telegram book, REL HQ papers, VHS; Field, "Campaign of 1864 & 1865," 556. Gregg's misunderstanding was only sorted out after he got three brigades in position shortly after midnight and went to report that fact to a sleeping Gen. Richard Anderson. Field, "Campaign of 1864 & 1865," 556. The exact location of Lee's camp is not known; E. Porter Alexander noted only that it was "at a house on the Osborne Turnpike, near Cornelius Creek." Gallagher, *Fighting for the Confederacy*, 479. Moxley Sorrel recalled that it was at the Chaffin house itself, but that seems to be where Ewell's HQ was located. Sorrel, *Recollections*, 265; McDonald, *Make Me a Map*, 241. According to a Union informant, Lee's HQ was "at James Taylor's farm, near and northwest of Chaffin's Bluff." OR 42, pt. 3, 226.

37   Manarin, *Henrico County: Field of Honor*, vol. 2, 680, 691; Sorrel, *Recollections*, 264-5, 268; J. A. H. Granbury, "That Fort Gilmer Fight," *CV*, vol. 13, 413; Moore, *Story of a Cannoneer*, 265; Sommers, *Richmond Redeemed*, 144; Dowdey, *Wartime Papers*, 860; Krick, *CW Weather*, 140. Fort Harrison was originally open to the rear, but the Federals spent the night of the 29/30 digging a western face to protect against a counterattack from that direction. As they had done at Petersburg on June 24, Hoke and Field failed to coordinate their attacks against Harrison. Fort Gilmer was north of Fort Harrison, north of Mill Road; a portion of it remains today, although much of it has been lost to a residential neighborhood. As with many anecdotes, Sorrel did not record the exact date that the incident with Ewell occurred, but most modern writers put it on the 30th. One Ewell biographer, however, puts it after the failed attack while Lee was scouting for a new line to bypass Harrison. Pfanz, *Ewell*, 418. One history of the battle put the Ewell incident on the morning of Oct. 1. Manarin, *Henrico County: Field of Honor*, vol. 2, 696. The exchange with John Pemberton can be interpreted two ways: Sorrel—who was either present for it or learned of it very soon thereafter—wrote that Lee intended it as a rebuke; Freeman took it to mean that Lee honestly wanted a plan from Pemberton if he had one. Sorrel's interpretation is used here. Sorrel, *Recollections*, 268; Freeman, *Lee*, vol. 3, 504. One recent historian suggested that Lee placed so much importance upon retaking the fort that in rallying the survivors for another attempt, "He may . . . have so put himself at risk as to have caused another 'Lee to the rear' incident." Sommers, *Richmond Redeemed*, 144.

October 1864

U. S. Grant's ability to shift large numbers of troops and supplies across the James River at will across the pontoon bridge at Deep Bottom was an endless headache for Gen. Lee, and he decided the time had come to eradicate his bridgehead on the north bank. Although Gens. Robert Hoke and Charles Field had twice failed to coordinate their attacks, Lee turned to them (and to Gen. Richard Anderson) to destroy the Army of the James. In a repetition of past failures like Fort Harrison and at Petersburg, the lack of coordination doomed the effort on October 7 and there was little or nothing to show for the losses sustained.

Lee spent hours each day inspecting the works north of the James, resigned to the fact he would have to keep a much larger force in the trenches around Richmond than he wanted. Hoke often rode with him. A legend arose that during one of their rides Lee told Hoke he wanted the North Carolinian to take command of the Army of Northern Virginia should something happen to him.[1]

On one tour of Hoke's lines, Lee paused in the sector held by Gen. William W. Kirkland's brigade. One of Kirkland's staffers remembered the visit:

> General Lee gave orders that the earthworks should be strengthened and the camp carefully policed. He rode along the line almost daily. One day he halted on our line and sent for General Kirkland. I rode up with the latter to meet our chief. He asked Kirkland for some couriers and sent for the other generals of the corps. When they came up he pointed to our camp and works and said "Gentlemen, this is the only brigade that has obeyed my instructions. I wish you to make your camp and line conform to this one. General Kirkland I am glad to see the condition of your command." Kirkland, flushed with pride, thanked General Lee for the compliment to his brigade, but added that its high state of efficiency was due to its former commander, General Martin, and he had only tried to maintain the command as he found it.[2]

Lee's last hope for the Valley went up in flames in October, as Sheridan's horsemen burned mills, barns, and in some instances, houses. Jubal Early could do little but watch and harass him from afar. When he spotted an opportunity to strike, Early attacked at Cedar Creek outside Winchester on October 19. His initial assault was wildly successful, but the tables turned and Sheridan crushed him. The defeat effectively ended the 1864 Valley Campaign. With Early no longer a threat, Lee knew it was only a matter of time before much of Sheridan's command was transferred to Petersburg.

In the latter half of the month James Longstreet returned to duty. Lee gave his old "Old War Horse" responsibility for the lines north of the James. Now more comfortable that his left wing was in much better hands than it was with either Dick Ewell or Richard Anderson, Lee intended to return south to Petersburg, where Grant was once again extending his lines westward.

* * *

[1] Barefoot, *General R. F. Hoke*, 231, 360-6. By all accounts Hoke was trustworthy and honorable, so it is likely he did not fabricate the story outright; rather, he misinterpreted some remark of Lee's. This is examined briefly in Hoke's obituary and in greater detail by his biographer. "Maj. Gen. Robert F. Hoke," *CV*, vol. 20, 437-9; Barefoot, *General R. F. Hoke*, 360-6. Supporters of the less-scrupulous William Mahone advanced a similiar story that swaps out Hoke for Mahone. Suffice it to say that neither man would have been advanced over the heads of the scores of generals who outranked them. If such a thing became necessary, the most obvious options were Joe Johnston, P. G. T. Beauregard, or James Longstreet.

[2] Charles G. Elliot, "Martin's Brigade, of Hoke's Division, 1863-64," *SHSP*, vol. 23, 196.

October 1, Saturday (Chaffin's Farm): Lee proposes to Grant a prisoner exchange. He requests clarification from Richmond on Lt. Col. John Pemberton's exact command, and informs Secretary of War Seddon of a victory by John H. Morgan in southwest Virginia yesterday and of Phil Sheridan's occupation of the central Shenandoah Valley. He also sends word to Secretary of War Seddon of Heth's successful attack on the enemy south of Petersburg yesterday, netting several hundred prisoners and several flags. Showers during the day.[3]

October 3, Monday (Chaffin's Farm): Lee informs Grant that he is willing to exchange "all captured soldiers of the United States of whatever nation and color under my control" but will not include "deserters from our service and negroes belonging to our citizens." Showers during the day.[4]

October 4, Tuesday (Chaffin's Farm): Lee sends Sec. Seddon a very bleak outlook on the situation: "The enemy's numerical superiority enables him to hold his lines with an adequate force, and extend on each flank with numbers so much greater than ours that we can only meet his corps, increased by recent recruits, with a division reduced by long and arduous service. We cannot fight to advantage with such odds, and there is the gravest reason to apprehend the result of every encounter. . . . We may be able, with the blessings of God, to keep the enemy in check to the beginning of winter." If the strength of the ANV is not increased, "the result may be calamitous," he warns. He also informs Secretary Seddon about Grant's refusal to exchange prisoners and encloses the letters between him and Grant. Lee learns of Federals at Brandy Station possibly moving to raid Gordonsville, so orders all supplies removed from there and for Mosby to interfere with enemy efforts to rebuild the Orange & Alexandria railroad.[5]

He congratulates John Breckinridge for the victory at Saltville on the 2nd, and informs Early of that victory as well as the possible threat east of the Blue Ridge. Lee notifies Richmond of Early's operations, Breckinridge's victory, and the enemy presence at Brandy Station and along the O&A. He congratulates Hampton on the cavalry's recent successes and instructs him and A. P. Hill to work together to attack Grant's left flank to keep him from stretching farther to the west. Showers continue.[6]

October 5, Wednesday (Chaffin's Farm): Lee forwards to the War Department several communications from Gen. W. H. C. Whiting regarding Wilmington and recommends reinforcements be transferred there from South Carolina. He informs Seddon of a cavalry raid into West Virginia and advises Breckinridge and Early to work together so Kershaw's Division can be returned to Petersburg.[7]

October 6, Thursday (Chaffin's Farm): Lee has a conference in the morning with President Davis and Gens. Ewell, Anderson, Field, Hoke, and Martin Gary to discuss an offensive to drive the Army of the James south of its namesake river tomorrow. In late afternoon Lee meets with Porter Alexander to go over artillery preparations for tomorrow's attack; Lee informs everyone present that he will personally be on the move at 2:00 a.m. and he requests

---

3   *OR* 7, Series 2, 906-7; *OR* 42, pt. 3, 1130; *OR* 39, pt. 3, 778-9; *OR* 43, pt. 2, 885; *OR* 42, pt. 1, 852; Manarin, *Henrico County: Field of Honor*, vol. 2, 707. Grant replied on the 2nd that he would exchange only those captured during the Chaffin's farm action of the previous three days (which included a number of black soldiers) and he wanted to know how the black troops would be addressed. *OR* 7, Series 2, 909. It is not known when Lee received this reply.

4   *OR* 7, Series 2, 914; Manarin, *Henrico County: Field of Honor*, vol. 2, 707. Grant denied the POW exchange because escaped slaves were not included. *OR* 7, Series 2, 914.

5   *OR* 42, pt. 3, 1134; *OR* 7, Series 2, 914; *OR* 43, pt. 2, 885; REL to Cornelius Boyle, Oct. 4, 1864, telegram book, REL HQ papers, VHS; REL to James Corley, Oct. 4, 1864, telegram book, REL HQ papers, VHS; REL to Early, Oct. 4, 1864, telegram book, REL HQ papers, VHS.

6   *OR* 39, pt. 3, 786; REL to Early, Oct. 4, 1864, telegram book, REL HQ papers, VHS; *OR* 43, pt. 2, 885; *OR* 42, pt. 3, 1133; REL to Hill, Oct. 4, 1864, telegram book, REL HQ papers, VHS; Manarin, *Henrico County: Field of Honor*, vol. 2, 707.

7   *OR* 42, pt. 2, 1280-2, 1294-5; *OR* 43, pt. 1, 639; *OR* 43, pt. 2, 885; REL to Early, Oct. 5, 1864, telegram book, REL HQ papers, VHS.

Alexander to join his party as they pass by the artilleryman's camp. Lee requests engineer chief Jeremy Gilmer to acquire black laborers for Whiting to work on the Wilmington defenses, and again instructs Breckinridge and Early to pool their forces.[8]

October 7, Friday (Chaffin's Farm/Darbytown Road/Johnson Farm): Lee is up shortly after midnight and leaves camp at 1:00 a.m. without breakfast, under the mistaken notion he instructed everyone yesterday to be prepared at that hour, and is in a foul mood because his staff officers are not ready. The general arrives at Porter Alexander's headquarters at the Gunn house at 1:30 a.m. and sends Venable to fetch Alexander, who also is not expecting Lee at that hour. When he learns Alexander did not secure a guide—Lee had not requested him to do so, but expected he would—Lee tells Venable that Venable will serve as the guide. Venable does not hear Lee's command, so a courier named "Evans" is pressed into duty to lead the party. Passing a house, Lee rouses the occupant and orders him to serve as a guide—without telling him where they want to go.

Lee and Anderson, and possibly Alexander as well, remain on the Darbytown Road in rear of the Texas Brigade observing the attack of Field's Division. As the command party follows the progress of the attack to the Johnson farm, Porter Alexander notes that Lee's demeanor had improved greatly from the early morning hours.[9]

That evening Lee informs Sec. Seddon of the attack that drove the Federals off Charles City Road but failed to push them across the James, noting that Gen. John Gregg, commander of the Texas Brigade, was killed. He informs Richmond that Sheridan's army is withdrawing down the Valley with Early in pursuit, and that enemy cavalry destroyed a bridge over the Rapidan. Longstreet reports for duty, volunteering to serve in the Western Theater if no position is available with Lee's army.[10]

October 8, Saturday (Chaffin's Farm): Lee writes to North Carolina Gov. Vance and Gen. Theophilus Holmes stressing the need for men with the ANV and requests troops on garrison duty be sent to Petersburg and replaced with local reserves, and to small veteran units be swapped for Whiting's troops at Wilmington. Lee provides updated figures to the War Department for yesterday's battle and grants permission to the officers and men of the Texas Brigade to go to Richmond to attend Gregg's funeral the next day. Maj. Giles B. Cooke, formerly of Beauregard's staff, joins Lee's staff.[11]

---

8 Tower, *Lee's Adjutant*, 195; Manarin, *Henrico County: Field of Honor*, vol. 2, 710; Gallagher, *Fighting for the Confederacy*, 479-81; *OR* 42, pt. 3, 1136; *OR* 43, pt. 2, 886; REL to Early, Oct. 6, 1864, telegram book, REL HQ papers, VHS. Lee officially moved ANV HQ to Chaffin's farm from Violet Bank sometime between Sept. 30 and Oct. 5. Charles Marshall was very ill, which left only Taylor and Venable to run HQ. Tower, *Lee's Adjutant*, 194. Marshall's illness, diagnosed as dysentery, was severe enough that he was admitted to a Richmond hospital on the 7th. He remained there for three days, although he was quite ill for some time after his return to duty. Marshall CSR; Tower, *Lee's Adjutant*, 200.

9 Gallagher, *Fighting for the Confederacy*, 479-83; Manarin, *Henrico County: Field of Honor*, vol. 2, 731-3; Calvin L. Collier, *They'll Do to Tie to: 3rd Arkansas Infantry Regiment, C.S.A.* (Little Rock, AK, 1995), 205; Hagood, *Memoirs*, 309; Hampton Newsome, *Richmond Must Fall: The Richmond-Petersburg Campaign, October 1864* (Kent, OH, 2013), 48. No "Evans" appears on the roster of the 39th VA Cav. Battalion. E. P. Alexander recalled that Lee remained angry with Venable for several weeks after this incident and made it clear that contrary to popular belief, R. E. Lee had a temper. Gallagher, *Fighting for the Confederacy*, 482. The horse Moxley Sorrel's brother Francis was riding was killed very close to Lee during the early stages of the fighting. Several days later when Lee encountered Francis on another horse, the army commander joked about the replacement horse being pregnant, which had somehow escaped Sorrel's notice. Sorrel, *Recollections*, 267. One wounded young soldier approached Lee and said, "General, if you don't send some more men down there, our boys will get hurt sure." Lee supposedly detailed one of his staff to take the young man to a surgeon. Dawson, *Reminiscences*, 127.

10 *OR* 42, pt. 1, 852; Dowdey, *Wartime Papers*, 862; Freeman, *Lee's Dispatches*, 300-1; *OR* 42, pt. 3, 1140. This engagement marked yet another occasion when Gens. Field and Hoke could not or would not coordinate their movements. Although Anderson was in charge on the field, Lee may have been directing Hoke's movements. Newsome, *Richmond Must Fall*, 70-2.

11 *OR* 42, pt. 3, 1141-2; *OR* 42, pt. 1, 852; "Diary of Professor Fitzgerald," Oct. 8, 1864, EPA papers, UNC; Krick, *Staff Officers in Gray*, 102. A soldier in the 5th TX noted that Lee's order allowing them to attend Gregg's funeral was "an honor

October 9, Sunday (Chaffin's Farm): Lee meets with Alexander to discuss a new line of fortifications southeast of Richmond to replace the portions captured on the 29th; he orders construction of this new line to begin tomorrow. He informs Sec. Seddon of small victories by Thomas Rosser in the Valley and Mosby in northern Virginia, and issues orders that all absentees and detailed men who are physically fit for regular duty must return to the ranks. He writes to Mary mentioning that Custis is with him and passing along news of the former slaves at White House and Romancoke.[12]

October 10, Monday (Chaffin's Farm): Lee informs A. P. Hill at Petersburg that reports have Grant preparing for another movement westward toward the Southside Railroad; he wants Hill to put as many local reserves and militia in the trenches as possible to create a mobile force to react to enemy movements: "We must drive them back at all costs." Lee writes to Gov. Smith defending Early and wanting to know the identity of the anonymous accuser quoted by Smith in his charges against Early. He informs Seddon of a minor victory by Breckinridge in eastern Tennessee, and writes to Adjutant General Cooper regarding medical exemptions. Lee writes to Maj. James B. Ferguson in England thanking him for a uniform sent through the blockade.[13]

October 11, Tuesday (Chaffin's Farm): Lee receives several letters from Jubal Early as well as his report of the Valley Campaign, delivered by Capt. Mann Page.[14]

October 12, Wednesday (Chaffin's Farm/Darbytown Road): Lee rides to Gen. Field's front on the Darbytown Road when enemy cavalry appears there, and shifts troops to meet what he and Field perceive to be another attack against Richmond. Lee instructs John Breckinridge to send any spare troops he can to Early, and dispatches a lengthy letter to Early regarding the tenuous situation in the Valley. Rain during the night.[15]

October 13, Thursday (Chaffin's Farm/Charles City Road): Lee returns to Field's front in the Darbytown Road/Charles City Road sector in the morning and informs Sec. Seddon that the Federals attacked and were repulsed.[16]

October 14, Friday (Chaffin's Farm): Lee again informs Gov. "Extra Billy" Smith that he will not relieve Early, and forwards to Seddon the

---

allowed no brigade before and accorded to us . . . as a mark of estimation of our services." "Diary of Professor Fitzgerald," Oct. 8, 1864, EPA papers, UNC.

12 Gallagher, *Fighting for the Confederacy*, 486; OR 43, pt. 1, 552-3, 633; circular, Oct. 9, 1864, Thomas L. Clingman papers, UNC; REL to Mrs. REL, Oct. 9, 1864, REL papers, LOC. Porter Alexander and engineer chief Jeremy Gilmer spent much of the day charting out this new line; Alexander later called it "the most beautiful line of intrenchments which I saw during the whole war." Gallagher, *Fighting for the Confederacy*, 486. Custis returned from Georgia with President Davis and assumed command of the Richmond troops in the fortifications on or just before this date.

13 OR 42, pt. 3, 1144-5; OR 43, pt. 2, 895; OR 39, pt. 3, 811; REL to Ferguson, Oct. 10, 1864, REL papers, VHS. Ferguson, a Confederate purchasing agent in England, sent Lee a uniform and other items in November 1863 that were lost to the blockade. He sent this uniform to Lee in August 1864 and it is very likely the same one Lee wore at Appomattox on April 9, 1865. Edward D. C. Campbell, Jr., "The Fabric of Command: R. E. Lee, Confederate Insignia, and the Perception of Rank," *VMHB* (April 1990), 283.

14 OR 43, pt. 2, 891. Page, the scion of two of Virginia's leading families (the Pages and the Randolphs) was named after several ancestors prominent in the Commonwealth's history. He lived at Lower Brandon in Prince George Co. Krick, *Staff Officers in Gray*, 236; Richard Channing Moore Page, *Genealogy of the Page Family in Virginia* (New York, 1893), 90.

15 Manarin, *Henrico County: Field of Honor*, vol. 2, 747; Field, "Campaign of 1864 & 1865," 558; OR 43, pt. 2, 891-2; Krick, *CW Weather*, 140.

16 Newsome, *Richmond Must Fall*, 85; OR 42, pt. 1, 853. Longstreet also appeared during this fighting in civilian clothes and his arm in a sling. Newsome, *Richmond Must Fall*, 85. Lee and Longstreet almost certainly conferred on this occasion, and one of Longstreet's staff officers recalled that "Longstreet reported for duty" on this date, but does not provide any details. Dawson, *Reminiscences*, 202.

correspondence between him and "Extra Billy" regarding Early. He reviews Henry Heth's request to have the 22nd Virginia Battalion disbanded.[17]

October 15, Saturday (Chaffin's Farm): Lee places William Pendleton in charge of the artillery at Petersburg and Bermuda Hundred and Porter Alexander in command of the guns north of the James. Lee favorably endorses A. P. Hill's request for Moxley Sorrel's promotion to brigadier general to command the Georgia brigade in Mahone's Division.[18]

October 16, Sunday (Chaffin's Farm): Lee is away from headquarters until after sundown, and is accompanied by Jefferson Davis when he returns. The two remain in conference until late in the night, when the president returns to Richmond escorted by Walter Taylor. The general telegraphs Sec. Seddon that John Mosby attacked the B&O outside Martinsburg on the 14th.[19]

October 17, Monday (Chaffin's Farm): Gen. Lee dines with Gen. Pendleton, who neglects to bless the meal. Lee instructs John Breckinridge to reinforce both Early and Richmond, and issues orders for Longstreet to resume command of the First Corps, with Anderson taking Hoke's and Johnson's divisions.[20]

October 18, Tuesday (Chaffin's Farm): Lee notifies Breckinridge that he has no objection to a prisoner exchange including free blacks but instructs that "recaptured slaves of Confederate citizens will not be exchanged," and notifies Richmond of two minor skirmishes in Breckinridge's department. A "great fire" breaks out in Richmond during the night near the Capitol, which destroys several structures and threatens many homes along Franklin Street, including Lee's.[21]

October 19, Wednesday (Chaffin's Farm): Lee writes a long letter of complaint to U. S. Grant about the use of prisoners as laborers on the Dutch Gap Canal, and in a separate communication accepts a proposal to distribute relief articles to POWs. James Longstreet officially returns to duty, taking command on the north side of the James River; his aide, T. J. Goree, observes that "Lee seems delighted to have him back again."[22]

The general authorizes Gen. Breckinridge to exchange his prisoners, including black troops, and Lee notifies Sec. Seddon of Breckinridge's continued success in eastern Tennessee, putting the Federals to flight toward Knoxville. Lee approves disbanding the 22nd Virginia Battalion "for cowardly conduct on every battlefield from Gettysburg to the present time."[23]

---

17 OR 43, pt. 2, 893-8; Hewitt, ed., *OR Supplement*, pt. 2, vol. 71, 711-4. The 22nd VA Battalion had performed miserably on several occasions during the war and Gen. Heth wanted it broken up and the men assigned to other units. Lee asked for specific examples of misbehavior, which Heth provided on the 18th. Ibid.

18 WHT to WNP, Oct. 15, 1864, WNP papers, UNC; REL endorsement on A. P. Hill to REL, Oct. 13, 1864, Sorrel CSR. The brigade had been without a commander since the death of Victor Girardy at Fussell's Mill.

19 Tower, *Lee's Adjutant*, 197; OR 43, pt. 1, 663. Taylor did not mention where Lee went, but only noted when he returned to Chaffin's with President Davis. It is likely that Lee rode to Richmond for church in the morning.

20 Lee, *Memoirs of WNP*, 375-6; Johnson, *Lee the Christian*, 145-6; OR 43, pt. 2, 899; SO 248, Oct. 17, 1864, REL HQ papers, VHS. Pendleton was so bothered by his oversight that he wrote to Lee two days later to apologize. Johnson, *Lee the Christian*, 375-6. Longstreet officially resumed command on the 19th. OR 42, pt. 1, 871.

21 OR 7, Series 2, 1009; OR 39, pt. 1, 847; Charleston *Mercury*, Oct. 24, 1864.

22 OR 7, Series 2, 1009-12; Wert, *Longstreet*, 393; Freeman, *Lee*, vol. 3, 510; Thomas W. Cutrer, ed., *Longstreet's Aide: The Civil War Letters of Major Thomas J. Goree* (Charlottesville, VA, 1995), 137. Grant replied on the 20th that he stopped using POWs at Dutch Gap since the Rebels stopped using black POWs around Fort Gilmer. OR 7, Series 2, 1018-9.

23 OR 39, pt. 3, 830; Freeman, *Lee's Dispatches*, 301-2; Hewitt, ed., *OR Supplement*, pt. 2, vol. 71, 711-4; undated SO, WHT papers, SH. Gen. Heth told Lee of the battalion's poor performance at Gettysburg, Mine Run, Bethesda Church, and Weldon Railroad, adding that at the latter engagement, the recently returned Gen. James Archer stayed with the unit in

October 20, Thursday (Chaffin's Farm): Lee meets with a delegation of the prisoners forced to work at Dutch Gap; after they depart Lee informs Porter Alexander of their being forced to help with the digging and instructs him to ensure the accuracy of the artillery fire on the canal. He learns of Jubal Early's defeat at Cedar Creek yesterday and informs both Breckinridge and Sec. Seddon of it, instructing the former to aid Early however he can. Lee issues orders reiterating that fraternization with the enemy is strictly prohibited, and he receives a request from William Pendleton to establish regular courier service between the ANV's headquarters and his own at Petersburg. Custis is promoted to major general.[24]

October 21, Friday (Chaffin's Farm): Lee has salted mackerel for breakfast, after which he writes to Gen. Pendleton to allay his concerns over not blessing the food at their meal several days before. Lee provides the War Department with the figures for Early's loss at Cedar Creek, and recommends that the forts at Wilmington, North Carolina, be issued 30 days rations in case they are cut off from outside supply. Lee congratulates Breckinridge for his victory at Saltville, but sharply condemns the execution of black troops there and wants the guilty officers arrested and brought to trial. Steady rain during the night.[25]

October 22, Saturday (Chaffin's Farm/ Richmond): Lee and Longstreet meet with Capt. John K. Mitchell, commander of the James River fleet, in Richmond regarding how best for the Army and Navy to work together and how to prevent the enemy from placing torpedoes in the James.[26]

October 23, Sunday (Richmond/Chaffin's Farm): Lee attends church service at St. Paul's in Richmond with Longstreet and President Davis, after which he returns to Chaffin's farm. He informs Seddon of his recent communications with Grant regarding POWs being used at Dutch Gap, and receives a letter from Mary in the evening. Jed Hotchkiss arrives at headquarters shortly before midnight and "had a long talk about matters in the Valley."[27]

October 24, Monday (Chaffin's Farm): Lee meets again with Jed Hotchkiss after Ewell and Hotchkiss inspect the lines around Fort Gilmer. Lee submits a proposal to Capt. Mitchell on how his gunboats can keep the Federals from getting in rear of Pickett on the Howlett Line. He receives a letter from Nannie Peyton of Fauquier County informing him that the enemy arrested many civilians in her neighborhood, including her husband Dr. Robert Peyton, and deported them to Alexandria.[28]

October 25, Tuesday (Chaffin's Farm): Scout Frank Stringfellow brings Lee letters from President Davis

---

person and could not curb their bad behavior. Heth added that the 22nd's commander, Lt. Col. Edward Tayloe, confessed to him that he had no confidence in his men, a statement that Taylor later recounted. Hewitt, ed., *OR Supplement*, pt. 2, vol. 71, 711-4.

24 Gallagher, *Fighting for the Confederacy*, 489; *OR* 43, pt. 1, 553; *OR* 43, pt. 2, 901; circular, Oct. 20, 1864, Clingman papers, UNC; WNP order book, MOC; Custis CSR. The timing of the meeting with the prisoners seems odd if Lee wrote to Grant about them the day before, but Porter Alexander is almost always correct as to dates. It is not out of the realm of possibility that Lee complained to Grant about them before meeting with them, or Alexander was wrong about the date.

25 REL to unknown, Oct. 21, 1864, REL papers, W&L; REL to WNP, Oct. 21, 1864, REL papers, W&L; *OR* 43, pt. 1, 553; *OR* 42, pt. 3, 1156-7; *OR* 7, Series 2, 1020; Krick, *CW Weather*, 140.

26 *OR* 42, pt. 3, 1174; Richmond *Enquirer*, Oct. 24, 1864, REL newspaper references, DSF papers, LVA.

27 Richmond *Daily Dispatch*, Oct. 24, 1864, REL newspaper references, DSF papers, LVA; *OR* 7, Series 2, 1029-30; Dowdey, *Wartime Papers*, 865; McDonald, *Make Me a Map*, 241.

28 McDonald, *Make Me a Map*, 241; *OR* 42, pt. 3, 1175-6; Dowdey, *Wartime Papers*, 865. On this date Taylor declined an invitation to be best man in a friend's wedding, citing the amount of work he had at HQ: "You may see how utterly impossible it is for me to be absent from my post. This military dept. now embraces all of Virginia and North Carolina and all the troops in the two states report to Gen. Lee. I am his only Adjutant General. This is enough to give you a faint idea of what rests on my shoulders, and of the amount of labor which daily claims my attention. I cannot be absent even for one day." WHT to "Lucien," Oct. 24, 1864, WHT papers, VMI.

and Rev. Kensey Johns Stewart proposing some sort of clandestine operation apparently involving Confederate secret service operatives in Canada; Lee is not impressed with Rev. Stewart or the proposed operation and writes to Davis his opposition to the project. He writes to Mary advising against her return to Richmond, because of her physical condition and also the scarcity of supplies in the capital: "Everyone who has no business in Richmond, or who cannot do the State some good by being there ought to be away. It adds to the number to be fed, and otherwise may increase our difficulties."[29]

October 26, Wednesday (Chaffin's Farm): Lee forwards to Sec. Seddon a letter from Capt. Mitchell hoping that he can use his influence to create better harmony between the Army and the Navy. Lee informs Wade Hampton that he has no additional troops to send to the Petersburg front as requested, but he accedes to Hampton's request to have conscripts assigned to the cavalry.[30]

October 27, Thursday (Chaffin's Farm/ Darbytown Road): In the morning Lee goes to the front inspecting the defenses along New Market and Darbytown roads, meeting with Hoke and possibly Longstreet also. He later notifies Seddon of Longstreet's repulse of an attack on Williamsburg Road, Heth's attack at Burgess's Mill south of Petersburg, and Mosby's capture of Gen. Alfred Duffie. He adds that if Grant sends a force against Wilmington reinforcements should come from Charleston and vice versa. Heavy storm in the afternoon with rain continuing during the night.[31]

October 28, Friday (Chaffin's Farm): Lee provides Richmond with further details of Hill's engagement at Petersburg and Longstreet's fight east of Richmond. The Richmond *Examiner* publishes Lee and Grant's correspondence regarding treatment of black troops.[32]

October 29, Saturday (Chaffin's Farm): Lee writes Gov. Vance thanking him for his efforts at mobilizing North Carolina's reserves and requesting that troops from western North Carolina be sent to reinforce Wilmington. He requests John Mosby to make a raid on the Manassas Gap Railroad and sends a letter of condolence to Wade Hampton for the death of his son at Petersburg. He informs Seddon that Hampton pursued the enemy as they withdrew and also of victories by Lunsford Lomax at Milford.[33]

October 30, Sunday (Chaffin's Farm/Richmond): Lee attends church at St. Paul's in Richmond with James Longstreet.[34]

---

29 Freeman, *Lee's Dispatches*, 302-4; Dowdey, *Wartime Papers*, 865-6. Stringfellow was one of Jeb Stuart's most trusted scouts. Freeman could not determine exactly what Rev. Stewart and Stringfellow proposed, but Edwin Lee was also somehow involved. Freeman, *Lee's Dispatches*, 304 n1. Custis's biographer proposed that it involved some sort of special intelligence force that operated under Custis's direction. Yates, *Perfect Gentleman*, vol. 1, 310-1. The only study of Confederate secret service operations concludes that it was much more than that, and was somehow involved with the plot to kidnap Abraham Lincoln, and possibly the original kidnapping scheme itself. Tidwell, *Come Retribution*, 20-2.

30 OR 42, pt. 3, 1173-7.

31 Barefoot, *General R. F. Hoke*, 234; Newsome, *Richmond Must Fall*, 154; OR 42, pt. 1, 853; OR 42, pt. 3, 1177; Krick, *CW Weather*, 140. Lee departed HQ alone as Venable was on leave and Marshall was still quite sick; Taylor went after him and left the ailing Marshall to run HQ. Tower, *Lee's Adjutant*, 200. Hoke recalled that this was the only occasion during which he ever noticed nervousness on Lee's part. Barefoot, *General R. F. Hoke*, 234. Duffie, a French nobleman and decorated veteran of the French army, was captured by Mosby's men near Bunker Hill, WV, on the 20th. Warner, *Generals in Blue*, 131-2.

32 OR 42, pt. 1, 852-3; Richmond *Examiner*, Oct. 28, 1864, REL newspaper references, DSF papers, LVA.

33 OR 42, pt. 3, 1183; OR 43, pt. 2, 909; REL to Hampton, Oct. 29, 1864, REL papers, MOC; OR 42, pt. 1, 854; OR 43, pt. 1, 553. Burgess's Mill was especially costly for Hampton, whose eldest son Wade Jr. was wounded and his other son Thomas was killed. Krick, *Staff Officers in Gray*, 147.

34 Richmond *Examiner*, Oct. 31, 1864, REL newspaper references, DSF papers, LVA.

October 31, Monday (Chaffin's Farm): Lee writes to A. P. Hill and Wade Hampton concerning errors in Hill's report of Burgess's Mill regarding Hampton's role in the battle. Lee informs Sec. Seddon that a change is needed in the Valley cavalry: "As soon as opportunity offers I desire to reorganize the cavalry in the Valley. The men in my opinion are as good as any in the service. The want of efficient officers and the absence of proper discipline and instruction has been its ruin."[35]

The general requests that cavalry be sent to Wilmington from South Carolina, and notifies of a skirmish by Mahone yesterday. He forwards to the War Department a letter from Custis regarding desertions from his local reserves; Lee points out that this not only weakens the lines but also the Richmond workforce. He approves a recent recommendation from one of John Breckinridge's commanders to pardon all Unionist Tennesseans who lay down their arms. During the evening, Lee tells Walter Taylor that he intends to return to the Petersburg front very soon.[36]

---

[35] OR 42, pt. 1, 954; REL to Hill, Oct. 31, 1864, REL HQ papers, VHS; Robert K. Krick, *The Smoothbore Volley that Doomed the Confederacy: The Death of Stonewall Jackson and Other Chapters on the Army of Northern Virginia* (Baton Rouge, LA, 2002), 195. Hampton complained that his men were slighted in Lee's report to the War Department; Lee explained that his report was based on preliminary information from A. P. Hill, and that the telegrapher changed the punctuation in transmitting the report, which completely changed its tone. OR 42, pt. 1, 954.

[36] OR 42, pt. 3, 1179, 1185; OR 42, pt. 1, 854; OR 39, pt. 3, 847-8; Tower, *Lee's Adjutant*, 201.

November 1864

Jubal Early's defeat at Cedar Creek on October 19 and William T. Sherman's earlier progress through Georgia and the fall of Atlanta sealed Abraham Lincoln's reelection, and with it an assurance of the continuation of the war to its final conclusion. "We must therefore make up our minds for another four years of war," Lee lamented to his wife Mary.[1] Three days later Sherman burned part of the city and marched south and east out of Atlanta into the heart of Georgia.

Lee left the Richmond area and returned south of the James River to the Petersburg front, inspecting the Howlett Line on the way. A new headquarters site was needed because, with the trees devoid of their foliage, Violet Bank was fully visible to enemy guns. Picking the new location fell to Walter Taylor, who selected a home owned by the Beasley family in the western part of Petersburg. Lee dined at Dodson's Tavern two blocks away several times during this time, and made social calls to others in the city.[2]

A thorough inspection tour of the Petersburg lines was needed because of Lee's lengthy absence from that front. Judge Robert Ould, the Confederate agent for the exchange of prisoners who held the rank of colonel (and who had close ties to the Confederate secret service) accompanied the general on one of the inspection rides.[3] Engineer Charles Dimmock, who designed and oversaw the construction of ten miles of earthworks and more than 50 batteries around Petersburg (later known as the Dimmock Line) encountered Lee several times during this period. "Lately I have been much gratified by complimentary notices of my work by Gen. Lee," he wrote his wife. "The Gen. with Lt. Gen. A. P. Hill passed over my line and expressed great satisfaction at the amount of work done and the creditable manner of its execution . . ." Dimmock continued:

> A few days since the two Gens. mentioned were at Gen. Mahone's Head Qrs. Seeing them at Gen. M's tent [sic] I approached when Gen. Lee arose and advanced two steps towards me extending his hand. He inquired most kindly for mother and the girls and as to my health. He then said, "Captain you have done a great deal of work since I was last here and it is well done." This from one rarely given to expressions of approbation even where they are deserved may be esteemed the most highly prized notice that has been taken of me during the war. The manner from him was kinder than the utterances. . . . Gen. Mahone's Division has lately been removed from the trenches and another substituted in its place and I have been placed in charge of work more to the right and fortunately where no bullets nor shells are constantly flying and yet Gen. Lee again compliments me by desiring that the work left unfinished be completed according to my plans and that I supervise their completion.[4]

President Davis summoned Lee to meet with him in Richmond to discuss how to oppose Sherman, who, after refusing to follow Hood's Army of Tennessee into Alabama, was marching essentially unopposed across Georgia. Lee knew there were not enough soldiers to resist the

---

1 REL to Mrs. REL, Nov. 12, 1864, REL papers, LOC.

2 Calkins, *CW Petersburg*, 16.

3 OR 42, pt. 3, 521-2. A spy reported Ould's presence with Lee, but he did not state which date or the precise location, only that it occurred prior to Nov. 5. Ibid.

4 Dimmock to Elizabeth Selden Dimmock, Nov. 13, 1864, Dimmock papers, VHS.

Federals at every point, and cautioned the president that if his own lines were weakened it could be disastrous. If Sherman was going to be stopped, Gen. Beauregard as head of the Department of the West would have to do it.

When Lee returned to Petersburg, his headquarters was not where it was when he left. To his surprise, the commander of the Army of Northern Virginia had been evicted from his quarters by a couple newly wed. Taylor's selection of Edge Hill farm several miles west of the city put the headquarters much closer to the army's slowly extending right flank. According to one leading historian of the campaign, "Lee enjoyed commodious quarters here—the best he had ever experienced in the field."[5]

Still convinced the best position for Richard Ewell was an administrative post to organize the Confederacy's cavalry branch, Lee summoned Ewell to Petersburg during the month. The pair of generals discussed placing Ewell at the head of the new cavalry bureau over a lunch of sweet potatoes.[6]

The 39th Virginia Cavalry Battalion remained as the headquarters guard and was not transferred into regular service as some of the troopers feared. However, there was some sort of trouble in the unit. Its commander, Maj. J. H. Richardson was court-martialed for some unknown offense and temporarily removed from command. By late November he was back in charge, although docked three months' pay.[7]

By the end of the month the armies had settled in for what looked to be a long and cold winter.

* * *

---

[5] Greene, *CW Petersburg*, 226.

[6] Martin, *Road to Glory*, 339-40.

[7] G. M. Coiner to father, Nov. 26, 1864, Coiner family papers, VHS. Few details are known about this incident, including the nature of the infraction, and nothing about it appears in Richardson's CSR. Neither history of the 39th sheds any light on Richardson's situation. See, generally, Driver, *39th Virginia Cavalry Battalion*, and Michael C. Hardy, *Lee's Bodyguards: The 39th Virginia Cavalry Battalion* (Charleston, SC, 2019).

November 1, Tuesday (Chaffin's Farm/Howlett Line/Petersburg): Gens. Lee and Pickett inspect the Howlett Line in the morning, while Walter Taylor rides ahead to Petersburg to locate a new place for Lee's headquarters. Taylor secures the Beasley house on High Street to use for that purpose.[8]

Lee receives a letter from Davis regarding the resumed feud between Longstreet and Evander Law; he informs Seddon that enemy movements forced the evacuation of Plymouth and Washington, North Carolina. He writes to Ernestine Stevens of Richmond, sending a star from his uniform.[9]

November 2, Wednesday (Petersburg): Lee inspects the lines around Petersburg, and writes to President Davis regarding the shrinking of the army: "Unless we can obtain a reasonable approximation to [Grant's] force I fear a great calamity will befall us. On last Thursday at Burgess's Mill we had three brigades to oppose six divisions. . . . I always find something to correct on the lines, but the great necessity I observed . . . was the want of men." Rain in the afternoon.[10]

November 3, Thursday (Petersburg): Gen. Lee inspects the lines southwest of Petersburg and appoints David Weisiger to command of William Mahone's brigade. The general asks Harry Heth for his opinion regarding a request from Lt. Col. Tayloe of the 22nd Virginia Battalion to have his unit combined with a heavy artillery unit in the Richmond fortifications, rather than disbanded altogether. Rain continues.[11]

November 4, Friday (Petersburg/Dinwiddie Court House): Lee inspects the cavalry lines on the extreme right, accompanied by his sons Rooney and Rob. They also tour the battlefield at Burgess's Mill with Wade Hampton. Gen. Lee moves his headquarters to the vicinity of Dinwiddie Court House, and Rob spends the night the with his father. Rain continues.[12]

November 5, Saturday (Dinwiddie Court House/Petersburg): Gen. Lee goes back to Petersburg, sending Walter Taylor ahead to establish his headquarters. The staffer once again selects the Beasley house.[13]

---

8 REL to Pickett, Nov. 1, 1864, REL papers, W&L; Freeman, *Lee's Dispatches*, 305; Wise, *17th Virginia*, 204; Tower, *Lee's Adjutant*, 202; Calkins, *CW Petersburg*, 15. Lee could not return to his previous campsite on the lawn of Violet Bank because the lack of foliage exposed the home to artillery fire. Freeman, *Lee*, vol. 3, 515. The Beasley house is at 558 High Street and is a private residence. A small stone marker in the front notes that it once served as the ANV HQ. At least one historian believes HQ was actually in an outbuilding rather than the main house itself, a belief shared by the present owners in 2016. Calkins, *CW Petersburg*, 15. Taylor confided to Bettie that Lee was not at all pleased with his selection of the Beasley house: "I took possession of a fine house—had his room nicely cleaned out and arranged, with a cheerful fire, etc. It was entirely *too* pleasant for him, for he is never so uncomfortable as when comfortable." Tower, *Lee's Adjutant*, 203.

9 Dowdey, *Wartime Papers*, 868; OR 42, pt. 3, 1198; REL to Ernestine Stevens, Nov. 1, 1864, Raphael Semmes papers, VHS. Law did not want to serve under Longstreet because of their bitter falling out in Tennessee, and requested a transfer to Hoke's Division. Dowdey, *Wartime Papers*, 868. Ernestine Stevens was the sister of Gen. Louis Hebert.

10 Dowdey, *Wartime Papers*, 868; OR 42, pt. 1, 908; Wiley, *Norfolk Blues*, 171.

11 Dowdey, *Wartime Papers*, 868; OR 42, pt. 3, 1199; Hewitt, ed., OR *Supplement*, pt. 2, vol. 71, 714-9; Wiley, *Norfolk Blues*, 171.

12 Tower, *Lee's Adjutant*, 203; Lee, *Recollections and Letters of REL*, 139-40; REL Jr. to Agnes, Nov. 6, 1864, Lee family papers, VHS; Wiley, *Norfolk Blues*, 171. The location of Lee's HQ camp is not known. Rob wrote only that it was "near Dinwiddie." REL Jr. to Agnes, Nov. 6, 1864, Lee family papers, VHS. Lee instructed Taylor to pack up HQ and move it from the Beasley house to the cavalry lines in "the woods some 8 miles off;" Taylor expected to "remain at least several days" in the new location. Tower, *Lee's Adjutant*, 203.

13 Tower, *Lee's Adjutant*, 203. Taylor was not pleased at Lee's decision to go back to Petersburg. He complained to Bettie of the entire move from Petersburg to the flank and back: "To work I was compelled to go, packing up all my books and records and moving bag and baggage to the woods some 8 miles off. I pitched tents confident we would remain at least several days, when lo! The next morning he informed me he thought we had better move back and so back I came to Petersburg and as I could find no better place . . . I took possession of the same house we had vacated." Tower, *Lee's Adjutant*, 203.

November 6, Sunday (Petersburg): Lee writes to daughter Mildred of his visit with her brothers.[14]

November 7, Monday (Petersburg): Lee sends William Pendleton his comments on a proposed new artillery organization. Rain.[15]

November 8, Tuesday (Petersburg): Lee forwards to the War Department Gen. Lawrence Baker's report regarding the evacuation of Plymouth, noting "General Baker appears to have done all that he could under the circumstances." He comments on a request from Gov. Vance to have D. H. Hill given command in eastern North Carolina, fearing a "want of harmony" if Hill and Braxton Bragg have overlapping commands. He writes to Mary Fairfax regarding the promotion of her son Ethelbert, and explains to Secretary of War Seddon that he recommended that the 22nd Virginia Battalion be disbanded thus Lt. Col. Tayloe's request for it to be converted into a heavy artillery unit is not under consideration. Election Day in the North.[16]

November 9, Wednesday (Petersburg): Lee writes to Fitz regarding command vacancies in his division and how best to reorganize the Valley cavalry units: "I have always had a good opinion of Munford and had him in mind for Wickham's Brigade, but at present cannot recommend him. I hope Rosser will do well. . . . We must do something for the reorganization of the western cavalry." Sculptor Edward Valentine completes his statuette of Lee.[17]

November 10, Thursday (Petersburg): Lee inspects the trenches held by Bushrod Johnson's division.[18]

November 11, Friday (Petersburg): Lee visits a portion of the works occupied by Cadmus Wilcox's division. He writes to Mrs. B. F. Mills that Judge Robert Ould is attempting to get answers from his Union counterpart regarding Maj. Thomas S. Mills's status.[19]

November 12, Saturday (Petersburg): Lee tours the rest of the line of Wilcox's Division and a portion of Mahone's Division, accompanied by Gen. Richard Anderson. The general writes to his wife Mary and sends along several sweet potatoes. He comments on the recent election: "I think you may make up your mind that Mr. Lincoln is reelected President. I have heard nothing reliable on the subject, but I could not see before the election . . . how he could

---

14 REL to Mildred, Nov. 6, 1864, G. B. Lee papers, VHS. He likely attended church this day at Grace Episcopal as it was only a block away from the Beasley house.

15 OR 51, pt. 2, 1050; Tower, *Lee's Adjutant*, 203.

16 Hewitt, ed., OR *Supplement*, vol. 7, 529; OR 42, pt. 3, 1163; REL to Mary R. Fairfax, Nov. 8, 1864, Fairfax family papers, LVA; OR *Supplement*, pt. 2, vol. 71, 714-9; Long, *CW Day by Day*, 594. D. H. Hill was one of Braxton Bragg's most vocal critics after Chickamauga, thus Lee's concerns were not without merit. Bragg was assigned to command all of North Carolina east of the Blue Ridge Mountains three days after this letter was penned. OR 42, pt. 3, 1209. Fairfax was serving in the Signal Corps, assigned to Heth's HQ. REL to Fairfax, Nov. 8, 1864, Fairfax papers, LVA.

17 REL to Fitz, Nov. 9, 1864, REL papers, Duke; Eicher, *REL: A Life Portrait*, 102. Rosser and Munford were never on friendly terms, and the latter faulted the former for the defeat at Tom's Brook in October. Miller, *Decision at Tom's Brook*, 108, 173. Lee's comments regarding Munford may stem from the falling out between Rosser and Munford. Valentine's sculpture was based on images of Lee taken by Vannerson and sent through the blockade in the spring; the work was intended for the Liverpool Bazaar but was completed too late to be included in the exhibition. Eicher, *REL: A Life Portrait*, 102. The Bazaar included a Bible and sword purchased for Lee. Unknown clipping in Charles C. Jones scrapbook, vol. 2, p. 97, REL papers, Duke.

18 Earl J. Hess, *In the Trenches at Petersburg: Field Fortifications & Confederate Defeat* (Chapel Hill, NC, 2009), 207-8. Lee recommended that a second parallel trench be constructed along the portion held by Wise's Brigade. Ibid.

19 A. M. Scales to wife, Nov. 12, 1864, Scales papers, NC Archives; REL to Mills, Nov. 11, 1864, REL papers, VHS. According to Gen. Alfred Scales, on this occasions Gen. Lee "was in fine spirits and more disposed to joke than I ever saw him." Scales to wife, Nov. 12, 1864, Scales papers, NC Archives. Mills was an aide to Richard H. Anderson and was captured at Petersburg on June 21, 1864. After his exchange in Feb. 1865, Mills was assigned to Mahone's staff. Krick, *Staff Officers in Gray*, 222.

fail. . . . We must therefore make up our minds for another four years of war."[20]

November 13, Sunday (Petersburg): Lee attends church at St. Paul's with Taylor. He informs the War Department of Early's recent movements in the Valley.[21]

November 14, Monday (Petersburg/Dinwiddie Court House): Lee goes to the right to inspect the cavalry positions around and past Dinwiddie, and meets with Gen. and Mrs. Hampton. He informs Sec. Seddon that the commander of the POW camp at Salisbury, North Carolina, thinks that several thousand foreign-born prisoners there could be brought into the Confederate army. He declines an offer from Mrs. Shippen to return headquarters to Violet Bank.[22]

November 15, Tuesday (Petersburg): Lee informs Seddon of a small victory by Breckinridge in east Tennessee and instructs Pendleton to deal with a group of artillerymen near Beaver Dam Station about whom the locals complained. He writes a brief note to Mary, after which he receives a letter from her.[23]

November 16, Wednesday (Petersburg): Lee writes to Walter Taylor's brother, Capt. Robert Taylor, sending him an autographed photograph and wishing him a quick recovery from his wound. Lee writes another letter to Mary with family news and requesting that she have some clothing and bedding repaired, and dispatches these along with his note of last night.[24]

November 18, Friday (Petersburg): Lee informs Seddon that Pickett seized a portion of the enemy's picket line last night, and also forwards to him a note from Longstreet concerning the excessive number of deserters from Pickett's Division; Pickett blames the reprieves on sentences of execution for this high number and Lee adds, "The great want in our army is firm discipline."[25]

November 19, Saturday (Petersburg): Lee informs President Davis that the only additional troops that can be sent to oppose William Sherman are those of William Hardee at Charleston and Savannah.[26]

November 20, Sunday (Petersburg): Lee writes to Agnes with a host of family news.[27]

November 21, Monday (Petersburg): Lee writes to Longstreet and Hampton soliciting their views of stripping the Petersburg lines and recalling Early's corps for an offensive against Grant. Lee writes to engineer chief Jeremy Gilmer about the organization

---

20 Wiley, *Norfolk Blues*, 173; REL to Mrs. REL, Nov. 12, 1864, REL papers, LOC. Lee and Anderson were accompanied by others, presumably Wilcox and Mahone and their brigadiers; an artilleryman only recorded Lee and Anderson with "others of lesser note." Wiley, *Norfolk Blues*, 173.

21 Tower, *Lee's Adjutant*, 205; *OR* 43, pt. 1, 553-4.

22 Dowdey, *Wartime Papers*, 869-70; *OR* Series 4, vol. 3, 822-3; REL to Shippen, Nov. 14, 1864, REL papers, MOC. Lee complained later that it is "a ride of over 30 miles when I visit that part of the line." Dowdey, *Wartime Papers*, 869.

23 *OR* 45, pt. 1, 1208; WHT endorsement on WNP to WHT, Nov. 14, 1864, WNP papers, UNC; Dowdey, *Wartime Papers*, 868-9.

24 REL to Robert Taylor, Nov. 16, 1864, Lee papers, SH; Dowdey, *Wartime Papers*, 869. Robert Taylor was Walter's younger brother and an aide to Mahone; he was wounded at the Wilderness and served in an administrative role in Richmond after his recuperation. Krick, *Staff Officers in Gray*, 283.

25 *OR* 42, pt. 1, 854; *OR* 42, pt. 3, 1213.

26 *OR* 44, 869. Hood's Army of Tennessee was no longer directly opposing Sherman. Hood had moved north in an effort to draw Sherman after him, and for a time it worked. When Sherman realized the game being played, he turned the responsibility for stopping Hood over to Gen. George Thomas and returned to Atlanta to prepare for a march across Georgia. Hood, meanwhile, moved west into Alabama in preparation for a move into Tennessee.

27 Dowdey, *Wartime Papers*, 870-1.

of black work gangs for the army, and forwards to Mosby the War Department's approval for him to hang prisoners from George Custer's command in retaliation for the hanging of Mosby's men. President Davis summons Lee to Richmond; Lee informs him that he will come tomorrow morning since the last train for the capital already left. Pvt. William Bell of the Norfolk Light Artillery Blues is assigned to duty as a clerk at ANV headquarters.[28]

November 22, Tuesday (Richmond/Petersburg): Lee meets with President Davis regarding opposing Sherman, and informs the War Department that Early retains control of the central Valley. Light snow.[29]

November 23, Tuesday (Petersburg/Richmond/Edge Hill): While Lee continues his meetings in Richmond, likely including Secretary of War Seddon and commander of Virginia's reserve forces Maj. Gen. James Kemper, Taylor relocates headquarters to the Turnbull house, Edge Hill, several miles west of Petersburg. Lee takes the train to Petersburg, arriving there in the evening to discover the new location of his headquarters; a passenger on the same train observes Lee help a wounded soldier with an arm in a sling put on his overcoat.[30]

November 24, Thursday (Edge Hill): Gen. Lee writes to James Longstreet regarding the potential for an offensive north of the James River.[31]

November 25, Friday (Edge Hill): Lee writes to Mary requesting that she and the girls resume their sock-making as the quartermaster has none to issue, and telling of his discovery of headquarters being moved to Edge Hill; he complains that his door does not shut which allows a number of dogs and cats to seek the warmth of the fireplace in his room.[32]

---

28 *OR* 42, pt. 3, 1222-4; *OR* 3, Series 4, 838-9; *OR* 43, pt. 2, 922-3; *OR* 51, pt. 2, 1053; Wiley, *Norfolk Blues*, 246. Lee originally intended to meet with Hampton in person, but other matters prevented it. *OR* 42, pt. 3, 1223. He almost certainly discussed the idea of a grand offensive with A. P. Hill as well, although no documentation of it survives. Longstreet favored an offensive north of the James River the next time Grant moved against the Southside RR. *OR* 42, pt. 3, 1224. Bell drafted many of the "official" copies of Lee's "Farewell Order" at Appomattox. Wiley, *Norfolk Blues*, 246.

29 *OR* 42, pt. 3, 1222; *OR* 43, pt. 1, 554; Krick, *CW Weather*, 142. Lee may have met with Longstreet to discuss a possible offensive north of the James, as Longstreet requested such a meeting before Lee returned to Petersburg; it is not known whether it took place. If it did, it may also have been on the morning of the 23rd. *OR* 42, pt. 3, 1224.

30 *OR* 3, Series 4, 847; Tower, *Lee's Adjutant*, 207; Dowdey, *Wartime Papers*, 871; Richmond *Whig*, Nov. 28, 1864, REL newspaper references, DSF papers, LVA. Taylor wrote Bettie of the rather odd reason for the relocation of HQ: "A young married couple was waiting impatiently for us to vacate the house we then occupied, and had given a gentle hint for us to depart." He noted that Edge Hill was "the only house available" and had been offered up for that purpose "some time previous." Since Lee was not present, Taylor took it upon himself to arrange the new HQ and took the finest room in the house for his own use at the urging of Mr. Turnbull: "Here I am finely fixed in the parlor with piano, sofas, lounges, pictures, rocking chair, etc., everything as fine as possible for a winter campaign." He noted also Lee's reaction to Taylor's choice of rooms upon touring the venue: "I believe the General was pleased with his room and on entering mine remarked, 'Ah! You are finely fixed; couldn't you find any other room?' 'No,' said I, 'but this will do. I can make myself tolerably comfortable here.' He was struck dumb with amazement at my impudence and soon vanished." Tower, *Lee's Adjutant*, 207. Lee told his wife Mary, "The house that we were occupying was wanted, indeed had been rented by a newly married couple, and they had ejected Col. Taylor that day." Dowdey, *Wartime Papers*, 871. Edge Hill was located at the intersection of the Long Ordinary Road (US 1) and Cox Road (VA 226). The home was burned during the fighting on April 2, 1865. Although the account of Lee on the train is undated, it must refer to this trip because it was the only time he rode the train to Petersburg in the time frame covered by the letter. The unidentified passenger observed a young soldier with his arm in a sling struggling to put on his overcoat, "but in the midst of his efforts, an officer rose from his seat . . . and very carefully and tenderly assisted him, drawing the coat gently over his wounded arm and buttoning it up comfortably, then with a few kind and pleasant words returning to his seat. . . . He was no other than our chief General Robert E. Lee." Richmond *Whig*, Nov. 28, 1864, REL newspaper references, DSF papers, LVA.

31 *OR* 42, pt. 3, 1229. This letter has never been found, but is referenced by Longstreet in a subsequent letter to Lee. Ibid. The fact that Lee expressed his views on this topic to Longstreet in writing suggests the two officers did not meet in Richmond as Longstreet requested.

32 Dowdey, *Wartime Papers*, 871-2.

November 26, Saturday (Edge Hill): Custis is formally placed in command of the local reserve troops manning the lines from Chaffin's Bluff to Fort Gilmer. The New York *Sun* publishes an 1852 letter from Lee to Custis supposedly found at Arlington, which reads in part: "Do your duty in all things like the old Puritan. You cannot do more, you should never wish to do less."[33]

November 27, Sunday (Edge Hill/Petersburg): Gen. Lee and Walter Taylor attend church at St. Paul's.[34]

November 28, Monday (Edge Hill): Lee informs the War Department of the capture of two enemy steamers in the Big Sandy River in West Virginia, and notifies Early of reports that the Federals plan to build a new railroad connecting Winchester and Harrisonburg—if true Lee wants it destroyed and the rails removed for use on Southern railways.[35]

November 29, Tuesday (Edge Hill): Lee learns of the capture of former Gen. Roger Pryor and informs Pryor's wife at her nearby residence. Lee warns Longstreet that the enemy is reported to be preparing for an attack against his lines, and notifies Seddon that several Union ironclads attacked the Howlett battery in the morning. He receives a letter from Mary.[36]

November 30, Wednesday (Edge Hill): Gen. Lee writes to President Davis regarding the state of Wilmington, North Carolina. Gov. Vance wants a portion of Lee's army sent to garrison the city, which Lee does not think is necessary at the present time because no force directly threatens Wilmington. If an attack appears imminent, Lee will react then: "Troops are as much required here as at Wilmington. It is the want all over the country." He informs Adjutant General Cooper that he has no reports of Grant sending troops from Petersburg to Charleston and that Bragg can spare nothing at Wilmington to go to Charleston; he recommends that the roads by which Sherman will approach be barricaded and fords and bridges guarded.

He writes to wife Mary regarding family news and socks for the army, and enclosing money to have his overcoat repaired. He addresses the possibility of meeting with portrait artist Hector Eaches, telling her "I am not in my quarters longer than necessary to transact the business of the office, when I go on the lines," so it would be difficult to find the time to meet with him.[37]

---

33 Custis CSR; Charles A. Graves, *The Forged Letter of General Robert E. Lee* (Richmond, VA, 1914), no pagination. UVA law professor Charles Graves proved this so-called "Duty Letter" to be a forgery, and published several reports in the 1910s to prove his case. The letter, however, continues to be presented as authentic, something even Custis denied.

34 Tower, *Lee's Adjutant*, 209.

35 OR 43, pt. 1, 650; OR 43, pt. 2, 925.

36 Sarah Pryor, *My Day: Reminiscences of a Long Life* (New York, 1909), 216-7; REL to Longstreet, Nov. 29, 1864, REL HQ papers, VHS; OR 42, vol. 3, 1231; Dowdey, *Wartime Papers*, 872. Upset at not having a command, Roger Pryor had resigned his commission in the fall of 1863 and was serving as a cavalry scout around Petersburg. Jeffry D. Wert, "Roger Atkinson Pryor," *Confederate General*, vol. 5, 65. At the time, the Pryors resided at Cottage Farm, the home of Robert McIlwaine west of Petersburg. Cadmus Wilcox, under whom Pryor had served earlier in the war, had his HQ in the yard at Cottage Farm and informed Mrs. Pryor earlier in the day of her husband's capture. Lee sent one of the staff to tell Mrs. Pryor while he waited in the yard. Pryor, *My Day*, 210-7.

37 OR 42, pt. 3, 1214-5, 1235; Dowdey, *Wartime Papers*, 872-3. Eaches was the son of Alexandria mayor Joseph Eaches, and served in the 17th VA until disabled by wounds and captured at Glendale in 1862. He was unfit for field service thereafter and spent the rest of the war detailed to the engineer bureau as a draftsman. R. Lewis Wright, *Artists in Virginia Before 1900* (Charlottesville, VA, 1983), 49; Philip Slaughter, *A Sketch of the Life of Randolph Fairfax* (Baltimore, MD, 1878), 35; Eaches CSR. Eaches's portrait of Lee may have been complete by this time and he wanted to show it to Lee. When he began painting it, and whether Lee sat for it in person, is not known. Eaches bragged to his sister in late October, when he was putting the finishing touches on the portrait, that it was met with the "unqualified approbation of most of the Richmond critics, several gentlemen of the press and also a number of Gen. Lee's intimate personal friends and staff officers. They have done me the honor to pronounce it the best picture of the General that has been painted." Barb Winters, ed., *Letters to Virginia: Correspondence from Three Generations of Alexandrians Before, During, and After the Civil War* (Morley, MO, 2010), 45.

December 1864

Winter slowed but did not bring a complete stop to military operations around Petersburg, as Union forces raided the Weldon Railroad at Hicksford and engaged in smaller actions north of the James River. The campaign against Wilmington, North Carolina, seemed to be ramping up though now that the Shenandoah Valley was no longer in play. Reluctantly, General Lee dispatched Robert Hoke's division to reinforce Braxton Bragg on the Cape Fear River to help protect the invaluable seaport.[1]

Out in the Western Theater, John Bell Hood's Army of Tennessee was all but destroyed in front of Nashville and was retreating, freeing up still more Union troops to join either Gen. U.S. Grant at Richmond/Petersburg, or Gen. William T. Sherman in Georgia. Savannah fell to Sherman, who offered it to President Lincoln as a Christmas present, but its garrison escaped intact and slipped north into the Carolinas.

Keeping the army fed and supplied once again posed larger problems than the enemy. The Army of Northern Virginia teetered on the brink of running out of rations, and its supply of winter clothing was once more so inadequate that Lee enlisted the help of family and friends at home to make socks and gloves. Desertions increased despite Lee's best efforts to curtail them; he believed the lack of supplies was the main motivating factor driving them from the ranks.

The lack of enemy activity allowed Lee to enjoy some semblance of a social life. He visited often with A. P. Hill's wife Dolly, and dined with the Bannister family at their house at Washington and Jefferson streets after attending church.[2] "Gen. Lee comes very frequently to see me," wrote Mrs. Hill. "He is the best and greatest man on earth, brought me the last time some delicious apples."[3]

Around Christmas, a rumor began circulating that Lee had been placed in overall command of all Confederate forces.

* * *

---

1 Bragg was sent to take command at Wilmington in October. When his reassignment was announced, the Richmond *Examiner* famously crowed, "Bragg has been sent to Wilmington. Goodbye Wilmington." Rod Gragg, *Confederate Goliath: The Battle of Fort Fisher* (Baton Rouge, LA, 2006), 27.

2 Greene, *CW Petersburg*, 225.

3 Robertson, *A. P. Hill*, 308.

December 1, Thursday (Edge Hill/Petersburg): Gen. Lee and Gen. Matt Ransom inspect Ransom's portion of the line and he forwards to Richmond a report from A. P. Hill regarding desertions from his corps during past two weeks; Lee notes "scarce provisions, continuous duty in trenches is probably the cause." He informs Mary's physician Dr. Alfred Hughes that he can provide a pass to get his wife through Confederate lines but Hughes will need to get permission from Grant to enter Union lines to go to their home in Wheeling. He makes a donation of $200 for the relief of the citizens of Petersburg.[4]

December 2, Friday (Edge Hill): Lee informs Sec. Seddon that enemy cavalry raided Stony Creek Station on the Weldon Railroad yesterday, capturing the garrison and destroying the depot. He also informs Seddon that Thomas Rosser's cavalry raided the B&O, destroying the railroad shops at Piedmont, West Virgina. The Richmond *Whig* prints Lee's "Duty Letter."[5]

December 3, Saturday (Edge Hill): The Richmond *Daily Dispatch* publishes an article recounting Brig. Gen. Archibald Gracie saving Lee's life by pulling him down from atop the trenches.[6]

December 4, Sunday (Edge Hill/Petersburg): Lee attends church at St. Paul's accompanied by Walter Taylor and Gen. Heth's wife Harriet, riding with her and others back to headquarters afterwards.[7]

December 5, Monday (Edge Hill): Lee alerts John Breckinridge that he may have to take command in the Shenandoah Valley, and updates President Davis on enemy movements from the Valley to Petersburg, noting with no little understatement, "All we want to resist them is men."[8]

December 6, Tuesday (Edge Hill): Gen. Lee informs President Davis that the Union VI Corps is reported to be leaving the Shenandoah Valley for Petersburg, and therefore Lee will begin recalling Jubal Early's troops to rejoin the main army. Lee's son Rob comes to visit his father and spends the night at headquarters. Also visiting Lee is Col. John S. Mosby, who dines with the general.[9]

December 7, Wednesday (Edge Hill): Lee informs the Richmond War Department that the Federals are moving in force on the Jerusalem Plank Road, but he is unsure what this movement means. He requests that Early's Shenandoah Valley troops be brought back to the capital area as quickly as possible. Enemy gunboats once again fire on the Howlett battery, prompting Lee to order that Longstreet reinforce the Howlett Line and that E. Porter Alexander go there

---

4   Pearce, *Chambers Diary*, 232; *OR* 42, pt. 3, 1249; REL to Hughes, Dec. 1, 1864, Heritage Auctions, lot # 25440, Dec. 1-2, 2006 auction; Greene, *CW Petersburg*, 224.

5   *OR* 42, pt. 1, 854; *OR* 43, pt. 1, 667; Graves, *Forged Letter*.

6   Richmond *Daily Dispatch*, Dec. 3, 1864. Archibald Gracie was born into a prominent family in New York City and married into the wealthy Mayo family of Richmond before the war. He rose from major of the 11th AL to command of one of Bushrod Johnson's brigades and was killed Dec. 2 at Petersburg. William C. Davis, "Archibald Gracie, Jr.," *Confederate General*, vol. 3, 21-2. The date of the Lee-Gracie incident is not known, but one witness put it shortly before the Battle of the Crater (July 30, 1864). George N. Saussy, "Generals Lee and Gracie at the Crater," *CV*, vol. 17, 160. A recent Petersburg study puts the incident much later, happening sometime in November. Hess, *In the Trenches*, 211. Gracie's son survived the sinking of the *RMS Titanic* and wrote a book about the ordeal, as well as one about the Battle of Chickamauga.

7   Tower, *Lee's Adjutant*, 208.

8   *OR* 43, pt. 2, 936; *OR* 42, pt. 3, 1254-5.

9   *OR* 42, pt. 3, 1256; Dowdey, *Wartime Papers*, 876; Mitchell, *Mosby Letters*, 125, 235. Dinner consisted of a mutton leg. Lee joked that one of the staff must have stolen it, given the scarcity of such items at HQ. Mitchell, *Mosby Letters*, 125. Years later, Mosby wrote that Lee told him on this occasion that Joe Johnston should never have moved from the Rapidan to Richmond in 1862, but rather should have moved immediately against Washington once McClellan moved to the Peninsula. Russell, *Mosby Memoirs*, 105.

in person to oversee it. Rob departs headquarters, borrowing Lee's horse Ajax to do so. Rain.[10]

December 8, Thursday (Edge Hill): Lee meets with Pendleton in the morning about the Union force moving toward Hicksford and informs Sec. Seddon of the latest intelligence on the enemy column, noting Gens. Hill and Hampton are in pursuit. He requests troops be sent to Weldon, thinking the enemy may be preparing to invade North Carolina. He also writes to Seddon regarding Rosser's raid into West Virginia and encloses captured letters outlining the measures the enemy are taking to eliminate John McNeil's partisans there.[11]

December 9, Friday (Edge Hill): Gen. Lee instructs Longstreet to assist in retaking ground lost on Pickett's front, and requests W. H. C. Whiting to send whatever troops he can from Wilmington to help defend the Weldon Railroad. Sleet.[12]

December 10, Saturday (Edge Hill): Lee requests Longstreet to make a reconnaissance in his front, and meets with William N. Pendleton regarding shifting artillery from Petersburg to Drewry's Bluff. Lee briefs Sec. Seddon of A. P. Hill's operations in pursuit of the Federals around Hicksford, and of minor moves at Hatcher's Run and on Longstreet's front. Lee orders all officers at Camp Lee to rejoin their units. Snow and sleet.[13]

December 11, Sunday (Edge Hill/Petersburg): Lee and Taylor attend church in the morning; afterwards Taylor goes to visit friends and does not return to headquarters until nightfall. Lee informs Seddon that while he is grateful for an extension allowing longer use of black laborers, he laments that he still doesn't have enough to even replace all the army's white teamsters. He sends a letter of condolence to Gen. Gracie's widow.[14]

December 12, Monday (Edge Hill): Lee issues orders condemning depredations done to local civilians, calling for better behavior by the men and better diligence by their officers in keeping control.[15]

December 13, Tuesday (Edge Hill): Lee informs Richmond that the Federals raided along the Weldon Railroad to Hicksford, ripping up several miles of track; at the same time they also launched movements up the Roanoke River and against Kinston but have since fallen back. He requests that "every available man" be sent to Savannah to oppose Sherman, and if Grant should weaken his forces in front of Petersburg, he will send a portion of the ANV to Georgia. He writes to Custis, apologizing for not being able to come to Richmond to see him but enemy movements have prevented it; he jokes that Lee has promised photos of himself to several young ladies but Custis has not gotten him the images and he thinks Custis is sullying the family name: "I am afraid that you will ruin my character with the young ladies, and may cause that of the family for fidelity to be suspected. . . . I am taxed with breach of promise."[16]

December 14, Wednesday (Edge Hill/Richmond): Lee informs President Davis that the army is out of meat

---

10 OR 42, pt. 3, 1256-7; Gallagher, *Fighting for the Confederacy*, 500; REL to Longstreet, Dec. 7, 1864, REL HQ papers, VHS; Dowdey, *Wartime Papers*, 876.

11 Lee, *Memoirs of WNP*, 378; OR 42, pt. 3, 1259; OR 43, pt. 1, 667-9.

12 REL to Longstreet, Dec. 9, 1864, REL HQ papers, VHS; OR 42, pt. 3, 1263; Hagood, *Memoirs*, 315.

13 REL to Longstreet, Dec. 10, 1864, REL HQ papers, VHS; WNP to James Corley, Dec. 10, 1864, WNP papers, UNC; OR 42, pt. 1, 855; SO 302, Dec. 10, 1864, REL HQ papers, VHS; Latrobe diary, Dec. 10, 1864, VHS.

14 Tower, *Lee's Adjutant*, 211; OR 42, pt. 3, 1267; Archibald Gracie, Jr., "Gen. Archibald Gracie," *CV*, vol. 5, 429-30. Taylor did not specify whether they went to Grace or St. Paul's.

15 OR 42, pt. 3, 1270. Longstreet references a message from Lee on this date, but Lee's message is lost. Based on Longstreet's context, it likely concerned a report of enemy troops arriving. Ibid.

16 OR 42, pt. 3, 1271; Freeman, *Lee's Dispatches*, 306-7; Dowdey, *Wartime Papers*, 876. Jefferson Davis referenced a communication from Lee on this date, but it is has not been found. It was likely about the Valley. OR 42, pt. 3, 1272.

rations, and there may be enough in Richmond for a day or two; there is rumored to be a supply in Wilmington. He tells Davis also that both sides are removing troops from the Valley, and the recent Union expeditions in North Carolina failed; "I do not know what may be General Grant's next move," but he fears Savannah will fall. He writes to Gov. Vance regarding "illicit trade" with the enemy in eastern North Carolina, and instructs John Breckinridge to send his cavalry into the Kanawha Valley if the Federals have reduced their strength there. Lee goes to Richmond to meet with Commissary General Lucius Northrop regarding the food crisis facing the army.[17]

December 15, Thursday (Richmond/Edge Hill): Lee returns to Petersburg, where he receives a box from his wife with clothes and a large supply of apples.[18]

December 16, Friday (Edge Hill): The Richmond *Sentinel* reprints the "Duty Letter."[19]

December 17, Saturday (Edge Hill): Lee advises Richmond that the XIX Corps is reported to have arrived at Petersburg from the Valley, but that Breckinridge reports the enemy threat to the lead mines in southwest Virginia gone. He writes to Mary thanking her for the recent care package but directing her to send any such packages to him via Maj. D. H. Wood to ensure prompt delivery.[20]

December 18, Sunday (Edge Hill/Petersburg): Lee and Taylor attend church service at St. Paul's in the morning. Later in the day Lee learns of a large enemy force leaving Hampton Roads and warns Seddon, Vance, and Bragg that it is likely bound for Wilmington; accordingly he instructs Longstreet to prepare Hoke's Division to go to Wilmington.[21]

December 19, Monday (Edge Hill): Lee informs President Davis that Beauregard and Hardee alone can determine if Savannah must be evacuated without a fight, in which case the troops can be saved; Lee can send no aid: "If Hoke and Johnson are sent south it will necessitate the abandonment of Richmond with the present opposing force." He orders Breckinridge to gather all the local reserves and fortify along New River, and requests a meeting with Longstreet tomorrow. Lee writes to Col. Henry Cabell that he received a request from the "friends of Mr. Leigh Robinson" of the Richmond Howitzers for him to have a furlough over Christmas and Lee hopes Cabell will send a formal request for it. He also writes to Lucy Minnegerode regarding Robinson, advising that he looks favorably upon the request, and includes a personal note of sympathy, "The death of every man in this Army cuts me to the heart." He writes to his brother Smith, enclosing a pass through the lines for a friend of Smith's.[22]

---

17 Dowdey, *Wartime Papers*, 877; OR 42, pt. 3, 1272; REL to Vance, Dec. 14, 1864, Lee papers, SH; OR 43, pt. 2, 938; Lee, *General Lee's City*, 128; Willard E. Wright, "Some Letters of Lucius Bellinger Northrop, 1860-1865," *VMHB* (Oct. 1960), 470-1.

18 Dowdey, *Wartime Papers*, 877. Very little is known regarding this apparently short trip to Richmond, other than that he met with Commissary General Lucius Northrop.

19 Graves, *Forged Letter*.

20 OR 42, pt. 3, 1278; Freeman, *Lee's Dispatches*, 309; Dowdey, *Wartime Papers*, 877-8. Wood was responsible for procuring transportation for soldiers in Richmond. Krick, *Staff Officers in Gray*, 308.

21 Tower, *Lee's Adjutant*, 212; OR 42, pt. 3, 1278-80; Carmichael, *Audacity Personified*, 119; REL to Bragg, Dec. 18, 1864, REL papers, NC Archives. Taylor noted that Lee was in ill-humor this day, apparently because Taylor went to visit friends after church rather than returning to HQ to handle paperwork. Tower, *Lee's Adjutant*, 212. Venable also commented on his chief's demeanor, noting that he intended to ask Lee for permission to go on leave, but told his wife, "If you had the pleasure of Gen. Lee's acquaintance you would debate with yourself about asking him for anything." Venable to wife, Dec. 18, 1864, in Margaret C. M. Venable memoirs, UVA.

22 OR 44, 966; OR 45, pt. 2, 711; REL to Longstreet, Dec. 19, 1864, REL HQ papers, VHS; REL to Cabell, Dec. 19, 1864, REL papers, UVA; REL to Minnegerode, Dec. 19, 1864, Raab Collection; REL to S. S. Lee, Dec. 19, 1864, Davis collection, Tulane. Cabell was chief of artillery of McLaws/Kershaw's Division. Krick, *Lee's Colonels*, 79.

December 20, Tuesday (Edge Hill/Richmond): Lee meets with Longstreet and Hoke in Richmond in the morning. The Richmond *Sentinel* publishes a letter "from a source entitled to know" repudiating the "Duty Letter." Rain during the evening.[23]

December 21, Wednesday (Richmond): Lee's stay in Richmond continues. Rain in the morning.[24]

December 22, Thursday (Richmond/Edge Hill): Lee returns to Petersburg and meets with Pendleton. He learns that Bragg's force at Wilmington exhausted its meat rations and advises President Davis of the supply situation there. He instructs Longstreet to send a force to Gordonsville to oppose an enemy raiding force, and shifts Rodes's Division across the James to reinforce Longstreet, afterwards requesting Seddon to expedite the movement of Longstreet's men to Gordonsville. The Senate votes 8-7 in favor of having the Committee on Military Affairs meet with Lee and Johnston.[25]

December 23, Friday (Edge Hill): Lee informs Richmond that an attack on Fort Branch on the Roanoke River in North Carolina was repulsed, and Lomax drove the Federals away from Gordonsville.

Lee telegraphs Gov. Vance asking if he can do anything to aid Bragg at Wilmington, and he declines an invitation from the Danville Female College to attend a concert.[26]

December 24, Saturday (Edge Hill): Lee informs Richmond that the Union Navy opened fire on Fort Fisher near Wilmington today and that one boat ran aground and exploded last night. He also sends the details of Lomax's fight yesterday and also that Breckinridge reports that the Federals did significant damage to the Virginia & Tennessee Railroad but that the injury to the salt works is minor.[27]

December 25, Sunday (Edge Hill/Petersburg): Lee attends church in the morning with Col. T. M. R. Talcott, then goes to the Bannister home with Talcott for dinner of turkey and potatoes. He informs Seddon that the enemy gunboats in the Roanoke went back downriver, probably to Plymouth, and also sends details of the fighting at Fort Fisher.[28]

December 26, Monday (Edge Hill): Lee writes to Seddon regarding the local reserves in the Richmond defenses: "I shall be very glad to relieve all the local

---

[23] OR 42, pt. 3, 1280-1; Graves, *Forged Letter*; Krick, *CW Weather*, 144. It seems the meeting with Longstreet and Hoke occurred at 707 Franklin, as Hoke was informed they would meet "at 9 o'clock ... at [Lee's] quarters in Richmond." OR 42, pt. 3, 1281. The identity of the author of the "Repudiation Letter" has never been determined. See Graves, *Forged Letter*. War Department clerk John B. Jones encountered Lee on this date and noted the general "looking robust, though weather-worn. He complains that the [War] Department is depleting his army by details, often for private and speculative purposes, to the benefit of private individuals – speculators." Jones, *War Clerk's Diary*, vol. 2, 360.

[24] Lee, *Memoirs of WNP*, 380-1; Krick, *CW Weather*, 144. Lee almost certainly met with President Davis and/or Secretary of War Seddon on this date.

[25] Venable to WNP, Dec. 22, 1864, WNP papers, UNC; Freeman, *Lee's Dispatches*, 310; REL to Longstreet, Dec. 22, 1864, REL HQ papers, VHS; OR 42, pt. 3, 1291; *Journal of the Congress of the CSA*, vol. 4, 402. The War Department officially disbanded the 22nd VA Battalion on this date per Lee's request. Hewitt, ed., OR *Supplement*, pt. 2, vol. 71, 714-9.

[26] OR 42, pt. 1, 855; OR 43, pt. 1, 679-80; Carmichael, *Audacity Personified*, 119; REL to Danville Female College, Dec. 23, 1864, REL papers, MOC.

[27] OR 42, pt. 1, 856; OR 43, pt. 1, 680; OR 45, pt. 2, 728-9. The Federals loaded the USS *Louisiana* with gunpowder and ran it ashore near Fisher hoping the explosion would breach Fisher's seawall; while the vessel exploded, it did absolutely no damage to the fort.

[28] Dowdey, *Wartime Papers*, 880; Greene, *CW Petersburg*, 228; Freeman, *Lee's Dispatches*, 311-2; OR 42, pt. 1, 856; OR 42, pt. 3, 1305. Mrs. Bannister noticed that Lee did not eat much of his turkey and asked if he preferred dark meat, to which Lee replied that he was saving his portion to take to Marshall, who was ill and remained at Edge Hill. She prepared a serving for Lee to take to him, which Marshall later credited for his recovery. Greene, *CW Petersburg*, 228. Lee wrote that only Talcott accompanied him to dinner at the Bannisters, with Taylor and Venable going elsewhere. Decades later, however, Taylor wrote that Lee and the staff all had Christmas dinner together at HQ. There may have been a second large meal, but it is more likely that Taylor's distant memory was incorrect. WHT to J. W. Jones, Jan. 3, 1904, WHT papers, NPL.

troops now in the trenches . . . but I don't know where to get troops to replace them." With Hoke gone to Wilmington, there are even fewer troops to man the lines and Early reports that more Federals are leaving the Valley for Petersburg: "I do not see where I am to get troops to meet him [Grant], as ours seem to diminish rather than to increase." Snow.[29]

December 27, Tuesday (Edge Hill): Lee forwards to Seddon the latest from Bragg regarding Fort Fisher and complains about the continuing desertions from Petersburg: "Scant fare, light clothing, constant duty, no recruits have discouraged" the men. Snow continues.[30]

December 28, Wednesday (Edge Hill): Lee writes to Gov. Vance regarding the condition of the railroads in North Carolina and how it nearly caused disaster at Wilmington by delaying Hoke's arrival there. The Richmond *Dispatch* publishes a rumor that Gen. Lee has been "appointed . . . generalissimo of the land and naval forces of the Confederacy." Snow continues.[31]

December 29, Thursday (Edge Hill): Lee notifies Seddon that the Federal fleet off Wilmington disappeared but they offloaded at least a division of infantry near Fort Fisher. He issues a circular requesting suggestions as to regiments that could be consolidated and for any officers unfit for command. Snow continues.[32]

December 30, Friday (Edge Hill): Lee writes to Bragg regarding Hoke and the situation at Wilmington, and receives a summons from the President. In the morning, artist Hector Eaches visits headquarters regarding his portrait of Lee, and during the afternoon Gen. John Pegram meets with Lee. In the evening Lee calls on Rev. Platt's wife Eleanor with a Christmas present for her newborn daughter. He receives a letter from his wife as well as boots from daughter Mary and a fur robe from the Lyons family; he writes back to Mary telling of his Christmas dinner.[33]

December 31, Saturday (Edge Hill): Snow.[34]

---

29 OR 42, pt. 3, 1310-1; Driver, *39th Virginia Cavalry Battalion*, 76.

30 OR 42, pt. 1, 856; OR 42, pt. 3, 1311; Driver, *39th Virginia Cavalry Battalion*, 76.

31 OR 42, pt. 3, 1334-5; Richmond *Daily Dispatch*, Dec. 28, 1864, REL newspaper references, DSF papers, LVA; Driver, *39th Virginia Cavalry Battalion*, 76.

32 OR 42, pt. 3, 1343; Driver, *39th Virginia Cavalry Battalion*, 76.

33 REL to Bragg, Dec. 30, 1864, REL papers, VHS; OR 51, pt. 2, 1055; Dowdey, *Wartime Papers*, 879-80; Williams, *Stonewall's Prussian Mapmaker*, 222; Eleanor B. M. Platt to mother, Dec. 31, 1864, E. B. M. Platt papers, VHS. Mrs. Platt wrote of this visit: "He and I sat cozily over the fire chatting. Oh I do so love, honor, [and] revere him. Indeed language fails to express all I feel for that noble man." Platt to mother, Dec. 31, 1864, Platt papers, VHS.

34 Driver, *39th Virginia Cavalry Battalion*, 76. Lee may have gone to Richmond on this date; he vanishes from the historical record almost entirely for several days straddling the New Year.

January 1865

The Confederacy was unraveling by the turn of the calendar into 1865. Fort Fisher guarding the river approach to Wilmington, North Carolina—the last major open port left—fell after a prolonged fight. Union forces moved inland against the city. Wilmington was doomed. Gen. William T. Sherman appeared to be targeting the Carolinas in general, and likely Charleston in particular. With Gen. John B. Hood's Army of Tennessee no longer an effective fighting force, Gen. George Thomas's army at Nashville was rumored to be joining Gen. U. S. Grant. The numerical odds facing the South had always been high; now it looked as though they would be impossible to overcome.

People across the South, in and out of the Army and government, looked to Robert E. Lee to somehow avert the end that was looking increasingly inevitable to nearly everyone except Jefferson Davis. Congress created the position of "General in Chief" and bestowed it upon Lee. The general wanted no part of it, pointing out that he had more on his plate than he could handle presently, and heaping more responsibilities on his shoulders would simply overtax his abilities and resources.[1]

In an attempt to salvage some sort of political victory while the Confederacy still had a few meager chips to play, a peace delegation was dispatched to meet with President Lincoln and Secretary of State William Seward at Hampton Roads.

In the midst of all this Lee continued about his routine. Roger Pryor's wife noted that she saw Lee pass by her residence almost daily on his rides to survey the lines.[2] Brig. Gen. William Terry, commander of the Stonewall Brigade, and one of his aides called upon Lee at Edge Hill one evening. "[H]is reception and entertainment of us was as natural, dignified, and interesting as if we had been seated under the roof of his beloved Arlington," recalled Terry.[3]

Large gaps exist in the records for Lee during this time, largely because Walter Taylor went on leave and no one else at headquarters came close to Taylor as far as documenting Lee's activities.

* * *

---

1 Dowdey, *Wartime Papers*, 884-6.

2 Pryor, *My Day*, 242.

3 Colt, *Defend the Valley*, 362.

January 1, Sunday (Richmond): Walter Taylor goes on furlough for several weeks, leaving Charles Venable in charge of headquarters.[4]

January 2, Monday (Richmond): Lee meets with Early to discuss the Valley.[5]

January 3, Tuesday (Richmond): Snow.[6]

January 4, Wednesday (Richmond): Lee writes to Early regarding procurement of horses for his cavalry. Snow continues.[7]

January 7, Saturday (Richmond/Edge Hill): Lee returns to Petersburg and writes to Longstreet regarding the consolidation of regiments and replacement of officers.[8]

January 8, Sunday (Edge Hill): Lee informs Bragg and Seddon of a large force of enemy infantry on transports in the James likely bound for Wilmington. He also informs Beauregard that any decisions regarding Charleston will have to be made there as Beauregard is much more familiar with the situation than Lee is at Petersburg. Lee notifies Adjutant General Samuel Cooper that Lee's instructions regarding an inspector general for southwest Virginia several months earlier were apparently misunderstood: rather than an officer being permanently assigned to that department, one was sent merely to make an inspection and then returned to Richmond. He writes to Mary Jerdone of Bloomsbury in Orange County thanking her for an unspecified gift and encloses a photo of himself.[9]

January 9, Monday (Edge Hill): Lee writes to the War Department concerning the condition of the Piedmont Railroad, enclosing letters from several other officers including Gen. Robert Hoke about its deteriorating state. He writes to Wade Hampton regarding the cavalry's weapons, and assigns Seth Barton to command of Field's Brigade. He requests North Carolina Gov. Vance to use his influence to keep the Raleigh newspapers from mentioning the contraband trade occurring in eastern North Carolina, and asks William Hardee if he has a position for Capt. Stephen Winthrop, whom Lee wants put in command of a regiment. In the afternoon, three young girls from the Northern Neck and their maid bring Lee several baskets of food and sundries. Rain during the night.[10]

January 10, Tuesday (Edge Hill): Lee writes to President Davis regarding Hardee's plans to resist Sherman's advance into South Carolina; he doesn't know Hood's intentions or even what he could do with the remnant of the Army of Tennessee other than to attempt to keep George Thomas's forces occupied in Tennessee. Lee proposes to send Matthew Butler's cavalry division to South Carolina, and possibly sending Hampton himself as well; he

---

4 Venable to wife, Jan. 1, 1865, in Margaret C. M. Venable memoirs, UVA. Taylor was absent almost all of January.

5 Early, *Memoirs*, 459.

6 Brooke, *Ironclads and Big Guns*, 199.

7 REL to Early, Jan. 4, 1865, REL papers, W&L; Osmun Latrobe diary, Jan. 4, 1865, VHS.

8 WNP to wife, Jan. 7, 1865, WNP papers, UNC; REL to Longstreet, Jan. 7, 1865, REL HQ papers, VHS.

9 *OR* 46, pt. 2, 1023; Freeman, *Lee's Dispatches*, 312-4; REL to Cooper, Jan. 8, 1865, Brand collection, Duke; REL to Jerdone, Jan. 8, 1865, REL papers, W&L. Lt. Col. Daniel T. Chandler was the officer Lee wanted sent to southwest Virginia. He resigned in late February 1865. REL to Cooper, Jan. 8, 1865, Brand collection, Duke; Krick, *Staff Officers in Gray*, 95.

10 *OR* 46, pt. 2, 1025-8; Carmichael, *Audacity Personified*, 121; REL to Hardee, Jan. 9, 1865, REL papers, Duke; Fitz Lee, *General Lee*, 366; Giles Cooke diary, Jan. 10, 1865, VHS. Winthrop, an officer in the British Army prior to joining the Confederate Army in 1863, served as an aide to Longstreet and Porter Alexander; both generals recommended Winthrop be given a regiment in the field. REL to Hardee, Jan. 9, 1865, REL papers, Duke; Krick, *Staff Officers in Gray*, 307. Lee identified his guests only as "the daughters of a Mrs. Nottingham, a refugee from Northampton County.... I have not had so pleasant a visit for a long time." Fitz Lee, *General Lee*, 366. Rev. Jones for some reason placed this incident on Dec. 29. Jones, *Life and Letters of REL*, 348.

advises that Grant sent troops from Petersburg to Wilmington. He instructs Breckinridge to work with the commanders in western North Carolina to clear out "deserters, traitors, [and] . . . bandetti" who are causing problems for the citizens in the mountains of North Carolina, and requests Gov. Vance to provide whatever aid he can to Gen. Bragg at Wilmington. Lee writes to his wife Mary recounting the visit of the three girls yesterday. Rain continues.[11]

January 11, Wednesday (Edge Hill): Lee informs Sec. Seddon that the ANV has "but two days supplies" left, and that the surrounding country has been swept clean; he is dependent on whatever reaches Petersburg by rail. Lee writes to Virginia Senator Andrew Hunter justifying the need to enlist black troops, recommending immediate freedom for those who enlist and freedom for their families at the end of the war. Lee informs Gov. Vance of the army's dire supply situation in hopes that he may be able to assist. He meets with Gen. Pendleton who notes that the pressure on Lee was apparent: "The burden on him is so heavy that those on whom he leans ought to help him to bear it as well as they can."[12]

January 12, Thursday (Edge Hill): Gen. Lee issues an appeal "To the Farmers east of the Blue Ridge" to send whatever food they can to help feed his army, and authorizes the impressment of supplies.[13]

January 13, Friday (Edge Hill): Lee sends an urgent request to Gov. Vance to send every available man to reinforce Wilmington.[14]

January 14, Saturday (Edge Hill): The Senate votes 14-2 in favor of assigning Lee to overall command.[15]

January 15, Sunday (Edge Hill): Lee briefs the president on his plans to send Butler's Division to South Carolina and that an enemy force came ashore between Bragg's forces at Wilmington and Fort Fisher, cutting off the fort; Bragg chose not to attack, but Lee ordered him to do so or they will lay siege to Fisher. He informs Seddon of Rosser's capture of an enemy force at Beverly, West Virginia.[16]

January 16, Monday (Edge Hill): Lee learns of the fall of Fort Fisher and reports it to Richmond, although he does not yet know any details. He writes to Seddon again on the question of supply, enclosing a copy of his appeal to farmers, and continuing to complain about illicit trade of contraband items in eastern North Carolina. Further, he sends Gov. Vance a report by the supply officer on the Chowan River regarding interference in his efforts by local citizens and state officers. He forwards to the War Department a request from Gen. William Wofford to be reassigned to duty in Georgia, noting that he regrets to lose Wofford's services.[17]

Upon inquiry from Butler, Lee informs the War Department that elements of his division currently in South Carolina on recruiting detail need not return to Virginia, they can simply rejoin their commands when Butler's Division is transferred there. Lee writes to Gen. William Terry enclosing $100 "sent by a friend to the Stonewall Brigade" and hoping the brigade is not suffering any more than the rest of the

---

11 Freeman, *Lee's Dispatches*, 314-6; Dowdey, *Wartime Papers*, 880; Carmichael, *Audacity Personified*, 120-1; Fitz Lee, *General Lee*, 366; Williams, *Stonewall's Prussian Mapmaker*, 228.

12 OR 46, pt. 2, 1035; OR 3, Series 4, 1012-3; Carmichael, *Audacity Personified*, 121; Lee, *Memoirs of WNP*, 386.

13 OR 46, pt. 2, 1075; Carmichael, *Audacity Personified*, 121. The already critical supply situation was made worse by recent rains that damaged the Piedmont Railroad. OR 46, pt. 2, 1075.

14 Carmichael, *Audacity Personified*, 121.

15 *Journal of the Congress of the CSA*, vol. 4, 453-4. The bill also included assignments for Gens. Joe Johnston and Beauregard.

16 Dowdey, *Wartime Papers*, 881-2; OR 46, pt. 1, 452.

17 OR 46, vol. 2, 1074-5; Carmichael, *Audacity Personified*, 121-2; Smith, *Most Daring of Men*, 135. Fort Fisher fell on the night of the 15th. Wofford, one of Kershaw's brigade commanders, was assigned to command the Department of North Georgia on Jan. 23. Warner, *Generals in Gray*, 344.

army. He thanks a namesake, R. E. L. Wilfong of Newton, North Carolina, for a recent care package.[18]

January 17, Tuesday (Edge Hill): Lee meets with Pendleton in the morning regarding the disposition of artillery in the Second Corps and the cavalry. He requests that the War Department order all men from Butler's Division to rejoin their units upon arrival in South Carolina. He writes to Mary regarding the socks she and the girls made for the army, and also mentions that Custis is visiting at headquarters. Both houses of the Virginia General Assembly unanimously pass a resolution calling for Lee to be made general in chief.[19]

January 18, Wednesday (Edge Hill): Lee explains in a lengthy letter to the president that the fall of Fort Fisher and closing of Wilmington as a port all but necessitates making official the practice of exchange with the North that has occurred for some time, for it is the only way to keep the armies supplied. He informs Seddon that Bragg was not able to save the artillery from the lower Cape Fear forts and needs additional guns to defend against ascent up the river to Wilmington. Davis offers Lee the position of overall commander of the Confederate armies. Rain begins early and continues all day.[20]

January 19, Thursday (Edge Hill): Lee's 58th birthday. Lee receives the president's letter and writes back his opposition to increasing his responsibility: "I do not think that while charged with my present command . . . I could direct the operations of the armies in the South Atlantic States. If I had the ability I would not have the time. The arrangement of the details of this army extended as it is, providing for its necessities and directing its operations engrosses all my time and still I am unable to accomplish what I desire and see to be necessary. I could not therefore propose to undertake more." He also informs Congressman William Porcher Miles that "It will be impossible for me to send sufficient troops from this army to oppose Sherman's and at the same time resist Grant. Sherman's army alone is equal to this, and I can see no benefit from inviting disaster at both places." He points out that he is sending Butler's cavalry to Hardee and he does not concur in the opinion that the capture of Charleston means the cause is lost.

The general continues corresponding with the War Department concerning the detachment of Butler's cavalry division, adding that he would like it returned for spring operations in Virginia. He notes that a shortage of soap is causing illness within the ranks. Lee writes to James Longstreet regarding desertions and the overall poor conditions in Pickett's command: "I desire you to correct the evils in Pickett's division . . . by every means in your power." Lee is paid $1,308 for November and December.[21]

January 20, Friday (Edge Hill): Lee writes to President Davis regarding the Piedmont Railroad and also the need for a commander for western North Carolina: Lee wants the region to be a separate district and Gen. James Martin given command and if he is unsuccessful then Col. John B. Palmer can be promoted and given command. In

---

18 OR 46, pt. 2, 1003-4; Dowdey, *Wartime Papers*, 883; REL to Wilfong, Jan. 16, 1864, REL papers, LVA. The Senate confirmed Custis's promotion to major general and attempted hold a re-vote on the bill passed on the 14th regarding Lee's overall command of the army; the motion failed a second time. Yates, *Perfect Gentleman*, vol. 1, 295; *Journal of the Congress of the CSA*, vol. 4, 456. Presumably a unanimous decision was desired.

19 Venable to WNP, Jan. 16, 1864, WNP papers, UNC; OR 46, pt. 2, 1083-4; OR 47, pt. 2, 1019; Dowdey, *Wartime Papers*, 884. The dates and purpose of Custis's visit are not known.

20 Freeman, *Lee's Dispatches*, 318-22; OR 46, pt. 2, 1091; G. M. Coiner to Kate Coiner, Coiner family papers, VHS. Davis's letter offered Lee three different larger commands in addition to the Army of Northern Virginia: (1) Virginia, the Carolinas, Georgia, and Florida; (2) Everything east of the Mississippi River; (3) "[Y]our former position of commander of all the armies of the Confederate States." Nowhere in the message, however, did Davis use the title "General in Chief," a position that did not yet officially exist. OR 46, pt. 2, 1091.

21 Dowdey, *Wartime Papers*, 884-6; OR 46, pt. 2, 1099-1101; Selcer, *Lee vs. Pickett*, 66; Pay Voucher, Jan, 18, 1865, REL CSR.

order to remove absent, incompetent, and otherwise unfit officers, Lee requests that the War Department create officer examining boards.²²

January 21, Saturday (Edge Hill): Lee informs President Davis he will defer to Hardee's judgment regarding Charleston, and notifies Seddon that Bragg repulsed an attack at Sugar Loaf between Fort Fisher and Wilmington but enemy gunboats are in the Cape Fear River in force. Davis requests a meeting with Lee as soon as possible. Lee sends to the Texas Brigade nine gold stars he received from "a young lady of Texas" which she requests to be presented to deserving soldiers of the brigade. Rain.²³

January 22, Sunday (Edge Hill/Richmond): Lee goes to Richmond to meet with President Davis. Rain continues.²⁴

January 23, Monday (Richmond): Congress approves the creation of the general in chief position. Rain continues.²⁵

January 24, Tuesday (Richmond/Edge Hill): Lee inquires of Bragg what he intends to do about an enemy raiding force near Weldon. He has tea with Richmond attorney James Lyons in the afternoon and afterwards returns to Petersburg. He finds at headquarters a complaint from Gen. Zebulon York regarding interference in his efforts to recruit for the Louisiana brigade, and forwards this to the War Department requesting an explanation.²⁶

January 25, Wednesday (Edge Hill): Lee issues an open call to the people for weapons for the cavalry, and instructs Bragg to make whatever dispositions necessary to meet the enemy along the Chowan River and to use his entire force in doing so.²⁷

January 26, Thursday (Edge Hill): Lee requests a copy of the War Department orders assigning the 8th and 14th Virginia Cavalry regiments to Jubal Early's cavalry. Rain.²⁸

January 27, Friday (Edge Hill/Richmond): Lee writes to Secretary of War Seddon and Adjutant General Cooper that the lack of supplies and no pay is causing mass desertions from the army and encloses a letter from Charles Field about conditions in Anderson's Brigade. He goes to Richmond in the evening. Rain.²⁹

January 28, Saturday (Richmond/Edge Hill): Lee returns to Petersburg and writes to President Davis suggesting that all cotton, tobacco, and naval stores be destroyed rather than left behind to be captured by the enemy when exposed points are evacuated.

---

22 Freeman, *Lee's Dispatches*, 324-6; *OR* 42, pt. 3, 1251-3; *OR* 46, pt. 2, 1110.

23 Freeman, *Lee's Dispatches*, 327; *OR* 46, pt. 2, 1118; Richmond *Examiner*, Feb. 17, 1865, REL newspaper references, DSF papers, LVA; Williams, *Stonewall's Prussian Mapmaker*, 232. The stars were presented to the selected men in February following a speech by Texas Senator Louis T. Wigfall, who commanded the brigade briefly early in the war. Polley, *Hood's Texas Brigade*, 285-7.

24 *OR* 46, pt. 2, 1118; Krick, *CW Weather*, 147. Lee's going to Richmond is inferred from Davis's summons on the 21st and the lack of any evidence to the contrary.

25 *OR* 5, Series 3, 688; Krick, *CW Weather*, 147.

26 *OR* 46, pt. 2, 1089-90, 1131; Jones, *War Clerk's Diary*, vol. 2, 398. Lee's telegram to Bragg is headlined Richmond, but the note to Seddon regarding York is headlined ANV HQ, which suggests Lee left Richmond after his appointment with Lyons, although this is not certain.

27 *OR* 46, pt. 2, 1134-7.

28 *OR* 46, pt. 2, 1140; Krick, *CW Weather*, 148.

29 *OR* 46, pt. 2, 1125-6, 1143; Mrs. REL to Abby L. Cook, Jan. 27, 1865, LJF papers, W&L; Krick, *CW Weather*, 148. Lee may have gone to Richmond regarding his appointment as general in chief. See Seddon to Cooper, Jan. 28, 1865, REL CSR. The only known source for this brief trip to Richmond is Mrs. Lee, who wrote a friend: "My husband arrived tonight; I see him quite often." Mrs. REL to Cook, Jan. 27, 1865, LJF papers, W&L.

He writes to Longstreet regarding the non-payment of the troops, and forwards to Early a complaint from the inspector general's office about Early's policy of allowing furloughed men to take artillery horses with them—it is feared that this will make the animals unfit for field service. Rain continues.[30]

January 29, Sunday (Edge Hill): Lee informs Richmond of reports from Early's scouts that a portion of George Thomas's army from Tennessee passed over the B&O en route to Grant; Lee bemoans that he will be unable to defend Richmond if true. He also writes to Mary, with updates on the number of socks provided and complaining about the bitter cold: "If our men had only clothes and abundant food, I should not care for the cold."[31]

January 30, Monday (Edge Hill): Lee writes to President Davis that additional scouts as well as northern newspapers confirm Thomas's army joining Grant, and he thinks that the peace delegation has been prevented from going to Hampton Roads in an attempt to hide the presence of these reinforcements, and forwards a letter from one of the commissioners. Lee requests that the remains of Hood's army be ordered to Virginia and he informs Bragg that Grant is being reinforced by Thomas's army from Tennessee and requests reinforcements from North Carolina.[32]

January 31, Tuesday (Edge Hill): The Senate confirms Lee's nomination as general in chief. He meets with Pendleton in the morning and instructs Longstreet to strengthen the Richmond defenses as he expects an attack once Thomas's troops arrive.

Lee informs President Davis that Grant will allow the peace delegation through the lines and encloses a message from Vice President Stephens.[33]

---

30 Freeman, *Lee's Dispatches*, 328-9; REL to Longstreet, Jan. 28, 1865, REL HQ papers, VHS; *OR* 46, pt. 2, 1135; Krick, *CW Weather*, 148. Lee may have been at the War Department in the morning, as Seddon requested that Lee's nomination as general in chief be submitted to the department in the morning. Seddon to Cooper, Jan. 28, 1865, REL CSR. Lee's letter to Davis mentions meeting with the president to discuss this topic, but does not give a hint as to when this occurred; it was likely on this recent trip to the capital. Freeman, *Lee's Dispatches*, 328-9. Jubal Early responded that he adopted this policy because sending the animals away from the army was the only way to feed them. *OR* 46, pt. 2, 1135.

31 Freeman, *Lee's Dispatches*, 329-30; Dowdey, *Wartime Papers*, 887.

32 Freeman, *Lee's Dispatches*, 330-3; *OR* 46, pt. 2, 1164. On Jan. 28, Davis appointed Vice President Alexander Stephens, Virginia Senator R. M. T. Hunter, and Assistant Secretary of War (and former Supreme Court justice) John Campbell as peace commissioners. They hoped to meet with Federal authorities at Hampton Roads to discuss an end to the war.

33 *Journal of the Congress of the CSA*, vol. 4, 510-1; REL CSR; Venable to WNP, Jan. 30, 1865, WNP papers, UNC; REL to Longstreet, Jan. 31, 1865, REL HQ papers, VHS; Freeman, *Lee's Dispatches*, 334-5.

February 1865

The war had turned decidedly against the South, and February saw a host of changes directly affecting the conflict. James Seddon was all but ousted as secretary of war, a scapegoat for the battlefield reversals over which he had little control. In his stead came an individual familiar to Robert E. Lee as well as many of the other commanders in both Virginia and the Western Theater: John C. Breckinridge. Lee and Breckinridge had great respect for one another, a professional appreciation that only grew over the ensuing weeks. "He is a great man," Lee said of the new secretary. "I was acquainted with him as a Congressman and Vice-President and as one of our generals, but I did not know him till he was Secretary of War, and is a lofty, pure, strong, man."[1]

"For the last year of the war," wrote Breckinridge of Lee,

> it was my fortune to be thrown much with him, and during the two months immediately preceding the fall of Richmond our respective duties made our intercourse close and constant. It was under these trying circumstances that I came fully to know and appreciate his heart and character. In those long and painful interviews he stood revealed to me a considerate, kind, gentle, firm, Christian gentleman.[2]

The same day Breckinridge assumed the reins at the War Department, Lee's appointment as general in chief was announced. Lee was not alone in wondering what the expectations were for him in this new role. The most prevalent rumors involved Lee either taking command in the Carolinas and Joe Johnston or Beauregard taking command the Army of Northern Virginia, or one of those two generals taking over the ANV under Lee with the latter assuming a U. S. Grant-like role.[3] Like Lee, Johnston had long-since realized the South could no longer win the war militarily. "Do not expect much of Lee in this [new] capacity," wrote Johnston. "He cannot give up the command of the Army of Northern Virginia without becoming merely a minor official."[4]

President Davis, and to some extent perhaps Lee as well, lost confidence in Beauregard's ability to resist William T. Sherman in the Carolinas. Lee could not (or would not) go there himself, so he turned to Joseph E. Johnston, one of his trusted old friends—despite the president's objections. Johnston was being asked to play a losing hand: Sherman was approaching from the south while elements of George Thomas's army under John Schofield were moving inland from the coast, while his own forces were scattered across the Carolinas.

Lee and Breckinridge met often, but their discussions were not always about battlefields and strategy. More and more the topic shifted to how to end the war.[5] They also began planning the evacuation of Richmond, which was something Jefferson Davis refused to believe would ever be necessary.

---

1 Gallagher, *Lee the Soldier*, 30.

2 Unknown clipping, Jones scrapbook, vol. 2, p. 158, REL papers, Duke.

3 Tower, *Lee's Adjutant*, 222.

4 Gallagher, *Lee the Soldier*, 178.

5 Davis, *Breckinridge*, 490.

Some hope remained in the trenches and at home. The officers and men of former Governor Henry Wise's brigade adopted a resolution to continue fighting until the end, and the citizens of Powhatan County—including Gen. Lee's brother Carter—also passed a resolution to maintain the fight until independence was gained.[6]

* * *

---

6 Richmond *Dispatch*, Feb. 17, 1865, REL newspaper references, DSF papers, LVA; Charles Carter Lee, *Resolutions Adopted by a Meeting of the People of Powhatan, Held in the Courthouse on February Court Day, 1865* (Richmond, VA, 1865), no pagination.

February 1, Wednesday (Edge Hill/Petersburg): Lee and John Gordon watch the dress parade of John Pegram's brigade. Adjutant General Samuel Cooper informs Lee that his nomination as general in chief was confirmed by the Confederate Senate and that his commission is at the War Department—does Lee wish it sent to Petersburg or will he pick it up himself in Richmond? James Seddon resigns his position as as the secretary of war.[7]

February 2, Thursday (Edge Hill/Petersburg): Lee and Gordon review Pegram's Division, accompanied by Mrs. Pegram, and inspect the division. John Mosby visits Lee at headquarters, and Lee requests the War Department put Collett Leventhorpe in command of Clingman's Brigade per Hoke's request.[8]

February 3, Friday (Edge Hill): Lee writes to Longstreet regarding the use of black laborers on the Richmond defenses, and forwards to the War Department a complaint from Early about Jesse McNeill's partisan rangers with the request that McNeill's command be done away with. Lee reassigns some of the headquarters duties to ease the burden on Taylor, giving more tasks to Venable and Marshall. He writes to his wife mentioning the review yesterday, and thanking a friend for compiling the family genealogy. Rain and sleet.[9]

February 4, Saturday (Edge Hill): Gen. Lee acknowledges his appointment as general in chief but is unsure of what it means and what his new responsibilities include, so he asks for clarification from the adjutant general. Lee informs Bragg that Beauregard is concentrating against Sherman at Columbia and asks if Bragg can spare any of his force; he later informs the president that Beauregard is on his own—nothing can be spared from Petersburg, Richmond, or North Carolina to reinforce him.[10]

Lee learns of a possible enemy cavalry raid against Salisbury, North Carolina, and informs the War Department of a skirmish by Early's cavalry in the Valley. Lee writes to the War Department about the breakup of Bradley Johnson's cavalry brigade—he refuses to allow them to serve solely in their home locales as it is unfair to the rest of the army and to set this precedent would encourage mutiny among other units desiring to do the same. He thanks Gen. Henry Wise for the resolution adopted by his brigade to continue the struggle.[11]

---

7 Williams, ed., *Stonewall's Prussian Mapmaker*, 238; *OR* 46, pt. 2, 1188; Long, *CW Day by Day*, 632. They may have also inspected Johnston's Brigade (Hinrichs is unclear). Seddon tried to resign on Jan. 18 due to his declining health and public perception he was responsible for the declining fortunes of war, but Davis did not accept it. Davis, *Honorable Defeat*, 17.

8 Dowdey, *Wartime Letters*, 888; Douglas, *I Rode with Stonewall*, 311; Williams, *Stonewall's Prussian Mapmaker*, 238; Mitchell, *Mosby Letters*, 36; *OR* 42, pt. 3, 1254. Douglas claimed that Longstreet, Hill, Anderson, and Heth were present for the review, but Hinrichs mentioned none other than Lee and Gordon. Mosby made no mention of the review, and no witness accounts place him there; whether he visited with Lee before or after the review is not known. Longstreet wrote to Lee on this date requesting that Joe Johnston be given command of the Army of Tennessee to "restore that army to organization, morale, and efficiency." *OR* 47, pt. 2, 1078-9. The British-born Leventhorpe was a brigadier in the North Carolina state forces, but resigned his Confederate Army commission after Gettysburg; he had to be commissioned in the Confederate Army before he could take command of anything other than NC state troops. He received this appointment on Feb. 18, but declined it several weeks later. Warner, *Generals in Gray*, 185.

9 REL to Longstreet, Feb. 3, 1865, REL papers, VHS; *OR* 51, pt. 2, 1060-1; Tower, *Lee's Adjutant*, 220; Dowdey, *Wartime Papers*, 888; Krick, *CW Weather*, 150. Taylor's month-long absence caused a considerable backlog of paperwork at HQ, despite Venable handling most of his duties. Taylor bragged to Bettie about how Lee finally appreciated how much work fell on his shoulders: "Whilst away the General had a taste of what I had to do and since my return has insisted on dividing the labor. He told me he had often thought I had too much to do and he did not wish me to do all the work. The difficulty heretofore has been that they would not allow me to decide how the work should be divided, but [today] it was arranged as I desired it and . . . I will have at least two hours less hard work daily than formerly. Poor Venable is considerably disgruntled." Tower, *Lee's Adjutant*, 220.

10 REL CSR; *OR* 46, pt. 2, 1199; *OR* 47, pt. 2, 1098; Freeman, *Lee's Dispatches*, 370-1.

11 *OR* 49, pt. 1, 961; *OR* 46, pt. 2, 1199-1200; Richmond *Dispatch*, Feb. 17, 1865, REL newspaper references, DSF papers, LVA.

February 5, Sunday (Edge Hill/ Petersburg/ Hatcher's Run): Admiral Raphael Semmes and the president's aide, Col. Joseph Ives, come to headquarters in the morning. Lee and Semmes meet alone; Ives stays with the staff and is subjected to Venable's diatribe about the supply situation. The meeting makes Lee and Taylor late for service at St. Paul's, where Gen. Pendleton assists Rev. Platt. Lee, sitting beside Pendleton's daughter, receives a message about fighting at Hatcher's Run, and the general sends Taylor to headquarters while he partakes of Communion (the first to do so) before leaving for Edge Hill.[12]

The general telegraphs Richmond of the enemy offensive along Hatcher's Run, then departs around 3:00 p.m. for the front with Venable and Marshall, leaving Taylor at headquarters. Lee arrives at the battlefield as Henry Heth's and Clement Evans's divisions are arrayed for battle; he orders the two divisions forward and personally rallies some of Heth's men. Adm. Semmes spends the night at Edge Hill. Rain and sleet.[13]

February 6, Monday (Edge Hill): Lee's appointment as general in chief is announced by the War Department and read to the troops. Lee writes to Richmond again regarding contraband trade and reports on the action at Hatcher's Run yesterday and today, including John Pegram's death. John C. Breckinridge replaces Seddon as the Confederate secretary of war. Rain and sleet.[14]

February 7, Tuesday (Edge Hill): Maj. Giles Cooke spends the day with William Mahone's division and spends several hours with Gen. Lee in the evening reporting on the situation on Mahone's front. He remains with the general until 9:00 p.m. Mixture of rain, sleet, and snow all day.[15]

February 8, Wednesday (Edge Hill): Lee informs Richmond that he committed all the troops he can spare to the fighting along Hatcher's Run and notes that the enemy has not advanced from their position today. He laments that the army's food supply is exhausted so he has sent his commissary chief to Richmond to make arrangements to get rations, providing a very grim outlook: "If some change is not made and the Commissary Department reorganized, I apprehend dire results. The physical strength of the men, if their courage survives, must fail under this treatment. Our cavalry has to be dispersed for want of forage.... Taking these facts in connection with the paucity of our numbers, you must not be surprised if calamity befalls us." He asks Bragg if the 2nd South Carolina Cavalry can be sent to Hardee, and writes to Mary regarding the recent

---

12 Tower, *Lee's Adjutant*, 218; Frederick M. Colston, "Recollections of the Last Months in the Army of Northern Virginia," *SHSP*, vol. 38, 4; Raphael Semmes, *Memoirs of Service Afloat During the War Between the States* (Secaucus, NJ, 1987), 801-2; Lee, *Memoirs of WNP*, 389. Capt. Frederick Colston escorted Semmes and Ives from the James River to Edge Hill; both Colston and Semmes incorrectly date this incident "near the end of January." Colston, "Recollections," 4; Semmes, *Memoirs*, 801-2. Lee never went first for Communion, so his doing so on this occasion must have raised some eyebrows. Freeman, *Lee*, vol. 3, 535 n64.

13 Bearss, *Petersburg Campaign*, vol. 2, 185-6; OR 46, pt. 1, 381; Tower, *Lee's Adjutant*, 218; Freeman, *Lee*, vol. 3, 535-6; Semmes, *Memoirs*, 801-2; Krick, *CW Weather*, 150. According to one account, Lee "wept like a child" at seeing his men break under fire at Hatcher's Run. Bearss, *Petersburg Campaign*, vol. 2, 238-9. Unfortunately, Semmes's diary does not begin until Feb. 19, but in his memoirs he wrote that he and Lee discussed the condition of the country and the overall outlook of the war. Semmes diary, Duke; Semmes, *Memoirs*, 801-2. Taylor told Bettie he expected the announcement making Lee general in chief to be made tomorrow, but he wasn't sure what affect it would have on ANV HQ: "I do not see how he can attend to all the administrative duties of this army and also direct military operations elsewhere. Then if he leaves, or rather if another immediate commander [of the ANV] is appointed, what becomes of the staff?" Tower, *Lee's Adjutant*, 218-9. No account mentions Semmes accompanying Lee to Hatcher's Run, and the admiral's whereabouts during that time are unknown.

14 OR 46, pt. 2, 1205-6; Warfield, *Manassas to Appomattox*, 166; OR 46, pt. 1, 381; G. M. Coiner to Kate Coiner, Feb. 6, 1865, Coiner papers, VHS; Long, *CW Day by Day*, 635. One of Pickett's men recalled that news of Lee's appointment "gave great satisfaction to the soldiers and was hailed with delight by everyone." Warfield, *Manassas to Appomattox*, 166.

15 Cooke diary, Feb. 7, 1865, VHS; Walter Clark to parents, Feb. 12, 1865, Clark letters, NCMOH. Lee wrote that this was "the most inclement day of the winter." Bearss, *Petersburg Campaign*, vol. 2, 230.

fighting and Pegram's death. President Davis requests a meeting with Lee and Bragg as soon as possible.[16]

February 9, Thursday (Edge Hill): Gen. Lee officially announces his assumption of the role of general in chief, and advises Richmond of his action. He also proposes a pardon for all deserters and absentees in an almost last-ditch effort to fill the army's ranks. Lee requests James Longstreet to inspect a portion of the lines deemed by the engineers to be vulnerable to a quick rush by the enemy, and notifies President Davis that Gen. Bragg will leave for Richmond tomorrow. Lee advises Gov. William Smith that only 500 of the 5,000 laborers he requested in December arrived, and that it is imperative that they be provided because he can no longer pull troops off the line to perform manual labor. Lee informs Congressman William Miles that he destroyed Miles's letter and the enclosed letter from South Carolina Gov. Magrath after reading them and is thus is unable to return them as requested.[17]

February 10, Friday (Edge Hill): Gen. Lee writes to Charles F. Suttle of Danville thanking him for a pair of riding gloves.[18]

February 11, Saturday (Edge Hill): Gen. Lee meets with his nephew, Gen. Fitz Lee, and puts him in command of the army's cavalry corps. Lee orders a pardon for all absentees who return to their units within 20 days, and he forwards to Richmond Gordon's report of the fight on Hatcher's Run. He replies to a letter from several prominent citizens of South Carolina requesting him to dispatch an infantry corps for service in the the state against Sherman—Lee has already sent everything and every man he can spare—and adds that the Army of Tennessee was ordered to the Carolinas. Secretary of State Judah Benjamin proposes to Lee the idea of enlisting slaves to serve in the military, and asks how best to remove public opposition to the idea. Lee sends his condolences to Gen. John Pegram's widow, and writes a short note to his wife Mary.[19]

February 12, Sunday (Edge Hill): Lee writes to Mary declining an offer of a dog, recommending instead he be sent to Bremo: "He would be very out of place following me in a campaign. He would be exposed to danger, hunger, and thirst, and I think he would be equally miserable cooped up in Richmond." He encloses a letter from Mrs. Stiles and mentions some clothing and food she sent him recently.[20]

February 13, Monday (Edge Hill/Richmond): Gen. Lee answers a letter from Vice President Alexander Stephens regarding the assignment of Joe Johnston to command the forces in the Carolinas. Lee explains that a revolving door of commanders would be very bad for troop morale, and with battle imminent no change should be made unless absolutely necessary. Further, he adds that he does not think it his decision to make but rather that of the War Department. Lee notifies Sec. Breckinridge that he warned the commanders in western North Carolina and southwest Virginia about Stoneman's Union cavalry

---

16 *OR* 46, pt. 1, 381-2; *OR* 47, pt. 2, 1129-30; REL to Mrs. REL, Feb. 8, 1865, Wellford papers, VHS. Both messages to Richmond were addressed to James Seddon, who was no longer secretary of war (Breckinridge took over the duties on the 7th). Davis, *Breckinridge*, 482. The rest of Lee's correspondence to the secretary of war for the first week of February was addressed to the "Honorable Secretary of War," suggesting that he knew of Seddon's departure, or planned departure, but was not aware of when the changeover would take place, or it was simply addressed to Seddon personally out of habit. The letter to wife Mary was dated January 8, but the context—specifically the mention of John Pegram's death—makes it clear it was written in February.

17 *OR* 46, pt. 2, 1226-7; *OR* 51, pt. 2, 1082-3; Freeman, *Lee's Dispatches*, 336; REL to Smith, Feb. 9, 1864, Lee papers, SH; Dowdey, *Wartime Papers*, 891.

18 REL to Charles F. Suttle, Feb. 10, 1864, REL papers, W&L.

19 Dowdey, *Wartime Papers*, 893; SO 40 Feb. 11, 1865, REL HQ papers, VHS; *OR* 46, pt. 2, 1229-31; *OR* 46, pt. 1, 390-1; *OR* 44, 1011-2; REL to Hetty C. Pegram, Feb. 11, 1865, REL papers, VHS.

20 Dowdey, *Wartime Papers*, 893.

raid. In the afternoon Lee travels to Richmond to meet with President Davis and Sec. Breckinridge.[21]

February 14, Tuesday (Richmond): Lee meets with Breckinridge at the War Department; clerk J. B. Jones observes Lee "walking about briskly, as if some great event was imminent. His gray locks and beard have become white, but his countenance is cheerful, and his health vigorous."[22]

February 15, Wednesday (Richmond): Lee continues his meetings in Richmond. Ordnance chief Josiah Gorgas encounters the general in the capital and observes in his diary that Lee appears "very much troubled and received me somewhat sternly." Rain and sleet.[23]

February 16, Thursday (Richmond): Lee meets again with Sec. Breckinridge in the morning. He notifies Gov. Vance that troops from George Thomas's Union army operating under John Schofield have landed at Fort Fisher at Wilmington. Rain.[24]

February 17, Friday (Richmond): Gen. Lee orders Gen. Theophilus Holmes, in command of reserve forces in North Carolina, to send Union prisoners north from Raleigh to Richmond via Danville so they can be properly exchanged. Rain continues.[25]

February 18, Saturday (Richmond/Edge Hill): Lee returns to Petersburg to "find my table as usual filled with letters which I must try and work off." The general notifies Bragg that he thinks reports of enemy strength at New Bern to be greatly inflated, thus Bragg should gather all available state troops and strike a strong blow. He answers a letter from U. S. Grant regarding holding civilians as hostages; Lee does not know what Grant references. Lee issues a circular that no leaves, furloughs, etc. will be granted "to go south of North Carolina," and writes Congressman Ethelbert Barksdale regarding the use of slaves as Confederate soldiers. Lee thanks Norma Stewart of Brook Hill in Henrico County for the socks and sends a short note to wife Mary advising of his safe arrival at Petersburg.[26]

February 19, Sunday (Edge Hill): Gen. Lee informs President Davis and Sec. Breckinridge of the "unfavorable" reports from both Gen. Beauregard and Gen. Bragg, and that the former is reported to be ill, as is Gen. Hardee, so Lee would like Joe Johnston put in overall command in North Carolina. Lee tactfully cautions that the end of the war is drawing near, and he recommends that preparations begin for the eventual evacuation of Richmond. Davis— who is no fan of Joe Johnston's— "suggests" that Lee meet with Beauregard in person to assess the situation in South Carolina. Lee requests that Hoke report on enemy strength at Wilmington, and warns Gov. Vance that William T. Sherman may head for Charlotte and link up with the forces from the coast

---

21 Dowdey, *Wartime Papers*, 894; *OR* 49, pt. 1, 970; Tower, *Lee's Adjutant*, 222; REL to James Corley, Feb. 13, 1865, REL papers, MOC. Despite his stature in the Confederacy, Lee apparently still needed tickets to travel by rail, for he requested his quartermaster, Lt. Col. James Corley, to procure tickets to Richmond for that afternoon for him. REL to Corley, Feb. 13, 1865, REL papers, MOC.

22 Historian William C. Davis recently wrote that Lee and Breckinridge met at Lee's HQ at Edge Hill. William C. Davis, *An Honorable Defeat: The Last Days of the Confederate Government* (New York, 2001), 32. Walter Taylor, however, noted that his chief was in Richmond on this date, something that was also confirmed by the chatty War Department clerk John B. Jones. Jones, *Rebel War Clerk's Diary*, vol. 2, 422. Davis, however, got the location correct in his earlier Breckinridge biography. Davis, *Breckinridge*, 490.

23 Vandiver, *Gorgas Diary*, 169; Krick, *CW Weather*, 150. Roswell Ripley was in Richmond during this time period to meet with Lee and give his views on Charleston; when they met is not known. *OR* 47, pt. 2, 1120.

24 Davis, *Breckinridge*, 490; Jones, *Rebel War Clerk's Diary*, vol. 2, 423; Carmichael, *Audacity Personified*, 123; Krick, *CW Weather*, 150.

25 *OR* 8, Series 2, 244; Krick, *CW Weather*, 150.

26 Dowdey, *Wartime Papers*, 895; *OR* 47, pt. 2, 1220; *OR* 8, Series 2, 261; *OR* 46, pt. 2, 1240; Richmond *Dispatch*, Feb. 24, 1865; REL to Norma Stewart, Feb. 18, 1865, Bryan family papers, VHS.

at either Raleigh or Weldon, so supplies in his path should be moved or destroyed.[27]

February 20, Monday (Edge Hill): Lee expands Early's area of responsibility to include southwest Virginia and east Tennessee, and instructs Ewell to remove all cotton and tobacco from Richmond. He forwards to Richmond a letter from Gordon that very little opposition exists in his corps to enlisting blacks. He instructs Bragg to forward POWs to be exchanged to Wilmington and tells Taylor to have headquarters ready to move tomorrow.[28]

February 21, Tuesday (Edge Hill): Lee meets with Pendleton just after breakfast, likely to discuss the details of evacuating Petersburg. He informs Breckinridge that he will concentrate the forces from Petersburg and Richmond at Burkeville should he be forced to abandon his lines, and renews his request for Johnston to command in North Carolina. Lee writes to Grant regarding the POW exchange at Wilmington complaining that, despite Grant's agreement, John Schofield—in command in eastern North Carolina—refuses to accept them, so Lee asks Grant to order Schofield to allow the exchange to occur as previously agreed upon; he informs Breckinridge and Bragg of his communications with Grant and points out the logistical problems of having to move the prisoners elsewhere. He instructs Bragg to "destroy all cotton, tobacco, and naval stores that would otherwise fall into the hands of the enemy," and urges him to include Lafayette McLaws's force in his small army if possible.[29]

Trying to maximize his manpower, Lee cancels all furloughs and notifies the War Department that he has 10,000 surplus small arms on hand to arm incoming recruits. He thanks the new commissary general, Isaac St. John, for his plea to the public for supplies, and informs Breckinridge of a victory by Mosby on the 18th. He writes Mary with a grim outlook for the coming campaign: "Gen. Grant will move against us soon . . . and no man can tell what may be the result. Sherman and Schofield are both advancing and seem to have everything their own way, but trusting in a Merciful God, who does not always give the battle to the strong, I pray we may not be overwhelmed. I shall however endeavor to do my duty and fight to the last." He asks what she intends to do if Richmond is evacuated, and also forwards a letter for Gen. Gracie's widow.[30]

February 22, Wednesday (Edge Hill): Lee orders Johnston to take command of the Army of Tennessee and Department of South Carolina, Georgia, and Florida and to "concentrate all forces and drive back Sherman;" Johnston is free to assign Beauregard to whatever role he chooses. Recognizing that Bragg cannot stop Schofield with his small force, Lee directs him to remove everything of value from his path, to "be bold and judicious" and

---

27 OR 47, pt. 1, 1044; OR 53, 412-3; OR 47, pt. 2, 1222, 1227; Carmichael, *Audacity Personified*, 123. The concerns over Beauregard arose largely over several of his grandiose and unrealistic plans, starting Feb. 3, and his lack of a grasp on the overall situation. On the 21st he would propose marching on Washington with 35,000 "to dictate a peace." OR 47, pt. 2, 1237-8. Davis explained later to Gen. Jeremy Gilmer that Beauregard "seemed to be crazy [and] the anxiety I felt . . . caused me first to seek Gen. Lee's services and those not being available to turn to you to prevent so fatal a blunder" as leaving Beauregard in command. On or about the 20th, Lee ordered Gilmer to meet with Beauregard. His report convinced Davis of the necessity of acceding to Lee's request for Joe Johnston to be put in command. Davis to Gilmer, April 2, 1880, Gilmer papers, UNC.

28 OR 46, pt. 2, 1243, 1261; OR 51, pt. 2, 1063; OR 8, Series 2, 275; Tower, *Lee's Adjutant*, 225. Lee did not indicate where he planned to go, but he may have intended to go to Beauregard as requested. Taylor lamented to Bettie that he, Marshall, and Venable were now responsible for the staff work of not just the ANV but all of the Confederate armies. Worse, Marshall was ill once again, making more work for Taylor and Venable. Tower, *Lee's Adjutant*, 225.

29 WHT to WNP, Feb. 20, 1865, WNP papers, UNC; OR 46, pt. 2, 1244-5; OR 8, Series 2, 282, 285-7; OR 47, pt. 2, 1241-2. The topic of discussion with Pendleton given in the text is an educated guess based on Lee's focus on beginning preparations to evacuate Richmond and Petersburg.

30 GO 5 Feb. 21, 1865, REL HQ papers, VHS; OR 46, pt. 2, 1245-6; Dowdey, *Wartime Papers*, 907; REL to Mrs. REL, Feb. 21, 1865, REL papers, LOC. St. John was previously head of the Nitre and Mining Corps and replaced Northrop as commissary general on Feb. 16. Warner, *Generals in Gray*, 267.

harass his flanks. He replies to a suggestion from Longstreet to pay for supplies with gold, pointing out that there is no gold to be had for this purpose. He also presents several options for meeting Sherman, including withdrawing from the lines around Richmond and Petersburg to unite with Johnston and strike a blow before the three Federal armies unite; Lee wants to discuss this in person but does not think that he can get to Richmond. He writes also to Breckinridge about the need to concentrate all available forces to defeat Sherman, Schofield, and Grant in detail; he is willing to cede the temporary loss of the mountain regions to accomplish this. He warns again that Richmond will likely have to be evacuated, and notes he ordered supplies concentrated at Burkeville in anticipation of a withdrawal to the west. Lee adds that Bragg has left the Cape Fear and that all remaining POWs in North Carolina are being sent to Richmond.

To boost morale, Lee issues a circular reminding the men that the ANV's seasoned veteran troops are superior in battle to the raw recruits comprising much of the enemy's ranks, and that offsets Grant's superiority in numbers. Lee abolishes the election of officers in favor of promoting those deserving of it. He forwards to Breckinridge a report from John Echols on the status of Breckinridge's former department, specifically mentioning the lack of horses. The general asks if government cotton and tobacco can be used to barter for horses.[31]

February 23, Thursday (Edge Hill): Lee updates President Davis on the situation in North Carolina, including the assignment of Johnston to command and that Jeremy Gilmer has been sent to meet with Beauregard; he again advises that all preparations be made to evacuate Richmond. The general sends detailed instructions to Johnston of what he hopes can be done in North Carolina and Virginia; if the Federals reach the Roanoke River Lee will move to unite with Johnston. Lee informs Sec. Breckinridge and Gen. Bragg that the POW exchange at Wilmington has been sorted out with Grant and Schofield, so the prisoners are to move to Wilmington as previously directed. Lee writes to Col. S. R. Johnston thanking him for naming his newborn son after him. He writes to Mary with the latest sock numbers and enclosing currency for her to use should she again be behind enemy lines, and also sends apples for her and the girls. Heavy rain during the day and night.[32]

February 24, Friday (Edge Hill): President Davis and Sec. Breckinridge come to Petersburg to meet with Lee at Edge Hill. Either before or after their meeting, Lee sends a flurry of correspondence to Breckinridge on several topics: desertion; Jesse McNeill's capture of Gens. George Crook and Benjamin Kelley at Cumberland, Maryland; small skirmishes near Knoxville; and the POW exchange at Wilmington.[33]

He also sends Davis an update on the situation in North Carolina as well as Richard Taylor's command in Mississippi. He instructs Johnston to have Hardee remove all supplies from Sherman's projected path, and requests the adjutant general to

---

31 OR 47, pt. 2, 1247-9; OR 46, pt. 2, 1250-1; OR 49, pt. 1, 989. Upon receipt of Lee's order, Johnston fatalistically replied, "It is too late to expect me to concentrate troops capable of driving back Sherman." OR 47, pt. 1247. Knowing Beauregard's fragile ego, Lee informed him of Johnston's appointment as gently as he could, adding, "Together I feel assured you will beat back Sherman." OR 47, pt. 2, 1248. His tact seemed to work, as Beauregard replied, "In the defense of our common country I will at all times be happy to serve with or under so gallant and patriotic a soldier as General Johnston." Ibid. Because Johnston was awaiting orders at the time of his assignment to command, he had no staff so Lee's staffers had to find the officers Johnston wanted so they could be reassigned to him. See OR 47, pt. 2, 1263.

32 OR 53, 414; OR 47, pt. 2, 1256-7; OR 8, Series 2, 297-9; REL to Johnston, Feb. 23, 1865, Heritage Auctions lot #43463, Sept. 17, 2016 auction; REL to Mrs. REL, Feb. 23, 1865, REL papers, LOC; Krick, *CW Weather*, 151. Camp rumor among the HQ guard had Johnston taking command of the ANV while Lee went to the Carolinas to oversee operations there. One of them wrote, "It is said also that Gen. Beauregard is insane and that S. D. Lee has taken command of his army." G. M. Coiner to Kate Coiner, Feb. 24, 1865, Coiner papers, VHS. There seems to have been at least some truth to this rumor, as Taylor confided, "Now that Gen. Johnston has been placed in command by Gen. Lee, I don't think that we will go to South Carolina—at any rate just now." Tower, *Lee's Adjutant*, 227.

33 Davis, *Breckinridge*, 490; OR 46, pt. 2, 1254; OR 3, Series 4, 1121-2; OR 46, pt. 1, 471-2; OR 49, pt. 1, 47; OR 8, Series 2, 803-4. The timing of their meeting is not known; Lee does not seem to have known in advance they were coming.

have the staff of the Army of Tennessee assigned to Johnston. He writes to Gov. Vance asking for his assistance in curtailing the alarming number of desertions from North Carolina regiments.[34]

February 25, Saturday (Edge Hill/Richmond): Lee writes to Longstreet regarding the concentration of forces in case of a junction of Grant and Sherman, and defending Lynchburg. He instructs Beauregard to use his own judgment as to Hardee's movements, and instructs Ewell to remove or destroy the cotton and tobacco in Richmond. He reluctantly suspends the execution of a Private Huddleston for desertion but informs the War Department that the man is not entitled to clemency: "Hundreds of men are deserting nightly, but I cannot keep the army together unless examples are made of such cases." In the evening Lee receives a summons from an apparently displeased President Davis. "Rainy raw day."[35]

February 26, Sunday (Richmond): Lee and Longstreet meet with President Davis, Sec. Breckinridge, Gov. Smith, and Richmond Mayor Joseph Mayo at the Executive Mansion for much of the day. Lee tells them that the evacuation of the capital will be necessary but that he can probably provide 10 or 12 days advance notice. They also discuss another approach to peace: Longstreet meeting with his friend Union Gen. Edward O. C. Ord, commander of the Army of the James, in a sort of back-channel approach to Grant and Lincoln.[36]

February 27, Monday (Richmond): Lee and Jefferson Davis address recently exchanged POWs at Camp Lee, encouraging them not to take the furlough they are entitled to but rather to return to the ranks immediately.[37]

February 28, Tuesday (Richmond/Edge Hill): Lee returns to Petersburg in the evening, Rooney and Rob accompanying him on the train from Richmond. He orders Bragg to unite his force with Johnston's army for a combined strike at Sherman, and appoints Bryan Grimes to command Rodes's division. He answers a letter from Breckinridge about preparing for the evacuation of the capital, noting that he already discussed this in person and so will not repeat himself in writing. He also provides the latest desertion figures, noting that they are the worst in North Carolina units and Bushrod Johnson's division. He informs the war secretary that lack of funds is preventing the purchase of animals for the army's transportation needs; he recommends selling government cotton and tobacco to get the money for this. Periods of light rain.[38]

---

34 Freeman, *Lee's Dispatches*, 336-7; OR 47, pt. 2, 1266, 1270-1.

35 Longstreet, *From Manassas to Appomattox*, 645-6; REL to Longstreet, Feb. 25, 1865, REL papers, VHS; OR 47, pt. 2, 1272; OR 46, pt. 2, 1256-60; Tower, *Lee's Adjutant*, 228; Semmes diary, Feb. 25, 1865, Duke. Davis's telegram read: "Rumors assuming to be based on your views have affected the public mind, and it is reported obstructs needful legislation. A little further progress will produce panic. If you can spare the time I wish you to come here." OR 46, pt. 2, 1256. This was almost certainly the instance Venable later described involving a message from Davis that, according to Venable, read in part: "Your counsels are no longer wanted in this matter" in connection with the evacuation of Richmond: "On receiving this, Gen. Lee ordered his horse, rode over to Swift Creek and went on the train to Richmond. That day nothing was done about the tobacco or the removal of the Archives. Gen. Lee returned deeply depressed and I do not think he ever told anyone anything of this interview with the President." Venable to WHT, March 29, 1878, WHT papers, SH.

36 Davis, *Breckinridge*, 494; OR 46, pt. 2, 786, 1275-6; Longstreet, *From Manassas to Appomattox*, 582-9.

37 Jones, *War Clerk's Diary*, vol. 2, 435. This idea of forgoing the entitled furlough was not well received on this or any other occasion it was proposed. Ibid.

38 REL to Mrs. REL, March 1, 1865, REL papers, LOC; Tower, *Lee's Adjutant*, 228; OR 47, pt. 2, 1292; OR 46, pt. 2, 1262-6; Semmes diary, Feb. 28, 1865, Duke.

March 1865

Robert E. Lee's Army of Northern Virginia was melting away along with the winter snow. The rate of desertion was alarming, especially for units composed of men from North Carolina. Lee was unable to stop the bleeding regardless of what he tried. Out of sheer desperation Congress authorized the enlistment of slaves into the army to fight as soldiers in exchange for their freedom, but the measure was too little and far too late to matter.

Lee anticipated that U. S. Grant would take the offensive as soon as the roads dried sufficiently to move his men and wagons, and thus needed his army in fighting trim as soon as possible. He ordered an increase in the hours devoted to drill.[1] In the first part of the month Lee attended a morale-building competition between Sam McGowan's and John R. Cooke's brigades to see which was the better drilled. Much of the army's brass, including Henry Heth, Cadmus Wilcox, and John Gordon, turned out to witness the event.[2]

By most accounts Lee displayed few signs of the tremendous pressure he was under. A staff officer in Gordon's corps who was also a frequent visitor to Edge Hill recorded his observations of the general. Lee, he began,

> must have known that the end was not far distant, and yet no one could have thought so from any indications made in his manner and demeanor. He was always perfectly self-possessed and did not indicate by word or action anything that he may have been thinking of. Often I have seen him walking up and down the piazza of the Turnbull house, and, while apparently calm and serene, he no doubt was sadly contemplating the result which he well knew must soon come. His calm demeanor did not show any symptom or sign of the cares and responsibilities which were then so greatly oppressing and distressing him.[3]

Roger Pryor's wife Sara remembered that Lee routinely passed her residence, and on Sundays attended "a little wooden chapel nearer his quarters than St. Paul's Church."[4] In early March Lee was able to tell Mrs. Pryor that her husband had been exchanged and would soon rejoin her at Cottage Farm.[5]

British observer Lt. Col. Arthur Fremantle provided one of the best non-combatant accounts of Gettysburg, and one of his countrymen did the same for the final days at Petersburg and Richmond.

---

1 Caldwell, *Brigade of South Carolinians*, 202.

2 Greene, *Final Battles*, 71. The competition took place at Heth's HQ, the Pickrell house. Ibid.

3 H. A. London, "A Tribute to General Lee," *Wake Forest Student* (Jan. 1907), vol. 26, no. 5, 314.

4 Pryor, *My Day*, 235-6.

5 Ibid., 243-4. Roger Pryor, as fiery an advocate for secession as he was inept as a general, had been serving as a private and scout for the 3rd VA Cav., one of Fitz Lee's regiments, when he was captured on November 28, 1864. Exactly when the former general was returned is unclear. He had been held for months as a suspected spy at Fort Lafayette in New York, but was released with a parole signed by President Lincoln and at City Point in late February. He was still in Federal custody as of March 1. Pryor CSR. War clerk and diarist J. B. Jones, still writing from Richmond, mentions Pryor as late as April 8, 1865 (the day before Lee surrendered at Appomattox): "Roger A. Pryor is said to have remained voluntarily in Petersburg, and announces his abandonment of the Confederate States cause." Jones, *Rebel War Clerk's Diary*, vol. 2, 473.

Thomas Conolly, a member of the British Parliament, was a frequent guest of Gen. Lee's headquarters and also with wife Mary and the girls in Richmond.

Agnes, who did not seem to understand the seriousness of the military situation, traveled from Richmond to Petersburg in the closing days of March to visit her father. She stayed with friends in the city, which must have caused the general no little anxiety.

The first few days of the month saw Union cavalry general Phil Sheridan destroy the tiny remainder of Jubal Early's Valley Army at Waynesboro. The Union horsemen thereafter advanced unopposed across central Virginia, destroying railroads and the Kanawha Canal and eventually threatening Lee's lines from the rear.

Farther south in the Carolinas, Joe Johnston tried to stop William T. Sherman by attacking his divided army at Bentonville. The initial attack routed the Union column, but the tide turned and the defeated Confederates retreated to Raleigh. Johnston dispatched Lt. Gen. Theophilus Holmes to meet with Lee to discuss the details of uniting their respective armies.[6] In order to do that, however, Lee must first slip away from Richmond and Petersburg and the large Federal host gathered against him.

Grant was not about to let the Army of Northern Virginia slip out of its trenches unopposed and march south to unite with Johnston. In a last-ditch measure, Lee tasked John Gordon with determining the best part of the Union lines to attack to force Grant to contract his lines and thus provide some window of opportunity. Gordon chose Fort Stedman east of Petersburg as his target. Although the initial thrust on the early morning of March 25 was successful and part of the line captured, enemy numbers dictated the outcome once again and Gordon's heavily outnumbered men withdrew.

Grant took the opportunity to assume the offensive. Sheridan's troopers arrived from the Valley and Grant sent them with heavy infantry support around Lee's right flank to Dinwiddie Court House. Lee quickly scraped together a stopgap force under Maj. Gen. George Pickett in an effort to keep Grant from severing Lee's line of retreat.

* * *

---

6 Johnston, *Narrative*, 394-5; Carmichael, *Audacity Personified*, 158. Holmes' biographer was unable to determine the exact dates of this mission, but determined it occurred after Bentonville. He noted that Holmes may not have gotten an audience with Lee and met only with Davis and Breckinridge in Richmond. Hilderman, *T. H. Holmes*, 180.

March 1, Wednesday (Edge Hill): Gen. Lee notifies Sec. Breckinridge that Jubal Early reports enemy cavalry moving in force on Staunton, and provides a brief update on troop positions in North Carolina. Lee orders that March 10 will be a day of fasting and prayer in accordance with a proclamation from President Davis, and writes to Margaret B. Daingerfield of Amelia County to thank her for her kind letter and knit socks. He takes some time to write to wife Mary, mentioning his ride back to Petersburg. The general includes a pair of drawers that he needs let out. Intermittent bouts of cold rain.[7]

March 2, Thursday (Edge Hill): Lee receives a letter from James Longstreet regarding meeting with Union Gen. Ord to discuss the possibility of peace. Lee writes to Longstreet and to President Davis requesting that they meet to discuss this prospect, and he also writes to U. S. Grant suggesting a meeting for that purpose. The general sends a second letter to Grant regarding prisoner exchanges, and also warns both Longstreet and Breckinridge of the possible approach of Phil Sheridan's command from the Shenandoah Valley. To meet this potential threat, Lee sends nephew Fitz Lee's division to operate north of the James River. He informs Johnston and Gov. Vance of the need to widen the gauge of the Piedmont Railroad to match that of the Richmond & Danville.[8]

March 3, Friday (Edge Hill/Richmond): Lee meets with John Gordon in the early hours of the morning to discuss the strategic situation and the various options available. He updates Secretary Breckinridge on Sherman's movements and also requests that the newspapers remain silent on his approach through the Carolinas. Late in the day the general goes to Richmond, and from there urges Johnston to expedite the march of the Army of Tennessee to unite with Bragg.[9]

March 4, Saturday (Richmond): Gen. Lee meets with President Davis, Secretary Breckinridge, Quartermaster General Alexander Lawton, and Commissary General Isaac St. John for several hours. He sends instructions to Johnston to take command of all the troops operating in North Carolina.[10]

---

7   OR 46, pt. 1, 510; *OR* 47, pt. 1, 1044; GO 6, March 1, 1865, REL newspaper references, DSF papers, LVA; REL to M. B. Daingerfield, March 1, 1865, LJF papers, W&L; REL to Mrs. REL March 1, 1865, REL papers, LOC; Semmes diary, March 1, 1865, Duke. The force referenced by Early was the remnants of Sheridan's Army of the Shenandoah, which Grant wanted use to destroy the Virginia Central RR and James River & Kanawha Canal; Sheridan occupied Staunton on March 1 and destroyed what remained of Early's force at Waynesboro the next day. See Richard L. Nicholas, *Sheridan's James River Campaign of 1865 through Central Virginia* (Scottsville, VA, 2012), 10.

8   Dowdey, *Wartime Papers*, 911; REL to Longstreet, (1 letter, 1 telegram) March 2, 1865, REL HQ papers, VHS; *OR* 46, pt. 2, 824-5, 1227; *OR* 47, pt. 2, 1312; Semmes diary, March 2, 1865, Duke. The Piedmont RR connected two railroads of differing gauges: the R&D (5-ft.) and the North Carolina RR (4-ft., 8 1/2 inch) with the Piedmont built to match the NC RR. See Black, *Railroads of the CSA*. Venable wrote what essentially was a "last letter" to his son on this date, which the child's mother hid from him for years; in it he mentioned sending the boy a letter signed by Lee as well as a compass given him by the general. Venable to son, March 2, 1865, Margaret C. M. Venable memoirs, UVA.

9   Freeman, *Lee*, vol. 4, 7-9; *OR* 47, pt. 1, 1045; *OR* 46, pt. 2, 1279; *OR* 47, pt. 2, 1316. Gordon left a detailed account of this meeting but he could not recall the date it occurred. Freeman concluded it was held on the early morning of March 3, but that is not definite. Gordon, *Reminiscences*, 385-9; Freeman, *Lee*, vol. 4, 7-9. One topic that Lee and Gordon may have discussed was a proposal by engineer Capt. Oscar Hinrichs to go to New York City to foment an insurrection within the city's German element. Hinrichs wrote this proposal on Feb. 25, and he and Gordon discussed it on March 1, with Gordon promising to speak with Lee about it. Williams, *Stonewall's Prussian Mapmaker*, 251. Petersburg historian Wil Greene has the meeting with Gordon occurring on the morning of the 4th and Lee traveling to Richmond immediately thereafter, but based on the telegram to Johnston (which was sent from Richmond) Lee went to the capital sometime on the 3rd. A. Wilson Greene, *The Final Battles of the Petersburg Campaign: Breaking the Backbone of the Rebellion* (Knoxville, TN, 2008), 107. Taylor volunteered to accompany the general to Richmond to assist him, but Lee preferred that Taylor remain at Edge Hill to run HQ and took Charles Marshall instead. Taylor did not say specifically when Lee left. Tower, *Lee's Adjutant*, 229-31.

10 Davis, *Breckinridge*, 495; Jones, *Rebel War Clerk's Diary*, vol. 2, 439-40; *OR* 47, pt. 2, 1320. It was possibly this evening when Lee complained to Custis at dinner: "I have been up to see the Congress and they do not seem to be able to do

March 5, Sunday (Richmond): Lee attends church in the morning at St. Paul's with President Davis and Secretary of the Treasury George Trenholm. He directs Johnston not to interrupt supply trains when moving his troops by rail and that supplies stored at depots in North Carolina are for the ANV's use, so he must gather his own from the countryside; Lee grants him discretion to strike at either Sherman or Schofield first once united with Bragg.[11]

March 6, Monday (Richmond): Lee meets with Maj. Lewis Ginter, commissary of Thomas's Brigade, about procuring supplies for the army.[12]

March 7, Tuesday (Richmond/Edge Hill): Lee meets with Breckinridge to discuss how to convince President Davis to end the war. He also meets with Longstreet and Fitz Lee regarding Sheridan's approach, and with Col. Thomas Carter, whom he sends to Lynchburg to take command of the remnants of Early's artillery.[13]

Lee returns to Petersburg late in the day and informs Breckinridge, Lawton, and Longstreet that Phil Sheridan has reached Charlottesville and split his forces, with part riding toward Lynchburg and the other portion moving toward Columbia near the confluence of the James and Rivanna rivers; Lee wants all government property removed from threatened points and he instructs Longstreet to send out cavalry scouts to provide easrly warning of Sheridan's approach.[14]

March 8, Wednesday (Edge Hill): Lee forwards to Richmond a report of an enemy raid on Fredericksburg, and the desertion figures for the past 10 days noting that they "have diminished, but are still distressingly large." He also sends a letter from Beauregard reporting that Richard Taylor expects to be "overrun" in Mississippi and Alabama; Lee adds that he directed Taylor to remove all supplies and machinery from exposed points. He instructs Fitz Lee to guard High Bridge against Sheridan. Heavy rain.[15]

March 10 Friday (Edge Hill): Lee writes to Gov. Vance thanking him for his efforts to curb desertion

---

anything except to eat peanuts and chew tobacco, while my army is starving. I told them the condition the men were in and that something must be done at once, but I can't get them to do anything, or they are unable to do anything." Emory Thomas put this episode on this date, but he was uncertain because he included a question mark. *REL*, 348. Lee met with Senator R. M. T. Hunter while in Richmond "almost immediately after" meeting with Breckinridge; whether this was on the 4th or 5th is not known. Davis, *Honorable Defeat*, 36.

11 Sallie B. Putnam, *Richmond During the War* (Alexandria, VA, 1983), 356; *OR* 47, pt. 2, 1324-5. Freeman wrote that Lee returned to Petersburg after church, but Taylor stated that Lee was still in Richmond on the evening of the 5th. Venable also went to Richmond after Lee and Marshall, leaving Taylor alone at Edge Hill. Freeman, *Lee*, vol. 4, 10; Tower, *Lee's Adjutant*, 229-31.

12 GO 60, March 6, 1865, Lewis Ginter CSR; Royall, *Some Reminiscences*, 43-4. Ginter was one of the wealthiest businessmen in Richmond and would play a major role in the city's economic rebirth after the war. He designed the city's magnificent Jefferson Hotel and owned what is now the city's botanical garden bearing his name. Lee dispatched Ginter to NC to look for supplies. When he returned, he informed Lee there were abundant supplies to be had, but they could not be transported due to monopolization of the railroads by sutlers and speculators. Brian Burns, *Lewis Ginter: Richmond's Gilded Age Icon* (Charleston, SC, 2011), 62. March 6 was the date Lee proposed to meet with Grant to discuss peace terms, but the meeting did not occur. Dowdey, *Wartime Papers*, 911.

13 Davis, *Honorable Defeat*, 39; *OR* 46, pt. 2, 1291, 1303; Dozier, *Gunner in Lee's Army*, 293. It was possibly on this date when Lee traded in his Mexican War-era prayer book to an unknown bookseller for a new copy, and was also given a dozen additional copies to be distributed to the army. Jones, *Christ in the Camp*, 53.

14 *OR* 46, pt. 1, 510; REL to A. R. Lawton, March 7, 1865, Lawton papers, UNC; REL to Longstreet, March 7, 1865 (2 messages), REL HQ papers, VHS. Presumably Marshall accompanied Lee back to HQ; the date of Venable's return is not known as he may not have been in Richmond on official business (Taylor was unclear on this). This was Lee's last known trip to Richmond prior to his surrender at Appomattox on April 9, 1865.

15 *OR* 46, pt. 1, 544-5; *OR* 46, pt. 2, 1292-4; *OR* 49, pt. 1, 1035; Krick, *CW Weather*, 153. High Bridge carried the Southside RR over the Appomattox River just east of Farmville. It was completed in 1853, stood 125 feet above the river, and was 2,400 feet long. The ANV would cross the Appomattox there and partially destroy the bridge during the Appomattox Campaign. Jo D. Smith, *A History of High Bridge* (Farmville, VA, 1987), 5.

from North Carolina units, and informing him a detail was sent to guard the crossing points of the Roanoke River to further curtail deserters. He informs Breckinridge that Gen. Bragg attacked John Schofield at Kinston yesterday, and that Tom Rosser attempted to free the prisoners taken at Waynesboro, twice attacking the column escorting them north.

In the evening Lee receives a request from Breckinridge to put into writing his views on the military situation, as they discussed recently. Lee replies that lack of supply is the greatest hindrance to the Army of Northern Virginia's operations and the forces in the field elsewhere are vastly outnumbered. "Unless the men and animals can be subsisted, the army cannot be kept together, and our present lines must be abandoned. Nor can it be moved to any other position where it can operate to advantage without provisions to enable it to move in a body." He stoically concludes, "While the military situation is not favorable, it is not worse than the superior numbers and resources of the enemy justified us in expecting from the beginning. Indeed the legitimate military consequences of that superiority have been postponed longer than we had reason to anticipate." Lee rides along the lines and spends a long day inspecting the front. He does not return to his headquarters until after midnight.[16]

March 10, Friday (Edge Hill): Gen. Lee attends church at St. Paul's in observance of President Davis's proclaiming today a day of fasting and prayer; Gens. Richard Anderson, Bushrod Johnson, and Matt Ransom are also in the audience, but "owing to the bad weather, the congregation was small."

Lee meets with John Gordon regarding a breakout attempt from Petersburg. He instructs Gordon to examine the Federal lines and determine the best location for the attack. Lee recommends to Davis that action be taken immediately to put blacks in uniform; he notes that Gov. Smith supports this and that Gen. Ewell is already working on the formation of black units and is just waiting for the authorization. He informs Breckinridge that Wade Hampton's cavalry attacked Sherman's near Fayetteville, North Carolina, yesterday. Finally, Lee writes to wife Mary with a request to have his laundry done, and bemoans his late hour return yesterday. Rain all day.[17]

March 11, Saturday (Edge Hill): Lee informs Breckinridge that Bragg reports the enemy in his front entrenched and stopped for the present; Sherman is approaching Fayetteville; and Sheridan's cavalry is on the James at Columbia. He writes to Johnston that if the road to Raleigh is interdicted, he cannot remain at Petersburg and if Johnston is pushed much farther north "both armies would certainly starve." He urges Johnston to attack Sherman if even the slightest possibility of success presents: "A bold and unexpected attack might relieve us." He writes to Longstreet of rumors that the rest of George Thomas's army reached Virginia under Thomas himself. Lee receives a live turkey as a gift from an unknown Petersburg resident.[18]

March 12, Sunday (Edge Hill): Lee receives a message from Johnston asking if he is justified in defending the railroad through Raleigh, to which Lee replies that he cannot hold Petersburg or Richmond without it. Lee sends a short note to Mary. Thomas

---

16 OR 47, pt. 2, 1353-4; OR 47, pt. 1, 1045; OR 46, pt. 1, 540-1; OR 46, pt. 2, 1292, 1295-6; REL to Mrs. REL, March 10, 1865, REL papers, LOC. The dates of this correspondence with Breckinridge are open to question. Breckinridge's letter is dated the 8th, but Lee dated his reply as the 9th and began, "I have received tonight your letter of this date requesting my opinion..." It is possible that one of the dates printed in the OR is incorrect, or that Lee misdated his letter or incorrectly referred to Breckinridge's letter. William C. Davis, who has studied this series of correspondence more closely than anyone, concluded that Lee received Breckinridge's letter on the evening of the 8th and began a response immediately, but did not finish or send it until the 9th. Davis, *Honorable Defeat*, 39-40. Lee did not provide the details behind his late return to HQ.

17 Pearce, *Chambers Diary*, 249; Freeman, *Lee*, vol. 4, 12 n44; Davis, *Rise and Fall*, vol. 2, 650-1; Dowdey, *Wartime Papers*, 914; OR 47, pt. 1, 1045; REL to Mrs. REL, March 10, 1865, REL papers, LOC.

18 OR 47, pt. 1, 1045; OR 47, pt. 2, 1372; REL to Longstreet, March 11, 1865, John W. Fairfax papers, VHS; Nelson D. Lankford, ed., *An Irishman in Dixie: Thomas Conolly's Diary of the Fall of the Confederacy* (Columbia, SC, 1988), 56.

Conolly of Parliament meets Mary and Agnes in Richmond.[19]

March 13, Monday (Edge Hill): Congress passes and President Davis signs a bill authorizing blacks to serve in the army; Davis writes to Lee asking for his suggestions in putting this into effect. Lee receives several bottles of wine from Mary; when Gen. Bryan Grimes calls at headquarters to report his division present, Lee notices that Grimes is unwell and insists he partake of this wine. Rob comes for a visit and spends the night at his fathers's headquarters.[20]

March 14, Tuesday (Edge Hill): Lee advises the president of his correspondence with Johnston and what he knows of his plans to meet Sherman, but he cautions that the loss of Raleigh is likely. He provides Breckinridge with the names of officers wishing to recruit black troops, and updates him on Fitz's progress to intercept Sheridan. Rob returns to his command, and Lee writes to Mary thanking her for the wine and mentioning his visit with their son.[21]

March 15, Wednesday (Edge Hill/Petersburg): Lee sends a lengthy explanation to Johnston of the situation in Virginia, pointing out that there are no supplies to be had in Virginia and that he is dependent upon North Carolina to keep his army fed, thus the railroad connections must be held and if he withdraws west of Raleigh the area of supply for both armies will thus be lost. He directs that Johnston must unite with Bragg but he leaves it to Johnston's discretion as to whether they attack Sherman or Schofield, but whichever it must be quickly done. Lee tells Breckinridge that now is not the time to consolidate units as Congress authorized, as Johnston's army is actively campaigning and Lee's will be so within days. Lee sends an aide to Cottage Farm to ask if Thomas Conolly of Parliament can stay there during his visit to the ANV. Showers.[22]

March 16, Thursday (Edge Hill): Lee forwards to Breckinridge several letters from British Foreign Secretary Lord John Russell sent through the lines by Grant; Lee wants to know how to respond to them. Gen. Wilcox brings Thomas Conolly to Edge Hill to meet Lee and they spend about 30 minutes talking; Lee invites them back for dinner. Lee gives Conolly a photo of himself and a Confederate flag. Rain during the night.[23]

March 17, Friday (Edge Hill): Lee meets with Early at headquarters, discussing affairs in western Virginia; as a result of their conference, Tom Rosser's and John McCausland's cavalry is transferred to the ANV. Lee sends Breckinridge a lengthy synopsis of the situation in Alabama, North Carolina, southwest Virginia, and the Shenandoah Valley; he notes that Sheridan's recent raid has badly crippled his ability to provide sustenance for his cavalry.[24]

March 18, Saturday (Edge Hill): Lee advises Breckinridge in the morning that Hardee temporarily halted Sherman's advance elements at Averasboro on the 16th. He informs Texas Congressman John R.

---

19 Dowdey, *Wartime Papers*, 914-5; REL to Mrs. REL, March 12, 1865, REL papers, LOC; Lankford, *Irishman in Dixie*, 44. Conolly reached the Confederacy on one of the successful last blockade runners and planned to run the blockade to his home country with a shipment of cotton; instead he arrived in time to experience firsthand the collapse of Lee's Army of Northern Virginia. Lankford, *Irishman in Dixie*, 3.

20 Long, *CW Day by Day*, 651; OR 46, pt. 2, 1308; REL to Mrs. REL, March 14, 1865, REL papers, LOC; Cowper, *Grimes Letters*, 100.

21 OR 53, 414; REL to Breckinridge, March 14, 1865, REL HQ papers, VHS; OR 46, pt. 2, 1312; REL to Mrs. REL, March 14, 1865, REL papers, LOC.

22 OR 47, pt. 2, 1395-6; OR 3, Series 4, 1143-4; Pryor, *My Day*, 235-6; Lankford, *Irishman in Dixie*, 51; Krick, *CW Weather*, 153. A spy sighted Lee in Petersburg during the day, but provided no details. OR 46, pt. 3, 29.

23 OR 46, pt. 3, 1315-6; Lankford, *Irishman in Dixie*, 52-7; Krick, *CW Weather*, 153. Conolly wrote that dinner consisted of vegetable soup, wine, rice, vegetables, and a turkey that Lee had been keeping in anticipation of a visit from President Davis. Lankford, *Irishman in Dixie*, 56.

24 Early, *Memoirs*, 466; OR 46, pt. 3, 1318-9.

Baylor that he will not detach the Texas Brigade as requested for a campaign into Arizona Territory, and warns Roberta L. Parker of Dinwiddie County of the dangers of staying there as Grant's troops threaten that region. Breckinridge comes to Edge Hill in the afternoon and stays the night at headquarters.[25]

March 19, Sunday (Edge Hill): Lee continues to meet with Breckinridge at headquarters, and Lee gives him a letter from Gen. James Martin in western North Carolina regarding desertions and overall disloyalty in that region; Martin requests a regiment from Lee to restore order, but Lee informs him he can spare no one. He also pens a letter to Breckinridge concerning conditions at Mobile. He informs Longstreet that Anderson reports enemy movements in his front. Lee sends the staff to bed early in anticipation of rising early tomorrow, and writes to Mary a short note with the latest family news. Thomas Conolly again visits Mary and the girls in Richmond.[26]

March 20, Monday (Edge Hill): Lee congratulates Johnston for his victory over Sherman at Bentonville yesterday, and informs Richmond that William Mahone has orders to cooperate with Adm. Semmes's flotilla should he attempt a breakout with his ships.[27]

March 21, Tuesday (Edge Hill): Lee informs Breckinridge that Joe Johnston is withdrawing from Bentonville because Sherman's entire army is now on the field and Johnston can make no further advantageous moves there. The general adds that George Thomas's Union army is advancing from Knoxville. Lee informs Longstreet that all signs indicate that Gen. Grant is ready to begin his spring offensive, and inquires if Gen. Richard Taylor can organize a force in Georgia or Alabama to move into Tennessee and draw Thomas and Stoneman back in his direction.[28]

March 22, Wednesday (Edge Hill/Hatcher's Run): Lee informs Richmond that Thomas is at Knoxville and Stoneman near Knoxville; all available troops in that region are moving to intercept. Lee rides out to the lines on Hatcher's Run and Breckinridge comes to headquarters again.[29]

March 23, Thursday (Edge Hill): Gen. Lee meets with William Pendleton after breakfast, presumably to discuss getting the army's artillery out of Petersburg. Lee acknowledges Joe Johnston's withdrawal from Bentonville, congratulating him on the performance of the Army of Tennessee. Lee also asks Johnston where they should meet to face Sherman. He relays a message from Johnston to the War Department: "Sherman's course cannot be hindered by the small force I [Johnston] have. I can do no more than annoy him. I respectfully suggest that it is no longer a question whether you [Lee] leave

---

25 *OR* 47, pt. 1, 1046; REL to J. R. Baylor, March 18, 1865, Heritage Auctions lot # 42062, March 12, 2011 auction; REL to R. L. Parker, March 18, 1865, REL papers, MOC; Jones, *Rebel War Clerk's Diary*, vol. 2, 454.

26 Davis, *Honorable Defeat*, 47; *OR* 49, pt. 1, 1034-5; REL to Breckinridge, March 19, 1865, REL HQ papers, VHS; REL to Longstreet, March 19, 1865, REL HQ papers, VHS; Tower, *Lee's Adjutant*, 232-4; REL to Mrs. REL, March 19, 1865, REL papers, LOC; Lankford, *Irishman in Dixie*, 59. Breckinridge biographer William C. Davis wrote that his subject remained with Lee until the 20th, but it appears that he returned to Richmond sometime on the 19th based on Lee writing to him. Davis, *Honorable Defeat*, 47.

27 *OR* 47, pt. 2, 1441; *OR* 46, pt. 3, 1327. Mahone's Division replaced Pickett's command on the Howlett Line during the winter.

28 Dowdey, *Wartime Papers*, 915-6; *OR* 47, pt. 1, 1046; REL to Longstreet, March 21, 1865, REL papers, VHS; *OR* 49, pt. 2, 1136.

29 *OR* 49, pt. 2, 1141; Owen, *In Camp and Battle*, 366-7; Davis, *Honorable Defeat*, 47. It may have been on this date that Rev. J. William Jones encountered Lee with A. P. Hill, Heth, and Gordon inspecting the lines along Hatcher's Run. Jones was delivering religious tracts to the men when Lee and the others approached him. Hill joked that rations were needed much more than religious pamphlets just then, and Lee told Jones that he had a dozen prayer books given him by a Richmond bookseller to distribute to the men. The Reverend later visited HQ to retrieve the books but Lee was absent. When one of the staff brought the books to him, Jones discovered that Lee had signed them all. Jones, *Christ in Camp*, 52-3.

present position. You have only to decide where to meet Sherman."[30]

Lee answers a letter from U. S. Grant about the reported murder of several officers while being held as prisoners of war; Lee explains that he knows nothing of any murders and that if it occurred, it was without the sanction of the government. Lee also points out that rumors of Federal troops doing the same thing have reached Richmond. Lee notifies James Longstreet of reported enemy movements and that he is to work with Semmes's gunboats if possible. He issues orders for troops not to destroy crops during military operations. During the evening Lee meets with John Gordon regarding an offensive; Gordon recommends targeting Fort Stedman, and the discussion and planning of the operation lasts into the early hours of the 24th.[31]

March 24, Friday (Edge Hill): Lee requests that President Davis call upon Gov. Smith for all slaves between 18 and 45 years of age for military service: "The services of these men are now necessary to enable us to oppose the enemy." He informs Johnston that he doesn't think Sheridan is bound for North Carolina as Johnston thinks but rather will join Grant around Petersburg; he fears that Sherman intends to move on Weldon thus all supplies need to removed to safety. He tells Breckinridge that the reports of 60 enemy gunboats—15 of them monitors—in the James River near Bermuda Hundred must be greatly exaggerated, and he requests that the War Department order Gen. Mansfield Lovell to report to Lee. He asks Longstreet for the latest desertion figures from his side of the James and instructs him to have his command ready to support Gordon's attack tomorrow. He writes to Eliza Stiles, thanking her for the cherries and pickles she sent, noting that he shared them with her son and Mr. Turnbull.[32]

March 25, Saturday (Edge Hill/Petersburg): Gen. Lee rises well before dawn and meets with Gens. Gordon and Pendleton at Second Corps headquarters to discuss the upcoming attack on Fort Stedman, and then rides with Pendleton to Blandford Cemetery to observe Gordon's assault. Lee sends several messages to Longstreet to hurry his troops up to support Gordon's apparent breakthrough, but once it becomes obvious the attack has failed, he cancels those orders.[33]

Later in the day Lee rides to the right to investigate firing in that sector and comes under artillery fire at the Boisseau farm. In the evening he notifies Gen. Breckinridge that although Gordon had initial success against Stedman, his attack ultimately failed. He also recommends to Breckinridge that paroled prisoners not be considered exchanged until agreed upon by the POW commissioners on both sides. At some point during the day Lee acquires maps of Charlotte and Campbell counties, likely indicating where he envisions the army will operate in the near future.[34]

---

30 WHT to WNP, March 22, 1865, WNP papers, UNC; *OR* 47, pt. 2, 1454; Freeman, *Lee's Dispatches*, 339.

31 *OR* 8, Series 2, 425; REL to Longstreet, March 23, 1865, REL HQ papers, VHS; *OR* 46, pt. 2, 1287; Gordon, *Reminiscences*, 405; Eckert, *John Brown Gordon*, 110. The often dramatic Gordon described the meeting thusly: "With the exception of the last council of war on the night before the surrender, I believe this conference . . . was the most serious and impressive in my experience." *Reminiscences*, 405.

32 *OR* 46, pt. 3, 1339-40; *OR* 47, pt. 3, 682; Freeman, *Lee's Dispatches*, 340; REL to Longstreet, March 24, 1865 (2 messages), REL HQ papers, VHS; REL to Eliza Stiles, March 24, 1865, REL papers, LOC.

33 WHT to WNP, March 24, 1865, WNP papers, UNC; Gordon, *Reminiscences*, 410; Clark, *Histories of NC Regts*, vol. 4, 450; Thomas P. Devereux memoirs, UNC; WHT to Longstreet, March 25, 1865 (3 messages), REL HQ papers, VHS. Both Rooney and Rob reported to their father just as the attack faltered. Rob later wrote of the encounter: "I have often recalled the sadness of his face, its careworn expression. When he caught sight of his two sons, a bright smile at once lit up his countenance, and he showed very plainly his pleasure at seeing us. He thanked my brother for responding so promptly to his call upon him, and regretted that events had so shaped themselves that the division would not then be needed, as he had hoped it would be." Lee, *Recollections and Letters of REL*, 146-7.

34 Wiley, *Norfolk Blues*, 211; Caldwell, *McGowan's Brigade*, 205; *OR* 46, pt. 1, 382-3; *OR* 8, Series 2, 431; Venable to Alfred Rives, March 25, 1865, Venable CSR. An artilleryman at the Boisseau farm observed: "All this time the enemy were

March 26, Sunday (Edge Hill): Lee sends President Davis a lengthy explanation for his decision to attack Fort Stedman: "I fear now it will be impossible to prevent a junction between Grant and Sherman, nor do I deem it prudent that this army should maintain its position until the latter shall approach too near."[35]

March 27, Monday (Edge Hill/Petersburg): Lee instructs Early to send a portion of what remains of his force to Petersburg and to gather what he can to resist the enemy advance from Knoxville; to make up for the lack of strength in the Valley he charges John Mosby with the defense of that region. He updates Breckinridge on the latest desertion figures, noting the large number of Georgians leaving Longstreet's command to join local reserve units at home—Lee is concerned that the commanders of those local units are encouraging the men to desert. In a last attempt to curb desertion, Lee publishes orders that the penalty for advising comrades to desert is death.[36]

The general informs ANV Quartermaster James Corley of a complaint by the Virginia legislature concerning damage done by the army's supply wagons, and forwards to the War Department a letter from the officers of the 49th Georgia proposing to bring their regiment up to strength with black recruits. He informs Johnston that Beauregard was responsible for a portion of the Army of Tennessee being sent to Mississippi rather than North Carolina, so Lee cannot answer why it was done. Lee goes out on the lines and returns to headquarters after dark to find Rooney and Rob there, and they have a late dinner together. He receives a letter from Agnes and writes a short note to Mary that he does not know when he will get to Richmond again.[37]

March 28, Tuesday (Edge Hill): Lee tells Early that enemy strength in east Tennessee and southwest Virginia cannot possibly be as great as reported, so to gather what force he can "and use them to best advantage." Lee informs Breckinridge of the situation in Early's department and admits that Early may not be the best officer to command there given the lack of public confidence in him; given Breckinridge's familiarity with the department, who does he recommend? Lee forwards to Richmond more details on the Fort Stedman attack, and sends Corley's answer to the complaint about damage from supply wagons noting "every exertion has been made to correct the evil complained of."[38]

Lee writes to Longstreet regarding the use of the local reserves and enlisting blacks into their ranks. After lunch, Thomas Conolly comes to headquarters, spending about an hour talking with Lee on a variety of topics including the origins of the war and Gen. Winfield Scott; Lee autographs the flag he previously gave to Conolly. The general writes to daughter Agnes, mentioning that he would be glad to see her tomorrow, but is not sure that he will be able to do so because of the start of active campaigning. He also writes to wife Mary with family news and sock count, and sends her his copy of Scott's memoirs to read.[39]

---

keeping up a heavy artillery fire on our line, one of which passed within eight or ten feet of General Lee's head, who was riding by at the time." Wiley, *Norfolk Blues*, 211.

35 Dowdey, *Wartime Papers*, 916-8.

36 OR 46, pt. 3, 1353-9; OR 49, pt. 2, 1165-6.

37 OR 46, pt. 2, 1286, 1315-7; OR 47, pt. 3, 699; Dowdey, *Wartime Papers*, 919; REL to Mrs. REL, March 27, 1865, REL papers, LOC. The proposal from the 49th GA was approved at brigade, division, and corps level; Lee concurred but suggested that the current regiment be condensed to six companies and four new ones of black troops be created. OR 46, pt. 2, 1315-7.

38 OR 46, pt. 3, 1362; OR 49, pt. 2, 1166; OR 46, pt. 1, 383; OR 46, pt. 2, 1286-7. Lee sent a telegram to Breckinridge on this date inquiring if Edward Johnson could be exchanged, so he likely wanted Johnson to replace Early. OR 8, Series 2, 443.

39 REL to Longstreet, March 28, 1865, Fairfax papers, VHS; Lankford, *Irishman in Dixie*, 70-2; Dowdey, *Wartime Papers*, 918-9. According to Conolly, "Gen. Lee explains how slavery was not the object of the war! Virginia first agreed not to

March 29, Wednesday (Edge Hill): Lee learns that a large Federal force is headed west toward Hatcher's Run, and that enemy cavalry occupies Dinwiddie Court House. In the afternoon he directs George Pickett to move with his command to Sutherland's Station to guard the Southside Railroad. As Lee drafts the orders to Pickett, Fitz Lee reports at headquarters; Lee directs him to take command of all three cavalry divisions and join Pickett at Sutherland's. Lee remains in close communication with Longstreet to determine if Grant is again making concurrent moves on both sides of the James.[40]

Lee relieves Early of command in southwest Virginia, advising him to return to his home where he will find an explanatory letter from Lee. He informs Breckinridge of Early's relief with Lunsford Lomax and John Echols to temporarily command until a permanent replacement is appointed; Lee asks Breckinridge for suggestions for a replacement and notes that he thinks John Bell Hood's health removes him from consideration. He updates Richmond on affairs in Mississippi and Alabama and the latest reports regarding Stoneman's raid, cautioning both the War Department and Johnston that while the local reserves from southwest Virginia are necessary to oppose Stoneman if too many men are taken from the ammunition works it will cripple munitions production.[41]

Lee informs President Davis that logistics prevent Kirby Smith from bringing his forces east, but it would be just as beneficial if he could move into Missouri and draw pressure off of Lee and Johnston. Lee informs Richmond that Anderson attacked the Federals at Dinwiddie Court House during the late afternoon but could not drive them away. Agnes comes to Petersburg to visit friends; Lee sends her a note that he cannot see her due to the situation at Dinwiddie. Heavy rain during the night.[42]

March 30, Thursday (Edge Hill/ Sutherland's Station/ Burgess Mill): Lee rises very early and leaves Edge Hill around 3 a.m. for the right, where he meets with Anderson, Pickett, Heth, Pendleton, and several brigadiers near Sutherland's Station. He draws a plan of attack in the mud with a stick to drive the Federals back from Dinwiddie Court House; Conolly joins the discussion in progress and remains with Lee for the ensuing battle, sharing a snack of bread and sardines. Lee goes with Anderson, Pendleton, and Conolly to Burgess Mill placing artillery along the defensive works.[43]

Lee remains on the field until 6 p.m. when he returns to Edge Hill where he dines with Conolly. Lee advises Richmond of the fighting at Dinwiddie and cavalry skirmishing at Five Forks. Lee sends a personal letter to Early explaining the reasons for his removal, and asks Johnston if he can spare Beauregard to replace Early. Agnes attempts to visit her father at Edge Hill while he is at the front. Constant rain all day.[44]

---

secede but entered the movement when Lincoln demanded that it was to be put down by force." Lankford, *Irishman in Dixie*, 72.

40 *OR* 46, pt. 1, 1263; Giles Cooke diary, March 29, 1865, VHS; Hewitt, ed., *OR Supplement*, vol. 8, 467; Bearss, *Petersburg Campaign*, vol. 2, 337; REL to Longstreet, March 29, 1865 (3 messages), REL HQ papers, VHS.

41 *OR* 46, pt. 3, 1362-3, 1366; *OR* 49, pt. 2, 1171; Freeman, *Lee's Dispatches*, 349-51; *OR* 3, Series 4, 1164-5, 1175-6.

42 Freeman, *Lee's Dispatches*, 347-8; *OR* 46, pt. 1, 1263; Coulling, *Lee Girls*, 142; Dowdey, *Wartime Papers*, 920; Caldwell, *McGowan's Brigade*, 207.

43 Lankford, *Irishman in Dixie*, 73-7; Wise, *17th Virginia*, 219; Harrison, *Pickett's Men*, 135-6; Cadmus Wilcox, "Defense of Batteries Gregg and Whitworth, and the Evacuation of Petersburg," *SHSP*, vol. 4, 21-2. Conolly came to HQ around 7:00 a.m. to meet Lee but found only Charles Marshall and Mr. Turnbull present, Lee, Taylor, and Venable having ridden to Sutherland's Station. After taking breakfast with Marshall and Turnbull, Conolly was joined by Giles Cooke and John Esten Cooke and together they rode in search of Lee, joining him at Sutherland's around 9:00 a.m. Lankford, *Irishman in Dixie*, 73-6.

44 Giles Cooke diary, March 30, 1865, VHS; Lankford, *Irishman in Dixie*, 77; Dowdey, *Wartime Papers*, 921; *OR* 49, pt. 2, 1174-5; *OR* 47, pt. 3, 718; Coulling, *Lee Girls*, 142. Freeman wrote that Lee returned to HQ immediately after wrapping up his meeting at Sutherland's, but Giles Cooke and Thomas Conolly stated that he remained in the field until early evening.

March 31, Friday (Edge Hill/Burgess Mill): Lee is again in the saddle before dawn, and sends a note to Agnes apologizing that he again must go to the front and cannot see her. Along the White Oak Road fortifications he learns from Bushrod Johnson that the Federal left flank is vulnerable, and organizes an attacking force with elements from three divisions. Lee personally commits Wise's Brigade to the fighting, and Walter Taylor attempts to seize the colors of a South Carolina regiment and lead McGowan's Brigade in a charge. Lee and McGowan make a personal reconnaissance of the terrain before an enemy counterattack drives the Confederates back to their jump-off point, where Lee is waiting for them.[45]

After the battle Lee encounters Gen. Eppa Hunton who has several bullet holes in his clothes as well as a bullet-damaged sword scabbard. Lee tells him to have the holes in his coat mended, to which Hunton replies that he will be glad to return home for his wife to repair them; Lee replies, "The idea of…going to see wives, it is perfectly ridiculous sir." Returning to Edge Hill after the fighting, Lee informs Breckinridge of the day's action. He also notifies Richmond that the Federals laid siege to Mobile and are approaching Selma; he also advises that he requested the services of Gen. John T. Morgan of Alabama, possibly to raise black troops in Alabama. He receives a letter from Agnes, who is still in Petersburg, in the evening. Heavy rains.[46]

Lee, vol. 4, 31; Cooke diary, March 30, 1865, VHS; Lankford, *Irishman in Dixie*, 76-7. Beauregard informed Johnston that he did not wish the southwest Virginia command because there were no troops there, and in his opinion absolutely nothing could be accomplished there. OR 47, pt. 3, 719.

45 Dowdey, *Wartime Papers*, 921; Caldwell, *McGowan's Brigade*, 208, 212-3; Bearss, *Petersburg Campaign*, vol. 2, 411, 419; Norfolk *Landmark*, June 16, 1876, WHT papers, NPL. Lee placed the attacking force under the command of Bushrod Johnson and Richard Anderson, but neither seems to have exercised much if any direction over the action. See Cummings, *Yankee Quaker*, 316-7. Oscar Hinrichs observed A. P. Hill with Lee at some point during the fighting, making for a very top-heavy command structure for a mere four brigades. Williams, *Stonewall's Prussian Mapmaker*, 263.

46 Hunton, *Autobiography*, 119; Dowdey, *Wartime Papers*, 922-4; Freeman, *Lee's Dispatches*, 353-7; Freeman, *Lee*, vol. 4, 34. Lee's message regarding Morgan gives no details and Freeman made no attempt to provide context, but Morgan's last assignment was "to raise and organize black troops in Alabama and Mississippi," so Lee's message is probably in relation to that. Arthur W. Bergeron, Jr., "John Tyler Morgan," *Confederate General*, vol. 4, 191.

April 1865

Robert E. Lee knew that U.S. Grant's operations around Dinwiddie at the end of March posed a serious threat to his ability to hold Richmond and Petersburg. Unfortunately for the Confederacy, he did not have the manpower and resources he needed to effectively counter the threat to his right flank. Grant had been edging westward for months, stretching Lee's lines to the breaking point. On the first day of April, the forces under Gens. George Pickett and Fitz Lee at Five Forks were overwhelmed and scattered, clearing the way for Union troops to strike and cut the Southside Railroad—Lee's last supply line into the capital.[1]

The moment Lee had been warning President Davis and the War Department about for many weeks was now at hand: Petersburg and Richmond must be evacuated to save the army. By this time, however, Grant had the initiative and Lee could no longer influence the flow of events. Evacuating his lines on his own terms was now impossible.

Early on the morning of April 2 Grant launched a general assault all along the lines and breached the fortifications southwest of Petersburg. Gen. A. P. Hill was killed trying to contain the breakthrough, and Lee put himself in harm's way as his men attempted to keep the enemy from capturing his own headquarters at Edge Hill. As everything was collapsing at Petersburg Lee's thoughts turned to his daughter Agnes. He made sure she caught a train out of the city—it was the last to leave. Almost comically, Walter Taylor asked the general for permission to go marry his sweetheart in Richmond.

Thus began the final campaign of the Army of Northern Virginia. The various commands from Petersburg, Bermuda Hundred, Drewry's Bluff, and Richmond converged at Amelia Court House as Lee headed west. He hoped to somehow outrun Grant, turn south, and unite with Joe Johnston's army in North Carolina. It was a forlorn hope.[2]

The supply problems that had plagued the Virginia army—and the entire Confederacy—for the last year resurfaced at Amelia: the rations Lee expected to find were not there. While his men scoured the countryside in search of food, Grant's troops arrived and blocked Lee's path. Rather than attack, as he would have done in the past, Lee detoured north around Grant's flank in an effort to escape. All the while, his army was falling apart.

On the 6th almost two of his infantry corps (which were greatly reduced in numbers by this time) and much of the army's wagon train were lost in the fighting at Sailors Creek near Farmville. Lee's son Custis was among the captured, as was the rest of the Richmond garrison. The next day much of the headquarters baggage was jettisoned, including order books, returns, and other official

---

1 Pickett and Fitz were guests of Tom Rosser at a shad bake well to the rear when Sheridan attacked; they did not inform their lieutenants they were leaving the field, but their presence at the front likely would have made no difference in the outcome of the battle.

2 At Amelia Lee encountered Pickett for the first time since Five Forks. Much has been made of Lee's supposed remark directed at Pickett after Sailors Creek: "Why is that man still with the army?" or words to that effect. One eyewitness to their meeting at Amelia noted that it was quite cordial, with Lee telling him "I am glad to see you." Todd memoirs, p. 292, UNC.

papers. That evening Grant sent a message asking for Lee's surrender. The general declined, but did not shut the door entirely.[3]

Two days later Lee discovered his route of escape was blocked and he was all but surrounded at Appomattox Court House. Heavily outnumbered and out of supplies, Lee had little choice but to meet with Grant. He agreed to surrender the Army of Northern Virginia, and three days later his men stacked their arms and furled their flags for the last time. The end found Lee reunited with former friends in blue he had not seen since before the war. Lee said farewell to his officers and men and headed for Richmond, where his wife and daughters waited in anxiety for his safe return.[4]

When he rode away from Appomattox on the 12th he was escorted by Union cavalry—not as a prisoner, but as a show of respect to the general. When he reached Richmond on the 15th civilians and soldiers—both blue and gray—gathered to watch him ride in the rain through the streets of the burned-out city to his house on Franklin Street, where his wife and daughters waited. Although other armies were still in the field, Robert E. Lee's war was at an end.[5]

* * *

[3] Freeman, *Lee*, vol. 4, 141 n81, WHT to Edwin D. Newton, May 11, 1903, WHT papers, NPL. As the keeper of "the headquarters archives, including order books, letter-copy books, and other valuable documents," Walter Taylor was especially chagrined over their loss. Taylor, *General Lee*, 280-1. Some of these records were saved; the ANV Order Book for April 23–Oct. 28, 1862 at the MOC bears the notation "Capt. A. M. Chappell [14th Virginia] picked it up when the army passed through Amelia"—almost certainly a survivor of the HQ purge. It was later given to the Amelia chapter of the United Daughters of the Confederacy.

[4] At some point while at Appomattox Lee's headquarters flag—a Second National pattern—was cut up to prevent it from falling into Federal hands, the fragments distributed for safe keeping and kept as souvenirs. Several fragments of this flag are in the collection of the Museum of the Confederacy, including one with the notation. "When the soldiers knew that Gen. Lee was going to surrender at Appomattox, to keep the flag floating over his headquarters from falling into the hands of the enemy, they took it down and cut it into small pieces and distributed them to the soldiers. This fragment was given to Mr. Samuel Fox and brought home by him to Leesburg." MOC flag fragment, acc. # 985.13.01950. No "Samuel Fox" is listed among the soldiers paroled at Appomattox, nor does he appear on the roster of the 39th VA Cav. Battalion. William G. Nine and Ronald G. Wilson, *The Appomattox Paroles, April 9-15, 1865* (Lynchburg, VA, 1989).

[5] Agnes wrote of the first weeks of April: "It seems such an age of sorrow, each succeeding event more crushing than the last." Agnes to Hattie Powell, April 27, 1865, Powell family papers, W&M.

April 1, Saturday (Edge Hill): Lee advises President Davis that Sheridan's presence at Dinwiddie poses a great threat to the Southside and Richmond & Danville railroads and forces "us to prepare for the necessity of evacuating our position on James River at once," and he requests a meeting with Davis or Breckinridge at Petersburg. He writes to Agnes that he cannot see her today and advises her to return to Richmond. Lee also instructs Beauregard to take command in western North Carolina to oppose Stoneman and informs Richmond and Johnston of his orders.[6] He learns from Pickett that he was forced back from Dinwiddie Court House, prompting Lee to order him to "hold Five Forks at all hazards." Lee goes to Richard Anderson's headquarters to await developments from Pickett's front, where he learns that the enemy appears to be concentrating against Five Forks and also receives a report from Longstreet that Grant is stripping troops from north of the James.

While still at Anderson's headquarters in late afternoon or early evening Lee learns that Pickett was overwhelmed at Five Forks, with much of his command captured. He orders Longstreet to come to Petersburg himself with Field's Division and for Mahone to send at least a brigade from the Howlett Line, and he notifies Breckinridge that disaster befell Pickett today. He agrees to a meeting with Johnston at Petersburg as requested, and meets with Pendleton during the evening to discuss the evacuation of the lines.[7]

April 2, Sunday (Edge Hill/Mayfield/Cottage Farm/Petersburg): In the early hours of the morning A. P. Hill comes to headquarters to confer with Lee, whom he finds in his chambers in his bedclothes, unwell and unable to sleep. The two are soon joined by Longstreet, who has ridden ahead of his troops, and are looking over a map around dawn when Venable bursts into the room and announces that the Federals broke through Hill's lines nearby. All three go to the door from where troops are faintly visible in the dim light across the fields; Hill immediately mounts up and goes to investigate and Lee sends Venable to do likewise.[8]

Lee gets dressed and mounts Traveller. As he reaches the front gate to Edge Hill, Col. William Palmer and Sgt. George W. Tucker, two of Hill's aides, arrive to inform Lee that Hill was killed shortly after leaving HQ. Lee sends Col. Palmer to break the news to Hill's wife. Lee summons Henry Heth to take command of the Third Corps, but Heth is cut-off on the other side of the breakthrough so Lee gives the corps to Longstreet.[9]

Gen. Nathaniel Harris reports to Lee near Edge Hill soon after sunrise with a brigade from the Howlett Line and Lee sends him to Wilcox at Fort Gregg. Lee remains at Edge Hill for as long as possible, observing the approaching enemy through

---

6 Dowdey, *Wartime Papers*, 922-4; Roman, *Operations of Beauregard*, vol. 2, 385; *OR* 47, pt. 3, 736-7. Gen. P. G. T. Beauregard thought that Greensboro was a more important strategic point to hold than Salisbury and ordered his available forces to concentrate there, ceding the loss of Salisbury; he intended to meet with both Lee and Johnston to discuss how best to resist the tightening noose around their forces, but Lee surrendered before they could meet. Roman, *Operations of Beauregard*, vol. 2, 385.

7 Freeman, *Lee*, vol. 4, 36-41; Bernard, *War Talks*, 425; *OR* 46, pt. 1, 1263-4; *OR* 47, pt. 3, 737; WHT to WNP, April 1, 1865, WNP papers, UNC. In a note to Gen. Richard Ewell (at an unknown time on this date) Charles Marshall wrote with considerable understatement, "the General is much occupied now." *OR* 46, pt. 3, 1375-6. Pendleton later recalled, "Contemplating the then thinness of his own line, its vast extent and the feebleness of his entire force, [Lee] said 'General, if our cause fails its epitaph may be written, Died of Congress and the Newspapers.'" Clipping from "Banner of the South and Planters Journal," Augusta, GA, Jan. 23, 1871, in Charles C. Jones scrapbook, vol. 2, REL papers, Duke.

8 Robertson, *A. P. Hill*, 315; Longstreet, *From Manassas to Appomattox*, 604-5; Greene, *Final Battles*, 261-3; J. William Jones, "Further Details of the Death of General A. P. Hill," *SHSP*, vol. 12, 185-7. Venable wrote that Gen. Longstreet arrived at HQ "about one o'clock" and slept for several hours in an adjacent room; however, this is at odds with Longstreet's recollections and no other account mentions this. Jones, "Further Details of the Death of A. P. Hill," 185-6.

9 George W. Tucker, "Death of General A. P. Hill," *SHSP*, vol. 11, 569; William H. Palmer to WHT, June 25, 1905, WHT papers, SH; Henry Heth, Appomattox Campaign report, April 11, 1865, Heth papers, MOC. Lee reportedly cried at the news of Hill's death, remarking, "He is at rest now, and we who are left are the ones to suffer." Freeman, *Lee*, vol. 4, 47; Jones, "Further Details of the Death of A. P. Hill," 184.

his field glasses, joined by Gen. Pendleton and Col. William Poague, whose guns unlimber in the yard in front of the house, drawing enemy fire while the staff hastily pack up headquarters.[10]

Forced from Edge Hill, which is subsequently destroyed by artillery fire, Lee goes to Mayfield on the bank of Rohoic Creek to observe the fighting at Fort Gregg and Fort Whitworth. Around this time Lee warns Breckinridge, "I see no prospect of doing more than holding our position here till night. I am not certain I can do that. . . . I advise that all preparation be made for leaving Richmond tonight." Ewell joins Lee from Richmond in late morning or early afternoon, to discuss the details of evacuating the capital; Lee gives him two sweet potatoes for the return train ride.[11]

In early afternoon, Lee moves his command post to Cottage Farm, where he is joined by Longstreet, Wilcox, and Heth, where he announces his intention to withdraw from the Petersburg lines during the night and move to Amelia Court House. He sends several more communications to Richmond, advising that he thinks he can hold Petersburg until nightfall, but that Richmond must be evacuated tonight and that the Richmond & Danville Railroad is "safe until tomorrow." Taylor drafts the evacuation orders around 3:00 p.m., assisted by Palmer. Upon receipt of a message from President Davis complaining about having to evacuate Richmond tonight, Lee explodes "I am sure I gave him sufficient notice;" soon after he replies "it will be necessary to retire tonight."[12]

Lee goes to inspect what is left of the lines around the city and upon his return to Cottage Farm finds the mayor and several of the city council who want to know Lee's intentions; he is too busy to meet with them and tells them he will communicate with them at 10:00 p.m. During the night Lee informs Johnston that he has instructed all the local reserves to be sent to Danville. Lee sends Giles Cooke to meet with the city delegation while he attends to the evacuation personally. As Lee meets with the staff during the night to handle the logistics of the evacuation, Taylor asks permission to go to Richmond to marry Bettie Saunders, which Lee surprisingly grants. Late that night Lee crosses the

---

10 Nathaniel H. Harris, "Nineteenth Mississippi Regiment," *CV*, vol. 6, 70; John Esten Cooke, *Wearing of the Gray: Being Personal Portraits, Scenes, and Adventures of the War* (Baton Rouge, LA, 1997), 551-2; Lee, *Memoirs of WNP*, 396-7; Poague, *Gunner with Stonewall*, 110-3; Anthony J. Gage, *Southside Virginia in the Civil War: Amelia, Brunswick, Charlotte, Halifax, Lunenburg, Mecklenburg, Nottoway, & Prince Edward Counties* (Lynchburg, VA, 1999), 50. One witness remarked on how easily the Federals could have captured HQ and Lee with it before the arrival of Poague's guns: "They were advancing with a heavy skirmish line, but in a very uncertain, undetermined, and cautious manner, evidently expecting to receive resistance, and being surprised at not finding it, were overcautious in their movements. It was then, and is now, my opinion that had they . . . made a direct and determined charge, they could have easily captured General Lee's headquarters." Percy G. Hawes, "Last Days of the Army of Northern Virginia," *CV*, vol. 27, 341. The Federals approached so close to Edge Hill before it was evacuated that some of them reportedly observed Lee in rear of the guns; after carrying the position, they asked prisoners for the identity of the officer. Gage, *Southside Virginia*, 50. One of William Turnbull's neighbors, Smith Nottingham, rode to Edge Hill as the enemy approached to ask Lee if troops could arrive from Richmond in time, to which Lee unhesitatingly replied "no." Greene, *Final Battles*, 311. As HQ was being evacuated Lee gave his camp bed to Turnbull, who hid it in a ravine behind the house. B. J. Turnbull to WHT, Oct. 28, 1894, WHT papers, NPL. He also returned a chair he had borrowed from Rev. Theodorick Pryor. Greene, *Final Battles*, 250.

11 Taylor, *General Lee*, 273; Wyatt, *Plantation Houses*, 37; W. H. Palmer to WHT, June 25, 1905, WHT papers, SH; *OR* 46, pt. 1, 1264; Pfanz, *Ewell*, 327. Col. Palmer of Hill's staff "found General Lee on the bluff above Town Creek [Rohoic Creek] in the hottest place to be found, exposed to the fire of batteries this side of his former headquarters and the bluff near the Whitworth House." When Palmer informed Lee that Longstreet was requesting reinforcements, Lee lost his temper and shot back that he was tired of receiving requests for troops that he simply did not have. Palmer to WHT, June 25, 1905, WHT papers, SH. Mayfield, one of the oldest surviving structures in Dinwiddie County, dates to sometime in the 18th century. It has been moved from its wartime location and today sits only a few hundred yards east of the site of Edge Hill. Wyatt, *Plantation Houses*, 37.

12 Wilcox, "Defense of Batteries Gregg & Whitworth," 32; Heth report, Heth papers, MOC; *OR* 46, pt. 1, 1265; *OR* 46, pt. 3, 1378-1380; Dowdey, *Wartime Papers*, 926-8; Freeman, *Lee*, vol. 4, 54-5; Venable to WHT, March 29, 18/8, WHT papers, SH; Freeman, *Lee's Dispatches*, 375. Gen. and Mrs. Pryor fled Cottage Farm that morning. Greene, *Final Battles*, 247. Taylor noted that Lee dictated orders for the army to rendezvous at Amelia, but did not issue written orders for supplies to meet it there. WHT to Gordon McCabe, Dec. 8, 1906, WHT papers, NPL.

Appomattox on the Battersea bridge and personally directs traffic at the intersection of River and Hickory roads; it is not known where he stops for the night. Agnes escapes Petersburg on the last train out of the city that evening, escorted by Capt. James L. Clark of the 12th Virginia Cavalry.[13]

April 3, Monday (Summit/Hebron Church): Lee accompanies Longstreet's command on its march through Chesterfield County by way of Chesterfield Court House. He and Longstreet are at Summit Station on the Clover Hill Railroad in the early afternoon when Judge James H. Cox, of nearby Clover Hill plantation, invites them and their staff officers to his home for dinner; they stay about an hour. Lee learns that the road leading to Bevill's Bridge, where Longstreet and Gordon were to cross, is flooded and inaccessible, forcing a detour several miles to the north to Goode's Bridge.

Lee camps for the night at Hebron Church, from where he advises Ewell that not only is Bevill's Bridge flooded, but that the pontoon bridge Ewell was to use at Mattoax is not ready thus Ewell will have to get to Amelia via Goode's Bridge. Walter Taylor and Bettie Saunders are married in the early morning hours by Rev. Minnegerode at the Louis Crenshaw house on Main Street in Richmond; following the ceremony, Taylor leaves to catch up to Lee as fires from the destruction of military supplies grow out of control and consume much of the city, and rejoins the general in the morning.[14]

April 4, Tuesday (Hebron Church/Amelia Court House): Lee's courier to Ewell regarding the changes to the line of march returns in the morning, having been unable to find Ewell or any of his command. Lee then changes Ewell's instructions to get to Amelia however he can. Lee crosses the Appomattox at Goode's Bridge between 7:30 and 8:00 a.m. and rides to Amelia Court House where he discovers not the rations he expected for his hungry men but more artillery ammunition than his army can possibly use. He issues an appeal to the citizens of Amelia County to provide food for his army, and scouts in the direction of Burkeville where he witnesses a clash between the 14th Virginia Cavalry and elements of Sheridan's cavalry on Avery Church Road. Lee establishes headquarters in the yard of Mrs. Francis L. Smith and orders all excess wagons and artillery to Danville, and plots out the army's line of march upon making contact with Ewell's column.[15]

---

13 Greene, *Final Battles*, 247-8; *OR* 47, pt. 3, 741; Taylor, *General Lee*, 276-7; Freeman, *Lee*, vol. 4, 57; Thomas C. DeLeon, *Belles, Beaux, and Brains of the '60s* (New York, 1909), 399-400. It is possible that Lee spent the night at Chesterfield Court House, as an officer in the HQ guard—which did not travel with Lee on most of the retreat—noted that Lee left there when the 39th arrived, but the officer did not state what time of day this occurred. Driver, *39th Virginia Cavalry Battalion*, 44-5. Agnes arrived back in Richmond at 2:00 a.m.; Clark was on parole awaiting exchange and was not able to participate in the fighting. DeLeon, *Belles, Beaux, and Brains*, 399-400. As Clark had both Savannah and Baltimore connections, it is possible that either Lee or Marshall knew him or his family. See Krick, *Staff Officers in Gray*, 97.

14 Driver, *39th Virginia Cavalry Battalion*, 44-5; Lily Logan Morrill, *My Confederate Girlhood: The Memoirs of Kate Virginia Cox Logan* (Richmond, VA, 1932), 69-73; *OR* 46, pt. 3, 1382; Freeman, *Lee*, vol. 4, 65 n27; Tower, *Lee's Adjutant*, 242; Taylor, *General Lee*, 279. The Clover Hill RR carried coal from mines in western Chesterfield Co. to Petersburg via a connection with the Richmond & Petersburg at Chester; little remains of it today. Clover Hill dates to the late 1780s and is a private residence today. Judge Cox was a Union representative at Virginia's secession convention. Wyatt, *Plantation Houses*, 33; O'Dell, *Chesterfield County*, 213. Gen. Mahone's family stopped at Clover Hill only hours before Lee's visit on their way from Petersburg to their home in Clarksville. Morrill, *My Confederate Girlhood*, 68-9; Nelson M. Blake, *William Mahone of Virginia: Soldier and Political Insurgent* (Richmond, VA, 1935), 65-6. Hebron Church was located between Skinquarter and Winterpock south of the Richmond Zoo. O'Dell, *Chesterfield County*, 386. Although much of Richmond was consumed by fire, the Lee residence and most of the buildings on West Franklin Street escaped the flames. After Union forces occupied the city Mary complained when a black sentry was posted outside the house as a guard; a white soldier was substituted instead to appease her. A. A. and Mary Hoehling, *The Last Days of the Confederacy: An Eyewitness Account of the Fall of Richmond, Capital City of the Confederate States* (New York, 1981), 223, 235. Bettie Saunders wrote a detailed account of the events leading to the wedding. Tower, *Lee's Adjutant*, 241-3.

15 Dowdey, *Wartime Papers*, 929; Freeman, *Lee*, vol. 4, 66-70; Gage, *Southside Virginia*, 53; *OR* 46, pt. 3, 1384-5. Lee described this delay to scour the countryside for provisions as "fatal, and could not be retrieved." Jones, *Personal Reminiscences*, 311. Lee reportedly saved the life of an enemy officer on a runaway horse in this skirmish, ordering the

April 5, Wednesday (Amelia Court House/Jetersville/Amelia Springs): Lee meets with Longstreet in the morning, dressed "in full uniform . . . wearing his best clothes and equipments, his gold spurs and magnificent sword;" they are soon joined by William Mahone, whose division was bringing up the rear of the column, Gordon, Heth, and Wilcox. Around midday Lee, Longstreet, and Porter Alexander set off in the direction of Jetersville, where Sheridan's force is discovered blocking their path; after consulting Longstreet, Mahone, and Rooney he determines not to attack but to divert his line of march north to follow the Southside Railroad to Farmville.[16]

He orders a night march by way of Amelia Springs, but poor roads, enemy cavalry, and eventually a broken bridge over Flat Creek slows progress to a crawl. During this night march, Charles Marshall sets part of Mahone's Division in motion without notifying Mahone; as a result, the division becomes strung out along the road for which Lee reprimands Mahone. When Mahone discovers that Marshall was responsible for the "improper" orders to his men, he has a very heated confrontation with the staff officer. Lee dines with the Anderson family at Selma, then personally oversees the repair to the Flat Creek bridge. Lee spends the night at Amelia Springs. Several of the headquarters wagons are captured or destroyed when Union cavalry raids the wagon train at Paineville. Periods of rain.[17]

April 6, Thursday (Amelia Springs/Deatonville/Rice/Farmville): Lee outlines the order of march before dawn and meets with Commissary General Isaac St. John who explains that he was unable to get rations from Richmond to Amelia as requested but that a huge stockpile is at Farmville. Lee has breakfast at the Jeter home, Mill Grove, near Amelia Springs and shortly after dawn he heads west to Rice, arriving before midday; while awaiting the rest of the army he reconnoiters the area. He soon encounters Mahone, whom he censures for his treatment of Marshall earlier; as they are talking Venable arrives with word that much of the wagon train was captured. Lee,

---

troopers to hold their fire as the man's horse rode frantically toward their lines. Samuel M. Gaines, "How General R. E. Lee Save the Life of a Federal Officer," *SHSP*, vol. 33, 375-6. Francis L. Smith was a prominent Alexandria lawyer (not to be confused with VMI Superintendent Francis H. Smith) who assisted Lee with settling the Custis estate and later the seizure of Arlington; Smith's wife relocated to Amelia to escape the Union occupation. Jones, *Personal Reminiscences*, 230; Colston, "Efficiency of Gen. Lee's Ordnance," 23. The residence used by Mrs. Smith no longer stands. Chris Calkins, *Lee's Retreat: A History and Field Guide* (Richmond, VA, 2000), 41. Another account stated Lee stayed at the home of a "Mrs. Masters" in Amelia. W. A. Watson, "The Fighting at Sailor's Creek," *CV*, vol. 25, 449. This was almost certainly Evenholm, the residence of Leander and Jane Masters, but it appears that Lee did little more than visit with Mrs. Masters and declined her offer to stay at the house. Mary A. Jefferson, *Old Homes and Buildings in Amelia County, Virginia* (Amelia, VA, 1964), 61-2, 72. One postwar account by Col. William Cheek of the 1st NC Cavalry stated that Union "Jessie Scouts"—cavalrymen clad in Confederate uniforms—scoured the countryside in an attempt to capture Lee, searching every house around Amelia during the night of April 4/5; this account placed his HQ "in a piece of woods a short distance north of Amelia Court House and east of the railroad." Cheek was taken prisoner near Amelia and claimed to have heard his captors talking about this attempt. Clark, *Histories of the Several Regiments*, vol. 1, 782.

16 Newsome, *CW Talks*, 427; Maurice S. Fortin, ed., "History of the Eighth Alabama Volunteer Regiment, CSA," *Alabama Historical Quarterly*, vol. 39, no. 1-4, pg. 185; Gallagher, *Fighting for the Confederacy*, 521; *OR Supplement*, vol. 7, 766; William A. McClendon, *Recollections of War Times by an Old Veteran While Under Stonewall Jackson and Lieutenant General James Longstreet* (Tuscaloosa, AL, 2010), 254. Mahone was struck by Lee's appearance and "impressed with the idea that he anticipated some accident to himself and desired to be found in that dress." Newsome, *CW Talks*, 427. Alexander noted that he "never saw Gen. Lee seem so anxious to bring on a battle in my life" as on this occasion in front of Jetersville. Gallagher, *Fighting for the Confederacy*, 521.

17 Newsome, *CW Talks*, 428; Freeman, *Lee*, vol. 4, 77-9; T. M. R. Talcott, "From Petersburg to Appomattox," *SHSP*, vol. 32, 69; Ramsey, *7th South Carolina Cavalry*, 182. There were two estates known as Selma in relatively close proximity: the Anderson residence, which Lee visited, and another near Deatonsville where the Southall family lived. Michael F. Whitaker (Amelia County Historical Society) email to author, March 25, 2019. Some writers have Lee at the larger Southall Selma, but this was out of his line of march on the 5th and too close to Grant's troops around Jetersville. The definitive history of Amelia County states that Lee spent the night at the Anderson Selma. Kathleen H. Hadfield, ed., *Historical Notes on Amelia County, Virginia* (Amelia, VA, 1982), 85, 89. Amelia Springs was an elaborate resort dating to the 1820s. Almost no trace of it remains today, and the wartime road by which it was accessed is no longer passable. Jefferson, *Old Homes in Amelia*, 89-90.

Mahone, and Venable ride to high ground overlooking the valley of Sailors Creek where they observe the remnants of Anderson's and Ewell's corps fleeing in disorder. Lee reportedly remarks to Mahone, "My God, has the army been dissolved?" and seizes a flag to rally the survivors.[18]

Lee directs Mahone to cover the army's withdrawal to Farmville and instructs him to destroy High Bridge after crossing to the north side of the Appomattox. Lee returns to Rice about sundown where Marshall drafts orders for the move to Farmville. Before leaving Rice Lee informs the commander at Lynchburg that he can send no aid to that point but to resist as best as possible against enemy cavalry approaching from the west. He also telegraphs President Davis at Danville to communicate with him at Farmville tonight. Around midnight Lee rides into Farmville and spends the remainder of the night at the home of Patrick Jackson. Custis is captured with his division at Sailors Creek.[19]

April 7, Friday (Farmville/Cumberland Church): After but few hours rest Lee has only a cup of tea for breakfast at the Jackson house and meets with Breckinridge and St. John regarding his plans which he requests Breckinridge to relay to president Davis. He pays his respects to the widow of Col. John T. Thornton of the 3rd Virginia Cavalry, and learns from Richard Manson, one of Custis's couriers, of

---

18 OR 46, pt. 3, 599, 1387; Davis, *Honorable Defeat*, 100-1; Hadfield, *Historical Notes on Amelia Co.*, 88; Gallagher, *Fighting for the Confederacy*, 522-4; Freeman, *Lee*, vol. 4, 82-5; Newsome, *CW Talks*, 428-30. Breckinridge, QM General Alexander Lawton, and the army's chief engineer Jeremy Gilmer were likely also with St. John. Davis, *Honorable Defeat*, 100; Freeman, *Lee*, vol. 4, 81 n18; Davis, *Breckinridge*, 507. On April 4 Breckinridge was observed in company with Lawton, Brig. Gens. Joseph Davis and Walter H. Stevens, and Judge Robert Ould. Festus P. Summers, ed., *A Borderland Confederate* (Pittsburg, PA, 1962), 95. There were many Jeters living in Amelia, but the Jeters at Mill Grove were the closest and most likely. The tray on which Lee was served is in the collection of the Amelia Co. Historical Society. A notation with the tray states that Lee was served lunch on the 6th by Jim Washington, one of the Jeter slaves; however, Lee was gone from that area by midday, thus breakfast seems much more likely. Hadfield, *Historical Notes on Amelia Co.*, 88; Michael F. Whitaker email to author, March 25, 2019. Gen. Sheridan reportedly arrived at Mill Grove later in the day, but was not recognized by the family. Jefferson, *Old Homes of Amelia*, 29-30. Lee was sighted at Deatonsville around 7:00 a.m. Chris M. Calkins, "Final March to Appomattox: The 12th Virginia Infantry, April 2-12, 1865, an Eyewitness Account," *Civil War Regiments*, vol. 2, no. 3, p. 242. While witnessing the battle at Sailors Creek, Lee is said to have told Gen. Pendleton, "half of our army is destroyed." Lee, *Memoirs of WNP*, 401. The ever-creative John S. Wise penned a version of Sailors Creek that claims Lee said, "A few more Sailors Creeks and it will all be over—ended just as I expected it would end from the first." After the war Taylor described Wise's account a complete fabrication, especially that particular remark. Undated memo by WHT, WHT papers, NPL. As with much of his writing Mahone's account is likely also embellished, but it has been cited by historians for decades. A North Carolina soldier passed Lee attempting to rally the troops on the hill above Sailors Creek and recalled he was by himself with no aides. John C. Scarborough, "A Confederate Private's Reminiscences," *Wake Forest Student* (Jan. 1907), vol. 26, no. 5, 348-9.

19 Newsome, *CW Talks*, 431; Gallagher, *Fighting for the Confederacy*, 524; Freeman, *Lee* vol. 4, 94-5; REL to R. E. Colston, April 6, 1865, REL HQ papers, VHS; *OR* 46, pt. 3, 1386; Custis CSR. Mahone claimed that Lee assigned Col. Talcott's engineers to destroy High Bridge. There were two bridges there—the famed railroad bridge and a small wagon bridge on the valley floor. Newsome, *CW Talks*, 431. John Wise claimed long after the war that he "found General Lee . . . in an open field north of Rice's Station" after midnight, but the veracity of many incidents related in Wise's memoirs is questionable. Wise, *End of an Era*, 428. Prominent Norfolk resident Dr. William B. Selden wrote to Taylor long after the war regarding Wise's memoirs: "Capt. Wise's reputation has followed him here and people, since he attempted to masquerade as an ex-Governor of Virginia, have been rather wary of accepting his version of anything." W. B. Selden to WHT, Jan. 18, 1908, WHT papers, NPL. Jackson's house was located at 304 Beech St. Today, it is a private residence. Venable's childhood home, where his mother lived during the war, was on the eastern outskirts of Farmville; today, it is used as the Longwood University president's house. Lee and the staff passed it in the darkness on their way into the town. It is rather odd that they did not rest there, which suggests Lee was specifically seeking the Jackson house (see April 7). Longwood House, National Register of Historic Places nomination form, March 8, 1984. Coincidentally, the Venable house site was previously owned by the Johnston family and was the birthplace of Joseph E. Johnston. Johnston's home burned, and the Venable house was the rebuilt structure. Craig L. Symonds, *Joseph E. Johnston: A Civil War Biography* (New York, 1994), 10. Ewell, Kershaw, and most of their men were also captured at Sailors Creek. It became a matter of some debate over who exactly captured Custis, with Pvt. Harris S. Hawthorn, Co. F, 121st New York, and Pvt. David D. White, Co. E, 37th Massachusetts both claiming credit. OR 46, pt. 1, 937, 947. See Frank E. White, Jr., *Sailor's Creek: Major General G. W. Custis Lee, Captured with Controversy* (Lynchburg, VA, 2008) for detailed analysis.

Custis's capture yesterday. He meets with Porter Alexander at the bridge north of town across the Appomattox River and instructs Alexander to oversee its destruction, and encounters his nephew George T. Lee who was separated from his command and trying to rejoin it.[20]

He learns that although High Bridge itself was destroyed, the smaller wagon bridge below escaped destruction causing him to lose his temper, and instructs Mahone and Alexander to defend against the Federals coming from High Bridge while the rest of the army draws rations and crosses at Farmville.

He is very nearly captured when an enemy cavalry column fords the river and strikes the wagon train near Piedmont Coal Pits; he attempts to lead a counter-attack himself but is talked out of it. He encounters Rooney after this skirmish and tells his son "Keep your command together and in good spirits. . . . Don't let it think of surrender. I will get you out of this."[21]

Around the time of the brush with Gregg's cavalry, Pendleton meets with Lee to relay that many of the generals think the time to surrender is at hand; Lee replies "Oh no, I trust it has not come to that."[22]

---

20 Freeman, *Lee*, vol. 4, 95-7; Davis, *Breckinridge*, 507; Gage, *Southside Virginia*, 60-1; *OR* 47, pt. 3, 767; Gallagher, *Fighting for the Confederacy*, 525; Yates, *Perfect Gentleman*, vol. 1, 324-8. The sequence of events on the morning of the 7th is difficult to establish, as is the location for some of these events, most notably the meeting or meetings with Breckinridge and St. John. Freeman concluded that Lee met with St. John in Farmville but met with Breckinridge some time later north of the Appomattox at the home of Richard D. Thaxton. *Lee*, vol. 4, 95-7. Although biographer William C. Davis did not provide a location for the meeting with Breckinridge in his study of the general, his later book on the collapse of the Confederate government states they conferred several times during the short stay in Farmville, likely both at the Jackson house and north of the river. It is possible they both spent the night at the Jackson house. Davis, *Honorable Defeat*, 101-2, 105-6. Another version of the Farmville stop states that Lee met with Breckinridge, St. John, and Lawton in the Jackson house in the morning. And after Lee departed, the others remained in the house until the Federals were on the outskirts of the town. The enemy opened fire and a shell struck the house while they were still inside. Gage, *Southside Virginia*, 60-1. The conference with Breckinridge was the last known communication Lee had with any member of the Confederate government before his surrender. The Thornton house is at 309 Beech St.; Col. Thornton was killed at Sharpsburg on September 17, 1862. Krick, *Lee's Colonels*, 372. George Lee, the son of Charles Carter Lee, recalled of this meeting with his uncle: "There I saw General Lee, who was dismounted and in conversation with some officers. . . . I left my horse and went towards him. He saw me and . . . took a few steps in my direction. When I got close enough, without other salutation, he asked 'My son, why did you come here?' He looked very grave and tired, and there was a tone of distress in his voice as he made the inquiry. I replied that I thought it my duty to come. 'You ought not to have come. You can't do any good here,' he replied." Yates, *Perfect Gentleman*, vol. 1, 328.

21 Long, *Memoirs of REL*, 413-5; Freeman, *Lee*, vol. 4, 97-102; Chris Calkins, *Thirty-Six Hours Before Appomattox: The Battles of Sailor's Creek, High Bridge, Farmville and Cumberland Church* (Farmville, VA, 2006), 53; E. V. White to J. W. Daniel, June 5, 1905, John W. Daniel papers, Duke. Henry Wise provided Lee a much-needed laugh in the morning when he reported at the head of the remnants of Johnson's Division. Wise had washed his face in a puddle that morning, and the soil in that part of Virginia is mostly red clay so his face was covered in red and orange streaks. "I looked like a Comanche Indian and when I was telling [Lee] how we cut our way out," recalled Wise, the general "broke into a smile and said 'General go wash your face!'" Wise, *End of an Era*, 432. Wise also claimed that Lee, fed up with Bushrod Johnson's poor performance, placed the former governor in command of the remnants of Johnson's Division; Freeman's father witnessed a portion of this exchange. Henry A. Wise, "The Career of Wise's Brigade, 1861-1865," *SHSP*, vol. 25, 18-9; Freeman, *Lee*, vol. 4, 97 n31. Col. Elijah White, who commanded one of the cavalry brigades that drove back the Federals from the wagons, recalled Lee's close call: "We met Gen. [J. Irvin] Gregg's people in a piece of woods above the bridge. They were charging rapidly and were within (I do not think) over 100 yards of Lee. He was off his horse leaning against a tree looking at a map." Gregg was captured in this skirmish. White to J. W. Daniel, June 5, 1905, Daniel papers, Duke. The skirmish occurred just south of the intersection of routes 600 and 637 north of Farmville. Freeman noted that Lee's remark to Rooney about not thinking of surrender is the first recorded instance of Lee mentioning capitulation as a possible outcome of the situation. Freeman, *Lee*, vol. 4, 101.

22 Poague, *Gunner with Stonewall*, 119; Lee, *Memoirs of WNP*, 401-2; Long, *Memoirs of REL*, 417; Taylor, *General Lee*, 282-3. Gordon approached Pendleton near Farmville on the morning of the 7th and suggested that Pendleton meet with Lee. Clipping from "Banner of the South and Planters Journal," Augusta, GA, Jan. 23, 1871, in Charles C. Jones scrapbook, vol. 2, REL papers, Duke. Long wrote that Pendleton met with Lee the evening of the 7th, but Venable remembered nothing of the sort occurring that night. Long, *Memoirs of REL*, 416-7; Venable to WHT, March 9, 1864, WHT papers, SH. The time for the meeting with Pendleton is taken from William Poague, who encountered Pendleton in the afternoon as the latter returned from his meeting with Lee. Poague, *Gunner with Stonewall*, 119. In his history of the Appomattox Campaign, William Marvel put the meeting with Pendleton the morning of the 8th, apparently based on Alexander's

Lee establishes headquarters for the night at either Cumberland Church or the home of John Blanton across the road, and is joined by Longstreet. Around 9:30 p.m. he receives a note from Grant suggesting the surrender of the Army of Northern Virginia, which Lee passes to Longstreet who comments only "Not yet." Lee replies to Grant that he does not view the situation as hopeless but "I reciprocate your desire to avoid useless effusion of blood," and asks what terms Grant would offer. Periods of rain.[23]

April 8, Saturday (Cumberland Church/ Curdsville/ Appomattox Court House): Lee rises early and travels with Longstreet's column, causing a stir when he and his entourage approach William Poague's artillery at the head of the column; in the darkness Poague initially thinks them to be enemy cavalry and is ready to surrender his guns to them. At New Store Lee further consolidates what remains of the army, removing Lt. Gen. Richard Anderson, Maj. Gen. George Pickett, and Maj. Gen. Bushrod Johnson from command and assigning the remnants of their commands to others.[24]

During the afternoon Lee receives another message from Grant, giving his terms for surrender and offering to meet with Lee to discuss laying down arms. Lee replies "I do not think the emergency has arisen to call for the surrender of this army" and proposes to meet Grant at 10 o'clock tomorrow

---

recollections. William Marvel, *Lee's Last Retreat: The Flight to Appomattox* (Chapel Hill, NC, 2002), 143-4. Little is known of the meeting on the 7th at which the generals proposed that Lee surrender, but it became a heated point of contention after the war as to who was included. Both Longstreet and Gordon denied being party to it; Pendleton called Longstreet a liar: "You . . . inform me that when at Farmville, in agreement with other chief men I suggested to you the contingency of surrender, you were 'struck with the impression that I had lent myself to an offense, the penalty of which was death.' Permit me to suggest to you now, Sir, that your opinion on the subject of surrender must subsequently have undergone a radical change." WNP to Longstreet, April 14, 1875, in WNP order book, MOC. Longstreet claimed Pendleton provided Lee or his staff with a list of the officers involved, likely based on the phrasing used in Armistead Long's account of the event. Thirty years after the fact this was still a sore subject with Longstreet. Longstreet to WHT, March 6, 1894, WHT papers, SH. One account states that Richard Anderson was the preferred messenger to Lee. Elliott, *R. H. Anderson*, 125. The best overall analysis of the Pendleton meeting is in Frank P. Cauble, *The Surrender Proceedings: April 9, 1865, Appomattox Court House* (Lynchburg, VA, 1987), 9-12.

23 Calkins, *36 Hours*, 55-6; Freeman, *Lee* vol. 4, 103-6; Longstreet, *From Manassas to Appomattox*, 408-12; OR 46, pt. 3, 619; Fletcher L. Elmore, Jr., ed., *Diary of J. E. Whitehorne, 1st Sergt., Co. F, 12th Virginia Infantry, A. P. Hill's 3rd Corps, A.N.V.A.* (Louisville, KY, 1995), 73. Freeman concluded that HQ was at the Blanton house, but evidence exists that it may have been Cumberland Church itself (where Mahone had his HQ). Calkins, *36 Hours*, 55, 64 n69. T. M. R. Talcott wrote that HQ was at New Store several miles to the west, but he may have been referring only to his engineer regiment and not the Army of Northern Virginia's HQ. Hewitt, ed., *OR Supplement*, vol. 7, 766. Grant wrote the note to Lee at 5:00 p.m. and attempted to get it to Lee in the afternoon, but one of Moxley Sorrel's aides was fired on when he tried to answer the flag of truce. According to Sorrel, "That ended the truce business for that afternoon." Around 9:00 p.m. another flag of truce was displayed and Gen. Seth Williams delivered Grant's message, which was in Lee's hands in approximately 30 minutes. OR 46, pt. 3, 619; Sorrel, *Recollections*, 308-12. Venable kept as a souvenir the candle Lee used to read Grant's message (although he wrongly referred to this as being connected with Grant's message of April 8). Venable to WHT, March 9, 1894, WHT papers, SH.

24 Chris M. Calkins, *The Battles of Appomattox Station and Appomattox Court House, April 8-9, 1865* (Lynchburg, VA, 1987), 7-9; Poague, *Gunner with Stonewall*, 120; Newsome, *CW Talks*, 435; Henry A. London, "Last at Appomattox," *Five Points in the Record of North Carolina in the Great War of 1861-5* (Goldsboro, NC, 1904), 60, 63. Anderson left the army immediately, intending to make his way to join Johnston in NC. Elliott, *R. H. Anderson*, 125. Johnson's men were assigned to Maj. Gen. Bryan Grimes. London, "Last at Appomattox," 60, 63. Pickett's survivors were assigned to Mahone. Newsome, *CW Talks*, 435. Despite instructions to return home and await orders, both Pickett and Johnson remained with the ANV and were paroled at Appomattox. Calkins, *Battles of Appomattox*, 9. Pickett's relief became a contested point after the war, as did the assignment of his men to Mahone. Taylor described the Pickett situation as "a rather delicate matter," and informed Fitz Lee that Pickett had not been "dismissed," but rather orders were issued "relieving him from duty with the army." WHT to C. A. Culberson, Dec. ? 1904, WHT papers, SH; WHT to Fitz Lee, Jan. 15, 1904, WHT papers, NPL. Decades after the war Mahone found the order signed by Taylor assigning Pickett's men to him; its current location is not known. Mahone to WHT, Nov. 29, 1891, WHT papers, SH. According to Taylor, Col. William Palmer made the three copies of the orders sent to the three generals. WHT to Palmer, June 17, 1911, WHT papers, SH. For an in-depth analysis of the Lee-Pickett relationship at this point in the war, see Selcer, *Lee vs. Pickett*, 70-82. For information on the controversy surrounding the relief of these three officers, see Marvel, *Lee's Last Retreat*, 214-7.

morning on the Richmond Stage Road to discuss peace. By nightfall Lee reaches a ridge overlooking the Appomattox River and sets up headquarters on a wooded knoll less than two miles from Appomattox Court House, where he has a crude dinner with Longstreet.[25]

During the evening Gen. Lee sends Taylor to oversee the wagon train, and instructs the staff to dispose of everything that is not absolutely necessary in order to lighten their baggage. In the late evening the general hears artillery to the front and learns that Phil Sheridan's Union cavalry had attacked the artillery and wagons at Appomattox Station and blocked the road west. Shortly before midnight Lee meets with Gens. Longstreet, Gordon, and Fitz Lee to discuss a breakout attempt in the morning. They decide that Gordon and Fitz will attempt to open the road to the west and, if not successful, Fitz will escape with the cavalry to join Joe Johnston and Lee will surrender the rest of the army.

After the meeting concludes Gordon sends an aide to ask Lee where he should camp tomorrow night to which Lee replies, "Tell General Gordon I should be glad for him to halt just beyond the Tennessee line."[26]

April 9, Sunday (Appomattox Court House): Lee gets little if any sleep during the night and meets with Pendleton around 1:00 a.m., who finds Lee dressed in his finest uniform explaining "I have probably to be Gen. Grant's prisoner, and thought I must make my best appearance." He does not eat before going to the front, arriving in rear of Gordon's lines around 3:00 a.m. He sends Venable to ask Gordon his opinion for success, to which Gordon replies "Tell Gen. Lee I have fought my corps to a frazzle, and I fear I can do nothing unless I am heavily supported by Longstreet's corps." Upon receipt of Gordon's message Lee supposedly remarks "Then there is nothing left me but to go and see Gen. Grant, and I had rather die a thousand deaths."[27]

He then confers with Longstreet and Mahone around sunrise, both of whom advise against further attacks if Gordon cannot break through. As Gordon attacks, Porter Alexander meets with Lee, arguing not for surrender but dispersing the army to continue the war as a guerrilla struggle to which Lee is vehemently opposed because of the devastation such warfare would bring to the people and the countryside. Gen. Wise reports to Lee as his conversation with Alexander concludes; Lee informs the former governor that in the event of surrender

---

25 Cauble, *Surrender Proceedings*, 7-8; *OR* 46, pt. 3, 641; Longstreet, *From Manassas to Appomattox*, 623; Latrobe diary, April 8, 1865, VHS. Grant's second message to Lee has long been thought to reach Lee after dark, in part because of Freeman's penchant for taking Lee literally: Lee replied to Grant that the message was received "at a late hour," which Freeman interpreted to mean late at night. Freeman, *Lee*, vol. 4, 112-3. However, Federal communications reveal that it was sent in the morning and taken into Confederate lines before noon, and that Lee's answer was received "at dusk." *OR* 46, pt. 3, 643; Andrew A. Humphreys, *The Virginia Campaign, 1864 and 1865* (New York, 1995), 392. See Cauble, *Surrender Proceedings*, 7-9, for detailed analysis of when Grant's message reached Lee. Lige White's Comanches were the rear guard and his men accidentally killed several Federal soldiers attempting to deliver the message under flag of truce, not realizing their mission until it was too late. Marcellus French, "Second Dispatch from Grant to Lee," Marcellus French papers, LVA. The HQ site is part of the NPS property at Appomattox.

26 Taylor, *General Lee*, 287; Giles Cooke, "Just Before & After Lee surrendered," WHT papers, NPL; Freeman, *Lee*, vol. 4, 114-6; Maurice, *Lee's Aide de Camp*, 259; Fitz Lee, *General Lee*, 392-3. Years later Fitz Lee said of this last council of war, "It was a picture for an artist." Fitz to John Esten Cooke, no date, Cooke papers, Duke. A soldier observing the scene from afar recalled, "Lee was standing around a small bivouac fire. He had no tent, no camp stools, nothing but blankets, saddles and roots of trees to sit on. Only by the light of the bivouac fire could be seen the anguished faces as they looked upon the calm, resolute countenance of their great commander." Calkins, *Battles of Appomattox*, 55.

27 Lee, *Memoirs of WNP*, 404; Maurice, *Lee's Aide de Camp*, 259-60; Jones, *Personal Reminiscences of REL*, 143; Gordon, *Reminiscences*, 437-8; Cauble, *Surrender Proceedings*, 19-20. It is often written that Gordon's "fought to a frazzle" comment was made *after* he attacked that morning, largely because of the way he phrased it in his memoirs, which Freeman interpreted to mean the break-out attempt had already failed by the time he spoke with Venable. Gordon, *Reminiscences*, 437-8; Freeman, *Lee*, vol. 4, 120. Venable's own recollections make it clear that this exchange took place *before* any attack was made, Gordon and Fitz Lee were making final arrangements to attack when he arrived, and Taylor noted that the attack began around 5:00 a.m. Gordon, *Reminiscences*, 437-8; Taylor, *General Lee*, 285. See Cauble, *Surrender Proceedings*, 19-21 for detailed analysis; Cauble's timeline is followed here.

Wise may wish to escape as the Federals may intend to prosecute him. Taylor returns from his overnight mission with the wagon train and Lee informs him of his intent to surrender the army.[28]

Around 8:30 Lee, Taylor, Marshall, and Sgt. Tucker leave for the 10 a.m. meeting with Grant on the Stage Road. With Tucker in the lead, the party passes through the rear guard and soon encounters the skirmish line of the pursuing II Corps. Lt. Col. Charles Whittier approaches the party and gives Marshall a note from Grant explaining that he is not authorized to discuss peace, only the surrender of Lee's army. Marshall reads the note to Lee, who then instructs Marshall to draft a note to Grant proposing to surrender the Army of Northern Virginia.[29]

During this exchange Col. John Haskell gallops up to Lee to report that Fitz Lee found an unguarded road to allow the army to escape; Lee replies for Longstreet to use his own discretion regarding making the attempt. Another messenger arrives soon after, reporting that Fitz was mistaken. Lee requests a truce but Whittier replies that an attack has been ordered on this front and cannot be stopped; while Whittier seeks approval for a temporary cessation of hostilities, Federal troops approach and request Lee and his party to return to their lines ahead of their ordered attack. With a temporary cease-fire in effect, Lee and the others return within Confederate lines around 11:00 a.m. to an apple orchard near the Sweeney home to await Grant's response.[30]

Alexander instructs several nearby soldiers to arrange some fence rails for Lee to sit upon in the orchard, and Longstreet soon joins them among the apple trees. One of Gordon's aides brings Lt. Col. James Forsyth of Sheridan's staff to the orchard, seeking permission to pass through Confederate lines to communicate with Meade regarding the truce; Lee grants permission and details Taylor to accompany Forsyth. Not long after Taylor returns from this mission, Lt. Col. Orville Babcock and Lt. William Dunn of Grant's staff arrive, accompanied by Col. John Fairfax of Longstreet's staff, to escort Lee to meet Grant. As Lee rises to speak with Babcock, Longstreet advises him "Unless [Grant] offers you liberal terms, let us fight it out."[31]

Babcock informs Lee that Grant is en route to meet with Lee wherever Lee chooses, and at Lee's request extends the cease-fire for several hours. Lee,

---

28 Longstreet, *From Manassas to Appomattox*, 624-5; Newsome, *CW Talks*, 435-7; Gallagher, *Fighting for the Confederacy*, 530-3; Taylor, *General Lee*, 287. How close Lee got to Gordon's lines is a matter of debate. Freeman implied that he was immediately behind the troops, in which case it would be odd that he sent Venable to Gordon rather than simply meeting with the Georgian himself. Alexander wrote that he met with Lee on a hill about one and one-half miles from town, which seems a more probable location. Cauble, *Surrender Proceedings*, 21.

29 Alexander, *Military Memoirs*, 606; Taylor, *General Lee*, 288-9; Maurice, *Lee's Aide de Camp*, 262-6; OR 46, pt. 3, 664-6. C. C. Taliaferro of the 39th VA Cav. Battalion claimed that he had "the mournful duty of carrying the flag of truce," but Marshall wrote that it was Hill's courier Sgt. Tucker who had that role. Driver, *39th Virginia Cavalry Battalion*, 78; Maurice, *Lee's Aide de Camp*, 262. Taylor did not mention the flag bearer's name in any of his writings, and had to remind Marshall that Taylor also accompanied Lee on this ride. Taylor, *General Lee*, 288; WHT to Marshall, Jan. 26, 1894, WHT papers, NPL. As far as is known this was the first time Lee personally appeared under a flag of truce. Freeman, *Lee*, vol. 4, 125.

30 J. C. Haskell memoirs, Duke; Maurice, *Lee's Aide de Camp*, 264-6; Freeman, *Lee* vol. 4, 129; OR 46, pt. 3, 665-6; Gallagher, *Fighting for the Confederacy*, 533. It is not known exactly how much danger Lee was in personally while between the lines dealing with Whittier, but Longstreet confessed "the situation was embarrassing," as the Federals prepared for an attack on his lines while Lee was attempting to surrender the army. *From Manassas to Appomattox*, 625. Taylor informed Fitz Lee years later that he did not fear Lee would be fired upon, "as we had practically sheathed our swords and were under the protection of a flag of truce." WHT to Fitz Lee, Dec. 4, 1894, WHT papers, NPL. Gen. George Meade was unwell and confined to an ambulance some distance to the rear, which complicated the negotiations for a truce at the front. George R. Agassiz, *Meade's Headquarters, 1863-1865: Letters of Colonel Theodore Lyman from the Wilderness to Appomattox* (Salem, NH, 1987), 355-6.

31 Alexander to WHT, Aug. 10, 1896, WHT papers, NPL; Alexander to Longstreet, Aug. 26, 1892, Longstreet papers, NCA; Taylor, *General Lee*, 289; Freeman, *Lee*, vol. 4, 131; Charles F. Adams, *Lee at Appomattox and Other Papers* (New York, 1902), 28. According to Marshall, Lee napped while Taylor was away with Forsyth, and did not wake until Babcock's arrival. Maurice, *Lee's Aide de Camp*, 267. One of Alexander's couriers left a highly questionable account in which he claimed that George Custer met with Lee in the orchard shortly before Forsyth's arrival. This is extremely unlikely. John H. Sharp memoirs, Henry T. Sharp papers, UNC.

Marshall, and Pvt. Joshua O. Johns accompany Babcock and his orderly up the hill into the village, where Marshall goes in search of a meeting place; he meets Wilmer McLean in the street who shows Marshall one unacceptable house completely devoid of furniture then offers his own residence. Lee, Marshall, and Babcock wait for Grant in McLean's parlor for about 30 minutes, while Johns tends to the horses outside.[32]

Around 1:30 p.m. the Federal commander arrives accompanied by Gens. Phil Sheridan and Edward Ord and a number of aides. After brief initial talk of Mexico and the "Old Army," Lee and Grant discuss the surrender terms, which are then written out by Marshall and Grant's aide, Col. Ely Parker. As the staff officers draft copies of the agreement, Lee is reunited with his former West Point adjutant Gen. Seth Williams. Grant offers to provide rations for Lee's soldiers. The meeting concludes around 3:00 p.m., with Grant and the others raising their hats in salute to Lee as he, Marshall, and Pvt. Johns ride slowly away from the McLean house.[33]

Returning to the orchard, Lee briefly and emotionally addresses the troops who crowd around him, telling them they are surrendered and to return to their homes. Lee then goes into the orchard, which Col. Talcott's engineer regiment guards to keep onlookers at a distance. During the late afternoon Lee designates Longstreet, Gordon, and Pendleton "to carry into effect the stipulations" of the surrender. Around sunset Lee returns to the headquarters camp on hillside a mile away, riding past "two solid walls of men . . . along the whole distance," some cheering, others crying. During the evening Lee directs Marshall to draft a farewell order to the troops.[34]

April 10, Monday (Appomattox Court House): Around 10:00 a.m. Lee asks Marshall for the draft of

---

32 *OR* 46, pt. 3, 665-6; Horace Porter, "The Surrender at Appomattox Court House," *B&L*, vol. 4, 735; Coffeyville *Weekly Journal*, March 11, 1876; Patrick A. Shroeder, *Thirty Myths about Lee's Surrender* (Lynchburg, VA, 2016), 11; Maurice, *Lee's Aide de Camp*, 268-9. Freeman wrote that Sgt. Tucker was the orderly who accompanied Lee and Marshall to the McLean house, citing Marshall as his source; nearly every account of the surrender followed suit. Freeman, *Lee*, vol. 4, 133. However, in none of his accounts of the surrender did Marshall identify the orderly who rode into town to the actual surrender. He did name Tucker as the one who carried the flag to the 10:00 a.m. meeting on the Stage Road, and it seems Freeman inferred that Tucker must have done so on this occasion as well. A postwar account by another member of the 39th VA claimed that Johns was the one on this occasion, which is reinforced by an account of the surrender in the NY *Herald* that also named an "Orderly Johns." See Michael C. Hardy, "Who Rode with Lee at Appomattox?" http://michaelchardy.blogspot.com/2018/09/who-rode-with-lee-at-appomattox.html, and Shroeder, *Thirty Myths*, 11 Catlett Taliaferro's claim of carrying the flag of truce cannot fully be discounted on this occasion either. Driver, *39th Virginia Cavalry Battalion*, 78. It is worth noting that Tucker's obituary does not mention anything about his going to the McLean house with Lee, although other highlights of his military service are included; certainly if he accompanied Lee and Marshall as is commonly believed, it would have been included. Baltimore *Sun*, Dec. 5, 1905. NPS Appomattox historian Patrick Schroeder concluded that it was Johns at the McLean house. Schroeder, *Thirty Myths*, 11. Lee wanted Taylor to accompany him as well, but the aide did not wish to be present for the surrender and was allowed to stay behind, citing exhaustion from being in the saddle. Taylor, *Four Years*, 152-3.

33 Porter, "Surrender at Appomattox," 735-43; Ulysses S. Grant, *Personal Memoirs of U. S. Grant* (New York, 1995), 435; *OR* 46, pt. 3, 665-6; Maurice, *Lee's Aide de Camp*, 268-74. Many detailed accounts of the surrender proceedings exist, so the discussions between Lee and Grant about terms and other matters are not included here. Marshall wrote that the proceedings lasted approximately one hour. Maurice, *Lee's Aide de Camp*, 273. Earlier in the day, Seth Williams sent word to Lee that Custis was a prisoner and unharmed. Ibid, 270.

34 Gallagher, *Fighting for the Confederacy*, 539-40; Blackford, *War Years*, 292-5; *OR* 46, pt. 3, 666-7; Albert H. Campbell to Custis, Jan. 25, 1875, Cowan Auctions lot #35, Nov. 17, 2017 auction; Maurice, *Lee's Aide de Camp*, 275-8. Lt. Col. Blackford of the engineers noted at the orchard that "Lee seemed to be in one of his savage moods and when these moods were on him it was safer to keep out of his way, so his staff kept to their tree except when it was necessary to introduce the visitors." Blackford, *War Years*, 292. A popular myth soon arose, although dispelled by many including Grant and Marshall, that Lee surrendered under an apple tree in this orchard. As a result, the tree disappeared within hours, completely destroyed by souvenir hunters, as noted by one of Alexander's couriers: "I found that the Federal and Confederate soldiers had cut that tree down (the tree was about 12 inches in diameter), and torn even the roots up for relics, leaving nothing but a hole in the ground to evidence that it ever stood there." J. H. Sharp memoirs, H. T. Sharp papers, UNC.

the farewell order, but Marshall has not completed it due to constant interruptions so Lee orders him into the headquarters ambulance and posts a guard so he can work without disruption. Lee meets with Grant on a knoll just east of the town for about half an hour, discussing how best to achieve peace and how the actual laying down of arms and paroling of Lee's men is to proceed.

As Lee returns to camp, he is met by George Meade and several of his staff. Meade jokingly accuses Lee of being the source for his own gray hair. Henry Hunt, the chief of artillery for the Army of the Potomac, calls upon Lee after Meade departs and visits with the general for about 30 minutes until Henry Wise and Cadmus Wilcox arrive at headquarters; Wilcox takes Hunt to visit with Armistead Long. Some time after Meade's visit, William Mahone calls on Lee and the two discuss what should be done with the war all but over.[35]

Lee requests reports from his commanders and bureau chiefs for the period March 29— April 8, and receives paroles for himself and the staff with permission to travel to Richmond. Marshall completes the farewell order, which is approved by Lee with revisions and given to the headquarters clerks to be copied and distributed as General Orders #9. Lee has Grant's orders granting permission for all Confederate soldiers paroled at Appomattox to pass through Union lines distributed throughout his army, and he writes a letter of recommendation for Porter Alexander. Lee dines with his staff that evening. Rain.[36]

April 11, Tuesday (Appomattox Court House): Lee and Marshall work on the preliminary Appomattox Campaign report, requesting that all troop returns be submitted by tonight and that duplicate copies of officer paroles be forwarded to him in Richmond. He writes a recommendation letter for Col. Talcott and dines with Longstreet. The band of the 4th North Carolina serenades Lee in the evening; he emerges from his tent to compliment them after their performance of "When the Swallows Fly Homeward." Fitz Lee surrenders in Farmville in the evening.[37]

April 12, Wednesday (Appomattox Court House/ Buckingham Court House): Lt. Samuel C. Lovell and a detail of 16 men from the 4th Massachusetts Cavalry report to Lee soon after daybreak; they have been sent by Federal Gen. John Gibbon to escort Lee to Richmond. As Lee is not yet ready to depart, he instructs the Federals to wait until he and the staff have breakfast—which consists of hard tack, fried pork, and coffee around a "table made from a hardtack box"—and make their final arrangements to take their final leave from the Army of Northern Virginia. He completes his campaign report, noting that there were fewer than 8,000 infantry in the ranks on April 9, and bids his farewell to many of his

---

35 Maurice, *Lee's Aide de Camp*, 278; Porter, "Surrender at Appomattox," 745-6; Freeman, *Lee*, vol. 4, 152-4; Long, *Memoirs of REL*, 425-6; Mahone to James Longstreet, undated [1890], William Mahone papers, Auburn University. Much to Lee's dismay, Grant was stopped by Confederate pickets and refused entrance into Lee's lines; several markers just east of town on the old roadbed indicate the site of their meeting, which was the last time Lee saw Grant until May of 1869. Freeman, *Lee*, vol. 4, 150-1. Meade was escorted by Charles Field, but Field apparently handed off Meade to Lee when they met in the road and did not continue with them to Lee's tent. Field, "Campaign of 1864 & 1865," 562.

36 Freeman, *Lee*, vol. 4, 152; Taylor, *General Lee*, 294-6; *OR* 46, pt. 3, 686, 1392; Maurice, *Lee's Aide de Camp*, 278; REL to no recipient, April 10, 1865, EPA papers, UNC; Giles Cooke, "Just Before & After Lee Surrendered," WHT papers, NPL. The official parole return for ANV HQ lists 11 officers of all ranks (including Lee) and 87 enlisted men. *OR* 46, pt. 1, 1277. The individual paroles for all the HQ staff were signed by Taylor except for Taylor's, which Lee signed. Taylor, *General Lee*, 296. Two HQ clerks (Norman Bell of the Norfolk Light Artillery Blues and William H. Cantzon of the Washington Artillery) made at least 12 and almost certainly more "official" copies of GO 9, and many more were copied later as souvenirs, some of which were autographed by Lee. Marshall's personal copy with Lee's signature resides at Stratford Hall. Isabel Marshall to REL Memorial Foundation, Sept. 29, 1939, SH.

37 Freeman, *Lee*, vol. 4, 156-7; WHT to WNP, April 11, 1865 (3 messages), WNP papers, UNC; REL to no recipient, April 11, 1865, REL papers, MOC; Wert, *Longstreet*, 404; Devereux memoirs, UNC; *OR* 46, pt. 3, 719. Much confusion arises regarding events of the next few days due to an error made by Maj. Giles Cooke in his diary, who wrote the date "April 10" twice, thus throwing off events from the 11th onward by one day. Marvel's *Lee's Last Retreat* uses Giles's incorrect dates, thus his chronology of events is wrong by 24 hours.

officers including Longstreet, telling the Georgian's aide T. J. Goree "I am going to put my Old War Horse under your charge. I want you take good care of him." Although Lee stays in the area until the formal surrender and stacking of arms is under way, he takes no part in it.[38]

In the afternoon Lee departs for Richmond, accompanied by Taylor, Marshall, Venable, and Giles Cooke. They have one wagon in which the ill Cooke travels, and Lee's personal ambulance driven by cook Bryan Lynch and likely Pvt. Anthony S. Butt of the 39th Virginia Cavalry Battalion. The Massachusetts cavalrymen accompany them through the camps and for a short distance beyond before Lee bids them to return. After only a short time Venable leaves the party and rides for his mother's home in Farmville. The others camp several miles east of Buckingham Court House in woods near the home of Martha Sheppard, who extends an invitation for them to stay in her house, but Gen. Lee declines the offer.[39]

April 13, Thursday (Buckingham Court House/Walton's Mill): Lee and his party continue riding eastward on the road. His horse Traveller throws a shoe and is re-shod during the evening. They camp for the night at Walton's Mill, near Morning Side, the home of Dr. Richard P. Walton several miles west of Cartersville. Learning that the general is nearby, Mrs. Walton offers Lee and the others the use of her house for the night, but Lee declines.[40]

April 14, Friday (Walton's Mill/Fine Creek Mills): In the morning Gen. Lee pays his respects to Mrs. Walton while the others pack up the camp equipment. Cooke departs the party to join his family nearby, while the others ride to Lee's brother Charles Carter Lee's estate Windsor at Fine Creek Mills. When they find his brother's house completely full,

---

38 William B. Arnold, Edward T. Bouve, and LaSalle Corbell Pickett, *The Fourth Massachusetts Cavalry in the Closing Scenes of the War for the Maintenance of the Union, from Richmond to Appomattox* (Boston, 1910), 31-2; OR 46, pt. 1, 1265-7; Wert, *Longstreet*, 404; Cutrer, *Longstreet's Aide*, 167; Freeman, *Lee*, vol. 4, 157-8; Marvel, *Lee's Last Retreat*, 190. One of the Massachusetts troopers got a good look at Lee and left this observation: "He was dressed in a neat, gray uniform and was a splendid looking soldier. Commanding officers of corps and divisions of the Confederate army and other officers . . . came to take leave of him. . . . Almost every one of the officers went away in tears." Arnold, *Fourth Massachusetts Cavalry*, 32. This was the last time Lee and Longstreet ever saw each other, although they would correspond after the war. Wert, *Longstreet*, 404.

39 WHT to Charles M. Graves, Nov. ? 1904, WHT papers, NPL; Cooke, "Just Before & After Lee Surrendered," WHT papers, NPL; Arnold, *Fourth Massachusetts Cavalry*, 32; Freeman, *Lee*, vol. 4, 159. Freeman and others wrote that the name of the driver was "Britt," almost certainly a misreading of Taylor's handwriting as there was no Britt in the 39th, whereas Anthony Southgate Butt was a teamster, who surrendered at Appomattox and took the Oath of Allegiance in Richmond; he is almost certainly the driver. Freeman, *Lee*, vol. 4, 158; Driver, *39th Virginia Cavalry Battalion*, 133. Surgeon Lafayette Guild's wife Pattie claimed that she and her husband were also part of Lee's party, but none of the others mention them. See Pattie Guild, "Journey to and from Appomattox," *CV*, vol. 6, no. 1, 11-12. A Massachusetts trooper wrote of the reception Lee's men gave him as he passed through the camps for the final time: "Then commenced an ovation that seemed to me a wonderful manifestation of confidence and affection for this great military chieftain. From the time we left his camp till we passed the last of his regiments, the men seemed to come from everywhere and the "Rebel Yell" was continuous." Arnold, *Fourth Massachusetts Cavalry*, 32. Their campsite was in the vicinity of Lee Wayside Road east of Buckingham. During the afternoon Union Gen. Seth Williams saw Custis at City Point and learned from him that Rob was thought to be wounded in the arm and in a hospital at Burkeville; he notified Gibbon of the status of Lee's two sons with the request that Lee be informed, but Lee had already left Appomattox when the message was received. Williams added that Custis was paroled for 10 days to go to Richmond; it is not known when this information reached Lee. OR 46, pt. 3, 722-3.

40 Freeman, *Lee*, vol. 4, 160; "Robert E. Lee at Washington College—Notes from the papers of my father, Reverend E. C. Gordon, D.D., arranged by Frank N Gordon, M.D.," E. C. Gordon papers, Duke. The campsite was close to the intersection of Columbia Road and Flannagan Mill Road, just west of the Willis River. The mill was known variously as Walton's Mill, Flannagan's Mill, and Trice's Mill; although it appears on an 1864 map as "Walton's Mill," Freeman and most accounts, including the historical marker at the location, refer to it as "Flannagan's Mill." See Virginia Department of Historic Resources, *Historical Architectural Survey of Cumberland County, Virginia* (Richmond, VA, 1994), 81. Gordon did not identify "Mrs. Walton," but she seems to have been the wife of Dr. Thomas Walton. For this Walton family history, see Henry M. Woodson, *Historical Genealogy of the Woodsons and Their Connections* (Memphis, TN, 1915), 312-9.

they camp out on the lawn of John Gilliam's house next door.[41]

April 15, Saturday (Fine Creek Mills/ Richmond): Lee has breakfast with the Gilliams, befriending their young daughter Polly. His nephew John Lee and Rooney join for the last leg of the journey to Richmond, and Maj. Lewis Ginter joins them before they reach the capital. They arrive in the city around 3:00 p.m., crossing the James on a Federal pontoon bridge at the foot of 17th Street. A small crowd gathers outside Lee's Franklin St. residence to pay their respects as word of his return spreads. An eyewitness recorded his arrival: "As he descended from his horse, a large number of persons pressed forward and shook hands with him. This ceremony being gotten through with by the General as quietly and unostentatiously as possible, he retired into his house and the crowd dispersed." Heavy rain.[42]

[41] Gordon, "REL at Washington College," Gordon papers, Duke; Cooke, "Just Before & After Lee Surrendered," WHT papers, NPL; Taylor, *General Lee*, 297; Freeman, *Lee*, vol. 4, 160; Templeman, *Virginia Homes of the Lees*, 28. They reportedly encountered a barefoot soldier on the road for whom Lee procured shoes at Windsor. Freeman, *Lee*, vol. 4, 160. Their campsite was on Route 711 west of Fine Creek, probably near the intersection with Riverglade Road. Windsor is a private residence today and not visible from the road. Their route took them very close to Derwent, where the Lees resided for several months before moving to Lexington later in 1865.

[42] Freeman, *Lee*, vol. 4, 160-1; Taylor, *General Lee*, 297; Burns, *Lewis Ginter*, 70; Richmond *Whig*, April 17, 1865; Krick, *CW Weather*, 155. Federal Gen. Edward Ord, in command in Richmond, notified Grant of Lee's arrival and asked if orders to arrest former Confederate government officials (because of Lincoln's assassination) applied to Lee, cautioning "I think the rebellion here would be reopened" if Lee were arrested. OR 46, pt. 3, 762.

Epilogue

The Civil War effectively ended with the surrender of Lee's Army of Northern Virginia, but the war officially dragged on more than two months. It took time for news of the Appomattox surrender to filter across the Confederacy. Gen. Joseph E. Johnston's forces in North Carolina surrendered 17 days later on April 26. Farther west in the Department of Alabama, Mississippi, and East Louisiana, Lt. Gen. Richard Taylor capitulated on May 4, Lt. Gen. E. Kirby Smith surrendered the Trans-Mississippi troops on May 26, and the men under Brig. Gen. Stand Watie, a Cherokee who had thrown his lot in with the Confederacy, put down their arms on June 23. Thousands of men simply left the ranks and headed for home.[1]

Lee distanced himself from it all, preferring to remain out of sight in the Franklin Street house in Richmond. Visitors, friends and well-wishers, however, could not be kept away. One visitor whose persistence paid off was photographer Matthew Brady. Initially rebuffed in his attempt to photograph the general, Brady enlisted the aid of his friend Judge Robert Ould to lean on Mrs. Lee, who eventually convinced her husband to pose for the photographer. Lee allotted the photographer a single hour on April 20, during which six images were taken on the back porch of the house, including two with Custis and Walter Taylor.[2]

When Lee did venture out it was after dark when the streets were mostly empty; daughter Mildred usually accompanied him on these nighttime walks.[3] On one of their walks the pair visited the home of Robert Chilton, Lee's former chief of staff. To his surprise, one of John Mosby's officers was there in search of orders or advice on what course Mosby and his men—who had not yet given up the fight—should do. Honor-bound by his Appomattox parole not to issue any orders, Lee advised the young officer: "Go home, all you boys who fought with me, and help to build up the shattered fortunes of our state."[4]

The day after his return to the city following his surrender Lee learned of the assassination of Abraham Lincoln—an act he strongly condemned.[5] The same day he posed for Brady, Lee sent his last official communication to Jefferson Davis. The report provided him with the numbers paroled at Appomattox, but more importantly tried to convince the president to give up the effort and surrender. "A partisan war may be continued, and hostilities protracted, causing individual suffering

---

1 Long, *Civil War Day by Day*, 682, 685, 690, 693.

2 Nelson Lankford, *Richmond Burning: The Last Days of the Confederate Capital* (New York, 2002), 229-30; Hopkins, *Robert E. Lee in War and Peace*, 73-80; Marshall W. Fishwick, *Lee After the War* (New York, 1963), 36. Nearly every account has the Brady photographs taken on the 17th, however the April 21 edition of the Richmond Whig stated that Lee posed for Brady "yesterday," i.e. the 20th. Richmond Whig, April 21, 1865. William Frassanito concluded that they were taken on the 16th based on an interview Brady gave 26 years later. William A. Frassanito, *Grant and Lee: The Virginia Campaigns, 1864-1865* (New York, 1983), 416-8. The Whig date is used here as that newspaper reported on Brady in detail over a span of several days.

3 Charles B. Flood, *Lee: The Last Years* (Boston, 1981), 45.

4 Ibid, 46. Initially, Grant and Secretary of War Edwin Stanton specifically excluded Mosby from Lee's surrender. Grant, however, changed his mind and sent word to Mosby that his men would be offered the same terms as Lee's army. In doing so, he hoped to bring an end to hostilities as quickly as possible. Caroline E. Janney, ed., *Petersburg to Appomattox: The End of the War in Virginia* (Chapel Hill, NC, 2018), 198-9, 205-6.

5 Pryor, *Reading the Man*, 427; Flood, *Last Years*, 49.

and the devastation of the country," wrote Lee, "but I see no prospect by that means of achieving a separate independence. . . . To save useless effusion of blood, I would recommend measures be taken for suspension of hostilities and the restoration of peace."[6]

Lee fully recognized that the best thing everyone could now do was put the war behind them and begin the process of rebuilding the nation and healing the wounds of war. "The conciliatory manner in which President [Andrew] Johnson spoke of the South must have been particularly agreeable to one who has the interest of its people so much at heart as you," he wrote former Governor John Letcher. "I wish that spirit would become more general," he continued, adding:

> It would go far to promote confidence, and to calm feelings which too long existed. . . . The duty of [Virginia's] citizens, then, appears to me too plain to admit of doubt. All should unite in honest efforts to obliterate the effects of war, and to restore the blessings of peace. They should remain . . . in the country; promote harmony and good feeling; qualify themselves to vote; and elect to the State and general Legislatures wise and patriotic men, who will devote their abilities to the interests of the country, and the healing of all dissensions.[7]

In May, Lee told his former aide Armistead Long, "I am looking for some quiet little house in the woods. . . . I wish to get Mrs. Lee out of Richmond as soon as practicable."[8] At the end of June he got his wish, leaving the capital for a small farmhouse in Powhatan County known as Derwent.[9] His sojourn in the countryside proved but a brief one. In late August he began the final chapter of his life when he accepted the presidency of Washington College in Lexington, Virginia.[10] In Lee's mind there was perhaps no greater way to help the South recover than to help educate its youth. Son Rob theorized his father "saw at Washington College . . . [the chance] for helping, by his experience and example, the youth of his country to become good and useful citizens."[11]

As he had done for the past four years, Lee would give his all to that new duty.

---

6 Dowdey, *Wartime Papers*, 938-9.

7 Joseph H. Crute, Jr., Robert E. *Lee's Derwent Letters* (n.p., 2004), 29-30.

8 Fishwick, *Lee, After the War*, 50.

9 Crute, *Derwent Letters*, 13.

10 Franklin L. Riley, ed., *General Robert E. Lee after Appomattox* (New York, 1922), 5, 10.

11 Lee, *Recollections and Letters of REL*, 183.

Bibliography

Manuscripts

Auburn University, Ralph B. Draughton Library, Auburn, AL
    William Mahone papers
Thomas Balch Library, Leesburg, VA
    "General Lee's Visit to Leesburg and Harrison Hall"
Clarke County Historical Association, Berryville, VA
    Adams Express Company receipt
College of William & Mary, Earl G. Swem Library, Williamsburg, VA
    Joseph E. Johnston papers
    Gustavus A. Myers papers
    Powell family papers
Dabbs House Museum, Richmond, VA
    Robert E. Lee papers
Davidson University, E. H. Little Library, Davidson, NC
    William E. Ardrey diary
Duke University, David M. Rubenstein Library, Durham, NC
    Alexander R. Boteler papers
    Alfred and Elizabeth Brand collection of Civil War and Lee Family Papers
    Edward G. Butler papers
    John Esten Cooke diary
    John W. Daniel papers
    E. C. Gordon papers
    John C. Haskell papers
    Robert T. Hubbard papers
    Williamson Kelly papers
    Robert E. Lee papers
    William Mahone papers
    Green W. Penn papers
    Mary B. Seifer papers
    Raphael Semmes papers
    John W. Wayland papers
Georgia Historical Society, Savannah, Georgia
    Harrison family papers
    Stiles family papers
Gilder-Lehrman Institute of American History, New York, NY
    Gilder-Lehrman collection
Handley Library, Winchester, VA
    Thomas G. Lupton papers
Huntington Library, San Marino, CA
    Robert A. Brock collection
Library of Congress, Washington, DC
    Robert E. Lee papers
Library of Virginia, Richmond, VA
    Joseph R. Anderson papers
    Jane Eliza Carter Beverly reminiscences
    Fairfax family papers
    Douglas S. Freeman papers
    Marcellus French papers
    Jamestown Exhibit papers
    Lee family papers
    Robert E. Lee papers
    Executive papers of Governor John Letcher
    E. C. Moncure papers
    James Vass papers
    Franklin G. Walter papers
    John A. Washington papers
Missouri Historical Society, St. Louis, MO
    Robert E. Lee collection
Museum of the Confederacy, Richmond, VA
    Army of Northern Virginia Order Book
    Robert H. Chilton papers
    Henry Heth papers
    Stonewall Jackson papers
    Robert E. Lee papers
    William Nelson Pendleton order book
    Kate Mason Rowland papers
National Archives, Washington, DC
    Confederate Civilians File
    Confederate Compiled Service Records
    Records of the Adjutant General
    Records of the Virginia Forces
New York Public Library, New York, NY
    Ezra A. Carman papers
Norfolk Public Library, William H. Sargeant Memorial Collection, Norfolk, VA
    Walter H. Taylor papers
North Carolina Museum of History
    Walter J. Clark letters
Raab Collection, Ardmore, PA
    Robert E. Lee letter
South Carolina Historical Society, Charleston, SC
    Miscellaneous Manuscript Collection
State Archives of North Carolina, Raleigh, NC
    Walter J. Bone papers
    Lawrence O'B. Branch papers
    J. B. Clifton diary
    Robert E. Lee papers
    Alfred M. Scales papers
    Zebulon B. Vance papers

Stratford Hall, Stratford, VA
  Lee papers
  Walter H. Taylor papers
Tulane University, Howard-Tilton Memorial Library, New Orleans, LA
  George H. & Katherine M. Davis collection
U.S. Army War College, Carlisle, PA
  Robert E. Lee letter
University of Florida, George A. Smathers Library, Gainesville, FL
  David L. Yulee papers
University of Georgia, Hargrett Library, Athens, GA
  William S. Basinger collection
  Stephen A. & Margaret P. Corker papers
  Robert E. Lee collection
University of North Carolina, Southern Historical Collection, Louis R. Wilson Library, Chapel Hill, NC
  E. Porter Alexander papers
  Charles H. Andrews papers
  Thomas Bragg diary
  Thomas L. Clingman papers
  Raleigh E. Colston papers
  Montgomery D. Corse papers
  Telamon Cuyler papers
  Burke Davis papers
  Thomas P. Devereux papers
  Jeremy F. Gilmer papers
  James A. Graham papers
  Peter W. Hairston papers
  D. H. Hill papers
  Thomas J. Jackson papers
  Alexander R. Lawton papers
  Robert E. Lee papers
  Stephen D. Lee papers
  Armistead L. Long papers
  James Longstreet papers
  John N. Maffitt papers
  Stephen R. Mallory diary
  Lafayette McLaws papers
  Raphael J. Moses papers
  Joseph C. Norwood papers
  Charles H. Olmstead papers
  William N. Pendleton papers
  Polk-Ewell-Brown papers
  Henry T. Sharp papers
  Westwood A. Todd papers
  George L. Upshur papers
  Charles S. Venable papers
  Whitaker-Snipes papers
  Robert W. Winston papers
University of Virginia, Albert and Shirley Small Special Collections Library, Charlottesville, VA
  Robert E. Lee papers
  McDowell-Miller-Warner papers
Virginia Historical Society, Richmond, VA
  Bemiss family papers
  Bryan family papers
  Burwell family papers
  Cazenove family papers
  Cocke family papers
  Coiner family papers
  Confederate States Army papers
  Giles Cooke diary
  J. A. Cooke papers
  Coons family papers
  R. H. Cunningham papers
  John W. Daniel papers
  Charles H. Dimmock papers
  John W. Fairfax papers
  Fitzhugh family papers
  Jeremy Gilmer map collection
  John Guerrant papers
  William S. Harrison papers
  A. W. Hoge diary
  Conway R. Howard papers
  Hundley family papers
  J. Ambler Johnston papers
  Samuel R. Johnston papers
  Osmun Latrobe diary
  Lee family papers
  George B. Lee papers
  Robert E. Lee papers
  Robert E. Lee Headquarters papers
  Henry B. McClellan papers
  Hunter McGuire papers
  John S. Mosby papers
  Gabrielle Page papers
  Peyton family papers
  Eleanor Beverley Meade Platt papers
  Robertson family papers
  Robinson family papers
  Scott family papers
  Raphael Semmes papers
  Francis W. Smith papers
  Sara Smith papers
  Talcott family papers
  Charles S. Venable papers
  George W. Venable papers
  John A. Washington papers
  Beverly R. Wellford papers
  Wickham family papers

Virginia Military Institute, Lexington, VA
    Francis M. Boykin papers
    Thomas J. Jackson papers
    Robert E. Lee papers
    William Mahone papers
    Francis H. Smith papers
    Walter H. Taylor papers

Virginia Polytechnic Institute & State University, Blacksburg, VA
    Milton Koontz diary
    Robert T. Preston papers
    Thomas R. Sharp diary

Washington & Lee University, James G. Leyburn Library, Lexington, VA
    Mary P. Coulling papers
    Robert E. Lee papers
    Lee-Jackson Foundation papers
    Alexander S. Patton diary
    Louisa F. Washington papers

West Virginia University, West Virginia & Regional History Center, Morgantown, WV
    Roy Bird Cook papers

Newspapers

Baltimore (MD) *Sun*
Charleston (SC) *Mercury*
Coffeyville (KS) *Weekly Journal*
Norfolk (VA) *Landmark*
Orange (VA) *Review*
Richmond (VA) *Daily Dispatch*
Richmond (VA) *Examiner*
Richmond (VA) *Whig*
Savannah (GA) *Daily Morning News*
Savannah (GA) *Republican*

Published Materials

Primary Works

"A Member of the Bar" [John Carrigan]. *Cheat Mountain: Unwritten Chapter of the Late War*. Nashville, TN: Albert B. Tavel, 1885.

Agassiz, George R. *Meade's Headquarters 1863-1865: Letters of Colonel Theodore Lyman from the Wilderness to Appomattox*. Salem, NH: Ayer Company, 1987.

Allan, William. *The Army of Northern Virginia in 1862*. Boston: Houghton Mifflin, 1892.

Alexander, Edward P. *Military Memoirs of a Confederate: A Critical Narrative*. Dayton, OH: Morningside Books, 2005.

Andrews, Garnett. "A Battle Planned but not Fought," in *Confederate Veteran*, vol. 5, no. 6 (June 1897), pp. 293-295.

Arnold, William B., Bouve, Edward T. & Pickett, LaSalle Corbell. *The Fourth Massachusetts Cavalry in the Closing Scenes of the War for the Maintenance of the Union, from Richmond to Appomattox*. Boston: unknown, 1910.

Avary, Myrta L., ed. *Recollections of Alexander H. Stephens: His Diary Kept while a Prisoner at Fort Warren, Boston Harbour, 1865*. New York: Doubleday, Page & Company, 1910.

Bandy, Ken & Freeland, Florence, eds. *The Gettysburg Papers*. Dayton, OH: Morningside Books, 1986.

Barker, Walter B. "Two Anecdotes of General Lee," in *Southern Historical Society Papers*, vol. 12 (1884), pp. 328-329.

Bauer, K. Jack, ed. *Soldiering: The Civil War Diary of Rice C. Bull*. Novato, CA: Presidio Press, 1995.

Beale, R. L. T. *History of the Ninth Virginia Cavalry in the War Between the States*. Richmond, VA: B. F. Johnson Publishing, 1899.

Beck, Brandon H., ed. *Third Alabama: The Civil War Memoir of Brigadier General Cullen Andrews Battle, CSA*. Tuscaloosa, AL: University of Alabama Press, 2002.

Bernard, George S. *War Talks of Confederate Veterans*. Dayton, OH: Morningside Books, 2003.

Betts, Alexander D. *Experience of a Confederate Chaplain, 1861-1864*. Greenville, SC: W. A. Betts, no date.

Blackford, Susan L. & Blackford, Charles M., III, eds. *Letters from Lee's Army*. Lincoln, NE: Bison Books, 1998.

Blackford, William W. *War Years with Jeb Stuart*. New York: Charles Scribners's Sons, 1945.

Blakey, Arch Frederic, Lainhart, Ann Smith & Stephens, Winston Bryant, Jr., eds. *Rose Cottage Chronicles: Civil War Letters of the Bryant-Stephens Families of North Florida*. Gainesville, FL: University Press of Florida, 1998.

Bond, Christiana. *Memories of General Robert E. Lee*. Baltimore, MD: Norman, Remington, 1926.

Booth, George W. *A Maryland Boy in Lee's Army: Personal Reminiscences of a Maryland Soldier in the War Between the States, 1861 – 1865*. Lincoln, NE: Bison Books, 2000.

Brent, Joseph L. *Memoirs of the War Between the States*. New Orleans, LA: Fontana Printing, 1940.

Brooke, George M., Jr., ed. *Ironclads and Big Guns of the Confederacy: The Journal and Letters of John M. Brooke*. Columbia, SC: University of South Carolina Press, 2002.

Broun, Thomas L. "General R. E. Lee's War-Horse," in *Confederate Veteran*, vol. 6, no. 7 (July 1898), p. 292.

Buck, Samuel D. *With the Old Confeds: Actual Experiences of a Captain in the Line*. Staunton, VA: Lot's Wife Publishing, 2007.

Burgess, Rose. "General Lee in Orange County," in *Orange County Historical Society Newsletter*, Winter 2004-5.

Caldwell, J. F. J. *A History of a Brigade of South Carolinians Known First as "Gregg's" and Subsequently as "McGowan's Brigade."* Philadelphia, PA: King & Baird, 1866.

Casler, John O. *Four Years in the Stonewall Brigade*. Girard, KS: Appeal Publishing, 1906.

Chamberlaine, William W. *Memoirs of the Civil War Between the Northern and Southern Sections of the United States of America, 1861-1865*. Washington, DC: Byron S. Adams, 1912.

Cheney, Newel. *History of the Ninth Regiment, New York Volunteer Cavalry, War of 1861 to 1865*. Poland Center, NY: Martin, Merz & Son, 1901.

Childers, William C., ed. "A Virginian's Dilemma: The Civil War Diary of Isaac Noyes Smith in Which He Describes the Activities of the 22nd Regiment of Virginia Volunteers, Sept. to Nov., 1861," in *West Virginia History*, vol. 27, no. 3 (April 1966), pp. 173-200.

Claiborne, John H. *Seventy-five Years in Old Virginia*. New York: Neale Publishing, 1904.

Clark, Walter, ed. *The Histories of the Several Regiments and Battalions from North Carolina in the Great War, 1861-'65*. 5 vols. Raleigh, NC: State of North Carolina, 1901.

Clemens, Thomas G., ed. *The Maryland Campaign of September 1862*. 3 vols. El Dorado Hills, CA: Savas Beatie, 2010-2017.

Clopton, William I. "New Light on the Great Drewry's Bluff Fight," in *Southern Historical Society Papers*, vol. 34 (1906), pp. 82-98.

Colston, Frederick M. "Recollections of the Last Months in the Army of Northern Virginia," in *Southern Historical Society Papers*, vol. 38 (1910), pp. 1-15.

Cobb, Thomas R.R. "Extracts from Letters to his Wife, February 3, 1861-December 10, 1862," in *Southern Historical Society Papers*, vol. 28 (1900), pp. 280-301.

Cooke, Giles B. "Col. W. H. Taylor, A.A.G. Army of Northern Virginia: An Appreciation," in *Confederate Veteran*, vol. 24 (1916), pp. 234-5.

Cooke, Giles B. "When With General Lee," in *Confederate Veteran*, vol. 37 (1929), pp. 182-3.

Cooke, John E. *A Life of General Robert E. Lee*. New York: D. Appleton & Co., 1871.

Cooke, John E. *Wearing of the Gray: Being Personal Portraits, Scenes, and Adventures of the War*. Baton Rouge, LA: Louisiana State University Press, 1997.

Cortada, James W., ed. *1861 Diary of Miss Fannie Page Hume, Orange, Virginia*. Orange, VA: Orange County Historical Society, 1983.

Couture, Richard T. *Charlie's Letters: The Correspondence of Charles E. DeNoon*. Farmville, VA: R. T. Couture, 1982.

Cowper, Pulaski, ed. *Extracts of Letters of Major General Bryan Grimes to his Wife*. Raleigh, NC: Edwards, Broughton & Co., 1883.

Craven, Avery, ed. *"To Markie:" The Letters of Robert E. Lee to Martha Custis Williams*. Cambridge, MA: Harvard University Press, 1933.

Crist, Lynda L., et al, eds. *The Papers of Jefferson Davis*, 14 vols. Baton Rouge, LA: Louisiana State University Press, 1971-2015.

Crute, Joseph H., Jr., ed. *Robert E. Lee's Derwent Letters*. No place: Joseph H. Crute, Jr., 2004.

Cutrer, Thomas W., ed. *Longstreet's Aide: The Civil War Letters of Major Thomas J. Goree*. Charlottesville, VA: University Press of Virginia, 1995.

Dabney, Robert L. *Life and Campaigns of Lt. General T. J. (Stonewall) Jackson*. Harrisonburg, VA: Sprinkle Publications, 1983.

Davis, Jefferson F. *The Rise and Fall of the Confederate Government*. 2 vols. New York: Da Capo Press, 1990.

Davis, John E. "A Federal Soldier's Incident," in *Southern Historical Society Papers*, vol. 17 (1889), pp. 241-2.

Davis, Varina. *Jefferson Davis: A Memoir by his Wife*. 2 vols. Baltimore, MD: Nautical & Aviation Publishing, 1990.

Dawson, Francis W. *Reminiscences of Confederate Service 1861-1865*. Baton Rouge, LA: Louisiana State University Press, 1993.

deButts, Robert E. L., Jr., ed. "Mary Custis Lee's 'Reminiscences of the War,'" in *Virginia Magazine of History and Biography* vol. 109, no. 3 (2001), pp. 301-325.

DeLeon, Thomas C. *Belles, Beaux, and Brains of the '60s*. New York: G. W. Dillingham, 1909.

Denson, C. B. *An Address Delivered in Raleigh, NC, on Memorial Day 1895 Containing a Memoir of the Late Major General William Henry Chase Whiting of the Confederate Army*. Raleigh, NC: Edwards & Broughton Printers, 1895.

Dickert, D. Augustus. *History of Kershaw's Brigade*. Newberry, SC: Elbert H. Aull Co., 1899.

Dobbins, Austin C. *Grandfather's Journal: Company B, Sixteenth Mississippi Infantry Volunteers, Harris' Brigade, Mahone's Division, Hill's Corps, A.N.V.* Dayton, OH: Morningside Books, 1988.

Douglas, Henry K. *I Rode with Stonewall*. Marietta, GA: Mockingbird Books, 1995.

Dowdey, Clifford & Manarin, Louis H., eds. *The Wartime Papers of R. E. Lee*. New York: Little, Brown & Co., 1961.

Dozier, Graham T., ed. *A Gunner in Lee's Army: The Civil War Letters of Thomas Henry Carter*. Chapel Hill, NC: University of North Carolina Press, 2014.

Dunaway, Wayland F. *Reminiscences of a Rebel*. Baltimore, MD: Butternut and Blue, 1996.

Early, Jubal A. "A Review by Jubal Early," in *Southern Historical Society Papers*, vol. 4 (1877), pp. 241-302.

Early, Jubal A. *Jubal Early's Memoirs: Autobiographical Sketch and Narrative of the War Between the States*. Baltimore, MD: Nautical & Aviation Publishing, 1989.

Elliot, Charles G. "Martin's Brigade, of Hoke's Division, 1863-64," in *Southern Historical Society Papers*, vol. 23 (1895), pp. 189-198.

Elmore, Fletcher L., Jr., ed. *Diary of J. E. Whitehorne, 1st Sergt. Co. F, 12th Virginia Infantry, A. P. Hill's 3rd Corps, A. N. VA.* Louisville, KY: Fletcher L. Elmore, Jr., 1995.

Evans, Clement A., ed. *Confederate Military History.* 12 vols. Secaucus, NJ: Blue & Grey Press, 1975.

Everson, Guy R. & Simpson, Edward W., Jr., eds. *Far, Far from Home: The Wartime Letters of Dick and Tally Simpson, 3rd South Carolina Volunteers.* New York: Oxford University Press, 1994.

Field, Charles W. "The Campaign of 1864 and 1865," in *Southern Historical Society Papers*, vol. 14 (1886), pp. 542-563.

Fortin, Martin S. "History of the Eighth Alabama Volunteer Regiment, CSA," in *The Alabama Historical Quarterly*, vol. xxxix, #s 1-4 (1977), pp. 5-321.

Freeman, Douglas S., ed. *Lee's Dispatches: Unpublished Letters of General Robert E. Lee, C.S.A., to Jefferson Davis and the War Department of the Confederate States of America, 1862-1865.* Baton Rouge, LA: Louisiana State University Press, 1994.

Fremantle, Arthur J. L. *Three Months in the Southern States: April – June 1863.* Lincoln, NE: Bison Books, 1991.

French, Samuel G. *Two Wars: The Autobiography & Diary of Gen. Samuel G. French, CSA.* Huntington, WV: Blue Acorn Press, 1999.

Frey, Jerry, ed. *In the Woods Before Dawn: The Samuel Richey Collection of the Southern Confederacy.* Gettysburg, PA: Thomas Publications, 1994.

Fry, Birkett D. "Pettigrew's Charge at Gettysburg," in *Southern Historical Society Papers*, vol. 7 (1879), pp. 91-3.

Gaines, Samuel M. "How General R. E. Lee Saved the Life of a Federal Officer," in *Southern Historical Society Papers*, vol. 33 (1905), pp. 375-6.

Gallagher, Gary W., ed. *Fighting for the Confederacy: The Personal Recollections of General Edward Porter Alexander.* Chapel Hill, NC: University of North Carolina Press, 1989.

Gibson, J. Catlett. "The Battle of Spotsylvania Courthouse, May 12, 1864," in *Southern Historical Society Papers*, vol. 32 (1904), pp. 200-210.

Goldsborough, William W. *The Maryland Line in the Confederate Army, 1861-1865.* Baltimore, MD: Gugenheimer, Weil & Co., 1900.

Gordon, John B. *Reminiscences of the Civil War.* Dayton, OH: Morningside Books, 1985.

Granbury, J. A. H. "That Fort Gilmer Fight," in *Confederate Veteran*, vol. 13, no. 9 (Sept. 1905), p. 413.

Grant, Ulysses S. *Personal Memoirs of U. S. Grant.* New York: Dover Publications, 1995.

Guild, Pattie. "Journey to and from Appomattox," in *Confederate Veteran*, vol. 6, no. 1 (Jan. 1898), pp. 11-12.

Gwin, Minrose C., ed. *A Woman's Civil War: A Diary, with Reminiscences of the War, from March 1862.* Madison, WI: University of Wisconsin Press, 1992.

Hagood, Johnson. *Memoirs of the War of Secession.* Camden, SC: Jim Fox Books, 1997.

Hamby, William S. "Fourth Texas in Battle of Gaines Mill," in *Confederate Veteran*, vol. 14 (1906), pp. 183-5.

Hamlin, Percy G., ed. *The Making of a Soldier: Letters of General R. S. Ewell.* Richmond, VA: Whittet & Shepperson, 1935.

Harris, Nathaniel H. "General Lee to the Rear – The Incident with Harris' Mississippi Brigade," in *Southern Historical Society Papers*, vol. 8 (1880), pp. 105-110.

Harris, Nathaniel H. "Nineteenth Mississippi Regiment," in *Confederate Veteran*, vol. 6 (Feb. 1898), pp. 70-1.

Harrison, Constance C. *Recollections Grave and Gay.* New York: Charles Scribner's Sons, 1911.

Harrison, Walter. *Pickett's Men: A Fragment of War History.* Baton Rouge, LA: Louisiana State University Press, 2000.

Hassler, William W., ed. *One of Lee's Best Men: The Civil War Letters of General William Dorsey Pender.* Chapel Hill, NC: University of North Carolina Press, 1999.

Hawes, Percy G. "Last Days of the Army of Northern Virginia," in *Confederate Veteran*, vol. 27 (Sept. 1919), pp. 341-4.

Hildebrand, John R., ed. *A Mennonite's Journal, 1862-1865: A Father's Account of the Civil War in the Shenandoah Valley.* Shippensburg, PA: Burd Street Press, 1996.

Hoke, Jacob. *The Great Invasion of 1863: General Lee in Pennsylvania.* Gettysburg, PA: Stan Clark Military Books, 1992.

Hood, John B. *Advance and Retreat.* New York: Da Capo Press, 1993.

Hopkins, Luther W. *From Bull Run to Appomattox: A Boy's View.* No place: Timeless Classic Books, 2010.

Horn, Stanley F., ed. *The Robert E. Lee Reader.* New York: Konecky & Konecky, 1949.

Howard, McHenry. *Recollections of a Maryland Confederate Soldier.* Dayton, OH: Morningside Books, 1975.

Hubbs, G. Ward, ed. *Voices from Company D: Diaries by the Greensboro Guards, 5th Alabama Infantry Regiment, Army of Northern Virginia.* Athens, GA: University of Georgia Press, 2003.

Humphreys, Andrew A. *The Virginia Campaign, 1864 and 1865.* New York: Da Capo Press, 1995.

Hunton, Eppa. *Autobiography of Eppa Hunton.* Richmond, VA: William Byrd Press, 1933.

"J. B. M." "How the Seven Days' Battle Around Richmond Began," in *Southern Historical Society Papers*, vol. 28 (1900), pp. 90-97.

Jackson, Mary Anna. *Memoirs of Stonewall Jackson by his Widow.* Louisville, KY: Prentice Press, 1895.

Jacobs, Michael. *Notes on the Rebel Invasion of Maryland and Pennsylvania and the Battle of Gettysburg, July 1st, 2nd, and 3rd, 1863.* Philadelphia: J.B. Lippincott & Co., 1864.

Johnson, W. Gart. "Reminiscences of Lee and of Gettysburg," in *Confederate Veteran*, vol. 1 (Aug. 1893), p. 246.

Johnston, David E. *The Story of a Confederate Boy in the Civil War.* Portland, OR: Glass & Prudhomme Co., 1914.

Johnston, J. Stoddard. "Sketches of Operations of General John C. Breckinridge," in *Southern Historical Society Papers*, vol. 7 (1879), pp. 385-392.

Johnston, Joseph E. *Narrative of Military Operations during the Civil War.* New York: Da Capo Press, 1990.

Johnston, Preston. "Some Post War Letters from Jefferson Davis to his Former Aide de Camp, William Preston Johnston," in *Virginia Magazine of History and Biography* (April 1943), pp. 151-159.

Jones, Benjamin W. *Under the Stars and Bars: A History of the Surry Light Artillery.* Dayton, OH: Morningside Books, 1975.

Jones, J. William. *Christ in the Camp: The True Story of the Great Revival during the War Between the States.* Harrisonburg, VA: Sprinkle Publications, 1986.

Jones, J. William. "Further Details of the Death of A. P. Hill," in *Southern Historical Society Papers*, vol. 12 (1884), pp. 183-7.

Jones, J. William. *Life and Letters of Gen. Robert Edward Lee, Soldier and Man.* Harrisonburg, VA: Sprinkle Publications, 1986.

Jones, J. William. *Personal Reminiscences, Anecdotes, and Letters of Gen. Robert E. Lee.* New York: D. Appleton & Company, 1875.

Jones, John B. *A Rebel War Clerk's Diary*, 2 vols. Philadelphia: J. B. Lippincott, 1866.

Jones, Terry L., ed. *Campbell Brown's Civil War with Ewell and the Army of Northern Virginia.* Baton Rouge, LA: Louisiana State University Press, 2001.

Kelley, Tom, ed. *The Personal Memoirs of Jonathan Thomas Scharf of the First Maryland Artillery.* Baltimore, MD: Butternut and Blue, 1992.

Lacy, J. Horace. "Lee at Fredericksburg," in *Century Magazine* (Aug. 1886), pp. 605-608.

Lankford, Nelson D. *An Irishman in Dixie: Thomas Conolly's Diary of the Fall of the Confederacy.* Columbia, SC: University of South Carolina Press, 1988.

Lanneau, John F. "Field Glimpses of Lee," in *Wake Forest Student*, vol. 26, no. 5 (Jan. 1907), pp. 321-329.

Lee, Charles C. *Resolutions Adopted by a Meeting of the People of Powhatan, Held in the Courthouse on February Court Day, 1865.* Richmond, VA: unknown, 1865.

Lee, Fitzhugh. "A Review of the First Two Days' Operations at Gettysburg and a Reply to General Longstreet," in *Southern Historical Society Papers*, vol. 5 (1878), pp. 162-194.

Lee, Fitzhugh. *General Lee: A Biography of Robert E. Lee.* New York: Da Capo Press, 1994.

Lee, Robert E., Jr. *Recollections and Letters of Robert E. Lee.* Old Saybrook, CT, n.d.

Lee, Sarah L. "War Time in Alexandria, Virginia," in *South Atlantic Quarterly* (Winter 1905), pp. 234-248.

Leigh, Benjmain W. "The Wounding of Stonewall Jackson – Extracts from a Letter of Major Benjamin Watkins Leigh," in *Southern Historical Society Papers*, vol. 3 (1877), pp. 230-4.

Leon, Louis. *Diary of a Tar Heel Confederate Soldier.* Charlotte, NC: Stone Publishing, 1913.

Lewis, Richard. *Camp Life of a Confederate Boy of Bratton's Brigade, Longstreet's Corps, C.S.A.* Charleston, SC: News & Courier Book Presses, 1883.

London, H. A. "A Tribute to General Lee," in *Wake Forest Student*, vol. 26, no. 5 (Jan. 1907), pp. 312-315.

Long, Armistead L. *Memoirs of Robert E. Lee: His Military and Personal History.* Secaucus, NJ: Blue & Grey Press, 1983.

Long, Armistead L. "Seacoast Defenses of South Carolina and Georgia," in *Southern Historical Society Papers*, vol. 1 (1876), pp. 103-107.

Longstreet, James. *From Manassas to Appomattox.* New York: Da Capo Press, 1992.

Lyman, George H. "Some Aspects of the Medical Service of the Armies of the United States during the War of the Rebellion," in *Papers of the Military Historical Society of Massachusetts*, vol. 13, Boston: Military Historical Society of Massachusetts, 1913, pp. 175-228.

Marshall, Charles. *Appomattox: An Address Delivered before the Society of the Army and Navy of the Confederate States in the State of Maryland, January 19, 1894.* Baltimore, MD: Gugenheimer, Weil & Co, 1894.

Maurice, Frederick, ed. *Lee's Aide de Camp: Charles Marshall.* Lincoln, NE: Bison Books, 2000.

Maury, Dabney H. *Recollections of a Virginian in the Mexican, Indian, and Civil Wars.* New York: Charles Scribner's Sons, 1894.

McCabe, W. Gordon. "Defence of Petersburg," in *Southern Historical Society Papers*, vol. 2 (1876), pp, 257-306.

McClellan, H. B. *The Campaigns of Stuart's Cavalry.* Secaucus, NJ: Blue & Grey Press, 1993.

McClendon, William A. *Recollections of War Times by an Old Veteran While Under Stonewall Jackson and Lieutenant General James Longstreet.* Tuscaloosa, AL: University of Alabama Press, 2010.

McDonald, Archie P., ed. *Make Me a Map of the Valley: The Civil War Journal of Stonewall Jackson's Topographer, Jedediah Hotchkiss.* Dallas: Southern Methodist University Press, 1973.

McDonald, William N. *A History of the Laurel Brigade.* Baltimore, MD: Johns Hopkins University Press, 2002.

McGuire, Judith W. *Diary of a Southern Refugee During the War, by a Lady of Virginia.* New York: E. J. Hale & Son, 1867.

McKim, Randolph H. *A Soldier's Recollections: Leaves from the Diary of a Young Confederate.* New York: Longmans, Green & Co., 1910.

McKim, Randolph H. "General J.E.B. Stuart in the Gettysburg Campaign," in *Southern Historical Society Papers*, vol. 37 (1909), pp. 210-231.

Mills, George H. *History of the Sixteenth North Carolina Regiment in the Civil War.* Rutherfordton, NC: John C. Mills, 1901.

Minor, J. B. "General Robert E. Lee Under Fire," in *Confederate Veteran*, vol. 17 (1909), p. 333.

Mitchell, Adele H., ed. *The Letters of John S. Mosby.* Richmond, VA: Stuart-Mosby Historical Society, 1986.

Mitchell, Adele H., ed. *The Letters of Major General James E. B. Stuart.* Richmond, VA: Stuart-Mosby Historical Society, 1990.

Montague, Ludwell Lee, ed. "Memoir of Mrs. Harriotte Lee Taliaferro Concerning Events in Virginia, April 11-21, 1861," in *Virginia Magazine of History and Biography*, vol. 57, no. 4 (Oct. 1949), pp. 416-420.

Moore, Edward A. *The Story of a Cannoneer under Stonewall Jackson.* New York, Neale Publishing, 1907.

Morrill, Lily Logan, ed. *My Confederate Girlhood: The Memoirs of Kate Virginia Cox Logan.* Richmond, VA: Garrett & Massie, 1932.

Morrison, James L., ed. *The Memoirs of Henry Heth.* Westport, CT: Greenwood Press, 1974.

Morton, Thomas C. "Anecdotes of General R. E. Lee," in *Southern Historical Society Papers*, vol. 11 (1883), pp. 517-20.

Moyle, Seth, ed. *The Heart of a Soldier: Intimate Wartime Letters from General George E. Pickett, C.S.A., to his Wife.* Gettysburg, PA: Stan Clark Military Books, 1995.

Mumper, James, A. *I Wrote You Word: The Poignant Letters of Private Holt, John Lee Holt, 1829-1863.* Lynchburg, VA: H. E. Howard, Inc., 1993.

Myers, Frank M. *The Comanches: A History of White's Battalion, Virginia Cavalry.* Baltimore, MD: Kelly, Piet, & Co., 1871.

Neese, George M. *Three Years in the Confederate Horse Artillery.* New York: Neale Publishing, 1911.

Newsome, Hampton, Horn, John & Selby, John G., eds. *Civil War Talks: Further Reminiscences of George S. Bernard and his Fellow Veterans.* Charlottesville, VA: University of Virginia Press, 2012.

Noll, Arthur H., ed. *Doctor Quintard: Chaplain C.S.A. and Second Bishop of Tennessee.* Sewanee, TN: University Press, 1905.

North Carolina Literary and Historical Society, ed. *Five Points in the Record of North Carolina in the Great War of 1861-5.* Goldsboro, NC: Nash Brothers, 1904.

Oates, William C. *The War Between the Union and the Confederacy and its Lost Opportunities.* New York: Neale Publishing, 1905.

Oeffinger, John C., ed. *A Soldier's General: The Civil War Letters of Major General Lafayette McLaws.* Chapel Hill, NC: University of North Carolina Press, 2002.

Oldaker, Glenn C. *Centennial Tales: Memoirs of Colonel "Chester" S. Bassett French, Extra Aide-de-Camp to Generals Lee and Jackson, The Army of Northern Virginia, 1861-1865.* New York: Carlton Press, 1962.

Owen, William M. *In Camp and Battle with the Washington Artillery of New Orleans.* Baton Rouge, LA: Louisiana State University Press, 1999.

Park, Robert E. "War Diary of Capt. Robert Emory Park, Twelfth Alabama Regiment," in *Southern Historical Society Papers*, vol. 26 (1898), pp. 1-31.

Paxton, John G., ed. *The Civil War Letters of General Frank "Bull" Paxton, CSA: A Lieutenant of Lee & Jackson.* Hillsboro, TX: Hill Junior College Press, 1978.

Pearce, T. H., ed. *Diary of Captain Henry A. Chambers.* Wendell, NC: Broadfoot Books, 1983.

Pearson, Johnnie P., ed. *Lee and Jackson's Bloody Twelfth: The Letters of Irby Goodwin Scott, First Lieutenant, Company G, Putnam Light Infantry, Twelfth Georgia Volunteer Infantry.* Knoxville, TN: University of Tennessee Press, 2010.

Pierson, William W., Jr., ed. *The Diary of Bertlett Yancey Malone.* Chapel Hill, NC, University of North Carolina, 1919.

Poague, William T. *Gunner with Stonewall: Reminiscences of William Thomas Poague.* Lincoln, NE: Bison Books, 1998.

Pollard, Edward A. *Lee and His Lieutenants Comprising the Early Life, Public Services, and Campaigns of General Robert E. Lee and His Companions in Arms.* New York: E. B. Treat & Co., 1867.

Polley, Joseph B. *Hood's Texas Brigade: Its Marches, Its Battles, Its Achievements.* New York: Neale Publishing, 1910.

Porter, Horace. *Campaigning with Grant.* New York: Mallard Press, 1991.

Pryor, Sarah. *My Day: Reminiscences of a Long Life.* New York: MacMillan Co., 1909.

Putnam, Sallie B. *Richmond During the War.* Alexandria, VA: Time-Life Books, 1983.

Rawley, James A., ed. *The American Civil War: An English View – The Writings of Field Marshal Viscount Wolseley.* Mechanicsburg, PA: Stackpole Books, 2002.

Reagan, John H. *Memoirs with Special Reference to Secession and the Civil War.* New York: Neale Publishing, 1906.

Roberts, William P. "General Lee's Recognition of Valor," in *Wake Forest Student*, vol. 26, no. 5 (Jan. 1907), p. 356.

Robertson, Margaret Briscoe Stuart. *My Childhood Recollections of the War: Life in the Confederate Stronghold of Staunton,*

Virginia, during the War Between the States. Staunton, VA: StauntonHistory.com, 2013.

Robertson, Mary D., ed. "The Journal of Nellie Kinzie Gordon," in *Georgia Historical Quarterly*, vol. 70, no. 3 (Fall 1986), pp. 477-517.

Roman, Alfred. *The Military Operations of General Beauregard*. 2 vols. New York: Da Capo Press, 1994.

Ross, Fitzgerald. *Cities and Camps of the Confederate States*. Urbana, IL: University of Illinois Press, 1997.

Rouse, Parke, Jr., ed. *When the Yankees Came: Civil War and Reconstruction on the Virginia Peninsula*. Richmond, VA: Dietz Press, 1987.

Rowland, Dunbar, ed. *Jefferson Davis, Constitutionalist: His Letters, Papers, and Speeches*. 10 vols. Jackson, MS: Mississippi Department of Archives & History, 1923.

Royall, William L. *Some Reminiscences*. New York: Neale Publishing, 1909.

Royster, Charles & Lee, Robert E., eds. *The Revolutionary War Memoirs of General Henry Lee*. New York: Da Capo Press, 1998.

Russell, Charles W., ed. *The Memoirs of Colonel John S. Mosby*. Boston: Little, Brown & Co., 1917.

Saussy, George N. "Generals Lee and Gracie at the Crater," in *Confederate Veteran*, vol. 17 (April 1909), p. 160.

Savage, John H. *The Life of John H. Savage: Citizen, Soldier, Lawyer Congressman*. Nashville, TN: self-published, 1903.

Scarborough, John C. "A Confederate Private's Reminiscences," in *Wake Forest Student*, vol. 26, no. 5 (Jan. 1907), pp. 347-349.

Scarborough, William K. ed., *The Diary of Edmund Ruffin*. 3 vols. Baton Rouge, LA: Louisiana State University Press, 1972-1977.

Scheibert, Justus. *Seven Months in the Rebel States During the North American War, 1863*. Tuscaloosa, AL: Confederate Publishing Co., 1958.

Schiller, Herbert M., ed. *A Captain's War: The Letters and Diaries of William H. S. Burgwyn, 1861-1865*. Shippensburg, PA: White Mane Publishing, 1993.

Schuricht, Hermann. "Jenkins' Brigade in the Gettysburg Campaign," in *Southern Historical Society Papers*, vol. 24 (1896), pp. 339-350.

Scott, W. W. "Some Personal Memories of General Robert E. Lee," in *William and Mary Quarterly* (Oct. 1926), pp. 277-288.

Semmes, Raphael. *Memoirs of Service Afloat During the War Between the States*. Secaucus, NJ: Blue & Grey Press, 1987.

Sieburg, Evelyn, & Hansen, James E., eds. *Memoirs of a Confederate Staff Officer: From Bethel to Bentonville*. Shippensburg, PA: White Mane Books, 1998.

Slaughter, Philip. *A Sketch of the Life of Randolph Fairfax*. Baltimore, MD: Innes & Co., 1878.

Smith, Gustavus W. *The Battle of Seven Pines*. New York: C. G. Crawford, 1891.

Smith, James P. "With Stonewall Jackson in the Army of Northern Virginia," in *Southern Historical Society Papers*, vol. 43 (1920), pp. 1-109.

Smith, John D. *The History of the Nineteenth Regiment of Maine Volunteer Infantry, 1862-1865*. Minneapolis, MN: Great Western Printing, 1909.

Snow, William P. *Lee and His Generals*. New York: Gramercy Books, 1996.

Sorrel, G. Moxley. *Recollections of a Confederate Staff Officer*. Dayton, OH: Morningside Books, 1978.

Stewart, William H. *A Pair of Blankets: Wartime History in Letters*. Wilmington, NC: Broadfoot Publishing, 1990.

Stiles, Robert. *Four Years Under Marse Robert*. Dayton, OH: Morningside Books, 1988.

Styple, William B., ed. *Writing & Fighting the Confederate War: The Letters of Peter Wellington Alexander, Confederate War Correspondent*. Kearny, NJ: Belle Grove Publishing, 2002.

Summers, Festus P, ed. *A Borderland Confederate*. Pittsburg, PA: University of Pittsburgh Press, 1962.

Swank, Walbrook D., ed. *Raw Pork and Hardtack: A Civil War Memoir from Manassas to Appomattox*. Shippensburg, PA: Burd Street Press, 1996.

Swank, Walbrook D., ed. *Stonewall Jackson's Foot Cavalry: Company A, 13th Virginia Infantry*. Shippensburg, PA: Burd Street Press, 2001.

Talcott, T. M. R. "From Petersburg to Appomattox," in *Southern Historical Society Papers*, vol. 32 (1904), pp. 67-72.

Talcott, T. M. R. "General Lee's Strategy at the Battle of Chancellorsville," in *Southern Historical Society Papers*, vol. 34 (1906), pp. 1-27.

Taylor, Richard. *Destruction and Reconstruction*. Waltham, MA: Blaisdell Publishing, 1968.

Taylor, Walter H. *Four Years with General Lee*. Bloomington, IN: Indiana University Press, 1996.

Taylor, Walter H. *General Lee: His Campaigns in Virginia, 1861-1865*. Dayton, OH: Morningside Books, 1975.

Thomas, Henry W. *History of the Doles-Cook Brigade, Army of Northern Virginia, CSA*. Atlanta: Franklin Printing & Publishing, 1903.

Toler, John T., ed. *The Civil War Diary of Betty Fanny Gray, Fauquier County, Virginia*. Warrenton, VA: Fauquier Historical Society, 2015.

Tombes, Robert M., ed. *When the Peaches Get Ripe: Letters Home from Lt. Robert Gaines Haile, Jr., Essex Sharpshooters, 55th Virginia, 1862*. Richmond, VA: Tizwin Publishing, 1999.

Tompkins, Ellen W., ed. "The Colonel's Lady: Some Letters of Ellen Wilkins Tompkins, July-December 1861," in *Virginia Magazine of History and Biography*, vol. 69, no. 4 (Oct. 1961), pp. 387-419.

Toney, Marcus B. *The Privations of a Private*. Nashville, TN: Publishing House of the M. E. Church, South, 1907.

Tower, R. Lockwood, ed. *A Carolinian Goes to War: The Civil War Narrative of Arthur Middleton Manigault, Brigadier General, CSA*. Columbia, SC: University of South Carolina Press, 1992.

Tower, R. Lockwood, ed. *Lee's Adjutant: The Wartime Letters of Colonel Walter Herron Taylor, 1862-1865*. Columbia, SC: University of South Carolina Press, 1995.

Trimble, Isaac. "The Campaign and Battle of Gettysburg," in *Confederate Veteran*, vol. 25 (May 1917), p. 209-13.

Tucker, George W. "Death of General A. P. Hill," in *Southern Historical Society Papers*, vol. 11 (1883), pp. 564-569.

(unknown author). "Sketch of Maj. Ferguson," in *Confederate Veteran*, vol. 7, no. 3 (March 1899), pp. 99-100.

Vandiver, Frank E., ed. *The Civil War Diary of General Josiah Gorgas*. Tuscaloosa, AL: University of Alabama Press, 1947.

Venable, Charles S. "The Campaign from the Wilderness to Petersburg," in *Southern Historical Society Papers*, vol. 14 (1886), pp. 522-542.

Von Borcke, Heros. *Memoirs of the Confederate War for Independence*. Nashville, TN: J. S. Sanders & Co., 1999.

Warfield, Edgar., *Manassas to Appomattox: The Civil War Memoirs of Pvt. Edgar Warfield, 17th Virginia Infantry*. McLean, VA: EPM Publications, 1996.

Warren, Edward. *A Doctor's Experiences in Three Continents*. Baltimore, MD: Cushings & Bailey, 1885.

Watson, W. A. "The Fighting at Sailor's Creek," in *Confederate Veteran*, vol. 25 (Oct. 1917), pp. 448-452.

Wheeler, J. G. "Lee to the Rear," in *Confederate Veteran*, vol. 11 (March 1903), pp. 116-7.

Wilcox, Cadmus M. "Defense of Batteries Gregg and Whitworth, and the Evacuation of Petersburg," in *Southern Historical Society Papers*, vol. 4 (1877), pp. 18-33.

Wiley, Ken, ed. *Norfolk Blues: The Civil War Diary of the Norfolk Light Artillery Blues*. Shippensburg, PA: Burd Street Press, 1997.

Williams, Edward B. *Rebel Brothers: The Civil War Letters of the Truehearts*. College Station, TX: Texas A&M University Press, 1995.

Williams, Richard B., ed. *Stonewall's Prussian Mapmaker: The Journals of Captain Oscar Hinrichs*. Chapel Hill, NC: University of North Carolina Press, 2014.

Winters, Barb, ed. *Letters to Virginia: Correspondence from Three Generations of Alexandrians Before, During, and After the Civil War*. Morley, MO: Acclaim Press, 2010.

Wise, George. *Campaigns and Battles of the Army of Northern Virginia*. New York: Neale Publishing, 1916.

Wise, George. *History of the Seventeenth Virginia Infantry, CSA*. Baltimore, MD: Kelly, Piet & Co., 1870.

Wise, Henry A. "The Career of Wise's Brigade, 1861-1865," in *Southern Historical Society Papers*, vol. 25 (1897), pp. 1-22.

Wise, John S. *The End of an Era*. Boston: Houghton, Mifflin & Co., 1900.

Woodward, C. Vann, ed. *Mary Chesnut's Civil War*. New York: Book of the Month Club, 1994.

Worsham, John H. *One of Jackson's Foot Cavalry*. New York: Neale Publishing, 1912.

Wright, A. O. "Reminiscence of Holding Traveller," in *Confederate Veteran*, vol. 13 (June 1905), p. 266.

Wright, Robert. "Sinking of the *Jamestown*: How it was Done at Drewry's Bluff," in *Southern Historical Society Papers*, vol. 29 (1901), pp. 371-2.

Wright, Willard E. "Some Letters of Lucius Bellinger Northrop, 1860-1865," in *Virginia Magazine of History & Biography*, vol. 68, no. 4 (Oct. 1960), pp. 456-477.

Wyckoff, Mac, ed. *The Civil War Letters of Alexander McNeill, 2nd South Carolina Infantry Regiment*. Columbia, SC: University of South Carolina Press, 2016.

Younger, Edward, ed. *Inside the Confederate Government: The Diary of Robert Garlick Hill Kean*. New York: Oxford University Press, 1957.

Secondary Works

Adams, Charles F. *Lee at Appomattox and Other Papers*. New York: Houghton, Mifflin & Co., 1902.

Akers, Monte. *Year of Desperate Struggle: Jeb Stuart and his Cavalry, From Gettysburg to Yellow Tavern, 1863-1864*. Philadelphia: Casemate, 2015.

Allardice, Bruce S. *More Generals in Gray*. Baton Rouge, LA: Louisiana State University Press, 1995.

Allen, Juanita. "Agnes Lee's Sweetheart: William Orton Williams, CSA," in *UDC Magazine* (June/July 1992), pp. 27-9.

Andrews, Matthew P. *Virginia: The Old Dominion*. Richmond, VA: Dietz Press, 1949.

Anthony-Tolbert, Susan. *Lucy Long, Robert E. Lee's Other Warhorse: The Mare with Mysteries*. Heathsville, VA: Singing Cat & Mule Publishing, 2012.

Armstrong, Richard L. *The Battle of McDowell: March 11 – May 18, 1862*. Lynchburg, VA: H. E. Howard, Inc., 1990.

Aubrecht, Michael. *The Civil War in Spotsylvania County: Confederate Campfires at the Crossroads*. Charleston, SC: History Press, 2009.

Barefoot, Daniel W. *General Robert F. Hoke: Lee's Modest Warrior*. Winston-Salem, NC: John F. Blair Publishing, 2001.

Bearss, Edwin C. *The Petersburg Campaign*. 2 vols. El Dorado Hills, CA: Savas Beatie, 2012, 2014.

Bickel, Karl A. "Robert E. Lee in Florida," in *Florida Historical Quarterly*, vol. 27, no. 1 (July 1948), pp. 59-66.

Black, Robert C., III. *The Railroads of the Confederacy*. Chapel Hill, NC: University of North Carolina Press, 1998.

Blake, Nelson M. *William Mahone of Virginia: Soldier and Political Insurgent*. Richmond, VA: Garrett & Massie, 1935.

Bluford, Robert, Jr. *The Battle of Totopotomoy Creek: Polegreen Church and the Prelude to Cold Harbor*. Charleston, SC: History Press, 2014.

Bockmiller, Stephen R. *Hagerstown in the Civil War*. Charleston, SC: Arcadia Publishing, 2011.

Bragg, Lillian C. & Screven, Frank B. "Robert E. Lee in Georgia," in *Georgia Review*, vol. 16, no. 4 (Winter 1962), pp. 433-438.

Branch, Paul, Jr. *Fort Macon: A History*. Charleston, SC: Nautical & Aviation Publishing, 1999.

Branch, Paul, Jr. *The Siege of Fort Macon*. Morehead City, NC: Herald Printing Company, 1982.

Brandt, Nat. *The Congressman Who Got Away with Murder*. Syracuse, NY: Syracuse University Press, 1991.

Bridges, Hal. *Lee's Maverick General: Daniel Harvey Hill*. Lincoln, NE: Bison Books, 1991.

Bright, David L. *Locomotives up the Turnpike: The Civil War Career of Quartermaster Captain Thomas R. Sharp, C.S.A.* Harrisburg, NC: David L. Bright, 2017.

Brock, Robert A., ed. *General Robert E. Lee: Soldier, Citizen, and Christian Patriot*. Richmond, VA: B. F. Johnson Publishing, 1897.

Brooke, George M., Jr. *John M. Brooke: Naval Scientist and Educator*. Charlottesville, VA: University Press of Virginia, 1980.

Brooks, William E. *Lee of Virginia*. Indianapolis, IN: Bobbs-Merrill Co., 1932.

Burns, Brian. *Lewis Ginter: Richmond's Gilded Age Icon*. Charleston, SC: History Press, 2011.

Bushong, Millard K. *Historic Jefferson County*. Boyce, VA: Carr Publishing, 1972.

Calkins, Chris M. *Auto Tour of Civil War Petersburg 1861 – 1865*. Petersburg, VA: City of Petersburg, 2003.

Calkins, Chris M. *The Battles of Appomattox Station and Appomattox Court House, April 8-9, 1865*. Lynchburg, VA: H. E. Howard, Inc., 1987.

Calkins, Chris M. "Final March to Appomattox: the 12th Virginia Infantry, April 2-12, 1865, An Eyewitness Account," in *Civil War Regiments*, vol. 2, no. 3, pp. 236-251.

Calkins, Chris M. *Lee's Retreat: A History and Field Guide*. Richmond, VA: Page One History Publications, 2000.

Calkins, Chris M. *Thirty-Six Hours Before Appomattox: The Battles of Sailor's Creek, High Bridge, Farmville and Cumberland Church*. Farmville, VA: Farmville Herald, 2006.

Campbell, Edward D. C., Jr. "The Fabric of Command: R. E. Lee, Confederate Insignia, and the Perception of Rank," in *Virginia Magazine of History & Biography*, vol. 98, no. 2 (April 1990), pp. 261-290.

Carmichael, Peter S., ed. *Audacity Personified: The Generalship of Robert E. Lee*. Baton Rouge, LA: Louisiana State University Press, 2004.

Carse, Robert. *Department of the South: Hilton Head Island in the Civil War*. Hilton Head Island, SC: Impressions Printing, 1987.

Cauble, Frank P. *The Surrender Proceedings: April 9, 1865, Appomattox Court House*. Lynchburg, VA: H. E. Howard, Inc., 1987.

Cavanaugh, Michael A. *6th Virginia Infantry*. Lynchburg, VA: H. E. Howard, Inc., 1988.

Chaney, William F. *Duty Most Sublime: The Life of Robert E. Lee as Told through the Carter Letters*. Baltimore, MD: Gateway Press, 1996.

Chesson, Michael B. *Richmond After the War: 1865-1900*. Richmond, VA: Virginia State Library, 1981.

Cisco, Walter B. *States Rights Gist: A South Carolina General of the Civil War*. Gretna, LA: Pelican Publishing, 2008.

Cleave, Egbert. *Cleave's Biographical Cyclopaedia of Homeopathic Physicians and Surgeons*. Philadelphia: Galaxy Publishing, 1873.

Clemmer, Gregg S. *Old Alleghany: The Life and Wars of General Ed Johnson*. Staunton, VA: Hearthside Publishing, 2004.

Coddington, Edwin B. *The Gettysburg Campaign: A Study in Command*. New York: Touchstone Books, 1997.

Collier, Calvin L. *They'll Do to Tie to: 3rd Arkansas Infantry Regiment, C.S.A.* Little Rock, AK: Democrat Printing & Lithograph, 1995.

Collins, Darrell L. *Major General Robert E. Rodes of the Army of Northern Virginia: A Biography*. El Dorado Hills, CA: Savas Beatie, 2008.

Colt, Margaretta B. *Defend the Valley: A Shenandoah Family in the Civil War*. New York: Oxford University Press, 1999.

Conrad, W. P. & Alexander, Ted. *When War Passed this Way*. Greencastle, PA: White Mane Publishing, 1987.

Cooling, Benjamin F. *Jubal Early's Raid on Washington, 1864*. Baltimore, MD: Nautical & Aviation Publishing, 1989.

Coski, John M. *Capital Navy: The Men, Ships, and Operations of the James River Squadron*. Campbell, CA: Savas-Woodbury Publishers, 1996.

Coulling, Mary P. *The Lee Girls*. Winston-Salem, NC: John F. Blair, 1987.

Crenshaw, Douglas. *Fort Harrison and the Battle of Chaffin's Farm: To Surprise and Capture Richmond*. Charleston, SC: History Press, 2013.

Crooks, Daniel J., Jr. *Lee in the Low Country: Defending Charleston & Savannah, 1861-1862*. Charleston, SC: History Press, 2008.

Crute, Joseph H., Jr. *Confederate Staff Officers, 1861-1865.* Powhatan, VA: Derwent Books, 1982.

Cummings, Charles M. *Yankee Quaker, Confederate General: The Curious Career of Bushrod Rust Johnson.* Rutherford, NJ: Fairleigh Dickinson University Press, 1971.

Daughtry, Mary B. *Gray Cavalier: The Life and Wars of General W. H. F. "Rooney" Lee.* New York: Da Capo Press, 2002.

Davis, Burke. *Gray Fox: Robert E. Lee and the Civil War.* New York: Wings Books, 1956.

Davis, James A. *51st Virginia Infantry.* Lynchburg, VA: H. E. Howard, Inc., 1984.

Davis, Margaret G. *Madison County, Virginia: A Revised History.* Madison, VA: Madison County Board of Supervisors, 1977.

Davis, William C. *An Honorable Defeat: The Last Days of the Confederate Government.* New York: Harcourt Books, 2001.

Davis, William C. *Breckinridge: Statesman, Soldier, Symbol.* Baton Rouge, LA: Louisiana State University Press, 1992.

Davis, William C., ed. *The Confederate General,* 6 vols. Harrisburg, PA: National Historical Society, 1990.

Davis, William C. *Jefferson Davis: The Man and His Hour.* New York: Harper Collins, 1992.

Dederer, John M. "In Search of the Unknown Soldier: A Critique of 'The Mystery in the Coffin,'" in *Virginia Magazine of History and Biography,* vol. 103, no. 1 (Jan. 1995), pp. 95-112.

Dederer, John M. "Robert E. Lee's First Visit to His Father's Grave," in *Virginia Magazine of History and Biography,* vol. 102, no. 1 (Jan. 1994), pp. 73-88.

Delauter, Roger U. *18th Virginia Cavalry.* Lynchburg, VA: H. E. Howard, Inc., 1985.

Dew, Charles B. *Ironmaker to the Confederacy: Joseph R. Anderson and the Tredegar Iron Works.* Richmond, VA: Library of Virginia, 1999.

Dowdey, Clifford. *Lee.* Gettysburg, PA: Stan Clark Military Books, 1991.

Driver, Robert J., Jr. *52nd Virginia Infantry.* Lynchburg, VA: H. E. Howard, Inc., 1986.

Driver, Robert J., Jr. *The Staunton Artillery – McClanahan's Battery.* Lynchburg, VA: H. E. Howard, Inc., 1988.

Driver, Robert J., Jr. & Ruffner, Kevin C. *1st Battalion Virginia Infantry, 39th Battalion Virginia Cavalry, 24th Battalion Virginia Partisan Rangers.* Lynchburg, VA: H. E. Howard, Inc., 1996.

Dubbs, Carol K. *Defend this Old Town: Williamsburg During the Civil War.* Baton Rouge, LA: Louisiana State University Press, 2002.

Duncan, Alexander M. *Roll of Officers and Members of the Georgia Hussars.* Savannah, GA: Morning News, 1906.

Eckert, Ralph L. *John Brown Gordon: Soldier, Southerner, American.* Baton Rouge, LA: Louisiana State University Press, 1989.

Elliott, Joseph C. *Lt. Gen. Richard Heron Anderson: Lee's Noble Soldier.* Dayton, OH: Morningside Books, 1985.

Evans, Eli P. *Judah P. Benjamin: The Jewish Confederate.* New York: Free Press, 1988.

Farrar, Emmie Ferguson. *Old Virginia Houses Along the James.* New York: Bonanza Books, 1957.

Fenn, R. W. D. & Ellis, J. E. *This Very Desirable Estate: The History of Hayfield in Caroline County in the Commonwealth of Virginia.* Bardon Hall, Leicestershire, England: self-published, 2007.

Fishwick, Marshall W. *Lee After the War.* New York: Dodd, Mead & Co., 1963.

Flood, Charles B. *Lee: The Last Years.* Boston: Houghton Mifflin, 1981.

Fox, John J., III. *Red Clay to Richmond: Trail of the 35th Georgia Infantry Regiment, CSA.* Winchester, VA: Angle Valley Press, 2006.

Fox, John J., III. *Stuart's Finest Hour: The Ride around McClellan, June 1862.* Winchester, VA: Angle Valley Press, 2014.

Fraser, Walter J., Jr. *Charleston! Charleston! The History of a Southern City.* Columbia, SC: University of South Carolina Press, 1989.

Frassanito, William A. *Grant and Lee: The Virginia Campaigns, 1864-1865.* New York: Charles Scribners' Sons, 1983.

Freeman, Douglas S. *A Calendar of Confederate Papers with a Bibliography of Some Confederate Publications.* Richmond, VA: Confederate Museum, 1908.

Freeman, Douglas S. *Lee's Lieutenants: A Study in Command,* 3 vols. New York: Charles Scribners' Sons, 1970.

Freeman, Douglas S. *R. E. Lee: A Biography,* 4 vols. New York: Charles Scribners' Sons, 1934-5.

Freeman, Douglas S. *The South to Posterity: An Introduction to the Writing of Confederate History.* Baton Rouge, LA: Louisiana State University Press, 1998.

French, Steve. *Imboden's Brigade in the Gettysburg Campaign.* Berkeley Springs, WV: Morgan Messenger, 2008.

Furguson, Ernest B. *Not War But Murder: Cold Harbor, 1864.* New York: Vintage Books, 2001.

Gabbert, John M. *Military Operations in Hanover County, Virginia, 1861-1865.* Roanoke, VA: Gurtner Graphics, 1989.

Gage, Anthony J. *Southside Virginia in the Civil War: Amelia, Brunswick, Charlotte, Halifax, Lunenburg, Mecklenburg, Nottoway, & Prince Edward Counties.* Lynchburg, VA: H. E. Howard, Inc., 1999.

Gallagher, Gary W., ed. *The Antietam Campaign.* Chapel Hill, NC: University of North Carolina Press, 1999.

Gallagher, Gary W., ed. *Lee the Soldier.* Lincoln, NE: University of Nebraska Press, 1996.

Gallagher, Gary W. "Robert E. Lee at Cumberland Island and on the Analyst's Couch," in *Virginia Magazine of History and Biography*, vol. 103, no. 1 (Jan. 1995), pp. 117-123.

Gallagher, Gary W. *Stephen Dodson Ramseur: Lee's Gallant General*. Chapel Hill, NC: University of North Carolina Press, 1995.

Gamble, Robert S. *Sully: The Biography of a House*. Chantilly, VA: Sully Foundation, 1973.

Gardiner, Mabel H. *Chronicles of Old Berkeley: A Narrative History of a Virginia County from its Beginnings to 1926*. Durham, NC: Seeman Press, 1938.

Gaughan, Anthony J. *The Last Battle of the Civil War*. Baton Rouge, LA: Louisiana State University Press, 2011.

Gibson, Langhorne, Jr. *Cabell's Canal: The Story of the James River and Kanawha*. Richmond, VA: Commodore Press, 2000.

Gold, Thomas D. *History of Clarke County, Virginia, and its Connection with the War Between the States*. Berryville, VA: C. R. Hughes, 1914.

Gordon, Lesley J. *General George E. Pickett in Life & Legend*. Chapel Hill, NC: University of North Carolina Press, 1998.

Gracie, Archibald, Jr. "Gen. Archibald Gracie," in *Confederate Veteran*, vol. 5 (Aug. 1897), pp. 429-433.

Gragg, Rod. *Confederate Goliath: The Battle of Fort Fisher*. Baton Rouge, LA: Louisiana State University Press, 2006.

Graves, Charles A. *The Forged Letter of General Robert E. Lee*. Richmond, VA: Richmond Press, 1914.

Gray, Arthur. "The White House: Washington's Marriage Place," in *Virginia Magazine of History and Biography*, vol. 42, no. 3 (July 1934), pp. 229-240.

Greene, A. Wilson. *A Campaign of Giants: The Battle for Petersburg*. Chapel Hill, NC: University of North Carolina Press, 2018.

Greene, A. Wilson. *Civil War Petersburg: Confederate City in the Crucible of War*. Charlottesville, VA: University of Virginia Press, 2006.

Greene, A. Wilson. *The Final Battles of the Petersburg Campaign: Breaking the Backbone of the Rebellion*. Knoxville, TN: University of Tennessee Press, 2008.

Hadfield, Kathleen H., ed. *Historical Notes on Amelia County, Virginia*. Amelia, VA: Amelia County Historical Society, 1982.

Hale, Laura V. *Four Valiant Years in the Lower Shenandoah Valley, 1861-1865*. Strasburg, VA: Shenandoah Publishing House, 1973.

Hall, Harry H. *A Johnny Reb Band from Salem: The Pride of Tarheelia*. Raleigh, NC: North Carolina Department of Archives & History, 2006.

Hanover County Historical Society. *Old Homes of Hanover County, Virginia*. Hanover, VA: County Historical Society, 2015.

Hardy, Michael C. *Lee's Body Guards: The 39th Battalion Virginia Cavalry*. Charleston, SC: History Press, 2019.

Harrison, Noel G. *Chancellorsville Battlefield Sites*. Lynchburg, VA: H. E. Howard, Inc., 1990.

Harrison, Noel G. *Fredericksburg Civil War Sites*. 2 vols. Lynchburg, VA: H. E. Howard, Inc., 1995.

Harsh, Joseph L. *Confederate Tide Rising: Robert E. Lee and the Making of Southern Strategy, 1861-1862*. Kent, OH: Kent State University Press, 1998.

Harsh, Joseph L. *Sounding the Shallows: A Confederate Companion for the Maryland Campaign of 1862*. Kent, OH: Kent State University Press, 2000.

Harsh, Joseph L. *Taken at the Flood: Robert E. Lee & Confederate Strategy in the Maryland Campaign of 1862*. Kent, OH: Kent State University Press, 1999.

Hartwig, D. Scott. *To Antietam Creek: The Maryland Campaign of September 1862*. Baltimore, MD: Johns Hopkins University Press, 2012.

Hassler, William W. *A. P. Hill: Lee's Forgotten General*. Chapel Hill, NC: University of North Carolina Press, 1995.

Henderson, G. F. R. *Stonewall Jackson and the American Civil War*. 2 vols. New York: Longmans, Green & Co., 1898.

Henderson, William D. *12th Virginia Infantry*. Lynchburg, VA: H. E. Howard, Inc., 1984.

Henderson, William D. *Petersburg in the Civil War: War at the Door*. Lynchburg, VA: H. E. Howard, Inc, 1998.

Henderson, William D. *The Road to Bristoe Station: Campaigning with Lee and Meade, August 1 – October 20, 1863*. Lynchburg, VA: H. E. Howard, Inc., 1987.

Hennessy, John J. *Return to Bull Run: The Campaign and Battle of Second Manassas*. New York: Simon & Schuster, 1993.

Hess, Earl J. *In the Trenches at Petersburg: Field Fortifications & Confederate Defeat*. Chapel Hill, NC: University of North Carolina Press, 2009.

Hess, Earl J. *Into the Crater: The Mine Attack at Petersburg*. Columbia, SC: University of South Carolina Press, 2010.

Hilderman, Walter C. *Theophilus Hunter Holmes: A North Carolina General in the Civil War*. Jefferson, NC: McFarland Publishing, 2013.

Hoehling, A. A. & Hoehling, Mary. *The Last Days of the Confederacy: An Eyewitness Account of the Fall of Richmond, Capital City of the Confederate States*. New York: Fairfax Press, 1981.

Hood, Stephen M. *John Bell Hood: The Rise, Fall, and Resurrection of a Confederate General*. El Dorado Hills, CA: Savas Beatie, 2013.

Hoover, Sallie W. S. "John Augustine Washington, C.S.A.," in *Confederate Veteran* (Jan. 1926), pp. 96-98.

Hopkins, Donald A. *Robert E. Lee in War and Peace: Photographs of a Confederate and American Icon*. El Dorado Hills, CA: Savas Beatie, 2013.

Horn, John. *The Destruction of the Weldon Railroad: Deep Bottom, Globe Tavern, and Reams Station, August 14-25, 1864.* Lynchburg, VA: H. E. Howard, Inc., 1991.

Horn, Jonathan. *The Man Who Would Not be Washington: Robert E. Lee's Civil War and His Decision that Changed American History.* New York: Scribner, 2015.

Howe, James L. "George Washington Custis Lee," in *Virginia Magazine of History and Biography*, vol. 48 (Oct. 1940), pp. 315-327.

Hurst, Patricia J. *Soldiers, Stories, Sites and Fights: Orange County, Virginia 1861-1865 and the Aftermath.* Rapidan, VA: Patricia J. Hurst, 1998.

Hurst, Patricia J. *The War Between the States, 1862-1865: Rapidan River Area of Clark Mountain, Orange County, Virginia.* Rapidan, VA: Patricia J. Hurst, 1989.

Iobst, Richard W. *The Bloody Sixth: The Sixth North Carolina Regiment, Confederate States of America.* Raleigh, NC: North Carolina Confederate Centennial Commission, 1965.

Janney, Caroline E., ed. *Petersburg to Appomattox: The End of the War in Virginia.* Chapel Hill, NC: University of North Carolina Press, 2018.

Jefferson, Mary A. *Old Homes and Buildings in Amelia County, Virginia.* Vol. 1. Amelia, VA: Mary A. Jefferson, 1964.

Jensen, Les. *32nd Virginia Infantry.* Lynchburg, VA: H. E. Howard, Inc., 1990.

Jett, Carolyn H. *Lancaster County, Virginia: Where the River Meets the Bay.* Lancaster, VA: Lancaster County History Book Committee, 2003.

Johnson, Clint. *In the Footsteps of Robert E. Lee.* Winston Salem, NC: Robert F. Blair Publishing, 2001.

Johnson, David E. *Douglas Southall Freeman.* Gretna, LA: Pelican Publishing, 2002.

Johnson, Gerald W. *Mount Vernon: The Story of a Shrine.* Mount Vernon, VA: Mount Vernon Ladies' Association, 1991.

Johnson, R. Winder. *The Ancestry of Rosalie Morris Johnson: Daughter of George Calvert Morris and Elizabeth Kuhn.* Philadelphia: Ferris & Leach, 1905.

Johnson, Robert U. & Buel, Clarence C., eds. *Battles and Leaders of the Civil War*, 4 vols. Secaucus, NJ: Castle Books, n.d.

Johnson, William J., *Robert E. Lee the Christian.* Arlington Heights, IL: Christian Liberty Press, 1993.

Johnston, Angus J., II. *Virginia Railroads in the Civil War.* Chapel Hill, NC: University of North Carolina Press, 1961.

Johnston, J. Ambler. *Echoes of 1861-1961.* Richmond, VA: J. Ambler Johnston, 1971.

Jones, Charles C., Jr. *The Life and Services of Commodore Josiah Tattnall.* Savannah, GA: Morning News Stream Printing House, 1878.

Jones, Jacqueline E. *Saving Savannah: The City and the Civil War.* New York: Alfred E. Knopf, 2008.

Jones, Virgil C. *Eight Hours Before Richmond.* New York: Henry Holt, 1957.

Jordan, Michael L. *Hidden History of Civil War Savannah.* Charleston, SC: History Press, 2017.

Kauffman, Michael W. *American Brutus: John Wilkes Booth and the Lincoln Conspiracies.* New York: Random House, 2004.

Keen, Hugh C. & Mewborn, Horace. *43rd Battalion Virginia Cavalry: Mosby's Command.* Lynchburg, VA: H. E. Howard, Inc., 1993.

Keller, S. Roger. *Crossroads of War: Washington County, Maryland in the Civil War.* Shippensburg, PA: Burd Street Press, 1997.

Kimball, Fiske. "The Building of Bremo," in *Virginia Magazine of History & Biography*, vol. 57, no. 1 (Jan. 1949), pp. 3-13.

Kimmel, Stanley. *Mr. Davis's Richmond.* New York: Bramhall House, 1958.

Kleese, Richard B. *49th Virginia Infantry.* Lynchburg, VA: H. E. Howard, Inc., 2002.

Knight, Charles R. "Strangers in a Strange Land: Capt. Charles H. Woodson & His Missouri Cavalry in the Valley," in *Shenandoah at War* (Spring 2018), pp. 58-63.

Knight, Charles R. *Valley Thunder: The Battle of New Market and the Opening of the Shenandoah Valley Campaign, May 1864.* El Dorado Hills, CA: Savas Beatie, 2010.

Krick, Robert E. L. *A Survey of Civil War Sites in Hanover County, Virginia.* Richmond, VA: National Park Service, 2002.

Krick, Robert E. L. *Staff Officers in Gray: A Biographical Register of the Staff Officers in the Army of Northern Virginia.* Chapel Hill, NC: University of North Carolina Press, 2003.

Krick, Robert K. *Civil War Weather in Virginia.* Tuscaloosa, AL: University of Alabama Press, 2007.

Krick, Robert K. *Lee's Colonels: A Biographical Register of the Field Officers of the Army of Northern Virginia.* Dayton, OH: Morningside Books, 1996.

Krick, Robert K., ed. *The Smoothbore Volley That Doomed the Confederacy: The Death of Stonewall Jackson and Other Chapters on the Army of Northern Virginia.* Baton Rouge, LA: Louisiana State University Press, 2002.

Kundahl, George G. *Alexandria Goes to War: Beyond Robert E. Lee.* Knoxville, TN: University of Tennessee Press, 2004.

Laboda, Lawrence R. *From Selma to Appomattox: The History of the Jeff Davis Artillery.* New York: Oxford University Press, 1996.

Laine, J. Gary & Penny, Morris M. *Law's Alabama Brigade in the War Between the Union and the Confederacy.* Shippensburg, PA: White Mane Publishing, 1996.

Lancaster, Robert A. *Historic Virginia Homes and Churches.* Philadelphia: J. B. Lippincott, 1915.

Land & Community Associates. *Survey of Historic Resources, Hanover County, Virginia*. Charlottesville, VA: Land & Community Associates, 1992.

Lankford, Nelson. *Richmond Burning: The Last Days of the Confederate Capital*. New York: Penguin, 2002.

Lattimore, Ralston B. *Fort Pulaski National Monument, Georgia*. Washington, DC: U. S. Government Printing Office, 1954.

Lee, Edmund Jennings. *Lee of Virginia, 1642-1892: Biographical and Genealogical Sketches of the Descendants of Colonel Richard Lee*. Philadelphia: Franklin Printing Co., 1895.

Lee, Richard M. *General Lee's City: An Illustrated Guide to the Historic Sites of Confederate Richmond*. McLean, VA: EPM Publications, 1987.

Lee, Susan P. *Memoirs of William Nelson Pendleton, DD*. Harrisonburg, VA: Sprinkle Publications, 1991.

Lesser, W. Hunter. *Rebels at the Gate: Lee and McClellan on the Front Line of a Nation Divided*. Naperville, IL: Sourcebooks, 2004.

Lesser, Hunter. *The First Campaign: A Guide to Civil War in the Mountains of West Virginia, 1861*. Charleston, WV: Quarrier Press, 2011.

Lindsay, Mary. *Historic Homes and Landmarks of Alexandria, Virginia*. Alexandria, VA: Landmarks Society, 1962.

Long, E. B. *The Civil War Day by Day: An Almanac 1861-1865*. New York: Da Capo Press, 1971.

Longacre, Edward G. *Pickett, Leader of the Charge: A Biography of General George E. Pickett, C.S.A.* Shippensburg, PA: White Mane Publishing, 1998.

Longstreet, Helen D. *Lee and Longstreet at High Tide*. Wilmington, NC: Broadfoot Publishing, 1989.

Loth, Calder, ed. *The Virginia Landmarks Register*. Charlottesville, VA: University Press of Virginia, 1986.

Lowry, Terry D. *22nd Virginia Infantry*. Lynchburg, VA: H. E. Howard, Inc., 1988.

MacDonald, Rose M. *E. Mrs. Robert E. Lee*. Arlington, VA: Robert B. Poisal, 1973.

Mackall, William S. *A Son's Recollections of his Father*. New York, E. P. Dutton, 1930.

Mackowski, Chris & White, Kristopher D. *Chancellorsville's Forgotten Front: The Battles of Second Fredericksburg and Salem Church, May 3, 1863*. El Dorado Hills, CA: Savas Beatie, 2013.

Maffitt, Emma M. "The Confederate Navy," in *Confederate Veteran*, vol. 25, no. 5 (May 1917), pp. 217-221.

Manarin, Louis H. *Henrico County: Field of Honor*, 2 vols. Richmond, VA: Henrico County Division of Recreation and Parks, 2004.

Manarin, Louis H. & Dowdey, Clifford. *The History of Henrico County*. Charlottesville, VA: University Press of Virginia, 1984.

Mansfield, James R. *A History of Early Spotsylvania*. Orange, VA: Green Publishers, 1977.

Martin, David G. *Gettysburg: July 1*. Conshohocken, PA: Combined Books, 1996.

Martin, Samuel J. *The Road to Glory: Confederate General Richard S. Ewell*. Indianapolis, IN: Guild Press of Indiana, 1991.

Marvel, William. *Lee's Last Retreat: The Flight to Appomattox*. Chapel Hill, NC: University of North Carolina Press, 2002.

Mason, Emily V. *Popular Life of General Robert E. Lee*. Baltimore, MD: J. Murphy & Co., 1872.

Matter, William D. *If It Takes All Summer: The Battle of Spotsylvania*. Chapel Hill, NC: University of North Carolina Press, 1988.

Maurice, Frederick. *Robert E. Lee: The Soldier*. New York: Houghton Mifflin, 1925.

McCarthy, Clara S. *The Foothills of the Blue Ridge in Fauquier County, Virginia*. Warrenton, VA: The Fauquier Democrat, 1974.

McCartney, Martha W. *Nature's Bounty, Nation's Glory: The Heritage and History of Hanover County, Virginia*. Hanover, VA: Heritage & History of Hanover County, Inc., 2009.

McCartney, Martha W. *With Reverence for the Past: Gloucester County, Virginia*. Richmond, VA: Dietz Press, 2001.

McCaslin, Richard B. *Lee in the Shadow of Washington*. Baton Rouge, LA: Louisiana State University Press, 2001.

McCue, John N. *The McCues of the Old Dominion*. Mexico, MO: Missouri Printing & Publishing, 1912.

McKinney, Tim. *The Civil War in Fayette County, West Virginia*. Charleston, WV: Quarrier Press, 1988.

McKinney, Tim. *Robert E. Lee at Sewell Mountain: The West Virginia Campaign*. Charleston, WV: Pictorial Histories Publishing, 1990.

McMurray, Richard M. *John Bell Hood and the War for Southern Independence*. Lincoln, NE: University of Nebraska Press, 1992.

Meredith, Roy. *The Face of Robert E. Lee in Life and in Legend*. New York: Charles Scribner's Sons, 1947.

Mewborn, Horace. "Herding Yankee Cattle: The Beefsteak Raid, September 14-17, 1864," in *Blue & Gray* (Summer 2005), pp. 7-17-, 44-50.

Miller, Ann L. *Antebellum Orange: The Pre-Civil War Homes, Buildings and Historic Sites of Orange County, Virginia*. Orange, VA: Orange County Historical Society, 1988.

Miller, J. Michael. *The North Anna Campaign: "Even to Hell Itself" May 21 – 26, 1864*. Lynchburg, VA: H. E. Howard, Inc., 1989.

Mingus, Scott L., Sr. *Confederate General William "Extra Billy" Smith: From Virginia's Statehouse to Gettysburg Scapegoat*. El Dorado Hills, CA: Savas Beatie, 2013.

Mink, Eric J. "Southern Exposure: Stonewall Sells: The 1863 Jackson Photograph," in *Fredericksburg History & Biography*, vol. 11 (2012), pp. 177-83.

Moger, Allen W. "Letters to General Lee after the War," in *Virginia Magazine of History and Biography*, vol. 64, no. 1 (Jan. 1956), pp. 30-69.

Morton, Oren F. *A History of Highland County, Virginia*. Monterey, VA: Oren F. Morton, 1911.

Musick, Michael P. *6th Virginia Cavalry*. Lynchburg, VA: H. E. Howard, Inc., 1990.

Nelligan, Murray H. *Custis-Lee Mansion: The Robert E. Lee Memorial*. Washington, DC: Government Printing Office, 1962.

Newell, Clayton R. *Lee vs. McClellan: The First Campaign*. Washington, DC: Regnery Publishing, 1996.

Newsome, Hampton. *Richmond Must Fall: The Richmond-Petersburg Campaign, October 1864*. Kent, OH: Kent State University Press, 2013.

Newton, Steven H. *Joseph E. Johnston and the Defense of Richmond*. Lawrence, KS: University Press of Kansas, 1998.

Nicholas, Richard L. *Sheridan's James River Campaign of 1865 through Central Virginia*. Scottsville, VA: Historic Albemarle, 2012.

Nightingale, N. B. "Dungeness," in *Georgia Historical Quarterly*, vol. 22, no. 4 (Dec. 1938), pp. 369-383.

Nine, William G. & Wilson, Ronald G. *The Appomattox Paroles, April 9-15, 1865*. Lynchburg, VA: H. E. Howard, Inc., 1989.

Nolan, Alan T. "Grave Thoughts," in *Virginia Magazine of History and Biography*, vol. 103, no. 1 (Jan. 1995), pp. 113-116.

Nolan, Alan T. *Lee Considered: General Robert E. Lee and Civil War History*. Chapel Hill, NC: University of North Carolina Press, 1991.

O'Dell, Jeffrey M. *Chesterfield County: Early Architecture and Historic Sites*. Chesterfield, VA: County of Chesterfield, 1983.

Osborne, Charles C. *Jubal: The Life and Times of General Jubal A. Early, CSA, Defender of the Lost Cause*. Baton Rouge, LA: Louisiana State University Press, 1994.

Page, Richard Channing Moore. *Genealogy of the Page Family in Virginia*. New York: Publishers Printing, 1893.

Page, Thomas N. *Robert E. Lee: Man and Soldier*. New York: Charles Scribners's Sons, 1911.

Parramore, Thomas C. *Southampton County, Virginia*. Charlottesville, VA: University Press of Virginia, 1978.

Parrish, James W. *Wiregrass to Appomattox: The Untold Story of the 50th Georgia Infantry Regiment, CSA*. Winchester, VA: Angle Valley Press, 2009.

Parrish, T. Michael. *Richard Taylor: Soldier Prince of Dixie*. Chapel Hill, NC: University of North Carolina Press, 1992.

Patchan, Scott C. *Second Manassas: Longstreet's Attack and the Struggle for Chinn Ridge*. Washington, D.C.: Potomac Books, 2011.

Patterson, Gerard A. *From Blue to Gray: The Life of Confederate General Cadmus M. Wilcox*. Mechanicsburg, PA: Stackpole Books, 2001.

Pendleton, Robert M. *Traveller: General Robert E. Lee's Favorite Greenbrier War Horse*. Lutz, FL: Robert M. Pendleton, 2005.

Perry, John. *Mrs. Robert E. Lee: The Lady of Arlington*. Colorado Springs, CO: Multnomah Books, 2001.

Peters, J. T. & Carden, H. B. *History of Fayette County, West Virginia*. Parsons, WV: McClain Printing, 1972.

Petruzzi, J. David. *The Complete Gettysburg Guide*. El Dorado Hills, CA: Savas Beatie, 2009.

Pfanz, Donald C. *Richard S. Ewell: A Soldier's Life*. Chapel Hill, NC: University of North Carolina Press, 1998.

Pfanz, Harry W. *Gettysburg: Culp's Hill & Cemetery Hill*. Chapel Hill, NC: University of North Carolina Press, 1993.

Pitts, Hugh D. *High Meadow: Where Robert E. Lee Drew his Sword*. Richmond, VA: Henrico County Historical Society, 1998.

Poole, Robert M. *On Hallowed Ground: The Story of Arlington National Cemetery*. New York: Walker & Company, 2009.

Porter, John W. H. *A Record of Events in Norfolk County, Virginia, from April 19th, 1861, to May 10th, 1862*. Portsmouth, VA: W. A Fiske, 1892.

Priest, John M. *Antietam: The Soldier's Battle*. New York: Oxford University Press, 1993.

Priest, John M. *Before Antietam: The Battle for South Mountain*. New York: Oxford University Press, 1992.

Priest, John M. *Nowhere to Run: The Wilderness, May 4th & 5th, 1864*. Shippensburg, PA: White Mane Publishing, 1995.

Pryor, Elizabeth B. *Reading the Man: A Portrait of Robert E. Lee Through His Private Letters*. New York: Penguin Books, 2008.

Pryor, Elizabeth B. "Thou Knowest Not the Time of Thy Visitation," in *Virginia Magazine of History and Biography*, vol. 119, no. 3 (2011), pp. 276-296.

Quarles, Garland R. *Occupied Winchester, 1861-1865*. Winchester, VA: Winchester-Frederick County Historical Society, 1991.

Quarstein, John V. *Hampton and Newport News in the Civil War*. Lynchburg, VA: H. E. Howard, Inc., 1998.

Quinn, Silvanus J. *The History of the City of Fredericksburg, Virginia*. Richmond, VA: Hermitage Press, 1908.

Ramey, Emily G., & Gott, John K., eds. *Years of Anguish: Fauquier County, Virginia, 1861-1865*. Annandale, VA: Bacon Race Books, 1987.

Ramsey, Marc., *The 7th South Carolina Cavalry: To the Defense of Richmond*. Wilmington, NC: Broadfoot Publishing, 2011.

Rankin, Thomas M. *23rd Virginia Infantry*. Lynchburg, VA: H. E. Howard, Inc., 1985.

Reardon, Carol & Vossler, Tom. *A Field Guide to Gettysburg*. Chapel Hill, NC: University of North Carolina Press, 2013.

Rhea, Gordon C. *Cold Harbor: Grant and Lee May 26 – June 3, 1864*. Baton Rouge, LA: Louisiana State University Press, 2002.

Rhea, Gordon C. *The Battles for Spotsylvania Court House and the Road to Yellow Tavern, May 7 – 12, 1864*. Baton Rouge, LA: Louisiana State University Press, 1997.

Rhea, Gordon C. *The Battle of the Wilderness: May 5 – 6, 1864*. Baton Rouge, LA: Louisiana State University Press, 1994.

Rhea, Gordon C. *To the North Anna River: Grant and Lee May 13 – 25, 1864*. Baton Rouge, LA: Louisiana State University Press, 2000.

Rhoades, Jeffrey L. *Scapegoat General: The Story of Major General Benjamin Huger, C.S.A.* Hamden, CT: Archon Books, 1985.

Riggs, David F. *Embattled Shrine: Jamestown in the Civil War*. Shippensburg, PA: White Mane Publishing, 1997.

Riley, Franklin L, ed. *General Robert E. Lee After Appomattox*. New York: MacMillan Co., 1922.

Robertson, James I., Jr. *General A. P. Hill: The Story of a Confederate Warrior*. New York: Vintage Books, 1992.

Robertson, James I., Jr. *Stonewall Jackson: The Man, The Soldier, The Legend*. New York: MacMillan Publishing, 1997.

Robertson, James I., Jr. *The Stonewall Brigade*. Baton Rouge, LA: Louisiana State University Press, 1991.

Rose, Rebecca A. *Colours of the Gray: An Illustrated Index of Wartime Flags from the Museum of the Confederacy's Collection*. Richmond, VA: Museum of the Confederacy, 1998.

Rosen, Robert N. *Confederate Charleston: An Illustrated History of the City and the People during the Civil War*. Columbia, SC: University of South Carolina Press, 1994.

Ruffner, Kevin C. *44th Virginia Infantry*. Lynchburg, VA: H. E. Howard, Inc., 1987.

Scheel, Eugene M. *Culpeper: A Virginia County's History through 1920*. Culpeper, VA: Culpeper Historical Society, 1982.

Schildt, John W. *Frederick in the Civil War: Battle & Honor in the Spired City*. Charleston, SC: History Press, 2010.

Schildt, John W. *Stonewall Jackson Day by Day*. Chewsville, MD: Antietam Publications, 1980.

Schmidt, Lewis G. *The Civil War in Florida: A Military History*. 4 vols. Allentown, PA: self-published, 1991.

Schroeder, Patrick A. *Thirty Myths about Lee's Surrender*. Lynchburg, VA: Schroeder Publications, 2016.

Schultz, David L., & Mingus, Scott L., Sr. *The Second Day at Gettysburg: The Attack and Defense of Cemetery Ridge, July 2, 1863*. El Dorado Hills, CA: Savas Beatie, 2015.

Scott, Mary W. *Houses of Old Richmond*. Richmond, VA: Valentine Museum, 1941.

Scott, W. W. *A History of Orange County, Virginia, From its Formation in 1734 to the End of Reconstruction in 1870*. Richmond, VA: Everrett Waddey Co., 1907.

Seale, William. *Virginia's Executive Mansion*. Richmond, VA: Virginia State Library and Archives, 1988.

Sears, Stephen W. *To the Gates of Richmond: The Peninsula Campaign*. New York: Ticknor & Fields, 1992.

Selcer, Richard F. *Lee vs. Pickett: Two Divided by War*. Gettysburg, PA: Thomas Publications, 1998.

Shaffner, Randolph P. *The Father of Virginia Military Institute: A Biography of Colonel J. T. L. Preston, CSA*. Jefferson, NC: McFarland & Co., 2014.

Shalf, Roseanne G. *Ashland, Ashland: The Story of a Turn-of-the-Century Railroad Town*. Lawrenceville, VA: Brunswick Publishing, 1994.

Sherrill, Lee W. *The 21st North Carolina Infantry: A Civil War History with a Roster of Officers*. Jefferson, NC: McFarland & Co., 2015.

Shingleton, Royce G. *High Seas Confederate: The Life and Times of John Newland Maffitt*. Columbia, SC: University of South Carolina Press, 1994.

Shingleton, Royce G. *John Taylor Wood: Sea Ghost of the Confederacy*. Athens, GA: University of Georgia Press, 1979.

Shultz, Gladys D. & Lawrence, Daisy G. *Lady from Savannah: The Life of Juliette Low*. New York: Girl Scouts of the U.S.A., 1988.

Slotkin, Richard. *No Quarter: The Battle of the Crater, 1864*. New York: Random House, 2009.

Smith, Derek. *Civil War Savannah*. Savannah, GA: Frederick C. Beil Publisher, 1997.

Smith, Gerald J. *One of the Most Daring of Men: The Life of Confederate General William Tatum Wofford*. Murfreesboro, TN: Southern Heritage Press, 1997.

Smith, Jo D. *A History of High Bridge*. Farmville, VA: Farmville Printing, 1987.

Smith, Timothy H. *The Story of Lee's Headquarters, Gettysburg, Pennsylvania*. Gettysburg, PA: Thomas Publications, 1995.

Sommers, Richard J. *Richmond Redeemed: The Siege at Petersburg*. El Dorado Hills, CA: Savas Beatie, 2014.

Speed, Thomas. *Records and Memorials of the Speed Family*, Louisville, KY: Courier-Journal Printing Co, 1892.

Stewart, George R. *Pickett's Charge: A Microhistory of the Final Attack at Gettysburg, July 3, 1863*. Boston: Houghton Mifflin, 1987.

Stone, H. David, Jr. *Vital Rails: The Charleston & Savannah Railroad and the Civil War in Coastal South Carolina*. Columbia, SC: University of South Carolina Press, 2008.

Stuart, Meriwether. "Samuel Ruth and General R. E. Lee: Disloyalty and the Line of Supply to Fredericksburg, 1862-1863," in *Virginia Magazine of History and Biography*, vol. 71, no. 1 (Jan. 1963), pp. 35-109.

Stuart, Meriwether. "The Military Orders of Daniel Ruggles, Department of Fredericksburg, April 22-June 5,

1861," in *Virginia Magazine of History and Biography,* vol. 69, no. 2, (April 1961), pp. 149-180.

Sutherland, Daniel E. *Seasons of War: The Ordeal of a Confederate Community 1861-1865.* New York: Free Press, 1995.

Symonds, Craig L. *Joseph E. Johnston: A Civil War Biography.* New York: W. W. Norton & Co., 1994.

Taylor, Jaquelin P. "Meadow Farm, Orange County, Virginia," in *Virginia Magazine of History and Biography,* vol. 46, no. 3 (July 1938), pp. 231-233.

Templeman, Eleanor Lee. *Virginia Homes of the Lees.* Annandale, VA: Charles Baptie Studios, n.d.

Thomas, Emory M. *Bold Dragoon: The Life of J.E.B. Stuart.* New York: Vintage Books, 1988.

Thomas, Emory M. *Robert E. Lee: A Biography.* New York: W. W. Norton & Company, 1995.

Thomson, J. Anderson, Jr., & Santos, Carlos Michael. "The Mystery in the Coffin: Another View of Lee's Visit to His Father's Grave," in *Virginia Magazine of History and Biography,* vol. 103, no. 1 (Jan. 1995), pp. 75-94.

Tidwell, William A. *Come Retribution: The Confederate Secret Service and the Assassination of Lincoln.* Jackson, MS: University Press of Mississippi, 1988.

Trask, Benjamin H., *16th Virginia Infantry.* Lynchburg, VA: H. E. Howard, Inc., 1986.

Trout, Robert J., ed. *In the Saddle with Stuart: The Story of Frank Smith Robertson of Jeb Stuart's Staff.* Gettysburg, PA: Thomas Publications, 1998.

Trudeau, Noah A. *Bloody Roads South: The Wilderness to Cold Harbor, May – June 1864.* Boston: Little, Brown, 1989.

Trudeau, Noah A. *Robert E. Lee.* New York: Palgrave Macmillan, 2009.

Tucker, George H. *Norfolk Highlights: 1584-1881.* Norfolk, VA: Norfolk Historical Society, 1972.

Tucker, Glenn. *Lee and Longstreet at Gettysburg.* Dayton, OH: Morningside Books, 1982.

Tucker, Glenn. *Robert E. Lee: Recollections and Vignettes with an Appraisal by Glenn Tucker.* No place: Eastern Acorn Press, no date.

(unknown author). *Biographical and Historical Memoirs of Louisiana,* 2 vols. Chicago: Goodspeed Publishing, 1892.

(unknown author). "The Retirement of Mr. Tree," in *The Telegraph Age,* vol. 20, no. 17 (Sept. 1903), pp. 433-5.

Vandiver, Frank E. *Jubal's Raid: General Early's Famous Attack on Washington in 1864.* Lincoln, NE: Bison Books, 1992.

Walker, Cornelius I. *The Life of Lieutenant General Richard Heron Anderson, of the Confederate States Army.* Charleston, SC: Art Publishing, 1917.

Walker, Frank S. *Remembering: A History of Orange County, Virginia.* Orange, VA: Orange County Historical Society, 2004.

Wallace, Lee A. *3rd Virginia Infantry,* Lynchburg, VA: H. E. Howard, Inc., 1986.

Warner, Ezra J. *Generals in Blue: Lives of the Union Commanders.* Baton Rouge, LA: Louisiana State University Press, 1999.

Warner, Ezra J. *Generals in Gray: Lives of the Confederate Commanders.* Baton Rouge, LA: Louisiana State University Press, 1959.

Welsh, Jack D. *Medical Histories of Confederate Generals.* Kent, OH: Kent State University Press, 1995.

Wert, Jeffry D. *A Glorious Army: Robert E. Lee's Triumph, 1862-1863.* New York: Simon & Schuster, 2011.

Wert, Jeffry D. *Cavalryman of the Lost Cause: A Biography of J. E. B. Stuart.* New York: Simon & Schuster, 2008.

Wert, Jeffry D. *General James Longstreet: The Confederacy's Most Controversial Soldier,* New York: Simon & Schuster, 1993.

Wheat, Thomas A. *A Guide to Civil War Yorktown.* Knoxville, TN: Bohemian Brigade Bookshop and Publishers, 1997.

White, Frank E., Jr. *Sailor's Creek: Major General G. W. Custis Lee, Captured with Controversy.* Lynchburg, VA: Schroeder Publications, 20008.

Williams, Ames W. *Washington & Old Dominion Railroad, 1847-1966.* Alexandria, VA: Meridian Sun Press, 1977.

Williams, Kimberly P., ed. *A Pride of Place: Rural Residences of Fauquier County, Virginia.* Charlottesville, VA: University of Virginia Press, 2003.

Williams, T. Harry. *P.G.T. Beauregard: Napoleon in Gray.* Baton Rouge, LA: Louisiana State University Press, 1995.

Wise, Jennings C. *The Military History of the Virginia Military Institute from 1839 to 1865.* Lynchburg, VA: J. P. Bell, 1915.

Wittenberg, Eric J. *Glory Enough for All: Sheridan's Second Raid and the Battle of Trevilian Station.* Washington, DC: Brassey's, 2002.

Wittenberg, Eric J. *Like a Meteor Blazing Brightly: The Short but Controversial Life of Colonel Ulric Dahlgren.* Roseville, MN: Edinburgh Press, 2009.

Wittenberg, Eric J. *The Union Cavalry Comes of Age: Hartwood Church to Brandy Station, 1863.* Washington, DC: Potomac Books, 2003.

Wittenberg, Eric J., Petruzzi, J. David, & Nugent, Michael F. *One Continuous Fight: The Retreat from Gettysburg and the Pursuit of Lee's Army of Northern Virginia, July 4-14, 1863.* El Dorado Hills, CA: Savas Beatie, 2008.

Wittenberg, Eric J. & Petruzzi, J. David. *Plenty of Blame to Go Around: Jeb Stuart's Controversial Ride to Gettysburg.* El Dorado Hills, CA: Savas Beatie, 2006.

Wood, John S., *The Virginia Bishop: A Yankee Hero of the Confederacy.* Richmond, VA: Garrett & Massie, 1961.

Woodson, Henry M. *Historical Genealogy of the Woodsons and their Connections.* Memphis, TN: H. M. Woodson, 1915.

Wright, R. Lewis. *Artists in Virginia Before 1900*. Charlottesville, VA: University Press of Virginia, 1983.

Wyatt, Edward A., IV. *Plantation Houses Around Petersburg in the Counties of Prince George, Chesterfield, and Dinwiddie, Virginia*. Petersburg, VA: Petersburg Progress-Index, 1955.

Yates, Bernice-Marie. *The Perfect Gentleman: The Life and Letters of George Washington Custis Lee*, 2 vols. Maitland, FL: Xulon Press, 2003.

Young, Rogers W. *Robert E. Lee and Fort Pulaski*. Washington, DC: Government Printing Office, 1941.

Young, Rogers W. "Two Years at Fort Bartow, 1862-1864," in *Georgia Historical Quarterly*, vol. 23, no. 3 (Sept. 1939), pp. 253-264.

Official Records

The War of the Rebellion: A Compilation of the Official Records of the Union and Confederate Armies. 128 vols. Washington, D.C.: Government Printing Office, 1880-1901.

Supplement to the Official Records of the Union and Confederate Armies. 100 vols. Wilmington, NC: Broadfoot, 1996.

Journal of the Congress of the Confederate States of America, 1861-1865. 7 vols. Washington, D.C.: Government Printing Office, 1904-5.

Unpublished Theses

Chappo, John F. "William H. Mahone of Virginia: An Intellectual Biography," Ph.D. Thesis, University of Southern Mississippi, 2007.

Lee, Dorothy. "Mary Anne Randolph Custis Lee: Wife of General Robert E. Lee," Honors Thesis, University of Richmond, 1930.

McGehee, C. Coleman. "I've Been Working on the Railroad: The Saga of the Richmond, Fredericksburg and Potomac Railroad Company," Master's Thesis, University of Richmond, 1992.

Sidwell, Robert W. "Sacrificing for the Lost Cause: General Robert E. Lee's Personal Staff," Ph.D. Thesis, Kent State University, 2018.

Websites

Valley of the Shadow, http://valley.lib.virginia.edu

Brandy Station Foundation, http://www.brandystationfoundation.com

Dictionary of Virginia Biography, www.lva.virginia.gov/public/dvb

Essential Civil War Curriculum, www.essentialcivilwarcurriculum.com

Index

Adams, Pearson B., 42, 42n15

Aiken's Landing, 216

Alabama Military Units: 6th Infantry, 200; 8th Infantry, 58, 428n21; 10th Infantry, 113n8; 11th Infantry, 457n6; 13th Infantry, 292n1; 15th Infantry, 292n11; 26th Infantry, 108, 282n30, 349

Albemarle, CSS, 80n22

Alexander, Edward Porter, 167, 168, 197, 197n28, 203n52, 211n33, 216n12, 236, 248n26, 251, 259, 259n33, 259n35, 444, 446n24; Lee's arrival and assumption of ANV command, 146n10; to provide men to man the railroad gun, 156; views battlefield from a balloon, 167n16; Sharpsburg Campaign, 198-199,199n36; commands an artillery battalion, 213, 216; Fredericksburg Campaign, 219 n27; 1862 winter quarters, 230; Chancellorsville, 266n21; Gettysburg, July 3, 295; retreat from Gettysburg, 297n33; winter of 1863-64, 370, 373; Overland Campaign, 382-382n25, 391-391n58, 394-394n72, 398n9, 403n29, 403n31; Petersburg Campaign, 408n46, 429, 438-439, 440n36, 442, 443-443n9, 444n12, 445-446; theory that the Federals are digging a mine under the lines, 413; the war's final winter, 457, 463n10; Appomattox Campaign, 493-493n16, 495, 497-498, 498n28, 498n31, 499n34, 500

Alexandria, Loudoun & Hampshire Railroad, 20-23, 28, 31

Allen, James, 12, 56, 56n25

Allen, Judge John J., 3

Allen, L.W., 165

Allen, William, 15, 163

Allston, Benjamin, 107

Alston, Charles, 86

Ambrose, Chaplain Thomas L., 267

Amelia Court House, Virginia, 488, 488n2, 489n3, 491, 491n12, 492, 493n15, 494n18

Amelia Island, Florida, 82

Amissville, engagement at, 216-217

Anderson Archer, 63n12

Anderson, George B., 190, 194n17

Anderson, J. Patton, 115

Anderson, Joseph R., 7, 21n42, 28, 34, 34n26, 63, 93, 94n5, 106-107, 121, 123-124, 128, 131-132, 136, 163, 170

Anderson, Richard H., 150, 178, 186, 233, 271, 341, 347n23, 367n7, 395n72, 399; promoted by Lee after the Seven Days Battles, 163; Lee recommends for promotion, 169; Anderson to command Huger's former division, 170; division ordered to return to main army, 179; Harpers Ferry operation, 195; Sharpsburg Campaign, 195n21; pickets on the lookout for enemy activity, 258; ordered to move to Chancellorsville, 260; Chancellorsville, 264, 264n14, 266, 268; the march to Gettysburg, 281, 283-284, 287; Gettysburg, July 1, 292, 292n9; Gettysburg, July 3, 295; reviewing Hill's corps, 313; Overland Campaign, 381, 382n24, 383, 383n29, 384, 387n45, 389, 391, 391n58, 392, 392n63, 394, 394n72, 395, 398, 398n8, 399n11, 404n31, 405; takes over Longstreet's corps, 383; Lee lacks confidence in, 398n6; ordered to fill abandoned lines at Bermuda Hundred, 403, 403n31, 404; ordered to Petersburg, 406; Petersburg Campaign, 408n45, 409, 413, 413n9, 417, 419-420, 423-425, 425n8, 426, 430, 430n33, 431, 433, 436-437, 439, 439n32, 440n36, 441-443, 443n10, 445, 452, 452n19, 453n20; the Crater, 421; Fort Harrison, 440; the war's final winter, 470n8, 481, 486; enemy movements in his front, 483; the war's final winter, 487n45; Five Forks, 490; Appomattox Campaign, 493, 496n22, 496n24; Sailors Creek, battle of, 494; removed from command, 496

Anderson, Dr. S.B., 271

Anderson, Samuel R., 53, 53n14, 64, 71

Andrews, William H., 190n5

Appomattox Campaign, 488, 492, 495n22, 500

Appomattox Court House, 497

Appomattox Court House, surrender at, 433n3, 444n13, 489, 489n4, 496n24, 503

Appomattox River, 408, 492, 494-495, 497, 480n15

Archer, James J., 147n12, 172, 265, 292n10, 425, 425n12, 431, 431n37, 445n23

Arkansas Military Units: 3rd Infantry, 45, 62n11, 63n14

Arlington House, home of Robert E. Lee, 11, 11n8, 22, 24, 25n56, 262, 262n6, 272, 311, 327, 333, 338, 342, 344-345, 387, 387n44, 401, 403, 455, 462, 493n15

Armistead, Lewis, 67n29, 165, 165n11, 193n14, 314n23, 354n24

Ashby, Turner, 45, 64n16, 130, 150, 150n24

Athey, William, 210n29

Atkinson, George, 56n26

Atlanta, Georgia, loss of, 432, 434n7

Atlantic & Gulf Railroad, 87

Atlee's Station, 393, 393n68, 393n69, 395

Augusta & Savannah Railroad, 80n22, 98

Augusta Arsenal, 79n17, 97

Averasboro, North Carolina, battle of, 482

Averell, William W., 340, 342, 359, 371, 373, 379, 385, 388

Aylett, William, 314n23, 431n34

Babcock, Orville, 498, 498n31, 499

Baker, Lawrence, 440, 452

Baldwin, Briscoe, 58n38, 216, 216n12, 217, 222, 225, 236, 306, 354, 354n27

Baldwin, J.B., 15, 49, 49n43, 49n45, 56-57

Baldwin, James W., 58

Ball, M. Dulaney, 38, 38n40
Ball, W.B., 218, 218n25, 219, 219n26
Baltimore & Ohio Railroad, 8, 13n13, 14, 63, 181, 203, 209-211, 251, 254, 285, 299, 301, 306, 317, 320, 328, 328n10, 360, 367, 369, 416-417, 430, 445, 457, 467
Banks, Nathaniel, 120-121, 130, 135, 137, 226, 229
Barbour, James, 16, 16n24, 281n27
Barbour, John, 329
Barksdale, Ethelbert, 473
Barksdale, William, 260, 304
Barnes, Surgeon General Joseph, 20n41
Barron, Samuel, 33
Barton, Seth, 354, 354n24, 359, 359n10, 430, 431n34, 463
Basinger, William S., 95n5
Battery Dantzler, 405, 405n35
Battle, Cullen, 386n39
Bayless, Dr. George W., 56
Baylor, Eugene W., 38
Baylor, John R., 483
Baylor, W.T.H., 12
Beale, R.L.T., 418n27, 225
Beaufort, South Carolina, 81, 117
Beauregard, Pierre G. T., 25n55, 25n57, 33, 38n40, 79n19, 82, 110, 115, 117, 154, 232n2, 255, 268, 272-273, 276, 280, 285-286, 296, 324, 337, 337n1, 338, 338n7, 340n14, 355n30, 370, 374n36, 378, 380, 388, 392, 392n64, 393, 394, 394n71, 395, 406, 419, 436, 436n22, 438n27, 441n1, 450, 464n15; shot furnaces from Charleston, 5; Lee discusses conditions in Virginia, 25; assigned to command northern Virginia, 28; possible spies, 28; commands northern Virginia, 31; plan to clear Yankees from Northern Virginia, 39, 44; no formal exchange agreement exists, 41; requested Francis W. Smith, 43n19; requests for commissions go to the secretary of war, 46; victory at First Manassas, 46; Lee's congratulations for victory at Manassas, 47; confirmed rank as full general, 58n41; replaced A.S. Johnston after Shiloh, 111; informed that six regiments will be sent to Corinth, 116; Sam Jones and Trapier ordered to report to him, 116; Kirby Smith's planned move against Nashville, 118; all available troops in Florida sent to him, 119; one of his coded letters is printed in the New York Herald, 121-122; reinforcements from Finegan, 134; 4th Florida being sent to him, 135; rifles are being sent from Florida, 136; Lee tries to prod into action, 139; winter of 1863-64, 366, 374; Bermuda Hundred, 388n49; Petersburg is his shining moment, 397; Overland Campaign, 398, 398n6, 401, 402, 403n29, 403n30, 403n31, 404n32, 405, 406n38, 406n39, 406n40; abandoned lines at Bermuda Hundred to concentrate at Petersburg, 403-404; Grant's army is south of the James River, 405; rapidly deteriorating situation at Petersburg, 405; Petersburg Campaign, 408, 408n46, 408n47, 413, 413n9, 416n18, 420, 420n38, 423, 423n1, 428, 428n24, 429-430, 430n31, 431, 435, 435n13, 437, 443; the Crater, 412n4, 421, 421n41, 421n42, 422; reassigned to Charleston, 432, 437; the war's final winter, 459, 463, 468, 470, 473, 474n27, 474n28, 475, 475n31, 475n32,
476, 480, 486, 486n44, Appomattox Campaign, 490, 490n6
Beckley, Alfred, 42, 53-54, 57
"Beefsteak Raid," 435n12, 436
Bell, Adam, 64n20
Bell, H.M., 210
Bell, Norman, 500n36
Bell, William, 454, 454n28
Bellona Arsenal, 24, 24n53, 41
Belvoir, 251, 251n41, 252, 254, 258, 278
Bemiss, Dr. S.M., 251, 252, 252n3, 255, 255n15, 256n20
Benjamin, Judah P., 61n5, 78n15, 95, 177n7, 210n26, 472; meets with Lee to discuss strategy, 75, 78; Lee sends report of activities since arriving in Charleston, 80; Lee's report about enemy occupation of Tybee Island, 83; Lee writes of poor recruiting in South Carolina, 85; Lee sends an update about Charleston, 87; notified of the "stone fleet" sunk in Charleston, 87; notified that Trapier is to expect landing of blockade runners, 92; Lee warns of pending expired enlistments for Georgia units, 96; Lee orders that Jekyll Island and Saint Simon's Island be abandoned, 97; ordered to withdraw all troops from coastal Florida, 99; Lee is stripping Florida and sending troops to Tennessee, 102; one of many civilians to come watch the battle, 157; suspicious foreigner, 209
Benning, Henry, 249
Bentonville, North Carolina, battle of, 478, 478n6, 483
Berkeley, Dr. Thomas A., 23-24, 24n52
Bermuda Hundred, engagements at, 147n13, 378, 380, 395, 400, 402, 404, 404n32, 405, 412, 414, 420, 420n40, 427, 439, 445, 484, 488
Bethesda Church, battle of, 370n17, 395, 395n72, 445n23
Beverly, William, 185
Big Bethel, battle of, 29n9, 32
Bird, H.D., 35
Blackford, Charles, 170n27
Blackford, William W., 192, 281, 293n13, 335n42, 338, 342, 435n15, 499n34
Blair, Francis P., 2, 2n5
Blair, William B., 21, 21n43, 22
Blanchard, A.G., 15, 15n21
Blandford Cemetery, 421, 421n41, 484
Blanton, John, 496, 496n23
Bloomsbury estate, 333-334, 346
Blue Sulphur Springs, 74n29
Boatswain's Swamp, 158
Bocock, Thomas, 340
Bolling, Robert, 186, 186n41
Bondurant, Miss Rosa, 36
Bonham, Milledge Luke, 21, 21n42, 22-25, 47n35, 314
Boonsboro, Maryland, 196-197, 197n28
Booth, John Wilkes, 82n33
Boswell, J.K., 259, 263, 263n11
Boteler, Alexander R., 148, 148n16, 153, 201, 240, 341, 379, 380n15
Boteler's Ford, 199, 201, 209
Botts, John Minor, 141
Boykin, Francis M., 8, 8n20, 17-18

Index | 525

Bradford, Edward M., 18, 18n31

Brady, Matthew, 503

Bragg, Braxton, 98n22, 109, 172, 193n14, 202, 207n12, 212n37, 213, 256, 286, 291, 309-310, 311n10, 314-317, 320, 320n10, 323, 341, 341n22, 354, 355n32, 368-370, 370n19, 376, 379, 383, 390n57, 393, 393n68, 394, 399-400, 403n29, 438, 452n16, 455-456, 456n1, 459-461,467; rumors Lee was going to replace him, 337-338, 340n14; resigns as commander of the Army of Tennessee, 350; becomes military advisor to Davis, 355; winter of 1863-64, 355n30, 361, 361n24, 372; Overland Campaign, 401, 406; abandoned lines at Bermuda Hundred to concentrate at Petersburg, 403n31; Lee will not move army closer to Richmond, 403; Petersburg Campaign, 408-409, 414, 420, 420n38, 425n8, 434, 434n7, 439, 446, 452; the war's final winter, 464-466, 466n26, 470-476, 479-482, 485

Bragg, Thomas, 98n22, 99, 103n17

Branch, James R., 15

Branch, Lawrence, 61n5, 129, 131, 138, 148, 148n15, 152, 153n34, 172

Brandy Station, Virginia and battle of, 183, 276, 281, 281n28, 283, 304, 318, 324, 324n31, 326

Bratton, John, 409

Brawner farm, battle of, 175

Brawner, W.G., 217n18

Breathed, James, 414, 414n12

Breckinridge, John C., 118n30, 349, 349n36, 351, 351n3, 353, 369, 371-373, 373n31, 374, 378-381, 383, 385, 387-389, 389n53, 390n57, 392-393, 393n68, 394, 400, 436, 438n28, 444, 453, 457, 479, 494; promoted to major general, 118; winter of 1863-64, 373; Overland Campaign, 390-391, 394n71, 397, 398, 398n10, 399, 399n15, 401; Petersburg Campaign, 438, 442-443; no objection to prisoner exchange, 445; Saltville, 446; pardons all Unionist Tennesseans who lay down their arms, 448; the war's final winter, 459-460, 464, 472, 472n16, 473, 473n22, 475, 478n6, 479, 480n10, 481, 481n16, 482-483, 483n26, 485, 485n38, 486-487; becomes Secretary of War, 468; replaces Seddon, 471; discussing details to evacuating Petersburg, 474; how to convince Davis to end the war, 480; Hampton's cavalry attacked Sherman at Fayetteville, 481; gunboats in the James River, 484; Appomattox Campaign, 490,494, 494n18, 495n20

Breeden, Mrs. J.A., 34

Brent, G.W., 438n27

Brent, Joseph, 133n32, 160-161, 166n11, 166n13

Bridgford, D.B., 279

Bristoe Station, capture of, 184, 318, 322, 322n19, 324, 328-329, 332

Brock Road, 381-382

Brockenbrough, John, 294

Brooke, John M., 6, 7n17, 11n2, 23, 27-28, 29n6, 35, 37, 47, 149, 149n19, 168n21, 437

Brooks, John S., 385n36

Broun, Joseph, 84, 94, 94n4, 89n31

Broun, Thomas L., 60

Brown, Dr. Bedford, 74n29

Brown, Campbell, 292-293, 299n42, 380, 385n35, 440n35

Brown, J. Thompson, 179

Brown, John, 1

Brown, Joseph (Governor, Georgia), 23, 80, 80n22, 97-98, 131n26, 141, 313, 359; any requests for troops should be sent to him, 88; did not like Davis, 94; refused to allow state troops to serve outside Georgia, 94n1; artillery to guard obstructions on the Savannah River, 97; requested to send a regiment to Knoxville, 108; Lee calls for troops to be sent to North Carolina, 113; state troops be retained for duration, 113; enemy prisoners on the way, 119; Milledgeville prisoners to be held in Atlanta, 120; weapons being sent to him, 123; Lee asks for martial law at Augusta and Savannah, 129; a new shipment of weapons, 134; death of T.R.R. Cobb, 228

Brown, Samuel B., 432, 432n2

Browne, William M., 218n21, 332-334

Brunswick, Georgia, 82, 82n30

Buchanan, James, 61n5

Buckland, battle of, 323

Buckner, Simon B., 118, 118n31, 283, 286, 346, 348, 354, 369-370, 370n19, 372n25, 390n57

Bull, Gustavus A., 171, 171n33

Bull, Rice, 266n20

Burgess's Mill, battle of, 447, 447n33, 448, 451

Burkesville, Virginia, 474-475, 492

Burks, Jesse, 42, 45, 54, 55n19

Burnside, Ambrose, 104n25, 128, 139, 149, 154, 169, 178n12, 188, 190, 214, 217, 233, 237, 237n29, 238n34, 243, 259, 280n20, 314-315, 317, 354, 370, 379, 392; captures New Bern, North Carolina, 101; remains at New Bern, 105; might move on Norfolk, 113; Holmes should try to arrange a POW exchange, 116; moved to Fort Monroe, 154; troops from North Carolina have gone to reinforce Pope, 178; leaving Fredericksburg, 181; army joins AOP, 196; made commander of the AOP, 213, 216, 216n15; Fredericksburg Campaign, 218-220, 222, 222n38, 223, 225, 227-229, 232, 234-236; meets Lincoln at Aquia, 225; "Mud March," 232; might be moving again, 237; British officials, 238; at Hampton Roads, 247; Burnside's corps sent west on the B&O, 251; Burnside and IX Corps are in Kentucky, 254; Knoxville, 333; winter of 1863-64, 367; moved to Alexandria, 374; The Crater, 412n4, 422; troops still at Petersburg, 414; rumor his troops are digging a mine, 418n30; Petersburg Campaign, 420n40

Burwell, Nat, 340

Burwell's Bay, 9, 33, 33n21, 37

Butler, Benjamin F., 62n8, 129n13, 326, 333, 359, 378, 384, 386, 388, 388n49, 395, 397, 400, 419, 423n2

Butler, Matthew C., 427n16, 463-465

Butt, Anthony S., 501, 501n39

Cabell, Henry, 459, 459n22

Cameron, Simon, 2, 2n5, 65n20

Cameron, S.F., 353

Camp Defiance, 67-69

Campbell, Ella, 222

Campbell, Francis L., 33, 33n21

Campbell, John A., 42, 42n15, 45, 467n32
Cantzon, William H., 500n36
Capers, Henry D., 371, 371n24
Caperton, Allen, 53-54
Cardwell, Lucy A., 202
Carter, A.V., 73
Carter, Hill (Lee's cousin), 21, 128, 270, 390n57
Carter, Robert R., 34, 34n25
Carter, Shirley T., 92
Carter, Thomas, 200, 200n40, 201n44, 255n14, 315, 480
Cashtown, Pennsylvania, 292
Caskie, James, 282, 309, 312
Castle Pinckney, South Carolina, 81n25
Castleberry, W.A., 292n10
Catlett, Richard H., 41, 41n8
Catlett's Station, skirmish at, 183-184, 184n34, 370-371
Catterton, William, 69n35
Causton's Bluff, Savannah, Georgia, 93
Cedar Creek, battle of, 441, 446, 449
Cedar Mountain, battle of, 175, 180, 184, 205, 255n16, 257
Cercopoly, Francis J., 80, 80n22
Chaffin's Bluff, Virginia, and engagements at, 132, 134, 151, 154, 168, 371n25, 403, 404n31, 405, 407, 413, 415, 418, 427n19, 428n24, 433, 439-440, 440n36, 442n3, 443n8, 445n19, 455
Chambersburg, Pennsylvania, 207, 208n14, 287, 287n49, 287n51, 288n53, 288n55, 290
Chambliss, John, 42n11, 216, 219
Chambliss, Robert, 210
Chancellorsville, Virginia, and battle of, 227n15, 233, 253, 260-266, 266n20, 268-271, 282, 282n30, 335, 359, 376, 383
Chandler, Daniel T., 463n9
Chandler, Thomas C., 225n9
Chapman, Augustus A., 54, 54n18, 57
Chappell, A.M., 489n3
Charleston 1861 fire, 86n15
Charleston & Savannah Railroad, 79, 79n18, 79n19, 80-81, 85, 91, 93, 96, 96n9, 98-99, 102, 178
Charleston *Mercury*, 70, 100, 113n6, 302, 341, 363n35
Charleston, South Carolina, 75, 88, 90, 211, 217, 228, 240-241, 247, 250, 258n28, 273, 306-307, 307n27, 321, 328, 337n1, 338n7, 347, 349, 370, 432, 435-437, 447, 462-463, 465-46, 467n2
Charleston, western Virginia, 208
Charlestown, western Virginia, 209
Chattanooga, Tennessee, 314, 320, 323, 350-351
Cheat Mountain, western Virginia, battle of, 45, 54, 60, 62n11, 63, 63n14, 64, 64n19, 65-66, 71, 75
Cheek, William, 493n15
Chesapeake & Ohio Canal, 14, 31, 195n21
Chesnut, James R., 44-45, 341
Chesnut, Mary, 315n25, 353n20
Chesterfield Court House, 492, 492n13
Cheves, Langdon, 156
Chew, R. Preston, 391
Chichester, C.E., 81n25

Chickamauga, Georgia, battle of, 310, 315-316, 320, 324, 346n21
Chilton, Laura, 230
Chilton, Robert H., 20, 20n41, 86n13, 161, 166n11, 178n13, 197, 198n31, 207n12, 210, 210n26, 227n16, 248n25, 255n14, 257, 257n27, 258n27, 259n33, 264, 264n15, 313n16, 328, 332, 357n4, 362n30, 503; commands the Recruiting Service, 12; lost Special Order 191, 21n41; unluckiest staff officer, 21n41; joins Lee's staff, 148; poorly written orders, 165n11; moves to inspector general, 205; ANV inspector general, 209, 211, 216; no furloughs to be granted, 248; nominated for promotion to brigadier general, and denied, 255n16; court of inquiry about rejection as a brigadier general, 259, 259n32; Chancellorsville, 268; court of inquiry about Magruder, 271; winter of 1863, 341, 341n2; winter of 1863-64, 349n34, 353, 355, 355n34, 356n35, 357, 359n10, 362, 363n34, 367n4, Lee regrets losing his services, 363
Chisholm, A.R., 405
Christman, William H., 387n44
City Point, Virginia, 136, 178n12, 361, 417n21
Clark, Henry T., (Governor, North Carolina), 109-110, 127, 128, 134, 136, 138, 140, 172-173, 179
Clark, James L., 41, 492, 492n13
Clark, M.L., 115-116
Clarke, J.G., 316, 316n30, 320, 320n10
Clarke, W.L., 12
Clarke, William J., 72, 72n16
Clarksville, Virginia, 492n14
Clay, Hugh L., 55
Cleary, F.D., 71
Clingman, Thomas, 134, 134n34, 361n23, 470
Clover Hill Railroad, 492, 492n14
Cobb, Howell, 73n26, 107, 114, 138, 150-153, 153n34, 167, 167n15, 168-169, 229, 235
Cobb, Thomas R.R., 73, 73n26, 116n25, 138n51, 150n25, 177, 178n10, 221n37, 228-229, 229n27
Cobb's Legion, 115, 177n5
Cocke, Cary C., 31, 31n15
Cocke, H.H., 8, 18, 18n32
Cocke, John H. (father of Philip St. George Cocke), 13-14, 14n19, 15-16, 18, 18n30, 19, 21
Cocke, Philip St. George, 5, 5n14, 12-14, 31n15
Cockspur Island, Georgia, 75, 80
Coiner, George, 432
Cold Harbor, 1862 battle of, 158, 371n24, 378, 395, 395n76, 396-398, 398n10, 399, 399n15, 401, 411
Cole, Archibald, 123, 133
Cole, Rev. John, 283, 427
Coleman, Samuel, 210n29
Collins, C.R., 283
Colquitt, Alfred H., 271-273
Colston, Frederick, 471n12
Colston, Raleigh, 250, 254, 258, 265, 265n19, 266n20, 274n52, 314, 314n23, 439
Compton, William A., 385n38
Confederate Military Units: 1st Engineer Regiment, 6n15, 364, 367

Conn, R.M., 37, 37n36
Conolly, Thomas, 478, 481-482, 482n23, 483, 485, 485n39, 486, 486n43, 486n44
Conoway, James E., 58, 62-63
Conrad, Robert Y., 313n17
Conrad's Mill, skirmish at, 64, 64n18
Conrad's Store, 135
conscription bill, 111, 113n5, 118
Conway, Moncure, 220n29
Cook, William H., 73, 73n26
Cooke, Giles B., 406, 406n38, 406n39, 443, 471, 486n43, 486n44, 491, 500n37, 501
Cooke, John Esten, 227n17, 284n39, 486n43
Cooke, John R., 477
Coolidge, Richard H., 192
Cooper, Adj. Gen. Samuel, 33, 33n21, 37n37, 44-45, 50, 53, 53n12, 54-55, 58, 63, 69, 71, 91, 97, 105, 179-180, 206, 209-210, 215, 218n24, 219-220, 220n29, 228-229, 236, 247-248, 248n26, 250, 281, 284n38, 300, 304-305, 313, 320, 320n10, 321, 328, 333, 338, 345, 345n14, 409, 417, 463; Lee complains about Wise, 57; confirmed rank as full general, 58n41; Lee complains about weather, 58; writes Lee about Davis' satisfaction with, 62; 20th Mississippi and Philips Legion available to Lee, 66n23; Cheat Mountain battle, 66; Lee informs of Rosecrans's withdrawal, 72; Lee's update on situation in western Virginia, 73; letter from Lee regarding G.S. Magruder and A.V. Carter, 73; Lee sends report of inspection trip along the coast, 82; Lee says Navy unable to prevent enemy from removing river obstructions, 93; balance of Johnston's army to the Peninsula, 117; Holmes's forces in North Carolina, 118; one of Beauregard's coded letters is printed in the New York *Herald*, 122; Sharpsburg Campaign, 202; Fredericksburg Campaign, 227; Lee does not oppose resignation of Toombs, 246; Toombs' resignation, 246n10; Jackson and Hill file complaints about the other, 249; Lee's Seven Days report, 249; Burnside's corps sent west on the B&O, 251; Lee writes about reinforcing Bragg in Tennessee, 256; three enemy corps moving toward Germanna and Ely's fords, 259; post-Chancellorsville, 273; Vance complains about NC units serving under Virginia officers, 274; Meade's summer 1863 operations, 315; Stuart's victory at Buckland, 323; Sam Jones ordered to send his cavalry to Longstreet, 334; winter of 1863-64, 351, 354, 359-360; Chilton taking a position on his staff, 363; sends copies of the Dahlgren papers to Lee, 365; Lee recommends all partisan units except Mosby be disbanded, 367; writes Meade regarding the Dahlgren papers, 368; medical exemptions for soldiers, 444; confirms Lee's appointment as general in chief, 470
Coosawhatchie, South Carolina, 76
Corker, Margaret, 306, 306n23
Corley, James L., 155, 404, 473n21, 485
Corrick's Ford, battle of, 39, 44
Corse, Montgomery D., 200n40, 282, 285, 289n57, 316-317, 347
"Council of Three," 3, 4n10, 4, 7n18
Coward, Asbury, 427, 427n19

Cox, Jacob, 47n36, 73n19
Cox, James H., 492, 492n14
Crampton's Gap, battle of, 196-197
Craney Island, 23n47, 44
Crater, battle of the, 313n17, 412, 412n4, 420-421, 421n41, 421n42, 422, 422n44, 424, 424n3, 426, 457n6
Crenshaw, James R., 6, 7n17, 8, 30, 30n12, 234
Crenshaw, William G., 182, 182n26
Critcher, John, 217, 260, 273
Crook, G.W.L., 20
Crook, George, 67n27, 385, 388, 419n36, 475
Cross Keys, battle of, 150
Crump, Charles A., 36, 36n34
Crutchfield, Stapleton, 40, 135, 136n41, 166n12, 243
Culpeper, Virginia, 203, 205, 211, 211n33, 212, 212n36, 213-215, 216n14, 219, 221, 227-228, 271, 280, 280n19, 281, 283n34, 284n38, 291, 300, 300n45, 300n46, 304n8, 314, 321, 322n18, 330, 425, 425n8, 426-427, 427n18
Cummings, Alfred C., 31, 31n14
Cummings, Dr. J.C., 47
Custis, George Washington Parke, 91-92, 97, 231
Cuthbert, George B., 238n35

Dabbs, Josiah and Catherine (owners of High Meadows), 143, 146, 146n11, 163
Dabney, R.L., 161n66, 256
Dahlgren, Ulric, 357, 359n9, 360, 360n15, 361, 365, 367-368
Daingerfield, Henry, 3
Dance, Willis J., 329
Daniel, F.V., 122
Daniel, John M., 70
Daniel, Junius, 271, 281n26, 363, 393
Daniel, Jr., Peter V., 6, 248
Danville, Virginia, 492
Davis, George D., 36
Davis, President Jefferson, 7n18, 8n21, 15, 30, 3010n, 35n30, 37, 39, 45, 48n41, 61n5, 64, 70, 78n13, 79n19, 102-103, 111, 125, 130, 131n26, 134n37, 137-138, 141, 151, 157-158, 160, 160n62, 161, 163, 178, 196n24, 203, 203n53, 205n2, 212-213, 215, 218, 229n28, 233n8, 235, 235n16, 235n18, 236, 243, 247, 249n28, 273n49, 281, 282n30, 284-285, 295n24, 296-299, 299n41, 300, 301-302, 305, 305n12, 306, 307n24, 308n28, 308n30, 308n34, 311, 311n11, 313-314, 316, 316n29, 317, 323, 326, 326n6, 330, 332n32, 333, 334n38, 334n40, 336-338, 349, 352, 358, 362, 364n39, 369, 374n34, 384, 387, 389n53, 390, 390n57, 393-394, 394n71, 395-396, 398n8, 399, 399n15, 400-402, 402n26, 404, 407, 409-410, 410n54, 414, 424-425, 428-429, 435-436, 436n22, 437, 437n25, 442, 445-446, 449, 454, 462, 464, 467n30, 472; arrives in Richmond, 11, 24; assigns Beauregard to Manassas, 25n57; Lee discusses conditions in Virginia, 25; officers of the provisional army, 28n4; observes drill of the Washington Artillery, 35; reviewing troops in Richmond, 37n35; reviews the 6th North Carolina, 44; illness, 45n23; goes to the front at First Manassas, 46-47; Lee meets with and discusses western Virginia, 48; proposed prisoner exchange, 53; satisfaction with Lee's efforts in western Virginia, 62; Lee briefs on western Virginia operations, 75,

78; Lee's new assignment, 78; Beauregard's report about Manassas, 82; Gov. Brown did not like him, 94n1; Davis considers recalling Lee to Richmond, 99; a new role for Lee, 100; appoints Lee as military advisor, 100; does not want martial law declared in Mobile, 105; Johnston to send Longstreet to North Carolina, 106; 17 regiments are being sent east from Winchester, 107; Huger's military government, 107; travels to Fredericksburg with Lee, 107; long, frequent meetings with Lee, 112; wants Johnston to go to the Peninsula, 114; Kirby Smith to remain in command in east Tennessee, 116; does not have authority to commission state officers, 118; declares martial law at Charleston, 124; on hand to observe Johnston's Fair Oaks fiasco, 126; wants to know Johnston's plans, 137; watches artillery duel at Mechanicsville, 138, 138n50; informs Lee he will be commander of the ANV, 142; rides back to Richmond with Lee, 142; appoints Lee to command the ANV, 143; Johnston does not reveal any plans, 144; Lee always kept Davis informed of plans, 144; formal orders appointing Lee in command of the ANV, 146; Lee will be the commander of the ANV, 146; strategy for the Seven Days battles, 147n13; too ill to visit Lee in the field, 147; Lee is preparing a fortified line in front of Richmond, 149; possible promotion of Richard Anderson, 150; wants troops brigaded by state, Lee will comply, 150; Lee says Huger can be sent to Charleston, 154; plans for Lee's offensive, 155; letter regarding unpopular John Pemberton, 156; Lee announces victory and hundreds of prisoners, 159; Lee's plan to trap McClellan at Glendale, 162; from Lee, McClellan is gone from Lee's front, 166; gets results of Lee's reconnaissance, 167; wants to reconnoiter McClellan's position, 167; warns Lee about personal exposure, 168; Lee recommends Richard Anderson and Micah Jenkins for promotion, 169; Jackson to guard the Virginia Central Railroad, 171; update on Hill's POW exchange, 171; Lee gives intel update regarding Pope, 172; Lee looking for a replacement for Beverly Robertson, 173; William F. "Extra Billy" Smith, 173; communicating with McClellan, 177; McClellan is leaving the Peninsula, 181; update on Pope, 181; D.H. Hill's fitness for independent command, 182; Lee's comments on D.H. Hill, 182n26; ANV across the Rapidan, 183; Catlett's Station, 183; Lee's desire to remain north of Richmond, 183; Bristoe Station Campaign, 184, 324, 328; Manassas Junction, 184; Lee provides info about August 29 attack, 186; Lee tells of Pope's defeat, 186; Lee asks approval to cross the Potomac, 188; Lee sends report of Second Manassas, 192; intent to cross the Potomac, 193; entire army has crossed the Potomac, 194; Davis wants to join Lee's army in Maryland, 195n21; returned to Richmond, 195n22; wants to join Lee's army in Maryland, 195; copy of Special Order 191, 196; Sharpsburg Campaign, 199, 201-202; post-Sharpsburg lull, 206; Lee wants to keep part of his army in the Valley and part on the Rappahannock, 210; Fredericksburg Campaign, 219, 222, 222n38; Lee feels Burnside to advance on Richmond via Fredericksburg, 221; Lee sends a copy of the New York *Herald*, 222; Federals still opposite across from Fredericksburg, 225; Lee's report about a Federal army being organized in New York, 226; Lee's concern about North Carolina, 232-233; Lee wrote to Halleck about Milroy, 234; Charleston or Wilmington attacks, 240; update on Pickett and Hood, 242; Lee travels to Richmond to meet with, 244; proposed reorganization of the artillery, 244n2, 246, 248; Lee wants to reorganize the staff and support positions in the army, 249; Burnside and IX Corps are in Kentucky, 254; Lee wants the beef cattle in Florida rounded up and sent to ANV, 257; Lee provides strength and location of enemy, 258; Lee notifies about enemy crossing at Deep Run, 259; three enemy corps moving toward Germanna and Ely's fords, 260; worried about deteriorating situation in the Western Theater, 261; Chancellorsville, 264, 265n19, 266n21, 267, 267n24, 268; Lee's message of victory at Chancellorsville, 265; Jackson wounded, 266; death of Stonewall Jackson, 269; does not want Lee to fall back to Richmond, 269; meets with Davis regarding reinforcing Vicksburg, 270, 270n35, 270n38; Lee's proposed reorganization of the ANV, 271; promotions for Heth and Pender, 272, 274; D.H. Hill, 275; post-Chancellorsville, 275; Lee needs more cavalry, 278; the march to Gettysburg, 280, 283; Stuart's Brandy Station report, 283; Lee writes about prisoner exchange and enemy movements, 286; Gettysburg, July 4, 295; Lee submits resignation, Davis refuses it, 303, 305, 307; Meade's army moving toward Culpeper, 304; situation in Tennessee, 309; detachment of Longstreet's corps to Tennessee, 312; Meade's summer 1863 operations, 315, 315n25; Lee confirms two Union corps have gone to Tennessee, 320; Rappahannock Station, battle of, 331; New Bern, 344; approves Thanks of Congress to Lee, 345; Lee's concern about troops recruited for local service only, 347; vulnerability of southwest Virginia, 348; names Bragg as military advisor to Davis, 350; two options for the Spring Campaign, 351; Longstreet's proposal to attack Knoxville, 354; winter of 1863-64, 355, 361n21, 361n24, 367; Kilpatrick-Dahlgren Raid, 357, 360; greets Rooney Lee returning from prison, 361; Lee has no indication of new enemy offensive in Virginia, 363; Lee has many conflicting reports on enemy intentions, 366; Meade says no one authorized his assassination, 367n4; Edward O'Neal, 368; Lee has reliable reports no large units have joined the AOP, 368; Lee reports that enemy dispositions are becoming clearer, 371; Field replaces Hood, 372n25; Winchester citizens arrested by both sides, 372; Lee asks to visit the army, 373; Burnside on the Rappahannock with Meade, 374; Lee complains about army's current situation, 388-389; army is in position along the North Anna River, 391; Lee will not move army closer to Richmond, 403; Lee is looking for answers about Grant's location, 405; Lee moved headquarters to Petersburg, 406; Petersburg Campaign, 407n43; Early's operations in the Valley, 409; wants to sack Joe Johnston, 411; Lee recommends Wade Hampton should command cavalry, 413; Early's raid having an effect on the northern population, 415; Point Lookout operation, 415n15; replaces Joe Johnston with John B. Hood, 416, 416n18; difficulty of getting adequate supplies, 418; Lee doubts anything would force Grant to abandon Petersburg, 419n32; Lee's lengthy analysis, 434; on way to meet with Hood in Georgia, 438n28, 439n34; returns from Georgia, 444n12; Lee's opinion of Kensey

Stewart, 447; feud between Longstreet and Law, 451; no available troops to send to oppose Sherman, 453; status of Wilmington, 455; operations in the Shenandoah Valley, 457; the army is out of meat, 458; the war's final winter, 459-460, 466, 472-473, 474n27, 475-476, 480, 484; Hardee's plans to resist Sherman, 463; offers Lee command of all armies, 465; Lee says Thomas' army is joining with Grant, 467; peace delegation, 467; picks Alexander Stephens, R.M.T. Hunter and John Campbell as peace commissioners, 467n32; lost confidence in Beauregard, 468; tells Lee his counsels are no longer wanted regarding Richmond, 476n35; Longstreet's meeting with General Ord to discuss peace, 479; March 10 a day of fasting and prayer, 479, 481; authorizes blacks to serve in the army, 482; reason for the Fort Stedman attack, 485; Kirby Smith cannot join Lee, 486; moment Lee had been warning about, 488; Petersburg and Richmond must be evacuated, 488; Lee advises that Sheridan is at Dinwiddie, 490; Lee advises that Richmond must evacuate tonight, 491; at Danville, 494; Lee sends his last official communication to, 503

Davis, Joseph R., 37n35, 38n40, 166, 279, 279n16, 344n17, 494n18
Davis, Richard, 379n12
Davis, Robert W., 3
Davis, Samuel B., 367, 367n5
Davis, William G.M., 137, 137n47
Dawson, Francis, 228n20, 382n25, 439n32
Dearing, James, 437
Dearing, St. Clair, 258, 258n28
Deas, George, 33, 33n21, 47n35, 63n15, 78n15, 259n32
Debaws, J.H., 19, 19n33
Deep Bottom, 407n43, 414, 419-420, 420n40, 423, 429, 441
DeLeon, Surgeon General David C., 35, 148, 159
Department of South Carolina, Georgia and East Florida, 78-79, 102, 104
Deshler, James, 46, 46n30
Dimmock Line, 449
Dimmock, Charles, 5, 7, 7n18, 8, 11n4, 12, 12n11, 17, 19, 21-22, 24, 24n53, 33, 35, 36, 37n35, 41, 43, 45, 48, 49n42, 435, 435n15, 449
Dinwiddie Court House, Virginia and battle of, 429, 451, 478, 486, 488, 490
Dix, John, 177, 235
Dix-Hill POW agreement, 177
Donelson, Daniel, 64, 64n19, 86n16, 116
Doswell, Benjamin T., 153
Douglas, Henry Kyd, 269, 183n33, 187n44, 194, 194n17, 199n34, 273n50
Dranesville, Virginia, 193, 193n14
Drayton, Thomas F., 79, 79n19, 89, 96, 96n9, 99n30, 221
Dreux, Charles, 43, 43n16
Drewry, Augustus, 104
Drewry's Bluff, and engagements at, 43n19, 114, 125-127, 131, 132n27, 134n37, 135, 135n39, 136, 137n48, 138, 138n51, 139, 149, 153-154, 164, 170, 172-173, 178-179, 271, 354n24, 355, 403, 403n30, 404n33, 405, 406n38, 433, 435n11, 458, 488

Driscoll, Dennis, 340n20
Dudley, Alexander, 128
Duffie, Alfred, 67n27, 447, 447n31
Dulany, W.H., 19
Dumont, Ebenezer, 44n22
Duncan, D.G., 6, 22
Dungeness, home of Nathaniel Greene, 90n2, 92n16
Dunn, William, 498
Dunovant, John, 91, 91n8
DuPont, Samuel, 79n18
Dutch Gap Canal, 129n13, 405n35, 423, 423n2, 425, 425n11, 426-427, 445, 445n22, 446

Eaches, Hector, 455, 461
Early, Jubal A., 21, 24, 32, 160n62, 162, 165, 221, 221n36, 255n14, 258-260, 271n41, 290, 290n2, 318, 320, 333, 336, 399, 403, 406, 414, 416, 418, 423n1, 426n14, 430, 430n33, 441, 453-454, 479; Shenandoah Valley Campaign, 14, 16-17, 344-345, 351, 355n34, 362, 370-371, 371n25, 372n28, 373, 373n33, 382n26, 383, 383n27, 383n28, 383n30, 384-385, 387, 389, 389n55, 390, 390n57, 394, 394n72, 397, 411, 411n1, 413, 420, 443, 443-444, 455; 24th Virginia Infantry, 30; reports for duty, 160; William F. Smith's brigade assigned to Early's Division, 173; upset by new brigade, 178; Sharpsburg Campaign, 201; post-Sharpsburg lull, 208; recommends Hoke's promotion, 234; promoted, 236; Chancellorsville, 263-264, 264n15, 265, 265n19, 266; post-Chancellorsville, 273, 273n50, 274; the march to Gettysburg, 284; Gettysburg, July 1, 292; Gettysburg, July 2, 293, 293n12; retreat from Gettysburg, 297; post-Gettysburg, 301, 305; reviewing Ewell's corps, 312; Bristoe Station Campaign, 329, 329n16; Rappahannock Station, battle of, 330n19; post-Rappahannock Station, 332, 332n26, 332n30, 333; Mine Run, 334-335, 335n44, 336n45, 336n46; ordered to take command in the Valley, 340; winter of 1863, 341-342; ordered to acquire any supplies he can find, 347; potential commander for southwest Virginia, 348; winter of 1863-64, 352; Imboden's request for court of inquiry, 353; Overland Campaign, 401; departs for the Valley, 402; repulsed an attack at Lynchburg, 407; ordered to move down the Valley to threaten Washington, 409; Point Lookout operation, 413n8; Early's raid having an effect on the northern population, 415; Union troops leaving Petersburg for Washington D.C., 415; able to operate as he chooses, 416; Lee congratulates on the move on Washington, 417; Petersburg Campaign, 417, 419n36, 425n9, 429, 438, 440, 442; victory at Snicker's Gap, 418; Kernstown, 419; requests Tom Rosser to lead his cavalry, 420n39; presence concerned Lincoln, 423; Union forces in Washington, 424; Grant sends additional troops to oppose him, 425; Lee alerts that Sheridan is new enemy commander, 426; Winchester and Fisher's Hill, 432; his opinion on reorganizing the cavalry in the Valley, 436; Fisher's Hill, 437-438, 438n29, 439; Third Winchester, 437; Cedar Creek, 441, 446, 449; Lee defends his actions to Governor Smith, 444-445; the war's final winter, 457, 463, 480, 482, 485, 485n38; operations in the Shenandoah Valley, 461, 470, 474; complaint about policy of furloughed men taking

horses with them, 467, 467n30; complaint about Jesse McNeill's partisan raiders, 470; remainder of the Valley Army destroyed at Waynesboro, 478, 479n7; relieved by Lee, 486

East Tennessee & Virginia Railroad, 110
Echols, John, 14, 14n18, 41n8, 208n20, 209-210, 390n57, 392, 398, 398n8, 399, 438, 475, 486
Edisto Island, 85, 89, 97
Edmonds, Elias, 46, 47n32
Elizabeth City, North Carolina, 119, 123
Ellerson, Andrew R., 159n59
Elliott, Bishop Stephen, 98, 243
Elliott, Granville G., 363, 363n33
Ellis, John (Governor of North Carolina), 19, 19n35, 21, 21n43, 23, 25, 28, 36
Ellis, Thomas H., 47-48
Eltham's Landing, engagement at, 130, 130n22
Ely's Ford, 259, 334, 340-341, 359-360, 373, 379, 383
Elzey, Arnold, 24, 24n52, 162, 237, 247-248, 249n27, 254-255, 266, 271-273, 278n11, 281-283, 316, 318, 321, 324-325, 348, 350-352, 352n13, 353, 354n24, 359, 361n23, 364, 364n39, 401
Etowah Iron Works, 232n2
Evans, Clement, 388, 388n51, 471
Evans, Nathan G. "Shanks," 35, 35n29, 79, 87-88, 92, 97-98, 109, 117, 134, 250
Ewell, Benjamin S., 12, 12n9, 17, 19n33, 21-22, 28-29, 32-34, 42
Ewell, Richard S., 12n9, 19n33, 20-21, 25, 73, 121, 124, 126, 160, 166, 281, 284, 290n2, 310-311, 312n14, 313, 317, 320-321, 321n16, 329, 345, 377, 403, 419, 428n20; promotion in Virginia forces, 6; go on offensive to give the enemy pause, 118; joins with Jackson to attack Banks, 120; requested to join with Jackson against Banks, 122; ordered to join Jackson in the Valley, 127; Branch's Brigade ordered to join Ewell, 129; Swift Run Gap, 129; it seems Banks is leaving the Valley, 30; Lee approves plan to remain at Conrad's Store, 133; Lee urges a junction with Jackson, 135; authorized to link with Jackson to defeat Banks, 137; ordered to Louisa Court House with Jackson, 170; promoted to lieutenant general, 261; post-Chancellorsville, 270n37, 273-275; recommended for corps command, 271; led the march into the Valley, 276; poised to capture Harrisburg, PA, 277; Lee's planning meeting for the move north, 278, 280; the march to Gettysburg, 278n9, 279, 281n27, 282-283, 285, 287n54, 288n55; Gettysburg, July 1, 292-293; Gettysburg, July 2, 293, 293n12, 293n13, 293n15; Gettysburg, July 3, 295; Gettysburg, July 4, 295n23; retreat from Gettysburg, 296-297, 298n37, 299; post-Gettysburg, 301, 304-307, 307n24; Lee reviews his corps, 312; Meade's summer 1863 operations, 315n27; Bristoe Station Campaign, 322, 322n19, 323, 324n28, 329n16; post-Rappahannock Station, 332n26, 332n30; Mine Run, 335, 336n45, 336n46; winter of 1863, 338, 338n6, 339, 339n9, 339n13, 340n15, 341n22; status of ability to command, 346; winter of 1863-64, 347, 347n23, 347n24, 351-354, 355n28, 355n34, 356n35, 362n25, 363, 372n28, 373, 374n34; temporary in command of ANV, 350; illness, 377, 394; Overland Campaign, 380-382, 382n24, 382n26, 383, 383n28, 383n28, 384-385, 385n35, 385n37, 385n38, 386, 386n39, 386n40, 387-389, 391, 392n64, 393, 394n70, 395, 397; Harris Farm, 389n52; Lee lacks confidence in, 398n7, 400n17; sent to Richmond to command the troops, 398; tries to resume command, 398; commands Richmond defenses, 401; Petersburg Campaign, 413, 415, 419-420, 425, 427, 427n17, 431, 433, 439, 440n36, 440n37, 442, 446; authorized to place torpedoes in the James River, 416; local reserves, 416; torpedoes were captured, 418; the Crater, 421; Lee trying to get him to stop the Federal canal on the James River, 423; won't attack the enemy, 426; Dutch Gap Canal, 427; Fort Harrison, 440; Lee's plan to make Ewell head of the cavalry bureau, 450; the war's final winter, 474; Lee orders Bragg to destroy all stores that might fall into enemy hands, 476; working on formation of black units, 481; Appomattox Campaign, 490n7, 491-492; captured at Sailors Creek, 494, 494n19

Fair Oaks/Seven Pines, battle of, 126, 161
Fairfax, John, 288n56, 498
Fairfax, Dr. Orlando, 230, 230n37
Fairfax, Randolph, 230
Falling Waters, 202n46, 298, 298n37, 300
Falmouth, 213, 219-220
Farinholt, Benjamin, 409n49
Farmville, Virginia, 480n15, 488, 493-494, 494n19, 495, 495n20, 495n21, 495n22, 496n22, 500-501
Farrand, Ebenezer, 135n39
Farrar, Fernandes R., 35n28
Farrar, Robert E., 35
Fauntleroy, Thomas, 20, 20n41, 57
Ferguson, James B., 372, 372n27, 444, 444n13
Fernandina, Florida, 76, 81-82, 86-87, 89
Field, Charles, 48, 117-118, 118n30, 119-121, 123, 246, 259n32, 264n16, 372n25, 381, 395, 404, 404n31, 405, 406n40, 408, 417, 424, 427, 427n17, 428, 428n21, 428n22, 429-430, 439-440, 440n37, 441-443, 443n10, 444, 463, 466, 490, 500n35
Finegan, Joseph, 115, 115n19, 119-120, 122-123, 134-135, 138, 140, 148-149, 155
Fingal (blockade runner), 81-82
Finley, Samuel B., 68
Fisher's Hill, Virginia, battle of, 432, 437, 439
Fitzhugh, Thaddeus, 367
Five Forks, Virginia, battle of, 486, 488, 488n2, 49
Flippo, Dr. Joseph A., 390
Florida Military Units: 1st Cavalry, 137; 2nd Infantry, 148; 4th Infantry, 92n14, 135; 6th Infantry, 148
Florida, CSS, 80n22
Floyd, John B., 13n14, 50, 50n46, 53, 55-57, 57n31, 58, 60, 60n3, 62-63, 66-67, 67n28, 68, 68n33, 69-71, 71n12, 72-74, 118n31, 128
Fontaine, Edmund, 43, 72
Forney, John H., 113, 113n8, 116, 122, 129, 132, 134, 170
Forney, William H., 305
Forrest, French, 13
Forsyth, James, 498, 498n31

Fort Bartow, 93n27, 94, 94n4, 94n5
Fort Beauregard, 79n18
Fort Boykin, 33n22, 38, 113
Fort Clinch, 76, 76n8
Fort Donelson, 102
Fort Fisher, 138, 460, 460n27, 461-462, 464, 464n17, 465-466, 473
Fort Gaines, 134, 440, 445n22, 446, 455
Fort Gregg, 490-491
Fort Harrison, 433, 439, 439n34, 440, 440n35, 440n37, 441
Fort Huger, 33n22, 105, 105n31
Fort Jackson, 94n5, 98, 98n26
Fort Lowry, 104
Fort Macon, 117, 117n29
Fort Magruder, 29
Fort Monroe, 18, 23, 101, 106-108, 111, 113-114, 136n44, 154, 241, 288, 304, 326, 331, 333
Fort Morgan, 134
Fort Moultrie, 79n18
Fort Nelson, 19
Fort Norfolk, 19, 40
Fort Powhatan, 8, 18, 23, 29, 29n7, 29n8, 33, 36, 113, 173, 177
Fort Pulaski, 75, 80, 95, 95n5, 97
Fort Stedman, battle of, 478, 484-485
Fort Sumter, 1, 76, 79n18, 79n19, 116n24
Fort Walker, 79n18
Foster, Thomas J., 349
Fox, Thomas H., 391, 391n58
Franklin, William B., 130n22, 237n29
Frederick, Maryland, 193, 193n14, 194, 194n17, 195n22
Fredericks Hall, 359-360
Fredericksburg Campaign, 214, 216-219, 219n27, 221-223, 225, 225n8, 226-229, 229n27, 232, 235-236, 251n41, 252, 256
Fredericksburg, Virginia, 114, 117, 121, 173, 178, 213-214, 219-220, 231, 244n4, 253, 259n34, 260, 264-265, 265n19, 267-268, 280-281, 301-302, 304n6, 329, 335, 380
Fremantle, Arthur J.L., 285, 288n53, 289, 292, 294-295, 295n22, 296, 296n26, 477
Fremont, John, 131n25, 133, 151
French, S. Bassett, 44n20, 73, 152, 179, 179n17, 180n17, 183n32, 192n12, 194, 194n18, 324
French, Samuel G., 104, 104n25, 105, 121, 133, 138, 173, 182, 215, 222, 270n37, 271n42, 274, 274n52
Front Royal, Virginia, and battle of, 126, 139, 206, 212, 212n35, 216, 300, 300n45, 344
Fry, Birkett, 295n21
Furman, Charles M., 92
Fussell's Mill, engagement at, 418n28, 423, 428, 428n22, 428n23, 429n27, 445n18

Gaines, Dr. William, 159, 159n59
Gaines's Mill, battle of, 158
Galena, USS, 135
Galt, Alexander, 307, 307n24

Gardner, William M., 439n34
Garland, Maurice, 198n30
Garland, Samuel M., 16, 16n23, 34, 34n26, 198n30
Garnett, Richard, 129, 129n18, 193
Garnett, Robert S., 7n17, 8n21, 11n2, 14, 14n15, 24, 24n55, 25n56, 29n7, 36-37, 41n7, 42, 50, 65n21; Lee's new adjutant, 6; promotion in Virginia forces, 6; becomes Lee's adjutant, 7n18; reassigned to northwestern Virginia, 27; given command of western Virginia, 29, 29n9, 32; communications between Staunton and Philippi, 34; killed at Corrick's Ford, 39, 44; takes command in western Virginia, 39; Lee approves plans for western Virginia, 40; Lee says three additional regiments to be assigned, 41; enemy intentions around Parkersburg, 43; Laurel Hill, 44n22; Rich Mountain, 44n22
Garrett, Thomas, 200
Gary, Martin, 402, 414, 418, 431, 437, 442
General Order #1, 4
General Orders #9, 500
General Orders #61, 269
George, Lee's cook, 239, 246, 240, 240n
Georgia Military Units: 1st Infantry, 47, 55n19, 56, 190n5; 1st Volunteers, 80n22; 8th Cavalry, 439n34; 12th Artillery Battalion, 371n24; 12th Infantry, 361n21; 18th Infantry, 106, 221, 221n37; 20th Infantry, 157n52; 21st Infantry, 200; 31st Infantry, 388n51; 35th Infantry, 171; 44th Infantry, 187; 49th Infantry, 359, 485, 485n37; 50th Infantry, 374n35; Cobb Legion, 235; Phillips Legion, 66n23; Savannah Volunteer Guards; 95n5; Troup Artillery, 49n44, 73
Georgia Railroad, 98
Germanna Ford, 259-260, 283, 311, 334, 373, 376, 379
Gettysburg, Pennsylvania, 288n55, 289-290, 297n32
Gettysburg, Pennsylvania, battle and Campaign, 272n43, 277, 284n38, 288n55, 289, 291-292, 292n9, 293, 293n12, 294-296, 300n47, 301-306, 307n27, 315n25, 348n28, 382n23, 445n23
Gibbon, John, 501n39
Gibson, Rev. Churchill, 435n15
Gilham, William, 45, 45n26
Gill, E.H., 32, 32n17
Gill, William G., 79, 79n17, 79n19, 87
Gillmore, Quincy A., 100, 401n22
Gilmer, Jeremy, 139, 139n54, 171, 177-178, 178n10, 179, 184, 205n2, 246, 250, 395n75, 415n13, 418, 443, 444n12, 453, 474n27, 475, 494n18
Gilmor, Harry, 146, 313, 313n17, 315, 320
Ginter, Lewis, 480, 480n12, 502
Girardy, Victor, 313, 313n17, 416, 416n17, 418, 418n28, 445n18
Gist, States Rights, 96, 89, 89n34, 109, 115
Gladney, John R., 89n32
Glendale, Virginia, battle of, 162-163
Globe Tavern, battle of, 423, 428n24, 429, 429n27
Glorietta Pass, New Mexico, battle of, 121n47
Gloucester Point, 13, 20-21, 29-31, 36, 41, 43-44, 113
Godwin, A.C., 424
Goode, Edmond, 55

Goode's Bridge, 492

Gordon, Eleanor Lytle, 101, 101n7

Gordon, H.A., 334

Gordon, John B., 215, 221, 269; Sharpsburg Campaign, 198n31, 200; to command Lawton's Brigade, 255; post-Chancellorsville, 273; potential commander for southwest Virginia, 348; winter of 1863-64, 373; Overland Campaign, 382n26, 383, 383n28, 383n30, 385, 385n38, 386, 388, 389n55; Petersburg Campaign, 413, 414n10; the war's final winter, 470, 470n8, 474, 477, 479, 479n9, 481, 483n29, 484; Hatcher's Run, 472; Fort Stedman, 478, 484, 484n31; last council of war, 484n31; Appomattox Campaign, 492-493, 495n22, 496n22, 497n27, 498, 498n28; Lee meets with to discuss a breakout, 497; ordered to carry out the surrender, 499

Gordon, William, 101n7

Gordonsville, Virginia, 106, 173, 182, 196, 203, 206, 212, 212n35, 212n36, 212n37, 215, 218, 259, 283, 311, 331, 381n22, 387n47

Goree, T.J., 346n20, 445, 501

Gorgas, Josiah, 36-37, 37n35, 44-45, 48n41, 94n5, 221, 306, 370, 399, 399n12, 417, 436, 473; ordered to send ammunition to Wise's command, 47; C.S. ordnance manual, 71; Lee requests additional heavy guns, 92; Lee requests more heavy artillery, 96; ordered to send addition artillery to Drewry's Bluff, 114, 120; 1,000 pikes to Jackson in the Shenandoah Valley, 116; requested to send an ordnance officer to Wilmington, 122; informed that Johnston does not need any more heavy guns, 123; issues new weapons to Mahone's and Branch's brigades, 138; Lee's railroad gun, 149; 1862 winter quarters, 225

Gosport Navy Yard, 10, 10n1, 13

Gracie, Archibald, 457, 457n6

Grafton, Virginia, 24

Graham, A.G., 19

Grant, Ulysses S., 291, 338n7, 346, 357, 377-378, 388, 403, 429, 433, 442, 446n24, 461; rumors of commanding the AOP, 362; Longstreet's opinion of, 364; Overland Campaign, 376, 383-385, 385n37, 387n43, 388n48, 389-390, 390n56, 392, 392n64, 393-396, 399n16, 400-404, 404n32, 405; has not learned from Hooker's experience in the Wilderness, 380; Lee thinks he will march on Spotsylvania, 383n28; Lee thinks he will move to the right again, 387; Cold Harbor, 398; truce to allow Grant to recover bodies, 400; planning to cross the James River, 402; army is south of the James River, 405; army is present at Petersburg, 406; Petersburg Campaign, 409, 412, 413n6, 418, 419n32, 420, 423, 425-426, 431n34, 436, 441, 442n3, 442n4, 444, 445n22, 446, 453, 454n28, 455; the Crater was a "stupendous failure," 412; Wadsworth's effects, 415; thinks Lee is with Early, 416; Vicksburg, 425n11; overwhelming numbers, 434; Lee complains about using prisoners to build a canal, 445; the war's final winter, 456-458, 462-463, 465, 467-468, 473, 475-478, 479n7, 484-486; peace delegation, 467; Lee writes about a POW exchange at Wilmington, 474; Lee writes about a peace meeting, 479; Lee supposed to meet about peace terms, 480n12; ready to begin spring offensive, 483; Dinwiddie, 488; has the initiative, Lee can't influence events, 488; asks for Lee's surrender, 489; stripping troops from north of the James, 490; sends Lee a note requesting the surrender of the ANV, 496, 496n23; sends Lee his terms, offers to meet Lee, 496; Appomattox Campaign, 497, 497n25, 498, 499n34; will meet Lee wherever he chooses, 498; meets with Lee to discuss surrender proceedings, 499, 499n33, 500; Confederate pickets refuse to let him pass, 500n35; notified of Lee's arrival in Richmond, 502n43; excluded Mosby from surrender terms, 503n4

Graves, R.H., 334

Gray's Point, 45n24, 46-48

Green, William, 42, 42n14

Greene, Nathaniel, 902n

Gregg, John, 382, 401, 440, 440n36, 443, 443n11, 495

Gregg, Maxcy, 120, 120n44, 123, 158-159, 229, 229n27, 251n41

Grimes, Bryan, 387, 393, 476, 482, 496n24

Groveton, battle of, 175, 185

Guild, Lafayette, 159, 169, 251, 252n3, 255, 256n20, 501n39

Gwathmey, Fannie Lewis, 244

Gwynn, Walter, 6, 7n17, 8, 12-13, 13n13, 14-15, 17-18, 18n30, 20n37, 21, 21n43, 22

Hagerstown, Maryland, 196, 196n24, 284, 286, 290-291, 291n7, 296, 296n28

Hagood, Johnson, 116, 430n31

Haile, Robert G., 151n30, 152n30

Hairston, Peter S., 11n3Hale, F.S., 48, 48n41

Half Sink estate, 141, 153, 153n38

Hall, Addison, 35

Halleck, Henry W., 154, 175, 177, 177n7, 178, 181, 234-236, 273, 339

Hamilton's Crossing, 380n17

Hampton Roads, Virginia, 106, 111, 127

Hampton, Virginia, 124n61

Hampton, Wade, 231, 236-237, 406, 448; senior to Fitz Lee, 173; Fredericksburg Campaign, 222, 227-229; captured flags, 225n7; 1862 winter quarters, 230; a move against Milroy, 241; lack of forage, 243; supplies at Staunton, 247; English Blakely rifled cannons, 251; the march to Gettysburg, 278; post-Gettysburg, 304; Mine Run, 336; winter of 1863-64, 345n14, 347-348, 351-352, 354, 354n24, 361; Overland Campaign, 387n45, 390n57, 404, 406n38; chasing Sheridan, 401; defeats Sheridan at Trevilian's Station, 402, 402n26; Lee congratulates for victory over Sheridan, 408; Petersburg Campaign, 409, 418, 418n27, 424-425, 427, 427n16, 428-430, 432, 434, 437-438, 442, 447, 448n35, 451, 453, 454n28; Lee recommends he should command cavalry, 413; suggests raid on City Point, 417; named ANV cavalry commander, 426; proposal to create a cavalry bureau, 427; Ream's Station, 430; "Beefsteak Raid," 435, 435n12, 436; loss of son at Petersburg, 447-448; son Thomas killed, son Wade Jr. wounded at Burgess's Mill, 447n33; the war's final winter, 458, 463

Hancock, Winfield S., 391n58, 399n16, 404, 404n32, 427

Hanover Junction, 179, 182, 218, 265, 274, 278, 281-282, 287n50, 314, 325, 329, 334, 338, 351-353, 353n18, 354-355, 359-360, 379, 388-390, 390n57, 391
Hardee, William J., 342, 403n30, 416, 453, 459, 463, 465-466, 471, 473, 475-476, 482
Harman, John, 109, 201, 270
Harman, Michael G., 16, 30, 30n11, 34, 38, 42, 44, 46, 49, 49n45, 53, 55, 57, 62-63, 67-68, 71, 74, 148
Harman, William H., 12
Harney, William S., 7, 8n19
Harper, Kenton, 7, 7n17, 7-8, 12
Harpers Ferry, western Virginia, 1, 6-8, 10, 12n11, 19, 21-22, 22n45, 24, 24n52, 25, 28, 37, 188-189, 194n17, 196-197, 199, 203, 206, 208, 227, 237n27, 284, 430
Harpers Ferry operation, 195, 195n20, 195n21, 197-198
Harris Farm, engagement at, 389n52
Harris, Nathaniel, 386, 490
Harrisburg, Pennsylvania, 277, 285, 287n59
Harrison, Henry T., 193, 288, 288n56
Harrison's Landing, 163, 166-168, 173, 175, 178, 178n13, 180, 378
Hartwood Church, 246, 246n9
Harvie, Edwin J., 146n11, 202, 202n47, 220, 220n30
Haskell, John, 498
Hatcher's Run, battle of, 458, 471, 471n13, 472, 483, 483n29, 486
Hawthorn, Harris S., 494n19
Haxall, Burton, 181, 181n24
Haxall, Lou, 340
Haxall's Landing, engagement at, 177n5
Hays, Harry, 330n17, 330n19, 331n23, 383n30
Hebert, Louis, 139, 139n56
Hebert, Paul O., 139,139n56, 141
Heck, J. M., 24
Heintzelman, Samuel P., 136n44, 137n49, 272
Herold, David, 82n33
Heth, Henry, 8n21, 55n20, 72, 82, 96, 103-104, 108, 122, 128, 137, 221, 221n35, 242, 246, 246n13, 272; promotion in Virginia forces, 6; quartermaster general, 8; thinks Floyd is completely incompetent, 71n12; meets with Lee to discuss strategy, 71; wants to swap a cavalry regiment for an infantry regiment, 105; Lee approves his defensive measures, 107; warned Staunton may be lost, 118; ordered to Wytheville, 129; post-Chancellorsville, 273-274; the march to Gettysburg, 279n16, 289, 289n58; Gettysburg, July 1, 292; Gettysburg, July 2, 293-294; Gettysburg, July 3, 294; post-Gettysburg, 302, 306n20; reviewing Hill's corps, 313; Bristoe Station Campaign, 322; Mine Run, 335; blamed for starting fight at Gettysburg, 348n28; winter of 1863-64, 348, 359; Overland Campaign, 381, 381n20, 384n33, 385, 385n37, 386, 402n28; Petersburg Campaign, 408-409, 417, 419, 428n24, 429n27, 431n37, 432, 438n29, 442, 451, 452n16; wants the 22nd Virginia Battalion broken up, 445, 445n17, 445n23; Burgess's Mill, 447; the war's final winter, 457, 470n8, 477, 477n2, 483n29, 486; Hatcher's Run, 471; replaces Hill, 490; Appomattox Campaign, 491, 493

Hickory Hill, 276-277, 281, 287, 287n50, 289, 291n6
High Bridge, 480, 480n15, 494, 494n19, 495
High Meadow estate, 143, 146, 146n11, 148, 169
Hildebrand, Jacob, 301
Hill, Ambrose P., 61n5, 163, 165, 169n26, 172n39, 182n27, 234n15, 246, 276, 310, 312n14, 318, 320, 338, 362-383, 498n29; Light Division, 118n30, 120n44; attack at Mechanicsville put McClellan on his heels, 145; planning meeting with officers for the attack on McClellan, 155; attacks without Jackson who is not on the field, 157; immediate assault on Cold Harbor, 159; ordered to join Jackson to attack Pope, 172; under arrest by Jackson, 172; reduce wagons, they are needed in Richmond, 173; Sharpsburg Campaign, 189, 200-202; feud with Jackson, 205, 205n3; post-Sharpsburg lull, 206; Fredericksburg Campaign, 220, 225; Maxcy Gregg, 229n27; continuing issues with Jackson, 234; reviews Rooney's brigade, 236; complaint against Jackson, 249; Jackson files formal complaint, 258n29; promoted to lieutenant general, 261; Chancellorsville, 263-264, 264n14, 265n20, 267, 267n25, 268, 268n28; wounded at Chancellorsville, 265; death of Stonewall Jackson, 269; recommended for corps command, 271; post-Chancellorsville, 272-275; arrives at Chambersburg, 277; the march to Gettysburg, 278, 278n9, 281, 281n27, 282, 283n36, 284-287, 287n55, 288-289; ordered to hold Fredericksburg, 279; Federals leaving Fredericksburg, 283; retreat from Gettysburg, 290, 296-299; Gettysburg, July 1, 292, 292n9; Gettysburg, July 2, 293, 293n13, 294; Gettysburg, July 3, 294-295, 295n21; Gettysburg, July 4, 295; reviewing Ewell's corps, 312; reviewing Hill's corps, 313; Bristoe Station Campaign, 322, 322n19, 322n20; Rappahannock Station, battle of, 331; post-Rappahannock Station, 332; Mine Run, 335, 336; winter of 1863, 338, 341; winter of 1863-64, 363, 372; Overland Campaign, 376, 380-381, 381n19, 381n20, 382, 382n24, 383n28, 384n33, 385, 385n37, 388, 388n49, 389, 389n55, 391, 392n64, 393, 396, 400, 402, 402n28, 405; illness, 377; baptism of daughter Lucy, 379; Tapp Farm, 381; ordered to cross the James River, 405; Petersburg Campaign, 408n45, 414, 417, 423, 429, 429n27, 430n31, 431n37, 434-435, 438n29, 439, 440n35, 442, 444, 445, 447-448, 448n35, 449, 454n28; the Crater, 420, 421n41, 422; Ream's Station, 430; the war's final winter, 456-458, 470n8, 483n29, 487n45; death of, 488, 490, 490n9, 491n11
Hill, Daniel H., 16n23, 23, 40-41, 151-152, 153n34, 156, 158, 173, 173n40, 178-179, 179n17, 180, 196, 198n30, 233, 254, 260-261, 270, 271n42, 273-274, 274n52, 275, 278, 280, 316, 452, 452n16; Lee's opinion on how to proceed with officers in higher command in former state units, 30; holding the Yorktown line, 125; planning meeting with officers for the attack on McClellan, 155; "if McClellan is there [Malvern Hill] in force, we had better leave him alone," 165; troops leave wounded and dead at Malvern Hill, 167; Hill will be in charge of POW exchange, 170; update on the POW exchange, 171; deal with any threats in North Carolina, 172; prisoner agreement with John Dix, 177; recent night attack on the James, 177; fortifications around Petersburg, 179; Lee's comments on, 182n26; sent to North Anna, 182; division ordered to join Lee, 184; Sharpsburg Campaign, 194n18, 197n27, 197n29, 200-201;

McClellan's quick moves, 196; post-Sharpsburg lull, 206; Fredericksburg Campaign, 228; where best to place him, 230n32; reassigned to North Carolina, 232; ordered to North Carolina, 235; arrest of six "disloyal citizens," 257; sent to North Carolina, 261n3, 269; Chancellorsville, 267; Colquitt's Brigade enroute, 272

Hindman, Thomas C., 118, 118n30

Hinrichs, Oscar, 324, 324n28, 479n9, 487n45

Hoge, Rev. Moses D., 26, 26n58, 361

Hoke, Robert, 234, 311, 314, 347, 368, 385, 456, 461, 463; Chancellorsville, 266, 266n22; post-Gettysburg, 307; Rappahannock Station, battle of, 330n17, 331, 331n23; Mine Run, 334; winter of 1863-64, 354n24, 361n23, 364, 366, 369, 372-373; Overland Campaign, 387, 390-391, 395, 398, 398n9, 399, 399n15, 402n28, 403; ordered to Drewry's Bluff, 402; Petersburg Campaign, 408, 414n10, 424, 438n29, 439, 439n31, 440, 440n37, 441, 441n1, 442, 443n10, 445, 447, 447n31; plan to command the Point Lookout prisoners, 413; prepare to send Hoke's Division to Wilmington, 459; the war's final winter, 459-460, 460n23, 470, 473

Hollins, George N., 43

Holmes, Theophilus, 45, 106, 114, 116, 119, 123, 131, 138, 148, 151, 158, 162, 170, 173n40, 179, 414-416, 443; Lee suggests using railroad rails as armor, 31; replaces Ruggles, 31n14; officers assigned to his regiments, 33; ordered not to reduce forces at Fredericksburg, 33; organization of the 30th Virginia, 34; Mathias Point, 35; forms a regiment, 37; troops firing on enemy from Mathias Point, 43; Lee's irritation with over Mathias Point, 45n24; ordered to construct a battery at Gray's Point, 45; rebuked for having companies not mustered into service, 48; status of Fort Lowry, 104; Fredericksburg, 105; ordered to Goldsboro, North Carolina, 107; ordered to hold troops at Goldsboro, 107; requests Lee come to North Carolina, 108; convinced that interior North Carolina was threatened, 111; hold troops to go to Suffolk or Weldon, 113; McClellan's move to Fort Monroe, 113; allowed to keep the horses from Cobb's Legion cavalry, 115; enemy troops landing at Elizabeth City, 115; should try to arrange a POW exchange with Burnside, 116; Fort Macon garrison to be evacuated, 117; enemy at Elizabeth City, North Carolina, 119; enemy won't advance from New Bern, 120; poor behavior from the 2nd NC Cavalry, 121; shipment of arms received in Wilmington, 122; transfer the Cobb Legion cavalry to Fredericksburg, 122; a brigade can be sent to him if needed, 127; notified that Norfolk is being evacuated, 127; be prepared to strike Burnside if Norfolk falls, 128; ordered to guard Weldon, 130; reports Union reinforcements at New Bern, 133; McClellan's approach requires reduction of this forces, 134; now responsible for the protection of Weldon, 137; defense of the Weldon Railroad, 139; Lee requests Holmes send as many wagons as possible to Richmond, 139; Lee says Burnside is going to move to the James River, 139; ordered to follow Burnside wherever he goes, 139; brigades to be stationed at Petersburg, 140; main focus is on Burnside, 140; ordered to defend the Southside or join Johnston's army, 141; ordered to bring his men to Petersburg, 149; ordered to bring his men to Richmond, 150; Burnside moved to Fort Monroe, 154; ordered to bring everything to Petersburg, 154; protect Drewry's Bluff, 154; on alert to join the ANV, 157; time with ANV at an end, 163; monitor Burnside's army in North Carolina, 169; defense of Weldon and Goldsboro, North Carolina, 413; the war's final winter, 473, 478, 478n6

Hood, Alexander B., 47

Hood, John Bell, 23, 130n22, 159, 179-180, 197, 211n30, 241-242, 248, 248n26, 249, 268, 271, 312, 314, 316n29, 372n25, 411, 432, 436n22, 438n28, 449, 453n26, 456; meeting with Lee, 14n17; reports for duty, 14; Smith's Farm, 45; has 18th Georgia added to his Texas brigade, 106; ordered to Gordonsville to link up with Jackson, 181; Lee's high spirits after Longstreet's attack, 186; released from arrest, 198n30; Sharpsburg Campaign, 199, 199n36; Lee reviews Hood's command, 210; promoted to major general, 215; Fredericksburg Campaign, 228; division and the Suffolk Campaign, 239n2; two murdered civilians by his command, 254; Gordonsville, 269; post-Chancellorsville, 273; Lee's planning meeting for the move north, 280; Gettysburg, July 2, 293, 293n14, 294; Meade's summer 1863 operations, 316; promoted to lieutenant general and made corps commander in Tennessee, 346, 346n21; winter of 1863-64, 361n23; replaces Joe Johnston, 416, 416n18; appointed to command the Army of Tennessee, 417; Lee will not send any troops to Hood in Georgia, 436; the war's final winter, 462-463, 486

Hooker, Joseph, 237n29, 238n34, 239n1, 240, 241n11, 244, 250, 276, 279-280, 283, 284, 316; Sharpsburg Campaign, 199n35; new commander of the AOP, 239; is up to something, but Lee doesn't know what, 242; bans truces and trading along the Rappahannock River, 247n16; sends Lee notice of death of Edwin V. Sumner, 250; the quiet after Fredericksburg, 252n4; Benjamin Scott, 254; not likely to uncover Washington, 256; Lee has no news on his intentions, 257; a feint at Port Royal, 258; Lee determines his left is being turned, 260; defeated by Lee at Chancellorsville, 261, 265; Chancellorsville, 263-264, 266-267, 267n24, 267n25, 268; families retrieving bodies from Chancellorsville, 269; post-Chancellorsville, 271; potential cavalry raid, 275; replaced by Meade, 277; the march to Gettysburg, 281, 285; winter of 1863-64, 369n16

Hotchkiss, Jed, 187n44, 207, 215, 215n10, 226n13, 247, 254n7, 258n31, 259n34, 264, 265n18, 267n24, 272, 278n9, 279, 279n17, 293n15, 296, 296n28, 297, 301, 304n8, 306, 320, 320n12, 332, 332n26, 369, 385, 390, 446; is he subject to the draft?, 247n15; Chancellorsville, 266-267; post-Gettysburg, 307n26; Overland Campaign, 390n57, 391, 391n59, 392n62, 392n63, 395n75, 400-401

Houchin, Ellis, 64

Howard, Conway, 220, 220n30

Howard, James, 248, 248n26

Howard, McHenry, 32, 32n18

Howlett Line, 404, 405, 405n35, 407, 407n43, 419-420, 423, 425-426, 426n13, 427n16, 439, 446, 449, 451, 455, 457, 483n27, 490

Hubbard, Robert T., 259n34

Huger, Benjamin, 22-23, 32-33, 48, 105, 129n13, 136, 138, 166n11; commands Harpers Ferry Arsenal, 22n45; officers from Virginia's provisional army, 28; officers of the provisional army, 28n4; strengthen Craney Island, 31; deserters from Fort Monroe, 36; ordered to move Pryor's regiment to Fort Boykin, 38; swapping guns at fort Norfolk, 40; VMI cadets, 42; Norfolk fortifications, 48; held responsible for loss of Roanoke Island, 103n17; Lee orders militia to assist, 106; enemy landing troops at Fort Monroe, 107-108; scattered condition of his command, 107; Magruder must be ready to reinforce if needed, 108; about a prisoner exchange with John Wool, 109; ordered to abolish his military government at Norfolk, 109; expected attack from McClellan, 111; enemy landing at Newport News, 113; defenses on the Nansemond River improved, 115; send non-serviceable weapons to Richmond Armory, 115; department placed under Johnston's command, 116; engagement at South Mills, North Carolina, 119-120; Elizabeth City movements are feints, 123; South Mills, 123; might be cut off and captured, 125; ordered to secure all boats around Norfolk, 128; evacuation instructions from Lee, 130; Lee approves his evacuation plans, 131; ordered to send Mahone's Brigade to Drewry's Bluff, 134; ordered to destroy warehouses and wharves if enemy approaches Petersburg, 135; ordered to obstruct the Appomattox River, 136; Petersburg & Weldon Railroad, 136; relocating to Richmond, 137; arrives at Drewry's Bluff, 139; command to be reunited, 140; asks Longstreet for return of his brigades, 148; can be sent to Charleston, 154; ordered to remain with his troops, 156; Lee's lack of confidence in, 157n52; Lee sends a message with routes of march, 158; ordered to loan two of his brigades to Magruder, 161; time with ANV at an end, 163; relieved of command and made inspector of artillery, 169n26

Hughes, Dr. Alfred, 400, 400n17, 457

Hundley, Larkin, 247

Hunt, Henry, 500

Hunter, David, 397, 401, 401n21, 409, 413, 415, 417

Hunter, Robert M.T., 15, 34, 34n27, 41, 283, 348, 467n32, 480n10

Hunter, Robert W., 385Huntersville, Virginia, 53

Hunton, Eppa, 25, 28, 31, 31n14, 285, 487

Hutt, J. Warren, 35, 35n30

Ida (steamer), 80

Imboden, John D., 141, 204, 209, 211, 221, 234, 236, 247, 247n19, 249, 255n14, 256, 273, 275, 313, 321, 323, 328, 328n10, 334, 378, 380-381, 398; raid against the B&O Railroad, 181; post-Sharpsburg lull, 207; 1862 winter quarters, 225; working with "Grumble" Jones, 226, 229-230; Lee congratulates on promotion, 240; Jones-Imboden raid, 250, 254-255; Lee congratulates on recent raid, 272; the march to Gettysburg, 278, 280-281, 283, 285; Gettysburg, July 1, 292; Gettysburg, July 4, 295; retreat from Gettysburg, 297-300; post-Gettysburg, 301, 305, 306, 307; Meade's summer 1863 operations, 315-317; Lee congratulates for victory at Charlestown, 324; Bristoe Station Campaign, 329; Rappahannock Station, battle of, 330n18, 331; post-Rappahannock Station, 332; winter of 1863, 339-340; winter of 1863-64, 344-345, 347, 359-360, 362, 362n25, 364n39, 369, 371-374; Lee denies request for court of inquiry filed against Early, 353; Overland Campaign, 379, 388, 392, 395

Indiana Military Units: 3rd Cavalry, 417n24; 7th Infantry, 44n22; 17th Infantry, 65n20

Ingraham, D.N., 34, 81

Irwin, J.W., 229

Island No. 10, 207n12

Iverson, Alfred, 297, 299, 299n39, 299n42, 320-321

Ives, Joseph C., 79, 79n19, 81, 86, 102, 104n25, 471, 471n12

Izard, Allen Smith, 76

Jackson, George, 78, 78n15

Jackson, Henry R., 44, 44n22, 45, 47, 49, 53, 55-56, 63n14, 91, 91n6

Jackson, Dr. Samuel K., 193

Jackson, Thomas J. "Stonewall," 7n18, 7, 13, 15, 19, 24, 24n52, 52n8, 121, 126-127, 151, 153-154, 161n66, 162n68, 165, 165n9, 166, 166n12, 167, 167n14, 182-183, 185n37, 193, 193n15, 194, 207, 216, 224-225, 230n32, 236, 237n27, 240, 248n25, 251n41, 253, 256, 258, 260, 263n11, 270n34, 271n41, 276, 279n14, 316n29; ordered to command Harpers Ferry, 7; replaces militia general at Harpers Ferry, 10; calls for volunteers, 12; orders to defend Martinsburg, 14; holding Harpers Ferry, 16n23; ordered not to cross into Maryland, 16; asked not to request weapons if he doesn't need them, 17; commander of troops around Harpers Ferry, 17; VMI cadets, 19n35; promoted to brigadier general, 40; Shenandoah Valley, 108; drawing attention away from the Peninsula, 111; falling back toward Staunton, 118; joins with Ewell to attack Banks, 120; probable fall of Fredericksburg, 120; requested to join with Ewell against Banks, 122; other than Ewell, there are no troops for Jackson, 123; nothing in Fredericksburg can be sent him, 124; charges against Richard Garnett, 129, 129n18; enemy concentrates at Fredericksburg, 129; it seems Banks is leaving the Valley, 130; victory at McDowell, 131n25; ordered not to overextend his pursuit of Fremont, 132; pursuit of Fremont, 133; Banks is leaving the Valley, 135; Lee congratulates on victory at McDowell, 135; Lee urges a junction with Ewell, 135; authorized to link with Ewell to defeat Banks, 137; sees opportunity to attack Banks, 137; recent victories at Front Royal and Winchester, 139; Lee congratulates Jackson on victories in the lower Valley, 140, 140n58; historians have debated Jackson's performance for Seven Days battles, 144n7; Lee plans for Jackson to move from the Valley to attack McClellan, 144n4; failed to turn Porter's flank, 145; Lee massed three divisions to cooperate with Jackson, 145; sends Boteler to Lee with info about affairs in the Valley, 148; getting reinforcements from Georgia, 149; Lee sends congratulations to Jackson, 150; Whiting ordered to reinforce with two brigades, 152; with three new brigades, is to attack McClellan's right flank, 152; planning meeting with officers for the attack on McClellan, 155; Lee sends orders for march to Richmond, 156; meets Lee for the first time, 156n49; hours behind schedule, did not communicate with A.P. Hill, 157n54; notifies Lee he is running behind schedule, 157; performance on the Peninsula was not that great, 157n54; conversation with A.P. Hill, 158; no word from, 158; ordered to move to Cold Harbor, 158; meets with Lee at Gaines's Mill, 160; can't support Magruder's attack at Savage's Station, 161; Lee's plan to trap McClellan at Glendale, 162; ordered to Louisa Court House with two divisions, 170; Lee is sending Stuart to Gordonsville, 171; Lee sending A.P. Hill's division to him, 172; looking to replace as cavalry commander, 173; beats Pope there, 175; Lee orders to suppress Pope, 175; reluctance to attack Pope, 178; ordered to work with Stuart, 179; congratulations from Lee for victory at Cedar Mountain, 180; S. Bassett French, 180n17; Longstreet and Hood to link up with at Gordonsville, 181; how to strike Pope, 182; visits Clark's Mountain, 182n27; Second Manassas Campaign, 183, 185-186, 186n42, 190, 192; Bristoe Station Campaign, 184; Cedar Mountain, 184; Manassas Junction, 184; Groveton, 185; to lead pursuit of Pope, 187; Lee's plan to cross the Potomac, 193; Sharpsburg Campaign, 194n18, 197, 199, 199n34, 200-202; commands forces in the Harpers Ferry operation, 195n21; Harpers Ferry operation, 195-196, 198; McClellan's quick moves, 196; capture of Harpers Ferry, 198, 198n31; feud with A.P. Hill, 205, 205n3; Lee recommends for promotion, 206; grand review after Sharpsburg, 208; nearly captured around Leetown, 209; post-Sharpsburg lull, 210; remains in lower Valley, 211; promoted to lieutenant general, 213, 215; Hotchkiss, 215n10; Fredericksburg Campaign, 216-219, 221-222, 222n38, 223, 227, 227n19, 228; Jubal Early, 220; 1862 winter quarters, 224; death of, 225n9, 270-271; loss of arm, 227n15; post-Fredericksburg, 230; court martial against Hill, 234; did not like Taliaferro, 235n17; wants to court martial Taliaferro, 235; reviews Rooney's brigade, 236; send "unfit for duty" men to Richmond to serve in hospitals, 241; promotions in the artillery, 242; complaint about Crutchfield, 243; Hayfield, 244; temporarily in command of ANV, 247n20; William Pendleton as artillery chief, 247; Hill's complaint about, 249; the quiet after Fredericksburg, 250, 252, 255; meets with Lee to discuss temporary command, 251; Longstreet senior to Jackson, but was away on assignment, 252n4; makes changes to the Fredericksburg report, 255; formal complaint against A.P. Hill, 258n29; Hooker's feint, 258; latest intel on Hooker's army, 259; Chancellorsville, 261, 263-264, 264n14, 265, 267n24, 268, 268n28; wounded at Chancellorsville, 264, 264n17, 265, 265n17, 266-267, 269; bust by Alexander Galt, 307n24

Jackson, William L. "Mudwall," 42, 42n15, 52, 52n8

James River, 403, 403n30, 403n31, 404-405, 405n35, 406n38, 407n43, 408-409, 414-415, 418-419, 419n32, 420-425, 425n11, 427, 429, 433-434, 439, 440n35, 441, 443, 445-446, 449, 454n29, 456, 460, 463, 471n12, 479-480, 486, 490, 502

James River & Kanawha Canal, 236, 267, 479n7

Jamestown CSS, 134n37

Jamestown, Virginia, 29n8

Janney, John, 4, 192-193

Jekyll Island, 98

Jenkins, Albert G., 123, 209, 268, 272-275, 279-282, 289n57, 307, 314

Jenkins, Micah, 169, 169n25, 171, 238, 278n10, 282, 382, 382n25, 409

Jerdone, Francis, 333, 342

Jerdone, Mary, 346, 376n2, 463

Jericho Mills, 391

Jesse, W.G., 389

Jetersville, Virginia, 493, 493n16, 493n17

John A. Moore, (steamer), 99

Johns, Bishop John, 154, 271, 278, 279n13

Johns, Joshua O., 499

Johnson, Andrew, 504

Johnson, Bradley T., 193, 193n14, 314, 334, 409, 426, 470

Johnson, Bushrod, 408n47, 413, 420-421, 421n41, 421n42, 422n43, 427, 431n34, 431n37, 452, 457n6, 476, 481, 487, 487n45, 495n21, 496, 496n24Johnson, Edward "Allegheny," 105, 105n28, 109, 118, 121, 123-124, 126-127, 137, 146, 210, 210n28, 260, 333n33, 359, 362, 372n28; promoted to major general, 258n27; Chancellorsville, 266, 268; post-Chancellorsville, 272, 272n43, 273n50, 274; Gettysburg, July 2, 293n12; retreat from Gettysburg, 299; post-Gettysburg, 305, 307; reviewing Ewell's corps, 312; post-Rappahannock Station, 332, 332n26, 333; Mine Run, 335, 335n43; potential commander for southwest Virginia, 348; winter of 1863-64, 353, 363, 372-373; Overland Campaign, 383, 383n30, 385, 387, 389n55; captured, 386; Petersburg Campaign, 426n14, 437, 437n25, 445; the war's final winter, 485n38

Johnson, Marmaduke, 4n12, 159, 159n58

Johnston, Albert Sidney, 58n41, 94, 99, 102, 111, 207n12

Johnston, J.S., 390, 390n57

Johnston, Joseph E., 10, 18n30, 24n52, 24n55, 40n3, 99n30, 103, 114, 114n11, 115, 119n35, 123, 132n27, 137, 140, 147, 202n47, 203n53, 207n12, 255, 280, 324n28, 337, 340n17, 341, 353, 355n30, 360, 366n3, 367, 370, 403, 403n30, 411, 441n1, 457n9, 472-473, 474, 476, 488, 490, 490n6, 491, 494n19, 496n24, 497; promotion in Virginia forces, 6; appointed to command Richmond, 7n17; recommended to command Richmond, 7; illness, 15; Arnold Elzey assigned as ordnance officer, 24; about 36,000 troops in the state, 25n56; Lee writes of dispositions he made in northern Virginia, 25; lack of percussion caps, 26; holding Harpers Ferry, 27; ordered to hold the Shenandoah Valley, 30; condition of troops sent to Harpers Ferry, 35; formation of the 43rd Infantry, 37; George Meem's militia unit, 40; victory at First Manassas, 46; Lee's congratulations for victory at Manassas, 47; confirmed rank as full general, 58n41; Davis considers recalling Lee to Richmond, 98; can he spare James Longstreet to take command in North Carolina, 105; Fredericksburg, 105; Davis to meet in Gordonsville, 106; send Longstreet to North Carolina, 106; Lee asks what troops can be sent to the Peninsula, 107; travels to Fredericksburg, 107; troops are being sent from Winchester, 107; Jackson is threatened in the Valley, 108; ordered to begin withdrawing army to Richmond, 109; arrives in Richmond, 110n53; army moved to east of Richmond, 111; Lee says he must shift to the Peninsula,

114; arrives on the Peninsula front on April 12, 116n25; arrives on the Peninsula front on April 13, 117; not in favor of reinforcing Magruder or holding the Peninsula, 117n27; departs Richmond for the Peninsula, 118; more ammunition being sent to him, 119; enemy is in front of Fredericksburg, 120; weakness of Field's forces at Fredericksburg, 121; heavy artillery being sent from Richmond, 122; defensive efforts on the Peninsula bought time, 125; heated exchanges with Lee, 125; reveals to Lee the plan to attack McClellan at Mechanicsville, 126; showed no signs of a serious battle, 126; wounded at Fair Oaks, 126; ordered to hold the Yorktown/Warwick River line longer, 127; plan to advance to the Potomac proposed to Davis, 127; abandons the Yorktown/Warwick River line, 128n10; Lee learns of Johnston's withdrawal from Yorktown, 128; Lee reminds that ordnance officers at unit levels, 128; retreat from Yorktown, 129n13; instructions about retreat, 130; news of Jackson's victory at McDowell, 131; Winder ordered to round up troops in Richmond and send to Johnston, 132; Washington Artillery being sent to him, 134; Lee gives intel on movements in the Valley, 136; Lee warns that McClellan will resume siege operations, 136; make sure troops respect private property, 136; has authorized Jackson to link with Ewell to defeat Banks, 137; Lee says Davis wants to know Johnston's plans, 137; meets Lee at Davis's request, 138; large deduction in Union troops at New Bern, 139; plans to attack McClellan on the 29th, 139; calls off attack on McClellan, 140, 140n61; rebukes Jackson for communicating directly with Lee, 140n58; gratification that Lee is willing to help, 141; wounded, carried off the field, 141, 146; secrecy contributed to poor relationship with Davis, 144; biggest failure was keeping Davis in the dark, 149n19; Lee happy that he is recovered, 220, 220n30; Lee has no indication of new enemy offensive in Virginia, 363; winter of 1863-64, 373, 374; replaced by Hood, 416n18; the war's final winter, 460, 464n15, 468, 470n8, 474n27, 475n31, 475n32, 479, 481-482, 485-486, 486n44; Bentonville, 478, 483; Lee offers discretion to strike Sherman or Schofield, 480; surrenders in North Carolina, 503

Johnston, Robert, 9, 368, 372, 379

Johnston, Samuel R., 160-161, 178, 178n11, 180, 293, 293n14, 381n22, 475

Johnston, William P., 398

Jones, Alexander C., 55, 55n21

Jones, B.M., 17

Jones, Rev. C.C., 77

Jones, Catesby ap R., 2n7, 8, 29

Jones, Charles Lee (Lee's cousin), 5, 5n14, 316

Jones, David R., 167, 167n15, 200n40, 201, 210

Jones, Rev. J. William, 351, 483n29

Jones, James, 85

Jones, John B., 236n21, 270, 270n37, 308n28, 308n33, 460n23, 473, 473n22, 477n5

Jones, John M., 272, 272n43, 381

Jones, John R., 152, 152n32

Jones, Roger, (Lee's cousin), 2, 2n7

Jones, Samuel, 105n28, 110, 113, 123, 230, 234n12, 247, 249-250, 255n14, 256, 260, 268, 270, 272, 278-279, 307, 314, 317, 318, 321, 328, 333, 348, 350-351; promotion in Virginia forces, 6; commands the Department of Alabama and West Florida, 105n28; Davis does not want martial law declared in Mobile, 105; promoted to brigadier general, 109; ordered to join Beauregard, 116; can't leave Mobile until his replacement arrives, 118; ordered to send artillery from Mobile to New Orleans, 120; needed with Beauregard, 122; prepare to remove everything from Pensacola, 112; Jones-Imboden raid, 255; the march to Gettysburg, 280, 282, 285-286; retreat from Gettysburg, 297, 299-300, 300n47; post-Gettysburg, 305-306, 308n28; Meade's summer 1863 operations, 315-316; Bristoe Station Campaign, 323, 328n12, 329; Rappahannock Station, battle of, 330n18; ordered to send his cavalry to Longstreet, 334; winter of 1863-64, 344-345, 349n36, 351; ordered to acquire any supplies he can find, 347; replaced by Breckinridge, 351n3

Jones, William E.; 1862 winter quarters, 225; working with Imboden, 226, 229, 230; Lee congratulates for Hardy County raid, 235; follow Milroy if he moves, 237; ordered to gather provisions in the Valley, 237; a complaint by Alexander Boteler, 240; Burnside's corps sent west on the B&O, 251; Jones-Imboden raid, 254; Chancellorsville, 268; report on the West Virginia raid, 270; the march to Gettysburg, 283; can't get along with Stuart, 320; Overland Campaign, 388, 395, 398-399; death of, 399, 401n21

Jones-Imboden raid, 250, 254-255

Kanawha Valley, 8, 13, 203, 208, 208n20, 209
Kautz, August, 409n49
Kearny, Philip, 192, 192n13, 206, 206n9, 207n9
Kelley, Benjamin, 475
Kelly's Ford, 260, 304, 318, 323, 326, 329
Kelly's Ford, battle of, 244, 244n4, 248-249, 251
Kemper, James L., 41n8, 147n12, 210, 221n34, 295, 349, 349n35, 434, 454
Kemper, William, 409
Kernstown, Virginia, battles of, 55n19, 129n18, 419, 419n36
Kershaw, Joseph, 211, 211n31, 238, 238n35, 247, 247n16, 257, 257n24, 258, 265n19, 391, 395, 399, 405, 406n40, 413, 418, 419, 423, 424, 425n8, 433, 436, 437, 438, 442, 494n19
Keyes, Erasmus, 1
Kilpatrick, Judson, 359-360, 357, 359n9, 367n4
Kilpatrick-Dahlgren Raid, 321n15, 351, 356-357, 359n9, 360n15, 361, 378
Kinloch, R.A., 87
Kinston, North Carolina, battle of, 481
Kirker, William H., 54n15
Kirkland, William W., 409, 441
Knox, Thomas S., 16
Knoxville, Tennessee, 108, 317, 328, 333-334, 345n14, 346n21, 354, 367, 369, 445, 483, 485

Lacy, Rev. Beverly T., 226n14, 255, 258, 258n31, 264, 267, 269, 272, 275, 279, 306-307, 351
Lacy, J. Horace, 226, 226n14, 227, 280n19

Lamar, D.G., 32
Lamkin, James, 421
Land, Mrs. Bettie, 362
Lane, James, 235-236, 386, 400
Langhorne, D.A., 6, 7n17, 14, 16-17, 32, 42-43
Latham, Woodville G., 129, 129n15
Latrobe, Osmun, 201n44, 269n29, 280n21
Law, Evander, 151, 370, 370n19, 373, 373n32, 374, 374n34, 374n35, 392, 451, 451n9
Lawley, Francis, 213, 226n11, 267, 268n26, 295, 297, 413
Lawton, Alexander, 80, 80n22, 94, 102n13, 110, 148, 153, 209, 255, 269, 313, 323, 347, 349, 371; accompanies Lee at Brunswick, 82n30; Lee has no troops to send, 88; with Lee on Green Island, 90; inspects Fort Pulaski, 91; meets with Lee to discuss strategy, 102; ordered to Tennessee, 109; Georgia troops be retained for duration, 114; enemy prisoners on the way, 119; Milledgeville prisoners to be held in Atlanta, 120; Union prisoners have arrived in Atlanta, 121; no heavy artillery available, 129; ordered to send troops to Atlanta to guard supplies, 133; enroute to Jackson with a brigade, 152; Sharpsburg Campaign, 199; shortage of everything, 346; the war's final winter, 479-480; Appomattox Campaign, 494n18, 495n20
Lay, George W., 47, 47n35
Leadbetter, Danville, 127, 127n7
Ledlie, James, 392
Lee, Agnes (Lee's daughter), 1, 3n9, 15, 27, 32, 36, 40, 58, 72, 82, 101, 122, 180n21, 204, 210n26, 224n5, 230, 240, 242, 254-255, 255n14, 256n17, 258, 271-272, 282n32, 283n32, 301, 305n13, 307, 312n14, 314, 331, 333, 339n11, 341n27, 343, 367, 379-380, 390, 424, 426, 453, 478, 482, 485-488, 489n5, 490, 492, 492n13
Lee, Annie (Lee's daughter), 30, 58, 72, 82, 101-103, 135, 180n18, 204, 210, 210n26, 211n32, 212n34, 217, 220
Lee, Cassius (Lee's cousin), 3, 4n11, 6-7, 7n19, 100
Lee, Charles Carter (Lee's brother), 104, 211, 230, 250, 272, 354, 426, 469, 495n20, 501
Lee, Charlotte (Lee's daughter-in-law), 72, 147, 177, 184, 209, 230, 246, 282, 288, 290, 291n6, 300, 301, 304, 312n14, 319-320, 325, 328, 337, 342-343, 354, 358n8
Lee, Edwin Gray, (Lee's cousin), 48, 48n38, 229, 229n29, 317, 329, 356, 436, 447n29
Lee, Fitzhugh, 3n9, 9n23, 11n14, 14, 14n19, 30, 30n10, 40, 40n5, 45, 54, 58, 60, 62, 64, 64n19, 64n20, 65n20, 72, 84, 85, 87-89, 100-101, 114, 141, 145, 147, 162, 164, 167n14, 168, 170, 173, 193, 219-220, 225, 234, 234n14, 243, 248n25, 249, 257, 280n43, 290n1, 328, 328n9, 340, 344, 364, 409, 425, promotion, 174; authorized to move from Hanover Court House, 180; requests Rob be assigned his ordnance officer, 181; jaded horses, 182; a move against Milroy, 241; skirmish at Hartwood Church, 246, 246n9; Lee compliments on action at Kelly's Ford, 251; report on Kelly's Ford, 251; brigade going to Loudoun County to gather supplies, 254; Chancellorsville, 263; passes to go through the lines, 320; winter of 1863, 338, 342; winter of 1863-64, 373; Overland Campaign, 380n17; ordered to follow Sheridan, 388; enemy cavalry at White House, 390; ordered to guard against Sheridan, 391; guarding Cold Harbor, 395; guarding the Chickahominy, 399; 414, 414n10, 423-424, 425n8, 433, 452; ordered to command all cavalry north of the James, 420; placed in command of the cavalry corps, 472; ordered to watch for Sheridan, 479; ordered to guard High Bridge, 480; Sheridan's approach, 480; attempt to intercept Sheridan, 482; take command of all cavalry and join Pickett, 486; Five Forks, 488, 488n1; Appomattox Campaign, 488, 488n1, 496n24, 497, 497n26, 498, 498n30, 499n33, 500, 501n39, 503
Lee, George T., 495, 495n20
Lee, George Washington Custis (Lee's son), 3, 3n8, 15, 17, 40, 59n42, 62, 76, 89, 91, 101, 134n36, 170, 173, 180, 180n21, 181, 191, 204-206, 204n54, 205n2, 209, 211, 209, 212, 214, 217, 222, 222n38, 230n31, 233-234, 240-241, 243-244, 248n21, 251, 255, 281-282, 304-305, 305n13, 306, 309, 312, 314, 316-317, 326, 332-334, 334n40, 338n7, 341n28, 343, 357, 360n15, 364n39, 365, 368, 375, 424-425, 444, 447n29, 455, 455n33; trying to get his mother to leave White House, 126n2; Sharpsburg Campaign, 202; post-Sharpsburg lull, 205; 1862 winter quarters, 230; Lee fears Hooker is up to something, 241; meeting with Davis, 246; post-Chancellorsville, 270, 270n37, 272; the march to Gettysburg, 279, 286; death of Charlotte, 342; nominated to command Richmond, 364; long letter from father regarding need to hold a field command, 368; troops manning the Petersburg defences, 406; Petersburg Campaign, 407, 407n41, 419, 427, 431, 436, 448; Point Lookout operation, 411, 414; accompanying Davis to Georgia, 439n34; returns from Georgia, 444n12; promoted to major general, 446, 465n18; the war's final winter, 458, 465; captured at Sailors Creek, 488, 493; Appomattox Campaign, 495, 495n21, 502
Lee, Henry Carter, 328, 328n9
Lee, Henry "Light Horse Harry," (Lee's father), 902n
Lee, Hugh H., 62, 62n9
Lee, John (Lee's nephew), 502
Lee, John Mason, 328, 328n9
Lee, Mary (Lee's daughter), 2-3, 3n8, 3n9, 7n17, 14n16, 15, 17, 19, 29, 114, 119, 154, 180, 180n21, 181, 220, 221n33, 301, 307, 312n14
Lee, Mary (Lee's wife), 23-24, 40, 42, 53, 62, 62n6, 63, 66, 68, 71-73, 78, 84, 87, 107, 180-181, 181n24, 182, 184, 204, 208-209, 210n26, 212n37, 215n5, 219, 227, 229-230, 230n30, 234, 236-237, 238n33, 240, 243, 246-247, 248n21, 249, 251, 254, 257-258, 258n29, 261, 262n6, 270, 270n36, 271n39, 272, 275, 279, 281, 281n28, 282, 283, 288n56, 289, 291, 291n6, 296, 298, 299n38, 301, 304, 306-307, 309, 312, 312n14, 315, 318-319, 320n10, 325, 325n32, 328, 331, 334, 338-339, 339n11, 341, 341n26, 342-343, 345-346, 346n20, 348, 350-351, 353, 361n22, 362-365, 367-368, 372-373, 378-379, 388, 390, 393-394, 399-401, 407, 407n41, 408n47, 409-411, 414-415, 417, 419, 422, 422n46, 424-425, 427, 430-431, 434, 434n7, 436, 444, 446-447, 449, 452-454, 454n30, 455, 459, 461, 464-465, 467, 471-472, 472n16, 473-475, 479, 481-483, 485, 489, 492n14, 504; must leave Arlington, 6; Lee says she must leave Arlington, 9; gone to White House home, 72; Lee had not seen Mary since he had left Arlington, 82n33; at White House Plantation, 85n5; Lee writes about concern for Fort

Pulaski, 96; departs White House Plantation, 125; leaves White House, 132, 132n31; leaves a note on the White House door, 133n33; not pleased at what happened to Arlington, 137; discovered staying behind Union lines, 138; pass through the lines to go to Richmond, 151; Lee writes about the death of their grandson, 169; Appomattox Campaign, 503

Lee, Mildred (Lee's daughter), 68, 81, 102, 173, 215, 215n7, 217, 217n17, 219, 230, 255, 262, 270, 275, 286n45, 301, 312n14, 313, 325, 325n35, 334, 343, 343n5, 363, 372, 374n35, 378, 394, 409, 414, 452, 503

Lee, Jr., Robert E. (Lee's son), 9, 27, 32, 44, 74, 101, 104-105, 107, 160, 160n61, 193, 208, 211, 211n32, 212, 212n34, 214, 219-220, 230n37, 234, 260, 280n23, 301, 305, 307, 309, 313-314, 323, 329, 339n11, 346, 348, 353, 353n18, 401, 407n41, 434, 451, 451n12, 457, 476; visits his father, 31; Sharpsburg Campaign, 200, 200n40; post-Fredericksburg, 230; Point Lookout operation, 411, 413n8; Petersburg Campaign, 418n31, 419, 427; the war's final winter, 458, 482, 484n33, 485; Appomattox Campaign, 493, 501n39; wounded, 428n20

Lee, Robert E., 6, 10, 11n3, 15n22, 19n35, 30, 39, 54n16, 58, 68, 71-72, 102, 105, 122, 146, 150, 157, 165, 166n13, 168n19, 209, 296n26, 333, 339, 393, 404, 419; a most gifted officer, 1; pre-war, 1; meets with Blair, 2; resigns from the U.S. Army, 2; Virginia's secession, 2; will follow his native Virginia, 2; resignation causes a stir, 3; accepts command of Virginia's forces, 4, 4n11; defensive policy, 5n14; resignation from the Army, 5; Virginia's defensive only policy, 5; offered a family pew at St. Paul's Episcopal, 7; meets with William S. Harney, 8; building an army from scratch, 10; settles into role as commander, 10; size of staff starts to increase, 10; Arlington seized by Federal troops, 11n5; daily routine, 11; material at Harpers Ferry not moved, 12; orders all Georgia and Alabama troops to Norfolk, 13; Walter Taylor, 13n13; orders Georgia troops to Norfolk, 14; commands troops from other states, 15; orders commanders to deal only with Virginia troops, 15; construction of fortifications around Richmond, 16; in command of all troops from other states, 16; requests detachment of VMI cadets, 17; receives a map of Fairfax County, 19; inspects Norfolk, 20, 20n37; leaves Richmond the first time, 20; 18 is the minimum enlistment age, 22; briefs Richmond city council on city's defenses, 22; visits Tredegar Iron Works, 22; regimental adjutants must come from regimental lieutenants, 23; inspection tour of Manassas, 24; returns to Richmond after Manassas visit, 25; focusing on river defenses, 27; Huger can do whatever he wants with officers of provisional army, 28n4; new horse "Richmond," 28; officers of the provisional army, 28; inspection of James River defenses, 29; left without a command, 30; pondering future since he has no command in Confederate Army, 30; accepts commission in the Confederate Army, 32; commission as full general in the Confederate Army, 32; George Deas assigned to staff, 33; report on Virginia mobilization sent to Letcher, 33; observes drill of the Washington Artillery, 35; Richmond Armory, 35; reviewing troops in Richmond, 37n35; 30th wedding anniversary; 38, notifies Jackson of promotion to brigadier general, 40; no formal exchange agreement exists, 41; complains of incomplete returns from the field, 42; orders VMI cadets to the 9th Virginia, 42; Beauregard's plan to join forces with Joe Johnston, 44; under strength companies 44; remains in Richmond during the battle of First Manassas, 46; Northrop, 47n35; departs for western Virginia, 49, 50n46, 51; shared a tent with Washington and Taylor, 52; Cheat Mountain, Virginia and battle of, 54, 60, 63, 65-66, 75; difficulties between Wise and Floyd, 54; Valley Mountain headquarters, 54, 62-64, 66, 66n23; William H. Kirker, 54n15; Alexander C. Jones, 55; frustration with Wise, 55; Reynolds' prisoner exchange, 55; winter clothing, 55; orders Wise to cooperate with Floyd, 56; Lee complains about Wise, 57n29; confirmed rank as full general, 58; Lee congratulates for Gauley Bridge skirmish, 58; death of John Washington, 60; his horse "Traveller," 60; Conrad's Mill, 64n18; disgusted at Rust's failure, 64n19; Elkwater, 64-65; authorization to transfer Wise, 66; Deitz farm, 67, 67n27, 73-74; Meadow Bluff, 67; Sewell Mountain, 67n28, 68-69, 71-73, 75; Wise's disorganized force, 68n30; newspapers pronounce him a failure, 70; Federals abandon Sewell Mountain positions, 71; loans field glasses to a private soldier, 71n10; seeks authorization to hire black laborers, 71-72; reminds Mary she cannot go back to Arlington, 72; writes to Rooney, 72; orders withdrawal from Sewell Mountain, 73; arrives in Richmond, 74, 74n31; Charlottesville, 74; departs Meadow Bluff, 74; Staunton, 74; White Sulphur Springs, 74, 74n29; briefs Davis on western Virginia operations, 75, 78; departs for Charleston, 75, 78, 81; describes situation as another forlorn hope 75; finds new assignment in Charleston no better than western Virginia, 75; Department of South Carolina, Georgia and East Florida is created, 78; meets with Davis about his new assignment, 78; Wilmington, North Carolina, 78-79; assumes command of Department of South Carolina, Georgia and East Florida, 79; Charleston, South Carolina, 79, 86, 87, 93; Coosawhatchie, 80; inspects Fort Pulaski, 80; inspects Castle Pinckney, 81n25; inspects Green Island, 81n23; Savannah, Georgia, 81, 91, 96-99, 102; arrives in Brunswick, 82n30; Brunswick, 82; inspects defences at Fernandina, 82; no civilian can leave Charleston without written permission, 83; *déjà vu* in South Carolina, 84; inspection tour of Charleston, 84; hears that Annie and Agnes are reunited with Mary, 85; Port Royal, 85; receives a letter from Mary, 85; letter to the Soldiers Relief Association in Charleston, 86; observes large fire in Charleston, 86, 86n15; travels to Charleston, 86; complains about Perry, 87; learns Richmond has ordered reinforcements to his department, 87; writes Mary about the fire in Charleston, 87; writes Mary to expect that Arlington is gone, 88; requests heavy guns from Wilmington sent to Charleston, 89; writes Custis about finding temporary quarters, 89; January 1862 least documented period of Lee during the war, 90; travels to Fernandina, 90; travels to Green Island, 90; visits his father's burial site, 90; father's grave at Dungeness, 92n16; Federal fleet off Amelia Island, 92; Fernandina, Florida, 92, 92n15; writes Custis he fears economic ruin with loss of Arlington, 92; writes Mary about his visit to his father's gravesite, 92; observes the sinking of a stone fleet off Sullivan's Island, 93; Ripley that spies are planning to burn railroad bridges, 93; almost killed by an exploding cannon, 94; buys "Traveller" for $200, 94; rumors of being named secretary of war, 95; manumission of the Custis slaves, 97; congratulates Pemberton on promotion, 98; Davis considers recalling Lee to Richmond, 98-99; orders Lee to withdrawal of all troops from coastal Florida, 99; appointed military advisor to Davis, 100, 103; recalled to Richmond, 100; many crises when he arrives in Richmond, 101; meets up with Mary at White House, 101; meets with Pemberton and Lawton, 102; arrives in Richmond, meets with Davis and the cabinet, 103; meets with Davis regarding southwest Virginia, 103; assumes duty as military advisor, 104; advises Magruder that Johnston cannot send him cavalry, 106; Johnston to send Longstreet to North Carolina, 106; comments on Mary's poor abilities as a seamstress, 107; travels to Fredericksburg, 107; endorses Washington's application, 109n52; approves Huger's prisoner exchange plan, 110; daily visits to Drewry's Bluff, 111; not willing to concentrate until he knows McClellan's plans, 111; confident McClellan won't reach the capital, 112; long, frequent meetings with Davis, 112; obstructions placed in the Elizabeth River, 113; advises Mary to leave White House, 114, 121; Johnston to go to the Peninsula, 114; Virginia troops that do not reenlist are put into state service, 116; Lee, Davis, Johnston meeting, 117n27; displeased that Gov. Milton in Florida is keeping troops, 118; visits daughter Mary, 119; wants CSS *Virginia* to make a night sortie, 124; heated exchanges with Johnston, 125; no expectation of withstanding a siege at Yorktown, 125; Johnston showed no signs of a serious battle, 126; on hand to observe Johnston's Fair Oaks fiasco, 126; orders engineers to Drewry's Bluff, 127; orders evacuation of Norfolk, 127; denies a request from Loring to return troops, 128; learns of Johnston's withdrawal from Yorktown, 128; Jackson's charges against Richard Garnett, 129; urges completion of obstructions in the James, 129; letter to Johnston regarding Walter Taylor having signed Lee's orders, 130, 130n20; visits Drewry's Bluff, 132n27; "Richmond must not be given up; . . . ," 134; writes Mary about the loss of the *Virginia*, 134; congratulates Jackson on victory at McDowell, 135; inspection trip to Drewry's Bluff, 135, 135n37; urges attack on McDowell to prevent going to McClellan's aid, 136n41; trying to get Johnston to tell Davis his plans, 137n49; watches artillery duel at Mechanicsville, 138, 138n50; still trying to get Johnston to reveal his plans, 139; Charleston and Savannah to be defended to last extremity, 140; congratulates Jackson on victories in the lower Valley, 140; sends two regiments to Weldon to assist Holmes, 140; sorting out confusion over who is responsible for Petersburg, 140, 140n59; offensive in the works, no info from Johnston, 141; Davis informs him Lee will be the new commander of the ANV, 142; "Lee acted without the least display of ceremony," 143; Mary made Lee a personal flag for his headquarters, 143; meeting with senior generals to get their opinion of the state of affairs, 143; moved headquarters to High Meadow, a house on Nine Mile Road, 143; always kept Davis informed of plans, 144; plan is based on Jackson arriving at the right place at the right time, 144; massed three divisions to cooperate with Jackson, 145; command of armies in eastern Virginia and North Carolina, 146; orders from Davis appointing Lee in command of the ANV, 146; receives Gen. G. W. Smith's dispositions, 146; long council of war meeting, 147; officially assumes command of the ANV, 147; retained duties as Davis's military aide, 147n12; does not recommend abandoning Fort Sumter and Fort Moultrie, 148; orders creation of a pioneer corps in each division, 148-149; inspects lines occupied by Longstreet, D. H. Hill and Huger, 149; Lee tells Davis he is preparing a fortified line in front of Richmond, 149; Lee's railroad gun, 149, 149n19, 156; orders staff officers to stay with their commands unless ordered elsewhere, 149; recommends a POW exchange with McClellan, 149; reconnaissance of McClellan's position before Richmond, 149; consolidates cavalry under Stuart, 150; Davis wants troops brigaded by state, Lee will comply, 150; orders military roads from each division to Richmond, 150; requests that able-bodied troops not be detailed to hospital duty, 150; sends congratulations to Jackson, 150; proposes to send two brigades to help Jackson, 151; orders Stuart to explore McClellan's right flank, 152; Half Sink estate, 153; agreement with McClellan that medical personnel are non-combatants, 154; feels now is a good time for Bragg to attack Halleck, 154; orders deserters sent to Jackson for trial, 154; says Huger can be sent to Charleston, 154; sends McClellan a list of prisoners, 154; artillery is organized into battalions, 155; changes in command structure, 155; congratulates Stuart for his ride around McClellan, 155; planning meeting with officers for the attack on McClellan, 155; drafts the attack orders for the 26th, 156; issues written orders to prevent confusion, 156n50; meets Jackson for the first time, 156n49; Pemberton might have to be replaced, 156; watches enemy assault on Ransom at Oak Grove, 156; lack of confidence in Huger, 157n52; note from Jackson he is running behind schedule, 157; finds Jackson in conference with Hill, 158; orders Jackson to move to Cold Harbor, 158; orders Ripley's brigade into the fight, 158; sends Taylor to find Jackson, 158; war council meeting with Jackson, Longstreet and others, 159; conference with Longstreet at Watt house, 160; meets with Richard Taylor, 160; intercept McClellan before he reaches the James River, 161; news that White House has been destroyed, 161; investigates Malvern Hill, 162; meets captured general George McCall, 162; plans to trap McClellan at Glendale, 162; physically worn down, 163, 165, 165n11; sends Jackson to confront Pope, 163, 171; uncertain of McClellan's next move, 163; meets brother Sidney, 164; plagued by a lack of maps and poor leadership at Malvern Hill, 165n11; McClellan does not intend to operate against Petersburg, 166; message from McClellan concerning Federal wounded, 167; POW exchange desirable, 167; reconnoiters Harrison's landing, 167; reorganizes the army after the Seven Days Battles, 167; congratulates the ANV for recent victories, 168; Davis warns Lee about personal exposure, 168; withdraw closer to Richmond, let Stuart watch McClellan, 168; writes McClellan and Halleck about reported execution of two civilians, 168; learns of death of grandson, 169n23; needs all division commanders to submit their reports, Seven Days Battles, 169; recommends Richard Anderson and Micah Jenkins for promotion, 169; Anderson to command Huger's former division, 170; congratulates the ANV for recent victories, 170; to discuss Pope's movements near Manassas, 170; approves POW exchange Hill organized, 171; complains to McClellan about civilians arrested for not taking oath, 171; advises Davis that Jackson needs additional troops to attack Pope, 172; cavalry screen from Malvern Hill to Savage's Station, 172; congratulates Stuart on his promotion, 173; horse "Richmond" not well, 173; looking for a replacement for Beverly Robertson, 173; shell McClellan's army from the south side of the James River, 173; horse "Richmond" dies, 174, 177; almost captured, 175, 184, 184n36; completes strategic reversal of the war in Virginia, 175; did not like Pope, 175; injured wrists in a fall, 176, 181, 191, 194; visits Custis and daughter Mary, 176; advises Longstreet to tighten up discipline, 177; complains to Halleck about Pope's actions, 177; advises Davis about letter to Halleck, 178; meets Mosby, 178; suggests G.W. Smith replace Pemberton at Charleston, 178; tells Davis it would be easier to relieve Pemberton than replace him, 178; exchanged officers report to Cooper for assignment, 179; recon of Malvern Hill with Gilmer, 179; congratulates Jackson for Cedar Mountain, 180; arrives at Gordonsville, 181; division of the army at Gordonsville, 181; Clark's Mountain, 182; how to strike Pope, 182; issues orders for the attack on Pope, 182; visits Clark's Mountain, 182n27; Brandy Station, 183; Congress thanks for the victories over McClellan, 183; Jackson to Pope's rear, 183n33; Second Manassas Campaign, 183, 185, 185n37, 188, 190; August 29 meeting, 185; nearly killed at Groveton, 185, 185n38; "Traveller," 185, 187, 199; Longstreet attacks Pope's left flank, 186; denies Pope's request for a truce, 187; ends Pope's threat, 188; lost orders 191, 188; options after Second Manassas, 188; "Lucy Long," Lee's horse, 191n11; death of Phil Kearny, 192; crosses the Potomac, 192-193, 193n15; Kearny's body returned through the lines, 192; Ox Hill, 192; suggests Bragg's army join Lee, 192, 193n14; communications line through the Shenandoah Valley, 193; has come to Maryland to free the state from Lincoln's control, 194; proposes a permanent provost and IG, 194; Sharpsburg Campaign, 194n18, 201-202; both hands bandaged to the fingertips, 195; Columbus O'Donnell, 195n20; crosses South Mountain, 195; Davis wants to join Lee's army in Maryland, 195; Frederick, 195n22; Special Order 191, 195; Congress thanks for the victories at Second Manassas, 196; still traveling in his ambulance, 197n28; withdraws to Sharpsburg, 197; death of daughter Annie, 205, 210, 210n26, 211, 215, 217, 220; post-Sharpsburg lull, 206-207, 208; will not return Florida units to Florida, 207; grand review after Sharpsburg, 208; nearly captured around Leetown, 209; commends Stuart for his performance, 210; Lee does not want Whiting with his army, 210; sends Cooper the flags of the 11th Pennsylvania and 103rd New York, 210; wants to keep part of his army in the Valley an part on the Rappahannock for the winter, 210; Lee reviews Kershaw's command, 211; surprised by Burnside's appearance at Falmouth, 213; Fredericksburg Campaign, 214, 217, 220-222, 224, 225n8, 227-228; Federal demand that Fredericksburg surrender, 219; happy Joe Johnston is recovered, 220; orders Jackson to move toward Fredericksburg, 220; feels Burnside to advance on Richmond via Fredericksburg, 221; Briscoe Baldwin assigned chief of ordnance for ANV, 222; 1862 winter quarters, 223-225; grants freedom to all of the Custis slaves, 224; loss of second grandchild, 224, 226; melt down 6-lb guns and recast as 12-lb Napoleons, 225; courting Mary at Chatham, 227; Edwin G. Lee, 229n29; congratulates the army for the victory at Fredericksburg, 231; refused to meet with Northrop, 232, 232n1; struggling to find supplies, 232; army running low on beef, 235; denies Jackson's request to court martial Taliaferro, 235; Vance wants Lee to come to NC, 235; reviews Rooney's brigade, 236; Burnside might be moving again, 237; problems feeding the army, 237; wants G.W. Smith replaced with Elzey or Kirby Smith, 237; British officials passing through the lines, 238; Mr. "Mr. F.J. Hooker" as Lee calls him, 239; the quiet after Fredericksburg, 239, 244, 257; congratulates Imboden on promotion, 240; orders all detached cavalrymen return to their units, 240; enemy planning an assault on Charleston, 241; fears Hooker is up to something, but Lee doesn't know what, 241-242; Hayfield, 244; proposed reorganization of the artillery, 244n2, 248; travels to Richmond to meet with Davis, 244; possible heart attack, 245; toll on his health, moved into Belvoir, 245; does not oppose resignation of Toombs, 246; submits report on the Seven Days, 246; bans truces and trading along the Rappahannock River, 247n16; few details about trips to Richmond, 248n21; Seven Days report, 249; wants to reorganize the staff and support positions in the army, 249; congratulates Mosby on promotion, 250; have Tredegar produce Napoleon guns until all bronze guns replaced, 250; thanks Governor Vance for help in filling ranks of state regiments, 250; letter to Mary says he has been unwell for some time, 251; meets with Jackson to discuss temporary command of ANV, 251; remains at Belvoir for three weeks, 251n41, 252, 254; reviews reports on Fredericksburg and Cedar Mountain, 252; Lee shifting army west of Fredericksburg, set up camp at Chancellorsville, 253; allows Jewish troops to go to Synagogue when possible, 254; Seddon broached idea to send Longstreet to Tennessee, 254n11; sends Seddon a map of the Seven Days' battles, 254; to Seddon, the Virginia Central must be repaired, 254; a diversion by Elzey to draw attention from Longstreet, 255; best way to relieve pressure in other areas is to go on the offensive, 255; makes changes to the Fredericksburg report, 255; requests 350 foot pontoon bridge, 255; Second Manassas report, 255n16; battle report about Fredericksburg, 256; concern about absence of Longstreet, 256; forwards Mosby's report of several weeks, 256; proposes offensive around May 1, 256; submits report on Cedar Mountain, 257; availability of cavalry in North Carolina, 258; enemy cavalry in force around Warrenton, 258; pickets on the lookout for enemy activity, 258; enemy crossed the

Rappahannock at Fredericksburg, 259; three enemy corps moving toward Germanna and Ely's fords, 259; wants to know when Longstreet will return, 259; determines that Fredericksburg crossing is a feint, 260; determines that Hooker is turning his left, 260; orders pontoon train moved to Gordonsville, 260; shifted the army into the Wilderness, 260; his greatest victory, 261; outnumbered three-to-one at Chancellorsville, 261; Jackson wounded, 265-267; Chancellorsville, 267n24; requests Davis come to Fredericksburg, 268; death of Stonewall Jackson, 269; Seddon's plan to send Pickett's Division to Vicksburg, 269; the Stonewall Brigade asks to escort Jackson's body to Richmond, 269; Lee meets with regarding reinforcing Vicksburg, 270, 270n35, 270n38; must meet with Davis soon, 270; post-Chancellorsville, 271; congratulates Imboden on recent raid, 272; large number of desertions from North Carolina units, 272; enemy planning another raid, 273; POW paroles, 273; not satisfied with Colston's Chancellorsville performance, 274n52; announces the new three-corps organizational structure, 275; June 1863: planning another invasion, 276, 278; arrives at Chambersburg, 277; Gettysburg, 277; no news from Stuart, 277, 288, 292; orders the army to concentrate at Gettysburg, 277; Venable thinks he should leave Lee's staff, 277; Lee's planning meeting for the move north, 280; submits report on Second Manassas, 280; ANV starts to cross the Potomac, 285; the march to Gettysburg, 286, 287, 287n56; writes Davis about prisoner exchange and enemy movements, 286; Meade and his army have moved into Maryland, 288; on June 29, announces that the ANV will go to Gettysburg, 288; hears sound of battle coming from Gettysburg, 290; learns of Rooney's capture, 290, 296; "We must whip these people soon . . ." 290; Gettysburg, July 1, 292; Gettysburg, July 2, 293-294; illness at Gettysburg, 293, 293n13, 293n14, 294-295, 296n26; Gettysburg, July 3, 294-295, 295n21; Gettysburg, July 4, 295-296; retreat from Gettysburg, 297-298, 298n36, 299-300; post-Gettysburg, 301; Henry Heth, 302; concerned about Rooney, 303; submits resignation to Davis, it is refused, 303, 305; all troops AWOL will be pardoned if they return within 20 days, 305; Union threat to execute Rooney, 305; might execute deserters if they don't return, 306; bust of Stonewall Jackson (Galt), 307; Davis refuses to accept Lee's resignation, 307; situation in Tennessee, 309; arrangements made to ship Longstreet's corps to Bragg, 311; inspects the defenses of Richmond, 311; reviews Ewell's corps, 312; reviews Hill's corps, 313; Union cavalry near Culpeper, 314; Meade's summer 1863 operations, 315n25, 316n29, 317; illness, 318, 321, 323-324, 324n30, 326, 377-378, 396, 398n6; wants "Grumble" Jones sent elsewhere, 320; announces a major enemy offensive in Charleston, 321; Bristoe Station Campaign, 322; cannot pursue Meade at Bristoe Station Campaign, 323; congratulates for victory over Kilpatrick at Buckland, 323; congratulates for victory at Charlestown, 324; praises latest exploits, 325; no idea when Rooney will be exchanged, 326; reviews Stuart's cavalry at Brandy Station, 328; fired upon again, 329; Rappahannock Station, battle of, 330n19, 331; considers impressment to provision the army, 332; post-Rappahannock Station, 332n26; U.S. government plans to auction Arlington, 333; Meade preparing another move, 334; orders Sam Jones to send his cavalry to Longstreet, 334; Mine Run, 335-336; rumors he was going to replace Bragg, 337-338, 340n14; notifies Richmond that Meade has withdrawn, 338; preparing another move toward Lee, 338; will not use impressment as requested, 339; winter of 1863-64, 342, 347, 353, 361n21, 365, 368, 372; frustration with Northrop, 343-345; proposes an attack on New Bern, 344; Davis approves Thanks of Congress to Lee, 345; Longstreet requests to be relieved of command, 345; explains strategic situation to Longstreet, 346; status of Ewell's ability to command, 346; concern about troops recruited for local service only, 347; submits his Gettysburg Campaign report, 347, 347n26; plan to have several officers to recruit partisan units, 348; vulnerability of southwest Virginia, 348; shortage of shoes, 349; death of sister Anne, 350, 354; almost captured during the Kilpatrick-Dahlgren Raid, 350-351, 356; Breckinridge visits, 351; two options for the Spring Campaign, 351; annoyed by false alarms from Richmond, 354n24;; Longstreet's proposal to attack Knoxville, 354; watching the building of a pontoon bridge, 357; papers on Dahlgren's body ordering the execution of Davis and others, 360; sends a letter to Longstreet regarding issues in the Western Theater, 360; approves Breckinridge's plan to fortify southwestern Virginia, 363; Grant is with the AOP, 364; needs Longstreet and Hoke returned to the ANV, 364; Cooper sends copies of the Dahlgren papers to Lee, 365; has many conflicting reports on enemy intentions, 366; lobbying for return of Longstreet's corps, 367; recommends all partisan units except Mosby be disbanded, 367; black troops replace white troops around Washington, 368; complains about a lack of supplies, 369; desertions and AWOL soldiers, 369; Winchester citizens arrested by both sides, 372; asks Davis to visit the army, 373; declines offer to have VMI cadets serve with the ANV, 373; baptism of Lucy Hill, 379; Grant has not learned from Hooker's experience in the Wilderness, 380; Tapp Farm, 381; "Lee to the rear!," 382, 385n38; under fire at the Wilderness, 382; wounding of Longstreet at the Wilderness, 382n25; a bullet strikes Lee's saddle, 384; not favorably impressed with the army's position, 384; Overland Campaign, 384n32, 388, 402n28, 404; Spotsylvania, 384n32, will keep his army between Grant and Richmond, 384; the Mule Shoe, 385-386; almost killed by artillery fire, 387, 391; congratulates Breckinridge for victory at New Market, 387; no successor for Stuart is appointed, 387; complains about army's current situation, 388; does not want McLaws with ANV, 388n49; enemy have left the Spotsylvania earthworks, 389; crosses the North Anna River, 390; failing health, 391n60, 392, 392n63, 393n69, 394, 395n76; not well enough to organize an attack against Grant, 392n64; replaces Ewell with Early, 394n70; Cold Harbor, 396, 398n6; health improves, 399; truce to allow Grant to recover bodies, 400; enemy from north of the James River are at Petersburg, 402; knows Grant is on the James River, 402; orders the army across the Chickahominy, 402; abandoned lines at Bermuda Hundred to concentrate at Petersburg, 403n31; notifies

Bragg he will not move army closer to Richmond, 403; placed in overall command of forces in Virginia and North Carolina, 403; looking for answers about Grant's location, 404-405; all of the Bermuda Hundred line is retaken, 405; Grant's army is south of the James River, 405; rapidly deteriorating situation at Petersburg, 405; arrives in Petersburg, 406n40; artillery fire, 406; is now aware that Grant is at Petersburg, 406; moves headquarters to Petersburg, 406; bleak report to Davis about situation at Petersburg, 407; Early's operations in the Valley, 409; seems Grant has gone on the defensive, 409; Early's operations in the Shenandoah Valley, 411; Point Lookout operation, 414; does not recommend Hood as replacement for Joe Johnston, 416; Early is able to operate as he chooses, 416; Ewell authorized to place torpedoes in the James River, 416; recommends Hardee as replacement for Joe Johnston, 416; congratulates Early on move on Washington, 417; learns that Hood is appointed to command the Army of Tennessee, 417; does not think Lincoln will withdraw troops from the Valley, 418; congratulates Early on victory at Kernstown, 419; doubts anything would force Grant to abandon Petersburg, 419n32; orders Morgan not to make a planned raid, 420; the Crater, 420-421, 421n42, 422, 422n45; Meade requests truce to bury the dead from the Crater, 422; Dutch Gap Canal, 423, 427; Petersburg Campaign, 423n1, 439; flags captured at the Crater number 20, 424; Union forces in Washington, 424, Howlett Line, 426n14; inspects the Howlett Line, 426; Sheridan is the new enemy commander in the Valley, 426; under fire at Fussell's Mill, 428n21; quiet in Petersburg, Lee visits the front lines, 432; struggled to keep his men in the ranks, 432; photo taken at Rockwell's studio, 433, 433n4; acknowledges Dimmock, 435n15; conscription issues, 435; will not send any troops to Hood in Georgia, 436; suggests using Charleston as base for privateers, 437; pleads regarding details for noncombatant roles, 438; Fort Harrison, 440-441; last hope for the Valley goes up in flames, 441; proposed prisoner exchange, 442; defends Early's actions to Governor Smith, 444-445; approves disbanding the 22nd Virginia Battalion for cowardly conduct, 445; complains to Grant about using prisoners to build a canal, 445; ordered Longstreet to resume command of the First Corps, 445; pardons all Unionist Tennesseans who lay down their arms, 448; there needs to be a change in the Valley cavalry, 448; plan to make Ewell head of the cavalry bureau, 450; wants the 22nd Virginia Battalion broken up, 452; the war's final winter, 456, 462, 472; desertions becoming a huge problem, 457, 476; saved by Archibald Gracie, 457, 457n6; the army is out of meat, 458; prepare to send Hoke's Division to Wilmington, 459; Christmas dinner, 460; the 22nd Virginia Battalion is disbanded, 460n25; might somehow avert the end of the war, 462; Davis offers Lee command of all armies, 464; confirmed as general in chief, 467-468; peace delegation, 467; says Thomas' army is joining with Grant, 467; great respect for Breckinridge, 468; Cooper confirms Lee's appointment at general in chief, 470; appointment as general in chief announced, 471; announces assumption as general in chief, 472; discussing details to evacuating Petersburg, 474, 474n29; orders Bragg to destroy all stores that might fall into enemy hands, 474, 476; orders Joe Johnston to take command of the Army of Tennessee, 474; McNeill's capture of Crook and Kelley, 475; suggest uniting with Johnston's army, 475; warns that Richmond might have to be evacuated, 475; depressed after a meeting with Davis, 476n35; tells he will probably have to evacuate Richmond, 476; ANV is melting away, 477; Longstreet's meeting with General Ord to discuss peace, 479; March 10 a day of fasting and prayer, 479; last known trip to Richmond prior to Appomattox, 480n14; Lee supposed to meet Grant about peace terms, 480n12; request from Breckinridge to put into writing his views, 481; urges Johnston to attack Sherman if any probability of success, 481; continues meeting with Breckinridge, 483; comes under artillery fire again, 484; last council of war, 484n31; Sheridan is not bound for North Carolina, 484; autographs a flag for Thomas Conolly, 485; Fort Stedman, 485; he won't be able to prevent Grant and Sherman from joining, 485; Kirby Smith cannot join Lee, 486; relieved Early and sends him home, 486; sends Pickett to guard the Southside Railroad, 486; Petersburg and Richmond must be evacuated, 488; Southside Railroad cut, Lee's last supply line, 488; Grant asks for his surrender, 489; headquarters flag cut up, 489n4; death of Hill, 490n9; Five Forks, 490; intends to withdraw from Petersburg at night, 491; warns Breckinridge he cannot hold position beyond nightfall, 491; Chesterfield Court House, 492n13; crosses the Appomattox at Goode's Bridge, 492; arrives at Farmville, 494; learns of Custis' capture, 494; orders High Bridge destroyed, 494n19; Sailors Creek, battle of, 494n18; Alexander tells Lee time for surrender is at hand, 495, 495n22; Pendleton tells Lee time for surrender is at hand, 495n22; asks Grant what terms he would offer, 496; has Grant's terms, offers to meet Grant the next day, 496; note from Grant requesting the surrender of the ANV, 496; replies to Grant's surrender request, 496; Longstreet, Mahone, Gordon all advise against further attacks, 497; thinks he will be Grant's prisoner, 497; will not disburse the army to continue a guerrilla war, 497; departs for meeting with Grant, 498; Grant will meet with him, 498; proposes to surrender the ANV, 498; temporary cease-fire awaiting Grant's reply, 498; Appomattox Campaign, 499n32, 503; Marshall drafts the farewell speech, 499; meets with Grant, 499, 499n33, 500; rides to the McLean home, 499; escort to Richmond, 500; parts with Longstreet, they will never meet again, 500; departs for Richmond, 501; Lee sends his last official communication to Davis, 503; accepts presidency of Washington College, 504

Lee, Sidney Smith (brother), 2n7, 136, 153, 164, 174, 362, 424

Lee, Stephen D., 171, 186, 201, 207, 215-216, 216n12, 437n25, 475n32

Lee, W. Raymond, 162

Lee, William Henry Fitzhugh "Rooney," 2, 3n9, 11n8, 14, 30, 30n10, 54, 58, 60, 62, 64, 64n19, 64n20, 65n20, 84-85, 85n5, 87, 97, 114, 141, 145, 147, 164, 176-177, 184, 193, 206, 209, 212, 214, 217, 220, 229, 234, 236, 280n23, 281n27, 283, 287n50, 298, 301, 304-305, 312n14, 320, 328,

328n9, 342, 358n8, 362, 362n26, 363, 365, 373, 400, 400n17, 401, 409; commissioned, 45; asks to see about buying Stratford Hall, 88; Lee "grieved" about leaving him in western Virginia, 88; funeral for his son, 168; learns of death of son, 169n24; post-Sharpsburg lull, 205, 206n8; Fredericksburg Campaign, 218; loss of second child, 226; post-Fredericksburg, 230; wounded at Brandy Station, 276, 281-282; captured, while wounded, and sent to a Union prison, 277, 287; Union hospital at Fort Monroe, 288, his father learns of his capture, 290, 296; Fort Monroe, 303; possible exchange, 305; no idea when he will be exchanged, 325-326; leaves Fort Monroe for Fort Lafayette prison, 331; enters Fort Lafayette, 332-333, 333n34; Lincoln approves Rooney's exchange, 351; return from prison, 358; leaves Fort Lafayette for Fort Monroe, 359; arrives in Richmond from Union prison, 361; returns to duty, 364; promoted to major general, 372; Overland Campaign, 379, 389, 402; needs to help find the Federal troops, 405; Petersburg Campaign, 407n41, 418n31, 419, 431, 451; confirmation that the VI corps has departed Petersburg, 416-417; poison oak, 431n34; the war's final winter, 476, 484n33, 485; Appomattox Campaign, 495, 495n21, 502

Lee's Life Guard, 15, 15n22

Leesburg, Virginia, 227

Letcher, John, (Governor, Virginia), 1, 3-4, 4n11, 6, 13, 15, 18n32, 22, 24, 27, 32, 40, 44n20, 48, 58, 73, 152, 324-326, 329, 331, 504; Lee accepts command of the state forces, 4; Lee's defensive only policy, 5; meets with Lee, 5; Harpers Ferry, 7; strength of states forces, 8; orders Harney's release, 8n19; military council, 11; official call for volunteers, 12; Lee in command of all troops from other states, 15; Lee orders guards at all public places, 18; Lee forwards Dimmock's opinion, 22; application from Francis W. Smith, 23; about 36,000 troops in the state, 25; Lee's report on Virginia mobilization, 33; purchase of old weapons, 34; Briscoe Baldwin, 36; under strength companies, 44; Alexander C. Jones, 55; Washington's death, 66; Lee seeks authorization to hire black laborers, 72; Lee briefs on western Virginia operations, 75; Lee requests he issue a general draft of Virginia soldiers, 88; Lee forwards a complaint about Huger, 108; Virginia troops that do not reenlist are put into state service, 116; conscription bill, 118; concerns about civilians being detained, 121; Lee and Jackson meet with, 170; reviews Stuart's cavalry at Brandy Station, 328

Leventhorpe, Collett, 470, 470n8

Lewis, H.W., 184n36

Lewis, Ivey F., 342

Lewis, John R.C., 43

Lexington, Virginia, 397

Lincoln, President Abraham, 2, 5n14, 194, 227n15, 357n1, 411n1, 418, 430, 456, 462, 485n39; call for volunteers, 1; election of, 1; Jackson's Campaign forced Lincoln to hold McDowell in Fredericksburg, 126; brings Halleck to command all Union armies, 175; orders McClellan replaced, 216n15; Burnside at Aquia, 225; meets with Burnside, 237, 237n29; authorizes Federal government to purchase Arlington, 344; approves Rooney's exchange, 350-351; Fort Stevens, 411; Early's presence in the Valley concerned him, 423; plot to kidnap, 447n29; reelection of, 449, 452; the war's final winter, 477n5; assassination, 502n44, 503

Lockridge, James, 28

Logan, A.C., 65n21

Lomax, Lunsford, 6, 425-426, 431, 447, 460, 486

Long, Armistead L., 46, 46n30, 51, 53n11, 53n12, 54n16, 76, 94n5, 100, 102, 104n25, 141, 147, 149n19, 150n23, 150n25, 153n38, 156, 182n27, 182n28, 184n35, 184n36, 185, 185n37, 187n44, 190, 190n6, 190n9, 197, 223, 247, 250n37, 251n39, 282, 292-294, 297, 308n36, 310, 315n27, 316, 360, 376; assigned to Lee's staff, 86, 123; replaced Gill as ordnance officer, 87; to Richmond with Lee, 100; rejoins Lee's staff, 112; Lee requests his promotion, 119; Lee's staff, 132; "the relations between Lee and Davis are very friendly," 144; remains with Lee when he assumes command of the ANV, 146n11; reconnaissance around Mechanicsville, 150; Half Sink estate, 153; Sharpsburg Campaign, 200n38; sent to assist Grumble Jones, 251; Meade's summer 1863 operations, 315; winter of 1863-64, 351, 352n10, 359; Overland Campaign, 385, 385n37; Appomattox Campaign, 495n22, 496, 496n22, 500, 504

Longstreet, James, 111, 118n30, 131, 144, 144n4, 153n38, 156, 158, 160, 162, 165, 167, 167n14, 168n19, 169n25, 171, 180n18, 181n22, 181n25, 182, 182n28, 210-211, 234n12, 236n22, 239n2, 248, 248n26, 251n41, 261n3, 268, 269n29, 270n34, 270n36, 270n37, 274n52, 284, 287, 289, 290n2, 296n26, 309, 313, 313n16, 313n18, 314, 316n30, 320, 324n30, 346n20, 346n21, 351, 371, 382n25, 410n53, 416, 438n29, 441n1; can Johnston spare James Longstreet to take command in North Carolina, 105; Johnston to send to North Carolina, 106; is free to operate as Johnston allows, 114; ordered to send forces to Richmond, 114; no bread available in Richmond, 115; Lee is the new commander of the ANV, 146; Lee's arrival and assumption of ANV command, 146n10; request from Huger to return his brigades, 148; thinks highly of Richard H. Anderson, 150; meets Lee at Dabb's house, 153; given command of his and D.H. Hill's divisions, 155; planning meeting with officers for the attack on McClellan, 155; immediate assault on Cold Harbor, 159; conference with Lee at Watt house, 160; scout artillery positions at Malvern Hill, 165; ordered to take command of the right wing of the army, 171; advised to tighten up discipline, 177; Lee sends to Gordonsville, 180; ordered to Gordonsville to link up with Jackson, 181; Clark's Mountain, 182; how to strike Pope, 182; visits Clark's Mountain, 182n27; Second Manassas Campaign, 183n33, 184-186, 192; Lee's plan to cross the Potomac, 193; Sharpsburg Campaign, 194n17, 194n18, 195n20, 195n21, 195n22, 196, 197n28, 198-199, 199n33, 200n38, 201, 201n44, 202; Harpers Ferry operation, 195; Boonsboro, 197; post-Sharpsburg lull, 205, 210, 215; Lee recommends for promotion, 206; grand review after Sharpsburg, 208; nearly captured around Leetown, 209; promoted to lieutenant general, 215; Fredericksburg Campaign, 216-220, 220n29, 222-223, 227-228, 234; 1862 winter quarters, 230; temporarily in command of ANV, 235-236; sent to Southside Virginia after Fredericksburg, 239; Richmond, 241; takes command of Hood and Pickett's divisions, 242; enemy moving down the Potomac, 243; at Suffolk, 244; needs an engineer, 246; Armistead Long as artillery chief, 247; Suffolk Campaign, 247n20, 255-256; Lee wants to keep Hood and Pickett in North Carolina, 249; need to collect all possible supplies, 250; Alexander to be sent to him as requested, 251; Burnside's corps sent west on the B&O, 251; Longstreet senior to Jackson, but was on assignment at Suffolk, 252n4; Burnside and IX Corps are in Kentucky, 254; Seddon broached idea to send him to Tennessee, 254n11; cavalry in North Carolina, 258; latest intel on Hooker's army, 259; rejoined the army after Chancellorsville, 261; post-Chancellorsville, 274; the march to Gettysburg, 276, 278n9, 279-280, 283, 283n36, 284n39, 285-286, 287n49, 287n57, 288, 288n56; arrives at Chambersburg, 277; Lee's planning meeting for the move north, 278, 280; Gettysburg, July 1, 292, 292n9, 293; Gettysburg, July 2, 293, 293n14, 294, 294n16; Gettysburg, July 3, 294, 294n19; Gettysburg, July 4, 296; retreat from Gettysburg, 296-299; post-Gettysburg, 308n28; Chickamauga, 310; deserters in North Carolina, 311; in Tennessee, 311n10; Meade's summer 1863 operations, 316; congratulates for victory at Chickamauga, 324; Knoxville, 333, 339n9, 346; Sam Jones ordered to send his cavalry to Longstreet, 334; requests to be relieved of command, 345; winter of 1863-64, 345n14, 351, 353, 361, 361n21, 361n24, 367, 369, 369n14, 370n18, 370n19, 371n24, 371n25, 372n25, 374n34; Lee sends a letter regarding issues in the Western Theater, 360; Lee has no indication of new enemy offensive in Virginia, 363; Lee feels Longstreet's opinion of Grant is wrong, 364; Lee lobbying for return of his corps, 366-367; arrives in Virginia, 370; Evander Law, 373, 392, 451, 451n10; wounded at the Wilderness, 373n32, 382, 382n25; Lee to review troops at Gordonsville, 374-375; Overland Campaign, 376, 381-382; successor due to wounding, 383; returns to duty, 441; Petersburg Campaign, 443, 444n16, 446-447, 453, 454n31, 455; ordered to resume command of the First Corps, 445; resumes command of the First Corps, 445n20; offensive north of the James River, 454, 454n28, 454n29; the war's final winter, 457-458, 458n15, 460, 460n23, 463, 463n10, 470n8, 472, 476, 480-481, 484, 486; prepare to send Hoke's Division to Wilmington, 459; non-payment for the troops, 467; use of black laborers on Richmond defenses, 470; plan to pay for supplies with gold, 475; back-channel approach to Grant and Lincoln about peace, 476; meeting with General Ord to discuss peace, 479; enemy movements in his front, 483; Appomattox Campaign, 490, 490n8, 491-493, 496n22, 497-498, 498n30; Grant stripping troops from north of the James, 490; looking for reinforcements, 491n11; sees Grant's note regarding surrender of the ANV, 496; Lee meets with to discuss a breakout, 497; ordered to carry out the surrender, 499; parts with Lee, they will never meet again, 500

Loring, Alonzo, 8, 13

Loring, William W., 39, 46, 46n30, 48, 53, 53n11, 56, 63, 63n14, 64n18, 64n20, 65n21, 66-67, 69, 702n, 113n6, 131, 138-140, 171-172, 203, 208, 208n20, 210; leaves for western Virginia, 47; western Virginia, 48; joins Lee, 51; not pleased at Lee's arrival, 53; arrest of James Ramsey, 54; Kirker, William H., 54n15; tension with Henry Jackson, 56; James Conoway, 62; preparing for an attack that did not come, 70; disposition of his forces, 71; Lee loans field glasses to a private soldier, 71n10; may have to depart the area, 72; winter quarters for the army, 72; concern about Monterey and Huntersville lines, 73; ordered to Meadow Bluff, 73; Lee denies a request to return troops from Huger, 128; ordered to hold Suffolk, 130; approved troop dispositions in western Virginia, 146; enemy withdrawing from Kanawha Valley, 183-184; no place for him in the ANV, 209

Loudoun Rangers, 192

Louisiana Military Units: 1st Infantry, 15, 43n16; 3rd Infantry, 139n56; 13th Infantry, 33n21; Washington Artillery, 35, 134, 188, 199, 296n26

Louisiana, CSS, 117

Lovell, Mansfield, 130, 138, 140, 153-154, 484; ordered to raise a battalion, 117; to request weapons from the state of Louisiana, 118; artillery enroute from Mobile to New Orleans, 120; Lee requests information about Sibley's Campaign in New Mexico, 121; ordered to remove all of the funds from New Orleans banks, 121; ordered to gather all available forces to defend New Orleans, 122; preliminary report on the loss of New Orleans, 131; requests weapons from Beauregard, 132; only available weapons are pikes and knives, 133; ordered to recruit a partisan ranger command, 135; Ben Butler wants return of specie from New Orleans banks, 136; John Magruder is assigned to command west of the Mississippi, 151

Low, Andrew, 301n48

Low, Juliette Gordon, 101n7

Low, Mary Cowper Stiles, 301

Lowe, Enoch (Governor, Maryland), 188, 193, 193n14, 194-195, 195n21, 195n22, 196n23

Lowell, Samuel D., 500

"Lucy Long," Lee's horse, 191, 191n11

Lyman, Theodore, 399n16

Lynch, Bryan, (Lee's cook), 194, 330, 247, 501

Lynchburg, Virginia, 283, 340, 345, 438-439, 476, 480, 494

Lyons, James, 6, 6n16, 466, 466n26

MacBeth, Charles, (Mayor, Charleston), 83

MacFarland, W.H., 229

Mackall, William W., 94n5, 95n5, 207, 207n12

Mackay, George C., 79

Mackay, Jack, 75-76, 76n5, 79n18, 86n17

Maffitt, John N., 75, 80, 80n22, 84, 89, 122

Magrath, Judge A.G., 134

Magrath, William J., 99

Magruder, Allan B., 46

Magruder, G.S., 73

Magruder, John B., 15, 20, 23, 32, 34, 40, 47, 48n38, 105, 116n24, 133n32, 141, 152, 153n34, 156, 158, 161, 161n66, 162, 162n68, 163n2, 165, 166n11, 167n15, 180n18, 181n23, 210n26; promotion in Virginia forces, 6; ordered to command around Richmond, 15; placed in command of the Peninsula, 21; Lee does not think enemy will advance from Fort Monroe, 23; rations and other supplies sent, 30; Lee approves all measures taken on the Peninsula, 31; needs better soldiers as videttes, 36; Robert Johnston, 37n37; ordered not to place troops to far in advance of Yorktown, 40; plan to suppress raiding parties, 41; ordered to form the 32nd Virginia, 42; Charles Dreux, 43; Gloucester Point, 43, 113; additional heavy guns sent to Gloucester Point, 44; congratulations for Hood's recent victory at Smith's farm, 45; defenses at Jamestown Island, 45; requests for arms and ammunition must go through ordnance officer, 48; CSS *Virginia* has gone into dry dock, 103; ordered to fortify along the Warwick River, 104; Johnston cannot send him cavalry, 106; enemy landing troops at Fort Monroe, 107, 108; enemy concentrating at Fort Monroe, 108; reports to Lee that the enemy at Fort Monroe is advancing, 108; reinforcements from Johnston, 109; no more assistance until enemy attack is imminent, 110; expected attack from McClellan, 111; enemy landing at Newport News, 113; cautioned not to overreact, 114; enemy is heading up the Peninsula, 114; do not abandon Williamsburg lines, 115; reports an attack on the Warwick River line, 115; various reinforcements being sent, 115; department placed under Johnston's command, 116; Johnston not in favor of reinforcing him, 117n27; parts of Johnston's army ordered to Magruder, 117; supplies being sent to him, 118; defensive efforts on the Peninsula bought time, 125; assigned to command a department in Texas, 139; ordered not to yield ground, 149; is assigned to command west of the Mississippi, 151; requests Stephen D. Lee to be assigned, 153; ordered to hold his position at all costs, 158; McClellan abandoned his works in front of Magruder, 160; time with ANV at an end, 163; enemy abandoning Malvern Hill, 166; assigned to Trans-Mississippi, 167; Chilton's court of inquiry, 271; winter of 1863-64, 371n24

Mahone, William, 8n21, 9, 13n13, 18n31, 23n48, 43n19, 121, 121n48, 127n9, 135n37, 138, 140, 173, 221n34, 313n17; defense of the Norfolk & Petersburg Railroad, 23; ordered to join Ewell at Gordonsville, 130-131; ordered to take command at Drewry's Bluff, 135; ordered to send heavy artillery units away to be organized into a regiment, 136; at Drewry's Bluff, 138; Fredericksburg Campaign, 223; Chancellorsville, 264, 264n16, 265, 265n19; the march to Gettysburg, 287n58; winter of 1863-64, 347n23, 360, 360n18, 368; Overland Campaign, 382n25, 383n29, 386, 392, 395, 399-400, 400n17; Petersburg Campaign, 407-408, 408n45, 409, 410n53, 416, 416n17, 417-418, 426, 426n15, 427n16, 429, 429n27, 441n1, 445, 448-449, 451-452, 452n19, 453n20, 453n24, the Crater, 412, 412n4, 420-421, 421n41, 421n42, 422, 422n44; flags captured by his men at Jerusalem Plank Road, 415; the war's final winter, 471, 483, 483n27; Appomattox Campaign, 490, 492n14, 493, 493n16, 494, 494n18, 494n19, 495, 496n23, 496n24, 500

Mallory, Stephen (Navy Secretary), 33, 41, 108, 111, 113, 115, 118, 124n61, 130, 133, 137-138, 151n30, 155, 173, 177n7, 355, 355n32, 371n23

Malvern Hill, battle of, 162-163, 165, 165n11, 167, 169, 172, 177n5, 178n13, 179-180
Manassas Gap Railroad, 12, 13n13, 35, 41, 216, 284n37, 447
Manassas, First Battle of, 39, 46, 47
Manassas, Second battle of, 176, 188, 192, 192n13, 194, 210n29, 255n16
Manassas, Virginia, 10, 24, 25n55, 39
Manigault, Arthur, 75, 752n, 79, 79n19, 81, 105
Manigault, George E., 76
Manigault, Joseph, 79, 202
Manson, Richard, 494
Markell, Catherine, 195
Marsh, N.F., 165, 165n9
Marshall, Anne, 2, 350, 354
Marshall, Charles, 3n8, 112, 156, 166, 182n27, 182n28, 185, 185n37, 185n38, 192, 192n13, 194, 195n20, 197, 197n27, 197n28, 198, 198n30, 198n31, 236n22, 265, 265n18, 283n34, 284, 284n38, 289n57, 303, 332, 346n18, 347n26, 349, 389n53, 460n28; joins Lee's staff, 101, 106, 106n38; composed a conscription bill, 111, 113, 113n5; promoted to major, 119; Lee's staff, 132; remains with Lee when he assumes command of the ANV, 146n11; Sharpsburg Campaign, 200n40; explanation of how to write a battle report, 246n13; Lee makes changes to the Cedar Mountain report, 255, 255n16; Lee makes changes to the Fredericksburg report, 255; the quiet after Fredericksburg, 255; winter of 1863, 340n15; winter of 1863-64, 343, 355, 362; wounded, 388; the Crater, 421n41; Petersburg Campaign, 427n19, 432, 443n8, 447n31; the war's final winter, 470, 471, 474n28, 479n9, 480n11, 480n14, 486n43; Appomattox Campaign, 490n7, 492n13, 493-494, 498, 498n29, 498n31, 499, 499n32, 499n33, 499n34, 500, 500n36; drafts Lee's farewell speech; 499-500; departs for Richmond, 501
Marshall, Edward C., 12, 284n37
Marshall, Humphrey, 103, 103n22, 104-105, 108-109, 118-120, 122, 127, 131, 134, 172
Marshall, Louis, 173, 173n42, 184
Martin, James G., 104n25, 119, 121, 131, 134, 134n34, 140, 173, 180, 465, 483
Martinsburg, Virginia, 14, 225, 284-286, 286n45, 298-299
Maryland Military Units (Confederate): 1st Infantry, 24n52, 193n14; Maryland Line, 325
Mason, A.P., 146n11, 198n30, 212, 220, 220n30
Mason, George, 15
Mason, J. Stevens, 171
Mason, James, 21
Mason, Lucilla, 107
Mason, W. Roy, 151n30
Massachusetts Military Units: 4th Cavalry, 500; 20th Infantry, 171; 37th Infantry, 494n19
Mathias Point, 35, 37, 41, 43, 45n24
Maury, Dabney, 46
Maury, Matthew F., 3, 46n29
May, Robert, (Mayor, Augusta), 97
Mayo, Joseph (Mayor, Richmond), 4, 41, 44, 476
McCabe, Gordon, 387n43, 421n42, 421n43
McCall, George, 162, 162n69, 165-166

McCarthy, E.S., 264
McCausland, John, 8, 8n20, 13, 22, 56, 420, 426n14, 482
McClellan, Ellen, 288
McClellan, George B., 109, 125, 134, 136, 137n49, 139, 139n54, 141, 141n61, 147, 148n14, 151n30, 167, 168n19, 168n20, 171, 173, 178, 178n13, 179, 184, 188-189, 196, 198n31, 203; Laurel Hill, 44n22; Rich Mountain, 44n22; moves his army to the Virginia Peninsula, 111, 113; Lee is confident McClellan won't reach the capital, 112; changing bases from the James to the York rivers, 115; posted guards to protect White House, 126; plan to land a division at West Point, 129n13; orders White House Plantation to be protected, 133; arrives at White House Plantation, 136; failed to reposition his army after Johnston's attack, 144; attacked Lee's lines in front of Richmond, 145; great Campaign against Richmond was over, 145; recommends a POW exchange with Lee, 149; requests a POW exchange, 150; Mosby finds vulnerability of McClellan's right flank, 151; Lee proposes Cobb to represent for the POW exchange, 152; POW exchange set, 152; Stuart to explore McClellan's right flank, 152; Stuart does almost complete circuit of McClellan's army; 153n36, agreement with Lee that medical personnel are non-combatants, 154; Lee sends a list of prisoners taken, 154; has not detected Lee's plans; 156, Lee is concerned McClellan might know his plans 157; does he know Lee's plans?, 158; abandoned his works in front of Magruder, 160; intercept McClellan before he reaches the James River, 161; Lee's plan to trap McClellan at Glendale, 162; army sheltered at Harrison's Landing, 163; Lee uncertain of next move, 163, 165; McClellan is gone from Lee's front, 166; Stuart will watch him at Harrison's Landing, 168; Lee requests wagons for removal of Union wounded, 169; D. H. Hill will be in charge of POW exchange, 170; Robert Ould is new POW agent, 172; threatened a renewal of the offensive against Richmond, 175; Lee communicates with, 177; flag of truce violation, 178; McLaws ordered to pursue him, 179; McClellan leaving Harrison's Landing; 180, leaving the Peninsula to reinforce Pope, 181; a portion of army joined Pope, 183; Special Order 191, 196n25, 197, 197n27; Sharpsburg Campaign, 201; post-Sharpsburg lull, 205-206, 206n9, 215; rumor of another march on Richmond, 208; replaced as commander of AOP, 213; 216, 216n15
McClellan, Henry B., 207, 207n9, 336n46, 381, 398n9, 398n10
McCue, J. Marshall, 36, 316
McDonald, Angus, 63-64, 64n16
McDonald, Cornelia, 284n38
McDowell, Irvin, 22n45, 24, 25n56, 126, 140n61
McDowell, Virginia, battle of, 126, 131, 131n25, 136n41, 217, 210n28
McFarland, W.H., 229n28
McGowan, Samuel, 338n4, 381n22, 393, 477, 487
McGrath, William, 96n9
McGuire, Dr. Hunter, 161n66, 266-267, 271n40, 394, 394n70, 398
McGuire, Judith, 271

McKim, Randolph, 270, 274, 274n53
McLaws, Lafayette, 153n34, 165, 165n11, 167n15, 168, 177, 179, 197, 209, 211, 312, 314, 346n21, 388, 388n49, 399, 474; promoted by Lee after the Seven Days Battles, 163; lack of discipline in the army, 172; sent to North Anna, 182; Harpers Ferry operation, 195-196; Sharpsburg Campaign, 195n21, 197, 198, 198n30, 199; McClellan's quick moves, 196; post-Sharpsburg lull, 211n31, 212n34; Fredericksburg Campaign, 220n29, 227, 229n27; the quiet after Fredericksburg, 252n1; pickets on the lookout for enemy activity, 258; ordered to Fredericksburg, 260; Chancellorsville, 264-266, 266n21, 268; post-Chancellorsville, 270; Gettysburg, July 2, 293-294; retreat from Gettysburg, 298n37; winter of 1863-64, 345n14, 372n25; Overland Campaign, 383
McLean, Wilmer, 499
McNeill, Jesse, 475
McNeill, John, 316, 334, 458
McRae, William, 409
Meade, George G., 291n8, 313-314, 318, 320-321, 368, 418n30; replaces Hooker as commander of the ANV, 277; the march to Gettysburg, 287n4; AOP has moved into Maryland, 288; Gettysburg, July 4, 295; retreat from Gettysburg, 299; post-Gettysburg, 301-302, 304, 306; army moving toward Culpeper, 304; between the Rappahannock and Rapidan rivers, 315; Meade's summer 1863 operations, 316; Bristoe Station Campaign, 322-323, 326, 329; takes the offensive, 327; Rappahannock Station, battle of, 330-331; preparing another move toward Lee, 334, 338; Mine Run, 335, 336; calls off the Mine Run Campaign, 337; winter of 1863, 339; winter of 1863-64, 351, 352n10, 367n4, 369n16, 373-374; reply regarding Dahlgren papers, 371; Cooper sends copies of the Dahlgren papers to Lee, 365; Lee sends copies of the Dahlgren papers to Meade, 367; Overland Campaign, 376, 390n56, 397, 399n16; Petersburg Campaign, 413n6; requests a truce to bury the dead from the Crater, 422; army headed for Germanna and Ely's fords, 379; Appomattox Campaign, 498, 498n30, 500, 500n35
Meade, Richard K., 116, 116n24, 160, 161n64, 180, 180n18, 250
Meade, Bishop William, 18, 18n32, 19, 104, 104n24
Meadow Bluff, 66-67, 67n27, 68, 73-74
Mechanicsville, battle of, 145, 155-158, 172
Meem, Gilbert S., 36, 36n33, 40
Meem, John G., 18
Memminger, Christopher, 367, 367n7
Memminger, Robert W., 92
Meredith, Lee's valet, 49, 51, 72, 78, 84, 88, 96n10, 100, 102, 234n16, 246
Meriwether, Mrs. J.B., 236
Michelbacher, Rabbi Maximillian J., 58, 254, 437
Michigan Military Units: 16th Infantry, 171
Miles, William Porcher, 135, 156, 157n52, 465, 472
Milledgeville, Georgia, 119
Miller, John, 57
Mills, Thomas S., 452, 452n19
Milroy, Robert, 234, 231, 235, 237, 241, 271

Milton, John (Governor, Florida), 78, 98-99, 104, 115-116, 118, 120, 122-123, 128, 132, 311
Mine Run Campaign, 272n43, 326n6, 327, 332, 334-335, 335n43, 336-337, 376, 380n15, 380n118, 396, 445n23
Minnegerode, Rev. Charles, 360, 373, 492
Minnegerode, Lucy, 340, 459
Minor, Charles L. C., 123
Minor, Frances C., 123
Minor, George, 7, 7n18, 149
Mississippi Military Units: 3rd Infantry, 130; 10th Infantry, 38n40; 11th Infantry, 120, 333; 17th Infantry, 265; 18th Infantry, 294n19; 20th Infantry, 66n23, Jeff Davis Legion, 221, 342
Mitchell, John K., 439, 446-447
Mitchell, Julian, 307, 307n27
Mitchell, W.G., 399n16
Mobile, Alabama, 211
Moncure, Eustis C., 389, 390n55, 390n56, 390n57
Monitor, USS, 105, 135
Monocacy, battle of, 194n18
Monterey, Virginia, 53, 73
Moore, Alfred C., 45, 45n25
Moore, Andrew J., 64
Moore, John C., 139, 139n56
Moorman, Marcellus, 25, 25n56
Morgan, John Hunt, 346, 347, 361, 361n21, 413, 415-416, 420, 424, 442
Morgan, John T., 282, 283, 283n35, 487, 487n46
Morgantown, western Virginia, 203
Morris, Edmund T., 34, 34n25
Morris, Richard G., 31
Morrison, Emmett M., 29
Morrison, Joseph G., 435n11
Morrison, Dr. S.B., 32, 267
Morrison, William, 23
Morton, T.C., 68n30
Morton's Ford, 339, 350-351, 351n8, 352, 355n34
Mosby, John S., 178, 178n12, 247n18, 306-307, 332, 347, 347n26, 369, 409, 425, 425n11, 428, 442, 444-445, 447n31; vulnerability of McClellan's right flank, 151; capture of Edwin Stoughton, 247; Lee recommends he be promoted, 249; a skirmish, 250; Lee congratulates on promotion, 250; fight with 1st Vermont Cavalry, 254; the quiet after Fredericksburg, 256; post-Gettysburg, 301; Lee praises latest exploits, 325; winter of 1863-64, 348, 360, 368, 369n16; Lee congratulates on his successes, 437; captured Gen. Alfred Duffie, 447; authorized to hang prisoners from Custer's command, 454; the war's final winter, 457, 457n9, 470, 470n8, 474, 485; Appomattox Campaign, 503; excluded from Grant's surrender terms, 503n4
Moses, Raphael, 178n13, 190, 243, 366
"Mud March," 232
Mudd, Dr. Samuel, 82n33
Mulberry Island, Virginia, 104
Mule Shoe, 386-387
Munford, George W., 43, 106

Munford, Thomas, 150, 150n24, 192, 197-198, 198n30, 216, 409, 426, 452, 452n17
Murray, Edward, 231, 231n39, 239-240, 240n4, 308n35
Musser, William R., 36
Myers, A.C., 26n58, 108

Nash, Benjamin H., 426, 427n16
Nashville, battle of, 456
Nashville, Tennessee, 118
New Bern, North Carolina, 101, 104n25, 119, 139, 149, 233, 281, 344, 347, 352, 354, 354n24, 359, 415
New Hampshire Military Units: 12th Infantry, 267
New Market, battle of, 378, 387
New Mexico Campaign, 121
New Orleans, Louisiana, 131, 138
New York Military Units: 9th Cavalry, 184n36, 415n16; 12th Infantry, 181; 13th Infantry, 138, 210, 10n29; 93rd Infantry, 161n65; 121st Infantry, 494n19; 123rd Infantry, 266n20
Newport News, Virginia, 23, 25, 113
Nisbet, James, 200
Norfolk & Petersburg Railroad, 13n13, 20, 23, 130, 407
Norfolk & Petersburg Telegraph Co., 13n15, 130
Norfolk, Virginia, 6, 10, 14-15, 18-20, 20n37, 22, 106, 111, 113, 119, 123, 124n61, 125, 127-128, 132, 209, 226
Norris, Wesley, 311, 311n10
North Anna River, 213, 218, 225n8, 389-390, 390n55, 391-392, 392n64
North Anna River, battle of, 377-378, 391
North Carolina Military Units: 1st Artillery, 117, 200; 1st Cavalry, 151, 493n15; 1st Infantry, 23, 29, 274n52, 344n13; 2nd Cavalry, 121, 184, 430n31; 3rd Cavalry, 221, 420n38; 3rd Infantry, 274n52, 44n14; 4th Infantry, 500; 5th Infantry, 200; 6th Infantry, 44, 44n20; 16th Infantry, 60; 20th Infantry, 385n36; 24th Infantry, 72n16; 25th Infantry, 258n28; 26th Infantry, 134n34, 298, 374; 30th Infantry, 274n54; 33rd Infantry, 61n5; 37th Infantry, 297; 49th Infantry, 230n36; 53rd Infantry, 347n25; 55th Infantry, 344n16; 57th Infantry, 424, 435n11
North Carolina Railroad, 315n26, 479n8
Northeastern Railroad, 79, 79n17
Northrop, Lucius B., 26n58, 47, 47n35, 108, 122, 133, 178, 232, 232n1, 234, 237, 304, 332-333, 343-345, 346n18, 425, 459, 459n18, 474n30
Norwood, Thomas L., 297, 297n32

Oak Grove, battle of, 156, 156n50, 157n52
Oates, William, 292n11, 374n35
O'Donnell, Columbus, 194n20, 195n20
Ohio Military Units: 6th Infantry, 265n18; 17th Infantry, 264
Olmstead, Charles H., 55n19, 80, 80n22, 82n33, 97, 97n20
O'Neal, Edward, 282, 282n30, 283n35, 349, 349n36, 368
Orange & Alexandria Railroad, 3-4, 12, 16n24, 20-21, 41, 43, 217-218, 281n27, 323-324, 329, 442
Orange Turnpike, 280n19, 330, 330n19, 333n32, 380
Ord, Edward O.C., 476, 499, 502n42
O'Sullivan, John L., 283, 283n36

Otey, J.M., 438n27
Ould, Robert, 172, 172n37, 273, 316, 331, 449, 449n3, 452, 494n18, 503
Overland Campaign, 376-378, 380-382, 384-391, 393, 395, 403-404, 424
Owen, William, 200, 296n26
Ox Hill, battle of, 188, 192

Page, Mann, 444, 444n14
Page, Powhatan R., 8, 8n20, 11n2
Page Jr., Thomas J., 314n22
Paine, William G., 35
Palmer, John B., 465
Palmer, William H., 381n19, 382n24, 420, 490-491, 491n11, 496n24
Parker, Eli, 499
Parker's Store, 359, 380, 383
Parkersburg, Virginia, 43
Parks, Perry, (Lee's cook,) 2, 49, 51, 72, 78, 84, 87-88, 96n10, 100, 102, 204, 226, 234n15, 240n8, 242, 251n41, 252, 254, 318n2, 324, 351
Parks, William C., 34, 34n25
Patrick Henry CSS, 134n37
Patton, John M., 15
Paul, Samuel, 402-403, 403n29, 420
Paxton, Frank, 235, 235n17
Payne's Farm, Virginia, battle of, 272n43, 327, 335, 335n43
Pea Ridge, Arkansas, battle of, 131n24
peace delegation, 467
Peake, Benjamin F., 192
Pegram, John, 202, 307, 320, 321n16, 329, 361n23, 385, 425, 431, 461, 470-472, 472n16
Pegram, Willie, 386
Pelham, John, 166, 225, 228n20, 244, 244n4, 248n25, 248-250
Pemberton, John C., 79, 79n19, 92, 109, 116, 119, 127, 129, 129n15, 139, 262, 269n29, 291, 376; obstructions on the Combahee and Ashepoo rivers, 86; Lee orders reinforcements to, 88; Lee warns not to antagonize Drayton, 96, 96n9; promoted to major general, 97; Lee informs that steamer *John A. Moore* will run the blockade, 99; assumes command of Department of South Carolina, Georgia and East Florida, 102, 102n13; meets with Lee to discuss strategy, 102; troops being sent from South Carolina will be replaced, 105; hold Cole's Island in Charleston, 113, 114; Georgia troops be kept in service, 117; ordered to send a brigade from Charleston, 120; ordered to send Maxcy Gregg's brigade to Richmond, 120; privately-owned blockade runners free to carry any cargo, 121; Lee wants Virginia units in South Carolina sent back to Virginia, 123; Davis to declare martial law at Charleston, 124; Lee cannot send reinforcements to Charleston, 128; martial law in Savannah, 131, 131n26; setting up a POW exchange, 132; another brigade might be needed from Charleston, 133; Lee requests that Ripley be sent to Richmond, 137; ordered to send a brigade to Richmond, 138; Lee asks for status of defenses and troop morale, 140; no heavy artillery available, 141; Lawton wants to bring a brigade to Virginia, 148; Lee feels that ironclads cannot pass well-served land batteries, 148; people in South Carolina do not like him, 156, 157n52; ordered to send part of Hampton Legion to Virginia, 169; advised about Holmes's troop movements around Petersburg, 170; Pickens has continuing problems with, 178; deteriorating situation in the Western Theater, 261; Vicksburg, 303, 425n11; Petersburg Campaign, 425, 440, 440n37, 442
Pender, William Dorsey, 42n14, 147n12, 225, 235-236, 257n26, 258n27, 263, 267, 267n25, 272-274, 285, 294
Pendleton, Sandie, 166n13, 269, 272, 331, 380
Pendleton, William N., 16, 16n23, 48n38, 146, 160, 166n13, 168n18, 186, 194, 197, 209-211, 215, 233, 247, 249, 256, 258, 278-279, 279n13, 290n2, 304, 325, 333, 367, 417, 446; continues as chief of artillery, 147; ordered to place as many guns as possible along the lines, 155; ordered to send extra artillery to Richmond, 167; Pendleton to shell McClellan's army from the south side of the James River, 173; recent night attack on the James, 177; artillery ordered to return to main army, 179-180; division of the army at Gordonsville, 181; sets artillery covering the Potomac River, 198; Sharpsburg Campaign, 199, 201, 201n44, 202; post-Sharpsburg lull, 206, 206n8, 208; Fredericksburg Campaign, 217, 218, 220-221, 27; 1862; Christmas holiday dinner, 224; 1862 winter quarters, 230; Hayfield, 244; proposed reorganization of the artillery, 244n2; the quiet after Fredericksburg, 254; Lee notifies about enemy crossing at Deep Run, 259; post-Chancellorsville, 275; Lee's planning meeting for the move north, 280; the march to Gettysburg, 283, 285-286; Gettysburg, July 1, 293; Gettysburg, July 2, 293, 93n14; retreat from Gettysburg, 298; Meade's summer 1863 operations, 314n22, 316n29; Bristoe Station Campaign, 322, 329; Rappahannock Station, battle of, 331; inspection of the horse depot in Lynchburg, 353; winter of 1863-64, 359, 359n13, 367, 373, 73n31, 374n35; Overland Campaign, 379, 390n57, 394n70, 403, 403n30; build a road parallel to the Brock Road, 383; Petersburg Campaign, 417n24, 419-420, 424, 431, 431n35, 437, 439, 445, 445n20, 452, 453; the Crater, 421, 421n42, 422, 422n45; the war's final winter, 458, 460, 464-465, 467, 471, 474, 474n29, 483, 486; Fort Stedman, 484; Appomattox Campaign, 490, 490n7, 491, 495n22, 496n22, 497; Sailors Creek, battle of, 494n18; tells Lee time for surrender is at hand, 495, 495n22; ordered to carry out the surrender, 499
Pennsylvania Military Units: 1st Reserves, 381n19; 4th Cavalry, 165; 6th Cavalry, 139; 11th Cavalry, 287; 11th Infantry, 210, 210n29; 67th Infantry, 387n44
Pensacola & Georgia Railroad, 87
Perrin, Abner, 386
Perrin, James L., 24
Perry, Edward, 216-217, 341, 434
Petersburg & Weldon Railroad, 79n17, 109, 138-139, 170, 315, 407, 409, 416, 418, 423, 427n19, 428, 428n24, 429, 430n31, 436, 445n23, 456-458
Petersburg Campaign, 136, 397, 397n5, 401n22, 402-403, 403n31, 405-406, 406n38, 407, 411-413, 419n32, 428, 477
Petersburg, Virginia, 242, 380, 397, 400-401, 406n39, 407n42, 408

Pettigrew, Johnston, 123, 269, 272, 278, 298, 298n37, 299
Peyton, Henry, 205, 207, 207n11, 435, 435n14
Peyton, Dr. Robert, 364, 372n29, 409, 446
Peyton, Nannette Lee, 207, 372
Phelan, James (Senator, Mississippi), 355
Philippi, battle of, 29n9, 35n29, 41
Phillips, Dr. Dinwiddie B., 28
Pickens, Francis (Governor, South Carolina), 81, 81n25, 85, 87-88, 91, 91n8, 113, 135, 140, 154, 171, 178, 229
Pickett, George E., 67n29, 208n17, 248, 248n26, 249, 268-269, 269n30, 270n37, 278n10, 306, 312-313, 315; promoted to major general, 215; Fredericksburg Campaign, 227; criticizes condition of his division, 236; division and the Suffolk Campaign, 239n2; Richmond, 241-242; division sent to North Carolina, 254; Seddon's plan to send to Vicksburg, 269, 269n29; post-Chancellorsville, 273; the march to Gettysburg, 278, 278n11, 279, 281, 286, 287n49, 289n57; Gettysburg, July 1, 292; Gettysburg, July 3, 294-295; retreat from Gettysburg, 296-297; post-Gettysburg, 305; Meade's summer 1863 operations, 314n23; Mine Run, 334; winter of 1863-64, 347, 351, 354, 354n24, 359n10, 366, 369-370; Overland Campaign, 383, 390-391, 405, 405n37; ordered to fill abandoned lines at Bermuda Hundred, 403, 403n31, 404-405; Petersburg Campaign, 407, 409n49, 415, 416n18, 417n23, 419-420, 425-426, 426n13, 427, 428n24, 430, 430n32, 431n34, 438-440, 446, 451, 453; the war's final winter, 458, 465, 478, 483n27, 486; Five Forks, 488, 488n1, 488n2, 490; Appomattox Campaign, 496n24; removed from command, 496
Piedmont Railroad, 211, 315, 315n26, 463, 464n13, 465, 479, 479n8
Piedmont, battle of, 16n24, 399, 401n21
Pierpont, Francis, 372
Pifer, Augustus, 222
Pike, Albert, 131, 131n24
Pillow, Gideon, 118n31
Pitzer, Andrew L., 332
Plank Road, 334-335, 368n9, 382, 382n25
Platt, Rev. William H., 413n8, 415, 419, 422n45, 471
Poague, William, 160n61, 200n40, 293, 294n16, 295n22, 381-382, 382n23, 387n47, 491, 491n10, 495n22, 496
Podestad, Louis de, 131
Point Lookout operation, 411, 411n2, 413, 413n8, 414, 415n15
Point of Rocks, engagement at, 194n17
Polk, Leonidas, 42, 61n5, 374, 374n36, 403, 403n30
Pollard, James, 361
Pope, John, 163, 171, 173, 173n42, 181n22, 182, 318, 322n18, 401; Jackson and Hill join to attack him, 172; commands Army of Virginia, 175; Jackson beats Pope at Brawner Farm, 175; Jackson beats Pope at Cedar Mountain, 175; Lee orders Jackson to suppress him, 175; Second Manassas Campaign, 176, 183n29; Jackson's reluctance to attack, 178; communications disrupted by Stuart, 179; Catlett's Station, 183, 183n32; crushed by Longstreet's attack, 186; left flank in the air, 186; requests a truce, 187; ends advance, retreats to Washington, 188; removal of Union wounded at Manassas, 192
Port Royal, Virginia, 79, 79n18, 88, 91, 225, 228
Porter, Fitz John, 145, 148n15, 153n38, 162n69
Porter, Horace, 376
Porterfield, George, 13, 16, 19,-20, 22, 24, 29n9, 32, 35n29, 37, 41, 41n7
Portsmouth, Virginia, 132
Posey, Carnot, 215, 299
Post, Dr. William M., 58, 59n42
Powell, Charles L., 356, 356n35
Powell, John L., 57
Prentiss, Benjamin, 118
Preston, J.T.L., 16, 16n23, 40
Preston, John S., 45n23, 85, 345
Preston, Robert T., 17, 17n28
Preston, Rev. Thomas, 37
Price, Sterling, 396
Primrose, Cicero, 117
Pryor, Judge Robertson, 3n9
Pryor, Roger A., 34, 34n27, 38, 123, 215, 216-217, 221, 221n34, 222, 259n32, 455, 455n36, 462, 477, 477n5, 491n12

Raccoon Ford, 280, 332, 332n26
Radford, R.C.W., 16, 32
Raily, Gooch, 220, 220n32
Raines, George, 97, 98
Ramsay, John, 200
Ramseur, Stephen D., 279, 307, 311, 363, 364n37, 386, 395, 399
Ramsey, James, 54, 55n19, 56
Randolph, Charles, 354
Randolph, George, 111, 117, 120, 150-153, 154n39, 162, 167, 168n21, 178, 179n16, 180, 183, 203, 203n53, 204, 206n9, 207, 207n9, 207n13, 209, 211, 215-216, 218, 218n22, 218n24, 309, 312n13; appointed secretary of war, 107; Lee, Davis, Johnston meeting, 117n27; Johnston plans to withdraw to Williamsburg, 127; Turner Ashby's cavalry, 130; Lee feels McClellan reinforced by Burnside and troops from Halleck's army, 154; can Cobb still manage the POW exchange, 169; Lee complains about details sent from the army, 169; Lee asks that newspapers not print sensitive information, 173; Lee meets regarding Beverly Robertson and "Grumble" Jones, 179; Lee forwards the colors of the 12th New York, 181, McClellan is leaving the Peninsula, 181; send D.H. Hill's command to Lee's army, 182; update on the Campaign, 194; Sharpsburg Campaign, 202; post-Sharpsburg lull, 206; Lee sends flags of the 11th Pennsylvania and 103rd New York, 210
Ransom, Matt, 457, 481
Ransom, Robert, 150, 216, 225n9, 233, 233n5, 270, 271n42, 278n10, 282, 321, 321n14, 348, 420, 420n39, 430, 431n34; poor behavior from the 2nd NC Cavalry, 121; brigade ordered to Fredericksburg, 123; ordered to Drewry's Bluff, 149; ordered to move to Drewry's Bluff, 150; ordered to harass enemy shipping at Drewry's Bluff, 153; enemy assault at Oak Grove, 156; Oak Grove, 157n52;

Fredericksburg Campaign, 227; 1862 winter quarters, 230; G.W. Smith's fitness to command, 237; gets a division in North Carolina, 241; post-Chancellorsville, 270n37, 273-274; winter of 1863-64, 354n24; Overland Campaign, 399n15; Petersburg Campaign, 425

Rappahannock Station, battle of, 216, 247, 257, 304, 304n7, 323n23, 326, 329-331, 331n23

Reagan, Postmaster General John, 135n37, 141, 222, 270n38, 273n49, 398, 398n9, 399, 399n11, 420n38, 428, 428n22

Ream's Station, battle of, 430, 430n31, 430n32, 431, 435

Reynolds, Joseph J., 54-55, 64, 65n20

Rhett, Mathilda, 82

Rhett, Thomas G., 25, 138, 173

Rich Mountain, battle of, 44, 53

Richards, Adolphus "Dolly," 425n11

Richards, Thomas W., 425, 425n11

Richardson, George, 44

Richardson, John H., 203n49, 222, 450, 450n7

Richardson, William H., 4, 7n18, 44

Richmond & Danville Railroad, 5n14, 6n15, 13, 38, 315n26, 401, 407-409, 409n49, 414-415, 415n13, 417n22, 418, 429, 479, 479n8, 490-491

Richmond & Petersburg Railroad, 20, 38, 79n17, 404, 406-407, 492n14

Richmond & York River Railroad, 31, 35, 35n28, 42, 128-132, 128n10, 148-149, 149n19, 155, 399n15

Richmond, CSS, 181, 194, 257

Richmond *Dispatch*, 168, 182, 194, 201, 209, 226, 231n39, 260

Richmond *Enquirer* 153, 159

Richmond *Examiner*, 70

Richmond *Whig*, 183

Richmond Arsenal, 36, 115, 123

Richmond, Fredericksburg & Potomac Railroad, 6, 14, 43, 122, 217-218, 226, 226n12, 247n20, 248, 266, 271, 324, 329, 390, 390n57, 392n63

Ripley, Roswell, 79, 79n18, 82, 85, 88, 179, 473n23; reports enemy advance on his front, 82n30; concerned about enemy incursions on coastal islands, 83; construction of river defenses and obstructions, 86; enemy sank ships loaded with stone in the Charleston ship channel, 87; river obstructions, 88; friction between Lee and Ripley, 91; Lee reminds that the field commander must make judgments, 92; spies are planning to burn railroad bridges, 93; enemy landed on Edisto Island, 97; Lee tells to construct casemates around the water batteries, 98; a floating battery in Charleston, 107; allowed to issue furloughs to Hagood's brigade, 116; dispute with Pemberton, 135; Lee requests that Pemberton send Ripley to Richmond, 137; ordered into the fight, 158; commands D.H. Hill's former division, 179n17; ordered to Hanover Junction, 182; winter of 1863-64, 367n7

Rivas, A.L., 171

Rives, A.S., 109

Rives, Alfred M., 29n8

Rives, M.S., 250

Rives, William C., 271

Roberts, William P., 430n31

Robertson, Beverly, 173, 179, 193, 193n15, 272, 275, 304

Robertson, Francis, 40n4, 298n36, 40n4

Robertson, Jerome, 345n14

Robertson, Judge John, 3, 3n9, 4

Robinson, Cary, 339, 339n10, 340, 354

Rocketts Landing, 22n45

Rockwell, J.E., 433, 433n4

Rodes, Robert, 198n31, 266-267, 274n54, 281, 379, Chancellorsville, 268; post-Chancellorsville, 273-274; the march to Gettysburg, 282n30, 283n35, 284; Gettysburg, July 1, 292; Gettysburg, July 2, 293, 293n12; post-Gettysburg, 306-307, 307n27; reviewing Ewell's corps, 312; Bristoe Station Campaign, 329; post-Rappahannock Station, 332, 332n26; winter of 1863, 339; potential commander for southwest Virginia, 348; winter of 1863-64, 351-353, 355, 363; Overland Campaign, 384-386, 386n39, 400n17; Petersburg Campaign, 432, 437n25; death of, 437

Roller, P.S., 215

Roman, Alfred, 406, 406n38, 406n39

Romancoke, (Rooney Lee's estate), 30n10, 125, 331, 348, 444

Rosecrans, William S., 68n30, 70, 73, 73n19, 77, 249, 314

Ross, Fitzgerald, 288, 297, 342

Rosser, Thomas, 162, 340, 342, 347-348, 351, 351n7, 371, 374, 420, 420n39, 438, 444, 452, 452n17, 457-458, 464, 481-482, 488n1

Ruffin, Edmund, 18, 18n32, 29n7, 117n26, 132n31, 137n46, 138n52, 139, 152

Ruffin, Jr., Edmund, 23, 32, 32n18

Ruggles, Daniel, 5, 13-15, 17, 18n31, 23, 28, 31n14, 49, 49n45, 374

Rush, Benjamin, 139

Rust, Albert, 62n11, 63n14, 64, 64n19, 64n20, 78

Rust, Armistead T. M., 8n19

Ruth, Samuel, 226n12

Sackett, William, 415, 415n16

Sailors Creek, battle of, 488, 488n2, 494, 494n18, 494n19

Salem Church, battle of, 261, 266n21, 267

Saltville, battle of, 446

Sandford, Charles W., 22

Saunders, Bettie, 321n15, 491-492, 492n14

Savage's Station, battle of, 149n19, 161, 161n66, 162, 172

Savannah, (privateer), 41

Savannah, CSS, 80n22

Savannah, Georgia, 80, 90, 94, 131n26, 211, 247, 347, 456, 458-459

Sayre, William, 139

Scales, Alfred, 301, 344n18, 372, 402n28, 452n19

Scary Creek, engagement at, 47n36

Scheibert, Justus, 255, 255n13, 255n15, 257, 263n11, 265, 265n18, 265n20, 266n20, 269, 282, 294

Schofield, John, 468, 473-475, 480-482

Scott, Benjamin I., 241, 241n11, 242, 254, 257n23

Scott, Mrs. Fannie, 241-242, 254, 257, 257n23

Scott, Winfield, 1-2, 2n5, 3, 6, 8, 14, 14n16

Seaboard & Roanoke Railroad, 132
Seawall, John T., 20
Seddon, James, 220n30, 222, 225-226, 229n28, 231, 233-237, 242, 246, 250, 258, 269, 269n30, 275, 278, 282, 299, 301, 304, 305n11, 308n30, 312, 314, 322, 324, 330, 346, 351-353, 364, 373, 384, 388, 388n49, 389-390, 390n57, 391-392, 392n63, 393, 398-401, 403, 405, 405n38, 407-408, 408n45, 409, 413, 415n13, 416, 418, 420, 422, 424-425, 425n8, 426-431, 435-438, 440, 442-443, 445-447, 451, 452-455, 457-458, 461, 463, 465, 466n26, 472n16; Fredericksburg Campaign, 227-228;
post-Fredericksburg, 230; complaint about William "Grumble," Jones, 240; supply difficulties, 241; enemy moving down the Potomac, 243; Lee forwards orders received from Hooker regarding POW's, 249; supply difficulties, 250; broached idea to send Longstreet to Tennessee, 254n11; Virginia Central must be repaired, 254; short of rations making troops sick, 256; Chancellorsville, 267, 267n24, 268; death of Stonewall Jackson, 269; Lee advises of Milroy's movement at Front Royal, 271; large number of desertions from North Carolina units, 272; POW paroles, 273; enemy troops at Urbana, 279; Lee announces a major enemy offensive in Charleston, 321; Bristoe Station Campaign, 328; deserters, 328; Rappahannock Station, battle of, 331; Lee considers impressment to provision the army, 332; winter of 1863, 341; winter of 1863-64, 344, 355n32, 360-361, 369n16, 374; Lee's continuing supply problem, 347; plan to have several officers to recruit partisan units, 348; wants military courts reinstated, 363; officer examination boards, 367; Lee complains about a lack of supplies, 369; Lee recommends using Navy machinery to make railroad rolling stock, 371; need to keep the Virginia Central Railroad open, 413; Charles Talcott is doing nothing to repair the Richmond & Danville, 415; updates Early's operations, 417; victories in the Valley by Rosser and Mosby, 444; there needs to be a change in the Valley cavalry, 448; the war's final winter, 459; the army is out of meat, 464; the war's final winter, 466; Lee's nomination as general in chief, 467n30; resigned from office, replaced by Breckinridge, 468, 470, 470n7
Seddon, Thomas, 299
Sedgwick, John, 183n31, 261, 265n19, 266-267, 321, 353, 372
Segar, John F., 21
Selden, Joseph, 20
Selden, Dr. William B., 210n26, 494n19
Semmes, Raphael, 471, 471n12, 471n13, 483-484
Seven Days Campaign, 145, 147n13, 163, 167, 167n15, 169, 169n25, 175, 177, 180-181, 207, 210n26, 211n30, 246, 254-255, 271
Seven Pines/Fair Oaks, battle of, 141, 144, 148, 153n38
Seward, Secretary of State William, 2n5, 462
Sewell Mountain, 60, 67, 67n28, 68, 71-73, 75
Seymour, William J., 322n20
Shands, William B., 17
Sharp, Thomas, 237, 237n27

Sharpsburg, Maryland, battle of, 61n5, 79n18, 188-190, 197-198, 198n31, 199, 199n33, 199n34, 200, 200n40, 206, 208, 210n29, 241, 257, 260, 382n23
Sheffey, Judge H. W., 23, 24, 24n52
Shenandoah Valley, Virginia, and Campaigns, 8, 12, 189, 203, 205, 209, 215-219, 221, 226, 230-231, 235-236, 239, 239n2, 246, 256-257, 272, 274, 276, 281, 283, 291, 291n8, 299-300, 300n47, 301, 305, 307, 316, 323, 329, 332, 339-340, 344-345, 351-353, 354n24, 364, 364n39, 367, 370-372, 374, 378-381, 383, 385, 387-388, 392, 394n70, 395, 397, 399-402, 406, 411, 413n8, 417-418, 419n36, 420, 423, 423n1, 424-426, 428, 432-433, 436-439, 441-444, 446, 448, 453-454, 456-457, 459, 461, 470, 479,482, 485
Shepherdstown, 198, 200, 206n8, 208
Sheridan, Philip, 369n16, 377-378, 401, 406, 408, 423, 426, 430-443; Overland Campaign, 386n42, 388, 391, 404; heading to the Valley, 400; Trevilian Station, 402, 402n27; Petersburg Campaign, 414, 437-438; army arrives from the Valley, 478; the war's final winter, 478-479, 479n7, 482; arrives in Charlottesville, 480; will join Grant at Petersburg, 484; Five Forks, 488n1; Appomattox Campaign, 492-493, 494n18, 498-499; blocks the road west, 497
Sherman, Thomas W., 79n18
Sherman, William T., 411, 424, 449, 450, 453n26, 454-456, 458, 462-463, 465, 468, 470, 472-475, 475n31, 476, 478-479, 480-482, 484, 485
Shields, James, 148
Shiloh, battle of, 111
Shirley Plantation, 78n14, 78n15
Shomo, Jacob, 369, 370n17
Shorter, John G., (Governor, Alabama), 123, 127, 152
Shriver, R.K., 202
Sibley, Henry H., 121, 121n47, 141
Sickles, Daniel, 172n37
Sigel, Franz, 251, 373n31, 378, 387-388, 397
Skaggs, John F., 251
Skeen, William, 46
Slash Church, battle of, 148n15, 153, 153n34
Slaughter, Montgomery, 219-220, 220n29
Smith, Charles W., 32, 32n19, 165n10
Smith, Edmund Kirby, 104-105, 150, 206, 212n37, 213, 237, 503; hold all available troops in Chattanooga, 107; notification that regiments from Georgia enroute, 108; Lee warns of disloyalty of population in east Tennessee, 110; Lee approves his defensive measures, 114; martial law will be declared in east Tennessee, 115; Davis wants him to remain in command in east Tennessee, 116; authorized to move against Nashville, 117; planned move against Nashville, 118; ordered to send captured troops to Milledgeville, Georgia, 119; weapons being sent to him, 123; available troops in North Carolina and Alabama to join him, 127; instructed to make sure public supplies pass through Knoxville, 129; ordered to ship weapons to Georgia, 134; status of troops sent him from Georgia and Alabama, 140; have Alabama and Georgia have arrived, 148; no heavy artillery available to him, 149; unarmed regiments sent to him, 151; reinforcements being sent,

154; Lee suggests he move into Kentucky with Bragg, 172; victory at Richmond, Kentucky, 194
Smith, Francis H., 3, 7n18, 11n4, 17, 17n28, 23n48, 33, 40-41, 44, 141, 211, 373, 413, 413n9
Smith, Francis L., 493n15
Smith, Francis W., 10, 18n32, 19, 19n35, 20, 20n38, 23, 23n47, 24, 42-43, 43n19, 121, 121n48
Smith, George W., 106, 108, 117, 117n27
Smith, Gustavus W., 111, 131, 141-142, 146, 14610n, 147, 147n13, 170, 194, 198n33, 203, 209-212, 215-216, 218n22, 218n24, 220-222, 225, 233, 236, 242, 249n27; illness, 151; ordered to stay in Richmond to recover his health, 155; Lee suggests he replace Pemberton, 178; returns to duty, 180; placed in command around Richmond, 181; McLaws and D.H. Hill to North Anna, 182; send reserve artillery to Lee, 182; Lee needs troops asap, 183; covering force for wounded at Gordonsville, 196; gather wounded at Warrenton, 198; post-Sharpsburg lull, 206-207; Fredericksburg Campaign, 218-219; enemy transports at Norfolk, 226-227; Wilmington, 228; Lee removes from command, 232; resigned his commission, 232n2, 243; fitness to command, 237
Smith, Isaac N., 67n28, 69
Smith, James P., 259, 259n34, 263, 265n18, 288
Smith, Martin L., 120n40, 129n15, 365, 368, 368n11, 370, 385, 391-392, 418n28
Smith, W.A., 42
Smith, William D., 156, 157n52
Smith, William P., 255, 255n14
Smith, William, "Extra Billy," 45, 173, 271, 321n16, 380n17, 438, 438n29, 444-445, 472, 476, 481, 484
Smith's Farm, engagement at, 45
Snicker's Gap, 216, 299
Snicker's Gap, engagement at, 418
The Society of the Cincinnati, 19n34
Soldiers Relief Association in Charleston, 85-86
Sorrel, Francis, 94n5, 95n5, 9610n
Sorrel, G. Moxley, 187n44, 200n38, 298, 361n21, 382-383, 383, 409, 410n53, 440n36, 440n37, 443n9, 445, 496n23
South Carolina Military Units: 1st Rifles, 119, 120n44; 2nd Cavalry, 471; 2nd Infantry, 24, 238n35; 4th Cavalry, 76; 4th Infantry, 35n29; 5th Infantry, 427; 10th Infantry, 79n19; 12th Infantry, 85; 13th Infantry, 85; 14th Infantry, 85n11; 15th Infantry, 89; Hampton Legion, 169; Hart's Battery, 328; Palmetto Sharpshooters, 169n25
South Carolina Railroad, 98
South Mills, North Carolina, 119-123
South Mountain, battle of, 16n23, 188, 195-196, 197n29, 198n30, 199
Southern Historical Society, 46n29
Southside Railroad, 35, 397, 401, 408, 444, 454n28, 480n15, 486, 488, 490, 493
Sparrow, Edward, 249, 249n28
Special Order 146, 275
Special Order 191, 195, 195n21, 196, 196n25, 197, 197n27, 289n57

Speed, John M., 19
Spotsylvania Court House, battle of, 335, 377, 383, 383n28, 383n29, 384-385, 385n37, 390n55, 396
St. John, Isaac, 495n20, 474, 474n30, 479, 493-494
Stacy, G.B., 87
Stafford, Leroy, 320, 353, 381
Stanton, Edwin, 403
Starke, William E., 65, 65n21
Staunton River Bridge, engagement at, 408, 409n49, 417
Staunton, Virginia, 64, 68, 71, 206n9, 210, 218, 231, 236, 247, 279-280, 283, 301, 305, 340-341, 371, 379, 397, 401, 401n21, 479, 479n7
Stephens, Alexander (Confederate vice president), 5, 5n13, 467n32, 472
Stephenson's Depot, 190n9, 203n52, 205
Steuart, George H., 32n18, 150, 150n24, 202, 204, 209-210, 274, 274n52, 274n53, 344n15, 386, 425, 425n12, 430, 431n34, 431n37
Stevens, Walter H., 130, 130n22, 315, 365, 405, 418n28; ordered to lay out a line of defenses, 147; Lee approves plan for fortified line around Richmond, 148; Lee's railroad gun, 149; to lay out defenses for Wise at Chaffin's Bluff, 154; ordered to layout defenses in Petersburg, 177; Petersburg Campaign, 438; Appomattox Campaign, 494n18
Stevenson, Carter L., 46, 46n30, 49n43, 96
Stewart, John, 101n7, 138, 138n52
Stewart, Rev. Kensey Johns, 447, 447n29
Stewart, William, 287n52
Stiles, Elizabeth Mackay, 102-103, 301, 301n48, 334, 484
Stiles, Henry, 234
Stiles, Kitty, 77
Stiles, Robert, 265n19
Stiles, William, 86, 86n17
Stoughton, Edwin, 247, 247n18
Strasburg, Virginia, 13, 216, 229, 340
Stringfellow, Frank, 374, 446, 447n29
Stuart, Alexander H. H., 49, 49n45
Stuart, Caroline, 311-312, 314, 333, 362, 362n29
Stuart, George Washington, 268, 270
Stuart, James E.B. "Jeb," 45, 54n15, 138, 140n61, 151, 159, 167, 167n14, 168n19, 182, 182n28, 186, 194, 194n19, 208, 208n14, 217, 225, 227n19, 230n31, 234n12, 237, 240, 247, 248n25, 250, 257-258, 263n11, 290n2, 314, 320, 321, 321n16, 362, 379n13, 447n29; a large number of transports are headed down the Potomac, 114; reports McClellan's right flank was vulnerable, 144; Lee consolidates cavalry under Stuart, 150; almost complete circuit of McClellan's army, 153n36; needs help from Lee, 153; will picket in front of Chaffin's Bluff, 154; Lee congratulates for his ride around McClellan, 155; reports enemy is destroying the York River Railroad, 160; news that White House has been destroyed, 161; promoted by Lee after the Seven Days Battles, 163; giving chase to McClellan, 166; McClellan is at Harrison's Landing, 166; Lee will withdraw closer to Richmond, let Stuart watch McClellan, 168; Lee orders to send some units to Gordonsville, 171; Lee congratulates Stuart on his

promotion, 173; reorganized the cavalry, 173; P.M.B. Young, 177n5; disrupt Pope's communications, 179; ordered to work with Jackson, 179; division of the army at Gordonsville, 181; how to strike Pope, 182; Kelly's Ford, 182; ordered to move on August 19, 182; Catlett's Station, 183, 183n32, 184; Second Manassas Campaign, 183n33, 184-185, 191n11; Jackson's situation at Groveton, 185; Lee's horse "Lucy Long," 191; Ox Hill, 192; crosses the Potomac, 193n15; Lee's plan to cross the Potomac, 193; Sharpsburg Campaign, 194n18, 197n27, 198, 198n32, 199n35, 201; enemy advancing on Frederick, 196; enemy advancing quickly on South Mountain, 196; word of Federals arriving in Sharpsburg, 199; victory at Martinsburg, 206; post-Sharpsburg lull, 207, 210-211; nearly captured around Leetown, 209; Lee commends for recent activity, 210; Fredericksburg Campaign, 216, 221, 223, 227-228, 228n20, 233-234; captured flags, 225n7; Leeds Ferry action, 225; post-Fredericksburg, 230; reviews Rooney's brigade, 236; the quiet after Fredericksburg, 239, 239n2, 252, 256; ordered to take command in the Valley, 241; Hayfield, 244; Lee compliments on action at Kelly's Ford, 251; visits Lee at Belvoir, 254; from Stuart, enemy cavalry in force around Warrenton, 258; pickets on the lookout for enemy activity, 258; large enemy force crossing Kelly's Ford, 259; three enemy corps moving toward Germanna and Ely's fords, 259; Chancellorsville, 260, 263, 265, 265n18, 265n20, 266, 266n20, 267-268; death of Stonewall Jackson, 269; post-Chancellorsville, 270n37, 271-275; alerts Stuart, enemy planning another raid, 273; a potential cavalry raid, 275; Brandy Station, 276, 279n18, 281; ride around Hooker's/Meade's army, 277, 284-285, 288, 289n59, 292; the march to Gettysburg, 278, 280, 284n39; Lee's planning meeting for the move north, 280n20; Lee has no word from, 288; Gettysburg, July 1, 292n9; finally arrives in Gettysburg, 294, 294n18; Gettysburg, July 4, 295n25; retreat from Gettysburg, 297-298, 298n36, 299-300, 300n46; post-Gettysburg, 304, 306; reviewing Ewell's corps, 312; Meade's summer 1863 operations, 315; Bristoe Station Campaign, 322, 322n19, 324, 328, 328n12; Lee congratulates for victory at Buckland, 323; Lee writes praising Mosby, 325; Lee and Davis reviews Stuart's Cavalry at Brandy Station, 328; post-Rappahannock Station, 332; Mine Run, 334-335, 335n42, 335n44, 336; rumors Lee was going to replace Bragg, 337; warns Lee of Meade's army's movement, 338; winter of 1863, 339-340, 340n15, 341; winter of 1863-64, 347, 347n26, 348-349, 351, 355, 359, 365, 365n40, 368, 368n8, 368n9, 369-372; Overland Campaign, 376, 379-380, 380n15, 381n20, 384, 387n45, 388n48; wounded at Yellow Station, 386, 377-378; Tapp Farm, 381; finds Federals moving toward Chancellorsville, 383; death of, 386, 386n42, 387n43, 388; no successor is appointed, 387; order announcing his death, 389; Lee did not immediately appoint a replacement for, 413n7

Stuart, Julia C, 362
Stuart, Margaret (cousin), 240, 301, 309, 311-312, 312n13, 313, 313n18, 342, 362, 364, 368, 374
Stuart, Dr. Richard, 82, 82n33

Stuart, T.S., 32
Stuart, William, 49, 49n43
Stump, George W., 328, 328n10
Suesserott, Dr. J.L., 288
Suffolk, Virginia, 242, 252n4, 255, 257-259, 261, 272, 274n52
Sumner, Edwin V., 237n29, 250, 250n37
Sutherland's Station, 486, 486n43, 486n44
Sutherlin, William T., 35
Swift Run Gap, 129
Swinburne, Dr. John, 167
Sydnor, T.W., 156, 157

Talcott, Andrew, 5, 5n15, 6n15, 8, 13, 15, 17, 20n39, 21-22, 22n45, 23n47, 24, 28-29, 29n9, 30, 30n10, 36n32, 37-38, 40, 40n4, 45, 48, 57, 87, 87n18, 105n31, 112, 119, 414, 415, 415n13, 417n22
Talcott, Thomas Mann Randolph, 6n15, 21, 21n42, 112, 119, 123, 132, 146n11, 192, 197, 227n16, 256, 256n8, 257, 263, 263n10, 263n11, 300, 300n46, 367, 367n4, 391, 408, 409n49, 418, 460, 460n28, 494n19, 496n23, 499-500
Taliaferro, C.C., 381, 384n34, 498n29, 499n32
Taliaferro, William B., 13, 13n14, 15, 15n21, 17, 20-21, 23, 29, 35n29, 222, 235, 235n17, 254
Tapp Field, 381n20, 381n22, 382-383, 383n28, 385n38
Tattnall, Josiah, 80, 80n22, 93, 95, 102, 124n61
Tayloe, Edward, 445n23, 451-452
Taylor, Algermon S., 12, 12n11, 15
Taylor, Elizabeth, 306
Taylor, Erasmus, 181, 181n25, 304n8, 307
Taylor, John C., 127n9
Taylor, Richard, 160, 160n62, 172, 206, 440n35, 475, 480, 483, 503
Taylor, Robert, 453, 453n24
Taylor, Walter H., 6n16, 10n1, 13n13, 26, 27n1, 53n12, 54n15, 54n16, 63, 64n20, 66-67, 74-75, 79, 79n19, 86, 94n5, 96, 102, 108, 125, 127, 127n9, 132n27, 161, 161n66, 181, 182n25, 187n44, 189, 195n21, 195n22, 196n23, 203n52, 233n9, 240, 248n26, 259n34, 261, 289n57, 290n1, 294, 303, 304n6, 307n28, 315, 315n25, 316, 321n15, 321n17, 322n19, 323n23, 333, 377, 379, 406, 446n28, 457; joins Lee's staff, 10; Lee's aide de camp, 12; assigned to Lee's headquarters, 14; shares a tent with Lee, 39, 52; departs for western Virginia, 49; western Virginia, 51; Cheat Mountain, 54; death of John Washington, 60; Washington's death, 65n21; Deitz farm, 67n27; White Sulphur Springs, 74n29; departs for Charleston, 78; AAG Department of South Carolina, Georgia and East Florida, 79; promoted to captain, 86, 86n13, 89; to Richmond with Lee, 100; looking for quarters for Lee, 103n17; assumed many of Washington's duties, 112; requests office supplies, 115-116; promoted to major, 119; letter to Johnston regarding having signed Lee's orders, 130; signs Lee's orders, 130; enemy ships in the James River at City Point, 131; Lee's staff, 132; issues SO22 announcing Lee as commander of ANV, 146; remains with Lee when he assumes command of the ANV, 146n11; escorted Kearny's body, 192n13; has to meet Davis and prevent him from going to Maryland, 195; rejoins Lee, 198;

Sharpsburg Campaign, 199n33; post-Sharpsburg lull, 205; death of Lee's daughter Annie, 211n32; named AAG for the ANV, 221, 221n33; Lee's winter quarters, 223n2, 224; visits Mary Lee, 226n12; Lee's letter of recommendation, 233; several hours going over the strength of the army, 242; Gettysburg, July 1, 292; Meade's summer 1863 operations, 315n28; Bristoe Station Campaign, 324, 324n31, 325n32, 329; Lee's staff butting heads, 326; Rappahannock Station, battle of, 330n17, 330n19, 331; post-Rappahannock Station, 332; Mine Run, 334, 335n42; winter of 1863, 338n3, 338n7, 339-340, 340n15, 341, 341n22, 342; does not like Chilton, 341n23; promoted to lieutenant colonel, 346; winter of 1863-64, 349n34, 352, 352n13, 355, 355n28, 355n34, 356n35, 359n9, 359n10, 361, 362n25, 364, 367n6, 374, 374n34; hears of Grant commanding the AOP, has low opinion of, 362; Overland Campaign, 381, 383n28, 383n29, 384, 384n34, 393n68, 394n70, 394n72, 395n74, 395n75, 398n6, 398n7, 401n22, 404n31, 406n39; Petersburg Campaign, 415, 418n30, 419, 419n34, 424, 424n3, 427, 427n18, 427n19, 428n24, 430n31, 431, 431n35, 434n7, 434n8, 435, 435n15, 436n22, 438n29, 440n35, 443n8, 445, 445n19, 447n31, 448-451, 451n8, 451n12, 451n13, 453-454, 454n30, 455; the Crater, 421n41; the war's final winter, 457-458, 458n14, 459, 459n21, 460n28, 462, 471, 471n13, 473n22, 474, 474n28, 475n32, 479n9, 480n11, 480n14, 486n43, 487; goes on leave, 463; Lee reduces burden on him, 470, 470n9; returns from leave, 470n9; Appomattox Campaign, 488, 489n3, 491, 491n12, 494n18, 494n19, 496n24, 497, 497n25, 497n27, 498, 498n29, 498n30, 498n31, 499n32, 501n39; marries Bettie Saunders, 492; Lee signs his parole, 500n36; departs for Richmond, 501; Brady's photo with Lee and Custis, 503

Teaser, CSS, 33-34, 34n25, 167n16

Temple, Mrs. Lucy, 242

Terrett, George H., 16, 19-21

Terry, William, 389n55, 409, 462, 464

Texas Military Units: 1st Infantry, 38n40; 2nd Infantry, 139n56; 5th Infantry, 106; 443n11; Texas Brigade, 172, 221n37, 345n14, 382, 401, 440, 443, 466, 483

Theodosia, (steamer), 172

Thomas, George H., 453n26, 462-463, 467-468, 473, 481, 483

Thornton, John T., 494

Thornton, Richard D., 495n20

Thoroughfare Gap, 185, 185n37, 205

Tomlinson, A.A., 184

Tompkins, Charles, 45, 56, 57n31, 67

Tompkins, Christopher Q., 13, 13n14, 72

Tompkins, Ellen W., 72, 73n19

Tompkins, Sally Louisa, 13n14

Tom's Brook, battle of, 452n17

Toombs, Robert, 47n35, 178n13, 246, 246n10, 249

Torbert, A.T.A., 151n30

Totopotomoy Creek, engagement at, 378

Townsend, E.D., 2n5

Trapier, James H., 81, 87, 89, 91-92, 97-99, 102, 104, 115

"Traveller," (Lee's horse), 60, 94, 147, 185, 187, 187n44, 199, 264, 286, 321n15, 357, 378, 382, 382n23, 385- 386, 434n5, 490, 501

Tredegar Iron Works, 7, 22, 28, 48, 63, 63n12, 94, 94n5, 163, 170, 250

Tree, J.B., 13, 14n15

Trenholm, George, 480

Trent, Dr. Peterfield, 161n66

Trent's Reach, 405, 405n35

Trevilian's Station, battle of, 402, 402n27, 415n16, 420n39

Trimble, Isaac, 32n18, 63n12, 247, 249, 285, 286n45, 288; recommends for promotion, 211; promoted, 236; wounded at Second Manassas, 247n16; offered command of the Shenandoah Valley, 271; post-Chancellorsville, 274; his new command, 275; the march to Gettysburg, 280, 286, 288n53, 288n54; Gettysburg, July 2, 293; Gettysburg, July 3, 294

Thomas, F. J., 25

Thompson, William Butler, 28, 28n3

Tucker, Rev. Beverly, 263

Tucker, George W., 490, 498, 498n29, 499n32

Tucker, John R., 41

Turner, Edward (Lee's cousin), 30n13, 65, 185

Turner's Gap, 196-197, 197n28, 198n30

Tybee Island, 80, 80n22, 82n33, 83

Tygart Valley, 63n14

Tyler, Jr., John, 396

United States Troops: 6th Cavalry, 133

Upperville, Virginia, 210, 217n18

Valentine, Edward, 452, 452n17

Van Dorn, Earl, 105

Vance, Zebulon, (Governor NC), 233, 235, 250, 273, 311, 314n23, 331, 344, 344n12, 357, 363, 363n35, 364, 364n37, 365n40, 367, 368n8, 385n36, 418, 426, 431, 434-435, 435n13, 436-437, 443, 447, 452, 455, 459-461, 463-464, 473, 476, 479-480

Vass, James, 185n37

Venable, Charles S., 120, 129n15, 132n29, 153n37, 158-159, 167n16, 185n38, 186, 186n42, 186n43, 197, 198n31, 199n37, 212n36, 219n26, 228n23, 256n18, 259n34, 281-282, 285, 290n1, 293-294, 303, 322n19, 326, 326n6, 334n40, 340, 340n15, 374n35, 377, 381, 404n33; asked to join Lee's staff, 112; joins Lee's staff, 119; Lee asks to be an aide on his staff, 122; Lee's staff, 132; ordered to report to Lee's staff, 152, 152n32; arrives and reports for duty, 155; Sharpsburg Campaign, 200n40, 201; thinks he should leave Lee's staff, 277; the march to Gettysburg, 279; retreat from Gettysburg, 298, 298n36; winter of 1863, 341n23, 343; winter of 1863-64, 349n34, 354, 354n24, 355, 362; Overland Campaign, 382, 384n32, 386, 386n42, 392n63, 392n64, 393n69, 394n71, 403n30, 404n32, 406n40; Petersburg Campaign, 408n46, 420; the Crater, 421n41, 421n42, 422n44; Petersburg Campaign, 427n19, 443, 443n8, 443n9, 447n31; the war's final winter, 459n21, 460n28, 463, 470, 470n9, 471, 474n28, 480n11, 480n14, 486n43; Lee was depressed after a meeting with Davis,

476n35; last letter to his son, 479n8; Appomattox Campaign, 490, 490n8, 493, 494n19, 495n22, 496n23, 497, 497n27, 498n28; departs for Richmond, 501

Verdiersville, Virginia, 334, 335n42, 380, 380n18

Vermont Military Units: 1st Cavalry, 254

Vicksburg, Mississippi, 261, 273n49, 291, 303, 354n24, 425n11

Virginia & Tennessee Railroad, 19n34, 32, 32n17, 53-54, 119, 123, 209, 344, 371, 379, 385, 460

Virginia Central Railroad, 43, 45-46, 49, 65n21, 72, 74, 74n31, 109, 137, 148n15, 171, 181-182, 250, 254, 268, 320n12, 331, 340, 344, 350, 353n18, 356, 362n25, 374n35, 390n57, 402n27, 413, 422, 479n7

Virginia Military Institute, 7n18, 28, 31, 211, 373, 373n31, 378, 397, 413, 413n9

Virginia Military Units:1st Artillery Regiment, 419, 419n35; 1st Cavalry, 16n24, 279, 279n14; 1st Infantry, 221, 221n34; 2nd Cavalry, 123n57, 150n24, 274n53; 2nd Infantry, 31n14, 48n38, 56n25, 163; 3rd Cavalry, 9n23, 34n27, 259n34, 477n5, 494; 3rd Infantry, 17n28, 34, 34n27, 38; 4th Cavalry, 153, 156, 159n59, 184n36; 4th Infantry, 56; 5th Battalion, 9n23; 5th Cavalry, 127n9, 367; 5th Infantry, 7n17, 57; 6th Cavalry, 176, 192, 339; 6th Infantry, 18n31, 18n32, 23n48, 264; 7th Cavalry, 16n24, 64n16, 339, 339n10, 425n11; 8th Cavalry, 105, 179, 323, 328, 348, 425n11, 466; 8th Infantry, 31, 31n14; 9th Cavalry, 64n20, 65n21, 229, 361, 368, 386n43, 387, 389, 418, 418n27; 9th Infantry, 9n23, 16n23, 40n5, 42, 136n41; 10th Infantry, 31n14, 48n38, 274n52; 11th Cavalry, 38n40; 11th Infantry, 16n23; 12th Cavalry, 492; 12th Infantry, 264n16, 400n17, 494n18; 13th Infantry, 9n23; 14th Cavalry, 78n15, 323, 328, 348, 466, 492; 14th Infantry, 296, 489n3; 15th Cavalry, 217n18, 260, 273; 15th Infantry, 7n17, 283; 16th Infantry, 15n22, 36n34; 17th Infantry, 159, 171n33, 200n40, 210n29, 426n13, 427n16, 455n36; 18th Cavalry, 328n10; 18th Heavy Artillery, 248n26; 18th Infantry, 241, 257n23; 19th Cavalry, 52n8; 19th Infantry, 8n19, 33, 34n26; 20th Heavy Artillery, 248n26; 21st Infantry, 41n9, 45, 45n26, 53, 63n12, 159n58, 225n10; 22nd Infantry, 13n14, 30, 56, 57n31, 67, 67n28, 73n19; 22nd Infantry Battalion, 445, 445n17, 451-452, 460n25; 23rd Infantry, 13n14, 30n12, 58n41, 274n52; 24th Infantry, 30; 25th Cavalry, 236, 247, 247n19, 255n14, 256, 272, 278; 25th Infantry Battalion, 8n20, 24n54; 26th Infantry, 8n20, 36n34, 68n30; 27th Infantry, 14n18, 38; 28th Infantry, 17n28, 55n20; 29th Infantry, 45n25, 62, 62n10; 30th Infantry, 33, 41n9; 31st Cavalry, 236, 247, 247n19, 255n14, 256, 272, 278; 31st Infantry, 8n20, 42n15, 52, 52n8, 62n9; 32nd Infantry, 19n33, 42, 58; 32nd Militia, 21; 33rd Infantry, 31n14, 48n38, 152n32; 34th Infantry, 31, 31n15, 35, 37; 35th Infantry, 42, 53-54, 57, 57n33; 36th Infantry, 8n20, 56; 37th Infantry, 274n52; 39th Cavalry Battalion, 203n49, 209, 222, 226, 241n10, 286n45, 286n47, 292, 296n27, 333, 432, 432n3, 433, 433n3, 443n9, 450, 450n7, 489n4, 492n13, 498n29, 499n32, 501, 501n39; 39th Infantry, 2n19; 39th Militia, 40; 40th Infantry, 33; 41st Infantry, 43n19, 121n48, 325, 332n32, 400n17, 427n16; 42nd Infantry, 7n17, 42, 42n15, 54, 55n19; 43rd Infantry, 37, 37n36; 44th Infantry, 35n28, 55n21; 45th Infantry, 71, 118, 129n15; 46th Infantry, 71, 203n49; 47th Infantry, 42, 42n14, 44, 162, 162n69; 48th Infantry, 40n5, 42n15, 51, 57; 49th Infantry, 37, 46n28, 173, 370, 385n38; 50th Infantry, 71, 118, 129, 255n14, 256, 272, 279, 342; 51st Infantry, 73, 73n26, 118, 129, 129n15; 52nd Infantry, 30n11, 49n43, 49n45, 57, 62, 6210n, 301n51, 369, 385, 432n2; 53rd Infantry, 35n27, 46n30, 49n43, 431n34; 54th Infantry, 348; 55th Infantry, 151n30; 56th Infantry, 49n43; 57th Infantry, 67n29; 57th Militia, 8n19; 58th Infantry, 55n20, 136n41; 60th Infantry, 65n21, 84, 119-120; 61st Infantry, 218, 221, 221n34, 287n53, 368; 63rd Infantry, 348; 101st Militia, 35n27; 111th Militia, 35; A. P. Hill's Light Division, 61n5, 118n30, 120n44, 189; King & Queen Artillery, 31; Albemarle Artillery, 153; Bedford Light Artillery, 43n19; Blackhorse Cavalry, 184n36; Chew's Battery, 391; Goochland Light Artillery, 67n27; King William Artillery, 200; Lee's Life Guard, 15n22; Nansemond Rangers, 17, 17n28; Nelson Light Artillery, 129n15, 421; Norfolk Light Artillery Blues, 218, 454, 500n36; Richmond Howitzers, 264, 265n19, 386n39, 459; Rockbridge Artillery, 9n23, 16n23, 104, 107, 160, 160n61, 186, 200, 207, 230n37, 268; Southern Rights Guard, 34, 34n26; Staunton Artillery, 384; Staunton Hill Artillery, 129; Stonewall Brigade, 271n41; Tredegar Battalion, 21, 21n42, 28, 34n26; Varina Artillery, 33; White's Battalion Cavalry, 194n19; Wise Legion, 69, 73-74, 88, 121, 130, 254

Virginia, CSS, 27, 95, 103, 108, 111, 115, 124, 124n61, 125, 127, 129-131, 134, 134n36, 136, 149n19

Vizetelly, Frank, 342

von Borcke, Heros, 184, 184n34, 186, 193n15, 199n36, 209n22, 227, 230n31, 263, 265

Wadsworth, James, 382, 413n6, 415

Walker, John, 195, 195n20, 195n21, 196, 199, 210, 215-216

Walker, Dr. N.S., 187

Walker, George D., 172

Walker, James, 271, 271n41

Walker, Leroy Pope, 18, 22, 33, 58, 61

Walker, R. Lindsay, 294n16, 351, 352n10

Walter, Franklin, 433

Walthall, Virginia, 136

Walton, Dr. Richard P., 501

Ware, Josiah W., 31, 31n15, 35, 37, 56

Warrenton, Virginia, 203, 215-218, 301, 321-322, 328

Warwick Courthouse, 23

Warwick River line, 115, 125, 128

Washington, James, 386n43, 387, 387n43

Washington, III, John A., 13n14; 27n1, 391n, 49n45, 5310n, 54n15, 54n16, 55n21, 55n22, 58, 59n42, 64, 64n20, 78n15, 136n44, 211, 331; joins Lee's staff, 10; Lee's aide de camp, 13, 18; shares a tent with Lee, 39, 52; departs for western Virginia, 49; western Virginia, 51; Cheat Mountain, 54; death of, 60, 65, 65n20, 65n21, 66

Washington, Louisa, 65n20, 65n21, 211

Washington, Thornton A., 78n15, 86, 91n8, 96, 96n8, 96n10; assigned to Lee's staff, 78; AG Department of South Carolina, Georgia and East Florida, 79; joins Lee in Charleston, 86n16; promoted to major, 91; left behind in

Coosawhatchie, 93n25; to Richmond with Lee, 100; Lee needs him, 104n25; reports to Lee, 106; Lee endorses application for a commissary position, 109; departs Lee's staff, 112; becomes quartermaster on Lee's staff, 118; leaves Lee's staff, 120

Waynesboro, Virginia, battle of, 479n7

Weisiger, David, 31n15, 42n11, 451

Weldon, North Carolina, 132, 134, 137, 347

Welford, Dr. William, 183

Wells, Coleman, 328

Werth, William H., 34, 35n27

West Point, Virginia, 21

West Virginia Military Units: 10th Infantry, 231

West, George B., 78n14

Western & Atlantic Railroad, 123

Whaley, William, 307

Wharton, Gabriel, 129, 129n15, 300, 300n47, 301, 305, 307

Whitcomb, H.D., 320n12, 422

White House (Rooney Lee's estate), 30, 30n10, 78n15, 85, 85n5, 101, 114, 121, 125-126, 130, 132, 132n31, 133, 133n33, 136-137, 145, 160-161, 161n65, 222, 225, 251, 256, 331, 444

White Oak Swamp, 161

White Sulphur Springs, 69, 74n29

White, David D., 494n19

White, Elijah V. "Lige," 194n19, 195n21, 238, 312, 495n21, 497n25

White, Robert, 330

Whitfield, J.B., 78n14

Whiting, William H. Chase, 144n4, 147, 147n13, 153, 159, 166, 211, 211n30, 345, 347, 361n23, 410, 414, 435n13, 458; only temporarily commanding the division, 151; Lee recommends he be sent to fortify Charleston harbor, 178; asks Lee about promoting him to major general, 180; Lee does not want him with his army, 210; promoted to major general, 258n27; Lee's planning meeting for the move north, 280; Petersburg Campaign, 435, 442, 443; sent to reinforce Jackson, 152

Whittier, Charles, 498, 498n30

Whittle, W.C., 36

Wickham, Anne Carter, 217

Wickham, Williams C., 36n32, 217, 217n18, 233, 288n56, 301, 361, 452

Wigfall, Louis T., 37n35, 38n40, 172, 202, 466n23

Wilbourne, R.E., 264, 264n17

Wilcox, Cadmus M., 113, 208n17, 217, 304; ordered to support Magruder, 108; Fredericksburg Campaign, 217n19; Gettysburg, July 2, 294; Gettysburg, July 3, 295; reviewing Hill's corps, 313; potential commander for southwest Virginia, 348; winter of 1863-64, 372; Overland Campaign, 381, 381n22, 402n28; Petersburg Campaign, 408, 408n45, 428n24, 438n29, 452, 453n20, 455n36; the war's final winter, 477, 482; Appomattox Campaign, 490-491, 493, 500

Wilderness, battle of, 272n43, 279, 334, 359, 373n32, 376-377, 453n24

Williams, J.B., 161

Williams, Lawrence, 136n44, 137n49

Williams, Martha "Markie" Custis, 171, 206

Williams, Orton (cousin), 3, 3n7, 14, 14n16, 16, 42, 282, 282n32, 283, 283n32, 305, 306n21

Williams, Seth, 496n23, 499, 499n33, 501n39

Williamsburg, Virginia, 21, 28-29, 115, 125, 348

Williamson, Thomas H., 37, 37n38

Williamsport, Maryland, 203, 286, 286n45, 295-296, 296n28, 297-298, 298n37

Willis, Edward S., 361, 361n21

Wilmer, Rev. Joseph P., 379

Wilmington & Manchester Railroad, 79n17

Wilmington & Weldon Railroad, 79n17

Wilmington, North Carolina, 138, 227-228, 233, 240, 247, 345, 347, 368, 410, 410n54, 411, 413-414, 414n10, 418, 423, 435, 435n13, 436-437, 442, 443, 446-448, 455-456, 456n1, 458-466, 473, 475

Wilson, James H., 409n49

Wilson, John P., 8

Wilson, Samuel S., 132

Wilson-Kautz raid, 409

Winchester & Potomac Railroad, 12, 13n13, 35, 209-210

Winchester, Virginia, 13, 199, 202, 204-205, 205n2, 207n9, 209, 211n33, 215, 225, 283, 296-297, 300, 300n44, 301, 305, 372

Winchester, Virginia, battles of, 126, 139, 418, 429, 432, 437

Winder, Charles, 32n18, 37

Winder, Henry, 45

Winder, John H., 41, 41n8, 132, 138, 170-171, 367n5

Winthrop, Stephen, 248, 248n26, 463, 463n10

Wise, Henry, 22, 22n46, 28, 41, 43-44, 50n46, 53-54, 58, 63, 67, 74, 123, 130n21, 151, 401n22, 452n18; Tompkins's arrival, 45; Scary Creek, 47n36; Lee's frustration with, 55; Lee orders to cooperate with Floyd, 56; Wise Legion, 56; Lee complains about, 57; Lee congratulates for Gauley Bridge skirmish, 58; refused to aid Floyd, 60; sent West, 60n3; Lee's authorization to transfer, 66; Lee concerned he is too isolated, 67; Sewell Mountain, 67n28; departs for Richmond, 68; disorganized force, 68n30; no longer in western Virginia, 71; wants a brigade command, 118; lobbying to command the Wise Legion, 121; Lee is trying to find him an assignment, 127; assigned to command a brigade, 130; C.S. Navy to assume control of Chaffin's Bluff, 151; Chaffin's Bluff is under C.S. Navy command, 154; on alert to join the ANV, 157; ordered to hold his position at all costs, 158; Lee says to watch for a quick strike on Chaffin's Bluff, 168; Petersburg Campaign, 408n47, 418n30; the Crater, 421n42; the war's final winter, 469-470, 487; Appomattox Campaign, 494n18, 494n19; Appomattox Campaign, 495n21, 497, 500

Wofford, William, 313, 316, 316n29, 416, 464, 464n17

Wolseley, Garnet, 190, 190n9, 208, 208n14

Wood, D.H., 459, 459n20

Wood, John T., 346n20, 347, 368, 413-414, 414n10, 415n15

Woodson, Charles, 313n19

Woodward, P.W., 34

Wool, John, 109-110, 168

Worsham, John, 159n58, 312n14

Wortham, Rev. G.H., 43

Wright, Ambrose R., 147n12, 313, 313n17, 359, 388
Wroe, Dr. John A., 291, 291n8
Wynne, Thomas H., 38

Yankee USS, 15n21
Yellow Tavern, battle of, 378, 386n42
Yerby, Thomas, 251n41, 252
York, Zebulon, 466, 466n26
Yorktown, Virginia, 21, 23, 29, 29n9, 36, 40, 104, 125, 128
Young, Henry E., 239, 243,435, 435n14
Young, Pierce M.B., 177n5, 353
Yulee, David, 86, 86n17, 87, 90

About the Author

Charles Knight is a native of Richmond, Virginia, where he developed a love of history at an early age. He has worked at museums and historic sites for more than two decades, and has given historical presentations to audiences across the country. Charlie, the author of *Valley Thunder: The Battle of New Market and the Opening of the Shenandoah Valley Campaign, May 1864* (2010), is currently at work on a biography of Confederate general William Mahone. He resides with his wife and children in North Carolina.